THE NEW
COOKING SCHOOL
COOKBOOK

COOKBOOK

ADVANCED FUNDAMENTALS

AMERICA'S TEST KITCHEN

Library of Congress Cataloging-in-Publication Data has been applied for

ISBN 978-1-954210-12-7

America's Test Kitchen
21 Drydock Avenue, Boston, MA 02210

Printed in Canada

10 9 8 7 6 5 4 3 2

Distributed by Penguin Random House Publisher Services
Tel: 800.733.3000

Editorial Director, Books **Adam Kowit**

Executive Food Editor **Dan Zuccarello**

Deputy Food Editors **Leah Colins and Stephanie Pixley**

Executive Managing Editor **Debra Hudak**

Senior Editors **Valerie Cimino, Joseph Gitter, Sacha Madadian, and Sara Mayer**

Test Cooks **Sāsha Coleman, Olivia Counter, Jacqueline Gochenouer, Eric Haessler, and Hisham Hassan**

Associate Editor **Sara Zatopek**

Contributing Editor **Cheryl Redmond**

Editorial Support **Katrina Munichiello, April Poole, and Rachel Schowalter**

Design Director **Lindsey Timko Chandler**

Deputy Art Director **Katie Barranger**

Designers **Allison Boales and Jen Kanavos Hoffman**

Photography Director **Julie Bozzo Cote**

Senior Photography Producer **Meredith Mulcahy**

Senior Staff Photographers **Steve Klise and Daniel J. van Ackere**

Staff Photographer **Kevin White**

Additional Photography **Joseph Keller and Carl Tremblay**

Food Styling **Tara Busa, Isabelle English, Joy Howard, Sheila Jarnes, Catrine Kelty, Chantal Lambeth, Gina McCreadie, Kendra McKnight, Ashley Moore, Marie Piraino, Elle Simone Scott, Kendra Smith, and Sally Staub**

Illustration **John Burgoyne; Traci Daberko; Rose Flynn; Sophie Greenspan; Hannah Jacobs; Jay Layman; MGMT.design, LLC; Michael Newhouse; and Lauren Pettapiece**

Project Manager, Creative Operations **Katie Kimmerer**

Senior Print Production Specialist **Lauren Robbins**

Production and Imaging Coordinator **Amanda Yong**

Production and Imaging Specialists **Tricia Neumyer and Dennis Noble**

Copy Editor **Deri Reed**

Proofreader **Ann-Marie Imbornoni**

Indexer **Elizabeth Parson**

Chief Creative Officer **Jack Bishop**

Executive Editorial Directors **Julia Collin Davison and Bridget Lancaster**

CONTENTS

WELCOME TO AMERICA'S TEST KITCHEN

This book has been tested, written, and edited by the folks at America's Test Kitchen, where curious cooks become confident cooks. Located in Boston's Seaport District in the historic Innovation and Design Building, it features 15,000 square feet of kitchen space, including multiple photography and video studios. It is the home of *Cook's Illustrated* magazine and *Cook's Country* magazine and is the workday destination for more than 60 test cooks, editors, and cookware specialists. Our mission is to empower and inspire confidence, community, and creativity in the kitchen.

We start the process of testing a recipe with a complete lack of preconceptions, which means that we accept no claim, no technique, and no recipe at face value. We simply assemble as many variations as possible, test a half dozen of the most promising ones, and taste the results blind. We then construct our own recipe and continue to test it, varying ingredients, techniques, and cooking times until we reach a consensus. As we like to say in the test kitchen, "We make the mistakes so you don't have to." The result, we hope, is the best version of a particular recipe, but we realize that only you can be the final judge of our success (or failure). We use the same rigorous approach when we test equipment and taste ingredients.

None of this would be possible without a belief that good cooking, much like good music, is based on a foundation of objective technique. Some people like spicy foods and others don't, but there is a right way to sauté; there is a best way to cook a pot roast; and there are measurable scientific principles involved in producing perfectly beaten, stable egg whites. Our ultimate goal is to investigate the fundamental principles of cooking to give you the techniques, tools, and ingredients you need to become a better cook. It is as simple as that.

To see what goes on behind the scenes at America's Test Kitchen, check out our social media channels for kitchen snapshots, exclusive content, video tips, and much more. You can watch us work (in our actual test kitchen) by tuning in to *America's Test Kitchen* or *Cook's Country* on public television or on our websites. Listen to *Proof*, *Mystery Recipe*, and *The Walk-In* (AmericasTestKitchen.com/podcasts) to hear engaging, complex stories about people and food. Want to hone your cooking skills or finally learn how to bake—with an America's Test Kitchen test cook? Enroll in one of our online cooking classes. And you can engage the next generation of home cooks with kid-tested recipes from America's Test Kitchen Kids.

Our community of home recipe testers provides valuable feedback on recipes under development by ensuring that they are foolproof. You can help us investigate the how and why behind successful recipes from your home kitchen. (Sign up at AmericasTestKitchen.com/recipe_testing.)

However you choose to visit us, we welcome you into our kitchen, where you can stand by our side as we test our way to the best recipes in America.

facebook.com/AmericasTestKitchen
instagram.com/TestKitchen
youtube.com/AmericasTestKitchen
tiktok.com/@TestKitchen
twitter.com/TestKitchen
pinterest.com/TestKitchen

AmericasTestKitchen.com
CooksIllustrated.com
CooksCountry.com
OnlineCookingSchool.com
AmericasTestKitchen.com/kids

INTRODUCTION

One of the most rewarding aspects of cooking is that there is always something new to learn. If you are already a proficient cook, your understanding of the basics helps prepare you to explore new territory, and you can take any direction you please. Have you always wanted to make your own cheese? How about bake flaky croissants and authentic baguettes? Fry a turkey? Do you want to entice your family and friends with new dinner favorites from across the globe by serving Tunisian Tagine with White Beans, Okra and Shrimp Stew, Lasagne Verdi alla Bolognese, Plov, and Jamaican Oxtail? Our recipes and techniques will help you master all of these dishes and more—minus the intimidation and failure.

You'll keep your cooking skills as sharp as your knives by cooking through the courses of recipes in this book. It's like enrolling in culinary grad school, with 97 elective courses to choose from. The courses are organized around more than 400 recipes that teach 200 techniques, so you can indulge your curiosity by diving into topics as diverse as savory soufflés, pho, and Texas barbecue. You will acquire new skills and keep learning as you cook through the recipes while also building up your confidence in the kitchen.

America's Test Kitchen has been teaching home cooks how to cook for more than 25 years. Our goal is to pass along everything we know to you so that you will be fearless when attempting new challenges in the kitchen. We work hard to develop recipes that always work and relentlessly test them using techniques that make them failproof. Each course in the book is introduced by a longtime ATK cook and includes their invaluable behind-the-recipe tips and advice. Yes, these advanced courses tackle topics and recipes that may take some practice to master—flipping a French-style omelet, hand pulling noodles, fearlessly frying crunchy chicken—but you will succeed and that sense of accomplishment is your, and our, reward.

The recipe overviews explain how and why each recipe works and a recap of the recipe's keys to success helps to thoroughly explain the recipe and reinforce the important takeaways. We've woven core techniques, food science, and more resources into each course so that you'll acquire additional valuable information as you read and cook. You'll also find step-by-step technique tutorials that lead many of the courses and explain the main method that's covered along with photo series within the course to illustrate important aspects of the more exacting recipes. You'll easily learn many things, from how to care for your knives, to the best way to extract every bit of meat from a lobster, to grinding your own burger, to making the final course perfection by creating desserts like fresh fruit pie, cheesecake, and several kinds of candy.

Wherever you are on your culinary journey, this book will make you a better cook. So, jump into any course and take your cooking to a whole new level. We'll be right there with you in the kitchen with everything you need along the way.

COURSE INSTRUCTORS

JACK BISHOP
Chief Creative Officer
America's Test Kitchen

MORGAN BOLLING
Executive Editor, Creative Content
Cook's Country Magazine

LEAH COLINS
Deputy Food Editor
Books

JULIA COLLIN DAVISON
Executive Editorial Director
America's Test Kitchen

KEITH DRESSER
Executive Food Editor
Cook's Illustrated Magazine

STEVE DUNN
Senior Editor
Cook's Illustrated Magazine

ANDREA GEARY
Deputy Food Editor
Cook's Illustrated Magazine

JOSEPH GITTER
Senior Editor
Books

LAWMAN JOHNSON
Senior Photo Test Cook
Cook's Country Magazine

NICOLE KONSTANTINAKOS
Deputy Food Editor
Cook's Country Magazine

LAN LAM
Senior Editor
Cook's Illustrated Magazine

BRIDGET LANCASTER
Executive Editorial Director
America's Test Kitchen

ASHLEY MOORE
Food Stylist
America's Test Kitchen

CHRISTIE MORRISON
Deputy Editor, Culinary Content
and Curriculum
America's Test Kitchen

ANNIE PETITO
Senior Editor
Cook's Illustrated Magazine

STEPHANIE PIXLEY
Deputy Food Editor
Books

BRYAN ROOF
Editorial Director
Cook's Country Magazine

ELLE SIMONE SCOTT
Executive Editor and Food Stylist
America's Test Kitchen

DAN SOUZA
Editor in Chief
Cook's Illustrated Magazine

DAN ZUCCARELLO
Executive Food Editor
Books

LIST OF RECIPES

VEGETABLES

SALADS

CONTINUES >

SALADS (CONTINUED)

SOUPS

SEAFOOD

BREADS

DESSERTS

COOKING SMARTS

20 SKILLS TO IMPROVE YOUR COOKING

Try implementing these small doable tweaks in your kitchen; they will save you time and help make you a better cook.

1 Keep your work area tidy. Place a bowl or plastic produce bag for trimmings on your counter when you cook. It keeps you more organized and minimizes trips to the trash bin.

2 Use a bench scraper to scoop up crumbs and scraps. You can also use it to lift and transfer chopped food.

3 Anchor your cutting board: Place a damp paper towel or dish towel underneath the board to help keep it in place.

4 Organize your prep. Placing your prepped ingredients in little bowls makes it easy to grab an ingredient and add it at just the right moment.

5 Wash your dishes and wipe down your cutting board as you're cooking. Your future self will thank you.

6 Clean your kitchen sponge. A dirty kitchen sponge can breed bacteria and contaminate your kitchen. Always wring out your sponge and store it in a place where it can dry out between uses. To easily clean your sponge, dampen it and microwave it for at least 2 minutes or run it through your dishwasher on a setting that reaches at least 155 degrees and has a heated dry cycle.

7 When storing nonstick cookware, place paper plates between the pans to prevent them from getting scratched.

8 Get in the habit of labeling and dating your zipper-lock/vacuum-sealer bags before you fill them and store in the freezer.

9 Use an instant-read thermometer to test food for doneness. It's the difference between a good cook and a great cook.

10 Use a digital kitchen scale to measure your baking ingredients by weight, not volume. It's the difference between a good baker and a great baker.

11 Whisk side to side, not in a loop. The side-to-side stroke is an easier motion to repeat rapidly and with force, and you'll generate more whisk strokes per minute than with any other motion.

12 Measuring something sticky like honey or corn syrup? Spray the measuring cup with vegetable oil spray.

13 Before chopping beets, or anything else that might stain, spray your cutting board with vegetable oil spray.

14 When tackling a new recipe for the first time, read it all the way through twice before starting.

15 Always, always, always taste as you go.

16 Think your dish needs salt? Sugar? Acid? Sprinkle a little onto your tasting spoon before committing.

17 If you add salt to a dish and it still tastes under-seasoned, adding an acid such as vinegar or lemon juice should do the trick.

18 Always make sure to grind black pepper fresh.

19 Want stronger-tasting garlic? Grate it. Want more mellow garlic? Slice it.

20 Allow food to rest longer than you'd think. For meat, this allows juices to redistribute so that they don't end up on your cutting board.

KITCHEN EQUIPMENT: THE BASICS

Here is a refresher course on the pieces of kitchen equipment we think every home cook should have—nothing fancy, just the essentials. The names of the test kitchen's favorites appear in boldface. Instead of making do, it might be time to treat yourself to the best options.

COOKWARE

SAUCEPANS

Every kitchen should be equipped with two saucepans: one with a capacity of 3 to 4 quarts, and a 2-quart nonstick saucepan. The larger one is great for vegetables and sauces, while the smaller can be used for cooking foods that stick easily such as oatmeal. The test kitchen's favorite large saucepan is the **All-Clad 4-Quart Stainless Steel Sauce Pan with Loop Helper Handle,** and our best buy is the Cuisinart MultiClad Unlimited 4-Quart Saucepan with Cover. Our favorite small saucepan is the **Calphalon Contemporary Nonstick 2½ Quart Shallow Saucepan with Cover**.

DUTCH OVEN

A Dutch oven is a kitchen workhorse built for both stovetop and oven use. A good-quality heavy-bottomed Dutch oven conducts heat steadily and evenly. The most useful size is 6 to 8 quarts. Our winning heavier Dutch oven is the **Le Creuset 7¼ Quart Round Dutch Oven**. Our best buy is the Cuisinart Chef's Classic Enameled Cast Iron Covered Casserole.

RIMMED BAKING SHEETS AND WIRE RACKS

Rimmed baking sheets are used for everything from roasting vegetables and cooking meat to baking cookies and sheet cakes. Fitted with the right size wire cooling rack, a rimmed baking sheet can stand in for a roasting pan. We prefer baking sheets that are 18 x 13 inches and have a 1-inch rim all around. Buy at least two. Our favorite rack—the **Checkered Chef Cooling Rack**—fits snugly in our winning baking sheet, the inexpensive **Nordic Ware Baker's Half Sheet**.

TRADITIONAL SKILLET

We prefer traditional skillets made of stainless steel sandwiched around an aluminum core. The finish (which is *not* nonstick) helps develop fond, the brown bits that stick to the bottom of the pan. Our winning traditional skillet, the **All-Clad D3 Stainless Steel 12" Fry Pan with Lid**, also comes in 10-inch and 8-inch versions.

NONSTICK SKILLET

The coating on nonstick pans helps delicate foods such as eggs and fish release easily. The nonstick coating wears out over time so the skillet will need to be replaced, but our winning **OXO Good Grips Non-Stick Pro 12" Open Frypan** is relatively inexpensive.

KNIVES

CHEF'S KNIFE

From chopping onions to mincing herbs to butchering a chicken, a chef's knife will handle 90 percent of your ingredient prep. If you buy only one knife, make it a reliable chef's knife like the test kitchen's longtime favorite, the **Victorinox Swiss Army Fibrox Pro 8" Chef's Knife**.

PARING KNIFE

A paring knife is key for tasks that require more dexterity than a chef's knife can provide: peeling and coring apples, deveining shrimp, cutting citrus segments, and more. Our winning paring knife is the **Victorinox Swiss Army 3¼" Spear Point Paring Knife**.

SERRATED KNIFE

We like the modestly priced **Mercer Culinary Millennia 10" Wide Bread Knife**.

BAKEWARE

BAKING DISHES

A 13 x 9-inch glass baking dish is functional, inexpensive, and great for baked ziti or a large fruit crisp, but it can't go under the broiler to brown the top of a casserole. We found an alternative to our favorite **Pyrex Easy Grab 3-Quart Oblong Baking Dish** that was broiler safe and looked nice coming to the table for serving: **Mrs. Anderson's Baking Lasagna Pan with Handle (Rose)** has a large capacity and is easy to clean.

TOOLS

CUTTING BOARDS

Wood and bamboo cutting boards take some work to clean and maintain, but if properly cared for they can last a lifetime. Plastic boards are nearly as durable and less expensive to buy and replace. Our favorite large plastic cutting board is the **Winco Statik Board Cutting Board 15" x 20" x ½"**, and our favorite wood cutting board is the **Teakhaus by Proteak Edge Grain Cutting Board**.

DRY MEASURING CUPS

Dry ingredients such as flour, sugar, grains, and other foods should always be measured in a dry measuring cup. These straight-sided cups typically have flat tops that make leveling dry ingredients easy. We prefer the **OXO Good Grips Stainless Steel Measuring Cups**.

LIQUID MEASURING CUP

For the utmost precision, use a liquid measuring cup for liquids. Our winning glass cup is the **Pyrex 1 Cup Measuring Cup**, and winning plastic cup is the **OXO Good Grips 1 Cup Angled Measuring Cup**.

MEASURING SPOONS

We use these tiny tools to measure everything from baking soda to olive oil. We like the simple sturdy design of **Cuisipro Stainless Steel 5-Piece Measuring Spoons**.

MIXING BOWLS AND PREP BOWLS

Mixing bowls handle everything from mixing pancake batter to simply melting butter. Our winning stainless-steel bowls are **Vollrath Economy Stainless Steel Mixing Bowls** and our favorite glass ones are in the **Pyrex Smart Essentials Mixing Bowl Set with Colored Lids**. We also like to use small glass prep bowls to measure out the ingredients needed for a recipe. Our winning set is the **Anchor Hocking 6-Piece Nesting Prep Bowl Set**.

PEPPER MILL

Preground pepper doesn't compare with freshly ground, which is what just about all of our savory recipes call for. The test kitchen's winning mill, the **Cole & Mason Derwent Pepper Mill**, is easy to load and grinds pepper from very fine to very coarse.

SPATULAS

A good metal spatula is essential for flipping or transferring foods from metal cookware or bakeware. Our winner is the **Wüsthof Gourmet 7" Slotted Fish Spatula**. (You'll want two for flipping fish.) When cooking in nonstick pans, we prefer our winning all-purpose spatula, the **Di Oro Living Seamless Silicone Spatula—Large**.

INSTANT-READ THERMOMETER

An instant-read thermometer helps to ensure success since it takes the guesswork out of knowing when food is done. We love our longtime winning thermometer, the **ThermoWorks Thermapen ONE**. Our best inexpensive option is the ThermoWorks ThermoPop.

TONGS

A good pair of tongs is a cook's best friend and should feel like a natural extension of your hands. The **OXO Good Grips 12-Inch Tongs** are our favorite; they grip food well and are comfortable to hold.

WOODEN SPOON

Wooden spoons are useful for a variety of stirring and scraping tasks, such as mixing stiff cookie dough and scraping up fond. Our co-winning wooden spoons are **Jonathan's Spoons Spootle** and **FAAY 13.5" Teak Cooking Spoon**.

CAN OPENER

Our favorite can opener, the **EZ-DUZ-IT Can Opener**, requires almost no thought to operate—it's intuitive and easy to use in all respects.

KITCHEN EQUIPMENT: BEYOND THE BASICS

Once you have outfitted your kitchen with the basic pieces of equipment, you can consider adding upgrades that will help you to master more involved cooking projects. The test kitchen's buying recommendations are included in bold so that you know which brands we consider to be the best investment.

COOKWARE

CAST-IRON SKILLET

A cast-iron skillet excels at searing and, if well seasoned, releases food as well as a nonstick surface. However, it does require extra effort to build and maintain its seasoning, so keep that in mind. Our roomy preseasoned favorite is the **Lodge Classic Cast Iron Skillet, 12"**.

CARBON STEEL SKILLET

Like cast iron, carbon steel also needs to be seasoned, but once it is, it offers the versatility of a traditional pan, the heat retention of cast iron at a lighter weight, and the slick release of a good nonstick skillet. Our winner is the **Matfer Bourgeat Black Steel Round Frying Pan, 11⅞"**.

FLAT-BOTTOMED WOK

This versatile pan is made of carbon steel so it transfers heat efficiently and sears foods effectively. It is suited to stir-frying, frying, and steaming. It offers a big, flat cooking surface and its flat bottom is stable on a flat stovetop. Our winning wok is the **Taylor and Ng Natural Nonstick Wok Set 12153 14" Carbon Steel**.

ROASTING PAN

This holiday staple is incredibly useful year-round. Besides roasting the Thanksgiving turkey, this pan shows up whenever we want to roast large cuts of meat. Its low sides and open design provide roasts with maximum exposure to the oven's hot air for even browning. Our winning roasting pan comes with a rack: the **Calphalon Contemporary Stainless Roasting Pan with Rack**.

STOCKPOT

A heavy 12-quart pot is useful for handling a variety of big jobs, from making a double batch of chicken broth to steaming lobsters. Our winning pot is the **Cook N Home Stainless Steel Stockpot with Lid 12 Quart**.

BAKEWARE

SOUFFLÉ DISH

A classic soufflé dish is round with straight sides and not-too-thick side walls that allow soufflés to rise up tall and straight. Our favorite is the **HIC 64 Ounce Soufflé**.

SPRINGFORM PAN

Unlike a traditional cake pan, a springform pan consists of two pieces: a round, flat base and a circular collar that latches open and closed, allowing delicate cakes to be unmolded upright. A must for making cheesecake. Our co-winning leakproof 9-inch pans are made by **Williams Sonoma** and **Nordic Ware**.

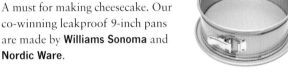

TART PAN

For making crisp-looking tarts, pans with a sharper, fluted design and a removable bottom have the edge. We highly recommend the **Matfer Steel Non-stick Tart Mold with Removable Bottom**.

BAKING STONE AND STEEL

A baking stone or steel conducts heat and transfers it evenly and steadily to the bottom of the pizza or bread being baked on it. To see a stone in action, see page 548. Our co-winning steels are **The Original Baking Steel** and the **Nerd Chef Steel Stone, Standard ¼"**. Our best buy and best light-weight option is the Outset Pizza Grill Stone Tiles, Set of 4.

BAKING PEEL

A baking peel is used to move pizza, bread, and other baked goods into, out of, and within a hot oven. Our winning peel, the innovative **EXO Polymer Sealed Super Peel**, is made of wood and has a cloth conveyor belt with a polymer coating to make it more moisture-proof.

KNIVES

CARBON STEEL CHEF'S KNIFE

Carbon steel knives are considered to be sharper and more durable than stainless. Our top pick, the **Bob Kramer 8" Carbon Steel Chef's Knife by Zwilling J.A. Henckels**, is a beautifully designed, hardy knife that will last a lifetime if you treat it right.

SANTOKU KNIFE

With its boxier build and curved tip, a santoku-style knife is a little shorter than a chef's knife. Is it a viable alternative to a chef's knife? It's really a matter of personal choice whether you prefer a smaller tool. A good santoku can mince, slice, and chop as well as any good chef's knife. The **Misono UX10 Santoku 7.0"** came out on top in our testing.

BONING KNIFE

A boning knife can make it easier to perform certain tasks, as its thin, narrow, razor-like blade is ideal for getting in between joints and for carving around larger bones. Our winner is the **Zwilling Pro 5.5" Flexible Boning Knife**.

MEAT CLEAVER

For tasks that require chopping power like splitting dense squash or a lobster and breaking down bone-in poultry and meat, reach for a cleaver. Its heft and size make it ideal for jobs that might otherwise damage or wear down your chef's knife. We like the **Shun Classic Meat Cleaver**.

TOOLS

DIGITAL SCALE

When baking, weighing the ingredients is the most accurate method of measurement. But a scale is also useful for tasks like portioning out ground meat and weighing vegetables and fruits. We highly recommend the **OXO Good Grips 11 lb Food Scale with Pull Out Display,** and our best buy is the Ozeri Pronto Digital Multifunction Kitchen and Food Scale.

BENCH SCRAPER

Bench scrapers aren't just for pastry. Along with scraping, trimming, or cutting dough, a scraper handily scoops up chopped herbs and diced vegetables and transfers them neatly to a pot. The **Dexter-Russell 6" Dough Cutter/ Scraper** is our winning scraper.

COARSE GRATER

Keep a grater on hand for smaller shredding jobs or for those times when you don't want to drag out your food processor. Our favorite, the **Rösle Coarse Grater,** is a flat paddle with grippy feet that can grate over any surface or bowl.

MANDOLINE

A good, sharp mandoline allows you to slice fruit and vegetables precisely, consistently, and quickly. Our co-winners are the **Super Benriner Mandoline Slicer** and **OXO Good Grips Chef's Mandoline Slicer 2.0.**

MEAT POUNDER

Since we prefer to pound uneven cutlets from the store or even out other pieces of meat, a meat pounder is an important tool. In the test kitchen we prefer a meat pounder with a vertical handle, which offers better leverage and control, and that weighs at least 1½ pounds. We recommend the **Norpro GRIP-EZ Meat Pounder.**

OYSTER KNIFE

The right oyster knife can make a difficult task a lot easier. Regular knives are unsuitable for opening oysters because they're too sharp and flexible; the thick, dull blades of oyster knives function as levers to pry shells apart without cutting into them. Our favorite is the **R. Murphy New Haven Oyster Knife with Stainless Steel Blade.**

PASTRY BRUSH

We use a pastry brush to paint crusts with egg wash before they enter the oven and to dab jam over fruit tarts. With a thick head of agile bristles, the **Winco Flat Pastry and Basting Brush, 1½ inch** is our winner. That said, it does contain BPA. For those who are concerned about BPA, our runner-up, the Ateco 1.5" Flat Stainless Steel Ferrule Pastry Brush, is a good choice.

PIE WEIGHTS

Many home bakers use rice or sugar or coins, but we have our best success with classic pie weights. We like **Mrs. Anderson's Baking Ceramic Pie Weights;** however, they come with just 1 cup of weights. We purchase four sets to completely fill an aluminum foil–lined pie shell. With weights piled up and pressing firmly against the dough walls, the edges of the pie shell remain high and the bottom turns out crisp, flaky, and golden brown.

PIPING SET

The best way to upgrade your decorating game is to use a piping bag outfitted with a decorating tip. We could not find a decorating kit that came with the right pastry bags and selection of tips so we put together the components we wanted from a craft store. Buy these essentials for your DIY set: twelve 16-inch disposable pastry bags, 4 reusable plastic couplers, and the following 6 Wilton tips: #4 round, #12 round, #70 leaf, #103 petal, #2D large closed star, and #1M open star. And remember, you can always use a ziplock bag with the tip cut off to do less precise work.

OFFSET SPATULA

For frosting a cake, there's no better tool than an offset spatula. The long, narrow blade is ideal for scooping and spreading frosting, and it is bent where it meets the handle for better leverage. We like to use the **OXO Good Grips Bent Icing Knife.**

SPIDER SKIMMER

When we're deep-frying, blanching, or boiling, we use a spider skimmer—a long-handled stainless-steel wire basket—to remove food from the pot. A spider has a larger capacity than a slotted spoon and more open area for faster, safer drainage. The **Rösle Wire Skimmer** is our favorite.

CLIP-ON PROBE THERMOMETER

A clip-on probe thermometer makes monitoring the temperature of hot oil easy. It displays the oil temperature and lets you know when it's hot enough to start frying. We like to use the feature-rich **ThermoWorks ChefAlarm**, which includes a low-temperature alarm, a timer, and a tracker that monitors the time elapsed since the target temperature was reached. Plus, it can be recalibrated.

KITCHEN TIMER

Timing is everything with recipes so a timer helps guarantee success in the kitchen. The best kitchen timers are simple and easy to read and hear. We especially like two models: The **ThermoWorks Extra Big & Loud Timer** is our top pick for cooks who want to track only one thing at a time. For cooks who want the ability to track multiple things with one timer, we recommend the **OXO Good Grips Triple Timer**.

SMALL APPLIANCES

FOOD PROCESSOR

If you are investing in one big-ticket appliance, it should be a food processor. It can chop foods that blenders can't handle, as well as slice and shred and mix up batters and doughs. Our winning **Cuisinart Custom 14 Cup Food Processor** is powerful and easy to operate.

STAND MIXER

If you are a serious cook or baker, a stand mixer is something you need to make breads and baked goods. Our winning **KitchenAid Pro Line Series 7 Quart Stand Mixer** is a powerful, smartly design machine that makes quick work of large and small volumes of food. Our best buy is the more reasonably priced KitchenAid Classic Plus Series 4.5 Quart Tilt-Head Stand Mixer.

SOUS VIDE CIRCULATOR

Sous vide cooking is easy if you have the right immersion circulator. Simple to set and easy to clip on a variety of vessels, it heats water rapidly and keeps the temperature right on target, whether you are cooking for 12 minutes or 20 hours. The **Breville Joule Sous Vide-White Polycarbonate** is our top pick.

MANUAL PASTA MACHINE

Pasta machines make the process of rolling out sheets of dough and cutting them into noodles faster and easier and the results more uniform. Hand-cranked pasta machines are the most prevalent and affordable options. Our longtime favorite is the **Marcato Atlas 150 Wellness Pasta Machine**.

ELECTRIC PASTA EXTRUDER

Easy to use, an electric pasta extruder is more expensive than a manual pasta machine but you'll want one if you want to make tubular shapes and round strands including penne, ziti, and spaghetti. They also mix the dough for you. Our favorite is the **Philips Pasta Maker**, which comes with four pasta shaping disks (more can be purchased).

ICE CREAM MAKER

A good electric ice cream maker makes it easy to produce customized ice cream, frozen yogurt, and sorbet at home. Our winning **Cuisinart Frozen Yogurt, Ice Cream & Sorbet Maker** is very easy to use, has a compact design, and is one of the quickest machines we tested.

CARING FOR YOUR KNIVES

Knives are vital kitchen workhorses and a sharp knife is a cook's best friend. It's important to keep them sharp, but what does that mean, and how do you accomplish that? Here's what you need to know to keep your knives at peak performance.

UNDERSTANDING DEGREES OF DULLNESS

It doesn't take months or weeks for a knife to lose its sharpness. Even a few minutes of cutting can cause the blade to feel slightly dull. That said, a knife that feels only a little dull probably does not need to be sharpened. The edge of a slightly dull knife is usually just misaligned and merely needs to be repositioned with a honing steel. A truly dull knife has an edge that is rounded and worn down and needs a sharpener to restore the standard Western 20- to 22-degree angle of each side of the edge.

Sharp
A sharp knife holds a 20-degree angle on each side of the edge.

Slightly Dull
The misaligned edge of a slightly dull knife is easily fixed with a steel.

Very Dull
A very dull, worn-down knife needs a sharpener to restore the edge.

HOW TO TELL IF YOUR KNIFE IS SHARP

In the test kitchen, we use a very simple test to see if knives need to be honed or sharpened: the paper test. Hold a sheet of paper by one end and drag your knife, from heel to tip, across it. If the knife snags or fails to cut the paper, it needs to be honed or sharpened. Try honing first. If the knife still fails the test, run it through a sharpener.

GOOD OPTIONS FOR KNIFE STORAGE

If you store your knives loose in a drawer, you're putting the sharp edge of your blades—not to mention your fingers—in danger.

Knife Guard

A knife guard is essentially a sheath that protects your blade and your fingers, keeping both safe and intact if the knife gets jostled around. It also keeps your knife from poking holes or slits in your knife roll when you're on the go. The best guards and cases fit snugly around your blade so that it can't knock around inside and get dull in transit.

Magnetic Knife Strip

A wall-mounted magnetic knife strip offers ample room to store knives without demanding drawer or counter space. It can accommodate even the longest knives.

Universal Knife Block

A universal knife block boasts a "slotless" frame filled with a nest of plastic rods to accommodate any arsenal of cutlery and holds knives in a compact footprint.

OUR RECOMMENDED SHARPENERS

While we typically recommend knives with a 15-degree angle, these Western-style sharpeners remain our top pick if you have 20-degree blades.

Electric
20-DEGREE

The **Chef'sChoice Model 130 Professional Sharpening Station** creates a sharp, polished edge on knives. Its spring-loaded blade guides allow no ambiguous wiggle room as they hold the blade against the sharpening wheels at the proper angle. One slot acts like a honing steel but removes all the guesswork.

15/20-DEGREE HYBRID

The **Chef's Choice 15/20 Angle Select Electric Knife Sharpener** is designed to sharpen both 15 and 20-degree edges. This sharpener is easy to use, and restores both styles to like-new sharpness in a matter of minutes. It can also sharpen single-beveled Japanese blades.

Manual

The **AccuSharp Knife and Tool Sharpener** makes admirably quick and thorough work of basic sharpening tasks at a fraction of the price of an electric sharpener.

DEGREES OF SHARPNESS

THE MORE ACUTE THE ANGLE, THE SHARPER THE BLADE WILL FEEL.

When manufacturers report that a knife has a 15- or 20-degree angle, they're referring to the angle of the bevel—the slim strip on either side of the blade that narrows to form the cutting edge.

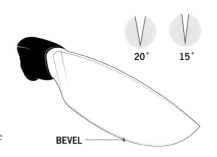

BEVEL

KNIFE SHARPENING KITCHEN HACK: USE A COFFEE MUG

Need to sharpen a small knife, but don't own a knife sharpener? If you find yourself with a dull knife but without a knife sharpener, you can use the unglazed bottom of a ceramic mug to sharpen small knives. Applying moderate pressure, hold the knife at a 15-degree angle and carefully draw the entire length of the blade across the rough surface.

KNIFE SHARPENING TAKEAWAYS

- Sharpen your knives regularly. Even the best knives will dull over time with regular use.
- A sharp knife is a safe knife. It is crucial to keep knives sharp so that they cut through food with less slippage.
- Using a sharp knife will make your food taste better. Get the thin slices or a fine dice you're looking for, not large or ragged hunks. Precisely cut food will cook at an even rate and produce a much more successful dish.

KEEPING KNIVES CLEAN

We recommend cleaning knives with a sponge, hot water, and soap. Scrub pads do a fine job of removing gunk from blades but can eventually damage the finish. Avoid a dishwasher: The knocking around can damage the edges, as can the corrosive nature of dishwasher detergent. If you have a carbon steel knife, we likewise recommend a sponge, hot water, and soap—just be sure to dry it or it will rust and blacken.

BOLSTER BLUES

If you have a knife with a full bolster, the band that joins the blade of the knife to its handle, we don't recommend using an electric sharpener: The thick end of the blade can't be run all the way through. Instead, use a manual sharpener.

MAKING THE MOST OF FRESH HERBS

One of the fastest, most economical ways to boost the flavor of food is to add fresh herbs. That's long been the philosophy in cuisines around the world, particularly in Southeast Asia and the Middle East, where fresh herbs are an essential component at meals (often, whole sprigs are heaped onto platters and eaten like vegetables alongside richer dishes). Happily, there are more varieties than ever available at farmers' markets and grocery stores. All the more reason to work them into your daily cooking repertoire.

8 HERBS YOU SHOULD BE COOKING WITH

We love the classic quartet of parsley, sage, rosemary, and thyme, but the herbs below are just as versatile and are worth snapping up if you come across them at the market or nursery.

1. Chervil
Profile: Grassy, anise-like sweetness
Try it in: Egg and fish dishes
Tip: Combine chervil with arugula, lettuce, and endive to make a classic mesclun mix.

2. Garlic Chives
Profile: Garlicky, crisp, juicy
Try them in: Stir-fries; as a substitute for scallions
Tip: Garlic chives are sometimes referred to as Chinese chives.

3. Curry Leaves
Profile: Lemony, cumin-y, menthol-y
Try them in: Curries; potato and rice dishes
Tip: Curry leaves are unrelated to curry powder.

4. Lavender
Profile: Floral, perfumy
Try it in: Syrups, custard, shortbread
Tip: Buy culinary, not ornamental, lavender, and use it sparingly.

5. Lemon Verbena
Profile: Minty lemon grass, menthol-y
Try it in: Infusions (drinks, syrups, jams, custards); salads (tender leaves only); with berries or stone fruit
Tip: Steeped in boiling water, it makes a fragrant tisane.

6. Makrut Lime Leaves
Profile: Tangy, bright, floral
Try them in: Thai curries and soups; cocktails and limeade; rice dishes; flavored salt
Tip: Use them as a fragrant garnish for proteins and vegetables by cutting out their tough spines and slicing the leaves very thin.

7. Shiso
Profile: Minty, citrusy, bitter, medicinal
Try it in: Spring rolls, cold noodle salads, green salads (tear tough leaves), fried rice
Tip: Red shiso tastes more bitter than the green variety.

8. Sorrel
Profile: Juicy, lemony, tart
Try it in: Creamy soups, salsa verde, salads; incorporated into a sauce; as a garnish for salmon or lamb
Tip: Sorrel can be cooked similarly to spinach or Swiss chard, but like those tender greens, it shrinks way down, so start with an ample amount.

TWO BASIC CATEGORIES: HEARTY AND DELICATE

We classify most herbs as either hearty or delicate. These adjectives refer not only to their textural qualities (leaves that are sturdy and tough versus delicate and tender) but also to the strength or volatility of their flavor compounds; in general, volatile flavor compounds in hearty herbs are somewhat more heat-stable than those in delicate varieties. These categories also help clarify the best ways to prep, store, and cook most herbs.

HEARTY HERBS
Rosemary, thyme, oregano, sage, marjoram

DELICATE HERBS
Basil, parsley, cilantro, dill, mint, chives, tarragon

NOT ALL HERBS CAN TAKE THE HEAT

Due to variability in the strength and volatility of their flavor compounds, hearty and delicate herbs behave differently when cooked. Here are general guidelines.

Hearty Add early in cooking to ensure maximum flavor extraction.
Delicate Use as a garnish or add for the last minute of cooking to preserve flavor and color.

PREP SCHOOL

Wash, Then Salad-Spin Dry

After rinsing delicate herbs, thoroughly dry them by spinning them in a paper towel–lined salad spinner. (Hearty herbs don't harbor much grit, but if they are dusty, you can give them a quick rinse.)

Pack Lightly When Measuring

Press down slightly on herbs in the measuring cup to remove air pockets; do not pack them down firmly.

Chop and Mince Like a Pro

Running your knife over a loose pile is inefficient. Here's a better way:

To chop: Gather leaves into tight pile and hold with your nonknife hand. Use rocking motion to slice thin. Turn sliced leaves 90 degrees and repeat.

To mince: Chop, then go over pile again by placing fingertips of your nonknife hand flat on top of knife spine and moving blade up and down with your knife hand while using knife tip as pivot.

SAVVY STORAGE

Proper herb storage is all about controlling the leaves' exposure to moisture. Hearty herbs are adapted to survive in dry weather by taking in moisture through their leaves, so it's important to keep them dry. Delicate herbs take in and release a lot of water and therefore must be kept moist lest they wilt (but they should not touch liquid, which encourages rot).

Favorite Storage Methods

When stored properly, many herbs will last at least a week.

Hearty Store in original packaging or open zipper-lock bag; refrigerate.

Delicate Wrap in slightly damp paper towels, place in open zipper-lock bag, and refrigerate.

USE SPRIGS FROM ROOT TO BLOSSOM

While some herbs don't have much use beyond their leaves, others (mostly delicate varieties) are edible up and down the sprig. Here's a breakdown of usable components besides leaves and their suggested applications.

Roots

Cilantro roots are aromatic, pungent, and citrusy. Cilantro stems with the roots attached are commonly found at Asian markets. The whole plant is increasingly available at conventional markets, too. Puree the roots into marinades and curry pastes; store unused roots in the freezer.

Seeds

Some herbs (such as cilantro and dill) produce aromatic seeds that can be used whole, crushed, or ground.

Stems

Some herbs (such as cilantro, parsley, and basil) have delicate stems that can be minced or chopped with the leaves or pureed into sauces (such as pesto), curry pastes, or soups.

Blossoms

In general, herb blossoms taste like their parent plants. Add them whole to salads or use them as an elegant garnish.

UPDATING YOUR SPICE COLLECTION

Put aside the usual preground powders and commercial blends. It's time to get more out of your spice collection. Spices provide aromatic warmth and vibrancy that can perk up even the simplest dish, from eggs to french fries to salads. But stocking a range of spices is only part of what will make you a better cook; you also need to understand how to eke out a spice's most dynamic flavors.

BROADEN YOUR SPICE PANTRY WITH THESE 8 ADDITIONS

As supermarket options continue to expand, so, too, should your spice collection. Here are a handful of our current favorites and a few ideas for how to use them.

Aleppo Pepper

What it is: Crushed dried red Halaby chiles from Syria and Turkey

Profile: Complex, raisiny sweetness; moderate, slow-to-build heat

How to use: Add to marinade for kebabs; braise with greens; sprinkle over avocado toast

Cardamom (Green)

What it is: Seed pods from *Elettaria cardamomum* plant in ginger family

Profile: Piney, floral; warm finish

How to use: Bake ground spice into cakes; sauté whole pods with onions for pilaf; braise crushed pods with lamb

Fennel Pollen

What it is: Pollen harvested from wild fennel; traditional to Tuscan cooking

Profile: Honey-like, savory, delicately crunchy

How to use: Add to dipping oil; sprinkle over lemony pasta, creamy soups, pork dishes

Gochugaru

What it is: Blend of crushed dried red Korean chiles that range in heat

Profile: Smoky-sweet, fruity, moderately spicy

How to use: Add to spice paste for kimchi; stir into chili oil; sprinkle over popcorn and caramelized onions

Mustard Seeds

What they are: Seeds from mustard plant; can be black, brown, or yellow

Profile: Crisp, bright, mild, sweet (yellow); pungent, bitter, spicy (brown, black)

How to use: Add to chutneys, brine for pickles, rubs for roast pork/ham

Smoked Paprika (Sweet) (Pimentón Dulce)

What it is: Sweet red peppers dried over oak and then ground

Profile: Rich, woodsy smoke; fruity sweetness

How to use: Mix into chorizo; sprinkle over fried or mashed potatoes, hummus, eggs

Sumac

What it is: Ground dried berries of sumac bush; usually processed with salt

Profile: Lemony, earthy tang

How to use: Add to za'atar; sprinkle over fattoush or roasted root vegetables

White Peppercorns

What they are: Fermented, ripe black peppercorns with skins removed before drying

Profile: Floral and earthy, with a delicate heat

How to use: Add to hot-and-sour soup, dry rubs, stir-fries, batter for gingerbread, flavorings for steamed fish

5 TIPS FOR BUYING AND STORING SPICES

1 Buy whole spices to grind as needed. Grinding releases the volatile compounds that give a spice its flavor and aroma; these dissipate over time.

2 Buy in small quantities so that you can replace spices in a timely manner. Replace whole spices after two years and ground spices after one year. (To keep track of freshness, label the jars with the purchase date.)

3 Keep away from heat, light, and moisture, all of which shorten shelf life.

4 Store ground spices in glass jars. Some spices (including cloves and star anise) contain high concentrations of oils that will soften and dissolve plastic. (It's OK to store whole spices in plastic, since it's only when spices are ground that enough oils are released to cause a problem.)

5 Check freshness before use. Crumble a pinch of whole spice or dried powder between your fingers and smell. If it releases a lively aroma, it's still good. If the aroma and color of the spice have faded, it's time to restock.

CRACK IT FOR CRUNCH

When you want the crunch of cracked or coarsely ground spices—think peppercorns, cumin, coriander, and fennel—for coating meat or sprinkling over finished dishes, here are two good ways to go about it.

Mortar and Pestle

Use circular grinding motion, maintaining downward pressure at all times until spices are ground.

Skillet/Pot

On baking sheet, rock bottom edge of skillet over 2 tablespoons of whole spices until spices crack.

THE FINEST GRINDER

A dedicated spice grinder such as our favorite, the **Krups Coffee and Spice Grinder,** grinds whole spices to a fine, even grind and makes it easy to capitalize on the richer flavors and aromas of freshly ground spices.

3 WAYS TO TREAT YOUR SPICES

The way you treat a spice can impact its flavor in a dish.

Blooming alters a spice's flavor, bringing out deeper, more complex notes. Dissolving the aromatic compounds in fat allows them to spread evenly throughout the dish and binds them so that they don't readily evaporate during cooking.
BEST FOR: Whole and ground spices

Toasting in a dry skillet applies dry heat directly to spices. It brings their oils to the surface, resulting in bolder aroma; it also causes desirable chemical transformations in the aroma compounds. It's a method we reserve for whole spices, since toasting preground spices drives off too many flavor compounds.
BEST FOR: Whole spices

Leaving spices raw preserves bright, clean top notes that get lost if you apply heat to them.
BEST FOR: Whole and ground spices

HARNESSING THE FLAVOR OF GARLIC

Sniff an intact clove of garlic, and you won't smell anything. But smash that same clove, and it comes to life, unleashing a ripe, complex pungency that defies its small size and plays an integral role in just about every cuisine around the world. That transformative nature, and its tremendous range of flavor and aroma, is what makes garlic so compelling to cooks. Depending on how you prepare it, garlic can be the hot sting in aioli and mojo; the aromatic depth in countless stir-fries, curries, and braises; or a mellow, creamy, caramelized spread for slathering on bread or mixing into doughs or sauces. It has been a culinary staple since as far back as ancient Mesopotamia—scholars have uncovered references to garlic and other alliums in recipes chiseled in cuneiform script on tablets—as well as a respected form of medicine and the subject of great lore and legend.

GARLIC GUIDELINES

DON'T BUY GARLIC THAT SMELLS LIKE GARLIC

A head of fresh garlic should not have any aroma, since its characteristic pungency is produced only when the cloves' cells are damaged. Strong-smelling garlic has likely been mishandled during transport or storage. To demonstrate this, we put a few heads of garlic in a plastic bag and whacked at them with a rolling pin (forcefully but not so much that it left visible damage). After a day in storage, they were pungent, while heads that we hadn't mistreated had no aroma at all.

KEEP GARLIC COOL, DRY, AND IN THE DARK

Garlic is highly sensitive to temperature and exposure to sunlight. Following harvest, garlic should be stored away from direct sunlight in low humidity to prevent sprouting and spoilage. Garlic should not be refrigerated, as the combination of low temperature and moisture will initiate spoilage.

PEEL GARLIC THE FAST, EASY WAY

Remove the outer papery skin of a garlic head, place the head in a 2-cup wide-mouth Mason jar, screw on the lid, and vigorously shake the jar for 30 seconds. Pour out the cloves and inspect them. If any still have skins, put them back in the jar and repeat.

TAKE ADVANTAGE OF PREPEELED CLOVES

If you go through a lot of garlic, using prepeeled cloves is a convenient alternative to peeling fresh ones, and their flavor can be perfectly acceptable. Just be wary of their shelf life, which tends to be shorter than that of a head of garlic stored in a cool, dry place (about two weeks versus several weeks, in our testing). Also make sure to carefully inspect what you buy: The cloves should look firm and white with a matte finish; avoid any that look yellow or shriveled or give off an overly pungent aroma.

DON'T DIS GARLIC POWDER

Garlic powder gets a bad rap—but it shouldn't. The sandy powder (which is simply dehydrated ground garlic) isn't meant to replace the fresh stuff but rather is a toasty, subtly sweet-savory seasoning that works well in concert with fresh garlic as well as alongside other spices in everything from dry rubs to chili, mashed potatoes, and garlic bread.

The trick to using garlic powder is to hydrate it before cooking, which can be done by mixing it with a little water before adding it to a dish—or it will happen naturally when it's applied to wet foods such as raw meat. Hydrating the powder before heating "awakens" the flavor-producing enzyme, alliinase, which goes dormant when producers dry the garlic (drying happens below 140 degrees to avoid deactivating the alliinase), whereas heating the powder before hydrating it would kill the enzyme—and any potential for garlic flavor.

HOW GARLIC FLAVOR WORKS

At the root of garlic flavor is an enzyme called **ALLIINASE**, which is released the moment the cloves' cells are damaged and jump-starts a pivotal chemical reaction. The alliinase acts on a sulfur-containing molecule called **ALLIIN**, converting it to a harsh-tasting molecule called **ALLICIN**. Allicin in turn immediately starts to change into a variety of other, often more mellow-tasting compounds, all of which in tandem are responsible for the flavor of garlic.

Manipulating garlic flavor is all about controlling the creation and subsequent evolution of allicin, and the following four variables are some of the tools cooks have to make that happen.

Knife Work

STRENGTHENS FLAVOR The more you break down garlic cells by chopping, the more allicin is produced. One minced clove of garlic has more flavor than one sliced clove of garlic, which has more flavor than one crushed clove of garlic.

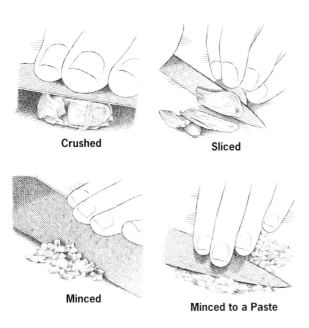

Crushed

Sliced

Minced

Minced to a Paste

Heat

MELLOWS FLAVOR AND INTRODUCES COMPLEXITY AND SWEETNESS Heating an intact clove of garlic to above 140 degrees deactivates the enzyme alliinase—the thing that starts the whole reaction in the first place—so cutting that garlic won't produce any additional garlic flavor. Heat also tames garlic's intensity after chopping, converting its raw-tasting compounds to mellower ones called polysulphides. Its sugars and amino acids undergo the Maillard reaction, turning the garlic flavor complex and sweet; just beware of overbrowning garlic, which will produce bitter-tasting compounds.

Time

INTRODUCES COMPLEXITY AND STRENGTHENS FLAVOR If you let cut garlic sit, more and more allicin will be produced and evolve into other compounds, making it taste more complex as well as stronger. Even a 10-minute rest before cooking will increase garlic's complexity. Just know that in raw garlic applications like aioli, while the allium's flavor will grow more complex with time, it will also intensify and may eventually become unpalatable.

Acid

MELLOWS FLAVOR Steeping just-minced garlic in an acidic liquid (such as lemon juice) inhibits the alliinase so that less harsh-tasting allicin is developed. This technique is especially handy when applied to preparations such as Caesar dressing and hummus, where there's no cooking to tame it and you want just a hint of raw-garlic bite.

ALL ABOUT OILS

Here's everything you need to know about selecting, using, and storing cooking oils.

VEGETABLE OIL

Best for: Baking, sautéing, and frying. "Vegetable oil" encompasses any edible oil made from plant sources, including nuts, seeds, and grains. Cooking oils labeled "vegetable oil" are usually made from soybeans. Most commercial vegetable oils have been refined, bleached, and deodorized so they have a neutral flavor and high smoking point.

CORN OIL

Best for: Frying and baking. Corn oil can taste sour when used in mayonnaise or dressings. When heated, its compounds change for the better, so food fried in corn oil tastes great.

EXTRA-VIRGIN OLIVE OIL

Best for: Sautéing, dressings, and finishing dishes. Extra-virgin olive oil, from the first cold-pressing of olives, is the highest grade and can taste grassy, peppery, buttery, or nutty. Uncooked applications let these flavors shine.

AVOCADO OIL

Best for: Finishing drizzles (unrefined); sautéing and frying (refined). Unrefined avocado oil has a buttery, grassy flavor. Refined avocado oil has a neutral taste and the highest smoking point of any cooking oil.

COCONUT OIL

Best for: Baking and sautéing. Unrefined coconut oil has a strong coconut flavor. We prefer refined coconut oil, which is versatile and virtually odorless—a great vegan alternative to butter.

CANOLA OIL AND SOYBEAN OIL

Best for: Baking, sautéing, and uncooked applications. Note that some cooks detect fishy or metallic aromas when these oils are heated.

PEANUT OIL

Best for: Baking, sautéing, and frying. Just be aware that it costs twice as much as canola or corn oil and is off-limits for people with peanut allergies.

TOASTED SESAME OIL

Best for: Dressings, sauces, sautéing, and finishing dishes. Toasted sesame oil is great for adding deep, nutty flavor to meat, fish, or vegetables. Don't substitute plain sesame oil (which is flavorless) for toasted sesame oil.

RICE BRAN OIL

Best for: Sautéing and frying. Refined rice bran oil has a high smoking point and mild flavor that make it ideal for cooking at high temperatures. We've found it to be a superior alternative to canola oil, though it's nearly twice as expensive.

WALNUT OIL

Best for: Sauces, vinaigrettes, and finishing dishes. Toasty unrefined walnut oil adds character when tossed with grains, pasta, or vegetables or incorporated into sauces or vinaigrettes. Avoid if you have tree-nut allergies.

BEST PURCHASING AND STORAGE PRACTICES

All oil will eventually go rancid. To ensure that your oil can be used—and for as long as possible—we have a few tips.

1 Look for a Harvest Date

The age of the oil is important. For many vegetable oils, it's not possible to find out when they were made. But when it comes to buying olive oil, you can often find the harvest date printed on the label of high-end oils and some supermarket olive oils such as our favorites, which are made by **Bertolli** and **California Olive Ranch**. Check this date to ensure that you're securing the freshest bottle possible. Alternatively, some labels cite an expiration date, which producers typically calculate as two years from harvesting.

2 Monitor How Long You've Had the Oil

Unopened olive oil can go rancid one year after the harvest date. Once opened, olive oil has a shelf life of about three months. Vegetable, canola, corn, and peanut oils have longer shelf lives; they should be replaced four months after opening.

3 Buy Only What You'll Use

Regardless of the type of oil, don't buy in bulk unless you plan to use all that oil within its shelf life.

4 Keep Oil in a Cool, Dark Place

To maximize shelf life, move oil containers off your countertop and away from the stove, as heat and sunlight can accelerate the oxidation process. It's better to keep oil in a cool, dark pantry or cupboard or, as Eric Decker, a professor in the Department of Food Science at the University of Massachusetts Amherst, recommends, in the refrigerator, where cold temperatures will really slow oxidation. Once refrigerated, oils keep for about six months after opening. Just be aware that some oils may solidify in the cold and must be warmed before use. A dark bottle can also help impede oxidation, so consider buying products that come in one.

VISUAL CUES FOR COOKING WITH OIL

The temperature of your oil can make a big difference in the flavor and texture of the food you cook in it. Here's a guide to the different terms we use when cooking in oil, what temperatures they correspond to, and some visual cues to help you see whether you've hit the mark.

Shimmering

Describes oil that has been heated to about 275 degrees. We heat oil to shimmering mostly when shallow-frying cutlets.
VISUAL CUE: Oil gleams and moves in ripples around the pan.

Bubbling

We generally deep-fry food at a starting temperature between 325 and 375 degrees—we've found that these temperatures are best for generating a light, crispy texture. Once the food is added to the oil, the temperature will drop; as the food cooks, the oil should remain somewhere between 250 and 325 degrees (depending on your recipe).
VISUAL CUE: Oil sizzles and fine bubbles appear when you drop in food.

PRO TIP: For the most accurate results, use a clip-on probe thermometer to monitor your oil temperature.

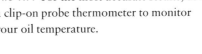

Smoking

Describes oil that has been heated to its smoking point, which can vary between 350 and 520 degrees. We heat oil to smoking when we want quick, even, and thorough browning while searing a steak or stir-frying. If the oil is below the smoking point when the food is added, browning will take too long and the food will overcook. Don't worry too much about overheating the oil; as long as you have your food at the ready, there's little risk since the oil will cool quickly once you add the food. If you have overheated it, you'll know because the oil will turn dark. In those cases, throw out the oil and start over.
VISUAL CUE: Multiple wisps of smoke rise from the pan.

GARNISHES YOU CAN'T LIVE WITHOUT

There's no better way to fend off dinner doldrums than keeping on hand a variety of ultraquick and vibrant sauces, seasonings, and toppings. Every cook needs an arsenal of finishing touches—tangy chutneys, piquant pastes, rich dressings, earthy spice blends, and seasoned salts—that can breathe new life into chicken breasts, jazz up vegetables, and add visual, textural, and flavor contrast to make a dish pop. Behold a larder's worth of our favorites, both familiar classics and modern riffs. We've organized them by flavor and texture profiles and offered suggested uses, but these are just starting points; use your imagination.

TANGY

Green Tomato Chutney

What it is: Sweet-sour preserve
Serve with: Rich meat, sausage, cheese, sandwiches
Total time: 3 hours **Yield:** 2 cups
Bring 2 pounds green tomatoes, cored and cut into 1-inch chunks; ¾ cup sugar; ¾ cup distilled white vinegar; 1 teaspoon coriander seeds; 1 teaspoon table salt; and ½ teaspoon red pepper flakes to simmer in saucepan. Cook until thickened, about 40 minutes. Let cool completely, about 2 hours. Stir in 2 teaspoons lemon juice just before serving.
Tip: To expedite cooling, spread the chutney into an even layer in a shallow dish.

Tangy Hoisin Sauce

What it is: Vinegary, gingery Asian soybean sauce
Serve with: Pork, chicken, rice, noodles, eggs
Total time: 5 minutes **Yield:** ½ cup
Stir ½ cup hoisin sauce, 2 thinly sliced scallions, 4 teaspoons rice vinegar, and 1 teaspoon grated fresh ginger in bowl until smooth.

CREAMY

Preserved-Lemon Aioli

What it is: Tangy garlic mayonnaise
Serve with: Vegetables, seafood, sandwiches
Total time: 5 minutes **Yield:** 1 cup
Process ¼ cup chopped preserved lemon, 3 large egg yolks, 1 tablespoon water, and 1 minced garlic clove in blender until well combined, about 30 seconds, scraping down sides of blender jar as needed. With blender running, slowly drizzle in ½ cup vegetable oil until aioli is emulsified and thickened, about 45 seconds, then drizzle in 1 tablespoon lemon juice and 2 tablespoons water.

Tahini Sauce

What it is: Middle Eastern sesame sauce
Serve with: Vegetables, french fries, falafel, grains, chicken, lamb
Total time: 5 minutes **Yield:** ⅓ cup
Whisk 2 tablespoons tahini, 2 tablespoons extra-virgin olive oil, 1 tablespoon lemon juice, 2 teaspoons honey, and pinch table salt together in small bowl.

FRESH

Tarragon-Lemon Gremolata

What it is: Italian herb garnish
Serve with: Soup, pasta, fish, vegetables
Total time: 5 minutes **Yield:** ¼ cup
Combine 2 tablespoons minced fresh tarragon, 2 tablespoons minced fresh parsley, 2 teaspoons grated lemon zest, and 1 minced garlic clove in bowl.
Tip: Prepare the gremolata just before serving to prevent the garlic flavor from becoming too sharp.

Mint Persillade

What it is: French herb sauce
Serve with: Meat, fish, vegetables
Total time: 5 minutes **Yield:** 1 cup
Pulse 1 cup fresh mint leaves; 1 cup fresh parsley leaves; 3 peeled garlic cloves; 3 anchovy fillets, rinsed and patted dry; 1 teaspoon grated lemon zest; ½ teaspoon table salt; and ⅛ teaspoon pepper in food processor until finely chopped, 15 to 20 pulses. Add 1 tablespoon lemon juice and pulse to combine. Transfer to bowl and whisk in ⅓ cup extra-virgin olive oil.

SEASONED SALTS

Salt infused with herbs, spices, or other flavorings delivers distinct, punchy flavor. Store-bought versions are expensive, but it's easy to make your own:
Combine ½ cup kosher salt and flavoring (see chart at right) in small bowl. Spread mixture on large plate and microwave, stirring every 60 seconds, until only slightly damp (mixture will continue to dry as it cools).

	FLAVORING	MICROWAVE
SRIRACHA SALT	⅓ cup sriracha	6–8 minutes
MUSTARD SALT	¼ cup Dijon mustard and ¼ cup whole-grain mustard	6–8 minutes
SMOKY SALT	1 teaspoon liquid smoke	1–2 minutes

SPICY

Spicy Honey

What it is: Spicy, tangy honey
Serve with: Vegetables, pizza
Total time: 15 minutes **Yield:** ¼ cup
Stir ¼ cup honey and 2 tablespoons hot sauce together in liquid measuring cup. Microwave until boiling, about 1 minute. Continue to microwave in 20-second intervals until reduced to ¼ cup, about 1 minute longer. Let cool for 10 minutes.

Korean Chile Sauce

What it is: Sweet and spicy sauce
Serve with: Stew, chili, rice bowls, noodles, macaroni and cheese, eggs
Total time: 5 minutes **Yield:** ⅔ cup
Whisk ¼ cup gochujang, 3 tablespoons water, 2 tablespoons toasted sesame oil, and 1 teaspoon sugar together in small bowl.
Tip: Store in a squeeze bottle for easy drizzling.

ONE-INGREDIENT FINISHERS

These minimalist seasonings enhance food without distracting from its flavor. Just be sure to use fresh, high-quality ingredients.

Citrus zest: Grate over vegetables, chicken, fish.
Grilled lemon halves: Squeeze over meat and seafood.
Extra-virgin olive oil: Drizzle over soup, salad, seafood, steak, pasta, grains.
Parmesan or Pecorino Romano cheese: Grate or shave over soup, salad, pasta, grains.
Vinegar: Drizzle a few drops over soup, stew, sauces, fried food.

CRISPY/CRUNCHY

Crispy Bread-Crumb Topping

What it is: Seasoned panko bread crumbs
Serve with: Vegetables, meat, fish, pasta
Total time: 10 minutes
Yield: 2 tablespoons
Grind 2 tablespoons panko bread crumbs in spice grinder or mortar and pestle to medium-fine crumbs. Transfer panko to 12-inch skillet, add 1 tablespoon vegetable oil, and stir. Toast over medium-low heat for 5 to 7 minutes. Off heat, add ¾ teaspoon kosher salt, ¼ teaspoon pepper, and ¼ teaspoon red pepper flakes.

Candied Bacon Bits

What it is: Sugar- and vinegar-glazed bacon bits
Serve with: Creamy soup, salad, pasta, eggs, dips
Total time: 10 minutes **Yield:** ¼ cup
Cut 4 slices bacon into ½-inch pieces and cook in 10-inch nonstick skillet over medium heat until crispy, 5 to 7 minutes. Remove bacon from skillet and discard fat. Return bacon to skillet and add 2 teaspoons packed dark brown sugar and ½ teaspoon cider vinegar. Cook over low heat, stirring constantly, until bacon is evenly coated. Transfer to plate and let cool completely.

Za'atar

What it is: Earthy, bright Middle Eastern spice blend
Serve with: Dips, meatballs, kebabs, roasted potatoes
Total time: 5 minutes **Yield:** ⅓ cup
Grind 2 tablespoons dried thyme and 1 tablespoon dried oregano in spice grinder or mortar and pestle until finely ground and powdery. Transfer to bowl and stir in 1½ tablespoons sumac, 1 tablespoon toasted sesame seeds, and ¼ teaspoon table salt.

Pistachio Dukkah

What it is: Egyptian nut, seed, and spice blend
Serve with: Olive oil as dip for bread, soup, seafood
Total time: 5 minutes **Yield:** ½ cup
Coarsely grind 1½ tablespoons toasted sesame seeds in spice grinder or mortar and pestle; transfer to bowl. Finely grind 1½ teaspoons toasted coriander seeds, ¾ teaspoon toasted cumin seeds, and ½ teaspoon toasted fennel seeds in grinder. Transfer to bowl with sesame seeds. Stir in 2 tablespoons shelled pistachios, toasted and chopped fine; ½ teaspoon table salt; and ½ teaspoon pepper.

Microwave-Fried Shallots, Garlic, or Leeks

Serve with: Soup, salad, stir-fries, rice, burgers
Total time: 20 minutes
Combine ½ cup vegetable oil and allium (see chart below) in medium bowl. Microwave for 5 minutes. Stir and continue to microwave 2 minutes longer. Repeat stirring and microwaving in 2-minute increments until beginning to brown, then repeat stirring and microwaving in 30-second increments until deep golden brown. Using slotted spoon, transfer to paper towel–lined plate; season with table salt. Let drain and crisp, about 5 minutes.

SHALLOTS Yield: ⅓ cup	3, sliced thin
GARLIC Yield: ½ cup	½ cup cloves, sliced or minced (After frying, dust garlic with 1 teaspoon confectioners' sugar to offset any bitterness before seasoning with salt.)
LEEKS Yield: 1 cup	1, white and light green parts only, halved lengthwise, sliced into very thin 2-inch-long strips, washed thoroughly, dried, and tossed with 2 tablespoons all-purpose flour (which accelerates browning)

Tip: Save the allium-infused oil for incorporating into dressings, mayonnaise, stir-fries, or curries or drizzling over soups or stews.

GETTING TO KNOW YOUR OVEN

Knowledge is power … and knowledge about how your oven works can make you a better cook.

OVEN BASICS

BROILER ELEMENT

UPPER-MIDDLE POSITION

LOWER-MIDDLE POSITION

HEATING ELEMENT
Heat is generated from here and rises

PREHEAT YOUR OVEN

Most ovens need at least 15 minutes to preheat fully. If you don't preheat your oven sufficiently, your food will spend more time in the oven and will suffer the consequences. Also, be sure to position the racks as directed.

Heating Patterns

The heating element for most standard ovens is located on the bottom. The heat from that element is carried to the food, in part, by moving air currents in a process called convection. The heat rises up around the food, reflects off the top of the oven, and circulates around the oven chamber. A convection setting, which could more accurately be called forced convection, uses a fan to accelerate the moving of the air and heat. Food generally dries, crisps, and browns more rapidly when cooked with the convection setting.

Rack Placement

Because the heat comes from the bottom, foods placed on lower oven racks will receive more direct heat on the bottom. Foods placed on higher oven racks will receive heat reflected off the oven ceiling onto the top of the food. So if you want to brown the bottom of something, place it on a lower rack; if you want to brown the top, place it on a higher rack. Foods placed on racks in the middle will have a balance of both.

Switch and Rotate

Even new or freshly calibrated ovens have hot and cool spots. Thus, you should rotate most foods you cook in your oven, and if you are placing food on more than one oven rack, you should switch the positions of the food halfway through baking/roasting to ensure even cooking and browning.

BROILING 101

With baking and roasting, indirect hot air circulating through the oven does the cooking. But in broiling, the cooking is accomplished through direct heat from above. And because the broiler's heat is generally more intense than that of the oven, it cooks foods faster, particularly on the exterior. Broiling is more akin to grilling than it is to oven roasting.

THREE TIPS FOR BROILING SUCCESS

1 When in doubt, go for "high." In our recipes, we don't specify broiler settings, but since the point of broiling is usually to expose food to intense heat, turn it up!

2 Measure the distance between the heating element and the oven rack; our broiling recipes specify this measurement rather than a rack position such as "middle" or "top."

3 When broiling on a rimmed baking sheet, set a wire rack inside it to elevate your food and prevent the bottom from steaming.

USE AN OVEN THERMOMETER

Unless you have your oven routinely calibrated, there is a good chance that its temperature readings may be off. Inaccurate temperatures will dramatically impact your food, leaving it underdone on the inside or over-browned and tough. To avoid such problems, we recommend purchasing an inexpensive oven thermometer like the **CDN Pro Accurate Oven Thermometer**, and checking it once the oven is preheated.

OVEN QUESTION

What is the self-cleaning function?

ANSWER

Most ovens have a self-cleaning function. When you activate it, the oven door locks and the heating element heats to its highest temperature, which is often up to 1,000 degrees. The supercharged heat incinerates caked-on matter, making it easy to remove with a damp cloth when the cycle is done and the oven has cooled.

TIP: Unless your oven's instructions specify otherwise, remove the oven racks before activating self-cleaning—they can warp in the intense heat.

KNOWING WHEN FOOD IS DONE

Don't flub a beautifully rosy steak or a perfectly chewy batch of cookies because you couldn't pinpoint the moment to stop cooking.

MEAT AND POULTRY

Don't Forget Carryover Cooking

The temperature of many proteins will continue to rise once they're taken off heat and allowed to rest before serving, a phenomenon known as carryover cooking. This is particularly true for thick roasts cooked at high temperatures, which must be removed from the heat as much as 10 to 15 degrees below the desired doneness. However, we've learned that carryover cooking is negligible in burgers, whole chickens, and whole fish; the loose grain of the burgers and the hollow cavities of the chicken and fish allow heat to escape, so these items should be cooked to the desired degree of doneness.

	COOK TO	SERVE AT
Beef/Lamb		
Rare	115°F–120°F	125°F
Medium-Rare	120°F–125°F	130°F
Medium	130°F–135°F	140°F
Medium-Well	140°F–145°F	150°F
Well-Done	150°F–155°F	160°F
Ground Beef		
Medium-Rare*	125°F	125°F
Medium*	130°F	130°F
Medium-Well*	140°F	140°F
Well-Done	160°+	160°+
Pork		
Medium	140°F–145°F	150°F
Well-Done	150°F–155°F	160°F
Chicken		
White Meat	160°F	160°F
Dark Meat	175°F	175°F

Pink Poultry and Pork Can Be Safe

Pink-tinted turkey and pork aren't necessarily undercooked. Often, the color is an indication that the pH of the meat is relatively high, which stabilizes the meat's pink pigment so that it doesn't break down when exposed to heat. As long as the meat registers the prescribed temperature, it's safe to eat.

*The USDA recommends cooking all ground beef to 160 degrees.

Cook Some Cuts Longer

Whereas most proteins are best cooked just to an internal temperature at which they're safe to eat, items like braised or slow-roasted dark-meat chicken, pork butt, and beef chuck often taste better when they're cooked longer. That's because these tough cuts are loaded with collagen, which breaks down into gelatin between 140 and 195 degrees and lubricates the muscle fibers, making them seem more moist and tender. It's also important to cook these cuts slowly; the longer they spend in that collagen breakdown window, the more tender the meat will be.

FISH AND SHELLFISH

	COOK TO
Salmon	
Farmed	125°F
Wild	120°F
Tuna	
Rare	110°F
Medium-Rare	125°F
Other	
White-Fleshed Fish	140°F
Sea Scallops	115°F
Lobster (tail)	140°F

SALMON: With less fat than farmed, wild salmon can dry out and overcook, so we cook it to a lower temperature.

SWORDFISH: The exterior of cooked swordfish should feel firm while the inside is just opaque but still moist.

SHRIMP: Cooked shrimp should look pink, feel just firm to the touch, and be slightly translucent at the center.

MUSSELS: An opened mussel is cooked, but one that remains closed might just need more cooking. Microwave it for 30 seconds; if it still doesn't open, discard it.

CLAMS: Open clams are done—and overcook quickly. Remove clams as they open and keep them warm in a covered bowl while the rest finish cooking.

BAKED GOODS AND SWEETS

We use a thermometer to gauge the doneness of not just proteins but also many baked goods and desserts. And when a food doesn't lend itself to temperature-taking, our visual guidelines can be just as helpful.

When to Use a Thermometer

YEAST BREADS

We have found that yeast bread can reach its recommended temperature for doneness well before the loaf is actually baked through. You should take the temperature of your bread as a backup, but stick to the recommended baking time and make sure the crust is well browned before removing the loaf from the oven and checking its temperature.

| Lean (e.g., sandwich bread) | 205–210°F |
| Enriched (e.g., brioche) | 190–195°F |

LOAF-PAN LOAVES: Insert the thermometer from the side, just above the pan edge, and direct it at a downward angle into the center of the loaf.

FREE-FORM LOAVES: Tip the loaf (cover your hand with a dish towel) and insert the probe through the bottom crust into the center.

CHEESECAKE

NEW YORK CHEESECAKE: The velvety consistency of this style is achieved when the center registers 165 degrees.

OTHER BAKED CHEESECAKES: For an all-over creamy consistency, we bake them to between 145 and 150 degrees.

CUSTARDS AND PUDDINGS

STOVETOP CUSTARDS: We cook custards like crème anglaise to a relatively low 175 degrees to prevent the egg proteins from curdling.

ICE CREAM BASES: Custard bases for ice cream should be thicker than conventional stovetop custards, so we cook them to 180 degrees.

BAKED CUSTARDS: Applications such as flan and crème brûlée should jiggle but not slosh when gently shaken and should register between 170 and 180 degrees (depending on the ratio of eggs to other ingredients).

When to Use Visual Cues

CAKES, MUFFINS, AND QUICK BREADS

THIN (LESS THAN ¾-INCH) ITEMS: Test for springback: Gently press the center of the food; it should feel springy and resilient. If your finger leaves an impression or the center jiggles, it's not done.

THICK (AT LEAST ¾-INCH) ITEMS: Use a skewer: Poke a wooden skewer or toothpick into the center; it should emerge with no more than a few crumbs attached. If you see moist batter or lots of crumbs, bake it longer.

COOKIES, BAR COOKIES, AND BROWNIES

For chewy centers, underbaking is key—but tricky to gauge. Look for these visual cues.

DROP COOKIES: Cookies should hang over the edge of a metal spatula blade.

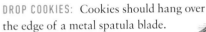

STAMPED AND SLICED COOKIES:
• Edges should be light brown and centers slightly moist.
• For uniformly crisp cookies, remove the cookies when the edges are deep golden brown and crisp, and the centers yield to slight pressure.

BROWNIES:
• For perfect brownies, poke a wooden toothpick into the center and look for a few moist crumbs; moist batter means they're not ready. Overbaking will yield dry results with diminished chocolate flavor.

PIE CRUST

Pastry should be well browned (deep color = deep flavor).

FRUIT PIES

Filling should bubble at the edges and in the vents.

FOR THE BEST RESULTS, GET OUT YOUR THERMOMETER

The axiom "knowledge is power" holds especially true in the kitchen—the more you know about what's going on inside your food as it cooks, the more you can control the result. That's why we're so gung ho about using an instant-read thermometer in the kitchen, as more control means less stress and better results.

CUTTING-EDGE TECHNIQUES

Here we go really granular on how to prep some everyday vegetables so that even cooks who already know the basics are sure to pick up a thing or two.

BROCCOLI

Here's how to cut broccoli so that its disparate parts cook evenly.

REMOVE FLORETS
Hold broccoli upside down on cutting board. Using tip of chef's knife, remove florets from stalk, cutting where floret stem meets larger stalk.

CUT FLORETS
Lay florets on cutting board. Hold chef's knife with pinch grip and 1 floret with other hand. Start with tip of knife at top of floret and cut down through floret and attached stem to divide each into even pieces. Repeat with remaining florets.

SQUARE STALK
Place stalk on cutting board. Trim off top and bottom. Hold chef's knife with pinch grip and stalk with claw grip. Starting with tip of knife at top of stalk, trim off woody outer layer. Repeatedly rotate stalk 90 degrees to trim other 3 sides.

PEEL AND CUT STALK
Use vegetable peeler to remove any tough outer part of stalk missed by chef's knife. Return stalk to cutting board. Hold chef's knife with pinch grip and stalk with claw grip, and slice stalk into oblong coins or planks, as directed in recipe.

TIP: Cutting florets close to where they meet the stalk will minimize waste, but you may need to trim the tough bottom (about ½ inch) of larger, outer florets.

BUTTERNUT SQUASH

Don't be daunted by butternut squash's bulbous shape and dense flesh. Follow our method, and you won't need to buy precut squash ever again.

BEST KNIFE GRIP: We employ the "pinch grip" for the cuts below. This means pinching the blade with your thumb and forefinger where it meets the handle, which gives you the most control and leverage over the whole length of the knife.

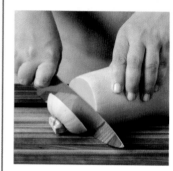

TRIM AND PEEL
Holding sharp chef's knife with pinch grip, position front part of blade on squash about ¼ inch from stem end. Push down and forward, using length of blade to cut through stem end. Rotate squash 180 degrees and repeat with bottom. Use vegetable peeler to peel skin.

TIP: For silky cooked squash, peel the white fibrous flesh just below the skin (about an ⅛-inch-thick layer) until the squash is completely orange.

DIVIDE
Holding bulb with 1 hand and continuing with pinch grip, cut in half where neck and bulb meet.

CUT NECK
Stand neck on 1 cut end for stability. Holding piece steady, place tip of knife on squash and apply gentle downward pressure to create even-size planks; thickness will depend on recipe. Rotate planks and cut into even-size pieces according to recipe.

TIP: If the squash neck is longer than 6 inches, cut it in half crosswise to create more-manageable pieces.

BUTTERNUT SQUASH (CONTINUED)

DESEED BULB
Stand bulb on 1 cut end for stability. Holding piece steady, apply gentle downward pressure to cut in half. Use spoon to scoop out seeds.

CUT BULB
Place each half cut side down. Hold squash with claw grip. Slice squash into even-size pieces according to recipe. As you cut, angle knife and follow curve of squash so each slice is an even thickness. (Knife blade won't be perpendicular to cutting board.) Rotate slices and cut into even-size pieces according to recipe.

CARROTS

The long, conical shape and dense texture of carrots make them a challenge to cut uniformly. Here's how to slice, dice, and julienne them into same-size pieces that look attractive and cook at the same rate.

How to Dice

CREATE FLAT SIDE
Cut peeled carrots into 2- to 3-inch lengths. With blade parallel to carrot, rest front of blade on end of carrot farthest away from you. Hold carrot with claw grip and apply downward pressure while moving blade forward to cut plank. Plank thickness will depend on desired size of dice.

CUT PLANKS

Lay piece on newly created flat side and slice more planks of equal thickness. As you cut, keep tip of knife blade in contact with cutting board using rocking motion: As heel of knife goes down, blade slices forward; then, blade slides back as heel is lifted up.

CARROTS (CONTINUED)

STACK
Stack several planks (including original plank sliced to create flat side). Using same cutting motion as above, cut sticks equal in thickness to planks.

TURN AND CHOP
Neatly bundle some sticks together, turn 90 degrees, and cut crosswise to complete size of dice desired.

TIP: Modified claw grip: To prevent stacked planks from slipping, use middle and index fingers to guide knife blade, and press pinkie and thumb against either end of stack.

How to Julienne

Cut carrots into lengths and create flat sides (see left). Then cut ⅛-inch-thick planks, and finally ⅛-inch-thick sticks, or julienne.

How to Slice

Basic slice: Hold whole carrot with claw grip and hold knife perpendicular to carrot. With tip of blade on cutting board and middle of blade on carrot, make even slices of desired thickness by pushing blade down and forward through carrot.

Bias cut: Use same motions as for slicing, but position knife at 45-degree angle relative to carrot. Change angle to vary length.

ONIONS AND SHALLOTS

Here's the best way to chop onions and mince shallots.

HALVE THROUGH ROOT END

First, create flat, stable surface: Using tip of chef's knife, cut off stem end of onion. Stand onion on cut surface with root end up. With front part of blade resting on root, push down and forward, using length of blade to cut onion in half from pole to pole. Peel onion, leaving root end intact.

TIP: We prefer a pinch grip when halving onions and prepping broccoli. Pinching the blade with your thumb and forefinger where it meets the handle allows you to choke up on the blade to get leverage over the whole length of the knife.

MAKE HORIZONTAL SLICES

Lay 1 half cut side down with poles parallel to edge of cutting board. If you cut with your right hand, root end of onion should be on left side. Place fingertips of your free hand on very top of onion and apply gentle pressure (you want enough pressure to hold onion in place but not so much that it squishes onion apart). With heel of knife resting on far side of onion, pull knife toward you while cutting inward toward root (a sharp knife is key here). Don't cut all the way through root end. For finely chopped onion, make closer cuts; for more coarsely chopped onion, space cuts farther apart.

TIP: Place the onion toward the front of the cutting board so that your fingers holding the knife handle don't hit the cutting board.

MAKE VERTICAL SLICES

Turn onion 90 degrees so root end is facing away from you. Using just tip of knife and pulling down and toward you, make evenly spaced vertical cuts. Cut up to—but not through— root end.

TIP: For more precision when cutting with the knife tip, use the finger grip, placing your thumb on the side of the blade and your forefinger on the spine.

CUT ACROSS SLICES

Rotate onion 90 degrees, returning it to original position with root end away from knife. Hold onion with claw grip. Start with front part of blade on onion and push down and forward; as heel of knife goes down, blade moves forward.

TIP: The "claw grip" allows your knuckles to help guide the side of the blade while your fingertips stay out of harm's way. After curving your fingers into a claw on top of the food, position your thumb behind them and press down to hold the food in place.

Mincing Shallots

A shallot's smaller size requires a slight adjustment to the onion technique.

MAKE HORIZONTAL AND VERTICAL SLICES

Use same strokes as for onions but switch to paring knife; its smaller size offers more control, and its thinner blade allows for more-precise cuts.

CUT ACROSS SLICES

Rock knife up and down with slight pivoting motion, without lifting knife tip off board, until shallot is evenly minced.

PEPPERS AND LARGE CHILES

Here's how to swiftly shave the ribs from bell peppers and large chiles and cut them into uniform pieces like a pro. Be sure to use a sharp knife, as the skin of peppers can be tough to cut through.

REMOVE TOP AND BOTTOM AND CORE

Remove ½ inch from stem end and from bottom. Set aside pieces. Stand pepper on its bottom so stem end is facing up. Using paring knife, cut around core through ribs. Pull core from pepper. Don't worry about removing all ribs and seeds at this point.

SLICE SIDE

Keeping pepper upright, use tip of chef's knife to make 1 vertical slice through side of pepper. Open up pepper and lay it on cutting board, skin side down.

REMOVE RIBS

Press gently so pepper lays as flat as possible. Hold end of pepper with 1 hand. Grasp chef's knife so blade is parallel to cutting board and you are cutting away from hand holding pepper. Slide knife along inside of pepper, cutting away any ribs and seeds.

SLICE OR DICE

Hold pepper with claw grip. Start with tip of knife on cutting board and front part of blade just above pepper, then push down and forward in rocking motion to cut strips. To dice, gather 6 strips, turn 90 degrees, and cut crosswise using same motion. Repeat with top and bottom pieces.

TIP: Use a modified pinch grip when holding the knife sideways. Turn the blade away from you 90 degrees. Instead of your thumb and forefinger pinching the blade, your thumb should be on the spine and your forefinger should be resting on the widest part of blade. Your middle finger should be against the bolster. This will allow you to follow the contours of the pepper.

POTATOES

Cutting potatoes into even pieces isn't the most challenging kitchen task, but it does take a little know-how. Be sure to use a pinch grip (i.e., pinch the blade with your thumb and forefinger where the blade meets the handle) for all these steps, as it gives you the most control over the entire length of the blade.

How to Slice

CUT FLAT BASE

Using chef's knife, cut thin slice from 1 side of potato to create stable base.

POSITION KNIFE

Rest potato on flat base. Hold knife blade parallel to length of potato for lengthwise slices and perpendicular for crosswise slices. For small potatoes, start with tip of knife on cutting board and middle of blade resting on potato. For larger potatoes such as russets, start with front of blade on potato.

CUT SLICES

Hold potato with claw grip and apply steady downward pressure with knife while moving blade forward to cut slices of desired thickness.

TIP: Starchy potatoes are notorious for clinging to the knife blade as you cut them. To prevent sticking, after each cut and before drawing back the blade, place the index finger of your claw hand on top of the piece(s) you cut to steady it (them), and then draw back the knife blade.

How to Dice

SLICE, THEN DICE

Cut slices as directed above; thickness should match desired size of dice (e.g., cut ½-inch slices for ½-inch dice). Stack several slices together and cut into batons, using claw grip and same motion as for slicing above. Turn 90 degrees and cut crosswise into dice.

CHAPTER 2

EGGS AND DAIRY

EGG BUYING AND STORAGE 101

When it comes to buying eggs, choosing between brown and white or large and jumbo is just the beginning. Here we clear up the confusion and give tips on how to store your eggs so that they stay their best, most delicious selves.

(Thank you to Professor Dianna Bourassa at the Department of Poultry Science at Auburn University in Alabama for her consultation.)

HERE'S WHAT MATTERS (AND WHAT DOESN'T) WHEN BUYING EGGS

Don't Sweat It: Five Things You Can Ignore

EGGSHELL COLOR While the most common shell colors are white and brown, you can find blue or even green eggs in some cartons. The good news: There's no nutritional or flavor difference between them, so pick whichever suits your fancy.

GRADES Grading indicates not only freshness but also the quality of the eggshell, with blemished or misshapen eggs given a lesser grade. Grade AA is the highest-quality egg you can get, but since it takes time to get eggs from farm to store, you'll find mostly Grade A on grocery shelves. Grade B eggs are often sent to food-processing facilities to be made into other egg products.

FARM FRESH This term is not regulated by the U.S. Department of Agriculture (USDA), so unless you're buying eggs from a local farmer, you can ignore it.

HORMONE-FREE This label is misleading. "It's illegal to give chickens hormones," says Bourassa. "So yes, they're hormone-free, but all eggs are."

VEGETARIAN FED This means that the hens are fed only vegetarian feed. This doesn't affect the flavor or nutritional value of the eggs, but since chickens are natural omnivores, a vegetarian diet "is actually not the best thing for their digestive system," says Bourassa.

It's Up to You: Terms You Might Care About

OMEGA-3 This means that the hens' feed contains omega-3 fatty acids, which could be in the form of fish oil, flaxseeds, or dehydrated alfalfa. Some people take omega-3 supplements to promote heart health.

PASTEURIZED Most eggs aren't pasteurized and are just washed and sanitized per USDA regulations. This washing removes bacteria and debris from the shell. In addition to being washed, pasteurized eggs are heated to kill bacteria such as salmonella. This can affect the protein structure of the egg white, which can in turn affect certain recipes that require stiffly whipped egg whites, like angel food cake. Those who are wary of using eggs in raw applications (such as in Caesar salad dressing) can use pasteurized eggs. However, they can be hard to find.

ORGANIC This means that the farm has been certified as organic by the USDA. The USDA requirements include feeding hens organic, non–genetically modified food; giving antibiotics only as needed; providing the hens with access to the outdoors; and using farming methods that "promote ecological balance and conserve biodiversity."

CERTIFIED HUMANE In order for eggs to be certified as humane, a nongovernmental third-party auditor checks to make sure that the hens are being treated humanely. Some requirements include providing access to perches and nest boxes, limiting flock density, and forbidding certain practices such as debeaking. Farmers are not required to provide outdoor access for the birds, but if they want a Certified Humane Pasture-Raised or Free-Range designation, they must meet further requirements set by the third-party auditor.

EGG SIZE: ONE THING THAT REALLY MATTERS IN TERMS OF COOKING

The USDA determines egg size by the weight of a dozen eggs. Common egg sizes include medium, large, extra-large, and jumbo. Peewee is the smallest size, but you would rarely, if ever, see peewee eggs in the grocery store. We use large eggs, which is a standard size and what we recommend for the best results when using our recipes, particularly when baking. But if you're just making yourself a fried egg, the size of the egg doesn't matter as much.

Egg Weights

If you bought jumbo eggs and a recipe calls for large, don't fret. Here's a formula to make your eggs work. Take the total weight of the eggs called for in the recipe and divide that number by the weight of the egg you have to get an approximate number of how many eggs to use.

LARGE IS STANDARD

We recommend using large eggs in our recipes, particularly when the amounts called for are precise, such as when baking.

SMALL	MEDIUM	LARGE	EXTRA-LARGE	JUMBO
1.3 ounces	1.6 ounces	1.8 ounces	2.0 ounces	2.2 ounces

* These weights do not include the weights of the shells.

HOW TO STORE EGGS

You're home with your eggs. Now what?

Do I need to refrigerate my eggs?

It all depends on if the eggs were washed. Standard supermarket eggs must be refrigerated because they are washed to clean off dirt and debris, a process that strips them of their protective cuticle and leaves them more vulnerable to bacteria; refrigeration prevents bacterial growth. Home-raised eggs, if they haven't been washed by their collector, still have this protective cuticle and don't need to be refrigerated. However, it is recommended that before using these eggs you give them a quick rinse and scrub to clean the shells of debris.

How long do eggs keep in the refrigerator?

The USDA recommends using refrigerated eggs no longer than three to five weeks after buying them, but Bourassa says there's no hard-and-fast rule. "I like to use my eggs within a couple of weeks, but I also might stretch that a little bit," she says. We tested two-, three-, and four-month-old eggs and found them palatable, though the four-month-old eggs had very loose egg whites and a slight refrigerator taste. The older eggs also deflated rapidly when whipped. While old eggs can be common, rotten eggs are rare. Eggs can become rotten, "but it's really only when there's been some sort of bacterial invasion, so it's not a time-sensitive thing," says Bourassa.

Should I use or discard a cracked egg?

Bourassa says to play it safe when it comes to using a cracked egg. "I wouldn't use any cracked eggs; that's an opening for any bacteria to get in there," she says. Our handy jingle: When in doubt, toss it out.

Should I keep my eggs in their carton?

Eggshells are porous and can absorb odors, which is why they should be stored in a container. "You want to minimize air exchange to keep them as fresh as possible," says Bourassa. As far as where to store eggs, keep them away from the refrigerator door, which exposes them to gusts of warmth when it's opened. Instead, store eggs on your refrigerator shelves, where they're kept consistently cool.

CLASSIC OMELETS

LAN LAM

Omelets are appealing and impressive; they can be delicate and sophisticated whether rolled in the French style or made light and soufflé-like using whipped egg whites. Making a great omelet can be easy once you know the right method. The learning curve is really just practicing the motions and coming to recognize the visual cues. Once you can do that, the process—which takes only minutes—becomes smooth and even fun, and the burst of satisfaction you feel when your omelet hits the plate never gets old. So, grab a skillet: Soon you'll be making omelets like a pro.

LAN'S PRO TIP: *An unscratched nonstick skillet or well-seasoned carbon steel skillet is critical for a great omelet. Whichever pan you choose, make sure to heat it carefully so that you don't have hot spots or cool spots which can lead to uneven cooking.*

THE METHOD
FRENCH-STYLE OMELET

The cooking of a French-style omelet goes very quickly and requires your full attention, so read through the steps before you start to ensure that you understand the process. Don't be discouraged if your first few omelets aren't perfect; you will get better with practice.

1 COOK
Cook, stirring constantly and scraping bits of egg from sides of skillet into middle.

2 SMOOTH
Remove from heat; scrape eggs from sides and smooth into even layer.

3 ADD CHEESE
Place cheese filling in center of eggs perpendicular to handle.

4 COVER
Cover skillet for 1 minute.

5 LOOSEN AND SLIDE
Loosen omelet and slide to rim opposite handle.

6 FOLD
Fold eggs partway over filling.

7 CHANGE GRIP
Grasp handle with nondominant hand; hold skillet over plate at 45-degree angle.

8 TILT
Slowly tilt skillet toward yourself while using spatula to roll omelet onto plate.

PERFECT OMELET WITH CHEDDAR AND CHIVES

Makes: 1 omelet
Total Time: 10 minutes

RECIPE OVERVIEW Rolling sunny, tender eggs around a tidy filling doesn't require much more skill or time than a hearty scramble—but the resulting French-style omelet is much more polished and satisfying. Filled with gooey cheddar and garnished with chives, this omelet is simple yet elegant. The technique does take some practice to master but practice makes perfect. Start by cooking three beaten eggs in an 8-inch nonstick skillet; this yields an omelet that is delicate but strong. Stirring constantly as the eggs cook breaks up the curds so that the texture of the finished omelet is even and fine. Once a small amount (about 10 percent) of liquid egg remains, it helps to cut the heat and smooth this "glue" over the curds so that the whole thing holds together in a cohesive round. The filling must be at serving temperature before being rolled into the omelet; briefly microwaving shredded cheddar cheese on a plate melts it just enough. Shaping the cheese filling into a 2-inch-wide strip and centering it in the omelet perpendicular to the handle makes it easy to roll the egg around the filling and out of the skillet. Briefly covering the skillet off the heat after adding the filling traps steam that helps the bottom of the eggs set enough to withstand rolling. (It also keeps the filling warm.) Using a rubber spatula to slide the eggs to the far side of the skillet and folding them partway over the filling starts the rolling process. Switching your grip so that you can tilt the skillet forward allows you to fully invert the omelet onto a plate below.

Read the recipe carefully and have your ingredients and equipment ready before you begin. To ensure success, work at a steady pace. For the best results, cook the omelet in a nonstick skillet that's in good condition (not scratched or worn). To serve two, make two three-egg omelets instead of a single six-egg omelet. Omelets can be held for 10 minutes in an oven set to the lowest temperature.

3	large eggs
	(Pinch) table salt
1	ounce extra-sharp cheddar cheese, shredded (¼ cup)
1½	teaspoons unsalted butter
1½	teaspoons chopped fresh chives

1. Beat eggs and salt in bowl until few streaks of white remain.

2. Sprinkle cheese in even layer on small plate. Microwave at 50 percent power until cheese is just melted, 30 to 60 seconds. Set aside.

3. Melt butter in 8-inch nonstick skillet over medium heat, swirling skillet to distribute butter across skillet bottom. When butter sizzles evenly across skillet bottom, add eggs. Cook, stirring constantly with rubber spatula and breaking up large curds, until eggs are mass of small to medium curds surrounded by small amount of liquid egg. Immediately remove skillet from heat.

4. Working quickly, scrape eggs from sides of skillet, then smooth into even layer. Using fork, fold cheese into 2-inch-wide strip and transfer to center of eggs perpendicular to handle. Cover for 1 minute. Remove lid and run spatula underneath perimeter of eggs to loosen omelet. Gently ease spatula under eggs and slide omelet toward edge of skillet opposite handle until edge of omelet is even with lip of skillet. Using spatula, fold egg on handle side of skillet over filling. With your nondominant hand, grasp handle with underhand grip and hold skillet at 45-degree angle over top half of plate. Slowly tilt skillet toward yourself while using spatula to gently roll omelet onto plate. Sprinkle chives over omelet and serve.

Variations
PERFECT HAM, PEAR, AND BRIE OMELET
Total Time: 15 minutes

You can make this omelet with any deli ham or even turkey.

1	tablespoon unsalted butter, divided
¼	cup chopped ripe peeled pear
2	pinches table salt, divided
¼	cup chopped thinly sliced deli ham
1	(1-ounce) slice Brie cheese, rind removed
3	large eggs

1. Melt 1½ teaspoons butter in 10-inch nonstick skillet over medium heat. Add pear and 1 pinch salt and cook, stirring occasionally, until pear begins to brown, 1 to 2 minutes. Add ham and cook, stirring constantly, until

ham is warmed through, about 1 minute. Remove skillet from heat. With rubber spatula, push pear-ham mixture to side of skillet opposite handle and top with Brie. Set aside.

2. Beat eggs and remaining pinch salt in bowl until few streaks of white remain. Melt remaining 1½ teaspoons butter in 8-inch nonstick skillet over medium heat, swirling skillet to distribute butter across skillet bottom. When butter sizzles evenly across skillet bottom, add eggs. Cook, stirring constantly with rubber spatula and breaking up large curds, until eggs are mass of small to medium curds surrounded by small amount of liquid egg. Immediately remove skillet from heat.

3. Working quickly, scrape eggs from sides of skillet, then smooth into even layer. Slide filling into center of eggs in 2-inch-wide strip perpendicular to handle. Cover for 1 minute. Remove lid and run spatula underneath perimeter of eggs to loosen omelet. Gently ease spatula under eggs and slide omelet toward edge of skillet opposite handle until edge of omelet is even with lip of skillet. Using spatula, fold egg on handle side of skillet over filling. With your nondominant hand, grasp handle with underhand grip and hold skillet at 45-degree angle over top half of plate. Slowly tilt skillet toward yourself while using spatula to gently roll omelet onto plate. Serve.

PERFECT KALE, FETA, AND SUN-DRIED TOMATO OMELET
Total Time: 15 minutes

Lacinato kale is also sold as cavolo nero, black, dinosaur, or Tuscan kale. Do not use other types of kale in this recipe, because they take longer to cook.

- 1 tablespoon unsalted butter, divided
- 1 garlic clove, minced
- ¼ teaspoon ground cumin
- 1½ ounces lacinato kale, stemmed and sliced thin (1½ cups)
- 2 pinches table salt, divided
- 2 tablespoons oil-packed sun-dried tomatoes, rinsed, patted dry, and sliced thin
- 2 tablespoons crumbled feta cheese
- 3 large eggs

1. Melt 1½ teaspoons butter in 10-inch nonstick skillet over medium heat. Add garlic and cumin and cook, stirring constantly, until fragrant, about 30 seconds. Add kale and 1 pinch salt and cook, stirring occasionally, until wilted, about 2 minutes. Add tomatoes and cook, stirring frequently, until tomatoes are warmed through and no liquid remains in skillet, 1 to 2 minutes. Remove skillet from heat. Push kale mixture to side of skillet opposite handle and top with feta. Set aside.

2. Beat eggs and remaining pinch salt in bowl until few streaks of white remain. Melt remaining 1½ teaspoons butter in 8-inch nonstick skillet over medium heat, swirling skillet to distribute butter across skillet bottom. When butter sizzles evenly across skillet bottom, add eggs. Cook, stirring constantly with rubber spatula and breaking up large curds, until eggs are mass of small to medium curds surrounded by small amount of liquid egg. Immediately remove skillet from heat.

3. Working quickly, scrape eggs from sides of skillet, then smooth into even layer. Slide filling into center of eggs in 2-inch-wide strip perpendicular to handle. Cover for 1 minute. Remove lid and run spatula underneath perimeter of eggs to loosen omelet. Gently ease spatula under eggs and slide omelet toward edge of skillet opposite handle until edge of omelet is even with lip of skillet. Using spatula, fold egg on handle side of skillet over filling. With your nondominant hand, grasp handle with underhand grip and hold skillet at 45-degree angle over top half of plate. Slowly tilt skillet toward yourself while using spatula to gently roll omelet onto plate. Serve.

KEYS TO SUCCESS
- **The right skillet:** Cooking 3 eggs in an 8-inch nonstick skillet yields an omelet that is delicate but strong enough to support the cheese filling.
- **Premelt the cheese:** Melting the cheese first is crucial as the filling sees very little heat.
- **Precook a cohesive filling:** Preheating the filling melts the cheese without overcooking the eggs.
- **Briefly cover the skillet:** This traps steam and helps the bottom of the eggs to set to reliably withstand rolling.
- **Switch your grip:** Tilting the skillet toward yourself allows the omelet to fully invert onto a plate below.

WHAT CAN GO WRONG

PROBLEM The omelet came out watery.

SOLUTION If you're looking for drier, firmer curds, you've got two options: You can increase the heat a tiny bit or stir leisurely.

PROBLEM Want to use different fillings.

SOLUTION You can change up the fillings quite easily. You want to cook the filling and have it at serving temperature before you start cooking the eggs. If making just one omelet, cook the filling in a second skillet and keep it warm on a burner while cooking the eggs. Slide the filling onto the eggs, and roll the omelet out of the pan. If making multiple omelets, keep the filling warm in a shallow pot and spoon the filling into place. Use about ½ cup of filling per 8-inch omelet. Try combining Swiss cheese and mushrooms or cheddar and avocado.

Whipping Egg Whites

BREAK CLEAN
For cleanest break (and fewest bits of shell), crack side of egg against flat surface.

KEEP WHITES WHITE
Using 3 bowls, separate egg over first bowl, letting white fall into bowl. Transfer yolk to second bowl. If white has no traces of yolk, pour it into third bowl.

START LOW AND SLOW
Whip egg whites and cream of tartar on medium-low until foamy. A slow start creates more volume.

FINISH HIGH
Increase speed to medium-high and continue to whip to soft or stiff peaks. If whites begin to look curdled or separated, you have gone too far and must start over.

Inside Whipped Egg Whites

Air bubbles whipped into the egg whites are coated with the unfurled egg proteins to make a foam.

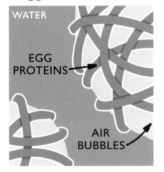

WATER

EGG PROTEINS

AIR BUBBLES

FLUFFY OMELETS
Serves: 2
Total Time: 30 minutes

RECIPE OVERVIEW A different breed than French-style rolled omelets or diner-style omelets folded into half-moons, fluffy omelets are made by baking whipped eggs in a skillet until they rise above the lip of the pan. You'll love their impressive height and delicate texture. Most recipes result in oozing soufflés or dry, bouncy rounds—or eggs that barely puff up at all. To give this omelet lofty height without making it tough, you fold butter-enriched yolks into stiffly whipped whites stabilized with cream of tartar. The whipped whites give the omelet great lift while the yolks and butter keep it tender and rich-tasting. For fillings that are light and flavorful and won't interfere with the cooking of the omelet, use one of the recipes below. Each filling can be sprinkled on top, along with the Parmesan cheese, in step 3. Be sure to make the filling before starting the omelet. A teaspoon of white vinegar or lemon juice can be used in place of the cream of tartar, and a hand-held mixer or a whisk can be used in place of a stand mixer.

4	large eggs, separated
1	tablespoon unsalted butter, melted, plus 1 tablespoon unsalted butter
¼	teaspoon table salt
¼	teaspoon cream of tartar
1	recipe filling (recipes follow) (optional)
1	ounce Parmesan cheese, grated (½ cup)

1. Adjust oven rack to middle position and heat oven to 375 degrees. Whisk egg yolks, melted butter, and salt together in bowl. Place egg whites in bowl of stand mixer and sprinkle cream of tartar over surface. Fit stand mixer with whisk attachment and whip egg whites on medium-low speed until foamy, 2 to 2½ minutes. Increase speed to medium-high and whip until stiff peaks just start to form, 2 to 3 minutes. Fold egg yolk mixture into egg whites until no white streaks remain.

2. Melt remaining 1 tablespoon butter in 12-inch ovensafe nonstick skillet over medium-high heat, swirling to coat bottom of skillet. When butter foams, quickly add egg mixture, spreading into even layer with spatula.

3. Off heat, gently sprinkle filling, if using, and Parmesan evenly over top of omelet. Transfer to oven and cook until center of omelet springs back when lightly pressed, 4½ minutes for slightly wet omelet or 5 minutes for drier omelet.

4. Run spatula around edge of omelet to loosen, shaking gently to release. Slide omelet onto cutting board and let stand for 30 seconds. Using spatula, fold omelet in half. Cut omelet in half crosswise. Serve immediately.

Variations

ASPARAGUS AND SMOKED SALMON FILLING

Makes: ¾ cup

1	teaspoon olive oil
1	shallot, sliced thin
5	ounces asparagus, trimmed and cut on bias into ¼-inch pieces
	Pinch table salt
	Pepper
1	ounce smoked salmon, chopped
½	teaspoon lemon juice

Heat oil in 12-inch nonstick skillet over medium-high heat until shimmering. Add shallot; cook until softened and starting to brown, 2 minutes. Add asparagus and pinch salt and season with pepper to taste. Cook, stirring frequently, until asparagus is crisp-tender, 5 to 7 minutes. Transfer asparagus mixture to bowl and stir in salmon and lemon juice.

MUSHROOM FILLING

Makes: ¾ cup

1	teaspoon olive oil
1	shallot, sliced thin
4	ounces white or cremini mushrooms, trimmed and chopped
⅛	teaspoon table salt
	Pepper
1	teaspoon balsamic vinegar

Heat oil in 12-inch nonstick skillet over medium-high heat until shimmering. Add shallot and cook until softened and starting to brown, about 2 minutes. Add mushrooms and salt and season with pepper to taste. Cook until liquid has evaporated and mushrooms begin to brown, 6 to 8 minutes. Transfer mixture to bowl and stir in vinegar.

ARTICHOKE AND BACON FILLING

Makes: ¾ cup

2	slices bacon, cut into ¼-inch pieces
1	shallot, sliced thin
5	ounces frozen artichoke hearts, thawed, patted dry, and chopped
⅛	teaspoon table salt
	Pepper
½	teaspoon lemon juice

Cook bacon in 12-inch nonstick skillet over medium-high heat until crisp, 3 to 6 minutes. Using slotted spoon, transfer bacon to paper towel–lined plate. Pour off all but 1 teaspoon fat from skillet. Add shallot and cook until softened and starting to brown, about 2 minutes. Add artichokes, salt, and pepper to taste. Cook, stirring frequently, until artichokes begin to brown, 6 to 8 minutes. Transfer artichoke mixture to bowl and stir in bacon and lemon juice.

KEYS TO SUCCESS

- **Cream of tartar:** This dry acid makes for a more stable egg foam and a lighter omelet.
- **Fold, don't beat:** Gently mix the yolks into the whipped whites to keep the air in them.
- **Spread evenly:** The egg mixture is quite stiff and needs to be spread in the pan.
- **Fill early:** Filling the omelet at the outset means that the eggs, cheese, and filling will all be piping hot.
- **Sub another cheese:** Pecorino, fontina, Gruyère, and sharp cheddar are good choices.

WHAT CAN GO WRONG

PROBLEM The omelet collapses quickly or isn't stable.

SOLUTION The egg whites weren't whisked long enough. It's important to whisk the egg whites until they have reached stiff peaks. Anything less than that won't provide the omelet with enough stability, eliminating the fluffiness from this omelet.

Whipping the egg whites to stiff peaks is part of what ensures stability; the other is adding a stabilizer such as cream of tartar. The acidic ingredient preserves that stability by slowing the formation of sulfur bonds in egg whites; if too many bonds form, the white's protein structure becomes too rigid, and the network that holds the whipped air and water in place begins to collapse. So before beating the whites, sprinkle some cream of tartar evenly over the surface to help the omelet hold its shape.

PROBLEM The omelet isn't as tall as it should be or deflates.

SOLUTION It's important to fold the yolks into the whites gently, just until no white streaks remain. If you stir too aggressively, the whites will lose some of their volume before the two are fully combined, and the resulting omelet will be less airy and soufflé-like.

PROBLEM The omelet sticks to the pan.

SOLUTION The omelet will stick to a traditional skillet, so it's imperative you use a nonstick pan.

THE TOOLS

Set yourself up for success by having everything—the equipment, eggs, and filling—ready to go.

8-INCH NONSTICK SKILLET A three-egg omelet made in this pan will be delicate but thick enough to support the filling. Make sure that the surface is slick; if the coating is scratched or worn, sliding the omelet out of the pan will be difficult.

TIGHT-FITTING LID Briefly covering the pan traps heat that helps the omelet set, making it easier to maneuver, and keeps the filling warm.

HEATPROOF RUBBER OR SILICONE SPATULA Any size or shape will work.

SERVING PLATE This is your landing pad for the omelet when you roll it out of the pan.

TIPS FOR FILLING OMELETS

Our Perfect Omelet with Cheddar and Chives (page 36) features extra-sharp cheddar, but you can fill an omelet with almost anything. That said, there are keys to avoiding mishaps such as ingredients spilling or leaking out of the omelet or being unpleasantly cold when you bite into them. Here are the best practices we follow in recipes such as our Perfect Ham, Pear, and Brie Omelet (page 36) and Perfect Kale, Feta, and Sun-Dried Tomato Omelet (page 37).

CUT SMALL Finely chopped pieces will cook through faster and pack more tightly, which means that you can add more filling (and flavor) to the omelet and that the pieces will hold together when you roll the omelet onto a plate.

PRECOOK This concentrates the filling's flavor, warms it up, and rids it of excess moisture that would otherwise leak from the omelet and mar the presentation.

KEEP WARM The filling should be at serving temperature when it meets the eggs, since it won't see much heat once it's rolled into the omelet. We like to sauté ingredients in a separate skillet just before we begin cooking the eggs in another pan or premelt the cheese in the microwave for cheese omelets.

MEASURE Each three-egg omelet can hold ½ cup of filling. In addition to that, you can add up to 2 tablespoons of shredded melty cheese (e.g., mozzarella, Jack, Colby, Muenster) to the hot filling; it will melt and fill in the gaps between the other chopped bits.

GOING THEIR SEPARATE WAYS

To create a fluffy omelet that doesn't taste like Styrofoam, we first need to separate the whites and yolks and treat them as separate entities. This is because the two components contribute different—and competing—qualities to the results: Whites build structure, while the rich-tasting fat in yolks weakens it. The next steps: Whip the whites with cream of tartar to add stability and stir a little melted butter into the yolks to enhance their rich flavor. We then gently recombine the two components. The extra fat keeps the omelet from tasting too lean, and the cream of tartar allows the omelet to stand tall and sturdy, despite the weakening effects of butter and yolks.

WHIP WHITES WITH CREAM OF TARTAR
Cream of tartar stabilizes the whipped egg whites, so the omelet stands tall.

SEPARATE WHITES AND YOLKS
Since these two components perform competing functions, they must be treated differently.

MIX YOLKS WITH BUTTER
Butter (melted first to make mixing easy) tenderizes the omelet and supplements the yolks' rich flavor.

EGG TORTILLAS AND TAJINES

NICOLE KONSTANTINAKOS

What do a Spanish tortilla, Egyptian eggah, and Tunisian tajine have in common? All are dense, creamy omelets boasting meltingly tender fillings of vegetables and meat. A Spanish tortilla de patatas (no relation to Mexican flour and corn tortillas) always contains potatoes while an egg tajine might contain potatoes along with a variety of hearty proteins, herbs, and spices. The eggah in this course is filled with ground beef and spinach while the tajine incorporates white beans instead of potatoes along with tender pieces of chicken. Each turns into an eggy, delicately sealed cake with rich flavor and a melt-in-your-mouth texture. Divided appropriately, all three egg dishes can be enjoyed as a meal or as an appetizer.

NICOLE'S PRO TIP: *Since the tortilla recipe is so simple, and the ingredients have nowhere to "hide", you'll get the most delicious results using a full-flavored and well-balanced olive oil, farm-fresh eggs, and good-quality vegetables. You can refrigerate the tortilla for up to 24 hours; serve it cold, at room temperature, or warmed slightly in the microwave (just take care not to overcook it when reheating).*

THE METHOD
EGG TORTILLA

This one-skillet method for making a Spanish tortilla or Egyptian eggah unites tender vegetables and creamy eggs. Using two plates to flip the eggs makes a messy task easier and foolproof.

1 COOK FILLING
Cook vegetables and meat in oil in nonstick skillet.

2 FOLD
Fold precooked filling into beaten eggs.

3 COOK EGG MIXTURE
Add egg mixture to nonstick skillet and cook, folding and shaking constantly.

4 SLIDE
After browning first side, loosen tortilla with heatproof rubber spatula and slide onto a large plate.

5 FLIP
Place second plate face down over tortilla and invert so that browned side is up.

6 SLIDE
Slide tortilla back into skillet, browned side up, then tuck edges into pan with rubber spatula.

CLASSIC SPANISH TORTILLA

Serves: 4 to 6
Total Time: 45 minutes

RECIPE OVERVIEW Tortilla Española (or tortilla de patatas), a well-loved tapas bar staple, also makes a simple satisfying dinner at home when the vegetable-filled omelet is sliced and served generously. It consists of potatoes and (usually) onion that are simmered in plentiful oil until meltingly tender and then bound with eggs for a dense but creamy omelet. Typical recipes call for simmering the potatoes in up to 4 cups of extra-virgin olive oil, but we found that cutting the amount of oil to 6 tablespoons worked just as well. You still get all of the flavor of the oil but none of the greasiness. Roasted red peppers and peas are distributed throughout the tortilla for more heartiness, texture, and complexity. Traditional recipes call for flipping the tortilla with the help of a single plate but we found a less intimidating way: Sliding the omelet onto a plate and then using a second plate to flip it and slide it back into the pan makes a once-messy task foolproof. We love the tortilla on its own but a dollop of Garlic Mayonnaise (recipe follows) ups its flavor ante. Serve the tortilla warm or at room temperature. For a more traditional tortilla, omit the roasted red peppers and the peas.

1½ pounds Yukon Gold potatoes, peeled, quartered, and sliced ⅛ inch thick
1 small onion, halved and sliced thin
6 tablespoons plus 1 teaspoon extra-virgin olive oil
1 teaspoon table salt, divided
¼ teaspoon pepper
8 large eggs
½ cup jarred roasted red peppers, rinsed, patted dry, and cut into ½-inch pieces
½ cup frozen peas, thawed

1. Toss potatoes, onion, ¼ cup oil, ½ teaspoon salt, and pepper in large bowl until potatoes are thoroughly separated and coated in oil. Heat 2 tablespoons oil in 10-inch nonstick skillet over medium-high heat until shimmering. Reduce heat to medium-low and add potato mixture to skillet. Cover and cook, stirring with heat-resistant rubber spatula every 5 minutes, until paring knife can be slipped into and out of potatoes with no resistance, 22 to 28 minutes (some potatoes may break into smaller pieces).

2. Meanwhile, whisk eggs and remaining ½ teaspoon salt in now-empty bowl until just combined. Using rubber spatula, fold hot potato mixture, red peppers, and peas into eggs until combined, making sure to scrape all of potato mixture out of skillet. Return now-empty skillet to medium-high heat, add remaining 1 teaspoon oil, and heat until just smoking. Add egg-potato mixture and cook, constantly shaking skillet and folding mixture, for 15 seconds. Smooth top of mixture with rubber spatula. Reduce heat to medium, cover, and cook, gently shaking skillet every 30 seconds, until bottom is golden brown and top is lightly set, about 2 minutes.

3. Using rubber spatula, loosen tortilla from skillet, shaking skillet back and forth until tortilla slides around freely. Slide tortilla onto large plate, invert onto second large plate, and slide, browned side up, back into skillet. Tuck edges of tortilla into skillet with rubber spatula. Return skillet to medium heat and continue to cook, gently shaking skillet every 30 seconds, until second side is golden brown, about 2 minutes longer.

4. Slide tortilla onto cutting board or serving plate and let cool for at least 15 minutes. Cut tortilla into cubes or wedges and serve.

Variation

SPANISH TORTILLA WITH CHORIZO AND SCALLIONS

Use a cured, Spanish-style chorizo sausage for this recipe or substitute Portuguese linguiça sausage.

In step 1, add 1 tablespoon oil and 4 ounces diced Spanish-style chorizo sausage to 10-inch nonstick skillet and cook over medium-high heat, stirring occasionally, until chorizo is browned and fat is rendered, about 5 minutes. Proceed with recipe, adding potato mixture to skillet with chorizo and rendered fat. In step 2, omit red peppers and peas and fold 4 thinly sliced scallions into eggs with potato mixture.

GARLIC MAYONNAISE

Makes: about 1¼ cups

2	large egg yolks
2	teaspoons Dijon mustard
2	teaspoons lemon juice
1	garlic clove, minced
¾	cup vegetable oil
1	tablespoon water
¼	cup extra-virgin olive oil
½	teaspoon table salt
¼	teaspoon pepper

Process egg yolks, mustard, lemon juice, and garlic in food processor until combined, about 10 seconds. With processor running, slowly drizzle in vegetable oil, about 1 minute. Transfer mixture to medium bowl and whisk in water. Whisking constantly, slowly drizzle in olive oil, about 30 seconds. Whisk in salt and pepper. (Mayonnaise can be refrigerated for up to 4 days.)

KEYS TO SUCCESS

- **Yukon Gold potatoes:** They are firmer and less starchy than russets.
- **A 10-inch nonstick skillet:** Prevents the tortilla from sticking to the pan
- **Less oil:** A mere 6 tablespoons replaces the traditional 3 to 4 cups to cook the potatoes.
- **Easy flipping:** The two-plate method makes flipping a snap.

The Wide World of Omelets

A Spanish tortilla is as much about the potatoes as it is the eggs. Its density and lack of cheese set it apart from other omelet styles.

American Omelet
This homey diner staple features a thin layer of egg folded over a loose pile of filling that can include vegetables, cheese, plus you-name-it.

Egyptian Eggah
Eggah is similar in texture to a frittata. The hearty filling ingredients are precooked before being added to beaten eggs. Eggah is cooked on the stovetop and flipped out and over in the skillet halfway through cooking.

French Omelet
Creamy, cigar-shaped French omelets are too delicate to hold anything more than a small amount of filling.

Italian Frittata
Like tortillas, frittatas are not folded. Instead they're finished in the oven for a dry, lightly souffléed texture with fillings from sausage to herbs.

Spanish Tortilla
A tortillla consists of tender potatoes and onions bound together with eggs for a dense but creamy omelet. It is flipped out of and over in the skillet not folded.

Tunisian Tajine
A tajine can be filled with a variety of hearty proteins such as chicken, beans, and cheese as well as herbs and spices. It is baked in a skillet and not folded or flipped.

EGYPTIAN EGGAH WITH GROUND BEEF AND SPINACH

Serves: 4 to 6
Total Time: 55 minutes

RECIPE OVERVIEW Eggah, the Arabic answer to the Spanish tortilla, often features boldly spiced fillings in a hearty egg base. We chose a traditional Egyptian filling of ground beef, spinach, and leeks. Using 90 percent lean ground beef ensures that the eggah doesn't turn out greasy, and precooking the spinach in the microwave eliminates any excess moisture that could leave the dish soggy. A mixture of cumin, cinnamon, and cilantro enhances the North African flavor profile. Precook the filling and let it cool slightly before adding it to the beaten eggs. To cook the eggah, we borrow a technique from our tortilla recipe and cook the egg mixture in a hot skillet, then flip it halfway through using two plates. Eggah can be served hot, warm, or at room temperature.

- 8 ounces (8 cups) baby spinach
- 6 tablespoons water, divided
- 4 teaspoons extra-virgin olive oil
- 1 pound leeks, whites and light green parts only, halved lengthwise, sliced thin, and washed thoroughly
- 8 ounces 90 percent lean ground beef
- 1 garlic clove, minced
- 1 teaspoon ground cumin
- ¼ teaspoon ground cinnamon
- 1 teaspoon table salt, divided
- ½ teaspoon pepper, divided
- 8 large eggs
- ¼ cup minced fresh cilantro

1. Place spinach and ¼ cup water in large bowl, cover, and microwave until spinach is wilted and decreased in volume by about half, about 5 minutes. Remove bowl from microwave and keep covered for 1 minute. Transfer spinach to colander and gently press to release liquid. Transfer spinach to cutting board and chop coarse. Return to colander and press again.

2. Heat 1 teaspoon oil in 10-inch nonstick skillet over medium heat until shimmering. Add leeks and cook until softened, about 5 minutes. Add ground beef and cook, breaking up meat with wooden spoon, until beginning to brown, 5 to 7 minutes. Stir in garlic, cumin, cinnamon, ½ teaspoon salt, and ¼ teaspoon pepper and cook until fragrant, about 30 seconds. Stir in spinach until heated through, about 1 minute; transfer to bowl and let cool slightly.

3. Beat eggs, remaining 2 tablespoons water, remaining ½ teaspoon salt, and remaining ¼ teaspoon pepper together with fork in large bowl until thoroughly combined and mixture is pure yellow; do not overbeat. Gently fold in spinach mixture and cilantro, making sure to scrape all of spinach mixture out of skillet.

4. Heat remaining 1 tablespoon oil in now-empty skillet over medium-high heat until just smoking. Add egg mixture and cook, shaking skillet and folding mixture constantly for 15 seconds. Smooth top of egg mixture, reduce heat to medium, cover, and cook, gently shaking skillet every 30 seconds, until bottom is golden brown and top is lightly set, about 3 minutes.

5. Off heat, run heat-resistant rubber spatula around edge of skillet and shake skillet gently to loosen eggah; it should slide around freely in skillet. Slide eggah onto large plate, then invert onto second large plate and slide back into skillet browned side up. Tuck edges of eggah into skillet with rubber spatula. Continue to cook over medium heat, gently shaking skillet every 30 seconds, until second side is golden brown, about 2 minutes. Slide eggah onto cutting board and let cool slightly. Slice and serve hot, warm, or at room temperature.

KEYS TO SUCCESS

- **A nonstick skillet with lid:** Nonstick helps eggs move around in the pan and the lid traps steam to gently cook eggs.

- **90 percent ground beef:** Cuts down the greasiness

- **Precooked filling:** Ensures that the omelet is evenly cooked

TUNISIAN TAJINE WITH WHITE BEANS

Serves: 4 to 6
Total Time: 1 hour

RECIPE OVERVIEW The word "tagine" (or "tajine" as in Tunisia) refers to the classic earthenware vessel—used to cook myriad North African dishes, especially the eponymous stews—with a unique conical shape that creates moist, delicious results. In Tunisia, the word "tajine" is also the name of a specific satiating egg dish that was originally made in the same pot, despite its looking nothing like a stew. Like tortillas (see page 44), these eggs are chock-full of a wide variety of hearty proteins, herbs, and spices. Nowadays, Tunisians commonly cook the meal in a baking dish; we choose a skillet. This recipe includes white beans, which become highly flavorful when cooked with spices and tomato paste, and tender pieces of sautéed chicken thighs. Stirring bread crumbs into the eggs absorbs extra moisture and sets the tajine's texture. Nuggets of mild Monterey Jack cheese melt into satisfying pools along the tajine's surface. The stuffed skillet bakes until the eggs are set up and browned. When purchasing ras el hanout, be sure that your blend features cumin, coriander, and turmeric. Turmeric will create the distinctive yellowish tone typical of traditional Tunisian tajines.

12 large eggs

½ cup panko bread crumbs, toasted, divided

½ cup minced fresh parsley

1 ounce Parmesan cheese, grated (½ cup)

3 tablespoons water

½ teaspoon table salt, divided

½ teaspoon pepper, divided

3 tablespoons extra-virgin olive oil

1½ pounds boneless, skinless chicken thighs, trimmed and cut into ½-inch pieces

1 tablespoon tomato paste

6 garlic cloves, minced

1 tablespoon ras el hanout

¼ teaspoon cayenne pepper

1 cup canned cannellini beans, rinsed

4 ounces Monterey Jack cheese, cut into ½-inch pieces (1 cup)

1. Adjust oven rack to upper-middle position and heat oven to 350 degrees. Whisk eggs, ¼ cup panko, parsley, Parmesan, water, ¼ teaspoon salt, and ¼ teaspoon pepper together in bowl; set aside.

2. Heat oil in 12-inch ovensafe nonstick skillet over medium-high heat until shimmering. Add chicken, tomato paste, remaining ¼ teaspoon salt, and remaining ¼ teaspoon pepper and cook, stirring occasionally, until chicken is well browned, 6 to 8 minutes. Stir in garlic, ras el hanout, and cayenne and cook until fragrant, about 1 minute. Stir in beans and cook until heated through, about 5 minutes.

3. Reduce heat to medium-low and stir in egg mixture. Cook, using spatula to scrape bottom of skillet, until large curds form but eggs are still very wet, about 2 minutes. Smooth egg mixture into even layer. Nestle Monterey Jack into egg curds and sprinkle top with remaining ¼ cup panko. Transfer skillet to oven and bake until tajine is slightly puffy and surface bounces back when lightly pressed, 10 to 12 minutes. Using oven mitt, remove skillet from oven. Being careful of hot skillet handle, use rubber spatula to loosen tajine from skillet and transfer to cutting board. Let sit for 5 minutes before slicing and serving.

KEYS TO SUCCESS

- **Canned cannellini beans:** A no-cook starchy option that hold their shape and replace potatoes

- **Panko bread crumbs:** Help to thicken the eggs and are also used as a garnish

- **An ovensafe nonstick skillet:** Dish is built in one pan that goes from stovetop to oven.

QUICHE

BRIDGET LANCASTER

It's handy to have a basic recipe for quiche, an elegant savory egg custard pie, in your repertoire since it can be served for breakfast, lunch, or dinner. And once you master the basic recipe, it's easy to vary it. The keys to a great quiche are having just the right proportion of dairy to eggs and parbaking the crust. We love classic quiche but sometimes crave a thick-crusted quiche brimming with a luxuriously creamy custard and a larger dose of perfectly suspended fillings. Our deep-dish quiche stands two inches tall and more than fills the bill.

BRIDGET'S PRO TIP: *Keeping the pie dough chilled at every step really is key here. Besides ensuring that the texture of the crust will be flaky, refrigerating the dough—both after making the dough and then rolling it out—will minimize any dough shrinkage. You want to avoid that shrinkage to make sure you can add every last drop of that delicious custard into the pie shell.*

THE METHOD
QUICHE

The pie crust and the custard of a quiche are both delicate. Parbaking the crust and filling it while it's warm are essential to keep it from getting soggy.

1 MAKE DOUGH
A food processor cuts in butter without overworking dough.

2 CHILL DOUGH
Room-temperature dough can be sticky and messy to work with. Chilling makes it easier to roll out.

3 MAKE AND CHILL PIE SHELL
Fit dough into pie plate, flute edges, and place in the freezer. Chilling dough before blind baking makes for flakier crust.

4 PREBAKE CRUST
Line chilled pie shell with aluminum foil or parchment, fill with pie weights, and bake.

5 WHISK CUSTARD TOGETHER
Make custard then add remaining ingredients.

6 FILL WARM PIE SHELL IN OVEN
Pour custard into large measuring cup and then fill pie shell in oven. That's easier and safer than transferring filled quiche to oven.

7 DON'T OVERBAKE
Pull quiche from oven before it has entirely set. It will continue to cook and set as it cools.

8 WAIT TO SLICE
Let quiche cool for at least an hour; it needs time to set up to become sliceable.

CLASSIC CHEESE QUICHE

Serves: 6 to 8
Total Time: 55 minutes, plus 1 hour cooling

RECIPE OVERVIEW The ideal quiche has a tender, buttery pastry crust that embraces a smooth eggy custard that is neither too rich nor too lean. We tested numerous combinations of dairy and eggs to find the perfect combination of 5 eggs and 2 cups of half-and-half. The baking temperature is equally important: 350 degrees is low enough to set the custard gently yet hot enough to brown the top without drying out the filling. To keep the crust from becoming soggy, parbake it before adding the filling. To avoid spilling the custard, set the parbaked crust in the oven before pouring the custard into the pastry shell. For perfectly baked quiche every time, pull it out of the oven when it is still slightly soft, which allows it to set up as it cools. Be sure to add the custard to the pie shell while the crust is still warm so that the quiche will bake evenly. You can substitute other fresh herbs for the chives, like thyme, parsley, or marjoram. You can substitute store-bought pie dough in this recipe. To prevent the crust from sagging during prebaking, make sure that the protruding crimped edge overhangs the edge of the pie plate slightly, and use plenty of pie weights (3 to 4 cups).

Crust

¼	cup ice water
4	teaspoons sour cream
1¼	cups (6¼ ounces) all-purpose flour
1½	teaspoons sugar
½	teaspoon salt
8	tablespoons unsalted butter, cut into ¼-inch pieces and frozen for 15 minutes

Filling

5	large eggs
2	cups half-and-half
¼	teaspoon table salt
¼	teaspoon pepper
4	ounces cheddar cheese, shredded (1 cup)
1	tablespoon minced fresh chives

1. FOR THE CRUST Combine ice water and sour cream in bowl. Process flour, sugar, and salt in food processor until combined, about 5 seconds. Scatter butter over top and pulse until butter is size of large peas, about 10 pulses. Add sour cream mixture and pulse until dough forms clumps and no dry flour remains, about 12 pulses, scraping down sides of bowl as needed.

2. Turn out dough onto sheet of plastic wrap and form into 4-inch disk. Wrap tightly in plastic and refrigerate for 1 hour. (Wrapped dough can be refrigerated for up to 2 days or frozen for up to 1 month. If frozen, let dough thaw completely on counter before rolling.)

3. Adjust oven rack to middle position and heat oven to 350 degrees. Let chilled dough sit on counter to soften slightly, about 10 minutes, before rolling. Roll dough into 12-inch circle on lightly floured counter. Loosely roll dough around rolling pin and gently unroll it onto 9-inch pie plate, letting excess dough hang over edge. Ease dough into plate by gently lifting edge of dough with your hand while pressing into plate bottom with your other hand.

4. Trim overhang to ½ inch beyond lip of plate. Tuck overhang under itself; folded edge should be flush with edge of plate. Crimp dough evenly around edge of plate using your fingers. Push protruding crimped edge so it slightly overhangs edge of plate. Wrap dough-lined plate loosely in plastic and freeze until dough is firm, about 15 minutes.

5. Place chilled pie shell on rimmed baking sheet. Line with double layer of parchment paper, covering edges to prevent burning, and fill with pie weights. Bake until edges are light golden brown, about 20 minutes. Remove parchment and weights, rotate plate, and bake until crust bottom dries out and turns light golden brown, 15 to 20 minutes. If crust begins to puff, pierce gently with tip of paring knife. Set aside. (Crust needn't cool completely before adding filling.)

6. FOR THE FILLING Adjust oven rack to lower-middle position and heat oven to 350 degrees. Whisk eggs, half-and-half, salt, and pepper together in large bowl. Stir in cheddar and chives. Transfer filling to 4-cup liquid measuring cup.

7. Place warm pie shell on rimmed baking sheet and place in oven. Carefully pour egg mixture into warm shell until it reaches about ½ inch from top edge of crust (you may have extra egg mixture).

8. Bake until top is lightly browned, center is set but soft, and knife inserted about 1 inch from edge comes out clean, 40 to 50 minutes. Let quiche cool for at least 1 hour or up to 3 hours. Serve slightly warm or at room temperature. (Let baked quiche cool completely, then cover with plastic wrap and refrigerate for up to 6 hours. [Crust of refrigerated quiche will be less crisp.] Quiche can be served slightly chilled, at room temperature, or warm; to serve warm, reheat in 350-degree oven for 10 to 15 minutes.)

Variations

LEEK AND GOAT CHEESE QUICHE

Melt 2 tablespoons unsalted butter in 10-inch skillet over medium-high heat. Add 2 finely chopped leeks, white and light green parts only, and cook until softened, about 6 minutes; transfer to plate. Substitute 1 cup crumbled goat cheese for cheddar, and stir leeks into eggs with cheese and chives.

SPINACH AND FETA QUICHE

Removing the excess moisture from the spinach is crucial here.

Omit chives and substitute 1 cup crumbled feta cheese for cheddar. Stir 1 (10-ounce) package frozen chopped spinach, thawed and squeezed dry, into eggs with cheese.

Rolling Out Any Pie Dough

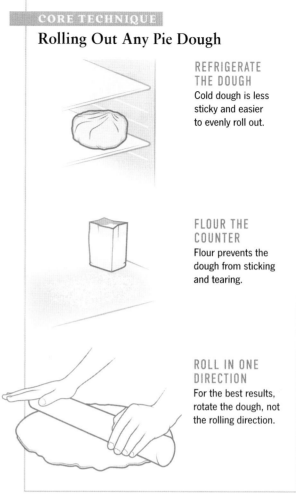

REFRIGERATE THE DOUGH
Cold dough is less sticky and easier to evenly roll out.

FLOUR THE COUNTER
Flour prevents the dough from sticking and tearing.

ROLL IN ONE DIRECTION
For the best results, rotate the dough, not the rolling direction.

ASPARAGUS AND GRUYÈRE QUICHE

Do not substitute precooked or frozen asparagus here.

Substitute Gruyère cheese for cheddar, and stir 1 bunch asparagus, sliced on bias into ¼-inch-thick pieces, into eggs with cheese and chives.

KEYS TO SUCCESS

- **Sour cream in the crust dough**: Adds flavor and makes the dough pliable
- **Chill the pie dough twice**: First chill makes it easier to roll out and second (before baking) makes for a flakier crust.
- **Prebake the crust**: Vital for getting a sturdy, crisp bottom crust when baked with wet custard
- **Rich, creamy custard**: Made with a perfect ratio of 5 eggs to 2 cups half-and-half
- **Let cool**: Quiche needs time to set to become sliceable. It can spend up to 3 hours cooling.

DEEP-DISH QUICHE LORRAINE

Serves: 8 to 10 (makes one 9-inch quiche)
Total Time: 3½ hours plus 1½ hours chilling, 20 minutes freezing, 2 hours cooling

RECIPE OVERVIEW A deep-dish quiche is a little unusual but offers a better ratio of custard to filling than a traditional one. Most recipes for quiche Lorraine are a fifty/fifty ratio of baked pie crust and custardy filling. This version highlights (and increases) the amount of savory bacon, cheese, and onion filling. It bakes in a deeper 9 by 2-inch cake pan rather than a regular 9-inch pie plate. The success of deep-dish quiche Lorraine recipe depends on the right ratio of eggs to liquid, plus gentle, even heat. The filling uses 8 large eggs plus an extra yolk, with whole milk and heavy cream to add richness. To add the quiche's fillings without affecting the perfect custard, we whisk a little cornstarch into the dairy component of the custard. This keeps it glossy and rich and allows you to bake the quiche Lorraine longer, which firms the custard. Finally, there are three ways to add insurance against leaks and tears in the crust of the quiche. To prevent the crust from sagging during blind baking, make sure it overhangs the pan's edge and use plenty of pie weights (3 to 4 cups).

Pastry Dough

- 1¾ cups (8¾ ounces) unbleached all-purpose flour, plus more for work surface
- ½ teaspoon table salt
- 12 tablespoons unsalted butter (1½ sticks), cold, cut into ½-inch cubes and frozen 10 minutes
- 3 tablespoons sour cream
- ¼–⅓ cup ice water
- 1 large egg white, lightly beaten

Filling

- 8 ounces bacon, preferably thick-cut, cut crosswise into ¼-inch pieces
- 2 medium onions, chopped fine (about 2 cups)
- 1½ tablespoons cornstarch
- 1½ cups whole milk
- 8 large eggs plus 1 large yolk
- 1½ cups heavy cream
- ½ teaspoon table salt
- ¼ teaspoon ground black pepper
- ⅛ teaspoon grated nutmeg
- ⅛ teaspoon cayenne
- 6 ounces Gruyère cheese, shredded (about 1½ cups)

CORE TECHNIQUE
Swapping a Pie Plate for a Cake Pan

MAKE A SLING
Unlike a pie plate, a deep cake pan requires a foil sling (fashioned from two lengths of foil) to remove the quiche.

ROLL OUT A BIGGER ROUND
Instead of a 12-inch round, roll out dough to a 15-inch circle big enough to fit in the cake pan with plenty of overhang.

UNROLL INTO CAKE PAN
Roll the dough loosely around a rolling pin and unroll it into the foil-lined cake pan.

EASE IN AND TRIM
Gently ease the dough into the pan. Trim, leaving a generous 1-inch overhang to anchor the dough.

1. **FOR THE DOUGH** Process flour and salt together in food processor until combined, about 3 seconds. Add butter and pulse until butter is size of large peas, about ten 1-second pulses.

2. Mix sour cream and ¼ cup ice water in small bowl until combined. Add half sour cream mixture to flour mixture; pulse for three 1-second pulses. Repeat with remaining sour cream mixture. Pinch dough with fingers; if dough is floury, dry, and does not hold together, add 1 to 2 tablespoons ice water and process until dough forms large clumps and no dry flour remains, three to five 1-second pulses.

3. Turn dough out onto work surface and flatten into 6-inch disk; cover disk in plastic wrap and refrigerate until firm but not hard, 1 to 2 hours, before rolling. (Dough can be refrigerated for up to 24 hours. Let thoroughly chilled dough stand at room temperature 15 minutes before rolling.)

4. Cut two 16-inch lengths of foil. Arrange foil pieces in round 9 by 2-inch cake pan so they are perpendicular, pushing them into corners and up sides of pan; press overhang against outside of pan. Spray foil lightly with nonstick cooking spray.

5. Roll out disk of dough on generously floured work surface to 15-inch circle (about ¼ inch thick). Roll dough loosely around rolling pin and unroll into cake pan. Working around circumference, ease dough into pan by gently lifting edge of dough with 1 hand while pressing into pan bottom with other. Trim any dough that extends more than 1 inch over edge of pan. Patch any cracks or holes with dough scraps as needed. Refrigerate any remaining dough scraps. Refrigerate dough-lined pan until firm, about 30 minutes, and then freeze for 20 minutes.

6. Adjust oven rack to lower-middle position and heat oven to 375 degrees. Line dough with parchment or foil and fill completely with pie weights or dried beans, gently pressing weights into corners of shell. Bake on rimmed baking sheet until exposed edges of dough are beginning to brown but bottom is still light in color, 30 to 40 minutes. Carefully remove parchment and pie weights. If any new holes or cracks have formed in dough, patch with reserved scraps. Return shell to oven and bake until bottom is golden brown, 15 to 20 minutes longer. Remove shell from oven and brush interior with egg white. Set aside while preparing filling. Reduce oven temperature to 350 degrees.

7. FOR THE FILLING Cook bacon in 12-inch skillet over medium heat until crisp, 8 to 12 minutes. Transfer to paper towel–lined plate and discard all but 2 tablespoons bacon fat from skillet. Return to medium heat, add onions, and cook, stirring frequently, until softened and lightly browned, about 12 minutes. Set onions aside to cool slightly.

8. Place cornstarch in large bowl; add 3 tablespoons milk and whisk to dissolve cornstarch. Whisk in remaining milk, eggs, yolk, cream, salt, pepper, nutmeg, and cayenne until mixture is smooth.

9. Scatter onions, bacon, and Gruyère evenly over crust. Gently pour custard mixture over filling. Using fork, push filling ingredients down into custard and drag gently through custard to dislodge air bubbles. Gently tap pan on counter-top to dislodge any remaining air bubbles.

10. Bake until top of quiche is lightly browned, toothpick inserted into center comes out clean, and center registers 170 degrees on instant-read thermometer, 1¼ to 1½ hours. Transfer to wire rack and let stand until cool to touch, about 2 hours.

11. When ready to serve, use sharp paring knife to remove any crust that extends beyond edge of pan. Lift foil overhang from sides of pan and remove quiche from pan; gently slide thin-bladed spatula between quiche and foil to loosen, then slide quiche onto serving plate. Cut into wedges and serve. The cooled quiche can be served warm or at room tempera-ture, or refrigerated for up to 3 days and reheated. (To reheat the whole quiche, place it on a rimmed baking sheet on the middle rack of a 325-degree oven for 20 minutes. Reheat slices at 375 for 10 minutes.)

KEYS TO SUCCESS

- **Sour cream in pastry dough**: Contributes some fat (more tenderness) as well as some milk solids (better browning)

- **Use a cake pan**: It's tall enough to contain all of the filling and won't leak.

- **Foil sling for dough**: Helps to extract pastry from the pan

- **A little cornstarch**: Mitigates the curdling effects of onions in the filling

WHAT CAN GO WRONG

PROBLEM   The pie shell is slumped and shallow.

SOLUTION   Deep-dish quiche depends on a tall prebaked pie shell. To ensure that the sides of the shell don't slump down during baking, be sure to use a layer of parchment or foil, topped with a good amount of pie weights.

PROBLEM   The quiche feels grainy.

SOLUTION   A small amount of cornstarch prevents the eggs from unraveling or separating during baking. While 1½ tablespoons of cornstarch may seem like an insignifi-cant amount, omitting this ingredient means that there's a risk of a grainy feel to the baked filling.

PROBLEM   The filling is tough around the exterior.

SOLUTION   The exterior rim of a quiche will be at a higher temperature than the center, so if left in the oven until the center is completely solid, the rim will be tough and over-cooked. The best way to check for doneness is to use an instant-read thermometer. A properly cooked quiche will register 170 degrees in the center.

SCIENCE LESSON   **Antidote to Curdled Custard: Cornstarch**

It's well known that too much heat can cause a custard to curdle. But onions are another culprit. They release a weak acid that produces an electrical charge on proteins, causing them to clump together so tightly that they squeeze out the moisture held between them. Starch granules in cornstarch interfere with this clumping and relax the proteins, which prevents them from squeezing out liquid and results in a smooth and creamy custard. Thanks to the cornstarch, we could add a full 2 cups of onions to our quiche with no ill effects.

Preventing Leaks in Pie Crust

Brushing the prebaked crust with lightly beaten egg white when it comes out of the oven helps seal any cracks. (The heat from the crust cooks the egg and creates a seal.) This trick will work with any blind-baked pie crust, though it is necessary only for custards or other wet fillings.

EGG SANDWICH PERFECTION

LAWMAN JOHNSON

These thoughtfully crafted egg sandwiches are hands-down better than any that you can buy out. What makes them special? They feature an "egg soufflé": tender, creamy, custardy eggs that stay neatly in place. The egg mixture bakes in a square metal baking pan with the added benefits that it makes four portions at a time and can be made ahead. Other components of the sandwiches include a well-seasoned savory ingredient, something rich and creamy, and a fresh accent or two, all of which adds up to a supremely satisfying package of flavors and textures that you'll want to eat for breakfast, lunch, and dinner.

LAWMAN'S PRO TIP: *Preparing the perfect egg sandwich is as much about perfectly cooked eggs as it is about pairing those eggs with complementing ingredients.*

BAKED EGGS FOR SANDWICHES

Serves: 4
Total Time: 1 hour

RECIPE OVERVIEW For an egg sandwich with tender, creamy eggs that stay put inside the bread, skip frying and scrambling. Inspired by a recipe from restaurateur and cookbook author Joanne Chang, we whisk water into eggs, season them lightly, and then gently bake them in a water bath. This hands-off method produces a custardy-smooth, silky egg filling. Tuck squares of the baked eggs into lightly toasted rolls or bread and add a carefully chosen selection of other ingredients to create egg sandwich nirvana. This recipe requires an 8-inch square metal baking pan. Avoid using a ceramic or glass dish, which will increase the cooking time and could cause the eggs to overcook during cooling. Each of our sandwich recipes calls for a salty component; if you omit it, you may want to season the eggs with additional salt after baking. For maximum efficiency, prepare your sandwich fillings while the eggs cook, and toast the bread while the eggs cool. Alternatively, let the eggs cool completely after cutting them, stack them in an airtight container, and refrigerate them for up to 3 days. To reheat, arrange the egg squares on a large plate and microwave at 50 percent power until they're warm (about 45 seconds for a single square or 2 to 3 minutes for four squares).

8 large eggs
¼ teaspoon table salt

1. Adjust oven rack to middle position and heat oven to 300 degrees. Whisk eggs and salt in large bowl until well combined. Whisk in ⅔ cup water. Spray 8-inch square baking pan with vegetable oil spray. Pour egg mixture into prepared pan and set pan on rimmed baking sheet. Add 1½ cups water to sheet. Transfer sheet to oven and bake until eggs are fully set, 35 to 40 minutes, rotating pan halfway through baking. Remove pan from sheet, transfer to wire rack, and let cool for 10 minutes.

2. Run knife around edges of pan and, using dish towel or oven mitts, invert eggs onto cutting board (if eggs stick to pan, tap bottom of pan firmly to dislodge). Cut into 4 equal squares.

KEYS TO SUCCESS

- **Use a square metal baking pan:** Metal heats up and cools down quickly, helping to prevent carryover cooking. An 8-inch square pan produces 4 neat squares of egg.

- **Keep the egg base neutral:** Allows for experimentation with highly seasoned toppings

- **Bake at a low oven temperature:** Keeps the eggs from overcooking

EGG, KIMCHI, AND AVOCADO SANDWICHES

Serves: 4
Total Time: 1¼ hours

We like the flavor and texture of kaiser rolls for these sandwiches, but you can substitute 4-inch bulkie rolls, English muffins, or burger buns, if desired. Blot the kimchi dry while the eggs bake.

¼ cup mayonnaise
4 kaiser rolls, halved and lightly toasted
¼ cup chopped fresh cilantro
1 recipe Baked Eggs for Sandwiches
1 ripe avocado, halved, pitted, and sliced thin
¾ cup cabbage kimchi, drained, chopped coarse, and blotted dry with paper towels

Spread mayonnaise on roll bottoms. Sprinkle cilantro over mayonnaise. Using spatula, transfer 1 egg square to each sandwich. Top each egg square with avocado and then kimchi. Set roll tops over kimchi and serve.

EGG, SMOKED SALMON, AND DILL SANDWICHES

Serves: 4
Total Time: 1¼ hours

We like the flavor and texture of rye bread for these sandwiches, but you can substitute 4-inch bulkie rolls, kaiser rolls, English muffins, or burger buns, if desired. Soak the onion while the eggs bake.

½ small red onion, sliced thin
Ice water
¼ cup plain Greek yogurt
8 slices hearty rye sandwich bread, lightly toasted
2 tablespoons chopped fresh dill
1 recipe Baked Eggs for Sandwiches
4 ounces smoked salmon

1. Place onion in bowl, cover with ice water, and let sit for 15 minutes. Drain onion well and pat dry.

2. Spread yogurt on 4 slices of toast. Sprinkle dill over yogurt. Using spatula, transfer 1 egg square to each sandwich. Top each egg square with smoked salmon and then onion. Set remaining 4 slices of toast over onion and serve.

EGG, HAM, AND PEPPERONCINI SANDWICHES

Serves: 4
Total Time: 1¼ hours

We like the flavor and texture of English muffins for these sandwiches, but you can substitute 4-inch bulkie rolls, kaiser rolls, or burger buns, if desired.

¼	cup apricot jam
4	English muffins, split and lightly toasted
1	recipe Baked Eggs for Sandwiches
4	slices deli cheddar cheese (4 ounces)
4	slices deli ham (4 ounces)
¼	cup pepperoncini, sliced and blotted dry

Spread jam on muffin bottoms. Using spatula, transfer 1 egg square to each sandwich. Top each egg square with cheddar, then ham, and then pepperoncini. Set muffin tops over pepperoncini and serve.

EGG, SALAMI, AND TOMATO SANDWICHES

Serves: 4
Total Time: 1¼ hours

We like the flavor and texture of bulkie rolls for these sandwiches, but you can substitute 4-inch kaiser rolls, English muffins, or burger buns, if desired.

¼	cup mayonnaise
4	bulkie rolls, halved and lightly toasted
¼	cup chopped fresh basil
1	recipe Baked Eggs for Sandwiches
12–16	thin slices salami (4 ounces)
4	thin tomato slices

Spread mayonnaise on roll bottoms. Sprinkle basil over mayonnaise. Using spatula, transfer 1 egg square to each sandwich. Top each egg square with salami and then 1 tomato slice. Set roll tops over tomato and serve.

Dilution Is the Solution

The proteins in raw eggs are coiled and don't interact with each other. But as eggs cook, the proteins unwind, entangle, and form a mesh. The tighter that mesh becomes, the firmer the eggs will be. But adding liquid puts space between the proteins, opening up the mesh. The result: tender, silky eggs.

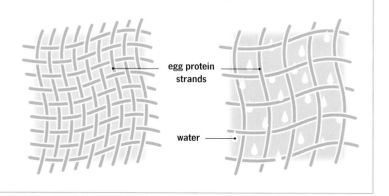

egg protein strands

water

PRINCIPLES FOR EGG SANDWICH PERFECTION

INGREDIENT SELECTION

Anchor the flavor
Build the sandwich around a well-seasoned, savory ingredient such as ham, smoked salmon, kimchi, or salami.

Add richness
Mayonnaise, cheese, Greek yogurt, or avocado contribute fat and creaminess.

Layer in accents
Acidic, pungent, and/or fresh choices such as herbs, tomatoes, onion, and jam work well.

ASSEMBLY

Mitigate moisture
Excess juices don't just drip; they also lubricate the other ingredients, making them prone to slipping out with every bite. Pat wet ingredients dry and avoid superjuicy ones in the first place.

Don't stack slippery ingredients Items such as multiple tomato slices will slide around and fall out of the sandwich.

Toast bread lightly
Crunchy, heavily toasted bread will cause ingredients to slide out when bitten.

Use creamy ingredients as glue They will hold lighter ingredients such as chopped herbs in place.

THE BENEFITS OF BAKING EGGS FOR SANDWICHES

Creamy, Custardy Texture
Beating some water into the eggs and baking them slowly in a water bath produces a luxuriously smooth consistency that pairs beautifully with crisp toast and multitextured sandwich fixings.

Make-Ahead Potential
Because the egg squares are relatively thin, they warm up quickly in the microwave and thus maintain their moisture and delicate texture.

If you'd like to plan for a meal on the go, prepare the eggs in advance, cut them into squares, and let them cool completely. Stack the squares in an airtight container and refrigerate them for up to three days.

To reheat, arrange the egg square(s) on a plate and microwave at 50 percent power until they're warm (about 45 seconds for a single square or 2 to 3 minutes for four squares).

COURSE
SAVORY SOUFFLÉS

ANNIE PETITO

A well-made cheese soufflé is a thing of beauty, tall and impressive. Seemingly complicated and finicky, a cheese soufflé is really nothing more than a sauce transformed through the addition of egg whites and air. This course begins with an Italian soufflé-like baked egg custard called a sformato. It's a great starter soufflé with pronounced cheese flavor and an elegant form. Next you can move on to master making a traditional towering cheese soufflé. Want to handily impress and feed a crowd? Serve a rolled soufflé that's stuffed with spinach and cheese. With the foolproof recipes in this course, you'll be whipping up light-as-air soufflés every time.

ANNIE'S PRO TIP: *I like to serve soufflés in a pretty classic manner: alongside lightly dressed salad leaves and a bright, tangy condiment like pickled mustard seeds.*

THE METHOD
SOUFFLÉ

The most foolproof way to test a soufflé for doneness is with an instant-read thermometer. To judge doneness without a thermometer, use two large spoons to pry open the soufflé so that you can peer inside it; the center should appear thick and creamy but not soupy.

1 COAT DISH WITH CHEESE
Grease soufflé dish and coat it evenly with grated Parmesan cheese.

2 MAKE BÉCHAMEL AND ADD TWO CHEESES
Make butter and milk sauce thickened with flour. Off heat, whisk in shredded Gruyère and more Parmesan until melted.

3 WHISK IN EGG YOLKS
When cool, whisk in egg yolks until incorporated.

4 WHIP EGG WHITES
Using stand mixer, whip egg whites and cream of tartar to stiff peaks (until they're glossy, firm, and hold their shape).

5 ADD CHEESE MIXTURE TO EGG WHITES
Add cheese mixture to whites and continue to whip.

6 LEAVE 1 INCH HEADROOM
Gently pour soufflé batter into prepared dish, leaving 1 inch headroom so batter can set before it rises above top of dish.

7 BAKE AND CHECK FOR DONENESS
Bake soufflé until surface is deep golden brown and it has risen 2 to 2½ inches above rim. To test for doneness, use an instant-read thermometer or two spoons to pull open top and check inside.

LEMON-HERB SFORMATI

Serves: 6
Total Time: 1¼ hours, plus 20 minutes cooling

RECIPE OVERVIEW A sformato is an elegant Italian baked egg custard with the light texture of a soufflé. Our individual sformati start with an egg-rich base that uses 8 eggs and then further enriches the custard by substituting half-and-half for some of the milk in the béchamel. To ensure that the custard bakes up silky but fully set, cook the sformati to between 175 and 180 degrees and then let them rest in the ramekins, by which point they will have cooled and set up enough to release cleanly. To flavor the custard, season the béchamel with salty-rich Pecorino as well as black and cayenne peppers and add fresh herbs and lemon zest to the custard. For a flavorful, texturally interesting garnish, enhance a classic Italian gremolata with butter-toasted panko bread crumbs and more cheese. The sformati will soufflé in the oven but will settle back to their original size while cooling. To take the temperature of the sformati, touch the probe tip to the bottom of the ramekin and pull it up about 1 inch. Fresh thyme can be used in place of fresh tarragon, if desired. The sformati can be served warm or at room temperature.

Sformati

- 8 large eggs
- 1 teaspoon salt
- 6 tablespoons unsalted butter
- 1 garlic clove, minced
- ¼ cup plus 2 tablespoons (1¾ ounces) all-purpose flour
- 1½ cups whole milk
- 1½ cups half-and-half
- 1½ ounces Pecorino Romano cheese, grated (¾ cup)
- ¼ teaspoon pepper
  Pinch cayenne pepper
- 2 tablespoons chopped fresh chives
- 2 teaspoons chopped fresh tarragon
- ½ teaspoon grated lemon zest

Gremolata

- 1 tablespoon unsalted butter
- 1 garlic clove, minced
- ¼ cup panko bread crumbs
- ¼ cup grated Pecorino Romano cheese
- ¼ cup chopped fresh chives
- 1 teaspoon finely grated lemon zest
  Table salt
  Pepper

1. FOR THE SFORMATI Adjust oven rack to upper-middle position and heat oven to 325 degrees. Grease six 6-ounce ramekins and place on wire rack set in rimmed baking sheet. Whisk eggs and salt together in bowl until homogeneous and set aside.

2. Melt butter in medium saucepan over medium heat. Add garlic and cook until fragrant, about 30 seconds. Stir in flour and cook for 1 minute. Slowly whisk in milk and half-and-half until smooth. Increase heat to high and bring to simmer, 2 to 4 minutes. Continue to cook, stirring constantly, 1 minute longer. Remove pan from heat and whisk in Pecorino, pepper, and cayenne until smooth. Let béchamel cool for 5 minutes.

3. Whisk chives, tarragon, lemon zest, and reserved eggs into béchamel until smooth. Divide mixture evenly among ramekins (¼ inch from top of each ramekin). Bake until centers register 175 to 180 degrees, 30 to 35 minutes.

4. FOR THE GREMOLATA While sformati are baking, melt butter in 8-inch skillet over medium-low heat. Add garlic and cook until fragrant, about 30 seconds. Add panko and cook, stirring frequently, until golden brown, 1 to 2 minutes. Let mixture cool for 2 minutes, then stir in Pecorino, chives, and lemon zest. Season with salt and pepper to taste.

5. Remove sformati from oven and let cool for 20 minutes. Invert sformati onto individual plates. Sprinkle evenly with gremolata and serve.

Variations
ROASTED RED PEPPER SFORMATI

Substitute Parmesan cheese for the Pecorino Romano in both the sformati and the gremolata. Omit chives and tarragon from sformati. Transfer cooled béchamel to blender along with ¾ cup rinsed and patted dry jarred roasted red peppers. Process until mixture is very smooth and homogeneous, 30 to 60 seconds. Transfer mixture to large bowl and whisk in lemon zest and reserved eggs until smooth. Continue with recipe as written.

SPINACH SFORMATI

Substitute Parmesan cheese for the Pecorino Romano in both the sformati and the gremolata. Omit chives and tarragon from sformati. Transfer cooled béchamel to blender along with 8 ounces thawed and squeezed dry frozen spinach. Process until mixture is very smooth and homogeneous, 30 to 60 seconds. Transfer mixture to large bowl and whisk in lemon zest and reserved eggs until smooth. Continue with recipe as written.

KEYS TO SUCCESS

- **An egg-rich base:** Contains 8 whole eggs

- **Half-and-half:** Adds extra richness to the béchamel

- **Let cool:** Sformati need to rest for 20 minutes before unmolding.

CHEESE SOUFFLÉ

Serves: 4 to 6
Total Time: 1¼ hours

RECIPE OVERVIEW This classic cheese soufflé has bold cheese flavor, good stature, and a light but not-too-airy texture, without the fussiness of most recipes. To bump up the cheese flavor without weighing it down, we add light-but-potent Parmesan cheese to the Gruyère. To get the texture just right while keeping the preparation simple, beat the egg whites to stiff peaks, and then—rather than carefully folding them into the cheese-béchamel—just add the sauce right to the mixer and beat everything until uniform. For well-rounded flavor, season with a little paprika, cayenne, white pepper, and nutmeg. Comté, sharp cheddar, or gouda cheese can be substituted for the Gruyère. To prevent the soufflé from overflowing the soufflé dish, leave at least 1 inch of space between the top of the batter and the rim of the dish; any excess batter should be discarded. The most foolproof way to test for doneness is with an instant-read thermometer. To judge doneness without a thermometer, use two large spoons to pry open the soufflé so that you can peer inside it; the center should appear thick and creamy but not soupy.

1	ounce Parmesan cheese, grated (½ cup), divided
¼	cup (1¼ ounces) all-purpose flour
¼	teaspoon paprika
¼	teaspoon table salt
⅛	teaspoon cayenne pepper
⅛	teaspoon white pepper
	Pinch ground nutmeg
4	tablespoons unsalted butter
1⅓	cups whole milk
6	ounces Gruyère cheese, shredded (1½ cups)
6	large eggs, separated
2	teaspoons minced fresh parsley, divided
¼	teaspoon cream of tartar

1. Adjust oven rack to middle position and heat oven to 350 degrees. Spray 8-inch round (2-quart) soufflé dish with vegetable oil spray, then sprinkle with 2 tablespoons Parmesan.

2. Combine flour, paprika, salt, cayenne, white pepper, and nutmeg in bowl. Melt butter in small saucepan over medium heat. Stir in flour mixture and cook for 1 minute. Slowly whisk in milk and bring to simmer. Cook, whisking constantly, until mixture is thickened and smooth, about 1 minute. Remove pan from heat and whisk in Gruyère and 5 tablespoons Parmesan until melted and smooth. Let cool for 10 minutes, then whisk in egg yolks and 1½ teaspoons parsley.

3. Using stand mixer fitted with whisk, whip egg whites and cream of tartar on medium-low speed until foamy, about 1 minute. Increase speed to medium-high and whip until stiff peaks form, 3 to 4 minutes. Add cheese mixture and continue to whip until fully combined, about 15 seconds.

4. Pour mixture into prepared dish and sprinkle with remaining 1 tablespoon Parmesan. Bake until risen above rim, top is deep golden brown, and interior registers 170 degrees, 30 to 35 minutes. Sprinkle with remaining ½ teaspoon parsley and serve immediately.

KEYS TO SUCCESS

- **Coat the dish with Parmesan**: This helps batter rise higher by not adhering to dish.

- **Two cheeses in the base**: Adds flavor without the weight

- **Add cream of tartar**: Makes the whites more stable

- **Beat don't fold**: Beating the egg whites into the base mixture delivers a light soufflé.

- **Use an instant-read thermometer**: The most reliable way to judge doneness

WHAT CAN GO WRONG

PROBLEM   The soufflé doesn't rise enough.

SOLUTION   Cleanly separate the eggs. If bits of yolk contaminate the whites, the whites won't whip properly. Separate the eggs straight from the fridge (when chilled, the yolks are taut and less likely to break), but let whites warm up a bit before beating them.

PROBLEM   The soufflé overflows the dish.

SOLUTION   As the soufflé bakes, the heat of the oven causes the moisture in the whipped egg whites to expand, giving the soufflé height. To prevent the soufflé from overflowing the soufflé dish, leave at least 1 inch of space between the top of the batter and the rim of the dish.

PROBLEM   The soufflé is dry and bland.

SOLUTION   Do not overbake the soufflé, thinking that more time will equal greater rise. During the final 10 minutes in the oven the soufflé isn't really rising as much as it is cooking through. Overbaking not only compromises the texture of the soufflé but also dulls the flavors.

ROLLED SPINACH AND CHEESE SOUFFLÉ FOR A CROWD

Serves: 10 to 12
Total Time: 1¾ hours, plus 30 minutes cooling

RECIPE OVERVIEW   A rolled soufflé, also known as egg roulade, is a white sauce–based egg dish leavened with whipped egg whites and stuffed with spinach and cheese. We liked the fluffy appearance of thicker roulades, but they tended to be tough and dry. Using flour and Parmesan in the egg base offers structure without toughness. Rolling the roulade on the baking sheet with the aid of the parchment paper lining helps make a perfect roulade without tearing. While a project piece, this flavorful roulade makes for an elegant brunch—and you can make it a day ahead.

Eggs
- ¾ cup all-purpose flour
- 6 tablespoons unsalted butter, melted
- 1 teaspoon table salt
- ½ teaspoon pepper
- 2¾ cups milk
- 1½ ounces Parmesan cheese, grated (¾ cup)
- 10 large eggs, separated
- ½ teaspoon cream of tartar

Filling
- 10 ounces frozen chopped spinach, thawed and squeezed dry
- 4 ounces Gruyère cheese, shredded (1 cup)
- 3 tablespoons minced fresh chives
- 2 tablespoons milk
- ½ teaspoon pepper
- ¼ teaspoon table salt

1. FOR THE EGGS   Adjust oven rack to middle position and heat oven to 375 degrees. Line 18 by 13-inch rimmed baking sheet with 18 by 16-inch sheet of aluminum foil, folding excess over sides of sheet, and spray foil and sides of sheet liberally with vegetable oil spray. Top foil with two 16½ by 13½-inch sheets of parchment paper, allowing parchment to overhang one long edge of baking sheet by 1 inch. Spray parchment liberally with vegetable oil spray.

2. Combine flour, butter, salt, and pepper in bowl and mash with fork to make smooth paste. Bring milk to boil in medium saucepan. Reduce heat to medium-low, whisk in flour mixture, and simmer, whisking constantly, until thickened, about 2 minutes. Off heat, whisk in Parmesan; reserve ⅓ cup of milk mixture for filling. Scrape remaining milk mixture into large bowl, let sit until slightly cooled, about 10 minutes, and then whisk in egg yolks.

Constructing a Rolled Soufflé

SPREAD AND BAKE
Gently spread egg base onto greased and lined rimmed baking sheet. Bake.

ADD FILLING
Carefully spread spinach-cheese filling over cooked, cooled egg base.

ROLL
Now roll two together using the parchment paper to help. Return roll to oven to warm.

3. Using stand mixer fitted with whisk, whip egg whites and cream of tartar on medium-low speed until foamy, about 1 minute. Increase speed to medium-high and whip until stiff peaks form, 3 to 4 minutes. Gently fold one-third of beaten egg whites into milk-yolk mixture. Using rubber spatula, fold in remaining egg whites until no white streaks remain. Spread mixture onto prepared baking sheet. Bake until golden brown and set, 22 to 24 minutes. Let cool in pan for 30 minutes. Reduce oven to 325 degrees.

4. FOR THE FILLING Combine reserved milk mixture, spinach, Gruyère, chives, milk, pepper, and salt in bowl and microwave until hot, 1 to 2 minutes. Spread spinach filling evenly over cooled egg sheet. Using parchment overhang, lift long edge of egg sheet and roll to opposite edge (parchment should encase roulade when rolling). With roulade still resting on edge of parchment, pull roulade to center of baking sheet, and finally roll it off seam side down onto foil; discard parchment. (Roulade can be wrapped in plastic wrap and refrigerated for up to 2 hours. To serve, discard plastic and proceed with step 5, increasing baking time to 35 minutes.)

5. Cover roulade with foil, and bake until hot throughout, about 25 minutes. Slice into 1-inch-thick slices and serve.

KEYS TO SUCCESS

- **Same base for the eggs and the filling:** Soufflé base binds the filling.
- **Grated Parmesan:** Provides just enough bulk to support a tall, tender roulade
- **Butter and flour paste:** Easier than making a roux to thicken the milk
- **Microwave the filling:** Makes for better spreadability

SOUFFLÉ MYTHS DEBUNKED

MYTH The soufflé will collapse from loud noises or sudden movements.

REALITY Steam will keep a hot soufflé fully inflated. No loud noise or slamming of the oven door can change that.

MYTH The egg whites must be gently folded into the base.

REALITY Egg whites whipped to stiff peaks will have ample structure to handle aggressive beating, even in a stand mixer.

MYTH Prodding to check doneness will make it collapse.

REALITY A soufflé is not a balloon; it's a matrix of very fine bubbles. No tool can pop enough of them to cause it to fall.

MYTH You can't make a fallen soufflé rise again.

REALITY Yes, your soufflé will fall after it's been out of the oven for about 5 minutes. But returning it to a 350-degree oven will convert the water back into steam and reinflate it (but it will lose about ½ inch of height).

FALLEN FROM GRACE

RETURNED TO GLORY

AVOIDING SOUFFLÉ MELTDOWNS

We developed a new approach for keeping soufflé spillovers at bay during cooking, eliminating the need for a parchment collar.

Soufflé recipes traditionally require attaching a greased parchment collar around the lip of the soufflé dish. Extending the collar several inches above the dish keeps the soufflé contained so that it rises up rather than spills over. But we found that the old-fashioned approach isn't necessary. The key is giving the fluid batter enough room to set up before it rises above the dish's lip. It takes about 20 minutes for the batter to reach the rim, at which point it's set and will continue to rise up, rather than spill over. In our Cheese Soufflé recipe (page 61), we call for leaving an inch of space between the top of the batter and the rim of the dish. Because soufflé dishes vary a bit in capacity, you may not need all the batter in our recipe, so discard any left over after filling your dish to the proper level.

SHOOT FOR BELOW THE RIM
Leaving 1 inch of space between the batter and the rim of the dish gives the batter room to set.

EGG-BASED SAUCES

CHRISTIE MORRISON

Rich and flavorful mayonnaise, hollandaise, béarnaise: These velvety-smooth classic sauces add an indispensable touch to whatever they are paired with. Mayonnaise needs no introduction. Hollandaise is one of the five classic French sauces, while béarnaise goes deeper into savory territory. These traditional French sauces can be finicky to make but in this course you will learn innovative techniques that turn finicky into foolproof, creating thick and creamy emulsions.

CHRISTIE'S PRO TIP: *When in doubt, add water. Hot egg-based sauces like Hollandaise and Béarnaise begin to curdle when the eggs get too hot and dry. A splash of water added to the mix can rescue a sauce if it hasn't gone too far. With cold sauces like mayonnaise, a little water can loosen a too-tight mayo and make it more spreadable.*

MAYONNAISE

Makes: 1½ cups
Total Time: 15 minutes

RECIPE OVERVIEW Mayonnaise is an egg-emulsified sauce made with vegetable oil instead of butter. This homemade mayo can be stored for one month because it's made with pasteurized egg yolks. Pasteurizing is as simple as heating the yolks to 160 degrees. Mixing in water and lemon juice keeps the base of the mayo fluid even though it has been heated. Immediately whisking oil into that base cools it and prevents it from thickening. At the same time, whisking breaks the oil into tiny droplets, the critical starting point for any mayo. With those droplets in place, blend the mixture in a food processor while slowly pouring in the rest of the oil to create a dense, creamy mayo. Since the oil is a major part of this recipe, use a freshly opened bottle for the best results. This recipe was designed for a food processor; we don't recommend substituting other appliances.

- 3 tablespoons water
- 2 large egg yolks
- 4 teaspoons lemon juice
- 1½ cups vegetable oil, divided
- ¾ teaspoon table salt
- ½ teaspoon Dijon mustard
- ¼ teaspoon sugar

1. Gently stir water, egg yolks, and lemon juice in bowl until no streaks of yolk remain. Microwave, stirring gently every 10 seconds, until mixture thickens slightly and registers 160 to 165 degrees, 1 to 2 minutes. Immediately add ¼ cup oil, salt, mustard, and sugar; whisk to combine. (Tiny droplets of oil will float to top of mixture.)

2. Strain mixture through fine-mesh strainer into bowl of food processor. With processor running, slowly drizzle in remaining 1¼ cups oil in thin stream, about 2 minutes. Scrape bottom and sides of bowl and process 5 seconds longer. Transfer to airtight container and refrigerate for up to 1 month.

Variations
AIOLI
Add 2 peeled and smashed garlic cloves to blender with egg yolks.

SMOKED PAPRIKA MAYONNAISE
Substitute lime juice for lemon juice. Add 1½ teaspoons smoked paprika, ¼ teaspoon ground cumin, and 1 small peeled and smashed garlic clove to blender with egg yolks.

HERBED MAYONNAISE
Add 2 tablespoons chopped fresh basil, 1 tablespoon chopped fresh parsley, and 1 tablespoon minced fresh chives to mayonnaise and pulse until combined but not smooth, about 10 pulses.

KEYS TO SUCCESS

- **Lemon juice and mustard:** Contribute rich, tangy flavor
- **Pasteurize the yolks:** Microwaving them gives the mayonnaise a longer shelf life.
- **Reliable method:** Whisking oil into microwaved yolk mixture cools it and creates a strong emulsion.

Ways to Use Mayonnaise

- To take sandwiches to the next level
- To make perfect deli salads
- As a dip for french fries and crudités
- As a garnish for hearty stews
- Dolloped on grilled or roasted poultry, meat, and fish

Mayo Under the Microscope

If you were to zoom in on a dense emulsion such as mayo, you would see tons of tiny oil droplets tightly packed together—but not actually touching. Keeping those droplets separate is the key to a stable emulsion. But it's a fragile business because the droplets are attracted to one another, and if they merge the emulsion fails. That's why emulsions contain emulsifiers (in mayonnaise, these are the lecithin in egg yolks and the polysaccharides in mustard), which form thin barriers around each oil droplet so that the droplets can coexist without coalescing into greasy pools.

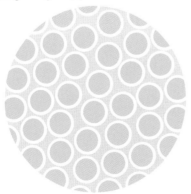

A DENSE EMULSION

HOLLANDAISE SAUCE

Serves: 4 to 6 (makes about 1¼ cups)
Total Time: 15 minutes

RECIPE OVERVIEW Although a stable hollandaise can be achieved the old-fashioned way with a double boiler, slow cooking, and constant monitoring, the best way to make this sauce recipe foolproof is to use the blender. Hollandaise is a notoriously finicky sauce that is prone to breaking because it requires butter to be emulsified into egg yolks. Slowly adding hot, melted butter (it needs to be 180 degrees to cook the eggs properly) into a mixture of egg yolks, lemon juice, and cayenne while the blender is running successfully creates a thick and creamy emulsion every time. For an unusual take on hollandaise, one variation goes in a distinctly savory direction with the addition of whole-grain mustard and fresh dill. We also created a delicate, aromatic saffron version and a tarragon-flecked béarnaise. The classic use for hollandaise is Eggs Benedict (page 68).

- 3 large egg yolks
- 2 tablespoons lemon juice
- ¼ teaspoon table salt
  Pinch cayenne pepper, plus extra for seasoning
- 16 tablespoons unsalted butter, melted and hot (180 degrees)

Process egg yolks, lemon juice, salt, and cayenne in blender until frothy, about 10 seconds, scraping bottom and sides of blender jar as needed. With blender running, slowly add hot butter and process until hollandaise is emulsified, about 2 minutes. Adjust consistency with hot water as needed until sauce drips slowly from spoon. Season with extra salt and cayenne to taste. Serve immediately.

Variations

MUSTARD-DILL HOLLANDAISE SAUCE

Add 1 tablespoon whole-grain mustard and 1 tablespoon minced fresh dill to hollandaise and blend until combined but not smooth.

SAFFRON HOLLANDAISE SAUCE

Add ⅛ teaspoon crumbled saffron threads to blender with egg yolks.

BÉARNAISE SAUCE

This sauce is a steakhouse classic, but it's just as versatile as hollandaise and is also great with burgers, grilled salmon, and roasted broccoli, just for starters.

Bring ½ cup white wine vinegar, 1 thinly sliced shallot, and 2 sprigs fresh tarragon to simmer in small skillet and cook until about 2 tablespoons of vinegar remain, 5 to 7 minutes; discard shallot and tarragon sprigs. Substitute seasoned vinegar for lemon juice. Add 1½ tablespoons minced fresh tarragon to hollandaise and pulse until combined but not smooth, about 10 pulses.

KEYS TO SUCCESS

- **A blender:** Vortex of the blender produces tinier suspended fat droplets for a better emulsion.
- **Hot 180-degree butter:** Needed to cook the egg yolks sufficiently
- **Adding butter very slowly:** Ensures that the sauce emulsifies properly

Ways to Use Hollandaise

- As a dip for poached shrimp

- Dolloped on grilled or roasted poultry, meat, and fish

- Drizzled onto blanched asparagus and broccoli and onto roasted root vegetables

- Drizzled on savory fritters

CORE TECHNIQUE
Adding Hot Butter to a Blender

MELT BUTTER
Melt butter and keep hot.

ADD HOT BUTTER
With blender running, slowly add hot butter and process until sauce is emulsified.

EGGS BENEDICT

Serves: 4
Total Time: 40 minutes

Our foolproof Hollandaise Sauce makes the fussiest part of this iconic brunch dish a breeze. For the best results, be sure to use the freshest eggs possible. Prepare the hollandaise after you have poached all 8 eggs in step 4. For two delicious takes on the classic, try replacing the bacon with smoked salmon and top with Mustard-Dill Hollandaise Sauce (page 67), or replace the bacon with roasted asparagus and top with Béarnaise Sauce (page 67).

- 8 slices Canadian bacon
- 4 English muffins, split and toasted
- 1 tablespoon distilled white vinegar
- 1 teaspoon table salt
- 8 large eggs
- 1 recipe Hollandaise Sauce (page 67)

1. Adjust oven rack to middle position and heat oven to 300 degrees. Place 1 slice Canadian bacon on each toasted English muffin half and arrange on rimmed baking sheet; keep warm in oven.

2. Bring 6 cups water to boil in Dutch oven, then add vinegar and salt. Fill second pot with water and heat until it registers 150 degrees; adjust heat as needed to maintain 150 degrees.

3. Crack 4 eggs, 1 at a time, into colander. Let stand until loose, watery whites drain away from eggs, 20 to 30 seconds. Gently transfer eggs to 2-cup liquid measuring cup. With lip of measuring cup just above surface of water, gently tip eggs into water, 1 at a time, leaving space between them. Cover pot, remove from heat, and let sit until whites closest to yolks are just set and opaque, about 3 minutes. If after 3 minutes whites are not set, let eggs continue to stand in water, checking every 30 seconds, until eggs reach desired doneness. (For medium-cooked yolks, let eggs sit in pot, covered, for 4 minutes, then begin checking for doneness.)

4. Using slotted spoon, carefully lift and drain each egg, then transfer to pot filled with 150-degree water and cover. (Eggs can be held in 150-degree water for up to 15 minutes.) Return Dutch oven used to cook eggs to boil, and repeat steps 2 and 3 with remaining 4 eggs.

5. Transfer prepared English muffins to individual plates. Using slotted spoon, carefully lift and drain eggs individually and lay on top of each Canadian bacon slice. Spoon hollandaise over top and serve.

MAKING MAYO THAT KEEPS

Pasteurize the yolks. Heating the yolks to 160 degrees (this takes just a minute or two in the microwave) kills common pathogens, and abundant lemon juice keeps the mayo food-safe for up to one month.

Emulsifying sensitive sauces like hollandaise (page 67) by hand is fussy at best, ineffective at worst. We often use a blender to create stable emulsions in a flash; the sharp blades break down the liquids into smaller droplets so they stay mixed.

THE MOST RELIABLE WAY TO MAKE MAYO

One of the biggest deterrents for making mayonnaise is that it can fail to form an emulsion, creating a greasy, runny mess. Here is our solution.

A. Whisk in Some Oil
Incorporating the first ¼ cup of oil by hand reliably establishes a base emulsion.

B. Process Remaining Oil
Slowly incorporating the rest of the oil using a food processor breaks the oil into tiny droplets that stay well emulsified.

HOW TO FIX FAILED MAYO

Because the success of making mayonnaise in the food processor depends on having enough volume in the bowl—and that can vary, depending on the shape of the bowl—there is always a chance that mayonnaise will not form a proper emulsion. We came up with an easy way to fix it if it doesn't.

Transfer mayonnaise mixture to 2-cup liquid measuring cup. Place 4 teaspoons water in bowl and, while whisking vigorously, very slowly drizzle in about ½ cup mayonnaise mixture (consistency should resemble heavy cream). Transfer to food processor and process, slowly drizzling in remaining mayonnaise. Once all mayonnaise has been added, scrape bottom and sides of bowl and process for 5 seconds. (Consistency will be slightly looser than unbroken mayonnaise but still thick and creamy.)

FAILED   RESCUED

SOUS VIDE EGGS

JOSEPH GITTER

Sous vide cooking is an incredibly simple, fool-proof method for cooking everything from eggs to meat to poultry. There's no getting around it: Eggs are tricky to cook. The white and the yolk behave differently when subjected to heat. Because they contain different proportions of proteins, fats, and water, the white and yolk coagulate and set at different temperatures, and they have different final textures. The low-temperature water bath with a sous vide circulator allows you to cook eggs with a precision absent from traditional methods and eliminate any guesswork. And with eggs in particular, this makes a huge difference. You'll learn the key elements of sous vide egg cooking to turn out soft-poached eggs, hard-cooked eggs, and a delicious runny egg yolk sauce.

JOE'S PRO TIP: *If you're planning on making our showstopping Runny Egg Yolk Sauce, it's worth investing in a squeeze bottle for plating. It's so easy to make precise, stunning presentations using that simple bit of kit. Serve the sauce with blanched asparagus and a squeeze of lemon for the ultimate make-ahead, fancy restaurant dish. It's also excellent on a burger or a steak.*

THE METHOD
SOUS VIDE

Here's how to cook in an automatic water bath using a sous vide circulator.

1 SET UP YOUR RIG
Attach your immersion circulator to a heat-safe 7-quart or 12-quart container. Fill it with water to about 1 inch above machine's minimum water level line.

2 PREHEAT WATER
Turn on machine and set temperature to desired cooking temperature. Typically the bath is set to the final internal temperature of the food. Food sits in the bath and slowly comes up to its ideal temperature without any danger of overcooking.

3 SEAL FOOD OTHER THAN EGGS IN A BAG
Place food as flat as possible in zipper-lock freezer bag and press out as much air as you can. Seal bag. If cooking above 158 degrees, double-bag food to prevent any water leakage.

4 SUBMERGE BAG
Once bath is up to temperature, gently lower bag into the bath.

5 CLIP BAG TO CONTAINER
Clip corner of bag to side of container with binder clip, allowing remaining air bubbles to rise to top of bag.

6 REMOVE LAST AIR BUBBLES
Open one corner of zipper and release any remaining air, then reseal bag. (Removing air gives food better contact with heated water, so it cooks more quickly and evenly.) To prevent cold spots on food, make sure bag isn't touching sous vide machine or cooking vessel.

7 COOK FOOD
Cover water with plastic wrap (or sous-vide specific lid for your container) during cooking. Do not cover the circulator. Cover helps to minimize evaporation and to keep temperature static after adding ingredients to bath.

8 REMOVE FOOD FROM BATH AND FINISH IF NEEDED
Remove food from bath. Eggs and some other foods are ready to enjoy straight out of bath.

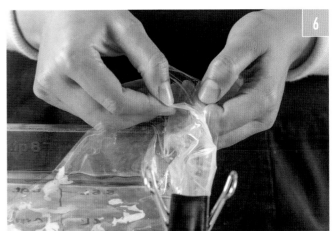

SOUS VIDE SOFT-POACHED EGGS

Makes: 1 to 16 eggs
Cooking Time: 20 minutes

RECIPE OVERVIEW Eggs are perhaps the poster child for sous vide cooking: The technique can produce eggs with unique texture; the method is hands-off; and the recipe is easily scalable. Typically, sous vide eggs are cooked at a low temperature (around 145 degrees) for at least an hour. This will give you a yolk that is slightly thickened but still runny and a barely set white. We found the white to be too loose when cooked in this temperature range, most of it running off when we cracked into the eggs. Some recipes call for cracking "63-degree eggs" such as these into simmering water to better set the whites. We opt to cook at a higher temperature for a shorter time to set more of the white. This method produces a traditional poached egg—right out of the shell. And with the ability to make these eggs ahead of time—just reheat them in a 140-degree water bath for anywhere from 15 to 60 minutes—this recipe is perfect for the brunch crowd. Be sure to use large eggs that have no cracks and are cold from the refrigerator. Fresher eggs have tighter egg whites and are better suited for this recipe. Serve with crusty bread or toast.

1–16 large eggs, chilled
Table salt and pepper

1. Using sous vide circulator, bring water to 167 degrees in 7-quart container. Using slotted spoon, gently lower eggs into prepared water bath, cover, and cook for 12 minutes.

2. Meanwhile, fill large bowl halfway with ice and water. Using slotted spoon, transfer eggs to ice bath and let sit until cool enough to touch, about 1 minute. To serve, crack eggs into individual bowls and season with salt and pepper to taste. (Eggs can be rapidly chilled in ice bath for 10 minutes and then refrigerated for up to 5 days. To reheat, lower eggs into water bath set to 140 degrees and cook until heated through, at least 15 minutes or up to 60 minutes. Crack into bowls as directed.)

SOUS VIDE HARD-COOKED EGGS

Makes: 1 to 18 eggs
Cooking Time: 20 minutes, plus chilling

RECIPE OVERVIEW Hard-cooked eggs are a breeze to make with a sous vide circulator. We like hard-cooked eggs that are easy to peel, with a set but not fudgy yolk. We found that cooking eggs in very hot water (194 degrees) rapidly denatured the outermost egg white proteins, causing them to form a solid gel that shrank and pulled away from the membrane. This translated to easy-peeling hard-cooked eggs with set but not overcooked yolks. (When we tested cooking eggs at lower temperatures for longer time periods, the egg whites stuck to the shell membrane, making peeling a frustrating task. And once we got those eggs peeled, their yolks were fudgy instead of firm.) Using sous vide to hard-cook eggs makes scaling the recipe up or down simple; the method and timing is the same for 1 to 18 eggs. So whether you're cooking a snack for yourself or preparing a large batch of deviled eggs for a party, this recipe has got you covered.

1–18 large eggs

1. Using sous vide circulator, bring water to 194 degrees in 7-quart container. Using slotted spoon, gently lower eggs into prepared water bath, cover, and cook for 20 minutes.

2. Meanwhile, fill large bowl halfway with ice and water. Using slotted spoon, transfer eggs to ice bath and let sit until chilled, about 15 minutes. Peel before serving. (Eggs can be rapidly chilled in ice bath for 15 minutes and then refrigerated for up to 5 days. They can be stored in their shells and peeled as needed.)

SOUS VIDE RUNNY EGG YOLK SAUCE

Makes: about 1 cup
Cooking Time: 20 minutes, plus chilling

RECIPE OVERVIEW Chefs are obsessed with emulsions because they combine something that is already delicious—rich fat—with a water-based ingredient to create something even more satisfying (think mayonnaise, butter, and cream—all emulsions). And egg yolks are one of nature's top-notch emulsions—a creamy mixture of water, protein, and fat (a full 34 percent). We love a good runny egg yolk, and this recipe provides the convenience of pasteurized, perfectly thickened yolks always ready to drizzle on toast, a burger, pasta carbonara, you name it. This recipe safely achieves pasteurization (144 degrees for at least 6 minutes) and then continues to heat the yolks to create a sauce with the ideal runny texture. Store-bought, in-shell, pasteurized eggs can also be used without any changes to the recipe. The cooking time depends on the number of yolks, so this recipe cannot be scaled up or down without making adjustments. Don't discard the whites—save them to make recipes such as angel food cake or meringue cookies. You can also freeze them for later use.

12 **large egg yolks**
¼ **teaspoon table salt**

1. Using sous vide circulator, bring water to 149 degrees in 7-quart container. Using spatula or ladle, push yolks through fine-mesh strainer into medium bowl; gently whisk yolks and salt until just smooth (do not overwhisk).

2. Pour mixture into 1-quart zipper-lock freezer bag. Seal bag, pressing out as much air as possible. Gently lower bag into prepared water bath until mixture is fully submerged, and then clip top corner of bag to side of water bath container, allowing remaining air bubbles to rise to top of bag. Reopen 1 corner of zipper, release remaining air bubbles, and reseal bag. Cover and cook for 32 minutes.

3. Meanwhile, fill large bowl halfway with ice and water. Transfer bag to ice bath and let sit until chilled, about 10 minutes. Transfer sauce to airtight container or squeeze bottle and refrigerate. (Sauce can be refrigerated for up to 1 week.)

CORE TECHNIQUE

Using an Ice Bath

If you're not serving food right away, it's important to rapidly chill the food before storage. Why? Food safety. Plunge the still-sealed bags into a large ice bath to stop the cooking, let sit until chilled, and then refrigerate it for later.

RESOURCES FOR SOUS VIDE COOKING

WHY YOU SHOULD SOUS VIDE

- It ensures perfectly and uniformly cooked food.
- The process is quiet, neat, and mostly hands-off.
- There is minimal cleanup because you're cooking your food in a bag.
- Vegetables are vibrantly colored and intensely flavorful because they're not cooked directly in water.
- Tough cuts of meat become fork-tender with long, slow, and gentle cooking.

HOW DO IMMERSION CIRCULATORS WORK?

The body of the machine houses a motor; a heating coil; one or more temperature sensors; and an impeller, which is like a propeller, that circulates water past the coil and throughout the vessel as the sensors monitor and adjust the heat.

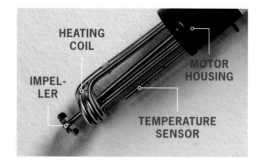

THE SOUS VIDE COOKING STARTER KIT

CHOOSE YOUR COOKING VESSEL

| Dutch Oven | Large Container | Large Saucepan | Stockpot | Cooler |

CHOOSE YOUR FOOD CONTAINER

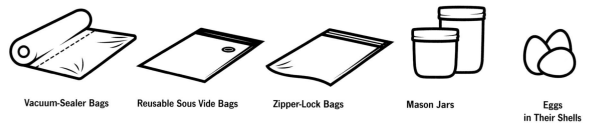

| Vacuum-Sealer Bags | Reusable Sous Vide Bags | Zipper-Lock Bags | Mason Jars | Eggs in Their Shells |

FOR LONGER COOKING:

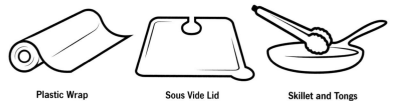

| Plastic Wrap | Sous Vide Lid | Skillet and Tongs |

Cover the vessel (but not the device) to prevent water evaporation. Choose plastic wrap or a reusable sous vide lid (be sure that it fits your device and vessel).

FOR FINISHING UP

After cooking meat, fish, or chicken sous vide, brown it on the stove for better appearance and better flavor.

Pro Tip Use binder clips. Large metal binder clips are handy for clipping the bag of food to the wall of the vessel and makes it easy to retrieve the bag once the food is cooked.

TIME AND TEMPERATURE CHART FOR SOUS VIDE EGGS

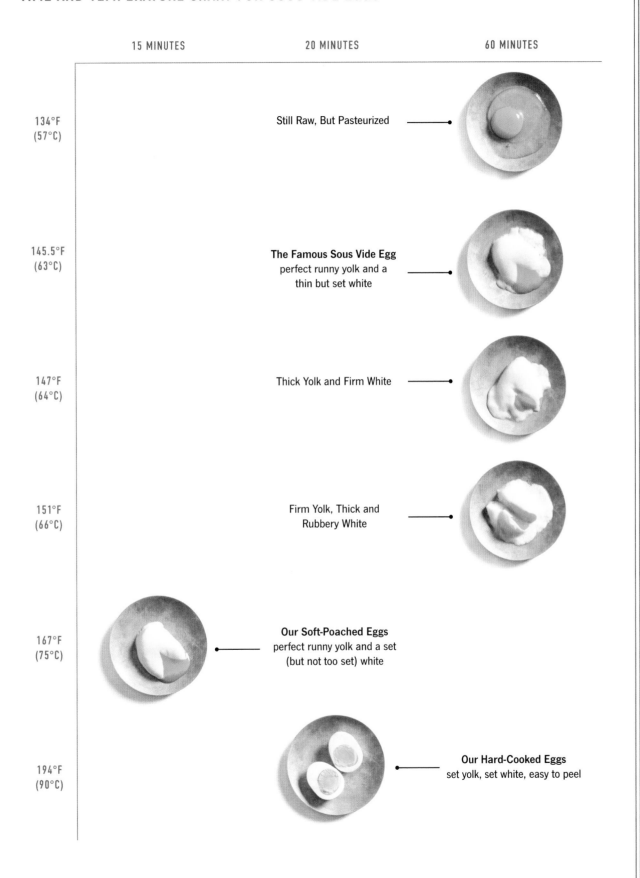

15 MINUTES	20 MINUTES	60 MINUTES

134°F (57°C) — Still Raw, But Pasteurized

145.5°F (63°C) — **The Famous Sous Vide Egg** perfect runny yolk and a thin but set white

147°F (64°C) — Thick Yolk and Firm White

151°F (66°C) — Firm Yolk, Thick and Rubbery White

167°F (75°C) — **Our Soft-Poached Eggs** perfect runny yolk and a set (but not too set) white

194°F (90°C) — **Our Hard-Cooked Eggs** set yolk, set white, easy to peel

Curing whole eggs or egg yolks in some combination of salt and sugar transforms them into something totally new that is full of incredible flavor.

SOY-MARINATED EGGS

Makes: 8 eggs

Total Time: 55 minutes, plus 3 hours marinating

These savory, runny-yoked eggs are great in ramen, on salads, or simply eaten on a piece of toast. To achieve easy-to-peel eggs with soft, jammy yolks, boil them for exactly 7 minutes in 3 quarts of water and then shock them in an ice bath. For perfectly seasoned eggs full of complex, savory flavor, marinate them for 3 to 4 hours in a mix of soy sauce, mirin, garlic, ginger, and scallions. A bit of sugar helps balance the salty soy sauce, and adding water to the potent marinade ensures that the eggs don't end up too salty. The soy marinade can be reused to marinate up to three batches of soft-cooked eggs; it can be refrigerated for up to 1 week and frozen for up to 1 month.

  1 **cup soy sauce**
  ¼ **cup mirin**
  2 **scallions, sliced thin**
  2 **tablespoons grated fresh ginger**
  2 **tablespoons sugar**
  2 **garlic cloves, minced**
  8 **large eggs**

   1. Combine soy sauce, mirin, scallions, ginger, sugar, and garlic in small saucepan and bring to simmer over medium-high heat. Remove from heat and stir in 1 cup cold water; set aside.

   2. Bring 3 quarts water to boil in large saucepan over high heat. Fill large bowl halfway with ice and water.

   3. Using spider skimmer or slotted spoon, gently lower eggs into boiling water and cook for 7 minutes. Transfer eggs to ice bath and let cool for 5 minutes.

   4. Working with 1 egg at a time, gently tap egg on counter to crack shell. Begin peeling off shell at wider end of egg, making sure to break membrane between shell and egg white. Working under gently running water, carefully peel membrane and shell off egg.

   5. Combine soy sauce mixture and eggs in large zipper-lock bag and place bag in medium bowl. Press out as much air as possible from bag so eggs are fully submerged in liquid, then seal bag. Refrigerate for at least 3 hours or up to 4 hours (any longer and eggs may become too salty). Remove eggs from marinade using slotted spoon. Serve. (Eggs, separated from marinade, can be refrigerated for up to 2 days.)

SOY SAUCE–CURED EGG YOLKS

Makes: 6 yolks

Total Time: 15 minutes, plus 8 hours chilling

One of our favorite Japanese egg preparations is shoyu tamago, a whole shelled hard-cooked egg marinated in soy sauce. For our take on that classic preparation, instead of a whole cooked egg, we cure raw yolks in a soy sauce mixture until they are just firm at the exterior. The high concentration of salt in the curing liquid draws water from the exterior of the yolk, forming a thin, intensely savory exterior shell around a gooey, runny interior. You can put them on anything—ramen, toast, salads—but they're perhaps best served simply on a hot bowl of rice.

  ⅓ **cup plus 1 tablespoon soy sauce or tamari**
  ¼ **cup plus 1 tablespoon sake**
  ¼ **cup sugar**
  6 **large eggs**

   1. Whisk soy sauce, sake, and sugar in medium bowl until sugar dissolves, about 30 seconds. Transfer mixture to loaf pan.

   2. Working with 1 egg at a time, crack eggs, separate yolks from whites, and carefully transfer yolks to pan with soy sauce mixture. Carefully lay 8 by 4-inch piece of paper towel directly on top of yolks (paper towel will absorb soy sauce mixture and coat tops of yolks). Wrap pan with plastic wrap and refrigerate until yolk exteriors are firm and translucent brown, at least 8 hours or up to 24 hours.

   3. Carefully remove paper towel from yolks. Using small spoon, gently lift each yolk from soy sauce mixture and serve.

SALT-CURED EGG YOLKS

Makes: 12 yolks

Total Time: 1 hour, plus 6 days chilling

Transforming inexpensive, readily available ingredients into something special is the key to making memorable dishes. One of the best examples of this practice is the salt-cured egg yolk. The process is dead simple: Separate yolks, pack in salt and sugar, wait, rinse, dry in the oven, and use. Just as with an aged hard cheese, grated cured yolks can quickly add savory depth and complexity to a wide range of foods: soups, salads, pastas, and even meats. Like all curing, this recipe relies on osmosis—water in the yolks travels through the yolk membrane to the surrounding cure. This recipe, which cures for a week, yields dry, firm yolks that lose almost 50 percent of their weight in water, which greatly concentrates fat and flavor.

1 pound kosher salt
1 pound sugar
12 large eggs

1. Pulse salt and sugar in food processor until evenly mixed and slightly ground, about 14 pulses. (Alternatively, salt and sugar can be processed in blender on high speed until evenly mixed and slightly ground, about 30 seconds.) Transfer 14 ounces salt mixture to 8-inch square baking pan and shake pan to create even layer. Using whole, in-shell egg, make 12 evenly spaced ¼-inch-deep indentations in salt bed by pressing bottom of egg gently into salt mixture.

2. Working with 1 egg at a time, crack eggs, separate yolks from whites, and transfer yolks to indentations in salt bed. Carefully pour remaining salt mixture evenly over yolks. Wrap pan with plastic wrap and refrigerate until yolks are firm and dry throughout, 6 to 7 days.

3. Adjust oven rack to middle position and heat oven to 200 degrees. Set wire rack in rimmed baking sheet. Fill medium bowl with cool water. Remove yolks from salt mixture, brushing off excess, and rinse gently in water. Pat yolks dry with paper towels and transfer to wire rack. Transfer sheet to oven and bake until exteriors of yolks are dry to touch, 30 to 40 minutes.

4. Grate or thinly slice yolks and sprinkle on your favorite dishes, from pasta and risotto to roasted vegetables and buttered toast. (Cured yolks can be refrigerated in airtight container for up to 2 weeks.)

Variation
BONITO AND BLACK PEPPER-CURED EGG YOLKS
Makes: 12 yolks
Total Time: 1 hour, plus 6 days chilling
Adding savory bonito flakes and plenty of spicy black pepper to our classic Salt-Cured Egg Yolks elevates these cured yolks to luxurious levels. Bonito flakes, one of the two primary ingredients in Japanese dashi broth, pack these yolks with supersavory glutamic acid, boosting them pretty high up on the umami scale.

1 pound kosher salt
1 pound sugar
3 tablespoons black peppercorns, ground fine in a spice grinder
1 ounce bonito flakes
12 large eggs

1. Pulse salt, sugar, pepper, and bonito flakes in food processor until evenly mixed and slightly ground, about 14 pulses. (Alternatively, ingredients can be processed in blender on high speed until evenly mixed and slightly ground, about 30 seconds.) Transfer 14 ounces salt mixture to 8-inch square baking pan and shake pan to create even

layer. Using whole, in-shell egg, make 12 evenly spaced ¼-inch-deep indentations in salt bed by pressing bottom of egg gently into salt mixture.

2. Working with 1 egg at a time, crack eggs, separate yolks from whites, and transfer yolks to indentations in salt bed. Carefully pour remaining salt mixture evenly over yolks. Wrap pan with plastic wrap and refrigerate until yolks are firm and dry throughout, 6 to 7 days.

3. Adjust oven rack to middle position and heat oven to 200 degrees. Set wire rack in rimmed baking sheet. Fill medium bowl with cool water. Remove yolks from salt mixture, brushing off excess, and rinse gently in water. Pat yolks dry with paper towels and transfer to wire rack. Transfer sheet to oven and bake until exteriors of yolks are dry to touch, 30 to 40 minutes.

4. Grate or thinly slice yolks and sprinkle on your favorite dishes, from pasta and risotto to roasted vegetables and buttered toast. (Cured yolks can be refrigerated in air-tight container for up to 2 weeks.)

HOMEMADE CHEESE

ANDREA GEARY

Cheese making is an art as well as a science. There are hundreds of different categories of cheese, but this course focuses on fresh cheese, meaning it can be eaten immediately after making it without any aging, ripening, or curing. It is cheese in its youngest, purest form. All you need to make fresh cheese at home is milk or buttermilk, lemon juice, vinegar, salt, a Dutch oven, a colander, and cheesecloth. Ricotta is surprisingly easy to make as is paneer once you have a failproof recipe in hand. They both taste amazing; make them once and you'll be hooked.

ANDREA'S PRO TIP: *Letting the ricotta drain too long can produce dry cheese, but if this happens to you don't lose heart. Reserve the drained whey and gently stir some in, 1 tablespoon at a time, until the desired consistency is achieved.*

THE METHOD
RICOTTA AND PANEER

Making Ricotta

1A HEAT MILK

Heat milk and salt to 185 degrees, stirring. Remove from heat and whisk in lemon juice and vinegar until curdled. Let sit undisturbed until mixture fully separates into curds and whey.

2A DRAIN

Pour mixture into cheesecloth-lined colander. Let sit, undisturbed, until whey has drained from edges of cheese but center is still very moist.

3A STIR

Quickly but gently transfer cheese to bowl, retaining as much whey in center of cheese as possible. Stir until smooth.

Making Paneer

1B CURDLE MILK

Bring milk to boil, stirring. Whisk in buttermilk, turn off heat, and let stand undisturbed for 1 minute. Pour mixture into cheesecloth-lined colander and let drain.

2B DRAIN CURDS

Pull edges of cheesecloth together to form pouch, twist edges together, and squeeze out as much liquid as possible.

3B PRESS CHEESE

Place cheese pouch between plates and weight down top plate. Let sit until cheese is firm and set. Unwrap cheese.

CREAMY RICOTTA CHEESE

Makes: about 2 pounds (4 cups)
Total Time: 40 minutes, plus 2 hours chilling

RECIPE OVERVIEW This fresh ricotta is luscious and creamy, with a distinct sweetness from the dairy and just a hint of tang. Begin by heating whole milk and salt to 185 degrees in a Dutch oven—just hot enough to enable the dairy to curdle after adding the curdling agents: lemon juice and white vinegar. Adding just enough vinegar keeps the ricotta from tasting sour. Stirring gently and then leaving the mixture alone once the curds appear allows the curds to separate from the whey. To finish, empty the pot into a cheesecloth-lined colander to drain and then transfer the ricotta to a bowl to break up the curds and incorporate some of the clear whey. For the best results, don't stir the milk too vigorously, and be very gentle with the curds once they form.

- ⅓ cup lemon juice (2 lemons)
- ¼ cup distilled white vinegar, plus extra as needed
- 1 gallon pasteurized (not ultra-pasteurized or UHT) whole milk
- 2 teaspoons table salt

1. Line colander with triple layer of cheesecloth and place in sink. Combine lemon juice and vinegar in liquid measuring cup; set aside. Heat milk and salt in Dutch oven over medium-high heat, stirring frequently to prevent scorching, until milk registers 185 degrees.

2. Remove pot from heat and stir in lemon juice mixture until fully incorporated and mixture curdles, about 15 seconds. Let sit undisturbed until mixture fully separates into solid curds and translucent whey, 5 to 10 minutes. If curds do not fully separate and there is still milky whey in pot, stir in extra vinegar, 1 tablespoon at a time, and let sit another 2 to 3 minutes, until curds separate.

3. Gently pour mixture into prepared colander. Let sit, undisturbed, until whey has drained from edges of cheese but center is still very moist, about 8 minutes. Working quickly, gently transfer cheese to large bowl, retaining as much whey in center of cheese as possible. Stir well to break up large curds and incorporate whey. Refrigerate ricotta until cold, about 2 hours. Stir cheese before using. (Ricotta can be refrigerated for up to 5 days.)

KEYS TO SUCCESS

- **Use fresh homogenized or pasteurized milk:** Ultra-pasteurized or ultra-heat-treated (UHT or long-life) milk will not curdle properly.

- **An accurate thermometer:** To be sure to hit the specified temperature

- **Don't drain for too long:** Otherwise the cheese will be too dry

LEMON RICOTTA PANCAKES

Makes: twelve 4-inch pancakes (serves 3 to 4)
Total Time: 45 minutes

An electric griddle set at 325 degrees can also be used to cook the pancakes. These pancakes are exceptionally rich and tender if you use homemade ricotta. You can use store-bought whole-milk ricotta; part-skim will work, too, but avoid nonfat ricotta. Serve with honey, confectioners' sugar, or a fruit topping.

- ⅔ cup (3⅓ ounces) all-purpose flour
- ½ teaspoon baking soda
- ½ teaspoon table salt
- 8 ounces (1 cup) Creamy Ricotta Cheese
- 2 large eggs, separated, plus 2 large whites
- ⅓ cup whole milk
- 1 teaspoon grated lemon zest plus 4 teaspoons juice
- ½ teaspoon vanilla extract
- 2 tablespoons unsalted butter, melted
- ¼ cup (1¾ ounces) sugar
- 1–2 teaspoons vegetable oil

1. Adjust oven rack to middle position and heat oven to 200 degrees. Spray wire rack set in rimmed baking sheet with vegetable oil spray and place in oven. Whisk flour, baking soda, and salt together in medium bowl and make well in center. Add ricotta, egg yolks, milk, lemon zest and juice, and vanilla and whisk until just combined. Gently stir in melted butter.

2. Using stand mixer fitted with whisk, whip egg whites on medium-low speed until foamy, about 1 minute. Increase speed to medium-high and whip whites to soft, billowy mounds, about 1 minute. Gradually add sugar and whip until glossy, soft peaks form, 1 to 2 minutes. Transfer one-third of whipped egg whites to batter and whisk gently until mixture is lightened. Using rubber spatula, gently fold remaining egg whites into batter.

3. Heat 1 teaspoon oil in 12-inch nonstick skillet over medium heat until shimmering. Using paper towels, wipe out oil, leaving thin film on bottom and sides of pan. Using ¼-cup measure or 2-ounce ladle, portion batter into pan in 3 places, leaving 2 inches between portions. Gently spread each portion into 4-inch round. Cook until edges are set and first side is deep golden brown, 2 to 3 minutes. Using thin, wide spatula, flip pancakes and continue to cook until second side is golden brown, 2 to 3 minutes longer. Serve pancakes immediately or transfer to prepared wire rack in preheated oven. Repeat with remaining batter, using remaining oil as needed.

PANEER

Makes: about 12 ounces
Total Time: 45 minutes, plus 45 minutes resting

RECIPE OVERVIEW Paneer is easy to make at home in not much more than an hour, using whole milk and buttermilk. The acidity in the buttermilk acts as the curdling agent, separating the curds and whey, which is drained off. The cheese is then squeezed to remove excess moisture and weighted down until firm enough to slice. Saag Paneer (recipe follows) is a classic and favorite use for paneer, but this is a super versatile fresh cheese: Since it doesn't melt like mozzarella does, you can cut it into slices and pan-fry, cut it into large cubes and roast with vegetables, or even skewer it onto kebabs to quickly grill. Whole milk will give you the best results. To ensure that the cheese is firm, wring it tightly in step 2 and use two plates that nestle together snugly.

- 3 quarts pasteurized (not ultrapasteurized or UHT) whole milk
- 3 cups buttermilk
- 1 tablespoon table salt

1. Line colander with triple layer of cheesecloth and place in sink. Bring milk to boil in Dutch oven over medium-high heat, stirring frequently to prevent scorching. Whisk in buttermilk and salt, turn off heat, and let stand undisturbed for 1 minute. Pour milk mixture into cheesecloth and let curds drain for 15 minutes.

2. Pull edges of cheesecloth together to form pouch. Twist edges of cheesecloth together, firmly squeezing out as much liquid as possible from cheese curds. Place taut, twisted cheese pouch between 2 large plates and weight down top plate with heavy Dutch oven. Set aside at room temperature until cheese is firm and set, about 45 minutes, then remove cheesecloth. (Paneer can be wrapped in plastic wrap and refrigerated for up to 3 days.)

> ### KEYS TO SUCCESS
> - **Use half buttermilk:** Its acid coagulates the milk
> - **Squeeze curds:** To remove excess water
> - **Press cheese between plates:** Helps cheese to drain

SAAG PANEER

Serves: 4 to 6
Total Time: 1½ hours, plus 45 minutes resting

RECIPE OVERVIEW Saag paneer, soft cubes of creamy fresh cheese in a spicy spinach puree, is an Indian restaurant classic. Re-creating this dish at home isn't difficult—even with making the fresh cheese. Instead of cooking the spinach in batches on the stovetop for the puree, it all gets wilted in the microwave. Adding mustard greens lends additional texture and a complexity that works well with the warm spices. Canned diced tomatoes brighten the dish, and buttery cashews—both pureed and chopped—give this Indian classic a subtle nutty richness. Use commercially produced cultured buttermilk in this recipe. Basmati rice is the traditional accompaniment. You will need a 12-inch skillet with a tight-fitting lid for this recipe.

- 1 (10-ounce) bag curly-leaf spinach, rinsed
- ¾ pound mustard greens, stemmed and rinsed
- 3 tablespoons unsalted butter
- 1 teaspoon cumin seeds
- 1 teaspoon ground coriander
- 1 teaspoon paprika
- ½ teaspoon ground cardamom
- ¼ teaspoon ground cinnamon
- 1 onion, chopped fine
- ¾ teaspoon table salt
- 3 garlic cloves, minced
- 1 tablespoon grated fresh ginger
- 1 jalapeño chile, stemmed, seeded, and minced
- 1 (14.5-ounce) can diced tomatoes, drained and chopped coarse
- ½ cup roasted cashews, chopped coarse, divided
- 1 cup water
- 1 cup buttermilk
- 1 recipe Paneer, cut into ½-inch pieces
- 3 tablespoons minced fresh cilantro

1. Microwave spinach in covered bowl until wilted, about 3 minutes. Let cool slightly, then chop enough spinach to measure ⅓ cup. Transfer remaining spinach to blender. Microwave mustard greens in covered bowl until wilted, about 4 minutes. Let cool slightly, then chop enough mustard greens to measure ⅓ cup; combine with chopped spinach. Transfer remaining mustard greens to blender with remaining spinach.

2. Meanwhile, melt butter in 12-inch skillet over medium-high heat. Add cumin seeds, coriander, paprika, cardamom, and cinnamon and cook until fragrant, about 30 seconds. Add onion and salt and cook, stirring frequently, until softened, about 3 minutes. Stir in garlic, ginger, and jalapeño and cook, stirring frequently, until lightly browned and just beginning to stick to pan, 2 to 3 minutes. Stir in tomatoes and cook mixture until pan is dry and tomatoes are beginning to brown, 3 to 4 minutes. Remove skillet from heat.

3. Transfer half of onion mixture, ¼ cup cashews, and water to blender with greens and process until smooth, about 1 minute. Stir puree, chopped greens, and buttermilk into skillet with remaining onion mixture and bring to simmer over medium-high heat. Reduce heat to low, cover, and cook until flavors have blended, 5 minutes. Season with salt and pepper to taste. Gently fold in paneer pieces and cook until just heated through, 1 to 2 minutes. Transfer to serving dish, sprinkle with remaining ¼ cup cashews and cilantro, and serve.

HOMEMADE YOGURT

ELLE SIMONE SCOTT

DIY yogurt has an incomparably fresh, milky taste—and it's entirely customizable. If you want full control over the finished product—pure, undoctored cultured dairy of the highest quality (no stabilizers, sweeteners, or additives)—as well as the ability to control the fat content, sourness level, and consistency, consider making yogurt at home. Whether you like it mild or tart, creamy or lean, the foolproof method you will learn in this course has you covered. You will also learn how to easily turn homemade yogurt into a rich yogurt cheese called labneh.

ELLE'S PRO TIP: *Yogurt is the quintessential condiment and probably the most well traveled. Within almost every culture you'll encounter an exciting yogurt variation. This means that from savory to sweet, from fruit to warm spices, you can enjoy yogurt for every meal of the day in almost every way.*

HOMEMADE YOGURT

Makes: 2 quarts
Total Time: 40 minutes, plus 13 hours fermenting and chilling

RECIPE OVERVIEW For tangy, creamy yogurt, you can skip the usual preliminary scalding and cooling steps by starting with ultra-pasteurized milk, which has already been rapidly heated and chilled. This lets bacterial cultures turn it into an especially thick and silky yogurt. Bring the milk to 115 degrees and stir in store-bought yogurt with live cultures, strains of bacteria that digest the lactose in milk, producing lactic acid. This acid is what gives yogurt its flavor and causes the proteins in milk to gradually form a gel, turning liquid milk into creamy yogurt. To provide those bacteria with a cozy environment to do their work, place the pot of warm water holding the jars of milk in the oven, then place a covered pot of boiling water beside it. This setup helps the oven maintain a temperature of 100 to 115 degrees for hours. After that, it is just a matter of tasting for tartness and thickness to decide when to pop the jars into the fridge to let the yogurt set. This recipe will work only with ultra-pasteurized milk. Most organic milk is ultra-pasteurized; this will be noted on the label. Be sure to use freshly opened containers of milk. Any type of plain yogurt (whole-milk, low-fat, Greek, etc.) that contains live cultures can be used. You can halve this recipe, if preferred. Be sure to save ½ cup of yogurt to use as the starter for a subsequent batch.

7½ cups ultra-pasteurized whole, 2 percent low-fat,
    1 percent low-fat, or skim milk
½ cup plain yogurt

1. Bring milk to 115 degrees in saucepan over medium heat, 2 to 5 minutes. (If your milk gets hotter than 115 degrees, let it cool to 115 degrees before proceeding. Higher temperatures can kill some cultures.) Off heat, whisk yogurt into milk until very well combined. Divide mixture evenly between two 1-quart Mason jars (they will be very full; a funnel can be helpful for this step). Add lids, then screw on rings until just finger-tight.

2. Adjust oven rack to lowest position and turn on oven light. Bring 5 quarts water to boil in large covered pot. Place jars in second large pot. Add water until jars are submerged to their necks. (If jars are taller than pot, add water to 1¼ inches from rim of pot.) Remove jars and bring water to 120 degrees over medium heat. Return jars to pot of 120-degree water. Transfer both pots to oven. Incubate yogurt, without opening oven door, for 5 hours.

3. Remove 1 jar from water bath. Using clean spoon, taste yogurt for tartness and consistency. If tarter, thicker yogurt is desired, return jar to water bath and shut oven door. (Bear in mind that yogurt will thicken significantly as it cools but can be loosened up by stirring prior to serving.) Set oven to 350 degrees and heat for 3 minutes (start your timer as soon as you set the dial; oven will not reach 350 degrees). Turn off oven and let incubate for up to 10 more hours, repeating heating step each time oven door is opened. Remove jars from water bath and refrigerate until fully cooled and set, about 8 hours. (Yogurt can be refrigerated for up to 2 weeks.)

LABNEH

Makes: ½ cup
Total Time: 15 minutes

RECIPE OVERVIEW Popular all over the Middle East, labneh is yogurt that's been drained of most of its whey so that it takes on a thick, lush consistency akin to that of whipped cream cheese. Drizzled with olive oil and sprinkled with za'atar, labneh can be part of a meze offering; it's also great spread on bread, spooned over granola, or dolloped anywhere else a lightly tart and creamy component would be welcome. Normally yogurt must be drained for several days to create labneh, but we found a much speedier approach. After straining yogurt through cheesecloth overnight, use paper towels to blot away enough moisture to create a spreadable consistency.

Making Labneh

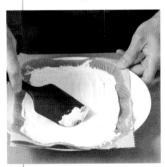

LINE AND SPREAD
Line large plate with triple layer of paper towels. Spread ⅔ cup homemade yogurt evenly over top; set aside and let sit for 10 minutes.

GRASP AND FOLD
Grasp paper towels and fold yogurt in half; peel back towels. Rotate plate 90 degrees and repeat folding and peeling 2 more times to consolidate yogurt into smaller, drier mass; you should have about ½ cup labneh.

Variations

LEMON-DILL LABNEH

You will need 1 cup labneh for this recipe. Serve with crudités or pita chips.

After yogurt has drained, stir in 1 tablespoon minced fresh dill, 2 teaspoons grated lemon zest, ⅛ teaspoon salt, and pinch pepper. Cover and refrigerate until flavors have blended, about 1 hour. Season with salt and pepper to taste before serving.

HONEY-WALNUT LABNEH

You will need 1 cup labneh for this recipe. Serve with pita bread.

After yogurt has drained, stir in 3 tablespoons toasted chopped walnuts, 1 tablespoon honey, and ⅛ teaspoon salt. Cover and refrigerate until flavors have blended, about 1 hour.

KEYS TO SUCCESS

- **Ultra-pasteurized milk:** Has already been heated and cooled so no need to scald and cool milk
- **A funnel:** Makes filling the jars a lot easier
- **Incubation time:** Controls the thickness and sourness of the finished yogurt

WHAT YOU'LL NEED

INGREDIENTS

Ultra-Pasteurized Milk Ultra-pasteurized milk leads to yogurt with a thick, uniform texture; it also saves time and effort. To understand, look at the usual first step in yogurt making: heating milk to 160 degrees or above. Along with killing unwanted microbes, this changes the milk's protein structure and gives the yogurt body. The scalding temperature affects the consistency of the final product. Lower temperatures produce a runnier gel, while higher ones make a thicker gel but can lead to separate curds and lots of whey if some of the proteins overcook. The ideal creamy, homogeneous texture is achieved when the milk is given only a very short, uniform exposure to high heat—which, as it happens, is how ultra-pasteurized milk is treated: It's heated to 275 degrees for less than 5 seconds and then rapidly chilled.

Store-Bought Plain Yogurt Use any commercial yogurt made with live, active cultures to initiate fermentation. Streptococcus thermophilus and Lactobacillus delbrueckii subspecies bulgaricus are the two (symbiotic) species of lactic acid bacteria mandated by the U.S. Food and Drug Administration because they "characterize yogurt." Almost all yogurts also contain these and other species and strains.

EQUIPMENT

You'll need two 1-quart glass Mason jars with metal lids to contain the yogurt while it incubates in hot water; one large saucepan; and two large pots (one with a lid) that will fit in your oven at the same time. A funnel is helpful for transferring the yogurt to the jars.

THE JOURNEY FROM MILK TO YOGURT

1. HEAT Warm milk on the stovetop until it reaches 115 degrees, an ideal temperature for bacterial proliferation.

2. INOCULATE Thoroughly whisk store-bought yogurt into the warm milk to begin the process of fermentation. Transfer the mixture to Mason jars.

3. INCUBATE Hold the milk mixture at a warm temperature to allow microbes in the starter to digest lactose (milk sugar) in the milk and produce lactic acid, creating tartness and causing the protein to gradually coagulate and form a gel. Do this by submerging the jars in a large pot of 120-degree water. Place the pot in a turned-off oven (with the light on) along with a second, lidded pot of boiling water. The second pot will emit heat so that it will take several hours for the oven temperature to fall from 115 to 100 degrees (the range where fermentation takes place).

HOW TO CUSTOMIZE

Making yogurt that you'll love begins with choosing a starter yogurt that you enjoy. Any variety (whole milk, Greek, Icelandic, etc.) will do the job, but keep in mind that different brands use different combinations of bacteria, and this accounts for variability in flavors ranging from buttery to cheesy to tangy to mild; textures can be firm, thin, gelatinous, ropy, or custardy. These qualities will transfer to your finished yogurt.

Then there's the milk. Any type (whole, low-fat, or skim) will work, but the more fat your milk contains, the richer your yogurt will be and the more structure it will have.

And yet, the starter and milk are only the beginning. Here are more ways to create a truly artisanal yogurt to suit your personal tastes.

TWEAK THE CONSISTENCY

RICHER Substitute ½ cup ultra-pasteurized heavy cream for ½ cup milk.

DENSER Whisk ¼ cup nonfat dry milk powder into cold milk before heating it.

STRAINED Place triple layer of cheesecloth over mouth of jar with chilled yogurt, screw on lid ring, and drain in refrigerator upside down in 2-cup measuring cup overnight. (See page 83 for how to make labneh.)

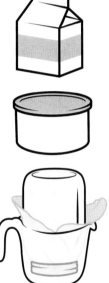

ADD FLAVORINGS

Extract Stir ¼ teaspoon extract (we like vanilla or almond) into milk along with starter.
Sweetener Garnish individual servings with white or brown sugar, honey, maple syrup, or fruit jam.

CONTROL SOURNESS AND THICKNESS

Adjust the incubation time to produce the effect you desire: The longer yogurt ferments, the more lactic acid is produced, and the more sour and thick it becomes. Chilling stops fermentation and allows the gel to set fully (it will loosen when stirred or served).

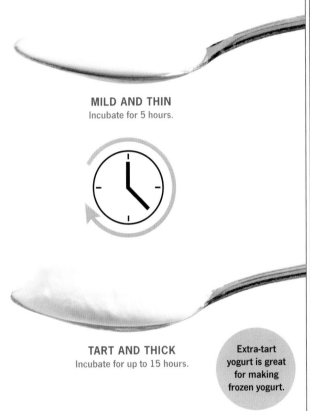

MILD AND THIN
Incubate for 5 hours.

TART AND THICK
Incubate for up to 15 hours.

> Extra-tart yogurt is great for making frozen yogurt.

THREE GOOD WAYS TO USE WHEY

If you strain your homemade yogurt (see above), don't pour the whey down the drain. The tart liquid has a number of good applications.

1. Buttermilk substitute: In drop biscuits, replacing all the buttermilk with whey yielded a batch just as tall, tender, and flavorful as the original.

2. Cocktail enhancer: The tartness of whey can complement or replace citrus in a cocktail, and the dairy protein produces a magnificent froth in shaken drinks. Try a whiskey sour using an ounce of whey in lieu of egg white.

3. Yogurt starter: Freeze whey in an ice cube tray. Then, whenever you want to make a new batch of yogurt, add two cubes to the milk as your starter.

COOKING WITH CHEESE

JULIA COLLIN DAVISON

Eaten by itself, cheese is of course delicious. When used as a main ingredient in a cooked application, cheese becomes even more irresistibly appealing. In this course you'll learn the secrets of melting cheese and how to put cheese to work in some of our favorite ways: cooked into a crunchy cheese wafer, melted into fondue, and transformed into a high-test nacho sauce. And by learning to select the right combination of cheeses, you'll level up everyday macaroni and cheese and grilled cheese sandwiches into sublime adult versions of themselves.

JULIA'S PRO TIP: *Always buy cheese in bulk and shred it yourself. Stay away from pre-shredded cheese, which is tossed with a variety of different things (often cellulose) to prevent it from clumping and melting in the package. If working with a softer cheese, try spraying the grater with a thin film of oil to prevent it from smearing.*

FRICO

Makes: 8 large wafers
Total Time: 25 minutes

RECIPE OVERVIEW Frico friabile is a one-ingredient wonder. Nothing more than shredded cheese that is melted and then browned to create a light, airy, crisp, and impressively sized wafer, this simple snack highlights the intense flavor of the cheese. But despite their simplicity, these wafers can turn out bitter, and too salty, without the crispness we prefer. Some recipes cook the cheese in butter or olive oil, but using a 10-inch nonstick skillet eliminates the need for any fat. To flip the round without it tearing or stretching, remove the pan from the heat for several seconds to cool; allowing a few moments for the cheese wafer to set up makes it easy to flip. Cooking the cheese at high heat causes it to brown too fast and become bitter, but at low heat it takes too long and dries out. A combination of medium and medium-high heat is best. Serve frico with drinks and other antipasto bites such as olives and tomatoes. Montasio cheese is worth tracking down; if you can't find it, use Asiago.

1 **pound Montasio or aged Asiago cheese, shredded (4 cups)**

Sprinkle ½ cup cheese over bottom of 10-inch nonstick skillet. Cook over medium-high heat, shaking skillet occasionally to ensure even distribution of cheese over bottom of skillet, until edges are lacy and toasted, about 4 minutes. As cheese begins to melt, use spatula to tidy lacy outer edges of cheese and prevent them from burning. Remove skillet from heat and allow cheese to set, about 30 seconds. Using fork and spatula, carefully flip cheese wafer over and return skillet to medium heat. Cook until second side is golden brown, about 2 minutes. Slide cheese wafer out of skillet onto plate. Repeat with remaining cheese. Serve.

KEYS TO SUCCESS
- **A nonstick skillet:** Cooks frico without adding butter or oil
- **Cool before flipping:** Lets the cheese set
- **Two heat settings:** Allows the cheese to brown without burning and drying out

CHEESE FONDUE

Serves: 4 as a main dish or 8 as an appetizer
Total Time: 30 minutes

RECIPE OVERVIEW Cheese fondue might seem dated, but it is an easy interactive meal that is made for cheese lovers. You don't even need a fondue pot to make this recipe, just the right ingredients and the right method. This Swiss-style fondue is made by melting at least two varieties of cheese—here Emmentaler and Gruyère, both classic fondue cheeses—in a dry white wine. Garlic and nutmeg are added to complement the cheese blend. Using room temperature cheese is key. That's because if cheese is overheated rapidly, it breaks down and separates into fat, water, and curdled protein. Cornstarch, tossed with the grated cheese and then activated by the simmering water, helps hold the cheese together and lends a silky texture. Serving in nested microwaveable bowls allows the fondue to stay creamy and to be reheated several times without becoming grainy. Do not substitute deli Swiss cheese for the Emmentaler—it will make the fondue stringy. Do use a crisp, un-oaked wine, such as Sauvignon Blanc. Along with the bread, serve with steamed broccoli and cauliflower florets, apple slices, and chunks of cured meats for dipping.

- 8 ounces Emmentaler cheese, shredded (2 cups), room temperature
- 8 ounces Gruyère cheese, shredded (2 cups), room temperature
- 2 tablespoons cornstarch
  Pinch ground nutmeg
- 1½ cups dry white wine
- 1 garlic clove, peeled and halved
- ¼ teaspoon pepper
- 1 (12-inch) baguette, cut into 1-inch pieces

1. Toss Emmentaler, Gruyère, cornstarch, and nutmeg together in bowl until well combined. Bring wine and garlic to boil in medium saucepan over high heat; discard garlic.

2. Reduce heat to medium-low and slowly whisk in cheese mixture 1 handful at a time. Continue to cook, whisking constantly, until mixture is smooth and begins to bubble, 2 to 4 minutes. Stir in pepper. Serve with bread.

KEYS TO SUCCESS

- **Use two cheeses:** For the best flavor and meltability

- **Start with room temperature cheese:** Prevents the cheese from overheating and breaking down

- **Cornstarch:** Keeps the cheese from separating

Reheating Fondue

Even our foolproof fondue eventually cools down and firms up. We tested dozens of ways to keep it warm and reheat it and found this method works best: To serve, fill a microwaveable bowl one-third full of boiling water, then nest a slightly smaller microwaveable bowl inside it. Pour the fondue into the smaller bowl and serve. To reheat, microwave the double-bowl setup for 2 to 3 minutes, stirring halfway.

NACHO CHEESE SAUCE WITH GOCHUJANG

Serves: 6 to 8
Total Time: 30 minutes

RECIPE OVERVIEW Classic nacho cheese sauce has a gooey, melty texture but can barely taste like cheese. Aged cheeses, such as cheddar, have rich, complex flavor but make for grainy sauces when melted. In 2011, *Modernist Cuisine* popularized the use of sodium citrate, an emulsifying salt, to defy cheese logic and make gooey nacho cheese from the good stuff. The base of this cheese sauce is a super-tasty combination of sharp aged cheddar and Swiss cheese. Inspired by cheesy ddukbokki, Korean rice cakes swimming in a spicy gochujang sauce topped with a mound of melty cheese, we made a quick gochujang sauce. Gochujang is a spicy fermented pepper paste essential to Korean cuisine. Gochugaru is a red chile powder made with dried Korean peppers. It is much less spicy than crushed red pepper flakes and adds sweet and smoky notes to the sauce. The gochujang sauce is folded into the cheese for a dip that's spicy, sweet, and salty. This sauce is best served warm. If you have a slow cooker, you can hold it in there on the warm setting. If not, serve the sauce in a microwave-safe bowl so that you can easily reheat it in the microwave as needed (15 to 30 seconds on high power will do the trick).

Gochujang Sauce

- 1 cup water
- 3 tablespoons gochujang
- 2 teaspoons gochugaru
- 2 teaspoons sugar
- 2 tablespoons corn syrup

Cheese Sauce

- 7 ounces sharp cheddar cheese, shredded (1¾ cups)
- 3½ ounces Swiss cheese, shredded (¾ cup plus 2 tablespoons)
- ⅔ cup water
- 1 tablespoon sodium citrate

1. **FOR THE GOCHUJANG SAUCE** Whisk water, gochujang, gochugaru, sugar, and corn syrup together in small saucepan. Bring to simmer over medium heat and cook, stirring occasionally with rubber spatula, until sauce has thickened and measures about 1 cup, 3 to 5 minutes. Remove from heat and set aside.

2. **FOR THE CHEESE SAUCE** Combine cheddar and Swiss in medium bowl. Whisk water and sodium citrate together in small saucepan until sodium citrate dissolves. Bring to simmer over medium heat. Whisking constantly, gradually add cheese mixture, about ¼ cup at a time, to simmering water, making sure each addition is fully incorporated before adding next, about 2 minutes. (Mixture will be very thick.)

3. Reduce heat to medium-low and, whisking constantly, gradually add gochujang sauce. Scrape down saucepan with rubber spatula and continue to cook, stirring constantly, until sauce is slightly thickened, about 45 seconds longer.

(Sauce will continue to thicken as it cools.) Remove saucepan from heat. If you like, make it extra-shiny with immersion blender. Transfer to serving bowl and serve warm, with plenty of tortilla chips. (The sauce can be refrigerated in airtight container for up to 1 week.)

KEYS TO SUCCESS

- **Korean condiments:** Punch up the flavor of the sauce
- **Two cheeses:** Combination of sharp cheddar and Swiss provides the best flavor.
- **Use sodium citrate:** Helps to emulsify the sauce

SCIENCE LESSON **The Secret Ingredient to Smooth Melted Cheese**

Not all cheese melts as graciously as a nice young Monterey Jack. A sharp, long-aged Gruyère, for instance, will tend to separate into a lumpy, chewy blob of protein sitting in a pool of liquid fat. The reason? Over the months that the Gruyère was aging, much of its water evaporated. That concentrated the cheese's wonderful flavor—one reason we love aged cheeses—and bumped up its relative fat content. An emulsion is a delicate thing, and with less water present to hold up its side of the arrangement, the fat is much more likely to break out of its emulsified state and puddle up when melted. Moreover, aging also causes the cheese's proteins to clump in little compact groups. Those tightly clustered tangles of aged proteins are too wrapped up in each other to emulsify well, and because they're so intertwined they don't come apart nearly as easily when heated. Instead, they stay put while the fat melts and drips out around them.

The solution: a salt solution. Sodium citrate is the best known of a few different ingredients known as melting salts, which facilitate the melting of old or stubborn cheeses. It's a white powder with a salty-sour taste, but in cheese, its taste isn't noticeable. The tight-knit proteins that hinder smooth melting are bonded to each other with the help of calcium ions. When you warm up a mixture of cheese with the addition of liquid and a small amount of sodium citrate, the sodium substitutes itself for some of the calcium that's helping the proteins cling. As the cheese is heated, the proteins separate from each other and again act as emulsifiers, strengthening the emulsion by holding fat and water together.

The result is a stable, smooth melt with no lumps and no leaks—perfect for fondues and cheese sauces. The chemical formula for sodium citrate even spells out "nacho." Behold: $Na_3C_6H_5O_7$.

GROWN-UP STOVETOP MACARONI AND CHEESE

Serves: 4
Total Time: 25 minutes

RECIPE OVERVIEW Inspired by an innovative macaroni and cheese recipe that calls for adding sodium citrate to cheese to keep it smooth when heated (instead of adding flour to make a béchamel), this sauce is based on American cheese, which contains a similar ingredient. Because American cheese has plenty of emulsifier but not a lot of flavor, we combine it with more-flavorful Gruyère and blue cheeses. A bit of mustard and cayenne pepper add piquancy. The macaroni cooks in a smaller-than-usual amount of water (along with some milk), so you don't have to drain it; the liquid that is left after the elbows are hydrated is just enough to form the base of the sauce. Rather than bake the mac and cheese, we sprinkle crunchy, cheesy toasted panko bread crumbs on top. This simplified mac and cheese recipe takes only about 25 minutes from start to finish. Because the macaroni is cooked in a measured amount of liquid, we don't recommend using different shapes or sizes of pasta. Use a 4-ounce block of American cheese from the deli counter rather than presliced cheese.

1¾	cups water
1	cup milk
8	ounces elbow macaroni
4	ounces American cheese, shredded (1 cup)
½	teaspoon Dijon mustard
	Small pinch cayenne pepper
3½	ounces Gruyère cheese, shredded (¾ cup)
2	tablespoons crumbled blue cheese
⅓	cup panko bread crumbs
1	tablespoon extra-virgin olive oil
⅛	teaspoon table salt
⅛	teaspoon pepper
2	tablespoons grated Parmesan cheese

1. Bring water and milk to boil in medium saucepan over high heat. Stir in macaroni and reduce heat to medium-low. Cook, stirring frequently, until macaroni is soft (slightly past al dente), 6 to 8 minutes. Add American cheese, mustard, and cayenne and cook, stirring constantly, until cheese is completely melted, about 1 minute. Off heat, stir in Gruyère and blue cheese until evenly distributed but not melted. Cover saucepan and let stand for 5 minutes.

2. Meanwhile, combine panko, oil, salt, and pepper in 8-inch nonstick skillet until panko is evenly moistened. Cook over medium heat, stirring frequently, until evenly browned, 3 to 4 minutes. Off heat, sprinkle Parmesan over panko mixture and stir to combine. Transfer panko mixture to small bowl.

3. Stir macaroni until sauce is smooth (sauce may look loose but will thicken as it cools). Season with salt and pepper to taste. Transfer to warm serving dish and sprinkle panko mixture over top. Serve immediately.

KEYS TO SUCCESS

- **Cook elbows in water and milk:** No need to drain pasta; leftover cooking liquid becomes the base of the sauce.

- **Use American cheese:** Prevents the sauce from clumping and separating

- **Gruyère and blue cheeses:** Bump up the flavor

SCIENCE LESSON

Why We Can Skip the Béchamel

Most versions of macaroni and cheese achieve a smooth consistency by starting with a béchamel, the classic sauce made by combining a flour-and-fat paste with milk. When combined with aged cheese, which is prone to breaking, the starches in the béchamel release elongated threads of amylose, which then wrap around the cheese's casein proteins, preventing them from squeezing out fat and recombining into curds. By using American cheese, we're able to skip the béchamel. Thanks to its emulsifying salts, American cheese stays smooth when melted and acts as a stabilizing agent for aged cheeses such as the Gruyère in our recipe.

GRUYÈRE ALONE = GRAINY
Without any stabilizing agent, the protein network in cheese breaks down when heated, fat breaks out, and proteins regroup in clumps. Aged (and thus drier) cheese is even more prone to breaking.

GRUYÈRE + AMERICAN = SMOOTH
American cheese contains emulsifying salts that replace calcium ions in dairy with sodium ions, stabilizing the cheese sauce so that it doesn't form curds and fat stays emulsified.

GROWN-UP GRILLED CHEESE SANDWICHES WITH CHEDDAR AND SHALLOT

Serves: 4
Total Time: 45 minutes

RECIPE OVERVIEW The grilled cheese conundrum: Young cheeses have no taste but melt perfectly, while aged cheeses have sophisticated flavor but turn grainy. This grilled cheese recipe provides the best of both worlds. Melty American cheese on fluffy white bread is a childhood classic, but we want a grilled cheese for adults that offers more robust flavor. Aged cheddar gives us the complexity we are after, but it makes for a greasy sandwich with a grainy filling. Adding a splash of wine and some Brie helps the aged cheddar melt evenly without separating or becoming greasy. Using a food processor to combine the ingredients ensures our cheese-and-wine mixture is easy to spread. A little bit of shallot ramps up the flavor without detracting from the cheese, and a smear of mustard butter livens up the bread. For the best flavor, look for a cheddar aged for about one year (avoid cheddar aged for longer; it won't melt well in this recipe). To quickly bring the cheese to room temperature, microwave the pieces until warm, about 30 seconds. The first two sandwiches can be held in a 200-degree oven on a wire rack set in a baking sheet while the second batch cooks.

- 7 ounces aged cheddar cheese, cut into 24 equal pieces, room temperature
- 2 ounces Brie cheese, rind removed
- 2 tablespoons dry white wine or dry vermouth
- 4 teaspoons minced shallot
- 3 tablespoons unsalted butter, softened
- 1 teaspoon Dijon mustard
- 8 slices hearty white sandwich bread

1. Process cheddar, Brie, and wine in food processor until smooth paste is formed, 20 to 30 seconds. Add shallot and pulse to combine, 3 to 5 pulses. Combine butter and mustard in small bowl.

2. Working on parchment paper–lined counter, divide mustard butter evenly among slices of bread. Spread butter evenly over surface of bread. Flip 4 slices of bread over and spread cheese mixture evenly over slices. Top with remaining 4 slices of bread, buttered sides up.

3. Preheat 12-inch nonstick skillet over medium heat for 2 minutes. (Droplets of water should just sizzle when flicked onto pan.) Place 2 sandwiches in skillet, reduce heat to medium-low, and cook until both sides are crisp and golden brown, 6 to 9 minutes per side, moving sandwiches to ensure even browning. Remove sandwiches from skillet and let stand for 2 minutes before serving. Repeat with remaining 2 sandwiches.

Why Young Cheese Melts Better Than Aged Cheese

Anyone who's melted cheese for a sandwich knows that some types melt better than others, turning creamy without releasing fat. During our testing for Grown-Up Grilled Cheese Sandwiches, we found that younger cheeses almost always performed better than aged ones. This is partly because aged cheeses have less moisture, making them prone to clump. But our science editor told us that there are other, more complicated factors at play as well, so we ran another test and controlled for moisture.

We purchased Cabot Creamery cheddars aged for 3, 16, and 24 months (all were sealed against evaporation during aging) and baked slices from each block on top of inverted metal cups that we preheated in a 175-degree oven until each slice had melted. The 3-month-old cheddar melted smoothly, evenly flowing down the cup's sides. Meanwhile, the 16-month-old cheddar showed signs of clumping as it slid down the metal, and the 24-month-old cheese actually broke into two large pieces and never melted.

Moisture plays a part in how cheese melts, but the state of its protein—specifically, its network of casein protein—affects it most. In freshly made cheeses, casein proteins are in tightly wound clusters, allowing for little interaction with one another. As cheese ages, it goes through a process called proteolysis, in which bonds between individual casein molecules are "snipped," allowing the clusters to unwind and bind with other casein molecules, forming a matrix. Early in this process, the matrix is flexible, allowing young cheeses to melt smoothly. With time, the proteins bond together more tightly, forming a stronger network that requires more heat to melt and is less flexible when melted. This can result in more separated fat and clumps, as with our older samples.

3-MONTH-OLD   **16-MONTH-OLD**   **24-MONTH-OLD**

Variations

GROWN-UP GRILLED CHEESE SANDWICHES WITH GRUYÈRE AND CHIVES

Substitute Gruyère cheese for cheddar, chives for shallot, and rye sandwich bread for white sandwich bread.

GROWN-UP GRILLED CHEESE SANDWICHES WITH ASIAGO AND DATES

Substitute Asiago cheese for cheddar, finely chopped pitted dates for shallot, and oatmeal sandwich bread for white sandwich bread.

GROWN-UP GRILLED CHEESE SANDWICHES WITH COMTÉ AND CORNICHON

Substitute Comté cheese for cheddar, minced cornichon for shallot, and rye sandwich bread for white sandwich bread.

GROWN-UP GRILLED CHEESE SANDWICHES WITH ROBIOLA AND CHIPOTLE

Substitute Robiola cheese, rind removed, for cheddar; ¼ teaspoon minced canned chipotle chile in adobo sauce for shallot; and oatmeal sandwich bread for white sandwich bread.

KEYS TO SUCCESS

- **Use a food processor:** Ensures that two cheeses become one
- **Add wine:** Adds moisture to help drier, older cheese melt more evenly and it tastes great
- **Butter the bread not the pan:** Buttering just the outside of the bread helps the bread to toast

You can't go wrong with cheese so a cheese board is always welcome at a gathering. The best cheese boards strike a perfect balance of textures and flavor, from cheese to accompaniments. With some thoughtful preparation you can make a spectacular spread.

BUILDING AN IMPRESSIVE CHEESE BOARD

1. Buy a variety For a mix of flavors and textures, choose one option from each profile: sharp and crumbly (like aged cheddar), soft and bright (like chèvre), firm and nutty (like Gruyère), tangy and funky (like blue), ripe and oozy (like Brie).

- **TIP:** Plan on serving 2 to 3 ounces of cheese per person.

2. Warm it up Most cheeses are best at room temperature, so remove them from the refrigerator at least 1 hour before serving. Keep them wrapped until party time to prevent them from drying out.

- **TIP:** You can quickly soften creamy varieties such as Brie by sealing them in a zipper-lock bag and letting them sit in 80-degree water.

3. Choose neutral bread and crackers Mild-tasting baguette (sliced on the bias into wide, elegant pieces) and water crackers allow the cheese to shine.

- **TIP:** Sliced bread stales quickly, so we brush the slices with extra-virgin olive oil, sprinkle them with salt, and toast them on a rimmed baking sheet in a 400-degree oven until golden brown.

4. Make your own accompaniments Homemade condiments will make the spread exceptional and personal. Fresh fruits, crunchy nuts, and briny olives also add contrast.

SLICING CHEESES

The way you slice the cheese actually impacts each bite—many cheeses change in flavor and texture from edge to center. With each slice, you want to keep a roughly equal ratio of interior and exterior (or rind). And different cuts add visual interest and make a cheese board easier to navigate. Here's how to slice it right.

SMALL BARK-WRAPPED WHEELS
Cheeses Harbison (pictured), Vacherin Mont d'Or, Winnimere, Rush Creek Reserve
What to do Using paring knife, start by making a shallow cut around the perimeter of the rind on top of the cheese, then make a shallow cut down the center of the wheel. Peel back both halves of the rind so guests can scoop out the cheese with a spoon or rounded knife.

SOFT WHEELS AND WEDGES
Cheeses Camembert, triple-crème cheeses such as Sugar Loaf (pictured, wheel), Brie Jouvence Fermier (pictured, wedge)
What to do Small wheels can be cut into equal-size wedges (imagine cutting a small cake). For larger wedges, make slices along the sides of the cheese that angle out from the tip of the wedge.

SEMISOFT AND HARD WEDGES
Cheeses Blue (pictured, semisoft), Manchego (pictured, hard), Drunken Goat
What to do Place the cheese cut-side down on the board. Make parallel slices off the sides, working towards the center. If you cut thick slices (like the blue), you can cut smaller pieces from each one.

RECTANGLES, SQUARES, AND BLOCKS
Cheeses Cheddar, softer cheeses such as Robiola, Taleggio (pictured, top), or Brebirousse d'Argental (pictured, bottom)
What to do If the cheese is fairly firm and relatively uniform in texture (like the Taleggio), you can simply slice straight across it, cutting each piece in half if you'd like.

If the cheese is softer and you can't get the whole cross section in a bite or two (like the Brebirousse d'Argental), start by cutting the cheese in half diagonally and then cut each half in half again to form triangles. Make small slices from the sides, from the exterior to the center, working towards the middle of the triangles.

LOGS
Cheese Goat (pictured)
What to do Slice the log into coins. For larger logs, position the coin so that it's flat and then cut into half-moons or little wedges.

LARGER FIRM AND SEMIFIRM WEDGES
Cheeses Alpine-style cheeses such as Challerhocker (pictured) and washed rind cheeses such as Morbier
What to do Place the cheese cut-side down on the board. Begin by cutting slices across the width of the cheese. When you work halfway or three-quarters of the way through the wedge, begin making slices along the length of the cheese instead. These wide wedges can be cut into smaller pieces.

Small Bark-Wrapped Wheels

Soft Wheels and Wedges

Semisoft Wedges

Hard Wedges

Rectangles, Squares, and Blocks

Logs

Larger Firm and Semifirm Wedges

VEGETABLES

DIPS AND SPREADS

STEPHANIE PIXLEY

Don't wait until the main meal to eat vegetables. Start your meal, or the party, with dips and spreads that are loaded with flavor and taste like their starring vegetable. In this course, you will learn how turn simple vegetables into irresistible versions of themselves that can be served with crudités or bread or used as a spread for sandwiches. Our flavor inspirations come from across the Middle East and the Mediterranean to bring you dips and spreads made from beets and roasted red peppers, carrots and habanero peppers, lemony garlicky potatoes, smoky eggplant, and earthy mushrooms.

STEPH'S PRO TIP: *If you're making a dip ahead, be sure to bring it to room temperature and then taste it for seasoning. I find that dips I've made ahead often benefit from the addition of a little extra salt or acid (usually in the form of lemon or lime juice) and thinning with just a touch of warm water.*

BEET MUHAMMARA

Serves: 8 (makes 2 cups)
Total Time: 30 minutes

RECIPE OVERVIEW Muhammara is a smoky red pepper dip from Syria that's enjoyed throughout the Middle East. This version incorporates beets, which bring out the best qualities of all of the traditional ingredients, heightening the sweetness of the red peppers and pomegranate molasses, bolstering the earthiness of the walnuts, and making the color all the more vibrant. Microwaving raw shredded beets softens them enough to blend into the creamy mixture while preserving their bright, fresh flavor. Some recipes thicken muhammara with bread, but we opt for toasted walnuts to do the job. Jarred roasted peppers add smokiness without any hassle and a touch of pomegranate molasses gives the dip its hallmark sweet yet slightly bitter flavor. You can use the large holes of a box grater or a food processor fitted with a shredding disk to shred the beets. Muhammara makes a delicious dip for crudités or pita, spread for sandwiches, or sauce for meat or fish.

- 8 ounces beets, trimmed, peeled, and shredded
- 1 cup jarred roasted red peppers, rinsed and patted dry
- 1 cup walnuts, toasted
- 1 scallion, sliced thin
- 2 tablespoons extra-virgin olive oil, plus extra for drizzling
- 2 tablespoons pomegranate molasses
- 2 teaspoons lemon juice
- 3/4 teaspoon table salt
- 1/2 teaspoon ground cumin
- 1/8 teaspoon cayenne pepper
- 2 tablespoons minced fresh parsley

1. Microwave beets in covered bowl, stirring often, until tender, about 4 minutes. Transfer beets to fine-mesh strainer set over bowl and let drain for 10 minutes.

2. Process drained beets, peppers, walnuts, scallion, oil, pomegranate molasses, lemon juice, salt, cumin, and cayenne together in food processor until smooth, about 1 minute, scraping down sides of bowl as needed.

3. Transfer mixture to serving bowl. Season with salt to taste. Drizzle with extra oil to taste and sprinkle with parsley before serving. (Dip can be refrigerated for up to 3 days; bring to room temperature before serving.)

KEYS TO SUCCESS

- **Microwave the raw shredded beets**: Softens them and keeps their color vibrant while keeping prep time short

- **Toast the walnuts**: Adds more flavor as they thicken the dip

- **Pomegranate molasses**: Gives the dip its hallmark sweet yet slightly bitter flavor

CARROT-HABANERO DIP

Serves: 10 (makes 2½ cups)
Total Time: 1¼ hours

RECIPE OVERVIEW This highly seasoned dip is packed with vibrant carrot flavor. To really bring out the fruity-earthy qualities of the carrots, a little (or a lot of) spicy heat in the form of habanero chiles works wonders. Cooking the carrots in a saucepan over an initial blast of heat quickly breaks down their cell walls and releases their sugars. To maintain their brilliant color, avoid browning and instead add water and simmer the carrots until tender. Toss in some Moroccan-inspired spices and minced habanero chile to provide a kick. Processing the mixture at the end produces a smooth dip reminiscent of hummus. Top with a drizzle of olive oil and some crunchy pepitas. To make this dip spicier, include the seeds from the chile.

  3 tablespoons extra-virgin olive oil, divided, plus extra for serving
  2 pounds carrots, peeled and sliced ¼ inch thick
  ½ teaspoon table salt
1–2 habanero chiles, seeded and minced
  2 garlic cloves, minced
  ¾ teaspoon ground coriander
  ¾ teaspoon ground cumin
  ¾ teaspoon ground ginger
  ⅛ teaspoon chili powder
  ⅛ teaspoon ground cinnamon
  ⅓ cup water
  1 tablespoon white wine vinegar
  1 tablespoon roasted, salted pepitas
  1 tablespoon minced fresh cilantro

1. Heat 1 tablespoon oil in large saucepan over medium-high heat until shimmering. Add carrots and salt and cook until carrots begin to soften, 5 to 6 minutes. Stir in habanero, garlic, coriander, cumin, ginger, chili powder, and cinnamon and cook until fragrant, about 30 seconds. Add water and bring to simmer. Cover, reduce heat to low, and cook, stirring occasionally, until carrots are tender, 15 to 20 minutes.

2. Transfer carrots to bowl of food processor, add vinegar, and process until smooth, scraping down sides of bowl as needed, 1 to 2 minutes. With processor running, slowly add remaining 2 tablespoons oil until incorporated. Transfer to serving bowl, cover, and refrigerate until chilled, 30 minutes to 1 hour. Season with salt and pepper to taste. Sprinkle with pepitas and cilantro and drizzle with extra oil. Serve.

KEYS TO SUCCESS

- **Soften carrots in oil then simmer**: Makes them tender and preserves their color

- **Customize the heat**: Control the heat with 1 or 2 habanero chiles, with or without their seeds.

- **Use a food processor**: Easily makes the dip smooth

CORE TECHNIQUE

Working with Habanero Chiles

Wear gloves when working with very hot peppers like habaneros to avoid direct contact with the oils that supply the heat. Wash your hands, knife, and cutting board well after prepping chiles.

SKORDALIA

Serves: 8 to 10 (makes 2 cups)
Total Time: 40 minutes

RECIPE OVERVIEW Skordalia is a heady, flavor-packed Greek potato puree that is garlic-forward, bright with lemon, and rich and smooth—just the thing to scoop up with crudités or spread on pita or crackers. We temper the bite of the garlic by soaking it in acidic lemon juice; this neutralizes its alliinase, the enzyme that creates the allium's harsh notes. Choosing an all-potato base rather than oft-used day-old bread helps to achieve a smooth texture. Sliced almonds not only add a touch of earthy sweetness but also contribute richness for a puree that is luxuriously

dense and creamy. Whizzing the ingredients in a blender produces a smooth, emulsified puree; adding water and olive oil yields a puree that remains dippable and spreadable even when cooled to room temperature. To make a puree with the smoothest texture, you'll need a potato ricer or food mill equipped with a fine disk; you can mash the potato thoroughly with a potato masher, but the dip will have a more rustic texture. We prefer a russet potato for its earthier flavor, but a Yukon Gold works well, too. It's fine to use two smaller potatoes that total 12 ounces in place of one big one. You can use either blanched or skin-on almonds. A rasp-style grater makes quick work of turning the garlic into a paste.

- 1 **large russet potato (12 ounces), peeled and sliced ½ inch thick**
- 4 **garlic cloves, peeled**
- 2 **teaspoons grated lemon zest plus ¼ cup juice (2 lemons)**
- ⅔ **cup sliced almonds**
- ½ **cup water**
- ½ **cup extra-virgin olive oil, plus extra for drizzling**
- ¾ **teaspoon table salt**
- 2 **teaspoons minced fresh chives or parsley**

1. Place potato in medium saucepan and add cold water to cover by 1 inch. Bring to boil over high heat. Adjust heat to maintain simmer and cook until paring knife can be easily slipped into and out of potato, 18 to 22 minutes.

2. While potato cooks, mince or grate garlic to fine paste. Transfer 1 tablespoon garlic paste to small bowl; discard remaining garlic paste. Combine lemon juice with garlic paste and let sit for 10 minutes.

3. Process garlic mixture, zest, almonds, water, oil, and salt in blender until very smooth, about 45 seconds.

4. Drain potato. Set ricer or food mill over medium bowl. Working in batches, transfer hot potato to hopper and process. Stir garlic mixture into potato until smooth. Season with salt and pepper to taste and transfer to serving bowl. Drizzle with extra oil and sprinkle with chives. Serve warm or at room temperature. (Skordalia can be refrigerated for up to 3 days. Let sit, covered, at room temperature for 30 minutes before serving.)

KEYS TO SUCCESS

- **Hydrate the potato:** Achieves a puree with a perfectly smooth texture that stays spreadable
- **Temper the garlic:** Lemon juice neutralizes the enzyme responsible for garlic's harsh flavor.
- **Use almonds:** Their richness makes the dip creamier and denser.

BABA GHANOUSH

Serves: 4
Total Time: 1¼ hours

RECIPE OVERVIEW Baba ghanoush originated in the Levantine region of the Middle East and is now popular worldwide. It is a deeply flavored dip made from fire-roasted eggplant that is enriched with tahini and seasoned with lemon and garlic. The bedrock technique is to cook the eggplant over an open flame until the skin is charred (it gets discarded) and the interior is meltingly tender. This simple, brilliant approach concentrates the eggplant's savory flavor, imparts alluring smokiness, and renders the flesh silky. Piercing the eggplants' skins before roasting encourages moisture to evaporate and prevents them from bursting open. You can roast them under the broiler or on the grill until they turn fully tender. Temper the pungency of the raw garlic with lemon juice and salt, and whisk in a generous amount of tahini, along with olive oil, to ensure that the dip is rich and creamy. To account for the eggplants' variable sizes and water content, season to taste with additional lemon juice and salt before serving. The finished product should be assertive but not overpowering.

- 2 **(12-ounce) eggplants**
- 1 **tablespoon lemon juice, plus extra for seasoning**
- 1 **garlic clove, minced to paste**
- 1 **teaspoon table salt**
- ¼ **cup tahini**
- ¼ **cup extra-virgin olive oil, divided**
- 1 **tablespoon chopped fresh parsley**

1. Poke each eggplant about 6 times with paring knife.

2A. FOR THE OVEN Adjust oven rack 8 inches from broiler element and heat broiler. Line rimmed baking sheet with aluminum foil.

2B. FOR A CHARCOAL GRILL Open bottom vent completely. Light large chimney starter filled with charcoal briquettes (6 quarts). When top coals are partially covered with ash, pour evenly over grill. Set cooking grate in place, cover, and open lid vent completely. Heat grill until hot, about 5 minutes.

2C. FOR A GAS GRILL Turn all burners to high; cover and heat grill until hot, about 15 minutes. Turn all burners to medium-high.

3. Place eggplants on prepared sheet (or directly on cooking grate) and broil (or grill, covered) for 20 minutes. Remove sheet from oven and flip eggplants (or flip eggplants on grill). Return sheet to oven and broil (or grill, covered) for 10 minutes. (Skin should be charred and have aroma of burning leaves.) Transfer eggplants to plate and let cool completely, about 30 minutes.

4. Meanwhile, combine lemon juice, garlic, and salt in medium bowl and let sit while eggplants cool.

5. Working with 1 eggplant at a time, split lengthwise on 1 side through skin and peel back skin to expose flesh. Using spoon, scoop out eggplant flesh; discard eggplant skin. Chop eggplant flesh fine with chef's knife and transfer to bowl with lemon juice mixture.

6. Add tahini and 2 tablespoons oil to eggplant mixture and whisk to combine. Let baba ghanoush sit for 20 minutes to allow flavors to blend, stirring occasionally. Season with extra lemon juice and salt to taste. Spread baba ghanoush in shallow bowl and drizzle with remaining 2 tablespoons oil. Sprinkle with parsley and serve.

KEYS TO SUCCESS

- **Poke holes in the eggplant:** Helps to release moisture during roasting

- **Temper the raw garlic:** Acidic lemon juice and salt soften its harsh favor.

Roasting Eggplant

POKE AND CHAR
Poke whole eggplants, then char under broiler or on grill.

COOL AND SCOOP
Allow eggplants to cool, then split lengthwise and scoop out soft flesh.

MUSHROOM PÂTÉ

Serves: 8 (makes 2 cups)
Total Time: 40 minutes, plus 2 hours chilling

RECIPE OVERVIEW To achieve a spread full of heady, earthy mushroom flavor, we supplement everyday white mushrooms with dried porcini, which are intensely flavored. Rehydrating the dried porcini before chopping them in the food processor is essential (it keeps the texture of the dish from ending up grainy), and utilizing some of the potent soaking liquid gives the pâté even more mushroom flavor. We get the best results by pulsing the mushrooms in a food processor until still slightly chunky. Cream cheese and some heavy cream provide a rich, creamy base; sautéed shallots, thyme, and garlic contribute deep flavor; and lemon juice and parsley offset the earthy flavors with some brightness. Serve with crackers or thinly sliced baguette.

1 cup water
1 ounce dried porcini mushrooms, rinsed
1 pound white mushrooms, trimmed and halved
3 tablespoons unsalted butter
2 large shallots, minced
¾ teaspoon table salt
3 garlic cloves, minced
1½ teaspoons minced fresh thyme
2 ounces cream cheese
2 tablespoons heavy cream
1 tablespoon minced fresh parsley
1½ teaspoons lemon juice

1. Microwave water and porcini mushrooms in covered bowl until steaming, about 1 minute. Let sit until softened, about 5 minutes. Drain porcini through fine-mesh strainer lined with coffee filter set over bowl. Reserve ⅓ cup liquid. Pulse porcini and white mushrooms in food processor until finely chopped and all pieces are pea-size or smaller, about 10 pulses, scraping down bowl as needed.

2. Melt butter in 12-inch skillet over medium heat. Add shallots and salt and cook until shallots are softened, 3 to 5 minutes. Stir in garlic and thyme and cook until fragrant, 30 seconds. Stir in processed mushrooms and cook, stirring occasionally, until liquid released from mushrooms evaporates and mushrooms begin to brown, 10 to 12 minutes.

3. Stir in reserved porcini liquid and cook until nearly evaporated, about 1 minute. Off heat, stir in cream cheese, cream, parsley, and lemon juice and season with salt and pepper to taste. Transfer to serving bowl and smooth top. Press plastic wrap flush to surface of pâté and refrigerate until firm, at least 2 hours or up to 3 days. Before serving, bring pâté to room temperature to soften.

KEYS TO SUCCESS

- **Mix of mushrooms:** Dried porcini and their soaking liquid add deep savory flavor.

- **Use a food processor:** Produces the best texture

CRUDITÉS MAKE A COMEBACK

Crudités, a haute French import (the French word means "raw" and the culinary term is plural), surfaced in U.S. cookbooks around the mid-20th century, and Americans latched on immediately. Homemakers and restaurant chefs appreciated how easy it was to platter up crisp vegetables with a dip or two and call it hors d'oeuvres. Even James Beard glorified crudités in one of his works, declaring the starter "the most appetizing dish imaginable."

With the advent of baby carrots in the 1980s and eventually prepackaged relish trays, the concept stopped feeling even remotely glamorous. But it's back on the upswing: Farm-fresh produce has never been more diverse, dips more inspired, and grazing boards more in vogue.

Start with the freshest seasonal vegetables you can get. Beyond that, it's all about treating the produce nicely, whipping up full-bodied dips, and plotting out an eye-catching display.

BUILD A CURATED BOARD

MAKE THE RIGHT AMOUNT Plan on 4 to 6 ounces vegetables and ¼ cup dip per person.

GO FOR LOTS OF COLOR Choose produce in a spectrum of colors, including rainbow carrots, Easter Egg radishes, and cherry tomato medleys.

MIX UP THE DIPS Serving multiple dips means that you can offer a range of flavors and consistencies. Garnishing them adds visual contrast; consider fresh herbs, crushed or ground spices, and olive oil.

CONSIDER THE CUTS Try making long and short cuts on the same item; quartering colorful cauliflower florets to see the gradient; and leaving the tops of root vegetables partially intact.

SIZE UP THE PLATTER Decide if you prefer the "wall-to-wall" look, where the surface is generously covered, or a more minimalist aesthetic.

MAKE VEGGIES EXTRA-CRISP While arranging the board, submerge raw vegetables in an ice bath to keep them hydrated and crisp.

ARRANGE THOUGHTFULLY Place the dips down first and the vegetables around them. If plating on a rectangular surface, flank the perimeter with longer items and cluster smaller pieces in the middle.

A CASE FOR BLANCHING

Blanching tenderizes tough vegetables and softens their raw bite; it also seasons them and brightens their color. Here are three keys to doing it well.

BLANCH IN SEA-SALTY WATER Supersalty water (½ cup of table salt per 2 quarts of water) not only seasons the vegetables and concentrates their flavors but also quickly softens pectin in their cell walls so that they turn tender before losing their vibrant color.

SHOCK IN ICE-COLD WATER Shocking halts cooking so that the vegetables don't oversoften or lose their bright color. The water bath will warm up quickly if you're blanching in batches, so be sure to use plenty of ice (and replenish as necessary) to keep it really cold.

COOK IN BATCHES Blanching each type of vegetable separately helps avoid over- or undercooking. Here's a cheat sheet of suggested cooking times for common produce for crudités, as well as a list of naturally tender items that shouldn't be blanched.

BLANCH		DON'T BLANCH
Asparagus	30–45 seconds, depending on thickness	Bell Peppers Cherry Tomatoes Cucumbers Endive Radishes Snow Peas
Broccoli	30–45 seconds	
Carrots	90 seconds	
Cauliflower	90 seconds	
Green Beans	30 seconds	
Snap Peas	60 seconds	

MAKE THE BEST OF THE BEST VEGETABLES

These tips will help maximize the vegetables' textures, flavors, and visual appeal.

GO FOR THIN-SKINNED, LESS-SEEDY CUCUMBERS
Slender English (also called European or hothouse) and petite Persian cukes boast thin, tender skins that are usually unwaxed and contain fewer bitter-tasting cucurbitacins than slicing cucumbers do. Plus, their tiny seeds go almost unnoticed.

CHOOSE RADISHES ACCORDING TO HEAT TOLERANCE
Common round red varieties pack a fiery punch, as do the streaky Purple Ninja kind. The heat in pastel Easter Egg radishes builds progressively as you eat them, and the tapered French Breakfast type are truly mild mannered.

KEEP COLOR IN COLORFUL CAULIFLOWER
Blanch purple cauliflower very briefly to prevent its water-soluble anthocyanin compounds from leaching out. As soon as the pieces are crisp-tender (after about 90 seconds), shock them in ice water to stop the cooking and set their color. (The carotenoids in orange cauliflower are not water-soluble and won't leach out; chlorophyll in the green variety will lose its bright color if overcooked, but not in a quick blanch.)

> Dips can be refrigerated for two to three days; if necessary, loosen with 1 tablespoon of warm water. Add garnishes just before serving.

PEEL—DON'T SNAP—ASPARAGUS
You'll throw away as much as half of each stalk's weight if you snap off the ends at their natural breaking point, and the uneven bunch won't plate nicely. Trimming 1 inch off the base and peeling the lower half of each stalk reduces waste and results in tender, refined spears.

BUY BUNCHED CARROTS, NOT BAGGED
Carrots with their feathery tops still attached aren't just prettier than bagged ones; they're fresher and richer-tasting, too, because they are sold within a few weeks of harvest when their greens are still vibrant and their flavor complex.

NO-FEAR ARTICHOKES

STEVE DUNN

A lot of people are daunted by the idea of preparing and serving artichokes. It's time to stop being intimidated. With the right instruction and recipes, whole artichokes are easy to prep and cook, impressive to serve, and fun to eat. This course covers all of the different ways to prepare and enjoy artichokes. You'll learn how to prep, then cook artichokes—from simply boiling, to roasting, to stuffing and braising, to frying, to grilling them in a matter of minutes.

STEVE'S PRO TIP: *While color and weight are usually reasonable indications of artichoke freshness, they can sometimes be misleading. When I buy an artichoke, I* always *listen to it too. I pick it up, hold it next to my ear and give it a good squeeze. If I hear a squeak, that's a good sign, and I know it still has ample moisture and crispness.*

THE METHOD
ARTICHOKES

Here's how to work with and prepare fresh artichokes for various recipes.

1 BUY BRIGHT GREEN AND TIGHT
Very fresh artichokes should feel heavy for their size and boast bright green, tightly closed leaves.

2 TRIM TOP AND BOTTOM
Using sharp chef's knife, cut away most of stem, leaving specified length attached. Cut off top quarter of leaves if specified in recipe.

3 SNAP OFF OUTER LEAVES
Pull tough outer leaves downward and break off at base. Repeat with leaves in first 3 or 4 rows from base as specified in recipe.

4 TIDY UP STEM
Use paring knife to trim away tough outer layer of stem and base, removing dark green parts.

5 SPLIT AND SCOOP
If required, halve artichoke lengthwise with chef's knife. Using spoon, scoop out fuzzy interior choke to get to the heart.

6 REMOVE LEAVES AROUND CHOKE
Use your fingers to pull out any purple-tinged leaves around choke, leaving small cavity.

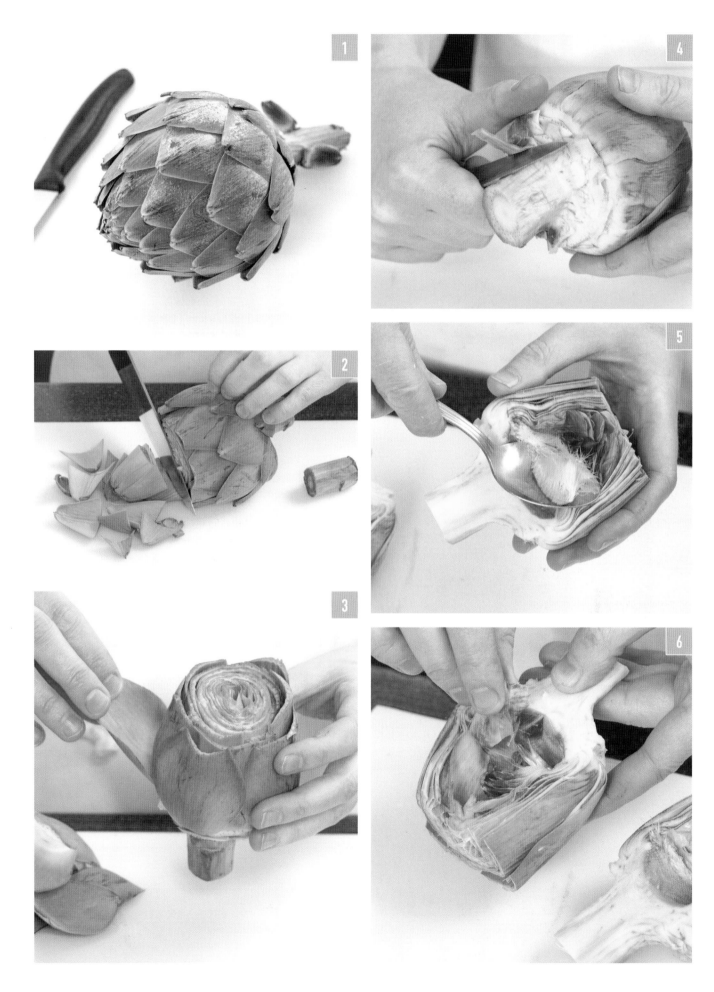

BOILED WHOLE ARTICHOKES

Serves: 4
Total Time: 1¼ hours

RECIPE OVERVIEW Boiling in salted water is not only the simplest, most hands-off way to cook artichokes but also the best way to make sure that they're well seasoned. We made the process even easier here by eliminating the traditional steps of removing the pointy ends, treating the cut artichokes with lemon juice to prevent discoloration, and weighing down the artichokes as they cook. (The artichokes may not be fully submerged, but the parts that need to cook will remain below the water line.) Serve with melted salted butter, mayonnaise (see our recipe on page 66), or vinaigrette. Have an empty bowl on hand for the spent leaves and chokes. This recipe can be halved.

> 4 artichokes (8 to 10 ounces each)
> Table salt for cooking artichokes

1. Bring 5 quarts water to boil in Dutch oven. Meanwhile, working with 1 artichoke at a time, use serrated knife to cut off stem so artichoke sits flat on counter. Cut off top inch of artichoke. Snap off any small leaves around base.

2. Add artichokes and 2½ tablespoons salt to boiling water and arrange artichokes stemmed side down. Adjust heat to maintain gentle boil. Cover and cook until outer leaf easily detaches from artichoke and paler flesh at bottom of leaf can be easily scraped off with your teeth, 40 to 55 minutes.

3. Using tongs or slotted spoon, transfer artichokes to wire rack set in rimmed baking sheet. Turn artichokes stemmed side up and let cool for 10 minutes. Transfer artichokes, stemmed side down, to platter or individual plates and serve.

4. TO EAT Pull off outer leaves one at a time. Pull leaf through your teeth to remove soft, meaty portion. Discard remainder of leaf. When only tender, purple-tipped leaves remain, grasp leaves and bite off tender lower sections. Pinch any remaining leaves together and pull away from base to reveal choke. Using small spoon, scrape out choke and discard. Cut heart into bite-size pieces and eat.

If Boiling Artichokes, Don't Bother...

REMOVING THE SPINES The pointy tips of the leaves are not terribly big or sharp, and they soften during cooking.

TREATING WITH LEMON Because artichokes are high in phenolic compounds, their cut surfaces discolor quickly. But cooking deepens their hue, hiding any oxidization.

WEIGHING DOWN It's not a problem if the artichokes bob around in the water; the edible portion will remain submerged without assistance.

ROASTED ARTICHOKES

Serves: 4
Total Time: 55 minutes

RECIPE OVERVIEW While artichokes are great boiled, roasting helps to accentuate their nutty flavor. This hybrid steam-and-roast method yields artichokes that are tender, deeply flavorful, and nicely browned. To prevent the artichokes from discoloring and drying out in the heat of the oven, we give them a quick dip in lemon water, toss them with olive oil and salt, and cover the roasting dish with foil. If your artichokes are larger than 8 to 10 ounces, strip away another layer or two of the toughest outer leaves. Serve the artichokes plain with a squeeze of lemon or pair them with Aioli (page 66). To eat, use your teeth to scrape the flesh from the cooked tough outer leaves. The inner tender leaves, heart, and stem are entirely edible.

1 lemon, plus lemon wedges for serving
4 artichokes (8 to 10 ounces each)
3 tablespoons extra-virgin olive oil, divided
¾ teaspoon table salt

1. Adjust oven rack to lower-middle position and heat oven to 475 degrees. Cut lemon in half, squeeze halves into 2 quarts water, and drop in spent halves.

2. Cut off most of stem of 1 artichoke, leaving about ¾ inch attached. Cut off top quarter. Pull tough outer leaves downward toward stem and break off at base; continue until first three or four rows of leaves have been removed. Using paring knife, trim outer layer of stem and rough areas around base, removing any dark green parts. Cut artichoke in half lengthwise. Using spoon, remove fuzzy choke. Pull out inner, tiny purple-tinged leaves, leaving small cavity in center. Drop prepped halves into lemon water. Repeat with remaining artichokes.

3. Brush 13 by 9-inch baking dish with 1 tablespoon oil. Remove artichokes from lemon water, shaking off some excess lemon water (some should be left clinging to leaves). Toss artichokes with remaining 2 tablespoons oil and salt and season with pepper to taste, gently working some oil and seasonings between leaves. Arrange artichoke halves cut side down in baking dish and cover tightly with aluminum foil.

4. Roast until cut sides of artichokes start to brown and both bases and leaves are tender when poked with tip of paring knife, 25 to 30 minutes. Transfer artichokes to serving dish. Serve artichokes warm or at room temperature, passing lemon wedges separately.

Variation

ROASTED ARTICHOKES WITH LEMON VINAIGRETTE

Cut very thin slices off both ends of 2 lemons and cut lemons in half crosswise. Place lemon halves, flesh side up, in baking dish with artichokes before covering with foil in step 3. Roast artichokes as directed. Once roasted lemon halves are cool enough to handle, squeeze into fine-mesh strainer set over bowl. Press on solids to extract all liquid; discard solids. Measure 1½ tablespoons strained lemon pulp into small bowl. Whisk in ½ teaspoon finely grated garlic, ½ teaspoon Dijon mustard, and ½ teaspoon salt and season with pepper to taste. Whisking constantly, gradually drizzle 6 tablespoons extra-virgin olive oil into lemon mixture. Whisk in 2 tablespoons minced fresh parsley. Serve with artichokes.

ROMAN-STYLE STUFFED BRAISED ARTICHOKES

Serves: 4
Total Time: 1½ hours

RECIPE OVERVIEW For this traditional Italian dish, a bright, robust stuffing is created with a blend of minced fresh parsley and mint, garlic, lemon zest, and bread crumbs moistened with extra-virgin olive oil. The stuffing infuses the artichokes with flavor as they braise. Cooking the artichokes takes little more than half an hour in a large Dutch oven filled with just enough water to cover the stems three-quarters of the way. (Any more liquid makes for sodden stems and a gummy filling.) If your artichokes are larger than 8 to 10 ounces, strip away another layer or two of the toughest outer leaves. To prevent the uncooked filling from spilling out, place each artichoke stem end down into a thickly cut onion ring. For even cooking, rotate the artichokes at the midway point so that the stem ends are facing up. Serve each artichoke with a spoon so that diners can coax out the stuffing.

1 slice hearty white sandwich bread, crust removed, cut into ½-inch pieces
1 lemon
4 artichokes (8 to 10 ounces each)
½ cup extra-virgin olive oil
¼ cup minced fresh parsley, stems reserved
¼ cup minced fresh mint
4 garlic cloves, minced
¾ teaspoon table salt, divided
1 onion, cut crosswise into ½-inch-thick slices and separated into rings

1. Pulse bread in food processor to fine crumbs, about 10 pulses; transfer to medium bowl. Grate 1 tablespoon zest from lemon and add to bowl; set aside. Cut lemon in half, squeeze halves into container filled with 2 quarts water, then add spent halves.

2. Working with 1 artichoke at a time, trim end of stem and cut off top quarter of artichoke. Break off tough outer leaves by pulling them downward until only light-colored core remains. Using kitchen shears, trim off top portion of outer leaves. Using paring knife, trim stem and base, removing any dark green parts. Spread leaves to reveal fuzzy choke at center. Using spoon, remove fuzzy choke. Rinse artichoke well, then submerge prepped artichoke in lemon water.

3. Add oil, parsley leaves, mint, garlic, and ½ teaspoon salt to bowl with bread crumbs and stir until well combined; season with pepper to taste. Using small spoon, divide filling evenly among artichokes, placing it in center of artichoke, where choke was.

4. Spread onion rings evenly over bottom of Dutch oven. Sprinkle reserved parsley stems and remaining ¼ teaspoon salt over onion rings. Set artichokes stem ends down into onion rings. Fill pot with enough cold water so that stems are three-quarters submerged.

WHAT CAN GO WRONG

PROBLEM The artichokes have tough, inedible sections.

SOLUTION When cooking fresh artichokes, most of the challenge is in the artichoke prep. Make sure to remove all the woody, tough, dark green portions of the artichoke during the cleaning process. What's left should be yellowish green in color and will be edible when the artichokes are cooked.

PROBLEM The filling tastes stale and bland with an unpleasant texture.

SOLUTION Don't try to take a shortcut by using store-bought dried bread crumbs. Commercial bread crumbs are so fine that they're dusty and have a stale "off" flavor. Fresh homemade bread crumbs are quick and easy to make in a food processor and have a flavor and texture that's superior to store-bought.

5. Cover and bring to boil over medium-high heat. Reduce heat to medium-low and simmer for 15 minutes. Using tongs, rotate artichokes so stem ends face up, using tongs to keep filling in place. Cover and cook until tip of paring knife is easily inserted into artichoke heart, about 15 minutes longer. Transfer artichokes to serving platter. Serve.

KEYS TO SUCCESS
- **Homemade bread crumbs:** Quick and easy to make, their flavor is fresher than store-bought.
- **Onion rings as pedestals:** They hold the stuffed artichokes above the water line so the filling stays dry.
- **Test for doneness:** Insert a paring knife into the heart, which is in the thickest part of the artichoke and the last part to finish cooking.

CARCIOFI ALLA GIUDIA
Serves: 4 as an appetizer
Total Time: 1¼ hours

RECIPE OVERVIEW Carciofi alla giudia are crunchy, crispy, creamy, and visually striking. To make the fried artichokes that Roman Jews have prepared for centuries during the thistle's spring harvest, cooks trim the thistles to expose their tender, inner leaves, and then deep-fry the artichokes a few at a time—twice. The first round softens up the vegetable's dense heart, and the second makes the petals unfurl and crisp. After plucking off the tough outer bracts, make four angled cuts with a sharp knife to remove the top half of the remaining leaves. Halving the artichoke exposes its hairy choke, which is scooped out with a spoon after the first fry, when it has softened considerably. Using very fresh, tightly closed blossoms minimizes the amount of leaves lost during prep. Double frying delivers a stunning range of textures: The first fry, done low and slow, renders the dense heart soft and creamy. The second, a 1-minute flash in hot oil, browns and crisps up the leaves so that they offer a range of potato chip–like crunch and crispness. The leaves also unfurl so that the finished product resembles a copper-dipped chrysanthemum. Frying in a combination of neutral canola oil and a small amount of olive oil minimizes cost and also allows the delicate artichoke flavor to stand out. Straining the used oil means that it can be reused more than half a dozen times. Look for artichokes that are uniformly green, have tightly closed leaves, feel heavy for their size, and squeak a little when squeezed—all indications of freshness; avoid any that are browning and dried out. Don't worry when the artichokes discolor as you prep them; any oxidation won't be visible after frying. If your large saucepan holds less than 4 quarts, use a large Dutch oven and add 2 cups more canola oil so that the artichokes are completely covered. We like to season these artichokes with flake sea salt. The stem makes a useful handle when prepping and cooking the artichokes but is usually too fibrous to eat.

4 artichokes (10 to 12 ounces each)
6 cups canola oil for frying
2 cups extra-virgin olive oil for frying
Lemon wedges

1. Working with 1 artichoke at a time, snap off tough outer leaves until you reach tender inner leaves (they'll be pale yellow at their base). Trim stem to 1½-inch length. Peel stem and base with paring or bird's beak knife to remove dark-green layer. Starting halfway up leaves, use chef's knife to make 45-degree angled cut toward top of artichoke to remove tips of leaves. Repeat same cut 3 more times, rotating artichoke quarter turn before each cut.

2. Set wire rack in rimmed baking sheet and line with double layer of paper towels. Heat canola oil and olive oil in large saucepan over medium-high heat to 275 degrees. Cut each artichoke in half through stem.

3. Using spider skimmer or slotted spoon, carefully add artichokes to oil. Cook until paring knife slipped into thickest part of base meets little resistance and leaves are medium brown, 10 to 12 minutes. Using spider skimmer or slotted spoon, transfer artichokes to prepared rack cut side down to drain. Remove saucepan from heat. Let artichokes cool for 15 minutes. (Artichoke halves can be wrapped well and refrigerated for up to 24 hours.)

4. Using spoon, scoop out choke from center of each artichoke half, being careful not to dislodge leaves attached to base. Replace paper towels with double layer of fresh paper towels. Heat oil over high heat to 350 degrees.

5. Place 2 artichoke halves cut side down in oil and, using spider skimmer or slotted spoon, lightly press on artichokes to submerge. Cook until outer leaves are dark brown, 45 to 60 seconds. Transfer to prepared rack cut side down to drain. Return oil to 350 degrees and repeat with remaining artichoke halves in 3 more batches. Sprinkle artichokes on both sides with flake sea salt to taste. Serve, passing lemon wedges separately.

Twice Fried ⟶ Three Textures

Carefully trimmed to expose the cone of inner leaves and fried twice, carciofi alla giudia boast stunning textural contrast. The first fry, which is more of a lazy, low-temperature oil poach, renders the vegetable's heart creamy and tender. The second fry is hotter and faster: a flash in shimmering oil that gives the thicker outer leaves kettle-chip crunch and the thinner interior ones lacy, Lay's-like crispness. (The first fry can be done in advance, making these great for parties since all you need is a 1-minute fry on serving day.)

KEYS TO SUCCESS
- **Simple prep:** Halving each artichoke exposes its fuzzy choke, making it easy to remove.
- **Double frying:** Delivers visual and textural contrast
- **Less olive oil:** Lets the artichoke flavor shine and is less expensive

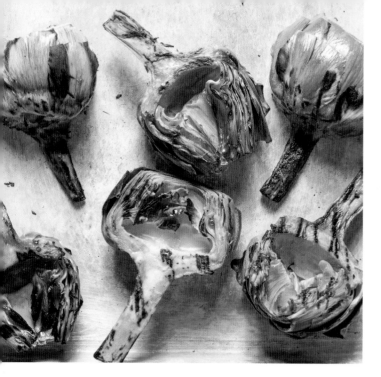

GRILLED ARTICHOKES WITH LEMON BUTTER

Serves: 4
Total Time: 1¼ hours

RECIPE OVERVIEW Grilling artichokes is an alternative preparation that brings a bit of smoky char and enhances their nutty flavor. Parboiling the artichokes in a broth with lemon juice, red pepper flakes, and salt ensures that they are completely tender and thoroughly seasoned. Brushing the chokes with extra-virgin olive oil helps them develop flavorful char marks on the grill. A simple blend of lemon zest and juice, garlic, and butter come together easily in the microwave and is perfect for dipping or drizzling. If your artichokes are larger than 8 to 10 ounces, strip away another layer or two of the toughest outer leaves.

- ½ teaspoon table salt, plus salt for parboiling artichokes
- ½ teaspoon red pepper flakes
- 2 lemons
- 4 artichokes (8 to 10 ounces each)
- 6 tablespoons unsalted butter
- 1 garlic clove, minced to paste
- ¼ teaspoon pepper
- 2 tablespoons extra-virgin olive oil

1. Combine 3 quarts water, 3 tablespoons salt, and pepper flakes in Dutch oven. Cut 1 lemon in half; squeeze juice into pot, then add spent halves. Bring to boil over high heat.

2. Meanwhile, working with 1 artichoke at a time, trim end of stem and cut off top quarter of artichoke. Break off bottom 3 or 4 rows of tough outer leaves by pulling them downward. Using kitchen shears, trim off top portion of outer leaves. Using paring knife, trim stem and base, removing any dark green parts.

3. Add artichokes to pot with boiling water mixture, cover, and reduce heat to medium-low. Simmer until tip of paring knife inserted into base of artichoke meets no resistance, 25 to 28 minutes, stirring occasionally.

4. Meanwhile, grate 2 teaspoons zest from remaining lemon; combine with butter, garlic, salt, and pepper in bowl. Microwave at 50 percent power until butter is melted and bubbling and garlic is fragrant, about 2 minutes, stirring occasionally. Squeeze 1½ tablespoons juice from zested lemon and stir into butter. Season with salt and pepper to taste.

5. Set wire rack in rimmed baking sheet. Place artichokes stem side up on prepared rack and let drain for 10 minutes. Cut artichokes in half lengthwise. Remove fuzzy choke and any tiny inner purple-tinged leaves using small spoon, leaving small cavity in center of each half.

6A. FOR A CHARCOAL GRILL Open bottom vent completely. Light large chimney starter filled with charcoal briquettes (6 quarts). When top coals are partially covered with ash, pour evenly over grill. Set cooking grate in place, cover, and open lid vent completely. Heat grill until hot, about 5 minutes.

6B. FOR A GAS GRILL Turn all burners to high, cover, and heat grill until hot, about 15 minutes. Leave all burners on high.

7. Clean and oil cooking grate. Brush artichokes with oil. Place artichokes on grill and cook (covered if using gas) until lightly charred, 2 to 4 minutes per side. Transfer artichokes to serving platter and tent with aluminum foil. Briefly rewarm lemon butter in microwave, if necessary, and serve with artichokes.

KEYS TO SUCCESS

- **Precook the artichokes:** Ensures their doneness and not burning on the grill
- **Single-level fire:** Hot coals provide a quick solid char

SCIENCE LESSON

Why Do Artichokes Turn Brown?

Artichokes are rich in phenolic compounds. When the cell walls of artichokes are cut or crushed, enzymes (polyphenol oxidase) in their tissues are exposed to oxygen and react with those phenols, producing unattractive black- or brown-colored pigments. Rubbing the exposed ends with acid slows the rate of browning. We found that vinegar (which is high in acetic acid) and parsley (which is high in ascorbic acid) each minimized darkening when added to cooking water. But lemon juice (which contains both citric and ascorbic acids) proved far more effective, limiting this enzymatic reaction almost completely.

ANATOMY OF A GLOBE ARTICHOKE

Artichokes are the flower buds of a huge Mediterranean plant from the thistle family. Small, medium, and large artichokes can all grow on a single plant. The artichoke itself is made up of four parts: the stem, which is edible in smaller artichokes but often stringy in larger ones; the outer and inner bracts (commonly referred to as "leaves" or "petals"), each of which has a pointed spine at the top and a nugget of delectable flesh at the bottom; the appropriately named choke, a central collection of wiry fibers that's always discarded; and the meaty heart, the prize of the artichoke.

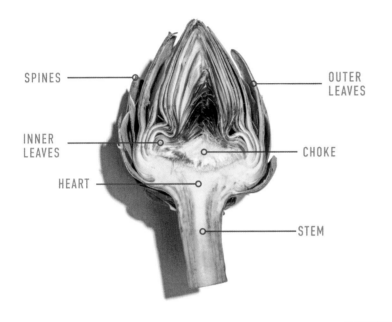

SPINES — OUTER LEAVES — INNER LEAVES — CHOKE — HEART — STEM

ASSESSING ARTICHOKES

While you will see artichokes throughout most of the year, springtime is high season. Then, artichokes of all sizes are widely available. When selecting fresh artichokes, examine the leaves for some clues that will help you pick the best specimens. The leaves should look tight, compact, and bright green. If you give an artichoke a squeeze, its leaves should squeak as they rub together (evidence that the artichoke still possesses much of its moisture). The leaves should also snap off cleanly. If the leaves bend rather than snap, or if they appear dried out or feathery at the edges, the artichoke is old.

Artichokes will keep in the refrigerator for up to five days if sprinkled lightly with water and stored in a zipper-lock plastic bag.

Buy this

Pass on this

HOW TO EAT A BOILED ARTICHOKE

PULL OFF OUTER LEAF
Pull outer leaf from artichoke.

SCRAPE WITH TEETH
Scrape leaf between your teeth to remove flesh.

PULL OFF SMALL LEAVES
Grasp and remove small, purple-tipped leaves. Bite off tender lower sections.

SCOOP OUT CHOKE
Once all leaves are removed, use small spoon to scrape out feathery choke and discard.

EAT HEART
Cut heart into bite-size pieces and eat.

POMMES DE TERRE

JACK BISHOP

Potatoes are a popular vegetable with countless preparations. In this course, you will learn three different methods for elevating the humble potato, French style. The course opens with a simple recipe for ultimate roasted potatoes made luxurious with the use of duck fat. It then proceeds with recipes for mashed potatoes rich with milk and two kinds of cheese and a classic layered potato cake made easier in a non-stick skillet.

JACK'S PRO TIP: *Potatoes need way more salt than you think so follow the seasoning recommendations in our recipes. There's nothing more disappointing than bland potatoes.*

DUCK FAT–ROASTED POTATOES

Serves: 6
Total Time: 1¼ hours

RECIPE OVERVIEW For the ultimate roasted potatoes, rethink the fat. This recipe calls for a richer option—duck fat—for potatoes that are crisp on the outside, moist on the inside, and exploding with meaty, savory flavor. Moist-yet-starchy Yukon Golds are the best potato option, peeled and cut into chunks to maximize their crispable surface area. We encourage thorough seasoning and deeper browning by boiling the chunks with a touch of baking soda and plenty of salt and then, after draining, vigorously stirring them to rough up their exterior before working in the duck fat. This added step is enough to coat the potatoes with a film of starchy, fatty paste for a rich, crisp shell. Preheating a baking sheet in a hot oven jump-starts the browning, and quickly turning the potatoes partway through roasting ensures even doneness. With minutes to go, stir in an extra tablespoon of duck fat, this time seasoned with fresh rosemary, and finish roasting the potatoes until they are well browned. These potatoes are aromatic, tender, and totally indulgent. You will have rendered duck fat to use here if you make Duck Confit (page 454).Or buy duck fat in the meat department at the supermarket. Alternatively, substitute chicken fat, lard, or a mixture of 3 tablespoons bacon fat and 3 tablespoons extra-virgin olive oil.

3½ pounds Yukon Gold potatoes, peeled and cut into 1½-inch pieces
1 teaspoon kosher salt, plus salt for cooking potatoes
½ teaspoon baking soda
6 tablespoons duck fat, divided
1 tablespoon chopped fresh rosemary

1. Adjust oven rack to top position, place rimmed baking sheet on rack, and heat oven to 475 degrees.

2. Bring 10 cups water to boil in Dutch oven over high heat. Add potatoes, ⅓ cup salt, and baking soda. Return to boil and cook for 1 minute. Drain potatoes. Return potatoes to pot and place over low heat. Cook, shaking pot occasionally, until surface moisture has evaporated, about 2 minutes. Remove from heat. Add 5 tablespoons fat and salt; mix with rubber spatula until potatoes are coated with thick paste, about 30 seconds.

3. Remove sheet from oven, transfer potatoes to sheet, and spread into even layer. Roast for 15 minutes.

4. Remove sheet from oven. Using thin, sharp, metal spatula, turn potatoes. Roast until golden brown, 12 to 15 minutes. While potatoes roast, combine rosemary and remaining 1 tablespoon fat in bowl.

5. Remove sheet from oven. Spoon rosemary-fat mixture over potatoes and turn again. Continue to roast until potatoes are well browned and rosemary is fragrant, 3 to 5 minutes. Season with salt and pepper to taste. Serve immediately.

KEYS TO SUCCESS

- **Yukon Gold potatoes**: Have the best balance of starchiness and waxiness so they crisp nicely
- **Quick brine potatoes with salt and baking soda**: Baking soda breaks down potatoes' pectin.
- **Preheated baking sheet**: Jump-starts browning

Saving Fat for Cooking

Saving the leftover fat from bacon, roasts, or poultry is easy to do. Pour the warm fat through a fine-mesh strainer into a Mason jar and discard any solids. (Alternatively, let the fat cool and harden and then scoop it into the jar, leaving any solids behind.) Put the lid on the jar, label it, and refrigerate for up to one month or freeze for up to six months, adding more fat as desired.

ALIGOT
Serves: 6
Total Time: 45 minutes

RECIPE OVERVIEW Aligot is a French mashed potato dish with a smooth slightly elastic texture and rich garlicky flavor. These potatoes get their elastic, satiny texture through prolonged, vigorous stirring that creates cheesy, garlicky mashed potatoes with the same signature stretch as the French original. Medium-starch Yukon Gold potatoes yield a puree with a mild, buttery flavor and a light, creamy consistency. We boil the potatoes, then use a food processor to "mash" them. Traditional aligot uses butter and crème fraîche to add flavor and creaminess and loosen the texture

The Science of Stretch: Rough 'Em Up

Normally we wouldn't dream of mashing potatoes in a food processor, let alone whipping them by hand for a protracted period—two techniques called for in our aligot recipe. Such rough handling causes the release of amylose, the tacky gel-like starch found in potatoes that spells the end of light, fluffy texture. But in these cheesy, garlicky French mashed potatoes, the release of amylose is actually a good thing. When combined with the cheese in the recipe, it helps produce aligot's signature stretch.

Here's how it works: When cheese is stirred vigorously into the hot boiled potatoes, this rough treatment causes the waterlogged starch granules in the spuds to burst, releasing sticky, gluey amylose. At the same time, the protein molecules in the melting cheese are uncoiling and stretching out like curly hair straightened by a flat iron. When amylose released from the potatoes comes into contact with the uncoiled proteins, it links them together into long, elastic fibers that give aligot its stretch.

Whip into Shape
For smooth, elastic texture,
stir potatoes for three to five minutes.

before mixing in the cheese. We substitute whole milk for the crème fraîche, which provides depth without going overboard. For the cheese, a combination of mild mozzarella and nutty Gruyère is just right. As for the stirring, you need to monitor the consistency closely: too much stirring and the aligot turns rubbery; too little and the cheese doesn't marry with the potatoes for that essential elasticity. The finished potatoes should have a smooth and slightly elastic texture. White cheddar can be substituted for the Gruyère. For richer, stretchier aligot, double the mozzarella.

    2   pounds Yukon Gold potatoes, peeled, cut into ½-inch-thick slices, rinsed well, and drained
  1½   teaspoons table salt, plus salt for cooking potatoes
    6   tablespoons unsalted butter
    2   garlic cloves, minced
1–1½   cups whole milk, divided
    4   ounces mozzarella cheese, shredded (1 cup)
    4   ounces Gruyère cheese, shredded (1 cup)

1. Place potatoes in large saucepan; add water to cover by 1 inch and 1 tablespoon salt. Partially cover saucepan with lid and bring potatoes to boil over high heat. Reduce heat to medium-low and simmer until potatoes are tender and just break apart when poked with fork, 12 to 17 minutes. Drain potatoes and dry saucepan.

2. Transfer potatoes to food processor; add butter, garlic, and 1½ teaspoons salt. Pulse until butter is melted and incorporated into potatoes, about ten 1-second pulses. Add 1 cup milk and continue to process until potatoes are smooth and creamy, about 20 seconds, scraping down sides halfway through.

3. Return potato mixture to saucepan and set over medium heat. Stir in cheeses, 1 cup at a time, until incorporated. Continue to cook potatoes, stirring vigorously, until cheese is fully melted and mixture is smooth and elastic, 3 to 5 minutes. If mixture is difficult to stir and seems thick, stir in 2 tablespoons milk at a time (up to ½ cup) until potatoes are loose and creamy. Season with salt and pepper to taste. Serve immediately.

KEYS TO SUCCESS

- **Yukon Golds:** Contribute mild buttery flavor and light creamy consistency due to less starch

- **Food processor:** Easily "mashes" the potatoes

- **Two cheeses:** Gruyère adds a sharp, nutty flavor and mozzarella gives the potatoes their stretchy texture.

- **Careful stirring:** Stirring is the key to aligot and 3 to 5 minutes is the magic number.

Tuber Testing for Aligot

RED POTATO
Red Bliss potatoes were overly dense.

RUSSET
Russet potatoes yielded a tacky texture.

YUKON GOLD
Yukon Golds had winning flavor and a lighter, creamier texture.

SCIENCE LESSON Seeing Rouge

Potato discoloration is of particular concern with pommes Anna since the peeled, sliced potatoes must wait to be layered into the skillet. We consulted spud expert Dr. Alfred Bushway, professor of food science at the University of Maine, to find out what causes potatoes to turn color. He explained that with peeling and slicing, potato cells are broken and enzymes and substrates are released. These enzymes and substrates combine with oxygen and react, causing discoloration. It's the same reaction that causes peeled apples to turn brown.

Tossing the potatoes with butter, as we do in our pommes Anna recipe, helps limit oxygen exposure and therefore retards discoloration. We had noted that certain potatoes discolor more rapidly than others. In our experience, russet potatoes seem to discolor most rapidly, so if you're a slow hand, opt for Yukon Golds or white potatoes for pommes Anna.

POMMES ANNA

Serves: 6 to 8
Total Time: 1¼ hours

RECIPE OVERVIEW Pommes Anna is a classic, elegant French potato cake. A few simple tricks help to achieve the best pommes Anna that boasts a crisp, deep brown potato cake with a glassine crust and soft, creamy layers within. Slicing the potatoes with the fine slicing disk of a food processor saves time and energy, then a nonstick ovenproof skillet ensures easy release every time. Tossing the potatoes with melted butter slows down discoloration while arranging the potatoes in the skillet as it heats accelerates cooking. Do not slice the potatoes until you are ready to start assembling, and start timing when you begin arranging the slices—no matter how quickly you arrange them, they will need 30 minutes on the stovetop to brown properly.

  3 **pounds russet potatoes, Yukon Gold potatoes, or white potatoes, peeled and sliced ¹⁄₁₆ to ⅛ inch thick**
  5 **tablespoons unsalted butter, melted**
  ¼ **cup vegetable oil or peanut oil, plus additional for greasing cookie sheet**
      Table salt

1. Toss potato slices with melted butter in large bowl until potatoes are evenly coated. Adjust oven rack to lower-middle position and heat oven to 450 degrees.

2. Pour oil into 10-inch heavy-bottomed ovenproof nonstick skillet; swirl to coat pan bottom and set skillet over medium-low heat. Begin timing, and arrange potato slices in skillet, starting in center to form first layer. Sprinkle evenly with scant ¼ teaspoon salt and pepper to taste. Arrange second layer of potatoes, working in opposite direction of first layer; sprinkle evenly with scant ¼ teaspoon salt and pepper. Repeat, layering potatoes in opposite directions and sprinkling with salt and pepper, until no slices remain (broken or uneven slices can be pieced together to form a single slice; potatoes will mound in center of skillet); continue to cook over medium-low heat until 30 minutes elapse from the time you began arranging potatoes in skillet.

3. Using bottom of 9-inch cake pan, press potatoes down firmly to compact. Cover skillet and place in oven. Bake until potatoes begin to soften, about 15 minutes. Uncover and continue to bake until potatoes are tender when paring knife is inserted in center and edge of potatoes near skillet is browned, about 10 minutes longer. Meanwhile, line rimless cookie sheet or back of baking sheet with foil and coat very lightly with oil. Drain off excess fat from potatoes by pressing potatoes into skillet with bottom of cake pan while tilting skillet to pour off fat.

4. Set foil-lined cookie sheet on top of skillet. With hands protected by oven mitts or dish towels, hold cookie sheet in place with one hand and carefully invert skillet and cookie sheet together. Remove skillet. Carefully slide potatoes onto platter; cut into wedges and serve immediately.

Constructing and Unmolding Pommes Anna

PLACE FIRST SLICE
Use nicest slices to form bottom layer. Start by placing one slice on bottom of skillet.

OVERLAP SLICES
Overlap slices in circle around center slice, then form outer circle of overlapping slices.

CONTINUE LAYERING
Continue layering, alternating the direction of the slices in each layer.

DRAIN OFF FAT
To drain off excess fat before unmolding, press cake pan against potatoes while tilting skillet. Be sure to use an oven mitt or dish towel over the hot handle.

INVERT SKILLET
To invert, set prepared baking sheet flat on top of skillet. Invert skillet and baking sheet together. Lift skillet off potatoes.

SLIDE ONTO PLATTER
Carefully slide pommes Anna from baking sheet onto serving platter.

KEYS TO SUCCESS

- **Toss potato slices with melted butter:** Limits oxygen exposure to slow down discoloration
- **Nonstick ovenproof skillet:** Essential to the successful release of the potatoes

FRENCH FRIES AND MORE

ANNIE PETITO

Many home cooks avoid frying because of the hot grease. But when done right, frying isn't that difficult. While every deep-frying recipe is a little different, most require a wide, deep pot; hot oil at the right temperature; a place to drain the crispy fried food; and the cook's full attention. Do you need a special frying pot? Absolutely not. You can deep-fry in a Dutch oven. In this course, you will learn how to make the best french fries you've ever had. Then you can move on to fry onion rings, asparagus, brussels sprouts, and incredible lightly battered and fried cauliflower that just may make you forget all about french fries.

ANNIE'S PRO TIP: *When frying lower-mass items, which absorb less energy, be sure to heat the oil more slowly. Hastily heated oil will continue to heat up, and you'll end up frantically adjusting the dial or, worse, burning your food.*

THE METHOD
DEEP FRYING

Cooking vegetables in hot oil deep enough to surround them takes some practice. When deep-frying, pay careful attention to every recipe step.

1 CUT FOOD EVENLY
Same-size pieces will cook at the same rate.

2 COAT FOOD
Toss food with starch or batter until evenly coated.

3 CLIP ON THERMOMETER
Clip candy/deep-fry thermometer onto side of heavy-bottomed Dutch oven of at least 6 quarts. Be sure end of thermometer is not touching bottom of pot. Use thermometer to monitor the oil's temperature.

4 HEAT OIL
Heat oil in Dutch oven over medium heat to correct temperature.

5 FRY BATCH 1
If batching is called for, add half of vegetables to hot oil.

6 DRAIN
Transfer food to paper towels or thick paper bag to drain.

7 RETURN OIL TO TEMPERATURE
Temperature drops when food is added so return oil to desired temperature before adding second batch.

8 FRY BATCH 2
Proceed with remaining food as necessary.

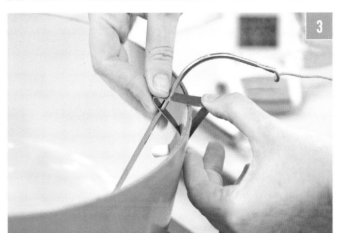

CLASSIC FRENCH FRIES

Serves: 4

Total Time: 1 hour, plus 30 minutes chilling

RECIPE OVERVIEW The ideal french fry should be long and crisp, with right-angle sides, a nice crunch on the outside, and an earthy potato taste. Russet potatoes are the best choice, but because they are starchy, it is important to rinse the starch off the surface after cutting the potatoes. Refrigerating the potatoes for at least 30 minutes in water makes for lighter, crispier fries and improves their browning. Coating the fries in a little cornstarch prior to cooking absorbs some of the surface moisture on the potatoes and creates a protective sheath that turns into a shatteringly crisp crust once fried. We prefer our fries cooked in peanut oil but vegetable oil is a good second choice. We fry the potatoes twice: The first fry is at a relatively low temperature to secure a soft and rich-tasting interior; the quick second fry is at a higher temperature to crisp and color the exterior. You will need a Dutch oven with at least a 6-quart capacity and a candy thermometer or other thermometer that registers high temperatures for this recipe.

2½ pounds russet potatoes (about 4 large), unpeeled, sides squared, and cut lengthwise into ¼-inch-thick fries

2 tablespoons cornstarch

3 quarts peanut or vegetable oil

1. Rinse cut potatoes in large bowl under cold running water until water turns clear. Cover with cold water and refrigerate for 30 minutes or up to 12 hours.

2. Pour off water, spread potatoes onto clean dish towels, and dry thoroughly. Transfer potatoes to large bowl and toss with cornstarch until evenly coated. Transfer potatoes to wire rack set in rimmed baking sheet and let rest until fine white coating forms, about 20 minutes.

3. Meanwhile, heat oil in large Dutch oven over medium heat to 325 degrees.

4. Add half of potatoes, a handful at a time, to hot oil and increase heat to high. Fry, stirring with mesh spider or large-hole slotted spoon, until potatoes start to turn from white to blond, 4 to 5 minutes. (Oil temperature will drop about 75 degrees during frying.) Transfer fries to thick paper bag or paper towels. Return oil to 325 degrees and repeat with remaining potatoes. Let fries cool, at least 10 minutes or up to 2 hours.

5. When ready to finish frying, increase heat to medium-high and heat oil to 375 degrees. Add half of fries, a handful at a time, and fry until golden brown and puffed, 2 to 3 minutes. Transfer to thick paper bag or paper towels. Return oil to 375 degrees and repeat with remaining fries. Season fries with salt and serve immediately.

KEYS TO SUCCESS

- **Rinsing and soaking potatoes**: Rinsing removes starch from the surface and a refrigerated soak allows for slower cooking.

- **Cornstarch coating**: Provides a protective sheath around fries to create a crispy crust

- **Two rounds of frying**: Par-frying helps the interior of the fries cook through while the second stage browns and crisps the exteriors.

WHAT CAN GO WRONG

PROBLEM The fries are undercooked or overcooked.

SOLUTION Make sure the fries are cut to the right size, using a ruler if necessary.

PROBLEM The fries are greasy and didn't brown properly.

SOLUTION Use a thermometer to monitor the oil's temperature and don't add the potatoes until the oil reaches the correct temperature. If the potatoes are added before the oil is ready, the fries will be greasy and won't brown or crisp properly.

PATATAS BRAVAS

Serves: 4 to 6
Total Time: 1 hour, plus 20 minutes cooling

RECIPE OVERVIEW Tapas bar versions of the Spanish favorite patatas bravas showcase crispy twice-fried potato pieces served with a smoky, spicy tomato-based sauce. To create an ultracrispy crust without having to fry the potato pieces twice, this version parboils them with baking soda, triggering a chain reaction that causes the pectin on the potatoes' surface to release a layer of starch that develops into a thick crust when fried. Tossing the parboiled pieces with kosher salt roughs up their surfaces, creating nooks and crannies through which steam escapes and oil is trapped, making for even more substantial crunch. Adding mayonnaise to the garlicky tomato sauce gives it an aioli element. You can use bittersweet or hot smoked paprika in place of sweet (but taste the sauce before deciding how much cayenne to add). For efficiency, get the water boiling while you make the sauce, and get the oil heating while you parboil the potatoes. Use a Dutch oven that holds 6 quarts or more.

Sauce

- 1 tablespoon vegetable oil
- 2 garlic cloves, minced to paste (2 teaspoons)
- 1 teaspoon sweet smoked paprika
- ½ teaspoon kosher salt
- ½–¾ teaspoon cayenne pepper
  Pinch red pepper flakes
- ¼ cup tomato paste
- ½ cup water
- 2 teaspoons sherry vinegar
- ¼ cup mayonnaise

Potatoes

- 2¼ pounds russet potatoes, peeled and cut into 1-inch pieces
- ½ teaspoon baking soda
- 1½ teaspoons kosher salt
- 3 cups peanut or vegetable oil for frying

1. FOR THE SAUCE Heat oil in small saucepan over medium-low heat until shimmering. Add garlic, paprika, salt, cayenne, and pepper flakes and cook until fragrant, about 30 seconds. Add tomato paste and cook for 30 seconds. Whisk in water and bring to boil over high heat. Reduce heat to medium-low and simmer until slightly thickened, 4 to 5 minutes. Transfer sauce to bowl, stir in vinegar, and let cool completely, about 20 minutes. Once cool, whisk in mayonnaise and set aside.

2. FOR THE POTATOES Meanwhile, bring 2 quarts water to boil in large saucepan over high heat. Add potatoes and baking soda. Return to boil and cook for 1 minute. Drain potatoes.

3. Return potatoes to now-empty saucepan and place over low heat. Cook, shaking saucepan occasionally, until any surface moisture has evaporated, 30 seconds to 1 minute.

Remove from heat. Add salt and stir with rubber spatula until potatoes are coated with thick, starchy paste, about 30 seconds. Transfer potatoes to rimmed baking sheet in single layer to cool.

4. Set wire rack in second rimmed baking sheet and line with triple layer of paper towels. Heat oil in large Dutch oven over high heat to 375 degrees. Add all potatoes (they should just be submerged in oil) and cook, stirring occasionally with spider skimmer or slotted spoon, until deep golden brown and crispy, 20 to 25 minutes.

5. Using spider skimmer or slotted spoon, transfer potatoes to prepared rack. Season with salt to taste. Spoon ½ cup sauce onto bottom of serving platter or 1½ tablespoons sauce onto individual plates. Arrange potatoes over sauce and serve immediately, passing remaining sauce separately.

KEYS TO SUCCESS

- **Russet potatoes:** Floury, starchy potatoes result in dry, fluffy interiors when fried.

- **Parboil potatoes with baking soda:** Causes the pectin on the potatoes to break down and release a starchy paste that fries up crispy

- **Toss with kosher salt:** Roughs up the surface of potatoes, making small holes that fill with hot oil and create a substantial crust

---

ULTIMATE EXTRA-CRUNCHY ONION RINGS

Serves: 6 to 8
Total Time: 1¾ hours

RECIPE OVERVIEW The best onion rings have a crunchy, craggy crust surrounding fully tender, sweet onions. To achieve that ideal, double-bread ½-inch-thick rings in a mixture of buttermilk, seasoned flour, and cornstarch. To streamline the process and avoid having to bread the onion rings in several batches, toss all the buttermilk-soaked onions with the flour mixture in a large paper shopping bag. (The double-bag setup ensures no blowouts or leaking.) To fry ultracrunchy onion rings in as few batches as possible, use plenty of oil and stir gently during frying for even cooking. With the generous amounts of breading, the rings can stay in the hot oil longer, ensuring that the onions themselves are fully cooked and tender. These rings fry up incredibly crunchy and taste even better dipped in a tangy stir-together horseradish sauce. Look for large onions (about 1 pound each) for this recipe. Be sure to use a double-bagged large paper shopping bag in step 2. Note that the onions are double-breaded, so don't discard the flour bag after the first shake. Buy refrigerated prepared horseradish, not the shelf-stable kind, which contains preservatives and additives.

Sauce

- ½ cup mayonnaise
- 2 tablespoons prepared horseradish
- 2 tablespoons Dijon mustard
- ¼ teaspoon cayenne pepper
- ¼ teaspoon pepper

Onion Rings

- 4 cups buttermilk
- 4 cups all-purpose flour
- ½ cup cornstarch
- 2 tablespoons Lawry's Seasoned Salt
- 2 tablespoons baking powder
- 2 teaspoons pepper
- ½ teaspoon table salt
- 2 large onions (1 pound each), peeled
- 3 quarts peanut or vegetable oil for frying

1. **FOR THE SAUCE** Whisk all ingredients together in bowl; set aside.

2. **FOR THE ONION RINGS** Adjust oven rack to middle position and heat oven to 200 degrees. Add buttermilk to large bowl. Combine flour, cornstarch, seasoned salt, baking powder, pepper, and salt in second large bowl. Transfer flour mixture to double-bagged large paper shopping bag. Slice onions crosswise into ½-inch-thick rounds. Reserve onion slices smaller than 2 inches in diameter for another use.

3. Separate remaining onion rounds into rings. Toss one-third of onion rings in buttermilk to thoroughly coat. Shake off excess buttermilk and transfer onion rings to flour mixture in bag. Repeat with remaining onion rings in 2 batches. Roll top of bag to seal and shake vigorously to coat onion rings in flour mixture. Remove onion rings from bag, shaking off excess flour mixture, and transfer to rimmed baking sheet.

4. Transfer one-third of onion rings back to buttermilk and toss to thoroughly coat. Shake off excess buttermilk and transfer onion rings back to flour mixture in bag. Repeat with remaining onion rings in 2 batches. Roll top of bag to seal and shake vigorously to coat onion rings in flour mixture. Pour contents of bag onto sheet. Separate any onion rings that stick together.

Bread Them in a Bag

Breading the onion rings twice is essential to getting the big crunch we want. But it can get messy—unless you do it in a bag, as we do here.

5. Line second rimmed baking sheet with triple layer of paper towels. Add oil to large Dutch oven until it measures about 2 inches deep and heat over medium-high heat to 375 degrees.

6. Add one-third of onion rings to hot oil and fry, without stirring, until breading is just set, 30 to 60 seconds. Stir gently with tongs or spider skimmer and continue to fry until dark golden brown, 3 to 5 minutes longer, flipping onion rings occasionally and separating any that stick together. Adjust burner, if necessary, to maintain oil temperature between 325 and 375 degrees. Transfer fried onion rings to paper towel–lined sheet and place in oven to keep warm.

7. Return oil to 375 degrees and repeat with remaining onion rings in 2 batches. Serve onion rings with sauce.

KEYS TO SUCCESS

- **Use large onions:** To make thicker rings
- **Bread the rings twice:** Leads to bigger crunch
- **Add seasoned salt:** Easily adds flavor to the flour coating

ASPARAGUS FRIES

Serves: 4 to 6
Total Time: 40 minutes

RECIPE OVERVIEW Asparagus fries are something special, crunchy on the outside, tender within. For the crispiest coating, we rely on a tried-and-true bound breading technique: dipping the asparagus spears in flour, then beaten eggs, and finally bread crumbs. To get the coating to adhere, rinse the spears under cold water before dipping them in the flour. The residual moisture is just enough to help the flour (and coating) stick. Use fresh bread to amplify the sweetness of the crumbs. A bright yet creamy sauce is the perfect accompaniment. Do not use asparagus that is thinner than ½ inch here. The bottom 1 ½ inches or so of asparagus is woody and needs to be trimmed. To know where to cut the spears, grip one spear about halfway down; with your other hand, hold the stem between your thumb and index finger about 1 inch from the bottom and bend the spear until it snaps. Using this spear as a guide, cut the remaining spears with your knife.

- ½ cup sour cream
- 1 tablespoon lemon juice
- 1 tablespoon Dijon mustard
- 1½ teaspoons table salt, divided
- ¾ teaspoon pepper, divided
- ¼ cup plus 3 tablespoons all-purpose flour, divided
- 3 large eggs
- 4 slices hearty white sandwich bread, torn into 1-inch pieces
- 1 pound (½-inch-thick) asparagus, trimmed
- 1 quart peanut or vegetable oil

1. Combine sour cream, lemon juice, mustard, ½ teaspoon salt, and ¼ teaspoon pepper in bowl; set aside sauce.

2. Place ¼ cup flour in shallow dish. Beat eggs in second shallow dish. Process bread, remaining 1 teaspoon salt, remaining ½ teaspoon pepper, and remaining 3 tablespoons flour in food processor until finely ground, about 1 minute. Transfer bread-crumb mixture to 13 by 9-inch baking dish.

3. Place asparagus in colander and rinse under cold water. Shake colander to lightly drain asparagus (asparagus should still be wet). Transfer one-third of asparagus to flour and toss to lightly coat; dip in egg, allowing excess to drip off; then transfer to bread-crumb mixture and press lightly to adhere. Transfer breaded asparagus to baking sheet. Repeat with remaining asparagus in 2 batches.

4. Line large plate with paper towels. Heat oil in large Dutch oven over medium-high heat to 350 degrees. Carefully add one-third of asparagus to hot oil and cook until golden brown, 1 to 2 minutes. Transfer to prepared plate. Repeat with remaining asparagus in 2 batches. Serve with sauce.

KEYS TO SUCCESS

- **Make fresh bread crumbs:** They have a clean flavor and softer texture when fried.

- **Add a little flour to the crumbs:** Makes the coating more uniform

Keys to Perfect Fried Asparagus

TRIM
Once you determine where the trimming point is (see recipe headnote), use that spear as a guide to trim the rest.

RINSE
Moisten the spears under cold running water to help the breading stick evenly.

BREAD
Toss the moistened spears in flour, dip them in beaten egg, and coat them in bread crumbs before frying.

GOBI MANCHURIAN

Serves: 4
Total Time: 1 hour

RECIPE OVERVIEW Gobi Manchurian, a multinational dish with roots in Chinese immigrant communities in Kolkata, India, features cauliflower florets battered and fried until crisp and then served with or tossed in a flavorful, spicy sauce. The dish has proven popular in Indian restaurants across the United States for its powerful flavors and mix of crisp and soft textures. Fans love it as a side dish or shared snack. For our "wet-style" version, we coat cauliflower florets in a light batter (of water, cornstarch, flour, baking powder, and salt) that turns wonderfully crisp when fried. The fried cauliflower stays crispy even after being dressed in the tangy sauce and enough freshly squeezed lime juice to brighten the whole dish. A whole 2½-pound head of cauliflower should yield 1 pound of florets. You can also buy precut florets if available. Use a Dutch oven that holds 6 quarts or more.

Sauce
- ¼ cup ketchup
- 3 tablespoons water
- 2 tablespoons soy sauce
- 1 tablespoon Asian chili-garlic sauce
- 2 teaspoons lime juice, plus lime wedges for serving
- ¾ teaspoon pepper
- ½ teaspoon ground cumin
- 2 tablespoons vegetable oil
- 3 scallions, white and green parts separated and sliced thin
- 1 tablespoon grated fresh ginger
- 3 garlic cloves, minced

Cauliflower

- 1 cup water
- ⅔ cup cornstarch
- ⅔ cup all-purpose flour
- 1 teaspoon table salt
- 1 teaspoon baking powder
- 1 pound (1½-inch) cauliflower florets (4 cups)
- 2 quarts peanut or vegetable oil for frying

1. **FOR THE SAUCE** Combine ketchup, water, soy sauce, chili-garlic sauce, lime juice, pepper, and cumin in bowl. Heat oil in small saucepan over medium-high heat until shimmering. Add scallion whites, ginger, and garlic and cook, stirring frequently, until fragrant, about 1½ minutes. Stir in ketchup mixture and bring to simmer, scraping up any bits of ginger mixture from bottom of saucepan. Transfer sauce to clean large bowl.

2. **FOR THE CAULIFLOWER** Whisk water, cornstarch, flour, salt, and baking powder in large bowl until smooth. Add cauliflower florets to batter and toss with rubber spatula to evenly coat; set aside.

3. Line baking sheet with triple layer of paper towels. Add oil to large Dutch oven until it measures about 1½ inches deep and heat over medium-high heat to 375 degrees.

4. Using tongs, add florets to hot oil 1 piece at a time. Cook, stirring occasionally to prevent florets from sticking, until coating is firm and very lightly golden, about 5 minutes. (Adjust burner, if necessary, to maintain oil temperature between 300 and 325 degrees.) Using spider skimmer, transfer florets to prepared sheet. Let sit 5 minutes.

5. Add cauliflower and scallion greens to bowl with sauce and toss to combine. Transfer to platter and serve with lime wedges.

KEYS TO SUCCESS

- **Light but thick, sticky batter:** Clings to the cauliflower
- **Plenty of cornstarch in the batter:** Absorbs water during frying for a crisp crust
- **Flavorful sauce:** Adds sweetness, heat, and depth

SCIENCE LESSON Cold-Start Frying

Vegetables fried using the cold-start method spend more time in the oil than when using the more traditional frying method, but they don't turn out greasier—they are actually lower in fat. As the vegetables cook, they lose surface moisture, which is replaced by oil. Because the cold start cooks them more gently, less moisture is lost, and less oil is absorbed during frying.

FRIED BRUSSELS SPROUTS

Serves: 4 to 6
Total Time: 40 minutes

RECIPE OVERVIEW Fried brussels sprouts are delightfully crispy, nutty, and salty. Yet when we tried making them, the brussels sprouts splattered every time they hit the hot oil because of their high moisture content. This version uses an unconventional technique of submerging the sprouts in cold oil and heating the oil and the sprouts together over high heat. The sprouts slowly cook through as the oil heats and then develop a deep brown exterior as the oil gets really hot. You cook the sprouts a little longer than you might think necessary. An easy stir-together sriracha sauce offers a spicy, creamy counterpoint. Choose brussels sprouts similar in size to ensure even cooking. We prefer larger brussels sprouts here because they're easier to dip in the sauce. To keep the sprouts' leaves intact and attached to their cores, trim just a small amount from the stems before cutting the sprouts in half. To wash your sprouts before cooking, do so before trimming and halving them. Stir gently and not too often in step 1; excessive stirring will cause the leaves to separate from the sprouts.

- 2 pounds brussels sprouts, trimmed and halved through stem
- 1 quart vegetable oil
  Sriracha Dipping Sauce (recipe follows)

1. Line rimmed baking sheet with triple layer of paper towels or thick paper bag. Combine brussels sprouts and oil in large Dutch oven. Cook over high heat, gently stirring occasionally, until brussels sprouts are dark brown throughout and crispy, 20 to 25 minutes.

2. Using spider skimmer or slotted spoon, lift brussels sprouts from oil and transfer to prepared sheet. Roll gently so paper towels absorb excess oil. Season with kosher salt to taste and serve immediately with dipping sauce.

SRIRACHA DIPPING SAUCE

Total Time: 5 minutes

- ½ cup mayonnaise
- 1½ tablespoons sriracha
- 2 teaspoons lime juice
- ¼ teaspoon garlic powder

Whisk all ingredients together in bowl. Cover and refrigerate until ready to use.

KEYS TO SUCCESS

- **Trim sprouts carefully:** So they keep together
- **Cold oil start:** Sprouts and oil heat together without splattering.

WHAT HAPPENS WHEN A POTATO HITS HOT OIL?

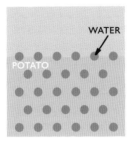 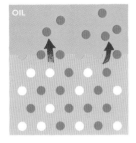 

Raw
Before hitting the oil, the potato holds moisture evenly spaced within.

Frying
While frying the potato fries in hot oil, the moisture turns to steam and exits, leaving holes in its wake.

After
The craters on the surface fill with oil, helping to create a crisp brown crust. The amount of oil absorbed is directly proportional to the amount of water lost.

OIL TEMPERATURE AND THE COLOR OF FRENCH FRIES

The temperature of the oil when cooking french fries makes a big difference. French fries cooked at 400 degrees brown far too quickly, verging on burnt before the inside of the fry can cook at all. French fries cooked at 275 degrees, on the other hand, cook through completely, but a crust is never able to form, and they grow limp and floppy. The magic temperature is 325 degrees. The heat is high enough to turn the water in the potato immediately to steam, to dry out the outer edge, and to form a brown, crispy crust, all the while cooking the potato for a moist and creamy center, too. Be sure to monitor the temperature of your oil!

Too Light
The crust is pale when cooked in 275-degree oil.

Perfect
The magic number for a crisp crust is 325 degrees.

Too Brown
Fries cook too fast (almost burnt) at 400 degrees.

DISPOSING OF USED OIL

Once the used oil is cool, you can filter it through a fine-mesh strainer lined with paper towels and return it to its original container. Refrigerate it, and use it three or four more times. When it's time to say goodbye, check with your municipality to see if recycling is available; if not, return the cooled oil to the original container, close it tightly, and toss it.

CORE TECHNIQUE
FROM HEAD TO FLORET

Here's how to prep cauliflower for frying.

1. Cut the stem flush with the base of the head, then snap off the leaves.

2. Place the head on the cutting board, rounded side down. Using a paring knife, cut down through the floret stems, rotating the head after each cut.

3. Pull off the loose florets, then continue cutting until all the florets are removed. Cut the florets into 1½-inch pieces.

SUPERGOOD ROOT VEGETABLES

JULIA COLLIN DAVISON

Humble root vegetables are very hard and fibrous, but our creative recipes and cooking methods turn them tender and extremely flavorful. There's a wide world of root vegetables to explore that includes more than carrots, parsnips, and beets. This course focuses on other members of the family—celery root, kohlrabi, yuca, and rutabaga. We bring out their best by employing pureeing, roasting, deep frying, and combining a medley of vegetables into a gratin.

JULIA'S PRO TIP: *Having a sharp, sturdy chef's knife is key when prepping hard root vegetables. I like to drape a clean kitchen towel over the tip of the knife when pushing through a tough cut, in order to give my non-knife-holding hand a safe place to hold on.*

CELERY ROOT PUREE

Serves: 4 to 6
Total Time: 40 minutes

RECIPE OVERVIEW Pureed cooked celery root is earthy, buttery, and elegant. For celery root puree with a clean, pure flavor, process chunks of the peeled root, along with russet potato for body, in the food processor to create tiny pieces that cook quickly in a small amount of water and butter. To help the vegetables cook even more quickly, add a bit of baking soda to the cooking liquid. This creates an alkaline cooking environment that speeds up their breakdown. Once the vegetables and water have cooked into a thick mush, return the mixture to the processor and buzz with some heavy cream to form a smooth puree. When buying celery root, look for one with few roots for easy peeling and minimal waste. Once it's prepped, you should have about 1½ pounds of celery root. If desired, garnish the puree with Bacon, Garlic, and Parsley Topping or Shallot, Sage, and Black Pepper Topping (recipes follow); make the topping while the celery root cooks. (If you're making the puree in advance, make the topping as close to serving as possible.) Alternatively, garnish the puree with 1 tablespoon of minced fresh herbs such as chives, parsley, chervil, or tarragon.

1¾–2	pounds celery root, peeled and cut into 2-inch chunks
1	(6-ounce) russet potato, peeled and cut into 2-inch chunks
2	tablespoons unsalted butter
1	cup water
½	teaspoon table salt
¼	teaspoon baking soda
⅓	cup heavy cream

1. Working in 2 batches, pulse celery root and potato in food processor until finely chopped, about 20 pulses per batch; transfer to bowl. (You should have about 4½ cups chopped vegetables.)

2. Melt butter in large saucepan over medium heat. Stir in celery root–potato mixture, water, salt, and baking soda. Cover and cook, stirring often (mixture will stick but cleans up easily), until vegetables are very soft and translucent and mixture resembles applesauce, 15 to 18 minutes.

CORE TECHNIQUE

Peeling Celery Root

TRIM AND PEEL
Using a chef's knife, trim off top and bottom of celery root. To remove thick skin, cut down around sides of vegetable, working from top to bottom and angling knife as needed.

3. Uncover and cook, stirring vigorously to further break down vegetables and thicken remaining cooking liquid, about 1 minute. Transfer vegetable mixture to clean, dry food processor. Add cream and process until smooth, about 40 seconds. Season with salt to taste. Transfer to bowl and serve. (Puree can be cooled and refrigerated for up to 2 days. Before serving, microwave puree on medium-high power in covered bowl, stirring often, until hot throughout, 7 to 10 minutes.)

BACON, GARLIC, AND PARSLEY TOPPING

Makes: about ¼ cup
Total Time: 15 minutes
If desired, freeze the bacon for 15 minutes to make it easier to chop.

- 2 slices bacon, chopped fine
- ¼ cup water
- 4 garlic cloves, sliced thin
- 1 tablespoon minced fresh parsley

Combine bacon, water, and garlic in 8-inch nonstick skillet and cook over medium-high heat until water has evaporated and bacon and garlic are browned and crispy, 8 to 10 minutes. Off heat, stir in parsley.

SHALLOT, SAGE, AND BLACK PEPPER TOPPING

Makes: about 3 tablespoons
Total Time: 15 minutes
For the best results, do not substitute dried sage.

- 2 tablespoons unsalted butter
- 1 small shallot, minced
- 1 tablespoon minced fresh sage
- ¼ teaspoon pepper
   Pinch table salt

Melt butter in 8-inch nonstick skillet over medium-high heat. Add shallot and sage; cook, stirring frequently, until shallot is golden and sage is crisp, about 3 minutes. Off heat, stir in pepper and salt.

KEYS TO SUCCESS

- **Using a food processor:** Finely chopped pieces of dense celery root and potato cook faster.

- **A bit of russet potato:** Adds body to the puree

- **Braising in butter and water:** Keeps the celery root flavor clean and pure

- **A bit of baking soda:** Helps to speed the vegetable's breakdown so it cooks faster

ROASTED KOHLRABI WITH CRUNCHY SEEDS

Serves: 4
Total Time: 35 minutes

RECIPE OVERVIEW Kohlrabi is a member of the turnip family with a flavor reminiscent of broccoli and celery root. A simple, quick roast with a trio of flavorful seeds is an excellent and crowd-pleasing way to bring mild-tasting kohlrabi to the dinner table. A hot oven (450 degrees) browns the kohlrabi beautifully, and the ¾-inch pieces cook in just 20 minutes. Usually seeds are toasted before being included in a dish, but here the high heat of the oven renders that extra step unnecessary. Lining the baking sheet with aluminum foil prevents the kohlrabi from sticking to the pan. (We initially tried using more oil, rather than foil, but that just made the kohlrabi greasy.) As the kohlrabi roasts, make sure to shake the pan once or twice to encourage even browning.

- 2 tablespoons extra-virgin olive oil
- 2 teaspoons sesame seeds
- 1 teaspoon poppy seeds
- ½ teaspoon fennel seeds, cracked
- ½ teaspoon table salt
- ¼ teaspoon pepper
- 2 pounds kohlrabi, trimmed, peeled, and cut into
   ¾-inch pieces

1. Adjust oven rack to middle position and heat oven to 450 degrees. Combine oil, sesame seeds, poppy seeds, fennel seeds, salt, and pepper in large bowl. Add kohlrabi and toss to coat.

2. Spread kohlrabi onto foil-lined rimmed baking sheet and roast, stirring occasionally, until browned and tender, about 20 minutes. Season with salt and pepper to taste. Serve.

KEYS TO SUCCESS

- **Proper prep:** Cutting the kohlrabi into small and even-size pieces means they roast faster and at the same rate.

- **A mix of seeds:** Adds crunch and flavor

CORE TECHNIQUE Peeling Kohlrabi

TRIM AND PEEL
Using a paring knife, trim off stalks and leaves from kohlrabi bulb. Remove outer ⅛ inch of thick skin and fibrous green parts underneath, so only white flesh remains.

FRIED YUCA WITH MOJO SAUCE

Serves: 4 to 6
Total Time: 1 hour

RECIPE OVERVIEW Yuca, also known as manioc and cassava, is the hard, starchy root of a woody shrub native to South America. Its starch is extracted and used to make tapioca, but this tuber is also used in many regions of the world just like potatoes: mashed, boiled, or fried for a comforting and hearty side dish. When parboiled and then fried, the wedges develop a dense, velvety texture within and a satisfyingly crisp shell on the outside. The delicate, potato-like flavor of yuca needs little more than salt to enhance it, but it's particularly delicious paired with a garlicky, citrusy Cuban mojo sauce, a classic accompaniment. Peeling yuca's tough skin is a job that calls for a sharp knife, not a vegetable peeler, but the effort pays off. Remove the woody core as well to ensure that the fried yuca wedges are tender throughout.

Mojo Sauce

- 2 tablespoons extra-virgin olive oil
- 6 garlic cloves, minced
- 1 teaspoon grated lime zest plus ¼ cup juice (2 limes)
- 1 teaspoon ground cumin
- 1 teaspoon dried oregano
- ¾ teaspoon table salt
- ½ teaspoon grated orange zest plus ½ cup juice
- ¼ teaspoon red pepper flakes

Fried Yuca

- 2 pounds yuca roots
  Table salt for cooking yuca
- 2 quarts vegetable oil

1. FOR THE SAUCE Combine all ingredients in small saucepan, bring to simmer over medium-high heat. Remove from heat and let cool completely before serving.

2. FOR THE YUCA Meanwhile, bring 3 quarts water to boil in Dutch oven over medium heat. Use sharp knife to remove 1 to 2 inches of woody stem from yuca. Cut remaining yuca crosswise into 3-inch lengths. Place pieces cut side down and use knife to remove skin in sections, cutting away any flesh that isn't pure white. Halve yuca pieces lengthwise. Pop out any woody core with spoon. Place each piece cut side down and cut lengthwise into ¾-inch-thick wedges.

3. Add yuca and 1 teaspoon salt to boiling water and cook, adjusting heat to maintain vigorous simmer, until yuca is tender and mostly translucent, 20 to 25 minutes. While yuca is cooking, place wire rack in rimmed baking sheet. Drain yuca well in colander. Spread on wire rack. Rinse Dutch oven and dry very well.

4. Heat oil in Dutch oven over medium-high heat to 350 degrees. Pat yuca wedges dry, then add to oil and cook, stirring occasionally, until evenly golden brown, 6 to 8 minutes. While yuca is cooking, remove wire rack and line baking sheet with paper towels. Transfer yuca to lined baking sheet. Season with salt to taste, and serve with mojo sauce.

KEYS TO SUCCESS

- **Boil then fry:** Boiling first softens the dense yuca flesh and ensures it cooks through during frying.
- **Pat dry:** Removing any surface moisture from the boiled yuca wedges means better browning in the hot oil.

CORE TECHNIQUE | **Prepping Yuca**

TRIM AND CUT
Use sharp knife to remove 1 to 2 inches of woody stem. Cut remaining yuca crosswise into 3-inch lengths.

REMOVE SKIN
Place yuca pieces cut side down and use knife to remove skin in sections, cutting away any flesh that isn't pure white.

CUT INTO WEDGES
Halve yuca pieces lengthwise. Pop out any woody core with spoon. Place each piece cut side down and cut lengthwise into ¾-inch-thick wedges.

ROOT VEGETABLE GRATIN

Serves: 6 to 8
Total Time: 1¾ hours, plus 25 minutes resting

RECIPE OVERVIEW Sweet rutabaga and herbal celery root complement the earthiness of potatoes in this root vegetable gratin. All these flavors come to the forefront by adding just a few aromatics: onion, garlic, thyme, and Dijon mustard. We add white wine to the gratin mixture because the wine's acidity strengthens the pectin in the potatoes, ensuring they remain intact while the denser, less-starchy rutabaga and celery root cook through; the wine also brightens the flavor of the vegetables. To help the top layers of the gratin cook through at the same rate as the bottom layers, cover the dish for the first portion of the cooking time. A layer of Parmesan-enhanced panko bread crumbs, added after removing the foil, toast to a golden brown while the gratin finishes cooking, resulting in a crispy, nutty, cheesy crust. Uniform thin slices of rutabaga, celery root, and potatoes are key to even cooking; use a mandoline, a V-slicer, or the slicing disk on a food processor.

1	tablespoon plus 1½ cups water, divided
2	teaspoons all-purpose flour
1½	teaspoons Dijon mustard
1½	teaspoons table salt
⅔	cup dry white wine
½	cup heavy cream
½	onion, chopped fine
1¼	teaspoons minced fresh thyme
1	garlic clove, minced
¼	teaspoon pepper
2	pounds large Yukon Gold potatoes, peeled and sliced ⅛ inch thick
1	pound rutabaga, trimmed, peeled, quartered, and sliced ⅛ inch thick
1	pound celery root, trimmed, peeled, quartered, and sliced ⅛ inch thick
¾	cup panko bread crumbs
1½	ounces Parmesan cheese, grated (¾ cup)
4	tablespoons unsalted butter, melted and cooled

1. Adjust oven rack to middle position and heat oven to 375 degrees. Grease 13 by 9-inch baking dish. Whisk 1 tablespoon water, flour, mustard, and salt in bowl until smooth. Add wine, cream, and remaining 1½ cups water, whisking to combine. Combine onion, thyme, garlic, and pepper in separate bowl.

2. Layer half of potatoes in prepared dish, arranging so they form even thickness. Sprinkle half of onion mixture evenly over potatoes. Arrange rutabaga and celery root slices in even layer over onions. Sprinkle remaining onion mixture over rutabaga and celery root. Layer remaining potatoes over onions. Slowly pour wine mixture over vegetables. Using rubber spatula, gently press down on vegetables to create even, compact layer. Cover tightly with aluminum foil and bake for 50 minutes. Remove foil and

continue to bake until knife inserted into center of gratin meets no resistance, 20 to 25 minutes.

3. Meanwhile, combine panko, Parmesan, and butter in bowl and season with salt and pepper. Remove gratin from oven and sprinkle evenly with panko mixture. Continue to bake until panko is golden brown, 15 to 20 minutes. Remove gratin from oven and let sit for 25 minutes. Serve.

KEYS TO SUCCESS

- **Using a mandoline:** Makes for quick and uniformly thin slices for a cohesive gratin
- **Adding dry white wine:** Keeps the potatoes from breaking down
- **Pressing down layers:** Compacts the gratin so that the slices cling together nicely

SCIENCE LESSON

Firming Up Potatoes with Wine

The wine in our root vegetable gratin brightens the flavor of this typically starchy-tasting dish, but more important, it also prevents the potatoes from breaking down and turning mushy while the denser celery root and rutabaga cook. Here's how it works: Potato cells have an abundance of starch granules; when these granules swell with water during cooking, they press against the cell walls, eventually causing them to burst and release starch. But when potatoes cook in water with wine, the wine lowers the pH, which strengthens the pectin in and around the cell walls, helping them resist bursting. The upshot is a pliable, not mushy, potato.

Of course, the acid also strengthens the pectin in the celery root and rutabaga, but since they contain less starch than potatoes, the acid's effect on them is less noticeable.

To demonstrate acid's effect on potatoes, we simmered two batches of ⅛-inch-thick potato slices, one in plain water and the other in 1½ cups of water acidulated with ⅔ cup of white wine. After just 10 minutes of simmering, the potatoes cooked in plain water fell apart, while those cooked in acidulated water remained whole and firm but pliable.

Pliable, Not Mushy
Cooking potatoes in water with wine strengthens their cell walls, so they resist bursting as they cook.

SPRING RADISH PRIMER

This guide looks at selecting and cooking radishes (and their greens), whether you want to enjoy them peppery and crisp or juicy-sweet and tender. In their crisp, peppery-hot raw state, these colorful roots can enhance salads or crudités platters or star in an elegant appetizer. If the fire of raw radishes is not your thing, then cooking them—whether sautéing, braising, or roasting—is the way to go.

Spring Radish Varieties

Radishes are divided into two main categories, spring and winter. The former are harvested in the spring, when the roots are small and tender; winter radishes, such as daikon and watermelon, are picked just before the ground freezes. Hundreds of types of radishes are grown worldwide; here are a few spring radishes you're likely to see in U.S. markets.

1. FRENCH BREAKFAST

These rosy-colored, tapered radishes with telltale white tips are especially mild.

2. ROUND RED

These are the most commonly grown radishes in the U.S.; there are many varieties, such as Cherry Belle and Scarlet Globe. They have a sharp flavor and a juicy crunch.

3. PURPLE NINJA

Slice these violet-red, oblong radishes to reveal a starlike matrix of lavender veins. They have a crisp texture and a spicy kick.

4. EASTER EGG

Not an actual variety of radish but a mix of pastel-colored varieties, these radishes are commonly harvested when quite small—about 1 inch in diameter. They are mild and crunchy, with bright-white flesh and subtle heat that builds.

RADISH RECOMMENDATIONS

SHOPPING Whenever possible, choose radishes with the greens attached; crisp, fresh-looking greens are a sign that the radishes are fresh. If the radishes come prebagged with the greens removed, make sure that they are firm and without cracks. Avoid very large radishes, which can have a woody texture and hollow cores.

STORAGE Remove the greens so that they don't pull moisture away from the radishes. Store separately—wrapped in paper towels in a loosely closed container, compost bag, or plastic produce bag—in the crisper drawer. The radishes will last for about a week; the greens will last for two to three days.

RADISH BUTTER

Makes: 1 cup
Total Time: 25 minutes

This easy appetizer is a riff on the venerable French nibble of radishes smeared with sweet butter and sprinkled with sea salt. We chop the radishes with vinegar to give their pungency staying power and then mix in horseradish to boost the spiciness. If your radishes have the greens attached, buy one small (9- to 10-ounce) bunch. Spread the butter on slices of baguette, rye toasts, crackers, or celery sticks.

- 6 ounces radishes, trimmed and quartered
- 2 teaspoons distilled white vinegar
- 4 tablespoons unsalted butter, softened
- 1–2 teaspoons prepared horseradish
- ¼ teaspoon table salt

1. Pulse radishes and vinegar in food processor until finely chopped, 10 to 15 pulses, scraping down sides of bowl as needed. Let stand for 10 minutes.

2. Transfer radishes to large plate lined with triple layer of paper towels and spread into even layer. Top with another layer of paper towels and press gently. Let stand for 5 minutes.

3. Combine butter, 1 teaspoon horseradish, and salt in bowl. Stir in radishes until well combined. Season with salt and up to 1 teaspoon additional horseradish to taste. Serve.

SAUTÉED RADISHES

Serves: 4 to 6
Total Time: 20 minutes

Here's a simple introduction to the mellow, sweet flavor of cooked radishes and their greens. Heat concentrates the natural sugars in radishes while downplaying many of the compounds responsible for their pungent, peppery flavor. To provide some textural variety and color, we cook the greens at the end, so they retain a slight crispness that complements the heartier radish pieces. If you can't find radishes with their greens, you can substitute baby arugula or watercress or skip step 2.

- 3 tablespoons unsalted butter, cut into 3 pieces, divided
- 1½ pounds radishes with their greens, radishes trimmed and quartered, 8 cups greens reserved
- ⅜ teaspoon table salt, divided
- ¼ teaspoon pepper, divided
- 1 garlic clove, minced
  Lemon wedges

1. Melt 2 tablespoons butter in 12-inch skillet over medium-high heat. Add radishes, ¼ teaspoon salt, and ⅛ teaspoon pepper and cook, stirring occasionally, until radishes are lightly browned and crisp-tender, 10 to 12 minutes. Stir in garlic and cook until fragrant, about 30 seconds; transfer to bowl.

2. Melt remaining 1 tablespoon butter in now-empty skillet over medium heat. Add radish greens, remaining ⅛ teaspoon salt, and remaining ⅛ teaspoon pepper; cook, stirring frequently, until wilted, about 1 minute. Off heat, stir in radishes and season with salt and pepper to taste. Serve with lemon wedges.

SCIENCE LESSON ### Radish's Zing—and How Heat Tames It

When radish cells are cut, an enzyme (mostly in the skin) called myrosinase (●) breaks down glucosinolate (▇) molecules in the vegetable, releasing pungent compounds called isothiocyanates (✳). It's these compounds that create radishes' sharp, assertive taste. Cooking radishes deactivates the enzyme, so they taste less pungent after they've been cooked.

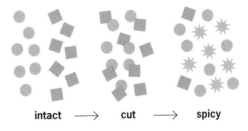

intact ⟶ cut ⟶ spicy

TARTS AND PIES

STEPHANIE PIXLEY

Sweet fruit tarts and pies usually get most of the limelight, but savory versions deserve serious attention. In this course you will learn how to combine vegetables with different crusts to create stunning tarts and pies. You will use store-bought frozen puff pastry to make an upside-down tomato tart and crisp beet and onion turnovers, store-bought phyllo dough for a flaky eggplant and tomato pie, and prepare a buttery dough to encase an Italian Swiss chard pie packed with hearty greens and Parmesan.

STEPH'S PRO TIP: *Don't stress if your phyllo dough cracks or rips when preparing a vegetable tart. With so many layers, any rips will be hidden once the whole thing is baked.*

UPSIDE-DOWN TOMATO TART

Serves: 4 to 6
Total Time: 2¼ hours

RECIPE OVERVIEW Tarte Tatin is a traditional dessert made by caramelizing apples and then baking them under a pie dough top. After cooking, it's inverted and the juices seep deliciously into the crust. This recipe uses the formula as a framework for tomatoes. The savory-sweet fruit pairs beautifully with the buttery pastry and a tangy-sweet sherry vinegar syrup (in lieu of the tarte Tatin's caramel) to produce a dish that's great as a light lunch or an appetizer. To ensure a crisp—not soggy—crust, start by removing the jelly and seeds from plum tomatoes, which have a low moisture content. Reducing a sherry vinegar and sugar syrup develops some caramelized notes and then it's finished with butter, shallot, and thyme. Roasting the tomatoes in the syrup for a full hour not only evaporates any excess moisture but also concentrates the tomatoes' fruity taste, gives their edges some flavorful browning, and enhances their meaty texture. Finally, top the tomatoes with puff pastry, a convenient alternative to pie or biscuit dough that needs only to be thawed, rolled, and cut before it is ready to go into the oven. After about 30 minutes of baking, the pastry is puffed, crisp, and golden brown. This tart is best eaten within a couple hours of baking.

⅓	cup sherry vinegar or cider vinegar
2½	tablespoons sugar
¾	teaspoon table salt, divided
½	teaspoon pepper, divided
1	shallot, chopped fine

1 tablespoon unsalted butter

2½ teaspoons minced fresh thyme, divided

2 pounds plum tomatoes (about 10), cored, halved lengthwise, seeds and gel removed

1 sheet puff pastry, thawed but still cool

1. Adjust oven rack to middle position and heat oven to 400 degrees. Bring vinegar, sugar, ½ teaspoon salt, and ¼ teaspoon pepper to simmer in 10-inch ovensafe skillet over medium-high heat, swirling skillet to dissolve sugar. Simmer vigorously, swirling skillet occasionally, until consistency resembles that of maple syrup, about 2 minutes. Add shallot, butter, and 2 teaspoons thyme and whisk until butter is fully incorporated, about 1 minute.

2. Remove skillet from heat; add tomatoes and toss to coat lightly with syrup. Arrange tomatoes cut side up in as close to single layer as possible (some overlap is OK; tomatoes will shrink as they cook) and sprinkle with remaining ¼ teaspoon salt and remaining ¼ teaspoon pepper. Transfer skillet to oven and cook until liquid has evaporated and tomatoes are very lightly browned around edges and softened but not fully collapsed, about 1 hour. While tomatoes cook, prepare pastry.

3. Roll pastry into 10-inch square on lightly floured counter. Using plate, bowl, or pot lid as template, cut out 10-inch round. Discard trimming. Transfer pastry round to large plate and refrigerate until needed. Remove skillet from oven and place pastry round over tomatoes. Bake until pastry is puffed, crisp, and deep golden brown, about 30 minutes, rotating skillet halfway through baking.

4. Let tart cool for 8 minutes. Run paring knife around edge of crust to loosen, then invert plate over skillet. Using pot holders, swiftly and carefully invert tart onto plate (if tomatoes shift or stick to skillet, arrange with spoon). Let cool for 10 minutes, then sprinkle with remaining ½ teaspoon thyme. Serve warm or at room temperature.

KEYS TO SUCCESS

- **Remove the tomato jelly and seeds**: Prevents moisture from leaching into the crust.

- **Oven-roast the tomatoes**: Fully evaporates any excess moisture

- **Use store-bought puff pastry**: Only needs to be rolled out and cut for an easy crust

---

CORE TECHNIQUE

Coring and Seeding Plum Tomatoes

CORE

Hold tomato in one hand with stem scar facing out. Insert tip of paring knife at an angle into tomato at edge of stem scar, about ½ to 1 inch deep. Using sawing motion, cut around stem scar while rotating tomato until core is cut free.

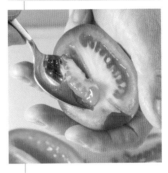

EXCAVATE

Use fingers or spoon to get deep into crevices on either side of core to remove seeds and gel. Save this flavorful jelly—which is packed with savory glutamates—to spoon over crusty bread and then top with a sprinkling of flake salt.

A Tart with Ultra-Tomatoey Flavor and a Crisp Crust

Parcooking the tomatoes in the oven is the key to our tart's success.

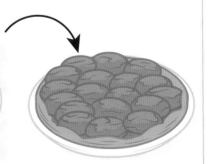

Roast Tomatoes

After reducing the tangy syrup, we add the tomatoes to the skillet and roast them for a full hour, concentrating their flavor.

Bake with Pastry

With much of the fruit's moisture driven off, the store-bought puff pastry placed over the top bakes up golden brown and crisp.

Invert Tart

Turning out the finished tart reveals lightly caramelized fruit gleaming with a sweet-tart glaze crowning the flaky, buttery base.

BEET AND CARAMELIZED ONION TURNOVERS WITH BEET-YOGURT SAUCE

Serves: 8 (makes 8 turnovers)
Total Time: 1¾ hours, plus 15 minutes cooling

RECIPE OVERVIEW It's rare that the humble beet gets to be the star of a dish. And you might not think of it as a baking ingredient at all. In these turnovers, however, this sweet, earthy root vegetable's true colors and flavors shine through—times two. You barely need to precook shredded beets before using them—just add to the skillet with the caramelized onions to wilt them. Then mix in woodsy fresh thyme and tangy mustard to create a gorgeous ruby-colored filling, which you'll use to stuff rectangular pockets of puff pastry. A sprinkling of everything bagel seasoning on top is an attractive finish; its toasted garlic and onion flakes echo the savory onions in the filling. Each turnover bakes up flaky and crisp, with a tender filling that almost fools your eyes into thinking it's a sweet jam when you cut into them. For a contrast in textures and temperatures, use additional shredded beets to make a tangy pink yogurt sauce that's as pretty as it is delicious and perfect for dunking or dolloping. Use the large holes of a box grater or a food processor fitted with a shredding disk to shred the beets. You can substitute 8 ounces cooked beets for the 10 ounces raw beets in the filling. See page 133 for more information on thawing frozen puff pastry.

Beet-Yogurt Sauce
- ¾ cup plain yogurt
- 2 ounces shredded raw or cooked beets (½ cup)
- ¼ teaspoon table salt
- ⅛ teaspoon pepper

Turnovers
- 2 tablespoons vegetable oil
- 2 onions, chopped fine
- ¼ teaspoon table salt
- ¼ teaspoon pepper
- 10 ounces beets, trimmed, peeled, and shredded
- 1 tablespoon minced fresh thyme
- 1 tablespoon Dijon mustard
- 2 (9½ by 9-inch) sheets puff pastry, thawed
- 1 large egg beaten with 1 teaspoon water
- 5 teaspoons everything bagel seasoning

1. FOR THE BEET-YOGURT SAUCE Combine all ingredients in bowl. Refrigerate until ready to serve.

2. FOR THE TURNOVERS Adjust oven rack to middle position and heat oven to 400 degrees. Line rimmed baking sheet with parchment paper. Heat oil in 12-inch nonstick skillet over medium heat until shimmering. Add onions, salt, and pepper and cook, stirring often, until onions soften and are dark brown, about 20 minutes, adjusting heat if onions begin to scorch. Stir in beets and cook until just wilted, 2 to 3 minutes. Stir in thyme and cook until fragrant, about 30 seconds. Transfer beet mixture to bowl, stir in mustard, and let cool completely, about 20 minutes.

3. Dust counter lightly with flour. Working with 1 piece puff pastry at a time, unfold pastry and roll into 10-inch square. Cut into four 5-inch squares. Space pastry squares evenly on prepared sheet. Divide beet filling evenly among pastry squares, mounding about 3 tablespoons in center of each square, then brush edges of pastry with egg wash (reserve remaining egg wash). Fold pastry over filling to form rectangle. Using fork, crimp edges of pastry to seal. Cut two 1-inch slits on top of each turnover (do not cut through filling). (Unbaked turnovers can be frozen in airtight container for up to 1 month.)

4. Brush tops of turnovers with remaining egg wash and sprinkle with everything bagel seasoning. Bake turnovers until well browned, 22 to 25 minutes, rotating sheet halfway through baking. Let turnovers cool on wire rack for 15 minutes. Serve warm or at room temperature with sauce.

KEYS TO SUCCESS
- **Shredded beets:** Only need to be wilted before baking
- **Store-bought puff pastry:** Convenient to use
- **Everything bagel seasoning:** Makes an easy, superflavorful topping

EGGPLANT AND TOMATO PHYLLO PIE

Serves: 4 to 6
Total Time: 2¾ hours

RECIPE OVERVIEW Eggplants and tomatoes live together famously in a number of satisfying dishes across the Mediterranean. Here the two are combined with cheese, garlic, and fresh herbs and baked in a shatteringly crisp phyllo crust. To bring out the best in the tomatoes' flavor, capture their juiciness, and avoid a soggy pie, salt the slices and let them sit in a colander to draw out excess moisture before building the tart. Broiling the eggplant first gives it deeper flavor and a delightful char. Shredded fresh mozzarella melts beautifully into the crust for a satisfying cheesy layer that keeps the bottom from getting soggy. Thaw phyllo in the refrigerator overnight or on the counter for 4 to 5 hours; don't thaw it in the microwave. Allow phyllo to come to room temperature before using.

1	pound tomatoes, cored and sliced ¼ inch thick
1¼	teaspoons table salt, divided
1	pound eggplant, sliced into ¼-inch-thick rounds
½	cup extra-virgin olive oil, divided
12	sheets (14 by 9-inch) phyllo, thawed, room temperature
3	garlic cloves, minced
2	teaspoons minced fresh oregano
¼	teaspoon pepper
6	ounces mozzarella cheese, shredded (1½ cups)
2	tablespoons grated Parmesan cheese
1	tablespoon chopped fresh basil

1. Adjust oven rack 6 inches from broiler element and heat broiler. Line rimmed baking sheet with aluminum foil. Toss tomatoes and ¾ teaspoon salt together in colander and set aside to drain for 30 minutes.

2. Meanwhile, arrange eggplant in single layer on prepared sheet and brush both sides with 2 tablespoons oil. Broil eggplant until softened and beginning to brown, 10 to 12 minutes, flipping eggplant halfway through broiling. Set aside to cool slightly, about 10 minutes.

3. Heat oven to 375 degrees. Line second rimmed baking sheet with parchment paper. Place ¼ cup oil in small bowl. Place 1 phyllo sheet on prepared sheet then lightly brush phyllo with prepared oil. Turn baking sheet 30 degrees and place second phyllo sheet on first phyllo sheet, leaving any overhanging phyllo in place. Brush second phyllo sheet with oil. Repeat turning baking sheet and layering remaining 10 phyllo sheets in pinwheel pattern, brushing each with oil (you should have 12 total layers of phyllo).

4. Shake colander to rid tomatoes of excess juice. Combine tomatoes, garlic, oregano, pepper, 1 tablespoon oil, and remaining ½ teaspoon salt in bowl. Sprinkle mozzarella evenly in center of phyllo in 9-inch circle. Shingle tomatoes and eggplant on top of mozzarella in concentric circles, alternating tomatoes and eggplant as you go. Sprinkle Parmesan cheese over top.

5. Gently fold edges of phyllo over vegetable mixture, pleating every 2 to 3 inches as needed, and lightly brush edges with remaining 1 tablespoon oil. Bake until phyllo is crisp and golden brown, 30 to 35 minutes. Let pie cool for 15 minutes then sprinkle with basil. Slice and serve.

KEYS TO SUCCESS

- **Thaw phyllo properly:** Makes it easier to work with
- **Salt the tomatoes:** Draws out moisture
- **Broil the eggplant:** Turns it tender and flavorful

Making Eggplant and Tomato Phyllo Pie

PLACE SHEET ONE
Line rimmed baking sheet with parchment paper. Place 1 phyllo sheet on prepared sheet then lightly brush phyllo with oil.

PLACE SHEET TWO
Turn baking sheet 30 degrees and place second phyllo sheet on first phyllo sheet, leaving any overhanging phyllo in place. Brush second phyllo sheet with oil.

PLACE REMAINING SHEETS
Repeat turning baking sheet and layering remaining 10 phyllo sheets in pinwheel pattern, brushing each with oil (you should have 12 total layers of phyllo).

FOLD AND PLEAT
Gently fold edges of phyllo over vegetable mixture, pleating every 2 to 3 inches as needed, and lightly brush edges with remaining 1 tablespoon oil.

ERBAZZONE

Serves: 12

Total Time: 2¾ hours, plus 2 hours chilling

RECIPE OVERVIEW Hailing from central Italy, this savory Swiss chard pie packs several pounds of hearty greens between layers of flaky golden pie crust, with additional flavor provided by pancetta and plenty of Parmigiano Reggiano cheese. First brown the pancetta and set it aside so you can cook the aromatics and the chard in its flavorful rendered fat. Ricotta is a controversial ingredient in erbazzone; many recipes don't include it. We like the cleaner, earthier taste of the erbazzone without the ricotta, but if you prefer a cheesier filling we've provided the option to include it. A buttery pie crust wraps the whole thing up in an irresistible package. This dough will be moister than most pie doughs; as the dough chills, it will absorb any excess moisture, leaving it supple and workable.

Crust

- 20 tablespoons (2½ sticks) unsalted butter, chilled
- 2½ cups (12½ ounces) all-purpose flour, divided
- 1 teaspoon table salt
- ½ cup ice water, divided

Filling

- 1 tablespoon extra-virgin olive oil
- 3 ounces pancetta, chopped fine, divided
- 1 onion, chopped fine
- 4 garlic cloves, minced
- 3 pounds Swiss chard, stemmed and cut into 1-inch pieces
- 4 ounces Parmigiano Reggiano cheese, grated (2 cups)
- 6 ounces (¾ cup) whole-milk ricotta cheese (optional)
- 1 large egg, lightly beaten

1. **FOR THE CRUST** Grate half stick butter using coarse holes on box grater and place in freezer. Cut remaining 2 sticks butter into ½-inch pieces.

2. Pulse 1½ cups flour and salt in food processor until combined, about 4 pulses. Add butter pieces and process until homogeneous dough forms, about 30 seconds. Using your hands, carefully break dough into 2-inch pieces and redistribute evenly around processor blade. Add remaining 1 cup flour and pulse until mixture is broken into pieces no larger than 1 inch (most pieces will be much smaller), 4 or 5 pulses. Empty mixture into medium bowl. Add grated butter and toss until butter pieces are separated and coated with flour.

3. Sprinkle ¼ cup ice water over mixture. Toss with rubber spatula until mixture is evenly moistened. Sprinkle remaining ¼ cup ice water over mixture and toss to combine. Press dough with spatula until dough sticks together. Divide dough in half and transfer to sheets of plastic wrap. Draw edges of plastic wrap over first dough half and press firmly on sides and top to form compact fissure-free mass. Flatten to form 5-inch square. Repeat with second dough half. Refrigerate for at least 2 hours or up to 2 days. Let chilled dough sit on counter to soften slightly, about 10 minutes, before rolling.

4. **FOR THE FILLING** Adjust oven rack to lower-middle position and heat oven to 400 degrees. Cook oil and ⅓ cup pancetta in Dutch oven over medium-low heat until pancetta is browned and fat is rendered, 5 to 7 minutes. Using slotted spoon, transfer pancetta to bowl. Pour off all but 1 tablespoon fat from pot.

5. Add onion to fat left in pot and cook over medium heat until softened, about 5 minutes. Stir in garlic and cook until fragrant, about 30 seconds. Increase heat to high. Add chard, 1 handful at a time, and cook until beginning to wilt, about 1 minute. Cover and continue to cook, stirring occasionally, until chard is wilted but still bright green, 2 to 4 minutes. Uncover and continue to cook until liquid evaporates, about 5 minutes. Transfer chard to large bowl and let cool completely, about 30 minutes.

6. Grease rimmed baking sheet. Stir Parmigiano; ricotta, if using; and cooked pancetta into chard. Roll 1 dough square into 14 by 10-inch rectangle on well-floured counter. Roll dough loosely around rolling pin and unroll it onto prepared sheet. Spread chard mixture evenly over crust, leaving 1-inch border around edges. Brush edges of crust with egg.

7. Roll remaining dough square into 14 by 10-inch rectangle on well-floured counter. Roll dough loosely around rolling pin and unroll it over filling. Press edges of crusts together to seal. Roll edges inward and use your fingers to crimp. Using sharp knife, cut through top crust into 12 equal squares (do not cut through filling). Brush with remaining egg and sprinkle with remaining pancetta.

8. Bake until pie is golden brown and pancetta is crispy, 30 to 35 minutes, rotating sheet halfway through baking. Transfer sheet to wire rack and let pie cool completely, about 30 minutes. Transfer pie to cutting board, cut into squares, and serve.

KEYS TO SUCCESS

- **Three pounds of Swiss chard:** Packs the pie with tender greens
- **Rendered pancetta fat:** Adds meaty flavor to the aromatics and chard

THAWING PUFF PASTRY

Homemade puff pastry is laborious and time-intensive to make, but luckily, convenient frozen puff pastry is readily available in grocery stores. Still, store-bought puff pastry can present the uninitiated with some minor obstacles, particularly when it comes to temperature.

For the perfect puff, the pastry should never come to room temperature. Most cooks thaw puff pastry on the counter, but it can quickly get too warm with this method. We recommend letting the pastry defrost slowly in the refrigerator, where it can't overheat. When rolling or cutting the pastry on the counter, do so as quickly as possible. If the dough becomes too soft, return it to the refrigerator for 5 minutes or so to firm up. Once the puff pastry has been shaped, make sure to chill the dough thoroughly before baking—15 minutes in the freezer or 30 minutes in the refrigerator will do the trick.

SCIENCE LESSON

REFREEZING THAWED PUFF PASTRY DOUGH

When you can't use an entire box of store-bought puff pastry, is it OK to refreeze dough that's already been thawed? Whether store-bought or homemade, puff pastry is made by laminating fat between multiple layers of dough. When puff pastry is baked, the water in the dough turns to steam, creating flaky pockets.

To find out if we could reuse leftovers, we purchased two common brands: Dufour Pastry Kitchens, made with butter, and Pepperidge Farm, made with butter and shortening. We allowed a sheet from each brand to thaw overnight in the refrigerator (per the package directions). We then cut rounds of dough with a cookie cutter from half of each sheet and baked them until bronzed and cooked through. Meanwhile, we rewrapped the leftover doughs (being sure not to compress the layers) and put them back in the freezer. Two days later, we thawed the doughs and baked more rounds.

We couldn't tell the difference between the once and twice-frozen Pepperidge Farm pastry, made with butter and shortening. But we did notice that the refrozen all-butter Dufour pastry didn't rise quite as high as the control sample when baked. Why? Butter has a lower melting point than shortening. This means that during the freeze-thaw-freeze-thaw cycle, butter melts more readily than shortening does. And when the butter melts, the pastry layers adhere, so refrozen all-butter dough is unable to rise quite as high.

That said, the effect is fairly minimal, and in the future we'll feel comfortable refreezing thawed pastry dough, even when it's made with just butter.

ALL ABOUT PHYLLO DOUGH

Phyllo dough, tissue-thin layers of pastry dough used for sweet and savory pastries in Greece and the Middle East, is available in two sizes: full-size sheets that are 18 by 14 inches (about 20 per box) and half-size sheets that are 14 by 9 inches (about 40 per box). The smaller sheets are more common, so we use those in our recipes like Eggplant and Tomato Phyllo Pie (page 131). If you buy the large sheets, simply cut them in half. Below are some other pointers that make working with this delicate dough easier.

- Thaw the phyllo dough completely before using. Frozen phyllo must be thawed before using. This is best achieved by placing the phyllo in the refrigerator for at least 12 hours.
- Keep the phyllo covered when using. Phyllo dries out very quickly. As soon as the phyllo is removed from its plastic sleeve, unfold the dough and carefully flatten it with your hands. Cover with plastic wrap, then a damp dish towel.
- Throw out badly torn sheets of dough. Usually each box has one or two torn sheets of phyllo that can't be salvaged. But if the sheets have just small cuts or tears, you can still work with them—put them in the middle of the pastry, where imperfections will go unnoticed. If all of the sheets have the exact same tear, alternate the orientation of each sheet when assembling the pastry.
- Don't refreeze leftover dough. Leftover sheets cannot be refrozen, but they can be rerolled, wrapped in plastic wrap, and stored in the refrigerator for up to five days.

VEGETABLE MAINS

NICOLE KONSTANTINAKOS

Vegetables often deserve center-of-the-plate status. Different preparation methods can expand vegetables' potential, making them main dish–friendly. With their hearty textures and deep flavors, the vegetables in this course are well-suited to take center stage. You'll learn how to prepare some vegetables as you would meat and make them the centerpiece of the meal. Salt and roast meaty mushrooms, roast and sear butternut squash steaks, and stuff eggplant, squash, or onions with ground meat and grains. You'll be really happy you did.

NICOLE'S PRO TIP: *After harvesting, and especially if stored for a long time or transported over great distances, vegetables can lose flavor and nutrients. If possible, look for locally grown vegetables that have a good shape, are unblemished, and have a fresh smell. Seek them out within a few days of when you plan to cook with them to be sure they're at their best and to cut down on food waste.*

WHOLE ROMANESCO WITH BERBERE AND YOGURT-TAHINI SAUCE

Serves: 4
Total Time: 30 minutes

RECIPE OVERVIEW Romanesco, cauliflower's dramatically beautiful cousin, makes for a showstopping vegetarian main dish. This key-lime green, fractal-looking vegetable is perfect for cooking whole, as happens in this recipe. For a tender interior and nicely charred exterior, start by partially cooking the romanesco in the microwave. Then brush with melted butter and transfer to the broiler to brown. Baste the broiled romanesco with more butter and berbere, a warmly aromatic and highly flavorful Ethiopian spice blend. A bright, cooling yogurt sauce with some nutty depth from tahini pleasantly offsets the warm spice coating, and pine nuts provide crunch against the just-perfectly-tender romanesco. If you can't find a 2-pound head of romanesco, purchase two 1-pound heads and reduce the microwaving time in step 2 to 5 to 7 minutes. You can substitute cauliflower for the romanesco.

Yogurt-Tahini Sauce
- ½   cup whole-milk yogurt
- 2   tablespoons tahini
- ½   teaspoon grated lemon zest plus 1 tablespoon juice
- 1   garlic clove, minced

Romanesco
- 1   head romanesco or cauliflower (2 pounds)
- 6   tablespoons unsalted butter, cut into 6 pieces
- ¼   teaspoon table salt
- ½   teaspoon paprika
- ¼   teaspoon cayenne pepper
- ¼   teaspoon ground coriander
- ⅛   teaspoon ground allspice
- ⅛   teaspoon ground cardamom
- ⅛   teaspoon ground cumin
- ⅛   teaspoon ground black pepper
- 2   tablespoons toasted and coarsely chopped pine nuts
- 1   tablespoon minced fresh cilantro

Vegetable Mathematics

The cruciferous vegetable romanesco goes by many names, including romanesco broccoli (a nod to its green color) and Roman cauliflower (a nod to its more cauliflower-like flavor). It has a striking fractal geography with spiraling cones of florets reaching from its core. Each bud consists of six smaller buds. And the total number of buds on a head represents a Fibonacci number. No matter the pattern, romanesco is a striking, delicious vegetable that deserves to be displayed.

1. **FOR THE SAUCE** Whisk all ingredients in bowl until combined. Season with salt and pepper to taste and set aside until ready to serve.

2. **FOR THE ROMANESCO** Adjust oven rack 6 inches from broiler element and heat broiler. Trim outer leaves of romanesco and cut stem flush with bottom florets. Microwave romanesco and 3 tablespoons butter in large, covered bowl until paring knife slips easily in and out of core, 8 to 12 minutes.

3. Transfer romanesco, stem side down, to 12-inch ovensafe skillet. Brush romanesco evenly with melted butter from bowl and sprinkle with salt. Transfer skillet to oven and broil until top of romanesco is spotty brown, 8 to 10 minutes. Meanwhile, microwave remaining 3 tablespoons butter, paprika, cayenne, coriander, allspice, cardamom, cumin, and pepper in now-empty bowl, stirring occasionally, until fragrant and bubbling, 1 to 2 minutes.

4. Using pot holder, remove skillet from oven and transfer to wire rack. Being careful of hot skillet handle, gently tilt skillet so butter pools to one side. Using spoon, baste romanesco until butter is absorbed, about 30 seconds.

5. Cut romanesco into wedges and transfer to serving platter. Season with salt to taste and sprinkle pine nuts and cilantro over top. Serve with sauce.

KEYS TO SUCCESS

- **A jump start in the microwave**: Parcooking the dense vegetable produces a fully tender interior.

- **A brush with melted butter**: Adds flavor and promotes browning

- **Homemade spice blend**: Adds fresh, complex flavor

ROASTED KING TRUMPET MUSHROOMS

Serves: 4
Total Time: 45 minutes

RECIPE OVERVIEW The king trumpet mushroom (or king oyster mushroom) is a popular variety native to the Mediterranean, the Middle East, North Africa, and many parts of Asia. These large, stumpy mushrooms have little aroma or flavor when raw, but cooking transforms them: They become deeply savory, with the meaty texture of squid or tender octopus. You can highlight this special quality by preparing the mushrooms almost like a piece of meat. Start by halving and crosshatching each mushroom, creating attractive "fillets," and then salting them and letting them sit briefly. Roasting the mushrooms cut side down in a hot oven results in plump and juicy, well-seasoned mushrooms with a nicely browned exterior crust. These mushrooms are delicious on their own, with just a squeeze of lemon. But to gild the lily, make one of two potent sauces (recipes follow) to serve with them. Look for trumpet mushrooms that are 3 to 4 ounces in size.

1¾ pounds king trumpet mushrooms
½ teaspoon table salt
4 tablespoons unsalted butter, melted
Lemon wedges

1. Adjust oven rack to lowest position and heat oven to 500 degrees. Trim bottom ½ inch of mushroom stems, then halve mushrooms lengthwise. Cut 1/16-inch-deep slits on cut side of mushrooms, spaced ½ inch apart, in crosshatch pattern. Sprinkle cut side of mushrooms with salt and let sit for 15 minutes.

2. Brush mushrooms evenly with melted butter, season with pepper to taste, and arrange cut side down on rimmed baking sheet. Roast until mushrooms are browned on cut side, 20 to 24 minutes. Transfer to serving platter. Serve with lemon wedges.

RED WINE–MISO SAUCE

Bring 1 cup dry red wine, 1 cup vegetable broth, 2 teaspoons sugar, and ½ teaspoon soy sauce to simmer in 10-inch skillet over medium heat and cook until reduced to ⅓ cup, 20 to 25 minutes. Off heat, whisk in 1 tablespoon unsalted butter and 5 teaspoons miso until smooth. Serve with mushrooms.

BROWN BUTTER–LEMON VINAIGRETTE

Melt 4 tablespoons unsalted butter in 10-inch skillet over medium heat. Cook, swirling constantly, until butter is dark golden brown and has nutty aroma, 3 to 5 minutes. Off heat, whisk in 2 tablespoons lemon juice, 1 teaspoon Dijon mustard, 1 teaspoon maple syrup, ¼ teaspoon salt, and ⅛ teaspoon pepper. Serve with mushrooms.

KEYS TO SUCCESS

- **Score the mushrooms**: Exposes more surface area

- **Salt the mushrooms**: Acts as a mini brine to draw out water and also seasons them

CHILE-RUBBED BUTTERNUT SQUASH STEAKS

Serves: 4
Total Time: 50 minutes

RECIPE OVERVIEW Butternut squash's dense texture gives it a meaty bite, and its mild flavor can handle bold seasonings. To create thick slabs, use the necks of large butternuts, carefully peeling them and slicing them lengthwise. Crosshatching the surface of the steaks creates more surface area for absorbing a spice rub, speeds up the process of drying out the exterior, and gives the steaks the appearance of grill marks. Roasting the squash steaks in the oven before searing them ensures the interior is tender, and it dries out the exterior so it can then develop a crust in a skillet. A bold-tasting Southwestern rub will make this squash remind you of blackened steak. Ranch dressing provides a refreshing foil to the spicy intensity of the steaks. Look for butternut squashes with necks at least 5 inches in length and 2½ to 3½ inches in diameter.

- ¼ cup extra-virgin olive oil, divided
- 2 teaspoons sugar
- 2 teaspoons smoked paprika
- 1½ teaspoons table salt
- 1 teaspoon garlic powder
- ½ teaspoon chipotle chile powder
- ½ teaspoon pepper
- 2 (3-pound) butternut squashes
  Ranch Dressing (recipe follows)

1. Adjust oven rack to middle position and heat oven to 450 degrees. Combine 3 tablespoons oil, sugar, paprika, salt, garlic powder, chile powder, and pepper in bowl; set aside.

2. Working with 1 squash at a time, cut crosswise into 2 pieces at base of neck; reserve bulb for another use. Peel away skin and fibrous threads just below skin (squash should be completely orange, with no white flesh), then carefully cut each piece in half lengthwise. Cut one, ¾-inch-thick slab lengthwise from each half. Repeat with remaining squash. (You should have 4 steaks; reserve remaining squash for another use.)

3. Place steaks on wire rack set in rimmed baking sheet. Cut ¹⁄₁₆-inch-deep slits on both sides of steaks, spaced ½ inch apart, in crosshatch pattern, and brush evenly with spice mixture. Flip steaks and brush second side with spice mixture. Roast until nearly tender and knife inserted into steaks meets with some resistance, 15 to 17 minutes; remove from oven.

4. Heat remaining 1 tablespoon oil in 12-inch nonstick skillet over medium-high heat until just smoking. Carefully place steaks in skillet and cook, without moving, until well browned and crisp on first side, about 3 minutes. Flip steaks and continue to cook until well browned and crisp on second side, about 3 minutes. Transfer steaks to platter and serve with ranch dressing.

RANCH DRESSING

Makes: ¾ cup

- ½ cup mayonnaise
- 2 tablespoons plain yogurt
- 1 teaspoon white wine vinegar
- 1½ teaspoons minced fresh chives
- 1½ teaspoons minced fresh dill
- ¼ teaspoon garlic powder
- ⅛ teaspoon table salt
- ⅛ teaspoon pepper

Whisk all ingredients in bowl until smooth. Refrigerate until serving. (Dressing can be refrigerated for up to 4 days.)

KEYS TO SUCCESS

- **Cut thick vegetable steaks:** From the necks of large squashes
- **Score both sides:** Creates more surface area for the spice rub and mimics grill marks
- **Roast, then sear:** For a substantial yet tender texture

CORE TECHNIQUE

Preparing Butternut Squash Steaks

HALVE NECK
Cut squash neck in half lengthwise.

CUT SLABS
Cut one ¾-inch-thick slab lengthwise from each squash half.

SCORE SIDES
Cut ¹⁄₁₆-inch-deep slits on both sides of steaks, spaced ½ inch apart, in a crosshatch pattern.

STUFFED EGGPLANT WITH BULGUR AND TOMATOES

Serves: 4
Total Time: 1½ hours

RECIPE OVERVIEW Stuffing is a simple way to make vegetables a main meal. Italian eggplant, with its boat-like shape when halved, is perfect for filling. This is a classic Turkish preparation known as imam bayildi and uses its flavors as inspiration for the warm-spiced tomato-based filling. The eggplants turn rich and creamy and the filling is hearty. Roasting the eggplants prior to stuffing is key to preventing them from being watery and tasteless. Letting the eggplants drain briefly gets rid of excess liquid before adding the stuffing. Bulgur makes a perfect filling base, plum tomatoes lend bright flavor and a bit of moisture, and Pecorino and pine nuts provide richness and depth. Do not confuse bulgur with cracked wheat, which has a much longer cooking time and will not work in this recipe.

4	(10-ounce) Italian eggplants, halved lengthwise
3	tablespoons extra-virgin olive oil, divided
¾	teaspoon table salt, divided
½	cup medium-grind bulgur, rinsed
¼	cup water
2	teaspoons minced fresh oregano or ½ teaspoon dried
¼	teaspoon ground cinnamon
	Pinch cayenne pepper (optional)
1	pound plum tomatoes, cored, seeded, and chopped
2	ounces Pecorino Romano cheese, grated (1 cup), divided
2	tablespoons pine nuts, toasted
2	teaspoons red wine vinegar
2	tablespoons minced fresh parsley

1. Adjust oven racks to upper-middle and lowest positions, place parchment paper–lined rimmed baking sheet on lowest rack, and heat oven to 400 degrees.

2. Score flesh of each eggplant half in 1-inch diamond pattern, about 1 inch deep. Brush scored sides of eggplant with 2 tablespoons oil and sprinkle with ½ teaspoon salt. Lay eggplant cut side down on hot sheet and roast until flesh is tender, 40 to 50 minutes. Transfer eggplant cut side down to paper towel–lined baking sheet and let drain.

3. Toss bulgur with water in bowl and let sit until grains are softened and liquid is fully absorbed, 20 to 40 minutes.

4. Cook remaining 1 tablespoon oil, oregano, cinnamon, and cayenne, if using, in 12-inch skillet until fragrant, about 30 seconds. Off heat, stir in bulgur, tomatoes, ¾ cup Pecorino, pine nuts, vinegar, and remaining ¼ teaspoon salt and let sit until heated through, about 1 minute. Season with salt and pepper to taste.

5. Return eggplant cut side up to rimmed baking sheet. Using 2 forks, gently push eggplant flesh to sides to make room for filling. Mound bulgur mixture into eggplant halves and pack lightly with back of spoon. Sprinkle with remaining ¼ cup Pecorino. Bake on upper rack until cheese is melted, 5 to 10 minutes. Sprinkle with parsley and serve.

KEYS TO SUCCESS

- **Preheat baking sheet:** The hot sheet slightly caramelizes the eggplant, adding flavor.
- **Roast then stuff:** Reduces moisture in the eggplant and softens the flesh

---

CORE TECHNIQUE

Preparing Eggplant for Stuffing

SCORE CUT SIDES
Using tip of knife, score eggplant half in 1-inch diamond pattern, about 1 inch deep. Brush cut sides with oil and roast cut side down on preheated baking sheet.

MOVE FLESH TO SIDES
Using 2 forks, gently press eggplant flesh to sides making room for filling. Mound filling into eggplant halves.

KOUSA MIHSHI

Serves: 4
Total Time: 2¼ hours

RECIPE OVERVIEW Kousa mihshi, zucchini stuffed with spiced lamb and rice and braised in cinnamon-accented tomato sauce, is one of the great Middle Eastern stuffed vegetable traditions. Dominique Khoury generously shares her version of the family recipe she grew up making in her Lebanese American home. The dish consists of hollowed-out zucchini filled with spiced ground lamb and rice that's slowly braised in tomato sauce until the meat is succulent and the rice tender. Soaking the rice before combining it with the lamb ensures that the grains cook evenly and thoroughly. Browning the stuffing and breaking it up creates small distinct pieces to pack into the squash cavities. To give the sauce a meaty underpinning, the aromatics are sautéed in the fatty lamb juices. Just 20 minutes of braising in the velvety sauce, and the zucchini are tender but not mushy and the filling cooked through. For this recipe, you'll need an apple corer, the type that removes the core only but does not slice the apple; the small end of a melon baller or long-handled bar spoon is also helpful. We like ground lamb here, but you can substitute 90 percent lean ground beef if preferred. Select zucchini that are similarly sized to ensure even cooking; and to make them easier to core, choose the straightest ones you can find. Use in-season tomatoes for the best flavor.

Hashweh

- ½ cup long-grain white rice
- 8 ounces ground lamb
- 1 teaspoon table salt
- ½ teaspoon pepper
- ¼ teaspoon ground cinnamon
- 2 tablespoons extra-virgin olive oil, divided

Sauce

- 2 tablespoons extra-virgin olive oil
- ½ teaspoon pepper
- ¼ teaspoon ground cinnamon
- 1 small onion, chopped coarse
- 2 garlic cloves, minced
- 2 pounds tomatoes, cored and chopped coarse
- 2 tablespoons tomato paste
- 2 teaspoons apple cider vinegar
- 1 teaspoon table salt

Zucchini

- 6 zucchini, 6 to 7 inches long and at least 1½ inches wide
- 2 tablespoons extra-virgin olive oil
- ¼ cup fresh parsley leaves
- 2 cups plain whole-milk yogurt

1. FOR THE HASHWEH Place rice in fine-mesh strainer and rinse under cold running water until water runs clear. Place rinsed rice in small bowl and cover with 2 cups hot tap water; let stand for 10 minutes. Drain rice in fine-mesh strainer. Mix rice, lamb, salt, pepper, cinnamon, and 1 tablespoon olive oil in bowl until rice is well dispersed (do not wash strainer). Heat remaining 1 tablespoon oil in 12-inch nonstick skillet over medium-high heat until shimmering. Add meat mixture to skillet (do not wash bowl) and, using heat-resistant spatula, mash to thin layer. Cook, stirring constantly and breaking up meat with side of spatula, until almost cooked through but still slightly pink, 3 to 4 minutes. Transfer mixture to now-empty fine-mesh strainer set over bowl (do not wash skillet). Return juices

and fat to now-empty skillet. Transfer meat mixture to now-empty bowl and, using fork, break up meat mixture until reduced to pieces no larger than ¼ inch.

2. FOR THE SAUCE Add oil to juices in skillet and cook over medium-low heat until sizzling. Stir in pepper and cinnamon and cook until just fragrant, about 30 seconds. Add onion and garlic and cook, stirring occasionally, until very soft and light golden, 7 to 9 minutes.

3. Transfer onion mixture to food processor (do not wash skillet). Add tomatoes, tomato paste, vinegar, and salt to processor, and process until smooth, 1½ to 2 minutes. Transfer tomato mixture to now-empty skillet. Bring to boil over medium-high heat. Reduce heat to simmer and cook, uncovered and stirring occasionally, until sauce is thickened and a heat-resistant spatula dragged across bottom of skillet leaves trail, 25 to 30 minutes. While sauce cooks, prepare zucchini.

4. FOR THE ZUCCHINI Remove stem end of one zucchini, and discard. Holding zucchini with one hand, insert apple corer into stem end and press and turn until cutting end of corer is about ½ inch from bottom of squash (or as far as corer will go), being careful not to damage walls of zucchini. (If stem end is too narrow to accommodate corer without damaging walls, remove additional inch of stem end). Remove corer. Using melon baller or long, thin spoon, scoop out core in pieces until furthest part of hollow is ½ inch from bottom of squash. Repeat with remaining zucchini. Rinse hollows and drain squash on towel.

5. Hold one zucchini stemmed side up on work surface. Using hand or small spoon, drop small portions of stuffing into hollow, tapping bottom of zucchini lightly on work surface to help filling settle, until stuffing is ½ inch from top of zucchini. Do not compact stuffing. Repeat with remaining zucchini and stuffing.

6. Remove sauce from heat. Gently arrange stuffed zucchini in skillet in single layer. Return skillet to medium-high heat and bring to boil. Adjust heat to low simmer,

CORE TECHNIQUE **Coring Zucchini**

CORE
Core zucchini with apple corer, pressing it into squash as far down as it will go.

SCOOP
Scoop out more pieces of core with melon baller until hollow is ½ inch from bottom. Rinse cavity to remove seeds and debris clinging to walls, and drain on towel.

cover, and cook for 20 minutes (small wisps of steam should escape from beneath skillet lid, but sauce should not boil). Turn zucchini over gently. Cover and continue to simmer until rice and meat are fully cooked and zucchini are tender but not mushy, 20 to 25 minutes. Drizzle zucchini and sauce with olive oil, sprinkle with parsley, and serve, passing yogurt separately.

KEYS TO SUCCESS

- **Soak the rice:** Ensures that the grains cook evenly
- **Use the lamb juices:** Sauté the aromatics in the lamb fat to add meaty flavor to the dish.

A Stuffing That Doubles as a Meal

Hashweh, the filling for kousa mihshi, dates back to ancient Greece and Persia and is the same stuffing of warm-spiced rice and minced lamb (or beef) that's rolled into grape leaves and spooned into countless fruits, vegetables, and proteins in Middle Eastern cooking. But many cooks make it for its own sake, too, often bejeweling it with dried fruit and crispy toasted nuts. Some serve hashweh warmed in a bowl with yogurt, mint, and toasted almonds or fold it into creamy scrambled eggs.

MEHSHI BAZAL

Serves: 4 to 6
Total Time: 2 hours

RECIPE OVERVIEW Syrian Jewish cook Sheila Sutton introduces us to an impressive vegetable dish particular to the cuisine—stuffed onion petals. The layers of onion are simmered in pomegranate juice, pomegranate molasses, and Aleppo pepper. This braising medium reduces down to a fruity-sweet-sour sauce that's enriched by the juices of a warm-spiced meat (and rice) filling. The sauce lacquers the onions with its ruby-hued shine. In order to easily separate the onion leaves and render them pliable enough for wrapping around filling, the onions are blanched whole (partially cut so the boiling water can reach the interior). Sometimes the rice (medium-grain for its binding quality) is soaked in advance to prevent the raw rice from wicking away all the moisture from the meat, turning it tough. We give the rice a quick dunk in the onion-blanching water for 5 minutes, which is enough to hydrate it and allow the filling to remain tender. Look for large onions that are approximately 12 to 16 ounces each. If medium-grain rice is unavailable, short grain rice can be substituted; do not use long-grain rice here. Serve onions warm or let rest longer in step 5 and serve at room temperature.

3 large red onions (about 1 pound each)
⅓ cup medium-grain rice, rinsed
12 ounces 85 percent lean ground beef
¾ teaspoon baharat
1 teaspoon table salt
  Pinch cinnamon
2 cups pomegranate juice
1 tablespoon pomegranate molasses
½ teaspoon ground dried Aleppo pepper
½ cup pomegranate seeds
2 tablespoons chopped fresh parsley

1. Bring 4 quarts of water to boil in Dutch oven. Trim ends of onions and arrange on cutting board with 1 cut side down. Starting at top of each onion with tip of knife at core, cut through 1 side. (Onion should remain intact; do not halve onion completely.) Add onions to boiling water and cook, turning occasionally, until onion layers begin to soften and separate, about 15 minutes.

2. Using slotted spoon, transfer onions to cutting board. Once cool enough to touch, gently separate first 7 layers from each onion. Some layers may tear slightly; only 15 layers are needed. Reserve remaining onion cores for another use.

3. Meanwhile, add rice to water left in pot and let sit, off heat, for 5 minutes; drain. Using your hands, gently knead rice, beef, baharat, salt, and cinnamon together in bowl until combined. Arrange 1 onion layer on counter with short side facing you. Place 2 tablespoons of rice mixture about ½ inch from bottom and roll up onion to form torpedo shape with tapered ends. Transfer stuffed onion to plate, seam side down. Repeat with 14 more onion layers and remaining rice mixture. (Stuffed onions can be refrigerated for up to 24 hours.)

4. Whisk pomegranate juice and pomegranate molasses together in 12-inch nonstick skillet. Evenly space 12 stuffed onions seam side down around edge of skillet and place three in center. Sprinkle with Aleppo. Bring to vigorous simmer over medium-high heat. Cover, reduce heat to medium-low, and cook for 25 minutes.

5. Using 2 forks, carefully flip onions. Continue to cook, uncovered, until onions are softened and glaze has thickened slightly, 10 to 15 minutes. Off heat, let rest for at least 10 minutes. Gently turn onions to coat with glaze, then transfer to serving platter. Spoon glaze over top and sprinkle with pomegranate seeds and parsley. Serve.

KEYS TO SUCCESS

- **Cut through onions on only one side:** Allows boiling water to reach the interior leaves
- **Dunk the rice:** Hydrates the grains and adds a little allium flavor
- **Pomegranate juice and molasses:** Bring a perfect tart-sweet balance

THE CHARMS OF OKRA

LAN LAM

Finger-shaped okra is the edible seedpod of a plant that thrives in the American South. It's fresh green vegetal flavor and delicate crunch is something like a cross between green beans and zucchini. Okra is one of those vegetables that fall into Love It or Hate It categories. Where it really belongs is in the I've Never Had It Cooked Properly category. This course is designed to let fresh okra shine in preparations designed to bring out its best. These velvety pods offer remarkable range and versatility, depending on how they're prepared. Learn okra's many charms as you sauté, stir-fry, roast, deep-fry, pickle, and stew this unique vegetable to perfection.

LAN'S PRO TIP: *Okra's unique texture can be challenging for some folks but with the proper introduction it's an easy vegetable to love. I find that the combination of a high heat cooking method (roasting or grilling) and a rich creamy sauce are a nice way to offer okra to the uninitiated.*

SAUTÉED OKRA

Serves: 4
Total Time: 15 minutes

RECIPE OVERVIEW As okra is boiled or braised, the inside can become gelatinous (or, to put it another way, slimy). For some, that can be a deal breaker but quickly sautéing whole pods over medium-high heat is a great way to minimize their slipperiness and maximize their fresh flavor and crisp texture. This side dish makes a perfect accompaniment to chicken or fish, such as halibut or catfish. Do not substitute frozen okra here.

2 tablespoons plus 1 teaspoon extra-virgin olive oil, divided
1 pound okra, stemmed
1 garlic clove, minced
   Lemon wedges

1. Heat 2 tablespoons oil in 12-inch skillet over medium-high heat until just smoking. Add okra and cook, stirring occasionally, until crisp-tender and well browned on most sides, 5 to 7 minutes.

2. Push okra to sides of skillet. Add garlic and remaining 1 teaspoon oil to center and cook, mashing mixture into pan, until fragrant, about 30 seconds. Stir mixture into okra, season with salt and pepper to taste, and serve immediately with lemon wedges.

KEYS TO SUCCESS

- **Simple and quick stovetop method:** Keeps the okra fresh and crisp
- **A little garlic:** Adds a hint of flavor

CORE TECHNIQUE   Stemming Okra

To stem okra, trim stems from okra pods, making sure to leave top "cap" on each pod intact. This minimizes slip and prevents okra from becoming gooey as it cooks.

ROASTED OKRA

Serves: 4
Total Time: 45 minutes

RECIPE OVERVIEW Roasted okra is a revelation: The pods emerge from the oven tender, brown, and lightly crisp at the edges, with a nutty-sweet, green bean–esque flavor. The high, dry heat of the oven concentrates the pods' nuanced vegetal flavors and encourages browning reactions that create even more complexity. Heat also dehydrates the okra's mucilage (the technical term for the slimy substance within the cells of its pod and seeds), so it becomes nearly undetectable. Roasting is also simple by nature. Split similar-size pods lengthwise, toss them with oil and salt, and arrange the pods cut sides down on a rimmed baking sheet. Cover with foil so that the thicker parts can steam and turn tender before the thin tips wither and scorch. Finally, uncover the okra to allow their cut sides, which rested flush against the baking sheet, to brown and crisp lightly. Do not substitute frozen okra here. For even cooking and browning, select okra pods that have approximately the same diameter. If you use a dark baking sheet, the browning time after removing the foil will be on the shorter end of the range. If desired, serve with Spicy Red Pepper Mayonnaise (recipe follows) by spreading the mixture onto a serving platter and arranging the okra on top. Alternatively, squeeze lemon or lime juice onto the roasted okra and/or sprinkle it with your favorite spice blend.

 1 **pound fresh okra, caps trimmed and halved lengthwise**
 2 **teaspoons vegetable oil**
 ½ **teaspoon table salt**

1. Adjust oven rack to middle position and heat oven to 425 degrees.

2. Toss okra with oil and salt in bowl until well combined. Arrange okra, cut sides down, in single layer on rimmed baking sheet. Cover tightly with aluminum foil and roast until okra is bright green, 12 to 15 minutes (cut sides of a few pieces may be beginning to brown). Remove foil and roast until cut sides are well browned, 7 to 12 minutes.

3. Let okra rest on sheet for 5 minutes. Serve.

KEYS TO SUCCESS

- **Oven roasting:** Enhances okra's nutty flavor and minimizes its slick texture

- **Foil on, foil off:** Helps okra roast evenly given its shape

SPICY RED PEPPER MAYONNAISE

Serves: 4
Total Time: 25 minutes

For a less spicy mayonnaise, use just a pinch of cayenne pepper.

 2 **teaspoons vegetable oil**
 5 **garlic cloves, minced**
 ¾ **teaspoon smoked paprika**
 ¾ **teaspoon ground coriander**
 ¾ **teaspoon ground cumin**
   Pinch to ⅛ teaspoon cayenne pepper
 ⅓ **cup jarred roasted red peppers, patted dry and minced**
 ½ **teaspoon table salt**
 ¼ **teaspoon sugar**
 3 **tablespoons mayonnaise**
 ¼ **teaspoon grated lime zest plus ½ teaspoon juice**

1. Heat oil in 8-inch skillet over medium heat until shimmering. Add garlic and cook, stirring frequently, until garlic just starts to brown, about 2 minutes. Add paprika, coriander, cumin, and cayenne and cook, stirring constantly, until fragrant, about 30 seconds. Immediately transfer to bowl. Stir in red peppers, salt, and sugar and refrigerate for at least 5 minutes.

2. Stir mayonnaise and lime zest and juice into red pepper mixture and serve.

CHARRED SICHUAN-STYLE OKRA

Serves: 4
Total Time: 30 minutes

RECIPE OVERVIEW Since okra stands up so well to the heat and punch of Creole cuisine, it makes sense that it would also pair well with a spicy Sichuan flavor profile. Start by making a concentrated chile oil, with the tingle-inducing flavor of Sichuan peppercorns. Broad bean chili paste gives the sauce heat and the distinct umami of fermented beans. Hoisin sauce and rice wine bring sweetness, acidity, and body to the sauce. Last but not least, scallions provide fresh balance. Charring the okra pods whole before cloaking them with the sauce lends a beautiful sear to the exterior and keeps good texture on the inside. Altogether, this is a sumptuous showstopper of a dish. If you can't find dried bird chiles (Thai red chiles), you can substitute ground red pepper flakes. Use a spice grinder to grind the bird chiles and Sichuan peppercorns. Do not substitute frozen okra here.

- ⅓ cup plus 2 tablespoons vegetable oil, divided
- 2 garlic cloves, sliced thin
- 1 (½-inch) piece fresh ginger, peeled and sliced into thin rounds
- 5 dried bird chiles, ground fine (1½ teaspoons)
- 1 teaspoon Sichuan peppercorns, ground fine (½ teaspoon)
- 1 star anise pod
- 6 tablespoons Shaoxing wine or dry sherry, divided
- ¼ cup hoisin sauce
- 3 tablespoons Asian broad bean chili paste or sauce
- 1 pound okra, stemmed
- ¼ cup water
- 6 scallions, white parts sliced thin on bias, green parts cut into 1-inch pieces
- 12 sprigs fresh cilantro, chopped coarse

1. Combine ⅓ cup oil, garlic, ginger, ground chiles, ground Sichuan peppercorns, and star anise in small saucepan and cook over medium-high heat until sizzling, 1 to 2 minutes. Reduce heat to low and gently simmer until garlic and ginger are softened but not browned, about 5 minutes. Let cool off heat for 5 minutes, then stir in 2 tablespoons Shaoxing wine, hoisin, and chili paste until combined; set aside.

2. Heat remaining 2 tablespoons oil in 12-inch skillet over medium-high heat until just smoking. Add okra and cook, stirring occasionally, until okra is crisp-tender and well browned on most sides, 5 to 7 minutes.

3. Stir remaining ¼ cup Shaoxing wine, water, and scallion greens and whites into skillet with okra, reduce heat to medium, and cook until liquid is reduced by half and scallion greens are just wilted, about 15 seconds. Off heat, stir in garlic-hoisin mixture until combined. Discard star anise and sprinkle with cilantro. Serve immediately.

Charring Okra

BROWN PODS
Cook whole okra in hot oil over medium-high heat until pods are well-browned on most sides and still crisp-tender.

ADD LIQUID AND REDUCE
Add Shaoxing wine, water, and scallions to okra, lower heat, and cook until liquid is reduced by half and scallion greens are wilted.

STIR IN SAUCE
Remove skillet from heat and stir Sichuan sauce into okra. Remove star anise pod.

DEEP-FRIED OKRA

Serves: 4 to 6
Total Time: 30 minutes, plus 30 minutes chilling

RECIPE OVERVIEW Hailed as a Southern staple, fried okra is an indulgent treat that, for many, is simply the only way to eat okra. For the ultimate crunchy bite, cut the pods into pieces so that the interior mucilage will evaporate when it hits the hot oil. For a light and crispy fried exterior that won't crumble and fall off the okra when you bite into it, you make a "glue" of buttermilk and egg to dip the pieces in before dredging in a cornmeal mixture. The ratio of cornmeal to cornstarch to all-purpose flour is key in creating a crunchy outer fried shell that adheres well. The cornmeal is crucial for the classic Southern fried flavor profile, the cornstarch adds a light crispy effect, and the flour adds the glutinous structure needed to ensure that the coating stays put. Add a final flavorful stir-in of garlic powder and cayenne to the blend before dredging and frying. While we prefer the flavor and texture of fresh okra in this recipe, you can substitute frozen cut okra, thawed and thoroughly patted dry, for fresh. We recommend frying in three batches if using frozen okra.

2/3 cup buttermilk
1 large egg
3/4 cup cornmeal
1/2 cup cornstarch
1/4 cup all-purpose flour
1 teaspoon garlic powder
1/2 teaspoon cayenne pepper
1 1/2 teaspoons table salt
1/4 teaspoon pepper
1 pound okra, stemmed and cut into 1-inch pieces
3 quarts peanut or vegetable oil
    Lemon wedges
    Hot sauce

1. Adjust oven rack to middle position and heat oven to 200 degrees. Line rimmed baking sheet with parchment paper. Set wire rack in second rimmed baking sheet and line with triple layer of paper towels.

2. Whisk buttermilk and egg together in shallow dish. Whisk cornmeal, cornstarch, flour, garlic powder, cayenne, salt, and pepper together in second shallow dish. Working in batches, dip okra in buttermilk mixture, letting excess drip back into dish. Dredge in cornmeal mixture, pressing firmly to adhere; transfer to parchment-lined sheet. Refrigerate, uncovered, for at least 30 minutes or up to 4 hours.

3. Add oil to large Dutch oven until it measures about 2 inches deep and heat over medium-high heat to 375 degrees. Carefully add half of okra to oil and fry, stirring as needed to prevent sticking, until okra is golden and crisp, 2 to 4 minutes. Adjust burner if necessary to maintain oil temperature between 350 and 375 degrees. Using wire skimmer or slotted spoon, transfer okra to prepared rack. Season with salt and transfer to oven to keep warm.

4. Return oil to 375 degrees and repeat with remaining okra. Serve immediately with lemon wedges and hot sauce.

KEYS TO SUCCESS

- **Cut okra into pieces:** Turns interior crunchy
- **Deep frying:** Hot oil eliminates okra's interior viscous liquid.

CAJUN PICKLED OKRA
Makes: two 1-pint jars
Total Time: 30 minutes

RECIPE OVERVIEW For an okra pickle packed with punchy Cajun flavor, you need a spicy, aromatic brine. This one includes a hefty dose of cayenne pepper and smoked paprika for both bright fiery heat and some slightly sweet smoky flavor. Oregano adds a nice roundness to the red spices. Spooning raw minced garlic straight into the jars alongside the okra (rather than steeping it in the brine first) builds the sharp, peppery backbone needed to make these pickles the ultimate Cajun treat. This pickle needs one week for the brine to fully penetrate the okra and for the flavors to develop, but it will continue to get more crisp as it sits in the refrigerator. Do not substitute frozen okra here.

1 1/2 cups white wine vinegar
1 cup water
2 tablespoons sugar
2 tablespoons kosher salt
1 teaspoon smoked paprika
1 teaspoon dried oregano
1/2 teaspoon cayenne pepper
6 garlic cloves, minced
14 ounces okra, stemmed

1. Bring vinegar, water, sugar, salt, paprika, oregano, and cayenne to boil in medium saucepan over medium-high heat; cover and remove from heat.

2. Fill two 1-pint jars with hot water to warm. Drain jars, then portion garlic into warm jars. Tightly pack okra vertically into jars, alternating the pods upside down and right side up for best fit.

3. Return brine to brief boil. Using funnel and ladle, pour hot brine over okra to cover. Let jars cool to room temperature, cover with lids, and refrigerate for 1 week before serving. (Pickled okra can be refrigerated for at least 6 months; okra will become crisper and flavor will mature over time.)

KEYS TO SUCCESS

- **Add smoky heat and spice to the brine:** With cayenne, smoked paprika, and raw garlic
- **Pickling:** The salt pulls out moisture, creating crunchy pods.

OKRA AND SHRIMP STEW

Serves: 8 to 10
Total Time: 4 hours 50 minutes

RECIPE OVERVIEW When Amethyst Ganaway makes this thick okra and shrimp stew it reminds her of her childhood home. The stew, well-known in the Carolina Lowcountry, is a long-simmered, complexly flavored mix of vegetables and seafood that takes a bit of time, but the investment is well worth it. Okra and shrimp stew is a gumbo-style dish. In fact, the word "gumbo" is derived from the West African word "gombo," which literally means "okra." But unlike the more familiar Louisiana-style gumbos, Lowcountry gumbos do not rely upon a deep-brown roux or filé powder for flavor and texture. Bright-green okra, with its sticky, slimy character, serves as a natural thickener; and the stew starts with a flavorful, slow-simmered broth made from a large smoked ham bone. If you can find medium shrimp (41 to 50 per pound), use those and leave them whole. Look for meaty ham hocks. If you buy the test kitchen's preferred brand of sausage, Jacob's World Famous Andouille, which is thicker than other products, halve it lengthwise before slicing it crosswise. You can substitute frozen okra here.

4	quarts water
1–1¼	pounds smoked ham hocks
1	onion, quartered
1	bay leaf
1	tablespoon vegetable oil
12	ounces andouille sausage, sliced ¼ inch thick
1	pound fresh okra, stemmed and cut crosswise ½ inch thick
1	(14.5-ounce) can diced tomatoes
1½	cups frozen baby lima (aka butter) beans
4	garlic cloves, minced
2	teaspoons table salt
1	teaspoon pepper
1	teaspoon granulated garlic
1	teaspoon onion powder
½	teaspoon paprika
1	pound large shrimp (26 to 30 per pound), peeled, deveined, and tails removed, cut into thirds
	Cooked white rice

1. Combine water, ham hocks, onion, and bay leaf in large Dutch oven and bring to boil over high heat. Reduce heat to medium-low; cover, with lid slightly ajar; and simmer until ham hocks are fork-tender, 2½ to 3 hours.

2. Remove pot from heat and transfer ham hocks to cutting board. Let ham hocks rest until cool enough to handle; discard onion and bay leaf from broth. Transfer broth to large bowl; measure out 8 cups broth (add enough water to equal 8 cups if necessary; reserve any excess for another use). Remove ham from bones, discard bones, and cut ham into bite-size pieces. (Broth and chopped ham can be refrigerated separately for up to 2 days. If fat solidifies on top of broth after chilling, you can discard fat before proceeding, if preferred.)

3. Heat oil in now-empty pot over medium-high heat until shimmering. Add sausage and cook until lightly browned on both sides, about 5 minutes. Add okra, tomatoes and their juice, beans, minced garlic, salt, pepper, granulated garlic, onion powder, paprika, 8 cups broth, and ham to pot. Bring to boil over high heat.

4. Reduce heat to medium and cook at strong simmer, uncovered, until reduced by about half and thickened to stew-like consistency, 55 minutes to 1 hour 5 minutes, stirring occasionally. Reduce heat to low; stir in shrimp; and cook until shrimp are just cooked through, about 3 minutes. Remove from heat and season with salt and pepper to taste. Serve over rice.

KEYS TO SUCCESS

- **Potent ham hock broth:** Serves as the base for the stew

- **Ham hock meat and andouille sausage:** Add an assertive, smoky meaty flavor

- **Frozen baby lima beans:** Cook up soft and creamy and soak up the rich broth

Making Okra and Shrimp Stew

CREATE BROTH
Simmer ham hocks, onion, and bay leaf in water to create rich broth.

CHOP HAM
When cool enough to handle, chop ham into bite-size pieces.

BROWN SAUSAGE
Brown sausage, then add vegetables, ham, and 8 cups reserved broth.

ADD SHRIMP
Simmer stew until thickened, then add shrimp at end of cooking.

SHOPPING AND STORAGE

Okra has become more available throughout the country, not just in the South, but its best season is summer and into the fall. When shopping for the varietal of okra most commonly found in American markets, size is an important consideration. Look for firm, unblemished fresh okra pods that are no longer than 3 inches in length. Pods larger than that will often be tough, and no cooking method will prevent them from becoming slimy. Okra is more perishable than most vegetables; store the fresh pods in a paper bag in the refrigerator for just a day or two.

Frozen Can Be A-OK

Although we typically prefer fresh okra to frozen, there are certain times when using frozen okra provides higher convenience and greater accessibility without sacrificing anything in the way of flavor. Namely, if you are making stewy types of dishes, like our Okra and Shrimp Stew (page 144), frozen works as well as fresh. For okra cooked using dry, high heat, such as Sautéed Okra (page 140), fresh is still best.

IT'S ALL USABLE!

Chris Smith, gardener and author of *The Whole Okra* (2019), thinks his muse deserves more recognition: "[Okra has] all these benefits that no one is currently recognizing on any kind of scale." For one thing, he says, most parts of the lush plant—not just the seed pods—can be consumed: The eye-catching flowers can be enjoyed straight from the garden or dried and steeped to make tea; the nutritious young leaves are wonderful braised; and the protein-rich mature seeds are "so, so delicious" when roasted and ground into a flour that "is nutty and smells like coffee." Even the stalks, he said, can be used as a fiber crop.

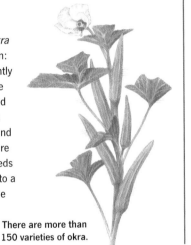

There are more than 150 varieties of okra.

WHY DOES OKRA TURN SLIMY?

Okra contains a substance called mucilage, which is a naturally occurring pectin-like substance also found in seaweeds, aloe and other cacti, and flaxseed. It's made up of chains of sugar molecules (called exopolysaccharides) secreted outside the okra pod's cells and glycoproteins. Just like other food gels we're more familiar with, like gelatin and cornstarch slurry, okra's starches need both heat and water to fully form a gel. The molecules are loosened by the heat, and they then form a microscopic network that retains the water. This is why okra's mucilage viscosity increases with exposure to heat and water—in other words, this is why cooked okra is sometimes unpalatably slimy.

Dry heat above 190°F damages the sugar-molecule chains so that they're less able to turn viscous. For this reason, many okra recipes call for dry, high heat (like Deep-Fried Okra, page 142), which keeps the okra as crisp as possible with minimal sliminess.

USING SCIENCE TO DICTATE TEXTURE

Okra can have two distinctly different characters, depending on how it's cooked. Its slick texture is formed by polysaccharides that dissolve in water to make a slippery gel. Thus, slowly stewing the vegetable exploits its gooey properties, eventually releasing most of its polysaccharides to create a thick, silky consistency. Conversely, a dry cooking method such as roasting bypasses slipperiness: In the heat of the oven, okra's mucilage dehydrates and clings to the inside of the pod. When the okra is chewed, this mucilage doesn't have time to dissolve and form a gel.

H$_2$O Is Key
Add or limit water, depending on the outcome you desire.

FERMENTED VEGETABLES

NICOLE KONSTANTINAKOS

Though fermented foods are particularly hot these days, fermenting has been around for millennia. The preserving process of fermentation relies on the cultivation of microorganisms, including beneficial bacteria. Fermented vegetables rely on the help of good bacteria and storage conditions to create the proper acidic environment. The acids "pickle" the vegetables and provide a fascinating array of fermented flavors and taste sensations. The process is simple: Cut up vegetables, submerge in salt brine, store at room temperature, and wait. The reward? Crispy, crunchy, sour pickles with very little work. You'll learn how to use this technique to make sauerkraut, kimchi, dill pickles, and beets.

NICOLE'S PRO TIP: *Since the optimal temperature for fermentation—50 to 70 degrees Fahrenheit—is warmer than your refrigerator, and likely to be cooler than your kitchen, if you plan to prepare a lot of fermented vegetables you might consider investing in a small refrigerated wine cooler. It would allow you to easily control the temperature and help contain the heady aromas of all of your projects.*

THE METHOD
SAUERKRAUT

Here are the steps that show how to ferment cabbage the traditional way.

1 SHRED CABBAGE
Cut cabbage into similar-size shreds to ensure jar will ferment at same rate. To easily shred cabbage, quarter and core cabbage then make smaller stacks of leaves. Press leaves flat to counter and carefully slice them into thin, uniform strips.

2 SALT CABBAGE
Toss cabbage with kosher salt, then knead with your hands until cabbage has softened and released some liquid. You need this liquid to start fermentation process and keep cabbage submerged in jar.

3 PACK JAR
As you fill jar with salted cabbage, use your fist to pack it as tightly as possible and remove any air pockets. When done, press a parchment round flush against cabbage.

4 SUBMERGE CABBAGE
To help cabbage stay fully submerged, place bag of brine on top to weigh it down. Use brine, not water, in case bag breaks; that way it won't ruin the balance of salinity in jar.

5 COVER JAR
Place triple layer of cheesecloth over mouth of jar to help fermentation gases escape while keeping out debris. Be sure to re-cover jar with cheesecloth every time you check it.

6 AIM FOR 65 DEGREES
It is crucial to monitor temperature of fermentation environment. Use a good thermometer to keep track of temperature of room. A fermentation temperature of about 65 degrees is best.

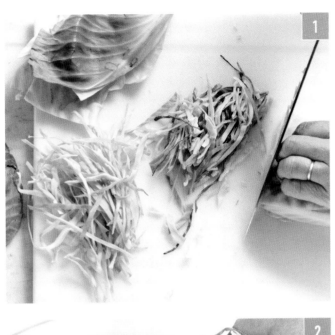

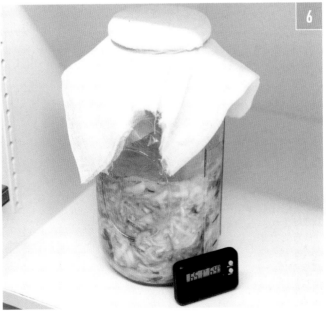

SAUERKRAUT

Makes: about 1½ quarts
Total Time: 20 minutes, plus 6–13 days fermenting

RECIPE OVERVIEW Sauerkraut packs a big flavor punch, and yet it's nothing more than shredded cabbage and salt that have been left to ferment. Naturally occurring bacteria do all the work: They devour sugars in the cabbage, producing lactic acid. This acidity and the complex flavor compounds they produce lend their trademark flavor. The kosher salt keeps bad bacteria at bay, so the salinity here is crucial. Too little salt, and the kraut wilts and spoils too quickly. Too much salt and the fermentation slows to a halt; this means that the sauerkraut won't become acidic enough and bad bacteria are free to take over. A fermentation temperature of about 65 degrees is best; too cool and the cabbage won't ferment, too hot and the sauerkraut will be mushy and overly funky. To keep the cabbage submerged, place a bag of brine on top. We like to use brine rather than water, because if the bag breaks it won't ruin the careful balance of salinity inside the jar. This sauerkraut cannot be processed for long-term storage.

2½ pounds green cabbage (1 head), quartered, cored, and sliced into ⅛-inch-thick shreds (7 cups)
2 tablespoons Diamond Crystal kosher salt, divided
1½ teaspoons juniper berries
2 cups water

1. Cut out parchment paper round to match diameter of ½-gallon wide-mouth jar. Toss cabbage with 4 teaspoons salt in large bowl. Using your hands, forcefully knead salt into cabbage until it has softened and begins to release moisture, about 3 minutes. Stir in juniper berries.

2. Tightly pack cabbage mixture and any accumulated liquid into jar, pressing down firmly with your fist to eliminate air pockets as you pack. Press parchment round flush against surface of cabbage.

3. Dissolve remaining 2 teaspoons salt in water and transfer to 1-quart zipper-lock plastic bag; squeeze out air and seal bag well. Place bag of brine on top of parchment and gently press down. Cover jar with triple layer of cheesecloth and secure with rubber band.

4. Place jar in 50- to 70-degree location away from direct sunlight and let ferment for 6 days; check jar daily, skimming residue from surface and pressing to keep cabbage submerged. After 6 days, taste sauerkraut daily until it has reached desired flavor (this may take up to 7 days longer; sauerkraut should be pale and translucent with a tart and floral flavor).

5. When sauerkraut has reached desired flavor, remove cheesecloth, bag of brine, and parchment, and skim off any residue. Serve. (Sauerkraut and accumulated juices can be transferred to clean jar, covered, and refrigerated for up to 6 weeks; once refrigerated, flavor of sauerkraut will continue to mature.)

KEYS TO SUCCESS

- **Proper prep:** Cut cabbage into even shreds so that they ferment at the same rate.
- **Foolproof preserving:** Method produces crunchy, pleasantly sour-tasting kraut.

KIMCHI

Makes: about 2 quarts
Total Time: 30 minutes, plus 1 hour salting, plus 9–20 days fermenting

RECIPE OVERVIEW There are many kinds of kimchi, the Korean pickle of fermented vegetables. This recipe uses napa cabbage, scallions, and carrots. It's the fermentation process that gives kimchi its signature flavor. First salt napa cabbage to remove excess water. For flavor, make a paste of garlic, ginger, gochugaru (Korean chili powder), sugar, fish sauce, and soy sauce—this brings complexity and heat. To eliminate air pockets and keep the cabbage submerged in its juices, place a plastic bag of water on top; use two bags to help prevent leaking. (We use water instead of brine in the bag here because there is so much salt in the kimchi.) The ideal environment for fermenting is between 50 and 70 degrees (do not ferment above 70 degrees). The fermentation temperature will affect the timing and flavor of the kimchi; warmer temperatures will ferment more quickly and produce sharper flavors. For a balanced flavor, we prefer a fermentation temperature of 65 degrees. If you can't find gochugaru (which has a mild, fruity flavor), you can substitute ⅓ cup red pepper flakes. This kimchi cannot be processed for long-term storage.

1 (2½-pound) head napa cabbage, cored and cut into 2-inch pieces
5 teaspoons Diamond Crystal kosher salt
20 garlic cloves, peeled
1 (2-inch) piece fresh ginger, peeled and chopped coarse
½ cup gochugaru
⅓ cup sugar
¼ cup low-sodium soy sauce
3 tablespoons fish sauce
16 scallions, cut into 2-inch pieces
1 carrot, peeled and cut into 2-inch matchsticks

1. Toss cabbage with salt in bowl, cover, and let sit at room temperature for 1 hour. Transfer cabbage to colander, squeeze to drain excess liquid, and return to now-empty bowl. Cut out parchment paper round to match diameter of ½-gallon wide-mouth jar.

2. Process garlic, ginger, gochugaru, sugar, soy sauce, and fish sauce in food processor until no large pieces of garlic or ginger remain, about 20 seconds. Add garlic mixture, scallions, and carrot to cabbage and toss to combine. Tightly pack vegetable mixture into jar, pressing down firmly with your fist to eliminate air pockets as you pack. Press parchment round flush against surface of vegetables.

3. Fill 1-quart zipper-lock bag with 1 cup water, squeeze out air, and seal well. Place inside second zipper-lock bag, squeeze out air, and seal well. Place bag of water on top of parchment and gently press down. Cover jar with triple layer of cheesecloth and secure with rubber band.

4. Place jar in 50- to 70-degree location away from direct sunlight and let ferment for 9 days; check jar daily, skimming residue from surface and pressing to keep mixture submerged. After 9 days, taste kimchi daily until it has reached desired flavor (this may take up to 11 days longer; cabbage should be soft and translucent with a pleasant cheesy, fishy flavor).

5. When kimchi has reached desired flavor, remove cheesecloth, bag of water, and parchment, and skim off any residue. Serve. (Kimchi and accumulated juice can be transferred to clean jar, covered, and refrigerated for up to 3 months; once refrigerated, kimchi will continue to soften and develop flavor.)

KEYS TO SUCCESS

- **Salt the cabbage**: To rid it of excess water which helps it stay crisp
- **Pack the jar tightly**: Helps the vegetables stay submerged

SOUR DILL PICKLES

Makes: 12 pickles
Total Time: 15 minutes, plus 3 hours salting, plus 7–14 days fermenting

RECIPE OVERVIEW When it comes to "full sour" dill pickles, it's all about the tangy flavor and the crunch. For assertive flavor, add fresh dill, dill seeds, garlic, and peppercorns to the pickling jar along with the cucumbers and brine. It is crucial that the brine be completely cool before pouring it into the jar, since warm brine could hinder the fermentation process. Also, if the brine is warm, it will soften the cucumbers and make the pickles mushy. To get crisp pickles, we attempted every technique we could find. We tried adding a grape leaf and a black tea bag; these contain tannic acid that deactivates the enzymes responsible for softening. We also used pricey sea salts containing minerals that inhibit softening. While delivering slightly more crisp pickles than if we didn't use these ingredients, these methods either added off-flavors or were too expensive. Then we tried salting the cucumbers with regular kosher salt for 3 hours before pickling. These pickles were significantly crunchier, without tasting off. Trim off both ends of the cucumbers. One of the ends (the nonstem end) can be responsible for making cucumber pickles lose their crispness when left intact. For the most balanced flavor, we prefer a fermentation temperature of 65 degrees. These pickles cannot be processed for long-term storage.

12 small pickling cucumbers (3 to 4 ounces each),
 ends trimmed
3 tablespoons Diamond Crystal kosher salt, divided
7 cups water
20 sprigs fresh dill
5 garlic cloves, smashed and peeled
1 tablespoon dill seeds
1½ teaspoons black peppercorns

1. Toss cucumbers with 1 tablespoon salt in bowl and refrigerate for 3 hours. Drain cucumbers in colander; do not rinse.

2. Meanwhile, bring water and remaining 2 tablespoons salt to boil in medium saucepan over high heat. Remove from heat and let cool completely.

3. Cut out parchment paper round to match diameter of ½-gallon wide-mouth jar. Tightly pack cucumbers, dill sprigs, garlic, dill seeds, and peppercorns into jar, leaving 2½ inches headspace. Pour cooled brine over cucumbers to cover. Press parchment round flush against surface of brine.

4. Fill 1-quart zipper-lock bag with ½ cup brine, squeeze out air, and seal well; discard excess brine. Place bag of brine on top of parchment and gently press down to submerge cucumbers. Cover jar with triple layer of cheesecloth and secure with rubber band.

5. Place jar in 50- to 70-degree location away from direct sunlight and let ferment for 7 days; check jar daily, skimming residue from surface and pressing to keep pickles submerged. After 7 days, taste pickles daily until they have reached desired flavor (this may take up to 7 days longer; pickles will look darker and have an earthy and tangy flavor).

6. When pickles have reached desired flavor, discard cheesecloth, bag of brine, and parchment; skim off any residue. Serve. (Pickles and brine can be transferred to clean jar, covered, and refrigerated for up to 1 month; once refrigerated, flavor of pickles will continue to mature.)

KEYS TO SUCCESS
- **Salt the cucumbers:** The long salting time helps the pickles achieve a good crisp texture.
- **Let the brine cool completely:** Warm brine will make the pickles soft and mushy and might inhibit fermentation.

BEETS AND BEET KVASS

Makes: about 3 cups fermented beets and 2½ cups beet kvass
Total Time: 15 minutes, plus 7–9 days fermenting

RECIPE OVERVIEW Most people associate pickled beets with the cloyingly sweet, soft, and syrupy product sold in grocery stores. Those descriptors don't jibe with the things we value in a good pickle—crispiness, crunch, salt, acidity, and refreshment. Here beets redeem themselves, with fermentation. As a bonus, the brine is imparted with sweetness from the sugar in the beets, making a delicious product on its own,

known in Eastern Europe as kvass (and containing a healthy dose of probiotics). You will need a container of at least 3 quarts so you have enough room for both the beets and the bag of brine that will sit on top of them. We found that a 9-day fermentation produced our favorite pickle.

1 pound red beets (2 large beets), rinsed and peeled
5 cups water
7½ teaspoons Diamond Crystal kosher salt

1. Using mandoline, slice beets ¹⁄₁₆-inch thick. Whisk water and salt in clean 3-quart (or larger) container until salt is dissolved. Transfer 2 cups brine to 1-quart zipper-lock bag; squeeze out air and seal bag well. (This bag of brine acts as a weight, keeping the beet slices submerged so that they ferment properly.) Add beets to remaining brine in 3-quart container and press down to submerge. Cut piece of parchment paper to match surface area of beets; press parchment flush against surface of beets. Place bag of brine on top of parchment and gently press down. Cover container tightly with 3 layers of cheesecloth. Secure cheesecloth in place with rubber bands and place container in 50- to 70-degree location away from direct sunlight.

2. Let beets ferment for 7 days; check container daily, skimming residue from surface and pressing to keep beets submerged. (When fermenting pickles, a white mold-like substance can quickly accumulate on the surface of the brining liquid. This is not mold but a harmless accumulation called kahm yeast that needs to be removed.) After 7 days, taste beets daily until they have reached desired flavor. They should be sweet, sour, and crisp.

3. Discard bag of brine and parchment and skim off any residue. Drain beets, reserving pickling liquid (kvass). Serve. (Leftover beets and kvass can be combined in clean airtight container and refrigerated for up to 1 month; once refrigerated, flavor of beets will continue to mature.)

KEYS TO SUCCESS
- **Peel beets and slice thin:** Makes for crisp pickles
- **A plastic bag of brine keeps the beets submerged:** If the bag breaks, brine won't dilute the salinity of the pickling brine.

A Word About Pickling Salt

When fermenting vegetables, it is important to use salt that is free of additives (iodine or anticaking agents), which can produce off-flavors and hazy brines and can inhibit the growth of good microbes. Diamond Crystal kosher salt contains only salt. You can also seek out pickling salt. Pickling salt can be substituted for Diamond Crystal kosher salt 1 for 1 by mass (grams). If measuring by volume, use 50 percent as much Morton Canning & Pickling Salt.

SALADS

COURSE

GREEN SALADS BEYOND LETTUCE

JACK BISHOP

It's always exciting to explore new specimens from the wide world of greens and use them to create an interesting salad in your bowl. This course will help you to expand your salad green options. You can choose bitter greens like frisée and escarole, fresh herbs, or wild greens like purslane. Purslane grows readily in the wild but is most likely available at your local farmers' market, a great place to investigate and source all kinds of salad materials.

JACK'S PRO TIP: *My kids call me the salad whisperer. My secrets? I get the greens really, really dry before dressing them. I spin them dry and then use towels to remove the last traces of moisture. And I add the dressing in two batches. I hate overdressed salad, and until you toss the greens with the first batch of dressing it can be hard to tell if you need more.*

MÂCHE SALAD WITH CUCUMBER AND MINT

Serves: 6 to 8
Total Time: 20 minutes

RECIPE OVERVIEW Mâche, also called lamb's lettuce, is a soft, tender green that grows in delicate rosettes and is beloved in French kitchens for its sweet, nutty flavor. Turn this baby lettuce into an elegant side salad by pairing it with the crisp, fresh flavor of thinly sliced cucumber. Fresh mint adds brightness, and crunchy pine nuts reinforce the mâche's buttery notes. Keep the dressing simple with just lemon juice, fresh herbs, and minced garlic, plus capers for some briny contrast. Mâche is a very delicate green, so be sure to handle it gently and make sure it is thoroughly dry before tossing it with the vinaigrette. If you can't find mâche, you can substitute either baby spinach or mesclun.

- 12 ounces (12 cups) mâche
- 1 cucumber, sliced thin
- ½ cup chopped fresh mint or parsley
- ⅓ cup pine nuts, toasted
- ¼ cup extra-virgin olive oil
- 1 tablespoon lemon juice
- 1 tablespoon minced fresh parsley or cilantro
- 1 tablespoon capers, rinsed and minced
- 1 teaspoon minced fresh thyme or rosemary
- 1 garlic clove, minced
- ¼ teaspoon table salt
- ¼ teaspoon pepper

Gently toss mâche, cucumber, mint, and pine nuts together in large bowl. Whisk oil, lemon juice, parsley, capers, thyme, garlic, salt, and pepper together in small bowl. Drizzle dressing over salad and toss gently to coat. Season with salt and pepper to taste. Serve.

KEYS TO SUCCESS

- **Delicate greens:** Buttery soft lettuce makes for a tender salad.
- **Herby lemony vinaigrette:** Provides a bright counterpoint to the greens
- **Toasted pine nuts:** Add light crunchy contrast

HERB SALAD

Serves: 4 to 6
Total Time: 10 minutes

RECIPE OVERVIEW Tender herbs can be more than an accent in salads; in many cuisines, whole or torn leaves are lightly dressed and served as a refreshing, intensely flavorful accompaniment to grilled, fried, and roasted dishes. All we need to take herbs from garnish to refreshing salad is a simple vinaigrette of lemon juice and olive oil to perfectly complement the herbs' bold flavors. Be sure to use vibrant, high-quality herbs; to wash and dry them thoroughly (excess liquid can wilt the leaves or dilute the dressing); and to dress them lightly. For the mixed tender herb leaves, we suggest any combination of dill, chives, chervil, and tarragon. To introduce more dynamic color and texture, add up to ½ cup of thinly sliced vegetables, such as radishes, shallots, fennel, or celery.

- 3 tablespoons extra-virgin olive oil
- ¼ teaspoon grated lemon zest plus 1 tablespoon juice
- ¼ teaspoon kosher salt
- 2 cups fresh parsley leaves
- 2 cups mixed tender herb leaves

Add oil, lemon zest and juice, and salt to large bowl. Season with pepper to taste and whisk to thoroughly combine. Add parsley and herb leaves and toss until evenly coated with dressing. Season with salt to taste. Serve immediately.

KEYS TO SUCCESS

- **Superfresh herbs:** Since the herbs are this salad, seek out the best ones.
- **Vegetable additions:** Add-ins such as radishes and fennel add crunch as well as color.
- **Superlight dressing:** Using just EVOO and lemon juice keeps the focus on the greens.

BITTER GREENS SALAD WITH OLIVES AND FETA

Serves: 4 to 6
Total Time: 20 minuutes

RECIPE OVERVIEW This recipe re-creates a salad traditionally eaten in Greece that is composed of a seasonal blend of pleasantly peppery, bitter greens—it's a far cry from the neighborhood pizza shop version of Greek salad. Romaine, an obvious choice to create a nice neutral base for a salad, doesn't have enough bitterness, even when mixed with peppery chicory greens. But a combination of escarole and frisée, which have crisp bite and plenty of spicy, bitter flavor, works well. Dill is a classic component of many bitter greens salads, so we include a full ⅓ cup to allow its clean, slightly sweet flavor to really shine. We then accent the greens with a bright lemon vinaigrette, a mix of briny feta and kalamata olives, and tangy, slightly spicy pepperoncini peppers. If you prefer more heat, do not seed the pepperoncini.

- 1 head escarole (1 pound), trimmed and cut into 1-inch pieces
- 1 small head frisée (4 ounces), trimmed and torn into 1-inch pieces
- ½ cup pitted kalamata olives, halved
- 2 ounces feta cheese, crumbled (½ cup)
- ⅓ cup pepperoncini, seeded and cut into ¼-inch-thick strips
- ⅓ cup chopped fresh dill
- 2 tablespoons lemon juice
- 1 garlic clove, minced
- ¼ teaspoon table salt
- ⅛ teaspoon pepper
- 3 tablespoons extra-virgin olive oil

Gently toss escarole, frisée, olives, feta, and pepperoncini together in large bowl. Whisk dill, lemon juice, garlic, salt, and pepper together in small bowl. Whisking constantly, slowly drizzle in oil. Drizzle dressing over salad and gently toss to coat. Serve.

> ## KEYS TO SUCCESS
> - **Escarole and frisée:** Their assertive flavor makes an authentic Greek salad.
> - **A lot of dill:** Complements the bitter greens
> - **Bring the briny:** Feta and olives add salty tang.

PURSLANE AND WATERMELON SALAD

Serves: 4 to 6
Total Time: 45 minutes

RECIPE OVERVIEW Purslane has crisp, juicy-sweet stems, tart, tangy, slightly peppery leaves, and the highest omega-3 fatty acid content of any plant, making it the perfect base for a salad. We pair it with watermelon because both are at their best in the summer. To start, we cube watermelon into 1-inch pieces, toss the pieces with sugar, and let them drain of any excess liquid. To gently balance the melon's sweetness and the purslane's tangy bite, we add thinly sliced shallot for delicate onion flavor. Tearing the fresh purslane into 1½-inch pieces ensures that every bite of salad has its flavor. Basil leaves bring freshness, torn fresh mozzarella adds creamy substance, and a simple vinaigrette of olive oil, cider vinegar, and lemon marries all the elements in delicate, savory harmony. This salad benefits from a liberal sprinkling of salt and pepper, so don't be shy when seasoning the salad at the end of step 2.

- 4 cups watermelon cut into 1-inch pieces
- 2 teaspoons sugar
- 2 tablespoons extra-virgin olive oil, plus extra for drizzling
- 1 tablespoon cider vinegar
- ½ teaspoon grated lemon zest plus 1 tablespoon juice
- ½ teaspoon table salt
- ¼ teaspoon pepper
- 6 ounces purslane, trimmed and torn into 1½-inch pieces (6 cups)
- ¼ cup fresh basil or parsley leaves, torn
- 1 shallot, sliced thin
- 6 ounces fresh mozzarella cheese, torn into 1-inch pieces

1. Toss watermelon with sugar in colander set over bowl; set aside and let sit for 30 minutes.

2. Whisk oil, vinegar, lemon zest and juice, salt, and pepper together in large bowl. Add purslane, basil, shallot, and drained watermelon and toss gently to combine. Transfer to serving platter and scatter mozzarella over top. Drizzle with extra oil and season with salt and pepper to taste. Serve.

> ## KEYS TO SUCCESS
> - **Sugaring the melon:** Draws out and removes extra moisture so melon stays firm
> - **Fresh basil:** Enhances the flavor of the purslane
> - **Easy lemon vinaigrette:** Unites the salad ingredients

WILTED SALADS

MORGAN BOLLING

Wilting sturdy greens or spinach with bacon fat for a warm salad is only the delicious beginning. This course ventures to bacon and beyond to explore different warm dressings and the greens that pair best with them. Citrus-infused olive oil and browned butter are just two of the fresh alternatives. Spinach is the typical choice for tossing with a warm vinaigrette, but there are plenty of other contenders to try: green leaf lettuce, frisée, arugula, chicory, endive, and pea greens. Happy wilting.

MORGAN'S PRO TIP: *I feel like there are times in life when it is worth splurging for expensive bacon. Killed salad is one of those times: The bacon plays a huge role, both with drippings in the vinaigrette and crisp bacon as a garnish. So use the best quality meat you can find.*

KILLED SALAD

Serves: 4
Total Time: 25 minutes

RECIPE OVERVIEW Far from "killed," this wilted mountain favorite (also called kilt salad, wilted salad, and smothered lettuce) is vibrant and lively. At its simplest, the traditional Appalachian dish is made by pouring hot bacon grease over greens to warm and barely wilt them. Six slices of bacon and 3 tablespoons of bacon fat enhance rather than overpower our sturdy green leaf lettuce, which holds up well under the hot dressing and wilts nicely. Cider vinegar cuts the richness of the bacon fat, and sugar tempers the acidity of the vinegar. Other firm greens, such as escarole, romaine, or red leaf lettuce, can be substituted for the green leaf lettuce, if desired.

1	head green leaf lettuce (12 ounces), torn into bite-size pieces
4	scallions, sliced thin
6	slices bacon, cut into ½-inch pieces
½	cup cider vinegar
3	tablespoons sugar
1	teaspoon table salt
½	teaspoon pepper

1. Combine lettuce and scallions in large bowl. Cook bacon in 10-inch nonstick skillet over medium heat until crispy, 6 to 8 minutes. Using slotted spoon, transfer bacon to paper towel–lined plate. Pour off all but 3 tablespoons fat from skillet (if you don't have 3 tablespoons, supplement with vegetable oil).

2. Return skillet to medium heat. Whisk in vinegar, sugar, salt, and pepper and bring to boil.

3. Once boiling, immediately pour hot dressing over lettuce-scallion mixture and toss to combine. Season with salt and pepper to taste. Serve, sprinkled with bacon.

KEYS TO SUCCESS

- **Use the bacon fat:** It becomes an integral part of the dressing.

- **Firm greens work best:** Green leaf lettuce stands up to the dressing.

- **Boiled dressing:** Cider vinegar adds tang and a bit of fruity sweetness.

1. Place goat cheese on plate and freeze until slightly firm, about 15 minutes.

2. Heat oil, grapefruit zest, shallot, and sugar in Dutch oven over medium-low heat until shallot is softened, about 5 minutes. Off heat, discard zest, stir in grapefruit juice, and add spinach. Cover and allow spinach to steam until just beginning to wilt, about 30 seconds.

3. Transfer spinach mixture to large bowl. Add strawberries, almonds, and goat cheese and toss to combine. Season with salt and pepper to taste. Serve.

KEYS TO SUCCESS

- **Freeze the cheese:** Keeps it from melting in the warm dressing
- **Use a Dutch oven:** Easy to both make the dressing and wilt the spinach
- **Use curly-leaf spinach:** It is the sturdiest spinach, so withstands the heat best.

Selecting Spinach

Tender flat-leaf and baby spinaches become soft and mushy when tossed with hot dressing. The heartier curly-leaf variety, wilted until just tender, stands up to the heat just fine.

Curly Spinach
Wilted winner

WILTED SPINACH SALAD WITH STRAWBERRIES, GOAT CHEESE, AND ALMONDS

Serves: 4 to 6
Total Time: 30 minutes

RECIPE OVERVIEW A bacon dressing tastes great in spinach salad, but here is a lighter approach to that typically rich salad. Tender flat-leaf and baby spinaches become soft and mushy when tossed with a hot olive oil dressing. The heartier curly-leaf variety, wilted until just tender, stands up to the heat just fine. Instead of the traditional bacon and bacon fat, we build this salad on a base of fruity extra-virgin olive oil and swap out the sharp vinegar usually called for in favor of tart grapefruit juice—and add a strip of zest to the hot oil to infuse the dressing with even more citrus flavor. Soft crumbled cheese beefs up the salad without bogging it down, especially after we quickly freeze the cheese to prevent it from melting in the heat of the dressing. Preparing the dressing in a Dutch oven and allowing the spinach to cook off the heat, covered with the dressing, for just 30 seconds produces a perfect, evenly wilted spinach salad. A handful of crunchy nuts adds a welcome textural contrast.

1½	ounces goat cheese or feta, crumbled (⅓ cup)
¼	cup extra-virgin olive oil
1	(3-inch) strip grapefruit zest plus 1½ tablespoons juice
1	shallot, minced
2	teaspoons sugar
10	ounces curly-leaf spinach, stemmed and torn into bite-size pieces
6	strawberries, hulled and sliced ¼ inch thick
¼	cup sliced almonds or chopped hazelnuts, toasted

FRISÉE SALAD WITH WARM BROWNED BUTTER–HAZELNUT VINAIGRETTE

Serves: 4 to 6
Total Time: 40 minutes

RECIPE OVERVIEW Frisée is a classic component in composed bistro salads but rarely gets to star in its own right. It has a distinct peppery-bitter flavor and a chewy texture that can be overwhelming if not treated correctly. A warm browned butter–hazelnut vinaigrette is ideal: It softens the greens, and its opulent flavor highlights and contrasts with the pepperiness of the frisée. Baby arugula both complements and tempers the frisée's natural flavor and texture. Cap this sophisticated salad with a few shavings of Manchego—its firm, crystalline texture and nutty flavor work perfectly.

3	tablespoons lemon juice
1	tablespoon whole-grain mustard
1	teaspoon sugar
¼	teaspoon table salt

1 shallot, halved through root end and sliced thin crosswise
¼ cup dried cranberries, chopped
5 tablespoons unsalted butter
⅓ cup hazelnuts, toasted, skinned, and chopped
2 heads frisée (10 ounces), torn into bite-size pieces
2 ounces (2 cups) baby arugula
2 ounces Manchego cheese, shaved

1. Whisk lemon juice, mustard, sugar, and salt together in small bowl. Add shallot and cranberries, cover tightly with plastic wrap, and microwave until steaming, 30 to 60 seconds. Stir briefly to submerge shallot. Let cool to room temperature, about 15 minutes.

2. Melt butter in 12-inch skillet over medium heat. Add hazelnuts and cook, stirring frequently, until butter is dark golden brown and fragrant, 3 to 5 minutes. Stir microwaved shallot mixture into butter mixture and let sit until heated through, about 30 seconds.

3. Gently toss frisée with warm vinaigrette in large bowl until evenly coated and wilted slightly. Add arugula and toss to combine. Season with salt and pepper to taste. Sprinkle with Manchego and serve.

KEYS TO SUCCESS

- **Use the microwave:** Easily heats the vinaigrette
- **Frisée and arugula:** This combo of greens makes a robust salad.
- **Warm vinaigrette:** Gently tenderizes the frisée

PEA GREEN SALAD WITH WARM APRICOT-PISTACHIO VINAIGRETTE

Serves: 4 to 6
Total Time: 40 minutes

RECIPE OVERVIEW Pea greens (also known as pea shoots or pea tendrils) are the young and tender leafy tips of the pea plant. Initially a farmers' market find in the spring and summer, they are increasingly appearing in the produce aisle of large supermarkets. Both the stems and the leaves of the pea plant are edible, making these delicate greens a lovely choice for a light salad. Complement the grassy pea greens with fresh peas, endive, and a warm, fruity vinaigrette that both offsets the faintly bitter quality of the pea greens and lightly wilts them. Steam the fresh peas in a skillet until just tender. In the same skillet, toast pistachios in oil and then take the skillet off the heat to add the rest of the dressing, as the hot oil will sizzle otherwise. The last step is simply to toss the warmed vinaigrette with the pea greens, cooked peas, and a bit of Belgian endive for crunch. You can substitute thawed frozen peas for the fresh peas; if using frozen peas, skip step 1.

Salad
1 pound shell-on English peas, shelled (1¼ cups)
8 ounces (8 cups) pea greens or microgreens
2 heads Belgian endive (8 ounces), trimmed, halved lengthwise, and sliced ¼ inch thick

Vinaigrette
3 tablespoons white wine vinegar
2 teaspoons whole-grain mustard
½ teaspoon sugar
¼ teaspoon table salt
½ cup dried apricots, chopped
1 small shallot, halved and sliced thin
3 tablespoons extra-virgin olive oil
⅓ cup shelled pistachios, chopped

1. FOR THE SALAD Bring peas and ¼ cup water to simmer in 10-inch skillet over medium-high heat. Cover, reduce heat to medium-low, and cook, stirring occasionally, until peas are tender, 5 to 7 minutes. Drain peas and set aside. Wipe skillet clean with paper towels.

2. FOR THE VINAIGRETTE Whisk vinegar, mustard, sugar, and salt together in medium bowl. Add apricots and shallot, cover, and microwave until steaming, 30 seconds to 1 minute. Stir to submerge shallot, then let cool completely, about 15 minutes. Heat oil in now-empty skillet over medium heat until shimmering. Add pistachios and cook, stirring frequently, until toasted and fragrant, 1 to 2 minutes. Off heat, stir in shallot mixture and let sit until heated through, about 30 seconds.

3. Gently toss cooked peas, pea greens, and endive with warm vinaigrette in large bowl until evenly coated and wilted slightly. Season with salt and pepper to taste. Serve.

- **Fresh peas:** Sweet and full of green pea goodness—when you can find them
- **Toasted pistachios:** Add nutty flavor and crunch to the salad
- **Warm vinaigrette:** Slightly wilts the greens

Early Growth of a Pea Plant

PEA SHOOTS
Pea shoots, or pea sprouts, are the first growth of a pea plant. If you spot them, buy them; delicate, sweet, and mild, they're around only briefly and are delicious raw. Sprinkle them over a dressed salad like you would alfalfa sprouts or microgreens.

PEA TENDRILS If you leave pea shoots alone, you'll soon have pea tendrils, the long, thin coils and leaves that spring out in every direction. Pea tendrils are more intense in flavor than pea shoots, but they add color and fresh spring flavor to salads and make a great garnish, too.

PEA GREENS In the third stage of growth, you get pea greens, which you can harvest for use in our salad on the facing page. The rounded, bright-green, faintly bitter leaves taste of fresh peas but without their sweetness, and they are delicious in pesto, too.

BITTER GREENS, CARROT, AND CHICKPEA SALAD WITH WARM LEMON DRESSING

Serves: 4
Total Time: 40 minutes

RECIPE OVERVIEW Sometimes drizzling a hot vinaigrette over greens isn't enough to wilt them. This recipe warms the greens with the dressing in a Dutch oven. Curly frisée, ruffled escarole, and/or frilly chicory are showcased. Alone or in combination, these greens make a robust, textured canvas for bold, flavorful ingredients. We warm up a Dutch oven by sautéing the colorful salad mix-ins (carrots, raisins, and almonds), let it cool slightly, and then add the greens and lemon vinaigrette off the heat. A few turns of the tongs and the greens have just the right slightly softened texture. Nutty chickpeas and salty feta add savory heft and dried fruit a little sweetness. The volume measurement of the greens may vary depending on the variety or combination used.

Vinaigrette
- 1 tablespoon grated lemon zest plus 6 tablespoons juice (2 lemons)
- 1 tablespoon Dijon mustard
- 1 tablespoon minced shallot
- ½ teaspoon ground cumin
- ½ teaspoon ground coriander
- ¼ teaspoon smoked paprika
- ¼ teaspoon cayenne pepper
- ¼ teaspoon table salt
- ¼ teaspoon pepper
- 2 tablespoons extra-virgin olive oil

Salad
- 1 (15-ounce) can chickpeas or white beans, rinsed
  Pinch table salt
- 1 tablespoon extra-virgin olive oil
- 3 carrots, peeled and shredded
- ¾ cup raisins or dried cranberries, chopped
- ½ cup slivered almonds or chopped hazelnuts
- 12 ounces (10–12 cups) bitter greens, such as escarole, chicory, and/or frisée, torn into bite-size pieces
- ⅓ cup mint or cilantro, chopped
- 1½ ounces feta or goat cheese, crumbled (⅓ cup)

1. FOR THE VINAIGRETTE Whisk lemon zest and juice, mustard, shallot, cumin, coriander, paprika, cayenne, salt, and pepper together in medium bowl. Whisking constantly, slowly drizzle in oil until emulsified.

2. FOR THE SALAD Toss chickpeas with 1 tablespoon vinaigrette and salt in bowl; set aside. Heat oil in Dutch oven over medium heat until shimmering. Add carrots, raisins, and almonds and cook, stirring frequently, until carrots are wilted, 4 to 5 minutes. Let cool off heat for 5 minutes.

3. Add half of remaining vinaigrette to pot, then add half of greens and toss for 1 minute to warm and wilt. Add mint and remaining greens, followed by remaining vinaigrette, and continue to toss until greens are evenly coated and warmed through, about 2 minutes longer. Season with salt and pepper to taste. Transfer greens to serving platter, top with feta and chickpeas, and serve.

KEYS TO SUCCESS

- **Use a Dutch oven:** Residual heat perfectly wilts the greens.
- **Dried fruit:** Adds a touch of sweetness
- **Nuts:** Add complementary crunch

SHAVED SALADS

STEVE DUNN

Feel like you are in a salad rut? Give some vegetables a shave. This simple technique will take your salads from blah to beautiful. Thin shaving eliminates the need to cook the vegetables, and using them raw adds fresh texture and more delicate vegetable flavor. In this course you will learn how to prepare celery and celery root, zucchini, brussels sprouts, jicama, and cucumber, transforming them into light and refreshing salads.

STEVE'S PRO TIP: *Shaving and slicing vegetables for a salad can take a little time, especially if you're making a large one for guests. When that's the case, I'll often do my prep work in advance and store all the sliced and shaved veggies in a large bowl of ice water for up to a couple of hours in my fridge. When I'm ready to serve, I drain them and spin them in a salad spinner to dry before finishing my salad.*

SHAVED CELERY SALAD WITH HONEY-POMEGRANATE VINAIGRETTE

Serves: 4 to 6
Total Time: 30 minutes

RECIPE OVERVIEW This fresh, light salad employs both celery ribs and celery root. Shaving the celery root thin with a vegetable peeler eliminates any need to cook the root, and the celery leaves plus chopped frisée give the salad more substance. The combination of sweet-tart pomegranate seeds and rich, salty Pecorino Romano cheese boosts the flavors and textures of the celery elements while toasted walnuts add more crunch. For the dressing, we echo the flavor of the pomegranate seeds by whisking pomegranate molasses with red wine vinegar, honey, shallot, and olive oil. Use the large holes of a box grater to shred the Pecorino Romano. A mandoline can also be used to shave the celery root in step 2.

    2 tablespoons pomegranate molasses
    1 tablespoon red wine vinegar
    1 small shallot, minced
    2 teaspoons honey
   ¼ teaspoon table salt
      Pinch pepper
    2 tablespoons extra-virgin olive oil
   14 ounces celery root, trimmed, peeled, and quartered
    4 celery ribs, sliced thin on bias, plus ½ cup celery leaves
    1 head frisée (6 ounces), trimmed and cut into
       1-inch pieces
  1½ ounces Pecorino Romano cheese, shredded (½ cup)
   ¼ cup pomegranate seeds, divided
   ½ cup walnuts, toasted and chopped coarse

1. Whisk pomegranate molasses, vinegar, shallot, honey, salt, and pepper together in large bowl. While whisking constantly, slowly drizzle in oil until combined.

2. Using sharp vegetable peeler, shave celery root into thin ribbons. Add celery root, celery ribs and leaves, frisée, Pecorino, and 2 tablespoons pomegranate seeds to bowl with dressing and toss gently to coat. Season with salt and pepper to taste. Sprinkle with walnuts and remaining 2 tablespoons pomegranate seeds. Serve.

KEYS TO SUCCESS

- **Shaved celery root:** Doesn't require cooking

- **Celery stalks and shaved celery root:** Make a crisp, fresh mélange of vegetables

- **Sweet-tart pomegranate:** Contributes the one-two punch of seeds plus molasses

SHAVED ZUCCHINI SALAD WITH PEPITAS

Serves: 4 to 6
Total Time: 20 minutes

RECIPE OVERVIEW   One of the great things about zucchini is that it's a blank canvas for flavor. To make the most of it, we shave it into long ribbons with a vegetable peeler, providing ample surface area for the flavorful dressing to coat. Tangy queso fresco, crunchy toasted pepitas, and fresh cilantro add textural contrast. Using in-season zucchini and good olive oil is crucial here. Look for small zucchini, which are younger and have thinner skins. Be ready to serve this dish quickly after it is assembled.

1½	pounds zucchini or summer squash
2	tablespoons extra-virgin olive oil
½	teaspoon grated lime zest plus 1 tablespoon juice
1	garlic clove, minced
¾	teaspoon table salt
¼	teaspoon pepper
½	cup chopped fresh cilantro or parsley
2	ounces queso fresco or feta, crumbled (½ cup)
¼	cup pepitas or sunflower seeds, toasted

Using vegetable peeler, shave zucchini lengthwise into very thin ribbons. Whisk oil, lime zest and juice, garlic, salt, and pepper together in large bowl. Add zucchini, cilantro, and queso fresco and toss to combine. Season with salt and pepper to taste. Sprinkle with pepitas and serve immediately.

KEYS TO SUCCESS

- **Long thin ribbons:** Look elegant and help the zucchini stay crunchy

- **Simple dressing:** Easy to make and superflavorful

- **Toast the seeds:** Gives them more flavor

CORE TECHNIQUE
Making Zucchini Ribbons

Using a vegetable peeler or mandoline, slice zucchini lengthwise into very thin ribbons.

SHAVED BRUSSELS SPROUT SALAD WITH WARM BACON VINAIGRETTE

Serves: 6
Total Time: 50 minutes

RECIPE OVERVIEW Raw brussels sprouts make a terrific base for a complex slaw-like salad. Slicing them thin and dressing them with a warm dressing help to tenderize the tough leaves and brighten their pungent flavor. Sprouts also take well to punchy dressings and bold additions like toasted almonds, shaved Parmesan, and smoky, salty bacon. We streamline the shredding process with an assembly-line approach: Work through all the trimming before moving onto the halving before moving onto the slicing. After crisping a few chopped slices of bacon, you build the rest of the dressing in the same skillet and then add the shaved sprouts, which are warmed not just by the dressing but also by the pan's residual heat. We prefer to thinly slice sprouts by hand, since the blades of a food processor tend to cut the leaves unevenly. The processor can be used, but the salad will be less tender.

¼	cup red wine vinegar
1	tablespoon whole-grain mustard
1	teaspoon sugar
¼	teaspoon table salt
1	shallot, halved through root end and sliced thin crosswise
4	slices bacon, cut into ½-inch pieces
1½	pounds brussels sprouts, trimmed, halved, and sliced thin
1½	cups finely shredded radicchio, long strands cut into bite-size lengths
2	ounces Parmesan, shaved into thin strips using vegetable peeler
¼	cup sliced almonds, toasted

1. Whisk vinegar, mustard, sugar, and salt together in bowl. Add shallot, cover tightly with plastic wrap, and microwave until steaming, 30 to 60 seconds. Stir briefly to submerge shallot. Cover and let cool to room temperature, about 15 minutes.

2. Cook bacon in 12-inch skillet over medium heat, stirring frequently, until crisp and well rendered, 6 to 8 minutes. Off heat, whisk in shallot mixture. Add brussels sprouts and radicchio and toss with tongs until dressing is evenly distributed and sprouts darken slightly, 1 to 2 minutes. Transfer to serving bowl. Add Parmesan and almonds and toss to combine. Season with salt and pepper to taste and serve immediately.

KEYS TO SUCCESS

- **Raw brussels sprouts:** Make a great salad green
- **Shreds of tender radicchio:** Lighten the salad's texture
- **Salad in a skillet:** Easily dressed on the stovetop instead of in a bowl

Slicing Brussels Sprouts by Hand

TRIM GENEROUSLY
Trim base from sprouts, cutting high enough so that each sprout is roughly as tall as it is wide. This will allow tough outer leaves to fall away; pull off and discard any that remain.

HALVE
Pile trimmed sprouts at one end of board. Cut each in half, pushing halved sprouts to opposite end of board.

SLICE
Divide cutting board into three regions: Keep halved sprouts at one end near nondominant hand, reserve center for slicing, and pile shredded sprouts on remaining third of board.

1 jalapeño or serrano chile, stemmed, halved, seeded, and sliced thin crosswise
1 teaspoon table salt, divided
¼ teaspoon pepper
6 tablespoons extra-virgin olive oil, divided
1 tablespoon honey
2 teaspoons grated lime zest plus ¼ cup juice (2 limes)
¼ cup fresh cilantro or parsley leaves
3 tablespoons roasted pepitas or sunflower seeds

1. Place scallops on clean dish towel, then top with second clean dish towel and gently press to dry. Let scallops sit between towels at room temperature for 10 minutes.

2. Meanwhile, gently toss jicama, mango, cucumbers, mesclun, radishes, shallot, and jalapeño in large bowl, then arrange attractively on individual plates.

3. Line large plate with double layer of paper towels. Sprinkle scallops with ½ teaspoon salt and pepper. Heat 1 tablespoon oil in 12-inch nonstick skillet over medium-high heat until just smoking. Add half of scallops in single layer, flat side down, and cook, without moving them, until well browned, 1½ to 2 minutes. Using tongs, flip scallops and continue to cook until sides of scallops are firm and centers are opaque, 30 to 90 seconds longer. Transfer scallops to prepared plate. Wipe out skillet with paper towels and repeat with 1 tablespoon oil and remaining scallops.

4. Divide scallops evenly among salad on prepared plates. Whisk honey, lime zest and juice, and remaining ½ teaspoon salt together in bowl. Whisking constantly, slowly drizzle in remaining ¼ cup oil until emulsified. Drizzle salad and scallops with dressing, then sprinkle with cilantro and pepitas. Serve.

KEYS TO SUCCESS

- **Raw jicama:** Adds slightly nutty, sweet crunch and its white flesh does not discolor
- **Large sea scallops:** Turn salad into dinner
- **Cilantro leaves:** Add a final layer of fresh flavor

SHAVED JICAMA, MANGO, AND CUCUMBER SALAD WITH PAN-SEARED SCALLOPS

Serves: 4
Total Time: 1 hour

RECIPE OVERVIEW Mexican salads inspired this combination of sweet mango, crisp cucumber, jicama, peppery radish, and spicy jalapeño. They all are shaved or sliced thin, then the ribbons make a bed for sweetly meaty scallops. Lime dressing, cilantro, and toasted pepitas pull this elegant main course salad together. We recommend buying "dry" scallops, which don't have chemical additives and taste better than "wet." Dry scallops look ivory or pinkish; wet scallops are bright white. Persian cucumbers (also called mini cucumbers) are similar to seedless cucumbers in flavor and texture. Use a sharp Y-shaped vegetable peeler or mandoline to shave the jicama and cucumbers. For more spice, reserve, mince, and add the ribs and seeds of the jalapeño.

1½ pounds large sea scallops, tendons removed
1 pound jicama, peeled and shaved into ribbons
1 mango, peeled, pitted, and sliced thin
3 Persian cucumbers or 8 ounces English cucumber, shaved lengthwise into ribbons
4 ounces (4 cups) mesclun
2 radishes, trimmed and sliced thin
1 shallot, sliced thin

WINTER FRUIT SALADS

KEITH DRESSER

Creating a vibrant fruit salad with peak summer produce is a cinch. But what about the rest of the year? This course is the answer to that question, focusing on salads made from winter fruits and vegetables. Prepare juicy flavorful salads by combining abundant citrus fruits with the likes of crisp raw fennel and crunchy red cabbage and jicama. And our delicious Caprese-style salad using ripe persimmons and burrata in the dead of winter is guaranteed to have you dreaming about summer.

KEITH'S PRO TIP: *Since the sweetness of winter citrus can vary, I like to have some sugar handy when seasoning citrus salads. I find a pinch or two of sugar (in addition to salt) boosts the citrus's flavor and balances out any excess bitterness.*

FENNEL, ORANGE, AND OLIVE SALAD

Serves: 4 to 6
Total Time: 30 minutes

RECIPE OVERVIEW This light and bright classic salad from Sicily celebrates ingredients that are abundant in the dead of winter. Citrus fruits, in particular, flourish then and come in many varieties. Beautiful blood oranges are a prized variety, so they are the star of this salad. Fennel is best when it is sliced as thin as possible; this ensures its texture is delicate and crisp rather than tough and chewy, making it an ideal pairing with the sweet, juicy oranges. To ensure that they are evenly distributed in the salad, cut the oranges into bite-size pieces and toss the salad gently to keep the segments from falling apart. To finish the salad, add some oil-cured black olives (to add briny contrast), plus fresh mint, lemon juice, olive oil, salt, and pepper.

- 2 blood oranges
- 1   fennel bulb, stalks discarded, bulb halved, cored, and sliced thin
- ¼ cup pitted brine-cured black olives, sliced thin
- 3 tablespoons extra-virgin olive oil
- 2 tablespoons coarsely chopped fresh mint
- 2 teaspoons lemon juice

Cut away peel and pith from oranges. Quarter oranges, then slice crosswise into ½-inch-thick pieces. Combine oranges and any accumulated juices, fennel, olives, oil, mint, and lemon juice in bowl. Season with salt and pepper to taste. Serve.

KEYS TO SUCCESS

- **Raw fennel**: Sliced thin, it's crisp and crunchy with a flavorful hint of anise.
- **Juice from the oranges**: Adds fresh flavor to the dressing

CORE TECHNIQUE

Preparing Fennel

TRIM
Cut off stems and fronds. Trim thin slice from base. Remove any tough or blemished outer layers from bulb.

CORE
Cut bulb in half through base, then use paring knife to remove core.

SLICE
Cut each half into thin strips, cutting from base to stem end.

1 red grapefruit
¼ cup extra-virgin olive oil
1½ tablespoons white wine vinegar
1 tablespoon honey
1½ teaspoons table salt
½ teaspoon pepper
6 cups thinly sliced red cabbage
1 cup thinly sliced red onion, rinsed
½ cup fresh cilantro leaves
⅓ cup roasted pepitas

1. Using rasp-style grater, grate 1½ teaspoons zest from grapefruit; transfer zest to large bowl. Cut away peel and pith from grapefruit. Holding grapefruit over separate bowl, use paring knife to slice between membranes to release segments; set aside grapefruit segments. Squeeze 2 tablespoons juice from remaining grapefruit pulp and add to bowl with zest.

2. Add oil, vinegar, honey, salt, and pepper to bowl with zest mixture and whisk to combine. Add cabbage, onion, cilantro, and grapefruit segments and toss to combine. Let sit for 30 minutes to allow flavors to meld.

3. Add pepitas and toss to combine. Season with salt and pepper to taste. Serve.

KEYS TO SUCCESS

- **Grapefruit juice**: Becomes the lively base for the vinaigrette
- **Let the dressed salad sit**: A half-hour rest softens the cabbage.
- **Roasted pepitas**: Provide a bit of crunch in every bite

RED CABBAGE AND GRAPEFRUIT SALAD

Serves: 4 to 6
Total Time: 25 minutes, plus 30 minutes sitting

RECIPE OVERVIEW An unlikely pairing of ingredients makes for a stellar winter salad that is fresh, crunchy, and bold. It starts with half a head of thinly sliced red cabbage and adds in another wintertime favorite: grapefruit. To make the fruit easier to eat, cut it into supremes (wedges freed from their bitter membranes). Then squeeze the juice from the remaining pulp and use it as the base for a vinaigrette with grapefruit zest, white wine vinegar, olive oil, and honey. Red onion and cilantro add pungency and sweet herbal freshness. Let the dressed salad sit for 30 minutes before serving to soften the cabbage and allow the flavors to meld. For a finishing touch and welcome crunch, sprinkle the salad with roasted pepitas (pumpkin seeds). You will need about half of a 2-pound cabbage to yield 6 cups. Green cabbage works here, too, but we prefer the slightly sweeter flavor and brighter color of red cabbage.

CORE TECHNIQUE

Cutting Grapefruit Supremes

REMOVE PEEL AND PITH
Use boning knife to remove peel and pith of grapefruit.

CUT BETWEEN MEMBRANES
Holding fruit over bowl, use paring knife to cut between membranes.

1. Cut away peel and pith from grapefruits and oranges. Cut each fruit in half from pole to pole, then slice crosswise into ¼-inch-thick pieces. Transfer fruit to bowl and toss with sugar and ½ teaspoon salt. Set aside for 15 minutes.

2. Melt butter in 8-inch skillet over medium heat. Add pecans and remaining ½ teaspoon salt and cook, stirring often, until lightly browned and fragrant, 2 to 4 minutes. Transfer pecans to paper towel–lined plate and set aside.

3. Drain fruit in colander, reserving 2 tablespoons juice. Transfer fruit to platter, arrange in even layer, and drizzle with oil. Whisk reserved juice, shallot, and mustard in medium bowl. Add watercress, ⅓ cup cranberries, and ¼ cup reserved pecans and toss to coat. Arrange watercress mixture over fruit, leaving 1-inch border around edges. Sprinkle with remaining ⅓ cup cranberries and remaining ¼ cup reserved pecans. Season with salt and pepper to taste. Serve immediately.

Variations

CITRUS SALAD WITH ARUGULA, GOLDEN RAISINS, AND WALNUTS
Substitute coarsely chopped walnuts for pecans, arugula for watercress, and ½ cup golden raisins for cranberries.

CITRUS SALAD WITH RADICCHIO, DATES, AND SMOKED ALMONDS
Substitute coarsely chopped smoked almonds for pecans, omitting butter and step 2. Substitute 1 small head radicchio, halved, cored, and sliced ¼ inch thick, for watercress, and chopped pitted dates for cranberries.

CITRUS SALAD WITH NAPA CABBAGE, DRIED CHERRIES, AND CASHEWS
Substitute coarsely chopped salted, roasted cashews for pecans, napa cabbage for watercress, and dried cherries for cranberries.

KEYS TO SUCCESS
- **Half-moon slices:** Easier prep than making membrane-free supremes
- **Sugar and salt fruit:** Draws out juices and tempers the sourness of the grapefruit

CITRUS SALAD WITH WATERCRESS, DRIED CRANBERRIES, AND PECANS
Serves: 4 to 6
Total Time: 55 minutes

RECIPE OVERVIEW Savory salads made with oranges and grapefruit are an impressive way to showcase colorful winter fruit—but only if you can work with the bitterness of the grapefruit and prevent the fruit's ample juice from drowning the other components. Start by treating the fruit with salt to counter its bitter notes (a technique we've used in the past with eggplant). But since the salt pulls even juice out of the fruit, you then drain the seasoned fruit to remove the excess juice, which is then used in the dressing. Salted nuts add richness that contrasts nicely with the fruit and the assertively flavored greens, and dried fruit adds texture and sweetness. You may substitute tangelos or Cara Caras for the navel oranges. Valencia and blood oranges can also be used, but since they are smaller, increase the number of fruit to four.

- 2 red grapefruits
- 3 navel oranges
- 1 teaspoon sugar
- 1 teaspoon table salt, divided
- 1 teaspoon unsalted butter
- ½ cup pecans, chopped coarse
- 3 tablespoons extra-virgin olive oil
- 1 small shallot, minced
- 1 teaspoon Dijon mustard
- 4 ounces (4 cups) watercress, torn into bite-size pieces
- ⅔ cup dried cranberries, divided

CORE TECHNIQUE | **Salting Fruit**

To remove extra moisture from fruit, toss with table salt in a colander set in a large bowl.

MANGO, ORANGE, AND JICAMA SALAD

Serves: 4 to 6
Total Time: 35 minutes, plus 20 minutes cooling

RECIPE OVERVIEW For a fresh, vibrant fruit salad in the late winter, start with a selection of tropical fruits, which boast plenty of sweetness and nuanced flavor. To provide juiciness and acidity, pair the fruits with a lime syrup to tie all the flavors together. A final addition of mildly flavored, crisp jicama, which softens slightly in the syrup, gives the salad just the right amount of texture without masking the bright fruit flavor. Make sure that the syrup has cooled before pouring it over the fruit.

- 3 tablespoons sugar
- ¼ teaspoon grated lime zest plus 3 tablespoons juice (2 limes)
- ¼ teaspoon red pepper flakes
  Pinch table salt
- 12 ounces jicama, peeled and cut into ¼-inch dice (1½ cups)
- 2 oranges
- 2 mangos, peeled, pitted, and cut into ½-inch dice (4 cups)

1. Bring sugar, lime zest and juice, pepper flakes, and salt to simmer in small saucepan over medium heat, stirring constantly, until sugar is dissolved, 1 to 2 minutes. Remove pan from heat, stir in jicama, and let syrup cool for 20 minutes.

2. Meanwhile, cut away peel and pith from oranges. Slice into ½-inch-thick rounds, then cut rounds into ½-inch pieces. Place oranges and mangos in large bowl.

3. When syrup is cool, pour over oranges and mangos and toss to combine. Refrigerate for 15 minutes before serving.

Variation
PAPAYA, CLEMENTINE, AND CHAYOTE SALAD

Chayote, also called mirliton, is often sold with other tropical fruits and vegetables. If you can't find chayote, substitute an equal amount of jicama.

Substitute 2 teaspoons grated fresh ginger for red pepper flakes; 1 chayote, peeled, halved, pitted, and cut into ¼-inch dice, for jicama; 3 clementines, peeled and each segment cut into 3 pieces, for oranges; and 2 large papayas, peeled, seeded, and cut into ½-inch dice, for mangos.

KEYS TO SUCCESS

- **Jicama:** Contributes crunch to contrast with the soft fruit

- **A 1:4 ratio:** One part citrus to 4 parts tropical fruit produces perfectly juicy salads.

- **The magic of salt:** Brings all of the flavors into focus

PERSIMMON AND BURRATA SALAD WITH PROSCIUTTO

Serves: 4 to 6
Total Time: 30 minutes

RECIPE OVERVIEW Caprese salad is at its peak in late summer when juicy sweet-tart tomatoes are paired with aromatic basil and slices of soft, creamy fresh mozzarella. But in the winter, it's hard to find sweet tomatoes. Turns out, persimmons are great with mozzarella and basil. We love the idea of being able to enjoy this interplay of flavors and textures in the fall and winter and found that you can achieve the sweet-tart balance with juicy honey-scented persimmons and punchy pomegranate seeds. To add richness to this cooler-season salad, use chunks of creamy burrata instead of mozzarella and add pieces of prosciutto, some crisped up in the microwave, for meaty saltiness. A drizzle of pomegranate molasses balances the sweetness and acidity of the salad. The skins of Fuyu persimmons can be tough; if yours are particularly tough we recommend peeling them before slicing.

- 2 ounces thinly sliced prosciutto, divided
- 2 tablespoons extra-virgin olive oil, divided
- 2 teaspoons lemon juice
- ⅛ teaspoon table salt
  Pinch pepper
- 1 pound ripe but firm Fuyu persimmons, stemmed, peeled if desired, and sliced ¼ inch thick
- 8 ounces burrata cheese, room temperature
- ½ cup fresh basil leaves, torn
- ¼ cup pomegranate seeds
- 2 teaspoons pomegranate molasses
  Flake sea salt

1. Place half of prosciutto in single layer between 2 layers of paper towels on plate and microwave until rendered and beginning to crisp, 2 to 4 minutes. Let cool slightly, then crumble into bite-size pieces.

2. Whisk 1 tablespoon oil, lemon juice, salt, and pepper together in large bowl. Add persimmons and gently toss to coat.

3. Arrange persimmons on serving platter, then drizzle any remaining dressing from bowl over top. Tear remaining half of prosciutto into bite-size pieces and arrange on top of persimmons. Cut burrata into 1-inch pieces, collecting creamy liquid, and arrange with liquid on top of persimmons and prosciutto. Sprinkle with basil, pomegranate seeds, and crispy prosciutto. Drizzle with pomegranate molasses and remaining 1 tablespoon oil. Season with sea salt and pepper to taste. Serve.

KEYS TO SUCCESS

- **Juicy persimmons:** A great substitute for tomatoes in a Caprese-style salad

- **Crisp prosciutto:** Adds salty richness

BREAD SALADS

ASHLEY MOORE

Traditionally, bread was mixed with cut-up vegetables and vinaigrette as a thrifty way to use up stale or leftover bread. Bread salads are now so popular that recipes call for turning bread stale on purpose. The pieces of bread absorb the salad's dressing and become highly flavorful. In this course you learn how to prepare the components of several interpretations of two of the most well-known Mediterranean bread salads: panzanella and fattoush.

ASHLEY'S PRO TIP: *Once I notice my family is no longer eating a fresh loaf of bread, I slice it and put it in the freezer in a zipper-lock bag—this way I always have some on hand. Not only is it great for using up in salads, but it also makes for a great slice of toast in a pinch.*

GREEK BREAD SALAD

Serves: 4 to 6
Total Time: 55 minutes, plus 30 minutes marinating

RECIPE OVERVIEW   You may know Italian bread salad, panzanella, but do you know its Greek cousin? The Greeks call this dakos, a salad of vibrant chopped Mediterranean ingredients that includes toasty pieces of pita. To add a spicy pop to the vegetables, make a marinade with red wine vinegar, the brine from jarred pepperoncini, and a spoonful of mustard. To flavor the pita and head off a soggy situation, toss the torn pieces with olive oil, garlic, and oregano and toast them in the oven. The vegetables become more flavorful as they marinate: We prefer a 30-minute marinade before serving; any longer and the vegetables become mushy.

- ¼ cup chopped jarred pepperoncini, plus 1½ tablespoons pepperoncini brine
- 1½ tablespoons red wine vinegar
- 1 teaspoon dried oregano, divided
- ½ teaspoon Dijon mustard
- 6 tablespoons extra-virgin olive oil, divided
- 1 pint cherry tomatoes, halved
- 1 (16-ounce) can chickpeas, drained and rinsed
- 1 cucumber, peeled, halved lengthwise, seeded, and sliced thin
- 1 cup crumbled feta cheese
- ¾ cup pitted kalamata olives, halved
- ½ small red onion, halved and sliced thin
- 2 (10-inch) pita breads, torn into 1-inch pieces
- 1 garlic clove, minced
- ⅓ cup chopped fresh parsley

1. Adjust oven rack to upper-middle position and heat oven to 400 degrees. Combine pepperoncini brine, vinegar, ½ teaspoon oregano, and mustard in medium bowl. Slowly whisk 5 tablespoons oil into vinegar mixture. Add pepperoncini, tomatoes, chickpeas, cucumber, feta, olives, and onion and toss to combine. Let sit 30 minutes.

2. Meanwhile, toss pita with remaining 1 tablespoon oil, remaining ½ teaspoon oregano, and garlic in medium bowl. Bake pita on rimmed baking sheet until golden brown, about 10 minutes, stirring halfway through baking. (Toasted pita can be stored at room temperature in an airtight container for up to 2 days.) Stir toasted pita and parsley into salad. Let stand 5 minutes. Season with salt and pepper. Serve.

KEYS TO SUCCESS

- **Pepperoncini brine:** Punches up the dressing
- **Marinate the vegetables in the dressing:** To absorb a lot of flavor
- **Toast the pita:** To help keep it crisp

FATTOUSH WITH BUTTERNUT SQUASH AND APPLE

Serves: 4 to 6
Total Time: 1½ hours

RECIPE OVERVIEW Flatbreads are a mainstay of tables across the Mediterranean, but the thin breads stale quickly, so creative dishes designed to use them up abound. Such recipes are called fatteh, derived from the Arabic word "fatta," meaning "to crumble." Pita bread salad, or fattoush, is a common example—and its appeal goes far beyond leftovers. The vibrant mix is simple but a textural marvel, combining crumbled toasted, fried, or day-old bread with summertime produce (tomatoes and cucumbers), fresh herbs, and greens, all simply dressed with lemon juice and olive oil and lavished with sumac. We thought about how to carry the experience into the colder months, when tomatoes and cucumbers aren't at their peak, and conjured a combination with distinctly fall flavors that still boasts fantastic contrasts in texture. Crisp sweet apples and slightly bitter radicchio provide fresh crunch, while roasted butternut squash gives the salad complexity and is a caramelized, soft, creamy foil to the crisp pieces of pita. We prefer a sweeter crisp apple like Pink Lady or Fuji to complement the bright lemony dressing.

- 2 (8-inch) pita breads
- ½ cup extra-virgin olive oil, divided
- ⅛ plus ¾ teaspoon table salt, divided
- ⅛ teaspoon pepper
- 2 pounds butternut squash, peeled, seeded, and cut into ½-inch pieces

- 3 tablespoons lemon juice
- 4 teaspoons ground sumac, plus extra for serving
- 1 garlic clove, minced
- 1 apple, cored and cut into ½-inch pieces
- ¼ head radicchio, cored and chopped (1 cup)
- ½ cup chopped fresh parsley
- 4 scallions, sliced thin

1. Adjust oven racks to middle and lowest positions and heat oven to 375 degrees. Using kitchen shears, cut around perimeter of each pita and separate into 2 thin rounds. Cut each round in half. Place pitas smooth side down on wire rack set in rimmed baking sheet. Brush rough sides of pitas evenly with 3 tablespoons oil, then sprinkle with ⅛ teaspoon salt and pepper. (Pitas do not need to be uniformly coated with oil.) Bake on upper rack until pitas are crisp and pale golden brown, 8 to 12 minutes. Let cool completely.

2. Increase oven temperature to 450 degrees. Toss squash with 1 tablespoon oil and ½ teaspoon salt. Spread in even layer on rimmed baking sheet and roast on lower rack until browned and tender, 20 to 25 minutes, stirring halfway through. Set aside to cool slightly, about 10 minutes.

3. Whisk lemon juice, sumac, garlic, and remaining ¼ teaspoon salt together in small bowl and let sit for 10 minutes. Whisking constantly, slowly drizzle in remaining ¼ cup oil.

4. Break cooled pitas into ½-inch pieces and place in large bowl. Add roasted squash, apple, radicchio, parsley, and scallions. Drizzle dressing over salad and toss gently to coat. Season with salt and pepper to taste. Serve, sprinkling individual portions with extra sumac.

KEYS TO SUCCESS

- **Contrasting textures of ingredients:** Make the salad especially appealing
- **Healthy amount of sumac:** Adds bright, citrusy flavor

Sumac: Spice with Sour

Ground sumac is made from dried berries that are harvested from a shrub grown in southern Europe and the Middle East. It's bright, with a clean, citrusy flavor and a slight raisiny sweetness— both more balanced and more complex-tasting than lemon juice. Try adding it when dishes need pucker. Sumac can be used as an ingredient in spice rubs or sprinkled over foods as a finishing touch. Liven up dry rubs and dressings or sprinkle it over vegetables, grilled meats, stews, eggs, and even popcorn so as not to mute its bright flavor. You can find both ground sumac and sumac berries, which you can grind yourself.

PANZANELLA WITH FIDDLEHEADS

Serves: 4 to 6
Total Time: 50 minutes

RECIPE OVERVIEW While one thinks of panzanella as a salad of fresh tomatoes and bread, early versions didn't include tomatoes. It was originally a way for Tuscans to extend the use of their precious loaves of bread; the stale bread was simply soaked in water and any vegetables on hand were tossed in. Here is a new variation, a bread salad abundant with bright green fiddleheads that showcases the spiraled vegetable's arresting appearance and unique flavor and texture and moves tomatoes to a supporting role. Blanching the fiddleheads first ensures that they're fully clean and also turns them a vivid green. Toss them with rich, chewy-crispy croutons, sweet grape tomatoes, and a simple vinaigrette; the sweetness and tang complement the fiddleheads. Fresh basil and creamy goat cheese finish this beautiful, hearty salad. Be sure to set up the ice water bath before cooking the fiddleheads; plunging them into the cold water immediately after blanching retains their bright green color and ensures that they don't overcook.

1   pound fiddleheads, trimmed and cleaned
½   teaspoon table salt, divided, plus salt for blanching fiddleheads
6   ounces ciabatta or sourdough bread, cut into ¾-inch pieces (4 cups)
3   tablespoons water
½   cup extra-virgin olive oil, divided
1   garlic clove, minced to paste
½   teaspoon pepper, divided
¼   cup red wine vinegar
5   ounces grape tomatoes, halved
2   ounces goat cheese, crumbled (½ cup)
¼   cup chopped fresh basil

1. Bring 4 quarts water to boil in large pot. Fill large bowl halfway with ice and water. Add fiddleheads and 1 tablespoon salt to boiling water and cook until crisp-tender, about 5 minutes. Using spider skimmer or slotted spoon, transfer fiddleheads to ice bath and let sit until cool, about 2 minutes. Transfer fiddleheads to plate lined with triple layer of paper towels and dry well.

2. Toss bread, water, and ¼ teaspoon salt together in large bowl, squeezing bread gently until water is absorbed. Cook bread mixture and ¼ cup oil in 12-inch nonstick skillet over medium-high heat, stirring often, until browned and crisp, 7 to 10 minutes.

3. Off heat, push bread to sides of skillet. Add 1 tablespoon oil, garlic, and ¼ teaspoon pepper; cook in residual heat of skillet, mashing mixture into skillet, until fragrant, about 10 seconds. Stir bread into garlic mixture, then transfer croutons to bowl to cool slightly, about 5 minutes.

Fiddleheads

Fiddleheads are the most beautiful of foraged greens. These tightly coiled ferns are so-named for their resemblance to the scroll of a violin. Their brief annual appearance (two to three weeks in any given area) signals the true beginning of spring. Find these coiled greens at farmers' markets and, increasingly, supermarkets. Look for fiddleheads that are tightly coiled, bright green, and with no browning, with bits of their brown, papery sheath clinging to them. Store them in a plastic produce bag in the refrigerator for just a few days. Never eat fiddleheads raw; they should always be blanched before they're used in a recipe.

4. Whisk vinegar, remaining 3 tablespoons oil, remaining ¼ teaspoon salt, and remaining ¼ teaspoon pepper in large bowl until combined. Add fiddleheads, croutons, and tomatoes and toss gently to coat. Season with salt and pepper to taste. Transfer to serving platter and sprinkle with goat cheese and basil. Serve.

KEYS TO SUCCESS

- **Fiddleheads**: This foraged green adds fresh asparagus-like flavor to the salad.
- **Homemade croutons**: Using ciabatta makes them hearty and chewy.
- **Fresh basil**: Enhances the vegetal flavor of the fiddleheads

CHICKEN AND WHITE BEAN PANZANELLA

Serves: 4 to 6
Total Time: 30 minutes

RECIPE OVERVIEW With its pieces of toasted French bread and tender chicken, this bread salad is a treat. Incorporating the chicken (and beans) into the salad is surprisingly streamlined when you make everything in a skillet. Then a quick red onion–basil vinaigrette marinates the tomatoes and beans as well as permeating the toasted bread. It might come as a pleasant surprise that the salad can sit: With the toasted bread it is flavorful—but not soggy—the next day. Do not discard the seeds or juice as you chop the tomatoes because they add important moisture.

6 ounces French or Italian bread, cut or torn into ½- to ¾-inch pieces (about 4 cups)
½ cup extra-virgin olive oil, divided
½ teaspoon table salt, divided
   Pinch pepper
3 (5- to 6-ounce) boneless, skinless chicken breasts, trimmed and pounded to uniform thickness
3 tablespoons red wine vinegar
1½ pounds tomatoes, cored and chopped, seeds and juice reserved
1 (15-ounce) can cannellini beans, rinsed
1 small red onion, halved and sliced thin
¼ cup chopped fresh basil
3 ounces (about 3 cups) baby arugula
2 ounces (½ cup) Parmesan cheese, shaved with vegetable peeler

1. Adjust oven rack to lowest position and heat oven to 450 degrees. Toss bread cubes with 1 tablepoon oil, ¼ teaspoon salt, and pepper.

2. Pat chicken dry with paper towels and sprinkle with salt and pepper to taste. Heat 1 tablespoon oil in 12-inch ovensafe skillet over medium-high heat until just smoking. Carefully add chicken and brown lightly on both sides, about 2 minutes per side; transfer to plate.

3. Off heat, spread bread cubes evenly into skillet. Lay chicken on top of bread and transfer skillet to oven. Bake until chicken registers 160 to 165 degrees and bread is browned in spots, 12 to 15 minutes.

4. Meanwhile, whisk remaining 6 tablespoons oil, vinegar, and remaining ¼ teaspoon salt together in large bowl. Stir in tomatoes with their seeds and juice, beans, onion, and basil and set aside to allow flavors to develop.

5. Transfer chicken to carving board, let cool slightly, then cut into 1-inch chunks. Gently fold chicken, toasted bread cubes, and arugula into tomato mixture. Season with salt and pepper to taste, sprinkle with Parmesan, and let sit 5 to 10 minutes. Serve warm or at room temperature. (Panzanella can be refrigerated for up to 1 day.)

KEYS TO SUCCESS

- **Marinate the tomatoes and beans in the dressing**: Infuses them with great flavor
- **Use high-quality bread**: Adds both flavor and texture to the salad

PASTA AND NOODLE SALADS

ANNIE PETITO

We've all encountered a disappointing pasta salad at some point. Pasta and noodle salads can be a challenge because the texture of the pasta has to be just right, not too hard or rubbery and definitely not mushy. This course rises to that challenge with methods to cook each kind of pasta or noodle perfectly and turn them into fresh and appealing salads. With the addition of proteins as diverse as salami, smoked fish, crab, shrimp, and steak, these cold noodle salads are hearty enough to call dinner.

ANNIE'S PRO TIP: *Always take the time to drain pasta or noodles really well to avoid salads that are watery or diluted in flavor.*

ITALIAN PASTA SALAD

Serves: 8 to 10 as a side dish
Total Time: 1 hour

RECIPE OVERVIEW This hearty pasta salad is chock-full of antipasto ingredients. For a better, more worthwhile salad, use corkscrew-shaped fusilli, which has plenty of surface area for capturing dressing. Cook the pasta until it is a little too soft—as it cools and firms up, it will have just the right tender texture. Rather than toss raw vegetables into the mix, we took inspiration from Italian antipasto platters and use intensely flavored jarred ingredients. Sun-dried tomatoes, kalamata olives, and pepperoncini offer up a mix of textures but don't overshadow the pasta. For heartiness, include salami, and to balance the salt and tang, add chunks of creamy mozzarella, fresh basil, and peppery arugula. To ensure that the pasta itself is just as flavorful as the rest of the dish, make a thick, punchy dressing by processing some of the salad ingredients themselves—capers and pepperoncini plus some of the tangy pepperoncini brine—with olive oil infused with garlic, red pepper flakes, and anchovies. The pasta firms as it cools, so overcooking is key to ensuring the proper texture. We prefer a small, individually packaged, dry Italian-style salami such as Genoa or soppressata, but unsliced deli salami can be used. If the salad is not being eaten right away, don't add the arugula and basil until right before serving.

1 pound fusilli
  Table salt for cooking pasta
¼ cup extra-virgin olive oil
3 garlic cloves, minced
3 anchovy fillets, rinsed, patted dry, and minced
¼ teaspoon red pepper flakes
1 cup pepperoncini, stemmed, plus 2 tablespoons brine
2 tablespoons capers, rinsed

2 ounces (2 cups) baby arugula
1 cup chopped fresh basil
½ cup oil-packed sun-dried tomatoes, sliced thin
½ cup pitted kalamata olives, quartered
8 ounces salami, cut into ⅜-inch dice
8 ounces fresh mozzarella cheese, cut into
  ⅜-inch dice and patted dry

1. Bring 4 quarts water to boil in large pot. Add pasta and 1 tablespoon salt and cook, stirring often, until pasta is tender throughout, 2 to 3 minutes past al dente. Drain pasta and rinse under cold water until chilled. Drain well and transfer to large bowl.

2. Meanwhile, combine oil, garlic, anchovies, and pepper flakes in liquid measuring cup. Cover and microwave until bubbling and fragrant, 30 to 60 seconds. Set aside.

3. Slice half of pepperoncini into thin rings and set aside. Transfer remaining pepperoncini to food processor. Add capers and pulse until finely chopped, 8 to 10 pulses, scraping down sides of bowl as needed. Add pepperoncini brine and warm oil mixture and process until combined, about 20 seconds.

4. Add dressing to pasta and toss to combine. Add arugula, basil, tomatoes, olives, salami, mozzarella, and reserved pepperoncini and toss well. Season with salt and pepper to taste. Serve. (Salad can be refrigerated for up to 3 days. Let come to room temperature before serving.)

KEYS TO SUCCESS

- **Overcook the noodles:** The softer pasta firms up to the perfect texture when cooled.

- **Zap the oil:** Infusing the oil with garlic, anchovy, and pepper flakes adds flavor to the pasta.

Al Dente Pasta Is So Retro(grade)

Just as leftover rice hardens when it is refrigerated, al dente pasta tastes overly firm once it cools. Retrogradation is to blame: As pasta cooks, its starch granules absorb water and swell. The chain-like starch molecules that formerly stuck together separate, allowing water to seep in among them. Then, as the pasta cools, the starch chains creep back together, forming tight microscopic crystals. The water that was keeping the molecules separate becomes bound up inside the crystals, and the pasta becomes overly firm because the starch is more rigidly compacted and the water is trapped.

OUR SOLUTION: When serving pasta cool, cook it until it is a little too soft. This way, when it retrogrades, it will firm up to just the right texture.

COUSCOUS SALAD WITH SMOKED TROUT, TOMATOES, AND PEPPERONCINI

Serves: 4 to 6
Total Time: 1 hour

RECIPE OVERVIEW Flaking smoked trout into quick-cooking couscous gives this dinner-worthy salad not only a little extra good-for-you protein but also a smoky flavor that complements the semolina pasta. Pepperoncini and cherry tomatoes add spiciness and freshness for a complexly flavored dish that's remarkably simple. A tangy vinaigrette, tossed with the grains while still warm, livens up the couscous, providing a refreshing counterpoint to the smoky richness of the trout. Much of the punch comes from an ingredient that often goes to waste as we use the brine from the pepperoncini instead of vinegar in the dressing. Hot-smoked mackerel or hot-smoked salmon also works well here.

2 cups water
1½ cups couscous
¾ teaspoon table salt
⅓ cup extra-virgin olive oil, plus extra for drizzling
1 cup pepperoncini, stemmed and sliced into
  thin rings, plus 3 tablespoons brine
1 garlic clove, minced
8 ounces cherry tomatoes, halved
½ cup fresh parsley leaves
3 scallions, sliced thin
6 ounces hot-smoked trout, skin and
  pin bones removed, flaked
  Lemon wedges

1. Bring water to boil in medium saucepan. Remove pot from heat, then stir in couscous and salt. Cover and let sit for 10 minutes. Fluff couscous with fork.

2. Whisk oil, pepperoncini brine, and garlic together in large bowl. Transfer couscous to bowl with dressing and toss to combine. Let sit until cooled completely, about 20 minutes.

3. Add cherry tomatoes, parsley, scallions, and pepperoncini rings to cooled couscous and gently toss to combine. Season with salt, pepper, and extra olive oil to taste. Divide salad among individual serving dishes and top with smoked trout. Serve with lemon wedges.

KEYS TO SUCCESS

- **Toss and cool:** Allowing cooked couscous to cool in the dressing lets it absorb maximum flavor.

- **Buy unflavored smoked trout:** It's convenient and buying it without added flavorings means it won't interfere with the recipe.

SUMMER RAMEN SALAD

Serves: 4 to 6
Total Time: 35 minutes

RECIPE OVERVIEW When the temperature rises, ramen noodles need a cooldown just as much as you do. Hiyashi chuka or summer ramen is that fix. It's a dish of brothless ramen noodles that are tossed in a sweet-sour soy sauce dressing and served chilled with crabmeat and an array of toppings that provide textural contrast and visual appeal. The noodles are tossed with a soy sauce–based dressing perked up with rice vinegar, sesame oil, chili oil, and scallion. While vegetables, eggs, and meat are most often found on the noodles, summer ramen presents a perfect opportunity for customizing based on what you have in the fridge or what you just brought home from the farmers' market. Crisp cucumbers, rich avocado, and crunchy, spicy radishes fill the bill. To this elegant base, add seafood and bright citrus, tossing crab with both orange juice and zest. You could use cooked shrimp or salmon instead. If using crab, be sure to purchase high-quality, fresh lump or jumbo lump crabmeat. For a milder vinaigrette, omit the chili oil. Note that this recipe uses unseasoned rice vinegar; we don't recommend using seasoned rice vinegar in its place. Serve with pickled ginger and cilantro leaves.

Sesame-Scallion Vinaigrette
- 2 tablespoons soy sauce
- 1 tablespoon unseasoned rice vinegar
- 1 tablespoon mirin
- 1 tablespoon water
- ½ teaspoon chili oil (optional)
- ¼ teaspoon toasted sesame oil
- ½ scallion, minced

Salad
- 2 teaspoons vegetable oil
- ¼ teaspoon grated orange zest plus ¼ cup juice
- 12 ounces lump crabmeat, picked over for shells and pressed dry between paper towels
- 4 (3-ounce) packages ramen noodles, seasoning packets discarded
- 1 avocado, sliced thin
- ½ English cucumber, cut into 2-inch-long matchsticks
- 4 radishes, trimmed, halved, and sliced thin
- 2 scallions, green parts only, sliced thin on bias
- 2 teaspoons toasted black sesame seeds

1. FOR THE SESAME-SCALLION VINAIGRETTE Whisk all ingredients together in bowl. (Vinaigrette can be refrigerated for up to 3 days; whisk to recombine before using.)

2. FOR THE SALAD Whisk oil and orange zest and juice together in medium bowl. Add crabmeat, tossing to coat, then season with salt and pepper to taste; refrigerate until ready to serve.

3. Bring 4 quarts water to boil in large pot. Add noodles and cook, stirring frequently, until tender. Drain noodles and rinse under cold water until chilled. Drain well, toss noodles with vinaigrette, and season with salt and pepper to taste. Divide among individual plates. Serve, topping individual portions with crabmeat mixture, avocado, cucumber, and radishes. Sprinkle with scallions and sesame seeds.

KEYS TO SUCCESS
- **Store-bought ramen noodles:** They're inexpensive, easy, and work great.
- **Robust dressing:** Made from superflavorful vinegar and oils
- **Crunchy toppings:** Include cucumber, radish, and sesame seeds

CHILLED SOMEN NOODLE SALAD WITH SHRIMP

Serves: 4 to 6
Total Time: 50 minutes, plus 3 hours chilling

RECIPE OVERVIEW Served in ice water with a bowl of dipping sauce and pickled ginger, somen noodles are perfect to help you cool off on a scorching day. For our version, cooled somen is tossed with a chilled savory broth turned sauce. The simple dashi sauce of simmered kombu (dried kelp) and dried bonito flakes seasoned with soy sauce, mirin, and sugar is chilled for 3 hours. After cooking the somen, rinse them in cold water to remove extra starch that would make them gummy, then toss with the sauce. Top individual bowls with sautéed shrimp, sliced cucumber, pickled ginger, and fresh cilantro and scallions for a refreshing dish. Do not substitute other types of noodles for the somen noodles here.

- 12 ounces extra-large shrimp (21 to 25 per pound), peeled, deveined, and tails removed
- ¼ teaspoon table salt
- ¼ teaspoon pepper
- 1 tablespoon extra-virgin olive oil
- 1½ cups water
- 1 (2-inch) piece kombu
- ¼ cup dried bonito flakes
- ½ cup soy sauce
- ¼ cup mirin
- 1 teaspoon sugar
- 12 ounces somen noodles
- ½ English cucumber, halved lengthwise and sliced thin
- ¼ cup pickled ginger, chopped coarse
- ¼ cup fresh cilantro or mint leaves
- 2 scallions, sliced thin on bias

1. Pat shrimp dry with paper towels and sprinkle with salt and pepper. Heat oil in 12-inch nonstick skillet over medium-high heat until just smoking. Add shrimp in single layer and cook, without stirring, until spotty brown and edges turn pink on bottom, about 1 minute. Flip shrimp and continue to cook until all but very center is opaque, about 30 seconds; transfer shrimp to plate and let cool slightly. (Shrimp can be refrigerated for up to 2 days.)

2. Bring water and kombu to boil in large saucepan over medium-low heat. Off heat, stir in bonito flakes and let sit for 3 minutes. Strain broth through fine-mesh strainer into large bowl, pressing on solids to extract as much broth as possible. Whisk in soy sauce, mirin, and sugar until sugar is dissolved. Cover and refrigerate until well chilled, about 3 hours.

3. Bring 4 quarts water to boil in large pot. Add noodles, and cook, stirring often, until tender. Drain noodles and rinse under cold water until chilled, then drain again, leaving noodles slightly wet. Toss noodles with sauce in large bowl. Top individual portions with shrimp, cucumber, pickled ginger, cilantro, and scallions. Serve.

KEYS TO SUCCESS

- **Freshly cooked shrimp**: Can be made quickly and ahead

- **Homemade dashi**: Creates an umami-rich broth

- **Leave noodles wet**: Keeps them from becoming gummy

BUN BO XAO

Serves: 4
Total Time: 40 minutes

RECIPE OVERVIEW This Vietnamese dish is a savory, aromatic salad of rice noodles topped with pickled and fresh vegetables, lemongrass beef, herbs, and peanuts. It's all about the contrasting hues and textures of the ingredients when they're layered in the bowl. Raw vegetables add color and crunch, peanuts add even more textural contrast, and the Thai basil and mint leaves add freshness and brightness. The dish is served at room temperature, which makes it forgiving for weeknight cooks. We prefer the unique flavor of Thai basil, but Italian basil can be used in its place. Be sure to drain the noodles thoroughly in step 2 to avoid diluting the flavors of the sauce.

¼ cup fish sauce, divided
1 lemongrass stalk, trimmed to bottom 6 inches and minced (5 teaspoons), divided
4 teaspoons vegetable oil, divided
1 tablespoon sugar, divided

1½ teaspoons Asian chili-garlic sauce, divided
1 pound skirt steak, trimmed and cut with grain into 3 equal pieces
8 ounces rice vermicelli
1 carrot, peeled and shredded
1 cucumber, peeled, seeded, and cut into 2-inch-long matchsticks
2 ounces (1 cup) bean sprouts
¼ cup lime juice (2 limes), plus lime wedges for serving
¼ cup fresh Thai basil leaves
¼ cup fresh mint leaves
2 tablespoons chopped dry-roasted peanuts

1. Whisk 1½ teaspoons fish sauce, 1 tablespoon lemongrass, 1 tablespoon oil, 1 teaspoon sugar, and ½ teaspoon chili-garlic sauce together in medium bowl. Add steak and toss to coat. Transfer steak to cutting board, cover with plastic wrap, and pound ¼ inch thick; return to bowl.

2. Bring 2 quarts water to boil in large saucepan. Off heat, add noodles to hot water and let stand until tender, about 5 minutes. Drain noodles in colander and rinse under cold running water until water runs clear. Drain well and divide among 4 individual serving bowls. Divide carrot, cucumber, and bean sprouts evenly over noodles in serving bowls.

3. Heat remaining 1 teaspoon oil in 12-inch skillet over medium-high heat until just smoking. Cook steak until well browned and meat registers 130 degrees, 2 to 3 minutes per side. Transfer steak to cutting board and tent with aluminum foil.

4. While steak is resting, whisk lime juice, remaining 3½ tablespoons fish sauce, remaining 2 teaspoons lemongrass, remaining 2 teaspoons sugar, and remaining 1 teaspoon chili-garlic in bowl until sugar is dissolved; set aside.

5. Slice steak thin against grain and divide evenly over noodles and vegetables in bowls. Whisk any accumulated juices from steak into sauce and drizzle 2 tablespoons sauce evenly over each bowl. Sprinkle with basil, mint, and peanuts. Serve with lime wedges.

KEYS TO SUCCESS

- **Drain the rice noodles well**: Avoids a watery sauce

- **Marinate and pound**: Give the steak a quick dip and pound it thin.

- **Thai basil and mint**: Add a finishing freshness

COURSE
SPICY SALADS

LAWMAN JOHNSON

The course is made up of piquant and vibrant salads that pack a punch and are sure to awaken your taste buds. Made from base vegetables such as lettuce, cucumbers, carrots and beets, and papaya, the heat and spice come from peppercorns, raw garlic, chiles (Thai and serrano), and a traditional Tunisian spice blend tempered with the delicate floral essence of both dried rose petals and rose water.

LAWMAN'S PRO TIP: *When creating a spicy salad, balance is the name of the game. The right combination of bright-bold flavors and nuanced seasoning is key.*

WEDGE SALAD WITH CREAMY BLACK PEPPER DRESSING

Serves: 6
Total Time: 30 minutes

RECIPE OVERVIEW Creamy peppercorn dressing is an unsung hero, adding unique intrigue and heat to salads, and we particularly like it on a classic wedge. To tame the intensity of fiery black pepper, we turn on the stove: After crisping bacon in a skillet, we simmer coarsely ground peppercorns in the fat left in the pan. Gently cooking peppercorns in fat tames their heat by pulling out the fat-soluble compound piperine, which packs that heat, and leaving a more mellow pepper flavor but plenty of presence. We drain the subdued peppercorns before adding them to a creamy and tangy—but not gloppy—base of olive oil, sour cream, mayo, buttermilk, Dijon mustard, and red wine vinegar. If you don't have buttermilk, substitute 2 tablespoons milk and increase the vinegar to 2½ teaspoons.

4	slices bacon, chopped
1	tablespoon coarsely ground black peppercorns
¼	cup extra-virgin olive oil
¼	cup sour cream
¼	cup mayonnaise
2	tablespoons buttermilk
2	teaspoons Dijon mustard
2	teaspoons red wine vinegar
1	garlic clove, minced
1	head iceberg lettuce (2 pounds), cored and cut into 6 wedges
12	ounces cherry tomatoes, halved

1. Cook bacon in 10-inch skillet over medium heat until crispy, 5 to 7 minutes. Using slotted spoon, transfer bacon to paper towel–lined plate; set aside.

2. Add pepper to fat in skillet and cook over low heat until faint bubbles appear. Continue to cook, swirling skillet occasionally, until pepper is fragrant, 7 to 10 minutes. Drain pepper in fine-mesh strainer over bowl. Discard fat and wipe bowl clean. Add drained pepper to bowl, along with oil, sour cream, mayonnaise, buttermilk, mustard, vinegar, and garlic and whisk to combine. Season dressing with salt to taste.

3. Arrange lettuce wedges on individual plates and top evenly with dressing, bacon, and tomatoes. Season with pepper to taste and serve.

KEYS TO SUCCESS

- **Tame the peppercorns:** Cooking them in bacon fat subdues their harshness and adds flavor.

- **Make the dressing creamy and tangy:** With a base of sour cream, mayo, and buttermilk

2. While cucumbers sit, whisk vinegar and garlic together in small bowl; let stand for at least 5 minutes or up to 15 minutes.

3. Whisk soy sauce, oil, and sugar into vinegar mixture until sugar has dissolved. Transfer cucumbers to medium bowl and discard any extracted liquid. Add dressing and sesame seeds to cucumbers and toss to combine. Serve immediately.

KEYS TO SUCCESS
- **Use English cucumbers:** Their skins are thin yet crisp and easy to smash.
- **Smash away with a skillet:** Creates the most surface area
- **Briefly salt cukes:** To expel their excess water

PAI HUANG GUA
Serves: 4
Total Time: 35 minutes

RECIPE OVERVIEW For a refreshing take on cucumber salad, put down your knife and pick up your skillet. Pai huang gua, or smashed cucumbers, is a Sichuan dish that is typically served with rich, spicy food. This recipe starts with English cucumbers, which are nearly seedless and have thin, crisp skins. Placing them in a zipper-lock bag and smashing them into large, irregular pieces speeds up the salting step that helps expel excess water. The craggy pieces also do a better job of holding on to the dressing. Using black vinegar, an aged rice-based vinegar, adds a mellow complexity to the soy and sesame dressing. We recommend using Chinese Chinkiang (or Zhenjiang) black vinegar in this dish for its complex flavor. If you can't find it, you can substitute 2 teaspoons rice vinegar plus 1 teaspoon balsamic vinegar. A rasp-style grater makes quick work of turning the garlic into a paste. We like to drizzle the cucumbers with Sichuan chili oil when serving them with milder dishes such as grilled fish or chicken.

2	(14-ounce) English cucumbers
1½	teaspoons kosher salt
4	teaspoons Chinese black vinegar
1	teaspoon garlic, minced or grated to paste
1	tablespoon soy sauce
2	teaspoons toasted sesame oil
1	teaspoon sugar
1	teaspoon sesame seeds, toasted

1. Trim and discard ends from cucumbers. Cut each cucumber crosswise into three equal lengths. Place pieces in large zipper-lock bag and seal bag. Using small skillet or rolling pin, firmly but gently smash cucumbers until flattened and split lengthwise into 3 or 4 spears each. Tear spears into rough 1- to 1½-inch pieces and transfer to colander set in large bowl. Toss cucumbers with salt and let stand for at least 15 minutes or up to 30 minutes.

Smashing Cucumbers

Cut cucumbers into thirds and place them in zipper-lock bag before gently pounding them with small skillet or rolling pin.

SHREDDED CARROT AND SERRANO CHILE SALAD
Serves: 4
Total Time: 45 minutes

RECIPE OVERVIEW This spicy carrot salad delivers big flavor powered by lime zest and juice, fish sauce, and the heat of serrano chile. Shredding carrots transforms their texture and exposes more surface area to the flavors of the bold dressing. To make quick work of shredding, opt for the shredding disk on a food processor; this creates finer shreds (which in turn soak up more dressing). For the dressing, potent fish sauce gives a salty, complex umami boost that amplifies the flavor of the earthy, sweet carrot shreds. Serrano chiles cut into thin rings add a bit of heat with good pepper flavor while chopped cilantro, mint, and scallions provide a range of fresh notes and a touch of color. Toasted sesame oil brings a savory, toasted element that anchors the bright flavors, and chopped peanuts add nutty crunch. If you don't have a shredding disk for your food processor, shred the carrots on the large holes of a box grater. If you're spice averse, use only one chile and consider halving it and removing the ribs and seeds. We recommend wearing rubber gloves when handling the chiles.

1 pound carrots, peeled
½ cup dry-roasted peanuts, chopped
⅓ cup chopped fresh mint
⅓ cup chopped fresh cilantro
¼ cup thinly sliced scallions
1–2 serrano chiles, stemmed and sliced into thin rings
1 tablespoon fish sauce
1 tablespoon sugar
1 tablespoon toasted sesame oil
2 teaspoons grated lime zest plus 3 tablespoons juice (2 limes)
1 garlic clove, minced
1 teaspoon table salt

1. Fit food processor with shredding disk and shred carrots.

2. Combine carrots, peanuts, mint, cilantro, scallions, serranos, fish sauce, sugar, oil, lime zest and juice, garlic, and salt in bowl and toss to thoroughly combine. Let sit for 30 minutes for flavors to meld. Serve. (Salad can be refrigerated for up to 24 hours.)

KEYS TO SUCCESS

- **Finer carrot shreds:** Create more interesting texture

- **Brown in place of white sugar:** It's OK to sub brown sugar for the granulated.

- **Heat from the serranos:** Powers the salad

SOM TAM

Serves: 4 to 6
Total Time: 30 minutes

RECIPE OVERVIEW Som tam (som=sour, tam=pounding), a northeastern Thai classic, is a crunchy, tart-spicy salad made with green papaya. In Thailand, papaya is often held in the hand and shredded with a machete-size knife, but for us grating the fruit with a box grater works. Its firm flesh can be hard to chew, so traditionally, a mortar and pestle are used to pound the shredded papaya to soften it, which also allows the dressing to penetrate easily. We simply macerate the papaya in a garlic, lime juice, fish sauce, palm sugar, and Thai chile dressing for 30 minutes. Dried shrimp adds a savory, fishy flavor. We add green beans and tomatoes for crunch, finishing the dish with crunchy peanuts. Do not use ripe, orange papaya; it will not work here. You can swap in 1½ pounds jicama (peeled, quartered, and shredded) for the papaya, if desired. You can substitute 1 to 2 serranos or ½ to 1 jalapeño for the Thai chiles. For a spicier dish, use the larger number of chiles.

2 tablespoons palm sugar or packed brown sugar, divided
2–4 Thai chiles, stemmed and sliced thin
2 tablespoons minced dried shrimp (optional)
1 garlic clove, minced

3 tablespoons lime juice (2 limes), plus extra for seasoning
2 tablespoons fish sauce, plus extra for seasoning
1 green papaya (2 pounds), peeled, halved lengthwise, and seeded
4 ounces green beans, trimmed and cut on bias into 1-inch lengths
3 ounces cherry or grape tomatoes, quartered
3 tablespoons chopped dry-roasted peanuts

1. Using mortar and pestle (or on cutting board using flat side of chef's knife), mash 1 tablespoon sugar, Thai chiles, shrimp (if using), and garlic to fine paste. Transfer to large bowl. Whisk in lime juice, fish sauce, and remaining 1 tablespoon sugar until sugar has dissolved. Quarter each papaya half. Using large holes of box grater or shredding disk of food processor, shred papaya. Transfer papaya to bowl with dressing and toss to coat. Let sit until flavors meld, at least 30 minutes or up to 1 hour, tossing occasionally.

2. Microwave green beans and 1 tablespoon water in covered bowl, stirring occasionally, until tender, about 4 minutes. Drain green beans and immediately rinse with cold water. Once cool, drain again and dry thoroughly with paper towels. Add green beans and tomatoes to papaya mixture and toss to combine. Season with extra lime juice and fish sauce to taste. Transfer salad to serving platter and sprinkle with peanuts. Serve.

KEYS TO SUCCESS

- **Don't pound:** Let papaya soak in the dressing.

- **Fish sauce and dried shrimp:** Add savory flavor

The Difference Between Green and Orange Papaya

Though very different in taste, texture, and appearance, green and orange papaya are actually the same fruit picked at different stages of development. The tender, creamy, orange-fleshed papaya is harvested when fully mature (though the exterior may still be green). Tasters describe it as "sweet," "melon-y."

Immature green papaya has crisp white flesh with very little flavor. It is prized mostly for its crunch and used primarily as a base for salads, most notably in the Thai classic som tam, where it serves as a bland backdrop for more powerful flavors. Tasters characterize green papaya as "clean-tasting" and "like cucumber or jicama."

CARROT AND BEET SALAD WITH ROSE HARISSA

Serves: 4 to 6
Total Time: 50 minutes

RECIPE OVERVIEW Sometimes the Tunisian spicy red pepper paste harissa gets the floral treatment with the addition of dried rosebuds and rose water. They add delicate floral aroma and sweetness that counterbalance the chiles' heat and the spices' warmth. Rose harissa shows off in this colorful salad of roasted beets, carrots, and shallots. Roasting the harissa-coated vegetables coaxes out their natural sweetness while deepening the harissa's complementary sweet heat. Tossing the still-warm vegetables with lemon zest and juice, parsley, and a fresh hit of harissa results in a beautifully balanced salad. Hard-cooked eggs and olives are traditional additions to Tunisian dishes and they make this salad substantial enough to be a light meal. Toasted almonds add textural contrast, and a scattering of dried rose petals gives the salad a fresh floral finish.

- 1 pound beets, peeled and cut into ½-inch wedges
- 1 pound carrots, peeled and cut ¼ inch thick on bias
- 6 shallots, peeled and halved lengthwise
- 3 tablespoons Rose Harissa (recipe follows), divided
- 2 tablespoons extra-virgin olive oil
- 1 tablespoon grated lemon zest plus 2 tablespoons juice
- ½ teaspoon table salt
- ¼ teaspoon pepper
- 2 large eggs
- ¼ cup pitted oil-cured olives, halved
- 3 tablespoons chopped fresh parsley
- ¼ cup whole almonds, toasted and chopped
- 3 tablespoons crumbled rose petals

1. Adjust oven racks to upper-middle and lower-middle positions and heat oven to 450 degrees. Toss beets, carrots, and shallots with 1 tablespoon rose harissa, oil, lemon zest, salt, and pepper in large bowl. Spread in single layer over 2 rimmed baking sheets. (Do not wash bowl.) Roast until vegetables are tender and well browned on one side, 20 to 25 minutes (do not stir during roasting).

2. Meanwhile, bring 1 inch water to rolling boil in medium saucepan over high heat. Place eggs in steamer basket and transfer basket to saucepan. Cover, reduce heat to medium-low, and cook eggs for 13 minutes. When eggs are almost finished cooking, combine 2 cups ice cubes and 2 cups cold water in second bowl. Using tongs or slotted spoon, transfer eggs to ice bath and let sit for 15 minutes. Peel and quarter eggs. (Hard-cooked eggs can be refrigerated, peeled or unpeeled, for up to 3 days.)

3. Whisk lemon juice and remaining 2 tablespoons rose harissa in now-empty bowl. Transfer roasted vegetables to bowl with rose harissa mixture and toss to combine. Stir in olives and parsley and season with salt and pepper to taste. Transfer vegetables to serving platter, sprinkle with almonds and rose petals, and arrange egg quarters over top. Serve.

ROSE HARISSA

Makes: about ½ cup

Rose, a traditional addition to harissa in Tunisia, adds further complexity to this favorite condiment; it's served with everything from grilled meats and couscous to roasted vegetables. The rose flavor comes from dried petals and rose water. Be sure to use food-grade dried rosebuds, which you can find at spice shops and specialty markets. This recipe can be easily doubled.

- 6 tablespoons extra-virgin olive oil
- ¼ cup paprika
- 1½ tablespoons ground dried Aleppo pepper
- 1 tablespoon ground coriander
- 3 garlic cloves, minced
- ½ teaspoon ground cumin
- ½ teaspoon caraway seeds
- ½ teaspoon table salt
- 2 tablespoons crumbled dried rosebuds, stems removed
- 1¼ teaspoons rose water

Combine oil, paprika, Aleppo pepper, coriander, garlic, cumin, caraway, and salt in bowl and microwave until bubbling and very fragrant, about 1 minute, stirring halfway through microwaving. Whisk in rosebuds and rose water; let cool completely. (Rose harissa can be refrigerated for up to 4 days.)

KEYS TO SUCCESS

- **Roasted beets and carrots:** These root vegetables have compatible flavors and textures.
- **Hard-cooked eggs:** You can make them ahead.
- **Dried rose petals and buds:** Provide floral flavor

COURSE
CRISPY SALADS

BRIDGET LANCASTER

You're probably thinking, Aren't all salads crisp? Well, there's crisp and then there's crispy. This course investigates how to prepare the starring ingredient in each of three salads so that it becomes light and crunchy and stays that way when mixed with the rest of the components, especially the dressing. You'll learn how to crisp jarred artichokes, eggplant, shallots, rice, and lentils for maximum impact.

BRIDGET'S PRO TIP: *Water is the destroyer of anything that's fried to a crisp, so for vegetables, which are plump and juicy due to their high water content, it pays to take that extra step to minimize that water before frying. The step of dehydrating the eggplant in the microwave is genius. A couple of minutes in the microwave forces out just enough water so that after frying the pieces retain that beautiful fried-crisp texture. I've used this method to prepare eggplant again and again.*

CRISPY ARTICHOKE SALAD WITH LEMON VINAIGRETTE

Serves: 4
Total Time: 40 minutes

RECIPE OVERVIEW Taking inspiration from irresistible recipes like the ultracrispy Jewish fried artichokes of Rome (page 106), we bring these textural marvels to the table and turn them into a light meal that's easy and unintimidating. In Mediterranean countries, the artichoke might be so revered because of the work that goes into preparing the delicacy; here, however, we savor the taste without the work by using jarred baby artichokes. We toss them in cornstarch and fry them until crispy but still moist. The salad gets a lot of its different flavors from vegetables alone, with the fried artichokes sitting on a bed of spicy, mustardy mizuna leaves and sweet peas in a lemony dressing. A finishing sprinkle of za'atar adds more tartness and a bit more crunch. The salad's careful balance of richness with freshness makes it a lovely light meal, or it can serve as a side to roast chicken or fish for a lively spring dinner.

- 3 cups jarred whole baby artichokes packed in water, halved, rinsed, and patted dry
- 3 tablespoons cornstarch
- 1 cup extra-virgin olive oil for frying
- 1 tablespoon lemon juice
- ¾ teaspoon Dijon mustard
- ¾ teaspoon minced shallot
  Pinch table salt
- 4 teaspoons extra-virgin olive oil
- 2 ounces (2 cups) mizuna or baby arugula
- ¾ cup frozen peas, thawed
- 1 teaspoon Za'atar (recipe follows)

1. Toss artichokes with cornstarch in bowl to coat. Heat 1 cup oil in 12-inch skillet over medium heat until shimmering. Shake excess cornstarch from artichokes and carefully add to skillet in single layer. Cook, stirring occasionally, until golden and crisp all over, 5 to 7 minutes. Using slotted spoon, transfer artichokes to paper towel–lined plate to cool slightly, about 10 minutes.

2. Whisk lemon juice, mustard, shallot, and salt together in bowl. Whisking constantly, slowly drizzle in 4 teaspoons oil until emulsified. Toss mizuna, peas, and 2 tablespoons vinaigrette together in large bowl. Transfer to serving platter and top with artichokes, drizzle with remaining vinaigrette, and sprinkle with za'atar. Serve.

ZA'ATAR

Makes: about ½ cup

Za'atar is an aromatic eastern Mediterranean blend of herbs, spices, and seeds that is used as both a seasoning for cooked dishes and a raw condiment. Try sprinkling it on almost anything that could use a bright, lemony punch.

½ cup dried thyme, ground

2 tablespoons sesame seeds, toasted

1½ tablespoons ground sumac

Combine all ingredients in bowl. (Za'atar can be stored in airtight container at room temperature for up to 1 month.)

KEYS TO SUCCESS

- **Jarred artichokes:** They're no-prep, tender, and deliver crispy results.
- **Cut whole artichokes in half:** More surface area means more crispiness.
- **Coat artichokes with cornstarch to shallow fry:** Keeps them crisp but juicy

CRISPY EGGPLANT SALAD

Serves: 2 to 3

Total Time: 45 minutes

RECIPE OVERVIEW For this salad, we take elements from Sicilian caponata—eggplant, tomatoes, herbs, and vinegary notes—and marry them with intense Thai flavors. We first dehydrate the eggplant pieces in the microwave then shallow-fry them before tossing them in nam prik—a bright Thai condiment made with lime juice, fish sauce, rice vinegar, ginger, garlic, and chiles. We toss in juicy cherry tomatoes and a healthy amount of fresh herbs, and top with crispy fried shallots for a dish that delivers all of the five tastes and as many different textures. Japanese eggplant is our unanimous favorite, but globe or Italian eggplant can be substituted if necessary. Traditional Genovese basil is a fine substitute for the Thai basil. Depending on the size of your microwave, you may need to microwave the eggplant in two batches. Be sure to remove the eggplant from the microwave immediately so that the steam can escape. Serve this salad with sticky rice, grilled steak, or both.

2 tablespoons fish sauce

2 tablespoons unseasoned rice vinegar

2 tablespoons lime juice

2 tablespoons palm sugar or packed light brown sugar

1 (1-inch piece) ginger, peeled and chopped

2 garlic cloves, chopped

½ red Thai chile, seeded and sliced thin

6 ounces cherry tomatoes, halved

2 large Japanese eggplants (1½ pounds), halved lengthwise, then cut crosswise into 1½-inch pieces

1 teaspoon kosher salt

2 cups vegetable oil for frying

½ cup fresh cilantro leaves

½ cup fresh mint leaves

½ cup fresh Thai basil leaves

1 recipe Microwave-Fried Shallots (recipe follows)

1. Process fish sauce, vinegar, lime juice, palm sugar, ginger, garlic, and chile in blender on high until dressing is mostly smooth, about 1 minute. Transfer to large serving bowl and stir in tomatoes; set aside.

2. Toss eggplant with salt in medium bowl. Line entire surface of large plate with double layer of coffee filters and lightly spray with vegetable oil spray. Spread eggplant in even layer on coffee filters. Microwave until eggplant is dry and shriveled to one-third of its original size, about 10 minutes, flipping halfway through to dry sides evenly (eggplant should not brown). Transfer eggplant immediately to paper towel–lined plate.

3. Heat oil in large Dutch oven over medium-high heat to 375 degrees. Add eggplant to oil and cook until flesh is deep golden brown and edges are crispy, 5 to 7 minutes. Using skimmer or slotted spoon, transfer to paper towel–lined plate and blot to remove excess oil. Transfer to bowl with dressing and tomatoes.

4. Toss cilantro, mint, and basil together in small bowl. Add half of herb mixture to bowl with eggplant, tossing to combine, then sprinkle remaining herb mixture and fried shallots over top. Serve.

MICROWAVED-FRIED SHALLOTS

    3 shallots, sliced thin
    ½ cup vegetable oil

Combine shallots and oil in medium bowl. Microwave for 5 minutes. Stir and continue to microwave 2 minutes longer. Repeat stirring and microwaving in 2-minute increments until beginning to brown (4 to 6 minutes). Repeat stirring and microwaving in 30-second increments until deep golden brown (30 seconds to 2 minutes). Using slotted spoon, transfer shallots to paper towel–lined plate; season with salt to taste. Let drain and crisp, about 5 minutes.

KEYS TO SUCCESS

- **Dry, then fry:** For crispy edges and silky interiors
- **Sub peanuts for shallots:** You can substitute ½ cup chopped roasted peanuts for the shallots.
- **Varied colors, tastes, and textures:** Exemplifies Thai cooking

CRISPY RICE SALAD

Serves: 4 to 6
Total Time: 50 minutes

RECIPE OVERVIEW Nam khao is a popular Laotian rice salad featuring a plethora of contrasting flavors and textures: crunchy and soft, tangy and salty, spicy and sweet, nutty and herbal. The traditional dish features rice balls deep-fried until they develop a crunchy crust, an appealing contrast to their soft, chewy interior. The balls are broken into pieces and tossed with fermented pork sausage, fresh herbs, peanuts, and a citrusy-spicy dressing. Instead of forming the rice into balls, this version has you fry half of the cooked rice in clusters until they're light golden and crisp throughout. This creates a rougher surface with crunchier nooks and crannies. Tossing this fried rice with the remaining cooked rice creates an irresistible crunchewy quality. Sweet-salty Chinese sausage is a good substitute for the dish's traditional, hard-to-find fermented pork sausage. You can substitute long-grain white rice for the jasmine rice; do not use basmati. Use a Dutch oven that holds 6 quarts or more.

    2¼ cups water
    1½ cups jasmine rice, rinsed
     3 tablespoons lime juice (2 limes)
     2 tablespoons fish sauce
     1 tablespoon Thai red curry paste
    1½ tablespoons sugar
     1 teaspoon grated fresh ginger
     2 shallots, sliced thin
     1 teaspoon vegetable oil
     2 ounces Chinese sausage, cut into ½-inch pieces
    1½ quarts peanut or vegetable oil for frying
     ½ cup fresh cilantro leaves
     ½ cup fresh mint leaves, torn
     4 scallions, sliced thin on bias
     ¼ cup dry-roasted peanuts, chopped coarse

1. Bring water and rice to simmer in large saucepan over high heat. Reduce heat to low, cover, and simmer gently until rice is tender and water has been fully absorbed, about 10 minutes. Off heat, lay clean dish towel underneath lid and let sit for 10 minutes. Spread rice onto large greased plate and let cool for 10 minutes.

2. Meanwhile, whisk lime juice, fish sauce, curry paste, sugar, and ginger in large bowl until sugar has dissolved. Stir in shallots and set aside.

3. Heat vegetable oil in large Dutch oven over medium heat until shimmering. Add sausage and cook until spotty brown, about 3 minutes; transfer to separate bowl. Wipe pot clean with paper towels.

4. Line rimmed baking sheet with triple layer of paper towels. Add peanut oil to now-empty pot until it measures about 1 inch deep and heat over medium-high heat to 400 degrees. Break half of rice into rough 2-inch clusters. Carefully add half of rice clusters to hot oil and cook, without stirring, until light golden brown, about 5 minutes. (Adjust heat as needed to maintain oil temperature between 375 and 400 degrees.) Using spider skimmer or slotted spoon, transfer fried rice to prepared sheet. Return oil to 400 degrees and repeat with remaining rice clusters; transfer to sheet and let drain for 10 minutes.

5. Using your fingers, break fried rice into bite-size pieces. Add fried rice, remaining cooked rice, sausage, cilantro, mint, and scallions to dressing and toss gently to combine. Transfer salad to serving platter and sprinkle with peanuts. Serve.

KEYS TO SUCCESS

- **Cook then fry:** Cooked rice stays firm while frying.
- **You can substitute ham:** For the Chinese sausage
- **Potent dressing:** Contains lime juice, fish sauce, curry paste, and fresh ginger

ROASTED SALADS

LEAH COLINS

Roasting vegetables concentrates their flavor as well as adding attractive browning. They're delicious by themselves when served as a side dish, but reach new heights in this course when combined with other ingredients to create earthy colorful salads. Get ready to roast beets, winter and pattypan squash, cauliflower, and small Italian onions to perfection, then use them as a base for hearty inviting salads.

LEAH'S PRO TIP: *For a good hard sear and welcomed roasty flavor, leave those veggies alone! Don't be tempted to open the oven or toss the veggies too much, as leaving them mostly undisturbed will promote the best browning. To turn roasted vegetables from a humble side dish into a reimagined salad, pair them with other fresh ingredients with a range of textures, colors, and flavors (think fresh crunchy greens, sweet dried fruit, toasty nuts, or a bright acidic dressing) that all come together in one harmonious bite.*

CHARRED BEET SALAD

Serves: 4 to 6
Total Time: 1¾ hours

RECIPE OVERVIEW This charred salad reinvents and reinvigorates the pairing of earthy, sweet beets and creamy, salty goat cheese. After roasting foil-wrapped beets, we slice and quickly char them on the stovetop. This step essentially burns some of the sugar, adding pleasantly complementary bitterness. We amplify that with crisp radicchio and toss it all with a dressing made from the beet cooking liquid. A simple spread of feta and Greek yogurt replaces the usual goat cheese. A final flourish of tart pomegranate seeds provides pops of bright acidity (and stays on message with the ruby color scheme). Be sure to scrub the beets clean before roasting as the roasting liquid forms the basis of the dressing.

4	ounces feta cheese, crumbled (1 cup)
½	cup plain Greek yogurt, divided
1½	pounds beets, trimmed
3	tablespoons extra-virgin olive oil
2	tablespoons water
2	tablespoons sherry vinegar
1½	teaspoons table salt
1	teaspoon pepper
1	tablespoon vegetable oil
4	ounces radicchio, cut into 2-inch pieces
½	cup pomegranate seeds
1	tablespoon roughly chopped fresh dill
1	tablespoon roughly chopped fresh tarragon

1. Adjust oven rack to middle position and heat oven to 375 degrees. Set wire rack in rimmed baking sheet. Combine feta and ¼ cup yogurt in small bowl and mash to form coarse spread; refrigerate until ready to serve.

2. Toss beets, olive oil, water, vinegar, salt, and pepper in bowl to combine. Stack two 16 by 12-inch pieces of aluminum foil on prepared rack. Arrange beets in center of foil and lift sides of foil to form bowl. Pour liquid over top and crimp foil tightly to seal.

3. Roast until beets can be easily pierced with paring knife, 1 to 1½ hours for small beets and 1½ to 2½ hours for medium to large beets. Open foil packet and set beets aside, then pour cooking liquid into large bowl (you should have about ½ cup). Whisk remaining ¼ cup yogurt into beet cooking liquid until smooth; set aside. Once beets are cool enough to handle, rub off skins with paper towels and cut into ½-inch-thick rounds.

4. Heat vegetable oil in 12-inch skillet over medium-high heat until just smoking. Arrange beets in skillet in single layer and cook until both sides are well charred, about 3 minutes per side. Transfer to cutting board and cut into 1½-inch pieces, then add to bowl with yogurt-beet dressing.

5. Add radicchio to bowl with beets and toss to combine. Season with salt and pepper to taste. Spread yogurt-feta mixture in even layer on large serving plate. Arrange beets and radicchio over top, then sprinkle with pomegranate seeds, dill, and tarragon. Serve.

KEYS TO SUCCESS
- **Roast, then char:** Ensures beets are perfectly cooked
- **Beet cooking liquid:** Adds intense flavor to the dressing
- **Feta and Greek yogurt:** Add plenty of creaminess in place of the expected goat cheese

ROASTED BUTTERNUT SQUASH SALAD WITH ZA'ATAR AND PARSLEY

Serves: 4 to 6
Total Time: 1½ hours

RECIPE OVERVIEW The sweet nuttiness of a roasted winter squash pairs best with flavors bold enough to balance it. In this hearty salad, that boldness comes from a traditional eastern Mediterranean spice blend, za'atar (a pungent combination of toasted sesame seeds, thyme, and sumac). High heat and placing the oven rack in the lowest position produce perfectly browned, tender squash in about 30 minutes. Dusting the za'atar over the hot squash works much like toasting the spice blend, boosting its flavor. For a foil to the tender squash, pepitas provide the textural accent the dish needs and reinforces the squash's flavor. Pomegranate seeds add a burst of tartness and color.

We prefer to use our homemade za'atar here, but you can substitute store-bought. You can also substitute chopped red grapes or small blueberries for the pomegranate seeds.

3	pounds butternut squash, peeled, seeded, and cut into ½-inch pieces (8 cups)
¼	cup extra-virgin olive oil, divided
1¼	teaspoons table salt, divided
½	teaspoon pepper
1	teaspoon Za'atar (page 182)
2	tablespoons lemon juice
2	tablespoons honey
1	small shallot, minced
¾	cup fresh parsley or cilantro leaves
⅓	cup roasted pepitas or sunflower seeds
½	cup pomegranate seeds

1. Adjust oven rack to lowest position and heat oven to 450 degrees. Toss squash with 1 tablespoon oil and sprinkle with 1 teaspoon salt and pepper. Arrange squash in single layer on rimmed baking sheet and roast until well browned and tender, 30 to 35 minutes, stirring halfway through roasting. Sprinkle squash with za'atar and let cool for 15 minutes.

2. Whisk lemon juice, honey, shallot, and remaining ¼ teaspoon salt together in large bowl. Whisking constantly, slowly drizzle in remaining 3 tablespoons oil until emulsified. Add squash, parsley, and pepitas and toss gently to coat. Transfer salad to serving platter and sprinkle with pomegranate seeds. Serve.

KEYS TO SUCCESS
- **Smaller pieces of squash:** They roast and brown relatively quickly.
- **Za'atar:** The spice blend adds complex flavor.

ROASTED CAULIFLOWER AND GRAPE SALAD

Serves: 4

Total Time: 50 minutes

RECIPE OVERVIEW Heady with cilantro, brightened with lots of lemon juice, and deepened with warm spices, the North African herb sauce chermoula is most often a marinade for meat and fish, but here it paints a cauliflower canvas with tremendous flavor. We start by roasting cauliflower until it's caramelized. Instead of discarding the core, we blitz it in the food processor and add it to the salad for a contrasting rice-like texture. Then we make the chermoula in the empty food processor. We balance its flavor in the salad with sweetness, roasting red onion and plenty of grapes as well. Fresh cilantro leaves and crunchy walnuts are the finishing touches to this substantial roasted vegetable salad. This salad is satisfying enough to be a meal but also nice as a side dish to hearty grains or rich meat.

Salad

1 head cauliflower (2 pounds), core chopped coarse, florets cut into 1-inch pieces (6 cups)

1 cup seedless red grapes

½ small red onion, sliced thin

2 tablespoons extra-virgin olive oil

½ teaspoon table salt

¼ teaspoon pepper

2 tablespoons fresh cilantro or parsley leaves

2 tablespoons coarsely chopped toasted walnuts or sliced almonds

Chermoula

1 cup fresh cilantro or parsley leaves

5 tablespoons extra-virgin olive oil

2 tablespoons lemon juice

4 garlic cloves, minced

½ teaspoon ground cumin

½ teaspoon paprika

¼ teaspoon table salt

⅛ teaspoon cayenne pepper

1. FOR THE SALAD Adjust oven rack to lowest position and heat oven to 475 degrees. Toss cauliflower florets, grapes, onion, oil, salt, and pepper together in bowl. Transfer to rimmed baking sheet and roast until vegetables are tender, florets are deep golden, and onion slices are charred at edges, 12 to 15 minutes, stirring halfway through roasting. Let cool slightly, about 15 minutes.

2. Meanwhile, pulse cauliflower core in food processor until finely ground into ⅛-inch pieces, 6 to 8 pulses, scraping down sides of bowl as needed; transfer to large bowl.

3. FOR THE CHERMOULA Process all ingredients in now-empty processor until smooth, about 1 minute, scraping down sides of bowl as needed. (Chermoula can be refrigerated for up to 2 days.) Transfer to bowl with cauliflower core.

4. Add roasted cauliflower mixture to chermoula mixture in bowl and toss to combine. Season with salt and pepper to taste. Sprinkle with cilantro and walnuts. Serve.

KEYS TO SUCCESS

- **Cauliflower x 2:** Roasted florets and the riced core contribute different textures to the salad.
- **Roasted red onion and grapes:** Their caramelized sweetness offsets the intense chermoula.
- **Toasted nuts:** Add a crunchy finish

ROASTED PATTYPAN SQUASH SALAD WITH DANDELION GREEN PESTO

Serves: 4 to 6

Total Time: 1 hour

RECIPE OVERVIEW Pattypan squash tastes like zucchini but with a unique shape that is an advantage when it comes to providing texture. We like baby pattypan squashes for their tender skin and vibrant flavor (some say the squash loses flavor as it matures). Before roasting the diminutive squashes, we cut them horizontally to make flower-shaped slabs, which we toss with just-off-the-cob corn in oil and maple syrup. We counter these fresh ingredients with an earthy-tasting pesto made from dandelion greens and roasted sunflower seeds. You can use baby arugula or watercress instead of dandelion greens. Pattypans come in different sizes; for this salad, we look for baby pattypans that measure between 1½ and 2 inches in diameter. If you can't find baby pattypan squash, you can use zucchini or summer squash cut crosswise into 1-inch-thick rounds.

Pesto

1 ounce dandelion greens, trimmed and torn into bite-size pieces (1 cup)

3 tablespoons roasted sunflower seeds

3 tablespoons water

1 tablespoon maple syrup

1 tablespoon cider vinegar

1 garlic clove, minced
¼ teaspoon table salt
⅛ teaspoon red pepper flakes
¼ cup extra-virgin olive oil

Salad
2 tablespoons extra-virgin olive oil
2 teaspoons maple syrup
½ teaspoon table salt
⅛ teaspoon pepper
1½ pounds baby pattypan squash, halved horizontally
4 ears corn, kernels cut from cob
1 pound ripe tomatoes, cored, cut into ½-inch-thick wedges, and wedges halved crosswise
1 ounce dandelion greens, trimmed and torn into bite-size pieces (1 cup)
2 tablespoons roasted sunflower seeds

1. **FOR THE PESTO** Adjust oven rack to lowest position, place rimmed baking sheet on rack, and heat oven to 500 degrees. Process dandelion greens, sunflower seeds, water, maple syrup, vinegar, garlic, salt, and pepper flakes in food processor until finely ground, about 1 minute, scraping down sides of bowl as needed. With processor running, slowly drizzle in oil until incorporated. (Pesto can be refrigerated for up to 2 days.)

2. **FOR THE SALAD** Whisk oil, maple syrup, salt, and pepper together in large bowl. Add squash and corn and toss to coat. Working quickly, spread vegetables in single layer on hot sheet, arranging squash cut side down. Roast until cut side of squash is browned and tender, 15 to 18 minutes. Transfer pan to wire rack and let cool slightly, about 15 minutes.

3. Combine roasted squash and corn, half of pesto, tomatoes, and dandelion greens in large bowl and toss gently to combine. Drizzle with remaining pesto and sprinkle with sunflower seeds. Serve.

> ### KEYS TO SUCCESS
> - **Roasting the squash:** Intensifies its flavor
> - **Maple syrup:** Flavors the oil and helps the squash brown
> - **Double dose of dandelions:** As the base of the pesto and as a salad green

ROASTED CIPOLLINI AND ESCAROLE SALAD

Serves: 4 to 6
Total Time: 1¼ hours

RECIPE OVERVIEW In the world of onions, Italian cipollini are truly stellar. They're gentler and sweeter in flavor and aroma than regular yellow, white, or red onions, making them perfect for use in salads. With more residual sugars, they caramelize easily during roasting, creating a melt-in-your-mouth texture that contrasts beautifully with the crunch of crisp, slightly bitter escarole and frisée in this salad. Crispy prosciutto and creamy blue cheese add saltiness and make the salad a textured meal. A tangy dressing with cracked caraway seeds (a common pairing with cipollini) balances all the flavors. You can use prepeeled cipollini onions in this recipe; simply halve them through the root end and proceed with step 2.

1½ pounds cipollini onions
6 tablespoons extra-virgin olive oil, divided
¼ teaspoon table salt
⅛ teaspoon pepper
4 ounces thinly sliced prosciutto
2 tablespoons apple cider vinegar
2 teaspoons Dijon mustard
1½ teaspoons caraway seeds, toasted and cracked
1 teaspoon honey
1 head escarole (1 pound), trimmed and cut into 1-inch pieces
½ head frisée (3 ounces), trimmed and cut into 1-inch pieces
2 ounces blue cheese, crumbled (½ cup)

1. Adjust oven rack to middle position and heat oven to 400 degrees. Bring 2 quarts water to boil in large saucepan. Add onions and cook for 30 seconds. Drain in colander and rinse with cold water until onions are cool enough to handle, about 1 minute. Transfer onions to paper towel–lined plate and pat dry. Trim root and stem ends, then peel and discard onion skins. Halve onions through root end and transfer to bowl.

2. Add 3 tablespoons oil, salt, and pepper to bowl with onions and toss to coat. Arrange onions, cut side down, on parchment paper–lined rimmed baking sheet and roast until well browned and softened, 35 to 40 minutes, rotating sheet halfway through roasting. Let cool, about 10 minutes.

3. Place prosciutto in single layer between 2 layers of paper towels on plate and microwave until rendered and beginning to crisp, 2 to 4 minutes. Let cool slightly, then crumble into bite-size pieces.

4. Whisk vinegar, mustard, caraway seeds, and honey together in large bowl. Whisking constantly, slowly drizzle in remaining 3 tablespoons oil until emulsified. Add escarole, frisée, roasted onions, and prosciutto and toss to combine. Season with salt and pepper to taste. Transfer to serving platter and sprinkle with blue cheese. Serve.

> ### KEYS TO SUCCESS
> - **Blanch the onions:** Makes them easier to peel
> - **Sweet and savory vinaigrette:** Adds the final flavor balance

GRILLED SALADS

STEPHANIE PIXLEY

Is it worth firing up the grill to use it to make a salad? We think so, and you will too once you taste the grilled salads in this course, their vegetables enhanced by the smoky char. Too often vegetables (and fruit) come off the grill crunchy and scorched or watery and soggy. We show you how to strategically cut and cook them for perfectly tender, lightly charred results.

STEPH'S PRO TIP: *Any grilled salad is instantly better when paired with grilled bread but that's especially true with the Grilled Peach and Tomato Salad. Just slice up any bread you have on hand, brush it with oil, rub it with a garlic clove if you're feeling fancy, and grill it for a few minutes on each side.*

GRILLED CAESAR SALAD

Serves: 6
Total Time: 1¼ hours

RECIPE OVERVIEW   We are intrigued by the idea of the flavors of a classic Caesar salad enriched with the smoky char of the grill. Start with compact romaine hearts, which hold their shape better than whole heads. Halve them lengthwise to increase their surface area, making sure to keep the core intact so the leaves don't fall apart on the grill. To prevent sticking, brush the leaves with dressing: You get twice the flavor by using the dressing before and after grilling. Just 1 to 2 minutes on a hot grill gives you a smoky and charred (not wilted) exterior. To keep things simple, we forego croutons for slices of crusty bread grilled just before the lettuce.

Dressing
- 1   tablespoon lemon juice
- 1   garlic clove, minced
- ½   cup mayonnaise
- ½   ounce Parmesan cheese, grated (¼ cup)
- 1   tablespoon white wine vinegar
- 1   tablespoon Worcestershire sauce
- 1   tablespoon Dijon mustard
- 2   anchovy fillets, rinsed
- ½   teaspoon salt
- ½   teaspoon pepper
- ¼   cup extra-virgin olive oil

Salad
- 1   (12-inch) baguette, cut on bias into
     5-inch-long, ½-inch-thick slices
- 3   tablespoons extra-virgin olive oil
- 1   garlic clove, peeled
- 3   romaine lettuce hearts (18 ounces),
     halved lengthwise through cores
- ½   ounce Parmesan cheese, grated (¼ cup)

1. FOR THE DRESSING   Combine lemon juice and garlic in bowl and let stand for 10 minutes. Process lemon-garlic mixture, mayonnaise, Parmesan, vinegar, Worcestershire, mustard, anchovies, salt, and pepper in blender for about 30 seconds. With blender running, slowly add oil. Reserve 6 tablespoons dressing for brushing romaine.

2A. FOR A CHARCOAL GRILL   Open bottom vent completely. Light large chimney starter filled with charcoal briquettes (6 quarts). When top coals are partially covered with ash, pour evenly over half of grill. Set cooking grate in place, cover, and open lid vent completely. Heat grill until hot, about 5 minutes.

2B. FOR A GAS GRILL   Turn all burners to high, cover, and heat grill until hot, about 15 minutes. Leave all burners on high.

3. **FOR THE SALAD** Clean and oil cooking grate. Brush bread with oil and grill (over coals if using charcoal), uncovered, until browned, about 1 minute per side. Transfer to platter and rub with garlic clove. Brush cut sides of romaine with reserved dressing; place half of romaine, cut side down, on grill (over coals if using charcoal). Grill, uncovered, until lightly charred, 1 to 2 minutes. Move to platter with bread. Repeat. Drizzle romaine with remaining dressing, sprinkle with Parmesan, and serve.

KEYS TO SUCCESS

- **Use hearts not heads**: More compact hearts withstand the heat better.

- **A hot fire**: Chars the romaine's exterior faster while keeping the interior crunchy

- **Grill just one side**: Improves the odds of getting softness and char

Prepping for Grilled Caesar

DRESS
Brush Caesar dressing onto halved romaine hearts before grilling.

GRILL
Grill dressed romaine halves on just 1 side to keep lettuce from wilting.

DRESS
Once charred lettuce comes off grill, finish with more Caesar dressing.

GRILLED VEGETABLE AND HALLOUMI SALAD

Serves: 4 to 6
Total Time: 50 minutes

RECIPE OVERVIEW Perfect for a summer supper, smoky charred vegetables pair nicely with briny halloumi cheese to create a warm and hearty salad. Halloumi, popular in Greece, has a solid consistency and high melting point, making it perfect for grilling. It becomes beautifully charred and crisp on the outside in contrast to its chewy warm interior. To keep with a Greek theme, we use eggplant, radicchio, and zucchini for the vegetables. After grilling the radicchio for just 5 minutes and the eggplant, zucchini, and cheese for 10 minutes, the vegetables and cheese are browned, tender, and redolent with smoky flavor. We simply chop all the grilled goodies before tossing everything with a sweet, herbaceous honey and thyme vinaigrette, a nice foil to the salty cheese and bitter radicchio. This salad is hearty enough to serve as a main dish and pairs well with grilled bread. The halloumi may appear to stick to the grill at first, but as it continues to brown it will naturally release and flip easily.

3   tablespoons honey
1   tablespoon minced fresh thyme
½   teaspoon grated lemon zest plus 3 tablespoons juice
1   garlic clove, minced
⅛   teaspoon table salt
⅛   teaspoon pepper
1   pound eggplant, sliced into ½-inch-thick rounds
1   head radicchio (10 ounces), quartered
1   zucchini, halved lengthwise
1   (8-ounce) block halloumi cheese, sliced into
     ½-inch-thick slabs
¼   cup extra-virgin olive oil, divided

1. Whisk honey, thyme, lemon zest and juice, garlic, salt, and pepper together in large bowl; set aside. Brush eggplant, radicchio, zucchini, and halloumi with 2 tablespoons oil and season with salt and pepper.

2A. FOR A CHARCOAL GRILL Open bottom vent completely. Light large chimney starter half filled with charcoal briquettes (3 quarts). When top coals are partially covered with ash, pour evenly over grill. Set cooking grate in place, cover, and open lid vent completely. Heat grill until hot, about 5 minutes.

2B. FOR A GAS GRILL Turn all burners to high, cover, and heat grill until hot, about 15 minutes. Turn all burners to medium.

3. Clean cooking grate, then repeatedly brush grate with well-oiled paper towels until grate is black and glossy, 5 to 10 times. Place vegetables and cheese on grill. Cook (covered if using gas), flipping as needed, until radicchio is softened and lightly charred, 3 to 5 minutes, and remaining vegetables and cheese are softened and lightly charred, about 10 minutes. Transfer vegetables and cheese to cutting board as they finish cooking, let cool slightly, then cut into 1-inch pieces.

4. Whisking constantly, slowly drizzle remaining 2 tablespoons oil into honey mixture. Add vegetables and cheese and gently toss to coat. Season with salt and pepper to taste. Serve.

KEYS TO SUCCESS

- **The right vegetables:** Their textures stand up to the heat of the grill which vaporizes moisture.

- **Halloumi:** It has a solid consistency so when it's heated it softens but doesn't melt.

GRILLED RADICCHIO SALAD WITH CORN, CHERRY TOMATOES, AND PECORINO

Serves: 4
Total Time: 1¼ hours

RECIPE OVERVIEW Grilled corn and radicchio have smoky-sweet char and a hint of bitterness that contrast nicely with crisp greens in this vibrant salad. The radicchio's leaves become lightly crisp and smoky, and the heat from the grill enhances corn's natural sweetness. We brush both vegetables with an aromatic dressing base that includes coriander, cumin, and garlic. For optimal browning, we flip the radicchio so that both cut sides come in direct contact with the heat. We also grill lime halves to lighten their acidity and add brightness to the dressing. Cherry tomatoes give an extra pop of sweetness, and the richness of shaved Pecorino Romano rounds out the salad. To keep the radicchio from falling apart on the grill, leave the core intact when cutting it into quarters. For extra crunch, top with spiced pepitas or crispy chickpeas.

½ cup extra-virgin olive oil
1 tablespoon ground coriander
3 garlic cloves, minced
1 teaspoon ground cumin
½ teaspoon chili powder
½ teaspoon table salt
½ teaspoon pepper
1½ tablespoons honey
1 head (10 ounces) radicchio, quartered through core
3 ears corn, husks and silk removed
2 limes, halved
8 ounces cherry tomatoes, halved
1 romaine lettuce heart (6 ounces), torn into bite-size pieces
1½ ounces Pecorino Romano cheese, shaved, divided
½ cup chopped fresh basil, divided

1. Microwave oil, coriander, garlic, cumin, chili powder, salt, and pepper in large bowl, stirring occasionally, until fragrant, about 1 minute. Set aside ¼ cup oil mixture for brushing radicchio and corn. Whisk honey into remaining oil mixture in bowl; set aside.

2. Place radicchio, corn, and lime halves on rimmed baking sheet. Whisk reserved ¼ cup oil mixture to recombine, then brush all over radicchio and corn on sheet.

3A. FOR A CHARCOAL GRILL Open bottom vent completely. Light large chimney starter filled with charcoal briquettes (6 quarts). When top coals are partially covered with ash, pour evenly over grill. Set cooking grate in place, cover, and open lid vent completely. Heat grill until hot, about 5 minutes.

3B. FOR A GAS GRILL Turn all burners to high, cover, and heat grill until hot, about 15 minutes. Leave all burners on high.

4. Clean and oil cooking grate. Place corn on grill and cook (covered if using gas), turning as needed, until lightly charred, 10 to 13 minutes. Return corn to sheet. Place radicchio and limes on grill and cook (covered if using gas), flipping radicchio as needed, until edges of radicchio are browned and wilted but centers are still slightly firm and lime halves are lightly charred, about 5 minutes. Return radicchio and limes to sheet with corn.

5. Once limes are cool enough to handle, squeeze to yield ¼ cup juice, then whisk into reserved honey-oil mixture in bowl until emulsified. Cut kernels from cobs and add to bowl with vinaigrette along with tomatoes, romaine, half of Pecorino, and half of basil. Toss gently to combine, then season with salt and pepper to taste. Transfer radicchio to serving platter and top with corn mixture, remaining Pecorino, and remaining basil. Serve.

KEYS TO SUCCESS

- **Cut radicchio into thick wedges:** Cutting through the core keeps them intact.

- **A taste of honey:** Its subtle sweetness in the dressing complements the vegetables.

GRILLED PEACH AND TOMATO SALAD WITH BURRATA AND BASIL

Serves: 4 to 6
Total Time: 1¼ hours

RECIPE OVERVIEW Grilling ripe peaches enhances their aroma and sweetness in this vibrant salad. To prevent the peaches from sticking to the grill and to add welcome browning, halve them and brush the cut sides with melted butter then grill over high heat to give the fruit a custardy-soft texture and subtle grill flavor. When grill marks form, move them to a covered baking pan over indirect heat until they are fully softened. Once the peaches are cool enough to handle, discard their skins, cut into wedges, and toss with tomato chunks in a simple vinaigrette of white wine vinegar and olive oil. Creamy burrata cheese adds texture and richness to this stunning dish, which is also fabulous made with nectarines or plums. For the best results, use high-quality, ripe, in-season tomatoes and peaches with a fragrant aroma and flesh that yields slightly when gently pressed. Using a metal baking pan on the cooler side of the grill won't harm the pan, but you can use a disposable aluminum pan if preferred; do not use a glass dish.

Peaches

- 1½ pounds ripe but slightly firm peaches (4 peaches), halved and pitted
- 2 tablespoons unsalted butter, melted

Salad

- 12 ounces ripe tomatoes, cored and cut into ½-inch pieces
- ¾ teaspoon table salt, divided
- 5 tablespoons extra-virgin olive oil, divided
- 1 tablespoon white wine vinegar
- 8 ounces burrata cheese, room temperature
- ⅓ cup chopped fresh basil or parsley

1. FOR THE PEACHES Brush cut sides of peaches with melted butter.

2A. FOR A CHARCOAL GRILL Open bottom vent completely. Light large chimney starter three-quarters filled with charcoal briquettes (4½ quarts). When top coals are partially covered with ash, pour evenly over half of grill. Set cooking grate in place, cover, and open lid vent completely. Heat grill until hot, about 5 minutes.

2B. FOR A GAS GRILL Turn all burners to high, cover, and heat grill until hot, about 15 minutes. Leave primary burner on high and turn off other burner(s).

3. Clean and oil cooking grate. Arrange peaches cut side down on hotter side of grill and cook (covered if using gas) until grill marks have formed, 5 to 7 minutes, moving peaches as needed to ensure even cooking.

4. Transfer peaches cut side up to 13 by 9-inch metal baking pan and cover loosely with aluminum foil. Place pan on cooler side of grill. If using gas, turn primary burner to medium. Cover and cook until peaches are very tender and paring knife slips in and out with little resistance, 10 to 15 minutes. When peaches are cool enough to handle, discard skins, then let cool completely.

5. FOR THE SALAD While peaches cool, toss tomatoes with ¼ teaspoon salt and let drain in colander for 30 minutes. Cut each peach half into 4 wedges and cut each wedge in half crosswise.

6. Whisk ¼ cup oil, vinegar, and remaining ½ teaspoon salt together in large bowl. Add peaches and tomatoes and toss gently to combine; transfer to shallow serving bowl. Place burrata on top of salad and drizzle with remaining 1 tablespoon oil. Season with pepper to taste and sprinkle with basil. Serve, breaking up burrata with spoon and allowing creamy liquid to meld with dressing.

KEYS TO SUCCESS

- **Brush peaches with butter:** Prevents them from sticking and promotes grill marks
- **Cover fruit on cool side:** Helps peaches retain heat and stay juicy while they soften
- **Sub in fresh mozzarella:** In place of the burrata

CORE TECHNIQUE **Achieving Perfectly Grilled Stone Fruit**

BRUSH WITH BUTTER
Brush cut side of halved, pitted fruit with melted butter.

GRILL CUT SIDE DOWN
Grill cut side down over direct heat until grill marks form.

TRANSFER TO PAN
Transfer cut side up to pan, cover, and cook over indirect heat until tender.

NAM TOK

Serves: 4 to 6
Total Time: TK

RECIPE OVERVIEW In this grilled-beef Thai salad, the cuisine's five signature flavor elements—hot, sour, salty, sweet, and bitter—shine in a light but satisfying dish. We prepared a standard half-grill fire to get a perfect medium-rare steak with a nicely charred crust. The five flavors come together in the dressing of fish sauce, lime juice, sugar, and hot spices, creating a counterpoint to the subtle bitter char of the meat. Kao kua (toasted rice ground in a spice grinder) adds extra body to the dressing. Don't skip the rice powder; it's integral to the texture and flavor of the dish. If fresh Thai chiles are unavailable, substitute half a serrano chile. Any variety of white rice can be used to make the rice powder. Toasted rice powder can also be found in many Asian markets: If desired, skip the toasting and grinding in step 1 and use 1 tablespoon store-bought rice powder instead.

- 1 teaspoon paprika
- 1 teaspoon cayenne pepper
- 1 tablespoon white rice
- 3 tablespoons lime juice (2 limes)
- 2 tablespoons fish sauce
- 2 tablespoons water
- ½ teaspoon sugar
- 1 (1½-pound) flank steak, trimmed
- ½ teaspoon table salt
- ¼ teaspoon white pepper
- 1 English cucumber, sliced on bias ¼ inch thick
- 1½ cups fresh mint or Thai basil leaves, torn
- 1½ cups fresh cilantro or mint leaves
- 4 shallots, sliced thin
- 1 Thai chile, stemmed, seeded, and sliced into thin rings

1. Combine paprika and cayenne in 8-inch skillet and cook over medium heat, shaking skillet, until fragrant, about 1 minute. Transfer to small bowl. Return skillet to medium-high heat; add rice and toast, stirring constantly, until deep golden brown, about 5 minutes. Transfer to second small bowl and let cool for 5 minutes. Grind rice using spice grinder, mini food processor, or mortar and pestle until it resembles fine meal, 10 to 30 seconds (you should have about 1 tablespoon rice powder).

2. Whisk lime juice, fish sauce, water, sugar, and ¼ teaspoon paprika mixture in large bowl and set aside.

3A. FOR A CHARCOAL GRILL Open bottom vent completely. Light large chimney starter filled with charcoal briquettes (6 quarts). When top coals are partially covered with ash, pour evenly over half of grill. Set cooking grate in place, cover, and open lid vent completely. Heat grill until hot, about 5 minutes.

3B. FOR A GAS GRILL Turn all burners to high, cover, and heat grill until hot, about 15 minutes. Leave primary burner on high and turn off other burner(s).

4. Clean and oil cooking grate. Pat steak dry with paper towels and sprinkle with salt and white pepper. Place steak on hotter side of grill and cook until beginning to char and beads of moisture appear on edges of meat, 5 to 6 minutes. Flip steak and continue to cook on second side until meat registers 120 to 125 degrees (for medium-rare), about 5 minutes. Transfer to cutting board, tent with aluminum foil, and let rest for 10 minutes (or let cool completely, about 1 hour).

5. Line large platter with cucumber slices. Slice steak against grain on bias ¼ inch thick. Transfer steak to bowl with lime juice mixture. Add mint, cilantro, shallots, Thai chile, and half of rice powder and toss to combine. Arrange steak over cucumber-lined platter. Serve, passing remaining rice powder and remaining paprika mixture separately.

KEYS TO SUCCESS

- **Flank steak**: A beefy, uniformly shaped cut is good for quick grilling.
- **Toast and grind the rice**: Gives the dressing fuller body and creates a crunchy topping

Unbeadable Trick: Knowing When to Flip

The salad's Thai name, nam tok (literally "water falling"), refers to the beads of moisture that form on the surface of the steak as it cooks—an age-old Thai cookery clue signifying that the meat is ready to be flipped. While this method sounded imprecise, during testing we found it to be a surprisingly accurate gauge of when flank steak is halfway done. Here's why: As this steak's interior gets hotter, its tightly packed fibers contract and release some of their interior moisture, which the fire's heat then pushes to the meat's surface. When turned at this point and cooked for an equal amount of time on the second side, the steak emerges deeply charred on the outside and medium-rare within. (Note: We do not recommend this technique across the board for steaks; since the thickness and density of the meat fibers vary from cut to cut, the time it takes for heat to penetrate and for beads of moisture to be pushed to the meat's surface differs.)

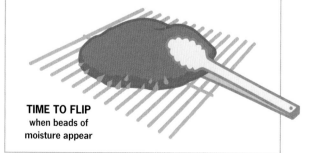

TIME TO FLIP
when beads of moisture appear

CHAPTER 5

SOUPS

ESSENTIAL BROTHS

JACK BISHOP

Making broth is a fundamental cooking technique that every cook should master; it's an important component in a wide variety of soups and stews, as well as in rice, bean, and pasta dishes. Nothing compares to the flavor of homemade broth: It brings everything you cook with it to a higher level. Use the broths in this course in any of our recipes that call for chicken or beef broth and you'll see; in fact, you may never want to go back to the commercial stuff. The good news is that making—and storing—broth is easy so you can always have it ready when you need it.

JACK'S PRO TIP: *Go lightly on the salt when making broth. You want to be able to use your home-made broth in recipes like risotto where it will be cooked down. It's easy to add more salt, but there's no fixing overly salty broth.*

THE METHOD
CHICKEN BROTH

This chicken broth recipe is basic, using just five ingredients and relatively easy to follow. It is an untraditional method that uses chicken parts to deliver maximum flavor in a minimal amount of time.

1 CUT UP CHICKEN
Use a meat cleaver to hack chicken parts into 2-inch pieces.

2 SAUTÉ CHICKEN
Lightly brown chicken to build flavor and help fond to form on bottom of pot.

3 ENHANCE FLAVOR
Only chopped onion is crucial to enhance the flavor of the broth.

4 SWEAT CHICKEN
Cook chicken pieces covered to extract their rich, flavorful juices.

5 SIMMER GENTLY
Add water, salt, and bay leaves, cover, and simmer gently.

6 STRAIN AND DEFAT
Pour broth through fine-mesh strainer, let broth settle, then skim off fat that rises to the surface.

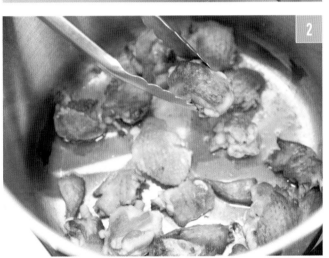

BASIC CHICKEN BROTH

Makes: 8 cups
Total Time: 1½ hours

RECIPE OVERVIEW Many recipes for homemade chicken broth simmer a whole chicken in water. For this broth we cut chicken parts into small pieces, which releases the chicken flavor in a shorter amount of time, since more surface area of the meat is exposed, and also exposes more bone marrow, which is key for both flavor and a thicker consistency. Sweating the chicken pieces for 20 minutes before adding the water further speeds along the release of flavor, keeping the cooking time relatively short. All this produces really chicken-y chicken broth in just about an hour and a half. The only vegetable you'll need for this recipe is onion. Use a meat cleaver or the heel of a chef's knife to cut the chicken into smaller pieces. Any chicken meat left over after you strain the broth will be very dry and flavorless; it should not be eaten. Chicken thighs can be substituted for the legs, backs, and wings in a pinch. Make sure to use a 7-quart or larger Dutch oven for this recipe.

- 1 tablespoon vegetable oil
- 3 pounds whole chicken legs, backs, and/or wings, hacked into 2-inch pieces
- 1 onion, chopped
- 8 cups water
- 2 teaspoons table salt
- 2 bay leaves

1. Heat oil in Dutch oven or stockpot over medium-high heat until just smoking. Brown half of chicken lightly on all sides, about 5 minutes; transfer to large bowl. Repeat with remaining chicken using fat left in pot, and transfer to bowl.

2. Add onion to fat left in pot and cook until softened, about 3 minutes. Return browned chicken and any accumulated juices to pot, cover, and reduce heat to low. Cook, stirring occasionally, until chicken has released its juices, about 20 minutes.

3. Add water, salt, and bay leaves and bring to boil. Cover, reduce heat to gentle simmer, and cook, skimming as needed, until broth tastes rich and flavorful, about 20 minutes longer.

4. Remove large bones from pot, then strain broth through fine-mesh strainer. Let broth settle for 5 to 10 minutes, then defat using wide, shallow spoon or fat separator. (Broth can be refrigerated for up to 4 days or frozen for up to 1 month.)

KEYS TO SUCCESS

- **Cut-up chicken:** Using chicken pieces exposes more of the bones and marrow, which add flavor and rich consistency to the broth; also releases flavorful juices more quickly.

- **Make a fond:** Browning the chicken pieces in the pot is a rapid flavor builder.

- **Keep it simple:** Onion and bay leaves support, not detract from, the chicken flavor.

RICH BEEF BROTH

Makes: about 8 cups
Total Time: 2½ hours

RECIPE OVERVIEW It will come as no surprise that the best recipes for beef broth use the most beef. This recipe calls for a generous 6 pounds of beef shanks to make 2 quarts of broth. The abundant connective tissue in shanks breaks down as the broth simmers and contributes a velvety richness. Browning and simmering the bones along with the meat builds more beefy flavor. Red wine, used to deglaze the pan after browning the beef, adds an extra layer of flavor. You can substitute 4 pounds of beef chuck, cut into 3-inch chunks, plus 2 pounds of small marrowbones for the beef shanks, if desired. For an accurate measurement of boiling water, bring a full kettle of water to a boil and then measure out the desired amount. To defat hot broth, we recommend using a ladle or fat separator. After the broth has been refrigerated, the fat hardens on the surface and is very easy to remove. See page 203 for storage information.

1 tablespoon vegetable oil, plus extra as needed
1 large onion
6 pounds cross-cut beef shanks, meat cut from bone in large chunks
½ cup dry red wine
2 quarts boiling water
2 bay leaves
½ teaspoon table salt

1. Heat oil in large stockpot or Dutch oven over medium-high heat until shimmering. Add onion and cook, stirring occasionally, until slightly softened, 2 to 3 minutes. Transfer to large bowl.

2. Brown beef and bones on all sides in 3 or 4 batches, about 5 minutes per batch, adding extra oil as necessary, up to 1 tablespoon. Transfer to bowl with onions.

3. Add wine to now-empty pot and cook, scraping up browned bits with wooden spoon, until reduced to about 3 tablespoons, about 2 minutes. Return browned beef, bones, and onion to pot and reduce heat to low. Cook, covered, until beef releases juices, about 20 minutes.

4. Increase heat to high. Add boiling water, bay leaves, and salt to pot; return mixture to boil and reduce heat to low. Simmer, covered, until meat is tender and broth is flavorful, 1½ to 2 hours, occasionally skimming foam off surface.

5. Strain, discarding bones and onion and reserving beef for another use. Skim fat from surface of broth before using.

KEYS TO SUCCESS

- **Lots of beef:** Six pounds of beef shanks give this broth big beef flavor.

- **Use shanks:** The connective tissue in beef shanks breaks down and adds richness.

- **Thorough browning:** Adds depth of flavor

BEEF BONE BROTH

Makes: about 8 cups
Total Time: 25 hours

RECIPE OVERVIEW This deeply flavorful, nuanced beef broth can be used in recipes or enjoyed as a drinking broth. We start with the most important ingredient: the beef. Many recipes call for roasting just beef bones, but those broths don't have much beefy flavor; and using meat alone produces thin broths that lack body. So we turn to oxtails—they are economical, widely available, and serve as all-in-one bundles of flavor-packed meat, fat, collagen-rich connective tissue, and bone marrow. Plus, since they're sold precut, oxtails don't require any special preparation. To extract the most flavor, brown them first to create fond and then simmer the broth for 24 hours for a broth with a beautiful mahogany color, rich beefy flavor, and luxurious, silky texture. An onion, a bit of tomato paste, and bay leaves enhance the broth's meaty flavor while adding a touch of aromatic sweetness, and white mushrooms play a crucial role in rounding out the overall flavor with their savory tones. We found that the long, slow simmer could be accomplished in a 200-degree oven or in a slow cooker set on low, keeping the recipe streamlined and hands-off. Try to buy oxtails that are approximately 2 inches thick and 2 to 4 inches in diameter; they will yield more flavor for the broth. Oxtails can often be found in the freezer section of the grocery store; if using frozen oxtails, be sure to thaw them completely before using. If using a slow cooker, you will need one that holds 5½ to 7 quarts.

2 tablespoons extra-virgin olive oil, divided
6 pounds oxtails
1 large onion, chopped
8 ounces white mushrooms, trimmed and chopped
2 tablespoons tomato paste
10 cups water, divided
3 bay leaves
1 teaspoon kosher salt
¼ teaspoon pepper

1. Heat 1 tablespoon oil in Dutch oven over medium-high heat until just smoking. Pat oxtails dry with paper towels. Brown half of oxtails, 7 to 10 minutes; transfer to large bowl. Repeat with remaining 1 tablespoon oil and remaining oxtails; transfer to bowl.

2. Add onion and mushrooms to fat left in pot and cook until softened and lightly browned, about 5 minutes. Stir in tomato paste and cook until fragrant, about 1 minute. Stir in 2 cups water, bay leaves, salt, and pepper, scraping up any browned bits.

3A. FOR THE OVEN Adjust oven rack to middle position and heat oven to 200 degrees. Stir remaining 8 cups water into pot, then return browned oxtails and any accumulated juices to pot and bring to simmer. Fit large piece of aluminum foil over pot, pressing to seal, then cover tightly with lid. Transfer pot to oven and cook until broth is rich and flavorful, about 24 hours.

3B. FOR THE SLOW COOKER Transfer browned oxtails and any accumulated juices and vegetable mixture to slow cooker. Stir in remaining 8 cups water. Cover and cook on low until broth is rich and flavorful, about 24 hours.

4. Remove oxtails, then strain broth through fine-mesh strainer into large container; discard solids. Let broth settle for 5 to 10 minutes, then defat using wide, shallow spoon or fat separator. (Cooled broth can be refrigerated for up to 4 days or frozen for up to 1 month.)

KEYS TO SUCCESS

- **Use oxtails:** A great source of collagen and marrow, oxtails are also economical—a plus, since they're discarded after cooking.

- **Cook for 24 hours:** For a rich, drinkable broth

RESOURCES FOR ESSENTIAL BROTHS

STORE-BOUGHT BROTHS 101

Store-bought broths can vary widely in flavor and quality, so it's important to choose wisely.

Chicken Broth

We most often reach for chicken broth (even for some vegetable soups and meat soups) because of its strong savory flavor. Look for broth with less than 700 milligrams of sodium per serving (the saltiness will increase as the broth simmers and evaporates). Our favorite is Swanson Chicken Stock. We also recommend a chicken broth concentrate, Better Than Bouillon Chicken Base.

Vegetarian Broth

Because commercial vegetable broths tend to be sweet, we sometimes mix vegetable broth with chicken broth for the best flavor. In fact, our favorite vegetarian broth, Orrington Farms Vegan Chicken Flavored Broth Base & Seasoning, has a savory flavor reminiscent of chicken broth.

Beef Broth

Beef broths can be short on beefy flavor, which is why we often combine beef and chicken broths in our soups. But with the right additions, a beef broth can pull off a deeply flavored beef soup. Since manufacturers put little actual beef in their broths, we focus on savoriness rather than beef flavor. We recommend Better Than Bouillon Roasted Beef Base, an economical concentrate that stores easily and dissolves quickly in hot water.

FREEZING BROTH IN PORTIONS

Portioning broth before freezing it makes it easy to defrost only as much as you need (from a few tablespoons for a sauce to a few cups for soup). Broth portions can be frozen for up to three months.

For Medium Amounts
Ladle the broth into nonstick muffin tins (each muffin cup will hold about one cup). After the broth has frozen, store the "cups" in a large zipper-lock bag. "Cups" are good for casseroles and braising/steaming/poaching liquid.

For Large Amounts
Line a 4-cup measuring cup with a zipper-lock bag (it holds the bag open so you can use both hands to pour) and pour in the cooled broth.

Seal the bag (double up if you wish) and lay it flat to freeze. This is a good option for soup, stew, rice, or gravy.

THE BEST WAY TO COOL BROTH

For safety reasons, the U.S. Food and Drug Administration (FDA) recommends cooling liquids to 70 degrees within 2 hours after cooking and 41 degrees within 4 hours after that.

We found that the best way to cool down the hot liquid—without raising the temperature of the refrigerator and risking the spoilage of other food—is to first let the liquid cool to 85 degrees on the counter, which takes about an hour. At that point, it's safe to transfer to the fridge, and the total time it takes to cool to 41 degrees is 4 hours and 30 minutes—well within the FDA's recommended range.

CHICKEN SOUPS

NICOLE KONSTANTINAKOS

Chicken soup is the epitome of comfort food, as the pair of recipes in this course shows. Whether you prefer light or dark meat, we have you covered: The first soup combines creamy corn and smoky ham with rich chicken thighs, then swirls in tender ribbons of egg. The second pairs clean-tasting chicken breast meat with nutty wild rice and jam-packs the broth with garlic and greens for a nutritious punch.

NICOLE'S PRO TIP: *To peel multiple cloves of garlic quickly and easily, start by breaking a head of garlic into its individual cloves. Remove the papery outer skins and place the cloves into a 2-cup wide-mouth jar. Seal the jar with the lid and shake vigorously until the skins have loosened, about 30 seconds. Remove the cloves from the jar and discard the skins. If any cloves still have their skins, return them to the jar and repeat shaking.*

CHINESE CORN AND CHICKEN SOUP

Serves: 6
Total Time: 45 minutes

RECIPE OVERVIEW   Classic Chinese corn and chicken soup is a hearty variant of egg drop soup. It was historically made with canned cream-style corn but this version uses fresh. Some of the kernels are pureed so that the vegetable's vibrant, sweet flavor suffuses the chicken broth base with freshness and color. Stirring in a few cups of whole kernels adds sweet, juicy bursts and gives the soup a hearty consistency. Per tradition, the broth base is bulked up with chicken thigh meat, a small amount of chopped smoky ham, and egg ribbons. We coat the pieces of thigh meat in a mixture of soy sauce, cornstarch, water, and baking soda that seasons and insulates the meat so that it cooks up tender and silky. White pepper and a scallion complement the sweetness of the fresh corn. To produce evenly delicate egg ribbons, dilute the beaten eggs with water to thin them out so that the eggs cook and set quickly in the hot soup, and pour the eggs through the tines of a fork to slow down the flow rate.

To make cutting the chicken easier, freeze it for 25 minutes. While this soup is best made with fresh, in-season corn, frozen corn kernels can be used; use 5 cups of thawed frozen corn kernels. Choose smoky ham, such as Virginia or Black Forest, from the deli.

 1   (3- to 4-ounce) boneless, skinless chicken thigh, trimmed and cut into ¼-inch pieces
 5   teaspoons plus ½ cup water, divided
 1   teaspoon plus 3 tablespoons cornstarch, divided
 1   teaspoon soy sauce
 ⅛   teaspoon baking soda
 2   large eggs
 4   cups chicken broth, divided
5–7   ears corn, kernels cut from cobs (5 cups), divided
 2   tablespoons finely chopped deli ham
 ¾   teaspoon table salt
 ¼   teaspoon white pepper
 1   scallion, sliced thin

1. Combine chicken, 1 tablespoon water, 1 teaspoon cornstarch, soy sauce, and baking soda in bowl. Let stand at room temperature while preparing other ingredients. In liquid measuring cup, beat eggs and 2 teaspoons water with fork until whites and yolks are thoroughly combined and color is pure yellow; set aside. Mix ½ cup chicken broth and remaining 3 tablespoons cornstarch in small bowl until thoroughly combined; set aside.

2. Process 2½ cups corn and remaining ½ cup water in blender on low speed until thick puree forms, about 30 seconds. Increase speed to high and continue to process until smooth, about 1 minute longer. Strain puree through fine-mesh strainer set over large saucepan. Using back of ladle or rubber spatula, push puree through strainer, extracting as much liquid as possible. Discard solids.

3. Add ham, salt, white pepper, remaining 3½ cups broth, and remaining 2½ cups corn to corn puree. Bring to boil over medium-high heat. Reduce heat to maintain simmer and add chicken, stirring to break up any clumps. Partially cover and simmer for 5 minutes (broth may look curdled as it comes to simmer). Stir broth-cornstarch mixture to recombine. Add to soup and cook, uncovered, stirring occasionally, until soup has thickened slightly, about 2 minutes.

4. Holding fork in your hand and measuring cup with egg mixture in your other hand, slowly pour egg mixture in slow, steady stream through tines of fork in concentric circles over saucepan until ribbons of coagulated egg form, about 1 minute. Season soup with salt and white pepper to taste. Gently ladle soup into bowls, sprinkle with scallion, and serve.

KEYS TO SUCCESS

- **Puree some kernels:** The puree suffuses the broth with fresh corn flavor and color.

- **Coat the chicken:** Cornstarch and baking soda help it cook up tender and silky.

- **Pour the eggs through a fork:** The tines slow down the flow rate to make thin, even ribbons.

"Ribboning" Eggs into Broth

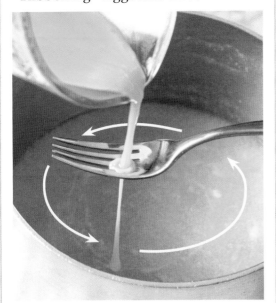

Holding fork in your hand and measuring cup with egg mixture in your other hand, pour mixture in slow stream through tines of fork in concentric circles over saucepan until ribbons of coagulated egg form.

GARLIC-CHICKEN AND WILD RICE SOUP

Serves: 6
Total Time: 1½ hours

RECIPE OVERVIEW There's nothing like a bowl of steaming chicken soup, especially when you're feeling under the weather. This recipe supercharges homemade chicken broth with a megadose of garlic before adding tender morsels of chicken. The soup includes a whopping ½ cup of minced garlic, which adds a bright yet balanced presence. To build flavor, we add aromatic vegetables, thyme, bay leaves, and tomato paste along with the broth. Nutty wild rice, cooked directly in the soup, is infused with its garlicky flavor. To keep the chicken tender, it simmers during the last few minutes of cooking. Finally, baby spinach and chopped fresh parsley add a vegetal boost.

- 3 tablespoons extra-virgin olive oil
- ½ cup minced garlic (about 25 cloves)
- 2 carrots, peeled and sliced ¼ inch thick
- 1 onion, chopped fine
- 1 celery rib, minced
- ¼ teaspoon table salt
- 2 teaspoons minced fresh thyme or ½ teaspoon dried
- 1 teaspoon tomato paste
- 6 cups chicken broth
- 2 bay leaves
- ⅔ cup wild rice, rinsed
- 8 ounces boneless, skinless chicken breasts, trimmed and cut into ¾-inch pieces
- 3 ounces (3 cups) baby spinach
- ¼ cup chopped fresh parsley

1. Heat oil and garlic in Dutch oven over medium-low heat, stirring occasionally, until garlic is light golden, 3 to 5 minutes. Add carrots, onion, celery, and salt, increase heat to medium, and cook, stirring occasionally, until vegetables are just beginning to brown, 10 to 12 minutes.

2. Stir in thyme and tomato paste and cook until fragrant, about 30 seconds. Stir in broth and bay leaves, scraping up any browned bits, and bring to simmer. Stir in rice, return to simmer, cover, and cook over medium-low heat until rice is tender, 40 to 50 minutes.

3. Discard bay leaves. Stir in chicken and spinach and cook over low heat, stirring occasionally, until chicken is cooked through and spinach is wilted, 3 to 5 minutes. Off heat, stir in parsley and season with salt and pepper to taste. Serve.

KEYS TO SUCCESS

- **Lots of garlic:** One-half cup delivers potent flavor; cooking tames any harshness.

- **Cook the rice in the soup:** It takes on savory flavor as it becomes tender.

- **Cut-up chicken:** Small pieces cook quickly.

JOSEPH GITTER

Vegetable soups can anchor a meal with as much heartiness as soups made with meat. The key is to build deep, multilayered flavor. Each soup in this course shows you how to coax extraordinary flavor out of ordinary vegetables such as mushrooms, artichokes, eggplants, onions, and corn. The way you prep the vegetables and cook them, the supporting ingredients you include—and sometimes what you leave out—all contribute to making a truly memorable vegetable soup.

JOE'S PRO TIP: *Vegetable soups generally reheat very well. Do so over low heat in a large saucepan; vigorous boiling can spoil the delicate texture of well-cooked vegetables. Reheated soup usually needs a little extra seasoning—a splash of vinegar and a sprinkle of salt will wake up a day-old soup no end. And sometimes the soup may need to be thinned out with a little extra warm broth or water.*

ARTICHOKE SOUP À LA BARIGOULE

Serves: 4 to 6
Total Time: 1¼ hours

RECIPE OVERVIEW Barigoule is a Provençal dish of braised artichokes, mushrooms, and root vegetables. Its ingredients translate well into a satisfying savory soup. To intensify their subtle flavor, the artichokes are seared first. Cooking the mushrooms covered and then sautéing them uncovered evaporates their excess moisture, and simmering the parsnips brings out their sweetness. Umami-rich anchovy fillets and garlic supply depth to the soup, and a leek adds sweetness and body. White wine and white wine vinegar add brightness, and a generous amount of tarragon contributes freshness. While we prefer the flavor and texture of jarred baby artichokes, you can substitute 18 ounces frozen artichoke hearts, thawed and patted dry.

- 3 tablespoons extra-virgin olive oil, divided
- 3 cups jarred whole baby artichokes packed in water, quartered, rinsed, and patted dry
- 12 ounces white mushrooms, trimmed and sliced thin
- 1 leek, white and light green parts only, halved lengthwise, sliced ¼ inch thick, and washed thoroughly
- 4 garlic cloves, minced
- 2 anchovy fillets, rinsed, patted dry, and minced
- 1 teaspoon minced fresh thyme or ¼ teaspoon dried
- 3 tablespoons all-purpose flour
- ¼ cup dry white wine
- 3 cups chicken broth
- 3 cups vegetable broth
- 6 ounces parsnips, peeled and cut into ½-inch pieces
- 2 bay leaves
- ¼ cup heavy cream
- 2 tablespoons chopped fresh tarragon
- 1 teaspoon white wine vinegar, plus extra for seasoning

1. Heat 1 tablespoon oil in Dutch oven over medium heat until shimmering. Add artichokes and cook until browned, 8 to 10 minutes. Transfer to cutting board, let cool slightly, then chop coarse.

2. Add 1 tablespoon oil and mushrooms to now-empty pot over medium heat, cover, and cook until they have released their liquid, about 5 minutes. Uncover and continue to cook until mushrooms are dry, about 5 minutes.

3. Stir in leek and remaining 1 tablespoon oil and cook until leek is softened and mushrooms are browned, 8 to 10 minutes. Stir in garlic, anchovies, and thyme and cook until fragrant, about 30 seconds. Stir in flour and cook for 1 minute. Stir in wine, scraping up any browned bits, and cook until nearly evaporated, about 1 minute.

4. Slowly whisk in chicken broth and vegetable broth, smoothing out any lumps. Stir in artichokes, parsnips, and bay leaves and bring to simmer. Reduce heat to low, cover, and simmer gently until parsnips are tender, 15 to 20 minutes. Off heat, discard bay leaves. Stir in cream, tarragon, and vinegar. Season with salt, pepper, and extra vinegar to taste. Serve.

KEYS TO SUCCESS

- **Seared artichokes:** Browning gives them more presence in the soup.
- **Anchovies:** Add umami depth
- **Tarragon:** Its anise notes freshen the soup.

Buying Processed Artichokes

Artichokes are served boiled, baked, stuffed, braised, and more (see page 102). They are used in everything from soups and stews to risotto, paella, and pasta. But while fresh artichokes have their place, they're limited by seasonality, so many recipes call for prepared artichokes as a flavorful alternative. When buying processed artichokes, avoid marinated versions; we prefer to control the seasonings ourselves. We also don't recommend canned hearts, which tend to taste waterlogged and have large, tough leaves. We think that smaller whole jarred artichoke hearts labeled "baby" or "cocktail" are best. (If the label doesn't say this, look for specimens no larger than 1½ inches in length.) If you can't find jarred baby artichokes, frozen artichoke hearts will work in certain recipes.

CLASSIC CORN CHOWDER

Serves: 6 to 8
Total Time: 1 hour

RECIPE OVERVIEW This silver-bullet recipe delivers all the best qualities of a great corn chowder: velvety texture, strong corn flavor, and plump, juicy kernels. For ultimate corn flavor, every element of the key ingredient—from kernel to cob—is included in every step, and canned corn boosts the flavor even more. For a sweet and smoky starting place, sauté chopped bacon to render its fat and reserve the crispy pieces to stir into the chowder at the end. Cooking the fresh corn kernels and onion in the fat creates a toasty, caramelized flavor base. Some canned corn pureed with chicken broth serves as a lush thickener that boosts the chowder's sweet corn flavors. Last, but certainly not least, the shucked cobs are simmered in the pot right alongside the potatoes for a subtle but significant final layer of corn flavor, perfectly finishing off this "nose-to-tail" corn chowder.

- 6 ears corn
- 2 (15-ounce) cans whole-kernel corn, drained
- 5 cups chicken broth, divided
- 3 slices bacon, chopped fine
- 1 onion, chopped
- ½ teaspoon table salt
- ¼ teaspoon pepper
- 1 pound red potatoes, unpeeled, cut into ½-inch pieces
- 1 cup heavy cream
- 4 scallions, sliced thin

1. Cut kernels from ears of corn by cutting cobs in half crosswise, then standing each half on its flat, cut end. Using chef's knife, cut kernels off ear, 1 side at a time. Reserve kernels and cobs separately. Puree canned corn and 2 cups broth in blender until smooth.

2. Cook bacon in Dutch oven over medium heat until crispy, about 8 minutes. Using slotted spoon, transfer bacon to paper towel–lined plate and reserve. Cook reserved corn kernels, onion, salt, and pepper in bacon fat until vegetables are softened and golden brown, 6 to 8 minutes.

3. Add reserved cobs, corn puree, remaining 3 cups broth, and potatoes to Dutch oven and bring to boil. Reduce heat to medium-low and simmer until potatoes are tender, about 15 minutes. Discard cobs and stir in cream, scallions, and reserved bacon. Season with salt and pepper to taste. Serve. (Soup can be refrigerated for up to 3 days.)

KEYS TO SUCCESS

- **Use corn cobs:** Simmered in the chowder (then removed), they reinforce the corn flavor.
- **Cook the onion and corn in bacon fat:** Creates a smoky flavor base for the chowder

MUSHROOM BISQUE

Serves: 6 to 10
Total Time: 1½ hours

RECIPE OVERVIEW This creamy mushroom bisque is a far more sophisticated version of cream of mushroom soup with an indulgent velvety texture and robust mushroom flavor. Using three kinds of mushrooms—white, cremini, and shiitake—produces deep, earthy mushroom flavor. Because mushrooms will exude moisture without being cut, you can cook them whole in the microwave until they release most of their liquid. The dehydrated mushrooms brown more efficiently in the pot, which is then deglazed with the reserved mushroom liquid. Additional ingredients are kept to a minimum so as not to distract from the mushrooms' flavor. A mixture of egg yolks and cream whisked in at the end gives the soup a texture that is luxurious without being cloying. To complement the lush texture and rich woodsy flavor of the soup, garnish each bowl with cream and a sprinkle of chives. Tying the thyme sprig with twine makes it easier to remove from the pot. For the smoothest result, use a conventional blender rather than an immersion blender.

SCIENCE LESSON

Yoking Together Yolks for Silky—and Flavorful—Bisque

The abundance of cream in bisques gives them their lush consistency, but it also makes most versions taste flat. While the fat droplets in cream thicken a liquid by getting in the way of water molecules, slowing their movement, they also mute flavor by coating the tongue and preventing flavor molecules from reaching taste receptors.

For a bisque with both pleasing body and a more pronounced mushroom flavor, we turned instead to an old-school French thickener—a so-called liaison, which replaces a large portion of the cream with egg yolks. As the bisque heats, proteins in the yolks unfold and bond together into long, tangled strands that, like the fat in cream, interfere with the movement of water molecules. Egg yolks also contain the powerful emulsifier lecithin, which has a twofold effect: It breaks up the fat droplets into smaller particles that disperse more completely throughout the liquid, obstructing more water molecules, for an even thicker consistency. It also keeps the bisque smooth by holding the fat droplets suspended in the liquid so they don't separate out.

If yolks can do all this, why even use cream? Because the fat it contains provides an appealing mouthfeel that yolks alone can't match.

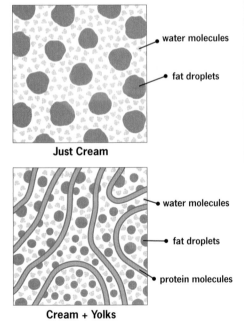

Just Cream

water molecules

fat droplets

Cream + Yolks

water molecules

fat droplets

protein molecules

1 pound white mushrooms, trimmed
8 ounces cremini mushrooms, trimmed
8 ounces shiitake mushrooms, stemmed
1½ teaspoons table salt
2 tablespoons vegetable oil
1 small onion, chopped fine
1 sprig fresh thyme
¼ teaspoon pepper
2 tablespoons dry sherry
4 cups water
3½ cups chicken broth
⅔ cup heavy cream, plus extra for serving
2 large egg yolks
1 teaspoon lemon juice
Chopped fresh chives

1. Toss white mushrooms, cremini mushrooms, shiitake mushrooms, and salt together in large bowl. Cover and microwave, stirring every 4 minutes, until mushrooms have released their liquid and reduced to about one-third their original volume, about 12 minutes. Transfer mushrooms to colander set in second large bowl and drain well, reserving liquid.

2. Heat oil in Dutch oven over medium heat until shimmering. Add mushrooms and cook, stirring occasionally, until mushrooms are browned and fond has formed on bottom of pot, about 8 minutes. Add onion, thyme sprig, and pepper and cook, stirring occasionally, until onion is just softened, about 2 minutes. Add sherry and cook until evaporated. Stir in reserved mushroom liquid and cook, scraping up any browned bits. Stir in water and broth and bring to simmer. Reduce heat to low and simmer for 20 minutes.

3. Discard thyme sprig. Working in batches, process soup in blender until very smooth, 1½ to 2 minutes. Return soup to now-empty pot.

4. Whisk cream and egg yolks together in medium bowl. Stirring slowly and constantly, add 2 cups soup to cream mixture to temper. Stirring constantly, slowly pour cream mixture into simmering soup. Heat gently, stirring constantly, until soup registers 165 degrees (do not overheat). Stir in lemon juice and season with salt and pepper to taste. Serve immediately, garnishing each serving with 1 teaspoon extra cream and sprinkle of chives.

KEYS TO SUCCESS

- **Don't chop**: Cooking the mushrooms whole saves time and works just as well.

- **Precook**: Microwave the mushrooms to eliminate moisture for more efficient browning.

Lots of Mushrooms, Little Work

Our bisque contains a full 2 pounds of mushrooms, but we found that there's no need to slice or chop them. Because mushrooms lack a thick outer layer, they give up moisture readily even when left whole. We simply toss them with salt and microwave them until most of their liquid is released. Then we brown the shriveled mushrooms to deepen their flavor and use the reserved mushroom liquid to help form the base of the soup.

Mega Mushrooms
A mix of white, cremini, and shiitake mushrooms gives our soup woodsy depth.

SMOKY EGGPLANT MISO SOUP

Serves: 4
Total Time: 6½ hours

RECIPE OVERVIEW Miso soup is traditionally based on the umami-rich Japanese stock called dashi. Dashi is made by briefly cooking katsuobushi (smoked, dried, and fermented skipjack tuna flakes) and a dried kelp called kombu in water. For this plant-based version, smoked and dehydrated eggplant replaces the katsuobushi. The dried eggplant, along with shiitake mushrooms, kombu, and aromatics, create a rich broth that is finished with a small amount of salty-sweet miso. As it flavors the broth, the smoky eggplant plumps up; you can then slice it and add it to the soup as a garnish. This recipe takes some time and effort, but don't skip it; the results are sublime.

1 large eggplant, sliced into ¼-inch-thick rounds
1 teaspoon kosher salt
2 cups wood chips
7 scallions, white and green parts separated and sliced thin
1 (1½-inch) piece ginger, peeled and sliced thin
1 (6-inch) piece lemongrass stalk, sliced thin
1 garlic clove, sliced thin
10 cups cold water
1 ounce dried shiitake mushrooms
2 (4-inch) pieces kombu
3 tablespoons soy sauce
1 tablespoon mirin
2½ tablespoons white miso
9 ounces soft tofu, cut into ½-inch pieces (1¼ cups)

1. Toss eggplant with salt in medium bowl; set aside for at least 15 minutes or up to 30 minutes. Meanwhile, using large piece of heavy-duty aluminum foil, wrap wood chips in 8 by 4½-inch foil packet. (Make sure chips do not poke holes in sides or bottom of packet.) Cut 2 evenly spaced, 2-inch slits in top of packet.

2A. FOR A CHARCOAL GRILL Open bottom vent completely. Light large chimney starter half filled with charcoal briquettes (3 quarts). When top coals are partially covered with ash, pour evenly over half of grill. Place wood chip packet on coals. Set cooking grate in place, cover, and open lid vent completely. Heat grill until hot and wood chips are smoking, about 5 minutes.

2B. FOR A GAS GRILL Remove cooking grate and place wood chip packet directly on primary burner. Set grate in place, turn all burners to high, cover, and heat grill until hot and wood chips are smoking, about 15 minutes. Turn primary burner to medium-high and turn off other burner(s). (Adjust primary burner as needed to maintain grill temperature around 325 degrees.)

3. Clean and oil cooking grate. Arrange eggplant pieces on cooler side of grill. Cook, covered, until eggplant flesh turns golden brown and smells deeply smoky, 30 to 45 minutes, flipping halfway through cooking. Transfer to wire rack set in rimmed baking sheet.

4. Preheat oven to 200 degrees. Transfer eggplant to oven and bake until pieces are shrunk, dry, and hard, about 4 hours. (If you have a convection option on your oven, now is a good time to use it. Start checking for doneness at the 3-hour mark.)

5. Place scallion whites, ginger, lemongrass, and garlic in center of small piece of cheesecloth; gather edges of cheesecloth and tie with kitchen twine to form sachet. Combine water, sachet, eggplant, shiitakes, and kombu in large saucepan and bring to gentle simmer over low heat, about 10 minutes. Cover and simmer gently for 30 minutes.

6. Remove and discard sachet and kombu. Strain liquid through coffee filter set in fine-mesh strainer, reserving eggplant and shiitakes. Rinse and dry saucepan; return strained broth to saucepan. Thinly slice 1 cup reserved eggplant and ¼ cup reserved shiitakes. Combine sliced eggplant and shiitakes in small bowl and season with salt to taste. Reserve any remaining eggplant and shiitakes for other use.

7. Whisk soy sauce, mirin, and miso into broth. Season with salt to taste. Add tofu and bring to simmer over medium-high heat. Turn off heat. Divide eggplant and shiitake mixture among 4 bowls. Pour soup over top, sprinkle with scallion greens, and serve.

KEYS TO SUCCESS

- **Smoke, then dry, the eggplant:** The dual grill-oven process gives the vegetable a deep umami quality reminiscent of katsuobushi.

- **Use soft tofu:** For a tender, silky texture

BEST FRENCH ONION SOUP

Serves: 6
Total Time: 4¾ to 5¼ hours

RECIPE OVERVIEW Great French onion soup is characterized by a rich broth, sweet-savory caramelized onions, and nutty Gruyère-topped toast—but it is really all about the onions. Forget constant stirring on the stovetop, which can take hours of active work. Cooking onions in the oven takes time but requires little attention, making this French onion soup recipe more hands-off. By starting the cooking in a 400-degree oven, you need to stir only periodically before moving the Dutch oven to the stovetop to deeply brown the onions. We let the onions recaramelize and then deglaze the pot several times with water before adding the broth and additional aromatics. Use yellow onions; sweet onions, such as Vidalia or Walla Walla, will make the soup overly sweet. Use broiler-safe crocks and keep the rims 4 to 5 inches from the broiler element to obtain a proper gratinée of cheese. If using ordinary soup bowls, sprinkle the toasted bread slices with Gruyère and broil them on the baking sheet until the cheese melts, then float them on top of the soup. Use a Dutch oven that holds 7 quarts or more for this recipe.

4	pounds yellow onions, halved and sliced through root end into ¼-inch-thick pieces
3	tablespoons unsalted butter, cut into 3 pieces
1½	teaspoons table salt, divided
2¾–3	cups water
½	cup dry sherry
4	cups chicken broth
2	cups beef broth
6	sprigs fresh thyme, tied with kitchen twine
1	bay leaf
1	(12-inch) baguette, cut into ½-inch slices
8	ounces Gruyère cheese, shredded (2 cups)

1. Adjust oven rack to middle position and heat oven to 400 degrees. Coat inside of Dutch oven with vegetable oil spray. Add onions, butter, and 1 teaspoon salt. Cover, transfer pot to oven, and cook until onions wilt slightly, about 1 hour.

2. Stir onions thoroughly, scraping bottom and sides of pot. Partially cover pot and continue to cook in oven until onions are very soft and golden brown, 1½ to 1¾ hours longer, stirring onions thoroughly after 1 hour.

3. Remove pot from oven and place over medium-high heat. (Do not turn off oven.) Continue to cook onions, stirring and scraping pot often, until liquid evaporates, onions brown, and bottom of pot is coated with dark crust, 20 to 25 minutes. (If onions begin to brown too quickly, reduce heat to medium.)

4. Stir in ¼ cup water, scraping up any browned bits. Continue to cook until water evaporates and pot bottom has formed another dark crust, 6 to 8 minutes. Repeat deglazing with ¼ cup water 2 or 3 more times, until onions are very dark brown.

5. Stir in sherry and cook until almost dry, about 5 minutes. Stir in 2 cups water, chicken broth, beef broth, thyme bundle, bay leaf, and remaining ½ teaspoon salt, scraping up any remaining browned bits, and bring to simmer. Reduce heat to medium-low, cover, and cook for 30 minutes. Discard thyme bundle and bay leaf and season soup with salt and pepper to taste.

6. Lay baguette slices on rimmed baking sheet and bake until dry, crisp, and lightly golden, about 10 minutes, flipping slices halfway through baking.

7. Position oven rack 8 inches from broiler element and heat broiler. Set individual broiler-safe crocks on separate rimmed baking sheet and fill each with about 1½ cups soup. Top each bowl with 1 or 2 baguette slices (do not overlap slices) and sprinkle evenly with Gruyère. Broil until cheese is melted and bubbly around edges, 3 to 5 minutes. Let cool for 5 minutes before serving.

KEYS TO SUCCESS

- **Choose the right onions:** Yellow onions have the most flavor and contribute the best color to the soup.
- **Cut them the right way:** Onions sliced pole to pole maintain their shape during long cooking.
- **Spray the pot:** So that the onions don't stick
- **Oven to stovetop:** A hybrid cooking method produces the best fond.
- **Triple deglaze:** Deglaze the pot at least three times to loosen the flavorful fond on the bottom.

WHAT CAN GO WRONG

PROBLEM The soup is too mild or too sweet.

SOLUTION Be sure to sure to use the right type of onion. Yellow onions offer the best sweet and savory notes.

PROBLEM The onions are stringy.

SOLUTION Slicing the onions against the grain results in cooked onions with a lifeless, stringy texture. Cutting the onions pole to pole—with the grain—helps the pieces maintain their shape through the long cooking process.

PROBLEM The soup lacks complexity.

SOLUTION The secret is in the fond. Don't skip deglazing, because it creates new layers of fond, helping the onions become very dark brown. The deeper the color of the onions, the better the flavor.

CORE TECHNIQUE

Caramelizing Onions in the Oven

RAW ONIONS
Add raw onions to a large Dutch oven.

AFTER 1 HOUR IN OVEN
Onions start to wilt and release moisture.

AFTER 2½ HOURS IN OVEN
Onions are golden, wilted, and significantly reduced in volume.

BEEFY SOUPS

DAN ZUCCARELLO

In this course, you'll learn how to use different cuts of beef to make a range of hearty, lively soups. Ground beef is brightened with kimchi and fortified with tofu for a spicy, yet comforting, soup. An Eastern European beef soup combines brisket with sauerkraut and dill. A fusion stew livens up chuck roast with Creole seasoning while oxtails are perfumed with star anise and ginger in a Hawaiian-style soup. And an old-fashioned beef and vegetable stew rounds out sirloin tips with plenty of carrots and mushrooms.

DAN'S PRO TIP: *How do you take your beef soups to the next level? Homemade broth. I store beef bones and scraps from steak night in my freezer until I have enough to fill my 6-quart pressure cooker, then top them off with water, vegetable odds and ends, and any umami-rich ingredients I have in my pantry such as tomato paste, soy sauce, or dried porcini mushrooms. After one hour under pressure...liquid gold!*

KIMCHI, BEEF, AND TOFU SOUP

Serves: 4
Total Time: 1 hour

RECIPE OVERVIEW Kimchi is a tangy, lightly spicy mix of pickled vegetables that's ubiquitous in Korean cuisine. Here it pushes a punchy, beefy soup to the top of the flavor podium. This warming, piquant, and deeply savory soup makes deft use of two proteins: Ground beef imbues the broth with tons of meaty flavor, while firm tofu absorbs all the soup's bold flavors and gives it even more staying power. Tangy, spicy kimchi adds complexity, and a dash of the kimchi's brine amps up its presence. Fresh ginger, mirin, and soy sauce give the broth more depth of flavor and a fantastic aroma. Using chicken broth instead of beef broth here helps support all those savory flavors without overwhelming them. A drizzle of toasted sesame oil lends pleasing nuttiness, and a sprinkling of scallions adds some welcome color. If there's not enough brine in the kimchi jar to yield ¼ cup, add water to compensate. Make sure to use firm (not soft) tofu here.

- 1 pound 85 percent lean ground beef
- ½ teaspoon table salt
- ½ teaspoon pepper
- 1 tablespoon grated fresh ginger
- ½ cup mirin
- 3 cups water
- 2 cups chicken broth
- 3 cups kimchi, drained with ¼ cup brine reserved, chopped coarse
- 8 ounces firm tofu, cut into ½-inch cubes
- 2 tablespoons soy sauce
- 4 scallions, sliced thin
- 1 tablespoon toasted sesame oil

1. Combine beef, salt, and pepper in Dutch oven; cook over medium-high heat, breaking up meat with wooden spoon, until moisture evaporates and beef begins to sizzle, 8 to 10 minutes.

2. Add ginger and cook until fragrant, about 30 seconds. Stir in mirin, scraping up any browned bits. Stir in water, broth, kimchi and reserved brine, tofu, and soy sauce and bring to boil. Reduce heat to low, cover, and simmer to allow flavors to meld, about 15 minutes.

3. Off heat, stir in scallions and oil. Serve.

KEYS TO SUCCESS

- **Chicken, not beef, broth:** Its milder flavor lets the other ingredients in the soup shine.

- **Firm tofu:** Adds protein and textural interest.

- **Kimchi brine:** Bolsters the bright, tangy flavor

BEEF AND CABBAGE SOUP

Serves: 4 to 6
Total Time: 2 hours

RECIPE OVERVIEW This hearty soup, popular in Eastern Europe, deserves a place on your table. Its marriage of tender chunks of beef brisket and crisp, tangy cabbage is a winner, not to mention the rich broth infused with aromatics. A mixture of beef and chicken broths provides just the right balance of flavor. Combining fresh cabbage with sauerkraut—an unconventional approach to the classic beef and cabbage soup—lends an extra level of flavor, and does so in minimum time. If you can't find savoy cabbage at your supermarket, you can substitute regular green cabbage; however, it has a less delicate texture. We tested store-bought sauerkraut and found that krauts packaged in shelf-stable jars and cans were fresher and brighter tasting than refrigerated products.

- 1 (1-pound) beef brisket, flat cut, trimmed and cut into ½-inch pieces
- 2 tablespoons vegetable oil, divided
- 1 onion, chopped
- 3 garlic cloves, minced
- 4 cups beef broth
- 4 cups chicken broth
- 2 bay leaves
- 2 carrots, peeled and cut into ½-inch pieces
- ½ small head savoy cabbage, quartered, cored, and shredded into ¼-inch-thick pieces
- ½ cup sauerkraut, rinsed
- 2 tablespoons minced fresh dill
   Sour cream

1. Pat beef dry with paper towels and season with salt and pepper. Heat 2 teaspoons oil in Dutch oven over medium-high heat until just smoking. Brown half of beef on all sides, 5 to 7 minutes. (Reduce heat if fond begins to burn.) Transfer browned beef to medium bowl. Repeat with 2 teaspoons oil and remaining beef; transfer to bowl.

2. Heat remaining 2 teaspoons oil in pot over medium heat until shimmering. Add onion and cook until softened, 5 to 7 minutes. Stir in garlic and cook until fragrant, about 30 seconds.

3. Stir in beef broth and chicken broth, scraping up any browned bits. Stir in bay leaves and browned meat with any accumulated juices. Bring to boil, then cover, reduce to gentle simmer, and cook for 30 minutes.

4. Stir in carrots, cabbage, and sauerkraut. Cover partially (leaving pot open about 1 inch) and simmer gently until beef and vegetables are tender, 30 to 40 minutes longer.

5. Off heat, discard bay leaves. Stir in dill, season with salt and pepper to taste, and serve, passing sour cream separately.

KEYS TO SUCCESS

- **Savoy cabbage plus sauerkraut:** Using both provides an extra level of flavor and delicate crispness.

- **Beef brisket:** This cut is tender and rich.

Slicing Brisket for Soup

CUT INTO PLANKS
Cut brisket against grain into ½-inch-wide planks.

CUT INTO STRIPS
Cut each plank horizontally into ½-inch strips.

CUT INTO PIECES
Slice each strip crosswise into ½-inch pieces.

BEEF AND VEGETABLE SOUP

Serves: 4 to 6
Total Time: 1¼ hours

RECIPE OVERVIEW This rich and hearty beef and vegetable soup has old-fashioned flavor and is a snap to make. It tastes like cooked-all-day versions but takes a whole lot less time. The key is using the right cut of meat, one that has great beefy flavor and cooks up tender in a reasonable amount of time. Tender cuts, like strip steak and rib eye, become tough, livery, and chalky when simmered in soup. Sirloin tip steak is the best choice—when cut into small pieces, the meat is tender and offers the illusion of being cooked for hours; plus, its meaty flavor imparts richness to the soup. Aromatics and chicken broth lighten the flavor profile of beef broth. To further boost the flavor of the beef, we add cremini mushrooms, tomato paste, soy sauce, and red wine, ingredients that are rich in glutamates, naturally occurring compounds that accentuate the meat's hearty flavor. A tablespoon of powdered gelatin mimics the body of a homemade meat broth (made rich through the gelatin released by the meat bones' collagen during the long simmering process). Choose whole sirloin tip steaks over ones that have been cut into small pieces for stir-fries. If sirloin tip steaks are unavailable, substitute blade or flank steak, removing any hard gristle and excess fat. White mushrooms can be used in place of the cremini, but with some trade-off in flavor. For a heartier soup, add 10 ounces red potatoes, cut into ½-inch pieces (2 cups), during the last 15 minutes of cooking. You could also add 1 cup frozen peas, frozen corn, or frozen cut green beans during the last 5 minutes of cooking.

1	pound sirloin tip steaks, trimmed and cut into ½-inch pieces
2	tablespoons soy sauce
1	teaspoon vegetable oil
1	pound cremini mushrooms, trimmed and quartered
1	large onion, chopped
2	tablespoons tomato paste
1	garlic clove, minced
½	cup red wine
4	cups beef broth
1¾	cups chicken broth
4	carrots, peeled and cut into ½-inch pieces
2	celery ribs, cut into ½-inch pieces
1	bay leaf
1	tablespoon unflavored gelatin
½	cup cold water
2	tablespoons minced fresh parsley

1. Combine beef and soy sauce in medium bowl; set aside for 15 minutes.

2. Heat oil in Dutch oven over medium-high heat until just smoking. Add mushrooms and onion; cook, stirring frequently, until onion is browned and dark bits form on pan bottom, 8 to 12 minutes. Transfer vegetables to bowl.

3. Add beef and cook, stirring occasionally, until liquid evaporates and meat starts to brown, 6 to 10 minutes. Add tomato paste and garlic and cook, stirring constantly, until fragrant, about 30 seconds. Add red wine, scraping bottom of pot to loosen any browned bits, and cook until syrupy, 1 to 2 minutes.

4. Add beef broth, chicken broth, carrots, celery, bay leaf, and browned mushrooms and onion; bring to boil. Reduce heat to low, cover, and simmer until vegetables and meat are tender, 25 to 30 minutes. While soup is simmering, sprinkle gelatin over cold water and let sit.

5. Remove pot from heat and discard bay leaf. Add gelatin mixture and stir until completely dissolved. Stir in parsley, season with salt and pepper to taste, and serve.

KEYS TO SUCCESS
- **Steak tips:** Cook quickly and taste beefy
- **Gelatin:** Adds the viscosity that would otherwise be provided by bones
- **Cremini mushrooms:** Have a stronger flavor than white mushrooms

BEEF YAKAMEIN
Serves: 6
Total Time: 3¼ hours

RECIPE OVERVIEW Yakamein (loosely translated from Chinese as "an order of noodles") originated in Chinese American restaurants all across the United States when chefs improvised with the ingredients they had on hand. Thanks mainly to the tireless efforts of chef Linda Green (aka the "Yakamein Lady"), a uniquely New Orleans version of yakamein has seen a surge in popularity. After trying Chef Green's delectable beef noodle soup boldly seasoned with soy sauce and Creole spices and several others from around the Crescent City, we created a recipe of our own to bring a taste of NOLA to home kitchens all around the country. Browning the beef chuck-eye roast before adding and sautéing aromatics (the "holy trinity" of onion, bell pepper, and celery) creates a deeply flavorful fond. Slowly simmering the roast in beef broth until it is meltingly tender creates a concentrated soup stock, and seasoning the broth with Creole spices, savory soy sauce, garlic, and a touch of monosodium glutamate makes it irresistible. To complete our classic beef yakamein, ladle the delicious broth over bowls of cooked spaghetti, the chopped beef, halved hard-cooked eggs, and sliced scallions, then finish the dish with dashes of more soy sauce and hot sauce. Smaller chuck-eye roasts (such as the one called for in this recipe) are sometimes sold prepackaged and labeled as chuck steak. If you can find only chuck roasts larger than 2 pounds, you can ask the butcher to cut a smaller roast for you or cut your own 2-pound roast and freeze the remaining meat for another use. Sriracha or Tabasco can be substituted for the Crystal Hot Sauce, if desired. We

developed this recipe with Kikkoman Soy Sauce and Better Than Bouillon Roasted Beef Base. Monosodium glutamate, an umami-enhancing seasoning that gives this yakamein broth a savory boost, is sold under the brand name Ac'cent. Look for it in the spice aisle next to the seasoning salts.

1 (2-pound) boneless beef chuck-eye roast, trimmed
2 teaspoons kosher salt
2 teaspoons pepper
2 tablespoons vegetable oil
1 onion, chopped
1 green bell pepper, stemmed, seeded, and chopped
1 celery rib, chopped
4 garlic cloves, minced
1 tablespoon Tony Chachere's Original Creole Seasoning
1 tablespoon sugar
1 teaspoon onion powder
½ teaspoon monosodium glutamate (optional)
8 cups beef broth
¼ cup soy sauce, plus extra for serving
12 ounces spaghetti
3 hard-cooked large eggs, halved
6 scallions, sliced ¼ inch thick
Crystal Hot Sauce

1. Pat beef dry with paper towels and sprinkle with salt and pepper. Heat oil in large Dutch oven over medium-high heat until shimmering. Add beef and cook until well browned on all sides, 8 to 12 minutes. Transfer beef to plate.

2. Add onion, bell pepper, and celery to fat left in pot and cook until softened, 5 to 7 minutes. Add garlic, Creole seasoning, sugar, onion powder, and monosodium glutamate, if using, and cook until fragrant, about 1 minute. Stir in broth and soy sauce, scraping up any browned bits. Return beef to pot and bring to boil over high heat. Cover, reduce heat to low, and simmer until beef is tender, 1½ to 2 hours.

3. Transfer beef to cutting board and let cool until easy to handle, at least 20 minutes. Use wide spoon to skim excess fat from broth. Set colander over large bowl. Strain broth through colander, pressing on solids to extract all liquid. Discard solids in colander. Return broth to pot; cover and keep warm over low heat.

4. Meanwhile, bring 3 quarts water to boil in large saucepan. Add pasta and cook until fully tender. Drain pasta and return it to saucepan. Cover and set aside.

5. Using chef's knife, chop beef into approximate ¾-inch pieces. Divide pasta evenly among 6 serving bowls. Divide beef, eggs, and scallions evenly among serving bowls on top of pasta. Ladle hot broth into serving bowls to cover pasta (about 1½ cups each). Serve, passing hot sauce and extra soy sauce separately.

KEYS TO SUCCESS

- **The holy trinity:** Bell pepper, celery, and onion put the NOLA stamp on this soup.
- **Generous seasoning:** Plenty of soy sauce, creole seasoning, garlic, salt, and a bit of MSG provide a bold, savory flavor profile.

Cutting Beef for Yakamein

CUT BEEF
Use chef's knife to cut beef into approximate ¾-inch pieces.

Building the Bowl

The components of yakamein are layered in sequentially, starting with the pasta and ending with the broth.

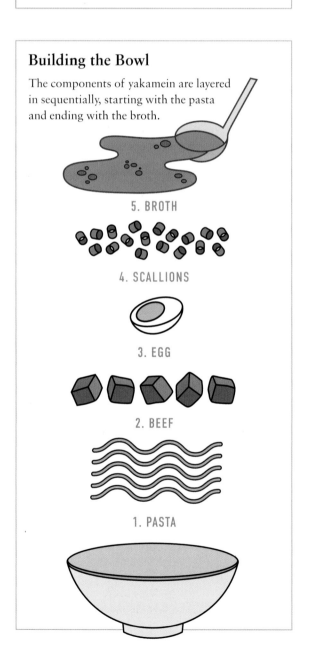

5. BROTH

4. SCALLIONS

3. EGG

2. BEEF

1. PASTA

MULTICOOKER HAWAIIAN OXTAIL SOUP

Serves: 4 to 6
Total Time: 2¼ Hours

RECIPE OVERVIEW Oxtail soup is a local Hawaiian favorite attributed to the islands' Chinese, Japanese, Okinawan, and Korean populations. One of the most popular versions draws from Cantonese traditions and boasts a clear broth perfumed by ginger, star anise, sweet-pungent chen pi (aged dried citrus peel), and fruity dried jujubes. The heady aromatics provide a counterpoint to the savory wallop of the oxtails, shiitakes, peanuts, and soy sauce. Peppery gai choy, scallions, and fresh cilantro offer bite. The multicooker saves some time but delivers lots of flavor. Look for oxtails that are approximately 2 inches thick. If certain ingredients are difficult to find, we have some substitutes, but the soup's flavor will be less nuanced as a result: You can substitute dry-roasted peanuts for the raw peanuts; four Medjool dates for the jujubes; 1½ tablespoons dried orange peel or three strips fresh orange zest for the chen pi; and 1 pound stemmed American mustard greens for the gai choy. This dish can also be cooked in a pressure cooker. Place the cooker on medium heat when instructed to use the "highest sauté function." For a complete Hawaiian-style meal, serve with two scoops of white rice.

8 ounces fresh ginger, sliced thin, plus 4 tablespoons peeled and grated for serving

5 star anise pods

¼ ounce chen pi

3 pounds oxtails, fat trimmed to ¼ inch or less

8 cups water

½ cup raw peanuts

8 dried jujubes

1 ounce dried whole shiitake mushrooms, stemmed and rinsed

¼ cup soy sauce, plus extra for serving

½ teaspoon table salt

1 pound gai choy, trimmed and cut into 2-inch pieces

1 cup fresh cilantro leaves

4 scallions, sliced thin on bias

1. Bundle sliced ginger, star anise, and chen pi in single layer of cheesecloth and secure with kitchen twine. Add cheesecloth bundle, oxtails, water, peanuts, jujubes, mushrooms, soy sauce, and salt to multicooker.

2. Lock lid into place and close pressure-release valve. Select high pressure-cook function and cook for 1 hour. Turn off multicooker and let pressure release naturally for 30 minutes. Quick-release any remaining pressure, then carefully remove lid, allowing steam to escape away from you.

3. Discard cheesecloth bundle. Using slotted spoon, transfer oxtails, peanuts, and mushrooms to large bowl, tent with aluminum foil, and let rest while finishing soup. Strain broth through fine-mesh strainer into large bowl or container, pressing on solids to extract as much liquid as possible; discard solids. Let broth settle for 5 minutes. Using wide, shallow spoon or ladle, skim excess fat from surface. (Broth can be refrigerated overnight before defatting to allow for easier skimming. Reheat oxtails, peanuts, and mushrooms in simmering broth before adding gai choy in step 4.)

4. Return defatted broth to now-empty pot. Using highest sauté function, bring broth to simmer, then turn off multicooker. Stir in gai choy and cook, using residual heat, until wilted, about 3 minutes. Season with extra soy sauce to taste.

5. Slice mushrooms thin, if desired. Divide oxtails, peanuts, and mushrooms among bowls, then ladle hot broth and gai choy over oxtails. Sprinkle each bowl with cilantro and scallions. Serve, passing grated ginger and extra soy sauce separately.

KEYS TO SUCCESS

- **The right size oxtails:** Two-inch-wide pieces will cook to just the right degree in the time given.

- **The right aromatics:** Ginger, star anise, chen pi, and dried jujubes give the broth a unique heady aroma.

Oxtails: Perfect for Pressure Cooking

There's hardly a better cut for imparting beefy flavor and lustrous body to broth than oxtail. This appendage from the posterior of a cow is full of connective tissue that transforms into gelatin during cooking, making the meat meltingly tender and the broth satiny. On the stovetop, that process can take 3 or 4 hours, but using the high setting of a multicooker, we were able to reduce the time to an hour, plus 30 minutes for releasing steam naturally. A note on shopping: Oxtails are sliced into sections that range greatly in diameter depending on whether they were cut from the top of the tail or the bottom. If possible, buy wider, 2-inch-thick pieces to help ensure that the meat doesn't overcook and stays attached to the bone. You can order oxtails from your butcher; they're also often found in the freezer section.

COURSE
CHILLED SOUPS

ELLE SIMONE SCOTT

An icy bowl of chilled soup is one of summer's great pleasures, a refreshing antidote to the heat. Although chilled soups might seem easy-breezy, they require some special consideration because cold temperatures mute flavors and, for the optimum texture and presentation, you can't just throw everything into a blender and expect perfection. The recipes in this course show you how to make chilled soups that are both flavorful and elegant.

ELLE'S PRO TIP: *Chilled soups are a nod to summer vegetable sophistication. They're also a great way to utilize any leftover goods from your garden or CSA box bounty before they go bad. Making cold soups and storing them in Mason jars labeled in the fridge can make for the best grab-and-go for entertaining or a nice summer afternoon snack.*

CHILLED BORSCHT

Serves: 4 to 6
Total Time: 1½ hours

RECIPE OVERVIEW Hot borscht is a grand affair, but chilled borscht is much simpler, with the beets taking center stage. For our chilled version, cooking beets in water is the best method because it produces the liquid base that you use to build the soup. Boil whole beets until tender so they retain as much of their flavor as possible. You don't need to bother to peel the beets until after cooking them, when you use a paper towel to rub the skins right off. In this recipe, water works better than broth, which overwhelms the flavor of the beets. This soup has a brilliant, deep pink broth that is thick with shreds of burgundy beets. The classic garnish of a little dill adds a bright green contrast. If possible, buy beets with the greens attached: Fresh tops mean fresh beets, and boiling the beets with some stem attached makes them even easier to peel. Medium-size beets are best for this recipe; small beets create more work, and large beets are sometimes tough.

7	cups water
2	pounds beets (6 medium), scrubbed and all but 1 inch of stems removed
1	small onion, peeled
¼	cup distilled white vinegar
¼	cup sugar
1½	teaspoons table salt
¾	cup heavy cream
¾	cup sour cream
1	tablespoon lemon juice
2	tablespoons chopped fresh dill

1. Combine water, beets, onion, vinegar, sugar, and salt in large saucepan. Bring to boil over high heat. Reduce heat to medium-low, cover partially, and simmer until beets are tender and can be easily pierced with skewer, about 45 minutes.

2. Remove and discard onion. Transfer beets to cutting board and let cool slightly. Strain liquid through strainer lined with paper towel and reserve.

3. Using paper towel, rub skin from beets. Grate half of beets on large holes of box grater or food processor fitted with shredding disk. Refrigerate grated beets until cold. Cut remaining beets into large chunks. Place half of cut beets in blender. Add just enough cooking liquid to cover them by 1 inch and blend until very smooth, about 2 minutes. Transfer to large container. Repeat with remaining beets. Stir remaining cooking liquid into pureed beets and refrigerate until cold, about 2 hours.

4. Remove pureed beets and grated beets from refrigerator. Whisk heavy cream and sour cream into pureed beets until smooth and fully blended. Stir in grated beets. (Soup can be refrigerated in airtight container for up to 3 days.) Stir in lemon juice and adjust seasonings. Ladle soup into bowls and garnish with dill and other garnishes as desired. Serve immediately.

KEYS TO SUCCESS

- **Medium-size beets:** They're big enough for easy handling, but small enough to be tender.
- **Cook the beets in water, not broth:** Water keeps the beet flavor front and center.
- **Fresh dill:** Adds a pop of contrasting color.

CORE TECHNIQUE

Peeling Cooked Beets

RUB OFF SKIN
To avoid stained hands when peeling cooked beets, when cool enough to handle, cradle beets in paper towel and gently rub off skin.

CHILLED FRESH TOMATO SOUP

Serves: 4
Total Time: 1 hour, plus 30 minutes cooling and 2 hours chilling

RECIPE OVERVIEW For the perfect full-flavored chilled tomato soup, even top-notch tomatoes need to be treated just right. The ideal soup should capture the essence of the fruit in silky-smooth liquid form: light yet satisfying, savory yet sweet, deeply flavorful yet simple. To get fresh yet complex flavor, we use a hybrid half-raw, half-cooked approach, using equal parts fresh and roasted tomatoes, plus a small dose of tomato paste for a tomatoey backbone. Adding olive oil gradually to the blender takes the tomatoes from a thin liquid to a rich, spoon-coating puree. Strained and chilled to let the flavors blend, the soup is velvety and delicious. A touch of sherry vinegar perks up all of the flavors. In-season, locally grown tomatoes and good-quality extra-virgin olive oil are ideal for this recipe. Serve the soup with Crostini (page 347) or Frico (page 86).

2	pounds tomatoes, cored
1	shallot, sliced thin
2	garlic cloves, unpeeled
2	teaspoons tomato paste
½	teaspoon table salt
⅛	teaspoon smoked paprika (optional)
	Pinch cayenne pepper
6	tablespoons extra-virgin olive oil, plus extra for drizzling
1	teaspoon sherry vinegar, plus extra as needed

1. Adjust oven rack to middle position and heat oven to 375 degrees. Line rimmed baking sheet with aluminum foil and lightly spray with vegetable oil spray.

2. Cut 1 pound tomatoes in half horizontally and arrange cut side up on prepared baking sheet. Arrange shallot and garlic cloves in single layer over 1 area of baking sheet. Roast for 15 minutes, then remove shallot and garlic cloves. Return baking sheet to oven and continue to roast tomatoes until softened but not browned, 10 to 15 minutes longer. Let cool to room temperature, about 30 minutes.

3. Peel garlic cloves and place in blender with roasted shallot and roasted tomatoes. Cut remaining 1 pound tomatoes into eighths and add to blender along with tomato paste, salt, paprika, if using, and cayenne. Puree until smooth, about 30 seconds. With motor running, drizzle in olive oil in slow, steady stream; puree will turn orange in color.

4. Strain puree through fine-mesh strainer into nonreactive bowl, pressing on solids in strainer to extract as much liquid as possible. Discard solids. Stir vinegar into soup. Cover and refrigerate until well chilled and flavors have blended, at least 2 hours or up to 24 hours.

5. To serve, stir soup to recombine (liquid separates on standing). Taste and adjust seasoning with salt and vinegar, as needed. Ladle soup into chilled bowls, drizzle sparingly with extra oil, and grind pepper over each, if desired. Serve immediately.

KEYS TO SUCCESS

- **Roasted tomatoes:** Add deep complex flavor
- **Raw tomatoes:** Provide freshness
- **Emulsify the oil:** Gradually blending in the oil gives the soup a rich consistency.

SPANISH CHILLED ALMOND AND GARLIC SOUP (WHITE GAZPACHO)

Serves: 6 to 8
Total Time: 40 minutes, plus 3 hours chilling

RECIPE OVERVIEW Spanish white gazpacho, or ajo blanco, is a chilled soup of almonds, bread, and garlic. It has a creamy sophisticated flavor that belies its short ingredient list. At its best, it is a study in contrasts: Some bites offer a nutty crunch, while others are sharply fruity and floral. To achieve the best texture, the order in which you add ingredients to the blender makes all the difference. First, grind the almonds, then add the bread (which has been soaked briefly in water), garlic, sherry vinegar, salt, and cayenne pepper. Finally, drizzle in olive oil and water. To get just a hint of almond flavor, mix a tablespoon of the pureed soup with almond extract, then stir just a teaspoon of the mixture back into the soup. Sliced green grapes and toasted almonds add fruitiness and crunch. An extra drizzle of good-quality extra-virgin olive oil makes for a rich finish and a beautiful presentation. This rich soup is best served in small portions (about 6 ounces).

6	slices hearty white sandwich bread, crusts removed
4	cups water
2½	cups (8¾ ounces) plus ⅓ cup sliced blanched almonds, divided
3	tablespoons sherry vinegar
1	garlic clove, peeled
¾	teaspoon table salt, divided
	Pinch cayenne pepper
½	cup extra-virgin olive oil, plus extra for drizzling
⅛	teaspoon almond extract
2	teaspoons vegetable oil
6	ounces seedless green grapes, sliced thin (1 cup)

1. Combine bread and water in bowl and let soak for 5 minutes. Process 2½ cups almonds in blender until finely ground, about 30 seconds, scraping down sides of blender jar as needed. Using your hands, remove bread from water, squeeze it lightly, and transfer to blender with almonds. Measure out 3 cups soaking water and set aside; transfer remaining soaking water to blender. Add vinegar, garlic, ½ teaspoon salt, and cayenne to blender and process until mixture has consistency of cake batter, 30 to 45 seconds. With blender running, add olive oil in thin, steady stream, about 30 seconds. Add reserved soaking water and process for 1 minute.

2. Season with salt and pepper to taste. Strain soup through fine-mesh strainer set in bowl, pressing on solids to extract liquid. Discard solids.

3. Measure 1 tablespoon soup into separate bowl and stir in almond extract. Return 1 teaspoon extract-soup mixture to soup; discard remaining mixture. Chill soup for at least 3 hours or up to 24 hours.

4. Heat vegetable oil in 8-inch skillet over medium-high heat until oil begins to shimmer. Add remaining ⅓ cup almonds and cook, stirring constantly, until golden brown, 3 to 4 minutes. Immediately transfer to bowl and stir in remaining ¼ teaspoon salt.

5. Ladle soup into shallow bowls. Mound grapes in center of each bowl, sprinkle with cooled almonds, and drizzle with extra olive oil. Serve immediately.

KEYS TO SUCCESS

- **Almonds go first:** Processing the nuts before adding the other ingredients helps make the smoothest soup.
- **Strain the soup:** To guarantee silkiness
- **A hint of extract:** Dilute the almond extract in a spoonful of soup before using to keep it subtle.

CHILLED CUCUMBER SOUP WITH MANGO AND MINT

Serves: 6
Total Time: ½ hour, plus 1 hour chilling

RECIPE OVERVIEW Both refreshing and elegant, this chilled soup is the perfect meal for a swelteringly hot summer's evening. The first step to a smooth, refined cucumber soup is to peel and seed the cucumbers; peels add bitterness and seeds can leave an acrid aftertaste. Scallion greens

provide a distinct but not overwhelming allium flavor. For mild flavor and richness, whole-milk yogurt is key; low-fat or nonfat yogurt turns out flat, acidic soup. A mixture of fresh mango, mint leaves, and lime juice adds bright color and flavor; make sure you wait to prepare the garnish until shortly before serving the soup. We prefer long, thin European cucumbers in this recipe, but regular American cucumbers can be used.

Soup

5	pounds cucumbers, peeled, seeded, and cut into 2-inch pieces (about 8 cups)
4	medium scallions, dark green parts only, chopped coarse (about ½ cup)
2½	cups cold water, divided
1	cup plain whole-milk yogurt
¼	teaspoon sugar
1	tablespoon lemon juice
1	teaspoon table salt
	Pinch pepper

Mango-Mint Garnish

1	large mango, peeled and cut into ¼-inch cubes (about 1½ cups)
2	teaspoons minced fresh mint leaves
½	teaspoon lime juice
¼	teaspoon table salt

1. FOR THE SOUP Toss cucumbers with scallions in medium bowl. Process half of cucumber-scallion mixture in blender with 1¼ cups cold water until smooth, about 1 minute. Transfer to large nonreactive bowl. Process remaining cucumber-scallion mixture with remaining 1¼ cups cold water and transfer to bowl with first batch. Whisk in yogurt, sugar, lemon juice, salt, and pepper. Cover tightly and refrigerate until chilled, at least 1 hour or up to 12 hours.

2. FOR THE GARNISH Toss mango, mint, lime juice, and salt in small bowl.

3. To serve, divide chilled soup among individual bowls. Sprinkle mango and mint mixture over each bowl, and serve immediately.

KEYS TO SUCCESS

- **Remove the seeds:** They can taste acrid.
- **Whole-milk yogurt:** Creates a rich texture
- **Mango garnish:** Enlivens the flavor and presentation of the soup

BEAN AND LENTIL SOUPS

ASHLEY MOORE

Dried beans and other legumes are humble, frugal foods, and soups based on them are everyday sustenance. But they don't have to be pedestrian. A great bean soup is one of the most soul-satisfying meals you can make. In this course, you'll learn how to get the ultimate flavor and texture out of dried beans for soups that are indulgent as well as nutritious.

ASHLEY'S PRO TIP: *Be sure to pick through your dried beans before cooking to check for loose stones. Even one small stone is enough to spoil an otherwise perfect batch of soup. To spot and remove the stones before cooking, spread the beans on a white plate or a cutting board.*

GREEK WHITE BEAN SOUP

Serves: 6
Total Time: 1¼ hours, plus 8 hours soaking

RECIPE OVERVIEW   Fasolatha, considered to be one of Greece's national dishes, is a soup of creamy white beans, peppery olive oil, and fresh vegetables. To avoid tough, exploded beans, we brine them overnight in salted water, which softens their skins, makes them less prone to bursting, and also results in creamier beans. Onion and celery create a flavorful base, and using broth instead of water gives additional depth. For a silkier and more cohesive texture, we blend 2 cups of the soup and mix it back into the pot. Lemon juice adds brightness, and stirring in Aleppo pepper at the end provides a hint of spice and warmth. Serving the soup with a drizzle of olive oil and a sprinkle of parsley creates an irresistibly fresh flavor and accents the rich, creamy beans. If you can't find Aleppo pepper, you can substitute ¼ teaspoon paprika plus ¼ teaspoon finely chopped red pepper flakes. For more information on soaking beans, see page 327.

3 tablespoons table salt for brining
1 pound (2½ cups) dried cannellini beans, picked over and rinsed
2 tablespoons extra-virgin olive oil, plus extra for serving
1 onion, chopped
½ teaspoon table salt
½ teaspoon pepper
2½ teaspoons minced fresh oregano or ¾ teaspoon dried
6 cups chicken or vegetable broth, plus extra as needed
4 celery ribs, cut into ½-inch pieces
3 tablespoons lemon juice
2 tablespoons chopped fresh parsley
1 teaspoon ground dried Aleppo pepper

1. Dissolve 3 tablespoons salt in 4 quarts cold water in large container. Add beans and soak at room temperature for at least 8 hours or up to 24 hours. Drain and rinse well.

2. Heat oil in Dutch oven over medium heat until shimmering. Add onion, salt, and pepper and cook until softened and lightly browned, 5 to 7 minutes. Stir in oregano and cook until fragrant, about 30 seconds. Stir in broth, celery, and soaked beans and bring to boil. Reduce heat to low, cover, and simmer until beans are tender, 45 minutes to 1 hour.

3. Process 2 cups soup in blender until smooth, about 30 seconds, then return to pot. Heat soup gently over low heat until hot (do not boil) and adjust consistency with extra hot broth as needed. Stir in lemon juice, parsley, Aleppo and season with salt and pepper to taste. Serve, drizzling individual portions with extra oil.

KEYS TO SUCCESS

- **Brine the beans**: Soaking in salted water produces creamy, intact beans.

- **Blend some soup**: Processing a portion of the soup makes the texture more cohesive.

BROWN BEAN SOUP
Serves: 4 to 6
Total Time: 2¼ hours, plus 8 hours soaking

RECIPE OVERVIEW Tepary beans are native to the American Southwest and northern Mexico. When dried, they are small and flat and look a bit more like lentils than common beans. This recipe plays on that similarity by substituting them for lentils in a take on the traditional Greek faki soupa. Soaking the beans overnight in water with a little salt and baking soda before simmering reduces the cooking time and makes them tender and creamy because both work to weaken cell-wall structure. In order to maintain the texture of the vegetables, sauté them separately and add them to the pot partway through cooking. The soup is finished with a healthy splash of red wine vinegar and some fresh parsley to brighten things up.

1½ teaspoons kosher salt, divided
¼ teaspoon baking soda
8 cups water
1¼ cups brown tepary beans, picked over and rinsed
6 tablespoons extra-virgin olive oil, divided
1 onion, cut into ½-inch pieces
2 carrots, peeled and cut into ½-inch pieces
1 celery rib, cut into ½-inch pieces
2 garlic cloves, chopped fine
2 cups vegetable broth
1 tablespoon tomato paste
2 bay leaves
3 tablespoons red wine vinegar
2 tablespoons finely chopped fresh parsley

1. Dissolve 1 teaspoon salt and baking soda in water in Dutch oven. Add beans, cover, and soak at room temperature for at least 8 hours or up to 24 hours. Bring beans (still in soaking liquid) to boil over high heat, skimming off any foam that rises to surface. Reduce heat to medium-low and simmer, uncovered, until beans are tender, about 45 minutes. Do not drain beans.

2. Meanwhile heat ¼ cup oil in 10-inch skillet over medium heat until shimmering. Stir in onion, carrots, celery, garlic, and remaining ½ teaspoon salt and cook until onion is translucent, 5 to 7 minutes. Remove from heat.

3. Add softened vegetables, broth, tomato paste, and bay leaves to pot and stir to combine. Bring to boil over high heat, then reduce heat to medium-low and simmer, uncovered, until soup has thickened and flavors have melded, about 30 minutes. Off heat, discard bay leaves, stir in vinegar, and season with salt to taste. Divide soup among warmed bowls, sprinkle with parsley, and drizzle with remaining 2 tablespoons oil. Serve.

KEYS TO SUCCESS

- **Baking soda bath**: Use baking soda as well as salt in the brine to tenderize the beans.

- **Red wine vinegar**: Enlivens the soup's flavor

- **It's OK to substitute**: If tepary beans aren't available use the same amount of kidney beans.

MINESTRA DI ORZO E FASIO
Serves: 4 to 6
Total Time: 2¾ hours, plus 8 hours soaking

RECIPE OVERVIEW In Italy, orzo—what Americans think of as a rice-shaped pasta—is the word for barley, and it's one of the most important ingredients in Friuli, where the high altitudes of the mountainous areas facilitate its cultivation. It's found in risotto-like dishes, but it's also frequently combined with hearty beans for a soup that makes a warming winter staple. This Friulian alternative to pasta e fagioli was once a peasant dish but has become a recognized culinary specialty of the region. We start with dried cranberry (aka borlotti) beans, a common Friulian ingredient, that we brine overnight in salted water so they cook up with soft skins. Next we render the fat from flavorful pancetta (cut into spoon-friendly bites) before adding onion, garlic, and bay leaves along with water and the soaked beans. We add the barley to the soup for the last hour of cooking and simmer until both the beans and grains are tender and thickened to a porridge-like consistency. This soup is traditionally served very thick; adjust consistency with additional hot water as needed. Do not substitute hulled, hull-less, quick-cooking, or presteamed barley (read the ingredient list on the package to determine this) in this recipe.

1½ tablespoons table salt for brining
8 ounces (1¼ cups) dried cranberry beans, picked over and rinsed
1 tablespoon extra-virgin olive oil, plus extra for serving
4 ounces pancetta, cut into ¼-inch pieces
1 onion, chopped fine
1 teaspoon table salt
3 garlic cloves, minced
12 cups water
2 bay leaves
1 cup pearl barley
¼ cup minced fresh parsley
1 tablespoon red wine vinegar

1. Dissolve 1½ tablespoons salt in 2 quarts cold water in large container. Add beans and soak at room temperature for at least 8 hours or up to 24 hours. Drain and rinse well.

2. Heat oil in large saucepan over medium-high heat until shimmering. Add pancetta and cook until browned and fat is rendered, 5 to 7 minutes. Add onion and salt and cook until softened and lightly browned, 5 to 7 minutes. Stir in garlic and cook until fragrant, about 30 seconds.

3. Stir in beans, water, and bay leaves and bring to boil. Reduce heat to medium-low and cover, leaving lid slightly ajar. Simmer, stirring occasionally, until beans are tender, about 1 hour.

4. Stir in barley and simmer, uncovered, stirring occasionally, until barley is tender, beans begin to break down, and soup has thickened, about 1 hour.

5. Discard bay leaves. Stir in parsley and vinegar and season with salt and pepper to taste. Adjust consistency with hot water as needed. Drizzle individual portions with extra oil before serving.

KEYS TO SUCCESS

- **Cook the aromatics in pancetta:** The onions and garlic meld with the pancetta fat for flavor that permeates the soup.

- **Check the barley:** This recipe works best with pearl barley; don't use other kinds.

MOONG DAL SOUP WITH COCONUT MILK AND SPINACH

Serves: 2
Total Time: 45 minutes

RECIPE OVERVIEW This aromatic, creamy soup made from moong dal (buttery split mung beans) is ready in no time. Split mung beans are ideal for soup because they contain protein, carbs, and fiber—and they cook down more quickly than other legumes. Coconut milk combines with warm spices and punchy fresh ingredients for creamy matrimony. If you can't find split mung beans, you can substitute split red lentils; do not use yellow lentils or split pigeon peas (toor dal). The leftover coconut milk can be frozen into cubes in an ice tray for use in other recipes. This recipe can easily be doubled in a Dutch oven.

1 tomato, cored and chopped
2 tablespoons chopped fresh cilantro
1 tablespoon lime juice, plus lime wedges for serving
1 jalapeño chile, stemmed, seeded, and minced, divided
2 tablespoons canola oil
1 small onion, chopped fine
1 tablespoon grated fresh ginger
2 garlic cloves, minced
1 teaspoon ground cumin
½ teaspoon turmeric
2½ cups chicken or vegetable broth
1 cup water
¾ cup split mung beans, picked over and rinsed
⅓ cup canned coconut milk
2 ounces frozen chopped spinach, thawed and squeezed dry

1. Combine tomato, cilantro, lime juice, and half of jalapeño in small bowl. Season with salt and pepper to taste; set aside.

2. Heat oil in large saucepan over medium heat until shimmering. Add onion and cook until softened and lightly browned, 5 to 7 minutes. Stir in ginger, garlic, cumin, turmeric, and remaining jalapeño and cook until fragrant, about 1 minute.

3. Stir in broth, water, and beans and bring to simmer. Reduce heat to low and cook, partially covered, until beans are beginning to break down, 10 to 12 minutes.

4. Whisk soup vigorously until beans are completely broken down and soup is thickened, about 30 seconds. Stir in coconut milk and spinach, return to simmer, and cook until spinach is heated through, about 2 minutes. Season with salt and pepper to taste. (Soup can be refrigerated for up to 3 days.) Top each portion with half of tomato mixture. Serve.

KEYS TO SUCCESS

- **Use a whisk:** To blend and thicken the soup
- **Coconut milk:** Creates a smooth backdrop for the spicy, savory, and acidic ingredients

HARIRA

Serves: 6 to 8
Total Time: 1¾ hours

RECIPE OVERVIEW Harira is an intensely flavored Moroccan soup of lentils, tomatoes, chickpeas, and often chicken or lamb. Our version uses lamb shoulder chops, and, after browning them, we bloom the aromatics in the rendered fat they leave behind. Begin with minced onion, next add a fragrant and warming combination of fresh ginger, cumin, paprika, cinnamon, cayenne, saffron, and black pepper. The result is a sweet, smoky, deeply flavorful base with just a touch of heat. Harissa, a superspicy paste of hot chiles, spices, garlic, and olive oil, is a critical finishing touch to every harira recipe. For the best and most potent flavor, we prefer to use our homemade harissa, but you can substitute store-bought harissa if you wish, though spiciness can vary greatly by brand. Large green or brown lentils work well in this recipe; do not use lentilles du Puy (French green lentils).

1	pound lamb shoulder chops (blade or round bone), 1 to 1½ inches thick, trimmed and halved
½	teaspoon table salt
½	teaspoon pepper, divided
1	tablespoon extra-virgin olive oil
1	onion, chopped fine
1	teaspoon grated fresh ginger
1	teaspoon ground cumin
½	teaspoon paprika
¼	teaspoon ground cinnamon
¼	teaspoon cayenne pepper
	Pinch saffron threads, crumbled
1	tablespoon all-purpose flour
10	cups chicken broth
¾	cup green or brown lentils, picked over and rinsed
1	(15-ounce) can chickpeas, rinsed
4	plum tomatoes, cored and cut into ¾-inch pieces
⅓	cup minced fresh cilantro
¼	cup Harissa (recipe follows), plus extra for serving

1. Adjust oven rack to lower-middle position and heat oven to 325 degrees. Pat lamb dry with paper towels and season with salt and ¼ teaspoon pepper. Heat oil in Dutch oven over medium-high heat until just smoking. Brown lamb, about 4 minutes per side; transfer to plate. Pour off all but 2 tablespoons fat from pot.

2. Add onion to fat left in pot and cook over medium heat until softened, about 5 minutes. Stir in ginger, cumin, paprika, cinnamon, cayenne, remaining ¼ teaspoon pepper, and saffron and cook until fragrant, about 30 seconds. Stir in flour and cook for 1 minute. Slowly whisk in broth, scraping up any browned bits and smoothing out any lumps, and bring to boil.

3. Nestle lamb into pot and add any accumulated juices, bring to simmer, and cook for 10 minutes. Stir in lentils and chickpeas, cover, and place pot in oven. Cook until fork slips easily in and out of lamb and lentils are tender, 50 minutes to 1 hour.

4. Transfer lamb to cutting board, let cool slightly, then shred into bite-size pieces using 2 forks, discarding excess fat and bones. Stir shredded lamb into soup and let sit until heated through, about 2 minutes. Stir in tomatoes, cilantro, and harissa and season with salt and pepper to taste. Serve, passing extra harissa separately.

HARISSA

Makes: about ½ cup

Harissa is a traditional Tunisian condiment that is great for flavoring soups, sauces, and dressings or dolloping on lamb, hummus, eggs, and sandwiches. It's a hot sauce and then some, with lots of warm spice aroma and a garlicky bite. If you can't find Aleppo pepper, you can substitute ¾ teaspoon paprika plus ¾ teaspoon finely chopped red pepper flakes.

6	tablespoons extra-virgin olive oil
6	garlic cloves, minced
2	tablespoons paprika
1	tablespoon ground coriander
1–3	tablespoons ground dried Aleppo pepper
1	teaspoon ground cumin
¾	teaspoon caraway seeds
½	teaspoon table salt

Combine all ingredients in bowl and microwave until bubbling and very fragrant, about 1 minute, stirring halfway through microwaving; let cool completely. (Harissa can be refrigerated for up to 4 days.)

KEYS TO SUCCESS

- **Lamb shoulder chops:** This cut adds richness.
- **Bloom the spices:** Cooking the spices in the rendered lamb fat amplifies their flavors.
- **Homemade harissa:** Adds a fresh spiciness and bite; store-bought is second best.

CREAMY SOUPS

LEAH COLINS

Cream soups seem luxurious but may also come across as overly rich and bland. The recipes in this course use creative ways to make soups that are not only creamy but also light and vibrant. Four take advantage of vegetables that are naturally smooth— sweet potatoes, kohlrabi, cauliflower, and chestnuts—and the fifth uses barley. Each one coaxes maximum flavor from its ingredients through careful cooking techniques. And though some include dairy products, none of these recipes need cream to achieve delicious results.

LEAH'S PRO TIP: *To blend a hot soup, follow a few basic tips to ensure success without a hot mess on your counter top. Blend in batches, making sure to fill the blender no more than halfway full. Start your blender on the slowest blending cycle, and slowly increase to ensure a blending vortex is created and maintained until smooth. Place a folded kitchen towel over the blender lid, making sure to hold securely in place the entire time you are blending.*

SWEET POTATO SOUP

Serves: 4 to 6 as a main dish or 8 as a starter
Total Time: 1 hour

RECIPE OVERVIEW Most sweet potato soup recipes call for so many other ingredients that the sweet potato flavor ends up muted and overpowered. By cutting back to shallot, thyme, and butter and using water instead of broth, this recipe keeps the focus on the main ingredient. For extra earthiness, we puree some of the potato skins into the soup. However, the real key to intensifying the sweet potato flavor is to use only a minimal amount of flavor-diluting water. To do so, let the sweet potatoes sit in hot water off the heat to make use of an enzyme that converts their starch content to sugar. Less starch means you can create a soup with less water, keeping the sweet potato flavor in the forefront. In addition to the chives, serve the soup with one of our suggested garnishes (recipes follow). The garnish can be prepared during step 1 while the sweet potatoes stand in the water.

4 tablespoons unsalted butter
1 shallot, sliced thin
4 sprigs fresh thyme
4¼ cups water
2 pounds sweet potatoes, peeled, halved lengthwise, and sliced ¼ inch thick, one-quarter of peels reserved
1 tablespoon packed brown sugar
½ teaspoon cider vinegar
1½ teaspoons table salt
¼ teaspoon pepper
   Minced fresh chives

1. Melt butter in large saucepan over medium-low heat. Add shallot and thyme and cook until shallot is softened but not browned, about 5 minutes. Add water, increase heat to high, and bring to simmer. Remove pot from heat, add sweet potatoes and reserved peels, and let stand uncovered for 20 minutes.

2. Add sugar, vinegar, salt, and pepper. Bring to simmer over high heat. Reduce heat to medium-low, cover, and cook until potatoes are very soft, about 10 minutes.

3. Discard thyme sprigs. Working in batches, process soup in blender until smooth, 45 to 60 seconds. Return soup to clean pot. Bring to simmer over medium heat, adjusting consistency if desired. Season with salt and pepper to taste. Serve, topping each portion with sprinkle of chives.

KEYS TO SUCCESS

- **Add some peels:** Including a small amount of sweet potato peels intensifies the vegetable's presence in the soup.

- **Garnish:** We recommend making at least one of the accompanying garnishes; the contrasting textures and temperatures elevate the soup.

BUTTERY RYE CROUTONS

Makes: 1½ cups

- 3 tablespoons unsalted butter
- 1 tablespoon olive oil
- 2 slices light rye bread, cut into ½-inch cubes (about 1½ cups)

Heat butter and oil in 10-inch skillet over medium heat. When foaming subsides, add bread cubes and cook, stirring frequently, until golden brown, about 10 minutes. Transfer croutons to paper towel–lined plate and season with salt to taste. (The croutons can be made ahead and stored in an airtight container for 1 week.)

CANDIED BACON BITS

Makes: about ¼ cup

Break up any large chunks before serving.

- 4 slices bacon, cut into ½-inch pieces
- 2 teaspoons dark brown sugar
- ½ teaspoon cider vinegar

Cook bacon in 10-inch nonstick skillet over medium heat until crisp and well rendered, 6 to 8 minutes. Using slotted spoon, remove bacon from skillet and discard fat. Return bacon to skillet and add brown sugar and vinegar. Cook over low heat, stirring constantly, until bacon is evenly coated. Transfer to plate in single layer. Let bacon cool completely.

MAPLE SOUR CREAM

Makes: ⅓ cup

Maple balances the sweet potatoes' earthiness.

- ⅓ cup sour cream
- 1 tablespoon maple syrup

Combine sour cream and maple syrup in bowl.

Putting Peels to Work

FLAVOR BOOST

Instead of discarding the sweet potato peels, we blend some of them into our soup to take advantage of an earthy-tasting compound they contain called methoxypyrazine. Because the compound in the peels is potent—it's detectable in water in levels as low as one part per trillion—we use only one-quarter of the peels in order to avoid overwhelming the soup.

SCIENCE LESSON **Thinning Sweet Potatoes with Less Liquid**

Creating a soup with prominent sweet potato flavor means using a minimal amount of water. The only catch? Sweet potatoes require more water than less starchy vegetables like squash or carrots to be thinned to a soupy consistency after boiling. That's because their large starch molecules form a loose mesh that traps added water, preventing the texture from turning runny. It takes a lot of water before the mesh can't hold any more liquid and the texture loosens and thins.

But we discovered a trick: We add the sweet potatoes to simmering water and then let them sit off the heat for 20 minutes before boiling them. This way, the large starch molecules are converted into much smaller sugar molecules that are unable to create a mesh. This means that we can puree the sweet potatoes with only 4¼ cups of cooking liquid to get just the right consistency. Another benefit: The conversion of starch to sugar makes the potatoes taste even better.

Usual way: Boil, then puree

Our way: Soak before boiling

CREAMY KOHLRABI SOUP

Serves: 4 to 6
Total Time: 1 hour

RECIPE OVERVIEW Here's a simple, deeply satisfying soup that utilizes nearly every part of the vegetable—root to leaf, so to speak. Similar to cauliflower, kohlrabi is particularly low in overall fiber, so it blends up perfectly into smooth soups and purees. This recipe highlights the delicate flavor of this brassica in a creamy, velvety soup. We start by cooking kohlrabi in an aromatic base of butter, onions, and water; using water helps to highlight the delicate flavor of the vegetable. To give more richness and body to the soup, we add a bit of milk to this base. A bit of dry mustard really amplifies the brassica flavor. (Brassicas like kohlrabi belong to the mustard family and share the same aromatic compounds that give mustard its characteristic zing.) Cooking the kohlrabi greens in the soup at the end adds a welcome element of contrast. Macadamia nuts and chives sprinkled on top make a crunchy garnish. You can substitute 4 ounces kale, stemmed and cut into 1-inch pieces, for the kohlrabi leaves.

4 tablespoons unsalted butter

1 onion, chopped

1¼ teaspoons table salt

4 pounds kohlrabi with their leaves, kohlrabi trimmed, peeled, and cut into ½-inch pieces (6 cups), leaves stemmed and cut into 1-inch pieces (2 cups)

2 cups water, plus extra as needed

1 cup whole milk

1½ teaspoons dry mustard

⅓ cup salted dry-roasted macadamia nuts, chopped coarse

1 tablespoon minced fresh chives

1. Melt butter in Dutch oven over medium heat. Add onion and salt and cook, stirring occasionally, until softened, about 5 minutes. Stir in kohlrabi pieces, water, and milk and bring to simmer. Cover, reduce heat to medium-low, and cook, stirring occasionally, until kohlrabi is tender (paring knife should slip easily in and out of pieces), 10 to 12 minutes.

2. Using slotted spoon, transfer 1½ cups kohlrabi to bowl. Continue to cook soup, covered, until remaining kohlrabi is very tender and easily breaks apart when poked with paring knife, 6 to 8 minutes. Stir in mustard.

3. Working in batches, process soup in blender until smooth, about 1 minute. Return soup to now-empty pot and bring to simmer over medium-low heat. Add kohlrabi leaves and cook, stirring occasionally, until tender and vibrant green, about 5 minutes. Off heat, stir in reserved cooked kohlrabi. Adjust consistency with extra hot water as needed. Season with salt to taste. Sprinkle individual portions with macadamia nuts and chives before serving.

KEYS TO SUCCESS

• **Chop some, puree some:** Pureed kohlrabi provides a creamy backdrop for kohlrabi pieces.

• **Use water and milk as the soup base:** Milk adds richness and body; water keeps it light and lets the kohlrabi take center stage.

CHESTNUT SOUP WITH MUSHROOMS AND BAHARAT

Serves: 4 to 6
Total Time: 1¼ hours

RECIPE OVERVIEW The appeal of chestnuts goes beyond roasting them plain, and in Turkey, the third-largest producer of chestnuts in the world, they're used in myriad ways. Here, we were inspired by kestane çorbasi, a pureed chestnut soup that can lean sweet or savory depending on who is at the stovetop. Along with the woodsy, rich chestnuts, our soup achieves an appealing sweet-savory balance from shallots and mushrooms (both classic ingredients). The addition of baharat manages to augment all the distinct flavors in the soup with its complex spice. For a strong mushroom backbone, we use dried porcini mushrooms and incorporate their soaking liquid as well to add depth. And we sauté shiitakes until nutty-brown and stir them in just before serving to add welcome texture. The mellow tanginess of creamy whole-milk yogurt gives the soup a smooth finish.

    2   cups water, divided
    ¼   ounce dried porcini mushrooms, rinsed
    2   tablespoons extra-virgin olive oil, divided,
        plus extra for drizzling
    1   pound shallots, quartered
    1   teaspoon table salt, divided
    ¾   teaspoon baharat
   14   ounces (3 cups) peeled and cooked chestnuts, chopped
    2   cups chicken or vegetable broth
   10   ounces shiitake mushrooms, stemmed and sliced thin
    ¼   teaspoon pepper
    ¾   cup plain whole-milk yogurt
    ½   cup plus 2 tablespoons minced fresh parsley, divided

1. Microwave ½ cup water and porcini mushrooms in covered bowl until steaming, about 1 minute. Let sit until softened, about 5 minutes. Drain mushrooms in fine-mesh strainer lined with coffee filter, reserving soaking liquid, and chop mushrooms fine.

2. Heat 1 tablespoon oil in Dutch oven over medium-low heat until shimmering. Add shallots and ½ teaspoon salt, cover, and cook until shallots are softened and beginning to brown, 12 to 15 minutes, stirring occasionally. Stir in minced porcini and baharat and cook until fragrant, about 30 seconds. Stir in chestnuts, broth, reserved porcini soaking liquid, and remaining 1½ cups water and bring to boil. Reduce heat to medium-low, cover, and simmer until chestnuts are very tender, about 20 minutes.

3. Meanwhile, heat remaining 1 tablespoon oil in 12-inch nonstick skillet over medium heat until shimmering. Add shiitake mushrooms, remaining ½ teaspoon salt, and pepper, cover, and cook until mushrooms are softened, about 5 minutes. Uncover and continue to cook, stirring occasionally, until liquid has evaporated and mushrooms begin to brown, 8 to 10 minutes longer; set aside.

4. Working in batches, process soup and yogurt in blender until smooth, about 1 minute. Return pureed soup to now-empty pot. Stir in all but ¼ cup reserved browned shiitakes and bring to gentle simmer over medium heat, adjusting consistency with hot water if desired. Stir in ½ cup parsley and season with salt and pepper to taste. Serve, sprinkling with reserved shiitakes and remaining 2 tablespoons parsley and drizzling with extra oil.

KEYS TO SUCCESS
- **Save the porcini liquid:** To flavor the broth
- **Convenient chestnuts:** Buying them already peeled and cooked saves time.
- **Sauté shiitakes:** The browned mushrooms add depth to the soup and texture as a garnish.

Chestnuts Roasting

You can purchase peeled and cooked chestnuts jarred or vacuum-packed, which makes easy work of using chestnuts in this recipe that purees the soft fruit. If you can't find them precooked, or if you're attracted to the baskets of raw chestnuts at the store in the winter months, you can prepare them at home. When purchasing, be sure to look for nuts with glossy shells, and avoid those that rattle when shaken, which indicates that they have dried out. For this recipe, cut 20 ounces of whole chestnuts in half crosswise, then blanch for 8 minutes in 8 cups of boiling water. Remove the pot from the heat, leaving the nuts in the water. One at a time, hold the chestnuts with a dish towel and squeeze the shell to extract the meat. Using a paring knife, trim any bits of husk.

CREAMY HAWAIJ CAULIFLOWER SOUP WITH ZHOUG
Serves: 4 to 6
Total Time: 1½ hours

RECIPE OVERVIEW A creamy cauliflower soup is a marvelous way to not only nourish yourself with all of the cruciferous vegetable's nutrients and fiber but also unlock its range of flavors—from bright and cabbage-like to nutty and even sweet. When well cooked, cauliflower quickly whips into a velvety soup—no flavor-diluting dairy required. We add the cauliflower to simmering water in two stages to bring out both the grassy flavor of just-cooked cauliflower and the nutty flavor of longer-cooked cauliflower. To enhance these two qualities, this recipe includes hawaij, a Yemeni spice blend also common to Israeli cuisine that boasts its own impressive range of flavors—earthy, sweet, and distinctly savory. Bloom the hawaij with the aromatics so its flavors flourish from the beginning. In addition to a countering topping of the grassy-hot cilantro-chile sauce zhoug and browned cauliflower florets, we also like to serve the soup with chopped pink pickled turnips.

1 head cauliflower (2 pounds)
¼ cup extra-virgin olive oil, divided, plus extra for serving
1 leek, white and light green parts only, halved lengthwise, sliced thin, and washed thoroughly
1 small onion, halved and sliced thin
1½ teaspoons table salt
1 tablespoon Hawaij (recipe follows)
4½ cups water
1 recipe Green Zhoug (recipe follows), divided
1 teaspoon white wine vinegar

1. Pull off outer leaves of cauliflower and trim stem. Using paring knife, cut around core to remove; slice core thin and reserve. Cut heaping 1 cup of ½-inch florets from head of cauliflower; set aside. Cut remaining cauliflower crosswise into ½-inch-thick slices.

2. Heat 3 tablespoons oil in large saucepan over medium-low heat until shimmering. Add leek, onion, and salt and cook, stirring often, until leek and onion are softened but not browned, about 7 minutes. Stir in hawaij and cook until fragrant, about 30 seconds. Stir in water, reserved sliced core, and half of sliced cauliflower. Increase heat to medium-high and bring to simmer. Reduce heat to medium-low and simmer gently for 15 minutes. Add remaining sliced cauliflower and simmer until cauliflower is tender and crumbles easily, 15 to 20 minutes.

3. Meanwhile, heat remaining 1 tablespoon oil in 8-inch skillet over medium heat until shimmering. Add reserved florets and cook, stirring often, until golden brown, 6 to 8 minutes. Transfer to bowl, add ¼ cup zhoug, and toss until well coated. Working in batches, process soup in blender until smooth, about 45 seconds. Return pureed soup to clean pot and bring to brief simmer over medium heat. Off heat, stir in vinegar and season with salt to taste. Spoon browned florets and remaining zhoug over individual serving bowls. Serve.

HAWAIJ

Makes: about ½ cup

This golden blend, found in Israeli cooking by way of its migration with Yemenite Jews, both warms and colors dishes. While a multipurpose blend, it has a rich history of use in soups, stews, and curries in Yemen. The color comes from the generous amount of turmeric, and the cloves, found only in some versions, add depth.

2½ tablespoons black peppercorns
2 tablespoons cumin seeds
1½ tablespoons coriander seeds
10 cardamom pods
6 whole cloves
1½ tablespoons ground turmeric

Process peppercorns, cumin seeds, coriander seeds, cardamom pods, and cloves in spice grinder until finely ground, about 30 seconds. Transfer to bowl and stir in turmeric. (Hawaij can be stored in airtight container at room temperature for up to 1 month.)

GREEN ZHOUG

Makes: about ½ cup

Zhoug is an Israeli hot sauce that can be either red or green. Our vibrant green version is made with fresh herbs, chiles, and spices. We like it with fish or drizzled on soups or sandwiches.

6 tablespoons extra-virgin olive oil
½ teaspoon ground coriander
¼ teaspoon ground cumin
¼ teaspoon ground cardamom
¼ teaspoon table salt
Pinch ground cloves
¾ cup fresh cilantro leaves
½ cup fresh parsley leaves
2 green Thai chiles, stemmed and chopped
2 garlic cloves, minced

1. Microwave oil, coriander, cumin, cardamom, salt, and cloves in covered bowl until fragrant, about 30 seconds; let cool completely.

2. Pulse oil-spice mixture, cilantro, parsley, chiles, and garlic in food processor until coarse paste forms, about 15 pulses, scraping down sides of bowl as needed. (Zhoug can be refrigerated for up to 4 days.)

KEYS TO SUCCESS

- **Cauliflower three ways:** Quick- and long-cooked cauliflower lend grassiness and nuttiness to the soup; browned florets make a flavorful topping.
- **Hawaij:** This easy-to-make blend adds warm spiciness.

Hawaij Blends

Spice blends of any origin are rarely a set formula. Some span cuisines and differ from country to country, state to state, town to town, or even household to household. Some are interpreted differently by different families, the blend at the hands of the cook of the household. The Yemeni spice blend hawaij, which means "mixture" in Arabic, is no exception. This warm, almost pungent, spice blend used for soup almost always contains cumin, black pepper, turmeric, and cardamom in differing amounts. Other spices such as caraway, ground cloves, coriander, fenugreek, nutmeg, ground onion, and saffron may make an appearance, each contributing significantly to the blend's profile and potency. Hawaij is popular among Yemenite Jewish cooks and so is common in Israeli cuisine. Don't confuse this savory blend with hawaij made for coffee and dessert, which is a blend of sweeter spices.

TANABOUR

Serves: 6
Total Time: 1½ hours

RECIPE OVERVIEW Yogurt brings milky tang—and an exceptional satiny texture—to the soothing Armenian soup known as tanabour. Tanabour, or spas, is a nourishing, filling, and thoroughly satisfying grain-and-yogurt soup. Though it can be made using a wide variety of grains, ours uses pearl barley, since—lacking hulls—it cooks to a tender, plump consistency without breaking down entirely. Greek yogurt gives the soup thickness and dairy richness without leaving it overly tart. An egg yolk contributes further richness and a silky consistency. Finally, we garnish the soup with cilantro and Aleppo pepper–infused melted butter. Dried mint is widely used in Middle Eastern cooking; its flavor is quite different from that of fresh mint, so if you can't find it, it's better to omit it than to substitute fresh. Chicken broth gives the soup added depth, but it can be replaced with water or vegetable broth. We prefer the richness of whole-milk Greek yogurt here, but low-fat can be used; avoid nonfat. If Aleppo pepper is unavailable, substitute 1 teaspoon of paprika plus a pinch of cayenne pepper. Fresh parsley or mint, or a combination of the two, can be substituted for the cilantro.

4	tablespoons unsalted butter, divided
1	onion, chopped fine
1	teaspoon dried mint
1	teaspoon table salt
½	teaspoon pepper
	Pinch baking soda
¾	cup pearl barley
4	cups chicken broth
2	cups water
1½	cups plain Greek yogurt
1	large egg yolk
¼	cup chopped fresh cilantro, divided
1	teaspoon ground dried Aleppo pepper

1. Melt 2 tablespoons butter in large saucepan over medium heat. Add onion, mint, salt, pepper, and baking soda. Cook, stirring occasionally, until onion has broken down into soft paste and is just starting to stick to saucepan, 6 to 8 minutes.

2. Stir in barley. Cook, stirring frequently, until grains are translucent around edges, about 3 minutes. Add broth and water. Increase heat to high and bring to boil. Adjust heat to maintain gentle simmer; cook, partially covered, until barley is very tender, 50 minutes to 1 hour, stirring occasionally. Meanwhile, whisk yogurt and egg yolk together in large bowl.

3. Remove saucepan from heat. Whisking vigorously, gradually add 2 cups barley mixture to yogurt mixture. Stirring constantly, add yogurt-barley mixture back to saucepan. Cover and let sit for 10 minutes to thicken.

4. Heat soup over medium heat, stirring occasionally, until temperature registers between 180 and 185 degrees (do not allow soup to boil or yogurt will curdle). Remove from heat. Soup should have consistency of buttermilk; if thicker, adjust by adding hot water, 2 tablespoons at a time. Stir in 2 tablespoons cilantro and season with salt to taste.

5. Melt remaining 2 tablespoons butter in small skillet over medium-high heat. Off heat, stir in Aleppo pepper. Ladle soup into bowls, drizzle each portion with 1 teaspoon spiced butter, sprinkle with remaining 2 tablespoons cilantro, and serve. (Leftovers can be refrigerated for up to 3 days; reheat gently, being careful not to allow temperature to exceed 180 degrees. If necessary, thin by adding water, 2 tablespoons at a time.)

KEYS TO SUCCESS

- **Barley:** Its texture is plump and soft, and it releases the right amount of starch into the soup, which helps prevent the yogurt from curdling.

- **Greek yogurt:** Provides good thickness and body without too much acidity

- **Temperature:** Keeping the soup between 180 and 185 degrees prevents it from curdling.

COURSE
SHELLFISH SOUPS

LAWMAN JOHNSON

Preparing shellfish soups can seem intimidating—from purchasing to dealing with the shells to determining when the fish is cooked properly. But if you're a seafood lover, you shouldn't have to go to a restaurant to experience stellar shellfish soup. The recipes in this course will walk you through a range of deliciously different soups that use clams, cockles, shrimp, scallops, and squid and show you that there's no mystery to shellfish soup—just good eating.

LAWMAN'S PRO TIP: *A great shellfish soup begins with quality ingredients, so be sure to source out the best you can.*

NEW ENGLAND CLAM CHOWDER

Serves: 6
Total Time: 1 hour

RECIPE OVERVIEW Good traditional clam chowder isn't hard to make, but the star ingredient can be finicky to work with. Medium-size hard-shell clams are the easiest to handle and guarantee the most clam flavor. Your first step will be to give them a good scrub to rid them of any sand. Rather than shucking the raw clams and adding them to the pot, steam the clams to open them and use the steaming liquid as the broth. Pull the steamed clams from the pot when they've just opened; if they've opened completely, they will overcook when returned to the soup to heat through. Waxy red potatoes cook up creamy without falling apart in the chowder. Bacon makes a nice substitute for the traditional salt pork and adds great smoky flavor. As for the creaminess factor, using a modest amount of heavy cream instead of milk means you can use less dairy for a rich, creamy chowder that tastes distinctly of clams.

- 3   cups water
- 7   pounds medium-size hard-shell clams, such as cherrystones, washed and scrubbed clean
- 5   ounces (about 3 slices) thick-cut bacon, cut into 1/4-inch pieces
- 1   large onion, chopped medium
- 2   tablespoons all-purpose flour
- 1½ pounds red potatoes (about 4 medium), cut into 1/2-inch chunks
- 1   bay leaf
- 1   teaspoon fresh thyme or 1/4 teaspoon dried
- 1   cup heavy cream
- 2   tablespoons minced fresh parsley

1. Bring water to boil in large Dutch oven. Add clams and cover with tight-fitting lid. Cook for 5 minutes, uncover, and stir with wooden spoon. Quickly cover pot and steam until clams just open, 2 to 4 minutes. (Don't let clams open completely.) Transfer clams to large bowl and cool slightly; reserve broth. Open clams with paring knife, holding clams over bowl to catch any juices. With knife, sever muscle that attaches clam to bottom shell and transfer meat to cutting board; discard shells. Mince clams and set aside. Pour clam broth into large bowl, holding back last few tablespoons of broth in case of sediment; set clam broth aside. (You should have about 5 cups. If not, add bottled clam juice or water to make this amount.) Rinse and dry pot, then return pot to burner.

2. Fry bacon in now-empty pot over medium-low heat until crisp, 5 to 7 minutes. Add onion and cook, stirring occasionally, until softened, about 5 minutes. Add flour and stir until lightly colored, about 1 minute. Gradually whisk in reserved clam broth. Add potatoes, bay leaf, and thyme and simmer until potatoes are tender, about 10 minutes. Add clams, cream, parsley, and salt and pepper to taste; bring to simmer. Remove from heat, discard bay leaf, and serve.

KEYS TO SUCCESS

- **Scrub those clams:** A bit of gritty sand can ruin a pot of chowder.
- **Steam briefly:** To avoid overcooked clams, pull them from the steam as soon as they open.
- **Bacon:** Adds smoky flavor

CORE TECHNIQUE | **Scrubbing Clams Clean**

To remove sand before cooking, simply scrub clams under cold running water using a soft brush.

SHELLFISH SOUP WITH LEEKS AND TURMERIC

Serves: 6 to 8
Total Time: 1 hour

RECIPE OVERVIEW For a succulent mixed shellfish soup bursting with flavor and chock-full of seafood, shrimp, scallops, and squid are an easy-to-eat trio. The shrimp shells are a valuable source of flavor, from which you can extract a potent and aromatic broth. After shelling the shrimp, sauté the shells and simmer them in white wine and water; just 10 minutes is enough time to extract their flavor. After straining out the shells, set aside the broth while you cook the soup base: a combination of leeks and spices reminiscent of North Africa—namely, ginger, coriander, and turmeric. A small bit of tomato paste and garlic reinforce the more savory aspects of the soup without being distracting. Deglaze the pan with the shrimp broth along with bottled clam juice for added dimension and natural sweetness. The resulting brothy soup base is the perfect medium for cooking the seafood. To avoid overcooking anything, add the seafood in stages: Scallops get a 2-minute head start on the shrimp, which cooks in mere minutes. Adding the squid last off heat gently poaches it and delivers a perfectly cooked, meaty shellfish soup. If desired, you can omit the squid in this recipe and increase the amount of shrimp to 1 ½ pounds.

- 2 tablespoons extra-virgin olive oil, divided, plus extra for serving
- 12 ounces large shrimp (26 to 30 per pound), peeled and deveined, shells reserved
- 1 cup dry white wine or dry vermouth
- 4 cups water
- 1½ pounds leeks, white and light green parts only, halved lengthwise, sliced thin, and washed thoroughly
- 4 ounces pancetta, chopped fine
- 3 tablespoons tomato paste
- 2 garlic cloves, minced
- 1 teaspoon table salt
- 1 teaspoon grated fresh ginger
- 1 teaspoon ground coriander
- ½ teaspoon ground turmeric
- ⅛ teaspoon red pepper flakes
- 2 (8-ounce) bottles clam juice
- 12 ounces large sea scallops, tendons removed
- 12 ounces squid, bodies sliced crosswise into ½-inch-thick rings, tentacles halved
- ⅓ cup minced fresh parsley

1. Heat 1 tablespoon oil in Dutch oven over medium heat until shimmering. Add shrimp shells and cook, stirring frequently, until beginning to turn spotty brown and pot starts to brown, 2 to 4 minutes. Add wine and simmer, stirring occasionally, for 2 minutes. Stir in water, bring to simmer, and cook for 4 minutes. Strain mixture through fine-mesh strainer into bowl, pressing on solids to extract as much liquid as possible; discard solids.

2. Heat remaining 1 tablespoon oil in now-empty pot over medium heat until shimmering. Add leeks and pancetta and cook until leeks are softened and lightly browned, about 8 minutes. Stir in tomato paste, garlic, salt, ginger, coriander, turmeric, and pepper flakes and cook until fragrant, about 1 minute. Stir in wine mixture and clam juice, scraping up any browned bits. Bring to simmer and cook until flavors meld, 15 to 20 minutes.

3. Reduce heat to gentle simmer, add sea scallops, and cook for 2 minutes. Stir in shrimp and cook until just opaque throughout, about 2 minutes. Off heat, stir in squid, cover, and let sit until just opaque and tender, 1 to 2 minutes. Stir in parsley and season with salt and pepper to taste. Serve, drizzling individual portions with extra oil.

KEYS TO SUCCESS

- **Use the shrimp shells:** A bonus ingredient, the shells provide intense shrimp flavor when browned and simmered.

- **Cook the aromatics:** A North African–inspired array of bold, warm spices blooms when cooked in pancetta fat.

- **Cook seafood in stages:** Add the different types of seafood to the pot according to how quickly they cook for perfect results.

FREGULA WITH CLAMS AND SAFFRON BROTH

Serves: 4
Total Time: 40 minutes

RECIPE OVERVIEW This soup of pasta and clams is a Sardinian classic that's all about simplicity. It relies chiefly on the flavor inherent in the soup's two main ingredients: chewy, toasty spherical fregula pasta, and arselle, the small, briny, succulent hard-shell clams found along the coast. Broth enriched with tomatoes (in various forms depending on the recipe), parsley, garlic, a touch of fragrant saffron, pepper flakes, and olive oil traditionally constitutes the soup base. We cook the pasta using the absorption method, right in the soup's base of chicken broth and water; this way, the fregula soaks up the flavorful broth during cooking. As a substitute for the Sardinian arselle, which aren't widely available in the United States, we landed on diminutive cockles, which are sweet and readily accessible. To cook the cockles perfectly, use our standard test kitchen method of steaming them in a shallow covered skillet and removing them as they open. Sun-dried tomatoes, which are found in some traditional versions of this recipe, are our tomato product; given the soup's quick cooking time, their deep, concentrated flavor is a bonus. Cockles are our preferred choice, but if they're unavailable, you can substitute small littleneck clams.

- 2 tablespoons extra-virgin olive oil, plus extra for drizzling
- 2 garlic cloves, minced
- ⅛ teaspoon red pepper flakes
- ⅛ teaspoon saffron threads, crumbled
- 2 cups chicken or vegetable broth
- 2 cups water
- ⅓ cup oil-packed sun-dried tomatoes, patted dry and chopped coarse
- ¼ cup minced fresh parsley, divided
- 1½ cups fregula
- 2 pounds cockles, scrubbed
- 1 cup dry white wine
- ¼ teaspoon grated lemon zest

1. Heat oil in Dutch oven over medium heat until shimmering. Add garlic, pepper flakes, and saffron and cook until fragrant, about 30 seconds. Stir in broth, water, tomatoes, and 2 tablespoons parsley and bring to boil. Stir in fregula and cook, stirring often, until al dente.

2. Meanwhile, bring cockles and wine to boil in covered 12-inch skillet over high heat. Cook, shaking skillet occasionally, until cockles have just opened, 6 to 8 minutes. Using slotted spoon, transfer cockles to large bowl. Discard any unopened cockles. Cover to keep warm.

3. Strain cockle cooking liquid through fine-mesh strainer lined with coffee filter into pot with fregula, avoiding any gritty sediment that has settled on bottom of pan. Stir in lemon zest and remaining 2 tablespoons parsley and season with salt and pepper to taste. Top individual portions with cockles and drizzle with extra oil before serving.

- **Absorption cooking:** Cooked right in the broth, the pasta soaks up savory flavor.
- **Cockles:** The small mollusks are a good substitute for Sardinian arselle (but you can also use small littleneck clams).

SHRIMP BISQUE

Serves: 6
Total Time: 1½ hours

RECIPE OVERVIEW Our stellar shrimp bisque is rich and velvety—delicate in character but deeply intense—with an almost sweet shrimp essence and an interplay of supporting flavors. Its texture is incredibly silky with tender pieces of poached shrimp. For incomparable shrimp flavor, grind the shrimp shells and half the shrimp, simmer them, and then strain them from the broth. Add the remaining shrimp at the last minute as a garnish. Before flambéing, be sure to roll up long shirtsleeves, tie back long hair, and turn off the exhaust fan and any lit burners.

2	pounds medium-large shrimp (31 to 40 per pound), divided
2	tablespoons vegetable oil
⅓	cup brandy or cognac, warmed
1	onion, chopped coarse
1	carrot, peeled and chopped coarse
1	celery rib, chopped coarse
1	garlic clove, peeled
2	tablespoons unsalted butter
½	cup all-purpose flour
1½	cups dry white wine
4	(8-ounce) bottles clam juice
1	(14.5-ounce) can diced tomatoes, drained
1	cup heavy cream
1	tablespoon lemon juice
1	small sprig fresh tarragon
	Pinch ground cayenne
2	tablespoons dry sherry or Madeira
2	tablespoons minced fresh chives
1	recipe Buttery Rye Croutons (page 227) (optional)

1. Peel and devein 1 pound of shrimp, reserving shells, and cut each shrimp into 3 pieces; refrigerate until needed.

2. Heat oil in 12-inch skillet over medium-high heat until just smoking. Add remaining 1 pound shrimp and reserved shrimp shells and cook until lightly browned, 3 to 5 minutes. Add brandy and let warm through, about 5 seconds. Wave lit match over pan until brandy ignites, then shake pan to distribute flames.

3. Transfer flambéed shrimp mixture to food processor and process until mixture resembles fine meal, 10 to 20 seconds. Transfer to bowl. Pulse onion, carrot, celery, and garlic in food processor until finely chopped, about 5 pulses.

4. Melt butter in Dutch oven over medium heat. Add processed shrimp and vegetables, cover, and cook until softened and fragrant, 5 to 7 minutes. Stir in flour and cook for 1 minute.

5. Gradually stir in wine and clam juice, scraping up any browned bits and smoothing out any lumps. Stir in tomatoes and bring to boil. Reduce to gentle simmer and cook until thickened and flavors meld, about 20 minutes.

6. Strain broth through fine-mesh strainer, pressing on solids to release as much liquid as possible. Clean pot and return it to stove.

7. Add strained broth, cream, lemon juice, tarragon sprig, and cayenne to pot and bring to simmer. Stir in reserved shrimp pieces and gently simmer until shrimp are bright pink, 1 to 2 minutes. Off heat, discard tarragon sprig, stir in sherry, and season with salt and pepper to taste. Sprinkle individual portions with chives and croutons, if using, before serving.

Variation
SEAFOOD BISQUE

Reduce shrimp to 8 ounces. Add 8 ounces large sea scallops, tendons removed, cut into quarters, to soup with reserved shrimp pieces in step 7. Add 8 ounces cooked lobster meat, cut into ½-inch pieces, to soup with sherry in step 7; cover and let heat through before serving.

Shell-On Shrimp

For a bisque with real shrimp flavor in record time, you need to use the shells, not just the meat. After peeling shrimp, sauté shells with vegetables and then simmer with water and wine to make a fast, flavorful shrimp stock.

KEYS TO SUCCESS

- **Grind the shells with the shrimp:** The shells add potent flavor.

- **Flambé prep:** Flambéing is important; make sure you follow directions to do it safely.

- **Strain the broth:** For a supersmooth texture

GUAY TIEW TOM YUM GOONG

Serves: 4 to 6
Total Time: 1¼ hours

RECIPE OVERVIEW This Thai soup contains generous amounts of shrimp and rice noodles—along with oyster mushrooms and cherry tomatoes—in a highly aromatic broth bursting with hot, sour, salty, and sweet flavors. Smashing galangal, scallions, lemongrass, makrut lime leaves, and Thai chiles releases their flavorful oils, and simmering them in chicken broth releases their vibrancy. We round out the classic flavor profile with more distinct ingredients: fish sauce, lime juice, cilantro, and Thai basil. Finally, add a dollop of homemade nam prik pao, a Thai chili jam that offers robust sweet, savory, and slightly spicy notes. Whole shrimp are traditional in this soup, but you can halve them crosswise before cooking to make them easier to eat. If galangal is unavailable, substitute fresh ginger. Makrut lime leaves add a lot to this soup. But if you can't find them, substitute three 3-inch strips each of lemon zest and lime zest. We prefer vermicelli made from 100 percent rice flour to varieties that include a secondary starch such as cornstarch. If you can find only the latter, soak them longer—up to 15 minutes.

- 4 ounces rice vermicelli
- 2 lemongrass stalks, trimmed to bottom 6 inches
- 4 scallions, trimmed, white parts left whole, green parts cut into 1-inch lengths
- 6 makrut lime leaves, torn if large
- 2 Thai chiles, stemmed (1 left whole, 1 sliced thin), divided, plus 2 Thai chiles, stemmed and sliced thin, for serving (optional)
- 1 (2-inch) piece fresh galangal, peeled and sliced into ¼-inch-thick rounds
- 8 cups chicken broth
- 1 tablespoon sugar, plus extra for seasoning
- 8 ounces oyster mushrooms, trimmed and torn into 1-inch pieces
- 3 tablespoons fish sauce, plus extra for seasoning
- 1 pound extra-large shrimp (21 to 25 per pound), peeled, deveined, and tails removed
- 12 ounces cherry tomatoes, halved
- 2 tablespoons lime juice, plus extra for seasoning and lime wedges for serving
- ½ cup fresh cilantro leaves
- ¼ cup fresh Thai basil leaves, torn if large (optional)
- 1 recipe Nam Prik Pao (recipe follows; optional)

1. Bring 4 quarts water to boil in large pot. Remove from heat, add vermicelli, and let sit, stirring occasionally, until vermicelli are fully tender, 10 to 15 minutes. Drain, rinse with cold water, drain again, and distribute evenly among large soup bowls.

½ cup vegetable oil

2 large shallots, sliced thin

4 large garlic cloves, sliced thin

10 dried arbol chiles, stemmed, halved lengthwise, and seeds reserved

2 tablespoons packed brown sugar

3 tablespoons lime juice, plus extra for seasoning (2 limes)

2 tablespoons fish sauce, plus extra for seasoning

1. Set fine-mesh strainer over heatproof bowl. Heat oil and shallots in medium saucepan over medium-high heat, stirring frequently, until shallots are deep golden brown, 10 to 14 minutes. Using slotted spoon, transfer shallots to second bowl. Add garlic to hot oil and cook, stirring constantly, until golden brown, 2 to 3 minutes. Using slotted spoon, transfer garlic to bowl with shallots. Add arbols and half of reserved seeds to hot oil and cook, stirring constantly, until arbols turn deep red, 1 to 2 minutes. Strain oil through strainer into bowl; reserve oil and transfer arbols to bowl with shallots and garlic. Do not wash saucepan.

2. Process shallot mixture, sugar, and lime juice in food processor until thick paste forms, 15 to 30 seconds, scraping down sides of bowl as needed.

3. Return paste to now-empty saucepan and add fish sauce and 2 tablespoons reserved oil. Bring to simmer over medium-low heat. Cook, stirring frequently, until mixture is thickened and has jam-like consistency, 4 to 5 minutes. Off heat, season with extra lime juice, extra fish sauce, and salt to taste. (Jam can be refrigerated for up to 1 month.)

2. Place lemongrass, scallion whites, lime leaves, whole Thai chile, and galangal on cutting board and lightly smash with meat pounder or bottom of small skillet until mixture is moist and very fragrant. Transfer lemongrass mixture to Dutch oven. Add broth and sugar and bring to boil over high heat. Reduce heat and simmer for 15 minutes. Using slotted spoon, remove solids from pot and discard.

3. Add mushrooms, fish sauce, scallion greens, and sliced Thai chile and simmer for 3 to 4 minutes. Stir in shrimp. Cover and let sit off heat until shrimp are opaque and cooked through, 4 to 5 minutes. Stir in tomatoes and lime juice. Season with extra sugar, extra fish sauce, and extra lime juice to taste.

4. Ladle soup into bowls of noodles; sprinkle with cilantro and Thai basil, if using. Serve, drizzled with nam prik pao, if using, and pass lime wedges and extra sliced Thai chiles, if using, separately.

NAM PRIK PAO

Makes: ¾ cup

The sweet, savory, and spicy condiment called nam prik pao is the classic garnish for guay tiew tom yum goong, but it's too good to be relegated to a single use. Thai cooks also use it on fried eggs, noodles, and white rice; in stir-fries; and even as a sandwich spread. Slice the shallots to a consistent thickness to ensure even cooking. For a spicier jam, add more chile seeds.

CORE TECHNIQUE

Smashing Aromatics

Use a meat pounder to crush aromatics; this allows them to release enough of their flavorful oils into the broth in just 15 minutes.

KEYS TO SUCCESS

- **Seek out the real thing:** Galangal, lime leaves, Thai chiles, and other ingredients give this soup incomparable flavor. We offer some substitutes but if you can find the real thing, use it.

- **Smash the aromatics:** This important step releases their oils.

CHAPTER 6

PASTA AND NOODLES

FRESH ITALIAN EGG PASTA

DAN ZUCCARELLO

Fresh pasta made with eggs is common throughout northern and central Italy; the eggs enrich and hydrate the dough. Our versatile egg pasta dough works well for making both strand pasta such as fettuccine and linguine and filled pastas such as ravioli and tortellini. Because it's superhydrated with egg yolks and olive oil, it's easy to roll out and cooks up supple and springy. Fresh egg pasta is more delicate than dried pasta, meaning the two aren't necessarily interchangeable, so we generally don't recommend substituting dried pasta for fresh in these recipes. But not to worry—with so many delicious recipes to go around, that's hardly a problem.

DAN'S PRO TIP: *This fresh egg pasta dough is extremely versatile and once you are comfortable with it, you can make things even more interesting with flavor modifications. I like to pulse 2 tablespoons of minced fresh leafy herbs into the flour before adding the eggs for fresh herb pasta. Or add 1 tablespoon grated lemon zest and 1 teaspoon pepper to the flour for fresh lemon-pepper pasta.*

THE METHOD
DOUGH SHEETS AND STRAND PASTA

Our failproof kitchen-tested methods and recipes make turning out fresh homemade pasta from scratch totally achievable.

1 CUT DOUGH INTO PIECES
Transfer rested dough to clean counter, divide into 6 pieces, and cover with plastic. Flatten 1 piece of dough into ½-inch-thick disk.

2 ROLL DOUGH SHEET
Using pasta machine with rollers set to widest position, feed dough through rollers twice.

3 ROLL DOUGH SHEET AGAIN
Bring tapered ends of dough toward middle; press to seal. Feed dough seam side first through rollers again. Repeat feeding dough tapered ends first through rollers set at widest position, without folding, until dough is smooth and barely tacky. (If dough sticks, lightly dust with flour and roll again.)

4 NARROW ROLLERS
Narrow rollers to next setting; feed dough through twice. Progressively narrow rollers, feeding dough through each setting twice, until dough is very thin and semitransparent. (If dough becomes too long to manage, halve crosswise.) Transfer sheet of pasta to dish towel and let air-dry for about 15 minutes; meanwhile, roll out remaining dough. Line 2 rimmed baking sheets with parchment paper and liberally dust with flour. Liberally dust pasta sheets with flour and cut into approximately 12-inch lengths.

5 CUT SHEETS INTO STRANDS
Fit pasta machine with desired noodle attachment and feed 1 pasta sheet through rollers to cut into strands.

6 SEPARATE STRANDS
Use fingers to unfurl pasta, liberally dust strands with flour, and arrange in small bundles on prepared sheet. Repeat with remaining pasta sheets.

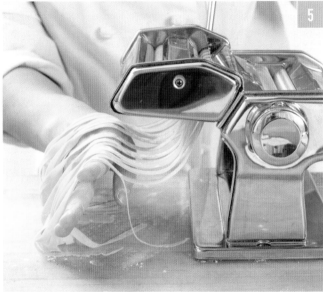

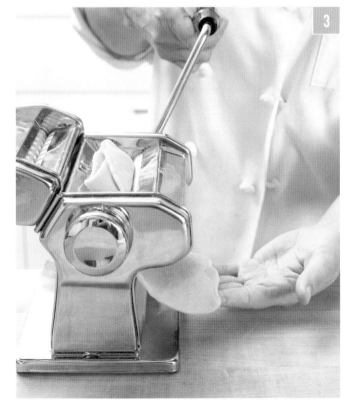

FRESH EGG PASTA DOUGH

Makes: 1 pound
Total Time: 10 minutes, plus 1 hour resting

RECIPE OVERVIEW Six egg yolks, in addition to two whole eggs and a couple tablespoons of olive oil, make this dough a dream to roll out while also enhancing its flavor. A food processor brings the dough together quickly, so only a quick knead by hand is necessary. Resting the dough allows the gluten—the protein network that forms when flour and liquid interact and which makes doughs chewy— time to relax so the dough won't contract after rolling out. You may cut the pasta either using the machine or by hand (see page 244). If using a high-protein all-purpose flour, such as from King Arthur, increase the number of egg yolks to seven.

2 cups (10 ounces) all-purpose flour, plus extra as needed
2 large eggs plus 6 large yolks
2 tablespoons extra-virgin olive oil

1. Process flour, eggs and yolks, and oil in food processor until mixture forms cohesive dough that feels soft and is barely tacky to touch, about 45 seconds. (If dough sticks to fingers, add up to ¼ cup flour, 1 tablespoon at a time, until barely tacky. If dough doesn't become cohesive, add up to 1 tablespoon water, 1 teaspoon at a time, until it just comes together; process 30 seconds longer.)

2. Transfer dough to clean counter and knead by hand until smooth, 1 to 2 minutes. Shape dough into 6-inch-long cylinder. Wrap tightly in plastic wrap and let rest for 1 hour or up to 4 hours.

KEYS TO SUCCESS

- **Use your scale:** To ensure proper dough texture, weigh the flour.
- **Size matters:** Using large eggs is crucial; extra-large or jumbo eggs will make the dough too moist.
- **Give it a rest:** Rest the dough for at least 1 hour before rolling. The longer it rests, the easier it will be to roll out.

CORE TECHNIQUE

Freezing Fresh Egg Pasta

To freeze fresh pasta strands, place on baking sheet and freeze until pasta is firm, then transfer pasta bundles to zipper-lock bag and freeze for up to 1 month. Do not thaw before cooking.

FETTUCCINE WITH OLIVADA

Serves: 4
Total Time: 50 minutes

RECIPE OVERVIEW Olivada could be described as a black pesto; it's similar to tapenade and is often used as a bruschetta topping in Italy, but it also makes a rich comple- ment to homemade pasta. Kalamata olives bring their powerful flavor to this olivada, supported by toasted garlic, shallot, fresh herbs, lemon, and plenty of Parmesan. Though some olivada recipes call for chopping by hand, we find that a food processor chops all of the ingredients to an ideal coarse but uniform texture in only about a minute. Make sure to use high-quality olives here. The anchovy adds an undertone of umami flavor without tasting fishy, and we recommend its inclusion.

3 medium garlic cloves, unpeeled
1½ cups pitted kalamata olives
1 ounce Parmesan cheese, grated (about ½ cup), plus extra for serving
6 tablespoons extra-virgin olive oil
¼ cup packed fresh parsley leaves
1 medium shallot, chopped coarse (about 3 tablespoons)
8 large basil leaves
1 tablespoon juice from 1 lemon
1 anchovy fillet, rinsed (optional)
Table salt for cooking pasta
1 recipe Fresh Egg Pasta Dough (at left), cut into fettuccine
Lemon wedges, for serving

1. Toast garlic in small skillet over medium heat, shaking pan occasionally, until garlic is softened and spotty brown, about 8 minutes; when cool, remove and discard skins.

2. Process garlic, olives, Parmesan, oil, parsley, shallot, basil, lemon juice, and anchovy (if using) in food processor, scraping down sides of workbowl as necessary. Transfer mixture to small bowl and season with salt and pepper to taste.

3. Bring 4 quarts water to boil in large pot. Add 1 tablespoon salt and pasta to boiling water and cook, stirring often, until al dente. Reserve ½ cup of cooking water, then drain pasta and return it to pot. Stir ¼ cup of reserved pasta cooking water into olivada and add olivada to pasta. Toss to combine, adjusting consistency of sauce with remaining reserved pasta cooking water as needed. Serve immediately, passing lemon wedges and extra Parmesan separately.

KEYS TO SUCCESS

- **Don't overcook:** Fresh pasta cooks very quickly, so start tasting for doneness after 2 minutes.

- **Toss with care:** Fresh pasta is more delicate than dried pasta, so the long strands will break more easily.

FETTUCCINE WITH TOMATO-BROWNED BUTTER SAUCE

Serves: 4
Total Time: 50 minutes

RECIPE OVERVIEW Let your fresh pasta really shine by cloaking it with a flavorful but simple tomato sauce. We start with butter, which mellows the acidity of the tomatoes and adds a velvety quality to the sauce. Browning the butter creates flavor complexity; we then add garlic for more depth. Processing whole canned tomatoes before incorporating them delivers a sauce with excellent texture. Don't forget to reserve some of the pasta cooking water so that you can adjust the final sauce consistency to your liking.

- 1 (28-ounce) can whole peeled tomatoes
- 4 tablespoons unsalted butter, divided
- 2 garlic cloves, minced
- ½ teaspoon sugar
- ½ teaspoon table salt, plus salt for cooking pasta
- 2 teaspoons sherry vinegar
- 1 recipe Fresh Egg Pasta Dough (page 242), cut into fettuccine
- 3 tablespoons chopped fresh basil
  Grated Parmesan cheese

1. Process tomatoes and their juice in food processor until smooth, about 30 seconds. Melt 3 tablespoons butter in 12-inch skillet over medium-high heat, swirling occasionally, until butter is dark brown and releases nutty aroma, about 1½ minutes. Stir in garlic and cook for 10 seconds. Stir in processed tomatoes, sugar, and salt and simmer until sauce is slightly reduced, about 8 minutes.

2. Off heat, whisk in remaining 1 tablespoon butter and vinegar. Season with salt and pepper to taste; cover to keep warm.

3. Bring 4 quarts water to boil in large Dutch oven. Add 1 tablespoon salt and pasta and cook until pasta is tender but still al dente. Reserve ½ cup pasta cooking water and drain pasta.

4. Add pasta and ¼ cup pasta cooking water to sauce in skillet and cook over medium heat, tossing to combine, just until well coated and hot. Add remaining cooking water as needed to adjust consistency. Stir in basil, season with salt and pepper to taste, and serve with Parmesan.

KEYS TO SUCCESS

- **Don't overcook:** Fresh pasta cooks very quickly, so start tasting for doneness after 2 minutes.

- **Reserve some cooking water:** This allows you to adjust the consistency of the sauce to your liking.

TAGLIATELLE WITH ARTICHOKES AND PARMESAN BREAD CRUMBS

Serves: 4
Total Time: 1¼ hours

RECIPE OVERVIEW Artichokes and pasta harmonize in this version of a favorite Italian dish. Rather than laboring to prep fresh artichoke hearts, we use jarred water-packed hearts. To offset any briny flavor from the acidified water the artichokes are packed in, we separate the leaves from the hearts and give the leaves a quick soak in fresh water. Cutting the hearts in half and patting them dry promotes deep browning, and then we stir in the leaves off the heat. Garlic, oregano, and anchovy combined with white wine, olive oil, and Parmesan make up the rest of the flavorful sauce, and the crunchy bread crumb and Parmesan topping adds great contrasting texture. Don't substitute marinated artichoke hearts for the water-packed hearts. We prefer jarred artichoke hearts labeled "baby" or "cocktail" that are 1½ inches or shorter in length. Larger artichoke hearts tend to have fibrous leaves. If you are using larger hearts, trim the top ¼ to ½ inch from the leaves.

Parmesan Bread Crumbs

    2   slices hearty white sandwich bread

    2   tablespoons extra-virgin olive oil

  ¼   cup grated Parmesan cheese

Pasta

    4   cups jarred whole baby artichoke hearts packed in water

  ¼   cup extra-virgin olive oil, divided, plus extra for drizzling

  ⅛   teaspoon table salt, plus salt for cooking pasta

    4   garlic cloves, minced

    1   tablespoon minced fresh oregano or 1 teaspoon dried

    2   anchovy fillets, rinsed, patted dry, and minced

  ⅛   teaspoon red pepper flakes

  ½   cup dry white wine

    1   recipe Fresh Egg Pasta Dough (page 242), cut into tagliatelle

    1   ounce Parmesan cheese, grated (½ cup), plus extra for serving

  ¼   cup minced fresh parsley

 1½ teaspoons grated lemon zest

1. FOR THE BREAD CRUMBS Pulse bread in food processor until finely ground, 10 to 15 pulses. Heat oil in 12-inch nonstick skillet over medium heat until shimmering. Add bread crumbs and cook, stirring constantly, until crumbs begin to brown, 3 to 5 minutes. Add Parmesan and continue to cook, stirring constantly, until crumbs are golden, 1 to 2 minutes longer. Transfer bread-crumb mixture to bowl and season with salt and pepper to taste.

2. FOR THE PASTA Cut leaves from artichoke hearts and place leaves in bowl. Cut hearts in half and pat dry with paper towels. Cover artichoke leaves with water and let sit for 15 minutes. Drain well.

3. Heat 1 tablespoon oil in 12-inch nonstick skillet over medium-high heat until shimmering. Add artichoke hearts and ⅛ teaspoon salt and cook, stirring frequently, until spotty brown, 7 to 9 minutes. Stir in garlic, oregano, anchovies, and pepper flakes and cook, stirring constantly, until fragrant, about 30 seconds. Stir in wine and bring to simmer. Off heat, stir in artichoke leaves.

4. Meanwhile, bring 4 quarts water to boil in large pot. Add pasta and 1 tablespoon salt and cook, stirring often, until pasta is tender but still al dente. Reserve 1½ cups cooking water, then drain pasta and return it to pot. Add artichoke mixture, Parmesan, parsley, lemon zest, 1 cup reserved cooking water, and remaining 3 tablespoons oil and toss to combine. Season with salt and pepper to taste and adjust consistency with remaining ½ cup reserved cooking water as needed. Serve, sprinkling individual portions with bread-crumb mixture and extra Parmesan and drizzling with extra oil.

KEY TO SUCCESS

- **Drain the leaves:** Draining them well after soaking removes excess moisture along with the acidic flavors.

No Machine? No Problem!

If you don't have a pasta maker, you can roll and cut dough by hand into sheets for strands or filled pasta:

CUT DOUGH

Shape dough into 6-inch cylinder; wrap in plastic and let rest for at least 1 hour. Divide into 6 equal pieces. Work with 1 piece at a time; rewrap remaining 5 pieces.

ROLL OUT SHEET

Dust both sides of piece with flour, then press cut side down into 3-inch square. With rolling pin, roll into 6-inch square, then dust both sides again with flour.

ROLL DOUGH AGAIN

Roll dough to 12 by 6 inches, rolling from center 1 way at a time; dust with flour. Continue rolling to 20 by 6 inches, lifting often to release from counter. Transfer to clean dish towel and air-dry for 15 minutes.

SHAPE DOUGH

A. For stuffed pasta, use sharp knife to trim and square off corners of pasta sheet, then proceed with recipe.

B. For strand pasta, starting with short end, gently fold sheet at 2-inch intervals to create flat roll.

CUT PASTA

Slice pasta crosswise to desired width (¼ inch for fettuccine, ⅜ inch for tagliatelle, or ¾ inch to 1 inch for pappardelle). Use fingers to unfurl pasta; transfer to baking sheet.

RESOURCES FOR FRESH ITALIAN EGG PASTA

FOUR STEPS TO PASTA DOUGH

1. Weigh flour: Use a digital scale to weigh the all-purpose flour.
Why? While the recipe will work using a volume equivalent, there is less room for error if you weigh the flour.

2. Process dough: Process the flour, eggs and yolks, and olive oil in a food processor until dough forms rough but cohesive ball, about 45 seconds.
Why? The efficient mechanical action of the processor brings the dough together quickly.

3. Check and adjust dough: Add either flour or water as needed to create a cohesive dough.
Why? The moisture content of this dough needs to be right in order to produce a workable dough.

4. Knead dough, then let rest: Knead until smooth, shape into a log, wrap with plastic, and let rest on the counter for at least 1 hour.
Why? Resting allows the gluten in the dough to relax, making for a malleable dough that won't spring back excessively.

WHAT CAN GO WRONG

PROBLEM Dough isn't coming together in food processor.

SOLUTION Add up to 1 tablespoon water, 1 teaspoon at a time, until dough forms cohesive mass that's barely tacky to touch.

PROBLEM Dough is too sticky.

SOLUTION Add up to ¼ cup flour, 1 tablespoon at a time, until dough is barely tacky.

FLOURS FOR ITALIAN PASTA

For egg-based fresh pasta, most Italians use type "00" flour, an extremely finely ground wheat flour. Because it is not widely available in the United States, we developed our recipe for Fresh Egg Pasta using all-purpose flour, which is made from a mix of hard and soft wheat and is slightly coarser. For egg-free pasta, semolina flour is the universal choice. It's ground using the endosperm of durum wheat and produces a dough that has less elasticity than one made with all-purpose or type "00" flour—perfect for making shapes like orecchiette that will hold their shape through the cooking process.

SEPARATING EGG WHITES

The two best tools for separating egg yolks from whites are your hands and the eggshells themselves.

Hand Method
Crack egg on flat surface and open shell so yolk and white fall into your cupped hand. Slightly open your fingers so white can slip into bowl below, leaving yolk in your hand.

Shell Method
Crack egg on flat surface and, working over bowl, tip contents of egg back and forth between pieces of shell, letting white fall into bowl and leaving yolk in 1 half of shell.

FRESH ITALIAN SEMOLINA PASTA

DAN SOUZA

In southern Italy, where eggs are historically more of a luxury, fresh pasta is usually made from just water and semolina flour. This flour, which is also a staple in dried pasta making, is made from the ground endosperm of durum wheat, a hard winter wheat that is high in gluten. Its deep yellow color comes from high concentrations of carotenoids (the same compounds responsible for the hues of carrots and mangos). Because of its higher gluten content, fresh semolina pasta is sturdier than fresh egg pasta.

DAN'S PRO TIP: *When working with fresh pasta, remember that time is on your side. If at any point the dough resists rolling or shaping, give it a rest to allow the gluten to relax.*

FRESH SEMOLINA PASTA DOUGH

Makes: 1 pound
Total Time: 20 minutes, plus 30 minutes resting

RECIPE OVERVIEW Using warm water rather than cold jump-starts gluten development in this dough, and the dough also gets a generous knead in a stand mixer. After a rest to let the gluten relax, you'll be able to create pasta shapes that cook up with appealing chew and springiness. You can find fine semolina in Italian markets and in many well-stocked supermarkets. The variation incorporates saffron for its aroma and golden color; this is the traditional dough for malloreddus (page 249). This recipe was developed using a 4.5-quart stand mixer. If using a 7-quart stand mixer, you will need to double the recipe so the dough is properly kneaded.

> 2 cups (11½ ounces) fine semolina flour
> 1 teaspoon table salt
> ⅔ cup warm water, plus extra as needed

1. Whisk flour and salt together in bowl of stand mixer, then stir in warm water. Using your hands, knead dough in bowl until shaggy, a dry ball forms, and no dry flour remains, about 3 minutes. If dry flour remains, add up to 2 teaspoons extra water, 1 teaspoon at a time, until flour is absorbed. (Dough will still be very dry and barely hold its shape.)

2. Using dough hook, knead dough on medium speed until smooth and elastic, 10 to 12 minutes. (Dough may break into smaller pieces while kneading.) Transfer dough to clean counter and knead by hand to form uniform ball. Wrap tightly in plastic wrap and let rest for 30 minutes or up to 4 hours.

Variation
FRESH SAFFRON SEMOLINA PASTA DOUGH

Combine the warm water and ½ teaspoon saffron in bowl and let steep for 15 minutes before adding to flour mixture in step 1.

KEYS TO SUCCESS

- **Warm it up:** Be sure to use warm water (110 degrees).

- **Don't substitute flours:** Be sure to use semolina flour; all-purpose flour will result in gummy pasta that tastes like boiled dough.

- **That's fine:** Conventional semolina is too coarse, so make sure to purchase fine semolina.

- **Let it rest:** At least 30 minutes of rest lets the gluten relax, making the dough easier to roll out and shape.

ORECCHIETTE ALLA NORCINA

Serves: 4 to 6
Total Time: 1¼ hours

RECIPE OVERVIEW Orecchiette, or "little ears," is a wonderful pasta for pairing with a chunky sauce since the little bowl shapes catch and hold sauce ingredients so well. Here we pair it with a pork sausage sauce from Umbria. The homemade sausage needs no meat grinder and allows for incorporating appropriate seasonings, including rosemary, nutmeg, and garlic. Since browning crumbled sausage makes it too easy to end up with overcooked, dry meat, we form the pork into one big patty, brown it on both sides, and chop it; the sausage pieces finish cooking in the sauce and stay moist and tender. Some browned chopped mushrooms bolster the earthy flavors. You may substitute dried orecchiette for the fresh.

½ teaspoon plus pinch table salt, divided, plus salt for cooking pasta
¼ teaspoon baking soda
8 ounces ground pork
3 garlic cloves, minced, divided
1¼ teaspoons minced fresh rosemary, divided
⅛ teaspoon ground nutmeg
1¼ teaspoons pepper, divided
8 ounces cremini or white mushrooms, trimmed
7 teaspoons extra-virgin olive oil
1 recipe Fresh Semolina Pasta Dough (left), shaped into orecchiette
½ cup dry white wine
¾ cup heavy cream
1½ ounces Pecorino Romano cheese, grated (¾ cup)
3 tablespoons minced fresh parsley
1 tablespoon lemon juice

1. Spray large plate with vegetable oil spray. Dissolve ½ teaspoon salt and baking soda in 4 teaspoons water in medium bowl. Gently fold in pork until combined, then let sit for 10 minutes. Add one-third of garlic, ¾ teaspoon rosemary, nutmeg, and ¾ teaspoon pepper and smear with rubber spatula until well combined and tacky, 10 to 15 seconds. Transfer sausage mixture to prepared plate and form into rough 6-inch patty. Pulse mushrooms in food processor until finely chopped, 10 to 12 pulses.

2. Heat 2 teaspoons oil in 12-inch skillet over medium-high heat until just smoking. Add patty and cook, without moving, until browned, 2 to 3 minutes. Flip and continue to cook until well browned on second side, 2 to 3 minutes (very center will be raw). Transfer patty to cutting board and chop into ⅛- to ¼-inch pieces.

3. Bring 4 quarts water to boil in large pot. Add pasta and 1 tablespoon salt and cook, stirring often, until al dente. Reserve 1½ cups cooking water, then drain pasta and return it to pot.

4. Meanwhile, heat 1 tablespoon oil in now-empty skillet over medium heat. Add mushrooms and remaining pinch salt and cook, stirring frequently, until browned, 5 to

7 minutes. Stir in remaining 2 teaspoons oil, remaining garlic, remaining ½ teaspoon rosemary, and remaining ½ teaspoon pepper and cook until fragrant, about 30 seconds. Stir in wine, scraping up any browned bits, and cook until completely evaporated, 1 to 2 minutes. Stir in sausage, cream, and ¾ cup pasta cooking water and simmer until meat is no longer pink, 1 to 3 minutes. Off heat, stir in Pecorino Romano until smooth.

5. Add sauce, parsley, and lemon juice to pasta and toss to coat. Adjust consistency with reserved cooking water as needed. Season with salt and pepper to taste. Serve immediately.

KEYS TO SUCCESS

- **Salt:** Letting the ground pork sit with salt and baking soda is important. The salt dissolves some of the pork's protein fibers.
- **Soda:** Baking soda raises the pH of the meat and improves its water-holding capacity so it stays juicy.

Shaping Orecchiette

CUT DOUGH
Liberally dust 2 rimmed baking sheets with fine semolina flour. Transfer dough to clean counter, divide into 8 pieces, and cover with plastic. Stretch and roll 1 piece of dough into ½-inch-thick rope, then cut rope into ½-inch nuggets.

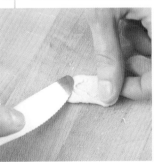

FORM OVAL
Arrange nugget cut side down and press into ⅛-inch-thick disk using tip of butter knife. Holding top of disk in place with thumb, position knife serrated side down on dough and drag toward you to form 1-inch-long oval with jagged surface.

FORM CUP SHAPE
Lightly dust smooth side of oval with flour. Using lightly floured fingers, place floured side of oval over tip of thumb and gently pull on sides to form even cup shape. Transfer to prepared sheets.

FILEJA WITH 'NDUJA TOMATO SAUCE

Serves: 4 to 6
Total Time: 40 minutes

RECIPE OVERVIEW Fileja hails from Calabria, so here we pair it with another Calabrian treasure: meltingly soft, assertively spicy 'nduja. This variety of salumi is often made from a mix of pork shoulder, belly, and fatback (among other cuts), liberally spiced to a fiery brick red with hot peppers, and slow-fermented so it takes on a tangy funk. Here, it makes a piquant and supersavory tomato sauce. Garnishes of chopped basil and grated Pecorino provide welcome bright, fresh, and salty counterpoints. You can find 'nduja in most Italian markets. You may substitute dried fileja for the fresh.

- 1 (15-ounce) can whole peeled tomatoes
- 2 tablespoons extra-virgin olive oil
- ½ onion, chopped fine
- ½ teaspoon table salt, plus salt for cooking pasta
- 1 garlic clove, minced
- 6 ounces 'nduja sausage, casings removed
- 1 recipe Fresh Semolina Pasta Dough (page 246), shaped into fileja
- 2 tablespoons chopped fresh basil
  Grated Pecorino Romano cheese

1. Pulse tomatoes and their juice in food processor until mostly smooth, 10 to 12 pulses.

2. Heat oil in large saucepan over medium heat until shimmering. Add onion and ½ teaspoon salt and cook until softened and lightly browned, about 4 minutes. Stir in garlic and cook until fragrant, about 30 seconds. Stir in tomatoes, bring to simmer, and cook, stirring occasionally, until thickened slightly, about 10 minutes. Add 'nduja, breaking up meat with wooden spoon, until fully incorporated. Season with salt and pepper to taste.

3. Meanwhile, bring 4 quarts water to boil in large pot. Add pasta and 1 tablespoon salt and cook, stirring often, until al dente. Reserve ½ cup cooking water, then drain pasta and return it to pot. Add sauce and toss to combine. Adjust consistency with reserved cooking water as needed. Sprinkle with basil and serve, passing Pecorino separately.

Freezing Fresh Semolina Pasta

To freeze fresh semolina pasta shapes, place on baking sheet and freeze until pasta is firm, then transfer pasta pieces to zipper-lock bag and freeze for up to 1 month. Do not thaw before cooking.

Shaping Fileja

CUT DOUGH
Liberally dust 2 rimmed baking sheets with fine semolina flour. Transfer dough to clean counter, divide into 16 pieces, and cover with plastic. Stretch and roll 1 piece of dough into ¼-inch-thick rope, then cut rope into 3-inch lengths.

ROLL COILS
Position dough length at 45-degree angle to counter edge. Place thin wooden skewer at top edge of dough, parallel to counter edge. Place palms of your hands at ends of skewer and roll evenly toward you to coil dough around skewer.

SLIDE COILS OFF SKEWER
Slide fileja off skewer onto prepared sheets. Dust skewer lightly with flour if dough begins to stick.

MALLOREDDUS WITH FAVA BEANS AND MINT

Serves: 6 to 8
Total Time: 1¼ hours

RECIPE OVERVIEW Tiny gnocchi-shaped malloreddus (meaning "fat bulls") are a beloved pasta specialty of Sardinia. Their ribbed shape traditionally comes from rolling them against the round reeds of a small basket. To make our own malloreddus, we infuse our semolina pasta dough with saffron, as is traditional, and roll individual pieces down the tines of a fork to create petite ridged dumplings. To let the texture, flavor, and color of our malloreddus shine, we pair them with a classic Sardinian spring combination of tender fava beans, tangy Pecorino cheese, and fresh mint. If you can't find fresh fava beans, you can substitute 2 cups thawed frozen fava beans, which have already had their waxy sheath removed.

- 2 pounds fava beans, shelled (2 cups)
  Table salt for cooking pasta
- 1 recipe Fresh Semolina Pasta Dough (page 246), shaped into malloreddus
- 3 tablespoons extra-virgin olive oil, divided
- ½ onion, chopped fine
- 2 garlic cloves, minced
  Pinch red pepper flakes
- 1 ounce Pecorino Romano cheese, grated (½ cup), plus extra for serving
- ½ cup chopped fresh mint

1. Bring 4 quarts water to boil in large pot. Fill large bowl halfway with ice and water. Add beans to boiling water and cook for 1 minute. Using slotted spoon, transfer beans to ice water and let sit until chilled, about 2 minutes; drain well. Using paring knife, make small cut along edge of each bean through waxy sheath, then gently squeeze sheath to release bean; discard sheath.

2. Return water to boil, add 1 tablespoon salt and pasta, and cook, stirring often, until al dente. Reserve 1½ cups cooking water, then drain pasta in colander. Toss pasta with 1 tablespoon oil in colander and set aside.

3. Heat remaining 2 tablespoons oil in 12-inch skillet over medium heat until shimmering. Add onion and cook until softened and lightly browned, 5 to 7 minutes. Stir in garlic and pepper flakes and cook until fragrant, about 30 seconds. Stir in beans and ½ cup reserved cooking water and cook until beans are tender and liquid has mostly evaporated, 3 to 4 minutes.

4. Stir in pasta, ½ cup reserved cooking water, and Pecorino and cook, stirring often, until cheese has melted and sauce has thickened slightly, 1 to 2 minutes. Adjust consistency with remaining ½ cup reserved cooking water as needed. Sprinkle with mint and serve, passing extra Pecorino separately.

Prepping Fresh Fava Beans

CUT THROUGH SHEATH
After blanching the beans, use a paring knife to make a small cut along the edge of each bean through the waxy sheath.

SQUEEZE OUT BEAN
Gently squeeze the sheath to release the bean; discard the sheath.

Shaping Malloreddus

CUT DOUGH
Liberally dust 2 rimmed baking sheets with fine semolina flour. Transfer dough to clean counter, divide into 8 pieces, and cover with plastic. Stretch and roll 1 piece of dough into ½-inch-thick rope, then cut rope into ½-inch nuggets. Dust lightly with flour.

STRETCH DOUGH
Place dough nugget cut side down on inverted tines of dinner fork. Press and stretch dough along tines into ⅛-inch-thick strip.

FORM CURLED SHAPE
Using lightly floured finger, gently roll dough strip down tines to form curled pasta shape with ridged exterior. Transfer to prepared sheets.

FILLED ITALIAN PASTA

JOSEPH GITTER

Presenting a platter of from-scratch stuffed pasta will make you feel as wise as an Italian nonna and will turn you into an instant legend with family and friends. There are countless varieties of filled pasta in Italy, with different shapes, fillings, and sauces; here we present a few of our favorite recipes, starting with simple ravioli and progressing to more intricately shaped tortellini. Using our fresh pasta dough on makes for supple, pillowy filled pasta morsels.

JOE'S PRO TIP: *When flouring a surface for finished pasta shapes, I love to use semolina flour. It's easier to handle and more cleanly separates from the pasta during cooking.*

THE METHOD
RAVIOLI

Cut and fill supple sheets of our malleable pasta dough to produce superb stuffed pasta such as ravioli and tortellini.

1 BRUSH WITH EGG WHITE
Lay 1 rolled pasta sheet on counter with long side parallel to edge. Using sharp knife, trim and square off corners. Brush bottom half with egg white.

2 PLACE FILLING AND CUT DOUGH
Starting 1½ inches from left edge of dough and 1 inch from bottom, evenly space 1-tablespoon mounds of filling to fit 6 mounds. Cut sheet at center points between filling mounds.

3 PRESS LAYERS TOGETHER
Lift top edge of dough over filling to line up with bottom edge. Holding top edge suspended with your thumbs, press layers together with your fingers.

4 SEAL CLOSED
Working around filling from back to front, press out air before sealing closed.

5 TRIM EDGES
Using fluted pastry wheel or sharp knife, cut away excess dough, leaving ¼- to ½-inch border around each mound. Place on parchment-lined baking sheet.

6 TASTE TEST
To test for doneness, pull one piece from pot, trim off corner without cutting into filling, and taste.

THREE-CHEESE RAVIOLI WITH TOMATO-BASIL SAUCE

Serves: 4 to 6
Total Time: 2¼ hours, plus 1 hour resting

RECIPE OVERVIEW Cheese-filled ravioli with tomato sauce is an all-ages pleaser. Our method for portioning the filling over a large piece of dough, cutting the dough into rectangles, and then folding the dough over the filling ensures that any air bubbles are removed from the ravioli—which means they won't burst during cooking. A blend of ricotta, fontina, and Parmesan delivers nuanced flavor and smooth texture to these ravioli, which are lightly coated with an herbed tomato sauce. If you don't have a pot that holds 6 quarts, cook the ravioli in two batches; toss the first batch with some sauce in a bowl, cover with foil, and keep warm in a 200-degree oven while the second batch cooks. The pasta will be the right level of thin and semitransparent for these ravioli when rolled to setting 7.

Filling

- 8 ounces (1 cup) whole-milk ricotta cheese
- 4 ounces Italian fontina cheese, cut into ¼-inch pieces (1 cup)
- 2 ounces Parmesan cheese, grated (1 cup), plus extra for serving
- 1 large egg
- ½ teaspoon pepper
- ¼ teaspoon table salt
- ⅛ teaspoon ground nutmeg

Pasta and Sauce

- 1 recipe Fresh Egg Pasta Dough (page 242)
- 2 tablespoons extra-virgin olive oil
- 2 garlic cloves, minced
- 1 (15-ounce) can tomato sauce
- 1 teaspoon sugar
- ¼ teaspoon pepper
- ¼ teaspoon dried oregano
- ½ cup fresh basil leaves, torn into ½-inch pieces

1. FOR THE FILLING Process ricotta, fontina, Parmesan, egg, pepper, salt, and nutmeg in food processor until smooth paste forms, 25 to 30 seconds, scraping down sides of bowl as needed. Transfer filling to medium bowl, cover with plastic, and refrigerate until needed.

2. FOR THE PASTA AND SAUCE Cut dough crosswise into 6 equal pieces. Working with 1 piece of dough at a time (keep remaining pieces covered), flatten into ½-inch-thick disk. Using pasta machine with rollers set to widest position, feed dough through rollers twice. Bring tapered ends of dough toward middle and press to seal. Feed dough seam side first through rollers again. Repeat feeding dough tapered end first through rollers set at widest position, without folding, until dough is smooth and barely tacky. (If dough sticks to fingers or rollers, lightly dust with flour and roll again.)

3. Narrow rollers to next setting and feed dough through rollers twice. Continue to progressively narrow rollers, feeding dough through each setting twice, until dough is very thin and semitransparent. (If dough becomes too long to manage, halve crosswise.) Transfer sheet of pasta to liberally floured sheet of parchment paper. Cover with second sheet of parchment, followed by damp dish towel, to keep pasta from drying out. Repeat rolling with remaining 5 pieces of dough, stacking pasta sheets between floured layers of parchment.

4. Line baking sheet with parchment. Lay 1 dough sheet on clean counter with long side parallel to counter edge (keep others covered). Trim ends of dough with sharp knife so that corners are square and dough is 18 inches long. Brush bottom half of dough with egg white. Starting 1½ inches from left edge of dough and 1 inch from bottom, deposit 1 tablespoon filling. Repeat placing 1-tablespoon mounds of filling, spaced 1½ inches apart, 1 inch from bottom edge of dough. You should be able to fit 6 mounds of filling on 1 dough sheet.

5. Cut dough sheet at center points between mounds of filling, separating it into 6 equal pieces. Working with 1 piece at a time, lift top edge of dough over filling and extend it so that it lines up with bottom edge. Keeping top edge of dough suspended over filling with your thumbs, use your fingers to press layers together, working around each mound of filling from back to front, pressing out as much air as possible before sealing completely.

6. Once all edges are sealed, use sharp knife or fluted pastry wheel to cut excess dough from around filling, leaving ¼- to ½-inch border around each mound (it's not necessary to cut folded edge of ravioli, but you may do so, if desired). (Dough scraps can be frozen and added to soup.) Transfer ravioli to prepared baking sheet. Refrigerate until ready to cook. Repeat shaping process with remaining dough and remaining filling.

7. Combine oil and garlic in 12-inch skillet. Cook over medium heat until garlic is fragrant and just beginning to turn golden, about 2 minutes. Carefully stir in tomato sauce, sugar, pepper, and oregano. Bring to simmer, then remove from heat. Stir in basil. Cover to keep warm.

8. Bring 6 quarts water to boil in large pot. Add ravioli and 1 tablespoon salt to boiling water. Cook, maintaining gentle boil, until ravioli are just tender, about 13 minutes. (To test, pull 1 ravioli from pot, trim off corner without cutting into filling, and taste. Return ravioli to pot if not yet tender.) Drain well. Using slotted spoon, transfer ravioli to warmed bowls or plates; top with sauce. Serve immediately, passing extra Parmesan separately.

KEYS TO SUCCESS

- **Avoid snapback:** When working with the dough, don't add too much flour, as this will cause it to dry out and become less flexible.

- **(Not) full of hot air:** Press out as much air as possible before sealing the ravioli.

SHORT RIB AGNOLOTTI
Serves: 8 to 10
Total Time: 3 hours, plus 4 hours chilling

RECIPE OVERVIEW Agnolotti, a specialty of the Piedmont region of Italy, are stuffed here with a comforting, meltingly tender braised meat filling, then tossed in hazelnut browned butter. We use boneless beef short ribs for their rich flavor and tender texture, while savoy cabbage, onion, garlic, rosemary, and red wine enhance the filling's texture and flavor. The traditional way of shaping agnolotti is also the simplest: Rather than cutting, filling, and shaping each piece, we pipe long rows of pasta with filling and then pinch and cut the pasta pieces at individual intervals. You can find Grana Padano at most well-stocked cheese counters; you can substitute Parmigiano Reggiano. The pasta will be the right level of thin and semitransparent for these agnolotti when rolled to setting 7.

Filling
- 1½ pounds boneless beef short ribs, trimmed and cut into 1½-inch pieces
- ½ teaspoon table salt
- ½ teaspoon pepper
- 2 tablespoons unsalted butter
- 2 cups chopped savoy cabbage
- 1 onion, chopped
- 3 garlic cloves, minced
- 2 teaspoons minced fresh rosemary
- ½ cup dry red wine
- 2 cups beef broth
- 1 ounce Grana Padano cheese, grated (½ cup)
- 1 large egg
- ⅛ teaspoon ground nutmeg

Pasta and Sauce
- 1 recipe Fresh Egg Pasta Dough (page 242)
- 8 tablespoons unsalted butter
- ¼ cup hazelnuts, toasted, skinned, and chopped coarse
- ¼ teaspoon table salt, plus salt for cooking pasta
- 2 teaspoons red wine vinegar
- 2 tablespoons minced fresh parsley

1. FOR THE FILLING Pat beef dry with paper towels and sprinkle with salt and pepper. Melt butter in Dutch oven over medium-high heat. Brown beef on all sides, 7 to 10 minutes; transfer to plate.

2. Add cabbage and onion to fat left in pot and cook over medium heat until softened, about 3 minutes. Stir in garlic and rosemary and cook until fragrant, about 30 seconds. Stir in wine, scraping up any browned bits, then stir in broth. Return beef and any accumulated juices to pot and bring to simmer. Reduce heat to medium-low, cover, and simmer until beef is tender, about 1 hour.

3. Drain beef mixture in fine-mesh strainer set over bowl. Reserve ¼ cup cooking liquid; discard remaining liquid. Transfer beef mixture and liquid to food processor; process until finely ground, about 1 minute, scraping down sides of

bowl as needed. Add Grana Padano, egg, and nutmeg and process until combined, about 30 seconds. Transfer filling to bowl; refrigerate for 30 minutes. (Filling can be refrigerated for up to 24 hours; bring to room temperature before proceeding with recipe.)

4. FOR THE PASTA AND SAUCE Transfer dough to clean counter, divide into 5 pieces, and cover with plastic wrap. Flatten 1 piece of dough into ½-inch-thick disk. Using pasta machine with rollers set to widest position, feed dough through rollers twice. Bring tapered ends of dough toward middle and press to seal. Feed dough seam side first through rollers again. Repeat feeding dough tapered end first through rollers set at widest position, without folding, until dough is smooth and barely tacky. (If dough sticks to fingers or rollers, lightly dust with flour and roll again.)

5. Narrow rollers to next setting and feed dough through rollers twice. Continue to progressively narrow rollers, feeding dough through each setting twice, until dough is very thin and semi-transparent. (If dough becomes too long to manage, halve crosswise.) Transfer sheet of pasta to liberally floured sheet of parchment paper. Cover with second sheet of parchment, followed by damp dish towel,

to keep pasta from drying out. Repeat rolling with remaining 4 pieces of dough, stacking pasta sheets between floured layers of parchment.

6. Liberally dust 2 rimmed baking sheets with flour. Transfer filling to 1-gallon zipper-lock bag. Snip off 1 corner of bag to create ¾-inch opening. Position 1 pasta sheet on lightly floured counter with long side parallel to counter edge (keep remaining sheets covered). Using pizza cutter or sharp knife, trim pasta into uniform 4-inch-wide sheet. Pipe filling lengthwise down center of sheet, leaving 1-inch border at each end. Lightly brush edges with water. Fold bottom edge of pasta over filling until flush with top edge. Gently press to seal long edge of pasta flush to filling; leave narrow edges unsealed. With index finger and thumb of both your hands facing downward, pinch filled portion of pasta together at 1-inch increments to create individual sections (about 15).

7. Using fluted pastry wheel or pizza cutter, trim excess dough from filled pasta strip, leaving ¼-inch border on ends and 1-inch border on top. Starting at bottom edge of strip, roll pastry wheel away from you in one motion between pinched sections to fold and seal dough and separate agnolotti. Pinch edges of each agnolotto to reinforce seal, then transfer to prepared sheets. Repeat with filling and shaping remaining pasta sheets (you should have about 75 agnolotti). Let agnolotti sit uncovered until dry to touch and slightly stiffened, about 30 minutes. (Agnolotti can be wrapped with plastic and refrigerated for up to 4 hours or chilled in freezer until firm, then transferred to zipper-lock bag and frozen for up to 1 month. If frozen, do not thaw before cooking; increase simmering time to 4 to 5 minutes.)

8. Cook butter, hazelnuts, and ¼ teaspoon salt in 12-inch skillet over medium-high heat, swirling skillet constantly, until butter is melted, has golden-brown color, and releases nutty aroma, about 3 minutes. Off heat, stir in vinegar; set aside. Bring 4 quarts water to boil in large pot. Add half of agnolotti and 1 tablespoon salt and simmer gently, stirring often, until edges of pasta are al dente, 3 to 4 minutes. Using slotted spoon, transfer agnolotti to skillet, gently toss to coat, and cover. Return cooking water to boil and repeat cooking remaining agnolotti; transfer to skillet. Add 2 tablespoons cooking water and gently toss to coat the agnolotti with sauce. Sprinkle with parsley and serve immediately.

Shaping Agnolotti

FOLD DOUGH OVER FILLING
Fold bottom edge of pasta sheet over filling until flush with top edge. Gently press to seal long edge of pasta flush to filling.

PINCH INTO PORTIONS
With index finger and thumb of both your hands facing downward, pinch filled portion of pasta together through filling at 1-inch increments.

TRIM EDGES
Trim excess dough from filled pasta strip. Starting at bottom edge of strip, roll pastry wheel away from you in one motion between pinched sections to fold and seal dough and separate agnolotti. Pinch edges of each agnolotto to reinforce seal.

KEYS TO SUCCESS
- **Shape gently:** Pinching the pasta too tightly when sealing the agnolotti may cause the final shape to burst when cooking.

- **Air-dry:** Letting the shaped agnolotti sit uncovered until dry to the touch and slightly stiffened will help them keep their shape.

SQUASH-FILLED CAPPELLACCI

Serves: 6
Total Time: 2¼ hours, plus 30 minutes drying

RECIPE OVERVIEW Similar in shape to jumbo tortellini, cappellacci ("big hats") sport a pointed top. Here we fill them with a luscious butternut squash filling enriched with Parmigiano Reggiano and accented with a touch of nutmeg. In their central Italian home, squash-filled cappellacci often incorporate mostarda (a fruit and mustard condiment) or crumbled amaretti cookies. To streamline the grocery list, we omit these additions, but in honor of the brightness that the assertive, acidic mostarda contributes, we add a drizzle of high-quality balsamic vinegar to finish, which brings a similar balance. Otherwise, all these tender pasta pillows need for sauce is a toss in sage-infused butter. The pasta will be the right level of thin and semitransparent for these cappellacci when rolled to setting 8.

Filling

1½ pounds butternut squash, peeled, seeded, and cut into 1-inch pieces (3½ cups)
6 tablespoons unsalted butter
2½ ounces Parmigiano Reggiano cheese, grated (1¼ cups)
¼ teaspoon table salt
⅛ teaspoon pepper
   Pinch ground nutmeg

Cappellacci

1 recipe Fresh Egg Pasta Dough (page 242)
6 tablespoons unsalted butter
1 tablespoon minced fresh sage
¼ teaspoon table salt, plus salt for cooking pasta
   Balsamic vinegar
   Shaved Parmigiano Reggiano cheese

1. FOR THE FILLING Microwave squash in covered bowl until very soft and easily pierced with fork, 15 to 18 minutes, stirring halfway through microwaving. Carefully remove cover, allowing steam to escape away from you, and drain squash.

2. Process squash, butter, Parmigiano, salt, pepper, and nutmeg in food processor until smooth, about 1 minute, scraping down sides of bowl as needed. Transfer filling to bowl and refrigerate for 30 minutes. (Filling can be refrigerated for up to 24 hours.)

3. FOR THE CAPPELLACCI Transfer dough to clean counter, divide into 6 pieces, and cover with plastic wrap. Flatten 1 piece of dough into ½-inch-thick disk. Using pasta machine with rollers set to widest position, feed dough through rollers twice. Bring tapered ends of dough toward middle and press to seal. Feed dough seam side first through rollers again. Repeat feeding dough tapered ends first through rollers set at widest position, without folding, until dough is smooth and barely tacky. (If dough sticks to fingers or rollers, lightly dust with flour and roll again.)

4. Narrow rollers to next setting and feed dough through rollers twice. Continue to progressively narrow rollers, feeding dough through each setting twice, until dough is paper thin, transparent, and delicate. (Pasta sheet should be about 5 inches wide; if not, fold sheet in half crosswise and roll again.) Transfer sheet of pasta to liberally floured sheet of parchment paper. Cover with second sheet of parchment, followed by damp dish towel, to keep pasta from drying out. Repeat rolling with remaining 5 pieces of dough, stacking pasta sheets between floured layers of parchment.

5. Liberally dust rimmed baking sheet with flour. Using pizza cutter or sharp knife, cut 1 pasta sheet into 5-inch squares on lightly floured counter (keep remaining sheets covered); discard scraps. Place 1 rounded tablespoon filling in center of each square. Working with 1 pasta square at a time, lightly brush edges with water. With one corner of pasta square facing you, fold bottom corner of pasta over filling until flush with top corner to form triangle shape. Press to seal edges flush to filling. Trim any uneven edges.

6. With folded edge of filled pasta facing you, pull corners together below filling until slightly overlapped to create cappellacci with cupped outer edge and dimpled center. Press to seal overlapping edges and transfer to prepared sheet. Repeat cutting and filling remaining pasta (you should have about 18 cappellacci). Let cappellacci sit uncovered until dry to touch and slightly stiffened, about 30 minutes. (Cappellacci can be wrapped with plastic and refrigerated for up to 4 hours or chilled in freezer until firm, then transferred to zipper-lock bag and frozen for up to 1 month. If frozen, do not thaw before cooking; increase simmering time to 6 to 8 minutes.)

7. Melt butter in 12-inch skillet over medium heat. Off heat, stir in sage and salt; set aside. Bring 4 quarts water to boil in large pot. Add half of cappellacci and 1 tablespoon salt and simmer gently, stirring often, until edges of cappellacci are al dente, 4 to 6 minutes. Using slotted spoon, transfer cappellacci to skillet, gently toss to coat, and cover to keep warm. Return cooking water to boil and repeat cooking remaining cappellacci; transfer to skillet and gently toss to coat. Drizzle individual portions with balsamic vinegar and top with Parmigiano before serving.

KEYS TO SUCCESS

- **Thin is in:** Roll the pasta until paper thin (translucent enough to see your hand through the dough). Otherwise the seams and folds where the dough is pinched together will be too thick and remain undercooked.

- **Squash that thought:** Be sure to use fresh, not frozen, squash here.

Shaping Cappellacci

FOLD INTO TRIANGLES
Fold bottom corner of pasta over filling until flush with top corner to form triangle shape. Press to seal edges flush to filling.

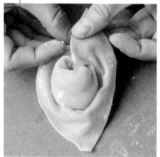

PULL TOGETHER AND SEAL
Pull corners together below filling until slightly overlapped to create cappellacci with cupped outer edge and dimpled center. Press to seal overlapping edges.

TORTELLINI IN BRODO

Serves: 8 to 10
Total Time: 1¾ hours, plus 30 minutes drying

RECIPE OVERVIEW Tortellini in brodo is a celebratory dish in Italy, traditionally served at Christmastime and sometimes over New Year's as well. The pasta shapes are tiny and intricately folded, the flavors inside are rich and meaty, and the broth has a delicately nuanced flavor. We opt for ground chicken for our tortellini filling because it offers a great balance of fatty and lean meat. Prosciutto and mortadella add robust richness (and are also traditional), while Parmigiano Reggiano, parsley, and nutmeg round out the flavors. Given that shaping tortellini is a time-consuming labor of love, we turn to store-bought broth here, creating superb flavor by infusing it with some of the ground chicken, onion, garlic, and more nutmeg. The pasta will be thin and semitransparent for these tortellini when rolled to setting 7.

Broth

- 8 ounces ground chicken
- 2 cups chicken broth
- ½ onion, peeled
- 3 garlic cloves, peeled and smashed
- 4 parsley stems
- ¼ teaspoon table salt
- ¼ teaspoon ground nutmeg

Tortellini

- 4 ounces ground chicken
- 2 ounces mortadella, chopped coarse
- 1 ounce prosciutto, chopped coarse
- 2 tablespoons grated Parmigiano Reggiano cheese
- 2 tablespoons chopped fresh parsley
- 2 tablespoons extra-virgin olive oil
- ¼ teaspoon ground nutmeg
- ½ recipe Fresh Egg Pasta Dough (page 242)
  Table salt for cooking pasta

1. FOR THE BROTH Bring all ingredients to simmer in small saucepan. Reduce heat to medium-low, cover, and cook until flavors meld, about 15 minutes. Strain broth through fine-mesh strainer into bowl, pressing on solids with rubber spatula to extract as much liquid as possible; discard solids. (Broth can be refrigerated for up to 24 hours.) Return broth to now-empty saucepan, cover, and keep warm over low heat.

2. FOR THE TORTELLINI Process ground chicken, mortadella, prosciutto, Parmigiano, parsley, oil, nutmeg, and 1 tablespoon warm broth in food processor until smooth, 30 to 45 seconds, scraping down sides of bowl as needed. Transfer mixture to bowl, cover, and refrigerate until chilled, about 30 minutes.

3. Transfer dough to clean counter, divide into 3 pieces, and cover with plastic wrap. Flatten 1 piece of dough into ½-inch-thick disk. Using pasta machine with rollers set to widest position, feed dough through rollers twice. Bring tapered ends of dough toward middle and press to seal. Feed dough seam side first through rollers again. Repeat feeding dough tapered end first through rollers set at widest position, without folding, until dough is smooth and barely tacky. (If dough sticks to fingers or rollers, lightly dust with flour and roll again.)

4. Narrow rollers to next setting and feed dough through rollers twice. Continue to progressively narrow rollers, feeding dough through each setting twice, until dough is very thin and semitransparent. (If dough becomes too long to manage, halve crosswise.) Transfer sheet of pasta to liberally floured sheet of parchment paper. Cover with second sheet of parchment, followed by damp dish towel, to keep pasta from drying out. Repeat rolling with remaining 2 pieces of dough, stacking pasta sheets between floured layers of parchment.

5. Liberally dust rimmed baking sheet with flour. Cut 1 pasta sheet into rounds on lightly floured counter using 2½-inch round cookie cutter (keep remaining sheets covered); discard scraps. Place ½ teaspoon filling in center of each round. Working with 1 pasta round at a time, lightly brush edges with water. Fold bottom edge of pasta over filling until flush with top edge to form half-moon shape. Press to seal edges flush to filling.

6. With folded edge of filled pasta facing you, pull corners together below filling until slightly overlapped to create tortellini with cupped outer edge and dimpled center. Press to seal overlapping edges and transfer to prepared sheet. Repeat cutting and filling remaining pasta (you should have about 60 tortellini). Let tortellini sit uncovered until dry to touch and slightly stiffened, about 30 minutes. (Tortellini can be wrapped with plastic and refrigerated for up to 4 hours or chilled in freezer until firm, then transferred to zipper-lock bag and frozen for up to 1 month. If frozen, do not thaw before cooking; increase simmering time to 3 to 4 minutes.)

7. Bring 4 quarts water to boil in large pot. Add tortellini and 1 tablespoon salt and simmer gently, stirring often, until edges of tortellini are al dente, 2 to 3 minutes. Using slotted spoon, transfer tortellini to individual bowls. Spoon warm broth over top and serve.

KEYS TO SUCCESS

- **The right chicken:** Be sure to use ground chicken, not ground chicken breast (also labeled 99 percent fat free).

- **Air-dry:** As with the agnolotti on page 253, letting the shaped tortellini dry for 30 minutes helps them hold their shape once cooked.

Shaping Tortellini

FOLD INTO HALF-MOONS

Fold bottom edge of pasta over filling until flush with top edge to form half-moon shape. Press to seal edges flush to filling.

PULL TOGETHER AND SEAL

Pull corners together below filling until slightly overlapped to create tortellini with cupped outer edge and dimpled center. Press to seal overlapping edges.

LONG-SIMMERED RAGUS

BRYAN ROOF

Meaty sauces are most often served with pasta or over polenta or used in lasagna. The secret of any great ragu can be found in its long cooking time, which allows for the development of sometimes bold, sometimes nuanced, always complex flavors. Although ragus usually include tomato, it may be in smaller amounts than for other sauces. And sometimes they contain no tomato at all. These chunky sauces pair well with tubular pastas since the sauce can coat the tubes inside and out. Ragus also work great with long, wide noodles like pappardelle and tagliatelle, as the luxurious sauce clings to their folds.

BRYAN'S PRO TIP: *Look for a high-quality bronze die–cut pasta to serve with your ragu. Bronze dies produce pasta shapes with uneven, pockmarked surfaces that are ideal for holding onto sauces. The packaging will usually indicate whether the pasta has been shaped with a bronze die.*

PORK RAGU

Makes: about 8 cups (enough for 2 pounds pasta)
Total Time: 3¼ hours

RECIPE OVERVIEW Southern Italian pork ragu promises rustic, bold flavor—and this version really delivers. Since today's pork is generally so lean, we use a fattier cut here to avoid dry meat. Though baby back ribs are an unconventional choice, they fit the bill, providing tender meat and lots of flavor and body from the bones. Browning the ribs first creates a flavorful fond, and a base of onion, carrots, and fennel lends traditional flavor. Braising the meat in the oven in broth, tomatoes, and wine renders it fork-tender, and cooking a whole head of garlic along with the meat requires less work than peeling and chopping a dozen cloves. We return the shredded meat to the savory cooking liquid along with the sweet, mellow garlic and toss it all together. This is great with ziti. Leftovers can be refrigerated for up to 3 days or frozen for up to 1 month.

- 2 (2¼- to 2½-pound) racks baby back ribs, trimmed and each rack cut into fourths
- 2 teaspoons ground fennel
- 4½ teaspoons kosher salt, divided
- 1 teaspoon pepper
- 3 tablespoons extra-virgin olive oil
- 1 large onion, chopped fine
- 1 large fennel bulb, stalks discarded, bulb halved, cored, and chopped fine
- 2 large carrots, peeled and chopped fine
- ¼ cup minced fresh sage, divided
- 1½ teaspoons minced fresh rosemary
- 1 cup plus 2 tablespoons dry red wine, divided
- 1 (28-ounce) can whole peeled tomatoes, drained and crushed
- 3 cups chicken broth
- 1 garlic head, outer papery skins removed and top fourth of head cut off and discarded

1. Adjust oven rack to middle position and heat oven to 300 degrees. Sprinkle ribs with ground fennel and season with 4 teaspoons salt and pepper, pressing spices to adhere. Heat oil in Dutch oven over medium-high heat until just smoking. Add half of ribs, meat side down, and cook, without moving them, until meat is well browned, 6 to 8 minutes; transfer to plate. Repeat with remaining ribs; set aside.

2. Reduce heat to medium and add onion, chopped fennel, carrots, 2 tablespoons sage, rosemary, and remaining ½ teaspoon salt to now-empty pot. Cook, stirring occasionally and scraping up any browned bits, until vegetables are well browned and beginning to stick to pot bottom, 12 to 15 minutes.

3. Add 1 cup wine and cook until evaporated, about 5 minutes. Stir in tomatoes and broth and bring to simmer. Submerge garlic and ribs, meat side down, in liquid; add any accumulated juices from plate. Cover and transfer to oven. Cook until ribs are fork-tender, about 2 hours.

4. Remove pot from oven and transfer ribs and garlic to rimmed baking sheet. Using large spoon, skim any fat from surface of sauce. Once cool enough to handle, shred meat from bones; discard bones and gristle. Return meat to pot. Squeeze garlic from its skin into pot. Stir in remaining 2 tablespoons sage and remaining 2 tablespoons wine. Season with salt and pepper to taste.

KEYS TO SUCCESS

- **Trim the ribs:** Trimming external fat from the ribs before browning prevents a greasy sauce.
- **Cut the ribs:** Cutting the racks into manageable pieces makes it easier to brown them, which creates a more flavorful fond.
- **Skim the fat:** Skimming the surface of the sauce after it comes out of the oven will prevent a greasy ragu.

LAMB RAGU

Makes: about 5 cups (enough for 1 pound pasta)
Total Time: 2¾ hours

RECIPE OVERVIEW Lamb ragu is a specialty and a staple of the Abruzzo region of Italy, where sheep abound. For our homage, braising large chunks of boneless lamb shoulder, shredding them, and then returning them to the cooking liquid yields meltingly tender and deeply flavorful results. Lamb ragu is often paired with chitarra pasta, so named for the guitar-shaped tool used to hand-cut long square strands; you can also serve this with regular spaghetti or linguine. You can substitute 2 pounds lamb shoulder chops (blade or round bone) for the lamb shoulder. Guanciale is traditional in this recipe, but an equal amount of salt pork, rind removed, rinsed, can be substituted. If it's difficult to chop the guanciale, put it in the freezer for 15 minutes to firm up. Leftovers can be refrigerated for up to 3 days or frozen for up to 1 month.

1½	pounds boneless lamb shoulder, trimmed and cut into 3-inch pieces
½	teaspoon table salt
½	teaspoon pepper
1	tablespoon extra-virgin olive oil
2	ounces guanciale, chopped fine
1	onion, chopped fine
1	carrot, peeled and chopped fine
1	celery rib, minced
3	garlic cloves, minced
1	tablespoon tomato paste
2	teaspoons minced fresh rosemary
½	teaspoon saffron threads, crumbled
¼	teaspoon red pepper flakes
½	cup dry white wine
1	(28-ounce) can whole peeled tomatoes

1. Adjust oven rack to lower-middle position and heat oven to 300 degrees. Pat lamb dry with paper towels and season with salt and pepper. Heat oil in Dutch oven over medium-high heat until just smoking. Brown lamb on all sides, about 8 minutes; transfer to plate. Pour off all but 1 tablespoon fat from pot and let pot cool slightly.

2. Add guanciale to fat left in pot and cook over medium-low heat until fat is rendered, about 2 minutes. Stir in onion, carrot, and celery, increase heat to medium, and cook until softened and lightly browned, 6 to 8 minutes. Stir in garlic, tomato paste, rosemary, saffron, and pepper flakes and cook until fragrant, about 30 seconds.

3. Stir in wine, scraping up any browned bits, and cook until reduced by half, about 3 minutes. Stir in tomatoes and their juice, breaking up tomatoes into rough 1-inch pieces with wooden spoon, and bring to simmer. Nestle lamb into pot along with any accumulated juices and return to simmer. Cover, transfer pot to oven, and cook until lamb is very tender, 2 to 2½ hours, turning lamb halfway through cooking.

4. Remove pot from oven. Transfer lamb to cutting board, let cool slightly, then shred into bite-size pieces using 2 forks; discard excess fat. Stir lamb and any accumulated juices into sauce and let sit until heated through, about 5 minutes. Season with salt and pepper to taste.

KEYS TO SUCCESS

- **Finely chop the guanciale:** This helps it render more effectively than if the pieces were larger.
- **Deglaze the pot:** Scraping the pot after adding the wine ensures that all the flavorful fond gets incorporated into the sauce.

CORE TECHNIQUE
Adjusting Sauce Consistency

When serving thick ragus with pasta, always reserve ½ cup of the cooking water before draining the pasta. Add the sauce to the cooked pasta and toss to combine, then adjust the final consistency with reserved cooking water as desired.

ULTIMATE RAGU ALLA BOLOGNESE

Makes: 6 cups (enough for 2 pounds pasta)
Total Time: 2¾ hours

RECIPE OVERVIEW   This rich, meaty interpretation of the famous ragu alla Bolognese has all the meats! We didn't stop at ground beef—or even at pork and veal, other traditional additions. To bolster the sauce's complex, savory flavor, we also packed in pancetta, mortadella, and chicken livers. A food processor makes quick work of finely chopping all these meats so that they incorporate smoothly into the ragu. If you can't find ground veal, use an additional 12 ounces ground beef. We love to serve this ragu with fresh tagliatelle or pappardelle, as is traditional. Leftovers can be refrigerated for up to 3 days or frozen for up to 1 month.

1   cup chicken broth
1   cup beef broth
8   teaspoons unflavored gelatin
1   onion, chopped coarse
1   large carrot, peeled and chopped coarse
1   celery rib, chopped coarse
4   ounces pancetta, chopped
4   ounces mortadella, chopped
6   ounces chicken livers, trimmed
3   tablespoons extra-virgin olive oil
12   ounces 85 percent lean ground beef
12   ounces ground pork
12   ounces ground veal
3   tablespoons minced fresh sage
1   (6-ounce) can tomato paste
2   cups dry red wine

1. Combine chicken broth and beef broth in bowl; sprinkle gelatin over top and set aside. Pulse onion, carrot, and celery in food processor until finely chopped, about 10 pulses, scraping down sides of bowl as needed; transfer to second bowl. Pulse pancetta and mortadella in now-empty processor until finely chopped, about 25 pulses, scraping down sides of bowl as needed; transfer to third bowl. Process chicken livers in now-empty processor until pureed, about 5 seconds; transfer to fourth bowl.

2. Heat oil in Dutch oven over medium-high heat until shimmering. Add beef, pork, and veal and cook, breaking up meat with wooden spoon, until all liquid has evaporated and meat begins to sizzle, 10 to 15 minutes. Add sage and pancetta mixture and cook, stirring frequently, until pancetta is translucent, 5 to 7 minutes, adjusting heat as needed to keep fond from burning. Add vegetable mixture and cook, stirring frequently, until softened, 5 to 7 minutes. Add tomato paste and cook, stirring constantly, until rust-colored and fragrant, about 3 minutes.

3. Stir in wine, scraping up any browned bits. Simmer until sauce has thickened, about 5 minutes. Stir in broth mixture and return to simmer. Reduce heat to low and cook at bare simmer until thickened (wooden spoon should leave trail when dragged through sauce), about 1½ hours.

4. Stir in pureed chicken livers, increase heat to medium-high, bring to boil, and immediately remove from heat. Season with salt and pepper to taste.

Trimming Chicken Livers

USE SCISSORS
Use kitchen shears to cut off heart if attached, then trim away fat and connective tissue. Rinse and pat dry.

- **Gelling:** Don't skip the powdered gelatin. It is key to creating the velvety texture that homemade bone stock traditionally contributes to this ragu.
- **Liver up:** The same goes for the chicken livers—they bring a critical flavor complexity to the sauce.
- **Mind the fond:** Adjust the heat as needed to keep the fond from burning, then deglaze the pot with the wine to scrape all that luscious fond back into the sauce.

RAGU BIANCO

Makes: about 5 cups (enough for 1 pound pasta)
Total Time: 2½ hours

RECIPE OVERVIEW Tomatoes didn't actually make their appearance in Italian ragus until the 1800s. To take things back, our white ragu skips tomatoes in favor of bright lemon and a touch of rich cream. We ensure plenty of savoriness in this meaty sauce by creating fond twice. We first brown finely chopped pancetta, onion, and fennel in a Dutch oven to create the initial fond, and then we add water and heavy cream to create a braising liquid. Into this liquid goes a pork shoulder, halved crosswise to make cooking faster and shredding easier, and the pot goes into the oven to simmer. During this braising time, a second fond forms on the sides of the pot. After scraping this second fond into the sauce, we add plenty of lemon juice along with some lemon zest. We like to toss this sauce with fresh pappardelle or tagliatelle with plenty of grated Pecorino Romano cheese. Because this ragu has less liquid than the ragus with tomato in this course, reserve extra pasta-cooking water (2 cups) to adjust the consistency of the finished dish. Pork butt roast is often labeled Boston butt in the supermarket. Leftovers can be refrigerated for up to 2 days.

4	ounces pancetta, chopped
1	large onion, chopped fine
1	large fennel bulb, stalks discarded, bulb halved, cored, and chopped fine
4	garlic cloves, minced
1½	teaspoons table salt
2	teaspoons minced fresh thyme
1	teaspoon pepper
⅓	cup heavy cream
1	(1½-pound) boneless pork butt roast, well trimmed and cut in half across grain
1½	teaspoons grated lemon zest plus ¼ cup juice (2 lemons)

1. Adjust oven rack to middle position and heat oven to 350 degrees. Cook pancetta and ⅔ cup water in Dutch oven over medium-high heat, stirring occasionally, until water has evaporated and dark fond forms on bottom of pot, 8 to 10 minutes. Add onion and fennel and cook, stirring occasionally, until vegetables soften and start to brown, 5 to 7 minutes. Stir in garlic, salt, thyme, and pepper and cook until fragrant, about 30 seconds.

2. Stir in cream and 2 cups water, scraping up any browned bits. Add pork and bring to boil over high heat. Cover, transfer to oven, and cook until pork is tender, about 1½ hours. Transfer pork to large plate and let cool for 15 minutes. Cover pot so fond will steam and soften. Using spatula, scrape browned bits from sides of pot and stir into sauce. Stir in lemon zest and juice.

3. Using 2 forks, shred pork into bite-size pieces, discarding any large pieces of fat or connective tissue. Return pork and any juices to Dutch oven and stir to combine.

KEYS TO SUCCESS

- **Trim the meat:** Trimming excess surface fat prevents a greasy sauce.
- **Double the fond:** Creating fond with the pancetta and then the pork butt ensures plenty of umami flavor in this ragu.
- **Tomato-free:** The heavy cream adds body and richness to the braising liquid here; don't substitute a different dairy product.

BAKED PASTA

CHRISTIE MORRISON

Rich casseroles of pasta, sauce, cheese, and sometimes meat or vegetables are as satisfyingly delicious as they are impressive looking. Turning out baked pastas that are both showstopping and crowd-pleasing requires time, patience, and care, but the outcomes speak for themselves. Here we start you off with a stovetop-to-oven four-cheese baked pasta that is elegant enough to be served to company before proceeding to two distinct lasagnas and finishing with pastitsio, a king among baked pastas.

CHRISTIE'S PRO TIP: *Undercook your noodles. Since most noodles will spend extra time baking with other ingredients in the sauce after boiling, it's important to cook them shy of al dente. Otherwise, you risk overcooked, mushy pasta in your bake.*

PASTA AI QUATTRO FORMAGGI

Serves: 4 to 6
Total Time: 1 hour

RECIPE OVERVIEW We start our version of this sophisticated Italian dish on the stovetop, parcooking the penne and whisking up a béchamel sauce, and then finish it in the oven to meld all the luscious flavors and brown the crispy bread-crumb topping. A roux-based béchamel in the French style—cooking butter with flour until smooth, then adding cream and simmering until thickened—only needs a minute to reach the proper consistency. For the best cheese flavor and texture, we use Italian fontina, Gorgonzola, Pecorino Romano, and Parmesan cheeses. Combining the hot béchamel and pasta with the cheeses (rather than melting the cheeses in the sauce) preserves the distinct flavors of the different cheeses. Knowing the pasta will spend some time in the oven, we drain it before it turns al dente so it won't overcook when baked under its topping of bread crumbs and more Parmesan. Make sure your baking dish is ovensafe to 500 degrees.

- 2 slices high-quality white sandwich bread, torn into quarters
- 1 ounce Parmesan cheese, grated (½ cup), divided
- ½ teaspoon table salt, divided, plus salt for cooking pasta
- ½ teaspoon pepper, divided
- 4 ounces Italian fontina cheese, rind removed, shredded (1 cup)
- 3 ounces Gorgonzola cheese, crumbled (¾ cup)
- 1 ounce Pecorino Romano cheese, grated (½ cup)
- 1 pound penne
- 2 teaspoons unsalted butter
- 2 teaspoons all-purpose flour
- 1½ cups heavy cream

1. Pulse bread in food processor to coarse crumbs, about 10 pulses. Transfer to bowl. Stir in ¼ cup Parmesan, ¼ teaspoon salt, and ¼ teaspoon pepper; set aside.

2. Adjust oven rack to middle position and heat oven to 500 degrees.

3. Bring 4 quarts water to boil in large pot. Meanwhile, combine remaining ¼ cup Parmesan, fontina, Gorgonzola, and Pecorino in large bowl; set aside. Add 1 tablespoon salt and pasta to boiling water and cook, stirring often.

4. While pasta is cooking, melt butter in small saucepan over medium-low heat. Whisk in flour until no lumps remain, about 30 seconds. Gradually whisk in cream, increase heat to medium, and bring to boil, stirring occasionally; reduce heat to medium-low and simmer for 1 minute. Stir in remaining ¼ teaspoon salt and remaining ¼ teaspoon pepper; cover and set béchamel aside.

5. When pasta is just shy of al dente, drain, leaving it slightly wet. Add pasta to bowl with cheeses; immediately pour béchamel over, then cover bowl and let stand for 3 minutes. Uncover and stir with rubber spatula, scraping bottom of bowl, until cheeses are melted and mixture is thoroughly combined.

6. Transfer pasta to 13 by 9-inch baking dish, then sprinkle evenly with reserved bread crumbs, pressing down lightly. Bake until topping is golden brown, about 7 minutes. Serve immediately.

KEYS TO SUCCESS

- **Cheesy goodness**: Combining the cheeses with the pasta off the heat ensures that the cheeses maintain all of their distinctive flavors.
- **The right dish**: Not all baking dishes are oven-safe to 500 degrees, so be sure to use one that is to prevent disaster.

CHEESE AND TOMATO LASAGNA

Serves: 8
Total Time: 2 hours, plus 20 minutes cooling

RECIPE OVERVIEW This southern Italian meat-free lasagna strips the dish down to its elemental components: dried curly-edged noodles, a blend of cheeses, and tomato sauce. No meat and no vegetables may make this less time-intensive to prep, but a lasagna with only cheese and tomato can easily turn out boring or unbalanced. So, we amp up the elements so that they offer bold flavor and substance of their own. Typical lasagna cheeses are a trio of ricotta, mozzarella, and Parmesan. However, we favor cottage cheese instead of ricotta because it's creamier and tangier; we also choose Pecorino Romano here, which is stronger in flavor than Parmesan. The tomato sauce includes three different types of tomatoes: crushed tomatoes, canned diced tomatoes to add texture, and tomato paste, which is an umami powerhouse. Another umami-rich ingredient is anchovies (which leave no trace of fishiness in the finished casserole). Alternating the noodle arrangement in step 4 keeps the lasagna level, which makes for even cooking and easier serving.

Cheese Sauce

- 4 ounces Pecorino Romano cheese, grated (2 cups)
- 8 ounces (1 cup) cottage cheese
- ½ cup heavy cream
- 2 garlic cloves, minced
- 1 teaspoon cornstarch
- ¼ teaspoon table salt
- ¼ teaspoon pepper

Tomato Sauce

- ¼ cup extra-virgin olive oil
- 1 onion, chopped fine
- 1½ teaspoons sugar
- ½ teaspoon red pepper flakes
- ½ teaspoon dried oregano
- ½ teaspoon table salt
- 4 garlic cloves, minced
- 8 anchovy fillets, rinsed, patted dry, and minced

- 1 (28-ounce) can crushed tomatoes
- 1 (14.5-ounce) can diced tomatoes, drained
- 1 ounce Pecorino Romano cheese, grated (½ cup)
- ¼ cup tomato paste

Lasagna

- 14 curly-edged lasagna noodles
- 8 ounces fontina cheese, shredded (2 cups), divided
- ⅛ teaspoon cornstarch
- ¼ cup grated Pecorino Romano cheese
- 3 tablespoons chopped fresh basil

1. FOR THE CHEESE SAUCE Whisk all ingredients in bowl until homogeneous. Set aside.

2. FOR THE TOMATO SAUCE Heat oil in large saucepan over medium heat. Add onion, sugar, pepper flakes, oregano, and salt and cook, stirring frequently, until onions are softened, about 10 minutes. Add garlic and anchovies and cook until fragrant, about 2 minutes. Stir in crushed tomatoes, diced tomatoes, Pecorino, and tomato paste and bring to simmer. Reduce heat to medium-low and simmer until slightly thickened, about 20 minutes.

3. FOR THE LASAGNA While sauce simmers, lay noodles in 13 by 9-inch baking dish and cover with boiling water. Let noodles soak until pliable, about 15 minutes, separating noodles with tip of paring knife to prevent sticking. Place dish in sink, pour off water, and run cold water over noodles. Pat noodles dry with clean dish towel; dry dish. Cut 2 noodles in half crosswise.

4. Adjust oven rack to middle position and heat oven to 375 degrees. Spread 1½ cups tomato sauce in bottom of dish. Lay 3 noodles lengthwise in dish with ends touching

1 short side, leaving space on opposite short side. Lay 1 half noodle crosswise in empty space to create even layer of noodles. Spread half of cheese sauce over noodles, followed by ½ cup fontina. Repeat layering of noodles, alternating which short side gets half noodle (alternating sides will prevent lasagna from buckling). Spread 1½ cups tomato sauce over second layer of noodles, followed by ½ cup fontina. Create third layer using 3½ noodles (reversing arrangement again), remaining cheese sauce, and ½ cup fontina.

5. Lay remaining 3½ noodles over cheese sauce. Spread remaining tomato sauce over noodles. Toss remaining ½ cup fontina with cornstarch, then sprinkle over tomato sauce, followed by Pecorino.

6. Spray sheet of aluminum foil with vegetable oil spray and cover lasagna. Bake for 35 minutes. Remove lasagna from oven and increase oven temperature to 500 degrees.

7. Discard foil, return lasagna to oven, and continue to bake until top is lightly browned, 10 to 15 minutes longer. Let lasagna cool for 20 minutes. Sprinkle with basil, cut into pieces, and serve.

KEYS TO SUCCESS

- **Use your noodle:** No-boil noodles are too thin for this recipe, so use regular ruffly lasagna noodles.

- **Layer up:** Our simple layering arrangement for the soaked noodles ensures that every portion of lasagna will be level.

CORE TECHNIQUE
Layering Lasagna Noodles

PLACE FIRST LAYER
Lay 3 soaked noodles lengthwise in baking dish over tomato sauce, with ends touching 1 short side.

USE A HALF NOODLE
Lay 1 half noodle crosswise in empty space at other short side to create even layer of noodles.

REPEAT LAYERS
After spreading layer of cheese on noodles, repeat layering of noodles, alternating which short side gets half noodle.

LASAGNE VERDI ALLA BOLOGNESE

Serves: 10 to 12
Total Time: 2 hours, plus 45 minutes cooling

RECIPE OVERVIEW This showstopping green lasagna with meat sauce hailing from Emilia-Romagna is a decadent combination of meaty ragu alla bolognese, creamy cheese sauce, and lots of Parmigiano Reggiano, all layered between thin sheets of homemade spinach pasta. For preparing the vibrant green pasta dough, convenient frozen spinach works just as well as fresh spinach; we simply puree it in a food processor with eggs. Knowing that the rich, flavorful meat sauce is a bit of a project (albeit well worth the work), we keep the cheese sauce simple by turning to our favorite unorthodox lasagna option: cottage cheese, since it turns creamy (instead of grainy like ricotta) in the oven. We whisk it with cream, Parmigiano, and a touch of cornstarch (to prevent curdling) for a lush no-cook sauce. We finish the lasagna with a sprinkling of Parmesan over a final layer of cheese sauce, which bakes into a crisp-edged, golden-brown top. The pasta will be thin but opaque when rolled to setting 6. For more information on rolling pasta sheets, see page 240.

Spinach Pasta Sheets
- 5 ounces frozen chopped spinach, thawed and squeezed dry
- 3 large eggs
- 2 cups (10 ounces) all-purpose flour, plus extra as needed
  Table salt for cooking pasta
- 1 tablespoon extra-virgin olive oil

Lasagna
- 6½ ounces Parmigiano Reggiano cheese, grated (3¼ cups), divided
- 8 ounces (1 cup) whole-milk cottage cheese
- 1 cup heavy cream
- 2 garlic cloves, minced
- 1 tablespoon cornstarch
- ½ teaspoon pepper
- ¼ teaspoon table salt
- 3 cups Ultimate Ragu alla Bolognese (page 260), room temperature, divided

1. FOR THE PASTA SHEETS Process spinach and eggs in food processor until spinach is finely chopped, about 30 seconds, scraping down sides of bowl as needed. Add flour and process until mixture forms cohesive dough that feels soft and is barely tacky to touch, about 45 seconds. (If dough sticks to fingers, add up to ¼ cup extra flour, 1 tablespoon at a time, until barely tacky.)

2. Transfer dough to clean counter and knead by hand to form smooth, round ball, about 2 minutes. Cover tightly with plastic wrap and let rest at room temperature for at least 15 minutes or up to 2 hours.

3. Transfer dough to clean counter, divide into 10 pieces (about 2¾ ounces each), and cover with plastic. Flatten 1 piece of dough into ½-inch-thick disk. Using pasta machine with rollers set to widest position, feed dough through rollers twice. Bring tapered ends of dough toward middle and press to seal. Feed dough seam side first through rollers again. Repeat feeding dough tapered end first through rollers set at widest position, without folding, until dough is smooth. (If dough sticks to fingers or rollers, lightly dust with flour and roll again.)

4. Narrow rollers to next setting and feed dough through rollers twice. Continue to progressively narrow rollers, feeding dough through each setting twice, until dough is thin but still sturdy; transfer to lightly floured counter. Using pizza cutter or sharp knife, trim pasta sheet into 11 by 3½-inch rectangle; discard scraps. Let lasagna noodle sit uncovered on counter while rolling remaining 9 pieces of dough (do not overlap noodles as they may stick together).

5. Bring 4 quarts water to boil in large pot. Add noodles and 1 tablespoon salt and cook, stirring often, until just tender, 2 to 3 minutes. Drain noodles and toss with oil. Using tongs, lay noodles flat over 2 rimmed baking sheets, overlapping as needed, and let cool slightly.

6. FOR THE LASAGNA Adjust oven rack to middle position and heat oven to 425 degrees. Grease 13 by 9-inch baking dish. Stir 3 cups Parmigiano, cottage cheese, cream, garlic, cornstarch, pepper, and salt together in bowl.

7. Spread 1 cup ragu in bottom of prepared dish. Lay 2 noodles lengthwise in dish, trimming edges as needed to fit. Spread 1 cup cheese sauce over top, followed by second layer of noodles. Spread 1 cup ragu over top, followed by third layer of noodles. Repeat layering of cheese sauce, noodles, and ragu, ending with fifth layer of noodles. Spread remaining cheese sauce over top and sprinkle with remaining ¼ cup Parmigiano. Spray sheet of aluminum foil with vegetable oil spray and cover lasagna. (Lasagna can be refrigerated for up to 24 hours.)

8. Bake until bubbling around edges, about 30 minutes. Remove foil and continue to bake until top is spotty brown, about 10 minutes. Let lasagna cool for 45 minutes. Cut into pieces and serve.

KEYS TO SUCCESS

- **Squeeze the spinach:** Squeezing out excess water prevents a too-wet pasta dough.

- **Room-temperature ragu:** If the ragu is right out of the fridge, it will affect the baking time of the lasagna; if it's too hot, it may overcook the noodles.

PASTITSIO

Serves: 6
Total Time: 2½ hours, plus 20 minutes cooling

RECIPE OVERVIEW A beloved Greek celebratory dish, pastitsio is as impressively stratified as it is delicious. For our rendition of this creamy, meaty macaroni casserole, we start by treating the raw ground beef with baking soda, which makes it better able to hold on to moisture, and we skip browning to avoid toughening the meat. Along with umami-rich tomato paste, other hallmark flavors of the savory meat sauce include red wine, cinnamon, oregano, mint, and paprika. We like the richness of whole milk for the béchamel, but you can substitute 2 percent low-fat milk, if desired. Do not use skim milk. Kasseri is a semifirm sheep's-milk cheese from Greece. If it's unavailable, substitute a mixture of 1½ ounces (¾ cup) grated Pecorino Romano and 3 ounces (¾ cup) shredded provolone, adding ½ cup to the ziti in step 4, ½ cup to the béchamel, and the remaining ½ cup to the top of the béchamel. We strongly recommend using a spider skimmer to transfer the pasta to the baking dish so that the finished dish will not be too wet, but a slotted spoon will work.

Meat Sauce

- 1 tablespoon plus ½ cup water, divided
- ¾ teaspoon table salt
- ¼ teaspoon baking soda
- 8 ounces 93 percent lean ground beef
- 1 tablespoon vegetable oil
- ½ cup finely chopped onion
- 3 garlic cloves, minced
- 1¼ teaspoons ground cinnamon
- 1 teaspoon dried oregano
- 1 teaspoon dried mint
- 1 teaspoon paprika
- ⅛ teaspoon red pepper flakes
- ⅛ teaspoon pepper
- ¼ cup red wine
- ⅓ cup tomato paste

Béchamel and Pasta

- 2 tablespoons unsalted butter
- 2 tablespoons all-purpose flour
- 1 garlic clove, minced
- ½ teaspoon table salt
- ¼ teaspoon grated nutmeg
- ⅛ teaspoon pepper
- 4 cups whole milk
- 8 ounces (2½ cups) ziti
- 4 ounces kasseri cheese, shredded (1 cup), divided
- 1 large egg, lightly beaten

1. **FOR THE MEAT SAUCE** Combine 1 tablespoon water, salt, and baking soda in medium bowl. Add beef and toss until thoroughly combined. Set aside.

2. Heat oil in medium saucepan over medium heat until shimmering. Add onion and cook, stirring frequently, until softened, about 3 minutes. Stir in garlic, cinnamon, oregano, mint, paprika, pepper flakes, and pepper and cook until fragrant, 1 to 2 minutes. Add wine and cook, stirring occasionally, until mixture is thickened, 2 to 3 minutes. Add tomato paste, beef mixture, and remaining ½ cup water and cook, breaking up meat into pieces no larger than ¼ inch with wooden spoon, until beef has just lost its pink color, 3 to 5 minutes. Bring to simmer; cover, reduce heat to low, and simmer for 30 minutes, stirring occasionally. Off heat, season with salt to taste. (Meat sauce can be refrigerated in airtight container for up to 3 days. Heat through before proceeding with step 3.)

3. **FOR THE BÉCHAMEL AND PASTA** Adjust oven rack to middle position and heat oven to 375 degrees. Spray 8-inch square baking dish with vegetable oil spray and place on rimmed baking sheet. Melt butter in large saucepan over medium heat. Add flour, garlic, salt, nutmeg, and pepper and cook, stirring constantly, until golden and fragrant, about 1 minute. Slowly whisk in milk and bring to boil. Add pasta and return to simmer, stirring frequently to prevent sticking. When mixture reaches simmer, cover and let stand off heat, stirring occasionally, for 15 minutes (pasta will not be fully cooked).

4. Using spider skimmer, transfer pasta to prepared dish, leaving excess béchamel in saucepan. Sprinkle ⅓ cup kasseri over pasta and stir to combine. Using spatula, gently press pasta into even layer. Add ⅓ cup kasseri to béchamel and whisk to combine. Whisk egg into béchamel. Spread meat sauce over pasta and, using spatula, spread into even layer. Top with béchamel. Sprinkle remaining ⅓ cup kasseri over béchamel. Bake until top of pastitsio is puffed and spotty brown, 40 to 50 minutes. Let cool for 20 minutes. Serve.

KEYS TO SUCCESS

- **Keep it lean**: Don't use ground beef that's less than 93 percent lean or else the pastitsio will be greasy.

- **A deep dish**: To accommodate all the components, use a baking dish that is at least 2¼ inches tall.

- **Pasta "pipes"**: Gently pressing the parcooked pasta into an even layer in the baking dish helps create the distinct layers in the finished dish; each slice should look like it contains rows of stacked pipes.

SCIENCE LESSON — Sauce and Pasta

Quid pro Quo

Most pastitsio recipes call for parcooking the pasta, tossing it with a portion of the béchamel, then thickening the remaining béchamel with enough roux to make it spreadable, not runny. But the pasta can actually cook right in the béchamel, so that its starch thickens the sauce. Briefly simmering and then steeping the ziti in the béchamel hydrates its starch just enough to ensure that it will be fully cooked after baking. As the pasta softens, it leaches starch that thickens the béchamel (without it, the béchamel would require twice as much roux to thicken up appropriately).

GNOCCHI AND GNUDI

ASHLEY MOORE

While gnocchi and gnudi aren't technically pasta, these little dumplings are treated and served just like pasta. The most familiar form of gnocchi are probably those made with potatoes, but other ingredients can be used, such as semolina flour for Roman gnocchi. Gnudi means "naked" in Italian, and these airy little dumplings are so named because they resemble ravioli without their pasta jackets. Traditionally gnudi are made with ricotta cheese, for a result that is much more ethereal than gnocchi. We'll also show you how to make gnudi from butternut squash.

ASHLEY'S PRO TIP: *You can freeze fresh gnocchi, but don't do it right away. Place the gnocchi on a heavily floured parchment-lined baking sheet and let them air-dry at room temperature for at least one hour before freezing. If you don't let them air-dry, they'll fall apart in the cooking water.*

POTATO GNOCCHI WITH SAGE BROWNED BUTTER

Serves: 4
Total Time: 1¼ hours

RECIPE OVERVIEW These little pillows created from dense, starchy ingredients seem like a culinary paradox. The method is straightforward enough: Knead mashed potatoes into a dough, shape, and boil. But despite the seeming simplicity, pitfalls lurk (lumpy mashed potatoes, too much or too little flour, a heavy hand when kneading). Microwaving and then baking russet potatoes makes an excellent start to the dough. To avoid lumps, which can cause the gnocchi to break apart, we use a ricer to create a smooth mash. While recipes often offer a range for the flour quantity, we use an exact amount based on the ratio of potato to flour so that the dough is mixed as little as possible, encouraging a light texture. And an egg, while untraditional, tenderizes our gnocchi further, delivering delicate dumplings beautifully showcased by an herbed browned butter sauce. After processing, you may have slightly more than the 3 cups (16 ounces) of potatoes required. Discard extra or set it aside for another use.

Gnocchi
- 2 pounds russet potatoes, unpeeled
- 1 large egg, lightly beaten
- ¾ cup plus 1 tablespoon (4 ounces) all-purpose flour, plus extra for baking sheets and counter
- 1 teaspoon table salt, plus salt for cooking gnocchi

Sage Browned Butter
- 4 tablespoons unsalted butter, cut into 4 pieces
- 1 small shallot, minced
- 1 teaspoon minced fresh sage
- 1½ teaspoons lemon juice
- ¼ teaspoon table salt

1. FOR THE GNOCCHI Adjust oven rack to middle position and heat oven to 450 degrees. Poke each potato 8 times with paring knife. Microwave potatoes until slightly softened at ends, about 10 minutes, flipping potatoes halfway through cooking. Transfer potatoes directly to oven rack and bake until skewer glides easily through flesh and potatoes yield to gentle pressure, 18 to 20 minutes.

2. Holding potatoes with dish towel, peel with paring knife. Process potatoes through ricer or food mill onto rimmed baking sheet. Gently spread potatoes into even layer and let cool for 5 minutes.

3. Transfer 3 cups (16 ounces) warm potatoes to bowl. Using fork, gently stir in egg until just combined. Sprinkle flour and 1 teaspoon salt over top and gently combine using fork until no pockets of dry flour remain. Press mixture into rough ball, transfer to lightly floured counter, and gently knead until smooth but slightly sticky, about 1 minute, lightly dusting counter with flour as needed to prevent sticking.

4. Line 2 clean rimmed baking sheets with parchment paper and dust liberally with flour. Divide dough into 8 equal pieces. Lightly dust counter with flour. Gently roll 1 piece of dough into ½-inch-thick rope, dusting with flour to prevent sticking. Cut rope into ¾-inch lengths.

5. Holding fork with tines upside down in your hand, press each dough piece cut side down against tines with thumb of your other hand to create indentation. Roll dough down tines to form ridges on sides. If dough sticks, dust thumb and/or fork with flour. Transfer formed gnocchi to prepared sheets and repeat with remaining dough.

6. FOR THE SAGE BROWNED BUTTER Melt butter in 12-inch skillet over medium-high heat, swirling occasionally, until butter is browned and releases nutty aroma, about 1½ minutes. Off heat, add shallot and sage, stirring until shallot is fragrant, about 1 minute. Stir in lemon juice and salt and cover to keep warm.

7. Bring 4 quarts water to boil in large pot. Add 1 tablespoon salt. Using parchment paper as sling, add half of gnocchi and cook until firm and just cooked through, about 90 seconds (gnocchi should float to surface after about 1 minute). Transfer gnocchi with slotted spoon to skillet with sage butter and cover to keep warm. Repeat with remaining gnocchi. Gently toss gnocchi with sage butter to combine and serve.

Variation
POTATO GNOCCHI WITH FONTINA SAUCE

Omit Sage Browned Butter. Melt 3 tablespoons unsalted butter in 12-inch skillet over medium heat. Whisk in ¼ cup gnocchi cooking water; 4 ounces fontina, shredded (1 cup); and ⅛ teaspoon grated nutmeg until cheese is melted and smooth. Using slotted spoon, transfer gnocchi to skillet and gently toss to coat; cover to keep warm.

KEYS TO SUCCESS

- **Use a scale:** Weigh the potatoes (before and after cooking) and the flour.
- **Rice it:** Using a ricer guarantees a lump-free mash.
- **Stick to the ratio:** Don't add extra flour to the dough, and use minimal flour as needed for dusting when shaping the gnocchi.

Making Ridges on Potato Gnocchi

Hold fork with tines facing down. Press each dough piece cut side down against the tines with your thumb to make an indentation. Roll the dumpling down the tines to create ridges on the sides.

ROMAN GNOCCHI
Serves: 4 to 6
Total Time: 1½ hours, plus 30 minutes chilling

RECIPE OVERVIEW Romans have made their gnocchi with semolina instead of potatoes for millennia. These dumplings are particularly comforting because they're appealingly creamy and slightly dense, similar to polenta. To make them, a sort of semolina porridge is cooked, spread into a thin layer, cooled, cut, and baked rather than boiled. The key is getting the ratio of liquid to semolina just right. If the mixture is too loose, it takes a long time to set up and cleanly cutting out the dumplings is difficult; plus, the gnocchi will fuse together in the hot oven. Instead of stamping out rounds, which wastes much of the semolina mixture, we portion dumplings straight from the pot using a measuring cup. Refrigerating them before baking allows a skin to form on the outside of each dumpling, ensuring that they hold their shape and can be lifted out of the dish cleanly to be served individually. An egg provides binding power and, along with a little baking powder, lift. A sprinkling of Parmigiano over the shingled dumplings before baking develops into an irresistible golden-brown top. You can find fine semolina in most Italian markets or in well-stocked supermarkets.

2½ cups whole milk
½ teaspoon table salt
Pinch ground nutmeg
1 cup (5¾ ounces) fine semolina flour
4 tablespoons unsalted butter, divided
1 large egg, lightly beaten
2 ounces Parmigiano Reggiano cheese, grated (1 cup), divided
1 teaspoon minced fresh rosemary
½ teaspoon baking powder

1. Adjust oven rack to middle position and heat oven to 400 degrees. Heat milk, salt, and nutmeg in medium saucepan over medium-low heat until bubbles form around edges of saucepan. Slowly pour semolina into milk mixture in steady stream while whisking constantly. Reduce heat to low and cook, stirring often with rubber spatula, until mixture forms stiff mass that pulls away from sides when stirring, 3 to 5 minutes. Remove saucepan from heat and let semolina mixture cool for 5 minutes.

2. Stir 3 tablespoons butter and egg into semolina mixture until incorporated. (Mixture will appear separated at first but will become smooth and somewhat shiny.) Stir in ¾ cup Parmigiano, rosemary, and baking powder until incorporated.

3. Fill small bowl with water. Moisten ¼-cup dry measuring cup with water and scoop even portion of semolina mixture. Invert gnocchi onto tray or large plate. Repeat, moistening measuring cup between scoops to prevent sticking. Refrigerate gnocchi, uncovered, for 30 minutes. (Gnocchi can be refrigerated, covered, for up to 24 hours.)

4. Grease 8-inch square baking dish with remaining 1 tablespoon butter. Shingle gnocchi in prepared dish, creating 3 rows of 4 gnocchi each. Sprinkle gnocchi with remaining ¼ cup Parmigiano and bake until tops of gnocchi are golden brown, 35 to 40 minutes. Let cool for 15 minutes before serving.

Making Semolina Gnocchi

FINISH DOUGH
Slowly whisk semolina into warm milk mixture. Cook over low heat until stiff dough forms. Add butter, egg, cheese, rosemary, and baking powder.

SHAPE GNOCCHI
Use moistened ¼ cup measure to portion gnocchi, inverting onto tray.

ARRANGE IN PAN
Shingle gnocchi in greased 8-inch square dish, then sprinkle with Parmesan and bake.

SPINACH AND RICOTTA GNUDI WITH TOMATO-BUTTER SAUCE

Serves: 4
Total Time: 1¼ hours

RECIPE OVERVIEW These verdant gnudi are cobbled together from ricotta and spinach, delicately seasoned with lemon zest and pepper, and bound with egg and flour. The trick to making them well is water management: Both the cheese and the greens are loaded with moisture, much of which needs to be either removed or bound up—but not too much, lest the dough requires so much binder that the dumplings turn out leaden instead of light. Drying the ricotta on a paper towel–lined rimmed baking sheet efficiently and quickly drains the cheese. Instead of blanching fresh spinach to break down its cells and release its water, we use frozen spinach, which readily gives up its water when it thaws and is easily squeezed dry. A combination of egg whites, flour, and panko bread crumbs (which lighten the mixture because they break up the structure) binds the mixture into a light, tender dough. You can substitute part-skim ricotta for the whole-milk ricotta. Frozen whole-leaf spinach is easiest to squeeze dry, but frozen chopped spinach will work. Squeezing should remove ½ to ⅔ cup liquid, leaving ⅔ cup finely chopped spinach.

Gnudi
- 12 ounces (1½ cups) whole-milk ricotta cheese
- ½ cup all-purpose flour
- 1 ounce Parmesan cheese, grated (½ cup), plus extra for garnishing
- 1 tablespoon panko bread crumbs
- ¾ teaspoon table salt, plus salt for cooking gnudi
- ½ teaspoon pepper
- ¼ teaspoon grated lemon zest
- 10 ounces frozen whole-leaf spinach, thawed and squeezed dry
- 2 large egg whites, lightly beaten

Sauce
- 4 tablespoons unsalted butter
- 3 garlic cloves, sliced thin
- 12 ounces cherry or grape tomatoes, halved
- 2 teaspoons cider vinegar
- ¼ teaspoon table salt
- ¼ teaspoon pepper
- 2 tablespoons shredded fresh basil

1. **FOR THE GNUDI** Line rimmed baking sheet with double layer of paper towels. Spread ricotta in even layer over towels; set aside and let sit for 10 minutes. Place flour, Parmesan, panko, salt, pepper, and lemon zest in large bowl and stir to combine. Process spinach in food processor until finely chopped, about 30 seconds, scraping down sides of bowl as needed. Transfer spinach to bowl with flour mixture. Grasp paper towels and fold ricotta in half; peel back towels. Rotate sheet 90 degrees and repeat folding and peeling 2 more times to consolidate ricotta into smaller mass. Using paper towels as sling, transfer ricotta to bowl with spinach mixture. Discard paper towels but do not wash sheet. Add egg whites to bowl and mix gently until well combined.

2. Transfer heaping teaspoons of dough to now-empty sheet (you should have 45 to 50 portions). Using your dry hands, gently roll each portion into 1-inch ball.

3. **FOR THE SAUCE** Melt butter in small saucepan over medium heat. Add garlic and cook, swirling saucepan occasionally, until butter is very foamy and garlic is pale golden brown, 2 to 3 minutes. Off heat, add tomatoes and vinegar; cover and set aside.

4. Bring 1 quart water to boil in Dutch oven. Add 1½ teaspoons salt. Using spider skimmer or slotted spoon, transfer all gnudi to water. Return water to gentle simmer. Cook, adjusting heat to maintain gentle simmer, for 5 minutes, starting timer once water has returned to simmer (to confirm doneness, cut 1 dumpling in half; center should be firm).

5. While gnudi simmer, add salt and pepper to sauce and cook over medium-high heat, stirring occasionally, until tomatoes are warmed through and slightly softened, about 2 minutes. Divide sauce evenly among 4 bowls. Using spider skimmer or slotted spoon, remove gnudi from pot, drain well, and transfer to bowls with sauce. Garnish with basil and extra Parmesan. Serve immediately.

"Towel-Drying" Ricotta

Letting ricotta sit in a paper towel–lined fine-mesh strainer is a common method for removing its whey, but it can take up to 10 hours to drain off just a few tablespoons. Creating more surface area by spreading the cheese in a thin layer on a paper towel–lined rimmed baking sheet removes just as much liquid in about 10 minutes. Ricotta without stabilizers such as locust bean, guar, and xanthan gums drains more readily.

The Scoop on Scooping

The texture of cooked ricotta gnudi can mostly be predicted by the consistency of the raw dough. A mixture that is firm enough to be rolled into ropes and cut into pieces (like gnocchi dough) tends to contain more binder and cook up rather dense. This dough, which is just cohesive enough to scoop and roll into balls, cooks up light and pillowy.

BUTTERNUT SQUASH GNUDI WITH KALE, PARMESAN, AND PEPITAS

Serves: 4
Total Time: 2 hours, plus 1 hour chilling

RECIPE OVERVIEW Using butternut squash instead of ricotta to make gnudi creates this ultimate fall dish, served on a bed of wilted kale and topped with pumpkin seeds and shaved Parmesan. The challenge in trying to make these dumplings is getting them to hold together without diluting the sweet squash flavor with large quantities of binders such as flour and eggs. So we use a little tapioca starch and egg white powder to effectively bind water and form a stable but supertender gel. Since this dough is too delicate to knead and roll out, we instead bake it in a water bath and then cut the gnudi by hand. You will need a 12-inch nonstick skillet with a tight-fitting lid for this recipe. A few gnudi will not be a perfect 1 by ¾-inch size. If you prefer, trim the whole block into a 6-inch square and then cut into 48 even pieces.

Gnudi
- 2½ pounds butternut squash, peeled, halved, seeded, and cut into 1½-inch pieces
- 1½ ounces Parmesan cheese, grated fine (¾ cup)
- 3 tablespoons plus 1 teaspoon egg white powder
- 3 tablespoons unsalted butter, cut into 4 pieces
- 2 tablespoons plus 2 teaspoons tapioca starch
- ½ teaspoon table salt

Kale
- 2 tablespoons extra-virgin olive oil, plus extra for drizzling
- 1 pound kale, stemmed and chopped
- 2 tablespoons water
- 5 tablespoons unsalted butter, divided
- 2 garlic cloves, minced
- 1 teaspoon sherry vinegar
- 2 tablespoons minced fresh sage, divided
- 2 tablespoons roasted, salted pepitas
- Finely grated lemon zest
- Parmesan cheese, shaved

1. **FOR THE GNUDI** Microwave squash in large bowl, covered, until tender when pierced with tip of paring knife, 15 to 20 minutes, stirring halfway through microwaving. Uncover squash, being careful of steam, and transfer to colander to drain; set aside to cool slightly.

2. Meanwhile, adjust oven rack to middle position and heat oven to 300 degrees. Line bottom of large roasting pan with dish towel, folding towel to fit smoothly; set aside. Spray 8-inch square baking pan with vegetable oil spray and line with plastic wrap, smoothing bottom.

3. Measure out 3 cups cooked squash and place in bowl of food processor, reserving remaining squash for another use. Process squash in food processor until smooth, about 1 minute, scraping down sides of bowl as needed. Add Parmesan, egg white powder, butter, tapioca starch, and salt and process until well combined, about 30 seconds, scraping down sides of bowl as needed. Transfer mixture to prepared baking pan, smooth top with spatula, and tap pan on counter to release air bubbles.

4. Cover pan tightly with aluminum foil and place in center of prepared roasting pan. Place roasting pan in oven and carefully pour boiling water into roasting pan to come halfway up sides of baking pan. Bake until center of mixture is set, no longer sticks to your fingers when gently pressed, and registers 170 to 180 degrees, 1 hour to 1 hour 10 minutes. Remove baking pan from water bath, discard foil, and let cool slightly, about 10 minutes. Refrigerate gnudi in pan until firm, about 1 hour. Carefully unmold gnudi onto cutting board, discarding plastic. Dip sharp knife in very hot water, wipe dry, and cut gnudi into 1 by ¾-inch rectangular pieces, rewetting and wiping knife clean between cuts. (You will have 50 to 60 pieces.)

5. **FOR THE KALE** Heat oil in large saucepan over medium-high heat until shimmering. Add kale and cook until slightly wilted, 1 to 2 minutes. Add water, 2 tablespoons butter, garlic, and vinegar and cook, stirring occasionally, until wilted and fragrant, 1 to 2 minutes. Season with salt and pepper to taste and divide among individual serving bowls.

6. Meanwhile, melt remaining 3 tablespoons butter in 12-inch nonstick skillet over medium heat. Add half of gnudi and 1 tablespoon sage, cover, and cook until browned on one side, 2 to 4 minutes. Season with salt and pepper to taste, and divide gnudi evenly between 2 serving bowls. Repeat with remaining gnudi and remaining 1 tablespoon sage. Sprinkle with pepitas, lemon zest, and Parmesan and drizzle with oil. Serve.

Shaping Squash Gnudi

SMOOTH INTO PAN
Transfer squash mixture to prepared pan, smooth top with a spatula, and tap pan on counter to release air bubbles.

BAKE
Cover pan with foil and place in center of prepared roasting pan. Place setup in oven and carefully pour boiling water into roasting pan. Bake as directed.

UNMOLD AND CUT
Remove baking pan from water bath, discard foil, let cool, and refrigerate until firm. Unmold gnudi onto a cutting board. Dip a sharp knife in hot water, wipe dry, and cut gnudi into 1 by ¾-inch rectangular pieces, rewetting and wiping knife clean between cuts.

KEYS TO SUCCESS

- **Take a powder:** Don't substitute raw egg whites for the egg white powder; the extra water will ruin the texture of the gnudi.

- **Elevate and anchor:** The dish towel raises the baking pan off the bottom of the roasting pan, preventing the gnudi from overcooking on the bottom while also providing traction for the baking pan so it doesn't slip when removing the roasting pan from the oven.

NOODLE STIR-FRIES

LAN LAM

Stir-fries aren't only about vegetables and meats (or even leftover rice). Stir-fried noodles, a popular street food and homestyle dish found throughout Asia, come in countless iterations using many types of noodles. After boiling the noodles until just shy of tender (or soaking them in the case of rice or cellophane noodles), the technique is similar to other stir-fries, and the cooking process goes very quickly. The parcooked noodles usually go into the wok or skillet near the end to finish cooking, meld with the other ingredients, and attain a bit of char. It's worth it to search out the noodle specified in the recipes; they each offer a certain texture and pick up the sauce in a specific way.

LAN'S PRO TIP: *As with all stir-fries, preparing your ingredients in advance will make the cooking process easier and more fun. When possible, I prep all of my vegetables first and then the proteins, so that I don't have pause prep to wash my cutting board.*

YAKISOBA WITH BEEF, SHIITAKES, AND CABBAGE

Serves: 4 to 6
Total Time: 1½ hours

RECIPE OVERVIEW Springy noodles in a bold, complex sauce make the Japanese dish yakisoba a standout among noodle stir-fries. Yakisoba noodles are made from wheat flour rather than the buckwheat flour used for soba noodles and have a pleasantly chewy elasticity. We undercook them slightly to enhance their chewy quality and rinse them with cold water to remove surface starches and make them appropriately slick. Tossing the sliced beef with baking soda raises the meat's pH, preventing its proteins from binding excessively and ensuring that each piece is tender and juicy. If you like, garnish the noodles with pickled ginger and the spice blend Shichimi Togarashi (recipe follows).

12	ounces flank steak, trimmed
⅛	teaspoon baking soda
¼	cup ketchup
¼	cup soy sauce
2	tablespoons Worcestershire sauce
1½	tablespoons packed brown sugar
3	garlic cloves, minced
3	anchovy fillets, rinsed, patted dry, and minced
1	teaspoon rice vinegar
1	pound fresh yakisoba, ramen, or lo mein noodles, or 8 ounces dried lo mein noodles
1	tablespoon vegetable oil, divided
6	ounces shiitake mushrooms, stemmed and sliced ¼ inch thick
1	carrot, peeled and sliced on bias ⅛ inch thick
¾	cup chicken broth, divided
6	cups napa cabbage, sliced crosswise into ½-inch strips
7	scallions, cut on bias into 1-inch pieces

1. Cut steak lengthwise with grain into 2- to 2½-inch strips. Cut each strip crosswise against grain into ¼-inch-thick slices. Combine 1 tablespoon water and baking soda in medium bowl. Add beef and toss to coat. Let stand at room temperature for 5 minutes.

2. Whisk ketchup, soy sauce, Worcestershire, sugar, garlic, anchovies, and vinegar together in second bowl. Stir 2 tablespoons sauce into beef mixture and set aside remaining sauce.

3. Bring 4 quarts water to boil in large pot. Add noodles and cook, stirring often, until almost tender (centers should still be firm with slightly opaque dot), 3 to 10 minutes (cooking times will vary depending on whether you are using fresh or dried noodles). Drain noodles and rinse under cold running water until water runs clear. Drain well and set aside.

4. Heat ½ teaspoon oil in 12-inch nonstick skillet or 14-inch flat-bottomed wok over high heat until just smoking. Add mushrooms and carrot and cook, stirring occasionally, until vegetables are spotty brown, 2 to 3 minutes. Add ¼ cup broth to skillet and cook until all liquid has evaporated and vegetables are tender, about 30 seconds. Transfer vegetables to third bowl.

5. Return skillet to high heat, add ½ teaspoon oil, and heat until beginning to smoke. Add cabbage and scallions and cook, without stirring, for 30 seconds. Cook, stirring occasionally, until cabbage and scallions are spotty brown and crisp-tender, 2 to 3 minutes. Transfer to bowl with mushrooms and carrot.

6. Return skillet to high heat, add 1 teaspoon oil, and heat until beginning to smoke. Add half of beef mixture in single layer. Cook, without stirring, for 30 seconds. Cook, stirring occasionally, until beef is spotty brown, 1 to 2 minutes. Transfer to bowl with vegetables. Repeat with remaining beef mixture and remaining 1 teaspoon oil.

7. Return skillet to high heat; add reserved sauce, remaining ½ cup broth, and noodles. Cook, scraping up any browned bits, until noodles are warmed through, about 1 minute. Transfer noodles to bowl with vegetables and beef and toss to combine. Season with salt to taste, and serve immediately.

SHICHIMI TOGARASHI

Makes: about ½ cup
This Japanese seven-spice blend is pungent and spicy from chile heat, aromatic from garlic and ginger, and fragrant from orange zest, which we microwave to dry.

1½	teaspoons grated orange zest
4	teaspoons sesame seeds, toasted
1	tablespoon paprika
2	teaspoons pepper
½	teaspoon garlic powder
½	teaspoon ground ginger
¼	teaspoon cayenne pepper

Microwave orange zest in small bowl, stirring occasionally, until dry and no longer clumping together, about 2 minutes. Stir in remaining ingredients. (Shichimi togarashi can be stored in airtight container for up to 1 week.)

KEYS TO SUCCESS

- **Coat the beef:** Letting the beef sit in a baking soda–water mixture raises the meat's pH and softens its chew.

- **Undercook the noodles:** Cook the noodles until almost tender.

- **Get more char:** Stirring occasionally rather than constantly helps to achieve better browning on the vegetables and the beef.

Chile Vinegar

- ⅓ cup distilled white vinegar
- 3 Thai chiles, stemmed and sliced into thin rings

Stir-Fry

- 8 ounces (¼-inch-wide) rice noodles
- 3 tablespoons vegetable oil, divided
- ⅛ teaspoon baking soda
- 12 ounces boneless, skinless chicken breasts, trimmed and sliced thin crosswise
- 1 tablespoon plus 2 teaspoons soy sauce, divided
- ½ teaspoon cornstarch
- ¼ cup oyster sauce
- 2 tablespoons packed dark brown sugar
- 1 tablespoon distilled white vinegar
- 1 teaspoon molasses
- 1 teaspoon fish sauce
- 3 garlic cloves, sliced thin
- 3 large eggs
- 10 ounces gai lan, trimmed, florets cut into 1-inch pieces, stalks cut ½ inch thick on bias

1. FOR THE CHILE VINEGAR Combine vinegar and Thai chiles in bowl; set aside for serving. (Chile vinegar can be refrigerated for up to 1 day; bring to room temperature before serving.)

2. FOR THE STIR-FRY Bring 4 quarts water to boil in large pot. Remove from heat, add noodles, and let sit, stirring occasionally, until soft and pliable but not fully tender. Drain noodles and rinse under cold running water until chilled. Drain noodles well again and toss with 2 teaspoons oil; set aside.

3. Combine 2 teaspoons water and baking soda in medium bowl. Add chicken and toss to coat; let sit for 5 minutes. Add 2 teaspoons soy sauce and cornstarch and toss until well combined. Whisk oyster sauce, sugar, vinegar, molasses, fish sauce, and remaining 1 tablespoon soy sauce in small bowl until sugar dissolves; set aside.

4. Cook 2 teaspoons oil and garlic in nonstick skillet or flat-bottomed wok over medium-low heat until garlic is deep golden brown, 1 to 2 minutes. Add chicken and increase heat to high. Cook, tossing chicken slowly but constantly, until no longer pink, 2 to 6 minutes; transfer to large bowl.

5. Heat 1 tablespoon oil in now-empty pan over high heat until shimmering. Add eggs and scramble quickly using rubber spatula. Continue to cook, scraping slowly but constantly along bottom and sides of pan, until eggs just form cohesive mass, 15 to 30 seconds (eggs will not be completely dry). Transfer to bowl with chicken and break up any large egg curds.

6. Heat remaining 2 teaspoons oil in now-empty pan over high heat until just smoking. Add gai lan and ¼ cup water (water will sputter) and cover immediately. Cook,

PAD SEE EW

Serves: 4 to 6
Total Time: 1 hour

RECIPE OVERVIEW Pad see ew, a Thai street food now popular around the world, is said to have been born out of the Chinese style of stir-frying but it is a distinctly Thai dish, with sweet-spicy-tart flavors and lightly chewy wok-charred flat rice noodles. For this version, we combine the rice noodles with tender chicken, crisp gai lan (Chinese broccoli), and moist egg, bound together by a sweet-salty soy sauce–based sauce. Chile vinegar is served separately, allowing diners to make their portion as spicy as they like. If fresh Thai chiles are unavailable, substitute one serrano or one-half jalapeño. You can substitute an equal amount of broccolini for the gai lan, but be sure to trim and peel the stalks before cutting. Do not substitute other types of noodles for the ¼-inch-wide rice noodles here. To make the chicken easier to slice, freeze it for 15 minutes. You will need a 12-inch nonstick skillet or a 14-inch flat-bottomed wok, each with a tight-fitting lid, for this recipe.

without stirring, until broccoli is bright green, about 2 minutes. Uncover and continue to cook, tossing occasionally, until all water has evaporated and broccoli is crisp-tender and spotty-brown, 1 to 3 minutes. Add noodles, oyster sauce mixture, and chicken-egg mixture and cook, tossing occasionally, until thoroughly combined and noodles are well coated and tender, 2 to 4 minutes. Serve, passing chile vinegar separately.

KEYS TO SUCCESS

- **No noodle clumps**: Draining the noodles well and tossing them with oil prevents them from turning into a stuck-together mess.

- **Baking soda magic**: Soaking the chicken briefly in a baking soda and water solution raises its pH, preventing the proteins in the meat from bonding together as tightly. This means it stays tender even when you cook it thoroughly.

SHRIMP PAD THAI

Serves: 4
Total Time: 1¼ hours

RECIPE OVERVIEW With its balance of salty, sweet, sour, and spicy flavors, pad thai is a quintessential and universally beloved Thai dish. This recipe incorporates its hallmark ingredients, including tamarind, dried shrimp, and salted preserved radish. Soaking the rice sticks in boiling water for 10 minutes before stir-frying makes for tender but not sticky noodles. The flavor profile of pad thai is created by combining fish sauce, sugar, ground chiles, and vinegar. For the bright, fruity taste that is essential to the dish, we use tamarind paste, which we soak in hot water and pass through a fine-mesh strainer to make a smooth puree. Tossed with fresh and dried shrimp, eggs, and preserved salted radish and garnished with scallions, peanuts, and cilantro, this dish is a delicious rendition of the Thai classic. If tamarind paste is unavailable, substitute ⅓ cup lime juice and ⅓ cup water and use light brown sugar instead of granulated sugar.

Sauce

- ¾ cup boiling water
- 2 tablespoons tamarind paste
- 3 tablespoons fish sauce
- 3 tablespoons sugar
- 2 tablespoons peanut or vegetable oil
- 1 tablespoon rice vinegar
- ¾ teaspoon cayenne pepper

Tamarind Paste

Sweet-tart, dark brownish-red tamarind is frequently used in Thai cuisine and is a necessary ingredient for an authentic-looking and -tasting pad thai. It's commonly sold in paste (also called pulp) as well as in concentrate form. The paste is firm, sticky, and filled with seeds and fibers, which is why we strain it. We favor tamarind paste because it has a fresher, brighter flavor than the concentrate.

Noodles, Shrimp, and Garnish

- 8 ounces dried rice stick noodles, ⅛ to ¼ inch wide
- 2 tablespoons peanut or vegetable oil, divided
- 12 ounces medium shrimp (41 to 50 per pound), peeled and deveined
  Table salt
- 1 medium shallot, minced (about 2 tablespoons)
- 3 garlic cloves, minced or pressed through a garlic press (about 1 tablespoon)
- 2 large eggs, lightly beaten
- 2 tablespoons chopped Thai salted preserved radish (optional)
- 1 tablespoon dried shrimp, chopped fine (optional)
- 3 cups bean sprouts
- ½ cup unsalted roasted peanuts, chopped coarse, divided
- 5 scallions, green parts only, sliced thin on the bias, divided
- ¼ cup loosely packed fresh cilantro leaves (optional)
  Lime wedges, for serving

1. FOR THE SAUCE Combine water and tamarind paste in small bowl and let sit until tamarind is softened and mushy, 10 to 30 minutes. Mash tamarind to break it up, then push it through fine-mesh strainer into medium bowl to remove seeds and fibers and extract as much pulp as possible. Stir in remaining sauce ingredients and set aside.

2. FOR THE NOODLES, SHRIMP, AND GARNISH Bring 4 quarts water to boil in large pot. Remove pot from heat, add rice noodles, and let sit, stirring occasionally, until almost tender, about 10 minutes. Drain noodles and set aside.

3. Heat 1 tablespoon oil in 12-inch nonstick skillet over high heat until just smoking. Add shrimp, sprinkle with ⅛ teaspoon salt, and cook without stirring until bright pink, about 1 minute. Stir shrimp and continue to cook until cooked through, 15 to 30 seconds longer. Transfer shrimp to clean bowl and cover with foil to keep warm.

4. Add remaining 1 tablespoon oil to skillet and return to medium heat until shimmering. Add shallot and garlic and cook, stirring constantly, until light golden brown, about 1½ minutes. Stir in eggs and cook, stirring constantly, until scrambled and barely moist, about 20 seconds.

5. Add noodles and salted radish and dried shrimp (if using) to eggs and toss to combine. Add sauce, increase heat to high, and cook, tossing slowly, until noodles are evenly coated, about 1 minute.

6. Add cooked shrimp, bean sprouts, ¼ cup peanuts, and all but ¼ cup of scallions and continue to cook, tossing slowly, until noodles are tender, about 2½ minutes. (If not yet tender, add 2 tablespoons water to skillet and continue to cook until tender.) Transfer noodles to serving platter, sprinkle with remaining ¼ cup peanuts, remaining ¼ cup scallions, and cilantro (if using) and serve with lime wedges.

Variation

SHRIMP AND TOFU PAD THAI

Add 4 ounces of extra-firm tofu or pressed tofu cut into ½-inch cubes (about 1 cup) to noodles along with bean sprouts.

> ### KEY TO SUCCESS
> - **Get prepped and ready:** Although the ingredient list is long, pad thai cooks very quickly, so have all the ingredients prepped and ready to go by the stovetop before starting to cook.

SWEET POTATO NOODLES WITH SHIITAKES AND SPINACH

Serves: 4 to 6
Total Time: 50 minutes

RECIPE OVERVIEW Japchae, one of Korea's beloved crowd-pleasing dishes, is made using sweet potato starch noodles, mixed vegetables, an egg garnish, and/or meat for a result that is both stunning and delicious. The flavorful sauce made from sesame oil, soy sauce, sugar, sesame seeds, and garlic makes it clear why Korean royalty kept this dish to themselves throughout much of history. Staggering the cooking times of the vegetables ensures that each is properly cooked. After soaking the noodles, stir-fry earthy shiitake mushrooms, onion, and carrots. Then add scallions and spinach, which need less time to cook. Last, in go the softened noodles to meld with everything else and make them fully tender. If you can't find sweet potato starch noodles, you can substitute another cellophane noodle. Toast the sesame seeds in a dry skillet over medium heat until fragrant, then quickly remove the seeds from the pan to prevent the seeds from scorching.

- 8 ounces (⅛-inch-wide) dried sweet potato starch noodles, broken into 12-inch lengths
- 2 tablespoons plus 2 teaspoons toasted sesame oil, divided
- 3 garlic cloves, minced, divided
- 2 tablespoons vegetable oil, divided
- ¼ cup soy sauce
- 3 tablespoons sugar
- 1 tablespoon sesame seeds, toasted
- 8 ounces shiitake mushrooms, stemmed and sliced thin
- 2 carrots, peeled and cut into 2-inch-long matchsticks
- 1 small onion, halved and sliced ½ inch thick
- 2 scallions, sliced thin
- 8 ounces (8 cups) baby spinach

1. Bring 4 quarts water to boil in large pot. Remove from heat, add noodles, and let sit, stirring occasionally, until noodles are soft and pliable but not fully tender, 8 to 10 minutes. Drain noodles and rinse under cold running water until chilled. Drain noodles again and toss with 2 teaspoons sesame oil; set aside.

2. Combine two-thirds garlic and 2 teaspoons vegetable oil in small bowl; set aside. Whisk soy sauce, sugar, sesame seeds, remaining 2 tablespoons sesame oil, and remaining garlic in second small bowl until sugar has dissolved; set aside.

3. Heat remaining 1 tablespoon vegetable oil in 12-inch skillet over high heat until just smoking. Add mushrooms, carrots, and onion and cook, stirring occasionally, until onion and carrots are crisp-tender, 4 to 6 minutes. Add scallions and spinach and cook until wilted, about 2 minutes.

4. Push vegetables to 1 side of skillet. Add garlic mixture to clearing and cook, mashing mixture into skillet, until fragrant, about 30 seconds. Stir garlic mixture into vegetables. Add noodles and sauce and cook, stirring constantly, until mixture is thoroughly combined and noodles are well coated and tender, 2 to 4 minutes. Serve.

KEYS TO SUCCESS

- **Prevent overcooking:** It's critical to drain and rinse the soaked noodles as soon as they are soft and pliable.
- **Prevent sticking:** Tossing the drained noodles with oil will prevent them from sticking together.

Cellophane Noodles

Korean sweet potato noodles belong to the cellophane noodle family, also called glass noodles because of their translucence. These types of noodles, which can be round or flat and vary in thickness, are made from the extracted starch of sweet or white potatoes, yams, beans (such as mung beans), tapioca (from the cassava plant), or even the flowering canna lily. Cellophane noodles have a soft, chewy texture (sometimes described as "bouncy").

HAND-PULLED NOODLES

JULIA COLLIN DAVISON

In Chinatowns across the country, the tradition of hand-pulled noodles thrives. The rustic homemade noodles, which can be flat and wide or thin and delicate, have a marvelous chew and elasticity. Though in noodle shops you might witness the cooks dramatically swinging ropes of dough through the air as part of the noodle-making process, we developed this recipe for wide, flat noodles that involves only pulling, stretching, and slapping pieces of dough on the counter. Once you master the technique, these noodles are a breeze to make.

JULIA'S PRO TIP: *Make sure you have a nice big, clean counter to work on when pulling these noodles. Getting the noodles into the water takes a little patience, since the noodles are long, sticky, and stretchy. I've found that pulling the noodles on a counter right next the stove works well.*

BIANG BIANG MIAN

Serves: 4
Total Time: 1¾ hours, plus 12 hours 20 minutes chilling and resting

RECIPE OVERVIEW Biang Biang noodles are a popular dish from the Shaanxi province of China. The name describes the sound made when the noodles are slapped against a counter to stretch them. To achieve optimum chew and texture, we use high-protein bread flour and an extended resting time to allow the strong gluten network to relax and make the stretching process easier. We dress the noodles simply in a Sichuan-inspired chili oil vinaigrette (a favorite way to serve them in the winter months). Bird chiles are dried red Thai chiles and are pretty spicy, which is why we give a wide range. Black vinegar, an important ingredient and condiment in Chinese cuisine, is a dark vinegar made from glutinous rice or sorghum with a fruity, slightly malty, and smoky flavor. It is critical to rest the dough for at least 12 hours (or up to 48 hours). Note that after 24 hours the surface of the dough may develop small black speckles. This oxidation has no impact on flavor or safety. In step 1, you can mix the dough in a food processor instead of a stand mixer: Process flour and salt in food processor until combined, about 2 seconds. With processor running, add water and oil and process until dough forms satiny ball that clears sides of workbowl, about 90 seconds.

Dough
2⅓	cups (12¾ ounces) bread flour
¾	teaspoon table salt
1	cup water
1	tablespoon vegetable oil

Chili Vinaigrette
10 to 20	bird chiles, ground fine
½	cup vegetable oil
2	garlic cloves, sliced thin
1	(1-inch) piece fresh ginger, peeled and sliced thin
1	tablespoon Sichuan peppercorns
½	cinnamon stick
1	star anise pod
2	tablespoons soy sauce
2	tablespoons black vinegar
1	tablespoon toasted sesame oil
1	teaspoon sugar

To Finish
4	quarts water
	Table salt for cooking noodles
12	fresh cilantro sprigs, trimmed and cut into 2-inch pieces
6	scallions, sliced thin on bias

1. **FOR THE DOUGH** Whisk flour and salt together in bowl of stand mixer. Add water and oil. Fit stand mixer with dough hook and mix on low speed until all flour is moistened, 1 to 2 minutes. Increase speed to medium and knead until dough is smooth and satiny, 10 to 12 minutes. (Alternatively, mix dough in food processor, following instructions in Recipe Overview.) Transfer dough to counter, knead for 30 seconds, and shape into 9-inch log. Wrap log in plastic wrap and refrigerate for at least 12 hours or up to 48 hours.

2. **FOR THE CHILI VINAIGRETTE** Place chiles in large heatproof bowl. Place fine-mesh strainer over bowl and set aside. Combine vegetable oil, garlic, ginger, peppercorns, cinnamon, and star anise pod in small saucepan and heat over medium-high heat until sizzling. Reduce heat to low and gently simmer until garlic and ginger are slightly browned, 10 to 12 minutes. Pour through strainer into bowl with chiles; discard solids in strainer. Stir chile oil to combine and let cool for 5 minutes. Stir in soy sauce, vinegar, sesame oil, and sugar until combined; set aside.

3. Unwrap dough, transfer to lightly oiled counter, and, using bench scraper or knife, divide into 6 equal pieces (each 1½ inches wide). Cover with plastic wrap and let rest for 20 minutes.

4. Oil both sides of 1 piece of dough and flatten into 7 by 3-inch rectangle, with long side parallel to edge of counter. With both hands, gently grasp short ends of dough. Stretch dough and slap against counter until noodle is 32 to 36 inches long (noodle will be between $1/16$ and $1/8$ inch thick). (If dough is hard to stretch to this length or is snapping back significantly, set aside on counter and let rest for 10 minutes. Meanwhile, continue stretching remaining portions of dough.)

5. Place noodle on counter. Pinch center of noodle with forefingers and thumbs of both hands and pull apart with even pressure in both directions to rip seam in middle of noodle and create 1 continuous loop. Cut loop to create 2 equal-length noodles. Set noodles aside on lightly oiled counter (do not let noodles touch) and cover with plastic wrap. Repeat stretching and cutting with remaining pieces of dough.

6. Meanwhile, bring 4 quarts water and 1 tablespoon salt to boil in large pot. Add half of noodles to water and cook, stirring occasionally, until noodles float and turn chewy-tender, 45 to 60 seconds. Using wire skimmer, transfer noodles to bowl with chili vinaigrette; toss to combine. Return water to boil and repeat with remaining noodles. Divide noodles among individual bowls, top with cilantro and scallions, and serve.

Pulling Flat Noodles by Hand

FLATTEN
Flatten 1 piece of oiled dough into 7 by 3-inch rectangle, with long side parallel to edge of counter.

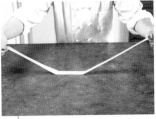

STRETCH AND SLAP
Gently grasp short ends of dough. Using quick repetitive flapping motion, stretch dough and slap center of dough strand against counter until noodle is 32 to 36 inches long.

PULL APART
Pinch center of noodle and pull apart to create 1 continuous loop. Cut loop into 2 equal noodles.

CHICKEN PHO, TWO WAYS

LAN LAM

In this course we present two expressions of phở gà, chicken phở. The northern version features a purely savory broth that is lightly seasoned, while the southern version incorporates more spices and a bit of sugar. Part of the pleasure of phở gà is how customizable it is, from which broth to make to which and what quantity of garnishes to place in your bowl. You can engineer each bite to be exactly the same or mix it up by favoring a different element with every taste.

LAN'S PRO TIP: *Phở broth can be made in advance and reheated but it must served as soon as it's assembled. Gather your sauces and toppings, bring the chicken to room temperature, and portion your noodles into deep bowls while the broth reheats. Once it's piping hot, ladle it into the bowls, making sure that the noodles and chicken are fully submerged. Serve immediately so that you can enjoy the noodles' tender-chewy texture before they absorb the broth and soften.*

PHỞ GÀ MIỀN BẮC

Serves: 6
Total Time: 2½ hours

RECIPE OVERVIEW We start our version of northern Vietnamese–style chicken phở by breaking down a whole chicken into parts that pack more snugly in a Dutch oven and lessen the amount of water needed to cover the chicken. This shortens the time needed to reduce the liquid to a concentrated broth. (With parts, you can also remove the white meat when it's cooked.) Covering the pot for the majority of the cooking time prevents evaporation. To keep the broth clear, we skim the scum from the broth, simmer the broth gently, and strain it through cheesecloth. In keeping with northern Vietnamese diners' preference for a savory and lightly spiced broth, we flavor ours with coriander seeds and cloves, adding the spices after we remove the chicken breasts. Before cooking, we soak rice noodles to remove starch from their surfaces so that they won't stick together. We like this phở served with shredded makrut lime leaves and nước mắm gứng, a gingery dipping sauce (which is not traditional, but some Vietnamese cooks like to include it). If you prefer a milder sauce, omit the Thai chile. Look for rice noodles labeled bánh phở; if they're unavailable, substitute ⅛-inch-wide flat rice noodles or rice vermicelli. The broth will taste overseasoned on its own but will be balanced by the unsalted noodles and garnishes.

Broth

- 1 (4-pound) whole chicken, neck and giblets reserved, liver discarded
- 12 cups water
- 1 onion, halved
- 1 (3-inch) piece ginger, peeled and halved lengthwise
- 2 teaspoons table salt
- 1 tablespoon coriander seeds
- 2 whole cloves
- ¼ cup fish sauce

Dipping Sauce

- ⅔ cup hot water
- ⅓ cup fish sauce
- ¼ cup lime juice (2 limes)
- 3 tablespoons sugar
- 1 tablespoon grated fresh ginger
- 2 garlic cloves, minced
- 1 Thai chile, stemmed and minced (optional)

Phở

- 12 ounces dried rice noodles
- ½ small onion, sliced thin
- 2 scallions, sliced thin
- 6 makrut lime leaves, middle vein removed and leaves sliced thin
  Fresh cilantro leaves and stems
  Thinly sliced serrano chiles

1. FOR THE BROTH Place chicken, breast side down, on cutting board. Using kitchen shears, cut through bones on either side of backbone. Reserve backbone. Using sharp chef's knife, cut straight down through breastbone to make 2 halves. Working with 1 half at a time, separate leg quarter and wing from each breast.

2. Transfer chicken parts, backbone, neck, and giblets to Dutch oven. Add water, onion, ginger, and salt and bring to boil over high heat. Reduce heat to maintain gentle simmer. Cook, skimming off any scum that rises to surface, until breasts register 160 to 165 degrees, 15 to 20 minutes. Transfer breasts to plate. Add coriander seeds and cloves to broth, cover, and continue to simmer 1 hour longer (check broth occasionally and adjust heat as necessary to maintain gentle simmer).

3. FOR THE DIPPING SAUCE While broth simmers, stir hot water, fish sauce, lime juice, sugar, ginger, garlic, and Thai chile, if using, in bowl until sugar dissolves.

4. Transfer leg quarters to plate with breasts. Discard wings, backbone, neck, giblets, and onion. Strain broth through fine-mesh strainer lined with double layer of cheesecloth. Rinse pot well and return broth to pot. (You should have about 12 cups broth.) Stir in fish sauce, cover, and keep warm over low heat.

5. FOR THE PHỞ Place noodles in large bowl and cover with water. Let sit until noodles are pliable, about 20 minutes. While noodles soak, shred chicken, discarding skin and bones. Bring 2 quarts water to boil in large pot. Drain noodles. Return broth to boil.

6. Add noodles to boiling water and cook, stirring frequently, until almost tender, 30 to 60 seconds. Drain immediately and divide among serving bowls. Place ⅓ cup chicken in each bowl (save remaining chicken for another use). Divide onion, scallions, and lime leaves among bowls. Add broth until chicken and noodles are covered by ½ inch, about 2 cups per bowl (save remaining broth for another use). Provide each diner with small bowl of dipping sauce and serve phở immediately, passing cilantro and serranos separately.

KEYS TO SUCCESS

- **Skim the broth**: Skimming the broth well as it comes to a boil removes the proteins that cause cloudiness.

- **Simmer and strain**: Simmering gently for the remaining cooking time and straining it through cheesecloth makes the broth especially clear.

Noodles That Don't Stick

For noodles that don't stick together and have droplets of broth clinging to each noodle's surface, soak them in tap water first, which removes the surface starches that would otherwise fuse the cooked noodles. Then give them a quick dunk in boiling water just to cook them through.

PHỞ GÀ MIỀN NAM

Serves: 6 to 8
Total Time: 2½ hours

RECIPE OVERVIEW For our southern Vietnamese–style chicken phở, we follow the same method for cooking the chicken, breaking down a whole bird into parts to pack them snugly in the Dutch oven and thus using less water to cover the chicken, which results in a concentrated broth in a shorter amount of time. Again, we treat the broth gently and strain it to keep it crystal clear, a hallmark of phở. Southern Vietnamese renditions of this dish usually feature a slightly sweet and highly spiced broth, so we flavor ours with sugar, star anise, cinnamon, coriander seeds, and cloves, adding the spices after we remove the chicken breasts from the pot to preserve more of their volatile flavor compounds. Southern diners also favor a wide assortment of garnishes so that every diner can personalize their bowl, so we offer several. Look for rice noodles labeled bánh phở; if they're unavailable, substitute ⅛-inch-wide flat rice noodles or rice vermicelli. The broth will taste overseasoned on its own but will be balanced by the unsalted noodles and garnishes.

Broth

- 1 (4-pound) whole chicken, neck and giblets reserved, liver discarded
- 12 cups water
- 1 onion, halved
- 1 (3-inch) piece ginger, peeled and halved lengthwise
- 2 teaspoons table salt
- 1 teaspoon sugar
- 1 tablespoon coriander seeds
- 1 cinnamon stick
- 1 star anise pod
- 2 whole cloves
- ¼ cup fish sauce

Phở

- 12 ounces dried rice noodles
- ½ small onion, sliced thin
- 2 scallions, sliced thin
- Bean sprouts
- Fresh cilantro leaves and stems
- Fresh Thai basil leaves
- Lime wedges
- Thinly sliced serrano chiles
- Hoisin sauce
- Sriracha

1. FOR THE BROTH Place chicken breast side down on cutting board. Using kitchen shears, cut through bones on either side of backbone. Reserve backbone. Using sharp chef's knife, cut straight down through breastbone to make 2 halves. Working with 1 half at a time, separate leg quarter and wing from each breast.

2. Transfer chicken parts, backbone, neck, and giblets to Dutch oven. Add water, onion, ginger, salt, and sugar and bring to boil over high heat. Reduce heat to maintain gentle simmer. Cook, skimming off any scum that rises to surface, until breasts register 160 to 165 degrees, 15 to 20 minutes. Transfer breasts to plate. Add coriander seeds, cinnamon stick, star anise, and cloves to broth, cover, and continue to simmer 1 hour longer (check broth occasionally and adjust heat as necessary to maintain gentle simmer).

3. Transfer leg quarters to plate with breasts. Discard wings, backbone, neck, giblets, and onion. Strain broth through fine-mesh strainer lined with double layer of cheesecloth. Rinse pot well and return broth to pot. (You should have about 12 cups broth; add water if necessary.) Stir in fish sauce, cover, and keep warm over low heat.

4. FOR THE PHỞ Place noodles in large bowl and cover with water. Let sit until noodles are pliable, about 20 minutes. While noodles soak, shred chicken, discarding skin and bones. Bring 2 quarts water to boil in large pot. Drain noodles. Return broth to boil.

5. Add noodles to boiling water and cook, stirring frequently, until almost tender, 30 to 60 seconds. Drain immediately and divide among serving bowls. Place ⅓ cup chicken in each bowl (save remaining chicken for another use). Divide onion and scallions among bowls. Add broth until chicken and noodles are covered by ½ inch, about 2 cups per bowl (save remaining broth for another use). Serve immediately, passing bean sprouts, cilantro, Thai basil, lime wedges, serranos, hoisin, and sriracha separately.

KEYS TO SUCCESS

- **Hold back the spice:** Delaying the addition of the spices until after you remove the chicken breasts from the pot ensures that their volatile compounds don't dissipate as much over the course of cooking.

- **Time management:** Prepare all the garnishes while the broth simmers.

WHAT CAN GO WRONG

PROBLEM The broth has off flavors or is muddy.

SOLUTION Pay close attention to these steps: Keeping the broth at a gentle simmer (don't boil it or let the simmer stop); skimming off the scum; and rinsing the pot well after making the broth.

DUMPLINGS

BRYAN ROOF

Nothing holds a candle to homemade dumplings. What's more, they are as fun to make as they are to eat. So it only makes sense that there are a great variety of dumplings prepared and consumed throughout the many provinces of China. Here we teach you versions of three classic Chinese-inspired dumplings, using a variety of wrappers (homemade and store-bought), fillings, shaping methods, and cooking methods.

BRYAN'S PRO TIP: *It's always best to buy and use untreated shrimp—those not treated with sodium or additives such as sodium tripolyphosphate (STPP). Most frozen shrimp have been treated (the ingredient list should tell you).*

SIMPLE DUMPLINGS
Makes: 24 dumplings
Total Time: 1¼ hours, plus 20 minutes standing and 30 minutes chilling

RECIPE OVERVIEW These soft, savory dumplings are filled with tender shrimp, crunchy cabbage, and scallions and spiked with garlic, ginger, and soy. For a light filling, we use a more-generous-than-normal amount of crunchy cabbage and incorporate a beaten egg. A sequence of browning, steaming, and cranking up the heat produces dumplings with a pleasing balance of ultra-appealing soft and crispy textures that are well complemented by a soy- and rice-vinegar–based dipping sauce. Dumplings are best served hot from the skillet, so we suggest serving the first batch immediately and then cooking the second batch. The simple folding instructions are for round gyoza wrappers, our preferred wrapper for these dumplings. See page 293 for information on how to work with other wrappers.

Scallion Dipping Sauce
- ¼ cup soy sauce
- 2 tablespoons rice vinegar
- 2 tablespoons mirin
- 2 tablespoons water
- 1 scallion, minced
- 1 teaspoon chili oil (optional)
- ½ teaspoon toasted sesame oil

Dumplings
- 3 cups minced napa cabbage
- ¾ teaspoon table salt
- 12 ounces large shrimp (26 to 30 per pound), peeled, deveined, and tails removed
- 4 scallions, minced
- 4 teaspoons soy sauce
- 1½ teaspoons grated fresh ginger
- 1 garlic clove, minced
- 1 large egg, lightly beaten
- ⅛ teaspoon pepper
- 24 round gyoza wrappers
- 4 teaspoons vegetable oil, divided

1. FOR THE SCALLION DIPPING SAUCE Combine all ingredients in bowl; set aside for serving. (Sauce can be refrigerated overnight.)

2. FOR THE DUMPLINGS Toss cabbage and salt in colander set over bowl. Let sit until cabbage begins to wilt, about 20 minutes; press cabbage gently with rubber spatula to squeeze out excess moisture. Meanwhile, pulse shrimp in food processor until finely chopped, about 10 pulses. Combine shrimp, cabbage, scallions, soy sauce, ginger, garlic, egg, and pepper in bowl. Cover and refrigerate until mixture is well chilled, at least 30 minutes or up to 24 hours.

- **Chill the filling:** Refrigerating the filling before filling the wrappers will help the filling hold together.
- **Clear the air:** Be sure to press out any air pockets when folding and sealing the dumplings.

Filling Simple Dumplings

ADD FILLING
Place 1 tablespoon filling in center of gyoza wrapper.

FOLD IN HALF
After moistening edge of wrapper, fold it in half to make half-moon shape.

PINCH CLOSED
With your forefinger and thumb, pinch dumpling closed, pressing out any air pockets.

GENTLY FLATTEN
Place dumpling on its side and press gently to flatten bottom.

3. Working with 4 wrappers at a time (cover others with damp paper towel), place 1 tablespoon filling in center of each wrapper, brush edges with water, fold wrapper in half, and pinch dumpling closed, pressing out any air pockets. Place dumpling on 1 side and gently flatten bottom. Transfer to baking sheet and cover with clean, damp dish towel. Repeat with remaining wrappers and filling. (Dumplings can be frozen in single layer until firm; transfer chilled dumplings to zipper-lock bag and store for up to 1 month. Do not thaw.)

4. Line large plate with double layer of paper towels. Brush 2 teaspoons oil over bottom of 12-inch nonstick skillet and arrange half of dumplings in skillet, flat side down (overlapping just slightly if necessary). Place skillet over medium-high heat and cook dumplings, without moving, until golden brown on bottom, about 5 minutes.

5. Reduce heat to low, add ½ cup water, and cover immediately. Continue to cook until most of water is absorbed and wrappers are slightly translucent, about 10 minutes. Uncover skillet, increase heat to medium-high, and continue to cook, without stirring, until dumpling bottoms are well browned and crisp, 3 to 4 minutes. Slide dumplings onto prepared plate, browned side down, and let drain briefly. Transfer dumplings to serving platter. Let skillet cool until just warm, then wipe clean with paper towels and repeat steps 4 and 5 with remaining dumplings, remaining 2 teaspoons oil, and another ½ cup water. Serve with dipping sauce.

PORK DUMPLINGS

Makes: 40 dumplings
Total Time: 4½ hours

RECIPE OVERVIEW A boiled dumpling is delicately chewy all over, while a pan-fried one boasts a single flat side that's contrastingly crisp and brown. A steaming, fragrant, homemade plateful of either kind, drizzled with soy sauce, chili oil, and vinegar, is simply irresistible—so here we show you both cooking methods, along with a more complex folding method than in the previous recipe. For the filling, we add vegetable oil and sesame oil to ground pork, mimicking the richness of the traditionally used fatty pork shoulder. Mixing the filling in the food processor develops myosin, a protein that helps the filling hold together when cooked. Keep all the dough covered with a damp towel except when rolling and shaping. A shorter, smaller-diameter rolling pin is ideal, but a conventional pin will also work. For an accurate measurement of boiling water, bring a full kettle of water to a boil and then measure out the desired amount. Our recipe makes 40 dumplings, so you can cook some right away and freeze some for later. To do this, freeze uncooked dumplings on a rimmed baking sheet until solid. Transfer them to a zipper-lock bag and freeze for up to 1 month. To pan-fry frozen dumplings, increase the water to ⅔ cup and the covered cooking time to 8 minutes. To boil, increase the cooking time to 8 minutes.

Dough

- 2½ cups (12½ ounces) all-purpose flour
- 1 cup boiling water

Filling

- 5 cups 1-inch pieces napa cabbage
- ½ teaspoon table salt, plus ½ teaspoon salt for salting cabbage
- 12 ounces ground pork
- 1½ tablespoons soy sauce, plus extra for dipping
- 1½ tablespoons toasted sesame oil
- 1 tablespoon vegetable oil, plus 2 tablespoons for pan frying (optional)
- 1 tablespoon Shaoxing wine or dry sherry
- 1 tablespoon hoisin sauce
- 1 tablespoon grated fresh ginger
- ¼ teaspoon ground white pepper
- 4 scallions, chopped fine
  Black or rice vinegar
  Chili oil

1. FOR THE DOUGH Place flour in food processor. With processor running, add boiling water. Continue to process until dough forms ball and clears sides of bowl, 30 to 45 seconds longer. Transfer dough to counter and knead with your hands until smooth, 2 to 3 minutes. Wrap dough in plastic wrap and let rest for 30 minutes.

2. FOR THE FILLING While dough rests, scrape any excess dough from now-empty processor bowl and blade. Pulse cabbage in processor until finely chopped, 8 to 10 pulses. Transfer cabbage to medium bowl and stir in ½ teaspoon salt; let sit for 10 minutes. Using your hands, squeeze excess moisture from cabbage. Transfer cabbage to small bowl and set aside.

3. Pulse pork, soy sauce, sesame oil, 1 tablespoon vegetable oil, wine, hoisin, ginger, pepper, and ½ teaspoon salt in now-empty food processor until blended and slightly sticky, about 10 pulses. Scatter cabbage over pork mixture. Add scallions and pulse until vegetables are evenly distributed, about 8 pulses. Transfer pork mixture to small bowl and, using rubber spatula, smooth surface. Cover with plastic and refrigerate.

4. Line 2 rimmed baking sheets with parchment paper. Dust lightly with flour; set aside. Unwrap dough and roll into 12-inch cylinder and cut cylinder into 4 equal pieces. Set 3 pieces aside and cover with plastic. Roll remaining piece into 8-inch cylinder. Cut cylinder in half and cut each half into 5 equal pieces. Place dough pieces on 1 cut side on lightly floured counter and lightly dust with flour. Using palm of your hand, press each dough piece into 2-inch disk. Cover disks with damp towel.

5. Roll 1 disk into 3½-inch round (wrappers needn't be perfectly round) and re-cover disk with damp towel. Repeat with remaining disks. (Do not overlap disks.) Using rubber spatula, mark filling with cross to divide into 4 equal portions. Transfer 1 portion to small bowl and refrigerate remaining filling. Working with 1 wrapper at a time (keep remaining wrappers covered), place scant 1 tablespoon filling in center of wrapper. Brush away any flour clinging to surface of wrapper. Lift side of wrapper closest to you and side farthest away and pinch together to form 1½-inch-wide seam in center of dumpling. (When viewed from above, dumpling will have rectangular shape with rounded open ends.) Lift left corner farthest away from you and bring to center of seam. Pinch to seal. Pinch together remaining dough on left side to seal. Repeat pinching on right side. Gently press dumpling into crescent shape and transfer to prepared sheet. Repeat with remaining wrappers and filling in bowl. Repeat dumpling-making process with remaining 3 pieces dough and 3 portions filling.

6A. TO PAN FRY Brush 12-inch nonstick skillet with 1 tablespoon vegetable oil. Evenly space 16 dumplings, flat sides down, around edge of skillet and place four in center. Cook over medium heat until bottoms begin to turn spotty brown, 3 to 4 minutes. Off heat, carefully add ½ cup water (water will sputter). Return skillet to heat and bring water to boil. Cover and reduce heat to medium-low. Cook for 6 minutes. Uncover, increase heat to medium-high, and cook until water has evaporated and bottoms of dumplings are crispy and browned, 1 to 3 minutes. Transfer dumplings to platter, crispy sides up. To cook second batch of dumplings, let skillet cool for 10 minutes. Rinse skillet under cool water and wipe dry with paper towels. Repeat cooking process with 1 tablespoon vegetable oil and remaining dumplings.

6B. TO BOIL Bring 4 quarts water to boil in large Dutch oven over high heat. Add 20 dumplings, a few at a time, stirring gently to prevent them from sticking. Return to simmer, adjusting heat as necessary to maintain simmer. Cook dumplings for 7 minutes. Drain well. Repeat with remaining dumplings

7. Serve dumplings hot, passing vinegar, chili oil, and extra soy sauce separately for dipping.

KEYS TO SUCCESS

- **Weigh the flour:** This ensures that the dough has the right moisture level.

- **Add minimal flour:** When working the dough, it should remain slightly tacky. This will ensure the dumplings seal properly.

- **A cold skillet:** If pan-frying, brushing the oil in a cold skillet ensures that it coats the pan evenly, which helps the dumplings crisp.

Shaping Dumplings

ADD FILLING AND SEAL EDGES
Place scant 1 tablespoon filling in center of wrapper. Seal top and bottom edges to form 1½-inch-wide seam.

PINCH TOGETHER
Bring far left corner to center of seam and pinch together.

SEAL SIDES
Pinch rest of left side to seal. Repeat process on right side.

PRESS INTO SHAPE
Gently press dumpling into crescent shape.

SHU MAI

Makes: 40 dumplings
Total Time: 45 minutes

RECIPE OVERVIEW The moist, intensely flavorful filling in our rendition of open-faced Chinese steamed dumplings boasts pork and shrimp, water chestnuts, shiitake mushrooms, cilantro, and ginger. To ensure proper flavor and consistent texture, we chop the pork (boneless country-style spareribs) in a food processor. Grinding half of the meat to a fine consistency and keeping the other half coarse ensures that the filling has great texture and holds together. To prevent the meat from drying out during steaming, we mix in a little powdered gelatin dissolved in soy sauce. We chop the shrimp in the food processor as well. For the wrappers, we use egg roll wrappers cut into 3-inch rounds with a biscuit cutter. Once we add the filling and gather the edges of the wrappers up around each one, we steam these full-flavored little parcels in a steamer basket. Use any size shrimp except popcorn shrimp; there's no need to halve shrimp smaller than 26 to 30 per pound.

- 2 tablespoons soy sauce
- ½ teaspoon unflavored gelatin
- 1 pound boneless country-style pork ribs, cut into 1-inch pieces, divided
- 8 ounces shrimp, peeled, tails removed, halved lengthwise
- ¼ cup chopped water chestnuts
- 4 dried shiitake mushroom caps (about ¾ ounce), soaked in hot water 30 minutes, squeezed dry, and chopped fine
- 2 tablespoons cornstarch
- 2 tablespoons minced fresh cilantro
- 1 tablespoon toasted sesame oil
- 1 tablespoon Shaoxing wine or dry sherry
- 1 tablespoon rice vinegar
- 2 teaspoons sugar
- 2 teaspoons grated fresh ginger
- ½ teaspoon table salt
- ½ teaspoon pepper
- 1 (1-pound) package 5½-inch square egg roll wrappers
- ¼ cup finely grated carrot (optional)
  Chili oil

1. Combine soy sauce and gelatin in small bowl. Set aside to allow gelatin to bloom, about 5 minutes.

2. Meanwhile, place half of pork in food processor and pulse until coarsely ground into ⅛-inch pieces, about 10 pulses; transfer to large bowl. Add shrimp and remaining pork to food processor and pulse until coarsely chopped into ¼-inch pieces, about 5 pulses. Add to more finely ground pork. Stir in soy sauce mixture, water chestnuts, mushrooms, cornstarch, cilantro, sesame oil, wine, vinegar, sugar, ginger, salt, and pepper.

Shaping Shu Mai

ADD FILLING
Brush the edges of the dumpling wrapper lightly with water. Place a heaping tablespoon of filling in the center of each wrapper.

PINCH SIDES
Pinch two opposing sides of the wrapper with your fingers. Rotate the dumpling 90 degrees, and, again, pinch the opposing sides of the wrapper with your fingers.

PINCH 8 TIMES
Continue to pinch the dumpling until you have eight equidistant pinches around the circumference of the dumpling.

SQUEEZE AT TOP
Gather up the sides of the dumpling and squeeze gently at the top to create a "waist."

PACK FILLING
Hold the dumpling in your hand and gently but firmly pack the filling into the dumpling with a butter knife or your finger.

3. Divide egg roll wrappers into 3 stacks. Using 3-inch biscuit cutter, cut two 3-inch rounds from each stack. Cover with moist paper towels to prevent drying.

4. Working with 6 rounds at a time, brush edges of each round lightly with water. Place heaping tablespoon of filling in center of each round. Form dumplings by pinching opposing sides of wrapper with your fingers until you have 8 equidistant pinches. Gather up sides of dumpling and squeeze gently to create "waist." Hold dumpling in your hand and gently but firmly pack down filling with butter knife or your finger. Transfer to parchment paper–lined baking sheet, cover with damp kitchen towel, and repeat with remaining wrappers and filling. Top center of each dumpling with pinch of grated carrot, if using.

5. Cut piece of parchment paper slightly smaller than diameter of steamer basket and place in basket. Poke about 20 small holes in parchment and lightly coat with vegetable oil spray. Place batches of dumplings on parchment, making sure they are not touching. Set steamer over simmering water and cook, covered, until no longer pink, 8 to 10 minutes. Serve immediately with chili oil.

KEYS TO SUCCESS

- **Fat equals flavor:** Don't trim the excess fat from the spareribs, as the fat contributes flavor and moistness to the shu mai.

- **Pull out the processor:** Pulsing the pork to two different consistencies—coarse and fine—ensures a consistently tender filling that will hold together and not crumble out of the dumpling when you take a bite.

- **Gelatin:** It's important for a juicy result.

COOKING FRESH AND FROZEN

The amounts of oil and water and the size of the skillet will change depending on the number of dumplings and whether they are fresh or frozen.

20 fresh	12"	1 tablespoon	½ cup
20 frozen	12"	1 tablespoon	⅔ cup
10 fresh	10"	2 teaspoons	⅓ cup
10 frozen	10"	2 teaspoons	½ cup

DIFFERENT WRAPPERS, DIFFERENT METHODS

For potstickers, we prefer the slightly chewy texture of gyoza wrappers, but you can also use wonton wrappers. The instructions given with the recipe are for using round wrappers. If using square wrappers, fold diagonally into a triangle after adding the filling and proceed with the recipe. For rectangular wrappers, fold in half lengthwise. Because smaller wrappers yield more dumplings, you'll need to cook them in multiple batches. Here's how to adjust the filling amount and steaming time.

WRAPPER	SIZE	FILLING AMOUNT	STEAMING TIME
Round wonton	3¾ inches (diameter)	1 tablespoon	6 minutes
Square wonton	3⅜ inches square	2 teaspoons	6 minutes
Rectangular wonton	3¼ by 2¾ inches	1 teaspoon	5 minutes

BAMBOO STEAMERS

Bamboo steamers are ideal for steaming any food that needs to sit flat during cooking, such as shu mai, or food that might break or become misshapen in a collapsible steamer with a curved base, such as fish fillets. They are most commonly available as sets of two or three 10-inch round bamboo tiers—a size that is compatible for use with a 14-inch wok or a 12-inch skillet. Each stackable tier provides about 68 square inches of surface area.

PERFECT PORTIONS OF FILLING

For our Pork Dumplings, rather than try to visualize mounds of filling as 40 equal portions, we devised this technique, which works no matter how many dumplings you are making.

Mark the filling with a cross to divide it into four portions.

Working with one portion at a time, divide each into tenths (approximately 1 scant tablespoon each).

ROLLS FRESH AND FRIED

ELLE SIMONE SCOTT

Rolls might not be the first items that come to mind when you think about Asian noodles, but their wrappers, whether made from rice flour or wheat flour, are essentially simple noodle sheets—a blank canvas just waiting to be filled. There are enough fresh and fried rolls from different countries in Asia to fill an entire book; here we offer four recipes to get you started. Two use rice paper wrappers and are fresh (that is, uncooked) rolls, while the other two use wheat flour wrappers and are fried.

ELLE'S PRO TIP: *When making rolls, the key to success is having a strategy if you're making more than one kind of roll and then having everything ready before you get started. The ingredients are often time-sensitive so walking into this exciting meal with your head in the game is the way to go.*

TOFU SUMMER ROLLS WITH SPICY ALMOND BUTTER SAUCE

Makes: 12 rolls
Total Time: 40 minutes, plus 1 hour resting

RECIPE OVERVIEW Probably the most commonly found ingredient in summer roll fillings is rice vermicelli, but these summer rolls are decidedly untraditional in that they don't include any noodles. Instead, we fill the fresh rolls with strips of marinated tofu, a rainbow of fresh vegetables, and loads of basil. The mix of red cabbage, red bell pepper, cucumber, and carrots delivers color and crunch. The basil adds herbal notes (essential in any summer roll), and strips of marinated tofu add heartiness. For further substance, we serve them with a sriracha-spiked almond butter sauce. Thick and rich, it clings nicely to the rolls. If Thai basil is unavailable, you can use Italian basil here. You can use smooth or chunky almond or peanut butter. These rolls are best served immediately.

Sauce

- 3 tablespoons almond or peanut butter
- 3 tablespoons water
- 1 tablespoon rice vinegar
- 1 tablespoon soy sauce
- 2 teaspoons grated fresh ginger
- 1 teaspoon sriracha
- 1 garlic clove, minced

Rolls

- 6 tablespoons rice wine vinegar, divided
- 1 tablespoon soy sauce
- 2 teaspoons sriracha
- 2 scallions, sliced thin on bias
- 7 ounces extra-firm tofu, cut into 3-inch-long by 1/2-inch-thick strips
- 3½ cups shredded red cabbage
- 12 (8½-inch) round rice paper wrappers
- 1 cup Thai basil leaves
- 1 red bell pepper, stemmed, seeded, and cut into 2-inch-long matchsticks
- ½ seedless English cucumber, cut into 3-inch-long matchsticks
- 2 carrots, peeled and shredded

1. FOR THE SAUCE Whisk all ingredients until well combined; set aside.

2. FOR THE ROLLS Whisk 2 tablespoons vinegar, soy sauce, sriracha, and scallions in small bowl until well combined. Place tofu in shallow dish, then pour soy sauce mixture over top and let sit for 1 hour. Toss cabbage with remaining 1/4 cup vinegar and let sit for 1 hour. Drain cabbage in fine mesh strainer, pressing gently with back of spatula to remove as much liquid as possible. Transfer to large plate and pat dry with paper towels.

3. Spread clean, damp dish towel on work surface. Fill large bowl with cold water. Submerge 1 wrapper in water until wet on both sides, no longer than 2 seconds. Shake gently over bowl to remove excess water, then lay wrapper flat on work surface (wrapper will be fairly stiff but will continue to soften as you assemble roll). Scatter 3 basil leaves over wrapper. Arrange 5 matchsticks each of bell pepper and cucumber horizontally on wrapper, leaving 2-inch border at bottom. Top with 1 tablespoon carrots, then arrange 2 tablespoons cabbage on top of carrots. Place 1 strip tofu horizontally on top of vegetables, being sure to shake off excess marinade.

4. Fold bottom of wrapper over filling, pulling back on it firmly to tighten it around filling, then fold sides of wrapper in and continue to roll tightly into spring roll. Transfer to platter and cover with second damp dish towel.

5. Repeat with remaining wrappers and filling. Serve with almond butter sauce.

KEYS TO SUCCESS

- **One at a time:** Be sure to make one roll at a time to keep the wrappers moist and pliable.

- **Enjoy right away:** The rolls will get soggy if made ahead, so plan to make them right before serving.

CORE TECHNIQUE
Hydrating Rice Paper Wrappers

USE COLD WATER
The hotter the water, the faster the wrapper hydrates and turns sodden and sticky. Cold water moistens the wrapper slowly, which gives you more time to work.

DON'T OVERSOAK
A 2-second dip is all that's needed; any longer and the wrappers will become soggy and tear easily when you add the fillings and roll the wrapper up. Wrappers will seem stiff but will soften as you assemble each roll.

GỎI CUỐN
Makes: 12 rolls
Total Time: 1¾ hours

RECIPE OVERVIEW These Vietnamese summer rolls contain rice vermicelli, along with plenty of fresh herbs, lettuce, pork, and shrimp. We use the same water for cooking the pork and the shrimp, which infuses a bit of porky flavor into the mild shrimp. Letting the shrimp cook off the heat keeps them from overcooking and turning tough. If Thai basil is unavailable, increase the mint and cilantro to 1½ cups each. A wooden surface will draw moisture away from the moist wrappers, so assemble the rolls directly on your counter or on a plastic cutting board. If part of the wrapper starts to dry out while you are forming the rolls, moisten it with your dampened fingers. These rolls are best served immediately. If you like, serve Nước Chấm (recipe follows) along with the Peanut-Hoisin Sauce.

Peanut-Hoisin Sauce
    1 Thai chile, sliced thin
    1 garlic clove, minced
    1 teaspoon kosher salt
  ⅔ cup water
  ⅓ cup creamy peanut butter
    3 tablespoons hoisin sauce
    2 tablespoons tomato paste
    1 tablespoon distilled white vinegar

Rolls
    6 ounces rice vermicelli
  10 ounces boneless country-style pork ribs, trimmed
        Kosher salt, for cooking pork
  18 medium-large shrimp (31 to 40 per pound), peeled, deveined, and tails removed
    1 cup fresh mint leaves
    1 cup fresh cilantro leaves and thin stems
    1 cup Thai basil leaves
  12 (8½-inch) round rice paper wrappers
  12 leaves red or green leaf lettuce, thick ribs removed
    2 scallions, sliced thin on bias

1. FOR THE PEANUT-HOISIN SAUCE Using mortar and pestle (or on cutting board using flat side of chef's knife), mash Thai chile, garlic, and salt to fine paste. Transfer to medium bowl. Add water, peanut butter, hoisin, tomato paste, and vinegar and whisk until smooth.

2. FOR THE ROLLS Bring 2 quarts water to boil in medium saucepan. Stir in noodles. Cook until noodles are tender but not mushy, 3 to 4 minutes. Drain noodles and rinse with cold water until cool. Drain noodles again, then spread on large plate to dry.

3. Bring 2 quarts water to boil in now-empty saucepan. Add pork and 2 teaspoons salt. Reduce heat, cover, and simmer until thickest part of pork registers 150 degrees, 8 to 12 minutes. Transfer pork to cutting board, reserving water.

4. Return water to boil. Add shrimp and cover. Let stand off heat until shrimp are opaque throughout, about 3 minutes. Drain shrimp and rinse with cold water until cool. Transfer to cutting board. Pat shrimp dry and halve lengthwise. Transfer to second plate.

5. When pork is cool enough to handle, cut each rib crosswise into 2-inch lengths. Slice each 2-inch piece lengthwise ⅛ inch thick (you should have at least 24 slices) and transfer to plate with shrimp. Tear mint, cilantro, and basil into 1-inch pieces and combine in bowl.

6. Fill large bowl with cold water. Submerge 1 wrapper in water until wet on both sides, no longer than 2 seconds. Shake gently over bowl to remove excess water, then lay wrapper flat on work surface (wrapper will be fairly stiff but will continue to soften as you assemble roll). Repeat with second wrapper and place next to first wrapper. Fold 1 lettuce leaf and place on lower third of first wrapper, leaving about ½-inch margin on each side. Spread ⅓ cup noodles on top of lettuce, then sprinkle with 1 teaspoon scallions. Top scallions with 2 slices pork. Spread ¼ cup herb mixture over pork.

7. Bring lower edge of wrapper up and over herbs. Roll snugly but gently until long sides of greens and noodles are enclosed. Fold in sides to enclose ends. Arrange 3 shrimp halves, cut side up, on remaining section of wrapper. Continue to roll until filling is completely enclosed in neat cylinder. Transfer roll to serving platter, shrimp side up, and cover with plastic wrap. Repeat with second moistened wrapper. Repeat with remaining wrappers and filling, keeping completed rolls covered with plastic. Uncover and serve with sauce. (Leftovers can be wrapped tightly and refrigerated for up to 24 hours, but wrappers will become chewier and may break in places.)

Rolling Gỏi Cuốn

COVER HERBS
Bring lower edge of wrapper up and over herbs.

ENCLOSE FILLING
Roll snugly but gently until greens and noodles are enclosed.

TUCK SIDES
Fold in sides to enclose ends.

ADD SHRIMP
Arrange 3 shrimp halves, cut side up, on remaining wrapper. Continue to roll until filling is completely enclosed in neat cylinder.

KEYS TO SUCCESS

- **Tender shrimp:** Cooking the shrimp gently off the heat keeps them tender, making the rolls easier to bite into.

- **Plenty of herbs:** Fresh herbs are a signature of these rolls, so don't skimp.

- **Stretchy wrappers:** Follow the instructions for hydrating wrappers on page 295; properly hydrated wrappers won't tear when you add the plentiful fillings.

NƯỚC CHẤM (VIETNAMESE DIPPING SAUCE)
Serves: 4 (makes 1 cup)
Hot water helps the sugar dissolve into the sauce.

- 3   tablespoons sugar, divided
- 1   small Thai chile, stemmed and minced
- 1   garlic clove, minced
- ⅔ cup hot water
- 5   tablespoons fish sauce
- ¼ cup lime juice (2 limes)

Using mortar and pestle (or on cutting board using flat side of chef's knife), mash 1 tablespoon sugar, Thai chile, and garlic to fine paste. Transfer to medium bowl and add hot water and remaining 2 tablespoons sugar. Stir until sugar is dissolved. Stir in fish sauce and lime juice.

EGG ROLLS

Makes: 8 rolls
Total Time: 55 minutes

RECIPE OVERVIEW A beloved mainstay in Chinese American restaurants, piping-hot egg rolls are crunchy, salty, sweet, savory, and meaty. Unlike summer roll wrappers (and spring roll wrappers), which are made from rice flour, egg roll wrappers are thicker and sturdier, made from wheat flour and eggs. For our egg rolls, we use bagged coleslaw mix and ground pork, which offer efficiency over hand-mincing cabbage and pork—without sacrificing any flavor. To that base we add scallions and shiitake mushrooms and flavor the filling with garlic, ginger, soy sauce, vinegar, and sugar. Another home cook–friendly adjustment is shallow-frying the rolls in a skillet rather than deep-frying them. This makes cooking easier and cleanup faster—and still produces excellent egg rolls. This recipe can easily be doubled: Extend the cooking time of the pork mixture by about 5 minutes in step 2 and fry the egg rolls in two batches. Besides the soy-vinegar dipping sauce, we like to serve the egg rolls with Chinese hot mustard.

Dipping Sauce

- 2 tablespoons soy sauce
- 1 tablespoon water
- 2 teaspoons distilled white vinegar
- 1 teaspoon sugar

Egg Rolls

- 8 ounces ground pork
- 6 scallions, white and green parts separated and sliced thin
- 3 garlic cloves, minced
- 2 teaspoons grated fresh ginger
- 3 cups (7 ounces) coleslaw mix
- 4 ounces shiitake mushrooms, stemmed and chopped
- 3 tablespoons soy sauce
- 1 tablespoon sugar
- 1 tablespoon distilled white vinegar
- 2 teaspoons toasted sesame oil
- 8 egg roll wrappers
- 2 cups vegetable oil for frying

1. FOR THE DIPPING SAUCE Whisk all ingredients in bowl until sugar is dissolved. Refrigerate for up to 4 days.

2. FOR THE EGG ROLLS Cook pork in 12-inch nonstick skillet over medium-high heat, breaking up meat with wooden spoon, until no longer pink, about 5 minutes. Add scallion whites, garlic, and ginger and cook until fragrant, about 1 minute. Add coleslaw mix, mushrooms, soy sauce, sugar, and vinegar and cook until cabbage is just softened, about 3 minutes.

Rolling Egg Rolls

PLACE AND SHAPE FILLING
Place a lightly packed ⅓ cup of filling on the lower half of the wrapper. Use your fingers to shape the filling into a cylinder.

MOISTEN WRAPPER EDGE
Dip your fingertips in water, and then moisten the entire border of the wrapper with a thin film of water.

FOLD UP BOTTOM THEN SIDES
Bring the bottom point of the wrapper over the filling and press down on the other side to seal. Then fold in the sides.

ROLL INTO CYLINDER
Roll into a log shape and press the edges to seal. Cover the egg roll with a moist paper towel while shaping the rest.

3. Off heat, stir in sesame oil and scallion greens. Transfer pork mixture to large plate, spread into even layer, and refrigerate until cool enough to handle, about 5 minutes. Wipe skillet clean with paper towels.

4. Fill small bowl with water. Working with 1 egg roll wrapper at a time, orient wrapper on counter so 1 corner points toward edge of counter. Place lightly packed ⅓ cup filling on lower half of wrapper and mold it with your fingers into neat cylindrical shape. Using your fingertips, moisten entire border of wrapper with thin film of water.

5. Fold bottom corner of wrapper up and over filling and press it down on other side of filling. Fold both side corners of wrapper in over filling and press gently to seal. Roll filling up over itself until wrapper is fully sealed. Leave egg roll seam side down on counter and cover with damp paper towel while shaping remaining egg rolls.

6. Line large plate with triple layer of paper towels. Heat vegetable oil in now-empty skillet over medium heat to 325 degrees. Using tongs, place all egg rolls in skillet, seam side down, and cook until golden brown, 2 to 4 minutes per side. Transfer to paper towel–lined plate and let cool slightly, about 5 minutes. Serve with dipping sauce.

KEYS TO SUCCESS

- **One at a time:** Egg roll wrappers are sturdier than summer roll wrappers, but you'll still get the best results working with one at a time.

- **Precook the pork:** Cooking the pork before filling these rolls ensures you'll only need a quick fry to finish them.

- **Shallow-fry:** Heating the oil to 350 degrees in a skillet and frying all the egg rolls at once produces rolls just as crunchy and golden as deep-frying would.

LUMPIANG SHANGHAI

Makes: 18 to 20 rolls
Total Time: 1½ hours

RECIPE OVERVIEW Despite their name, lumpiang Shanghai are a Filipino holiday staple. They evolved from a dish that early Chinese traders brought to the Philippines, possibly as far back as the ninth century. Today they are made with special lumpia wrappers (or spring roll wrappers), which are thinner than egg roll wrappers and generally contain just flour (rice or wheat) and water. Our version of these slender fried rolls features a savory vegetable and ground pork filling flavored with garlic, ginger, soy sauce, and pepper. We pulse the vegetables and aromatics in a food processor until finely chopped before pulsing in the pork along with beaten egg. The vegetable juices freed by the whirring blades of the processor, along with the egg, moisten the filling, making it easy to pipe into neat strips on the

wrappers (a zipper-lock bag is a convenient tool for this). We roll up the filling carefully, making sure to work out any air pockets; this prevents the lumpia from floating as they cook, which could cause them to cook unevenly. We seal the lumpia with beaten egg and then fry until their exteriors are golden brown and crisp all over. The dipping sauce is sukang maasim (white cane vinegar) seasoned with soy sauce, garlic, pepper, and sugar. You can substitute distilled white vinegar. Use a Dutch oven that holds 6 quarts or more. Crisp leftover lumpia by baking them in a 425-degree oven for 8 to 10 minutes. When removed from the oven, the rolls will be soft; they will crisp as they cool. Serve warm or at room temperature. Instead of the dipping sauce, you can serve the lumpia with a store-bought sweet chili sauce.

Dipping Sauce

⅔	cup sukang maasim
1	tablespoon soy sauce
1½	teaspoons pepper
1	teaspoon sugar
1	garlic clove, minced
	Pinch table salt

Lumpia

½	cup chopped onion
⅓	cup chopped carrot
⅓	cup chopped celery
4	garlic cloves, peeled
1	(½-inch) piece ginger, peeled
1	large egg
1	pound ground pork
1	tablespoon soy sauce
1	teaspoon pepper
¼	teaspoon table salt
18–20	(8-inch) square lumpia wrappers or spring roll wrappers
1½	quarts vegetable oil for frying

1. FOR THE DIPPING SAUCE Stir all ingredients together in bowl. Let stand at room temperature for at least 30 minutes to let flavors meld or refrigerate for up to 4 days.

2. FOR THE LUMPIA Process onion, carrot, celery, garlic, and ginger in food processor until finely chopped, scraping down sides of bowl as needed, about 20 seconds. Beat egg in small bowl until homogeneous. Add 2 tablespoons beaten egg to food processor, reserving remainder. Add pork, soy sauce, pepper, and salt and process until combined, scraping down sides of bowl as needed, 10 to 15 seconds. Transfer mixture to large heavy-duty zipper-lock bag and snip 1 corner to create 1-inch opening. Peel wrappers apart to separate; stack neatly and cover with very lightly dampened dish towel.

3. Place 1 wrapper on counter so 1 corner points to edge of counter. Pipe 5 by ¾-inch strip of filling parallel to counter, just below center of wrapper. Using pastry brush, apply light layer of egg wash onto upper 1½ inches of top

corner of wrapper, making sure to brush all the way to edges. Fold bottom corner of wrapper over filling and press gently along length of filling to remove air pockets. Fold side corners over to enclose filling snugly and gently roll to form tight cylinder. Transfer, egg-washed corner down, to rimmed baking sheet or large platter. (Do not stack.) Wipe any excess egg from counter and repeat with remaining wrappers and filling, filling two at a time if you feel comfortable with it. (Lumpia can be refrigerated in single layer in airtight container for up to 24 hours. Alternatively, freeze in single layer and then stack in airtight container and freeze for up to 1 month. Do not thaw before frying.)

4. Heat oil in Dutch oven over medium heat to 350 degrees. Set wire rack in rimmed baking sheet. Line rack with paper towels. Using tongs, transfer 6 lumpia to oil and fry, adjusting burner if necessary to maintain oil temperature of 340 to 360 degrees, until lumpia are golden brown, 5 to 7 minutes (frozen lumpia will take 1 to 2 minutes longer). Transfer to prepared rack. Repeat with remaining lumpia in 2 more batches. Let cool for at least 5 minutes before serving with dipping sauce.

Rolling Lumpia

PUT FILLING IN BAG
Load filling into large heavy-duty zipper-lock bag. Snip 1 corner to create 1-inch opening.

ADD FILLING TO WRAPPER
Pipe even 5 by ¾-inch strip of filling just below center of wrapper.

APPLY EGG WASH
Apply light layer of egg wash onto top corner of wrapper with pastry brush, making sure to brush all the way to edges.

FOLD AND PRESS OUT AIR
Fold bottom corner of wrapper over filling and gently press along length of filling to remove air pockets.

FOLD AND ROLL
Fold side corners over to enclose filling and gently roll to form tight cylinder.

KEYS TO SUCCESS

- **A tight roll:** Rolling up the filled wrappers tightly presses out any air pockets, which would cause the lumpia to float in the oil and cook unevenly.

- **Crisp shell:** These thin rolls get a raw pork filling, so deep-frying them in a Dutch oven cooks the pork while crisping up the lumpia wrappers.

CHAPTER 7

RICE, GRAINS, AND BEANS

COURSE

PILAF-STYLE RICE AND GRAINS

ANDREA GEARY

"Pilaf" is one of those words that refers both to the specific dish and to the cooking method used to achieve it, as demonstrated in this course. It draws together dishes from all over the world that employ the general pilaf technique of first sautéing aromatics and rice in fat, both to enhance flavor and to ensure that the grains cook up distinctly separate, never clumpy. As you'll see, this pilaf principle can also be applied to pasta and grains.

ANDREA'S PRO TIP: *Use this fun hack to reheat left-over rice pilaf: Spoon a portion of rice into a bowl, top it with an ice cube, and microwave until the rice is hot. Discard what's left of the ice and stir the rice gently before serving. (Microwaves can't directly heat up ice because the water is locked in a rigid crystal structure. As the waves heat up the remaining water in the rice, the heat from the rice warms up the surface of the ice cube, so it melts a little bit. Then that water released from the melting ice can be boiled by the microwave, so it turns to steam, and steams the rice.)*

THE METHOD
RICE PILAF

This pilaf method makes it easy to cook long-grain rice to light fluffiness. It uses less cooking liquid and tames the starchiness in the rice.

1 RINSE RICE
Rinse and drain rice to remove excess starch.

2 COOK ONION
Melt butter or heat oil in pan. Soften aromatics, such as onion and garlic.

3 SAUTÉ RICE
Add rice to pan and cook, stirring occasionally, until browned and aromatic.

4 USE LESS LIQUID
Add cooking liquid, cover, and bring to a boil. Reduce to a simmer and cook until liquid is absorbed.

5 STEAM OFF THE HEAT
Remove from heat, lay folded dish towel underneath lid, and let sit for 10 minutes. The dish towel absorbs excess moisture.

6 FLUFF AND SERVE
Fluff rice with fork to separate grains and serve.

RICE AND PASTA PILAF

Serves: 4 to 6
Total Time: 1¼ hours

RECIPE OVERVIEW This technique turns out buttery, perfectly cooked rice and pasta from the same pot. A fistful of pasta (usually vermicelli) is broken into short pieces and toasted in butter. Minced garlic and/or finely chopped onion is added, followed by long-grain rice. Once the grains are coated in fat, chicken broth is added and the pilaf is simmered. In a well-executed version, the cooked rice and pasta are tender and separate, boasting rich depth from the butter and nuttiness from the toasted noodles. But because of the different cooking times of rice and pasta, it's easy to end up with raw, crunchy rice and mushy pasta. The quicker-cooking vermicelli absorbs broth more rapidly than rice, thereby denying the rice sufficient liquid to cook through. To achieve uniform tenderness, the rice needs to be able to absorb broth at the same rate as the pasta. So rather than just rinsing it like we normally would for a pilaf, we soak the uncooked rice in hot tap water ahead of cooking, then rinse it a number times. This lets its starches absorb enough water so that the rice and pasta finish cooking at the same time with an ideal tender texture. Both long straight strands of vermicelli and coiled vermicelli nests will work in this recipe.

- 1½ **cups basmati or other long-grain white rice**
- 3 **tablespoons unsalted butter**
- 2 **ounces vermicelli, broken into 1-inch pieces**
- 1 **onion, grated**
- 1 **garlic clove, minced**
- 2½ **cups chicken broth**
- 1¼ **teaspoons table salt**
- 3 **tablespoons minced fresh parsley**

1. Place rice in medium bowl and cover with hot tap water by 2 inches; let stand for 15 minutes.

2. Using your hands, gently swish grains to release excess starch. Carefully pour off water, leaving rice in bowl. Add cold tap water to rice, then pour off water. Repeat adding and pouring off cold water 4 or 5 times, until water runs almost clear. Drain rice in fine-mesh strainer.

3. Melt butter in saucepan over medium heat. Add pasta and cook, stirring occasionally, until browned, about 3 minutes. Add onion and garlic and cook, stirring occasionally, until onion is softened but not browned, about 4 minutes. Add rice and cook, stirring occasionally, until edges of rice begin to turn translucent, about 3 minutes. Add broth and salt and bring to boil. Reduce heat to low, cover, and cook until all liquid is absorbed, about 10 minutes. Off heat, remove lid, fold dish towel in half, and place over saucepan; replace lid. Let stand for 10 minutes. Fluff rice with fork, stir in parsley, and serve.

Variations

HERBED RICE AND PASTA PILAF

Stir ¼ cup plain whole-milk yogurt, ¼ cup minced fresh dill, and ¼ cup minced fresh chives into pilaf with parsley.

RICE AND PASTA PILAF WITH GOLDEN RAISINS AND ALMONDS

Place ½ cup golden raisins in bowl and cover with boiling water by 1 inch. Let stand until plump, about 5 minutes. Drain and set aside. Add 2 bay leaves and 1 teaspoon ground cardamom to saucepan with broth. Just before serving, discard bay leaves. Stir in raisins and ½ cup slivered almonds, toasted and chopped coarse, with parsley.

RICE AND PASTA PILAF WITH POMEGRANATE AND WALNUTS

Omit onion and garlic. Add 2 tablespoons grated fresh ginger to saucepan with rice. Add ½ teaspoon ground cumin with broth. Omit parsley; instead, stir ½ cup walnuts, toasted and chopped coarse; ½ cup pomegranate seeds; ½ cup chopped fresh cilantro; and 1 tablespoon lemon juice into fluffed rice.

> ## KEYS TO SUCCESS
> - **Go beyond rinsing:** Soaking the rice in hot water hydrates it much more than just rinsing it, essentially giving it a jump start on cooking.
> - **Absorb steam:** A dish towel under the lid absorbs excess moisture, ensuring superfluffy results.

ARROZ CON TITOTÉ

Serves: 4
Total Time: 1 hour

RECIPE OVERVIEW Arroz con titoté, a tan-colored, brown-flecked coconut rice that is popular in beachside restaurants along the Caribbean coast of Colombia, is a knockout dish featuring a toasty aroma and a rich nutty flavor barely recognizable as coconut—a result of the unique treatment of the coconut milk. Here's how it works: Pour a can of coconut milk into a saucepan and boil it until all the water is gone, leaving only coconut oil and tiny particles of coconut solids. Then keep cooking until those solids darken to a toasty brown. Add the rice and coat well with the fat before stirring in water, brown sugar, salt, and raisins. Coating the rice grains with fat before adding the liquid is a classic pilaf strategy that ensures that the grains cook up separate and not gluey. And the browned coconut bits, which along with the rendered fat is known as titoté, imparts a rich toasty depth. The coconut solids may bond to the surface of your saucepan in step 2, but they will release as the rice cooks. The raisins heighten the dish's slight sweetness, while a spritz of lime, the traditional garnish, snaps all the flavors into focus—so don't omit the lime wedges.

1 (14-ounce) can coconut milk
1½ cups long-grain white rice
2¼ cups water, divided
⅓ cup raisins
2 tablespoons packed dark brown sugar
1 teaspoon table salt
Lime wedges

1. Pour coconut milk into large saucepan. Cover, leaving lid slightly ajar so steam can escape. Cook over medium-high heat, stirring occasionally, until coconut milk is reduced by about three-quarters and begins to sputter, 10 to 12 minutes. While coconut milk cooks, place rice in fine-mesh strainer set over bowl. Rinse under running water, swishing with your hands, until water runs clear. Drain thoroughly.

2. Reduce heat to medium. Uncover saucepan and cook, stirring frequently, until fat separates from coconut solids, about 2 minutes. Continue to cook, stirring frequently, until coconut solids turn deep brown (solids will stick to saucepan), about 3 minutes longer. Add rice and cook, stirring constantly, until grains are well coated with fat. Stir in ½ cup water (mixture may sputter) and scrape bottom and sides of saucepan with wooden spoon to loosen coconut solids. Stir in raisins, sugar, salt, and remaining 1¾ cups water. Bring mixture to boil. Adjust heat to maintain low simmer. Cover and cook until all liquid is absorbed, 18 to 20 minutes.

3. Remove saucepan from heat and let sit, covered, for 10 minutes. Mix rice gently but thoroughly and transfer to serving bowl. Serve with lime wedges.

KEYS TO SUCCESS

- **Pure, full-fat coconut milk:** The label should list only coconut and water. Brands with additives won't separate into fats and solids, and low-fat coconut milk doesn't have enough fat.

- **Have patience:** The oil will eventually separate out after the coconut milk reduces. Let the coconut solids get dark before adding the rice.

SCIENCE LESSON Coaxing Nutty Flavor from Coconut Milk

The fruity aroma and vanilla-like flavor of coconut milk come from volatile compounds called lactones. Simmering the milk causes some of the lactones to dissipate, but enough remain to make dishes taste coconutty. But simmering the milk until its water evaporates, the oil separates out, and the coconut solids brown drives off lactones and creates nutty, buttery flavor compounds. Some of these (pyrazines, pyrroles, and furans) are also found in true nuts such as pecans or almonds.

WILD RICE PILAF WITH PECANS AND DRIED CRANBERRIES

Serves: 6 to 8
Total Time: 1½ hours

RECIPE OVERVIEW Wild rice is tricky to cook: Sometimes it can turn out undercooked and difficult to chew, other times the rice can be overcooked and gluey. This method gets you properly cooked wild rice every time, presented in a delicious pilaf with long-grain white rice, aromatics, dried fruit, and nuts. The key is to cook the white rice pilaf-style, with onions, carrots, cranberries, and herbs, but slowly simmer the wild rice separately in plenty of liquid. Be sure to stop the cooking process and drain the wild rice at just the right moment by checking for doneness every couple of minutes past the 35-minute mark. For the simmering liquid, we use chicken broth—its mild yet rich profile tempers the wild rice's muddy flavor to a pleasant earthiness and affirms its subdued nuttiness. Just before serving, add the cooked wild rice to the mix and toss everything together for a winning pilaf.

1¾ cups chicken broth
2½ cups water, divided
2 bay leaves
8 sprigs fresh thyme, divided into 2 bundles, each tied together with kitchen twine
1 cup wild rice, rinsed and drained
1½ cups long-grain white rice, rinsed and drained
3 tablespoons unsalted butter
1 medium onion, minced
2 carrots, peeled and chopped fine
1 teaspoon table salt
¾ cup sweetened or unsweetened dried cranberries
¾ cup pecans, toasted and chopped coarse
1½ tablespoons minced fresh parsley leaves
Ground black pepper

1. Bring chicken broth, ¼ cup water, bay leaves, and 1 bundle thyme to boil in medium saucepan over medium-high heat. Add wild rice, cover, and reduce heat to low; simmer until rice is plump and tender and has absorbed most of liquid, 35 to 45 minutes. Drain rice in fine-mesh strainer. Return rice to saucepan; cover to keep warm and set aside.

2. Meanwhile, place white rice in medium bowl and add water to cover by 2 inches; gently swish grains to release excess starch. Carefully pour off water, leaving rice in bowl. Repeat 4 or 5 times, until water runs almost clear. Drain rice in fine-mesh strainer.

3. Melt butter in medium saucepan over medium-high heat. Add onion, carrots, and salt; cook, stirring frequently, until softened but not browned, about 4 minutes. Stir in rinsed white rice until coated with butter; cook, stirring frequently, until grains begin to turn translucent, about 3 minutes. Meanwhile, bring remaining 2¼ cups water to boil in small saucepan. Add boiling water and second thyme bundle to white rice and return to boil. Reduce heat to low, sprinkle cranberries evenly over rice, and cover. Simmer until all liquid is absorbed, 16 to 18 minutes. Remove saucepan from heat and let sit, covered, for 10 minutes. Fluff wild and white rice with fork and discard bay leaves and thyme bundles.

4. Combine wild rice, white rice mixture, pecans, and parsley in large bowl; toss with rubber spatula until evenly mixed. Season with salt and pepper to taste and serve.

KEY TO SUCCESS

- **Mind the timer:** Wild rice quickly goes from tough to pasty, so begin testing the rice at the 35-minute mark and drain the rice as soon as it is tender.

Carrots Two Ways

Carrots are as important to plov as the meat (the ratio is almost 1:1). To give them even more prominence, we use them in two ways. First, we grate the largest carrot and add it with the aromatics so that its earthy sweetness flavors the dish. Then we cut the others into chunky batons that we add in the last phase of cooking so that they retain their shape and add pops of color.

Shreds
Flavor cooking liquid

Batons
Retain their shape and add texture when stirred in during last phase of cooking

PLOV

Serves: 4
Total Time: 2¾ hours

RECIPE OVERVIEW Uzbekistan's celebratory rice pilaf is presented piled high on a platter for maximum effect. Onions, carrots, and spices are sautéed, then chunks of beef or lamb go into the pot, with water added to almost cover the meat. A head of garlic is placed in the center and everything is cooked over moderate heat until the meat is nearly tender. Then, cooks typically smooth long-grain rice into an even layer over the stew and crank up the heat, bringing the liquid to a hard boil so that it is forced through the rice to flavor it without disturbing the distinct layers. Last, the heat is lowered to let the rice finish cooking. And therein lies the challenge: The meat must turn tender at the exact time the rice is cooked and the moisture has been absorbed, leaving the pot neither scorched nor flooded. To achieve this, we braise the meat separately and add it to the rice at the end of cooking. Instead of cranking the heat, we stir the rice into the stew and gently simmer so that it cooks more slowly. If barberries are unavailable, combine 2 tablespoons dried currants and 1 tablespoon lemon juice in a small bowl. Microwave, covered, until very steamy, about 1 minute. Add the currants and juice as directed. Diners can mix individual cloves of the garlic into their pilaf.

5 carrots, peeled
1 pound boneless beef short ribs, trimmed
1½ teaspoons table salt, divided
1 tablespoon vegetable oil
2 onions, quartered through root end and sliced ¼ inch thick
2 tablespoons dried barberries, divided
3 garlic cloves, minced, plus 1 head garlic, outer papery skin removed and top ½ inch cut off
1 tablespoon ground cumin
2 teaspoons ground coriander
½ teaspoon pepper
1¾ cups water
1 cup basmati rice, rinsed and drained
2 scallions, sliced thin

1. Adjust oven rack to middle position and heat oven to 350 degrees. Grate largest carrot. Cut remaining 4 carrots into 2 by ½-inch pieces.

2. Pat beef dry with paper towels and sprinkle all over with ½ teaspoon salt. Heat oil in large ovensafe saucepan over medium-high heat until shimmering. Add beef and cook until well browned on all sides, 10 to 12 minutes. Using tongs, transfer beef to bowl.

3. Add onions and remaining 1 teaspoon salt to saucepan. Cover and cook, stirring occasionally and scraping up any browned bits, until onions are soft, about 5 minutes. Add grated carrot, 1 tablespoon barberries, minced garlic, cumin, coriander, and pepper and cook, stirring constantly, until garlic and spices are fragrant, 1 to 2 minutes. Spread

mixture into even layer. Return beef to saucepan, nestling it into vegetables. Add water and any accumulated beef juices. Place garlic head in center of saucepan. Increase heat to high and bring mixture to vigorous simmer. Remove saucepan from heat; place large sheet of aluminum foil over saucepan, crimp tightly to seal, and cover tightly with lid. Transfer saucepan to oven and cook until meat is fork tender, 1¼ to 1½ hours.

4. Transfer beef and garlic head to cutting board. Stir rice and remaining carrots into cooking liquid (saucepan handle will be hot). Bring to simmer over medium heat. Adjust heat to maintain simmer; replace foil, cover, and cook until liquid level has dropped below rice and rice is half cooked, about 10 minutes. While rice cooks, cut beef into ½-inch cubes. Gently fold beef into rice mixture, making sure to incorporate rice on bottom of saucepan. Replace foil, cover, and continue to cook until rice is tender and moisture is fully absorbed, 10 to 15 minutes longer. (Check rice every 5 minutes by sliding butter knife to bottom of center of saucepan and gently pushing rice aside; if bottom appears to be drying out, reduce heat slightly.)

5. Pile pilaf on platter. Sprinkle with scallions and remaining 1 tablespoon barberries. Garnish with garlic head and serve.

KEYS TO SUCCESS

- **Seal the pot**: Before transferring the beef and vegetables to the oven, cover the pot tightly with foil so that every bit of the flavorful cooking liquid is retained during braising.

- **Seal the pot again**: Be sure to tightly crimp the foil again when simmering the rice on the stovetop.

- **Gentle braise**: A long oven braise makes for more even heat, encouraging even evaporation of the liquid and perfectly tender rice.

CORE TECHNIQUE

Sealing the Pot with Foil

The rice in plov is cooked via the absorption method, which means there is just enough liquid in the pot to hydrate and gel the rice's starch. But a lid that doesn't provide a perfect seal can allow too much liquid to escape, leaving some of the grains dry and hard. Crimping a sheet of aluminum foil over the pot before topping it with the lid controls evaporation better, ensuring that every bit of the flavorful cooking liquid is retained and absorbed into the rice.

OAT BERRY PILAF WITH WALNUTS AND GORGONZOLA

Serves: 4 to 6
Total Time: 1¼ hours

RECIPE OVERVIEW Whole grains can get the pilaf treatment, too. While we think of oats mostly in cut or rolled form as part of a wholesome breakfast, oat berries (sometimes called oat groats) have a pleasant chewy texture and hearty, mildly nutty flavor that bring a new dimension to pilafs. Oat berries are whole oats that have been hulled and cleaned but not processed. (Other forms of oat are processed further, such as being ground, cut, or rolled flat.) Because they haven't been processed, oat berries retain a high nutritional value and take longer to cook than other types of oats. Thanks to their naturally nutty flavor, there's actually no need to toast them before using them in a pilaf, as you would with rice or other grains. Here, we add water and oat berries to a saucepan after sautéing minced shallot. Creamy, pungent Gorgonzola makes a nice balance to the earthy oat berries' flavor, and waiting to sprinkle the cheese over the oat berries just before serving prevents the pilaf from becoming too thick. The addition of tart dried cherries and tangy balsamic vinegar cut through the richness, while parsley gives the pilaf freshness.

1	tablespoon extra-virgin olive oil
1	shallot, minced
2	cups water
1½	cups oat berries (groats), rinsed and drained
¼	teaspoon table salt
¾	cup walnuts, toasted and chopped
½	cup dried cherries
2	tablespoons minced fresh parsley
1	tablespoon balsamic vinegar
2	ounces Gorgonzola cheese, crumbled (½ cup)

1. Heat oil in large saucepan over medium heat until shimmering. Add shallot and cook, stirring occasionally, until softened, about 2 minutes. Stir in water, oat berries, and salt and bring to simmer. Reduce heat to low, cover, and continue to simmer until oat berries are tender but still slightly chewy, 30 to 40 minutes.

2. Remove pot from heat and lay clean folded dish towel underneath lid. Let sit for 10 minutes. Fluff oat berries with fork and fold in walnuts, cherries, and parsley. Drizzle with vinegar. Transfer pilaf to serving bowl. Sprinkle Gorgonzola over top and season with salt and pepper to taste. Serve.

LAYERED GRAIN AND RICE DISHES

JOSEPH GITTER

Layering grains or rice with other ingredients can make for impressive multitextured dishes. And sometimes the grain itself can be formed into distinct layers during the cooking process, as with the paella and bibimbap dishes in this course, which are simply showstopping. We know that grains and rice are important everyday staples in most cuisines of the world, but as you'll see here, they also hold a place of honor when it comes to making more celebratory dishes and special-occasion party food.

JOE'S PRO TIP: *While you can buy preserved lemons, it's really worth making your own - they're almost incomparable. They work beautifully in vinaigrettes, salads, on seafood, and blitzed into a mayonnaise. Experiment with other citrus and use them interchangeably. I currently have jars of preserved Meyer lemons, key limes, and kumquats in my fridge.*

CHICKEN AND SPICED FREEKEH WITH CILANTRO AND PRESERVED LEMON

Serves: 4 to 6
Total Time: 1½ hours

RECIPE OVERVIEW Freekeh, also known as frikeh and farik, is made from green durum wheat that is roasted and rubbed to create its flavor and texture. This whole grain is often paired with chicken in the Middle East, especially in Lebanon. Freekeh's distinctly toasty flavors play well with both rich spices (like the smoked paprika and intensely floral cardamom) and bright preserved lemon. Here, we layer it with chicken thighs, making for a satiating meal. We first brown the chicken pieces in a Dutch oven, then remove them to cook aromatics and add the broth and freekeh. The thighs are placed on top of the grains and the pot goes into the oven to bake. To serve, we shred the chicken, add it back to the freekeh, and stir in cilantro and toasted pistachios for grassy notes along with a satisfying crunch. The fragrant preserved lemon is an important addition to this dish, so we don't recommend omitting it. Its bright, ultralemony flavor, balanced by brininess and sourness, adds great interest to stews, salad dressings, cooked grains, sautéed vegetables, and more. Look for cracked freekeh that is roughly the size of steel-cut oats.

4	(5- to 7-ounce) bone-in chicken thighs, trimmed
½	teaspoon table salt
¼	teaspoon pepper
1	tablespoon extra-virgin olive oil, plus extra for drizzling
1	onion, chopped fine
4	garlic cloves, minced
1½	teaspoons smoked paprika
¼	teaspoon ground cardamom
¼	teaspoon red pepper flakes
2¼	cups chicken broth
1½	cups cracked freekeh, rinsed
¼	cup plus 2 tablespoons chopped fresh cilantro, divided
½	cup shelled unsalted pistachios, toasted and chopped
2	tablespoons rinsed and minced Preserved Lemons (recipe follows)

1. Adjust oven rack to lower-middle position and heat oven to 350 degrees. Pat chicken thighs dry with paper towels and sprinkle with salt and pepper. Heat oil in Dutch oven over medium-high heat until just smoking. Add chicken and cook until well browned, 8 to 10 minutes.

2. Transfer chicken to plate and discard skin. Add onion to fat left in pot and cook over medium heat until softened, about 5 minutes. Stir in garlic, paprika, cardamom, and pepper flakes and cook until fragrant, about 30 seconds. Stir in broth, scraping up any browned bits, then stir in freekeh.

3. Nestle chicken into freekeh mixture and add any accumulated juices. Cover, transfer pot to oven, and cook until freekeh is tender and chicken registers 195 degrees, 35 to 40 minutes.

4. Remove pot from oven. Transfer chicken to cutting board, let cool slightly, then shred into bite-size pieces using 2 forks; discard bones.

5. Meanwhile, gently fluff freekeh with fork. Lay clean dish towel over pot, replace lid, and let sit for 5 minutes. Stir in chicken, ¼ cup cilantro, pistachios, and preserved lemon. Season with salt and pepper to taste. Sprinkle with remaining 2 tablespoons cilantro and drizzle with extra oil. Serve.

PRESERVED LEMONS

Makes: 4 preserved lemons

Once preserved in salt, lemon becomes an almost completely different ingredient. The rind becomes soft and aromatic and can be sliced thin or minced before adding to a dish. Look for Meyer lemons from August through March; regular lemons can be substituted. Wash, scrub, and dry the lemons well before preserving them. You will need a 1-quart glass jar with a tight-fitting lid for this recipe.

12 lemons, preferably Meyer
½ cup kosher salt

1. Wash and dry 4 lemons. Cut lengthwise into quarters, stopping 1 inch from bottom so lemons stay intact at base. Juice remaining 8 lemons to yield 1½ cups juice; set aside any extra juice.

2. Gently stretch 1 cut lemon open and pour 2 tablespoons salt into center. Working over bowl, gently rub cut surfaces of lemon together, then place lemon in 1-quart jar. Repeat with remaining cut lemons and remaining salt. Add any accumulated salt and juice in bowl to jar.

3. Pour 1½ cups lemon juice into jar and press gently to submerge lemons. (Add reserved extra juice to jar as needed to cover lemons completely.) Cover jar tightly with lid and shake. Refrigerate lemons, shaking jar once per day for first 4 days to redistribute salt and juice. Let lemons cure in refrigerator until glossy and softened, 6 to 8 weeks. (Preserved lemons can be refrigerated for at least 6 months.)

4. To use, cut off desired amount of preserved lemon. If desired, use knife to remove pulp and white pith from rind before using.

> ### KEY TO SUCCESS
> • **Cracked freekeh:** Buy cracked, not whole, freekeh, which will not cook through in time.

FARRO AND BROCCOLI RABE GRATIN

Serves: 4 to 6
Total Time: 1¼ hours

RECIPE OVERVIEW The tender chew and robust nuttiness of farro bring great personality to this gratin. Many gratins trade on the richness of dairy to create creaminess, but this one gets its magic from white miso. Added to the cooking liquid, it combines with the starch released by the simmering farro to create a lush, silky sauce that adds body and lightly binds all the ingredients. We first sauté onion in olive oil, then toast the farro in the oil to enhance its whole-grain nuttiness. We then simmer the grains in water, vegetable broth, and white miso until just tender. Next, we blanch broccoli rabe to tame its bite and lock in its vibrant color before sautéing it with garlic and red pepper flakes. White beans and sun-dried tomatoes add pops of sweet flavor. Last, we layer on a topping of toasted panko bread crumbs and Parmesan, which crisps up under the broiler.

3 tablespoons extra-virgin olive oil, divided
1 onion, chopped fine
¼ teaspoon table salt, plus salt for cooking broccoli rabe
1½ cups whole farro
2½ cups water
2 cups vegetable broth
2 tablespoons white miso
½ cup panko bread crumbs
¼ cup grated Parmesan cheese
1 pound broccoli rabe, trimmed and cut into 2-inch pieces
6 garlic cloves, minced
⅛ teaspoon red pepper flakes
1 (15-ounce) can small white beans or navy beans, rinsed
¾ cup oil-packed sun-dried tomatoes, chopped

1. Heat 1 tablespoon oil in large saucepan over medium heat until shimmering. Add onion and salt and cook until softened and lightly browned, 5 to 7 minutes. Stir in farro and cook, stirring occasionally, until lightly toasted, about 2 minutes. Stir in water, broth, and miso and bring to simmer. Cook, stirring often, until farro is just tender and remaining liquid has thickened into creamy sauce, 25 to 35 minutes.

2. Meanwhile, toss panko with 1 tablespoon oil in bowl and microwave, stirring occasionally, until golden brown, 1 to 2 minutes. Stir in Parmesan and set aside.

3. Bring 4 quarts water to boil in Dutch oven. Add broccoli rabe and 1 tablespoon salt and cook until just tender, about 2 minutes. Drain broccoli rabe and set aside. Combine remaining 1 tablespoon oil, garlic, and pepper flakes in now-empty pot and cook over medium heat until fragrant and sizzling, 1 to 2 minutes. Stir in reserved broccoli rabe and cook until hot and well coated, about 2 minutes. Off heat, stir in beans, tomatoes, and farro mixture. Season with salt and pepper to taste.

4. Adjust oven rack 10 inches from broiler element and heat broiler. Transfer bean-farro mixture to broiler-safe 3-quart gratin dish (or broiler-safe 13 by 9-inch baking dish) and sprinkle with reserved panko mixture. Broil until lightly browned and hot, 1 to 2 minutes. Serve.

KEY TO SUCCESS
- **Whole farro:** Be sure to use whole farro, not pearl, quick-cooking, or presteamed farro.

CHICKEN BIRYANI
Serves: 6
Total Time: 1½ hours

RECIPE OVERVIEW In a classic chicken biryani, spiced basmati rice is lavished with butter, studded with dried fruit and nuts, and layered with sauced bone-in chicken; it's all baked together before being topped with deep-fried onions and fresh herbs. For our version, we use chunks of boneless chicken thighs. We sauté the onion in butter rather than deep-frying it, then brown the chicken in the same skillet and stir in garam masala, ginger, garlic, and chile, followed by whole-milk yogurt to add moisture. Finally, rather than partially cooking the rice up front and then steaming it to doneness later—which can make it hard to get perfectly cooked rice—we cook it through in water spiced with cinnamon and cumin and then steam it briefly with the chicken at the end. We stir a fistful of dried currants into the cooked rice and pour over the butter from sautéing the onion. After spooning the flavorful rice on top of the chicken in the pan, we add saffron (bloomed in a little warm water), and then cover and steam it before adding the garnishes of fried onion, fresh mint and cilantro, and an herby yogurt sauce. To make this dish spicier, include the jalapeño seeds. You can substitute long-grain white rice for the basmati, but it will be less fluffy. Cook it for about 12 minutes in step 3.

Garnish and Yogurt Sauce
- ½ teaspoon saffron threads, crumbled
- 3 tablespoons warm water
- 1 cup plain whole-milk yogurt
- 2 tablespoons chopped fresh cilantro
- 2 tablespoons chopped fresh mint
- 1 garlic clove, minced
- ¼ teaspoon table salt
- ¼ teaspoon pepper

Biryani
- 6 tablespoons unsalted butter
- 2 cups thinly sliced onion
- 1¼ teaspoons table salt, divided, plus salt for cooking rice
- 1 cinnamon stick
- 2 teaspoons cumin seeds
- 2 cups basmati rice
- ⅓ cup dried currants
- 2 pounds boneless, skinless chicken thighs, trimmed and cut into 1½-inch chunks
- ½ teaspoon pepper
- 1 jalapeño chile, stemmed, seeded, and minced
- 1 tablespoon grated fresh ginger
- 1 tablespoon garam masala
- 3 garlic cloves, minced
- ½ cup plain whole-milk yogurt
- 2 tablespoons chopped fresh mint
- 2 tablespoons chopped fresh cilantro

1. **FOR THE GARNISH AND SAUCE** Combine saffron and water in bowl and set aside. Combine yogurt, cilantro, mint, garlic, salt, and pepper in second bowl and set aside.

2. **FOR THE BIRYANI** Set fine-mesh strainer in medium bowl. Melt butter in 12-inch nonstick skillet over medium heat. Add onion and cook, stirring often, until dark brown, 11 to 14 minutes. Transfer onion to prepared strainer and press with spatula to squeeze out excess butter (reserve butter). Spread onion on small plate and sprinkle with ¼ teaspoon salt. Set aside onion and butter (do not wash skillet).

3. Meanwhile, bring 12 cups water, cinnamon stick, and cumin seeds to boil in large saucepan over high heat. Add rice and 1 tablespoon salt and cook, stirring occasionally, until tender, about 10 minutes. Drain rice in fine-mesh strainer. Return rice to saucepan and stir in currants, reserved butter, and ¼ teaspoon salt; cover and set aside.

4. Combine chicken, pepper, and remaining ¾ teaspoon salt in now-empty skillet and cook over medium-high heat until browned and cooked through, about 10 minutes. Stir in jalapeño, ginger, garam masala, and garlic and cook until fragrant, about 1 minute. Off heat, stir in yogurt until combined.

5. Spoon rice over chicken mixture and spread into even layer. Drizzle saffron water evenly over rice, spiraling in from edge of skillet to center. Cover skillet, return to medium heat, and cook until heated through and steam escapes from under lid, about 5 minutes. Off heat, sprinkle biryani with reserved fried onion, mint, and cilantro. Serve with yogurt sauce.

KEYS TO SUCCESS

- **Drain the rice:** Drain the simmered rice well to avoid adding too much moisture to the finished dish.

- **Really brown those onions:** To get the sliced onion to express all its depth and sweetness, you need to sauté it past the "golden brown" stage until it turns fully dark brown.

PAELLA DE VERDURAS

Serves: 4
Total Time: 1¼ hours

RECIPE OVERVIEW Spanish paella is a historically flexible dish, ranging from the Valencian classic studded with snails, rabbit, and garrofón (the broad, white shell bean native to the region) to the dramatic arroz a la marinera teeming with shellfish to Grilled Paella (page 501). That flexibility is even more evident in paella de verduras. This approach to the beloved rice dish elevates the vegetables to showcase levels rather than relegating them to background status. It can go in countless directions based on locally available produce and personal taste. This hearty version features green and butter beans—tributes to the vegetables Valencians often add—plus chunky cauliflower florets. Making great paella is fundamentally about flavoring the rice, so in lieu of the meaty fond that lends a savory backbone to paellas containing meat, poultry, or seafood, here we retool a Spanish sofrito to make a complex flavor base. We brown bell pepper instead of just sautéing it, swap in umami-rich tomato paste for fresh tomato, load up on the garlic, and omit the sweet-tasting onion. Then we mix in smoked paprika, saffron, and nutty-tasting dry sherry for brightness and depth. To ensure that the rice at the surface cooks through, we cover the pan for part of the cooking time to trap moist heat, which hydrates the grains. Continuing to cook the rice after the liquid in the pan evaporates creates the caramelized, crisp-chewy layer on the bottom called a socarrat that adds even more complexity (it will sizzle and pop). Letting the paella rest for a few minutes before serving helps the socarrat layer firm up so that it turns even crispier and releases easily from the pan. If neither Spanish short-grain Calasparra nor Bomba rice is available, you can use arborio rice. For a vegetarian dish, use vegetable broth instead of chicken. It's worth seeking out butter beans for their large size; do not substitute small white beans.

3	tablespoons extra-virgin olive oil, divided
2½	cups 2- to 2½-inch cauliflower florets
¾	teaspoon table salt, divided
6	ounces green beans, trimmed and cut into 2- to 2½-inch pieces
1	red bell pepper, stemmed, seeded, and chopped fine
1	tablespoon tomato paste
3	garlic cloves, minced
1	teaspoon smoked paprika
¼	teaspoon saffron threads, crumbled
¼	cup dry sherry
1	cup Calasparra or Bomba rice
1	(15-ounce) can butter beans, rinsed
3½	cups chicken broth
	Lemon wedges (optional)

1. Heat 1½ tablespoons oil in 12-inch skillet over medium heat until shimmering. Add cauliflower and ¼ teaspoon salt and cook, stirring frequently, until cauliflower is spotty brown, 3 to 5 minutes. Add green beans and ¼ teaspoon salt. Continue to cook, stirring frequently, until green beans are dark green, 2 to 4 minutes longer. Transfer vegetables to bowl.

2. Heat remaining 1½ tablespoons oil in now-empty skillet over medium heat until shimmering. Add bell pepper and remaining ¼ teaspoon salt and cook, stirring occasionally, until bell pepper starts to brown, 7 to 10 minutes. Add tomato paste and cook, stirring constantly, until bell pepper pieces are coated in tomato paste, about 1 minute. Add garlic, paprika, and saffron and cook, stirring constantly, until fragrant, about 30 seconds. Stir in sherry and cook,

stirring frequently, until excess moisture has evaporated and bell pepper mixture forms large clumps, 1 to 2 minutes.

3. Add rice and stir until very well combined. Off heat, smooth into even layer. Scatter butter beans evenly over rice. Scatter cauliflower and green beans evenly over butter beans. Gently pour broth all over, making sure rice is fully submerged (it's OK if parts of vegetables aren't submerged).

4. Bring to boil over high heat. Adjust heat to maintain gentle simmer and cook until broth is just below top of rice, 12 to 17 minutes. Cover and cook until rice is cooked through, about 5 minutes. Uncover and cook until rice pops and sizzles and all excess moisture has evaporated (to test, use butter knife to gently push aside some rice and vegetables), 3 to 7 minutes. (If socarrat is desired, continue to cook, rotating skillet quarter turn every 20 seconds, until rice on bottom of skillet is well browned and slightly crusty [use butter knife to test], 2 to 5 minutes longer.) Let rest off heat for 5 minutes. Serve, passing lemon wedges separately, if using.

KEYS TO SUCCESS

- **Evenly cooked rice:** For rice that is neither blown out nor al dente, cover the pan for part of the cooking time. This traps moist heat that helps hydrate the grains of rice at the surface.

- **Crisp-chewy socarrat:** Continuing to cook the rice after the liquid in the pan has evaporated creates a caramelized, crisp-chewy layer that adds even more complexity.

WHAT CAN GO WRONG

PROBLEM The socarrat is soggy.

SOLUTION Socarrat benefits from a brief rest before serving. This allows the starch, which is flexible when the rice is hot, to crystallize and become rigid, so the socarrat crisps and easily releases from the pan. Think of a freshly baked cookie straight from the oven—right off the baking sheet, it's limp, but once it cools a bit, it firms up.

VEGETABLE BIBIMBAP WITH NURUNGJI

Serves: 6

Total Time: 1½ hours, plus 30 minutes chilling

RECIPE OVERVIEW Bibimbap is a classic Korean dish composed of tender-chewy short-grain rice with an array of garnishes, including sautéed vegetables, sometimes meat, and a fried egg. Bibim means "mixed," bap means "rice," and a dolsot is the heavy single-serving stone bowl in which the bibimbap is traditionally assembled. While bibimbap is widely served today, one of its theories of origin is that it was ceremonial food to honor ancestors. In the traditional preparation method, the dolsot is heated and then coated with sesame oil so the soft rice sizzles when it's piled in. While the garnishes are arranged on top, the heat retained in the stone crisps the bottom layer of rice, forming a browned crust called a nurungji. Our version of this dish takes some liberties, making it family-style in a large Dutch oven and paring back on the number of garnishes. Korean cooks use short-grain white rice because its clingy surface helps it form a more cohesive crust than smooth long-grain rice would. The primary component of the sauce is gochujang, along with toasted sesame oil and a bit of sugar. This version skips the meat, and for the vegetable garnishes, we use chopped spinach, shredded carrots, and sliced shiitake mushrooms, sautéing them sequentially in a skillet so that each cooks evenly and seasoning each batch with soy sauce, sugar, garlic, and scallions. We also make some pungent quick-pickled vegetables to top the bibimbap. (If you like, you can use store-bought kimchi instead.) To make sure everyone gets substantial pieces of crust, we mix the bibimbap in two stages, first combining the vegetables, eggs, and soft rice and then digging deep and scraping up the crust in big pieces that stay crunchy. You can prepare the pickles, chile sauce, and vegetables a day ahead of time (warm the vegetables to room temperature in the microwave before adding them to the rice). For a true bibimbap experience, bring the whole pot to the table before stirring the vegetables into the rice in step 10.

Pickles

 1 cup cider vinegar

 2 tablespoons sugar

1½ teaspoons table salt

 4 ounces (2 cups) bean sprouts

 1 cucumber, peeled, quartered lengthwise, seeded, and sliced thin on bias

Chile Sauce

¼ cup gochujang

 3 tablespoons water

 2 tablespoons toasted sesame oil

 1 teaspoon sugar

Rice

2½ cups short-grain white rice
2½ cups water
¾ teaspoon table salt

Vegetables

½ cup water
3 scallions, minced
3 tablespoons soy sauce
3 garlic cloves, minced
1 tablespoon sugar
1 tablespoon vegetable oil
3 carrots, peeled and shredded (2 cups)
8 ounces shiitake mushrooms, stemmed, caps sliced thin
1 (10-ounce) bag curly-leaf spinach, stemmed and chopped coarse

Bibimbap

2 tablespoons plus 2 teaspoons vegetable oil
1 tablespoon toasted sesame oil
4 large eggs

1. FOR THE PICKLES Whisk vinegar, sugar, and salt together in medium bowl. Add bean sprouts and cucumber and toss to combine. Gently press on vegetables to submerge. Cover and refrigerate for at least 30 minutes or up to 24 hours.

2. FOR THE CHILE SAUCE Whisk all ingredients together in small bowl. Cover and set aside.

3. FOR THE RICE Bring rice, water, and salt to boil in medium saucepan over high heat. Cover, reduce heat to low, and cook for 7 minutes. Remove saucepan from heat and let sit, covered, until rice is tender, about 15 minutes.

4. FOR THE VEGETABLES While rice cooks, stir together water, scallions, soy sauce, garlic, and sugar. Heat 1 teaspoon oil in Dutch oven over high heat until shimmering.

5. Add carrots and stir until coated. Add ⅓ cup scallion mixture and cook, stirring frequently, until carrots are slightly softened and moisture has evaporated, 1 to 2 minutes. Using slotted spoon, transfer carrots to small bowl.

6. Heat 1 teaspoon oil in now-empty pot until shimmering. Add mushrooms and stir until coated with oil. Add ⅓ cup scallion mixture and cook, stirring frequently, until mushrooms are tender and moisture has evaporated, 3 to 4 minutes. Using slotted spoon, transfer mushrooms to second small bowl.

7. Heat remaining 1 teaspoon oil in now-empty pot until shimmering. Add spinach and remaining ⅓ cup scallion mixture and stir to coat spinach. Cook, stirring frequently, until spinach is completely wilted but still bright green, 1 to 2 minutes. Using slotted spoon, transfer spinach to third small bowl. Discard any remaining liquid and wipe pot clean with paper towels.

8. FOR THE BIBIMBAP Heat 2 tablespoons vegetable oil and sesame oil in now-empty pot over high heat until shimmering. Carefully add cooked rice and gently press into even layer. Cook, without stirring, until rice begins to form crust on bottom of pot, about 2 minutes. Using slotted spoon, transfer carrots, spinach, and mushrooms to pot and arrange in piles that cover surface of rice. Reduce heat to low.

9. While crust forms, heat remaining 2 teaspoons vegetable oil in 10-inch nonstick skillet over low heat for 5 minutes. Crack eggs into small bowl. Pour eggs into skillet; cover and cook (about 2 minutes for runny yolks, 2½ minutes for soft but set yolks, and 3 minutes for firmly set yolks). Slide eggs onto vegetables in pot.

10. Drizzle 2 tablespoons chile sauce over eggs. Without disturbing crust, use wooden spoon to stir rice, vegetables, and eggs until combined. Just before serving, scrape large pieces of crust from bottom of pot and stir into rice. Serve in individual bowls, passing pickles and remaining chile sauce separately.

KEYS TO SUCCESS

- **Achieve the nurungji:** For the best crust, use an enameled cast-iron Dutch oven.
- **Two-stage mixing:** Using a wooden spoon to stir the soft portion of rice, vegetables, and eggs together, and only then scraping large pieces of the crust from the bottom of the pot, ensures that everyone gets substantial pieces of the crunchy crust.

THE SCIENCE OF RICE

All rice starts as brown rice, which is made up of the endosperm, germ, aleurone, bran, and hull or husk. Brown rices have simply been hulled and cleaned; since their bran layers are intact, they take longer to cook, boast nuttier flavor and more distinct chew, and cook up less sticky and/or creamy compared with equivalent white varieties. White rices are hulled and milled to remove the bran, aleurone, and germ.

THE LONG AND SHORT OF IT

The categories of long-grain, medium-grain, and short-grain rice are defined based on the grains' length-to-width ratio and are somewhat flexible. For example, you will variously see arborio referred to as either medium-grain or short-grain. These differences in categorization can be attributed to farmers growing different genetic strains of rice varieties. The length-to-width ratio and the starch composition determine whether the rice cooks up fluffy or sticky, tender or chewy, or somewhere in between.

STARCHES IN RICE

Rice contains two different starches, in varying proportions depending on the variety. Their relative amounts determine the texture of the cooked rice. Amylose is a straight molecule that organizes into a tight formation, helping each grain stay distinct and firm when cooked. Amylopectin has molecules with bushy branches that prevent it from organizing tidily, making the cooked rice clingier and stickier. Long-grain rices tend to have a higher proportion of amylose, while shorter-grain rices have a higher percentage of amylopectin.

Long-Grain includes conventional white and brown varieties, including the Carolina Gold cultivar, as well as basmati and jasmine rices
Starch about 22% amylose, 78% amylopectin
Typical Uses steamed, pilafs, puddings, biryani, fried rice

Medium-Grain includes conventional white and brown varieties and specialty rice cultivars such as arborio, carnaroli, and Valencia, as well as black (purple) rice varieties
Starch about 18% amylose, 82% amylopectin
Typical Uses risotto, paella, brothy rice dishes

Short-Grain includes conventional short-grain white and brown varieties and sushi rices, including the Calrose cultivar
Starch about 15% amylose, 85% amylopectin
Typical Uses sushi, rice bowls, fried rice

WHEN—AND WHEN NOT— TO RINSE RICE

Rinsing white rice removes excess surface starch that would otherwise absorb water and swell, causing the grains to stick together. Brown rice has its bran layer intact, so there is little to no exterior starch to wash away.
DO rinse for pilaf, steamed rice, and rice salads, where you want separate, distinct grains.
DON'T rinse for applications such as risotto or rice pudding; rinsing compromises the desirably creamy, sticky consistency.
Method Rinse rice in fine-mesh strainer under cold running water until water runs clear. (To check if water is starchy, capture some in bowl. If water is cloudy, keep rinsing and check again.)

UNDER CONTROL

The funny thing about rice is that though it has a reputation for being finicky, it's actually predictable in that, when cooked on its own, it always absorbs water in a 1:1 ratio by volume. What is finicky is how much water evaporates during cooking, since that can vary depending on the heat level, the diameter of your saucepan, how tightly its lid fits, and what other ingredients you are cooking along with the rice.

ARE ARBORIO RICE AND SUSHI RICE INTERCHANGEABLE?

Arborio rice and sushi rice are similar in shape and size and both have a relatively high amount of the starch component amylopectin, but arborio rice isn't a great choice for Asian dishes because of a characteristic called "chalk." During maturation, the starch structures at the arborio grain's core deform, making for a firm, toothy center when cooked. While this trait is great for risotto, giving the dish its signature al dente texture, it's less than ideal for sushi or for a rice that accompanies Asian dishes. Conversely, we've tried making risotto with sushi rice. Tasters reported that the resulting risotto was creamy, but "it wasn't risotto" because the grains lacked the quintessential al dente bite of arborio rice. The bottom line? Arborio rice and sushi rice are not interchangeable in recipes.

Sushi Rice
Typically either short- or medium-grain rice, it's both sticky and chewy.

Arborio Rice
The core of this creamy short-grain rice stays firm when cooked.

HOMINY AND MASA HARINA

LEAH COLINS

Hominy is oversize and deeply flavorful dried field corn kernels that have been degerminated and cooked in an alkaline solution until tender and chewy in a process called nixtamalization. This process unlocks nutrients and toasty flavors from the corn and is what gives oversize hominy its oversize corn flavor. The process is also what allows hominy—when dried and ground into the corn flour called masa harina—to be formed into a dough. The flavorful dough, masa, is then used to make corn tortillas (and thus tortilla chips), tamales, huaraches, pupusas, and more.

LEAH'S PRO TIP: *When working with masa harina, make sure to leave the dough well covered when not in immediate use, as it can dry out quickly and cause cracking in the shaping process. If your dough feels too dry or sticky when shaping, keep a small bowl of water on hand to moisten your hands for easier handling and shaping of the dough.*

CHICKEN POSOLE VERDE

Serves: 6 to 8
Total Time: 2 hours

RECIPE OVERVIEW Posole is the Mexican name for both hominy and the full-flavored stew made with hominy and meat. Forms of this stew date back to the Aztecs, and today no Mexican family celebration would be complete without it. The stew is made throughout Mexico in several distinct styles (with or without chiles). Our green chicken posole features the trademark tanginess of tomatillos, jalapeños, and cilantro. Using whole bone-in chicken thighs results in easy-to-shred, tender meat (chicken breasts tend to dry out and turn stringy), giving our stew a rustic texture. We brown the chicken and then sauté aromatics after removing the chicken, incorporating the flavorful fond. After returning the partially cooked chicken to the pot, we move the cooking from the stove to the more even, gentle heat of the oven. Once the chicken is tender, we set it aside and stir in canned hominy; the lightly sweet kernels turn pleasantly chewy after only a short simmer. Adding the tomatillo puree late in the cooking allows the flavors to meld without dulling the puree's bright freshness. Finally, we return the shredded chicken to the pot to warm briefly before serving the posole with lime wedges, diced avocado, and/or sliced radishes.

4	pounds bone-in chicken thighs, trimmed
1	teaspoon table salt, divided
¾	teaspoon pepper
2	tablespoons vegetable oil, divided
1	onion, chopped fine
3	garlic cloves, minced
1	tablespoon chopped fresh oregano or 1 teaspoon dried
4½	cups chicken broth, divided
12	ounces tomatillos, husks and stems removed, rinsed well and dried, quartered
2½	cups trimmed fresh cilantro leaves and stems (2 bunches)
2	jalapeño chiles, stemmed, halved, and seeded
2	(15-ounce) cans white or yellow hominy, rinsed

1. Adjust oven rack to lower-middle position and heat oven to 300 degrees. Pat chicken dry with paper towels and sprinkle with ¾ teaspoon salt and pepper. Heat 1 tablespoon oil in Dutch oven over medium-high heat until just smoking. Brown half of chicken, about 5 minutes per side; transfer to plate. Repeat with remaining 1 tablespoon oil and remaining chicken; transfer to plate. Let chicken cool slightly, then discard skin.

2. Pour off all but 1 tablespoon fat from pot. Add onion and remaining ¼ teaspoon salt and cook over medium heat until softened, about 5 minutes. Stir in garlic and oregano and cook until fragrant, about 30 seconds. Stir in 4 cups broth, scraping up any browned bits, and bring to simmer. Nestle chicken into pot along with any accumulated juices. Cover, transfer pot to oven, and cook until chicken is tender, about 1 hour.

3. Remove pot from oven. Transfer chicken to cutting board, let cool slightly, then shred into bite-size pieces using 2 forks; discard bones.

4. Meanwhile, process tomatillos, cilantro, jalapeños, and remaining ½ cup broth in blender until smooth, about 30 seconds. Stir tomatillo mixture and hominy into stew, bring to simmer over medium heat, and cook until flavors meld, 10 to 15 minutes. Stir in chicken and cook until heated through, about 2 minutes. Season with salt and pepper to taste. Serve.

KEY TO SUCCESS
- **Handling the hominy:** Rinse the hominy well to remove any excess starch, and be sure not to simmer it for too long or it will turn mushy.

PORK POSOLE ROJO

Serves: 8 to 10
Total Time: 3½ hours

RECIPE OVERVIEW Red posole is richer than its green cousin and has a deep, earthy flavor profile. Authentic versions boast a rich, porky flavor and body, thanks to bones from the head, neck, shank, and feet of a pig, supplemented with some boneless meat from the shoulder or loin. For our homage, we use more readily available bone-in pork butt roast. Splitting it into small chunks before cooking is the easiest method; the chunks cook faster than a whole roast and are easier to shred than smaller cubes. To avoid firming up the texture of the meat too much (which would inhibit shredding), we skip browning and instead parcook the meat gently with onions and garlic to develop flavor in the broth. Canned tomatoes add lively acidity and color. For the chiles, we like the rich, slightly sweet flavor of anchos, which we soak and puree into a thick paste. We mix most of the puree into the stew, saving the rest to add later for those who want extra heat. As in our green posole, we add the canned hominy only after the meat is removed from the pot; this gives the hominy enough time to absorb flavor from the broth and turn pleasingly chewy without overcooking. For an accurate measurement of boiling water, bring a full kettle of water to a boil and then measure out the desired amount. Serve with lime wedges, diced avocado, and/or sliced radishes.

1   (5-pound) bone-in pork butt roast
1¾   teaspoons table salt, divided
1   teaspoon pepper
2   tablespoons vegetable oil
2   large onions, chopped coarse
5   garlic cloves, minced
6   cups chicken broth
1   (14.5-ounce) can diced tomatoes

1   tablespoon minced fresh oregano or 1 teaspoon dried
3   dried ancho chiles, stemmed and seeded
1½   cups boiling water
3   (15-ounce) cans white or yellow hominy, rinsed

1. Adjust oven rack to lower-middle position and heat oven to 300 degrees. Trim thick skin and excess fat from meat and cut along muscles to divide roast into large pieces of various sizes; reserve bones. Sprinkle pork with 1 teaspoon salt and pepper.

2. Heat oil in Dutch oven over medium heat until shimmering. Add onions and ¼ teaspoon salt and cook until softened, 8 to 10 minutes. Stir in garlic and cook until fragrant, about 30 seconds. Add pork and bones and cook, stirring often, until meat is no longer pink on outside, about 8 minutes. Stir in broth, tomatoes and their juice, oregano, and remaining ½ teaspoon salt and bring to simmer, skimming foam from surface as needed. Cover, place pot in oven, and cook until pork is tender, about 2 hours.

3. Meanwhile, soak anchos in bowl with boiling water until softened, about 20 minutes. Process anchos and soaking liquid in blender until smooth, about 30 seconds. Strain through fine-mesh strainer into bowl, using rubber spatula to help pass chili mixture through strainer. Measure out and reserve ¼ cup ancho mixture for serving.

4. Remove pot from oven, transfer pork to cutting board, and let cool slightly; discard bones. While pork cools, stir hominy and remaining ancho mixture into pot and bring to simmer over medium heat. Reduce heat to low, cover, and simmer gently until flavors meld, about 30 minutes.

5. Using 2 forks, shred pork into bite-size pieces. Stir shredded pork into stew and cook until heated through, about 2 minutes. Season with reserved ancho mixture and salt and pepper to taste. Serve.

KEY TO SUCCESS
- **Don't brown the pork:** For shreddable meat, do not brown the chunks; cook them only until no longer pink on the outside.

Dried Hominy

We use canned hominy in both of our posole recipes here. You can use dried hominy, but you will need to presoak it in a manner similar to dried beans and then precook it before using in these recipes. Use 4 ounces dried hominy for each 15-ounce can of hominy. Soak the dried hominy in 1 quart cold water (per each 4-ounce portion) at room temperature for at least 8 hours or up to 24 hours. Drain and rinse, then add to a pot and cover with about 2 inches of water. Bring to a boil, then reduce the heat and simmer until the kernels are tender, about 2 hours. Drain well.

Making Corn Tortillas

STIR AND KNEAD

Stir masa harina, salt, warm water, and oil together with a rubber spatula, then knead the dough until it has the texture of Play-Doh.

ROLL AND PRESS FLAT

Pinch off a golf ball–size piece of dough, roll it into a ball, and gently press it flat. Divide dough into 18 equal rolled and flattened balls, keeping dough covered with damp paper towel.

PRESS INTO CIRCLE

Place a dough ball in the center of the prepared zipper-lock bag. Use a clear pie plate to press the dough into a flat 5½-inch circle.

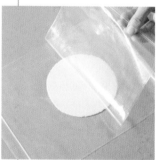

LIFT AND INVERT

Peel top layer of plastic away from tortilla. Lift tortilla from bottom layer of plastic and gently invert onto your palm.

COOK, FLIP, PRESS

Flip tortilla into skillet and cook until edges begin to dry and bottom edges start to brown. Flip and cook until second side starts to brown at edges. Flip again and press with spatula on center and edges of tortilla to create puff.

HOMEMADE CORN TORTILLAS

Makes: 18 tortillas
Total Time: 1½ hours

RECIPE OVERVIEW Fresh homemade tortillas are light and tender and bursting with corn flavor—and are worlds better than anything store-bought. Begin by making a stir-together dough of masa harina, warm water, vegetable oil, and salt. The warm water helps the dough hydrate quickly and fully while the oil makes the dough more tender and easier to work with. To press the tortillas, divide the dough into equal portions and place each, one by one, in a greased, cut-open zipper-lock bag and press flat with a clear pie plate into a 5½-inch circle. (The clear plate makes it easy to see the size of the circle as it expands. You can also use a tortilla press or a flat-bottomed skillet to press the tortillas.) Transfer each pressed tortilla to a hot nonstick skillet, then flip it twice and give it a final press with a spatula to cause it to puff. Puffing the tortillas in this manner creates a fluffy, light texture with a layered interior. Finally, to ensure that the tortillas remain tender and pliable, wrap the hot tortillas in a damp dish towel to steam them and keep them warm while finishing the batch. We recommend either placing the tortillas in a tortilla warmer or stacking them in a damp dish towel and microwaving for 2 minutes before serving.

> 3 cups (12 ounces) masa harina
> 2 teaspoons table salt
> 2–2½ cups warm water
> 2 tablespoons plus 1 teaspoon vegetable oil, divided

1. Whisk masa harina and salt together in medium bowl. Stir in 2 cups warm water and 2 tablespoons oil with rubber spatula until combined. Using your hands, knead dough in bowl until it is soft and tacky and has texture of Play-Doh. If necessary, add up to ½ cup more warm water, 1 tablespoon at a time, until proper texture is achieved. (You can test for proper hydration by gently flattening a golf ball–size piece of dough with your hands. If many large cracks form around edges, it is too dry.)

2. Divide dough into 18 equal portions, about a scant 3 tablespoons (1½ ounces) each. Roll each portion into smooth ball between your hands. Transfer dough balls to plate and keep covered with damp paper towel. Cut open seams along sides of 1-gallon zipper-lock bag, leaving bottom seam intact. Spray inside of bag lightly with vegetable oil spray; wipe excess oil spray from bag with paper towel.

3. Heat remaining 1 teaspoon oil in 12-inch nonstick skillet over medium heat until just smoking. Using tongs, wipe skillet with paper towels. Place 1 dough ball in center of prepared bag. Fold top layer of plastic over ball. Using clear pie plate, press dough flat into thin 5½-inch circle.

4. Peel top layer of plastic away from tortilla. Using plastic to lift tortilla from bottom, place exposed side of tortilla in palm of your hand and invert tortilla. Peel away plastic. Carefully flip tortilla into skillet and cook until bottom begins to brown at edges, about 1 minute.

5. Using thin spatula, flip tortilla and cook until second side is browned at edges, about 45 seconds. Flip tortilla again and press center and edges firmly with spatula so tortilla puffs, about 15 seconds.

6. Transfer cooked tortilla to tortilla warmer or wrap in damp dish towel. Repeat with remaining dough balls, lightly spraying bag with oil spray and wiping off excess as needed to keep tortillas from sticking. Serve. (If storing tortillas in damp dish towel, microwave for 2 minutes to rewarm before serving.)

KEY TO SUCCESS
- **Warm water:** Using 110-degree water will quickly hydrate the dough, ensuring that it will not crack significantly when flattened.

WHAT CAN GO WRONG

PROBLEM The tortillas don't puff.

SOLUTION Toward the end of cooking each tortilla, press on it with a spatula; this releases steam in the tortilla and causes it to puff in the middle.

TAMALES TWO WAYS
Makes: 18 tamales
Total Time: 2 hours

RECIPE OVERVIEW Traditional tamales are a labor of love, from boiling and grinding masa for dough, to soaking corn husks, to tying each tamale closed for steaming. They are often made for holidays and special occasions and are a group effort to divide and conquer the time-consuming steps. This rendition alters and streamlines the process while still capturing the essential elements of tamales—corn cakes that are hearty yet light in texture, with rich, flavorful fillings, all wrapped up in corn husks. Although masa dough made from a coarser corn flour is traditional for tamales, it can be difficult to find, so we use widely available masa harina. To add some granular texture and bigger corn flavor to the finely ground masa harina, we turn to grits. Incorporating some corn kernels gives the dough an even bigger boost of corn flavor. Then, choose your filling: The bold beef filling uses blade steak, smoky chipotles, and dried anchos. The more subtly spiced chicken filling uses chicken thighs along with dried New Mexican and ancho chiles. Soaking the corn husks before filling them rids them of any dirt and makes them pliable enough to roll around the tamale filling. To fold the tamales, most recipes require tying each one closed with either a strip of corn husk or

string. But here, we fold the soaked husks tightly around the tamales and place the parcels with the seam sides facing the edges of a steamer basket. This keeps them closed during cooking. For an accurate measurement of boiling water, bring a full kettle of water to a boil and then measure out the desired amount. To reheat six or fewer tamales, place them on a large plate with 1 tablespoon of water, cover them with damp paper towels, and then wrap them with plastic wrap; microwave the tamales at 50 percent power until they are hot throughout, about 4 minutes.

1	cup plus 2 tablespoons quick grits
1½	cups boiling water
1	cup (4 ounces) plus 2 tablespoons masa harina
20	large dried corn husks
1½	cups frozen corn, thawed
6	tablespoons unsalted butter, cut into ½-inch cubes and softened
6	tablespoons lard, softened
1	tablespoon sugar
2¼	teaspoons baking powder
¾	teaspoon table salt
1	recipe filling (recipes follow)

1. Place grits in medium bowl, whisk in boiling water, and let stand until water is mostly absorbed, about 10 minutes. Stir in masa harina, cover, and let cool completely, about 20 minutes. Meanwhile, place husks in large bowl, cover with hot water, and let soak until pliable, about 30 minutes.

2. Process masa dough, corn, butter, lard, sugar, baking powder, and salt in food processor until mixture is light, sticky, and very smooth, about 1 minute, scraping down sides of bowl as necessary. Remove husks from water and pat dry with clean dish towel.

3. Working with 1 husk at a time, lay on counter, cupped side up, with long side facing you and wide end on right side. Spread ¼ cup tamale dough into 4-inch square over bottom right-hand corner, pushing it flush to bottom edge but leaving ¼-inch border at wide edge. Mound 2 scant tablespoons filling in line across center of dough, parallel to bottom edge. Roll husk away from you and over filling so that dough surrounds filling and forms cylinder. Fold up tapered end, leaving top open, and transfer to platter, seam side down.

4. Fit large pot or Dutch oven with steamer basket, removing feet from steamer basket if pot is short. Fill pot with water until it just touches bottom of basket and bring to boil. Gently lay tamales in basket with open ends facing up and seam sides facing out. Cover and steam, checking water level often and adding water as needed, until tamales easily come free from husks, about 1 hour. Transfer tamales to large platter. Microwave remaining sauce from filling in covered bowl until hot, about 30 seconds, and serve with tamales.

CHIPOTLE BEEF FILLING

Makes: enough for 18 tamales

4	dried ancho chiles, stemmed, seeded, and torn into ½-inch pieces (1 cup)
3	tablespoons vegetable oil
1	large onion, chopped
6	garlic cloves, minced
1½	tablespoons minced canned chipotle chile in adobo sauce
1	teaspoon dried oregano
1	teaspoon sugar, plus extra as needed
1	teaspoon table salt
¾	teaspoon ground cumin
½	teaspoon ground cinnamon
⅛	teaspoon ground cloves
3	cups beef broth
1¾	pounds top blade steaks, trimmed
1½	tablespoons red wine vinegar

1. Toast anchos in 12-inch skillet over medium heat, stirring frequently, until fragrant, 2 to 6 minutes; transfer to bowl.

2. Heat oil in now-empty skillet over medium heat until shimmering. Add onion and cook until softened, 5 to 7 minutes. Stir in garlic, chipotle, oregano, sugar, salt, cumin, cinnamon, cloves, and toasted anchos and cook for 30 seconds. Stir in broth and simmer until slightly reduced, about 10 minutes. Transfer mixture to blender and process until smooth, about 20 seconds; return to skillet.

3. Season beef with salt and pepper, nestle into skillet, and bring to simmer over medium heat. Cover, reduce heat to low, and cook until beef is very tender, about 1½ hours.

4. Transfer beef to carving board and let cool slightly. Using 2 forks, shred beef into small pieces. Stir vinegar into sauce and season with salt, pepper, and extra sugar to taste. Toss shredded beef with 1 cup sauce.

RED CHILE CHICKEN FILLING

Makes: enough for 18 tamales

4	dried ancho chiles, stemmed, seeded, and torn into ½-inch pieces (1 cup)
4	dried New Mexican chiles, stemmed, seeded, and torn into ½-inch pieces (1 cup)
3	tablespoons vegetable oil
1	large onion, chopped
6	garlic cloves, minced
¾	teaspoon ground cumin
¾	teaspoon dried oregano
1	teaspoon table salt, divided
3	cups chicken broth
1¼	pounds boneless, skinless chicken thighs, trimmed
½	teaspoon pepper
1½	tablespoons cider vinegar
	Sugar

1. Toast anchos and New Mexican chiles in 12-inch skillet over medium heat, stirring frequently, until fragrant, 2 to 6 minutes; transfer to bowl.

2. Heat oil in now-empty skillet over medium heat until shimmering. Add onion and cook until softened, 5 to 7 minutes. Stir in garlic, cumin, oregano, ½ teaspoon salt, and toasted chiles and cook for 30 seconds. Stir in broth and simmer until slightly reduced, about 10 minutes. Transfer mixture to blender and process until smooth, about 20 seconds; return to skillet.

3. Sprinkle chicken with remaining ½ teaspoon salt and pepper, nestle into skillet, and bring to simmer over medium heat. Cover, reduce heat to low, and cook until chicken registers 160 degrees, 20 to 25 minutes.

4. Transfer chicken to carving board and let cool slightly. Using 2 forks, shred chicken into small pieces.

5. Stir vinegar into sauce and season with salt, pepper, and sugar to taste. Toss chicken with 1 cup sauce.

KEYS TO SUCCESS

- **The right grits:** Use quick, not instant, grits here.

- **Size the husks:** Use large corn husks that measure about 8 by 6 inches; if the husks are much smaller, you may need to use two per tamale and shingle them as needed to hold all the filling.

- **Roll 'em up:** It is important to roll the tamales tightly so they don't leak while cooking.

Making Tamales

MAKE DOUGH
Whisk boiling water into grits and let stand until absorbed. Stir in masa harina. Process cooled masa mixture with corn and remaining dough ingredients until very smooth.

SOAK CORN HUSKS
Place dried corn husks in large bowl and cover with hot water.

SPREAD DOUGH
Lay husk on counter with long side parallel to edge of counter. Spoon ¼ cup dough onto bottom right-hand corner of husk. Spread into 4-inch square, flush with bottom edge.

ADD FILLING
Place scant 2 tablespoons filling down center of dough, parallel to long side of husk. Roll husk away from you so that dough surrounds filling.

FOLD TAMALES
Fold tapered end of tamale up, leaving top open, and transfer to platter, seam side down.

STEAM TAMALES
Place tamales in steamer basket, with seams facing edge of pot and open ends facing up. Cover pot and steam tamales for about 1 hour.

TOMATILLO-CHICKEN HUARACHES

Serves: 4
Total Time: 2 hours

RECIPE OVERVIEW Generously sized and utterly delicious, huaraches are named for their doppelgänger, the iconic huarache woven leather sandal. The hearty huaraches of Mexico City consist of masa dough filled and topped with varying proteins, vegetables, cheeses, and sauces. This version features a stuffing of rich refried beans and a topping of shredded chicken mixed with tomatillo salsa; it's all garnished with radishes and queso fresco. Using convenient store-bought rotisserie chicken lets you focus your time and efforts on making the masa flatbreads. Hydrating the masa harina with boiling rather than room-temperature water allows the starches in the flour to absorb it more quickly and completely, resulting in a well-hydrated dough that's easy to work with and won't dry out. This is important because you need to shape and flatten the dough twice: once before adding the stuffing and then after you fold the dough around it. Properly hydrated masa dough should be tacky, requiring damp hands to keep it from sticking. For an accurate measurement of boiling water, bring a kettle of water to a boil and then measure out the desired amount.

- 3 cups (12 ounces) masa harina
- 1¾ teaspoons table salt, divided
- 4 cups boiling water, plus warm tap water as needed
- 1 (15-ounce) can pinto beans, rinsed
- ¼ cup chicken broth
- 5 tablespoons lard, divided
- ½ onion, chopped fine
- ½ jalapeño chile, stemmed, seeded, and minced
- 2 garlic cloves, minced
- 1 teaspoon ground cumin
- 1 tablespoon chopped fresh cilantro plus ¼ cup leaves
- 1 teaspoon lime juice
- 1 (2½-pound) rotisserie chicken, skin and bones discarded and meat shredded into bite-size pieces (3 cups)
- 3 cups tomatillo salsa
- 4 radishes, sliced thin
- 4 ounces queso fresco, crumbled (1 cup)

1. Whisk masa harina and 1¼ teaspoons salt together in large bowl. Add boiling water and mix with rubber spatula until soft dough forms. Cover with damp dish towel and let rest for 30 minutes.

2. Meanwhile, process beans and broth in food processor until smooth, about 30 seconds, scraping down sides of bowl as needed; set aside. Heat 1 tablespoon lard in 12-inch nonstick skillet over medium heat until shimmering. Add onion, jalapeño, and remaining ½ teaspoon salt and cook over medium heat until vegetables are softened and beginning to brown, 5 to 7 minutes.

3. Stir in garlic and cumin and cook until fragrant, about 30 seconds. Stir in reserved beans and cook, stirring often, until well combined and thickened slightly, about 5 minutes. Off heat, stir in chopped cilantro and lime juice and season with salt and pepper to taste; set aside to cool slightly. Once cool enough to handle, divide beans into 4 equal portions using greased ⅓-cup dry measuring cup. Transfer to large plate and set aside. Wipe out skillet.

4. Adjust oven rack to middle position and heat oven to 200 degrees. Set wire rack in rimmed baking sheet. Once dough has rested for 30 minutes, test dough's hydration by flattening golf ball–size piece. If cracks larger than ¼ inch form around edges, knead in warm tap water by hand, 1 teaspoon at a time, until dough is soft and slightly tacky. Transfer dough to counter, shape into large ball, divide into 4 equal pieces, and place on parchment-lined second rimmed baking sheet. Cover dough with wet dish towel. Cut open seams along both sides of 1-gallon zipper-lock bag, leaving bottom seam intact.

5. Working with 1 piece of dough at a time, repeat testing hydration and add extra water as needed. Shape dough into rough oval, about 4 inches long, then enclose in split bag (oval should be perpendicular to counter edge and seam of bag should be on your right). Press dough flat into ½-inch-thick, 6-inch-long oval using flat-bottomed pot or pie plate. Peel away plastic, smooth any cracks around edges of round, and place 1 reserved refried bean portion in center of dough oval. (If at any time dough feels dry, moisten hands to smooth out any cracks and make dough pliable.)

6. Grasping side edges of zipper-lock bag, lift to bring sides of dough up around filling and press edges of dough to seal. Remoisten your hands, unfold bag, and smooth any cracks with your damp fingers. Flip dough seam side down, enclose in split bag, and press flat into a 9-inch oval about ¼ inch thick using flat-bottomed pot or pie plate. Return shaped dough to sheet and cover with wet dish towel while shaping remaining dough.

7. Heat 1 tablespoon lard in clean, dry skillet over medium-high heat until shimmering. Gently place 1 dough oval in skillet and cook until dark spotty brown on first side, 4 to 6 minutes. Using 2 spatulas, gently flip huarache and continue to cook until second side is crispy and dark spotty brown, 4 to 6 minutes longer; transfer to prepared rack and hold in warm oven. Repeat with remaining lard and remaining dough ovals.

8. Meanwhile, microwave chicken and salsa in large bowl until warmed through, 1 to 3 minutes. Top huaraches with chicken-salsa mixture and sprinkle with radishes, queso fresco, and cilantro leaves. Serve.

Shaping Huaraches

SHAPE AND PRESS
Shape dough piece into 4-inch oval and enclose in split plastic bag. Using flat-bottomed pot or pie plate, press dough into 6-inch oval about ½ inch thick.

FILL AND SEAL
Smooth any cracks around edges of round and place bean mixture in center of masa. Grasping side edges of bag, lift to bring sides of dough up around filling; pinch top of dough to seal.

UNFOLD AND SMOOTH
Remoisten your hands, unfold bag, and smooth any cracks with your damp fingers.

FLIP AND PRESS
Flip dough seam side down, enclose in split bag, and press dough flat into 9-inch oval about ¼ inch thick using flat-bottomed pot or pie plate.

KEYS TO SUCCESS
- **Hydrated dough**: Let the dough rest, covered with a damp dish towel, for 30 minutes before trying to work with it.
- **Seal the dough**: Though some filling may show through the formed huaraches when cooking them, seal the edges well to prevent leaks.

WHAT CAN GO WRONG

PROBLEM The dough is dry and cracking.

SOLUTION Knead in warm water, 1 teaspoon at a time, until the dough feels tacky.

RICE AND BEANS

LAWMAN JOHNSON

Rice and beans is a familiar and favorite combination the world over, and here we present recipes with roots in the Caribbean, the United States, and the Middle East. In fact, rice-and-bean combinations are so integral to Caribbean and Latin American cooking that they are referred to as matrimonio (the marriage). While it may be more convenient to simply top boiled rice with canned beans, taking the time and effort to use dried beans, cook the rice with aromatics, and build layered flavor through longer cooking is well worth the effort, as the recipes in this course aptly demonstrate.

LAWMAN'S PRO TIP: *Perfectly cooked rice and beans make an excellent culinary base. Adding aromatics and spices can transform this simple marriage of ingredients into windows into various cultures.*

CUBAN-STYLE BLACK BEANS AND RICE

Serves: 6 to 8
Total Time: 1½ hours, plus 8 hours soaking

RECIPE OVERVIEW In Cuba, a traditional preparation called moros y cristianos features black beans and rice cooked with vegetables, spices, and pork to create either a flavorful main course or a hearty side dish. We first simmer half an onion, half a green pepper, half a garlic head, and bay leaves with dried beans so that both the beans and their cooking liquid are full-flavored (and later lend that quality to the rice). We then sauté salt pork in a pot until crispy, then lightly brown a sofrito (onion, green pepper, and garlic flavored with cumin and oregano) in the rendered fat. The uncooked rice is added, followed by the cooked black beans and their cooking liquid, and everything simmers until the flavorful bean liquid has been absorbed and the rice is tender. The traditional step of washing off the excess starch from the rice helps prevent it from turning sticky and clumping together and is particularly important here, since there is already starch in the bean cooking liquid. With so many different ingredients in one pot, it's tricky to get perfectly cooked rice on the stovetop. The bottom tends to scorch while the top remains undercooked. So we turn to our oven-baked rice technique, in which all-around, indirect heat allows for gentle, even cooking. We bring the rice, beans, and liquid to a simmer, give them a stir, cover the vessel, and slide it into the oven. After about the same time as it would take to cook on the stove, this method results in perfectly cooked rice from top to bottom. It is important to use lean—not fatty—salt pork. If you can't find it, substitute 6 diced slices of bacon and decrease the cooking time in step 4 to 8 minutes. You will need a Dutch oven with a tight-fitting lid for this recipe.

½   teaspoon table salt, plus salt for soaking and
     cooking beans
6½ ounces dried black beans (1 cup), picked over
     and rinsed
2   cups chicken broth
2   cups water
2   large green bell peppers, stemmed, seeded, and halved
1   large onion, halved at equator and peeled,
     root end left intact
1   head garlic, 5 medium cloves minced or pressed through
     a garlic press (about 5 teaspoons), remaining head
     halved at equator with skin left intact
2   bay leaves
1½ cups long-grain white rice
2   tablespoons olive oil, divided
6   ounces lean salt pork, cut into ¼-inch dice
4   teaspoons ground cumin
1   tablespoon minced fresh oregano leaves
2   tablespoons red wine vinegar
2   scallions, sliced thin, for serving
     Lime wedges, for serving

1. Dissolve 1½ tablespoons salt in 2 quarts cold water in large bowl or container. Add beans and soak at room temperature for at least 8 hours or up to 24 hours. Drain and rinse well.

2. In Dutch oven, stir together drained beans, broth, water, 1 bell pepper half, 1 onion half (with root end), halved garlic head, bay leaves, and 1 teaspoon salt. Bring to simmer over medium-high heat, cover, and reduce heat to low. Cook until beans are just soft, 30 to 35 minutes. Using tongs, remove and discard pepper, onion, garlic, and bay leaves. Drain beans in colander set over large bowl, reserving 2½ cups bean cooking liquid. (If you don't have enough bean cooking liquid, add water to equal 2½ cups.) Do not wash out Dutch oven.

3. Adjust oven rack to middle position and heat oven to 350 degrees. Place rice in large fine-mesh strainer and rinse under cold running water until water runs clear, about 1½ minutes. Shake strainer vigorously to remove all excess water; set rice aside. Cut remaining peppers and onion into 2-inch pieces and process in food processor until broken into rough ¼-inch pieces, about 8 pulses, scraping down bowl as necessary; set vegetables aside.

4. In now-empty Dutch oven, heat 1 tablespoon oil and salt pork over medium-low heat and cook, stirring frequently, until lightly browned and rendered, 15 to 20 minutes. Add

remaining 1 tablespoon oil, chopped bell peppers and onion, cumin, and oregano. Increase heat to medium and continue to cook, stirring frequently, until vegetables are softened and beginning to brown, 10 to 15 minutes longer. Add minced garlic and cook, stirring constantly, until fragrant, about 1 minute. Add rice and stir to coat, about 30 seconds.

5. Stir in beans, reserved bean cooking liquid, vinegar, and ½ teaspoon salt. Increase heat to medium-high and bring to simmer. Cover and transfer to oven. Cook until liquid is absorbed and rice is tender, about 30 minutes. Fluff with fork and let rest, uncovered, for 5 minutes. Serve, passing scallions and lime wedges separately.

KEYS TO SUCCESS

- **Rinse the rice:** This step is especially important here, since there will be plenty of starch in the cooking liquid thanks to the black beans.

- **Stovetop to oven:** Cooking the beans on the stovetop and transferring the Dutch oven to the oven after adding the rice ensures that the steady heat of the oven cooks the rice evenly.

RED BEANS AND RICE WITH OKRA AND TOMATOES

Serves: 6 to 8
Total Time: 1¾ hours, plus 8 hours soaking

RECIPE OVERVIEW Red beans and rice is a classic New Orleans Monday favorite; historically, since Sunday was a day of rest, all chores were pushed to Monday, and this was a dish that could simmer relatively unattended and be ready at the end of a busy day. Rice, beans, and meat (often leftover ham from Sunday's dinner) are traditional musts, along with the "holy trinity" (onion, celery, and green bell pepper), the city's version of a sofrito or mirepoix. For our own version of this dish, we boost the flavor profile by adding okra and tomatoes. Camellia-brand red beans—from the oldest dried bean company in America, founded in New Orleans—are what's used in New Orleans; these are available by mail order but can be hard to find otherwise, so we use small dried red beans. Instead of traditional tasso ham, we use bacon. To ensure the stewed okra keeps some crunchy bite, toss the whole okra pods in salt and let them sit for an hour before rinsing, cutting, and adding to the beans for the final half hour of cooking. While we prefer to use fresh okra in this recipe, you can substitute frozen cut okra, thawed and thoroughly patted dry. If using frozen, skip step 2. Serve the beans and rice with hot sauce.

Red Beans and Vegetables

Table salt for brining beans and salting okra

- 1 pound small red beans (2 cups), picked over and rinsed
- 1 pound okra, stemmed
- 4 slices bacon, chopped fine
- 1 onion, chopped fine
- 1 green bell pepper, stemmed, seeded, and chopped fine
- 1 celery rib, minced
- 3 garlic cloves, minced
- 2 bay leaves
- 1 teaspoon minced fresh thyme or ¼ teaspoon dried
- 1 teaspoon paprika
- ¼ teaspoon cayenne pepper
- ¼ teaspoon pepper
- 5 cups water
- 3 cups chicken broth
- 2 (14.5-ounce) cans diced tomatoes, drained
- 1 tablespoon red wine vinegar, plus extra for seasoning

Rice

- 1 tablespoon unsalted butter
- 2 cups long-grain white rice, rinsed
- 3 cups water
- 1 teaspoon table salt
- 3 scallions, sliced thin

1. FOR THE RED BEANS AND VEGETABLES
Dissolve 3 tablespoons salt in 4 quarts cold water in large bowl or container. Add beans and soak at room temperature for at least 8 hours or up to 24 hours. Drain and rinse well; set aside.

2. Toss okra with 1 teaspoon salt and let sit for 1 hour, stirring halfway through salting time. Rinse well, then cut into 1-inch pieces; set aside.

3. Cook bacon in Dutch oven over medium heat, stirring occasionally, until crispy, 5 to 7 minutes. Add onion, bell pepper, and celery and cook until vegetables are softened, 5 to 7 minutes. Stir in garlic, bay leaves, thyme, paprika, cayenne, and pepper and cook until fragrant, about 30 seconds.

4. Stir in water, broth, and beans and bring to boil over high heat. Reduce to vigorous simmer and cook, stirring occasionally, until beans are just softened and liquid begins to thicken, 45 minutes to 1 hour.

5. Stir in tomatoes, vinegar, and okra and cook until liquid is thickened and beans are fully tender and creamy, about 30 minutes.

6. FOR THE RICE While bean mixture cooks, melt butter in large saucepan over medium heat. Add rice and cook, stirring often, until edges begin to turn translucent, about 2 minutes. Stir in water and salt and bring to boil. Cover, reduce heat to low, and simmer until liquid is absorbed and rice is tender, about 20 minutes. Remove pot from heat, lay clean folded dish towel underneath lid, and let rice sit for 10 minutes. Fluff rice with fork.

7. Discard bay leaves from beans. Season with salt, pepper, and extra vinegar to taste. Top individual portions of rice with beans and sprinkle with scallions. Serve.

KEYS TO SUCCESS

- **Pilaf method:** Sautéing the rice in butter before adding the liquid ensures flavorful, fluffy grains.
- **Salt the okra:** Salting the stemmed pods removes enough moisture for them to retain crispness throughout the cooking process, while still releasing some of their mucilage to help thicken the rice and beans.

Soaking Dried Beans

LONG SOAK

Dissolve 3 tablespoons salt in 4 quarts cold water in large bowl or container. Add 1 pound dried beans and soak at room temperature for at least 8 hours, or up to 24 hours. Drain and rinse well; soaked beans can be refrigerated for up to 2 days.

QUICK SOAK

If pressed for time, you can "quick-brine" your beans. Combine salt, water, and beans in large Dutch oven and bring to boil over high heat. Remove pot from heat, cover, and let stand for 1 hour. Drain and rinse well; they can be refrigerated for up to 2 days.

Why Brine Your Beans?

We nearly always recommend brining dried beans before cooking them. The results—intact beans with tender, creamy exteriors—are worth the hands-off time it takes. The reason that soaking dried beans in salt water makes them cook up with softer skins has to do with how the sodium ions in salt water interact with the cells in the beans' skins. As the beans soak in salt water, sodium ions replace some of the calcium and magnesium ions in the skins. Because sodium ions are weaker than these mineral ions, they allow more water to penetrate the skins. This gives the skins themselves a softer, more malleable texture, making them less likely to break apart as the beans swell during cooking.

KOSHARI

Serves: 4 to 6
Total Time: 1¾ hours

RECIPE OVERVIEW Considered the national dish of Egypt, koshari evolved as a way to use up leftovers and is now a popular street food. This hearty dish usually features rice (often short-grain, but long-grain is used as well), small-shape pasta, lentils, and chickpeas smothered in a spiced tomato sauce and topped with crispy fried onions. The dish takes some time to put together, but the results are comforting and delicious. We cook the lentils and the pasta in pots of salted boiling water, then drain and set each aside while we prepare the rice and the sauce. Soaking the rice in hot water before cooking removes some of its excess starch so it doesn't clump. Even more important, the hot-water soak softens the grains' exteriors so that they can absorb water more easily. Without this soak, the parcooked lentils would absorb the bulk of the cooking liquid once the two are combined, robbing the rice of the liquid it needs to cook through. The tomato sauce is typically piquant with vinegar and can also be made spicy with cayenne or red pepper flakes; here we present a vinegar-spiked sauce with a little cayenne for warmth. Using the same spices (a blend of coriander, cumin, cinnamon, nutmeg, and cayenne) in both the sauce and the rice provides a complex and integrated flavor profile. We add canned chickpeas (you can substitute cooked dried chickpeas, if you like) directly to the sauce to infuse them with flavor. The finishing touch is a generous amount of ultrasavory, crunchy fried onions that bring concentrated, sweet-savory depth and texture to this classic Egyptian comfort food. Large green or brown lentils both work well in this recipe; do not use French green lentils or lentilles du Puy. Long-grain white, jasmine, or Texmati rice can be substituted for the basmati.

  1 cup elbow macaroni
  1 teaspoon table salt, divided, plus salt for cooking pasta and lentils
  1 cup green or brown lentils, picked over and rinsed
  1 recipe Crispy Onions, plus ¼ cup reserved oil (recipe follows)
  4 garlic cloves, minced, divided
1½ teaspoons ground coriander, divided
1½ teaspoons ground cumin, divided
 ¾ teaspoon ground cinnamon, divided
 ¼ teaspoon ground nutmeg, divided
 ¼ teaspoon cayenne pepper, divided
  1 (28-ounce) can tomato sauce
  1 (15-ounce) can chickpeas, rinsed
  1 cup basmati rice
  2 cups water
  1 tablespoon red wine vinegar
  3 tablespoons minced fresh parsley

1. Bring 2 quarts water to boil in Dutch oven. Add pasta and 1½ teaspoons salt and cook, stirring often, until al dente. Drain pasta, rinse with water, then drain again. Transfer to bowl and set aside.

2. Meanwhile, bring lentils, 4 cups water, and 1 teaspoon salt to boil in medium saucepan over high heat. Reduce heat to low and cook until lentils are just tender, 15 to 17 minutes. Drain and set aside.

3. Cook 1 tablespoon reserved onion oil, 1 teaspoon garlic, ½ teaspoon salt, ½ teaspoon coriander, ½ teaspoon cumin, ¼ teaspoon cinnamon, ⅛ teaspoon nutmeg, and ⅛ teaspoon cayenne in now-empty saucepan over medium heat until fragrant, about 1 minute. Stir in tomato sauce and chickpeas, bring to simmer, and cook until slightly thickened, about 10 minutes. Cover and keep sauce and chickpeas warm.

4. While sauce cooks, place rice in medium bowl, cover with hot tap water by 2 inches, and let sit for 15 minutes. Using your hands, gently swish grains to release excess starch. Carefully pour off water, leaving rice in bowl. Repeat adding and pouring off cold water 4 or 5 times, until water runs almost clear. Drain rice in fine-mesh strainer.

5. Cook remaining 3 tablespoons reserved onion oil, remaining garlic, remaining 1 teaspoon coriander, remaining 1 teaspoon cumin, remaining ½ teaspoon cinnamon, remaining ⅛ teaspoon nutmeg, and remaining ⅛ teaspoon cayenne in now-empty pot over medium heat until fragrant, about 2 minutes. Add rice and cook, stirring occasionally, until grain edges begin to turn translucent, about 3 minutes. Stir in water and remaining ½ teaspoon salt and bring to boil. Stir in lentils, reduce heat to low, cover, and simmer gently until all liquid is absorbed, about 12 minutes.

6. Off heat, sprinkle pasta over rice mixture. Cover, laying clean dish towel underneath lid, and let sit for 10 minutes.

7. Return sauce and chickpeas to simmer over medium heat. Stir in vinegar and season with salt and pepper to taste. Fluff rice and lentils with fork and stir in parsley and half of crispy onions. Transfer to serving platter and top with half of sauce and remaining onions. Serve, passing remaining sauce separately.

CRISPY ONIONS
Makes: 1½ cups

We remove a good bit of the onions' water before frying by tossing them with salt, microwaving for 5 minutes, and drying thoroughly. Be sure to reserve enough oil to use in the koshari. The remaining oil may be refrigerated in an airtight container for up to 1 month; it's great for sautéing vegetables and adding to salad dressings and pasta sauces. Sprinkle leftover onions on salads or sandwiches.

- **2** pounds onions, halved and sliced crosswise into ¼-inch-thick pieces
- **2** teaspoons table salt
- **1½** cups vegetable oil

1. Toss onions and salt together in large bowl. Microwave for 5 minutes. Rinse thoroughly, transfer to paper towel–lined baking sheet, and dry well.

2. Heat onions and oil in Dutch oven over high heat, stirring frequently, until onions are golden brown, 25 to 30 minutes. Drain onions in colander set in large bowl. Transfer onions to paper towel–lined baking sheet to drain. Serve.

KEYS TO SUCCESS

- **Soak the rice:** Soaking the raw rice in hot water prior to cooking softens the grains' exteriors so that they can absorb water more easily, putting them on a level playing field with the lentils. This also washes away excess starch, helping the rice cook up fluffy rather than sticky.

- **Use the right lentils:** Many lentil dishes benefit from the firm, distinct texture of lentilles du Puy. But in this dish, the softer (but still intact) texture of green or brown lentils pairs best with the tender rice.

SMALL BUT MIGHTY LENTILS

JACK BISHOP

Lentils in and of themselves are fairly simple to cook. Although they are available canned, dried lentils are by far the most commonly found form, and they cook quickly thanks to their small size and thin skins. So here we move beyond the basics to learn about cooking lentils and grains together so that each is perfectly tender, how to shallow-fry lentils to completely change their texture, and how to take advantage of the unique qualities of red lentils (which are actually hulled, split brown or green lentils) to make both vegetarian kofte and dal.

JACK'S PRO TIP: *I love lentils for salads because they pair so well with vegetables and soak up potent dressings. French green lentils hold their shape nicely and have a lovely nutty flavor. They are my go-to lentil for rice dishes, salads, and many soups.*

BARLEY AND LENTILS WITH MUSHROOMS AND TAHINI-YOGURT SAUCE

Serves: 4
Total Time: 50 minutes, plus 30 minutes resting

RECIPE OVERVIEW This superhearty dish is a great way to showcase the robust flavor of black lentils. Slightly smaller than brown lentils, black lentils have a great ability to hold their shape even when tender (which means we can cook them in the same pot as the barley). Here the lentils and barley are paired with porcini and portobello mushrooms, onion, and a creamy tahini-yogurt sauce enlivened with lemon and garlic. While the lentils simmer and stay warm in the pot, we sauté the onion and brown the portobellos in a large skillet. Then the umami-rich porcini and their flavorful soaking liquid go in, pairing beautifully with the meaty portobellos. Some fresh dill and strips of lemon peel brighten and balance the earthiness, and drizzling the garlicky Tahini-Yogurt Sauce over the barley and lentils before serving works perfectly to balance all the hearty flavors and textures. While we prefer black lentils here, lentilles du Puy, brown lentils, and green lentils can be substituted.

Tahini-Yogurt Sauce
- ⅓ cup tahini
- ⅓ cup plain Greek yogurt
- ¼ cup water
- 3 tablespoons lemon juice
- 1 garlic clove, minced
- ¾ teaspoon table salt

Barley and Lentils
- 1½ cups water
- ½ ounce dried porcini mushrooms, rinsed
- 1 cup pearl barley
- ½ cup black lentils, picked over and rinsed
- ½ teaspoon table salt, plus salt for cooking barley and lentils
- 2 tablespoons extra-virgin olive oil
- 1 onion, chopped fine
- 2 large portobello mushroom caps, cut into 1-inch pieces
- 3 (2-inch) strips lemon zest, sliced thin lengthwise
- ¾ teaspoon ground coriander
- ¼ teaspoon pepper
- 2 tablespoons chopped fresh dill

1. FOR THE SAUCE Whisk all ingredients in bowl until combined. Season with pepper to taste. Let sit until flavors meld, about 30 minutes. (Sauce can be refrigerated for up to 4 days.)

2. FOR THE BARLEY AND LENTILS Microwave water and porcini mushrooms in covered bowl until steaming, about 1 minute. Let sit until softened, 5 minutes. Drain in fine-mesh strainer lined with coffee filter, reserving liquid, and chop porcini.

3. Bring 4 quarts water to boil in Dutch oven. Add barley, lentils, and 1 tablespoon salt, return to boil, and cook until

tender, 20 to 40 minutes. Drain barley and lentils, return to now-empty pot, and cover to keep warm.

4. Meanwhile, heat oil in 12-inch nonstick skillet over medium heat until shimmering. Add onion and cook until softened, about 5 minutes. Stir in portobello mushrooms, cover, and cook until portobellos have released their liquid and begin to brown, about 4 minutes.

5. Uncover, stir in lemon zest, coriander, salt, and pepper, and cook until fragrant, about 30 seconds. Stir in porcini and porcini soaking liquid, bring to boil, and cook, stirring occasionally, until liquid is thickened slightly and reduced to ½ cup, about 5 minutes. Stir mushroom mixture and dill into barley-lentil mixture and season with salt and pepper to taste. Serve, drizzling individual portions with sauce.

KEYS TO SUCCESS

- **Use pearl barley:** Read the package carefully. Do not substitute hulled, hull-less, quick-cooking, or presteamed barley.
- **Proper draining:** Draining the porcini in a fine-mesh strainer lined with a coffee filter gives you flavorful, grit-free soaking liquid.

CRISPY LENTIL AND HERB SALAD

Serves: 4
Total Time: 35 minutes, plus 1 hour soaking

RECIPE OVERVIEW We take inspiration from preparations in countries including India, Lebanon, Syria, and Turkey for cooking these lentils. Soaking them in salted water for at least an hour softens them—something we often do with dried beans but not usually with quick-cooking dried lentils. The soaked and drained lentils are then ready for their star treatment: getting fried into tender-on-the-inside, crispy-on-the-outside little pearls. To make the most of the fried lentils' unique texture, we don't toss them with a dressing, which might cause them to lose their crispy quality. Instead, we use yogurt as an anchor, spreading it on a platter and topping it with a lightly dressed blend of fresh herbs tossed with the crunchy lentils and sweet dried cherries. Pita is a must for scooping everything up in perfect bites. The firm texture of lentilles du Puy works best here, though you can use brown lentils instead.

- 1 teaspoon table salt for brining
- ½ cup dried lentilles du Puy, picked over and rinsed
- ⅓ cup vegetable oil for frying
- ½ teaspoon ground cumin
- ¼ teaspoon plus pinch table salt, divided
- 1 cup plain Greek yogurt
- 3 tablespoons extra-virgin olive oil, divided
- 1 teaspoon grated lemon zest plus 1 teaspoon juice
- 1 garlic clove, minced

- ½ cup fresh parsley leaves
- ½ cup torn fresh dill
- ½ cup fresh cilantro leaves
- ¼ cup dried cherries, chopped
  Pomegranate molasses
  Pita, warmed

1. Dissolve 1 teaspoon salt in 1 quart water in bowl. Add lentils and let sit at room temperature for at least 1 hour or up to 24 hours. Drain well and pat dry with paper towels.

2. Heat vegetable oil in large saucepan over medium heat until shimmering. Add lentils and cook, stirring constantly, until crispy and golden in spots, 8 to 12 minutes (oil should bubble vigorously throughout; adjust heat as needed). Carefully drain lentils in fine-mesh strainer set over bowl, then transfer lentils to paper towel–lined plate. Discard oil. Sprinkle with cumin and ¼ teaspoon salt and toss to combine; set aside. (Cooled lentils can be stored in airtight container at room temperature for up to 24 hours.)

3. Whisk yogurt, 2 tablespoons olive oil, lemon zest and juice, and garlic together in bowl and season with salt and pepper to taste. Spread yogurt mixture over serving platter. Toss parsley, dill, cilantro, remaining pinch salt, and remaining 1 tablespoon olive oil together in bowl, then gently stir in lentils and cherries and arrange on top of yogurt mixture, leaving 1-inch border. Drizzle with pomegranate molasses. Serve with pita.

KEYS TO SUCCESS

- **Soak the lentils:** This ensures they turn crispy and cook through without burning.
- **A large saucepan:** The lentils will bubble and steam when you fry them.
- **Keep lentils separate:** Sprinkling them on top of the salad ensures they stay nice and crispy.

VOSPOV KOFTE

Serves: 4 to 6
Total Time: 1¼ hours, plus 1 hour chilling

RECIPE OVERVIEW Vospov (red lentil) kofte is the popular vegetarian analog to chi kofte, the canonical Armenian dish of minced raw beef or lamb that's bound with bulgur, seasoned with spices, formed into logs or balls, and served with a mixture of chopped herbs inside pita or lavash. We start by cooking red lentils in plenty of water until they break down into a smooth paste, then stir in an equal amount of fine-grind bulgur and let it sit while the bulgur hydrates and we sauté onion and spices to incorporate into the mixture. The combination of olive oil and butter develops nutty flavor as it softens the onions and blooms the spices. After a stint in the refrigerator to firm up, the mixture is ready for shaping. For the herb component, we mix a modest amount of chopped parsley into the kofte and then turn much more of it into a vibrant herb salad with mint, scallions, Aleppo pepper, sumac, lemon juice, and olive oil. If sumac is unavailable, increase the lemon juice to 1 tablespoon and the salt to ½ teaspoon in the salad. We like the gentle heat and raisiny sweetness of Aleppo pepper here, but if it's unavailable, substitute ¾ teaspoon paprika and ¼ teaspoon cayenne pepper in the kofte and ⅜ teaspoon paprika and ⅛ teaspoon cayenne in the salad. Serve the kofte on their own or with pita or lavash.

Kofte

- 3 cups water
- 1 cup dried red lentils, picked over and rinsed
- ¼ cup extra-virgin olive oil
- 1¼ teaspoons table salt, divided
- 1 cup fine-grind bulgur
- 4 tablespoons unsalted butter
- 1 onion, chopped fine
- 1 teaspoon ground dried Aleppo pepper
- 1 teaspoon ground cumin
- ¼ teaspoon pepper
- ¼ teaspoon ground allspice
- 2 tablespoons chopped fresh parsley

Salad

- ¾ cup chopped fresh parsley
- 4 scallions, sliced thin
- ¼ cup chopped fresh mint
- 1 tablespoon extra-virgin olive oil
- 2 teaspoons lemon juice
- 1 teaspoon ground sumac
- ½ teaspoon ground dried Aleppo pepper
- ¼ teaspoon table salt

1. FOR THE KOFTE Bring water, lentils, oil, and 1 teaspoon salt to boil in large saucepan over high heat. Adjust heat to maintain gentle simmer. Cover and cook, stirring occasionally, until lentils are fully broken down, 20 to 25 minutes. Place bulgur in large bowl.

2. Pour lentil mixture over bulgur, stir until uniform, and set aside. Wipe out saucepan with paper towel. Melt butter in now-empty saucepan over medium-high heat. Add onion, Aleppo pepper, cumin, pepper, allspice, and remaining ¼ teaspoon salt. Cook, stirring frequently, until onion is softened and just beginning to brown, 8 to 10 minutes. Add parsley and onion mixture to lentil mixture and stir until uniform. Transfer to bowl and let cool completely, 30 to 45 minutes. Refrigerate until stiffened enough to mold, about 30 minutes.

3. Using ¼-cup dry measuring cup sprayed with vegetable oil spray, divide mixture into 16 portions (respray cup if mixture starts to stick). Using your slightly moistened hands, press and roll each portion into 3-inch log. Arrange around perimeter of platter.

4. FOR THE SALAD Toss all ingredients together in bowl. Top kofte with salad; serve at room temperature.

KEYS TO SUCCESS

- **Fundamental ratio:** The ratio of water to lentils to bulgur (3:1:1) can't change. Drier mixtures result in starchy kofte that tend to crack and fall apart when you mold them, while wetter mixtures produce pasty kofte that are too soft to hold their shape.

- **Use fine-grind bulgur:** Using a coarser grind will result in unpleasant graininess in the kofte.

Grinding Fine Bulgur

Fine-grind (#1) bulgur is a must in vospov kofte, where the small particles seamlessly bind up the lentil mixture. This bulgur, which is roughly the size of semolina, can be hard to find unless you're shopping at a Middle Eastern market or online, but it's easy to make a facsimile by briefly grinding any-size bulgur in a blender. To get the right amount for this recipe, process ¾ cup plus 2 tablespoons in a blender for about 2 minutes.

PALAK DAL

Serves: 4 to 6
Total Time: 1¼ hours

RECIPE OVERVIEW There are nearly endless varieties of dal found throughout India. Here is our spinach version of the northern Indian dish. A typical recipe starts by simmering pulses in water, sometimes with turmeric and/or asafetida, the dried resin from the root of the Ferula assafoetida plant. Indian cooks often use a pressure cooker to expedite cooking time, but here we use red lentils, as they have their hulls removed and turn creamy quickly. A few vigorous turns of a whisk break down the cooked lentils even more and give them a porridge-like consistency. We then wilt baby spinach in the dal and make the tadka. This genius seasoning technique is central to Indian cuisine: Bloom whole spices in fat, and then use the fragrant, sizzling, visually stunning mixture as a glistening garnish. For less heat, remove the ribs and seeds of the serrano. Fresh curry leaves add a wonderful aroma, but if they're unavailable, you can omit them. Serve with naan and basmati rice.

4½	cups water
1½	cups (10½ ounces) dried red lentils, picked over and rinsed
1	tablespoon grated fresh ginger
¾	teaspoon ground turmeric
6	ounces (6 cups) baby spinach
1½	teaspoons table salt
3	tablespoons ghee
1½	teaspoons brown or yellow mustard seeds
1½	teaspoons cumin seeds
1	large onion, chopped
15	curry leaves, roughly torn (optional)
6	garlic cloves, sliced
4	whole dried arbol chiles
1	serrano chile, halved lengthwise
1½	teaspoons lemon juice, plus extra for seasoning
⅓	cup chopped fresh cilantro

1. Bring water, lentils, ginger, and turmeric to boil in large saucepan over medium-high heat. Reduce heat to maintain vigorous simmer. Cook, uncovered, stirring occasionally, until lentils are soft and starting to break down, 18 to 20 minutes.

2. Whisk lentils vigorously until coarsely pureed, about 30 seconds. Continue to cook until lentils have consistency of loose polenta or oatmeal, up to 5 minutes longer. Stir in spinach and salt and cook until spinach is fully wilted, 30 to 60 seconds longer. Cover and set aside off heat.

3. Melt ghee in 10-inch skillet over medium-high heat. Add mustard seeds and cumin seeds and cook, stirring constantly, until seeds sizzle and pop, about 30 seconds. Add onion and cook, stirring frequently, until onion is just starting to brown, about 5 minutes. Add curry leaves (if using), garlic, arbols, and serrano and cook, stirring frequently, until onion and garlic are golden brown, 3 to 4 minutes.

4. Add lemon juice to lentils and stir to incorporate. (Dal should have consistency of loose polenta. If too thick, loosen with hot water, adding 1 tablespoon at a time.) Season with salt and extra lemon juice to taste. Transfer dal to serving bowl and spoon onion mixture on top. Sprinkle with cilantro and serve.

KEYS TO SUCCESS

- **Whisk the lentils:** This is essential to achieve the right consistency for the dal.
- **Mind the tadka:** Monitor the spices and aromatics carefully during frying, reducing the heat if necessary to prevent scorching.

No Ghee? Browned Butter Works

Ghee is a type of clarified butter that is simmered until all its moisture has evaporated and its milk solids have browned, changing its flavor and the composition of its fat. The solids are strained out, leaving pure butterfat with a nutty flavor. To approximate real ghee, melt 6 tablespoons butter in a 10-inch skillet over medium-high heat. Cook, swirling skillet and stirring constantly with a rubber spatula, until the butter is dark golden brown and has a nutty aroma, 1 to 3 minutes longer. Slowly pour the butter into a small heatproof bowl, leaving as much of the browned milk solids behind as possible.

MAKING THE MOST OF CHICKPEAS

DAN ZUCCARELLO

Most of us probably keep a couple of cans of chickpeas in the pantry for topping salads. But here you will learn how (and why) to cook with dried chickpeas: They have a deeper, earthier flavor and cook up so much creamier and smoother than the canned variety. You'll also learn to use canned chickpeas in a whole new way. One is always told to rinse and drain canned beans, but the liquid in canned chickpeas, known as aquafaba, actually brings unique thickening, enriching qualities when used in stewy dishes.

DAN'S PRO TIP: *Toppings are not only pretty but also add complementary flavors and textures that make hummus a treat. And you don't need to go far to find them—just look in your pantry! Beyond a drizzle of high-quality oil, consider toasted nuts and seeds, dried spice blends such as Za'atar (page 21) or even everything bagel seasoning, or jarred olives, artichokes, or roasted peppers.*

ULTIMATE HUMMUS

Serves: 4 (makes about 2 cups)
Total Time: 1½ hours, plus 8½ hours soaking and resting

RECIPE OVERVIEW In Middle Eastern cuisine, hummus is traditionally made with dried beans and is silky smooth and ethereal in texture, with flavors balanced between chickpeas, tahini, lemon juice, garlic, and olive oil. And it's often served with toppings that turn it into a meal. To produce a smooth puree, first, after processing the chickpeas until almost ground, we add a mixture of bean cooking water and lemon juice. Grinding the chickpeas alone and then adding liquid—slowly—produces a smoother puree than processing everything at once. Second, we whisk together the olive oil and tahini and add them to the puree in a slow drizzle while processing, creating an emulsion right in the hummus. As the color of the dip changes with the dispersion of the oil, the ultimate hummus is born. Serve with pita and raw vegetables as is, or with one of our toppings at right.

- ½ cup dried chickpeas, rinsed and picked over
- ⅛ teaspoon baking soda
- 3 tablespoons lemon juice
- 6 tablespoons tahini
- 2 tablespoons extra-virgin olive oil, plus extra for drizzling
- 1 (14-ounce) can chickpeas, rinsed
- 1 small garlic clove, minced
- ½ teaspoon table salt
- ¼ teaspoon ground cumin
- Pinch cayenne pepper
- 1 tablespoon minced fresh cilantro or parsley

1. Place chickpeas in large container and cover with water by 2 to 3 inches. Soak at room temperature for at least 8 hours or up to 24 hours. Drain well.

2. Bring chickpeas, baking soda, and 1 quart water to boil in large saucepan over high heat. Reduce heat to low and simmer gently, stirring occasionally, until beans are tender, about 1 hour. Drain, reserving ¼ cup bean cooking water, and cool.

3. Combine bean cooking water and lemon juice in small bowl or measuring cup. Whisk together tahini and oil in second small bowl.

4. Process cooked and canned chickpeas, garlic, salt, cumin, and cayenne in food processor until almost fully ground, about 15 seconds. Scrape down bowl with rubber spatula. With machine running, add lemon juice mixture in steady stream. Scrape down bowl and continue to process for 1 minute. With machine running, add tahini mixture in steady stream; continue to process until hummus is smooth and creamy, about 15 seconds, scraping bowl as needed.

5. Transfer hummus to serving bowl, sprinkle cilantro over surface, cover with plastic wrap, and let stand until flavors meld, at least 30 minutes. Drizzle with olive oil and serve. (Hummus can be refrigerated for up to 5 days. When ready to serve, stir in approximately 1 tablespoon warm water if texture is too thick.)

CRISPY MUSHROOM AND SUMAC TOPPING

Serves: 4

Total Time: 35 minutes

When roughly shredded and then sautéed, oyster mushrooms take on lacy, crispy edges and become so delicious you'll want to eat them straight from the pan. Chickpeas tossed in sumac with a squeeze of caramelized lemon offer a bright flavor and texture counterpoint. More texture comes from a final sprinkling of chopped slightly sweet pistachios. You can substitute halved portobello mushrooms, sliced thin, for the oyster mushrooms.

- 12 ounces oyster mushrooms, trimmed and torn into 1½-inch pieces
- ¼ cup water
- 2 tablespoons extra-virgin olive oil, divided, plus extra for drizzling
- ⅛ teaspoon table salt
- 1 lemon, quartered
- 1 (15-ounce) can chickpeas, rinsed
- 2 teaspoons sumac, plus extra for serving
- ¼ cup fresh parsley leaves
- 2 tablespoons chopped toasted pistachios

1. Cook mushrooms and water in 12-inch nonstick skillet over high heat, stirring occasionally, until mushrooms begin to stick to bottom of skillet, 6 to 8 minutes. Reduce heat to medium-high and stir in 1 tablespoon oil and salt. Cook, stirring occasionally, until mushrooms are crisp and well browned, 8 to 12 minutes. Transfer to plate.

2. Add remaining 1 tablespoon oil and lemon quarters, cut sides down, to now-empty skillet and cook over medium-high heat, until well browned on cut sides, 2 to 3 minutes; transfer to plate with mushrooms. Add chickpeas to oil left in again-empty skillet and cook until lightly browned, about 2 minutes. Off heat, add sumac and toss to coat. Season with salt and pepper to taste. Serve warm over hummus, topping with parsley and pistachios, sprinkling with extra sumac, and drizzling with extra oil. Serve with seared lemon quarters.

KEYS TO SUCCESS

- **Baking soda:** Adding baking soda to the chickpeas helps them cook faster; the alkalines in the baking soda help break down the cell structure and turn the chickpeas tender.

- **Grind the chickpeas in two stages:** Grinding the chickpeas and then adding liquid and processing again, makes for a smoother puree.

- **Create an emulsion:** Drizzling in the tahini-oil mixture while processing further encourages a silky-smooth hummus.

BAHARAT-SPICED BEEF TOPPING

Serves: 4

Total Time: 40 minutes

This warmly spiced topping turns hummus into a hearty meal. Ground lamb can be used in place of the beef, if desired. Toast the pine nuts in a dry skillet over medium-high heat until fragrant, 3 to 5 minutes. Spoon the topping over the hummus, garnishing with additional pine nuts and chopped fresh parsley.

- 2 teaspoons water
- ½ teaspoon table salt
- ¼ teaspoon baking soda
- 8 ounces 85 percent lean ground beef
- 1 tablespoon extra-virgin olive oil
- ¼ cup finely chopped onion
- 2 garlic cloves, minced
- 1 teaspoon hot smoked paprika
- 1 teaspoon ground cumin
- ¼ teaspoon pepper
- ¼ teaspoon ground coriander
- ⅛ teaspoon ground cloves
- ⅛ teaspoon ground cinnamon
- ¼ cup pine nuts, toasted
- 2 teaspoons lemon juice

1. Combine water, salt, and baking soda in large bowl. Add beef and toss to combine. Let sit for 5 minutes.

2. Heat oil in 12-inch nonstick skillet over medium heat until shimmering. Add onion and garlic and cook, stirring occasionally, until onion is softened, 3 to 4 minutes. Add paprika, cumin, pepper, coriander, cloves, and cinnamon and cook, stirring constantly, until fragrant, about 30 seconds. Add beef and cook, breaking up meat with wooden spoon, until beef is no longer pink, about 5 minutes. Add pine nuts and lemon juice and toss to combine. Serve warm over hummus.

FALAFEL BURGERS WITH HERB-YOGURT SAUCE

Serves: 4
Total Time: 45 minutes, plus 8 hours soaking

RECIPE OVERVIEW Falafel are crispy on the outside, soft on the inside, packed with seasoning, and utterly irresistible. Here we essentially supersize the chickpea fritters to make a uniquely delicious burger. We start by soaking dried chickpeas overnight to soften before grinding them into coarse, textural bits along with onion, herbs, garlic, and spices. Traditional falafel recipes use flour and coarsely ground chickpeas to create a dough-like texture, but a large burger patty turns out too dry and bready when prepared in the same way. So, to keep the interiors of our burgers moist and soft, we mix up a microwaved paste of flour, water, and baking powder and incorporate that into the mixture. To ensure burger-size falafel, we use a dry measuring cup to drop scoops of the falafel mixture into a heated skillet, then use the back of a spoon to press each portion into a ¾-inch-thick patty. For condiments, we offer a sauce of Greek yogurt, lemon juice, and fresh herbs and sliced cucumber and pickled red onions for a burger so flavorful we may never go back to falafel wrapped in pita bread.

8	ounces dried chickpeas, picked over and rinsed
1	cup plain Greek yogurt
1	teaspoon grated lemon zest plus 2 tablespoons juice and more juice for seasoning
3	garlic cloves, minced, divided
2	tablespoons minced fresh cilantro plus ¾ cup leaves and stems, divided
2	tablespoons minced fresh mint
¾	cup fresh parsley leaves
½	onion, chopped fine
1½	teaspoons ground coriander
1	teaspoon ground cumin
1	teaspoon table salt
¼	teaspoon cayenne pepper
¼	cup all-purpose flour
⅓	cup water
2	teaspoons baking powder
2	tablespoons vegetable oil, plus extra as needed
4	hamburger buns, toasted if desired
¼	English cucumber, sliced thin
½	cup Quick-Pickled Red Onions (recipe follows)

1. Place chickpeas in large container and cover with water by 2 to 3 inches. Soak at room temperature for at least 8 hours or up to 24 hours. Drain well.

2. Whisk yogurt, lemon zest and juice, ⅓ of the minced garlic, minced cilantro, and mint in medium bowl until smooth. Season with salt and extra lemon juice to taste; set aside. (Sauce can be refrigerated for up to 4 days.)

3. Process remaining minced garlic, cilantro leaves and stems, parsley, onion, coriander, cumin, salt, and cayenne in food processor until mixture is finely ground, about 30 seconds, scraping down sides of bowl as needed. Add chickpeas and pulse 6 times. Continue to pulse until chickpeas are coarsely chopped and resemble sesame seeds, about 6 more pulses. Transfer mixture to large bowl and set aside.

4. Whisk flour and water in bowl until no lumps remain. Microwave, whisking every 10 seconds, until mixture thickens to stiff, smooth, pudding-like consistency that forms mound when dropped from end of whisk into bowl, 40 to 80 seconds. Stir baking powder into flour paste. Add flour paste to chickpea mixture and, using rubber spatula, mix until fully incorporated. (Falafel mixture can be refrigerated for up to 2 hours.)

5. Heat oil in 12-inch nonstick skillet over medium heat until shimmering. Using 1 cup measure, drop 4 even portions (about ¾ cup each) into skillet, then press each portion into ¾-inch-thick patty with back of spoon. Cook until golden brown and crisp on first side, 4 to 6 minutes. Using 2 spatulas, gently flip patties and cook until well browned and crisp on second side, 4 to 6 minutes, adding extra oil as needed if skillet looks dry. Serve burgers on buns, topped with cucumber, pickled onions, and herb-yogurt sauce.

QUICK-PICKLED RED ONIONS

Makes: about 1 cup

Look for a firm, dry onion with thin, shiny skin and a deep purple color.

1	cup red wine vinegar
⅓	cup sugar
¼	teaspoon table salt
1	red onion, halved and sliced thin through root end

Bring vinegar, sugar, and salt to simmer in small saucepan over medium-high heat, stirring occasionally, until sugar has dissolved. Off heat, stir in onion, cover, and let cool to room temperature, about 1 hour. (Pickled onions can be refrigerated in airtight container for up to 1 week.)

KEYS TO SUCCESS

- **Start with dried chickpeas:** Burgers made with canned chickpeas will have a mushy, mealy texture.

- **Make the paste:** The flour-water paste hydrates the chickpea mixture to create fluffy burgers that aren't dense.

ESPINACAS CON GARBANZOS

Serves: 4
Total Time: 40 minutes

RECIPE OVERVIEW A favorite in the Spanish city of Seville, this bean and vegetable dish is visually unassuming: a mound of butter-soft chickpeas interspersed with plenty of well-cooked spinach and perhaps a few crispy bits of fried bread sticking out of it like sails. But its enticing aroma stops you in your tracks, thanks to the smoky paprika, earthy cumin, spicy cinnamon and chile, and musky-sweet saffron, underpinned by garlic and fruity olive oil. Recipes often start with dried chickpeas that must be soaked and simmered, but some opt for canned; we use the latter here to take full advantage of the body-building and seasoning properties of aquafaba. Combining the aquafaba with some chicken broth creates a savory, robust simmering liquid. Many recipes also call for seasoning and thickening the dish with a picada, a paste of garlic and bread cooked in olive oil. We like the viscosity that a picada brings to the dish and the way it helps some of the sauce stay put within the spinach, giving it a desirable juicy quality. A small amount of tomatoes and some sherry vinegar add tang. For the spinach, the goal is lush, silky, well-cooked greens that wilt completely and disperse evenly. This is surprisingly hard to achieve with fresh spinach, which tends to clump up even when it's prechopped and always seems a bit chewy. But frozen spinach works beautifully; since freezing tenderizes the vegetable, it is soft even as it goes into the pot. Plenty of olive oil helps create an almost creamy consistency. Use a fruity, spicy, high-quality olive oil here. Red wine vinegar can be substituted for the sherry vinegar.

1	loaf crusty bread, divided
2	(15-ounce) cans chickpeas (1 can drained, 1 can shaken and undrained)
1½	cups chicken broth
6	tablespoons extra-virgin olive oil, divided
6	garlic cloves, minced
1	tablespoon smoked paprika
1	teaspoon ground cumin
¼	teaspoon table salt
⅛	teaspoon ground cinnamon
⅛	teaspoon cayenne pepper
1	small pinch saffron
2	small plum tomatoes, halved lengthwise, flesh shredded on large holes of box grater and skins discarded
4	teaspoons sherry vinegar, plus extra for seasoning
10	ounces frozen chopped spinach, thawed and squeezed dry

1. Cut 1½-ounce piece from loaf of bread (thickness will vary depending on size of loaf) and tear into 1-inch pieces. Process in food processor until finely ground (you should have ¾ cup crumbs). Combine chickpeas and broth in large saucepan and bring to boil over high heat. Adjust heat to maintain simmer and cook until level of liquid is just below top layer of chickpeas, about 10 minutes.

2. While chickpeas cook, heat ¼ cup oil in 10-inch nonstick or carbon-steel skillet over medium heat until just shimmering. Add bread crumbs and cook, stirring frequently, until deep golden brown, 3 to 4 minutes. Add garlic, paprika, cumin, salt, cinnamon, cayenne, and saffron and cook until fragrant, 30 seconds. Stir in tomatoes and vinegar; remove from heat.

3. Stir bread mixture and spinach into chickpeas. Continue to simmer, stirring occasionally, until mixture is thick and stew-like, 5 to 10 minutes longer. Off heat, stir in remaining 2 tablespoons oil. Cover and let stand for 5 minutes. Season with salt and extra vinegar to taste. Transfer to serving bowl and serve with remaining bread.

KEYS TO SUCCESS

- **Shake the can:** This ensures that none of the aquafaba is left clinging to the bottom of the can.

- **Use good bread:** A crusty loaf with some chew to it will make a texturally pleasing picada.

SCIENCE LESSON **Aquawhatta?**

Aquafaba is the starchy liquid that comes in a can of chickpeas—and it's aqua-fabulous. It's often used in vegan baked goods, since it whips up just like egg whites. But it's also a great binder used straight from the can, bringing rich body and thicker texture to dishes like stews. To get started using it, shake the unopened can of chickpeas well. The starches in the liquid settle in the can, so to take full advantage, you need them evenly distributed throughout the liquid. Drain the beans through a fine-mesh strainer over a bowl to capture the liquid. Whisk the liquid, and then measure. Aquafaba will keep in the refrigerator for 1 week. You can also freeze it in 1-tablespoon portions in ice cube trays. Once the bean liquid cubes are frozen solid, pop them into a freezer bag for future use. To speed things along, you can thaw the aquafaba in the microwave (don't cook it, though).

2 ounces pancetta, cut into ½-inch pieces
1 small carrot, peeled and cut into ½-inch pieces
1 small celery rib, cut into ½-inch pieces
4 garlic cloves, peeled
1 onion, halved and cut into 1-inch pieces
1 (14-ounce) can whole peeled tomatoes, drained
¼ cup extra-virgin olive oil, plus extra for serving
2 teaspoons minced fresh rosemary
1 anchovy fillet, rinsed, patted dry, and minced
¼ teaspoon red pepper flakes
2 (15-ounce) cans chickpeas (cans shaken and undrained)
2 cups water
1 teaspoon table salt
8 ounces (1½ cups) ditalini
1 tablespoon lemon juice
1 tablespoon minced fresh parsley
   Grated Parmesan cheese

1. Process pancetta in food processor until ground to paste, about 30 seconds, scraping down sides of bowl as needed. Add carrot, celery, and garlic and pulse until finely chopped, 8 to 10 pulses. Add onion and pulse until onion is cut into ⅛- to ¼-inch pieces, 8 to 10 pulses. Transfer pancetta mixture to Dutch oven. Pulse tomatoes in now-empty processor until coarsely chopped, 8 to 10 pulses. Set aside.

2. Add oil to pancetta mixture in pot and cook over medium heat, stirring frequently, until fond begins to form on bottom of pot, about 5 minutes. Add rosemary, anchovy, and pepper flakes and cook until fragrant, about 1 minute. Stir in tomatoes, chickpeas and their liquid, water, and salt and bring to boil, scraping up any browned bits. Reduce heat to medium-low and simmer for 10 minutes. Add pasta and cook, stirring frequently, until tender, 10 to 12 minutes. Stir in lemon juice and parsley and season with salt and pepper to taste. Serve, passing Parmesan and extra oil separately.

PASTA E CECI

Serves: 4 to 6
Total Time: 1 hour

RECIPE OVERVIEW Every Italian household has its own version of pasta and chickpeas, the stick-to-your-ribs stew that is a sibling to pasta e fagioli. It may be homestyle cooking, but it takes some finesse to get the thickness of the dish right and not end up with merely a macaroni soup. We start by sautéing a soffritto—finely chopped onion, carrot, celery, garlic, and pancetta—in olive oil. We then stir in tomatoes, water, and canned chickpeas along with their aquafaba, which contributes a thicker body and more seasoned flavor than water or another liquid would. Simmering the chickpeas before adding the pasta makes them creamy and, because they break down a bit, they add even more body to the cooking liquid. Ditalini is a great choice for the pasta, since it's similar in size to the chickpeas. We simmer the mixture for about 10 minutes, at which point the pasta becomes tender and releases some starch of its own to further thicken the stew. Lemon juice and parsley stirred in at the end add a touch of brightness. Other short pasta can be substituted for the ditalini; substitute by weight and not by volume.

KEYS TO SUCCESS

- **Fond builds flavor:** The pancetta and vegetable mixture adds layers of nuanced flavor to the pasta and chickpeas.

- **Shake the cans:** This ensures getting every last drop of the thickening power of aquafaba.

- **Stir the pasta:** Stirring frequently while it cooks encourages the release of starch to further thicken this stew.

COURSE
BAKED BEANS

CHRISTIE MORRISON

Just as beans themselves are a broad category, baked beans can encompass more than you might think. Yes, you'll learn here how to make the best Boston baked beans, but you'll also find Greek, French, and Brazilian takes on turning simple dried beans into hearty, warming, fantastic—even company-worthy—meals. Whereas canned beans would turn to mush in any of these long-cooking recipes, dried beans absorb the flavors surrounding them as they slowly tenderize to perfect creaminess in the steady, even heat of the oven.

CHRISTIE'S PRO TIP: *Don't skip the soak. You have to think ahead to plan your grocery list or thaw a steak for tomorrow's dinner. Thinking ahead to soak beans is just as easy, and the results are clear: Soaked beans cook up faster and more evenly than unsoaked beans, which results in a creamier texture.*

BOSTON BAKED BEANS
Serves: 4 to 6
Total Time: 5¼ hours

RECIPE OVERVIEW Heady with smoky pork and bittersweet molasses, authentic Boston baked beans are a true American original. Both sweet and savory, they are a unique combination of the simplest ingredients that are unified and refined during a long simmer—a fine example of the whole being greater than the sum of its parts. The development of intense flavor is by means of the judicious use of canonical ingredients (beans, pork, molasses, mustard, and sometimes onion) and long, slow cooking. The most important ingredient is, of course, the beans. The classic choice is standard dried white beans in one of three sizes: small white beans, midsize navy or pea beans, or large great northern beans. We like the small white beans for their dense, creamy texture and ability to remain firm and intact over the course of a long simmer. (Larger sizes tend to split.) Next up is the meat. Some type of cured pork is essential for depth and lush texture, though its flavor should never dominate. Traditionalists swear by salt pork, but its flavor can be mild. Bacon is a more modern choice, but on its own it can be overwhelming. The perfect solution comes when we put both into the pot. The bacon brings the desired smoky depth to the beans, while the salt pork tempers the bacon's hickory tang. In traditional recipes, the salt pork is cast raw into the beans (often as a large piece) and is supposed to melt into the sauce, but it often doesn't render completely. The simple step of first browning the salt pork jump-starts the fat rendering and makes the flavor of the beans significantly fuller and richer. Cooking the beans at 300 degrees allows them to cook a bit faster than at a lower temperature, without sacrificing any of the creaminess that long, slow cooking brings. Uncovering them for the last hour of cooking allows the liquid to reduce to a syrupy, intensified sauce that perfectly cloaks the beans. Do not use dark or blackstrap molasses; the flavor will overwhelm the beans.

4 ounces salt pork, rind removed, cut into ½-inch pieces
2 slices bacon, cut into ¼-inch pieces
1 onion, chopped fine
9 cups water
1 pound (2½ cups) dried small white beans, picked over and rinsed
½ cup plus 1 tablespoon molasses, divided
1½ tablespoons spicy brown mustard
1¼ teaspoons table salt
1 teaspoon cider vinegar

1. Adjust oven rack to lower-middle position and heat oven to 300 degrees. Cook salt pork and bacon in Dutch oven over medium heat, stirring occasionally, until lightly browned and most of fat is rendered, about 7 minutes. Add onion and continue to cook, stirring occasionally, until onion is softened, 5 to 7 minutes longer. Add water, beans, ½ cup molasses, mustard, and salt. Increase heat to medium-high and bring to boil. Cover pot and transfer to oven. Bake until beans are tender, about 4 hours, stirring halfway through baking.

2. Carefully remove lid and continue to bake until liquid has thickened to syrupy consistency, 1 to 1½ hours longer. Remove pot from oven. Stir in vinegar and remaining 1 tablespoon molasses, season with salt and pepper to taste, and serve. (Beans can be refrigerated for up to 4 days.)

KEYS TO SUCCESS

- **Render the salt pork:** Use fatty—not lean—salt pork and brown it to render most of its fat before adding more ingredients to the pot.
- **Wait on the vinegar:** Vinegar changes the acidity of the baked beans; adding it earlier will discourage the beans from softening properly.

WHAT CAN GO WRONG

PROBLEM Crunchy beans.

SOLUTION You might have extremely hard water. Hard water, recognizable by mineral deposits in pots and plumbing and green rings around the drains in porcelain tubs and sinks, contains high levels of calcium and magnesium. Calcium, for reasons not yet fully understood, toughens cellulose. Your safest bet is to use bottled water. On the other hand, you might have stale beans; this is impossible to detect until after cooking, but they will never soften.

GIGANTES PLAKI

Serves: 4 to 6
Total Time: 2½ hours, plus 8¼ hours soaking and cooling

RECIPE OVERVIEW Gigantes plaki is a popular dish often found both as meze at tavernas throughout Greece and on family dining tables, most often during Lent. The name refers to the type of bean (gigantes) and the style of cooking it in a baking dish in the oven (plaki). The beans absorb the juices and flavors of generous amounts of olive oil, tomatoes, and aromatics, becoming creamy, luxurious, and meaty textured within a scrumptious casserole with caramelized edges and an intoxicating aroma. Onion, celery, carrots, and garlic form the base of the aromatics along with beloved Greek oregano; hints of warmth from cinnamon and sweetness from a touch of honey balance the acidity of the tomato-heavy sauce. Gigantes plaki can be eaten warm or at room temperature, as a hearty side dish or a delicious main, with a hunk of bread to sop up all of the sauce. If you can't find gigante beans, you can substitute dried large lima beans.

3 tablespoons table salt for brining
1 pound (2½ cups) dried gigante beans, picked over and rinsed
¼ cup extra-virgin olive oil, plus extra for drizzling
1 onion, chopped
2 carrots, peeled and chopped
2 celery ribs, chopped
1 teaspoon table salt
2 tablespoons tomato paste
4 garlic cloves, minced
1 tablespoon chopped fresh oregano or 1 teaspoon dried
¼ teaspoon ground cinnamon
1 (14.5-ounce) can whole peeled tomatoes, drained with juice reserved, chopped
1¼ cups water
1 tablespoon honey
2 bay leaves
2 tablespoons chopped fresh dill

1. Dissolve salt in 4 quarts cold water in large container. Add beans and soak at room temperature for at least 8 hours or up to 24 hours. Drain and rinse well.

2. Bring beans and 3 quarts water to boil in Dutch oven. Reduce heat and simmer, stirring occasionally, until beans are tender, 1 to 1½ hours. (Skim any loose bean skins or foam from surface of liquid as beans cook.) Drain beans and set aside. Wipe out pot with paper towels.

3. Adjust oven rack to middle position and heat oven to 400 degrees. Heat oil in now-empty pot over medium heat until shimmering. Add onion, carrots, celery, and salt and cook until softened and beginning to brown, 7 to

10 minutes. Stir in tomato paste, garlic, oregano, and cinnamon and cook until fragrant, about 30 seconds. Add tomatoes and their juices and water, scraping up any browned bits. Stir in beans, honey, and bay leaves and bring to simmer. Season with salt and pepper to taste.

4. Transfer bean mixture to 13 by 9-inch baking dish, smoothing top with rubber spatula. Transfer dish to oven and bake until beans are cooked through and edges are golden brown and bubbling, 30 to 45 minutes. Let cool for 15 minutes, remove bay leaves, and sprinkle with dill and drizzle with extra oil. Serve.

KEY TO SUCCESS
- **A long soak:** These large beans are prone to blowouts, so soak them for at least 8 hours.

CASSOULET

Serves: 8 to 10
Total Time: 3 hours, plus 12 hours soaking

RECIPE OVERVIEW Hailing from the Languedoc, this revered French stew includes garlicky white beans, crispy-skinned duck confit, pork sausage, and a variety of other meats, capped off with a buttery bread-crumb topping. It originated as peasant food, making do with whatever was on hand, and so the heart and soul of cassoulet was (and remains) the beans. Dried white kidney-shaped beans that turn meltingly soft but still hold their shape are the key. We prefer flageolet beans, but dried cannellini or navy beans can be used. We love our stellar homemade duck confit, but you can use store-bought. To avoid the time-consuming step of having to slow-roast fresh meat before adding it to the pot, we sear chunks of pork butt and then essentially stew them in the pot with the other ingredients. We add the beans early, after the pork has browned, so they can cook through and soak up amazing flavor as the pork stews. For the topping, added to the cassoulet near the end of cooking, our croutons soak up the meaty juices while their tops stay buttery and crispy and form a proper crust.

Pork and Beans
- 2 pounds (5 cups) dried flageolet, cannellini, or navy beans, picked over and rinsed
- 1 tablespoon vegetable oil
- 1 pound boneless pork butt roast, trimmed and cut into 1-inch pieces
- 1 onion, chopped fine
- 9 garlic cloves, minced
- 2 tablespoons minced fresh thyme or 2 teaspoons dried
- ½ teaspoon table salt
- 1 cup dry white wine
- 1 tablespoon tomato paste
- 10 cups chicken broth, plus extra as needed
- 1 (28-ounce) can diced tomatoes, drained

Cassoulet
- 5 slices hearty white sandwich bread, cut into ½-inch cubes
- 3 tablespoons unsalted butter, melted
- ¼ teaspoon table salt
- ⅛ teaspoon pepper
- 1 pound (4- to 6-inch-long) garlic pork sausages
- 6 confit duck legs (page 454), scraped clean of confit fat

1. FOR THE PORK AND BEANS Combine beans and 2½ quarts cold water in large bowl and soak at room temperature for at least 12 hours or up to 24 hours. Drain beans and set aside.

2. Heat oil in large Dutch oven over medium-high heat until just smoking. Add pork and cook, stirring occasionally, until well browned, about 10 minutes, reducing heat if pan begins to scorch. Stir in onion, garlic, thyme, and salt and cook until onion begins to soften, about 3 minutes. Stir in wine and tomato paste, scraping up any browned bits. Stir in drained beans, broth, and tomatoes and bring to boil over high heat. Reduce heat to medium-low and simmer gently, uncovered, stirring occasionally, until beans and pork are just tender, about 1 hour (adjusting burner as needed to maintain gentle simmer).

3. FOR THE CASSOULET Meanwhile, adjust oven rack to middle position and heat oven to 400 degrees. Toss bread cubes with melted butter, salt, and pepper and spread over rimmed baking sheet. Bake until light golden and crispy, about 15 minutes, stirring bread cubes halfway through baking; set aside. Do not turn off oven.

4. Brown sausages in 12-inch nonstick skillet over medium heat until golden on all sides, 5 to 8 minutes; transfer to paper towel–lined plate and set aside.

5. When beans are just tender, level of broth and beans should be equal; if necessary, add extra broth. Nestle sausages into bean mixture and lay duck legs, skin side up, on top of beans (the duck skin should be exposed; do not nestle into beans). Bake, uncovered, until duck skin is golden and crispy and casserole is bubbling around edges, about 50 minutes.

6. Sprinkle croutons over top and continue to bake until they form crust, about 10 minutes longer. Let cassoulet cool and thicken slightly, 15 to 20 minutes, before serving.

KEYS TO SUCCESS
- **Avoid bean blowout:** You'll get the best results if you soak the beans for at least 8 hours.

- **Seek out sausage:** Look for Irish pork sausage if you can't source French garlic sausage. Italian sausage will work, but it contains fennel and other Italian seasonings that will affect flavor.

- **Season sparingly:** Many of the components are already well seasoned, so be sparing with salt.

1 tablespoon chili powder
1 teaspoon ground cumin
1 teaspoon ground coriander
7 cups water
1 pound (2½ cups) dried black beans, picked over and rinsed
2 bay leaves
⅛ teaspoon baking soda
1 pound linguiça sausage, cut into ½-inch pieces

Hot Sauce
2 tomatoes, cored, seeded, and chopped fine
1 onion, chopped fine
1 small green bell pepper, stemmed, seeded, and chopped fine
1 jalapeño chile, stemmed, seeded, and minced
⅓ cup white wine vinegar
3 tablespoons extra-virgin olive oil
1 tablespoon minced fresh cilantro
½ teaspoon table salt

FEIJOADA

Serves: 6 to 8
Total Time: 3 hours

RECIPE OVERVIEW Feijoada is as much an event as a meal. Considered one of Brazil's national dishes, this hearty black bean stew is typically loaded with a bevy of pork cuts (as well as pig parts such as feet, ears, tail, and snout) and flavored with molho apimentado, a fresh, salsa-like hot sauce. It's served with a slew of sides and garnishes, including white rice, sliced oranges, sautéed kale, and farofa, a dish made with toasted manioc flour. For our home rendition with creamy flavorful beans, intense smoky pork flavor, and tender juicy meat, we start with the beans. Since success in this recipe doesn't require the black beans to cook up entirely intact (some burst beans add more creaminess to the stew's consistency), there's no need for presoaking. We do add a tiny bit of baking soda to help them retain their dark, rich color after cooking. For the meat, we skip the offal and focus on three pork cuts that pack a punch and require little prep work: boneless pork butt roast, smoky bacon, and garlicky linguiça sausage. We simply sear the pork and brown the bacon in the Dutch oven before adding aromatics, spices, the beans, and water. The linguiça goes in near the end of the cooking time. Make the hot sauce soon after the stew goes into the oven so that the flavors have time to develop.

Stew
1 (3½- to 4-pound) boneless pork butt roast, pulled apart at seams, trimmed, and cut into 1½-inch pieces
3 tablespoons vegetable oil, divided
4 slices bacon, chopped fine
1 onion, chopped fine
½ teaspoon table salt, divided
4 garlic cloves, minced

1. **FOR THE STEW** Adjust oven rack to lower-middle position and heat oven to 325 degrees. Pat pork dry with paper towels and season with salt and pepper. Heat 1 tablespoon oil in Dutch oven over medium-high heat until just smoking. Add half of pork and brown well on all sides, 7 to 10 minutes; transfer to large bowl. Repeat with 1 tablespoon oil and remaining pork. Add bacon to fat left in pot and cook over medium heat until crispy, 5 to 7 minutes.

2. Stir in remaining 1 tablespoon oil, onion, and ¼ teaspoon salt and cook until onion is softened, about 5 minutes. Stir in garlic, chili powder, cumin, and coriander and cook until fragrant, about 30 seconds. Stir in water, beans, bay leaves, baking soda, remaining ¼ teaspoon salt, and pork and any accumulated juices and bring to simmer. Cover, transfer pot to oven, and cook for 1½ hours. Remove pot from oven and stir in linguiça. Cover, return pot to oven, and cook until meat and beans are fully tender, about 30 minutes.

3. **FOR THE HOT SAUCE** While the stew cooks, combine all ingredients in bowl and let sit at room temperature until flavors meld, about 30 minutes. (Sauce can be refrigerated for up to 2 days.)

4. Remove pot from oven and discard bay leaves. (Stew can be refrigerated for up to 2 days; add water as needed to loosen consistency when reheating.) Season with salt and pepper to taste. Serve with hot sauce.

KEYS TO SUCCESS
- **Skip the soak:** Though most recipes using dried beans require soaking, the feijoada turns out better if you don't soak them; some burst beans are what brings thickening power to this stew.
- **Wait to add linguiça:** Since it's already cooked, adding the sausage at the end keeps it tender and prevents it from turning rubbery.

FRESH LEGUMES

MORGAN BOLLING

The legume umbrella shelters both dried beans like kidney beans and fresh beans like the edamame, lima beans, and fava beans found in this course. Edamame are young (immature) soybeans, harvested while still green. Once only found in frozen food supermarket aisles, they are far more readily available fresh now-adays. Lima beans still are difficult to find fresh but are just as good (and easily found) in convenient frozen form. And fresh favas are a true highlight of spring, nutty and buttery, nestled in wonderfully fuzzy green pods.

MORGAN'S PRO TIP: *It's great if you remember to thaw frozen lima beans or fava beans the night before cooking. But if you forget, thaw them quickly by placing them in a fine-mesh strainer, and rinsing with warm water until thawed. Drain and pat them dry before using.*

EDAMAME SALAD

Serves: 4
Total Time: 30 minutes

RECIPE OVERVIEW The bright vegetable flavor and satisfying pop of texture found in edamame make them a great base for salads. However, keeping the focus on the edamame can be a challenge, as tart vinaigrettes or other bold ingredients can overpower the fresh beans' mildness. Baby arugula complements the beans well, thanks to its subtle peppery flavor and delicate leaves. Lots of mint and basil bring a light, summery element to the salad. Thinly sliced shallot adds mild onion flavor, and just a couple of radishes add crunch and color without too much spiciness. For the vinaigrette, rice vinegar has a mild acidity, and a little honey adds sweetness and helps emulsify the dressing. The finishing touch is a sprinkling of roasted sunflower seeds, which add crunch and nuttiness. Look for fresh edamame in late summer and early fall, or use frozen edamame that have been thawed and patted dry.

2	tablespoons unseasoned rice vinegar
1	tablespoon honey
1	small garlic clove, minced
1	teaspoon table salt
3	tablespoons extra-virgin olive oil
18	ounces shelled edamame beans (3 cups)
2	ounces (2 cups) baby arugula
½	cup shredded fresh basil
½	cup chopped fresh mint
2	radishes, trimmed, halved, and sliced thin
1	shallot, halved and sliced thin
¼	cup roasted sunflower seeds

Whisk vinegar, honey, garlic, and salt together in large bowl. While whisking constantly, slowly whisk in oil until combined. Add edamame, arugula, basil, mint, radishes, and shallot and toss to combine. Sprinkle with sunflower seeds and season with salt and pepper to taste. Serve.

KEY TO SUCCESS

- **Lots of herbs:** The basil and mint are treated like salad greens here, so don't skimp on them.

Fresh Edamame

If you find fresh edamame in a farmer's market or Asian market, you'll need to cook the beans before using them in a recipe (soybeans should not be eaten raw). Bring 2 cups water to a boil and cook the whole pods until tender, 6 to 8 minutes. Let cool, then shell the beans. Frozen edamame are already blanched, so there's no need to cook them before use.

SUCCOTASH SALAD WITH LIMA BEANS AND CILANTRO

Serves: 4 to 6
Total Time: 30 minutes, plus 30 minutes resting

RECIPE OVERVIEW Succotash—both the dish and the name—has Native American origins, and when seasonal produce is at its best, it should shine. The traditional medley has a base of sweet fresh corn and fresh shell beans (such as lima beans or butter beans); beyond that, other vegetables such as bell peppers, onion, tomatoes, and zucchini or summer squash might be added, and sometimes it's finished with butter or cream. In keeping with the seasonal spirit of the dish, we use fresh corn, which has a flavor far superior to that of frozen or canned. You could leave the kernels raw for succotash, but browning them in a skillet, as we do here, enhances their natural sweetness and adds a touch of caramelized complexity. Fresh lima beans can be hard to find outside of a farmers' market, so we call for frozen limas, to which we add zucchini, tomatoes, and scallions. And omitting the dairy makes for a fresher, brighter-tasting succotash. Fresh cilantro is a must here.

- ⅓ cup extra-virgin olive oil, divided
- ¼ cup white wine vinegar
- 1 tablespoon honey
- 2 teaspoons table salt, divided
- ¼ teaspoon red pepper flakes, plus extra for seasoning
- 1½ cups frozen lima beans, thawed
- 8 ounces cherry tomatoes, halved
- 1 zucchini, cut into ½-inch chunks
- 4 scallions, sliced thin
- 4 ears corn, kernels cut from cobs (3 cups)
- 1 garlic clove, minced
- 2 tablespoons chopped fresh cilantro

1. Whisk ¼ cup oil, vinegar, honey, 1½ teaspoons salt, and pepper flakes together in large bowl. Add lima beans, tomatoes, zucchini, and scallions and toss to combine.

2. Heat remaining oil in 12-inch nonstick skillet over medium-high heat until shimmering. Add corn and remaining ½ teaspoon salt and cook, stirring occasionally, until softened and just beginning to brown, 5 to 7 minutes. Add garlic and cook until fragrant, about 30 seconds.

3. Transfer corn mixture to bowl with lima bean mixture and toss to combine. Let sit for at least 30 minutes to allow flavors to meld. (Salad can be covered with plastic wrap and refrigerated for up to 2 days.)

4. Stir in cilantro and season with salt and extra pepper flakes to taste. Serve.

KEY TO SUCCESS
- **Fresh corn:** Don't substitute frozen or canned corn in this truly seasonal recipe.

Fresh Lima Beans

Fresh lima beans are not generally available in supermarkets, though you may find them in farmers' markets or specialty food stores. You should never eat raw lima beans, because they contain a compound called linamarin, which turns into cyanide when consumed. However, cooking the beans destroys these enzymes. If you do find fresh lima beans, shell them, bring 2 cups water to a boil, and simmer the beans until tender, about 20 minutes; then drain and proceed with the recipe.

VIGNOLE

Serves: 6
Total Time: 1 hour

RECIPE OVERVIEW This vibrant skillet braise hailing from the Abruzzo region of Italy celebrates springtime vegetables. The fava beans for this dish are traditionally shelled but cooked and served with their translucent waxy skin left on. Since the skins tend to be tough, we tenderize them by blanching them in water with baking soda. Don't be alarmed when the high pH of the water causes the favas to turn purple. All that's needed to restore their green hue is to rinse the beans well after cooking. We add baby artichokes to the skillet first to cook almost all the way through before adding delicate asparagus and peas, and then finally the blanched favas. We finish the dish with a handful of herbs and some lemon zest. This recipe works best with fresh vegetables, but you can substitute 1 cup frozen, thawed fava beans and 1¼ cups frozen peas; add the peas to the skillet with the beans in step 4.

- 1 lemon
- 4 baby artichokes (3 ounces each)
- 1 teaspoon baking soda
- 1 pound fava beans, shelled (1 cup)
- 1 tablespoon extra-virgin olive oil, plus extra for serving
- 1 leek, white and light green parts only, halved lengthwise, sliced thin, and washed thoroughly
- 1 teaspoon table salt
- 3 garlic cloves, minced
- 1 cup chicken or vegetable broth
- 1 pound asparagus, trimmed and cut on bias into 2-inch lengths
- 1 pound fresh peas, shelled (1¼ cups)
- 2 tablespoons shredded fresh basil
- 1 tablespoon chopped fresh mint

1. Grate 2 teaspoons lemon zest from lemon; set aside. Halve lemon and squeeze lemon halves into container filled with 4 cups water, then add spent halves. Working with 1 artichoke at a time, trim stem to about ¾ inch and cut off top quarter of artichoke. Break off bottom 3 or 4 rows of tough outer leaves by pulling them downward. Using paring knife, trim outer layer of stem and base, removing any dark green parts. Cut artichoke into quarters and submerge in water.

2. Bring 2 cups water and baking soda to boil in small saucepan. Add beans and cook until edges begin to darken, 1 to 2 minutes. Drain and rinse well with cold water.

3. Heat oil in 12-inch skillet over medium heat until shimmering. Add leek, 1 tablespoon water, and salt and cook until softened, about 3 minutes. Stir in garlic and cook until fragrant, about 30 seconds.

4. Remove artichokes from lemon water, shaking off excess water, and add to skillet. Stir in broth and bring to simmer. Reduce heat to medium-low, cover, and cook until artichokes are almost tender, 6 to 8 minutes. Stir in asparagus and peas, cover, and cook until crisp-tender, 5 to 7 minutes. Stir in beans and cook until heated through and artichokes are fully tender, about 2 minutes. Off heat, stir in basil, mint, and lemon zest. Season with salt and pepper to taste and drizzle with extra oil. Serve immediately.

KEY TO SUCCESS

- **Blanch the beans:** It's traditional for this dish to leave the skins on the fava beans, so blanching them in water with some baking soda tenderizes the tough skins.

CORE TECHNIQUE

Preparing Fresh Fava Beans

SHELL BEANS
To shell favas, use paring knife and thumb to snip off tip of pod and pull apart sides to release beans. Blanch beans and dry well.

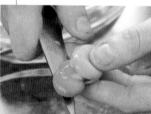

REMOVE WAXY SHEATH
Use paring knife to make small cut along edge of bean through waxy sheath, then gently squeeze sheath to release bean.

FAVA BEAN CROSTINI WITH MANCHEGO AND PINE NUTS

Serves: 8 to 10
Total Time: 1½ hours, plus 20 minutes cooling

RECIPE OVERVIEW Showcasing the rich flavor and buttery texture of fava beans, this sophisticated hors d'oeuvre is a surefire crowd-pleaser. Unlike the fava beans in our Vignole (page 346), the fresh favas here need to have their translucent waxy skins removed in addition to removing the outer shells, since the skins will not mash well. To preserve the creamy-tangy flavor of the beans, we simmer them with aromatic shallot, garlic, and cumin. Once the beans are softened and most of the water has evaporated, we use a potato masher to turn them into a smooth, creamy topping. Stirring in lemon juice and parsley adds a final fresh flavor punch. We spread the fava puree onto crispy thin toasted baguette slices and garnish them with Manchego cheese shavings and toasted pine nuts. This recipe works best with fresh fava beans, but if you can't find them, you can substitute 1 pound (3 cups) frozen shucked fava beans, thawed. Skip step 2 if using frozen favas. Be sure to set up the ice water bath before cooking the fava beans, as plunging them immediately in the cold water after blanching retains their bright green color and ensures that they don't overcook.

24 (¼-inch-thick) slices baguette (1 baguette)
5 tablespoons extra-virgin olive oil, plus extra for serving
3 pounds fava beans, shelled (3 cups)
1 shallot, minced
1 garlic clove, minced
½ teaspoon ground cumin
1 cup water
½ teaspoon table salt
3 tablespoons minced fresh parsley
1 tablespoon lemon juice
1 ounce Manchego cheese, shaved
2 tablespoons pine nuts, toasted

1. Adjust oven rack to middle position and heat oven to 400 degrees. Place baguette slices in single layer on rimmed baking sheet. Bake until golden and crisp, 8 to 10 minutes, flipping slices halfway through baking. Brush bread with 1 tablespoon oil and season with salt to taste. Let cool completely on sheet, about 30 minutes.

2. Meanwhile, bring 4 quarts water to boil in large pot. Fill large bowl halfway with ice and water. Add fava beans to boiling water and cook for 1 minute. Using slotted spoon, transfer fava beans to ice water and let cool, about 2 minutes. Transfer fava beans to triple layer of paper towels and dry well. Using paring knife, make small cut along edge of each bean through waxy sheath, then gently squeeze sheath to release bean; discard sheath.

3. Heat remaining ¼ cup oil in medium saucepan over medium heat until shimmering. Add shallot and cook until softened, about 3 minutes. Stir in garlic and cumin and cook until fragrant, about 30 seconds. Stir in fava beans, water, and salt and bring to simmer. Cook until fava beans are softened and most of liquid has evaporated, 12 to 15 minutes.

4. Off heat, using potato masher, mash bean mixture until mostly smooth. Stir in parsley and lemon juice and let cool to room temperature, about 20 minutes.

5. Spread fava bean mixture evenly over toasted baguette slices and top with Manchego and pine nuts. Drizzle with extra oil to taste. Serve.

KEYS TO SUCCESS

- **Skin the beans:** Removing the favas' waxy sheath takes some time but ensures a smooth puree.
- **Water bath:** Set it up beforehand so that you can quickly plunge the blanched beans into the bath to retain their color and stop their cooking.

TA'AMEYA WITH TAHINI-YOGURT SAUCE

Serves: 4
Total Time: 1 hour

RECIPE OVERVIEW Falafel (balls or patties) nestled into pita bread and adorned with vegetables and tahini sauce is a delectable street food across the Mediterranean. While a lot of falafel is made from ground chickpeas, falafel in Egypt, known as ta'ameya, uses sweet, nutty fava beans. The fried patties have a gorgeous green hue amplified by plentiful fresh herbs and scallions. They're flavored with warm spices and often coated with sesame seeds, which increase the crispness that encases the luscious, creamy interiors. Ground pita and an egg are key (and resourceful) binders, and baking powder gives the mash a soft fluffiness. No falafel is complete without toppings, and a creamy yogurt-tahini sauce with juicy tomatoes, crisp cucumbers, and onions add richness and freshness. You will have leftovers of the sauce, but it keeps in the refrigerator for several days and is delicious drizzled on any roasted vegetables. You can use ¼ of an English cucumber in place of the Persian cucumbers. We like to serve the falafel with Pink Pickled Turnips (recipe follows), a traditional Egyptian accompaniment. We prefer using fresh fava beans, but if you can't find them, you can substitute 21 ounces frozen shelled fava beans, thawed. Skip step 2 if using frozen favas. Be sure to set up the ice water bath before cooking the fava beans, as plunging them immediately in the cold water after blanching retains their bright green color and ensures that they don't overcook.

Tahini-Yogurt Sauce

- ⅓ cup tahini
- ⅓ cup plain Greek yogurt
- ¼ cup water
- 3 tablespoons lemon juice
- 1 garlic clove, minced
- ¾ teaspoon table salt

Ta'ameya

- 7 ounces fava beans, shelled
- ¾ cup torn pita; plus 2 (8-inch) pitas, halved
- ½ teaspoon fennel seeds, toasted and cracked
- ¼ cup chopped fresh cilantro and/or parsley
- 1 large egg
- 2 scallions, sliced thin
- 2 garlic cloves, minced
- ½ teaspoon baking powder
- ½ teaspoon ground coriander
- ½ teaspoon ground cumin
- ½ teaspoon table salt
- ¼ teaspoon pepper
- 2 teaspoons sesame seeds
- ½ cup extra-virgin olive oil for frying
- 1 tomato, cored and chopped
- 2 Persian cucumbers, halved lengthwise and sliced thin
- ½ red onion, sliced thin (½ cup)
- 1 teaspoon nigella seeds (optional)

1. FOR THE TAHINI-YOGURT SAUCE Whisk all ingredients in bowl until combined. Season with pepper to taste. Let sit until flavors meld, about 30 minutes. (Sauce can be refrigerated for up to 4 days.)

2. FOR THE TA'AMEYA Bring 4 quarts water to boil in large pot. Fill large bowl halfway with ice and water. Add fava beans to boiling water and cook for 1 minute. Using slotted spoon, transfer fava beans to ice water and let cool, about 2 minutes. Transfer fava beans to triple layer of paper towels and dry well. Using paring knife, make small cut along edge of each bean through waxy sheath, then gently squeeze sheath to release bean; discard sheath.

3. Process torn pita pieces and fennel seeds in food processor until finely ground, about 15 seconds. Add fava beans, cilantro, egg, scallions, garlic, baking powder, coriander, cumin, salt, and pepper and pulse until fava beans are coarsely chopped and mixture is cohesive, about 15 pulses, scraping down sides of bowl as needed. Working with 2 tablespoons mixture at a time, shape into 2-inch-wide patties (you should have 16 patties). Transfer patties to large plate, sprinkle evenly with sesame seeds, and press lightly to adhere.

4. Set wire rack in rimmed baking sheet and line with triple layer of paper towels. Heat oil in 12-inch nonstick skillet over medium heat to 350 degrees. Add 8 patties and cook until deep golden brown, 2 to 3 minutes per side, using 2 spatulas to carefully flip patties. Transfer falafel to prepared rack to drain and repeat with remaining falafel, adjusting heat as needed if falafel begins to brown too quickly. Stuff each pita half with falafel, tomato, cucumber, and onion and top with tahini-yogurt sauce and nigella seeds, if using. Serve.

PINK PICKLED TURNIPS
Makes: 4 cups

The turnips get their vibrant fuchsia hue from the beets that accompany them in the brine. The pickle needs to be refrigerated for 2 days to allow the brine to fully penetrate and pickle the vegetables. These pickled turnips cannot be processed for long-term storage.

- 1¼ cups white wine vinegar
- 1¼ cups water
- 2½ tablespoons sugar
- 1½ tablespoons canning and pickling salt
- 3 garlic cloves, smashed and peeled
- ¾ teaspoon whole allspice berries
- ¾ teaspoon black peppercorns
- 1 pound turnips, peeled and cut into 2 by ½-inch sticks
- 1 small beet, trimmed, peeled, and cut into 1-inch pieces

1. Bring vinegar, water, sugar, salt, garlic, allspice, and peppercorns to boil in medium saucepan over medium-high heat. Cover, remove from heat, and let steep for 10 minutes. Strain brine through fine-mesh strainer, then return to saucepan.

2. Place two 1-pint jars in bowl and place under hot running water until heated through, 1 to 2 minutes; shake dry. Pack turnips vertically into hot jars with beet pieces evenly distributed throughout.

3. Return brine to brief boil. Using funnel and ladle, pour hot brine over vegetables to cover. Let jars cool to room temperature, cover with lids, and refrigerate for at least 2 days before serving. (Pickled turnips can be refrigerated for up to 1 month; turnips will soften over time.)

KEYS TO SUCCESS

- **Ice bath:** Prevent overcooking (and mushy falafel) by plunging the fava beans into ice water immediately after blanching them.

- **Oil temperature:** Heat the oil to 350 degrees before frying, and bring it back to this temperature before frying the second batch. When taking the temperature of the frying oil, tilt the skillet so the oil pools on one side.

MEAT

ULTIMATE STEAKS AND CHOPS

ANNIE PETITO

A thick steak or pork chop is an unabashed display of meaty flavor and texture. The recipes in this course each start with a cut that's known for its flavor or tenderness. We make sure that the cut is treated right, that it's cooked to your liking, and that its flavor shines. The techniques you'll learn are foolproof: butter-basting a steak to develop a significant crust while keeping its interior rosy; sous-viding to achieve steak with no opportunity for error; grilling so you not only get a sear but you get a smoky char that complements the meat; and pan-searing a pork chop to perfection on the stovetop.

ANNIE'S PRO TIP: *Don't skip the resting period after cooking. Resting is all about controlling the meat's juices, which are proteins dissolved in water. Meat that has rested and cooled slightly has thicker juices that are less inclined to flow all over the plate when sliced, which means more flavorful proteins and fat in each bite.*

BUTTER-BASTED RIB STEAK

Serves: 2
Total Time: 35 minutes

RECIPE OVERVIEW There's steak, and then there's pan-seared, butter-basted rib steak. These two processes serve different purposes and the second isn't just for flavor. Searing means cooking the surface of meat at a high temperature to create a browned crust. Basting requires continuously spooning hot fat over the steak to continue cooking it evenly. To prevent a gray band from forming under the crust (an indicator of overcooked, dried-out meat), don't be afraid to repeatedly flip the steak as it sears. Why? A hot skillet cooks food from the bottom up. When a protein is flipped, some heat from the seared side dissipates into the air, but lingering residual heat continues to cook the protein from the top down. The more a protein is flipped, the more it cooks from both sides. Our hot basting liquid—butter infused with shallot, garlic, and thyme—also helps the steak to cook from the top down and boosts its rich flavor.

1 (1¼-pound) bone-in rib steak or (1-pound) boneless rib-eye steak, 1½ inches thick, trimmed
1 teaspoon pepper
½ teaspoon table salt
1 tablespoon extra-virgin olive oil
3 tablespoons unsalted butter
1 shallot, peeled and quartered through root end
2 garlic cloves, lightly crushed and peeled
5 sprigs fresh thyme

1. Pat steak dry with paper towels and sprinkle with pepper and salt. Heat oil in 12-inch skillet over medium-high heat until just smoking. Place steak in skillet and cook for 30 seconds. Flip steak and continue to cook for 30 seconds. Continue flipping steak every 30 seconds for 3 more minutes.

2. Slide steak to back of skillet, opposite handle, and add butter to front of skillet. Once butter has melted and begun to foam, add shallot, garlic, and thyme sprigs. Holding skillet handle, tilt skillet so butter pools near base of handle. Use metal spoon to continuously spoon butter and aromatics over steak, concentrating on areas where crust is less browned. Baste steak, flipping it every 30 seconds, until steak registers 120 to 125 degrees (for medium-rare), 1 to 2 minutes.

3. Remove skillet from heat and transfer steak to cutting board; tent with aluminum foil and let rest for 10 minutes. Discard aromatics from pan and transfer butter mixture to small bowl. Cut meat from bone (if bone-in), slice steak thin against grain, and serve with butter mixture.

Variation
BUTTER-BASTED RIB STEAK WITH COFFEE-CHILE BUTTER
Substitute 2 tablespoons whole coffee beans, cracked, for garlic and ½ teaspoon red pepper flakes for thyme.

- **Flip frequently**: Cooks the steak from the top down in addition to from the bottom up to prevent a gray band of meat
- **Spoon with hot melted butter**: Also helps the steak cook from the top down
- **Infuse the butter**: It's an opportunity to add extra flavor.

Butter-Basting Steak

INFUSE BUTTER
Slide the seared steak to the back of the skillet, then add the butter to the front of the skillet with the aromatics.

MELT BUTTER
Holding the skillet handle, tilt skillet so butter pools near base of handle.

BASTE
Using spoon, baste steak, flipping it every 30 seconds, until steak registers 120 to 125 degrees (for medium-rare), 1 to 2 minutes.

SPICE-CRUSTED STEAKS

Serves: 4 to 6
Total Time: 35 minutes

RECIPE OVERVIEW We like spice on rib-eye steaks; the steaks are rich and beefy enough to stand up to the bold (but not overly aggressive) spice crust and thick enough to provide the perfect ratio of interior meat to exterior spice, ensuring the right mix of flavors and textures in every bite. Spice blends have a tendency to burn and can fall off during cooking—but our crust is superflavorful, not superburnt. We continually flip the steaks, thus ensuring that each side is exposed to the heat in short intervals. And by not patting the steaks dry before applying the spice blend (as most

recipes call for), we let the moisture from the meat act as a glue to help the spices stick. For even more insurance, we use a fork to flip the steaks, rather than tongs or a spatula, to keep the spice crust in place.

  1 tablespoon black peppercorns
  2 tablespoons chopped fresh rosemary
  1 tablespoon kosher salt
  2 teaspoons ground coriander
  2 teaspoons grated lemon zest
1½ teaspoons dry mustard
  1 teaspoon red pepper flakes
  2 (1-pound) boneless rib-eye steaks, 1½ inches thick, trimmed
  1 tablespoon vegetable oil

1. Place peppercorns in zipper-lock bag and seal bag. Using rolling pin, crush peppercorns coarse. Combine peppercorns, rosemary, salt, coriander, lemon zest, mustard, and pepper flakes in bowl. Season steaks all over, including sides, with spice mixture, pressing to adhere. (Use all of spice mixture.)

2. Set wire rack in rimmed baking sheet. Heat oil in 12-inch nonstick skillet over medium heat until just smoking. Add steaks and cook, flipping steaks with fork every 2 minutes, until well browned and meat registers 120 to 125 degrees (for medium-rare), 10 to 13 minutes. Transfer steaks to prepared rack, tent with aluminum foil, and let rest for 5 minutes. Transfer steaks to cutting board. Slice against grain and serve.

KEYS TO SUCCESS

- **Flip steak continually for flavor:** Ensures the spices don't burn
- **Skip patting the steak dry:** Helps keep the crust in place
- **Flip with a fork:** Prevents disturbing the spice crust

Crushing Peppercorns

ROLL
Put the peppercorns in a zipper-lock bag and press and roll them until they're coarsely crushed.

until steaks are fully submerged, and then clip top corner of bag to side of water bath container, allowing remaining air bubbles to rise to top of bag. Reopen 1 corner of zipper, release remaining air bubbles, and reseal bag. Cover and cook for at least 1½ hours or up to 3 hours.

2. Transfer steaks to paper towel–lined plate and let rest for 5 to 10 minutes. Pat steaks dry with paper towels. Heat remaining 3 tablespoons oil in 12-inch skillet over medium-high heat until just smoking. Sear steaks until well browned, about 1 minute per side. Transfer to cutting board and slice ½ inch thick. Serve.

RED WINE–PEPPERCORN PAN SAUCE

Makes: about ½ cup (serves 4)

Note that this recipe is meant to be started after you have seared the steaks. Use a good-quality medium-bodied wine, such as a Côtes du Rhône or Pinot Noir, for this sauce.

	Vegetable oil, if needed
1	large shallot, minced
½	cup dry red wine
¾	cup chicken broth
2	teaspoons packed brown sugar
3	tablespoons unsalted butter, cut into 3 pieces and chilled
1	teaspoon coarsely ground pepper
¼	teaspoon balsamic vinegar

1. Pour off all but 1 tablespoon fat from skillet used to sear steak. (If necessary, add oil to equal 1 tablespoon.) Add shallot and cook over medium heat until softened, 1 to 2 minutes. Stir in wine, scraping up any browned bits. Bring to simmer and cook until wine is reduced to glaze, about 3 minutes.

2. Stir in broth and sugar and simmer until reduced to ⅓ cup, 4 to 6 minutes. Off heat, whisk in butter, 1 piece at a time, until melted and sauce is thickened and glossy. Whisk in pepper, vinegar, and any accumulated meat juices. Season with salt to taste.

SOUS VIDE SEARED STEAKS

Serves: 4
Total Time: 30 minutes, plus 1½ hours cooking

RECIPE OVERVIEW Cooking steaks sous vide is a game changer. The water bath technique takes all the guesswork and stress out of the dinner-preparation equation. Steaks are cooked to the same temperature, and thus the same doneness, all the way through. This eliminates the gray band of overcooked meat around the exterior of steaks that can occur with searing methods. Once your steaks are taken out of the water bath, all that's left to do is to give them a quick sear in a screaming-hot pan to create browning. You can use other tender steaks (rib eye, shell sirloin, top sirloin, and tenderloin) in this recipe; avoid tougher cuts such as top round, bottom round, blade, and flank, as they would require a longer cook time. Serve with Red Wine–Peppercorn Pan Sauce (recipe follows), if desired; prepare the sauce after searing the steak and spoon over steak immediately after making.

2	(1-pound) boneless strip steaks, 1 to 1½ inches thick, trimmed
7	tablespoons vegetable oil, divided

1. Using sous vide circulator, bring water to 130 degrees in 7-quart container (for medium-rare steaks). Season steaks with salt and pepper. Place steaks and ¼ cup oil in 1-gallon zipper-lock freezer bag and toss to coat. Arrange steaks in single layer and seal bag, pressing out as much air as possible. Gently lower bag into prepared water bath

KEYS TO SUCCESS

• **Use a tender cut:** Cooks quickly via circulator (tougher cuts need prolonged cooking to break down their collagen)

• **Cooking sous vide:** For more information, see pages 70 and 74.

• **Finish by searing:** Creates a crust after cooking

THICK-CUT PORTERHOUSE STEAKS

Serves: 6 to 8
Total Time: 2 hours

RECIPE OVERVIEW Mammoth porterhouse steaks make a spectacular centerpiece. But mammoth isn't easy to cook, and unevenly cooked steaks aren't all that spectacular. To help our porterhouse steaks stay pink, juicy, and tender throughout, we arrange the steaks on a wire rack set in a rimmed baking sheet and then roast them in a low, 275-degree oven to gradually bring them up to temperature before searing. Because the steaks are elevated on the rack, hot air circulates all around them and they cook more evenly from all sides. This method also dries the steaks' exterior so that the final sear in a ripping-hot pan is fast and furious, further reducing the chance of overcooking. You can substitute T-bone steaks.

- 2 (2½- to 3-pound) porterhouse steaks, 2 inches thick, trimmed
- 3 tablespoons vegetable oil

1. Adjust oven rack to middle position and heat oven to 275 degrees. Set wire rack in aluminum foil–lined rimmed baking sheet. Pat steaks dry with paper towels and season liberally with kosher salt and pepper. Place steaks side by side on prepared rack with tenderloins facing center, about 1 inch apart. Transfer steaks to oven. Cook until thermometer inserted sideways 3 inches from tip of strip side of steak registers 115 to 120 degrees (for medium-rare), 1 hour 10 minutes to 1½ hours, rotating sheet halfway through cooking.

2. Pat steaks dry with paper towels. Heat oil in 12-inch skillet over high heat until just smoking. Place 1 steak in skillet and sear until well browned, about 2 minutes per side, lifting occasionally to redistribute oil. Using tongs, stand steak upright to sear edges, 1 to 2 minutes. Return steak to wire rack, tent with foil, and repeat with remaining steak. Let steaks rest for 10 minutes.

3. Transfer steaks to carving board. Carve strip steaks and tenderloins from bones. Place T-bones on platter. Slice steaks thin against grain, then reassemble sliced steaks on both sides of bones. Season with salt and pepper to taste. Serve.

KEYS TO SUCCESS

- **Reverse-sear:** Needs only a short time in the scorching-hot skillet after coming up in temperature in the oven

- **Sear in a generous amount of oil:** Ensures the large pieces of meat brown evenly

- **Slice steak then reassemble around the bone:** Keeps the steak warm

BISTECCA ALLA FIORENTINA

Serves: 6 to 8
Total Time: 1¼ hours

RECIPE OVERVIEW Simple preparation as spectacular is a hallmark of Tuscan cooking. Take, for example, Tuscany's famous bistecca alla Fiorentina, a thick-cut porterhouse steak usually sourced from the Chianina cows of Valdichiana, that are grilled to perfection, drizzled with olive oil, and served with lemon. Our method for grilling porterhouses—starting on the hot side of the grill, with the delicate tenderloin portion facing the cooler side and the strip portion facing the hotter side, and then finishing on the cooler side—makes domestic steaks taste just as good. But in this recipe, the oil is almost as important as the steak; we drizzle on the oil after slicing—just before serving—to preserve its delicate flavors. A squeeze of lemon juice at the table cuts through the richness. Flare-ups may occur when grilling over charcoal. If the flames become constant, slide the steaks to the cooler side of the grill until the flames die down. You can substitute T-bone steaks.

- 2 (2½- to 3-pound) porterhouse steaks, 2 inches thick, fat trimmed to ¼ inch
- 4 teaspoons kosher salt
- 4 teaspoons extra-virgin olive oil (if using gas), plus extra for drizzling
- 2 teaspoons pepper
   Lemon wedges

1. Pat steaks dry with paper towels and sprinkle each side of each steak with 1 teaspoon salt. Transfer steaks to large plate and refrigerate, uncovered, for at least 1 hour or up to 24 hours.

2A. FOR A CHARCOAL GRILL Open bottom vent completely. Light large chimney starter filled with charcoal briquettes (6 quarts). When top coals are partially covered with ash, pour evenly over half of grill. Set cooking grate in place, cover, and open lid vent completely. Heat grill until hot, about 5 minutes.

2B. FOR A GAS GRILL Turn all burners to high, cover, and heat grill until hot, about 15 minutes. Leave primary burner on high and turn off other burner(s). (Adjust primary burner [or, if using 3-burner grill, primary burner and second burner] as needed to maintain grill temperature of 450 degrees.)

3. Pat steaks dry with paper towels. If using gas, brush each side of each steak with 1 teaspoon oil. Sprinkle each side of each steak with ½ teaspoon pepper.

4. Clean and oil cooking grate. Place steaks on hotter side of grill, with tenderloins facing cooler side. Cook (covered if using gas) until evenly charred on first side, 6 to 8 minutes. Flip steaks and position so tenderloins are still facing cooler side of grill. Continue to cook (covered if using gas) until evenly charred on second side, 6 to 8 minutes.

5. Flip steaks and transfer to cooler side of grill, with bone side facing hotter side. Cover and cook until thermometer inserted 3 inches from tip of strip side of steak registers 115 to 120 degrees (for medium-rare), 8 to 12 minutes, flipping steaks halfway through cooking. Transfer steaks to wire rack set in rimmed baking sheet, tent with aluminum foil, and let rest for 10 to 15 minutes.

6. Transfer steaks to carving board. Carve strips and tenderloins from bones. Place T-bones on platter. Slice steaks thin against grain, then reassemble sliced steaks around bones. Drizzle with extra olive oil and season with salt and pepper to taste. Serve with lemon wedges.

KEYS TO SUCCESS

- **Salt and refrigerate the steak:** Ensures the thick steaks are tender and juicy through the grilling process
- **Drizzle with olive oil and sprinkle with salt:** Highlights the flavor of the meat

ULTIMATE CHARCOAL-GRILLED STEAKS

Serves: 4
Total Time: 2¼ to 2¾ hours

RECIPE OVERVIEW For this recipe, a novel technique for cooking over a live fire relies on a charcoal chimney starter not to light the coals, but to actually do the final searing. This method creates a grilled steak with a killer crust and perfectly cooked meat from edge to edge. It involves finishing the steaks right over the chimney, stabilized with metal skewers. You will need a charcoal chimney starter with a 7½-inch diameter and four 12-inch metal skewers for this recipe. If your chimney starter has a smaller diameter, skewer each steak individually and cook in four batches. During cooking, the lit chimney can be placed on the grill grate or set on top of bricks.

- 2 (1-pound) boneless strip steaks, 1¾ inches thick, fat caps removed
- 2 teaspoons kosher salt

1. Adjust oven rack to middle position and heat oven to 200 degrees. Cut each steak in half crosswise to create four 8-ounce steaks. Cut ¹⁄₁₆-inch-deep slits, spaced ¼ inch apart, in crosshatch pattern on both sides of each steak. Sprinkle both sides of each steak with ½ teaspoon salt. Place two halves of 1 steak with tapered ends flat on counter and pass two 12-inch metal skewers, spaced 1½ inches apart, horizontally through steaks, making sure to keep ¼ inch space between halves. Repeat skewering with remaining steak halves.

2. Place skewered steaks on wire rack set in rimmed baking sheet, transfer to oven, and cook until centers of steaks register 120 degrees (for medium-rare), flipping

steaks halfway through cooking and removing them as they come to temperature, 1½ hours to 1 hour 50 minutes. Tent skewered steaks (still on rack) with aluminum foil.

3. Light large chimney starter half filled with charcoal briquettes (3 quarts). Place lit chimney on grill grate or on top of bricks. When top coals are completely covered with ash, uncover steaks (reserving foil) and pat dry with paper towels. Using tongs, place 1 set of steaks directly over chimney so skewers rest on rim of chimney (steaks will be suspended over coals). Cook until both sides are well browned and charred, about 1 minute per side. Using tongs, return first set of steaks to wire rack in sheet, season with pepper, and tent with reserved foil. Repeat with second set of skewered steaks. Remove skewers from steaks and serve.

KEYS TO SUCCESS

- **Trim the fat:** Prevents flare-ups from dripping fat
- **Start in the oven:** Brings the steaks up to temperature so they need only kiss the chimney
- **Cook over a chimney:** Mimics a steakhouse-caliber broiler so the steaks sear superfast
- **Suspend the steaks right over the chimney:** Increases access to high heat

Skewering Steaks

TRIM
Remove the steak's fat cap to prevent flare-ups, then slice the steak in half.

SKEWER
With the steaks flat on counter, pass two 12-inch metal skewers, spaced 1½ inches apart, horizontally through the steaks, making sure to keep ¼-inch space between steak halves.

2. Flip chops; reduce heat to medium; and continue to cook, flipping chops every 2 minutes, until exterior is well browned and meat registers 140 degrees, 10 to 15 minutes longer. (Chops should be sizzling; if not, increase heat slightly. Reduce heat if skillet starts to smoke.)

3. Transfer chops to carving board and let rest for 5 minutes. Carve meat from bone and slice ½ inch thick. (When carving chops, meat at tapered end near bone may retain slightly pink hue despite being cooked.) Season meat with coarse or flake sea salt to taste. Serve with bones.

KEYS TO SUCCESS

- **Choose a rib chop:** These are thick enough to brown before overcooking.

- **Nonstick solution, no oil needed:** The rendered fat from the chops is enough to prevent sticking.

- **Change the temperature:** Start in a cold pan to heat the chops gently, raise the heat to high to cook off moisture, lower the heat to medium to cook through evenly without smoking.

PAN-SEARED THICK-CUT PORK CHOPS

Serves: 4
Total Time: 30 minutes

RECIPE OVERVIEW Achieving deeply browned, juicy bone-in pork chops starts with choosing the right chop: 1½-inch-thick rib chops, which are thick enough to build up a browned exterior before cooking through. Then it's about temperature control: We start the chops in a cold (not preheated) nonstick skillet and place it over high heat, flipping the chops every 2 minutes so that the meat's temperature increases gradually and allowing a crust to build up on the outside without overcooking the interior. A nonstick pan means that no oil is necessary. We then turn the heat to high to drive off moisture and prevent the chops from steaming. Finally, we lower the heat to medium to encourage browning without smoking. A sprinkle of coarse or flake sea salt ensures that juicy slices of the pork are well seasoned. Make sure to include the bones when serving; they're great for nibbling.

- 2 **(14- to 16-ounce) bone-in pork rib chops, 1½ inches thick, trimmed**
- ½ **teaspoon pepper**

1. Pat chops dry with paper towels and sprinkle both sides with pepper. Place chops 1 inch apart in cold 12-inch nonstick or carbon-steel skillet, arranging so narrow part of 1 chop is opposite wider part of second. Place skillet over high heat and cook chops for 2 minutes. Flip chops and cook on second side for 2 minutes. (Neither side of chops will be browned at this point.)

Cold-Searing on an Electric Stovetop

Electric stoves can be slow to respond to a cook's commands. This can pose a problem with our cold-searing method, which requires an initial blast of high heat followed by a quick turndown to medium heat. However, there's a simple workaround: As you cook your chops on high heat on one burner, preheat a second burner to medium heat. After the initial sear, transfer the pan to the medium-heat burner and continue cooking.

DRY-AGING STEAK AT HOME

Sometimes an option at a high-end meat market, sometimes a way of leveling up at the steakhouse, "dry aging" is supposed to mean more valuable meat. In commercial dry-aging, butchers hold large primal cuts of beef (typically the rib or short loin sections) for as long as 120 days in humid refrigerators ranging between 32 and 40 degrees. (The humidity is necessary to prevent the meat's exterior from drying out too much.)

We tried replicating these results at home on a smaller scale. We bought rib-eye and strip steaks and stored them in the back of the refrigerator, where the temperature is coldest. Since home refrigerators are less humid, we wrapped the steaks in cheesecloth and put them on a wire rack to allow air to pass through while also preventing excessive dehydration, then checked them after four days (the longest length of time we felt comfortable storing raw beef in a home fridge). Their edges looked appropriately dried out, so we pan-seared the home-aged steaks and tasted them alongside a batch of the same commercially dry-aged cuts. Our findings? Sure enough, four days of dry-aging in a home fridge gave the steaks a comparably smoky flavor and dense, tender texture—and at a much lower price tag. Feel free to dry-age the steaks for any of our recipes.

GRILLING STEAK OVER A CHIMNEY STARTER

Most of us use a chimney starter only for lighting coals before we pour them into the grill. But the coals are actually at their hottest in the chimney—not in the grill, where airflow is restricted. So for Ultimate Charcoal-Grilled Steaks (page 356), we leave the coals in the chimney and finish the steaks over them for a deeply browned sear in minutes.

Steak
Remove the fat cap and divide each strip steak in half. Crosshatch the surface for maximum browned crust. Salt the steak and precook it in the oven, low and slow.

Chimney Design
The cylindrical shape concentrates the heat. The open ends maximize airflow, keeping the fire burning intensely.

Skewers
Use 12-inch metal skewers to suspend the halved steak across the chimney.

Vents
Located on both the sides and bottom (of our winning chimney), these allow even more air circulation.

Coals
Three quarts fill the chimney halfway.

Kettle Grill
What would make a safer base when cooking over a hot chimney?

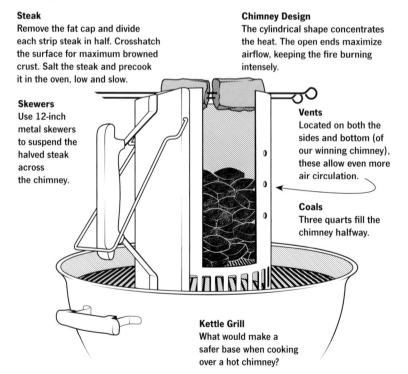

PORK RIB CHOPS

As the name suggests, pork rib chops are cut from the rib section of the pork loin, so they have a relatively high fat content and are unlikely to dry out during cooking. They're the most flavorful of pork loin chops and they're the most impressive to receive, seared golden, in the center of the plate. These chops are easily identifiable by the bone that runs along one side and the one large eye of loin muscle. Chops can be sold thick-cut and thin-cut. Be sure to seek out 1½-inch-thick chops for our Pan-Seared Thick-Cut Pork Chops (page 357); the extra weight allows for longer cooking and better browning. Note that rib chops are also sold boneless; in fact, most boneless chops you'll find are cut from the rib chop. Be sure to buy bone-in. Bone-in rib chops may be labeled as rib cut, end cut, or center cut.

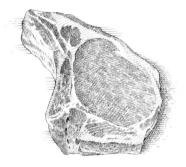

CONSIDERATIONS FOR COOKING THICK STEAKS

It can be difficult to keep the perimeter of thick steaks from overcooking (and a gray band from forming) while the very center of the steak comes up to the desired temperature. How do we achieve a good crust and a medium-rare center for the thick, satisfying, steakhouse-style steaks you find in this course?

METHOD #1: REVERSE SEARING

Searing thick-cut steaks quickly keeps the meat directly under the crust from turning gray. But although a quick, hot sear might get the outer rim in shape, it doesn't give the steak enough time in the pan to come to temperature at the center. So we start the steak in the oven to warm it up slowly to a temperature just shy of our desired doneness; this also dries the outside of the steaks thoroughly—more thoroughly than patting them dry with paper towels—so they are perfectly cooked in the flash it takes to then brown them in the skillet on the stovetop. See Thick-Cut Porterhouse Steaks (page 355).

METHOD #2: FAST FLIPPING

This searing method—flipping the steaks, often every 2 minutes, rather than patiently leaving the steaks alone—allows a crust to form without the steak sitting for too long in the same place. It cooks the steak from the bottom up and the top down so the interior warms evenly and the crust builds gradually for edge-to-edge rosiness. It requires a more watchful eye than reverse searing but takes less time. See Butter-Basted Rib Steak (page 352), Spice-Crusted Steaks (page 353), and Pan-Seared Thick-Cut Pork Chops (page 357).

METHOD #3: SOUS VIDE

The great thing about cooking sous vide is that no matter the thickness of the cut of meat, it cooks evenly from edge to edge in the controlled environment. The steak will emerge from the water perfectly cooked and then need just a short sear in a scorching-hot skillet. See Sous Vide Seared Steaks (page 354).

METHOD #4: LIVE-FIRE COOKING

A different twist on reverse-searing, cooking warmed steaks over a chimney starter is effective because that heat is superconcentrated—much more concentrated than you can get on the cooking surface of your grill. Skewer the steaks and flip them on top of the chimney for the best grilled steaks you've ever had, like with our Ultimate Charcoal-Grilled Steaks (page 356).

RIB VERSUS RIB-EYE

A rib-eye steak (see page 353), one of the most popular cuts, is a rib steak with the bone removed. The steaks are essentially a big slab of prime rib. A bone-in rib steak (see page 352) has a little extra flavor from the bone whereas a boneless rib-eye steak is tender, juicy, and easier to cook.

Rib-Eye Steak
aka beauty steak, Delmonico steak, Spencer steak, Scotch filet, entrecôte

Rib Steak
aka bone-in rib steak

NEXT-LEVEL BURGERS

JULIA COLLIN DAVISON

You can make a burger with any ground meat from the supermarket by forming it into patties, maybe with a binder, and applying heat. But if you're going to make a burger at home rather than getting one out, why not go the distance? In the home kitchen, you can control the fat content, meatiness, and juiciness for unforgettable burgers. For us, the first step is grinding our own meat. It sounds complicated—something for a professional butcher—but it's quite easy with a home food processor. The second step is forming the patties and cooking them right, of course. Finally, the third step is creating craveable, sometimes daring, combinations of meat and toppings. And don't stick to beef. There's a lot of flavor to be found in pork and lamb burgers.

JULIA'S PRO TIP: *Before shaping the burgers, spread the ground meat out on the baking sheet and remove any large pieces of gristle. Also, I find that letting the shaped patties chill in the refrigerator before cooking helps them hold their shape a bit better when cooking.*

THE METHOD
COOKING BURGER PATTIES

1 GRIND MEAT
Grind your meat according to your recipe and divide it into four lightly packed balls.

2 FORM PATTIES
Gently flatten balls of ground meat into ¾-inch-thick patties, about 4½ inches in diameter. Forming the patties gently helps prevent overworking the meat, which can make for tough burgers. Using your fingertips, gently press center of patty to create a slight divot.

3 SALT NOW
Sprinkle the patties with salt and pepper. Salting is essential for a well-seasoned burger, but salt also removes water from the meat—which is not a path to a tender burger, so don't salt too early.

4 SEAR
Cook the burgers briefly on each side over high heat until well browned. This will caramelize the exterior of the meat and form a flavorful crust.

5 BAKE
Transfer the burgers to a baking sheet and bake in a low, 300-degree oven until they reach the desired temperature. Searing on the stove and finishing in a low-heat oven ensures a well-browned crust and juicy center.

6 LET REST
Transfer the burgers to a plate and let rest for 5 minutes. Resting allows the juices to redistribute evenly throughout the patty.

SIRLOIN BURGER BLEND

Serves: 4

Total Time: 45 minutes, plus 35 minutes freezing

RECIPE OVERVIEW Although store-bought ground chuck makes a quick and satisfying burger, home-ground meat provides a loose, craggy texture and strong beefy flavor that make for a truly superior burger experience. We start with sirloin steak tips—which have good flavor, contain minimal gristly fat, and are available in small quantities—and turn to our trusty food processor to grind them. Butter gives the meat some much-needed moisture and fat for juicy, tender burgers. Sirloin steak tips are often sold as flap meat. When trimming the meat, remove any pieces of fat thicker than $\frac{1}{8}$ inch along with any silverskin. After trimming, you should have about 1 $\frac{1}{4}$ pounds of meat. To double this recipe, spread beef over two baking sheets in step 1 and pulse in food processor in eight batches.

- 2 pounds sirloin steak tips, trimmed and cut into $\frac{1}{2}$-inch pieces
- 4 tablespoons unsalted butter, melted and cooled
- $\frac{1}{2}$ teaspoon table salt
- $\frac{1}{4}$ teaspoon pepper

1. Arrange beef in single layer on rimmed baking sheet and freeze until very firm and starting to harden around edges but still pliable, 35 to 45 minutes.

2. Working in 4 batches, pulse beef in food processor until finely ground into $\frac{1}{16}$-inch pieces, about 20 pulses, stopping to redistribute meat as needed; return to sheet. Spread ground beef over sheet, discarding any long strands of gristle and large chunks of fat. Drizzle with melted butter and gently toss with fork to combine.

KEYS TO SUCCESS

- **Select steak tips:** They have good flavor, contain minimal gristly fat, and are available in small quantities.

- **Freeze chunks of meat:** Ensures the meat chops rather than mashes in the food processor

- **Drizzle butter into the meat mix:** Increases richness to just the right level

ULTIMATE BEEF BURGER BLEND

Serves: 4

Total Time: 45 minutes, plus 35 minutes freezing

RECIPE OVERVIEW This deluxe, home-ground blend is a perfect combination of intense flavor and rich, tender texture that will instantly elevate your burger into the big leagues. Skirt steak is a must for its deep, earthy flavor; boneless short ribs offer tender texture; and sirloin steak tips provide the bold beef flavor. If you can't find skirt steak, you can substitute flank steak, though the flavor will be slightly milder. When trimming the meat, remove any pieces of fat thicker than $\frac{1}{8}$ inch along with any silverskin. After trimming, you should have about 1 $\frac{3}{4}$ pounds of meat. To double this recipe, spread beef over two baking sheets in step 1 and pulse in food processor in eight batches.

- 1 pound skirt steak, trimmed and cut into $\frac{1}{2}$-inch pieces
- 8 ounces boneless beef short ribs, trimmed and cut into $\frac{1}{2}$-inch pieces
- 8 ounces sirloin steak tips, trimmed and cut into $\frac{1}{2}$-inch pieces
- $\frac{1}{2}$ teaspoon table salt
- $\frac{1}{4}$ teaspoon pepper

1. Arrange beef in single layer on rimmed baking sheet and freeze until very firm and starting to harden around edges but still pliable, 35 to 45 minutes.

2. Working in 4 batches, pulse beef in food processor until finely ground into $\frac{1}{16}$-inch pieces, about 20 pulses, stopping to redistribute meat as needed; return to sheet. Spread ground beef over sheet, discarding any long strands of gristle and large chunks of fat, and gently toss with fork to combine.

KEY TO SUCCESS

- **Use several cuts:** Creates a blend with the best balance of moisture and flavor

JUICY PUB-STYLE BURGERS

Serves: 4
Total Time: 20 minutes

RECIPE OVERVIEW These burgers really are premium. Lightly packing the patties gives the burgers enough structure without overworking the meat and making the burgers bouncy. We use a two-step cooking process to do the beef justice: The stovetop provides intense heat for searing, and the oven's ambient heat allows a gentle, even finish for the perfect juicy center. A quick pub sauce can jazz up the basic burger, and premium (but simple) additions make appealing variations. For the best flavor, season the burgers aggressively just before cooking. Use a food processor with a capacity of 7 to 14 cups. Serve with Pub-Style Burger Sauce (recipe follows), if desired.

- 1   recipe Burger Blend (page 362)
- 1   teaspoon vegetable oil
- 4   hamburger buns, toasted and buttered

1. Adjust oven rack to middle position and heat oven to 300 degrees. Divide meat into 4 lightly packed balls. Gently flatten into ¾-inch-thick patties, about 4½ inches in diameter. Refrigerate patties until ready to cook, or for up to 24 hours.

2. Season 1 side of patties with salt and pepper. Using spatula, flip patties and season second side. Heat oil in 12-inch skillet over high heat until just smoking. Using spatula, transfer patties to skillet and cook, without moving them, for 2 minutes. Flip patties and continue to cook 2 minutes longer. Transfer patties to rimmed baking sheet and bake until meat registers 125 degrees (for medium-rare), 3 to 5 minutes.

3. Transfer burgers to plate and let rest for 5 minutes. Transfer to buns and serve.

PUB-STYLE BURGER SAUCE

Makes: about 1 cup (enough to top 4 burgers)

- ¾   cup mayonnaise
- 2   tablespoons soy sauce
- 1   tablespoon dark brown sugar
- 1   tablespoon Worcestershire sauce
- 1   tablespoon minced chives
- 1   garlic clove, minced
- ¾   teaspoon ground black pepper

Whisk all ingredients together in bowl.

Variations

JUICY PUB-STYLE BURGERS WITH CRISPY SHALLOTS AND BLUE CHEESE

Heat ½ cup vegetable oil and 3 thinly sliced shallots in medium saucepan over high heat; cook, stirring frequently, until shallots are golden, about 8 minutes. Using slotted spoon, transfer shallots to paper towel–lined plate, season with salt, and let drain until crispy, about 5 minutes.

(Shallots can be stored at room temperature for up to 3 days.) Top each burger with ¼ cup crumbled blue cheese before transferring to oven. Top with shallots before serving.

JUICY PUB-STYLE BURGERS WITH PEPPERED BACON AND AGED CHEDDAR

Before cooking burgers, lay 6 slices of bacon in rimmed baking sheet. Sprinkle with 2 teaspoons coarsely ground pepper. Place second rimmed baking sheet on top of bacon. Bake in 375-degree oven until bacon is crisp, 15 to 20 minutes; transfer to paper towel–lined plate and let cool. Cut bacon in half crosswise. Before finishing burgers in oven, top with ¼ cup shredded aged cheddar cheese. Top with bacon before serving.

JUICY PUB-STYLE BURGERS WITH PAN-ROASTED MUSHROOMS AND GRUYÈRE

Heat 2 tablespoons vegetable oil in 12-inch skillet over medium-high heat until just smoking. Add 10 ounces thinly sliced cremini mushrooms, ¼ teaspoon table salt, and ¼ teaspoon pepper; cook, stirring frequently, until browned, 5 to 7 minutes. Add 1 minced shallot and 2 teaspoons minced thyme and cook until fragrant. Remove skillet from heat and stir in 2 tablespoons dry sherry. Top each burger with 1 ounce grated Gruyère cheese before transferring to oven. Top with mushrooms before serving.

KEYS TO SUCCESS

- **Sear then bake:** Starting the burger patties on the stove gives them a flavorful crust and finishing them in the oven gives them a juicy interior.

- **Let the patties rest:** To redistribute juices

BISTRO BURGERS WITH PÂTÉ, FIGS, AND WATERCRESS

Serves: 4
Total Time: 45 minutes

RECIPE OVERVIEW The pairing of a rich home-ground burger with pâté and a fig salad is truly extraordinary—a burger dressed to impress. Pâté is a rich, umami-dense paste generally made from duck or chicken liver. The beauty of pâté is that it adds intensely rich flavor but requires no prep beyond spreading a thick layer on the bun. A quick fig salad freshens and balances the flavors. Watercress, which needs no embellishment, lends texture and a pleasant vegetal flavor. We prefer to use one of our homemade beef burger blends here; however, you can substitute 1¾ pounds of 85 percent lean ground beef if desired. You can find pâté in the gourmet cheese section of most well-stocked supermarkets. Be sure to use a smooth-textured pâté, not a coarse country pâté.

- 8 ounces figs, stemmed and sliced thin
- 1 small shallot, halved and sliced thin
- 2 teaspoons balsamic vinegar
- 1 teaspoon honey
- 1 recipe Burger Blend (page 362)
- ½ teaspoon table salt
- ¼ teaspoon pepper
- 1 teaspoon vegetable oil
- 6 ounces chicken or duck liver pâté
- 4 hamburger buns, toasted if desired
- 2 ounces (2 cups) watercress

1. Adjust oven rack to middle position and heat oven to 300 degrees. Combine figs, shallot, vinegar, and honey in bowl; set aside for serving.

2. Divide burger blend into 4 lightly packed balls, then gently flatten into ¾-inch-thick patties. Using your fingertips, press center of each patty down until about ½ inch thick, creating slight divot.

3. Season patties with salt and pepper. Heat oil in 12-inch skillet over high heat until just smoking. Using spatula, transfer patties to skillet, divot side up, and cook until well browned on first side, 2 to 4 minutes. Gently flip patties and continue to cook until well browned on second side, 2 to 4 minutes. Transfer patties to rimmed baking sheet, divot side down, and bake until burgers register 120 to 125 degrees (for medium-rare) or 130 to 135 degrees (for medium), 3 to 8 minutes. Transfer burgers to platter and let rest for 5 minutes.

4. Spread pâté evenly over bun tops. Serve burgers on buns, topped with fig mixture and watercress.

KEY TO SUCCESS

- **Find balance:** Sweet figs, bright vinegar, and peppery watercress counterbalance the rich pâté and burger.

BREAKFAST PORK BURGERS

Serves: 4
Total Time: 50 minutes

RECIPE OVERVIEW This recipe features everything we love about breakfast in burger form: savory, salty pork with a little maple sweetness, a fresh soft-cooked egg, and a hearty English muffin to mop up any errant, oozing yolk. To keep the patties from drying out during cooking, we rely on the traditional meatball standby of a panade; mixing this paste of mashed bread and milk into the ground pork ensures a juicy patty that stays tender. A little soy sauce amps up the savoriness of the patty and seasons it throughout, while fresh sage makes the flavors pop. A touch of maple syrup adds a rich flavor that is just sweet enough and encourages beautiful browning. We weren't sure our decadent breakfast burger needed a topping of cheese, but after trying a couple of iterations, we loved how the tang of cheddar offset the burger's ample richness. Look for English muffins that are at least 4 inches in diameter. Serve with hot sauce.

- 1 slice hearty white sandwich bread, torn into 1-inch pieces
- 1 shallot, minced
- 2 tablespoons milk
- 2 tablespoons maple syrup
- 4 teaspoons soy sauce
- 2 teaspoons minced fresh sage
- ½ teaspoon plus ⅛ teaspoon pepper, divided
- 1½ pounds ground pork
- ½ teaspoon plus ⅛ teaspoon table salt, divided
- 4 teaspoons vegetable oil, divided
- 4 slices cheddar cheese (4 ounces)
- 4 large eggs
- 4 English muffins, toasted

1. Using fork, mash bread, shallot, milk, maple syrup, soy sauce, sage, and ½ teaspoon pepper to paste in large bowl. Break ground pork into small pieces and add to bowl with bread mixture. Gently knead with hands until well combined. Divide pork mixture into 4 equal portions, then gently shape each portion into ¾-inch-thick patty. Using your fingertips, press center of each patty down until about ½ inch thick, creating slight divot.

2. Season patties with ½ teaspoon salt. Heat 1 teaspoon oil in 12-inch nonstick skillet over medium heat until just smoking. Transfer patties to skillet, divot side up, and cook until well browned on first side, 4 to 6 minutes. Flip patties, top with cheddar, and reduce heat to medium-low. Continue to cook until browned on second side and meat registers 150 degrees, 5 to 7 minutes. Transfer burgers to platter and let rest for 5 minutes. Let skillet cool slightly, then wipe clean with paper towels.

3. Meanwhile, crack eggs into 2 small bowls (2 eggs per bowl) and season with remaining ⅛ teaspoon salt and remaining ⅛ teaspoon pepper. Add remaining 1 tablespoon oil to now-empty skillet and heat over medium-high heat

until shimmering. Swirl to coat skillet with oil, then working quickly, pour 1 bowl of eggs in 1 side of skillet and second bowl of eggs in other side. Cover and cook for 1 minute. Remove skillet from burner and let sit, covered, 15 to 45 seconds for runny yolks (white around edge of yolk will be barely opaque), 45 to 60 seconds for soft but set yolks, or about 2 minutes for medium-set yolks. Serve burgers on muffins, topped with eggs.

KEYS TO SUCCESS

- **Use a bread-milk panade:** Keeps the pork patties from drying out
- **Add a touch of soy sauce:** Gives the patties meaty depth

LAMB BURGERS WITH HALLOUMI AND BEET TZATZIKI

Serves: 4
Total Time: 55 minutes, plus 1 hour chilling

RECIPE OVERVIEW The rich flavor of lamb makes for an exceptional burger experience. We pair delicately spiced ground lamb patties with a colorful beet tzatziki, pan-seared halloumi cheese, and a drizzle of sweet honey for a truly unique burger that could transport us to the Greek islands any night of the week. To give the rich ground lamb a boost, we make a warm spice blend of coriander, oregano, and cinnamon. Slabs of firm, salty halloumi cheese develop a beautiful nutty brown crust when seared and offset the richness of the lamb. For a creamy tang, we top our burgers with a generous dollop of tzatziki, which we spike with earthy beets to turn it a vivid pink. A drizzle of honey helps pull all the flavors together.

- 1   beet, peeled and shredded (¾ cup)
- ¼   English cucumber, shredded
- 1   teaspoon table salt, divided
- ½   cup whole Greek yogurt
- 3   tablespoons plus 1 teaspoon extra-virgin olive oil, divided
- 1   tablespoon minced fresh mint or dill
- 1   small garlic clove, minced
- 1½ pounds ground lamb
- 1½ teaspoons ground coriander
- 1½ teaspoons dried oregano
- ⅛   teaspoon ground cinnamon
- ½   teaspoon pepper
- 1   (8-ounce) block halloumi cheese, sliced crosswise into ½-inch-thick slabs
- 4   hamburger buns, toasted if desired
- 1½ ounces (1½ cups) baby arugula
- 1   tablespoon honey

1. Toss beet and cucumber with ½ teaspoon salt in colander set over medium bowl and let sit for 15 minutes. Discard any drained juices and wipe bowl clean with paper towels. Whisk yogurt, 2 tablespoons oil, mint, and garlic together in now-empty bowl, then stir in beet mixture. Cover and refrigerate for at least 1 hour or up to 2 days. Season tzatziki with salt and pepper to taste.

2. Break ground lamb into small pieces in large bowl. Add coriander, oregano, cinnamon, and pepper and gently knead with hands until well combined. Divide lamb mixture into 4 equal portions, then gently shape each portion into ¾-inch-thick patty. Using your fingertips, press center of each patty down until about ½ inch thick, creating slight divot.

3. Season patties with remaining ½ teaspoon salt. Heat 1 teaspoon oil in 12-inch skillet over medium heat until just smoking. Transfer patties to skillet, divot side up, and cook until well browned on first side, 2 to 4 minutes. Flip patties and continue to cook until browned on second side and meat registers 120 to 125 degrees (for medium-rare) or 130 to 135 (for medium), 3 to 5 minutes. Transfer burgers to platter and let rest for 5 minutes. Wipe skillet clean with paper towels.

4. Pat halloumi dry with paper towels. Heat remaining 1 tablespoon oil in now-empty skillet over medium heat until shimmering. Arrange halloumi in single layer in skillet and cook until golden brown, 2 to 4 minutes per side. Serve burgers on buns, topped with halloumi, tzatziki, and arugula, and drizzled with honey.

KEYS TO SUCCESS

- **Incorporate warm spices:** They enhance the ground lamb.
- **Top with halloumi:** Salty cheese goes well with the richness of the lamb.
- **Drizzle with honey:** Sweetness provides a surprisingly fitting way to pull the burger together.

GOOD REASONS TO GRIND IT YOURSELF

The best ground meat is meat you grind yourself. (And you don't need a meat grinder; see how we do it in a food processor.) The second-best ground meat is meat your butcher grinds for you. And the third-best ground meat is meat you buy packaged at the supermarket. Buying ground meat at the supermarket is kind of a gamble; unless your butcher grinds to order, there's no way to know what you're actually getting. The cut, fat content, and texture of store-ground meat can vary widely. It's often overprocessed to a pulp, so it cooks up heavy and dense no matter how much care you take. But when grinding your own meat, you're in the driver's seat. The coarser texture you can achieve is great for burgers because it makes them looser and more tender. You know exactly what cut you're using and how marbled it is.

A serious reason to consider home-grinding for beef in particular is food safety: Regardless of where the meat is processed, ground pork, poultry, and beef are safe to eat as long as they are cooked to 160 degrees—the temperature at which potential pathogens are deactivated. But since ground beef is frequently served at temperatures lower than 160 degrees, foodborne illness can be an issue. Meat processing plants have stringent guidelines intended to prevent cross-contamination, but anyone who reads the news knows that outbreaks of salmonella and the harmful 0157:H7 strain of E. coli routinely occur. However, only ground beef—not whole cuts—is considered risky. This is because contaminants do not penetrate the surface of a steak or a roast, and any that may be present on the surface will be killed during cooking, making the meat safe even if the interior is served rare. The risk occurs during grinding, when the exterior of the meat is distributed into the interior, taking any potential pathogens along with it.

As long as you follow safe food-handling guidelines—including frequent and thorough hand washing, thorough cleaning of surfaces, and storing meat at or below 40 degrees—we believe that grinding beef at home is safer than buying ground beef at the store since the chance of a single cut of beef (that you then grind at home) being contaminated is relatively slim. Conversely, a single portion of preground store beef can be an amalgam of various grades of meat from different parts of many different cattle. In fact, a typical hamburger may contain meat from hundreds of different animals. And obviously, the more cattle that go into your burger the greater the odds of contamination.

GETTING THE RIGHT GRIND

Underprocessed meat will lead to gristly bits. If you're making burgers, this could also mean patties that don't hold together. Overprocessed meat becomes rubbery and dense as it cooks. Perfectly ground meat contains pieces that are fine enough to ensure tenderness but coarse enough that a burger patty will stay loose. Here are the steps to perfection.

1. Cut meat into ½-inch pieces.

2. Arrange ½-inch pieces of meat in single layer on rimmed baking sheet. Freeze until firm and starting to harden around edges but still pliable, about 35 minutes.

3. Working in batches, pulse meat in food processor, stopping to redistribute meat as needed for an even grind according to recipe. Spread ground meat over sheet and discard any long strands of gristle and large chunks of fat.

BUTCHERING, STUFFING, AND TYING

STEVE DUNN

There are many ways to elevate the presentation factor for meat, and these options open up to you when you become more confident with your butchering skills. Butchering doesn't have to apply only to large roasts you serve for company. Here you'll also learn how roulades add flavor to workaday pork tenderloins and that osso buco is a great way to put a veal shank on your plate. Take out the meat mallet. Dig out the twine. And learn how to manipulate cuts of meat.

STEVE'S PRO TIP: *One thing to keep in mind when tying a roast is to tie it snugly but not too tightly. The meat expands while cooking, and if the roast is tied too tight, it can lead to it buckling into an odd shape, or if it's stuffed, may lead to the filling being squeezed out of the roast. Tie it as though you would your shoe, snug but not uncomfortably tight.*

BRACIOLE

Serves: 6 to 8
Total Time: 4 hours

RECIPE OVERVIEW For our take on the Italian stuffed beef rolls, we use flank steak rather than top or bottom round (the other common choices) because its loose grain makes it easier to pound thin and its higher fat content means that it emerges from the oven tender and moist. Our filling is bold; it includes umami-rich prosciutto, anchovies, and fontina—which is also a good melter that brings much-needed fat to the dish. In addition, a gremolata-inspired mix within the filling provides a jolt of flavor and freshness. Incorporating beef broth into the tomato sauce integrates the beef and the sauce into a unified whole. Cut sixteen 10-inch lengths of kitchen twine before starting the recipe. You can substitute sharp provolone for the fontina, if desired. Serve the braciole and sauce together, with pasta or polenta; or separately, as a pasta course with the sauce followed by the meat.

- 7 tablespoons extra-virgin olive oil, divided
- 10 garlic cloves, minced, divided
- 2 teaspoons grated lemon zest
- 3 anchovy fillets, rinsed and minced
- 1/3 cup plus 2 tablespoons chopped fresh basil, divided
- 1/3 cup minced fresh parsley
- 1/3 cup grated Pecorino Romano cheese, plus extra for serving
- 1/3 cup plain dried bread crumbs
- 3 ounces fontina cheese, shredded (3/4 cup)
- 1 (2- to 2 1/2-pound) flank steak, trimmed
- 8 thin slices prosciutto (4 ounces)
- 1 teaspoon kosher salt
- 1/2 teaspoon pepper
- 1 large onion, chopped fine
- 1/4 teaspoon red pepper flakes
- 1/4 cup tomato paste
- 3/4 cup dry red wine
- 1 (28-ounce) can crushed tomatoes
- 2 cups beef broth

1. Adjust oven rack to lower-middle position and heat oven to 325 degrees. Stir 3 tablespoons oil, half of garlic, lemon zest, and anchovies together in medium bowl. Add 1/3 cup basil, parsley, Pecorino, and bread crumbs and stir to incorporate. Stir in fontina until evenly distributed and set aside filling.

2. Halve steak against grain to create 2 smaller steaks. Lay 1 steak on cutting board with grain running parallel to counter edge. Holding blade of chef's knife parallel to counter, halve steak horizontally to create 2 thin pieces. Repeat with remaining steak. Cover 1 piece with plastic wrap and, using meat pounder, flatten into rough rectangle measuring no more than 1/4 inch thick. Repeat pounding with remaining 3 pieces. Cut each piece in half, with grain, to create total of 8 pieces.

Assembling Braciole

HALVE

Lay 1 steak on the cutting board with the grain running parallel to the counter edge. Slice horizontally to create 2 thin pieces. Repeat with the second steak.

POUND

Cover 1 piece of meat with plastic wrap and pound into rough rectangle about ¼ inch thick. Repeat with the remaining 3 pieces.

SLICE

Cut each piece of meat in half, with grain, to create total of 8 pieces.

FILL

Arrange 4 pieces of meat so grain runs parallel to the counter edge. Distribute filling over each piece and top each with slice of prosciutto.

ROLL

Keeping the filling in place, roll each piece of meat away from you to form tight log.

TIE

Tie each roll with 2 pieces of kitchen twine to secure.

3. Lay 4 pieces on cutting board with grain running parallel to counter edge (if 1 side is shorter than the other, place shorter side closer to you). Distribute half of filling evenly over pieces. Top filling on each piece with 1 slice of prosciutto, folding to fit, and press firmly. Keeping filling in place, roll each piece away from you to form tight log. Tie each roll with 2 pieces kitchen twine to secure. Repeat process with remaining steak pieces, filling, and prosciutto. Sprinkle rolls on both sides with salt and pepper.

4. Heat remaining ¼ cup oil in large Dutch oven over medium-high heat until shimmering. Brown rolls on 2 sides, 8 to 10 minutes. Using tongs, transfer rolls to plate. Add onion to pot and cook, stirring occasionally, until softened and lightly browned, 5 to 7 minutes. Stir in pepper flakes and remaining garlic; cook until fragrant, about 30 seconds. Stir in tomato paste and cook until slightly darkened, 3 to 4 minutes. Add wine and cook, scraping up any browned bits. Stir in tomatoes and broth. Return rolls to pot; bring to simmer. Cover and transfer to oven. Braise until meat is fork-tender, 2½ to 3 hours, using tongs to flip rolls halfway through braising.

5. Transfer braciole to serving dish and discard twine. Stir remaining 2 tablespoons basil into tomato sauce and season with salt and pepper to taste. Pour sauce over braciole and serve, passing extra Pecorino separately.

KEYS TO SUCCESS

- **Choose flank steak:** Has a loose grain so it's easy to pound thin

- **Add umami-rich ingredients to the filling:** Lets the filling's savor shine through

- **Incorporate fontina cheese:** Melts well for a rich, seamless filling

- **Add beef broth to the tomato sauce:** Coheres its flavors with the meat

OSSO BUCO

Serves: 6
Total Time: 3¼ hours

RECIPE OVERVIEW In osso buco, slow, steady cooking renders veal shanks remarkably tender and turns a simple broth of carrots, onion, celery, wine, and stock into a velvety sauce. Each diner gets an individual shank; for some, the best part is the luscious bone marrow, extracted with a small spoon. Our recipe for this classic uses a flavorful braising liquid and cooking technique to produce a rich sauce that is true to the venerable recipe; aromatics deepen the flavor of store-bought stock. We oven-braise the shanks, which is the easiest cooking method, and the natural reduction that takes place leaves just the right amount of liquid in the pot. Tying the shanks around the equator keeps the meat attached to the bone for an attractive presentation. Many recipes suggest flouring the veal before browning it, but we found we got better flavor when we simply seared the meat after liberally seasoning with salt and pepper. We stir gremolata into the sauce to brighten the hearty dish, as well as using it to garnish the shanks.

Osso Buco
- 6 (14- to 16-ounce) veal shanks, 1½ inches thick
- 6 tablespoons extra-virgin olive oil, divided
- 2½ cups dry white wine, divided
- 2 onions, chopped
- 2 carrots, peeled and chopped
- 2 celery ribs, chopped
- 6 garlic cloves, minced
- 2 cups chicken broth
- 1 (14.5-ounce) can diced tomatoes, drained
- 2 bay leaves

Gremolata
- ¼ cup minced fresh parsley
- 3 garlic cloves, minced
- 2 teaspoons finely grated lemon zest

1. FOR THE OSSO BUCO Adjust oven rack to lower-middle position and heat oven to 325 degrees. Pat shanks dry with paper towels and season with salt and pepper. Tie piece of twine around thickest portion of each shank to keep meat attached to bone while cooking. Heat 2 tablespoons oil in Dutch oven over medium-high heat until just smoking. Brown half of shanks on all sides, 8 to 10 minutes; transfer to large bowl. Repeat with 2 tablespoons oil and remaining shanks; transfer to bowl. Off heat, add 1½ cups wine to now-empty pot and scrape up any browned bits. Pour liquid into bowl with shanks.

2. Heat remaining 2 tablespoons oil in again-empty pot until shimmering. Add onions, carrots, and celery and cook until vegetables are softened and lightly browned, 8 to 10 minutes. Stir in garlic and cook until lightly browned, about 1 minute. Stir in broth, tomatoes, bay leaves, and remaining 1 cup wine and bring to simmer. Nestle shanks into pot along with deglazing liquid. Cover pot, leaving lid slightly ajar, and transfer pot to oven. Cook until veal is tender and fork slips easily in and out of meat, but meat is not falling off bone, about 2 hours.

3. FOR THE GREMOLATA Combine parsley, garlic, and lemon zest in small bowl.

4. Remove pot from oven and discard bay leaves. Stir half of gremolata into braising liquid and season with salt and pepper to taste. Let sit for 5 minutes.

5. Transfer shanks to individual bowls and discard twine. Ladle braising liquid over shanks and sprinkle with remaining gremolata. Serve.

KEYS TO SUCCESS
- **Wrap twine around each shank:** Keeps them intact through braising and serving
- **Brown shanks in two batches:** Creates lots of rich fond to flavor the sauce
- **Leave the lid ajar:** Lets the braising liquid evaporate to just the right amount

Buying Veal Shanks

Cut crosswise from the front legs, the shanks, also known as osso buco after the exemplary dish, contain both meat and bone. Shanks can vary in thickness and diameter, so shop carefully. Although they're sometimes sold boneless, you want shanks with the marrow-packed bone, which adds flavor and body to the braising medium. Shanks become fall-off-the-bone tender, which is why we tie each one for a special presentation.

PORCHETTA

Serves: 8 to 10
Total Time: 1½ to 2 hours, plus 6 hours chilling

RECIPE OVERVIEW Porchetta—fall-apart tender, rich pieces of slow-cooked pork infused with the flavors of garlic, fennel, rosemary, and thyme and served with pieces of crisp skin on a crusty roll—is one of Italy's greatest street foods. To take it inside, we opt for accessible pork butt over the traditional whole pig. For extra-crispy "skin," we cross-hatch the fat cap, rub it with a mixture of salt and baking soda, and refrigerate the roast overnight to help dry it out. We cut the roast into two pieces and tie each into a compact cylinder before cooking the roasts in a covered roasting pan, trapping steam to cook the meat evenly and keep it moist. Finally, we uncover the pan to brown and crisp the outer layer. Look for a roast with a substantial fat cap. If fennel seeds are unavailable, substitute ¼ cup ground fennel. A longer refrigeration time is preferred.

- 3 tablespoons fennel seeds
- ½ cup fresh rosemary leaves (2 bunches)
- ¼ cup fresh thyme leaves (2 bunches)
- 12 garlic cloves, peeled
- 2 tablespoons plus 1 teaspoon kosher salt, divided
- 4 teaspoons pepper, divided
- ½ cup extra-virgin olive oil
- 1 (5- to 6-pound) boneless pork butt roast, trimmed
- ¼ teaspoon baking soda

1. Grind fennel seeds in spice grinder or mortar and pestle until finely ground. Transfer ground fennel to food processor and add rosemary, thyme, garlic, 2 teaspoons salt, and 1 tablespoon pepper. Pulse mixture until finely chopped, 10 to 15 pulses. Add oil and process until smooth paste forms, 20 to 30 seconds.

2. Using sharp knife, cut slits 1 inch apart in crosshatch pattern in fat cap of roast, being careful not to cut into meat. Cut roast in half with grain into 2 equal pieces. Turn each roast on its side so fat cap is facing away from you, bottom of roast is facing toward you, and newly cut side is facing up. Starting 1 inch from short end of each roast, use boning or paring knife to make slit that starts 1 inch from top of roast and ends 1 inch from bottom, pushing knife completely through roast. Repeat making slits, spaced 1 to 1½ inches apart, along length of each roast, stopping 1 inch from opposite end (you should have 6 to 8 slits, depending on size of roast).

3. Turn roast so fat cap is facing down. Rub sides and bottom of roasts with 2 teaspoons salt, taking care to work salt into slits from both sides. Rub herb paste onto sides and bottom of each roast, taking care to work paste into slits from both sides. Flip roast so that fat cap is facing up. Using 3 pieces of kitchen twine per roast, tie each roast into compact cylinder.

4. Combine baking soda, remaining 1 tablespoon salt, and remaining 1 teaspoon pepper in small bowl. Rub fat cap of each roast with salt–baking soda mixture, taking care to work mixture into crosshatches. Transfer roasts to wire rack set in rimmed baking sheet and refrigerate, uncovered, for at least 6 hours or up to 24 hours.

Preparing Porchetta

HALVE
Cut the roast in half with the grain into 2 equal pieces.

SLIT
Turn the roast on its side. Starting 1 inch from short end of roast, make a slit that starts 1 inch from top of roast and ends 1 inch from bottom.

SPACE OUT
Repeat making slits, spaced 1 to 1½ inches apart, along the length of each roast, stopping 1 inch from opposite end.

RUB
Turn the roast so the fat cap is facing down. Rub the sides and bottom of each roast with salt and work into slits. Repeat with herb paste.

TIE
Tie each roast into a compact cylinder.

5. Adjust oven rack to middle position and heat oven to 325 degrees. Transfer roasts, fat side up, to large roasting pan, leaving at least 2 inches between roasts. Cover tightly with aluminum foil. Cook until pork registers 180 degrees, 2 to 2½ hours.

6. Remove pan from oven and increase oven temperature to 500 degrees. Carefully discard foil and transfer roasts to large plate. Discard liquid in pan. Line pan with foil. Remove twine from roasts; return roasts to pan, directly on foil; and return pan to oven. Cook until exteriors of roasts are well browned and interiors register 190 degrees, 20 to 30 minutes. Transfer roasts to carving board and let rest for 20 minutes. Slice roasts ½ inch thick, transfer to platter, and serve.

KEYS TO SUCCESS
- **Cut slits in the roast:** Gets the herb paste flavor deep into the roast
- **Cut roast in half and tie into cylinders:** Results in attractive slices
- **Start cooking with a foil cover:** Keeps the meat moist for the first stage of cooking

PORK TENDERLOIN ROULADE WITH PANCETTA, PEAR, AND CHEDDAR
Serves: 4 to 6
Total Time: 1½ hours

RECIPE OVERVIEW A great way to bump up the flavor of mild pork tenderloin is to pack the meat with a pungent stuffing. To stuff it without leaking, we butterfly the meat, meaning we slice the tenderloin nearly in half lengthwise. We then pound the tenderloin to an even thickness, roll it around a mixture of salty pancetta and sweet pears, and tie it with kitchen twine. Cheddar cheese helps bind the pancetta-and-pear stuffing while adding sharp flavor and richness. You will need a 12-inch ovensafe nonstick skillet for this recipe.

Stuffing
- 3 ounces pancetta, chopped fine
- 1 ripe but firm Bosc pear, peeled, halved, cored, and chopped
- 1 shallot, minced
- 1 teaspoon minced fresh thyme
- 3 ounces sharp cheddar cheese, shredded (¾ cup)
- ½ teaspoon pepper

Pork
- 2 (1- to 1¼-pound) pork tenderloin, trimmed
- 1½ teaspoons kosher salt
- ½ teaspoon pepper
- 1 tablespoon extra-virgin olive oil

- **Bind the filling with cheddar cheese**: Adds both sharp flavor and more richness
- **Trim the pounded pork**: Makes rolling neat and easy

Preparing Pork Tenderloin Roulade

BUTTERFLY

Cut the tenderloins in half horizontally, stopping ½ inch from edge so the halves remain attached.

POUND

Open up the tenderloins, cover with plastic wrap, and pound to an even ¼-inch thickness.

TRIM

Trim and discard any ragged edges to create a neat rectangle.

FILL

With the long side of the tenderloin facing you, sprinkle half of the stuffing (scant 1 cup) over the bottom half of tenderloin, leaving 1-inch border around 3 edges.

ROLL

Roll the tenderloin away from you into a tight log.

TIE

Position the tenderloin seam side down and tie crosswise with kitchen twine at 1-inch intervals to secure.

1. FOR THE STUFFING Cook pancetta in 12-inch ovensafe nonstick skillet over medium heat until crispy, 5 to 7 minutes. Add pear, shallot, and thyme and cook until pear is softened, 4 to 6 minutes. Transfer to bowl and let cool for 10 minutes. Stir in cheddar and pepper. Wipe skillet clean with paper towels.

2. FOR THE PORK Adjust oven rack to middle position and heat oven to 350 degrees. Cut tenderloins in half horizontally, stopping ½ inch from edge so halves remain attached. Open up tenderloins, cover with plastic wrap, and pound to even ¼-inch thickness.

3. Working with 1 tenderloin at a time, trim and discard any ragged edges to create neat rectangle. With long side of tenderloin facing you, sprinkle half of stuffing (scant 1 cup) over bottom half of tenderloin, leaving 1-inch border around 3 edges. Roll tenderloin away from you into tight log.

4. Position tenderloins seam side down and tie crosswise with kitchen twine at 1-inch intervals to secure. (Stuffed tenderloins can be wrapped individually in plastic wrap and refrigerated for up to 24 hours.)

5. Sprinkle each tenderloin with ¾ teaspoon salt and ¼ teaspoon pepper. Heat oil in now-empty skillet over medium-high heat until shimmering. Add tenderloins and brown on all sides, 6 to 8 minutes. Transfer skillet to oven and roast until center of stuffing registers 140 degrees, 16 to 20 minutes. Transfer tenderloins to carving board, tent with aluminum foil, and let rest for 10 minutes. Remove twine, slice into 1-inch-thick medallions, and serve.

IMPRESSIVE ROASTS

DAN SOUZA

Depending on where they're cut from the animal, roasts come in a range of sizes, beefiness, and price points that makes them appropriate for many different occasions, even weeknights. But there are certain roasts that are big and beefy—and yes, a bit more pricey—that are distinctly special-occasion roasts, and therefore roasts you'll want to make sure turn out perfect. You'll learn techniques for handling a large prime rib roast so slices turn out rosy-red; you'll satisfy tenderloin fans with a pepper-crusted roast that lives up to its name; and you'll roast a flawless ham, a fresh one. Prepare to impress your guests with timeless recipes.

DAN'S PRO TIP: *For large roasts, planning is everything. Be sure to buy your roast early so you have plenty of time to prep, salt, and air-dry it days before popping it in the oven.*

BEST PRIME RIB

Serves: 8 to 10
Total Time: 4½ hours, plus 24½ hours salting and resting

RECIPE OVERVIEW Keep it simple: Roasting lets a prime rib's extraordinary flavor shine. Salt is even more essential with prime rib than other cuts. We salt our roast way in advance (as long as four days!); this seasons the thick roast to the core and dries out the exterior so that it develops a prized, deeply browned crust when seared. In our first feat, we remove the meat from the bones to make searing easier. Then we tie the roast back to the bones to ensure more even cooking. A very low oven temperature allows the meat's enzymes to act as natural tenderizers, and a quick trip under the broiler right before serving restores the glorious crispness the crust lost while the meat was resting. A longer salting time is preferable. If the roast has not reached the correct temperature in the time range specified in step 4, reheat the oven to 200 degrees for 5 minutes, shut it off, and continue to cook the roast until it reaches the desired temperature.

  1 (7-pound) first-cut beef standing rib roast (3 bones), with ½-inch fat cap
  2 tablespoons kosher salt
  2 teaspoons vegetable oil

1. Using sharp knife, cut beef from bones. Cut slits 1 inch apart in crosshatch pattern in fat cap of roast, being careful not to cut into beef. Rub salt thoroughly over roast and into slits. Place beef back on bones (to save space in refrigerator) and refrigerate, uncovered, for at least 24 hours or up to 4 days.

2. Adjust oven rack to middle position and heat oven to 200 degrees. Heat oil in 12-inch skillet over high heat until just smoking. Remove beef from bones. Sear top and sides of roast until browned, 6 to 8 minutes; do not sear side of roast that was cut from bones.

3. Fit roast back onto bones, let cool for 10 minutes, then tie together with kitchen twine between bones. Transfer roast, fat side up, to wire rack set in rimmed baking sheet and season with pepper. Roast until beef registers 110 degrees, 3 to 4 hours.

4. Turn oven off and leave roast in oven, without opening door, until beef registers 120 to 125 degrees (for medium-rare), 30 minutes to 1¼ hours. Remove roast from oven (leave roast on sheet) and let rest for at least 30 minutes or up to 1¼ hours.

5. Adjust oven rack 8 inches from broiler element and heat broiler. Place 3-inch aluminum foil ball under ribs to elevate fat cap. Broil until top of roast is well browned and crisp, 2 to 8 minutes. Transfer roast to carving board. Remove twine and remove meat from ribs. Slice roast ¾ inch thick. Serve.

KEYS TO SUCCESS

- **Salt up to 4 days in advance:** Deeply seasons the beefy cut and dries out its exterior for a dark crust

- **Remove the roast from the bones:** Makes searing easy (we tie it back together before roasting)

- **Finish cooking in an off oven:** Encourages enzymatic activity to naturally tenderize the meat

- **Finish the roast under the broiler:** Crisps it

Preparing Prime Rib

DEBONE
Using a sharp knife, cut the beef from the bones.

SALT
Cut slits 1 inch apart in a crosshatch pattern in fat cap. Rub 2 tablespoons salt thoroughly over the roast and into the slits. Refrigerate for at least 24 hours or up to 4 days.

SEAR
Remove the beef from the bones and sear the top and sides of the roast until browned, 6 to 8 minutes. (Do not sear the side that was cut from the bones.)

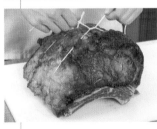

TIE
Fit the roast back onto the bones, let it cool for 10 minutes, then tie together with kitchen twine between the bones.

PEPPER-CRUSTED BEEF TENDERLOIN ROAST

Serves: 10 to 12
Total Time: 1½ hours

RECIPE OVERVIEW This tender, rosy roast boasts a spicy, yet not harsh-tasting, peppercorn crust that doesn't fall off. The tricks: Rubbing the raw tenderloin with an abrasive mixture of kosher salt, sugar, and baking soda transforms its surface into a magnet for the pepper crust. To tame the heat of the pepper crust, we simmer cracked peppercorns in oil, then strain. Then, to replace some of the subtle flavors we simmer away, we add some orange zest and nutmeg. With the crust in place, we gently roast the tenderloin until it is perfectly rosy, then serve it with a tangy, fruity Pomegranate-Port Sauce (recipe follows) to complement the rich beef. Not all pepper mills produce a coarse enough grind for this recipe. Coarsely cracked peppercorns are each about the size of a halved whole one.

4½	teaspoons kosher salt
1½	teaspoons sugar
¼	teaspoon baking soda
9	tablespoons olive oil, divided
½	cup coarsely cracked black peppercorns
1	tablespoon finely grated orange zest
½	teaspoon ground nutmeg
1	(6-pound) whole beef tenderloin, trimmed

1. Adjust oven rack to middle position and heat oven to 300 degrees. Combine salt, sugar, and baking soda in bowl; set aside. Heat 6 tablespoons oil and peppercorns in small saucepan over low heat until faint bubbles appear. Continue to cook at bare simmer, swirling pan occasionally, until pepper is fragrant, 7 to 10 minutes. Using fine-mesh strainer, drain cooking oil from peppercorns; discard cooking oil. Mix peppercorns with remaining 3 tablespoons oil, orange zest, and nutmeg.

2. Set tenderloin on sheet of plastic wrap. Sprinkle salt mixture evenly over surface of tenderloin and rub into tenderloin until surface is tacky. Tuck tail end of tenderloin under about 6 inches to create more even shape. Rub top and side of tenderloin with peppercorn mixture, pressing to make sure peppercorns adhere. Spray three 12-inch lengths kitchen twine with vegetable oil spray; tie head of tenderloin to maintain even shape, spacing twine at 2-inch intervals.

3. Transfer prepared tenderloin to wire rack set in rimmed baking sheet, keeping tail end tucked under. Roast until thickest part of meat registers about 120 degrees for rare or about 125 degrees for medium-rare (thinner parts of tenderloin will be slightly more done), 60 to 70 minutes. Transfer to carving board and let rest for 30 minutes.

4. Remove twine and slice meat into ½-inch-thick slices. Serve.

KEY TO SUCCESS.

• **Tuck and tie the tail:** Ensures even cooking

POMEGRANATE-PORT SAUCE

Makes: 1 cup

2	cups pomegranate juice
1½	cups ruby port
1	shallot, minced
1	tablespoon sugar
1	teaspoon balsamic vinegar
1	sprig fresh thyme
1	teaspoon table salt
4	tablespoons cold unsalted butter, cut into 4 pieces

Bring juice, port, shallot, sugar, vinegar, thyme sprig, and salt to simmer over medium-high heat. Cook until reduced to 1 cup, 30 to 35 minutes. Strain sauce through fine-mesh strainer and return to saucepan. Return saucepan to medium heat and whisk in butter, 1 piece at a time. Season with salt and pepper to taste.

Coating the Tenderloin with Peppercorns

SALT
Rub salt, sugar, and baking soda into the roast until the surface is tacky.

TUCK
Tuck the tail end of the tenderloin under about 6 inches to create a more even shape.

RUB
Rub the top and sides of the tenderloin with the peppercorn mixture, pressing so the peppercorns adhere.

TIE
Spray three 12-inch lengths of kitchen twine with vegetable oil spray; tie the head of the tenderloin crosswise at 2-inch intervals to maintain even shape.

Trimming Whole Beef Tenderloin

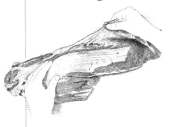

PULL AWAY FAT
Pull away the outer layer of fat to expose the fatty chain of meat.

CUT OFF CHAIN
Pull the chain of fat away from the roast, cut it off, and discard the chain.

SCRAPE SILVERSKIN
Scrape the silverskin at creases in the thick end to expose lobes.

TRIM SILVERSKIN
Trim the silverskin by slicing under it and cutting upward.

REMOVE SILVERSKIN
Remove the remaining silverskin in creases at thick end. Turn the tenderloin over and remove fat from underside.

ROASTED FRESH HAM

Serves: 12 to 14
Total Time: 4¾ to 6¼ hours, plus 12 hours marinating and 1⅓ hours resting

RECIPE OVERVIEW Unlike the hams that most people are familiar with, fresh ham is neither cured nor smoked. This big cut is basically just an oddly shaped bone-in, skin-on pork roast, and slow roasting turns it tender and flavorful. In order to make it easier to season the meat, we remove its thick skin, cut slits into the fat underneath and then one bigger pocket in the meat end of the ham, and rub it all over with salt, sugar, and herbs. Roasting the ham in an oven bag helps it retain plenty of moisture. A simple tangy glaze brushed on toward the end of roasting makes for a flavorful finish. This recipe requires a turkey-size oven bag. Be sure to cut a slit in the oven bag so it doesn't burst. A longer refrigeration time is preferable.

1 (8- to 10-pound) bone-in, skin-on shank-end fresh ham
⅓ cup packed brown sugar
⅓ cup kosher salt
3 tablespoons minced fresh rosemary
1 tablespoon minced fresh thyme
1 large oven bag
2 tablespoons maple syrup
2 tablespoons molasses
1 tablespoon soy sauce
1 tablespoon Dijon mustard
1 teaspoon pepper

1. Using sharp knife, remove skin from ham and trim fat to ½- to ¼-inch thickness. Cut slits 1 inch apart in cross-hatch pattern in fat, being careful not to cut into meat. Place ham on its side. Cut one 4-inch horizontal pocket about 2 inches deep in center of flat side of ham, being careful not to poke through opposite side.

2. Combine sugar, salt, rosemary, and thyme in bowl. Rub half of sugar mixture in ham pocket. Tie 1 piece of kitchen twine tightly around base of ham. Rub exterior of ham with remaining sugar mixture. Wrap ham tightly in plastic wrap and refrigerate for at least 12 hours or up to 24 hours.

3. Adjust oven rack to lowest position and heat oven to 325 degrees. Set V-rack in large roasting pan and spray with vegetable oil spray. Unwrap ham and place in oven bag flat side down. Tie top of oven bag closed with kitchen twine. Place ham, flat side down, on V-rack and cut ½-inch slit in top of oven bag. Roast until extremely tender and pork near (but not touching) bone registers 160 degrees, 3½ to 5 hours. Remove ham from oven and let rest in oven bag on V-rack for 1 hour. Heat oven to 450 degrees.

4. Whisk maple syrup, molasses, soy sauce, mustard, and pepper together in bowl. Cut off top of oven bag and push down with tongs, allowing accumulated juices to spill into roasting pan; discard oven bag. Leave ham sitting flat side down on V-rack.

5. Brush ham with half of glaze and roast for 10 minutes. Brush ham with remaining glaze, rotate pan, and roast until deep amber color, about 10 minutes. Move ham to carving board, flat side down, and let rest for 30 minutes. Pour pan juices into fat separator and let liquid settle for 5 minutes. Carve ham ¼ inch thick, arrange on serving dish, and moisten lightly with defatted pan juices. Serve, passing remaining pan juices separately.

KEYS TO SUCCESS

- **Select shank-end ham:** Easier to carve than sirloin-end
- **Make a pocket for a paste:** Seasons the ham deeply and evenly
- **Roast in an oven bag:** Helps retain moisture

Preparing Ham for Roasting

CUT
Slice one 4-inch horizontal pocket about 2 inches deep in the center of the flat side of the ham, being careful not to poke through the opposite end.

FILL
Rub half of the sugar mixture in the pocket.

SECURE
Tie 1 piece of kitchen twine tightly around the base of ham. Rub the exterior with remaining sugar mixture.

PRIME PRIME RIB

The USDA grades beef as prime, choice, or select. "Prime" rib doesn't mean a roast with a USDA prime designation, however, and is something of a misnomer. (That's why we prefer to call for "standing rib roast.") Prime rib was originally used to refer to the most desirable portions of the rib section. That means that prime-grade prime rib is the best of the best, costing more per pound, naturally, than choice prime rib. Additionally, some butchers offer dry-aged prime rib. (For more on dry aging, see page 358.) Dry aging adds even more cost per pound. To find out if prime-grade prime rib is worth the premium, we cooked several prime-grade, choice-grade, and dry-aged rib roasts. In the entire lot, there were no outright losers, but the experiment was telling. First, we don't recommend spending the extra cash on dry aging here; we found that its nuances were lost on this already great roast. On the other hand, in most cases the prime cuts beat out the choice cuts in terms of superior marbling and, thus, superior flavor and texture. Given that this meal will be a splurge no matter how you slice it, springing for prime beef makes sense, although a choice roast will be almost as good.

PURCHASING FRESH HAM

Most of us think of true ham as a pink haunch that's smoked, fully cooked, and ready to eat. Fresh ham is none of those things: It's simply the pig's upper hind leg, a big pork roast. And it might be your perfect pig cut if you like full-flavored pork. Whole fresh hams can weigh up to 25 pounds, so they're usually broken down into the sirloin end closer to the torso and the tapered shank end. The bone structure of the sirloin end makes carving tricky, so we favor a shank end fresh ham. The cut is usually covered with a thick layer of skin, which we remove before roasting.

Sirloin-Half Fresh Ham

Shank-End Fresh Ham

FIRST- OR SECOND-BEST RIB ROASTS

For a table-appropriate roast, butchers cut a rib roast into two distinct cuts, first and second cut. They're both prime rib, but the more desirable of the two cuts consists of ribs 10 through 12, the portion closer to the loin primal. It's considered more desirable because it contains the large, single rib-eye muscle and is less fatty than the second cut.

As in the case of prime rib, second-cut rib roast might be second best, but it's still pretty darn good. It consists of ribs 6 through 8 or 9; closer to the chuck end of the cow, the cut becomes more multi-muscled, and since muscles are surrounded by fat, this means a fattier roast. While the more regularly formed loin end is usually favored for its superior tenderness, we know that some fat, of course, is good and this cut is tremendously flavorful because of its more plentiful soft pockets of fat, as well as a more generous fat cap that bastes it as it cooks. Maybe you'll prefer the second best.

First-Cut Standing Rib Roast
aka large end rib roast; ribs 10 through 12

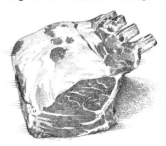

Second-Cut Standing Rib Roast
aka prime rib, beef rib roast, loin end,
small end, rib-eye roast, Newport roast

UNDER-THE-RADAR CUTS

LAN LAM

Steaks or large roasts are commonly desired cuts with their juicy meat and satisfying chew, but beyond the meaty body of the animal are cuts that make some of the richest, silkiest stews (and they're economical to boot). These sometimes forgotten parts require long braising because of the presence of fat and connective tissue and marrow-filled bone, but when the process is done, they turn from tough to meltingly tender and contribute to rich sauces and stocks. Learn how oxtails, beef shanks, and ham hocks create braises around the world.

LAN'S PRO TIP: *I'll take these "off-cuts" over a steak any day because they bring the flavor and are forgiving to prepare. These braising cuts can take an extra twenty minutes of cooking, whereas steaks and roasts can dry out if they aren't carefully monitored. And these braises reheat beautifully. In fact, they often taste better the next day. What's not to love?*

ETLI KURU FASULYE

Serves: 6 to 8
Total Time: 5 hours

RECIPE OVERVIEW Oxtails shine in our version of a Turkish dish, etli kuru fasulye, or "white beans with meat," when white beans are a creamy, nutty counterpoint to hearty oxtails. We start by roasting the oxtails in the oven for an hour, rather than browning them in a Dutch oven; in doing this, we repeatedly render and discard a significant amount of fat (about a half-cup!). The braising liquid gets its character from a simple yet flavorful trio: sweet whole tomatoes, warm and earthy Aleppo pepper, and pungent oregano. Try to buy oxtails that are approximately 2 inches thick and 2 to 4 inches in diameter. Oxtails can often be found in the freezer section of the grocery store; if using frozen oxtails, thaw them completely before using.

- 4 pounds oxtails, trimmed
- 4 cups chicken broth
- 2 tablespoons extra-virgin olive oil
- 1 onion, chopped fine
- 1 carrot, peeled and chopped fine
- 6 garlic cloves, minced
- 2 tablespoons tomato paste
- 2 tablespoons ground dried Aleppo pepper
- 1 tablespoon minced fresh oregano, divided
- 1 (28-ounce) can whole peeled tomatoes
- 1 (15-ounce) can navy beans, rinsed
- 1 tablespoon sherry vinegar

1. Adjust oven rack to lower-middle position and heat oven to 450 degrees. Pat oxtails dry with paper towels and season with salt and pepper. Arrange oxtails cut side down in single layer in large roasting pan and roast until meat begins to brown, about 45 minutes.

2. Discard any accumulated fat and juices in pan and continue to roast until meat is well browned, 15 to 20 minutes. Transfer oxtails to bowl and tent with aluminum foil; set aside. Stir chicken broth into pan, scraping up any browned bits; set aside.

3. Reduce oven temperature to 300 degrees. Heat oil in Dutch oven over medium heat until shimmering. Add onion and carrot and cook until softened, about 5 minutes. Stir in garlic, tomato paste, Aleppo pepper, and 1 teaspoon oregano and cook until fragrant, about 30 seconds.

4. Stir in broth mixture from roasting pan and tomatoes and their juice and bring to simmer. Nestle oxtails into pot, bring to simmer, and cover; transfer pot to oven. Cook until oxtails are tender and fork slips easily in and out of meat, about 3 hours.

5. Transfer oxtails to bowl and tent with foil. Strain braising liquid through fine-mesh strainer into fat separator; return solids to now-empty pot. Let braising liquid settle for 5 minutes, then pour defatted liquid into pot with solids.

6. Stir in beans, vinegar, and remaining 2 teaspoons oregano. Return oxtails and any accumulated juices to pot, bring to gentle simmer over medium heat, and cook until oxtails and beans are heated through, about 5 minutes. Season with salt and pepper to taste. Transfer oxtails to serving platter and spoon 1 cup sauce over top. Serve, passing remaining sauce separately.

KEYS TO SUCCESS

- **Roast the oxtails to brown them:** Renders lots of fat that can be discarded rather than incorporated into the bean dish
- **Spoon the sauce over oxtails in a serving vessel:** Keeps the ultratender meat from falling off the bone

All About Oxtails

You might not think of an animal's tail as edible, but when you cut it crosswise, you get oxtails—and we think they're highly underrated in the U.S. They're incredibly rich, full of marrow that's easily coaxed out, and cook to a tender softness—even more tender than short ribs. There was a time when humans were less wasteful, when we ate every portion of beef we could—eating oxtails is a holdover from that time. They are called oxtails and they can be the tails of oxen—castrated mature bulls that are mainly used for hard labor. What you're buying in the store, however, will generally be from regular beef cattle. You can find them in a good supermarket and surely at a butcher. But since they're mainly used for braising, you can substitute beef shanks, another beefy, tissue-abundant cut, in most recipes, and vice versa. Before cooking, trim any large chunks of excess fat surrounding the oxtails.

JAMAICAN OXTAIL

Serves: 6 to 8
Total Time: 5 hours, plus 4 hours marinating

RECIPE OVERVIEW This recipe comes from Jillian Atkinson, a photographer and food writer living in Brooklyn, New York, who absorbed this staple of Jamaican cuisine from watching her grandmother cook. A long cooking time tenderizes the oxtails, extracts gelatin from the bone, and delivers a treasured stickiness that requires you to lick your lips while you eat. The flavor foundation in this version is sweet and salty, a combination of what's called browning (caramelized sugar that the oxtails are cooked in) and savory dark soy sauce. Plan ahead: The oxtails need to marinate for at least 4 hours before cooking. Note that the oxtail marinade is reserved and added to the pot in step 9. We call for using dark soy sauce here, which is thicker and slightly sweeter than regular soy sauce. Butter beans are also called baby lima beans. If you can't find them canned, you can substitute 1½ cups (about 8 ounces) frozen beans. You can substitute a habanero chile for the Scotch bonnet chile, if desired. It's important to have the hot water called for in step 6 ready to add as soon as the sugar has properly browned. The wide time range for the reduction in step 10 takes into account the varying heating capabilities of different stove tops. Be sure to reduce the liquid until it has thickened and is just below the surface of the oxtails.

Stuffing

5	pounds oxtails, 2 to 2½ inches thick, trimmed
2	onions, halved and sliced thin
10	sprigs fresh thyme
2	scallions, crushed with side of knife, then chopped
2	tablespoons distilled white vinegar
1	tablespoon table salt
1	tablespoon pepper
1	tablespoon Worcestershire sauce
1	tablespoon dark soy sauce
3	garlic cloves, chopped
1	teaspoon onion powder
1	teaspoon granulated garlic
8	whole allspice berries
6	cups hot water
1	Scotch bonnet chile
1	(15.5-ounce) can butter beans, rinsed
¼	cup ketchup

Browning

¼	cup sugar
¼	cup hot water

1. **FOR THE OXTAIL** Place oxtails in large bowl and fill with cold water. Agitate to remove any loose bone and fat fragments. Drain and repeat, then drain again.

2. Add onions, thyme sprigs, scallions, vinegar, salt, pepper, Worcestershire, soy sauce, garlic, onion powder, granulated garlic, and allspice berries to bowl with oxtails and toss to thoroughly combine. Cover and refrigerate for at least 4 hours or up to 24 hours.

3. Brush marinade off oxtails and transfer oxtails to plate; reserve marinade to use in step 9.

4. **FOR THE BROWNING** Add sugar to center of large Dutch oven. Place pot over medium-low heat and cook, without stirring, until edges of sugar begin to liquefy and turn golden, about 4 minutes. Using long-handled wooden spoon or heat-resistant rubber spatula, pull edges of melted sugar inward to help melt remaining sugar.

5. Continue to cook until sugar turns dark chocolate brown, 4 to 6 minutes longer, stirring often for even cooking. (Browning will smoke; we recommend turning on your hood vent.)

6. Carefully add ¼ cup hot water to browning (mixture will sputter and let off steam) and stir to incorporate. Simmer until reduced by half and large bubbles break surface, 1½ to 2 minutes.

7. Add oxtails to browning and increase heat to medium-high (pot will be crowded). Cook, turning oxtails frequently, until oxtails have picked up significant color from sugar-based browning, some fond has begun to form on bottom of pot, and most moisture has cooked off to point where sizzling can be heard, 10 to 12 minutes.

8. Add 6 cups hot water to pot and bring to boil. Cover, reduce heat to medium-low, and cook at strong simmer for 2½ hours, stirring and turning oxtails occasionally.

9. Stir reserved marinade into pot. Poke small hole in Scotch bonnet with tip of paring knife and add to pot. Cover and continue to simmer until largest oxtails are fork-tender and meat begins to fall easily off bone, about 1 hour longer, stirring occasionally and being mindful to not burst Scotch bonnet as you stir.

10. Stir in butter beans and continue to simmer, covered, until meat falls easily off bone, about 30 minutes longer. Stir in ketchup and cook, uncovered, until liquid has thickened and reduced to just below surface of oxtails, 5 to 15 minutes. Serve.

KEYS TO SUCCESS

- **Marinate:** Flavors the oxtails with an umami depth

- **Make browning:** A dark caramel sauce used in Jamaican cooking to give the oxtails color during cooking

- **Add a pierced Scotch bonnet chile to the pot:** Infuses the whole dish with the perfect amount of heat rather than harsh bites

ALCATRA

Serves: 6
Total Time: 4½ hours

RECIPE OVERVIEW Alcatra, a simple and meaty Portuguese beef stew, features tender chunks of beef braised with onions, garlic, spices, and wine. Beef shanks are lean (which means the cooking liquid doesn't need to be skimmed) and full of collagen, which breaks down into gelatin and gives the sauce full body. Submerging the sliced onions completely in the liquid under the meat causes them to form a meaty-tasting compound that amps up the savory flavor of the broth, and smoky-sweet Spanish chorizo sausage matches up perfectly with the other flavors in the stew. You can substitute 4 pounds of bone-in cross-cut shanks if that's all you can find. Remove those marrow bones before cooking and save them for another use (see page 385). Cross-cut shanks cook more quickly, so check the stew for doneness in step 2 after 3 hours.

3 pounds boneless long-cut beef shanks
1 teaspoon table salt
5 garlic cloves, peeled and smashed
5 allspice berries
4 bay leaves
1½ teaspoons peppercorns
2 large onions, halved and sliced thin
2¼ cups dry white wine
¼ teaspoon ground cinnamon
8 ounces Spanish-style chorizo sausage, cut into ¼-inch-thick rounds

1. Adjust oven rack to middle position and heat oven to 325 degrees. Trim away any fat or large pieces of connective tissue from exterior of shanks (silverskin can be left on meat). Cut each shank crosswise into 2½-inch pieces. Sprinkle meat with salt.

2. Cut 8-inch square triple thickness of cheesecloth. Place garlic, allspice berries, bay leaves, and peppercorns in center of cheesecloth and tie into bundle with kitchen twine. Arrange onions and spice bundle in Dutch oven in even layer. Add wine and cinnamon. Arrange shank pieces in single layer on top of onions. Cover and cook until beef is tender, about 3½ hours.

3. Remove pot from oven and add chorizo. Using tongs, flip each piece of beef over, making sure that chorizo is submerged. Cover and let stand until chorizo is warmed through, about 20 minutes. Discard spice bundle. Season with salt and pepper to taste and serve.

KEYS TO SUCCESS

- **Select lean beef shank:** Gives the broth body without grease
- **Skip searing:** Focuses on the warm flavors as much as the meatiness of the beef
- **Submerge sliced onions in the liquid:** Causes them to form a meaty-tasting compound that enhances the broth

BULALO

Serves: 6 to 8
Total Time: 3½ hours

RECIPE OVERVIEW Bulalo, a Filipino soup of beef shanks and vegetables, is traditionally cooked in a cauldron until the beef's collagen and marrow melt to create luscious flavor. For our version, we start by frying sliced garlic in a Dutch oven and then browning the shanks in the flavorful leftover oil. Next we build a rich broth using onion, ginger, garlic, black peppercorns, fish sauce, and water. Letting everything simmer for about 2 hours helps break down the collagen and fats, producing ultratender meat. Corn and cabbage are traditional additions, but some recipes also add green beans, potatoes, and sweet onions; we landed on corn, napa cabbage, and potatoes. Adding the potatoes to the Dutch oven with the cabbage keeps them from becoming too mushy. We like serving bulalo with scallions, fish sauce, vinegar, and chili oil. White cane vinegar is a common Filipino vinegar that's made from sugarcane and boasts a balanced, versatile tart-sweetness. Look for beef shanks that are 2 inches thick and 2 to 4 inches in diameter. Use a Dutch oven that holds 6 quarts or more for this recipe.

¼ cup vegetable oil
12 garlic cloves, peeled (6 sliced thin, 6 crushed)
4 pounds cross-cut beef shanks, trimmed
1 tablespoon table salt, divided
1 onion, quartered
1 (4-inch) piece ginger, sliced into thin rounds
1 tablespoon black peppercorns
3½ quarts water
2 tablespoons fish sauce, plus extra for seasoning
2 ears corn, husks and silk removed, cut into 1-inch lengths
1 pound Yukon Gold potatoes, unpeeled, cut into 1-inch pieces
½ head napa cabbage, cored and sliced thin (8 cups)
2 scallions, sliced thin on bias
White cane vinegar or distilled white vinegar
Chili oil

1. Cook vegetable oil and sliced garlic in Dutch oven over medium heat, stirring frequently, until garlic is crisp and light golden brown, about 3 minutes. Using slotted spoon, transfer garlic to paper towel–lined plate and season with salt to taste; set aside for serving. Pour off and reserve oil left in pot.

2. Pat beef shanks dry with paper towels and sprinkle with 1 teaspoon salt. Heat 1 tablespoon reserved oil in now-empty pot over medium-high heat until just smoking. Brown half of shanks on all sides, about 8 minutes; transfer to bowl. Repeat with 1 tablespoon reserved oil and remaining shanks; transfer to bowl. Discard any remaining reserved oil.

3. Add onion, ginger, peppercorns, and crushed garlic to fat left in pot and cook until fragrant, about 1 minute. Return shanks and any accumulated juices to pot. Cover, reduce heat to low, and cook until beef releases additional juices, about 15 minutes, scraping bottom of pot occasionally to release fond.

4. Add water, fish sauce, and remaining 2 teaspoons salt and bring to boil. Reduce heat to low, partially cover, and simmer, skimming away foam as needed, until meat is tender and broth is flavorful, 1½ to 2 hours.

5. Transfer shanks to cutting board and let cool slightly. Using 2 forks, shred beef into bite-size pieces. Reserve shank bones and discard excess fat and connective tissue.

6. Set fine-mesh strainer over large bowl or container and line with triple layer of cheesecloth. Strain broth through prepared strainer and let settle for 5 minutes. Using wide, shallow spoon, skim excess fat from surface of broth. (You should have 12 cups broth; add extra water as needed to equal 12 cups. Broth, shredded beef, and reserved bones can be refrigerated separately for up to 4 days.)

7. Return broth to now-empty pot and bring to simmer over medium-high heat. Add corn and cook until tender, about 15 minutes. Stir in potatoes and cabbage and cook until tender, about 8 minutes. Off heat, stir in beef and

reserved bones and let sit until heated through, about 5 minutes. Season with extra fish sauce to taste. Sprinkle individual portions with scallions and reserved garlic chips and serve, passing vinegar and chili oil separately.

KEYS TO SUCCESS

- **Go wild with garlic:** Frying garlic cloves in oil creates a delicious garnish, and browning the shanks in the resulting garlic oil flavors the braise.
- **Garnish it:** Serving the soup with scallions, fish sauce, vinegar, and chili oil brightens and freshens it.

SOUTHERN-STYLE COLLARD GREENS WITH HAM HOCKS

Serves: 6 to 8
Total Time: 2½ hours

RECIPE OVERVIEW This Southern staple is made by braising collard greens with salty, smoky ham hocks. Over a long cooking time, the pork and greens intermingle and turn the cooking water into a supersavory pot liquor (or "pot likker"). We found that two smoked ham hocks provide the deepest, most smoky pork flavor. Plus, after a long braising time, it's easy to pull the savory little chunks of meat off the hocks to add back to the greens. Be sure to remove the rind from the ham before cutting it into pieces. Do not drain off the cooking liquid before serving. This flavorful, savory pot liquor should be sipped while eating the collards. Any leftover pot liquor can be used as a soup base. We like to serve the greens with cornbread.

- 2 pounds collard greens
- 2 tablespoons unsalted butter
- 1 onion, chopped
- 6 cups water
- 2 (12-ounce) smoked ham hocks
- 3 garlic cloves, smashed and peeled
- 2¼ teaspoons table salt
- 2 teaspoons sugar
- ⅛ teaspoon red pepper flakes
- Hot sauce

1. Adjust oven rack to lower-middle position and heat oven to 300 degrees. Trim collard stems to base of leaves; discard trimmings. Cut leaves into roughly 2-inch pieces. Place collard greens in large bowl and cover with water. Swish with your hand to remove grit. Repeat with fresh water, as needed, until grit no longer appears in bottom of bowl. Remove collard greens from water and set aside (you needn't dry them).

2. Melt butter in large Dutch oven over medium heat. Add onion and cook until lightly browned, 6 to 8 minutes. Add water, ham hocks, garlic, salt, sugar, and pepper flakes and bring to boil over high heat. Add collard greens (pot may be full) and stir until collard greens wilt slightly, about 1 minute. Cover, transfer to oven, and cook until collard greens are very tender, about 1½ hours.

3. Transfer ham hocks to cutting board and let cool for 10 minutes. Remove meat from ham hocks, chop, and return to pot; discard skin and bones. Season collard greens with salt to taste. Serve with hot sauce.

KEYS TO SUCCESS

- **Use two ham hocks:** Flavors the pot liquor deeply and provides enough meat to shred into the greens
- **Oven-braise:** Results in silky, evenly cooked greens
- **Remove the rind:** You don't want it in the greens.

CORE TECHNIQUE

Getting the Meat from Ham Hocks

Remove meat from ham hocks. Shred, discarding skin and bones.

Handling Ham Hocks

These joint areas contain a great deal of bone, fat, and connective tissue. They're used to lend complex flavor and a rich, satiny texture to soups. And they do contain a good amount of meat; they just need to be braised or slow-cooked for long periods of time to break down the connective tissue so you can access it. Once tender, the meat can be picked off the bone, shredded, and added to soups, stews, chilis, greens, or beans. Ham hocks are usually sold smoked or cured (what we call for) although fresh ones are available, too.

SAVE THOSE MARROW BONES

If you can only find cross-cut beef shanks for a recipe that calls for long-cut, you'll need to remove the bones before you begin. But don't throw them out; roast them. When roasted, the marrow inside the bones softens and becomes richly flavored. Simply scoop it out and spread it on toasted bread for a decadent appetizer or side dish. You can also use the roasted bones for making soup stock. Before roasting the marrow bones, we soak them in a brine and refrigerate them for up to two days. In addition to seasoning, brining dissolves proteins in the marrow that would otherwise turn an unattractive dark gray color during cooking.

To roast the marrow bones: Dissolve ¼ cup salt in 2 quarts water, add bones to brine, and refrigerate until marrow turns creamy in color, 1 to 2 days. Arrange bones cut side down on foil-lined baking sheet and roast on middle rack of 350-degree oven until skewer inserted in marrow slides in and out with ease, 20 to 25 minutes.

TWO CUTS OF BEEF SHANKS

This upper part of the cow's legs puts in a lot of work to make the cow move. Tough work means tough, sinewy meat—unless the cut is slowly braised. Then it breaks down into something incredibly tender and luscious, thanks to connective tissue that liquefies, lubricating the meat and imparting silky richness to the cooking liquid. While many cuts rich in connective tissue are also quite fatty, meaning that their cooking liquid requires careful defatting, beef shanks are actually quite lean so their sauce forms clean and clear. All this connective tissue means beef shanks don't cook quickly—but the wait is worth it. And for homemade beef broth (see page 200), they're your best bet, combining affordability with plentiful collagen that produces a broth with great body (and nourishment).

Beef shanks are sold as both long-cut (more connective tissue) and cross-cut (less connective tissue), as well as with or without the bone. We use both in different applications; cross-cut shanks provide valuable body to a braise when used.

Long-Cut Beef Shank

Cross-Cut Beef Shank

BUYING OXTAILS

Depending on which part of the tail they come from, oxtail pieces can vary in diameter from ¾ inch to 4 inches (see the range below). (Thicker pieces are cut close to the body; thinner pieces come from the end of the tail.) Try to buy oxtail packages with pieces approximately 2 inches thick and between 2 and 4 inches in diameter; they will yield more meat for your dish. Thicker pieces also lend more flavor to the broth with more marrow that can be extracted. It's fine to use a few small pieces; just don't rely on them exclusively.

GRILL-ROASTING

ASHLEY MOORE

What's the difference between grilling and grill-roasting? Grill-roasting is a technique you use for larger cuts of meat. You see, the oven isn't your only option for roasting meat. For tender cuts that don't require slow cooking over low heat, such as beef tenderloin, the grill works just as well. Grill-roasting relies on indirect heat between 300 and 400 degrees (in contrast to true grilling, which occurs at temperatures in excess of 500 degrees). Coals are banked on one side of the grill, and meat roasts on the "cool" side, with the lid kept down to trap heat and create an environment much like the oven. With a gas grill, the primary burner is kept on and the others are turned off. Give your roasts grill-enhancing flavor benefits with the techniques you learn in this course.

ASHLEY'S PRO TIP: *Use your grill not only to cook meat, but also char and cook vegetables, fruit, and herbs. Once grilled, they can be processed in a blender into a deliciously dynamic sauce.*

THE METHOD
SECRETS TO GRILL-ROASTING

1 SEASON OR BRINE
Season the meat and let stand 1 hour before grill-roasting. For lean cuts of pork, skip the salt and brine the meat before placing it on the grill.

2 SET UP HALF-GRILL FIRE
Many recipes recommend banking coals on both sides of the grill. We find the edges of large roasts can burn with this method. We prefer to transfer all coals to one side of the grill, leaving half of the grill free of coals so meat can cook without danger of burning. To ensure even cooking, it is a good idea to rotate the meat halfway through cooking.

3 USE VENTS
To help regulate heat, adjust vents on both the lid and grill bottom. We prefer to close vents partially to keep the coals from burning up too fast and to help the grill retain heat. Banking the coals on one side of the grill and rotating the roast will promote even cooking.

4 GRILL ON COOLER SIDE
Grill-roast meat, fat side up, on cooler side of grill with lid down until it reaches desired temperature.

5 MOVE TO HOTTER SIDE
Move meat to hotter side of grill and sear, fat side down, to create crust.

BONUS USE CHUNKS OR CHIPS
You can use wood chunks or chips to enhance smoky flavor. While charcoal will impart some flavor to the meat, wood chunks or chips are necessary to achieve true smokiness (especially with a gas grill). Place soaked, drained chunks directly on charcoal; wrap wood chips in a foil packet poked with holes (or place in a foil tray for a gas grill). To keep the fire burning as long as possible, we also prefer to use briquettes rather than hardwood charcoal.

GRILL-ROASTED BEEF TENDERLOIN

Serves: 6

Total Time: 2 hours, plus 30 minutes resting

RECIPE OVERVIEW Beef tenderloin isn't just for winter holidays and gatherings; it can be fancy summer fare, too. But it doesn't taste as smoky as other beef cuts on the grill. That's because much of the signature grilled flavor in fattier cuts is created as fat drippings break down into flavorful compounds that condense on the food above, and lean tenderloin doesn't generate those drippings. Our solution brings in the bacon. But we don't wrap the roast in it as you might guess—that is too distractingly porky. Instead, we lace strips onto a skewer and allowed their fat to render slowly near the beef while it roasts to create those drippings and thus a steady stream of smoke to flavor the beef. We like to serve the tenderloin with Chermoula (page 410).

- 2¼ teaspoons kosher salt
- 2 teaspoons vegetable oil
- 1 teaspoon pepper
- 1 teaspoon baking soda
- 1 (3-pound) center-cut beef tenderloin roast, trimmed and tied at 1½-inch intervals
- 3 slices bacon

1. Combine salt, oil, pepper, and baking soda in small bowl. Rub mixture evenly over roast and let sit while preparing grill.

2. Stack bacon slices. Keeping slices stacked, thread 12-inch metal skewer through bacon 6 or 7 times to create accordion shape. Push stack together to compact into about 2-inch length.

3A. FOR A CHARCOAL GRILL Open bottom vent halfway. Light large chimney starter two-thirds filled with charcoal briquettes (4 quarts). When top coals are partially covered with ash, pour evenly over half of grill. Set cooking grate in place, cover, and open lid vent halfway. Heat grill until hot, about 5 minutes.

3B. FOR A GAS GRILL Turn all burners to high, cover, and heat grill until hot, about 15 minutes. Turn primary burner to medium and turn off other burner(s). (Adjust primary burner as needed to maintain grill temperature of 300 degrees.)

4. Clean and oil cooking grate. Place roast on hotter side of grill and cook until lightly browned on all sides, about 12 minutes. Slide roast to cooler side of grill, arranging so roast is about 7 inches from heat source. Place skewered bacon on hotter side of grill. (For charcoal, place near center of grill, above edge of coals. For gas, place above heat diffuser of primary burner. Bacon should be 4 to 6 inches from roast and drippings should fall on coals or heat diffuser and produce steady stream of smoke and minimal flare-ups. If flare-ups are large or frequent, slide bacon skewer 1 inch toward roast.)

5. Cover and cook until beef registers 120 to 125 degrees (for medium-rare), 50 minutes to 1¼ hours. Transfer roast to carving board and let rest for 30 minutes. Remove twine from roast. Slice meat into ½-inch-thick slices and serve.

KEYS TO SUCCESS

- **Choose center-cut tenderloin:** Cylindric roast is easy to cook to even doneness on the grill.

- **Rub the roast with baking soda:** Causes it to brown before it can overcook

- **Cook skewers of bacon alongside roast:** Provides the smoky flavor lean tenderloin can't achieve on its own on the grill

CUBAN-STYLE GRILL-ROASTED PORK

Serves: 8 to 10

Total Time: 5 to 7 hours, plus 18 hours brining, and 2 hours resting

RECIPE OVERVIEW Roast pork in Cuba is perfection: crackling-crisp skin and tender meat infused with flavor. To achieve something similar, we use a combination cooking method: cooking the pork on the grill until our initial supply of coals dies down, and then finishing it in the oven. To flavor the pork, we again combine methods, first brining the pork in a powerful solution that includes two heads of garlic and orange juice, and then rubbing on a flavor paste. Let the meat rest for a full hour before serving or it will not be as tender. Serve with Mojo Sauce (recipe follows), if desired, black beans, rice, and/or fried plantains.

Pork

1 (7- to 8-pound) bone-in, skin-on pork picnic shoulder roast
3 cups sugar for brining
2 cups table salt for brining
2 garlic heads, unpeeled, cloves separated and crushed
4 cups orange juice (8 oranges) for brining

Paste

12 garlic cloves, chopped coarse
2 tablespoons ground cumin
2 tablespoons dried oregano
1 tablespoon table salt
1½ teaspoons pepper
6 tablespoons orange juice
2 tablespoons distilled white vinegar
2 tablespoons vegetable oil

1. FOR THE PORK Cut 1-inch-deep slits (1 inch long) all over roast, spaced about 2 inches apart. Dissolve sugar and salt in 6 quarts cold water in large container. Stir in garlic and orange juice. Submerge pork in brine, cover, and refrigerate for 18 to 24 hours. Remove pork from brine and pat dry with paper towels.

2. FOR THE PASTE Pulse garlic, cumin, oregano, salt, and pepper in food processor to coarse paste, about 10 pulses. With processor running, add orange juice, vinegar, and oil and process until smooth, about 20 seconds. Rub all over roast and into slits. Wrap roast in plastic wrap and let sit at room temperature for 1 hour.

3A. FOR A CHARCOAL GRILL Open bottom vent halfway. Light large chimney starter three-quarters filled with charcoal briquettes (4½ quarts). When top coals are partially covered with ash, pour into steeply banked pile against side of grill. Set cooking grate in place, cover, and open lid vent halfway. Heat grill until hot, about 5 minutes.

3B. FOR A GAS GRILL Turn all burners to high, cover, and heat grill until hot, about 15 minutes. Turn primary burner to medium-high and turn off other burner(s). (Adjust primary burner [or, if using 3-burner grill, primary burner and second burner] as needed to maintain grill temperature of 325 degrees.)

4. Clean and oil cooking grate. Make two ½-inch folds on long side of 18-inch length of aluminum foil to form reinforced edge. Place foil in center of cooking grate, with reinforced edge over hotter side of grill. Place roast, skin side up, on cooler side of grill so that it covers about one-third of foil. Lift and bend edges to shield sides of pork, tucking in edges. Cover (position lid vent over meat if using charcoal) and cook for 2 hours. During final 20 minutes of grilling, adjust oven rack to lower-middle position and heat oven to 325 degrees. Transfer pork to wire rack set in rimmed baking sheet. Roast pork in oven until skin is browned and crisp and meat registers 190 degrees, 3 to 4 hours.

5. Transfer roast to carving board and let rest for 1 hour. Remove skin in 1 large piece. Scrape off and discard fat from top of roast and from underside of skin. Cut meat away from bone in 3 or 4 large pieces, then slice ¼ inch thick. Cut skin into strips. Serve.

MOJO SAUCE

Makes: 1 cup (serves 8 to 10)

½ cup olive oil
4 garlic cloves, minced to paste
2 teaspoons kosher salt
½ teaspoon ground cumin
¼ cup distilled white vinegar
¼ cup orange juice
¼ teaspoon dried oregano
⅛ teaspoon pepper

Heat oil in medium saucepan over medium heat until shimmering. Add garlic, salt, and cumin and cook, stirring, until fragrant, about 30 seconds. Remove pan from heat and whisk in vinegar, orange juice, oregano, and pepper. Transfer sauce to bowl and let cool completely. Whisk sauce to recombine before serving

KEYS TO SUCCESS

- **Cut slits in the roast:** Lets the flavor of the rub run deep
- **Marinade and rub with garlic paste:** Gives pork tremendous flavor
- **Transfer from the grill to the oven:** Saves time since the coals die down

CORE TECHNIQUE

Cutting Slits in Pork Roast

SLIT
With sharp paring knife, cut 1-inch-deep slits (about 1 inch long) all over roast, spaced about 2 inches apart.

Picking the Perfect Pork Roast

What's the best cut for Cuban-style pork? We tried them all. Widely available Boston butt (the upper portion of the front leg) was an attractive option thanks to its high fat content. But it comes with no skin attached, and the crisp, flavorful skin is one of the highlights of this dish. Fresh ham (from the rear leg) has skin but is usually too lean. We settled on the picnic shoulder (also called pork shoulder), a flavorful cut from the lower portion of the front leg that almost always comes bone-in—and with a fair share of fat and rind to boot.

GRILLED BONE-IN LEG OF LAMB WITH CHARRED SCALLION SAUCE

Serves: 10 to 12
Total Time: 2½ to 3 hours, plus 12 hours marinating and 30 minutes resting

RECIPE OVERVIEW This grand cut is impressive enough for any celebration, but its tapered shape also means that even cooking is a challenge, especially over a live flame. To help avoid flare-ups while still giving the roast a charred exterior and medium-rare interior, set up a half-grill fire and start the leg of lamb on the cooler side of the grill before searing it over the hotter side. Smear a powerful paste of fresh thyme, dried oregano, garlic, lemon zest, and plenty of salt and pepper onto the leg of lamb and refrigerate it overnight to season the meat. The dish is finished with a rich sauce of charred scallions mixed with extra-virgin olive oil, red wine vinegar, parsley, and garlic. For an accurate temperature reading in step 5, insert your thermometer into the thickest part of the leg until you hit bone, then pull it ½ inch away.

Lamb

- 12 garlic cloves, minced
- 2 tablespoons vegetable oil
- 2 tablespoons kosher salt
- 1½ tablespoons pepper
- 1 tablespoon fresh thyme leaves
- 1 tablespoon dried oregano
- 2 teaspoons finely grated lemon zest
- 1 teaspoon ground coriander
- 1 (8-pound) bone-in leg of lamb, trimmed

Scallion Sauce

- ¾ cup extra-virgin olive oil
- ¼ cup chopped fresh parsley
- 1 tablespoon red wine vinegar
- 2 garlic cloves, minced
- 1 teaspoon pepper
- ¾ teaspoon kosher salt
- ¼ teaspoon red pepper flakes
- 12 scallions, trimmed

1. FOR THE LAMB Combine garlic, oil, salt, pepper, thyme, oregano, lemon zest, and coriander in bowl. Place lamb on rimmed baking sheet and rub all over with garlic paste. Cover with plastic wrap and refrigerate for at least 12 hours or up to 24 hours.

2. FOR THE SCALLION SAUCE Combine oil, parsley, vinegar, garlic, pepper, salt, and pepper flakes in bowl; set aside.

3A. FOR A CHARCOAL GRILL Open bottom vent completely. Light large chimney starter filled with charcoal briquettes (6 quarts). When top coals are partially covered with ash, pour evenly over half of grill. Set cooking grate in place, cover, and open lid vent completely. Heat grill until hot, about 5 minutes.

The Case for Bone-In

Would a boneless leg of lamb be easier to cook evenly and carve perfectly? Yes. So why go bone-in here? The practical reasons are that boneless roasts come in netting that you have to cut away (it is not grill-safe), necessitating retying with twine. Also, a bone-in leg gives you a range of doneness throughout the roast to please all tastes. But mostly it comes down to the grand, festive look of a whole bone-in leg. The cut is also a nod to earlier times when animals were butchered more simply and large cuts were cooked over a live fire, as in this recipe. Go all out—go for a bone-in leg of lamb.

3B. FOR A GAS GRILL Turn all burners to high, cover, and heat grill until hot, about 15 minutes. Leave primary burner on high and turn off other burner(s). (Adjust primary burner [or, if using 3-burner grill, primary burner and second burner] as needed to maintain grill temperature between 350 and 400 degrees.)

4. Clean and oil cooking grate. Place scallions on hotter side of grill. Cook (covered if using gas) until lightly charred on both sides, about 3 minutes per side. Transfer scallions to plate.

5. Uncover lamb and place fat side up on cooler side of grill, parallel to fire. (If using gas, it may be necessary to angle thicker end of lamb toward hotter side of grill to fit.) Cover grill (position lid vent directly over lamb if using charcoal) and cook until thickest part of meat (½ inch from bone) registers 120 degrees, 1¼ hours to 1¾ hours.

6. Transfer lamb, fat side down, to hotter side of grill. Cook (covered if using gas) until fat side is well browned, 7 to 9 minutes. Transfer lamb to carving board, fat side up, and tent with aluminum foil. Let rest for 30 minutes.

7. Cut scallions into ½-inch pieces, then stir into reserved sauce mixture. Season sauce with salt and pepper to taste. Slice lamb thin and serve with sauce.

KEYS TO SUCCESS

- **Make a half-grill fire:** Fat renders without flare-ups on the cooler side; meat sears on the hotter side.

- **Let the rubbed lamb rest in the refrigerator overnight:** Takes on great flavor

- **Char scallions:** Makes a sauce as smoky as the meat

Taking the Temperature

PROBE
For an accurate temperature reading, insert your thermometer into the thickest part of the leg until you hit bone, then pull it ½ inch away.

TEXAS THICK-CUT SMOKED PORK CHOPS

Serves: 8
Total Time: 2½ hours, plus 1 hour brining

RECIPE OVERVIEW Massive pork chops can deliver Texas-size pit-smoked flavor with the help of the grill and the right method. We roast extra-thick bone-in chops to help keep their lean meat from drying out on the grill; brining them in a saltwater solution with some sugar also helps (and promotes browning). A spice mixture of salt, pepper, onion powder, and granulated garlic sprinkled on before grilling adds flavor, and roasting the chops over mesquite chips infuses the meat's crust with fragrant smoke. A half-grill fire allows us to gently cook the chops through on the cooler side, so they retain most of their juices along the way. A homemade bacony barbecue sauce bright with vinegar reinforces the chops' smoky grilled taste. Each chop can easily serve two people. Grate the onion for the sauce on the large holes of a box grater. We prefer mesquite wood chips in this recipe.

Pork

- 3 tablespoons table salt for brining
- 3 tablespoons sugar for brining
- 4 (18- to 20-ounce) bone-in pork rib chops, 2 inches thick, trimmed
- 2 tablespoons pepper
- 1½ tablespoons table salt
- 2 teaspoons onion powder
- 2 teaspoons granulated garlic

Barbecue Sauce

- 2 slices bacon
- ¼ cup grated onion
- ⅛ teaspoon table salt
- ¾ cup cider vinegar
- 1¼ cups chicken broth
- 1 cup ketchup
- 2 tablespoons hot sauce
- ½ teaspoon liquid smoke
- ¼ teaspoon pepper
- 2 cups wood chips

1. FOR THE PORK Dissolve 3 tablespoons salt and sugar in 1½ quarts cold water in large container. Submerge chops in brine, cover, and refrigerate for 1 hour. Combine pepper, salt, onion powder, and granulated garlic in bowl; set aside.

2. FOR THE BARBECUE SAUCE Meanwhile, cook bacon in medium saucepan over medium heat until fat begins to render and bacon begins to brown, 4 to 6 minutes. Add onion and salt and cook until softened, 2 to 4 minutes. Stir in vinegar, scraping up any browned bits, and cook until slightly thickened, about 2 minutes.

3. Stir in broth, ketchup, hot sauce, liquid smoke, and pepper. Bring to simmer and cook until slightly thickened, about 15 minutes, stirring occasionally. Discard bacon and season with salt and pepper to taste. Remove from heat, cover, and keep warm.

4. Just before grilling, soak wood chips in water for 15 minutes, then drain. Using large piece of heavy-duty aluminum foil, wrap soaked chips in 8 by 4½-inch foil packet. (Make sure chips do not poke holes in sides or bottom of packet.) Cut 2 evenly spaced 2-inch slits in top of packet. Remove chops from brine and pat dry with paper towels. Season chops all over with reserved spice mixture.

5A. FOR A CHARCOAL GRILL Open bottom vent completely. Light large chimney starter three-quarters filled with charcoal briquettes (4½ quarts). When top coals are partially covered with ash, pour evenly over half of grill. Place wood chip packet on coals. Set cooking grate in place, cover, and open lid vent completely. Heat grill until hot and wood chips are smoking, about 5 minutes.

5B. FOR A GAS GRILL Remove cooking grate and place wood chip packet directly on primary burner. Set cooking grate in place, turn all burners to high, cover, and heat grill until hot and wood chips are smoking, about 15 minutes. Turn primary burner to medium-high and turn off other burner(s). (Adjust primary burner [or, if using 3-burner grill, primary burner and second burner] as needed to maintain grill temperature around 325 degrees.)

6. Clean and oil cooking grate. Arrange chops on cooler side of grill with bone ends toward fire. Cover (position lid vent over chops if using charcoal) and cook until chops register 140 degrees, 45 to 50 minutes, flipping halfway through cooking.

7. Transfer chops to serving dish and let rest for 10 minutes. Brush chops generously with warm sauce and serve, passing remaining sauce separately.

KEYS TO SUCCESS

- **Choose extra thick bone-in rib chops:** Achieves smoky flavor roasting on the grill without overcooking
- **Brine the pork chops:** Further ensures juiciness by retaining moisture
- **Make a barbecue sauce:** Complements the smoky pork

Make It Mesquite

Smoky, peaty mesquite is the wood of choice in Llano, Texas, and its unique flavor is key to these pork chops; hickory is too pungent, apple too sweet, and oak too mild. Mesquite chips are available at most hardware stores and online.

SHOULDER CHEAT SHEET

Still find pork shoulder confusing? Here's a simple list summarizing the differences and similarities between pork butt roast and picnic shoulder roast so you know what to buy.

PORK BUTT	PICNIC SHOULDER
Also known as "pork shoulder" or "Boston butt"	Also known as "pork shoulder" or "picnic roast"
Well marbled with fat	Typically has less intramuscular fat and marbling
Often has fat cap	Frequently sold with skin on
Rectangular, uniform shape	Tapered, triangular shape
Sold bone-in or boneless	Sold bone-in or boneless

WHEN TO USE PORK BUTT

Since pork butt has more fat marbling throughout the meat and a more uniform shape, it's the best cut for stewing and braising as well as for making fall-apart-tender pulled pork for a barbecue or for tacos. We also oven-roast it for our Porchetta (page 371). If a recipe calls for a choice between pork shoulder and pork butt, the butt will be more user-friendly.

WHEN TO USE PICNIC SHOULDER

Picnic shoulder is our cut of choice when making a pork roast that traditionally has crackling-crisp skin (such as our Cuban-Style Grill-Roasted Pork on page 388), since the cut is sold with the skin on. We only cook this roast whole—we don't cut it for stew, and we don't "pull it," as for pulled pork.

MAKING A FOIL PACKET FOR WOOD CHIPS

1. Soak wood chips in water for 15 minutes; spread drained chips in center of piece of heavy-duty aluminum foil. Fold to seal edges, then cut evenly spaced 2-inch slits in top of packet to allow smoke to escape.

2. Place aluminum foil packet of chips on lit coals of charcoal grill or over primary burner on gas grill.

BUILDING A FOIL SHIELD

We use this technique to protect Cuban-Style Grill-Roasted Pork (page 388) from getting too dark on the side closest to the heat without having to open the grill and rotate the roast.

1. Make two ½-inch folds on the long side of an 18-inch length of foil to form a reinforced edge. Place the foil on the center of the cooking grate, with the reinforced edge over the hot side of the grill. Position the roast, skin side up, over the cool side of the grill so that it covers about a third of the foil.

2. Lift and bend the edges of the foil to shield the sides of the roast, tucking in the edges.

BIG BARBECUE

MORGAN BOLLING

The United States is home to a number of regional styles of barbecue. We won't choose an allegiance; we love them all. The smoke, the spice, the sauce (thick, thin, sweet, tangy)—there's nothing to dislike about barbecue. But barbecue isn't a beginner's sport; distinct skills that surpass simple grilling are needed. The cuts are large and can be tough. The grill requires attention. The smoke flavor needs to be replicated in a backyard. This course is your companion to becoming your own backyard pit master. Upgrade your next cookout with tender brisket, juicy pulled pork, or satisfying ribs.

MORGAN'S PRO TIP: *Set up your charcoal snake the night before your barbecue. It takes some time and is one less thing to think about in the morning; you just have to light the coals and get smoking.*

TEXAS BARBECUE BRISKET

Serves: 12 to 15
Total Time: 6¼ to 8¼ hours, plus 12 hours salting and 2 hours resting

RECIPE OVERVIEW You can re-create a Texas-style smoked whole brisket with a tender, juicy interior encased in a dark, peppery bark at home on a charcoal grill. The key to success? A grill setup called a charcoal snake. This C-shaped array of smoldering briquettes provides low, slow, indirect heat to the center of the grill for upwards of 6 hours, so you need to refuel only once during the exceptionally long cooking time. Cooking the brisket fat side down gives it a protective barrier against the direct heat of the fire. And wrapping the brisket in foil toward the end of its cooking time, then letting it rest in a cooler for 2 hours before serving, helps keep it ultramoist and juicy. We developed this recipe using a 22-inch Weber Kettle charcoal grill.

- 1 (10- to 12-pound) whole beef brisket, untrimmed
- ¼ cup kosher salt
- ¼ cup pepper
- 5 (3-inch) wood chunks
- 1 (13 by 9-inch) disposable aluminum pan

1. With brisket positioned point side up, use sharp knife to trim fat cap to ½- to ¼-inch thickness. Remove excess fat from deep pocket where flat and point are attached. Trim and discard short edge of flat if less than 1 inch thick. Flip brisket and remove any large deposits of fat from underside.

2. Combine salt and pepper in bowl. Place brisket on rimmed baking sheet and sprinkle all over with salt mixture. Cover loosely with plastic wrap and refrigerate for at least 12 or up to 24 hours.

3. Open bottom vent completely. Set up charcoal snake: Arrange 58 briquettes, 2 briquettes wide, around perimeter of grill, overlapping slightly so briquettes are touching, leaving 8-inch gap between ends of snake. Place second layer of 58 briquettes, also 2 briquettes wide, on top of first. (Completed snake should be 2 briquettes wide by 2 briquettes high.)

4. Starting 4 inches from 1 end of snake, evenly space wood chunks on top of snake. Place disposable pan in center of grill. Fill disposable pan with 6 cups water. Light chimney starter filled with 10 briquettes (pile briquettes on 1 side of chimney). When coals are partially covered with ash, pour over 1 end of snake. (Make sure lit coals touch only 1 end of snake.)

5. Set cooking grate in place. Clean and oil cooking grate. Place brisket, fat side down, directly over water pan, with point end facing gap in snake. Insert temperature probe into side of upper third of point. Cover grill, open lid vent completely, and position lid vent over gap in snake. Cook, undisturbed and without lifting lid, until meat registers 170 degrees, 4 to 5 hours.

Making Texas Barbecue Brisket

PLACE BRIQUETTES
Set up the charcoal snake with 2 sets of 58 briquettes, 2 briquettes wide by 2 briquettes high. Starting 4 inches from 1 end of the snake, evenly space wood chunks on top.

POUR COALS
Place a disposable pan in the center of the grill; fill the pan with 6 cups of water. Pour the coals over only 1 end of the snake.

BARBECUE
Place the brisket, fat side down, directly over the pan of water, with the point end facing the gap in the snake. Insert the probe into the side of the upper third of the point. Cook to 170 degrees.

WRAP IN FOIL
Wrap the brisket tightly with a layer of foil. Rotate the brisket 90 degrees and wrap it with a second layer of foil so it is airtight.

REFUEL
Pour unlit briquettes halfway around perimeter of the grill over the gap and the spent coals. Return the brisket to the grill over the water pan with the point facing where the gap in the snake used to be.

FINISH
Reinsert the probe and cook to 205 degrees. Transfer the brisket to a cooler; cover and let rest for 2 to 3 hours.

Buy the Right Brisket

A full brisket is from the lower chest of the cow and ranges from 8 to 20 pounds in size. It's made up of both the "point" and "flat" cuts. While the flat alone is easier to find (it's what you're likely to find packaged in the meat case), special-ordering a full brisket from the butcher counter is well worth it. A full brisket allows you to offer diners both lean slices from the flat portion and "moist" (or fatty) slices from the point. The ideal brisket will have an even, ½-inch-thick fat cap. If you can't find a whole brisket in the 10- to 12-pound range, it's better to buy a slightly larger brisket and trim it down to size (smaller briskets are more prone to drying out on the grill).

Working with Wood

Adding wood chips to your grill imparts a deep, smoky flavor to food. In the test kitchen, we use wood in two different forms: chips and chunks. In either case, the wood usually needs to soak in water before being added to the grill in order to maintain a slow smolder rather than a quick burn.

We usually soak wood chunks for at least one hour before using. Place them directly on the coals for long, slow-smoking Southern-style recipes such as brisket or ribs. Just nestle the soaked chunks into the pile of charcoal, set the cooking grate in place, and cover the grill for 5 minutes. Once the grill is hot, clean it and start cooking.

If you have a gas grill, you'll want to use chips. Soak the chips for at least 30 minutes, then place them inside a foil pouch with holes cut into it for ventilation. You can also use a disposable aluminum tray. Place the aluminum pouch or tray directly over the primary burner, light the grill, cover it, and wait until the chips start smoking heavily, around 15 minutes or so. (See how to do this on page 393.)

If you're a barbecuing fanatic, you may want to keep a supply of presoaked wood chips on hand. We found that after the initial soaking, wood chips or chunks can be placed in a zipper-lock bag and stored in the freezer indefinitely. Pull them out of the bag and use as is—there is no need to thaw.

6. Place 2 large sheets of aluminum foil on rimmed baking sheet. Remove temperature probe from brisket. Using oven mitts, lift brisket and transfer to center of foil, fat side down. Wrap brisket tightly with first layer of foil, minimizing air pockets between foil and brisket. Rotate brisket 90 degrees and wrap with second layer of foil. (Use additional foil, if necessary, to completely wrap brisket.) Foil wrap should be airtight. Make small mark on foil with marker to keep track of fat/point side.

7. Remove cooking grate. Starting at still-unlit end of snake, pour 3 quarts unlit briquettes about halfway around perimeter of grill over gap and spent coals. Replace cooking grate. Return foil-wrapped brisket to grill over water pan, fat side down, with point end facing where gap in snake used to be. Reinsert temperature probe into point. Cover grill and continue to cook until meat registers 205 degrees, 1 to 2 hours longer.

8. Remove temperature probe. Transfer foil-wrapped brisket to cooler, point side up. Close cooler and let rest for at least 2 hours or up to 3 hours. Transfer brisket to carving board, unwrap, and position fat side up. Slice flat against grain ¼ inch thick, stopping once you reach base of point. Rotate point 90 degrees and slice point against grain (perpendicular to first cut) ⅜ inch thick. Serve.

KEYS TO SUCCESS
- **Snake briquettes around the grill:** Provides heat for 6 hours, so you only need to refuel once
- **Cook fat-side down:** Protects the meat from direct heat
- **Wrap the brisket in foil to finish cooking and cool:** Results in ultrajuicy meat at serving time

SOUTH CAROLINA PULLED PORK
Serves: 8
Total Time: 5¼ to 6¼ hours, plus 2 hours resting

RECIPE OVERVIEW In South Carolina, pit masters dress pulled pork in a savory mustard-based sauce nicknamed Carolina Gold. We rub a boneless pork butt with a spice rub that includes dry mustard to highlight the mustard in the sauce; the rub also helps the meat develop a flavorful crust. Brushing the pork with our mustardy sauce before it goes into a low oven produces a second hit of mustard bite. We found that a combination of grill smoking and oven roasting reduces the cooking time from all day to 4 or 5 hours. Tossing the shredded pork with the remaining sauce gives the meat a final layer of flavor. If you'd like to use wood chunks instead of wood chips with a charcoal grill, substitute four medium wood chunks, soaked in water for 1 hour, for the wood chip packets.

Pork

3	tablespoons dry mustard
2	tablespoons table salt
1½	tablespoons packed light brown sugar
2	teaspoons pepper
2	teaspoons paprika
¼	teaspoon cayenne pepper
1	(4- to 5-pound) boneless pork butt roast, trimmed
4	cups wood chips

Barbecue Sauce

½	cup yellow mustard
½	cup packed light brown sugar
¼	cup distilled white vinegar
2	tablespoons Worcestershire sauce
1	tablespoon hot sauce
1	teaspoon table salt
1	teaspoon pepper

1. FOR THE PORK Combine mustard, salt, sugar, pepper, paprika, and cayenne in bowl. Pat pork dry with paper towels and rub with spice mixture. Wrap meat in plastic wrap and let sit at room temperature for at least 1 hour, or refrigerate for up to 24 hours. (If refrigerated, let sit at room temperature for 1 hour before grilling.)

2. Just before grilling, soak wood chips in water for 15 minutes, then drain. Using large piece of heavy-duty aluminum foil, wrap 2 cups soaked chips in 8 by 4½-inch foil packet. (Make sure chips do not poke holes in sides or bottom of packet.) Repeat with remaining 2 cups chips. Cut 2 evenly spaced 2-inch slits in top of each packet.

3A. FOR A CHARCOAL GRILL Open bottom vent halfway. Light large chimney starter half filled with charcoal briquettes (3 quarts). When top coals are partially covered with ash, pour into steeply banked pile against 1 side of grill. Place wood chip packs on coals. Set cooking grate in place, cover, and open lid vent halfway. Heat grill until hot and wood chips are smoking, about 5 minutes.

3B. FOR A GAS GRILL Remove cooking grate and place wood chip packets directly on primary burner. Set cooking grate in place, turn all burners to high, cover, and heat grill until hot and wood chips are smoking, about 15 minutes. Turn primary burner to medium-high and turn other burner(s) off. (Adjust primary burner [or, if using 3-burner grill, primary burner and second burner] as needed to maintain grill temperature around 325 degrees.)

4. Clean and oil cooking grate. Place roast on cooler side of grill. Cover (positioning lid vent over roast if using charcoal) and cook until pork has dark, rosy crust, about 2 hours. During final 20 minutes of grilling, adjust oven rack to lower-middle position and heat oven to 325 degrees.

5. FOR THE BARBECUE SAUCE Whisk all ingredients in bowl until smooth. Measure out ½ cup sauce for cooking; set aside remaining sauce for tossing with pork.

6. Transfer pork to large roasting pan and brush evenly with the ½ cup sauce for cooking. Cover pan tightly with foil and transfer to oven. Roast until fork slips easily in and out of meat, 2 to 3 hours.

7. Remove pork from oven and let rest, still covered with foil, for 1 hour. When cool enough to handle, unwrap pork and pull meat into thin shreds, discarding excess fat and gristle. Toss pork with reserved sauce and serve.

KEYS TO SUCCESS

- **Use mustard powder in the rub**: Gives the roast spicy flavor and a good crust
- **Finish roast in the oven**: Reduces the cooking time to just 4 to 5 hours instead of all day
- **Use the fork test**: The roast is done when a fork goes in and out with little resistance.

Mustard Three Ways

So that our coating lives up to its name of Carolina Gold, we apply mustard to the pork in two forms and in three stages. First, rubbing the pork shoulder with a spice mixture that's heavy on the dry mustard ensures a mustardy crust. Second, brushing the pork with the mustardy barbecue sauce before it goes into the oven produces a second hit of mustard flavor. Finally, tossing the shredded pork with the remaining sauce gives the meat a final layer of mustard flavor.

MEMPHIS BARBECUE SPARERIBS

Serves: 8 to 12
Total Time: 6½ hours, plus 20 minutes resting

RECIPE OVERVIEW For these saucy Memphis wet ribs, a potent spice rub performs double duty, seasoning the meat and creating the backbone for our barbecue sauce. Tying two racks together means double the yield—four hefty racks—on one home grill. To keep the ribs moist, we grill them over indirect heat and baste them with a traditional "mop" of juice and vinegar. After a few hours of smoking on the grill, we then brush the ribs with the flavorful barbecue sauce and transfer them to the steady, even heat of the oven to finish tenderizing.

Spice Rub
- ¼ cup paprika
- 2 tablespoons packed brown sugar
- 2 tablespoons salt
- 2 teaspoons pepper
- 2 teaspoons onion powder
- 2 teaspoons granulated garlic

Barbecue Sauce and Mop
- 1½ cups ketchup
- 1¼ cups apple juice, divided
- ¼ cup molasses
- ½ cup cider vinegar, divided
- ¼ cup Worcestershire sauce
- 3 tablespoons yellow mustard, divided
- 2 teaspoons pepper

Ribs
- 4 (2½- to 3-pound) racks St. Louis–style spareribs, trimmed, membrane removed
- 2 cups wood chips, soaked in water for 15 minutes and drained
- 1 (13 by 9-inch) disposable aluminum roasting pan (if using charcoal) or 1 (8½ by 6-inch) disposable aluminum pan (if using gas)

1. FOR THE SPICE RUB Combine all ingredients in bowl.

2. FOR THE BARBECUE SAUCE AND MOP Combine ketchup, ¾ cup apple juice, molasses, ¼ cup vinegar, Worcestershire, 2 tablespoons mustard, and 2 tablespoons spice rub in medium saucepan and bring to boil over medium heat. Reduce heat to medium-low and simmer until thickened and reduced to 2 cups, about 20 minutes. Off heat, stir in pepper; set barbecue sauce aside. For the mop, whisk ¼ cup of the barbecue sauce with remaining ½ cup apple juice, ¼ cup vinegar, and 1 tablespoon mustard in bowl.

Removing the Membrane from Ribs

In some applications, the papery membrane on the underside of a rack of ribs is chewy and unpleasant to eat, and its protective qualities aren't necessary. The membrane is very thin, so removing it should not expose the rib bones. Here's how to easily remove it.

LOOSEN EDGE
Using tip of paring knife, loosen edge of membrane on rack.

GRIP AND PULL
Using paper towel for grip, pull membrane off slowly. (It should come off in single piece.)

3. FOR THE RIBS Pat ribs dry with paper towels and season with remaining spice rub. Place 1 rack of ribs, meaty side down, on cutting board. Place second rack of ribs, meaty side up, directly on top of first rack, arranging thick end over tapered end. Tie racks together at 2-inch intervals with kitchen twine. Repeat with remaining 2 racks of ribs for two bundles. Using large piece of heavy-duty aluminum foil, wrap soaked chips in foil packet and cut several vent holes in top.

4A. FOR A CHARCOAL GRILL Open bottom vent halfway and place disposable roasting pan on 1 side of grill. Fill pan with 2 quarts water. Arrange 3 quarts unlit charcoal briquettes on other side of grill. Light large chimney starter half filled with charcoal briquettes (3 quarts). When top coals are partially covered with ash, pour evenly over unlit coals. Place wood chip packet on coals. Set cooking grate in place, cover, and open lid vent halfway. Heat grill until hot and wood chips are smoking, about 5 minutes.

4B. FOR A GAS GRILL Place wood chip packet and disposable pan over primary burner and fill pan with 2 cups water. Turn primary burner to high (leave other burners off), cover, and heat grill until hot and wood chips are smoking, about 15 minutes. (Adjust primary burner as needed to maintain grill temperature of 275 to 300 degrees.)

5. Clean and oil cooking grate. Place ribs on cooler side of grill and baste with one-third of mop. Cover (positioning lid vent over ribs for charcoal) and cook for 2 hours, flipping and switching positions of ribs and basting again with half of remaining mop halfway through cooking.

6. Adjust oven racks to upper-middle and lower-middle positions and heat oven to 300 degrees. Line 2 rimmed baking sheets with foil. Cut kitchen twine from racks. Transfer 2 racks, meaty side up, to each sheet. Baste with remaining mop and bake for 2 hours, switching and rotating sheets halfway through baking.

7. Remove ribs from oven and brush evenly with ½ cup barbecue sauce. Return to oven and continue to bake until tender, basting with ½ cup barbecue sauce and switching and rotating sheets twice during baking, about 45 minutes. (Ribs do not need to be flipped and should remain meaty side up during baking.) Transfer ribs to carving board. Brush evenly with remaining ½ cup barbecue sauce, tent loosely with foil, and let rest for 20 minutes. Cut ribs in between bones to separate. Serve.

KEYS TO SUCCESS

- **Tie racks of ribs together**: Allows you to fit more on the grill

- **Spice two ways**: Using spices in the rub and in the barbecue sauce creates flavor that melds with the ribs.

- **Finish ribs in the oven**: Ensures smoky flavor and tender meat

Making Rib Bundles

STACK

Place 1 rack of ribs, meaty side down, on a cutting board. Place a second rack of ribs, meaty side up, directly on top of first rack, arranging thick end over tapered end.

TIE

Tie racks together at 2-inch intervals with kitchen twine. Repeat with remaining 2 racks of ribs. (You should have 2 bundles of ribs.)

TEXAS-SMOKED BEEF RIBS

Serves: 4
Total Time: 6½ to 7¼ hours, plus 30 minutes resting

RECIPE OVERVIEW Mammoth Texas-style beef ribs are so big they look like they came off a T. rex. But beneath the dark, peppery crust and pink smoke ring is succulent, tender beef so flavorful that barbecue sauce is unnecessary. To smoke these ribs on a humble charcoal grill rather than a huge smoker with temperature controls, we turn again

to the charcoal snake from our Texas Barbecue Brisket (page 395). This allows us to surround the thick ribs with indirect heat for upwards of 6 hours, and the wood chunks on top provided steady smoke to infuse the meat with flavor. Cooking the ribs all the way to 210 degrees, so that the meat hangs out above 180 degrees for a long time, ensures that the collagen melts properly. Wait and you're rewarded with ultratender, juicy, and, yes, mammoth ribs. We developed this recipe using a 22-inch Weber Kettle charcoal grill.

    3   tablespoons kosher salt
    3   tablespoons pepper
    2   (4- to 5-pound) racks beef plate ribs, 1 to 1½ inches of
        meat on top of bone, trimmed
    5   (3-inch) wood chunks
    1   (13 by 9-inch) disposable aluminum pan

1. Combine salt and pepper in bowl, then sprinkle ribs all over with salt-pepper mixture.

2. Open bottom vent completely. Set up charcoal snake: Arrange 60 briquettes, 2 briquettes wide, around perimeter of grill, overlapping slightly so briquettes are touching, leaving 8-inch gap between ends of snake. Place second layer of 60 briquettes, also 2 briquettes wide, on top of first. (Completed snake should be 2 briquettes wide by 2 briquettes high.)

3. Starting 4 inches from 1 end of snake, evenly space wood chunks on top of snake. Place disposable pan in center of grill so short end of pan faces gap in snake. Fill disposable pan with 4 cups water. Light chimney starter filled with 15 briquettes (pile briquettes on 1 side of chimney to make them easier to ignite). When coals are partially covered with ash, pour over 1 end of snake. (Make sure lit coals touch only 1 end of snake.)

4. Set cooking grate in place. Clean and oil cooking grate. Position ribs next to each other on cooking grate, bone side down, crosswise over disposable pan and gap in snake (they will be off-center; this is OK). Cover grill, position lid vent over gap in snake, and open lid vent completely. Cook undisturbed until rack of ribs overhanging gap in snake registers 210 degrees in meatiest portion, 5½ to 6¼ hours. Transfer ribs to carving board, tent with aluminum foil, and let rest for 30 minutes. Cut ribs between bones and serve.

KEYS TO SUCCESS

- **Let the rubbed ribs sit before smoking**: Results in more flavor

- **Chunks on a snake**: Create steady smoke for hours by arranging wood chunks on top of a C-shaped array of charcoal briquettes.

RESOURCES FOR BIG BARBECUE

EIGHT STEPS TO SENSATIONAL RIBS

We don't have a barbecue rig—you probably don't either—so we've come up with some universal steps to making great ribs on an everyday charcoal grill.

1. RUB
Rub both sides of the ribs with a spice mixture, pressing so it adheres.

2. PREPARE THE GRILL
Pour hot coals onto half of the grill, according to your recipe. This creates a low, slow oven out of your grill, perfect for cooking ribs.

3. ADD SMOKE
Place wood chips over the coals, cover the grill, and let them heat for 5 minutes for smoky flavor—without a smoker.

4. START COOL
Place the ribs on the cooler side of the grill to cook low and slow without the exterior burning before the interior is tender.

5. BRUSH
If you're mopping dry ribs or saucing wet ribs, this is the time to do it. The ribs will drink up the flavor in the remaining cooking time and caramelize slightly.

6. BAKE
You don't have a huge smoker so it's best to finish the ribs in the oven so they can fully tenderize without having to rebuild a burnt-out charcoal setup.

7. FORK
Insert a fork into the ribs to check that they are tender but not falling off the bone (195 to 200 degrees). If the fork pulls right out, the ribs are done. If not, the meat needs to cook longer.

8. RELAX
Let the ribs rest for 20 to 30 minutes when they come out of the oven. The juices will redistribute for moist ribs.

SLICING WHOLE BRISKET

A full brisket is made up of two overlapping muscles—the fatty, thicker point cut (on the left in photo) and the leaner, thinner flat cut—that are separated by a line of fat. Their grains run perpendicular to each other. When slicing the cooked brisket, we start by slicing the flat cut ¼ inch thick. When the slices show a line of fat running through the middle, we know we've reached the point, so we rotate the meat 90 degrees and cut the point into slightly thicker, ⅜-inch slices.

SHOPPING FOR BEEF RIBS

Beef ribs are located on the cow next to expensive cuts such as prime rib, so butchers often overtrim ribs to maximize the bulk on the pricier cuts. Buy slabs with a thick layer of meat. A three- or four-rib slab works best.

Where's the Beef?
These bony ribs are better suited for the stockpot than for the smoke pit.

Here's the Beef.
These meaty-but-manageable ribs are worth the time and effort.

Won't Fit
These mammoth ribs are hard to squeeze into a kettle grill.

PARSING PORK RIBS

When it comes to pork ribs, we much prefer St. Louis–style spareribs to baby back ribs. How are they different? Baby back ribs are cut from the section of the rib cage closest to the backbone. Loin center-cut roasts and chops come from the same part of the pig, which explains why baby back ribs can be expensive, and popular. But this location also explains why baby back ribs are much leaner (read: less flavorful) than spareribs and why they need special attention to keep from drying out on the grill. Whole spareribs from the underside of the pig are untrimmed, containing the brisket bone and surrounding meat, so each rack can weigh upward of 5 pounds. Some racks of spareribs are so big they barely fit on the grill. That's why we use this more manageable cut, called the St. Louis–style sparerib, because the brisket bone and surrounding meat are trimmed off to produce a narrower, rectangular rack that usually weighs in at a relatively svelte 3 pounds. Spareribs are larger and less lean than baby back ribs so they dry out far less quickly and cook more consistently.

Baby Back Ribs
aka loin back ribs, riblets

St. Louis–Style Spareribs
aka St. Louis spareribs, spareribs

The U.S. is home to numerous regional and subregional barbecue styles, each with nuances that make them unique. Some favor beef cuts, some pork. An easy entrée into the different styles is through the flavors and textures of the regional sauces. Here are a number of homemade barbecue sauces to try—the collection is exemplary but not exhaustive. You can also find South Carolina (see page 396) and Memphis styles (see page 399) in the course. Use sauces on smoked meats or simply spoon over small cuts of grilled or seared meat for a barbecue flavor punch.

KANSAS CITY BARBECUE SAUCE

Makes: about 4 cups

In Kansas City, barbecue is slathered with a thick, sweet, smoky, and sticky tomato-based sauce. Our Kansas City recipe combines the usual sauce ingredients—ketchup, vinegar, molasses, hot sauce, mustard—with two unexpected ingredients: dark corn syrup and root beer, which give the sauce the sticky, sweet, and smoky characteristics. But beware: We found that this sauce burns very quickly and should not be used over direct heat when grilling. We like our barbecue sauce extra-thick; if you like a thinner, smoother texture, strain it after it has finished cooking.

- 2 teaspoons vegetable oil
- 1 onion, minced
- 4 cups chicken broth
- 1 cup root beer
- 1 cup cider vinegar
- 1 cup dark corn syrup
- ½ cup molasses
- ½ cup tomato paste
- ½ cup ketchup
- 2 tablespoons brown mustard
- 1 tablespoon hot sauce
- ½ teaspoon garlic powder
- ¼ teaspoon liquid smoke (optional)

Heat oil in saucepan over medium-high heat until shimmering. Add onion and cook until softened, about 5 minutes. Whisk in remaining ingredients, except for liquid smoke, and bring to boil. Reduce heat to medium and simmer until mixture is thick and has reduced to 4 cups, about 1 hour. Stir in liquid smoke, if using. (Sauce can be refrigerated in airtight container for up to 1 week.)

OKLAHOMA BARBECUE SAUCE

Makes: about 1½ cups

Oklahoma barbecue sauce is all about restraint. As they say in Oklahoma, "If your pork is smothered in sauce, it means you're trying to cover something up." Serve the sauce as is traditional, on the side. It goes particularly well with pork.

- 1 tablespoon vegetable oil
- ½ small onion, chopped fine
- 1 tablespoon tomato paste
- 2 teaspoons paprika
- 1 cup ketchup
- ¾ cup cider vinegar
- 3 tablespoons brown sugar
- 1 tablespoon Worcestershire sauce
- ½ teaspoon celery salt

1. Heat oil in medium saucepan over medium heat until shimmering. Add onion and cook until softened, about 3 minutes. Stir in tomato paste and paprika and cook until paste begins to darken, about 1 minute.

2. Add ketchup, vinegar, brown sugar, Worcestershire, and celery salt and bring to boil. Reduce heat to medium-low and simmer until slightly thickened, 8 to 10 minutes. Transfer to bowl and let cool completely. Season with salt and pepper to taste. Serve. (Sauce can be refrigerated for up to 5 days.)

TEXAS BARBECUE SAUCE

Makes: about 2 cups

Texas-style barbecue is largely about the dry rub; sauces are served in bottles on the side for your own adornment. But why open a bottle when our tangy, peppery barbecue sauce is just as easy—and tastes much better. We combine the usual sauce ingredients—vinegar, brown sugar, molasses, etc.—with dry mustard, pepper, and chili powder for spiciness. Savory Worcestershire adds depth, while tomato juice (in place of ketchup) provides tangy flavor and helps thin the sauce out. This peppery, tangy barbecue sauce works well with beef, chicken, and pork.

- 2 tablespoons unsalted butter
- ½ small onion, chopped fine
- 2 garlic cloves, minced
- 1½ teaspoons chili powder
- 1½ teaspoons pepper
- ½ teaspoon dry mustard

2 cups tomato juice
6 tablespoons white vinegar
2 tablespoons Worcestershire sauce
2 tablespoons brown sugar
2 tablespoons molasses

1. Melt butter over medium heat in saucepan. Cook onion until softened, about 5 minutes. Stir in garlic, chili powder, pepper, and mustard and cook until fragrant, about 30 seconds.

2. Stir in tomato juice, vinegar, Worcestershire, sugar, and molasses and simmer until sauce is reduced to 2 cups, about 20 minutes. Season with salt. Serve at room temperature. (Sauce can be refrigerated for up to 1 week.)

EASTERN NORTH CAROLINA–STYLE BARBECUE SAUCE

Makes: about 2½ cups

In eastern North Carolina, the barbecue sauce should have a vinegary punch, a bit of spiciness, plenty of salt, and be thin enough to soak into finely chopped barbecued pork. Whisking together cider vinegar, Texas Pete hot sauce, salt, pepper, and red pepper flakes gives us a tangy base while some brown sugar balances the heat. One 12-ounce bottle of Texas Pete will yield more than enough for this recipe. Toss the sauce with pulled pork and serve more on the side.

1½ cups cider vinegar
1 cup Texas Pete Original Hot Sauce
¼ cup packed light brown sugar
2 teaspoons kosher salt
1 teaspoon pepper
1 teaspoon red pepper flakes

Whisk all ingredients together in bowl.

LEXINGTON-STYLE BARBECUE SAUCE

Makes: about 2½ cups

In Lexington, North Carolina, the barbecue sauce is tangy in flavor, ideal for soaking into rich, smoky barbecued pork. To mimic it, we simmer cider vinegar, ketchup, granulated garlic, pepper, red pepper flakes, and salt to meld their flavors. The ketchup makes the sauce redder, a touch sweeter, and a bit thicker. Toss with pulled pork and serve more on the side.

2 cups cider vinegar
1 cup ketchup
2 teaspoons granulated garlic
2 teaspoons pepper
1½ teaspoons kosher salt
1 teaspoon red pepper flakes

Combine all ingredients in small saucepan and bring to boil over medium-high heat. Reduce heat to medium-low and simmer for 5 minutes. Transfer sauce to bowl and let cool completely.

LOUISIANA SWEET BARBECUE SAUCE

Makes: about 2 cups

Louisiana barbecue sauce is uniquely wine-y and most often sweet with the heat of chili sauce. It's served warm and goes great brushed on ribs or chicken.

4 tablespoons unsalted butter
1 small onion, chopped
2 garlic cloves, minced
1 teaspoon paprika
1 tablespoon pepper
2 tablespoons lemon juice
1 teaspoon dry mustard
½ teaspoon hot pepper sauce
½ teaspoon table salt
1 tablespoon brown sugar, firmly packed
6 tablespoons cider vinegar
¼ cup molasses
2 tablespoons cream sherry
1 (15-ounce) can tomato sauce

Melt butter in a medium saucepan. Add onion and sauté until softened, 3 to 4 minutes. Stir in garlic, paprika, pepper, lemon juice, dry mustard, hot pepper sauce, and salt; cook over medium heat to blend flavors, about 5 minutes. Meanwhile, dissolve brown sugar in vinegar. Add vinegar-sugar mixture, molasses, sherry, and tomato sauce; bring to simmer. Simmer uncovered until sauce thickens slightly, about 15 minutes. Serve.

POULTRY

BUYING AND PREPPING CHICKEN

The road to serving juicy, flavorful chicken starts even before you turn on the stove or oven. Here's how to buy the right parts and prep them properly.

SHOPPING

Always Buy Air-Chilled

Chicken with an "Air-Chilled" label has been cooled after slaughter by being hung from a conveyor belt that circulates around a cold room. Conversely, water-chilled chicken sits in a chlorinated bath, where it absorbs water that inflates the chicken's price. Air-chilled chicken is typically more tender, likely because the slower temperature drop gives enzymes in the meat more time to tenderize muscle tissue.

Avoid Packaged Parts

The U.S. Department of Agriculture doesn't regulate the weight of chicken parts, so a package might contain pieces that vary dramatically in weight, which can make it hard to ensure that they cook at the same rate. In packages of split breasts and leg quarters, we found that the largest pieces could weigh twice as much as the smallest. Buy parts individually from the meat counter and select similar-size pieces.

Don't Freeze in Supermarket Packaging

We don't freeze chicken in its packaging (unless it is vacuum-sealed) because most packaging has air gaps that cause freezer burn. Instead, we wrap each chicken part in plastic wrap, place it in a zipper-lock freezer bag, press out the air, and freeze the parts in a single layer. And don't refreeze chicken: Its texture when cooked becomes significantly tougher.

SAFETY TIPS FOR HANDLING RAW CHICKEN

Season Safely

Though bacteria can't live for more than a few minutes in direct contact with salt (which dehydrates bacteria), it can live on the edges of a box or shaker. To avoid contamination, premeasure salt and pepper so you don't need to reach into a box or grab a grinder with dirty hands.

Don't Rinse

Avoid rinsing raw poultry. Contrary to what some cookbooks advise, rinsing is likely to spread bacteria around the sink (and perhaps onto nearby foods such as lettuce sitting on the counter). And our tests failed to demonstrate any flavor benefit to rinsing poultry before cooking.

Be Sure to Disinfect

Wash your hands, knives, cutting boards, and counters (and anything else that has come into contact with the raw bird, its juices, or your hands) with hot, soapy water. In lab tests, we found that hot, soapy water; a bleach solution; and undiluted vinegar were equally effective at reducing bacteria on non-dishwasher-safe cutting boards.

ONE BIRD, TWO KINDS OF MEAT

WHITE Cook breasts to 160 degrees.
Mild, lean canvas for other flavors; prone to overcooking easily if you're not careful; best cooked relatively quickly. Tips: Brine or salt in advance, and use a thermometer to gauge doneness.

DARK Cook thighs and drumsticks to at least 175 degrees. Richer flavor; harder to overcook; can have more fat, which can cause flare-ups or make sauces greasy; great for braising.

CHICKEN PARTS

We prefer buying a whole chicken and breaking it down into parts: two split breasts, two drumsticks, two thighs, and two wings. Bone-in parts cook relatively quickly, are flavorful (thanks to the skin and bones), and provide variety and interest on the plate.

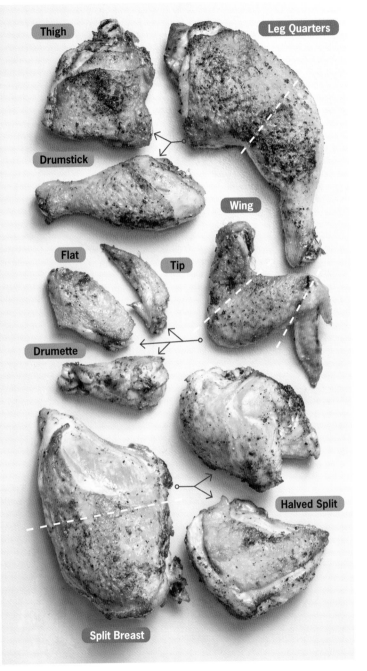

Thigh

Leg Quarters

Drumstick

Wing

Flat

Tip

Drumette

Halved Split

Split Breast

HOW TO BOOST FLAVOR IN CHICKEN PARTS

Brining, Salting, Marinating

Brining is soaking the chicken in a saltwater solution before cooking; the salt penetrates the meat, helping season it and encouraging it to hold on to its moisture when cooked.

Salting is applying salt (sometimes in combination with other dry seasonings/spices) to the exterior of the chicken and letting the chicken sit, refrigerated, for a period of time so that the salt can work its way into the meat. Salting provides the same benefits as brining.

Marinating is coating or soaking the chicken in a seasoned wet mixture; if the marinade is salty (via salty ingredients: soy sauce, fish sauce, Worcestershire sauce, etc.), it does some of the same work as brining and salting.

Slashing

Cutting slits through the skin and into the meat (typically about ½ inch deep) helps salt and other flavors get deeper into the chicken. Slashing also creates more surface area for seasonings to stick to. To see what this looks like, turn to the Smoked Citrus Chicken recipe on page 434.

Browning

Deep browning of the skin creates savory, complex flavor. For uncoated chicken skin to brown efficiently, some of the fat in the skin must be rendered out first. One trick for rendering that fat is to start chicken parts skin side down in a cold pan that is then placed on the heat; the cold start creates a gentle temperature ramp-up that helps render the fat.

Tip When you're looking for efficient browning, always make sure that the chicken (or anything else you want to brown) is as dry as possible before it goes on the heat; otherwise, the excess moisture has to evaporate before any browning can begin.

GET SKIN IN THE GAME

BRYAN ROOF

When you roast chicken, you want it to be moist through and through—except, of course, for the skin. There, the goal is a crackling crispness. The coexistence of dry skin and succulent meat, whether in a whole bird or in parts, depends on the methods for both seasoning and cooking. The recipes in this course will help you achieve that balance by showing you how and where to salt, how to render the fat, and how to handle the heat.

BRYAN'S PRO TIP: *It may seem like an unnecessary extra step, but patting poultry skin dry with paper towels removes excess water from the surface that would otherwise cause the skin to first steam before it can crisp during cooking. Drying the skin allows it to crisp more efficiently in the skillet or oven.*

CRISPY-SKINNED CHICKEN BREASTS WITH CHERMOULA

Serves: 4

Total Time: 1¼ hours

RECIPE OVERVIEW Achieving crisp skin and tender, well-seasoned meat when roasting bone-in chicken breasts is simple—if you deploy salt and heat in the right way. For direct contact, separate the skin from the flesh and sprinkle the meat underneath with salt to season it and help it retain moisture, and then prick the skin to allow it to render fat during cooking. Then slide the breasts into the oven to roast gently. Once the meat is cooked through, sear the breasts in a skillet on the stovetop to finish. The direct heat burnishes the skin and also gives the chicken a serious flavor boost. Be sure to remove excess fatty skin from the thick ends of the breasts when trimming. Though these chicken breasts taste great on their own, we love to serve them with chermoula, the North African sauce of herbs and warm spices.

- 4 (12-ounce) bone-in split chicken breasts, trimmed
- ¾ teaspoon table salt
- 1 tablespoon vegetable oil
- 1 recipe Chermoula (recipe follows)

1. Adjust oven rack to lower-middle position and heat oven to 325 degrees. Line rimmed baking sheet with aluminum foil. Working with 1 breast at a time, use your fingers or handle of spoon to carefully separate chicken skin from meat, leaving it attached at top and bottom of breast and at ribs. Sprinkle salt evenly over all chicken, then lay skin back in place. Using metal skewer or tip of paring knife, poke 6 to 8 holes in fat deposits in skin. Arrange breasts, skin side up, on prepared sheet. Roast until chicken registers 160 degrees, 35 to 45 minutes.

2. Heat 12-inch skillet over low heat for 5 minutes. Add oil and swirl to coat surface. Add chicken, skin side down, and increase heat to medium-high. Cook chicken, without moving it, until skin is well browned and crispy, 3 to 5 minutes. Using tongs, flip chicken and prop against side of skillet so thick side of breast is facing down; continue to cook until browned, 1 to 2 minutes longer. Transfer to serving dish and let rest for 10 minutes before serving with chermoula.

CORE TECHNIQUE
Roasting Bone-In Chicken Breasts

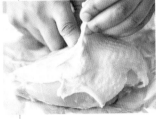

LOOSEN SKIN AND SALT
Use your fingers or handle of spoon to carefully peel skin from meat, leaving it attached. Sprinkle salt evenly over all chicken meat under skin.

REPLACE SKIN AND POKE
Lay skin back over salted chicken to help it retain moisture. Using metal skewer or paring knife, poke holes in fat deposits to allow fat to render.

ROAST AND SEAR
Roast chicken until it registers 160 degrees, then sear in a skillet until skin is crispy and browned.

CORE TECHNIQUE
Trimming Bone-In, Skin-On Breasts

Besides trimming fat and loose skin, we also trim the rib section so that the breast lies flat in the pan.

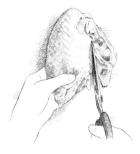

TRIM RIB SECTION
With breast skin side up, use kitchen shears to trim rib section, following contours of breast.

TRIM EXCESS FAT AND SKIN
With breast skin side down, use chef's knife to trim any excess fat and skin around edges of breast.

CHERMOULA

Serves: 4 to 6 (makes about 1 cup)

- 6 tablespoons chopped fresh cilantro
- 3 tablespoons extra-virgin olive oil
- 2 tablespoons grated fresh ginger
- 2 tablespoons smoked paprika
- 4 garlic cloves, minced
- 1 tablespoon grated lemon zest plus 2 tablespoons juice
- 1 tablespoon ground cumin
- ½ teaspoon red pepper flakes

Combine all ingredients in small bowl. Season with salt and pepper to taste.

KEYS TO SUCCESS

- **Salt the meat:** Applying the salt under the skin seasons the meat effectively.
- **Poke holes in the skin:** Small holes help the skin render fat more effectively as it cooks, which increases crispness.

The Bone-In Advantage

Why buy bone-in chicken breasts? First, the crisped skin adds flavor and nice textural contrast. Second, bone-in breasts are far less expensive than boneless. Lastly, unlike boneless, skinless breasts, which have no barrier against drying, bone-in breasts have built-in protection (skin and bone), making them more foolproof to cook.

Prone to Drying Out
Boneless, skinless breasts are entirely exposed to the heat.

Easier to Keep Moist
The skin and bone provide protection.

HERBED ROAST CHICKEN

Serves: 3 to 4
Total Time: 1½ hours, plus 1 hour 20 minutes brining and resting

RECIPE OVERVIEW One of the most appealing ways to prepare roast chicken is to flavor it with a mixture of fresh herbs and butter—but the skin, and the shape of the bird, can pose a challenge. Butterflying the chicken solves a couple of problems: It creates a flatter surface for the herb butter to stick to and it makes it easy to sear the chicken on the stove, which promotes crisp, brown skin. After brining the chicken, make shallow cuts in the dark meat to help the skin render its fat and create pockets to trap the herbs. For multiple layers of herb flavor, rub part of the butter under the skin on the breast and then brown the chicken in a skillet before moving it to the oven. Spread more butter over the chicken partway through roasting. Finally, add extra herb butter and lemon juice to the flavorful pan juices to make a quick sauce. You can substitute an equal amount of basil for the tarragon and replace the thyme with rosemary, oregano, or sage. Do not use dried herbs, which lose potency during cooking and turn the dish gritty. If using a kosher chicken, do not brine in step 1. The chicken may slightly overhang the skillet at first, but once browned it will fit.

Chicken

- 1 (5-pound) whole chicken, giblets discarded
- ½ cup table salt for brining
- 6 tablespoons unsalted butter, softened
- 6 scallions, green parts only, minced
- ¼ cup minced fresh tarragon
- 1 tablespoon minced fresh thyme
- 1 garlic clove, minced
- ¼ teaspoon table salt
- ¼ teaspoon pepper
- 1 tablespoon vegetable oil

Sauce

- 1–1½ cups chicken broth
- 2 teaspoons all-purpose flour
- 1 teaspoon lemon juice

1. FOR THE CHICKEN With chicken breast side down, use kitchen shears to cut through bones on either side of backbone and discard backbone. Flip chicken over and press on breastbone to flatten. Using sharp knife, cut 2 slashes, ⅛ inch deep, into skin of thighs and legs, about ¾ inch apart. Dissolve ½ cup salt in 2 quarts cold water in large container. Submerge chicken in brine, cover, and refrigerate for 1 hour.

2. Meanwhile, adjust oven rack to middle position and heat oven to 450 degrees. Combine softened butter, scallions, tarragon, thyme, garlic, salt, and pepper in bowl. Transfer 2 tablespoons herb butter to small bowl and refrigerate; set remaining herb butter aside.

3. Remove chicken from brine and pat dry with paper towels. Using your fingers, carefully loosen center portion of skin covering each side of breast. Place 1 tablespoon room-temperature herb butter underneath skin over center of each side of breast. Gently press on skin to distribute butter over meat. Season chicken with pepper.

4. Heat oil in 12-inch ovensafe skillet over medium-high heat until just smoking. Add chicken skin side down and reduce heat to medium. Cook until lightly browned, 8 to 10 minutes. Transfer skillet to oven and roast chicken for 25 minutes.

5. Using pot holder, remove chicken from oven. Using 2 large wads of paper towels, flip chicken skin side up. Using spoon or spatula, evenly coat chicken skin with remaining room-temperature herb butter and return to oven. Roast chicken until skin is golden brown, breast registers 160 degrees, and thighs register 175 degrees, 15 to 20 minutes. Transfer chicken to carving board and let rest, uncovered, for 20 minutes.

6. FOR THE SAUCE While chicken rests, pour pan juices into fat separator. Let liquid settle for 5 minutes, then pour juices into 2-cup liquid measuring cup. Add enough broth to measure 1½ cups. Heat 2 teaspoons fat from fat separator in now-empty skillet over medium heat until shimmering. Add flour and cook, stirring constantly, until golden, about 1 minute. Slowly whisk in broth mixture, scraping up any browned bits. Bring to rapid simmer and cook until reduced to 1 cup, 5 to 7 minutes. Stir in any accumulated chicken juices, return to simmer, and cook for 30 seconds. Off heat, whisk in lemon juice and reserved cold herb butter. Season with salt and pepper to taste. Carve chicken and serve, passing sauce separately.

KEYS TO SUCCESS
- **Slash the thighs:** The cuts help the skin render fat and create pockets to hold the herbs.
- **Pack on the herbs:** Use a paste of fresh herbs under the skin, on the skin, and in a sauce for potent, layered flavor.
- **Sear and roast:** Searing the chicken in a skillet before roasting starts the rendering process, which leads to crispier skin.

Herbs Three Ways
To ensure herbs in every bite, make a paste of tarragon, thyme, scallions, and butter and deploy it three ways.

UNDER SKIN
Before roasting, spread herb butter evenly under loosened skin of breast meat.

OVER SKIN
Midway through cooking, coat skin of entire bird with herb butter.

ON THE SIDE
Serve chicken with pan sauce enriched with herb butter.

Prepping Chicken for an Herbal Infusion

BUTTERFLY
Herbs will roll right off whole chicken. To help them stay put, flatten bird, first removing backbone.

PRESS
Use heel of your hand to press firmly on breastbone so chicken will lie flat, helping herbs stay on top.

SCORE
Make shallow cuts on legs and thighs to create pockets that can trap herbs.

CUMIN-CORIANDER RUBBED CORNISH GAME HENS

Serves: 4
Total Time: 1¼ hours, plus 4 hours chilling

RECIPE OVERVIEW Cornish game hens look elegant and are surprisingly easy, if you treat them right. They have a high skin-to-meat ratio, so the potential for a nice crispy exterior is strong. But their diminutive size means that the meat finishes cooking before the skin is fully rendered and crisp. We have a few techniques to address this problem. Splitting the birds in half provides even exposure to the heating element for even cooking and a combination of roasting and broiling maximizes browning. As for flavoring, a spice rub works better than a wet marinade or paste. Salt, potent and earthy cumin and coriander, some sweet paprika, and spicy cayenne make an easy rub that pairs nicely with the richness of the hens. We rub the underside of the split birds with half of this mixture; to the rest, we add baking powder and a bit of oil and rub it into the skin. The salt helps pull moisture to the skin's surface so that it can evaporate more quickly, and the baking powder further promotes crisping and browning. A 4-hour chill dries out the skin a bit more prior to cooking. If your hens weigh 1½ to 2 pounds, cook three instead of four and extend the broiling time in step 5 to 15 minutes. If your hens are frozen, be sure to thaw them in the refrigerator for 24 to 36 hours before salting.

- 4 (1¼- to 1½-pound) whole Cornish game hens, giblets discarded
- 2 tablespoons kosher salt
- 2 teaspoons ground cumin
- 2 teaspoons ground coriander
- 1 teaspoon paprika
- ¼ teaspoon cayenne pepper
- ¼ teaspoon vegetable oil
- 1 teaspoon baking powder
  Vegetable oil spray

1. Working with 1 hen at a time, use kitchen shears to cut along both sides of backbone to remove it. Flatten hens and lay breast side up on counter. Using sharp chef's knife, cut through center of breast to make 2 halves.

2. Using your fingers, gently separate skin from breast and thighs. Using metal skewer or tip of paring knife, poke 10 to 15 holes in fat deposits on top of breast halves and thighs. Tuck wingtips behind back. Pat hens dry with paper towels.

3. Combine salt, cumin, coriander, paprika, and cayenne in bowl. Sprinkle half of salt mixture on underside (bone side) of hens. Stir oil into remaining salt mixture until salt is evenly coated with oil. Stir in baking powder until well combined. Turn hens skin side up and rub oil mixture evenly over surface. Transfer hens, skin side up, to wire rack set in rimmed baking sheet and refrigerate, uncovered, for at least 4 hours or up to 24 hours.

4. Adjust oven racks to upper-middle and lower-middle positions, place second rimmed baking sheet on lower rack, and heat oven to 500 degrees. Once oven is fully heated, spray skin side of hens with oil spray and season with pepper. Carefully transfer hens, skin side down, to baking sheet and cook for 10 minutes.

5. Remove hens from oven and heat broiler. Flip hens skin side up. Transfer baking sheet with hens to upper rack and broil until well browned and breasts register 160 degrees and thighs register 175 degrees, about 5 minutes, rotating as necessary to promote even browning. Serve.

Variation
OREGANO-ANISE RUBBED CORNISH GAME HENS
Substitute 1 teaspoon dried oregano and ½ teaspoon anise seeds for cumin and coriander.

KEYS TO SUCCESS

- **Air-dry:** Chill the seasoned birds uncovered for 4 hours to dry the skin.

- **Roast and broil:** A high-heat dual cooking method crisps the skin in record time.

FEARLESS FRIED CHICKEN

MORGAN BOLLING

There's no arguing the point: Making even the simplest fried chicken is a kitchen production, one involving hot oil, thermometers, and a potential greasy mess. So when you do go through the trouble, the recipe had better deliver. The recipes in this course fry up chicken that is deeply bronzed with crisp and crunchy crusts using peanut oil, vegetable oil, or lard.

MORGAN'S PRO TIP: *After coating the chicken in flour, let it sit in the refrigerator at least 30 minutes before frying. This will help the coating adhere to the chicken after frying. (It also gives you time to clean up before guests arrive if frying for a party).*

I like to use leftover lard from frying lard fried chicken in biscuits. They will be ultratender and savory.

THE METHOD
FRIED CHICKEN

Follow these straightforward steps to successfully fry chicken.

1 BRINE
Soak the chicken parts in a tangy buttermilk brine.

2 MAKE COATING
Blend flour and spices with a little more buttermilk for a pebbly, craggy texture.

3 COAT CHICKEN
Dredge the soaked chicken parts in the coating, covering all sides and pressing to adhere.

4 HEAT OIL
Heat a quart of peanut or vegetable oil in a large Dutch oven to 375 degrees.

5 FRY COVERED
Add the chicken to the pot and cover it to contain spatters; fry until the first side is golden brown.

6 FRY UNCOVERED
Uncover the pot, turn the chicken pieces over, and fry until golden brown on the second side.

EXTRA-CRUNCHY FRIED CHICKEN

Serves: 4

Total Time: 1 hour, plus 1 hour brining

RECIPE OVERVIEW For well-seasoned, extra-crunchy fried chicken we start by brining the chicken in heavily salted buttermilk. For the crunchy coating, we combine flour with a little baking powder and then add buttermilk to make a thick slurry, which clings tightly to the meat. Frying the chicken with the lid on the pot for half the cooking time contains the spatter-prone oil and keeps it hot. Keeping the oil at the correct temperature is essential to producing crunchy fried chicken that is neither too brown nor too greasy. Use a Dutch oven that holds 6 quarts or more for this recipe. If you want to produce a slightly lower-fat version, you can remove the skin from the chicken before soaking it in the buttermilk; the chicken will be slightly less crunchy. Do not use kosher chicken for this recipe and don't let the chicken soak in the brine for longer than 1 hour or it will be too salty.

- 2 **tablespoons table salt for brining**
- 2 **cups plus 6 tablespoons buttermilk, divided**
- 3½ **pounds bone-in chicken pieces (split breasts halved crosswise, drumsticks, and/or thighs), trimmed**
- 1 **quart peanut or vegetable oil for frying**
- 3 **cups all-purpose flour**
- 2 **teaspoons baking powder**
- ¾ **teaspoon dried thyme**
- ½ **teaspoon pepper**
- ¼ **teaspoon garlic powder**

1. Dissolve salt in 2 cups buttermilk in large container. Submerge chicken in brine, cover, and refrigerate for 1 hour.

2. Line platter with triple layer of paper towels. Set wire rack in rimmed baking sheet. Add oil to large Dutch oven until it measures about ¾ inch deep and heat over medium-high heat to 375 degrees.

3. Meanwhile, whisk flour, baking powder, thyme, pepper, and garlic powder together in large bowl. Add remaining 6 tablespoons buttermilk; with your fingers rub flour and buttermilk together until buttermilk is evenly incorporated into flour and mixture resembles coarse, wet sand. Dredge chicken pieces in flour mixture and turn to coat thoroughly, gently pressing flour mixture onto chicken. Shake excess flour from each piece of chicken and transfer to prepared baking sheet.

4. Place chicken pieces skin side down in oil, cover, and fry until deep golden brown, 8 to 10 minutes. Adjust burner, if necessary, to maintain oil temperature between 300 and 325 degrees. (After 4 minutes, check chicken for even browning and rearrange if some pieces are browning

faster than others.) Turn chicken pieces over and continue to fry, uncovered, until chicken pieces are deep golden brown on second side and breasts register 160 degrees and thighs and drumsticks register 175 degrees, 6 to 8 minutes. Using tongs, transfer chicken to prepared platter; let stand for 5 minutes. Serve.

Variation

EXTRA-SPICY, EXTRA-CRUNCHY FRIED CHICKEN

Add ¼ cup hot sauce to buttermilk mixture in step 1. Substitute 2 tablespoons cayenne pepper and 2 teaspoons chili powder for dried thyme and garlic powder.

• KEYS TO SUCCESS

- **Brine the chicken:** A salted buttermilk soak keeps the chicken moist and well seasoned.

- **Add baking powder:** A modest amount mixed with the flour adds lightness and crunch.

- **Use the lid:** Covering the pot at the beginning of frying contains spatters and keeps the oil hot.

WHAT CAN GO WRONG

PROBLEM The chicken is too salty.

SOLUTION Do not let the chicken brine for much longer than an hour, because the chicken will absorb too much salt and will taste overseasoned.

PROBLEM The chicken is greasy and does not crisp and brown properly.

SOLUTION Use a thermometer to monitor the oil's temperature, and don't add the chicken until the oil reaches 375 degrees. If after 10 or 15 minutes, the oil refuses to come up to temperature, turn up the burner a bit and keep heating the oil. If the chicken is added before the oil is ready, the chicken will be greasy and won't crisp or brown properly.

PROBLEM The chicken doesn't cook through in the time indicated.

SOLUTION Make sure to cover the pot immediately after adding the chicken to the hot oil. The cover traps heat inside the pot so that the chicken cooks through in a timely fashion. The cover also helps the temperature of the oil recover faster. After turning the chicken pieces so that the browned side is facing up, continue cooking uncovered so that the crisp crusts won't soften.

LARD FRIED CHICKEN

Serves: 4

Total Time: 1¼ hours, plus 30 minutes chilling

RECIPE OVERVIEW In Indiana kitchens, chicken pieces are seasoned with salt and plenty of black pepper, dunked in a light coating of flour, and then cooked in bubbling lard. The resulting fried chicken is crisp (not craggy) in texture on the outside, superjuicy on the inside, and uniquely savory: If you're a fried chicken fan, it's a must-try. Dipping the chicken pieces in flour, then water, and then back in flour creates a substantial yet light crust. For fast frying, we cook the chicken all in one batch. Keeping the lard between 300 and 325 degrees ensures a golden brown coating without any off-flavors (which can happen when lard is heated to higher temperatures). Draining the fried chicken on paper towels wicks off any excess lard for juicy, not greasy, chicken. Use a Dutch oven that holds 6 quarts or more for this recipe. We developed this recipe using Morrell Snow Cap Lard, but you can substitute 1 quart peanut or vegetable oil, if desired, although the taste will be different. If you're breaking down a whole chicken for this dish, a 4½-pound chicken will yield the necessary pieces. If you're using table salt, reduce the amount by half. To take the temperature of the chicken pieces, first take them out of the oil and place them on a plate; this is the safest way and provides the most accurate reading.

3	pounds bone-in chicken pieces (2 split breasts cut in half crosswise, 2 drumsticks, and 2 thighs), trimmed
5	teaspoons kosher salt, divided
1	tablespoon pepper
1½	cups all-purpose flour
1½	teaspoons baking powder
2	pounds lard

1. Sprinkle chicken all over with 2 teaspoons salt and pepper. Whisk flour, baking powder, and remaining 1 tablespoon salt in large bowl until combined. Place 4 cups water in medium bowl.

2. Working with 1 piece of chicken at a time, dredge chicken in flour mixture, shaking off excess; dunk in water, letting excess drip off; then dredge again in flour mixture, pressing to adhere. Transfer to large plate and refrigerate for at least 30 minutes or up to 2 hours.

3. Set wire rack in rimmed baking sheet and line half of rack with triple layer of paper towels. Heat lard in large Dutch oven over medium-high heat to 350 degrees.

4. Add all chicken to lard, skin side down, in single layer (some slight overlap is OK) so pieces are mostly submerged. Fry for 10 minutes, rotating pot 180 degrees after 5 minutes. Adjust burner, if necessary, to maintain oil temperature between 300 and 325 degrees.

5. Carefully flip chicken and continue to fry until golden brown and breasts register 160 degrees and drumsticks/thighs register 175 degrees, 5 to 9 minutes longer. Transfer chicken to paper towel–lined side of prepared rack and drain for about 10 seconds per side, then move to unlined side of rack. Let cool for 10 minutes. Serve.

• **KEYS TO SUCCESS**

• **Season generously:** This chicken gets its savory flavor from plenty of pepper and salt.

• **Fry low:** With lard, it's best to fry at a moderate 300 to 325 degrees to prevent off-flavors.

• **Drain well:** Let the pieces drain after frying to preserve crispness.

How Frying Crisps Food

Fried foods crisp when their starch molecules absorb water; form a gel (a disorganized jumble of starch molecules holding water); and then eject that water as steam during frying, leaving behind an open, dry matrix that crisps and browns.

MOLE HOT FRIED CHICKEN

Serves: 4 to 6
Total Time: 1 hour, plus 2½ hours brining and chilling

RECIPE OVERVIEW Packed to the brim with cayenne pepper, Nashville hot fried chicken may have you in tears, but the incredibly crunchy, juicy fried chicken is worth the pain. The real star of Nashville hot chicken is the spicy oil (or lard) that gets lacquered onto the craggy crust after the chicken comes out of the fryer. Unlike buffalo sauce, which contains lots of water that quickly sogs out fried wings, the oil adds flavor without compromising crunch. For this recipe we take that brilliant technique and combine it with the rich flavors of Mexican mole—chipotle chile, cocoa, cinnamon, cumin—for an intense, dark chile oil that's brushed onto the crunchy crust after frying. To ramp up the crisp and crunch factor of the crust, we use a blend of all-purpose flour and potato starch (the secret ingredient in Japanese fried dishes such as chicken karaage) in the coating. Due to its unique composition, potato starch forms a dense, brittle exterior when fried and makes a coating that remains crisp for hours. After you dredge the chicken, a couple hours uncovered in the refrigerator allows the starches to hydrate so that the coating is thick and cohesive, not crumbly and dusty. This chicken is spicy and packed with deep, satisfying flavor. Make sure to buy potato starch, not potato flour; you can find it in your supermarket or online. We like to serve this chicken with Quick-Pickled Red Onions (page 337), dill pickle chips, crème fraîche, white bread or torta rolls, and fresh cilantro.

Brine

- 1 cup kosher salt
- ½ cup plus 3 tablespoons sugar
- 3½ pounds bone-in chicken pieces (split breasts cut in half, drumsticks, and/or thighs), trimmed

Coating

- 1¼ cups all-purpose flour
- ¾ cup potato starch
- 1 tablespoon cayenne pepper
- 2 teaspoons pepper, divided
- 1½ teaspoons kosher salt, divided
- 1 teaspoon baking powder
- 1 cup buttermilk

Spice Oil

- ⅓ cup vegetable oil
- 2 teaspoons sesame seeds
- 2 teaspoons cayenne pepper
- 1½ teaspoons chipotle chile powder
- ½ teaspoon garlic powder
- ¼ teaspoon kosher salt
- ⅛ teaspoon ground cinnamon
- ⅛ teaspoon cocoa powder
- ⅛ teaspoon ground cumin

- 3 quarts vegetable oil, for frying

1. FOR THE BRINE Dissolve salt and sugar in 2 quarts water in large bowl. Add chicken, cover with plastic wrap, and refrigerate for at least 30 minutes or up to 1 hour. Drain chicken.

2. FOR THE COATING Whisk flour, potato starch, cayenne, 1 teaspoon pepper, 1 teaspoon salt, and baking powder together in large shallow dish. Whisk buttermilk, remaining 1 teaspoon pepper, and remaining ½ teaspoon salt together in large bowl. Working with 3 pieces at a time, dunk chicken in buttermilk mixture, then dredge in flour mixture, pressing mixture onto chicken to form thick, even coating. Place chicken, skin side up, on wire rack set in rimmed baking sheet. Refrigerate, uncovered, for at least 2 hours or up to 24 hours.

3. FOR THE SPICE OIL Whisk all ingredients together in small saucepan. Bring mixture to simmer over medium-high heat. Reduce heat to medium-low and cook, stirring occasionally, until mixture is fragrant and slightly darkened, about 5 minutes. (Cooled spice oil can be refrigerated in airtight container for up to 3 days. Reheat over medium heat before using.)

4. Meanwhile, adjust oven rack to middle position and heat oven to 200 degrees. Heat oil in large Dutch oven over medium-high heat to 350 degrees. Place half of chicken in oil and fry until breasts register 155 degrees and drumsticks/thighs register 165 degrees, 13 to 16 minutes. (Adjust burner, if necessary, to maintain oil temperature between 300 degrees and 325 degrees.) Transfer chicken to second wire rack set in second rimmed baking sheet and place in oven to keep warm. Return oil to 350 degrees and repeat with remaining chicken. Stir spice oil to recombine and brush over both sides of chicken. Serve.

> ## • KEYS TO SUCCESS
>
> - **Use potato starch:** The starch helps create a coating with long-lasting crunch.
>
> - **Hydrate the coating:** Make sure the coating is evenly moistened to avoid dry, dusty patches.
>
> - **Spice it up:** A generous amount of cayenne and other spices makes the chicken both fiery and flavorful.

Plunging food into hot fat is actually an efficient way to cook. The entire surface gets exposed to the heat, so food cooks through quickly and uniformly. The oil can get really hot, so moisture evaporates, flavor is concentrated, and food develops unmatched crispness. And frying encourages browning and adds richness. To do the frying yourself, all you need is an organized setup and the right tools—most of which you probably already have.

SETTING UP A FRY STATION

Like most cooking tasks, frying is simple as long as you are organized. Setting up your station with prepped food and the right tools is the first step to success.

①

Baking Sheet Provides space to drain fried food in a single layer and to catch spills

Wire Rack Helps air circulate below the paper towels to wick away some moisture

Paper Towels Wick oil from fried food

Spider Skimmer/Slotted Spoon Helps you quickly remove batches of food from the oil

②

Clip-On Probe Thermometer: Displays oil temperature and lets you know when it's hot enough to start frying

③

Dutch Oven Minimizes splatter with tall sides; provides broad cooking surface that allows you to cook food in fewer batches

④

Tongs Let you add food to hot oil in a precise way

Prepped Food Is ready and easy to grab when spread out evenly

ALL ABOUT THE OIL

What to Buy Most foods are fried between 325 and 400 degrees, so it's important to use oil with a high smoking point (the temperature at which wisps of smoke appear when fat is heated, signaling that the fat is breaking down). Otherwise, the food will taste burnt or bitter. These oils are all good options.

Vegetable blend   **Corn**   **Peanut**

Also try: rice bran, safflower, avocado

DEEP-FRYING FUNDAMENTALS

These tips will help ensure success in any application.

Don't Crowd the Pot
Adding too much food will cause the oil temperature to plunge and not recover quickly enough to crisp the food before it cooks through. It can also cause sticking if the pieces don't have enough space.

Stir Sticky Items
In addition to shaking off excess coatings and not crowding the pot, stirring the contents can help prevent them from fusing.

Adjust the Heat to Maintain the Target Temperature
Oil temperature fluctuates as food cooks and when fresh food is added, so monitor it closely; a clip-on probe thermometer makes this easy.

Remove Debris Between Batches
Use a slotted spoon or spider skimmer to fish out bits of food, lest they burn and imbue the oil with an acrid, bitter flavor.

Let the Oil Temperature Recover Between Batches
Don't add more food to the pot between batches before the oil temperature has rebounded; otherwise, the food will cook up greasy and soggy instead of crisping.

Drain Well
Transfer cooked food to a wire rack lined with a triple layer of paper towels set in a rimmed baking sheet.

Salt Immediately
Salt sticks better to hot foods (the moisture from emitted steam helps salt cling to the surface), so sprinkle it on the food just after draining.

Hold the First Batch(es) in the Oven
When frying multiple batches, keep cooked food hot and crisp by transferring it (on the paper towel–lined wire rack set in a baking sheet) to a 200-degree oven.

WINGING IT

STEVE DUNN

Roasted, grilled, and fried, chicken wings are no longer just a snack at the bar in Buffalo. In this course we show you how to make three meal-worthy versions of wings. A minimalist, very chickeny recipe calls to mind the wings on a whole roast chicken. Spicy Korean wings are fried not once but twice to make them extracrispy. And from Louisiana, supersized turkey wings are stuffed with garlic and potent spices, braised, and served with a Cajun-style gravy.

STEVE'S PRO TIP: *Chicken and turkey wings are loaded with collagen, which, when converted to gelatin, adds great body and mouthfeel to broths. Do what I do, and rather than discard the wingtips from these recipes, save them in a large zipper-lock bag in your freezer for the next time you're making broth.*

ROASTED AND GLAZED CHICKEN WINGS

Serves: 4
Total Time: 1¼ hours

RECIPE OVERVIEW The wings plucked from a whole roast chicken deliver a couple glorious bites: They offer succulent, savory meat along with well-rendered, sweetly caramelized skin. An entire trayful of wings with those same attributes makes a tasty, informal meal when served with a crisp green salad and a crusty loaf of bread. To render the wings' fat and produce evenly browned skin, we roast the flats and drumettes with a baking sheet placed on top of them. The extra weight ensures that both sides of the wings are in close contact with hot metal for effective heating. As they cook, the flats and drumettes exude gelatin-rich juices; these are poured off and reduced to a syrupy glaze to brush onto the wings after a final skin-browning blast under the broiler. Roast the wingtips along with the flats and drumettes to boost the flavor and volume of the juices (but if you purchase chicken wings that are packaged without wingtips, it's OK to omit them). This recipe was developed with Diamond Crystal kosher salt; if you're using Morton, which is denser, decrease the amount to 2¼ teaspoons.

- 4 pounds chicken wings, cut at joints, wingtips reserved
- 1 tablespoon vegetable oil
- 1 tablespoon kosher salt
- 1 teaspoon pepper

1. Adjust oven racks to lowest and upper-middle positions and heat oven to 400 degrees. Spray rimmed baking sheet with vegetable oil spray and line with parchment paper. Pat chicken dry with paper towels and transfer to large bowl. Add oil, salt, and pepper. Toss well to combine.

2. Arrange drumettes along 2 long sides of prepared baking sheet. Place flats rounded side down in center. Tuck wingtips in to fill any gaps on sheet (discard any wingtips that don't fit). Top chicken with second sheet of parchment, then gently press second rimmed baking sheet on top of parchment to weigh down wings. Roast on lower rack for 45 minutes.

3. Remove sheet from oven and heat broiler. Carefully and gently tilt 1 corner of sheet over fat separator or liquid measuring cup and drain off as much liquid as possible; you should have ⅓ to ½ cup. Remove top baking sheet and parchment. Discard wingtips (or save for nibbling). Flip remaining pieces.

4. Transfer defatted drippings to small saucepan. Cook over medium heat, swirling saucepan occasionally, until juices are reduced to 2 to 3 tablespoons, 6 to 8 minutes. Cover to keep warm.

5. While juices are reducing, broil chicken on upper rack until evenly golden brown, 6 to 8 minutes, rotating sheet halfway through broiling. Brush chicken with reduced juices, transfer to platter, and serve.

- KEYS TO SUCCESS
- **Two sheets:** Sandwiching the wings between baking sheets puts both sides in close contact with hot metal, producing well-rendered skin.
- **Chicken-glazed chicken:** The drippings are reduced to a syrupy glaze and brushed back on the wings for potent chicken flavor.
- **Broil after roasting:** Sliding the wings under the broiler after roasting yields better browning.

Wings Like the Ones You Sneak from a Whole Bird (and Lots of 'Em)

To produce a full 4 pounds of golden-brown, well-rendered wings—just like the two delicacies you might nibble on while carving a whole roasted bird—we strategically arrange the flats, drumettes, and wingtips on a parchment paper–lined baking sheet. The thicker drumettes go on the outside edges of the sheet, which we found heated more quickly. The thinner flats occupy the center, with the collagen-rich wingtips (added to boost the flavor of the jus) filling in any empty spots. To promote even, deep browning and to encourage fat and juices to render, we weigh the parts down with a second baking sheet (after laying a sheet of parchment on top to prevent sticking).

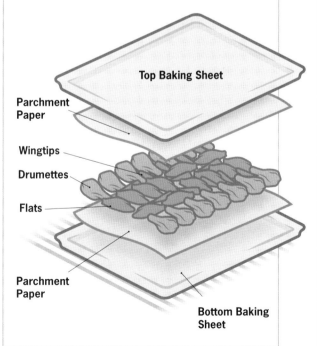

Top Baking Sheet

Parchment Paper

Wingtips

Drumettes

Flats

Parchment Paper

Bottom Baking Sheet

Cutting Up Chicken Wings

CUT THROUGH JOINT
Using kitchen shears or sharp chef's knife, cut through joint between drumette and flat.

CUT OFF WINGTIP
Cut off wingtip and reserve.

The Tastiest Part of a Roast Chicken

Wings have a fat content similar to that of dark meat: They contain about 3.5 percent fat, while thighs contain nearly 4 percent; breast meat, on the other hand, contains a mere 1.25 percent. Wings' large amounts of connective tissue and high skin-to-meat ratio mean that they're loaded with collagen, so wings roasted on a whole chicken become incredibly ten-

der and juicy. In the heat of the oven, the fat is slowly rendered from their abundant skin, leaving it lightly crisp and attractively browned. As they roast, the wings are also basted in the golden, savory jus that comes off the body of the bird, which adds even more umami richness.

DAKGANGJEONG

Serves: 4 to 6
Total Time: 1½ hours

RECIPE OVERVIEW   A thin, crispy exterior and a spicy-sweet-salty sauce are the hallmarks of Korean fried chicken. The biggest challenge is preventing the sauce from destroying the crust. With their high exterior-to-interior ratio, wings offer the potential for maximum crunch; and they cook quickly, making them the perfect chicken part for this dish. A loose batter of flour, cornstarch, and water clings nicely to the wings and fries up brown and crispy. To help the coating withstand a wet sauce, we double-fry the wings, which removes more water from the skin than a single fry does, making the coating extra-crispy. Gochujang, Korean chili paste, gives the sauce the proper spicy, fermented notes, while sugar tempers the heat and garlic and ginger—cooked briefly with sesame oil—provide depth. A rasp-style grater makes quick work of turning the garlic into a paste. Tailor the heat level of your wings by adjusting the amount of gochujang. If you can't find gochujang, substitute an equal amount of sriracha and add only 2 tablespoons of water to the sauce. Use a Dutch oven that holds 6 quarts or more for this recipe. If you buy chicken wings that are already split, with the tips removed, you will need only 2½ pounds.

1	tablespoon toasted sesame oil
1	garlic clove, minced to paste
1	teaspoon grated fresh ginger
1¾	cups water, divided
3	tablespoons sugar
2–3	tablespoons gochujang
1	tablespoon soy sauce
2	quarts peanut or vegetable oil for frying
1	cup all-purpose flour
3	tablespoons cornstarch
3	pounds chicken wings, cut at joints, wingtips discarded

1. Combine sesame oil, garlic, and ginger in large bowl and microwave until mixture is bubbly and garlic and ginger are fragrant but not browned, 40 to 60 seconds. Whisk in ¼ cup water, sugar, gochujang, and soy sauce until smooth; set aside.

2. Heat oil in Dutch oven over medium-high heat to 350 degrees. While oil heats, whisk flour, cornstarch, and remaining 1½ cups water in second large bowl until smooth. Set wire rack in rimmed baking sheet and set aside.

3. Place half of wings in batter and stir to coat. Using tongs, remove wings from batter one at a time, allowing any excess batter to drip back into bowl, and add to hot oil. Increase heat to high and cook, stirring occasionally to prevent wings from sticking, until coating is light golden and beginning to crisp, about 7 minutes. (Oil temperature will drop sharply after adding wings.) Transfer wings to prepared rack. Return oil to 350 degrees and repeat with remaining wings. Reduce heat to medium and let second batch of wings rest for 5 minutes.

4. Heat oil to 375 degrees. Carefully return all wings to oil and cook, stirring occasionally, until deep golden brown and very crispy, about 7 minutes. Return wings to rack and let stand for 2 minutes. Transfer wings to reserved sauce and toss until coated. Return wings to rack and let stand for 2 minutes to allow coating to set. Transfer to platter and serve.

- **KEYS TO SUCCESS**
- **Flour plus cornstarch:** This combo, mixed with water, makes a clingy, crispy coating.
- **Double frying:** This method drives more moisture from the skin, producing maximum crunch.
- **Fast cooking method:** Each batch takes just 7 minutes, and the second fry can be done in one large batch.

Winging It, Korean-Style

Dakgangjeong boast a big crunch and a complex sauce that make them appealing to eat, but they also employ a relatively quick and easy cooking method that makes them more appealing to prepare than many other styles of fried chicken.

Supercrispy
Double frying ensures that the skin stays crispy long after being sauced.

Complex Sauce
Gochujang chile paste, soy sauce, sesame oil, sugar, and aromatics make a savory, spicy, sweet sauce.

Lots of Skin
A high ratio of skin to meat protects the meat and keeps it moist—and also means crunch in every bite.

Cook Quickly
Because they're small, wings will be fully cooked by the time they're brown and crispy, 28 minutes in total for both rounds.

Temp Drops? Don't Worry

The oil temperature will drop when the chicken is added, but as long as it stays above 250 degrees (where there is enough energy to evaporate water and brown the exterior), the results will be fine.

Oil should stay within this range while frying.

350°

250°

STUFFED TURKEY WINGS

Serves: 4
Total Time: 3 hours

RECIPE OVERVIEW At Laura's II in Lafayette, Louisiana, they serve meaty stuffed turkey wings, beautifully browned and braised to tenderness, with a scoop of rice. For the "stuffing" part, the wings are slit open and stuffed with cloves of garlic and a powerful mix of spices. Our version re-creates their secret spice mix with a blend of paprika, cayenne, granulated garlic, onion powder, celery salt, and salt and pepper and envelops the wings in a deeply flavorful Cajun-style gravy. After making slits in the drumette and flat portions of the separated wings, we rub them inside and out with the spice mix and stuff halved garlic cloves inside. Browning the wings gives them beautiful color, creates flavorful fond in the pot, and tempers the cayenne's raw heat. From there, add a bit of flour to the fat left in the pot to make a caramel-colored roux and then soften a mix of onion, bell pepper, and celery (aka the "Cajun holy trinity") and aromatics in the roux. A nice even braise in the oven produces wings that are fall-off-the-bone tender and draped in an almost impossibly complex and delicious gravy. Serve with rice.

Spice Mix
1¾ teaspoons paprika
1 teaspoon granulated garlic
¾ teaspoon salt
¾ teaspoon pepper
½ teaspoon onion powder
½ teaspoon celery salt
¼ teaspoon cayenne pepper

Turkey
4 (12- to 16-ounce) whole turkey wings, cut at joints into flats and drumettes, wingtips discarded
12 garlic cloves, peeled (8 halved lengthwise, 4 smashed)
¼ cup vegetable oil
¼ cup all-purpose flour
1 cup finely chopped green bell pepper
1 cup finely chopped onion
¼ cup finely chopped celery
1 tablespoon chopped fresh thyme
3 cups chicken broth

1. **FOR THE SPICE MIX** Combine all ingredients in bowl. Measure out 1½ teaspoons spice mix and set aside.

2. **FOR THE TURKEY** Adjust oven rack to middle position and heat oven to 300 degrees. Make one 1-inch-long incision, about ½ inch deep, on either side of each drumette bone and one 2-inch-long incision, about ½ inch deep, between bones on underside of each flat. Sprinkle wings inside and out with remaining 4 teaspoons spice mix. Stuff 1 piece halved garlic into each pocket of each drumette and 2 pieces into pocket of each flat.

3. Heat oil in Dutch oven over medium-high heat until shimmering. Add wings and cook until browned on both sides, about 10 minutes. Transfer wings to plate. Reduce heat to medium and add flour to fat left in pot. Cook, stirring often, until roux is caramel-colored, about 3 minutes.

4. Add bell pepper, onion, celery, thyme, smashed garlic, and reserved spice mix and cook, stirring occasionally and scraping up any browned bits, until vegetables are just beginning to soften, about 5 minutes.

5. Stir in broth and bring to simmer. Nestle wings into broth mixture. Cover, transfer pot to oven, and cook for 1 hour. Remove pot from oven and flip wings. Cover, return pot to oven, and continue to cook until tender, about 45 minutes longer.

6. Transfer wings to clean plate. Bring gravy to boil over high heat and cook until slightly thickened, about 7 minutes. Off heat, season with table salt and pepper to taste. Return wings to pot and gently turn to coat with gravy. Serve.

- **KEYS TO SUCCESS**
- **Slit the wings**: Jumbo-size turkey wings take well to flavoring from within.
- **Make a roux**: The flavorful fond in the pot, combined with flour, is the base for a deeply savory gravy.
- **A long braise**: Cooking the wings low and slow makes them fall-off-the-bone tender.

Slits for Stuffing

We cut slits in both the flats and the drumettes and then season the wings with our potent spice mix before stuffing the slits with halved garlic cloves.

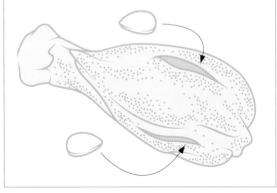

Americans may not eat as many chicken wings as chicken breasts, but when it comes to certain holidays—say, Super Bowl Sunday—wings are the top choice. And they deserve special attention, as wings are unique among poultry cuts in their ratio of meat to skin and bone. Interestingly, chicken wings are white, not dark, meat. But because they contain a good deal of collagen, when cooking they do not easily fall into either category.

SKIN

Chicken wings have the highest proportion of skin compared to other chicken parts—22 percent by weight, or twice the amount found in thighs. The skin itself is about 53 percent moisture, 37 percent fat, and 10 percent protein, of which around 70 percent is collagen.

MEAT

Contrary to popular belief, the meat in chicken wings is white meat, not dark meat, containing far less of the oxygen-holding protein myoglobin.

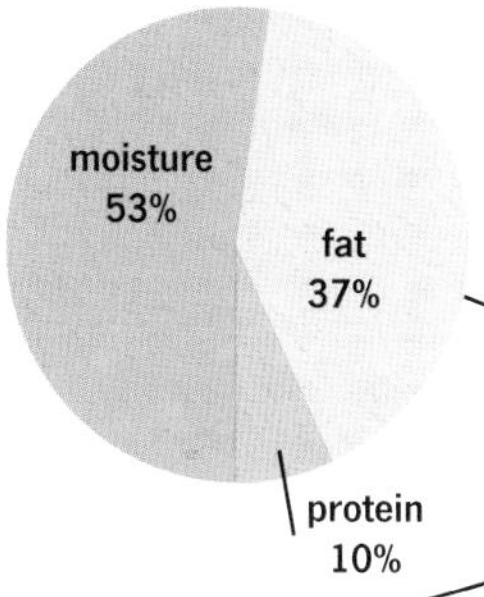

White Meat
Dark Meat

moisture 53%
fat 37%
protein 10%

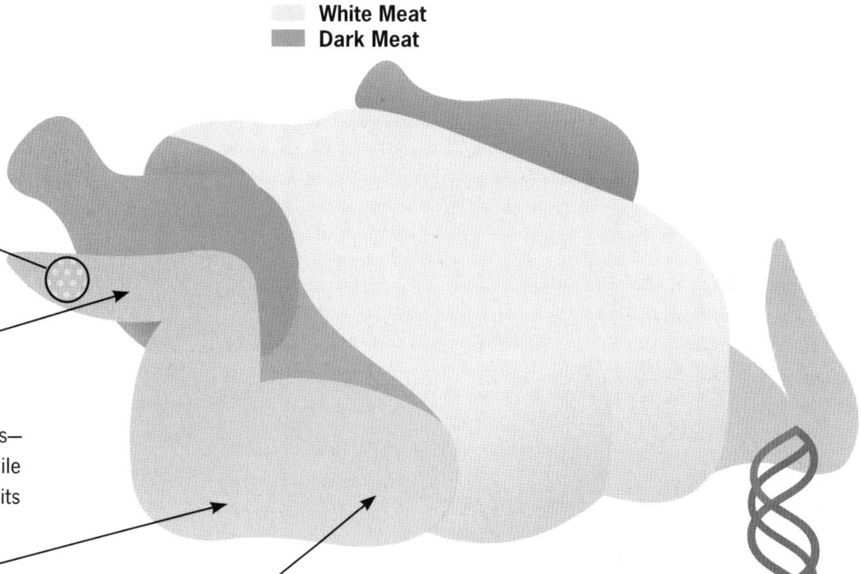

WINGTIP

The very ends of the wings—the wing-tips—consist mostly of skin and cartilage. While they can be cooked up into crunchy tidbits or saved to make stock, they are rarely served to diners in America.

collagen

FLAT

The flat is the middle section of the wing; it is smaller, thinner, and longer than the drumette. Chicken wings served in restaurants often consist of both the drumette and the flat.

DRUMETTE

The drumette is the piece of the wing closest to the body; it looks like a smaller version of a drumstick.

THE POWER OF COLLAGEN

The robust amount of collagen in chicken-wing skin unwinds into moisture-holding gelatin at temperatures as low as 135 degrees—20 degrees lower than the temperature at which collagen found in chicken muscle unwinds. Since the meat in chicken wings is lean and delicate white meat, the extra gelatin from the skin is extremely helpful when cooking because it provides the perception of juiciness thanks to its moisture-holding capacity. Interestingly, researchers found that marinating chicken wings in marinades containing both acid (lemon juice) and salt for 20 hours significantly lowered the denaturation temperature of the chicken-wing skin collagen even further—to as low as 122 degrees.

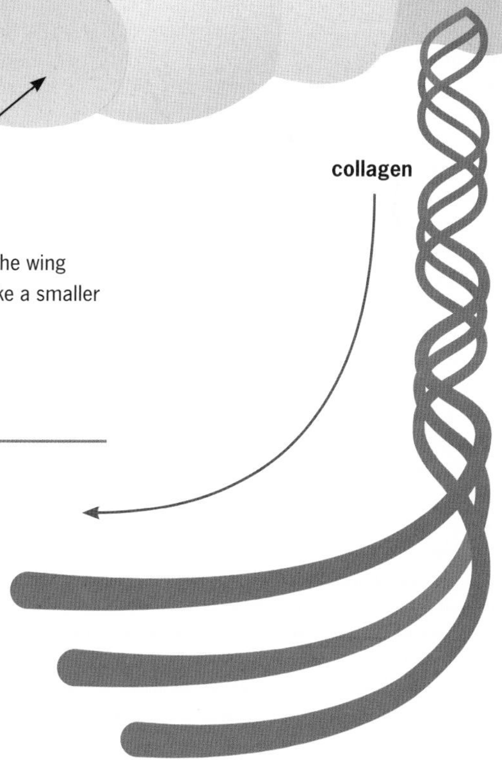

WITH HEAT
When collagen is heated, its triple helix structure unwinds into gelatin, which can hold up to 10 times its weight in water.

CHICKEN PIE

ASHLEY MOORE

Chicken pot pie should be satisfying but not overly rich, complex but not complicated, rustic but not messy. The three recipes in this course strike that balance, each in its own way. In the first, a classic pot pie, a buttery crust blankets a classic white-meat filling. For the second, we make a filling of boneless thighs and spring vegetables in a Dutch oven and top it with a puff-pastry lattice. And finally, chicken thighs stand in for pigeon in our take on Morocco's b'stilla, which envelops a savory filling in layers of flaky phyllo. All three recipes are generously sized; we know you'll want to share the delicious results.

ASHLEY'S PRO TIP: *Always let your pie rest before cutting into it. Pay close attention to the time mentioned in the recipe. If you get antsy and cut a slice too early, the filling will not be as cohesive as it is meant to be.*

CLASSIC CHICKEN POT PIE

Serves: 6 to 8
Total Time: 1½ hours with premade dough

RECIPE OVERVIEW This recipe yields moist meat, bright fresh vegetables, and a creamy but not excessively rich filling that is under a flaky pie crust. To simplify the cooking process, we use boneless, skinless chicken breasts, which are poached in broth before being shredded into bite-size pieces. For the sauce, sauté the aromatics and vegetables before adding flour to make a roux. Whisking in the reserved chicken poaching liquid along with milk builds rich flavor. A bit of sherry brightens up the filling. Stir in the shredded chicken, peas, and parsley just before topping the pie to ensure that these delicate ingredients don't overcook in the oven. You can use store-bought pie dough in place of homemade in this recipe.

- 1½ pounds boneless, skinless chicken breasts, trimmed
- 2 cups chicken broth
- 4 tablespoons unsalted butter
- 1 onion, chopped fine
- 3 carrots, peeled and sliced ¼ inch thick
- 2 celery ribs, sliced ¼ inch thick
- 1 teaspoon table salt
- 2 garlic cloves, minced
- 2 teaspoons minced fresh thyme or ½ teaspoon dried
- ½ cup all-purpose flour
- 1½ cups milk
- ¼ cup dry sherry
- 1 cup frozen peas
- 3 tablespoons minced fresh parsley
- 1 recipe Foolproof All-Butter Double-Crust Pie Dough (page 582)
- 1 egg, lightly beaten with 1 teaspoon water

1. Adjust oven rack to lower-middle position and heat oven to 400 degrees. Bring chicken and broth to simmer in Dutch oven over medium heat. Reduce heat to low, cover, and cook until chicken registers 160 degrees, 10 to 15 minutes. Transfer chicken to cutting board and broth to bowl.

2. Melt butter in now-empty pot over medium heat. Add onion, carrots, celery, and salt and cook until softened, about 5 minutes. Stir in garlic and thyme and cook until fragrant, about 30 seconds. Stir in flour and cook for 1 minute. Whisk in reserved broth and milk, scraping up any browned bits and smoothing out any lumps. Bring to simmer and cook until sauce is thickened, about 3 minutes. Season with salt and pepper to taste, then stir in sherry.

3. Once chicken is cool enough to handle, shred with 2 forks into bite-size pieces. Add to sauce, along with any accumulated juices, peas, and parsley. Transfer to 13 by 9-inch baking dish (or similar-size casserole dish). (Filling can be frozen for up to 1 month; to bake, thaw completely in refrigerator, then bring to gentle simmer, covered, stirring often, before transferring to baking dish and continuing with step 4.)

4. Roll each dough disk into 9-inch round on well-floured counter, then overlap by half, brushing with water where dough overlaps. Roll together to seal, then roll into 16 by 12-inch rectangle. Loosely roll dough around rolling pin and gently unroll it over filling in dish, letting excess dough hang over edge. Trim dough to ½ inch beyond lip of dish, then tuck overhang under itself; folded edge should be flush with edge of dish. Crimp dough evenly around edge of dish using your fingers. Cut five 2-inch slits in top of dough. (Assembled pot pie can be refrigerated for up to 24 hours; to bake, continue with step 5, increasing cooking time to 40 to 50 minutes.)

5. Brush surface with egg wash and bake until topping is golden and filling is bubbling, about 30 minutes, rotating dish halfway through cooking. Let cool for 20 minutes before serving.

- **KEYS TO SUCCESS**
- **Double-duty broth:** Use the same chicken broth to poach the breasts and make the sauce for extra flavor.
- **Roux:** Stir flour into the sautéed vegetables to give the sauce the right amount of cling.

DUTCH OVEN CHICKEN POT PIE WITH SPRING VEGETABLES

Serves: 6
Total Time: 1½ hours

RECIPE OVERVIEW In this one-pot approach to chicken pot pie, all of the cooking is completed within (and on top of!) a Dutch oven, starting it on the stovetop before transferring it to the oven to bake. Tomato paste and soy sauce boost savoriness in the sauce without being distinguishable in their own right. Boneless chicken thighs cook right in the sauce and stay moist and tender. Swapping in leeks for onions gives the filling a fresh spring flavor, which is further enhanced with fresh asparagus, peas, and tarragon. The crust is a simple yet stunning lattice made from convenient store-bought puff pastry. We bake the delicate lattice top separate from the filling to ensure that it holds its shape. Simply turn the lid of the Dutch oven upside down to act as a baking sheet before covering the pot and baking the pastry on top. To thaw frozen puff pastry, let it sit either in the refrigerator for 24 hours or on the counter for 30 minutes to 1 hour. You can place the baked pastry on top of the filling in the pot just before serving for an impressive presentation, or you can cut the pastry into wedges and place them over individual portions of the filling.

1 (9½ by 9-inch) sheet puff pastry, thawed
4 tablespoons unsalted butter
1 pound leeks, white and light green parts only, halved lengthwise, cut into ½-inch pieces, and washed thoroughly
4 carrots, peeled and cut into ½-inch pieces
1 teaspoon table salt
4 garlic cloves, minced
2 teaspoons tomato paste
½ cup all-purpose flour
3 cups chicken broth, plus extra as needed
¼ cup heavy cream
1 teaspoon soy sauce
2 bay leaves
2 pounds boneless, skinless chicken thighs, trimmed and cut into 1-inch pieces
1 large egg, lightly beaten
1 pound asparagus, trimmed and cut on bias into 1-inch lengths
1 cup frozen peas
2 tablespoons chopped fresh tarragon or parsley
1 tablespoon grated lemon zest plus 2 teaspoons juice

1. Cut sheet of parchment paper to match outline of Dutch oven lid and place on large plate or overturned rimmed baking sheet. Roll puff pastry sheet into 15 by 11-inch rectangle on lightly floured counter. Using pizza cutter or sharp knife, cut pastry widthwise into ten 1½-inch-wide strips.

2. Space 5 pastry strips parallel and evenly across parchment circle. Fold back first, third, and fifth strips almost completely. Lay additional pastry strip perpendicular to second and fourth strips, keeping it snug to folded edges of pastry, then unfold strips. Repeat laying remaining 4 pastry strips evenly across parchment circle, alternating between folding back second and fourth strips and first, third, and fifth strips to create lattice pattern. Using pizza cutter, trim edges of pastry following outline of parchment circle. Cover loosely with plastic wrap and refrigerate while preparing filling.

3. Adjust oven rack to lower-middle position and heat oven to 400 degrees. Melt butter in Dutch oven over medium heat. Add leeks, carrots, and salt and cook until vegetables are softened, 5 to 7 minutes. Stir in garlic and tomato paste and cook until fragrant, about 1 minute. Stir in flour and cook for 1 minute.

4. Slowly stir in broth, scraping up any browned bits and smoothing out any lumps. Stir in cream, soy sauce, and bay leaves. Bring to simmer and cook until mixture is thickened, about 3 minutes. Stir in chicken and return to simmer.

5. Off heat, cover pot with inverted lid and carefully place parchment with pastry on lid. Brush pastry with egg and sprinkle with salt. Transfer pot to oven and bake until pastry is puffed and golden brown, 25 to 30 minutes, rotating pot halfway through baking.

6. Remove pot from oven. Transfer parchment with pastry to wire rack; discard parchment. Remove lid and discard bay leaves. Stir asparagus into filling and cook over medium heat until crisp-tender, 3 to 5 minutes. Off heat, stir in peas and let sit until heated through, about 5 minutes. Adjust filling consistency with extra hot broth as needed. Stir in tarragon and lemon zest and juice. Season with salt and pepper to taste. Set pastry on top of filling and serve.

- **KEYS TO SUCCESS**
- **Secret sauce:** Small amounts of soy sauce and tomato paste add savory flavor.
- **Gentle cooking:** Add the asparagus and peas at the end to preserve their fresh flavor and color.

CHICKEN B'STILLA
Serves: 10 to 12
Total Time: 2½ hours

RECIPE OVERVIEW B'stilla is an impressive Moroccan tart whose savory filling is customarily made with pigeon and richly flavored with almonds and cinnamon sugar. The most cherished qualities of this dish are its many contrasts: crisp yet juicy, sweet yet savory, succulent yet wholesome. Cooked gently in a spiced broth, moist, flavorful chicken thighs are a worthy substitute for pigeon. The rich cooking liquid becomes the base of the traditional custard-like component of the pie. Although b'stilla is usually made with layers of a paper-thin dough called warqa, easy-to-find phyllo works perfectly. For ease of serving, we assemble the pie in the same skillet used to cook the chicken: Line the pan with phyllo and then add the almond mixture, followed by the chicken-egg mixture. Finally, top it with more phyllo. Encased in the pie, the almond mixture soaks up the rich juices from the chicken above it, and the wide, shallow shape makes this pie easy to serve. A customary sprinkling of cinnamon sugar on the baked pie drives home the sweet-savory contrasts. Phyllo dough is also available in larger 18 by 14-inch sheets; if using, cut them in half to make 14 by 9-inch sheets. Do not thaw the phyllo in the microwave; let it sit in the refrigerator overnight or on the counter for 4 to 5 hours. While working with the phyllo, cover the sheets with plastic wrap, then a damp dish towel to prevent drying.

½	cup extra-virgin olive oil, divided
1	onion, chopped fine
¾	teaspoon table salt
1	tablespoon grated fresh ginger

Making a Lattice Top

SPACE FIRST 5 STRIPS

Space 5 pastry strips parallel and evenly across parchment circle. Fold back first, third, and fifth strips almost completely.

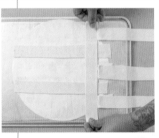

LAY STRIPS PERPENDICULAR

Lay pastry strip perpendicular to second and fourth strips, keeping it snug to folded edges of pastry, then unfold strips.

REPEAT

Repeat laying remaining 4 pastry strips evenly across parchment circle, alternating between folding back second and fourth strips and first, third, and fifth strips to create lattice pattern.

TRIM EDGES

Using pizza cutter, trim edges of pastry following outline of parchment circle.

½ teaspoon pepper
½ teaspoon ground turmeric
½ teaspoon paprika
1½ cups water
2 pounds boneless, skinless chicken thighs, trimmed
6 large eggs
½ cup minced fresh cilantro
1 pound (14 by 9-inch) phyllo, thawed
1½ cups slivered almonds, toasted and chopped
¼ cup confectioners' sugar, divided
1 tablespoon ground cinnamon, divided

1. Heat 1 tablespoon oil in 12-inch nonstick skillet over medium heat until shimmering. Add onion and salt and cook until softened, about 5 minutes. Stir in ginger, pepper, turmeric, and paprika and cook until fragrant, about 30 seconds. Add water and chicken and bring to simmer. Reduce heat to low, cover, and cook until chicken registers 175 degrees, 15 to 20 minutes. Transfer chicken to cutting board, let cool slightly, then shred into bite-size pieces using 2 forks; transfer to large bowl.

2. Bring cooking liquid to boil over high heat and cook until reduced to about 1 cup, about 10 minutes. Whisk eggs together in small bowl. Reduce heat to low. Whisking constantly, slowly pour eggs into broth and cook until mixture resembles loose scrambled eggs, 6 to 8 minutes; transfer to bowl with chicken. Stir in cilantro until combined. Wipe skillet clean with paper towels and let cool completely.

3. Adjust oven rack to middle position and heat oven to 375 degrees. Brush 1 phyllo sheet with oil and arrange in bottom of cooled skillet with short side against side of pan. Some phyllo will overhang edge of skillet; leave in place. Turn skillet 30 degrees. Brush second phyllo sheet with oil and arrange in skillet, leaving any overhanging phyllo in place. Repeat turning and layering with 10 more phyllo sheets in pinwheel pattern, brushing each with oil, to cover entire circumference of skillet (you should have total of 12 layers of phyllo).

4. Combine almonds, 3 tablespoons sugar, and 2 teaspoons cinnamon and sprinkle over phyllo in skillet. Lay 2 phyllo sheets evenly across top of almond mixture and brush top with oil. Rotate skillet 90 degrees and lay 2 more phyllo sheets evenly across top; do not brush with oil. Spoon chicken mixture into skillet and spread into even layer.

5. Stack 5 phyllo sheets on counter and brush top with oil. Fold phyllo in half crosswise and brush top with oil. Lay phyllo stack on center of chicken mixture.

6. Fold overhanging phyllo over filling and phyllo stack, pleating phyllo every 2 to 3 inches, and press to seal. Brush top with oil and bake until phyllo is crisp and golden, 35 to 40 minutes.

7. Combine remaining 1 tablespoon sugar and remaining 1 teaspoon cinnamon in small bowl. Let b'stilla cool in skillet for 15 minutes. Using rubber spatula, carefully slide b'stilla out onto cutting board. Dust top with cinnamon sugar, slice, and serve.

• KEYS TO SUCCESS
• **Bloom the spices:** Heating the spices brings out their flavor for a potent broth.
• **Enclose the almonds:** Cooking the almond mixture inside the pie, rather than on top, gives the pie flavor and prevents it from drying out.
• **Cinnamon sugar:** A sweet-savory contrast makes this dish special.

Assembling Chicken B'stilla

LAY FIRST PHYLLO SHEET
Brush 1 phyllo sheet with oil and arrange in bottom of skillet with short side against side of pan. Continue layering 11 more phyllo sheets in skillet in pinwheel pattern.

ADD ALMOND MIXTURE
Sprinkle almond mixture over phyllo in skillet, then lay 2 phyllo sheets across top and brush with oil. Rotate skillet 90 degrees and lay 2 more phyllo sheets across top.

ADD CHICKEN MIXTURE
Spoon chicken mixture into skillet and spread into even layer. Stack 5 phyllo sheets and brush with oil. Fold in half, brush top with oil, and lay on chicken mixture.

FOLD IN PHYLLO
Fold overhanging phyllo over filling and phyllo stack, pleating phyllo every 2 to 3 inches, and press to seal. Brush top with oil before baking.

BAKE AND SERVE
Bake b'stilla until phyllo is crisp and golden. Cool then slide pie out of skillet. Sprinkle with cinnamon sugar, slice, and serve.

GRILLED, BARBECUED, AND SMOKED

BRIDGET LANCASTER

Grilling, whether with charcoal or gas, works wonders with chicken, adding deep flavor and smoky intrigue to the mild-mannered protein. Grilled chicken parts offer something for everyone, but the irregular shapes and mixture of white and dark meat, as well as fat deposits, can all spell trouble. In this course you'll learn how to prep the chicken (and the grill) for grilling, barbecuing, and smoking—and get finger-licking-good results.

BRIDGET'S PRO TIP: *All good things come to those who wait. Marinating or seasoning the meat and then giving it plenty of time for all those flavors to make their way deeper into the meat will pay off. Starting foods on the cooler side of a grill will ensure that the meat is cooked through slowly, and not dried out or burnt to a crisp. Plus, slowing down the cooking process means you get to spend more time outside at the grill, which is always a very good thing.*

GRILLED CHICKEN WITH ADOBO AND SAZÓN

Serves: 4 to 6
Total Time: 1¾ hours, plus 3 hours marinating

RECIPE OVERVIEW This juicy, intensely flavored chicken gets its punch from two dried seasonings from the Puerto Rican pantry: adobo, a blend made from granulated garlic, salt, black pepper, and oregano; and sazón, which includes all the ingredients of adobo as well as achiote, dried onion, cumin, and more herbs. Breaking down a whole chicken yourself ensures that the leg and breast pieces are proportionately sized for even cooking, and you can enjoy the delicacy that is the grilled backbone. After tossing the parts in a mixture of vinegar and oil, we rub the adobo-sazón seasoning over and under the skin as well as into pockets that we had slashed into the leg quarters. Allow the chicken to marinate for at least 3 hours and then grill it mainly over indirect heat, browning the skin over high heat for the final few minutes of cooking. A punchy postmarinade made with lots of garlic and chopped cilantro adds more bright, savory flavor. Look for sazón with cilantro and achiote (also called annatto) at the supermarket, and avoid those without salt. If you prefer to make your own sazón, you'll need 4 teaspoons here. You can substitute garlic powder for the granulated garlic. If you don't want to break down a whole chicken, purchase 4 to 4½ pounds of bone-in leg quarters and split breasts.

Adobo and Sazón

- 4 teaspoons granulated garlic
- 2½ teaspoons Sazón (recipe follows) or commercial sazón
- 1 teaspoon table salt
- ½ teaspoon pepper
- ¼ teaspoon dried oregano

Chicken

- 1 (4- to 4½-pound) whole chicken, giblets discarded
- 5 tablespoons distilled white vinegar, divided
- 5 tablespoons extra-virgin olive oil, divided
- 6 garlic cloves, minced
- ½ teaspoon table salt
- 1 (13 by 9-inch) disposable aluminum roasting pan
- ¼ cup chopped fresh cilantro
- ½ teaspoon pepper

1. FOR THE ADOBO AND SAZÓN Combine all ingredients in bowl.

2. FOR THE CHICKEN Place chicken breast side down on cutting board. Using kitchen shears, cut through bones on either side of backbone. Reserve backbone. Using chef's knife, cut through breastbone to split chicken in half.

3. Working with 1 half of chicken, slice through skin connecting leg quarter to breast, cutting close to leg quarter to ensure skin completely covers breast and rib meat. Leave split breast whole and tuck wing behind back. Flip leg quarter and remove and discard any rib bone connected to the thigh bone. Repeat with second half of chicken.

4. Place 1 leg quarter skin side up on cutting board. Using sharp knife, make 3 slashes: 1 across thigh, 1 across joint, and 1 across drumstick (each slash should reach bone). Flip leg quarter and make 1 more diagonal slash across back of drumstick. Repeat with second leg quarter.

5. Toss chicken (including backbone) with 1 tablespoon vinegar and 1 tablespoon oil in large bowl, using your hands to loosen skin from meat. Sprinkle adobo-sazón mixture over chicken pieces. Toss with your hands, rubbing mixture all over chicken, into slashes, and under skin. Cover and refrigerate chicken for at least 3 hours or up to 24 hours.

6A. FOR A CHARCOAL GRILL Open bottom vent completely. Light large chimney starter filled with charcoal briquettes (6 quarts). When top coals are partially covered with ash, pour evenly over half of grill. Set cooking grate in place, cover, and open lid vent completely. Heat grill until hot, about 5 minutes.

6B. FOR A GAS GRILL Turn all burners to high, cover, and heat grill until hot, about 15 minutes. Turn primary burner to medium and turn other burner(s) to low. (Adjust primary burner as needed to maintain grill temperature between 400 and 425 degrees.)

7. While grill heats, place garlic on cutting board and sprinkle with salt. Mash to paste with side of knife. (This can also be done using mortar and pestle.) Transfer garlic paste to disposable pan. Add cilantro, pepper, remaining ¼ cup vinegar, and remaining ¼ cup oil and mix to form paste.

Big Flavor, Three Ways

This deeply flavored grilled chicken gets its punch from three separate sources.

Dry Adobo
A simple yet impactful mixture consisting of granulated garlic, salt, black pepper, and oregano, adobo brings a savory boost to countless Puerto Rican dishes.

Sazón
A frequent companion to adobo in Puerto Rican cooking, this blend features all of that seasoning's components along with achiote, dried onion, cumin, and more dried herbs. Many versions also include monosodium glutamate to further enhance savory taste.

Garlicky Postmarinade
A sauce with lots of garlic, cilantro, vinegar, and oil contributes more heat and bite to the finished chicken.

CORE TECHNIQUE **For More Flavor, Slash Seasoning Pockets**

To get flavor from a spice rub deep into chicken leg quarters, try this trick: On the skin side of each leg quarter, slash meat down to the bone across the thigh, joint, and drumstick, and make another diagonal slash across the back of the drumstick (not shown). Then massage seasoning into the slashes for superflavorful meat.

8. Clean and oil cooking grate. Place chicken (including backbone) on cooler side of grill, skin side up. Cover and cook until underside of chicken is lightly browned, 15 to 20 minutes. Flip chicken, cover, and continue to cook on cooler side of grill until thickest part of breast registers 150 degrees, 15 to 20 minutes longer. While chicken cooks, place disposable pan with paste on hotter side of grill and heat until liquid begins to simmer and garlic begins to cook, 2 to 3 minutes. Remove disposable pan from grill.

9. Transfer chicken to hotter side of grill, skin side down, and cook (covered if using gas) until skin is well browned, 2 to 3 minutes. As chicken browns, place disposable pan on cooler side of grill.

10. Flip chicken and cook until breasts register 155 degrees and leg quarters register 175 degrees, about 2 to 3 minutes. As chicken reaches temperature, transfer to disposable pan. Once all chicken is in disposable pan, cover with aluminum foil and slide to hotter side of grill. Cook until marinade is sizzling, 3 to 4 minutes. Let stand off heat for 10 minutes.

11. Cut each breast in half crosswise through the bone. Cut leg quarters through joint to separate thigh and drumstick. Place chicken, including backbone, on serving platter. Pour marinade from disposable pan into serving bowl. Serve, passing marinade separately.

SAZÓN

Makes: about ¼ cup
Total Time: 10 minutes

This recipe was developed with granulated garlic and onion, but you can substitute the powdered versions if that's what you have on hand. Monosodium glutamate gives the mixture a savory boost. You'll find it in the spice aisle under the brand name Ac'cent, but you can omit it, if desired. This will make more than you need for the Grilled Chicken with Adobo and Sazón, but the extra makes a great addition to meat, bean, and rice dishes. This recipe can easily be doubled. Achiote is also called annatto.

    1   tablespoon ground achiote
    1   teaspoon granulated garlic
    1   teaspoon granulated onion
    1   teaspoon monosodium glutamate (optional)
    1   teaspoon table salt
    ½   teaspoon pepper
    ½   teaspoon ground coriander
    ½   teaspoon dried cilantro
    ¼   teaspoon ground cumin
    ¼   teaspoon dried oregano

Combine all ingredients in bowl. Store in airtight container until needed.

KEYS TO SUCCESS

• **Marinate before:** Vinegar and oil help the adobo-sazon mixture stick to the chicken, and a 3-hour marinade flavors the meat.

• **And after:** Heating the cooked parts briefly in a bright, punchy marinade ups the flavor more.

SWEET AND TANGY BARBECUED CHICKEN

Serves: 6 to 8
Total Time: 2¼ hours, plus 6 hours brining

RECIPE OVERVIEW Barbecued chicken, cooked low and slow on a grill, can take a boldly flavored sauce, like this sweet-and-spicy version. For chicken that is well seasoned all the way to the bone, first apply a rub and let the chicken chill: Salt, onion and garlic powders, paprika, a touch of cayenne, and some brown sugar maintain a bold presence even after grilling. To ensure that all the chicken pieces cook at a slow, steady rate, we place a disposable aluminum pan opposite the coals in the grill setup and fill it partway with water, which lowers the temperature inside the grill. Wait to apply the sauce until after searing the chicken; this prevents the sauce from burning and gives the chicken skin a chance to develop color first. Applying the sauce in stages, rather than all at once, ensures that its bright tanginess isn't lost. When browning the chicken over the hotter side of the grill, move it away from any flare-ups. Use the large holes of a box grater to grate the onion for the sauce.

Chicken

    2   tablespoons packed dark brown sugar
    1½ tablespoons kosher salt
    1½ teaspoons onion powder
    1½ teaspoons garlic powder
    1½ teaspoons paprika
    ¼   teaspoon cayenne pepper
    6   pounds bone-in chicken pieces (split breasts and/or leg quarters), trimmed

Sauce

    1   cup ketchup
    5   tablespoons molasses
    3   tablespoons cider vinegar
    2   tablespoons Worcestershire sauce
    2   tablespoons Dijon mustard
    ¼   teaspoon pepper
    2   tablespoons vegetable oil
    ⅓   cup grated onion
    1   garlic clove, minced
    1   teaspoon chili powder
    ¼   teaspoon cayenne pepper
    1   large disposable aluminum roasting pan (if using charcoal) or 2 disposable aluminum pie plates (if using gas)

1. **FOR THE CHICKEN** Combine sugar, salt, onion powder, garlic powder, paprika, and cayenne in bowl. Arrange chicken on rimmed baking sheet and sprinkle both sides evenly with spice rub. Cover with plastic wrap and refrigerate for at least 6 hours or up to 24 hours.

2. **FOR THE SAUCE** Whisk ketchup, molasses, vinegar, Worcestershire, mustard, and pepper together in bowl. Heat oil in medium saucepan over medium heat until shimmering. Add onion and garlic; cook until onion is softened, 2 to 4 minutes. Add chili powder and cayenne and cook until fragrant, about 30 seconds. Whisk in ketchup mixture and bring to boil. Reduce heat to medium-low and simmer gently for 5 minutes. Set aside ⅔ cup sauce to baste chicken and reserve remaining sauce for serving. (Sauce can be refrigerated for up to 1 week.)

3A. **FOR A CHARCOAL GRILL** Open bottom vent halfway and place disposable pan filled with 3 cups water on 1 side of grill. Light large chimney starter filled with charcoal briquettes (6 quarts). When top coals are partially covered with ash, pour evenly over other half of grill (opposite disposable pan). Set cooking grate in place, cover, and open lid vent halfway. Heat grill until hot, about 5 minutes.

3B. **FOR A GAS GRILL** Place 2 disposable pie plates, each filled with 1½ cups water, directly on 1 burner of gas grill (opposite primary burner). Turn all burners to high, cover, and heat grill until hot, about 15 minutes. Turn primary burner to medium-high and turn off other burner(s). (Adjust primary burner as needed to maintain grill temperature of 325 to 350 degrees.)

4. Clean and oil cooking grate. Place chicken, skin side down, over hotter part of grill and cook until browned and blistered in spots, 2 to 5 minutes. Flip chicken and cook until second side is browned, 4 to 6 minutes. Move chicken to cooler part and brush both sides with ⅓ cup sauce. Arrange chicken, skin side up, with leg quarters closest to fire and breasts farthest away. Cover (positioning lid vent over chicken if using charcoal) and cook for 25 minutes.

5. Brush both sides of chicken with remaining ⅓ cup sauce and continue to cook, covered, until breasts register 160 degrees and leg quarters register 175 degrees, 25 to 35 minutes longer.

6. Transfer chicken to serving platter, tent with aluminum foil, and let rest for 10 minutes. Serve, passing reserved sauce separately.

Trimming a Leg Quarter

Some leg quarters come with the backbone still attached. To remove it, hold leg quarter skin side down, grasp backbone, and bend it back to pop thigh bone out of socket. Cut through joint and any attached skin.

KEYS TO SUCCESS

- **Apply a rub:** A pregrill coating of spices adds layered flavor.
- **Sear, then sauce:** Partially cook the chicken parts before applying the sauce so the skin browns and the sauce doesn't burn.

Packaged Parts Have a Weight Problem

Grabbing a package of chicken parts is usually a lot faster than standing in line at the meat counter to buy them individually. But that convenience may come at a cost. The same chicken parts aren't required to be the same weight and their size can vary dramatically. For example, the U.S. Department of Agriculture permits leg quarters sold together to weigh between 8.5 and 24 ounces; in other words, one leg quarter in a package can weigh almost three times as much as another. Breasts can come from chickens that weigh between 3 and 5.5 pounds—a difference that can't help but translate to the breasts themselves. Such a disparity can be a problem when you're trying to get food to cook at the same rate. This lack of standardization showed up in our own shopping. We bought 26 packages of split breasts and leg quarters (representing five brands) from five different Boston-area supermarkets. When we weighed each piece and calculated the maximum weight variation within each package, the differences were startling: The largest pieces were twice the size of the smallest. Worse, some leg quarters came with attached backbone pieces that had to be cut off and discarded (which means throwing away money). Lesson learned: Whenever possible, buy chicken parts individually from a butcher, who can select similar-size pieces.

Pass on Packaged Parts
These leg quarters came in the same package, yet the one on the left weighs twice as much as the one on the right—a discrepancy that can lead to uneven cooking.

CITRUS SMOKED CHICKEN

Serves: 4 to 6
Total Time: 1½ hours, plus 1 hour marinating

RECIPE OVERVIEW This char-grilled chicken infused with citrus and spice is inspired by the chicken made at El Pollo Loco, the restaurant chain founded by Juan Francisco "Pancho" Ochoa. Cutting slits into bone-in chicken pieces before marinating gives more surface area for a bold marinade of orange and lemon zest, cumin, garlic, cinnamon, and cayenne to cling to. Cooking the chicken over indirect heat on a hot grill outfitted with a packet of wood chips infuses the meat with a smoky flavor. Then charring it on the hotter side of the grill for the last few minutes gives it a deeper color. If you prefer, you can use two wood chunks in place of the wood chip packet if you're using a charcoal grill. We tested this recipe with applewood, cherrywood, and hickory wood chips, but feel free to use any type of wood chips you like.

- ¼ cup extra-virgin olive oil
- 4 garlic cloves, minced
- 1 tablespoon kosher salt
- 1½ teaspoons ground cumin
- 1½ teaspoons grated orange zest, plus orange wedges for serving
- 1 teaspoon grated lemon zest, plus lemon wedges for serving
- ¾ teaspoon ground cinnamon
- ½ teaspoon pepper
- ⅛ teaspoon cayenne pepper
- 3 pounds bone-in chicken pieces (split breasts cut in half crosswise, drumsticks, and/or thighs), trimmed
- 1 cup wood chips

1. Whisk oil, garlic, salt, cumin, orange zest, lemon zest, cinnamon, pepper, and cayenne together in large bowl. Cut two ½-inch-deep slits in skin side of each chicken breast half, two ½-inch-deep slits in skin side of each thigh, and two ½-inch-deep slits in each drumstick. Transfer chicken to bowl with marinade and turn to thoroughly coat. Cover and refrigerate for at least 1 hour or up to 24 hours.

2. Using large piece of heavy-duty aluminum foil, wrap wood chips in 8 by 4-inch foil packet. (Make sure chips do not poke holes in sides or bottom of packet.) Cut 2 evenly spaced 2-inch slits in top of packet.

3A. FOR A CHARCOAL GRILL Open bottom vent completely. Light large chimney starter mounded with charcoal briquettes (7 quarts). When top coals are partially covered with ash, pour evenly over half of grill. Place wood chip packet on coals. Set cooking grate in place, cover, and open lid vent completely. Heat grill until hot, about 5 minutes.

3B. FOR A GAS GRILL Remove cooking grate and place wood chip packet directly on primary burner. Set grate in place and turn all burners to high. Cover and heat grill until hot, about 15 minutes. Leave primary burner on high and turn off other burner(s). (Adjust primary burner [or, if using 3-burner grill, primary burner and second burner] as needed to maintain grill temperature between 350 and 400 degrees.)

4. Clean and oil cooking grate. Place chicken skin side up on cooler side of grill, with breast pieces farthest away from heat. Cover and cook until breasts register 160 degrees and drumsticks/thighs register 175 degrees, 22 to 28 minutes, transferring pieces to plate, skin side up, as they come to temperature. (Re-cover grill after checking pieces for doneness.)

5. Transfer chicken, skin side down, to hotter side of grill. Cook until skin is well browned, 2 to 5 minutes, moving pieces as needed for even browning. Transfer chicken to platter, tent with foil, and let rest for 10 minutes. Serve with orange and lemon wedges.

KEYS TO SUCCESS

- **Cut slits:** Slashing through the chicken skin makes more surface area for the marinade to cling to.
- **Char-grill:** A few minutes over direct heat gives the chicken pieces a bronzed finish.

CORE TECHNIQUE

Making a Foil Packet for Wood Chips

SEAL AND CUT SLITS
Spread chips in center of 15 by 12-inch piece of heavy-duty aluminum foil. Fold to seal edges, then cut 2 evenly spaced 2-inch slits in top of packet to allow smoke to escape.

PLACE PACKET
Place aluminum foil packet of chips on lit coals of charcoal grill or over primary burner on gas grill.

Smoky, but Not Too Smoky

When we make wood chip packets in the test kitchen, we often use a large amount of chips and soak them (so that they burn and smoke longer). But here we wanted a lighter smoke flavor to make sure that the bright citrus and spice flavors came through. So we use a relatively small amount of chips (1 cup) and don't soak them. The resulting chicken has just the right amount of smoke to balance—but not overwhelm—the other flavors.

SETTING UP A FIRE

The fire setup—how much charcoal or how many burners you're using and where the heat is located in relation to the food—allows you to control the heat level and the rate of cooking. Using the wrong setup can cause food to burn before it's cooked through or cook through without developing any flavorful browning or char.

Best Practice: Use the fire setup that's appropriate for the type of food you're grilling. We use three main fire setups, and follow these guidelines when choosing which to use.

FIRE TYPE	BEST FOR
Single-Level Fire	Small, quick-cooking foods such as burgers, sausages, shrimp, fish fillets, and some vegetables
Half-Grill Fire	Foods that you want to cook gently but also sear such as bone-in chicken parts, thin steaks, and some vegetables
Banked Fire	Large foods that require hours on the grill such as boneless pork butt roast

THREE BASIC FIRE SETUPS

SINGLE-LEVEL FIRE
Charcoal Setup Distribute lit coals in even layer across bottom of grill.

Gas Setup Turn all burners to high, cover, and heat grill until hot. Leave all burners on high.

HALF-GRILL FIRE
Charcoal Setup: Distribute lit coals in even layer over 1 half of grill.

Gas Setup Turn all burners to high, cover, and heat grill until hot. Leave primary burner on high and turn off other burner(s).

BANKED FIRE
Charcoal Setup: Bank lit coals steeply against 1 side of grill.

Gas Setup: Turn all burners to high, cover, and heat grill until hot. Adjust primary burner as directed in recipe and turn off other burner(s).

DON'T COOK ON A GUNKED-UP GRILL

Food debris, grease, and smoke that build up on various parts of the grill can cause sticking and impart off-flavors to food; full grease traps can ignite; and built-up grease on the interior basin and underside of the grill lid can carbonize and turn into a patchy layer that flakes off and lands on your food.

HOW TO CLEAN YOUR GRILL

Interior basin and lid: Lightly scrub the cool grill and lid with steel wool and water.

Ash catcher (charcoal only): Empty the cooled ash regularly.

Grease traps (gas only): Remove the cool shallow pan from under your grill and scrub it with hot soapy water. To make cleanup easier, line the pan with aluminum foil before use.

Cooking grate: After preheating the grill, scrape the cooking grate clean with a grill brush.

OILING THE COOKING GRATE

Most cooking grates are made of steel or cast iron and must be oiled before grilling to keep food from sticking.

Best Practice: Using tongs, dip a wad of paper towels in vegetable oil and thoroughly wipe the preheated, scrubbed cooking grate before adding food.

COURSE
KOJI MAGIC

DAN SOUZA

The secret behind some of the tastiest Asian foods and beverages—including soy sauce, miso, sake, and fermented bean paste—is a fungus called koji. From this fungus, you can make an enzyme-rich slurry, shio koji, that's used as a cure or marinade for all kinds of mean, seafood, and even vegetables. The enzymes in shio koji tenderize the meat and enhance its flavor. The process requires planning ahead but is otherwise supereasy. And as you'll see in this course, shio koji has a special affinity with poultry, making chicken and turkey tender and ultrasavory.

DAN'S PRO TIP: *The benefits and power of koji are hard to overstate. I recommend making a batch of shio koji and then experimenting with it as a marinade for all of your favorite foods. You'll be amazed at what it can do.*

SHIO KOJI

Makes: about 1 quart
Total Time: 7 days

RECIPE OVERVIEW Shio koji is a traditional use of koji, the ancient mold that gives us soy sauce, miso, fermented bean paste, and sake. It is made by combining rice koji (cooked rice that has been inoculated with koji spores and then dried), salt, and water and letting the mixture ferment for about a week, during which time it develops a sweet, fruity, slightly funky aroma. Shio koji is primarily used as a marinade. Because it is rich in protease enzymes (which break down proteins) and amylase enzymes (which break down starches), it can transform many foods. In our Koji Fried Chicken, it turns the chicken incredibly savory and tender. It helps our Koji Turkey (page 438) to retain juices and remain moist. We prefer using a plastic food storage container for this recipe, but any medium (1-quart or more) food-safe container will work. There are a few options for buying rice koji. Some well-stocked high-end supermarkets carry it, but for the majority of us, online is the best option.

1¾   cups water
2¼   cups firm granular rice koji
9   tablespoons kosher salt

In medium saucepan, heat water to 140 degrees. Combine hot water, koji, and salt in lidded container and whisk until salt is dissolved, about 30 seconds. Cover with lid and let ferment at room temperature until mixture is thickened and smells sweet, fruity, and slightly funky, at least 7 days or up to 14 days, stirring once per day. After initial fermentation, store in refrigerator for up to 6 months.

KEYS TO SUCCESS

- **Temp the water:** You want to be precise here.
- **Be patient:** It takes at least 7 days for the shio koji's flavor to develop fully.
- **Keeps forever:** Because shio koji is fermented

KOJI FRIED CHICKEN

Serves: 4 to 6
Total Time: 1 hour, plus 9½ hours chilling

RECIPE OVERVIEW Shio koji's tenderizing and flavor-boosting properties make for amazing fried chicken. The first step is to marinate chicken parts in about a half-cup of shio koji for a good long time. Next we dunk the chicken in buttermilk and dredge it in a mixture of cornstarch, flour, and dried granular rice koji. To prevent the sugar-rich rice koji in the coating from burning, we use a fry-then-bake method, producing deeply meaty and juicy chicken with a golden-brown, crunchtastic crust. This recipe improves with age: The longer you marinate the chicken (up to three days), the better and meatier it gets. And the longer you let the dredge sit on the chicken (up to 24 hours), the better and crispier the crust becomes. Use a Dutch oven that holds 6 quarts or more for this recipe.

3½ pounds bone-in chicken pieces (split breasts halved crosswise, drumsticks, and/or thighs), trimmed

7 tablespoons Shio Koji (page 436)

1 cup cornstarch

½ cup plus ⅓ cup all-purpose flour

½ cup plus 2 tablespoons firm granular rice koji

1 tablespoon kosher salt, divided, plus extra for seasoning

2 teaspoons pepper, divided

1 teaspoon baking powder

1 cup buttermilk

1½ quarts peanut or vegetable oil for frying

1. Combine chicken and shio koji in 1-gallon zipper-lock bag. Press out excess air, seal, and massage bag to evenly distribute shio koji. Refrigerate chicken for at least 8 hours or up to 3 days.

2. Combine cornstarch, flour, koji, 2 teaspoons salt, 1 teaspoon pepper, and baking powder in blender and process on high speed until finely ground, about 2 minutes. Transfer koji mixture to large shallow dish. Whisk buttermilk, remaining 1 teaspoon salt, and remaining 1 teaspoon pepper in large bowl. Working with 3 pieces at a time, dunk chicken in buttermilk mixture, then dredge in flour mixture, pressing mixture onto chicken to form thick, even coating. Place chicken, skin side up, on wire rack set in rimmed baking sheet. Refrigerate, uncovered, for at least 1½ hours or up to 24 hours.

3. Adjust oven rack to middle position and heat oven to 350 degrees. Set second wire rack in second rimmed baking sheet. Meanwhile, heat oil in large Dutch oven over medium-high heat to 375 degrees. Place half of chicken in oil, reduce heat to medium, and fry until first side is deep golden brown, 2 to 3 minutes. Flip chicken and continue to fry until second side is deep golden brown, 2 to 3 minutes longer. (Adjust heat as necessary to maintain oil temperature around 300 degrees.) Transfer chicken to clean wire rack. Return oil to 375 degrees and repeat with remaining chicken.

4. Bake chicken until breasts register 160 degrees and thighs/drumsticks register 170 degrees, 10 to 20 minutes, transferring pieces to platter as they reach correct temperature. Season chicken with salt to taste, and serve.

KEYS TO SUCCESS

- **Double koji:** Using a shio koji marinade and dry koji in the coating yields supersavory chicken.

- **Double cooking:** To prevent the sugar-rich koji from burning, fry the chicken just until brown and then finish cooking it in the oven.

KOJI TURKEY

Serves: 10 to 12
Total Time: 2½ hours, plus 12 hours brining

RECIPE OVERVIEW The tenderizing, flavor-enhancing properties of shio koji make it a natural treatment for turkey, and it's easily incorporated into a brine, along with sugar and salt. Using a turkey breast and two leg quarters saves space while brining and also simplifies cooking (you can remove the separate pieces from the oven as they come to temperature). A coat of shio koji–spiked butter, brushed on at the end of cooking, gives the turkey skin a burnished appearance and adds even more savory-sweet flavor. To take advantage of all the amazing koji-fied turkey drippings, we cook the turkey parts on a bed of potatoes, carrots, and shallots; the vegetables continue to roast and brown while the turkey rests. Shio koji takes at least a week to make, so start it well in advance of when you plan to make this recipe. We prefer the flavor of our homemade shio koji, but if time is short you can purchase ready-made shio koji. We call for one whole bone-in turkey breast, also known as a turkey crown, and two turkey leg quarters (thigh and drumstick attached), but you can also buy a 12- to 14-pound whole turkey and butcher it yourself into these same parts.

2	cups Shio Koji (page 436)
1½	cups sugar for brining
1½	cups kosher salt for brining
1	(6- to 7-pound) bone-in whole turkey breast, trimmed
2	(1½- to 1¾-pound) turkey leg quarters
2	pounds small red potatoes, quartered
1	pound carrots, peeled and sliced on bias 2 inches thick
10	shallots, peeled and halved
3	tablespoons vegetable oil, divided
1	teaspoon kosher salt
¾	teaspoon pepper, divided
1	bunch thyme sprigs
3	tablespoons unsalted butter, melted

1. Process shio koji in blender until smooth, about 30 seconds. Reserve 3 tablespoons blended shio koji in airtight container in refrigerator. Transfer remaining blended shio koji to large stockpot or large plastic container and whisk in 4 quarts water, sugar, and 1½ cups salt until dissolved. Add turkey parts to brine, cover, and refrigerate for at least 12 hours or up to 16 hours.

2. Remove turkey parts from brine and pat dry with paper towels; set aside at room temperature. Adjust oven rack to lower-middle position and heat oven to 400 degrees. Line rimmed baking sheet with aluminum foil.

3. Toss potatoes, carrots, shallots, 2 tablespoons oil, salt, and 2 tablespoons reserved shio koji in large bowl to combine. Sprinkle with ¼ teaspoon pepper. Arrange vegetables on prepared sheet and top with wire rack (rack will rest on vegetables). Arrange thyme sprigs in single layer on rack. Whisk melted butter and remaining 1 tablespoon shio koji until combined; set aside.

4. Place turkey parts on prepared rack, skin side up, and brush skin with remaining 1 tablespoon oil. Sprinkle with remaining ½ teaspoon pepper and cover loosely with foil. Roast for 30 minutes. Remove foil and continue to roast for 25 minutes. Rotate sheet, brush skin with shio koji–butter mixture (if butter mixture has solidified, reheat in microwave for 10 to 20 seconds), and roast until breast registers 155 degrees and thighs register 170 degrees, 25 to 45 minutes, removing pieces as they come to temperature. (If any portions of the turkey skin are browning too rapidly, re-cover them with foil.) Increase oven temperature to 450 degrees.

5. Transfer turkey to carving board, tent with foil, and let rest for 30 minutes. Remove rack and continue to roast vegetables until vegetables are tender and potatoes are spotty brown, about 30 minutes, stirring halfway through. Transfer vegetables to serving bowl. Carve turkey and transfer to serving platter. Serve.

KEYS TO SUCCESS

- **Brine:** Although shio koji is savory and sweet, you still need salt and sugar in the brine for the proper level of seasoning.

- **Butter:** Blending shio koji into the butter that you brush on the turkey parts makes for next-level crispy, savory skin.

UNFORGETTABLE TURKEY

DAN ZUCCARELLO

A bronzed and tender roast turkey is a classic thing of beauty, and many cooks never venture beyond this traditional version. But expand your turkey cooking repertoire and you'll be handsomely rewarded with celebratory meals that really up the "wow" factor. In this course you'll learn how to roll and stuff a turkey breast porchetta-style and confit a batch of rich-tasting thighs. We also cover using your charcoal grill to produce moist turkey with a delicately smoky accent, and take the ultimate plunge for rave-worthy deep-fried turkey.

DAN'S PRO TIP: *It's important to keep your ball of kitchen twine away from raw food to prevent cross contamination when tying and trussing items like turkey. I like to place the twine on the handle of a spoon or in a small bowl to prevent contamination of the entire spool.*

PORCHETTA-STYLE TURKEY BREAST

Serves: 6 to 8
Total Time: 3½ hours, plus 8 hours salting

RECIPE OVERVIEW Turkey porchetta, or turchetta, is a flavor-packed, visually impressive turkey breast preparation that takes its name, shape, and seasonings from the iconic Italian pork roast called porchetta. After deboning a crown roast (better than starting with a boneless turkey breast, since doing the butchery yourself guarantees that the skin and meat are intact), we toss the breast halves and tenderloins with a rosemary-scented herb-spice paste. When the meat is wrapped in the skin into a cylinder, the paste is evenly swirled throughout, lending each slice attractive marbling and loads of flavor. For rich, colorful flavor development, we salt the exterior of the roast so that it dries out as it rests in the fridge and brush melted butter over the surface just before cooking. Refrigerating the assembled roast for 8 hours (or up to two days) before cooking allows the salt in the paste to migrate into the meat, seasoning it and helping it retain its juices during cooking. Starting the roast in a low oven and pulling it out 15 degrees shy of the target temperature (160 degrees) means that carryover cooking can gradually raise its internal temperature so that it doesn't overshoot the mark. Briefly blasting the roast at 500 degrees deepens its color. We prefer a natural turkey breast here; if you're using a self-basting breast (such as Butterball) or kosher breast, omit the 4 teaspoons of salt in the herb paste. This recipe was developed using Diamond Crystal Kosher Salt; if you're using Morton Kosher Salt, which is denser, use 1 tablespoon in the herb paste and 1½ teaspoons on the exterior of the roast.

1 tablespoon fennel seeds
2 teaspoons black peppercorns
¼ cup fresh rosemary leaves, chopped
¼ cup fresh sage leaves, chopped
¼ cup fresh thyme leaves
6 garlic cloves, chopped
2 tablespoons kosher salt, divided
3 tablespoons extra-virgin olive oil
1 (7- to 8-pound) bone-in turkey breast
2 tablespoons unsalted butter, melted

1. Grind fennel seeds and peppercorns using spice grinder or mortar and pestle until finely ground. Transfer to food processor and add rosemary, sage, thyme, garlic, and 4 teaspoons salt. Pulse mixture until finely chopped, 15 to 20 pulses, scraping down sides of bowl as needed. Add oil and process until paste forms, 20 to 30 seconds. Cut seven 16-inch lengths and one 30-inch length of kitchen twine and set aside. Measure out 20-inch piece of aluminum foil and crumple into loose ball. Uncrumple foil and place on rimmed baking sheet (crinkled foil will insulate bottom of sheet and minimize smoking during final roasting step). Spray wire rack with vegetable oil spray and place on prepared sheet.

Assembling Turchetta

Almost all the hands-on work for turchetta happens up front—and is worth the effort.

CUT THROUGH RIBS
To remove back, place turkey breast skin side down on cutting board. Using kitchen shears, cut through ribs, following vertical lines of fat where breast meets back, from tapered ends of breast to wing joints.

POP JOINTS
Using your hands, bend back away from breast to pop shoulder joints out of sockets.

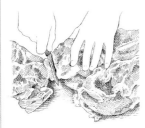

SEPARATE BACK
Using paring knife, cut through joints between bones to separate back from breast.

REMOVE SKIN
Flip breast skin side up. Starting at tapered side of breast and using your fingers to separate skin from meat, peel skin off breast meat and reserve.

REMOVE BREASTS
Using tip of chef's knife or boning knife, cut along rib cage to remove each breast half completely.

REMOVE TENDERLOINS
Reserve bones for making stock, or discard. Peel tenderloins from underside of each breast.

SLICE BREASTS
Lay 1 breast half on cutting board, smooth side down and with narrow end pointing toward your knife hand. Slice into breast starting where breast becomes thicker (about halfway along length). Stop ½ inch from edge of breast and open to create 1 long piece of even thickness. Repeat with remaining breast half.

LAY BREASTS ON SKIN
Pat exterior of skin dry and lay flat, exterior side down, with long side running parallel to counter. Lay 1 breast half on 1 side of skin with butterflied end closest to you. Lay second breast half next to first with butterflied end farthest away from you. Spread breast halves slightly apart and lay tenderloins between them with their thin ends overlapping in center.

TIE SKIN SHUT
Using skin as aid, fold up each breast half over tenderloins so skin meets directly over tenderloins. Slip one 16-inch length of twine under roast about 2 inches from 1 end and tie into simple knot, pinching skin closed as you tighten. Repeat tying at opposite end. Tie remaining five 16-inch lengths of twine evenly between 2 end pieces. Trim excess twine.

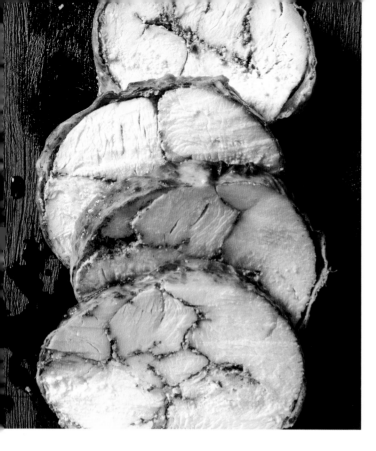

6. Using skin as aid, fold up each breast half over tenderloins so skin meets directly over tenderloins. Slip one 16-inch length of twine under roast about 2 inches from 1 end and tie into simple knot, pinching skin closed as you tighten. Repeat tying at opposite end. Tie remaining five 16-inch lengths of twine evenly between 2 end pieces. Trim excess twine.

7. Tie 1 end of 30-inch length of twine onto loop farthest from you. Working toward you, loop twine over top and around each successive strand until you get to bottom of roast. Flip roast and continue looping to bottom of roast. Flip roast again and tie off where you started. Sprinkle roast evenly with remaining 2 teaspoons salt and place on prepared rack. Refrigerate, uncovered, for at least 8 hours or up to 2 days.

8. Adjust oven rack to upper-middle position and heat oven to 275 degrees. Brush roast with melted butter. Cook until thickest part of roast registers 125 degrees, 1 ½ to 1 ¾ hours. Remove roast from oven and increase oven temperature to 500 degrees. When oven is up to temperature, remove twine from roast; return roast to oven; and cook until skin is browned and roast registers 145 degrees, 15 to 20 minutes.

9. Transfer roast to cutting board, tent with foil, and let rest for 30 minutes. Slice ½ inch thick and serve.

KEYS TO SUCCESS

- **Toss with herb-spice paste:** Tossing the turkey with the paste rather than spreading it over one side ensures that the paste is evenly swirled throughout the roast.

- **Let meat rest:** The salt in the paste migrates into the meat, seasoning it and helping it retain its juices.

- **Salt and butter the exterior:** Salt dries out the skin while it rests, and brushing with melted butter leads to rich, flavorful color.

Give It a Good, Long Rest

Don't be tempted to shortchange the turkey's half-hour sojourn on the counter at the end of cooking. The roast comes out of the oven when it is 15 degrees shy of its target temperature (160 degrees), and this time is built into the recipe to take advantage of the carryover cooking that inevitably occurs as the meat rests. Heat from the roast's surface will gradually migrate to its middle, raising its temperature until it hits the mark but doesn't exceed it.

2. To remove back, place turkey breast skin side down on cutting board. Using kitchen shears, cut through ribs, following vertical lines of fat where breast meets back, from tapered ends of breast to wing joints. Using your hands, bend back away from breast to pop shoulder joints out of sockets. Using paring knife, cut through joints between bones to separate back from breast.

3. Flip breast skin side up. Starting at tapered side of breast and using your fingers to separate skin from meat, peel skin off breast meat and reserve. Using tip of chef's knife or boning knife, cut along rib cage to remove each breast half completely. Reserve bones for making stock, or discard. Peel tenderloins from underside of each breast and use knife to remove exposed part of white tendon from each tenderloin.

4. Lay 1 breast half on cutting board, smooth side down and with narrow end pointing toward your knife hand. Holding knife parallel to cutting board, slice into breast starting where breast becomes thicker (about halfway along length). Stop ½ inch from edge of breast and open to create 1 long piece of even thickness. Repeat with remaining breast half. Transfer all meat to large bowl. Add herb paste and massage into meat to coat evenly.

5. Pat exterior of skin dry with paper towels and lay flat, exterior side down, on cutting board with long side running parallel to counter. Remove any loose pieces of fat. Lay 1 breast half on 1 side of skin with butterflied end closest to you. Lay second breast half next to first with butterflied end farthest away from you. Spread breast halves slightly apart and lay tenderloins between them with their thin ends overlapping in center.

TURKEY THIGH CONFIT WITH CITRUS-MUSTARD SAUCE

Serves: 6 to 8
Total Time: 5½ hours, plus 4 days salting

RECIPE OVERVIEW Before refrigeration, confit was a simple and effective way to prolong the shelf life of foods, including duck and goose parts. The poultry was cured in salt and then gently poached in its own fat before being buried beneath the fat and stored in an airtight crock. At serving time, all that was needed was a blast of heat to crisp the skin. This silky, supple turkey version starts with processing onion, salt, pepper, sugar, and thyme in a food processor. The turkey thighs are coated in this paste and left to cure in the refrigerator; as they sit, the salt, sugar, and some water-soluble compounds in the aromatics give the turkey a deeply savory flavor. After four to six days, you rinse away the cure and oven-poach the thighs in duck fat until tender. The thighs can then be refrigerated for up to six days or immediately browned and served with a bright and tangy citrus-mustard sauce. Start this recipe at least five days or up to 12 days before serving (almost all the time is hands-off). The proper measurement of salt is crucial here. Be sure to use table salt, not kosher salt, and measure it carefully. To ensure proper seasoning, make sure that the total weight of the turkey is within 2 ounces of the 4-pound target weight; do not use enhanced or kosher turkey thighs. Though duck fat is traditional, we found that chicken fat or even vegetable oil also works nicely. Reserve the remaining stock and the duck fat or chicken fat in step 5 for further use; used vegetable oil should be discarded. It is convenient to split up the cooking over several days, but if you prefer to do all the cooking in one day, go straight from step 2 to step 5 without letting the turkey cool.

3	large onions, chopped coarse (4¾ cups)
12	sprigs fresh thyme
2½	tablespoons table salt for curing
1½	tablespoons sugar
1½	teaspoons pepper
4	pounds bone-in turkey thighs
6	cups duck fat, chicken fat, or vegetable oil for confit
1	garlic head, halved crosswise
2	bay leaves
½	cup orange marmalade
2	tablespoons whole-grain mustard
¾	teaspoon grated lime zest plus 2 tablespoons juice
¼	teaspoon table salt
⅛	teaspoon cayenne pepper

1. TO CURE Process onions, thyme sprigs, 2½ table-spoons salt, sugar, and pepper in food processor until finely chopped, about 20 seconds, scraping down sides of bowl as needed. Spread one-third of mixture evenly in bottom of 13 by 9-inch baking dish. Arrange turkey thighs, skin side up, in single layer in dish. Spread remaining onion mixture evenly over thighs. Wrap dish tightly with plastic wrap and refrigerate for 4 to 6 days (whatever is most convenient).

2. TO COOK Adjust oven rack to lower-middle position and heat oven to 200 degrees. Remove thighs from onion mixture and rinse well (if you don't have a garbage disposal, do not allow onion pieces to go down drain). Pat thighs dry with paper towels. Heat fat in large Dutch oven over medium heat to 165 degrees. Off heat, add turkey thighs, skin side down and in single layer, making sure thighs are completely submerged. Add garlic and bay leaves. Transfer to oven, uncovered, and cook until metal skewer inserted straight down into thickest part of largest thigh can be easily removed without lifting thigh, 4 to 5 hours. (To ensure that oven temperature remains steady, wait at least 20 minutes before retesting if turkey is not done.) Remove from oven.

3. TO MAKE AHEAD Let turkey cool completely in pot, about 2 hours; cover pot and refrigerate for up to 6 days.

4. TO SERVE Uncover pot. Heat pot over medium-low heat until fat is melted, about 25 minutes. Increase heat to medium, maintaining bare simmer, and continue to cook until thickest part of largest thigh registers 135 to 140 degrees, about 30 minutes longer. (If turkey has been cooked in vegetable oil, heat pot over medium heat, maintaining bare simmer, until thickest part of largest thigh registers 135 to 140 degrees, about 30 minutes.)

5. Adjust oven rack to lower-middle position and heat oven to 500 degrees. While oven heats, crumple 20-inch length of aluminum foil into loose ball. Uncrumple foil, place in rimmed baking sheet, and top with wire rack. Using tongs, gently transfer thighs, skin side up, to prepared wire

CORE TECHNIQUE
Carving Turkey Thighs

EXPOSE THIGHBONE
Place thigh skin side down. Using tip of paring knife, cut along sides of thighbone, exposing bone.

REMOVE THIGHBONE
Carefully remove bone and any stray bits of cartilage. Flip thigh skin side up.

SLICE MEAT
Using sharp chef's knife, slice thigh crosswise ¾ inch thick.

rack, being careful not to tear delicate skin. Set aside. Strain liquid through fine-mesh strainer into large bowl. Working in batches, pour liquid into fat separator, letting liquid settle for 5 minutes before separating fat from turkey stock. (Alternatively, use bulb baster to extract turkey stock from beneath fat.) Transfer 4 teaspoons turkey stock to small bowl, add marmalade, and microwave until mixture is fluid, about 30 seconds. Stir in mustard, lime zest and juice, salt, and cayenne. Transfer to serving bowl.

6. Transfer thighs to oven and roast until well browned, 12 to 15 minutes. Transfer thighs to cutting board, skin side up, and let rest until just cool enough to handle, about 15 minutes.

7. Flip 1 thigh skin side down. Using tip of paring knife, cut along sides of thighbone, exposing bone. Carefully remove bone and any stray bits of cartilage. Flip thigh skin side up. Using sharp chef's knife, slice thigh crosswise ¾ inch thick. Transfer to serving platter, skin side up. Repeat with remaining thighs. Serve, passing sauce separately.

Confit at a Glance

One more reason to love turkey confit is its terrific make-ahead potential. The process takes at least five days, but almost all the preparation time is unattended.

Cure
Salt turkey (along with aromatics) for 4 to 6 days.

Cook
Oven-poach turkey in fat for 4 to 5 hours.

Hold
Refrigerate for up to 6 days.
(This step can be skipped.)

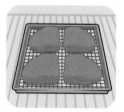

Brown
Warm through on stovetop, then brown in hot oven.

SOUS VIDE TURKEY THIGH CONFIT WITH CITRUS-MUSTARD SAUCE
Serves: 6 to 8
Total Time: 17½ hours, plus 4 days salting

Confit is well suited to sous vide cooking: You need only 1 cup of fat or oil instead of the 6 cups required for the oven method; it allows you to precisely control the cooking temperature; and as with traditional confit, the timing is flexible. Start this recipe at least five days or up to 12 days before serving (almost all the time is hands-off). We double-bag the turkey thighs to protect against seam failure, so you will need four 1-gallon zipper-lock freezer bags. If preferred, use a vacuum sealer and skip the double-bagging. This recipe calls for the same ingredients as Turkey Thigh Confit with Citrus-Mustard Sauce, with two exceptions: You need only 1 cup of fat or oil and ½ teaspoon of granulated garlic instead of a head of garlic.

1. Follow recipe for Turkey Thigh Confit with Citrus-Mustard Sauce through step 1.

2. Using sous vide circulator, bring 4 inches (about 6 quarts) water to 158 degrees in 12-quart stockpot or similar-size heatproof container. Remove thighs from onion mixture and rinse well (if you don't have a garbage disposal, do not allow onion pieces to go down drain). Pat thighs dry with paper towels. Fold back top of 1-gallon zipper-lock freezer bag. Place 2 thighs skin side up in single layer in bag. Add ½ cup fat, ¼ teaspoon granulated garlic, and 1 bay leaf. Seal bag, pressing out as much air as possible. Gently lower into prepared water bath until thighs are fully submerged, allowing air bubbles to rise to top of bag. Open 1 corner of zipper, release air bubbles, and reseal bag. Repeat bagging and resealing with second zipper-lock bag and remaining thighs, ½ cup fat, ¼ teaspoon granulated garlic, and bay leaf.

3. Seal each bag inside separate 1-gallon zipper-lock freezer bag. Gently lower 1 bag into prepared water bath until thighs are fully submerged, then clip top corner of bag to side of container, allowing remaining air bubbles to rise to top of bag. Open 1 corner of zipper of outer bag, release air bubbles, and reseal bag. Repeat with second bag. Cover container with plastic wrap and cook for at least 16 hours or up to 20 hours. Remove bags from water bath and let cool completely, about 1 hour. Refrigerate, still double-bagged, for up to 6 days.

4. TO SERVE Using sous vide circulator, bring 4 inches (about 6 quarts) water to 140 degrees in 12-quart stockpot or similar-size heatproof container. Fully submerge each bag in water bath, cover container with plastic, and cook for at least 1½ hours.

5. Continue with recipe for Turkey Thigh Confit with Citrus-Mustard Sauce from step 5.

- **Coat thighs with seasoning:** As the thighs sit, flavors permeate the meat. Salt helps them to hold on to moisture and gives them a firm, dense texture.

- **Gently poach:** Poaching in a 200-degree oven produces moist and meltingly tender meat.

- **Minimal work on serving day:** The confit can be prepared up to 12 days in advance.

- **Easy sauce:** The bright and zesty sauce complements the richness of the turkey.

Checking for Doneness

Don't wait until the meat is falling off the bone, which is an indication that it's overdone. Instead, gauge the turkey's doneness by inserting a metal skewer straight into the thickest part of the largest thigh. If the skewer can be easily removed without lifting the thigh with it, the meat is ready.

HOLIDAY SMOKED TURKEY

Serves: 10 to 12
Total Time: 4¾ hours, plus 30 minutes resting

RECIPE OVERVIEW Smoking a turkey is a pro holiday move. When done well, barbecuing keeps the relatively lean meat moist and juicy, and smoke adds a lot of flavor. This recipe is inspired by James Beard Award–winning pit master Rodney Scott and adapted from his book, *Rodney Scott's World of BBQ* (2021). It starts with a spatchcocked turkey, meaning the backbone is removed and the bird is laid out flat, so it cooks more evenly. While Scott's recipe was designed for a ceramic smoker, ours works in a kettle charcoal grill. We arrange the coals in a C shape around the perimeter of the bottom of the grill, a setup known as the charcoal snake. Lighting both sides of the snake allows the coals to slowly ignite in succession for a nice low, long burn from two directions, helping the spatchcocked turkey cook evenly. Wood chunks added on top of the charcoal provide bursts of smoke throughout cooking. Use a probe thermometer to determine when the breast hits 160 degrees, at which point you'll remove the turkey from the grill so that the meat doesn't dry out and the skin stays beautifully bronzed and not too dark. We developed this recipe using a 22-inch kettle charcoal grill. We recommend reading the entire recipe before starting. You can reserve the turkey neck and giblets for making gravy, if desired.

Mop
2 cups distilled white vinegar
¼ cup granulated sugar
2 thin lemon slices
1 tablespoon pepper
2 teaspoons cayenne pepper
½ teaspoon red pepper flakes

Rub
2 tablespoons kosher salt
1 tablespoon monosodium glutamate
1 tablespoon pepper
1 tablespoon paprika
1 tablespoon chili powder
1 tablespoon packed light brown sugar
1½ teaspoons garlic powder
1½ teaspoons onion powder
¼ teaspoon cayenne pepper

Turkey
1 (12- to 14-pound) turkey, neck and giblets discarded, spatchcocked
4 (3-inch) wood chunks
1 (13 by 9-inch) disposable aluminum pan

1. **FOR THE MOP** Combine all ingredients in medium saucepan and bring to simmer over medium-high heat. Cook until sugar is dissolved, about 2 minutes. Remove from heat and let cool completely. Discard lemon slices. (Mop can be refrigerated in airtight container for up to 2 months.)

2. **FOR THE RUB** Combine all ingredients in bowl.

3. **FOR THE TURKEY** Sprinkle rub all over both sides of turkey. Open bottom vent of charcoal grill completely. To make charcoal snake, arrange 50 charcoal briquettes, 2 briquettes wide, around perimeter of grill, overlapping slightly so briquettes are touching and leaving 9-inch gap between ends of snake. Place second layer of 50 briquettes, also 2 briquettes wide, on top of first. (Completed arrangement should be 2 briquettes wide by 2 briquettes high.)

4. Starting 2 inches from each end of charcoal snake, place wood chunks on top of charcoal about 2 inches apart. Slide disposable pan into charcoal gap, running lengthwise into arc of snake and touching grill wall on opposite side of snake. Pour 6 cups water into pan.

5. Light chimney starter filled with 20 briquettes (pile briquettes on 1 side of chimney so they catch). When coals are partially covered with ash, use tongs to pile 10 coals on each end of charcoal snake, where briquettes meet water pan, so both ends of snake ignite.

6. Set cooking grate in place, then clean and oil grate. Position turkey, skin side down, over water pan, with drumsticks pointing toward arc in charcoal snake. Cover grill, position lid vent over turkey, and open lid vent completely. Cook, undisturbed, for 2 hours.

7. Using small barbecue mop or basting brush, baste turkey liberally with mop. Using oven mitts or grill mitts, flip turkey skin side up, again positioning it over water pan with drumsticks pointing toward arc in charcoal snake. Baste skin side liberally with more mop (you may not need all of it; discard any extra).

8. Insert temperature probe into thickest part of breast. Cover grill and cook until breast registers 160 degrees (check temperature of both sides of breast) and thighs register 175 degrees, about 1 hour.

9. Transfer turkey to rimmed baking sheet. Let rest for 30 to 40 minutes. Carve turkey and transfer to serving platter. Serve.

KEYS TO SUCCESS

- **Spatchcock the turkey:** The flatter shape makes grilling the large bird much easier.

- **Make a snake:** Arranging the charcoal in a C shape around the grill creates a long, slow burn for even cooking.

Spatchcocking a Turkey

REMOVE BACKBONE
Use shears or cleaver to remove backbone from turkey; flip turkey over.

FLATTEN BIRD
Use heels of your palms to flatten turkey; apply rub and start smoking.

Grill Setup for Smoked Turkey

This "two-headed snake" (you light both ends simultaneously) provides hours of heat and smoke to gently cook and flavor the turkey.

SNAKE CONSTRUCTION
Two briquettes wide by two briquettes high

WOOD CHUNK PLACEMENT
About 2 inches apart for consistent smoke

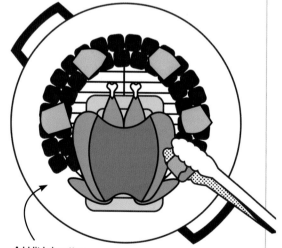

Add lit briquettes
to both ends.

TURKEY PLACEMENT
Skin side down over water pan, with drumsticks
pointing toward arc in charcoal snake

DEEP-FRIED TURKEY

Serves: 10 to 12
Total Time: 2½ hours, plus 13½ hours cooling, chilling, and resting

RECIPE OVERVIEW Fried turkey enthusiasts utter a common refrain: "It's the best turkey I've ever had." They rave about how deep frying produces beautifully browned skin and juicy meat. If you've never eaten a deep-fried turkey, you need to try it for yourself to understand. For guaranteed juiciness, make an ultratasty injected marinade of garlicky herb butter. To this mixture, add chicken broth, puree it all in the blender, and pour it through a fine-mesh strainer to ensure that the marinade is thin enough to keep from clogging up the injector. After letting the marinade cool, shoot it throughout the turkey, moving the needle around in each spot to make sure it's well distributed in the breast, legs, and wings. Then season the skin, truss the legs and the wings close to the bird, and place the turkey breast side up on the vertical turkey rack to keep the legs closer to the heat source and ensure that they cook to a higher temperature than the white meat. Fry at 300 degrees until the skin is browned and crisp and the breast registers 150 degrees. We developed this recipe with the Bayou Classic Stainless Steel 32-Quart Turkey Fryer and Gas One High Pressure Burner. If using a different turkey fryer, follow the manufacturer's instructions for determining the appropriate amount of frying oil. Many turkey fryers come with meat injectors, but if yours doesn't, you can often buy one online or at cooking supply stores. We used Butterball turkeys, but you can substitute another brand of prebrined or "self-basting" turkey if desired. Most supermarket turkeys are prebrined. To be sure, look for a label indicating that the turkey includes a percentage of salt solution. We suggest serving this fried turkey with our Cranberry Chimichurri (recipe follows), a lighter, brighter alternative to gravy.

Garlic-Herb Browned Butter Injection

6	garlic cloves, minced
4	teaspoons fresh thyme leaves
4	teaspoons chopped fresh sage
1	tablespoon chopped fresh rosemary
1	tablespoon kosher salt
2	teaspoons pepper
16	tablespoons unsalted butter
1	cup chicken broth

Turkey

1	tablespoon kosher salt
1	tablespoon light brown sugar
2	teaspoons pepper
1	(12- to 14-pound) prebrined turkey, giblets discarded
2	tablespoons peanut or vegetable oil
3½–4	gallons peanut or vegetable oil for frying

1. FOR THE GARLIC-HERB BROWNED BUTTER INJECTION Combine garlic, thyme, sage, rosemary, salt, and pepper in bowl. Melt butter in medium saucepan over medium-high heat. Continue to cook, stirring and scraping bottom of pan with heat-resistant spatula, until milk solids are dark golden brown and butter has nutty aroma, 2 to 5 minutes longer. Off heat, stir in garlic-herb mixture and cook for 30 seconds (mixture will bubble up). Stir in broth.

2. Transfer butter mixture to blender and blend until completely uniform and emulsified, about 2 minutes, scraping down sides of blender jar halfway through blending. Strain through fine-mesh strainer into 2-cup liquid measuring cup, pressing on solids to extract liquid. Set aside to cool for at least 1 hour or up to 3 hours.

3. FOR THE TURKEY Combine salt, sugar, and pepper in small bowl; set aside. Set wire rack in rimmed baking sheet. Pat turkey dry inside and out with paper towels. Place turkey breast side up on prepared rack. Using kitchen shears, remove all excess skin and fat around neck, making sure opening around neck is clear, and remove tail.

4. Stir reserved garlic-herb browned butter to recombine. Using marinade injector, inject each turkey breast in 3 places, working needle around in each injection site to distribute marinade throughout breast (using about 4 ounces marinade in each breast). Inject each drumstick in 3 places, aiming to inject meatiest parts of drumsticks (using about 1½ ounces marinade in each drumstick). Inject each thigh in 3 places, aiming to inject meatiest parts of thighs (using about 1½ ounces in each thigh). Inject wings in flat and drumette with remaining marinade. Using paper towels, wipe any marinade from exterior of turkey.

5. Rub turkey with 2 tablespoons oil and rub all over with reserved salt mixture. Tie legs together with butcher's twine. Tuck wings behind back and tie wings tightly to sides of turkey by tying single loop of twine around turkey at midline of breast. Refrigerate turkey for at least 12 hours or up to 24 hours.

6. Add enough oil to turkey fryer to reach max fill line and attach clip-on thermometer, making sure tip of thermometer is submerged in oil. When ready to light turkey fryer, bring turkey outdoors and arrange breast side up on vertical turkey rack. Insert temperature probe parallel to breast bone into thickest part of breast. Light turkey fryer and heat oil to 325 degrees over high heat.

7. When oil reaches 325 degrees, turn off heat to fryer and remove clip-on thermometer. Wearing protective grilling glove or oven mitt, very slowly lower turkey into hot oil until submerged. (Oil will bubble rapidly and very top of breast may remain exposed; this is OK). Return clip-on thermometer and return heat to high. Fry turkey until breast registers 150 degrees, adjusting heat as necessary to keep oil temperature between 300 and 315 and degrees, 35 to 50 minutes. If temperature probe reads 150 degrees before 35 minutes, tip of probe is likely not in thickest part of breast; remove bird, adjust probe, and continue to cook.

8. Turn off heat and remove clip-on thermometer. Carefully lift turkey, allowing excess oil to drip back into fryer, and transfer to clean rimmed baking sheet. Use instant-read thermometer to double check for temperature of at least 150 degrees in breast (if temperature is lower, return turkey to oil until lowest temperature you can find is 150 degrees). Leaving temperature probe in breast, bring turkey inside on vertical rack and monitor temperature until it reaches at least 160 degrees, 10 to 20 minutes.

9. Continue to let rest until cool enough to handle, about 20 minutes longer. Carve and serve.

CRANBERRY CHIMICHURRI

Makes: about 1½ cups
Total Time: 20 minutes, plus 30 minutes resting

- ¾ cup dried cranberries, minced
- ½ cup chopped fresh cilantro leaves and stems
- ½ cup chopped fresh parsley
- ⅔ cup extra-virgin olive oil
- 3 tablespoons red wine vinegar
- 1 shallot, minced
- 3 garlic cloves, minced
- 1½ teaspoons dried oregano
- ½ teaspoon table salt
- ½ teaspoon red pepper flakes
- ¼ teaspoon pepper

Combine all ingredients in bowl and let sit for at least 30 minutes to allow flavors to meld before serving.

Deep Frying Turkey

TRIM NECK
Trim neck cavity of raw bird of excess fat: the oil has to be able to flow freely through there or bad things happen.

INJECT
Inject marinade in each breast half, each drumstick, and each thigh in 3 places, and inject wing flats and drumettes.

RUB
Rub turkey with 2 tablespoons oil and then with reserved salt mixture.

TIE LEGS AND WINGS
Tie legs together with butcher's twine; tuck wings behind back and tie tightly to sides of turkey.

PLACE TURKEY
Arrange turkey breast side up on vertical turkey rack. Insert temperature probe parallel to breast bone into thickest part of breast.

LOWER TURKEY
Wearing protective grilling glove or oven mitt, very slowly lower turkey into hot oil until submerged.

RESOURCES FOR TURKEY

There are three main types of turkeys for sale in supermarkets; which kind you buy is a matter of personal preference.

SELF-BASTING/ PREBRINED	KOSHER	NATURAL/ UNTREATED
These birds have been injected with a salt solution, so they don't need to be brined or salted in advance.	Kosher birds are salted and processed in accordance to strict Jewish practices; they don't need to be salted or brined.	These birds are minimally processed, so we recommend brining or salting them.

DEALING WITH THE USED OIL

Let the oil cool completely. Once it's cool enough to handle, use a large liquid measuring cup to ladle it out of the pot and into a funnel placed in the original container you've saved. If you're planning to use the oil again—and you can, up to eight times—filter it through a fine-mesh strainer lined with cheesecloth.

WHY YOU SHOULD INVEST IN DUCK FAT

Some confit recipes call for vegetable oil or chicken fat instead of duck fat; all three fats produce confits that brown beautifully and taste similar—even though the fats taste very different on their own. That's because the meat doesn't absorb fat during the confit process; it emerges with just a bare coating on its surface. But we still recommend using duck fat if you can swing it. Duck fat is particularly delicious and the leftover fat from confit can be strained, frozen, and reused in a variety of ways: as the fat for gravy or making more confit, to sauté vegetables, or to drizzle over a simple soup for depth.

WHAT MAKES CONFIT SO DARN GOOD?

Deep, Complex Flavor
During a four-day cure, water-soluble compounds in onions, fresh thyme, and black pepper make their way into the turkey, seasoning it to the bone.

Tender Meat
Melted fat heats the turkey gently, evenly, and efficiently, giving its collagen time to break down into gelatin and turning the meat remarkably tender.

Moist, Firm, Dense Texture
Little water escapes during cooking, so the turkey stays moist. In addition, chloride ions from the salt push the muscle fibers apart from each other, causing them to draw in and retain moisture. After a while, the chloride also starts to denature and "cook" some of the proteins, giving the meat the satisfying firm, dense texture that is a hallmark of confit.

SAFETY TIPS FOR FRYING TURKEY

Here are a few pointers to ensure safe frying.

Watch the weather
It's best not to fry when it's raining, snowing, or windy.

Look up
Make sure there are no tree limbs, awnings, etc., overhead.

Keep clear
Set up the fryer in a stable, level area 10 feet away from buildings and leave 2 feet between the tank and the burner. Keep children and pets away.

Check for leaks
Check that all junctions connecting the tank to the fryer are secure and free from leaks.

Measure oil first
Overfilling the frying pot can cause oil to run into the flames.

Thaw turkey fully
Oil and water—even frozen water—don't mix; a partially frozen bird can cause oil to shoot out of the pot.

Mind the flame
Keep the burner centered under the pot so the flames don't touch any overflowing oil. And turn the burner off when putting the turkey in and taking it out.

Go slow
Lower and raise the turkey slowly—it will bubble vigorously when it first goes in—and use grill gloves to hold the hook.

COURSE

DUCK DEMYSTIFIED

KEITH DRESSER

To love duck is to understand its uniqueness: It's all dark meat, since both the breast and leg portions are well-exercised muscles with ample fat, and it's imbued with a sultry, bass-note richness that chicken and turkey just don't have. Duck is often eaten rare (like beef). The duck's breast is also relatively flat, which enables its skin to brown remarkably evenly, and it's versatile for entertaining. Here's the catch: The qualities that make duck special to eat also make it a challenge to cook well. The recipes in this course will give you the know-how and confidence to cook restaurant-quality duck at home.

KEITH'S PRO TIP: *Duck fat is phenomenal in cooking, so when prepping duck make sure to save all the trimmings and slowly render them over low heat until the fat has melted. Duck fat will keep for months in the refrigerator or freezer. Use it in place of butter or other fats to flavor everything from potatoes and vegetables to soups and stews.*

DUCK BREAST SALAD WITH BLACKBERRIES AND QUICK-PICKLED FENNEL

Serves: 4
Total Time: 50 minutes

RECIPE OVERVIEW Some pairings are so perfect that they become classics. This dinner party–worthy salad is based on one such pairing: duck and orange. It stars two duck breasts, which we cook slowly in a skillet skin side down to render the fat and create a perfectly crispy cap of skin covering succulent, rosy meat. Lacy, delicately bitter frisée and soft and peppery baby watercress stand up to the duck's substantial presence. The sweet acidity of oranges cuts through the duck's richness. This salad uses them in two ways: sliced into sweet, juicy triangles as well as juiced for a punchy orange-ginger vinaigrette. Blackberries add visual interest and pops of sweetness. Last, quick pickled fennel is an easy yet complexly flavored addition that adds crunch, subtle anise notes, and vinegary tartness. If you use mature watercress, trim its thicker, woodier stems before using and tear the leaves into bite-size pieces.

- 2 (8- to 10-ounce) boneless split duck breasts, trimmed
- ¼ teaspoon table salt
- ¼ teaspoon pepper
- 2 oranges
- 6 ounces (1¼ cups) blackberries, halved
- ½ head frisée (3 ounces), torn into bite-size pieces
- 2 ounces (2 cups) baby watercress or baby arugula
- 1 cup Quick-Pickled Fennel (recipe follows)
- 6 tablespoons Orange-Ginger Vinaigrette (recipe follows), divided

1. Using sharp knife, cut slits ½ inch apart in crosshatch pattern in duck skin and fat cap, being careful not to cut into meat. Pat breasts dry with paper towels and sprinkle with salt and pepper.

2. Heat 12-inch skillet over medium heat for 3 minutes. Reduce heat to low, carefully place breasts skin side down in skillet, and cook until fat begins to render, about 5 minutes. Continue to cook, adjusting heat as needed for fat to maintain constant but gentle sizzle, until most of fat has rendered and skin is deep golden and crispy, 10 to 15 minutes.

3. Flip breasts skin side up and continue to cook until duck registers 120 to 125 degrees (for medium-rare), 2 to 5 minutes. Transfer breasts to cutting board and let rest while finishing salad.

4. Meanwhile, cut away peel and pith from oranges. Quarter oranges, then slice crosswise ¼ inch thick. Slice breasts ¼ inch thick. Gently toss oranges, blackberries, frisée, watercress, fennel, and ¼ cup vinaigrette in large bowl to combine. Divide among individual plates. Serve, topping individual portions with duck and drizzling with remaining 2 tablespoons vinaigrette.

QUICK-PICKLED FENNEL
Makes: 2 cups

- ¾ cup seasoned rice vinegar
- ¼ cup water
- 1 (1-inch) strip orange zest
- 1 garlic clove, peeled and halved
- ¼ teaspoon fennel seeds
- ⅛ teaspoon black peppercorns
- ⅛ teaspoon yellow mustard seeds
- 1 fennel bulb, stalks discarded, bulb halved, cored, and sliced thin

Combine vinegar, water, orange zest, garlic, fennel seeds, peppercorns, and mustard seeds in 4-cup liquid measuring cup. Microwave until boiling, about 3 minutes. Stir in fennel until completely submerged and let cool completely, about 30 minutes. Drain and serve. (Drained pickled fennel can be refrigerated for up to 6 weeks; fennel will soften significantly after 6 weeks.)

ORANGE-GINGER VINAIGRETTE
Makes: about 1 cup

To avoid off-flavors, reduce the juice in a nonreactive stainless-steel saucepan.

- 2 cups orange juice (4 oranges)
- 1 tablespoon honey
- 3 tablespoons lime juice (2 limes)
- 1 tablespoon minced shallot
- 1 teaspoon grated fresh ginger
- ½ teaspoon table salt
- ½ teaspoon pepper
- 2 tablespoons extra-virgin olive oil

Bring orange juice and honey to boil in small saucepan over medium-high heat. Reduce heat to maintain simmer and cook until mixture is thickened and measures about ⅔ cup, 15 to 20 minutes. Transfer syrup to medium bowl and refrigerate until cool, about 15 minutes. Whisk in lime juice, shallot, ginger, salt, and pepper until combined. Whisking constantly, slowly drizzle in oil until emulsified. Season with salt and pepper to taste. (Vinaigrette can be refrigerated for up to 1 week; whisk to recombine before using.)

KEYS TO SUCCESS

- **Low heat:** Keeping the heat low allows plenty of time for the duck's ample fat to render.

- **Plenty of orange:** Using both orange sections and orange juice provides a bright counterpoint to the duck's richness.

DUCK BREASTS WITH PORT WINE–FIG SAUCE
Serves: 4
Total Time: 50 minutes, plus 6 hours salting

RECIPE OVERVIEW In this elegant dinner, a simple sauce made of port wine, dried figs, vinegar, and sugar pairs perfectly with duck. Preparing duck breasts is really a straightforward process. You first trim away excess fat and any gristly bits and then double-check for bone fragments. Just like with many roasts, you score the skin in a crosshatch pattern to help the subcutaneous fat render and the skin crisp. The breasts are then salted, wrapped, and refrigerated for at least 6 hours to firm them up, help them retain moisture, and season them deeply. Starting the breasts skin side down in a cold skillet and then cooking them over medium heat is an efficient way to render the fat, crisp the skin, and cook the meat gently. After flipping the breasts and lowering the heat, finish cooking them to the desired temperature on the stovetop (we prefer medium-rare or medium). If you can find only duck breasts that weigh 10 to 12 ounces each, they will also work here. They tend to come with more excess fat; once it's trimmed away, the breasts will weigh closer to 8 or 9 ounces. You may need to cook these larger duck breasts about 1 minute longer on the second side to reach the desired temperature.

Duck
- 4 (7- to 8-ounce) boneless duck breasts
- 2 teaspoons kosher salt
- 1½ teaspoons pepper

Sauce

- ½ cup ruby port
- ¼ cup dried Black Mission figs, halved through stem
- ¼ cup red wine vinegar
- 3 tablespoons sugar

1. **FOR THE DUCK** Pat duck breasts dry with paper towels. Place breasts skin side down on cutting board. Using sharp knife, trim away excess fat around edges of breasts, then remove any visible silverskin attached to meat.

2. Flip breasts and cut ½-inch crosshatch pattern in fat, being careful not to cut into meat. Sprinkle all over with salt and pepper. Place duck on large plate skin side up, cover tightly with plastic wrap, and refrigerate for at least 6 hours or up to 24 hours.

3. **FOR THE SAUCE** Meanwhile, combine all ingredients in small saucepan. Bring to boil over medium heat and cook until reduced to about ½ cup, about 15 minutes; set aside off heat. Sauce will thicken to syrupy consistency as it cools. (Cooled sauce can be stored in airtight container for up to 3 days or refrigerated for up to 2 weeks.)

4. Place breasts skin side down in cold 12-inch nonstick skillet. Cook over medium heat until copious amount of fat has rendered and skin is well browned and crispy, 17 to 20 minutes.

5. Flip breasts skin side up and reduce heat to medium-low. Cook until centers of breasts register 125 to 130 degrees (for medium-rare), 1 to 2 minutes; 130 to 135 degrees (for medium), 3 to 4 minutes; 135 to 140 degrees (for medium-well), 4 to 5 minutes; or 145 to 150 degrees (for well-done), 7 to 8 minutes.

6. Transfer breasts to wire rack set in rimmed baking sheet. Tent with aluminum foil and let rest for 10 minutes.

7. Transfer duck to carving board and slice 1/4 inch thick. Serve with sauce.

KEYS TO SUCCESS

- **Crosshatch the skin:** The cuts create escape routes for the rendered fat, and the edges become appealingly crispy as the skin cooks.

- **Salt:** A long salting period improves the duck meat's texture and moistness as well as flavor.

CORE TECHNIQUE

Crosshatching Duck Skin

SHALLOW CUTS
When crosshatching duck skin, be sure not to cut through to meat.

WHOLE ROAST DUCK WITH CHERRY SAUCE

Serves: 4

Total Time: 3 hours, plus 6 hours salting

RECIPE OVERVIEW A whole roasted duck makes an impressive presentation, and a few easy techniques make it manageable. Begin by trimming the bird thoroughly of excess fat around the neck and cavity, and then scoring the skin extensively to create channels for rendered fat to escape. Salting the duck for at least 6 hours helps keep it juicy and thoroughly seasons the rich meat to highlight its full flavor. When it's time to cook, we give the tougher legs a head start by submerging the bottom half of the duck in water in a Dutch oven and vigorously simmering it on the stove until the leg quarters register 145 to 160 degrees. Meanwhile, because the breast doesn't have contact with the water, it cooks more slowly. Move the bird to a V-rack and finish it in the oven, glazing it first with a soy sauce–maple syrup glaze for deep browning. While the duck rests, we make a bright, fruity cherry sauce to accompany and balance the rich meat. Pekin ducks may also be labeled as Long Island ducks and are typically sold frozen. Thaw the ducks in the refrigerator for 24 hours. This recipe was developed with Diamond Crystal kosher salt. If using Morton kosher salt, use 25 percent less. Do not thaw the cherries before using. If desired, pulse the cherries in a food processor until coarsely chopped. In step 4, the uncrumpled aluminum foil prevents the rendered fat from smoking. Even when the duck is fully cooked, its juices will have a reddish hue.

Duck

- 1 (5½- to 6-pound) Pekin duck, neck and giblets reserved if making stock
- 2 tablespoons kosher salt, divided
- 1 tablespoon maple syrup
- 1½ teaspoons soy sauce

Cherry Sauce

- 3 tablespoons maple syrup
- 2 tablespoons red wine vinegar
- 2 teaspoons soy sauce
- 1 teaspoon cornstarch
- ¼ teaspoon pepper
- 1 sprig fresh thyme
- 9 ounces frozen sweet cherries, quartered

1. FOR THE DUCK Use your hands to remove large fat deposits from bottom of cavity. Using kitchen shears, trim excess neck skin from top of breast; remove tail and first 2 segments from each wing, leaving only drumette. Arrange duck breast side up. With tip of sharp knife, cut slits spaced ¾ inch apart in crosshatch pattern in skin and fat of breast, being careful not to cut into meat. Flip duck breast side down. Cut parallel slits spaced ¾ inch apart in skin and fat of each thigh (do not crosshatch).

2. Rub 2 teaspoons salt into cavity. Rub 1 teaspoon salt into breast, taking care to rub salt into slits. Rub remaining 1 tablespoon salt into skin of rest of duck. Align skin at bottom of cavity so 1 side overlaps other by at least ½ inch. Use sturdy toothpick to pin skin layers to each other to close cavity. Place duck on large plate and refrigerate uncovered for 6 to 12 hours.

3. Place duck breast side up in Dutch oven. Add water until at least half of thighs are submerged but most of breast remains above water, about 6 cups. Bring to boil over high heat. Reduce heat to maintain vigorous simmer. Cook, uncovered, until thermometer inserted into thickest part of drumstick, all the way to bone, registers 145 to 160 degrees, 45 minutes to 1 hour 5 minutes. After 20 minutes of cooking, adjust oven rack to lower-middle position and heat oven to 425 degrees. Stir maple syrup and soy sauce together in small bowl.

4. Remove pot from heat. Crumple 20-inch length of aluminum foil into loose ball. Uncrumple foil and place in roasting pan. Set V-rack on foil and spray with vegetable oil spray. Using tongs and spatula, lift duck from pot, allow liquid to drain, and transfer to V-rack, breast side up. Brush breast and top of drumsticks with approximately one-third of maple syrup mixture. Flip duck and brush remaining mixture over back and sides. Transfer braising liquid to large bowl to cool. (Once cool, defat liquid and reserve liquid and/or fat for another use, if desired.) Roast duck until back is golden brown and breast registers 140 to 150 degrees, about 20 minutes.

5. Remove roasting pan from oven. Using tongs and spatula, flip duck breast side up. Continue to roast until breast registers 160 to 165 degrees, 15 to 25 minutes longer. Transfer duck to carving board and let rest for 20 minutes.

6. FOR THE SAUCE Whisk maple syrup, vinegar, soy sauce, cornstarch, and pepper together in small saucepan. Add thyme sprig and bring to simmer over medium-high heat, stirring constantly with rubber spatula. Continue to cook, stirring constantly, until mixture thickens, about 2 minutes longer. Stir in cherries and cook, stirring occasionally, until sauce has consistency of maple syrup, 3 to 5 minutes. Discard thyme sprig and season sauce with salt and pepper to taste. Transfer to serving bowl. Carve duck and serve, passing sauce separately.

KEYS TO SUCCESS

- **Score and salt:** Scoring lets excess fat escape and salting improves texture and flavor.
- **Simmer, then roast:** The tougher legs get a cooking jump-start so they'll finish roasting with the breast meat.

CORE TECHNIQUE

Prepping Duck

TRIM SKIN
Using kitchen shears, trim excess neck skin from top of breast.

REMOVE TAIL
Remove tail and first 2 segments from each wing, leaving only drumette.

CROSSHATCH
Cut crosshatch pattern in skin and fat of breast. Cut parallel slits in skin and fat of each thigh. Rub salt into cavity and deep into scored skin and fat.

CLOSE CAVITY
Align skin at bottom of cavity so 1 side overlaps other; use toothpick to pin layers to each other to close cavity. Refrigerate for 6 to 24 hours.

DUCK CONFIT

Serves: 6

Total Time: 4 hours, plus 8 hours chilling

RECIPE OVERVIEW Duck confit, which boasts a rich, concentrated flavor and tender, silky texture, is a French classic. The meat can be separated from the bone and used in casseroles or to top salads, or you can crisp up whole legs on the stovetop or in the oven to serve them intact in all their golden glory. The salting treatment for the duck legs acts like a brine without the water, seasoning the meat and helping it retain moisture while it cooks. Thyme and bay leaves bring a hint of aromatic herbal flavor to the duck. If possible, let the legs chill in the fat for a few days (or even a week) before serving; they will taste even better. When it's time to remove the legs from the fat, just be sure to allow the fat to soften; otherwise you may tear the meat from the legs. Duck fat can be found at high-end butcher shops, specialty shops, and online. Duck fat is crucial here for texture and flavor; however, if you are a little short, you can supplement it with vegetable oil. Duck fat can also be reused to make more confit, like our Turkey Thigh Confit (page 443) or in other recipes like our Duck Fat–Roasted Potatoes (page 110). To store for up to a year, simply remelt the fat, strain through a fine-mesh strainer, and refrigerate in an airtight container (discard the fat when it begins to smell off).

- 6 (11-ounce) duck legs, trimmed of excess fat
- 1 tablespoon kosher salt
- ¼ teaspoon pepper
- 10 sprigs fresh thyme
- 4 bay leaves, crumbled
- 6–8 cups duck fat

1. Sprinkle duck legs evenly with salt and pepper. Toss with thyme sprigs and bay leaves in large bowl, cover tightly with plastic wrap, and refrigerate for 8 to 24 hours.

2. Adjust oven rack to middle position and heat oven to 300 degrees. Lay legs, skin side up, in single layer in Dutch oven and arrange thyme sprigs and bay leaves over top. Melt duck fat in medium saucepan over medium heat until liquefied, 5 to 10 minutes. Pour melted duck fat over legs until they are just covered.

3. Transfer pot to oven and bake, without moving legs, until skin has rendered most of its fat, meat is completely tender, and leg bones twist easily away from meat, about 3 hours (fat will be bubbling gently). Being very careful of hot fat, transfer pot to wire rack and let cool completely, about 2 hours. (At this point, with legs covered completely in fat, pot can be wrapped in plastic wrap and refrigerated for up to 1 month; if desired, transfer cooled legs to smaller airtight container and pour cooled fat over top to cover completely.)

4. To serve duck legs on their own, remove them from fat and scrape off as much fat as possible. Lay legs, skin side down, in 12-inch nonstick skillet and cook gently over medium-low heat until skin is crispy, 8 to 10 minutes. Gently flip legs and continue to cook until heated through, 4 to 6 minutes. Serve immediately.

Confitting Duck

TRIM, SEASON, REFRIGERATE

Trim excess skin and fat from duck legs. Sprinkle with salt and pepper and toss with herbs. Cover tightly with plastic and refrigerate for 8 to 24 hours.

COVER WITH FAT

Arrange legs, skin side up, in single layer in Dutch oven and arrange herbs over top. Pour melted duck fat over legs until just covered.

BAKE

Bake duck until skin has rendered most of its fat, meat is completely tender, and leg bones twist easily away from meat (fat will be bubbling gently). Let duck and fat cool completely in pot.

REFRIGERATE

Once cooled, entire pot can be wrapped in plastic wrap and refrigerated for up to 1 month. Or transfer cooled legs to smaller air-tight container and pour cooled fat over top to cover completely.

KEYS TO SUCCESS

- **Duck fat:** There's no substitute for the flavor that duck fat brings to the table.

- **Time:** The confited legs improve over time and will last up to a month in the refrigerator.

- **Be gentle:** Let the duck fat soften, and remove the legs from the fat gently so they don't tear.

CARVING DUCK

Ducks have a blockier shape than chickens or turkeys, so carving our Whole Roast Duck with Cherry Sauce (page 452) is a little different from carving these other birds.

1. Use tip of knife to cut through skin and fat where leg meets breast.

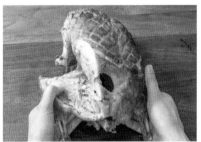

2. Pull leg quarter from breast while pushing up on joint. Cut through joint and skin to remove leg quarter. Repeat on other side.

3. Hold leg quarter upright so joint rests on cutting board. Cut down between drumstick and thigh until you reach bone.

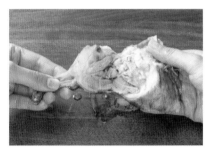

4. Using your hands, bend thigh and drumstick away from each other to expose joint; cut through joint. Repeat with second leg.

5. Arrange duck so cavity faces you. Draw tip of knife along side of breastbone, making sure knife stays against bone, to separate meat from breastbone. Rotate duck 90 degrees.

6. Starting at pointy (cavity) end of breast, draw knife along rib cage, lifting meat as you separate it from ribs. Repeat on other side.

7. Slice each breast half crosswise ½ inch thick.

8. Stand duck on cutting board with cavity end facing up and drumettes facing you. Using your hand to steady duck, cut through joint between wing and rib cage to separate drumettes.

DUCK VARIETIES

The duck breasts and whole ducks sold in supermarkets are usually White Pekin, or Long Island, ducks. Once raised on Long Island, these birds are now grown on farms around the country, and the largest producer is in Indiana, a long way from New York. White Pekins have a balanced meat-to-fat ratio and the breasts are typically more consistent in size. Most duck breasts are sold whole, with the skin on but without the bones. They can be split nicely into two halves, each weighing about 6 ounces. Since the Pekin duck is the breed found in supermarkets, we stuck with this variety when developing our recipes for duck.

SEAFOOD

GLOBAL SEAFOOD STARTERS

ANNIE PETITO

American shrimp cocktail will always be a classic. While its simple appeal has its place, this course treats you to dishes with a whole lot more personality. Learn how to easily poach shrimp to serve in a Mexican preparation full of spicy textural sensation. Pickle fresh mussels to enjoy in a lively Spanish-inspired creation. Find out how to use shrimp to make the best crab cakes that actually taste like crab. And turn dried salt cod into little fried fritters just looking for a party.

ANNIE'S PRO TIP: *When working with mussels, discard any with an unpleasant odor or with a cracked or broken shell or a shell that won't close. For shrimp, we prefer untreated (it will say on the package whether there is salt or additives such as sodium tripolyphosphate).*

CÓCTEL DE CAMARÓN

Serves: 4 to 6
Total Time: 45 minutes

RECIPE OVERVIEW Eaten ice-cold with a spoon and saltines, Mexican shrimp cocktail offers an incredible mix of flavors and textures: plump, tender poached shrimp, crisp bites of raw onion and cucumber, and cool, creamy avocado—all coated in a tangy, spicy-sweet tomato sauce. Success lies in nailing two key aspects: the cooking of the shrimp, and the sweetness and consistency of the sauce, which always contains ketchup. There are several ways to poach delicate proteins such as shrimp: Keep them at a low simmer or dump them into boiling water and pull the pot off the burner so that carryover cooking does the job. We opt for the residual heat method, which is not just easier but offers more consistent results. In fact, when 1¼ pounds of cold, raw shrimp is added to 3 cups of boiling water, the water temperature instantly drops to 155 degrees, ideal for poaching. Along with ketchup, the sauce for cóctel de camarón typically includes some kind of tomato juice (frequently Clamato) as well as hot sauce and fresh lime juice. Favoring a less sweet sauce, instead of Clamato we turn to V8, which also gives the sauce a slightly thicker texture that nicely coats the shrimp. As for hot sauce, the balanced flavor of Valentina, Cholula, or Tapatío hot sauce works best. If using a spicier, vinegary hot sauce such as Tabasco, start with half the amount called for and adjust to your taste. Saltines are a traditional accompaniment, but tortilla chips or thick-cut potato chips are also good.

1¼ pounds large shrimp (26 to 30 per pound),
      peeled, deveined, and tails removed
¼   teaspoon table salt, plus salt for cooking shrimp
1   cup V8 juice, chilled
½   cup ketchup
3   tablespoons lime juice (2 limes), plus lime wedges
      for serving
2   teaspoons hot sauce, plus extra for serving
½   English cucumber, cut into ½-inch pieces
1   cup finely chopped red onion
1   avocado, halved, pitted, and cut into ½-inch pieces
¼   cup chopped fresh cilantro
      Saltines

1. Bring 3 cups water to boil in large saucepan over high heat. Stir in shrimp and 1 tablespoon salt. Cover and let stand off heat until shrimp are opaque, about 5 minutes, shaking saucepan halfway through. Fill large bowl halfway with ice and water. Transfer shrimp to ice bath and let cool for 3 to 5 minutes. Once cool, cut each shrimp crosswise into 3 pieces.

2. Combine V8 juice, ketchup, lime juice, hot sauce, and salt in medium bowl. Add cucumber, onion, and shrimp and stir until evenly coated. Stir in avocado and cilantro. Portion cocktail into individual bowls or glasses and serve immediately, passing saltines, lime wedges, and extra hot sauce separately.

KEYS TO SUCCESS

- **Cook using residual heat:** Bringing the water to a full boil before adding the shrimp ensures that there will be enough heat in the saucepan to cook them through but not turn them rubbery.
- **Bite-size pieces:** Cutting the vegetables and shrimp small makes them easy to scoop up with a spoon and then enjoy a mix of textures in every bite.

Why Cóctel de Camarón Should Have a V8

The sweet ketchup in Mexican shrimp cocktail is often cut with Clamato, tomato juice, or V8. We thought Clamato had lots of character but was a little thin, while tomato juice was overly sweet and fruity. But V8's blend of tomato and vegetable juices and lack of added sweeteners gave the dish a welcome savory balance. Measuring viscosity on a DIY consistometer showed that V8 has a thicker consistency than the other choices; it produced a punchy sauce that was liquid-y but not watered down.

V8 (left) flowed the slowest down the slope of our DIY consistometer, indicating a thicker viscosity that we preferred to that of tomato juice (center) and Clamato (right).

MUSSELS ESCABÈCHE

Serves: 6 to 8
Total Time: 45 minutes

RECIPE OVERVIEW Escabèche has many variations in many cuisines, but the commonality is a spiced vinegar marinade that flavors and tenderizes anything from fish or meat (which are often cooked prior to marinating) to vegetables. For this Spanish-inspired version, we bathe briny mussels in an aromatic mixture of vinegar, olive oil, and fragrant spices for a unique addition to any appetizer spread. The first step here is cooking the mussels so they remain plump and tender. We use a high-heat method to cook them quickly, first bringing a mix of white wine and water to a boil, then adding the mussels and cooking for just 3 to 6 minutes before straining, to reduce the risk of overcooking. For the vinegar marinade we bloom aromatics in oil; a bay leaf offers depth, and smoked paprika provides earthy nuance. A healthy dose of sherry vinegar forms the vinegary base for pickling the mussels; its bright, bold flavor gives each small bite big impact. We suggest serving these mussels with toothpicks for grabbing, along with extra bread for dipping in the flavorful marinade. We prefer the bright flavor of the mussels after a quick pickling period of just 15 minutes, but they can be refrigerated for up to 2 days in their vinegar brine. Let the mussels come to room temperature before serving.

- ⅔ **cup dry white wine**
- 2 **pounds mussels, scrubbed and debearded**
- ⅓ **cup extra-virgin olive oil**
- ½ **small red onion, sliced ¼ inch thick**
- 4 **garlic cloves, sliced thin**
- 2 **bay leaves**
- 2 **sprigs fresh thyme**
- 2 **tablespoons minced fresh parsley, divided**
- ¾ **teaspoon smoked paprika**
- ¼ **cup sherry vinegar**
- ¼ **teaspoon table salt**
- ⅛ **teaspoon pepper**

1. Bring wine and ⅔ cup water to boil in Dutch oven over high heat. Add mussels, cover, and cook, stirring occasionally, until mussels open, 3 to 6 minutes. Strain mussels and discard cooking liquid and any mussels that have not opened. Let mussels cool slightly, then remove mussels from shells and place in large bowl; discard shells.

2. Heat oil in now-empty pot over medium heat until shimmering. Add onion, garlic, bay leaves, thyme, 1 tablespoon parsley, and paprika. Cook, stirring often, until garlic is fragrant and onion is slightly wilted, about 1 minute.

3. Off heat, stir in vinegar, salt, and pepper. Pour mixture over mussels and let sit for 15 minutes. (Mussels can be refrigerated for up to 2 days; bring to room temperature before serving.) Season with salt and pepper to taste and sprinkle with remaining 1 tablespoon parsley before serving.

KEYS TO SUCCESS

- **Watch the clock**: The mussels cook fast in the hot liquid; start checking after 3 minutes.
- **Bloom the spices**: The flavors in most spices are oil soluble, so just a minute of cooking in olive oil releases their flavor far more than if added directly to the cooking liquid.

CORE TECHNIQUE

Debearding Mussels

Occasionally, mussels will have a weedy but harmless piece, called a beard, protruding from their shells that needs to be removed before cooking. To remove it, grasp beard between your thumb and flat side of paring knife and tug. Don't debeard mussels until you are ready to cook them.

BEST CRAB CAKES

Serves: 4
Total Time: 1¼ hours, plus 20 minutes soaking and 30 minutes chilling

RECIPE OVERVIEW Crab cakes should taste like crab—sweet, plump meat held together with a binder that doesn't mask it. And you don't need to start with fresh crab meat, which can be hard to come by. In fact, good-quality pasteurized crabmeat found at the supermarket makes a surprisingly good alternative. For the best texture, we use jumbo lump or lump crabmeat, avoiding finer, flakier backfin meat. To rid the meat of any fishiness, there's a trick: Soak it briefly in milk to wash away the compound responsible for fishiness. To highlight the sweetness and bind our cakes, we

skip over traditional ingredients that mute crab's delicate flavor, and instead make a quick shrimp mousse; pureeing shrimp releases fragments of sticky muscle proteins that hold the pieces of crab together. Either fresh or pasteurized crabmeat can be used. With packaged crab, if the meat smells clean and fresh you can skip the soaking and straining in steps 1 and 5 and simply blot away any excess liquid. Serve with Classic Tartar Sauce (recipe follows).

1 pound lump crabmeat, picked over for shells
1 cup milk
1½ cups panko bread crumbs, divided
¾ teaspoon table salt, divided
¼ teaspoon pepper, divided
2 celery ribs, chopped
½ cup chopped onion
1 garlic clove, smashed and peeled
1 tablespoon unsalted butter
4 ounces extra-large shrimp (21 to 25 per pound), peeled, deveined, and tails removed
¼ cup heavy cream
2 teaspoons Dijon mustard
1 teaspoon lemon juice
½ teaspoon hot sauce
½ teaspoon Old Bay seasoning
¼ cup vegetable oil, divided
Lemon wedges

1. Line rimmed baking sheet with parchment paper. Place crabmeat and milk in bowl, making sure crab is totally submerged. Cover and refrigerate for 20 minutes.

2. Meanwhile, pulse ¾ cup panko in food processor until finely ground, about 15 pulses. Toast ground panko and remaining ¾ cup panko in 10-inch nonstick skillet over medium-high heat, stirring constantly, until golden brown, about 5 minutes. Transfer panko to shallow dish and stir in ¼ teaspoon salt and ⅛ teaspoon pepper; set aside. Wipe skillet clean with paper towels.

3. Pulse celery, onion, and garlic in now-empty processor until finely chopped, 5 to 8 pulses, scraping down sides of bowl as needed; transfer to large bowl. Wipe processor bowl and blade clean with paper towels. Melt butter in now-empty skillet over medium heat. Add processed vegetables, remaining ½ teaspoon salt, and remaining ⅛ teaspoon pepper and cook until vegetables are softened, 4 to 6 minutes. Return vegetables to large bowl and set aside to cool. Wipe skillet clean with paper towels.

4. Pulse shrimp in again-empty processor until finely ground, 12 to 15 pulses, scraping down sides of bowl as needed. Add cream and pulse to combine, 2 to 4 pulses; transfer to bowl with cooled vegetables.

5. Strain soaked crabmeat through fine-mesh strainer, pressing firmly to remove milk but being careful not to break up lumps of crabmeat. Add drained crab to bowl with vegetable mixture. Fold mustard, lemon juice, hot sauce, and Old Bay into mixture, being careful not to overmix or break up

lumps of crabmeat. Using your lightly moistened hands, divide crab mixture into 8 equal portions, then firmly shape each into ½-inch-thick cake. Transfer to prepared sheet, cover with plastic wrap, and refrigerate for 30 minutes.

6. Working with 1 cake at a time, dredge in panko, pressing lightly to adhere; return to sheet. Heat 1 tablespoon oil in now-empty skillet over medium heat until shimmering. Place 4 cakes in skillet and cook until first side is golden brown, about 3 minutes. Carefully flip cakes, add 1 tablespoon oil to skillet, and reduce heat to medium-low. Cook until second side is golden brown, 4 to 6 minutes. Transfer cakes to paper towel–lined plate and let drain, about 30 seconds per side; transfer to serving platter. Wipe skillet clean with paper towels and repeat with remaining 4 cakes and remaining 2 tablespoons oil. Serve with lemon wedges.

KEYS TO SUCCESS

- **Take the flavors off mute:** Pureed shrimp replace the flavor-dulling egg and mayo common to crab cakes. Any shrimp will do, so buy whatever is cheapest.

- **Give them a rest:** Thirty minutes of chilling makes the cakes noticeably sturdier so there is less risk of them falling apart.

- **Crush panko:** Traditional dry bread crumbs can be dusty, but panko pieces are too large and can fall off. Crushing just half in the food processor helps the mix adhere while maintaining plenty of crunchy bits.

Crab Cake Clarity

Most recipes resort to flavor-dulling binders like mayonnaise and eggs. Instead, we employ a two-step approach that enhances the meat's delicate flavor while providing just as much structure.

Bind with Shrimp
A puree of shrimp and cream holds the cakes together without dulling the meat's delicate flavor.

Firm Up in Fridge
Resting the cakes in the refrigerator for 30 minutes helps them set.

CLASSIC TARTAR SAUCE

Makes: about 1 cup
Total Time: 20 minutes

Be sure to rinse the capers before mincing them or else the sauce will have a strong, briny flavor. This is a classic with crab cakes and fried white fish, but it pairs nicely with baked fish, too.

    ¾   cup mayonnaise
    1½ teaspoons minced shallot
    2   tablespoons capers, rinsed and minced
    2   tablespoons sweet pickle relish
    1½ teaspoons white vinegar
    ½   teaspoon Worcestershire sauce

Combine all ingredients in bowl, let sit for 15 minutes, and season with salt and pepper to taste. (Sauce can be refrigerated for up to 5 days.)

SALT COD FRITTERS

Makes: 24 fritters (serves 6 to 8)
Total Time: 1¼ hours, plus 24 hours soaking

RECIPE OVERVIEW Drying and salting cod was once done as a preservation method but is now just plain desirable—cod becomes tender, buttery, and meaty with a firm, steak-like texture. Fritters using it are a popular bar snack in Portugal and Spain. They're small, deep-fried bites with supercrisp exteriors and creamy, briny insides—there's not much to dislike. Unlike croquetas, which are bound by a béchamel sauce, fritters are typically made from a simple base of potato and egg, along with aromatics and a bit of liquid (water, milk, or cream). We love the simplicity and keep things traditional, forgoing additions we've seen like bread crumbs to bind. Russet potatoes provide the perfect texture and their mild flavor doesn't interfere with the salt cod; an egg gives body and structure; and heavy cream adds just the right amount of richness for creamy contrast to the brininess. A touch of baking powder keeps this mixture light through frying. Look for salt cod in fish markets and some well-stocked supermarkets. It is shelf stable and typically packaged in a wooden box or plastic bag. Be sure to change the water when soaking the salt cod as directed in step 1, or the fritters will taste unpalatably salty.

    1   pound salt cod, checked for bones and rinsed thoroughly
    12 ounces russet potatoes, peeled and cut into 1-inch pieces
    6   garlic cloves, smashed and peeled
    ½   cup heavy cream
    2   tablespoons minced fresh chives
    1   large egg, lightly beaten
    2   teaspoons grated lemon zest, plus lemon wedges for serving
    ¼   teaspoon table salt
    ⅛   teaspoon pepper
    ⅛   teaspoon baking powder
    1   quart peanut or vegetable oil for frying

1. Submerge salt cod in large bowl of cold water and refrigerate until cod is soft enough to break apart easily with your fingers, about 24 hours, changing water twice during soaking.

2. Drain cod, transfer to large saucepan along with potatoes and garlic, and cover with water by 2 inches. Bring to boil, then reduce to medium heat and simmer until potatoes are tender, 15 to 20 minutes.

3. Drain cod mixture in colander, then transfer to large bowl. Using potato masher, mash until mixture is mostly smooth. Stir in heavy cream, chives, egg, lemon zest, salt, pepper, and baking powder until well incorporated. (Mixture can be refrigerated in airtight container for up to 2 days. Let sit at room temperature for 30 minutes before frying.)

4. Line serving platter with triple layer of paper towels. Pinch off and roll cod mixture into 24 balls (about 2 tablespoons each) and arrange on large plate. Add oil to large Dutch oven until it measures about ¾ inch deep and heat over medium-high heat to 375 degrees. Add half of fritters to oil and cook until golden all over, about 6 minutes, stirring to prevent sticking. Adjust burner, if necessary, to maintain oil temperature between 350 and 375 degrees. Using wire skimmer or slotted spoon, transfer fritters to prepared platter. Return oil to 375 degrees and repeat with remaining balls. Season with salt to taste. Serve immediately with lemon wedges.

KEYS TO SUCCESS

- **A long soak:** To properly hydrate, the salt cod requires 24 hours of soaking in 2 changes of cold water.

- **Starchy russets:** Their texture adds body to the fritters.

- **A bit of baking powder:** Helps to keep the fritters light

SEAFOOD IN THE RAW

KEITH DRESSER

From a bracing, briny oyster to a slice of buttery-smooth fish crudo, raw seafood brings the taste of the sea to your plate and is always a reason to celebrate. But despite the clear popularity (as evidenced by nearly 16,000 sushi restaurants in the United States), many cooks still don't eat raw fish at home. Yet plattering up some oysters or even your own raw bar is easy to do with a few skills under your belt. Here you'll learn how to successfully prepare and serve raw fish and shellfish (and well as fish that is partially "cooked" by acid), from shopping for the right fish to shucking an oyster.

KEITH'S PRO TIP: *When dealing with raw fish, to produce a product that both looks and tastes delicious, you must use a sharp knife. Use a long, thin blade and try to slice through the fish with one slice (don't use a sawing motion). For crudo, slice the fish across the grain to eliminate any stringiness or chewiness.*

FISH CRUDO WITH FURIKAKE

Serves: 4 to 6
Total Time: 15 minutes

RECIPE OVERVIEW At its simplest, fish crudo is nothing more than raw seafood topped with a contrasting garnish. Fruity olive oil, bright lemon juice, or a sprinkle of sea salt are all a great start but the options are endless. Try using tuna, sea bass, fluke, and/or scallops. Here we add flavor and texture with the Japanese seaweed–sesame seed spice blend known as furikake. You can purchase furikake or make your own. Inspect the fillets for bones and remove before slicing.

- 12 ounces skinless sushi-grade fluke fillets
- 1½ tablespoons extra-virgin olive oil
- 1 tablespoon lemon juice
- 1 tablespoon soy sauce
- 2 teaspoons Furikake (recipe follows)

1. Using sharp knife, cut fluke lengthwise into 2- to 3-inch-wide strips. Slice each strip crosswise on bias into ⅛-inch-thick slices. Arrange fluke attractively on individual chilled plates.

2. Whisk oil, lemon juice, and soy sauce together in small bowl. Drizzle sauce over fluke and sprinkle with furikake. Serve immediately.

FURIKAKE

Makes: about ½ cup
Total Time: 10 minutes

2	nori sheets, torn into 1-inch pieces
3	tablespoons sesame seeds, toasted
1½	tablespoons bonito flakes
1½	teaspoons sugar
1½	teaspoons flake sea salt, such as Maldon

Process nori in spice grinder until coarsely ground and pieces are no larger than ½ inch, about 15 seconds. Add sesame seeds, bonito flakes, and sugar and pulse until coarsely ground and pieces of nori are no larger than ¼ inch, about 2 pulses. Transfer to small bowl and stir in salt. (Furikake can be stored in airtight container for up to 3 months.)

KEYS TO SUCCESS

- **Freshness is key:** Look for fish labeled "sushi grade" or ask your fishmonger.

- **A clean slice:** Aim for ⅛-inch-thick slices. To make slicing easier, freeze fish for 15 minutes and be sure your knife is sharp.

- **Garnish judiciously:** Toppings should create contrast without overpowering the flavor of the fish.

Sushi-Grade Fish

What makes fish appropriate for eating raw? Unfortunately, there are no official standards for the label, although it is assumed that "sushi-grade" fish is suitable for raw applications. If a fish that's prone to parasites (salmon, wild cod, mackerel, and freshwater fish) is given this label, it means it was frozen to ensure these parasites were killed before the fish was sold. It is unlikely that farmed fish will have parasites because they are given parasite-free feed. When possible, research to find a purveyor that supplies local sushi or poke restaurants. Some wholesale purveyors will sell directly to individuals. Or look for a busy fish market (a sign of high turnover) and tell your fishmonger you mean to serve the fish raw. Ask them to slice fish to order, ideally pieces that have little to no connective tissue (which can be chewy) or thin belly portions (which can be tough and fatty when raw). When serving salmon raw, we call for farm-raised salmon, because wild-caught salmon can be prone to parasites; it must be commercially frozen to the FDA's standards to be safe for raw consumption.

FISH CEVICHE WITH RADISHES AND ORANGE

Serves: 6 to 8
Total Time: 35 minutes, plus 30 minutes resting

RECIPE OVERVIEW Ceviche, the Latin American dish in which pieces of raw fish are "cooked" in an acidic marinade until the flesh firms and turns opaque, allows the fresh, clean, delicate flavor of seafood to shine and awakens the palate for the meal to come. To create a flavorful yet balanced marinade and sauce, we make a Peruvian-inspired leche de tigre ("tiger's milk") by blending lime juice, ají amarillo chile paste, garlic, olive oil, and a small amount of fish. Once strained, the mixture becomes an intensely flavorful, silky emulsion. We then soak thinly sliced and briefly salted fish in the leche until it is just opaque and slightly firm. To complete the dish, we add sweet oranges, crisp peppery radishes, and chopped cilantro. We serve the ceviche with corn nuts and popcorn, both traditional in Latin America, which provide salty crunch. Black sea bass, halibut, or grouper can be substituted for the snapper. If you can't find ají amarillo chile paste, you can substitute 1 stemmed and seeded habanero chile. Serving the popcorn and corn nuts separately allows diners to customize their ceviche to suit their taste.

1 pound skinless red snapper fillets, ½ inch thick
3½ teaspoons kosher salt, divided
¾ cup lime juice (6 limes)
3 tablespoons extra-virgin olive oil, divided
1 tablespoon ají amarillo chile paste
2 garlic cloves, peeled
3 oranges
8 ounces radishes, trimmed, halved, and sliced thin
¼ cup coarsely chopped fresh cilantro
1 cup corn nuts
1 cup lightly salted popcorn

1. Using sharp knife, cut fish lengthwise into ½-inch-wide strips. Slice each strip crosswise ⅛ inch thick. Set aside ⅓ cup (2½ ounces) fish pieces. Toss remaining fish with 1 teaspoon salt and refrigerate for at least 10 minutes or up to 30 minutes.

2. Meanwhile, process reserved fish pieces, remaining 2½ teaspoons salt, lime juice, 2 tablespoons oil, chile paste, and garlic in blender until smooth, 30 to 60 seconds. Strain mixture through fine-mesh strainer set over large bowl, pressing on solids to extract as much liquid as possible. Discard solids. (Sauce can be refrigerated for up to 24 hours. It will separate slightly; whisk to recombine before proceeding with recipe.)

3. Cut away peel and pith from oranges. Holding fruit over bowl, use paring knife to slice between membranes to release segments. Cut orange segments into ¼-inch pieces. Add oranges, salted fish, and radishes to bowl with sauce and toss to combine. Refrigerate for 30 to 40 minutes (for more-opaque fish, refrigerate for 45 minutes to 1 hour).

4. Add cilantro to ceviche and toss. Portion ceviche into individual bowls and drizzle with remaining 1 tablespoon oil. Serve, passing corn nuts and popcorn separately.

KEYS TO SUCCESS

- **Blend thoroughly:** A blended marinade becomes an emulsion with enough body to coat and cling to each piece of fish. Combining the citrus with the blended ingredients also creates a less acidic marinade, so the fish "cooks" more slowly and has a longer serving window.

- **Marinate sufficiently:** Marinating between 30 and 40 minutes means the fish turns opaque and its texture is firm but easily yields as you bite into it—our sweet spot.

- **Don't omit garnishes:** Contrasting layers of flavor and texture is key to a successful ceviche.

How Acid "Cooks" Fish

Acids denature and coagulate fish proteins, firming fish and turning it opaque just as hot cooking methods do. However, acid doesn't change the fish's taste—its clean, delicate flavor still shines. It also does not kill microbes, which underscores the importance of using the freshest seafood. Our leche de tigre is about three times less acidic than straight lime juice, so it affects the fish more slowly, giving us some breathing room in the marinating time. We marinated thin slices of fish in our leche to demonstrate how it affects the flesh over time.

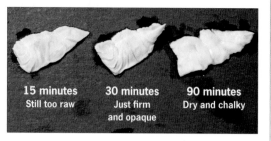

15 minutes
Still too raw

30 minutes
Just firm and opaque

90 minutes
Dry and chalky

WHAT CAN GO WRONG

PROBLEM The fish is dry and chalky.

SOLUTION The fish may have marinated for too long. By 45 minutes the fish will start to take on the texture of fully cooked fish, but becomes unpleasantly dry after 1 hour.

How to Buy the Freshest Fish

When making ceviche, using the freshest seafood possible is imperative for both flavor and food safety reasons. Here's what to look for:

CLEAN SMELL The seafood (and the store or counter) should smell like the sea, not fishy or sour.
SHINY SURFACE Fillets should look bright and shiny; whole fish should have bright, clear eyes.
FIRM TEXTURE Fresh fish is firm. Ask your fishmonger to press the flesh with their finger; it should spring back.
ADVICE Ask your fishmonger what's freshest that day, even if it's not what you originally had in mind. Ceviche works with many different varieties of fish.

SCALLOP CEVICHE WITH CUCUMBER AND GRAPEFRUIT

Serves: 6 to 8
Total Time: 45 minutes

RECIPE OVERVIEW As with our fish ceviche, we start by making a leche de tigre marinating liquid, here blending acidic grapefruit juice with jalapeño, garlic, shallot, ginger, cilantro, and olive oil. We include a small amount of scallops and their otherwise-discarded tendons to create a marinade that clings and serves as a sauce as well. After cutting the scallops into bite-size pieces and salting briefly, we soak them in the leche for just 5 minutes, until tender and slightly opaque. To complete the dish, we add pieces of grapefruit and crisp cucumber. We serve the ceviche with corn nuts and plantain chips, which provide salty crunch. It is imperative that you use the freshest scallops possible in this recipe. We recommend buying "dry" scallops, which don't have chemical additives and taste better than "wet." Dry scallops will look ivory or pinkish; wet scallops are bright white. Serving the plantain chips and corn nuts separately allows diners to customize the ceviche to their taste.

- 1 **pound large sea scallops, tendons removed and reserved**
- 3½ **teaspoons kosher salt, divided**
- 2 **red grapefruits**
- 20 **sprigs fresh cilantro, plus ¼ cup coarsely chopped**
- ⅓ **cup lime juice (3 limes)**
- 1 **jalapeño chile, stemmed and seeded**
- 1 **(1-inch) piece fresh ginger, peeled and sliced into ⅛-inch-thick rounds**
- 3 **tablespoons extra-virgin olive oil, divided**
- 1 **small shallot, peeled**
- 2 **garlic cloves, peeled**
- ½ **English cucumber, quartered lengthwise, seeded, and cut into ⅛-inch pieces**
- 2 **cups plantain chips**
- 1 **cup corn nuts**

1. Using sharp knife, cut scallops into ¼-inch pieces. Combine reserved tendons and enough scallop pieces to measure ⅓ cup (2½ ounces) and set aside. Toss remaining scallops with 1 teaspoon salt and refrigerate for at least 10 minutes or up to 30 minutes.

2. Juice 1 grapefruit and set aside ½ cup juice. Cut away peel and pith from remaining grapefruit. Holding fruit over bowl, use paring knife to slice between membranes to release segments. Cut grapefruit segments into ¼-inch pieces; set aside.

3. Process reserved ⅓ cup scallop pieces, remaining 2½ teaspoons salt, reserved grapefruit juice, cilantro sprigs, lime juice, jalapeño, ginger, 2 tablespoons oil, shallot, and zgarlic in blender until smooth, 30 to 60 seconds. Strain mixture through fine-mesh strainer set over large bowl, pressing on solids to extract as much liquid as possible. Discard solids. (Sauce can be refrigerated for up to 24 hours. It will separate slightly; whisk to recombine before proceeding with recipe.)

4. Add salted scallops, reserved grapefruit segments, and cucumber to bowl with sauce and toss to combine. Refrigerate for at least 5 minutes or up to 15 minutes.

5. Add chopped cilantro to ceviche and toss to combine. Portion ceviche into individual bowls and drizzle with remaining 1 tablespoon oil. Serve, passing plantain chips and corn nuts separately.

KEYS TO SUCCESS

- **Buy dry scallops:** Dry scallops don't have chemical additives and will have the best flavor. Dry scallops look ivory or pinkish (wet scallops, which contain chemical additives, look bright white).

- **Combine some raw scallops (and tendons) with citrus:** Creates a sauce with more body and less acid, allowing the ceviche to "cook" more slowly and creating a larger serving window

Add Some Crunch (and Pop)

In Peru and Ecuador, where many different types of corn are grown, popcorn and corn nuts are often served alongside ceviche. Their salty crunch is the perfect complement to ceviche's bright, fresh flavors. Plantain chips and tortilla chips are also popular accompaniments.

TUNA POKE

Serves: 4
Total Time: 25 minutes

RECIPE OVERVIEW Poke ("poh-KAY") translates from Hawaiian as "to cut or slice into pieces" and refers to a raw fish salad that's become increasingly popular across the rest of the United States. The earliest pokes were ultrasimple: just raw, shallow-water fish pulled straight from the ocean and tossed with sea salt, seaweed, and ground roasted kukui nuts. The poke here is a version of ahi shoyu poke—which has become Hawaii's most popular poke in the last half century, and is almost as simple as the original. It rests on a foundation of fresh, dense, meaty, clean-tasting yellowfin tuna dressed with a simple, savory soy sauce mixture. The macadamia nuts and (optional) furikake garnish take inspiration from the seaweed and kukui nuts in the original Hawaiian version. Vidalia, Maui, or Walla Walla sweet onions will all work here. If you can't find sweet onions, you can substitute a yellow onion by soaking thin slices in ice water for 20 minutes and then draining and patting dry. You can make furikake yourself (see page 465) or use store-bought. Serve this poke as a snack or an appetizer, or make it a meal by serving it over warm rice.

- 1 pound skinless yellowfin tuna, cut into ¾-inch cubes
- ¼ cup thinly sliced sweet onion (halved and sliced through root end)
- ⅓ cup finely chopped salted dry-roasted macadamia nuts
- 3 scallions, white and green parts separated and sliced thin on bias
- 3 tablespoons soy sauce
- 2 tablespoons vegetable oil
- 2 teaspoons toasted sesame oil
- 2 teaspoons grated fresh ginger
- 1 garlic clove, minced
- ¾ teaspoon red pepper flakes
  Furikake (page 465, optional)

Gently combine tuna, onion, macadamia nuts, scallion whites, soy sauce, vegetable oil, sesame oil, ginger, garlic, and pepper flakes in large bowl using rubber spatula. Season with salt to taste. Serve, sprinkled with furikake, if using, and scallion greens. (Poke can be refrigerated for up to 24 hours.)

KEYS TO SUCCESS

- **The freshest tuna:** The raw tuna should appear moist and shiny and feel firm. And it should smell clean, not fishy.

- **A simple dressing:** Soy sauce, vegetable oil, and toasted sesame oil, that's it.

- **A touch of heat:** From fresh ginger, garlic, and red pepper flakes

OYSTERS ON THE HALF SHELL

Serves: 2 or 3
Total Time: 15 minutes

RECIPE OVERVIEW There's nothing fancier than hosting an oyster raw bar shindig. But we've got you covered if you're unsure about how to shuck oysters (see below) or serve them at home. Plan on 4 to 6 oysters per person, or less if you're serving other seafood such as ceviche or crudo. To serve oysters on the half shell the way they are in restaurants and raw bars, the first step is to crush ice by hand (see page 471). You will also need an oyster knife, a few dish towels, a deep tray or a sheet pan, and lots of that crushed ice. The ice chills the oysters and condiments and keeps the oysters securely nestled on the platter so that they don't tip. If you're serving the oysters with accompaniments, embed the serving bowls in the ice before filling them. To better enjoy the oysters with your guests, get a head start and make the sauces and crushed ice ahead of time, but save the oyster shucking until you're ready to serve.

    3 pounds crushed ice
   12 oysters, well scrubbed

Arrange ice in even layer on chilled serving platter. Shuck 1 oyster and discard top shell; place oyster on ice, being careful not to spill much liquid. Repeat with remaining oysters.

LIME-AND-SOY-MARINATED SCALLIONS

Serves: 8 (makes about ½ cup)
Total Time: 20 minutes

    3 tablespoons lime juice (2 limes)
    2 scallions, sliced thin
    1 tablespoon water
    1 tablespoon soy sauce
   ½ teaspoon sugar

Stir all ingredients together and refrigerate for at least 15 minutes or up to 24 hours before serving.

RED WINE VINEGAR MIGNONETTE GRANITÉ

Serves: 8 (makes about ⅔ cup)
Total Time: 10 minutes, plus 1 hour freezing

We froze that tart-sweet mignonette you enjoy on oysters and made it into a topping of flavorful ice flakes. For a traditional mignonette, skip the freezing and scraping steps; simply refrigerate the mixed ingredients for at least 30 minutes or up to two days, and serve chilled.

   ½ cup red wine vinegar
    3 tablespoons water
    2 teaspoons finely grated shallot
   ¾ teaspoon sugar
    1 teaspoon coarsely ground pepper

In shallow bowl, stir together vinegar, water, shallot, and sugar. Freeze until fully frozen, at least 1 hour or up to 2 days. One hour before serving, place small serving bowl in freezer. To serve, scrape frozen mixture with fork to create ice crystals. Stir in pepper. Transfer to chilled serving bowl; serve, or cover and freeze until ready to use.

COCKTAIL SAUCE

Makes: 1¼ cups
Total Time: 5 minutes

    1 cup ketchup
   ¼ cup prepared horseradish
    1 teaspoon Worcestershire sauce
    1 teaspoon lemon juice
   ½ teaspoon Old Bay seasoning
   ⅛ teaspoon cayenne pepper

Whisk all ingredients in bowl until combined. (Sauce can be refrigerated for up to 4 days; bring to room temperature before serving.)

CORE TECHNIQUE
Shucking an Oyster

SET UP DISH TOWEL
Fold dish towel several times into thin, tight roll. Grip towel in fist of hand that will be holding oyster, wrapping 1 end over your thumb and tucking it between your thumb and forefinger.

INSERT OYSTER KNIFE
Using your towel-protected thumb, hold oyster in place with hinge facing away from thumb. Insert tip of oyster knife into hinge of oyster.

POP HINGE
Work tip of knife into hinge using twisting motion. When shells begin to separate, twist knife to pop hinge.

RELEASE OYSTER
Run knife along top shell, scraping abductor muscle from shell to release oyster. Slide knife under oyster to scrape abductor muscle from bottom shell.

BUYING OYSTERS

There are five species of commercially cultivated oysters farmed in North American waters: Eastern, Pacific, European flat (also known as Belon), Kumamoto, and Olympia.

In Person

Specimens should be heavy for their size (a sign of freshness) and shut tight (or close up when you touch them).

Online

Oysters are increasingly available online directly from farmers, and they tolerate shipping exceptionally well because they can survive out of water for days as long as they're kept fridge-cold. Here are a few of our favorite purveyors and the oysters they offer:

Bon Secour Fisheries (Eastern)
Real Oyster Cult (Eastern, Pacific)
Taylor Shellfish Farms (Pacific, Kumamoto)

MEET THE OYSTER FAMILY

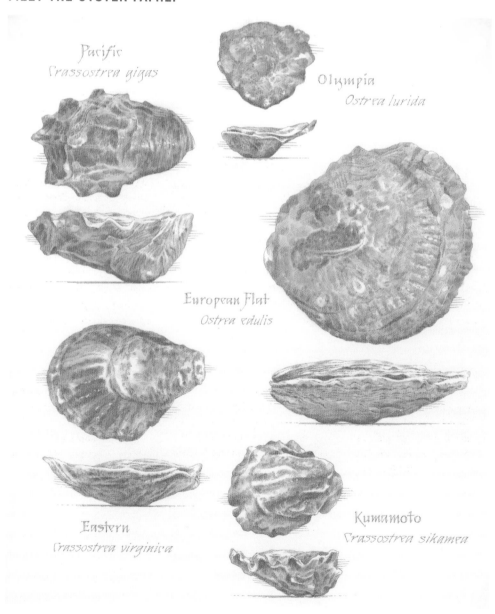

Pacific
Crassostrea gigas

Olympia
Ostrea lurida

European Flat
Ostrea edulis

Eastern
Crassostrea virginica

Kumamoto
Crassostrea sikamea

SERVING SEAFOOD ON A BED OF ICE

A frosty bed of crushed ice cradles your shucked oysters (and their valuable liquor) and keeps any sauces chilled. Set out just oysters or poached shrimp or any of the recipes in this course, placing small bowls of ceviche or poke directly atop the ice. Five pounds of crushed ice will create a 1½-inch-thick layer of ice in a rimmed baking sheet—enough to keep twenty-four 2½- to 3-inch oysters cold for about 30 minutes. Store extra ice in a colander set in a bowl in the fridge. Use this stash to refresh your platter as needed.

STORING OYSTERS

Depending on the variety and freshness, oysters keep anywhere from a few days to a week as long as they're refrigerated. (Online sources often specify shelf life.) Keep them in a bowl covered with a damp towel, remoistening it as needed to prevent the oysters from drying out. Do not store oysters directly on or underneath ice; they will die in fresh water. (It's OK to place them on ice for serving.)

FOR THE BEST CRUSHED ICE, GRAB A SKILLET

The best approach to crushing ice is the old-fashioned way: by hand. Fill a heavy-duty 1-gallon zipper-lock freezer bag about three-quarters full with ice cubes and press out as much air as possible before sealing. Wrap the bag tightly with a large dish towel. Then simply strike the wrapped bag with a mallet, skillet, or rolling pin to break the ice to the desired size. (Don't use a pin made of softwood or one with ball bearings, as it could be damaged by the ice.) You will need about 5 pounds to create a 1½-inch-thick layer of ice in a rimmed baking sheet. This will keep about twenty-four 2½- to 3-inch oysters cold for about 30 minutes. If you're using a smaller platter, store extra ice in a colander set in a bowl in the fridge. Use this stash to refresh your oyster platter as needed.

SLOW SHUCKING?

If your oyster shucking is progressing slowly, instead of placing shucked oysters directly on the ice as they're ready (where the ice will likely melt before you're finished), make a foil landing zone. Crumple up aluminum foil so there are hills and valleys, then place shucked oyster on top and press firmly until the foil flattens and the oyster stays full of liquid. Once you've shucked all oysters, put them on ice.

HOW TO EAT AN OYSTER

Sip some of the liquor. It's OK to pour off some and also OK if some spills during shucking.
Slurp the whole oyster into your mouth.
Chew it well so that you really get to taste it.

NEW WAYS WITH FILLETS

DAN SOUZA

Fish fillets are incredibly versatile. When they are cut at least one inch thick they are pretty sturdy and nearly any method of cooking works for them. They are also a wonderful blank canvas when it comes to adding flavor. Whether richly bathed in butter, salted and seared to crispy perfection in a skillet on the stovetop, poached in extra-virgin olive oil, or oven-steamed with ginger, you will learn how to cook fillets that turn out succulent and moist every time.

DAN'S PRO TIP: *Great fish meals start at the store, so always ask what fish came in most recently. And then be fearless: Buy that fish even if you haven't cooked with it before.*

BUTTER-BASTED FISH FILLETS WITH GARLIC AND THYME

Serves: 2
Total Time: 30 minutes

RECIPE OVERVIEW Butter basting sounds like music to the ears: The technique involves repeatedly spooning sizzling butter over food as it cooks. The butter bath, which is also a classic method for cooking big beef steaks, is great for mild, lean, flaky fish. The hot butter helps cook the top of the fillet as the skillet heats the bottom, allowing you to flip the delicate fish only once and early in the cooking process—before the flesh has become too fragile. Throughout the process, the butter browns and coats the mild fish in savory flavor, adding richness. We add thyme sprigs and crushed garlic cloves to the pan, which infuse the butter as it heats and makes for an aromatic dish. Lemon wedges are a must; the brightness of the lemon juice cuts through the butter's richness. Black sea bass, haddock, hake, red snapper, and pollock can be substituted for the cod.

- 2 (6- to 8-ounce) skinless cod fillets, 1 inch thick
- ½ teaspoon kosher salt
- ⅛ teaspoon pepper
- 1 tablespoon vegetable oil
- 3 tablespoons unsalted butter, cut into ½-inch cubes
- 2 garlic cloves, crushed and peeled
- 4 sprigs fresh thyme
   Lemon wedges

1. Pat all sides of fillets dry with paper towels. Sprinkle on all sides with salt and pepper. Heat oil in 12-inch non-stick skillet over medium-high heat until just smoking. Reduce heat to medium and place cod skinned side down in skillet. Using fish spatula, gently press on each fillet for 5 seconds to ensure good contact with skillet. Cook cod, without moving it, until underside is light golden brown, 4 to 5 minutes.

2. Using 2 spatulas, gently flip fillets and cook for 1 minute. Scatter butter around cod. When butter is melted, tilt skillet slightly toward you so that butter pools at front of skillet. Using large spoon, scoop up melted butter and pour over cod repeatedly for 15 seconds. Place skillet flat on burner and continue to cook 30 seconds longer. Tilt skillet and baste for 15 seconds. Place skillet flat on burner and take temperature of thickest part of each fillet. Continue to alternate basting and cooking until fillets reach 130 degrees. Add garlic and thyme sprigs to skillet at 12 o'clock position (butter will spatter). When spattering has subsided, continue basting and cooking until fillets reach 135 degrees at thickest point. (Total cooking time will range from 8 to 10 minutes.)

3. Transfer fillets to individual plates. Discard garlic. Top each fillet with thyme sprigs, pour butter over cod, and serve with lemon wedges.

and slow. When the fish is almost done, we flip the fillets, remove the pan from the heat, and let the residual heat finish cooking the fish all the way through. You can use any skin-on fish fillet that's 1 inch thick and has skin that is pleasant to eat, such as salmon, arctic char, bluefish, and red snapper. If using arctic char or wild salmon, cook the fillets to 120 degrees (for medium-rare). If using farmed salmon, cook the fillets to 125 degrees (for medium-rare). If using bluefish, cook the fillets to 130 degrees (for medium-rare). These crispy fillets can stand up to a bold sauce. In spring when wild ramps are available, we love to top the fillets with a deliciously bright and aromatic Ramp Pesto. Other times of year, we opt for a briny-citrusy Green Olive, Almond, and Orange Relish (recipes follow).

- ¾ teaspoon plus ⅛ teaspoon table salt, divided
- ¾ teaspoon sugar
- 4 (6- to 8-ounce) skin-on sea bass fish fillets, 1 inch thick
- 2 tablespoons extra-virgin olive oil
  Lemon wedges for serving

1. Combine ¾ teaspoon salt and sugar in small bowl. Using sharp knife, make 3 or 4 shallow slashes, about ½ inch apart, lengthwise in skin side of each fillet, being careful not to cut into flesh and stopping ½ inch from top and bottom edge of skin. Season flesh sides of fillets evenly with salt mixture and place skin side up on wire rack set in rimmed baking sheet. Sprinkle skin side with remaining ⅛ teaspoon salt. Refrigerate for 45 minutes or up to 1½ hours.

2. Pat fillets dry with paper towels. Heat oil in 12-inch nonstick skillet over high heat until just smoking. Place fillets skin side down in skillet. Immediately reduce heat to medium-low and, using fish spatula, firmly press fillets for 20 to 30 seconds to ensure contact between skin and skillet. Continue to cook until skin is well browned and flesh is opaque except for top ¼ inch, 6 to 12 minutes. (If at any time during searing, oil starts to smoke or sides of fish start to brown, reduce heat so that oil is sizzling but not smoking.)

3. Remove from the heat, flip fish, and continue to cook using residual heat of skillet until fish registers 135 degrees, about 30 seconds to 1 minute longer. Transfer fish skin side up to large plate. Serve fish with lemon wedges.

KEYS TO SUCCESS

- **Use a deep spoon**: To most easily gather up the hot butter to baste the fish

- **An "on-off" method**: Alternating between butter-basting for 15 seconds and letting the fish cook on a flat skillet for 30 seconds moderates the skillet's heat.

- **Temp frequently**: In between bastings, using an instant-read thermometer to temp the fish eliminates any guesswork as to when it's done.

- **Add the garlic and herbs to the far side of the skillet**: To keep any splattering away from your hands.

CRISPY SKIN-ON FISH FILLETS

Serves: 4
Total Time: 1¼ hours

RECIPE OVERVIEW Here is a master technique for cooking skin-on fish fillets such as sea bass and red snapper. Serving fish skin-on is a way to instantly elevate it, creating succulence and textural contrast as well as an elegant presentation. For potato-chip-thin crisp skin and ultramoist fish, we first score and dry-brine the fish with a salt-sugar mixture. The salt actually dissolves some of the proteins in the fish, forming a gel that can hold on to more moisture so the portions near the outside don't overcook. To get the skin incredibly crispy we do most of our cooking on the skin side, what the French dub "unilateral" cooking. We first get the skillet smoking hot, then lower the heat immediately after placing the fillets in the pan. This allows the skin to start to brown right away, while the fish cooks through low

KEYS TO SUCCESS

- **Score the skin**: Prevents the skin from buckling so that it stays flat to the surface of the skillet

- **Don't turn too soon**: It may seem like you're going to overcook one side, but the low heat and presalting prevents this.

- **Sizzle but no smoke**: You want to hear sizzling but not see smoke emerging from the skillet. If at any point the oil starts to smoke, reduce the heat.

RAMP PESTO

Makes: 1 cup
Total Time: 25 minutes

Processing a mix of cooked and raw ramps creates a balanced pesto with potent but not overwhelming allium bite. Extra pesto can be tossed with pasta or spread on bruschetta.

 6 ounces ramps, white parts sliced thin, green parts cut into 1-inch pieces
 6 tablespoons extra-virgin olive oil, divided
 3 tablespoons chopped toasted pistachios
 2 tablespoons water
 1 tablespoon lemon juice
 ¼ teaspoon table salt
 ¼ cup grated Parmesan cheese

1. Measure out ¼ cup ramp greens and set aside. Heat 2 tablespoons oil in 12-inch nonstick skillet over medium heat until shimmering. Add ramp whites and cook until softened, about 2 minutes. Stir in remaining ramp greens and cook until just wilted, about 1 minute. Transfer to food processor and let cool slightly, about 10 minutes.

2. Add remaining ¼ cup oil, pistachios, water, lemon juice, salt, and reserved ramp greens to food processor and process until smooth, about 30 seconds, scraping down sides of bowl as needed. Transfer to bowl and stir in Parmesan. Adjust consistency with additional water as needed; set aside until ready to serve. (Pesto can be refrigerated for up to 3 days).

GREEN OLIVE, ALMOND, AND ORANGE RELISH

Makes: 1 cup
Total Time: 10 minutes

This relish provides a trifecta of flavor: brininess, richness, and sweetness. If the olives are marinated, rinse and drain them before chopping.

 ½ cup slivered almonds, toasted
 ½ cup green olives, pitted and chopped coarse
 1 garlic clove, minced
 1 teaspoon grated orange zest plus ¼ cup juice
 ¼ cup extra-virgin olive oil
 ¼ cup minced fresh mint
 2 teaspoons white wine vinegar
   Cayenne pepper

Pulse almonds, olives, garlic, and orange zest in food processor until nuts and olives are finely chopped, 10 to 12 pulses. Transfer to bowl and stir in orange juice, oil, mint, and vinegar. Season with salt and cayenne to taste. (Relish can be refrigerated for up to 2 days.)

OVEN-STEAMED FISH FILLETS WITH SCALLIONS AND GINGER

Serves: 4
Total Time: 1 hour

RECIPE OVERVIEW Both Chinese and French cuisines have classic approaches to steaming fish, a delicate method for cooking a delicate protein that leads to supremely moist results. It's fast enough to do on a weeknight but also offers company-worthy elegance. We draw inspiration from both the Chinese method (bold, fresh flavors for the fish and a finishing drizzle of hot oil that sizzles, releasing aromas) and the French method (oven-steaming to produce a flavorful, concentrated fish jus) for a technique that's easy and impressive. We place skinless fillets on a foil sling in a baking pan that we cover, which allows the fish to flavor the cooking liquid (soy sauce, Shaoxing wine, and sesame oil), and vice versa. The sling makes it easy to transfer the fillets to a platter without them falling apart. Removing the fish from the oven before it's fully cooked— 130 degrees rather than the typical 135—prevents it from overcooking at the end, when we pour over the sizzling, ginger-infused oil (which raises the fish's temperature). If using a glass baking dish, add 5 minutes to the cooking time. Black sea bass, halibut, haddock, red snapper, and pollock can all be used here as long as the fillets are about 1 inch thick.

 8 scallions, trimmed, divided
 1 (3-inch) piece ginger, peeled
 3 garlic cloves, sliced thin
 4 (6- to 8-ounce) skinless cod fillets, 1 inch thick
 3 tablespoons soy sauce
 2 tablespoons Shaoxing wine or dry sherry
 1½ teaspoons toasted sesame oil
 1½ teaspoons sugar
 ¼ teaspoon table salt
 ¼ teaspoon white pepper
 2 tablespoons vegetable oil
 ⅓ cup fresh cilantro leaves and thin stems

1. Adjust oven rack to middle position and heat oven to 450 degrees. Chop 6 scallions coarse and scatter over bottom of 13 by 9-inch baking pan. Slice remaining 2 scallions thin on bias and set aside until ready to serve. Coarsely chop 2 inches ginger and add to pan with scallions, then sprinkle with garlic. Slice remaining 1 inch ginger into matchsticks; set aside.

2. Fold 18 by 12-inch piece of aluminum foil lengthwise to create 18 by 6-inch sling and spray lightly with vegetable oil spray. Place sling lengthwise on top of aromatics in pan, with extra foil hanging over ends of pan, then place cod on sling, spaced evenly apart. (If fillets vary in thickness, place thinner fillets in middle and thicker fillets at ends.)

3. Whisk soy sauce, Shaoxing wine, sesame oil, sugar, salt, and white pepper together in bowl, then pour around cod in pan. Cover pan tightly with foil and bake until fish registers 130 degrees, 12 to 14 minutes.

4. Grasping sling at both ends, carefully transfer sling and cod to deep platter. Place spatula at 1 end of fillets to hold in place and carefully slide out sling from under cod, leaving cod behind on platter. Strain remaining cooking liquid from pan through fine-mesh strainer set over bowl, pressing on solids to extract liquid; discard solids. Pour strained liquid over cod, then sprinkle with reserved scallions. Heat vegetable oil in 8-inch skillet over high heat until shimmering. Reduce heat to low, add reserved ginger, and cook, stirring, until ginger begins to brown and crisp, 20 to 30 seconds. Drizzle oil and ginger over cod (oil will crackle), then sprinkle with cilantro. Serve.

KEYS TO SUCCESS

- **A foil sling does double duty:** Placing the fillets on the sling allows the fish to flavor the sauce while cooking and makes it easy to transfer it to a serving platter without falling apart.

- **A hot oil finish:** We transfer the fish to a platter when it's just shy of its target temperature of 135 degrees. The final pour of hot ginger-infused oil finishes cooking the fish, releasing fragrant aromas and adding richness to the mostly lean dish.

Finish with a Sizzle

We transfer the fish to a platter when it's just shy of its target temperature of 135 degrees and then pour hot ginger-infused oil over it. The oil finishes cooking the fish, releasing fragrant aromas and adding some richness to this lean dish.

OIL-POACHED FISH FILLETS WITH ARTICHOKES AND TOMATO VINAIGRETTE

Serves: 4
Total Time: 1¼ hours, plus 20 minutes salting

RECIPE OVERVIEW If your experience with poached white fish fillets is limited to water poaching, you might be surprised to learn another technique: oil-poaching. Poaching fish in oil renders the delicate flesh silky and supple. The fish absorbs very little oil because in order for oil to penetrate the fish, moisture must exit. But because oil and water repel each other, it's difficult for moisture to enter the oil. Hence, more of the juices stay in the fish. In our recipe, the oil pulls triple duty: We use it to crisp artichokes and garlic for a fun-textured garnish, we poach the fish in it, and then we blend the oil into a creamy vinaigrette for serving. We place half an onion in the skillet to displace the oil so it comes up higher in the pan around the fish—so we can use less of it. Because the cold fish fillets rapidly cool the oil, we add the fish when the oil is at 180 degrees—well above target temperature—to compensate. We then transfer the fish to the oven to cook at a steadier temperature than could be achieved on the stovetop, flipping once, to slowly and evenly bring the fish to its ideal internal temperature of 130 to 135 degrees. While we prefer the flavor and texture of jarred whole baby artichokes, you can substitute 6 ounces frozen artichoke hearts, thawed and patted dry. You will need a 10-inch ovensafe nonstick skillet. Cod, halibut, mahi-mahi, striped bass, and swordfish can all be used in place of red snapper in this recipe.

Fish

    4 (4- to 6-ounce) skinless red snapper fillets, 1 inch thick
    ½ teaspoon table salt, divided
    1 cup jarred whole baby artichokes packed in water,
       quartered, rinsed, and patted dry
    1 tablespoon cornstarch
    ¾ cup extra-virgin olive oil, divided
    3 garlic cloves, minced
    ½ onion

Vinaigrette

    6 ounces cherry tomatoes, 4 ounces whole, 2 ounces
       cut into ⅛-inch-thick rounds, divided
    ½ small shallot
    4 teaspoons sherry vinegar
    ½ teaspoon pepper
    ¼ teaspoon table salt
    1 tablespoon minced fresh parsley

1. FOR THE FISH Adjust oven racks to middle and lower-middle positions and heat oven to 250 degrees. Pat snapper dry with paper towels and sprinkle each fillet with ⅛ teaspoon salt. Let sit at room temperature for 20 minutes.

2. Meanwhile, toss artichokes with cornstarch in bowl to coat. Heat ½ cup oil in 10-inch ovensafe nonstick skillet over medium heat until shimmering. Shake excess cornstarch from artichokes and add to skillet. Cook, stirring occasionally, until crisp and golden, 2 to 4 minutes. Add garlic and continue to cook until garlic is golden, 30 to 60 seconds. Strain oil through fine-mesh strainer into bowl. Transfer artichokes and garlic to paper towel–lined ovensafe plate and season with salt to taste. Do not wash strainer.

3. Return strained oil to now-empty skillet and add remaining ¼ cup oil. Place onion half in center of skillet. Let oil cool until it registers about 180 degrees, 5 to 8 minutes. Arrange fillets, skinned side up, around onion (oil should come roughly halfway up fillets) and spoon some oil over each fillet. Cover, transfer skillet to upper rack, and cook for 15 minutes.

4. Using pot holders, remove skillet from oven. Being careful of hot skillet handle, gently flip fillets using 2 spatulas. Cover, return skillet to upper rack, and place plate with artichokes and garlic on lower rack. Continue to cook until fish flakes apart when gently prodded with paring knife and registers 135 degrees, 9 to 14 minutes. Carefully transfer snapper to serving platter and tent loosely with aluminum foil; reserve oil in pan. Turn off oven, leaving plate of artichokes in oven.

5. FOR THE VINAIGRETTE Process ½ cup reserved fish cooking oil, whole tomatoes, shallot, vinegar, pepper, and salt in blender until smooth, about 2 minutes, scraping down sides of blender jar as needed. Add any accumulated fish juices and blend for 10 seconds. Strain sauce through fine-mesh strainer into bowl; discard solids. Season with salt and pepper to taste. Spoon vinaigrette around fish. Garnish each fillet with crisped artichokes and garlic, parsley, and tomato rounds. Serve.

Poaching Fish in Oil

PLACE ONION HALF
Bring oil in 10-inch skillet to 180 degrees and carefully place onion half in center of skillet to displace some oil.

PLACE FISH
Arrange fish fillets, skinned side up, around onion (oil should come roughly halfway up sides of fillets). Spoon a little oil over each fillet, cover skillet, and cook in 250-degree oven for 15 minutes.

FLIP FILLETS
Using 2 spatulas, carefully flip fillets. Cover skillet, return to oven, and cook until fish registers 135 degrees.

KEYS TO SUCCESS

- **Use a small pan:** A 10-inch skillet requires less oil to partially submerge the fish than a 12-inch one.

- **Use two fish spatulas:** To make turning fillets easier; one elevates the fish while the other steadies it during the flip.

- **Temp-check the oil:** You want it at 180 degrees when adding the fillets. Frying artichokes first means the oil will already be hot; adding ¼ cup more oil helps bring the temperature down.

SCIENCE LESSON Food Cooks Slower in Oil than in Water

Fish (and other food) cooks more gently in oil than in water, even when both liquids are exactly the same temperature. This is because oil has about half the heat capacity of water, which means it requires half the amount of energy to reach the same temperature as an equal volume of water. As a result, it has less energy to transfer to food and thus will cook the food more slowly than water.

WHY POACH IN OIL?

Poaching in oil allows fish to retain more of its juices than poaching in wine or broth, leading to remarkably moist, velvety results. This is because cooking in oil is inherently more gentle than cooking in water (see "Food Cooks Slower in Oil than in Water," opposite). And while you might expect that fish poached in fat would be greasy, it actually absorbs very little oil. Why? In order for oil to penetrate the fish, moisture must exit first. But because oil and water repel each other, it's very difficult for moisture inside the fish to readily enter the oil. Hence, more of the juices stay in the fish. In fact, in our tests, oil-poached fish lost just 14 percent of its weight during cooking, while water-poached fillets lost 24 percent.

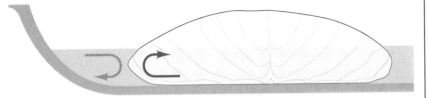

REMOVING FISH SKIN

If you buy skin-on fillets, some quick knife work can remove the skin. With a boning or other sharp knife, separate a corner of the skin from the fish. Using a paper towel to hold the skin, slide the knife between the fish and the skin to separate them.

BUTTER BASTING: EASY AS 1, 2, 3

1. BASTE
Tilt skillet toward you and repeatedly spoon butter over fish for 15 seconds.

2. REST
Place skillet flat on burner and cook fish for 30 seconds.

3. BASTE
Repeat steps 1 and 2 until fish registers 140 degrees.

USING A FOIL SLING

Steaming the fillets on top of an aluminum foil sling allows us to easily transfer them from the baking pan to the serving platter without breaking.

Grasping both ends, carefully lift sling so that fillets slide to center and are cradled in middle. Place sling gently on serving platter.

Place spatula at 1 end of fillets to hold in place. Carefully slide out sling from underneath fish.

SIDE OF SALMON DELICACIES

ANDREA GEARY

A whole side of salmon is super impressive and makes a great centerpiece for the table. Better yet, it's easy to make and easy to gussy up with a simple sauce. This makes it a winner in our book for serving company. Salmon's rich texture means it's also versatile, so here we show how to roast it, poach it, and hot-smoke it. You've got great options for a weeknight meal, Saturday night dinner party, and Sunday brunch.

ANDREA'S PRO TIP: *I eat salmon for its rich meatiness, but it's also a great source of omega-3 fatty acids. If you're into that, be sure to eat the gray-ish layer of fish right next to the skin; that's where most of those fats are concentrated.*

THE METHOD
OVEN-POACHED SALMON

Wrapping fish in a sealed foil packet with seasonings is the perfect way to poach it low and slow in the oven.

1 MAKE FOIL WRAPPING
Working with 2 pieces of foil, fold up 1 long side of each by 3 inches. Lay with folded sides touching, fold edges together and press flat.

2 PLACE FISH
Center third sheet of foil over seam. Lay salmon in center of foil.

3 ADD AROMATICS
Sprinkle fish with vinegar, then top with herb sprigs and lemon slices.

4 SEAL PACKET
Fold edges up over salmon and fold together; do not crimp too tightly.

5 PLACE ON RACK
Lay foil-wrapped fish directly on oven rack (without baking sheet). To check temperature, poke thermometer through foil and into fish.

6 CHILL AND SERVE
Once cold, unwrap salmon and brush away lemon and tarragon. Gently transfer to platter.

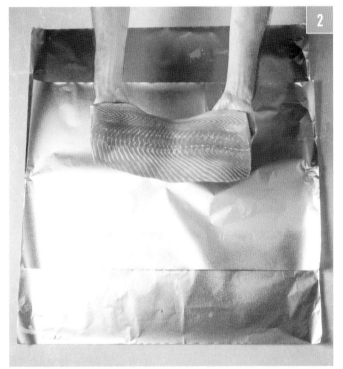

OVEN-POACHED SIDE OF SALMON

Serves: 8 to 10
Total Time: 1½ hours, plus 1 hour chilling

RECIPE OVERVIEW A poached whole side of salmon is admirable for several reasons. The moist, gentle poaching produces soft, supple salmon from end to end. Flavored with lemon and herbs and served cool, it's light and refreshing and looks elegant on a platter and works just as well at brunch or a summer dinner al fresco. And it's lovely served on its own, over a salad, or dressed up on a platter surrounded by cooked vegetables and grains, and of course a nice sauce. Cooks often poach a large fillet with a specialized fish poacher, as few other pots will hold one. We move the operation out of the pot by wrapping the side in layers of heavy-duty aluminum foil and placing it on the rack of a low oven to gently steam. Skipping the submersion in liquid means the salmon has more concentrated flavor, and the foil-encased fish can be transferred directly to the refrigerator to chill. The salmon is good with lemon wedges or any of the sauces on page 482. Use heavy-duty aluminum foil measuring 18 inches wide. You can cook two individually wrapped sides of salmon on the upper- and lower-middle racks without altering the cooking time.

- 1 (4-pound) center-cut skin-on salmon fillet, pin bones removed
- 1 teaspoon table salt
- 2 tablespoons cider vinegar
- 6 sprigs fresh tarragon or dill, plus 2 tablespoons minced
- 2 lemons, sliced thin, plus lemon wedges for serving

1. Adjust oven rack to middle position and heat oven to 250 degrees. Cut 3 pieces of heavy-duty aluminum foil 12 inches longer than side of salmon. Working with 2 pieces of foil, fold up 1 long side of each by 3 inches. Lay sheets side by side with folded sides touching, fold edges together to create secure seam, and press seam flat. Center third sheet of foil over seam. Spray foil with vegetable oil spray.

2. Pat salmon dry with paper towels and sprinkle with salt. Lay salmon, skin side down, in center of foil. Sprinkle with vinegar, then top with tarragon sprigs and lemon slices. Fold foil up over salmon to create seam on top and gently fold foil edges together to secure; do not crimp too tightly.

3. Lay foil-wrapped salmon directly on oven rack (without baking sheet). Cook until center registers 135 to 140 degrees, 45 minutes to 1 hour. (To check temperature, poke thermometer through foil and into fish.)

4. Remove salmon from oven and carefully open foil. Let salmon cool for 30 minutes. Pour off any accumulated liquid, then reseal salmon in foil and refrigerate until cold, at least 1 hour.

5. Unwrap salmon and brush away lemon slices, tarragon sprigs, and any solidified poaching liquid. Transfer fish to serving platter, sprinkle with minced tarragon, and serve with lemon wedges.

KEYS TO SUCCESS

- **Double up on foil:** Two layers of heavy-duty foil and our precise wrapping instructions prevent the fish's juices from leaking onto the bottom of your oven and creating a pesky mess.

- **Cook directly on the oven rack:** This keeps the fish's bottom from cooking more rapidly than the top (as would happen if placed on a baking sheet).

When Is Foil-Wrapped Food Done?

A thermometer is the best way to determine doneness in fish, chicken, and meat, but how do you take the temperature of food that's wrapped in foil? We simply poke an instant-read thermometer directly though the top of the foil into the center of the fish. To better locate the exact center of a food, write an "X" on the outside of the foil in marker at the center position before wrapping it tight.

ROASTED WHOLE SIDE OF SALMON

Serves: 8 to 10
Total Time: 45 minutes, plus 1 hour salting

RECIPE OVERVIEW Cooking a whole side of salmon demands different considerations than cooking individual fillets. The large fillet doesn't fit in a skillet, so you need to use the oven, where it can be a challenge to achieve ideal browning. The key is to brown the surface of the fish as quickly as possible under the broiler to develop a crust before dropping the heat so the salmon can cook gently for the bulk of the time. To do this, we hasten browning by brushing the salmon's surface with honey, which caramelizes in minutes (the fish will not taste sweet). Note that the surface will continue to brown after the oven temperature is reduced in step 4; if the surface starts to darken too much before the fillet's center registers 125 degrees, shield the dark portion with aluminum foil. If using wild salmon, which contains less fat than farmed salmon, remove it from the oven when the center of the fillet registers 120 degrees. Serve as is or with one of the sauces on page 482.

- 1 (4-pound) skin-on side of salmon, pin bones removed and belly fat trimmed
- 1 tablespoon kosher salt
- 2 tablespoons honey
  Lemon wedges

1. Sprinkle flesh side of salmon evenly with salt and refrigerate, uncovered, for at least 1 hour or up to 4 hours.

Going to Extremes for Perfection

Broiling can deeply brown a large piece of salmon, but it's not a good method for cooking the fish from start to finish because the intense heat overcooks the outermost layer. To achieve a deeply browned exterior and a silky interior, we used the broiler to jump-start browning and then a very low (250-degree) heat to bake the fish gently.

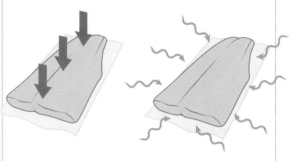

Broil to brown; bake at 250° to finish
A high-low cooking method guarantees perfectly cooked fish.

2. Adjust oven rack 7 inches from broiler element and heat oven to 250 degrees. Line rimmed baking sheet with aluminum foil and place wire rack in sheet. Fold 18 by 12-inch piece of foil lengthwise to create 18 by 6-inch sling. Place sling on wire rack and spray with vegetable oil spray.

3. Heat broiler. Pat salmon dry with paper towels and place, skin side down, on foil sling. Brush salmon evenly with honey and broil until surface is lightly but evenly browned, 8 to 12 minutes, rotating sheet halfway through broiling.

4. Return oven temperature to 250 degrees and continue to cook until center of fillet registers 125 degrees, 10 to 15 minutes longer, rotating sheet halfway through cooking. Using foil sling, transfer salmon to serving platter, then carefully remove foil. Serve, passing lemon wedges separately.

KEYS TO SUCCESS

- **Salt the fish:** This helps it retain moisture and prevents the white albumin from seeping out during cooking.

- **Rub on honey:** The sugars caramelize even more readily than white sugar, and honey can be brushed on more evenly.

- **Use three-step cooking:** Preheating to 250 degrees warms the entire oven. A quick broil browns the surface of the fish. Returning the heat to 250 degrees allows the fillet to gently cook through.

- **A foil sling:** Permits effortless transfer from counter to oven to platter.

Buying and Trimming a Side of Salmon

A side of salmon—that is, a single fillet that runs the length of the fish—typically weighs between 4 and 5 pounds. Most of the fillet is uniformly thick and will cook evenly; however, the tail end tapers, so we prefer to trim off that portion if the fillet weighs more than the recipe calls for. Ideally, your fishmonger will remove the tail portion for you, but you can easily do it yourself with a sharp knife. We also recommend trimming off the belly fat, which is a heavily marbled strip that runs most of the length of the fillet. If you trim the salmon yourself, save the excess for making salmon cakes or gravlax.

Removing Pin Bones

These small white bones run through the center of a side of fish or a fish fillet. They should be removed by your fishmonger, but it is important to check in case any were missed. Draping the fillet over an inverted bowl forces pinbones in salmon to stick out (or run fingers over surface to locate pinbones). Remove protruding bones with tweezers or needle-nose pliers.

Sauces for Salmon

FRESH TOMATO RELISH

Makes: about 1 cup
Total Time: 25 minutes
Be sure to use super-ripe tomatoes in this simple relish.

- 2   tomatoes, cored, seeded, and cut into ¼-inch pieces
- 1   small shallot, minced
- 1   small garlic clove, minced
- 2   tablespoons chopped fresh basil
- 1   tablespoon extra-virgin olive oil
- 1   teaspoon red wine vinegar

Combine all ingredients in bowl; let sit for 15 minutes. Season with salt and pepper to taste. (Relish can be refrigerated for up to 2 days.)

HORSERADISH CREAM SAUCE WITH CHIVES

Makes: about 2 cups
Total Time: 10 minutes

- 1   cup heavy cream, chilled
- ¼   cup minced fresh chives
- 1   (2-inch) piece fresh horseradish root, grated, or 2 tablespoons prepared horseradish
- 2   teaspoons lemon juice

Beat cream in deep bowl with hand-held mixer at medium speed until thick but not yet able to hold soft peaks, about 1½ minutes. Whisk in chives, horseradish root, and lemon juice until just combined. (Sauce can be covered and refrigerated for up to 2 hours; whisk briefly just before serving.)

CUCUMBER-GINGER RELISH

Makes: about 2 cups
Total Time: 15 minutes

- ½   cup rice vinegar
- 6   tablespoons extra-virgin olive oil
- ¼   cup lime juice (2 limes)
- 2   tablespoons whole-grain mustard
- 1   tablespoon grated fresh ginger
- ½   teaspoon kosher salt
- 1   English cucumber, seeded and cut into ¼-inch dice
- 1   cup minced fresh mint
- 1   cup minced fresh cilantro
- 1   serrano chile, stemmed, seeded, and minced

Whisk vinegar, oil, lime juice, mustard, ginger, and salt in bowl until smooth. Add cucumber, mint, cilantro, and serrano and stir to combine.

HOT-SMOKED WHOLE SIDE OF SALMON

Serves: 16
Total Time: 1½ hours, plus 8 hours curing and drying

RECIPE OVERVIEW Hot-smoked salmon offers the most flaky texture of perfectly roasted fish, a salty-sweet smoky flavor, and a delicately chewy exterior for subtle textural contrast. The silky fish deftly transitions from the brunch table (perhaps flaked into just-set scrambled eggs or mixed into a quiche) to dinner (maybe served as an entrée with salad or stirred into butter rice for a Scottish-style kedgeree, page 484). In fact, a benefit of cooking a whole side is that you can serve it to a large group or divide it into pieces and squirrel it away in the freezer for future uses. And the smoking can be achieved on a standard kettle grill. We start by seasoning the fish with sugar and salt to flavor it, draw out moisture, and firm up the texture. After 4 hours, we rinse off the cure and let the salmon dry in the refrigerator until a tacky film forms on the surface—which is ideal for capturing the flavorful vapors in the smoke. We then cook it over indirect heat with plenty of hardwood smoke from wood chips until it's fully cooked yet moist and succulent. We used Diamond Crystal kosher salt here. If using Morton kosher salt, which is denser, use only 6 tablespoons. If you would like to use wild salmon, we recommend king salmon; cook it to 120 degrees. We prefer hickory chips for our salmon, but any kind of hardwood chips will work. For tips on smoking on a gas grill, see page 485.

- ½   cup sugar for curing
- ½   cup kosher salt for curing
- 1   (4-pound) skin-on side of salmon, thin end of tail removed and reserved for another use, pin bones removed, and belly fat trimmed
- 1–1½ cups wood chips

1. Combine sugar and salt in small bowl. Place salmon on wire rack set in rimmed baking sheet. Spread sugar mixture evenly over surface of flesh, pressing gently to adhere. Refrigerate, uncovered, for 4 hours.

2. Rinse salmon under cold water and return to rack. Pat dry with paper towels. Refrigerate, uncovered, until surface of fillet is tacky and matte, 4 to 20 hours.

3. Using large piece of heavy-duty aluminum foil, wrap chips (1 cup if using charcoal; 1½ cups if using gas) in 8 by 4½-inch foil packet. (Make sure chips do not poke holes in sides or bottom of packet. If using gas, make sure there are no more than 2 layers of foil on bottom of packet.) Cut 3 evenly spaced 2-inch slits in top of packet.

4A. FOR A CHARCOAL GRILL Open bottom vent halfway. Light large chimney starter half filled with charcoal briquettes (3 quarts). Place 6 unlit briquettes on 1 side of grill. When top coals are partially covered with ash, pour into steeply banked pile over unlit briquettes. Place wood chip packet on coals with slits facing up. Set cooking grate in place, cover, and open lid vent halfway. Heat grill until hot and wood chips are smoking, about 5 minutes.

4B. FOR A GAS GRILL Remove cooking grate and place wood chip packet directly on primary burner. Set grate in place and turn primary burner to high (leave other burners off). Cover and heat grill until hot and wood chips are smoking, 15 to 25 minutes. Turn primary burner to medium. (Adjust primary burner as needed to maintain grill temperature between 275 and 300 degrees.)

5. Clean and oil cooking grate. Fold large piece of heavy-duty foil into 18 by 6-inch rectangle. Spray lightly with vegetable oil spray. Place foil rectangle on cooler side of grill (on gas grill arrange foil parallel to primary burner, spaced 8 to 10 inches from heat source) and place salmon on foil. Cover grill (positioning lid vent over salmon if using charcoal) and cook until center of thickest part of fillet registers 125 degrees and is still translucent when cut into with paring knife, 50 minutes to 1 hour 10 minutes.

6. Using foil as sling, transfer salmon to platter. Carefully slide foil out from beneath salmon. Serve. (Salmon can be cut into pieces, cooled completely, wrapped tightly in plastic wrap, and frozen for up to 2 months.)

KEYS TO SUCCESS

- **Air-dry in the fridge**: Anywhere from 4 to 20 hours dries out the surface just enough to ensure an admirably robust smoke flavor without overly drying the fillet.

- **A foil sling**: Helps you maneuver the fish on and off the grill without falling apart

- **Use indirect heat**: Building a moderate fire on one side of your grill and placing the salmon opposite lets the smoke and gentle heat waft over the fish until it's just cooked.

WHAT CAN GO WRONG

PROBLEM You test the temperature of your salmon but it's not quite done, so you cook it some more. When you temp it again, there's a bumpy, white streak on the surface.

SOLUTION Piercing the fish with a thermometer releases juices containing water and dissolved protein called albumin, which dries and turns semisolid and white. It's harmless, but to prevent it, after removing the thermometer probe, swab the puncture site with a paper towel before continuing to cook the fish.

HOT-SMOKED SALMON KEDGEREE

Serves: 6 to 8
Total Time: 45 minutes

RECIPE OVERVIEW Traditional British kedgeree, a comforting meal that can be served at any time of day, is a jumble of buttery rice and onions dotted with flakes of smoked fish, hard-cooked eggs, and herbs and infused with lemony brightness. Though many modern versions contain turmeric, curry powder, and coriander in homage to the dish's Indian origins, ours features just a pinch of cayenne to keep the focus on our succulent and savory hot-smoked salmon. We use precooked, cooled basmati rice so that each grain remains distinct and intact, contributing to the overall light feel of the dish, and we grate the hard-cooked eggs to imbue the rice with extra richness and a hint of sunny yellow color. Plenty of fresh parsley and chives stirred in right before serving provide a fresh finish to this comforting meal. We like basmati rice here for its delicate fragrance, but any long-grain white rice will work. This recipe works best with day-old rice; alternatively, cook the rice a couple hours ahead, spread it on a rimmed baking sheet, and let it cool completely before chilling for 30 minutes. Use the large holes of a box grater to grate the eggs.

- 5 tablespoons unsalted butter
- 1 large onion, chopped
- 1¼ teaspoons table salt, divided
  Pinch cayenne pepper (optional)
- 6 cups cooked basmati rice
- 8 ounces Hot-Smoked Whole Side of Salmon (page 482), broken into 1-inch flakes
- 6 hard-cooked large eggs, peeled and grated
- ⅓ cup chopped fresh parsley
- ⅓ cup chopped fresh chives
- 5 tablespoons lemon juice (2 lemons), plus lemon wedges for serving
- ½ teaspoon pepper

1. Melt butter in 12-inch nonstick skillet over medium-low heat. Add onion, ¼ teaspoon salt, and cayenne, if using. Cook, stirring occasionally, until onion is soft but not browned, 10 to 12 minutes. Add rice and remaining 1 teaspoon salt and increase heat to medium-high. Cook, stirring frequently to break up clumps and coat rice with butter, until rice is heated through, about 10 minutes. Add salmon and cook, stirring frequently, until salmon is heated through, about 5 minutes.

2. Transfer mixture to large bowl. Add eggs, parsley, chives, lemon juice, and pepper and toss to combine. Season with salt to taste. Transfer to platter and serve, passing lemon wedges separately.

Best Practices for Smoking on a Gas Grill

Grill smoking over charcoal is straightforward: Wrap the wood chips in foil to create a packet, cut some slits in the top, and place it atop your lit coals. But getting a packet of wood chips to smoke on a gas grill can be a bit more challenging. The first step is to place the chip packet directly on the heat diffusers so that it is as close as possible to the flame. But because these don't emit as much heat as burning coals, sometimes the chips still don't smoke enough—or even at all. The diffusers also don't offer the most stable place for the packet. Here are some tips for maximizing smoke and ensuring that the process goes smoothly.

1. DON'T OVERWRAP THE PACKET
Make sure you don't fold the foil in such a way that creates more than two layers; this will minimize layers of trapped air, which would otherwise insulate the chips from the heat and hinder smoking.

2. WIDEN SLITS IF NECESSARY
If the chips aren't smoking, use the tip of a paring knife to gently widen the slits on top of the packet to let in more oxygen and encourage smoking.

3. MOLD PACKET GENTLY OVER DIFFUSER
Heat diffusers are often shaped like inverted Vs. Take advantage of foil's flexibility so that the packet won't fall to the bottom of the grill.

4. IF NEED BE, DON'T REPLACE GRATE
If the packet doesn't fit easily under the cooking grate, don't bother putting the grate back. In most cases, smoked food doesn't sit directly above the chip packet, so the grate isn't needed.

SIMPLE WAYS WITH WHOLE FISH

JOSEPH GITTER

Roasting a fish whole shouldn't be intimidating. In fact, roasting whole fish is easier than fillets because there is less risk of overcooking. The skin and bones insulate the flesh, allowing for deeply flavorful, perfectly moist fish. While you can cook a whole fish using any cooking technique, here we focus on some of our favorites: roasting, baking, and grilling.

JOE'S PRO TIP: *Serving a whole fish is a bold and impressive move for any gathering. However there is less cover for substandard fish to hide behind. Make sure your whole fish is fresh by checking that it has clear (not cloudy) eyes, the flesh is firm to the touch, and it should definitely pass the nose test.*

WHOLE ROAST SNAPPER WITH CITRUS VINAIGRETTE

Serves: 4
Total Time: 1¼ hours

RECIPE OVERVIEW Here is a basic technique for roasting two medium whole fish such as red snapper weighing between 1½ and 2 pounds—just the right size for each person to enjoy a fillet. We start by making shallow slashes in the skin to ensure even cooking all the way to the bone, and to allow the seasoning to penetrate. The slashes also allow you to gauge the doneness of the fish easily. Applying an intense citrus salt to both the fish cavities and outside skin infuses the mild flesh with flavor, and a quick citrus vinaigrette makes a punchy accompaniment. We roast the fish on a rimmed baking sheet rather than a roasting pan for adequate air circulation above and

below. After a brief stint in a hot oven, they emerge firm, flaky, and very moist. Fish weighing more than 2 pounds will be hard to maneuver on the baking sheet and should be avoided. This recipe also works for branzino and black sea bass. If using black sea bass, cook the fish to 135 degrees in step 3.

6 tablespoons extra-virgin olive oil, divided
¼ cup minced fresh cilantro
1 small shallot, minced
2 teaspoons grated lime zest plus 2 tablespoons juice, divided
2 teaspoons grated orange zest plus 2 tablespoons juice, divided
⅛ teaspoon red pepper flakes
1½ teaspoons table salt
½ teaspoon pepper
2 (1½- to 2-pound) whole red snapper, scaled, gutted, and fins snipped off with scissors

1. Adjust oven rack to middle position and heat oven to 500 degrees. Line rimmed baking sheet with parchment paper and spray parchment with vegetable oil spray. Whisk ¼ cup oil, cilantro, shallot, lime juice, orange juice, and pepper flakes together in bowl. Season with salt and pepper to taste; set aside.

2. Combine lime zest, orange zest, salt, and pepper in bowl. Make 3 or 4 shallow slashes, about 2 inches apart, on both sides of each snapper. Open each cavity and sprinkle 1 teaspoon zest mixture on flesh. Brush 1 tablespoon oil on outside of each snapper and season with remaining zest mixture; transfer to prepared sheet and let sit for 10 minutes.

3. Roast until fish flakes apart when gently prodded with paring knife and registers 130 degrees, 15 to 20 minutes.

4. Carefully transfer snapper to cutting board and let rest for 10 minutes. Fillet each snapper by making vertical cut just behind head from top of fish to belly. Make another cut along top of snapper from head to tail. Starting at head and working toward tail, gently slide spatula between top fillet and bones to separate; transfer fillet, skin side up, to serving platter. Gently lift tail and peel skeleton and head from bottom fillet; discard head and skeleton. Transfer second fillet, skin side up, to platter. Whisk vinaigrette to recombine and serve with snapper.

KEYS TO SUCCESS

- **Slash the skin:** Ensures even cooking and deep seasoning

- **Season inside and out:** With a relatively quick cooking time, this allows flavor to penetrate the fish more fully.

- **Temp the fish:** To check doneness, insert the thermometer into the fillets through the opening by the gills.

WHOLE ROAST MACKEREL WITH PRESERVED LEMON

Serves: 4
Total Time: 1 hour

RECIPE OVERVIEW Mackerel is rich and pungent and maintains its tender, moist texture best when roasted whole. It impresses because each slender fish is enough to serve one person. Mackerel can stand up to anything, so we double down on flavor with a robust stuffing. Inspired by the aromatic ingredients in Moroccan cuisine, we tuck a combination of sweet red bell pepper, fragrant preserved lemon, and briny green olives into each fish. We line up our stuffed fish on a rimmed baking sheet for optimum air circulation and roast them in a hot oven. After just 10 minutes or so, we have four perfectly cooked, superflavorful fish. If you can't find preserved lemons, you can substitute 2 tablespoons finely grated lemon zest. To take the temperature, insert the thermometer into the fillets through the opening by the gills. You can substitute whole trout for the mackerel. The heads can be removed before serving, if desired.

3 tablespoons extra-virgin olive oil, divided
1 red bell pepper, stemmed, seeded, and chopped fine
1 red onion, chopped fine
½ preserved lemon, pulp and white pith removed, rind rinsed and minced (2 tablespoons)
⅓ cup pitted brine-cured green olives, chopped
1 tablespoon minced fresh parsley
4 (8- to 10-ounce) whole mackerel, scaled, gutted, and fins snipped off with scissors
1 teaspoon table salt, divided
1 teaspoon pepper, divided
   Lemon wedges

1. Adjust oven rack to middle position and heat oven to 500 degrees. Heat 2 tablespoons oil in 12-inch skillet over medium-high heat until shimmering. Add bell pepper and onion and cook until vegetables are softened and well browned, 8 to 10 minutes. Stir in preserved lemon and cook until fragrant, about 30 seconds. Off heat, stir in olives and parsley and season with salt and pepper to taste.

2. Grease rimmed baking sheet with remaining 1 tablespoon oil. Open cavity of each mackerel, sprinkle flesh with ¼ teaspoon salt and ¼ teaspoon pepper, and spoon one-quarter of filling into opening. Place mackerel on prepared sheet, spaced at least 2 inches apart. Roast until mackerel registers 135 degrees, 10 to 12 minutes. Carefully transfer mackerel to serving platter and let rest for 5 minutes. Serve with lemon wedges.

KEYS TO SUCCESS

- **Aromatic stuffing:** Stands up to the rich fish

- **Rimmed baking sheet:** Provides good air circulation

- **Superhot oven:** Cooks fish in just 10 minutes

2 teaspoons kosher salt
1 teaspoon ground fennel
1 teaspoon grated orange zest
4 (10- to 12-ounce) whole trout, scaled, gutted, and fins snipped off with scissors
¼ teaspoon pepper
2 tablespoons mayonnaise
½ teaspoon honey
1 (13 by 9-inch) disposable aluminum pan (if using charcoal)

1. Place salt, fennel, and orange zest on cutting board and chop until finely minced and well combined. Pat trout dry with paper towels inside and out. Open up each fish and sprinkle fennel mixture and pepper evenly over flesh. Close up fish and let sit for 10 minutes. Stir mayonnaise and honey together. Brush mayonnaise mixture evenly over entire exterior of each fish.

2A. FOR A CHARCOAL GRILL Using kitchen shears, poke twelve ½-inch holes in bottom of disposable pan. Open bottom vent completely and place disposable pan in center of grill. Light large chimney starter two-thirds filled with charcoal briquettes (4 quarts). When top coals are partially covered with ash, pour into even layer in disposable pan. Set cooking grate in place with bars parallel to long side of pan, cover, and open lid vent completely. Heat grill until hot, about 5 minutes.

2B. FOR A GAS GRILL Turn all burners to high, cover, and heat grill until hot, about 15 minutes. Leave all burners on high.

3. Fold paper towels into compact wad. Holding paper towels with tongs, dip in oil, then wipe grate. Dip paper towels in oil again and wipe grate for second time. Cover grill and heat for 5 minutes. Uncover and wipe grate twice more with oiled paper towels. Place trout on grill, perpendicular to grate bars (directly over disposable pan if using charcoal). Cook (covered if using gas) until skin is browned and beginning to blister, 2 to 4 minutes. Gently flip trout and cook until second side is browned and beginning to blister, and fish registers 135 degrees, 2 to 4 minutes. Serve.

GRILLED WHOLE TROUT WITH ORANGE AND FENNEL

Serves: 4
Total Time: 1¼ hours

RECIPE OVERVIEW Grill-roasting trout is a sensational way to prepare whole fish. The grill infuses the fish with complementary smoky flavor, and the skin crisps beautifully, a contrast to the moist flesh beneath. And because the skin acts as a buffer during cooking, it helps ensure that the interior cooks through gently. And the skin keeps the delicate flesh contained, making a whole fish easier to handle than fillets. With all of these pluses, you do have to contend with preventing the fish from sticking to the grill. Grilling over high heat is a good starting place, since the chemical bonds that cause foods to stick to iron grill grates break down when exposed to high enough heat for a long enough time. But at high heat, a whole trout will overcook before its skin can adequately crisp and brown. So, to speed up browning, we brush the fish lightly with a mix of honey and mayonnaise: The sugars in the honey promote quick browning, while the mayonnaise helps disperse the honey evenly across the fish (an emulsion of oil and water, mayo mixes more evenly with honey than pure oil would). The result is moist trout with perfectly crisp skin. To take the temperature, insert the thermometer into the fillets through the opening by the gills.

KEYS TO SUCCESS

- **Clean your grill grates:** This is critical to minimize sticking—see page 435 for more information.

- **For charcoal grills, build a concentrated fire:** An aluminum pan corrals the coals under the trout for maximum heat output.

- **Use two fish spatulas to flip:** A second spatula helps support the raw side of the fish while the first flips it over, helping the fish to stay together.

Why Browned Food Doesn't Stick

When cooking on the stovetop or grill, if you try to flip a piece of protein—whether fish, chicken, pork, or beef—too soon, the skin or the outer layer of meat will stick (or worse, with delicate fish, flake apart into shreds). But wait long enough and, as soon as the exterior browns, the protein releases from the pan. Why does this happen?

The food sticks because cysteine, an amino acid in the protein molecules, contains a sulfur atom that will bond at low temperatures with iron atoms that are present in the pan or grill grate. High heat will break these bonds, but getting your pan or grill ripping hot isn't enough—as soon as you put the food down, the temperature of the cooking surface will drop, and the food will stick. You have to wait patiently for the temperature to climb back up and then cook the exterior of the food to a high enough temperature to break the bonds.

But how do you know when that point has been reached? Conveniently, there is a visual cue: browning. Food browns when a series of chemical reactions take place, which generally happens at around the same high temperature that is required to break the sulfur-iron bonds between the food and pan. Voilà, the food releases.

Stuck
At low temperatures, proteins bond to a pan or grill grate and stick.

Released
At high temperatures, food browns and releases.

SALT-BAKED WHOLE BRANZINO
Serves: 4
Total Time: 1¼ hours

RECIPE OVERVIEW The tradition of baking whole fish in a thick salt crust goes at least as far back as fourth-century-BCE Sicily. Why (beyond awe-inspiring presentation) should you do this? Baking fish in a salt crust not only seasons the fish throughout—and perfectly—but it also cooks the entire body so evenly that it produces some of the most succulent fish we've tasted. In fact, when we measure the final temperature of the salt-crusted fish, there is virtually no discrepancy between the top and bottom fillets—something impossible to achieve in fish baked directly on a baking sheet. We combine the salt with a mixture of egg whites and water to create a workable paste. You can also bake black sea bass and red snapper following this method. Fish weighing more than 2 pounds will be hard to maneuver on the baking sheet and should be avoided. We developed this recipe using Diamond Crystal kosher salt. If using Morton kosher salt, the weight equivalence for 8 cups is 4½ pounds. To take the temperature, insert the thermometer into the fillets through the opening by the gills.

- 8 cups (3 pounds) kosher salt
- ⅔ cup water, plus extra as needed
- 4 large egg whites
- 2 (1½- to 2-pound) whole branzino, about 16 inches long, scaled, gutted, and fins snipped off with scissors
- 3 garlic cloves, minced, divided
- 1 lemon, sliced thin, divided, plus lemon wedges for serving

1. Adjust oven rack to upper-middle position and heat oven to 325 degrees. Line rimmed baking sheet with parchment paper. Stir salt, water, and egg whites in large bowl until well combined. (Mixture should hold together when squeezed; if necessary, continue to stir, adding extra water, 1 tablespoon at a time, until mixture holds.)

2. Working with 1 branzino at a time, open cavity, spread half of garlic on flesh, and stuff with half of lemon slices.

3. Divide 3 cups of salt mixture into 2 even mounds on prepared sheet. Pat mounds into 10 by 4-inch rectangles, spaced about 1 inch apart. Lay 1 branzino lengthwise across each mound. Gently pack remaining salt mixture evenly around each branzino, leaving heads and tails exposed. Roast until branzino registers 135 degrees, 40 to 45 minutes, rotating sheet halfway through roasting. Transfer sheet to wire rack and let branzino rest for 5 minutes.

4. Using back of serving spoon, gently tap top and sides of salt crusts to crack into large pieces and discard. Using spatula, transfer branzino to cutting board and brush away excess salt. Fillet each branzino by making vertical cut just behind head from top of fish to belly. Make another cut along top of branzino from head to tail. Starting at head

and working toward tail, gently slide spatula between top fillet and bones to separate; transfer fillet, skin side up, to serving platter. Gently lift tail and peel skeleton and head from bottom fillet; discard head, skeleton, and lemon slices. Transfer second fillet, skin side up, to platter. (See page 491.) Serve with lemon wedges.

KEYS TO SUCCESS

- **Kosher salt:** Given the quantity of salt needed, affordable kosher salt works just fine.
- **Encasing the fish in a salt crust:** Seasons the fish and also cooks it evenly
- **Stuffing with garlic and lemon:** Adds flavor from the inside out

Preparing Salt-Baked Branzino

MAKE SALT MOUNDS
Divide 3 cups of salt mixture into 2 even mounds on prepared sheet. Pat mounds into 10 by 4-inch rectangles.

PLACE FISH
Lay 1 branzino lengthwise across each mound.

PACK SALT AROUND FISH
Gently pack remaining salt around each, leaving heads and tails exposed.

RESOURCES FOR WHOLE FISH

FISH TO EAT WHOLE

We like cooking black sea bass, branzino, mackerel, red snapper, and trout whole, and all five of these are easy to find at a good fish counter. Here are some pointers to take the fear out of fish with fins.

Black sea bass, branzino (European sea bass), and red snapper are all of comparable size and should be filleted after cooking (see at right) to serve. Mackerel and trout are nice because each fish serves one.

Customarily, these fish will come to you scaled and gutted (certainly ask your fishmonger if this is not automatic); you may just need to snip off the fins with kitchen scissors before cooking.

Unless you're salt-crusting your branzino (see page 490), cooking whole fish by roasting or grilling is a fairly streamlined process; serving it as fillets is simple if you follow our steps (unless folks just want to dig in with their own forks and knives, which is fine, too). And be sure to look out for translucent pin bones when eating—part of the whole-fish experience.

STILL IN DOUBT? CHOOSE TROUT

Not only are whole trout almost always sold cleaned, scaled, and gutted, they often have their backbones and pinbones removed for even less fuss (although filleting a cooked fish isn't much more work as we show at right). And one fish serves one person for nice portioning.

FLIPPING WHOLE FISH ON THE GRILL

SLIDE UNDER AND LIFT

Slide spatula scant 1 inch under backbone edge and lift edge up. Slide second spatula under, then remove first spatula, allowing fish to ease onto second spatula.

FLIP

Place first spatula on top of fish so it's oriented in same direction as second spatula and flip fish over.

FILLETING WHOLE FISH

1. Make vertical cut just behind head from top of fish to belly.

2. Make another cut along back of fish from head to tail. Starting at head and working toward tail, use metal spatula to lift meat away from bones. Repeat on second side.

3. Gently lift tail and peel skeleton and head from bottom fillet; discard head and skeleton. Transfer second fillet, skin side up, to platter.

LUXURIOUS LOBSTER

ELLE SIMONE SCOTT

Lobster is the filet mignon of seafood, but it didn't start out as a delicacy: Until the mid-19th century, lobsters were so commonplace in the coastal states that they were used as bait and fertilizer. Today, wild American lobsters are caught from Maine down to North Carolina and often held in tanks, selling for upwards of $10 per pound. Lobster is eaten at high-end restaurants and with vats of melted butter by vacationers.

ELLE'S PRO TIP: *Don't let this crustacean fool you; lobster prep isn't as hard as it seems. It does take some time and patience, attention, and a good fresh lobster. The fresher it is, the easier it is to extract all the delicious meat that you've definitely paid for. Don't worry, it's worth all the effort.*

THE METHOD

LOBSTER MEAT

There's a lot more meat in a lobster than just the tails and claws—if you know how to get it. Here's our tried and true approach to extracting every last bit.

1 SEPARATE TAIL

Once cooked lobster is cool enough to handle, set it on cutting board. Grasp tail with your hand and grab body with your other hand and twist to separate.

2 FLATTEN TAIL

Lay tail on its side on counter and use both your hands to press down on tail until shell cracks.

3 REMOVE TAIL MEAT

Hold tail, flippers facing you and shell facing down. Pull sides back to open shell and remove meat. Remove green tomalley and dark vein. Slice tail lengthwise if desired for easy sharing.

4 SEPARATE KNUCKLES

Twist "arms" to remove claws and attached "knuckles." Twist knuckle and claw to separate. Break knuckles at joint using back of chef's knife or lobster-cracking tool. Use handle of teaspoon to push out meat.

5 SEPARATE CLAWS

Wiggle hinged portion of each claw to separate. If meat is stuck inside small part, remove with skewer.

6 CRACK CLAWS

Break open claws, cracking 1 side and then flipping to crack other side.

7 REMOVE CLAW MEAT

Remove meat from claws.

8 SEPARATE LEGS

Twist legs to remove. Lay flat on counter. Using rolling pin, roll toward open end, pushing out meat. Stop rolling before reaching end of legs; otherwise leg can crack and release pieces of shell.

BOILED LOBSTER

Serves: 4 (makes 1 pound meat)
Total Time: 45 minutes

RECIPE OVERVIEW Some cooks suggest steaming lobster, but that requires a steamer on a rack and can leave the lobsters slightly underseasoned. We prefer to boil ours in salt water. Freezing the lobsters briefly to sedate them before cooking renders them motionless before going into the pot. To determine doneness (who wants chewy lobster?), we take a cue from other meat cookery and poke a thermometer in the underside of the meaty tail. The target temperature turns out to be just a bit higher than for white fish: 140 degrees. To cook four lobsters at once, you will need a pot with a capacity of at least 3 gallons. If your pot is smaller, boil the lobsters in batches. Start timing the lobsters from the moment they go into the pot. Serve with melted butter and lemon wedges, or use the meat in a classic lobster roll (recipe follows).

4 (1¼-pound) live lobsters
⅓ cup table salt, for cooking lobsters

1. Place lobsters in large bowl and freeze for 30 minutes. Meanwhile, bring 2 gallons water to boil in large pot.

2. Add lobsters and salt to pot, arranging with tongs so that all lobsters are submerged. Cover pot, leaving lid slightly ajar, and adjust heat to maintain gentle boil. Cook for 8 minutes; then, holding lobster with tongs, insert thermometer through underside of tail into thickest part; meat should register 140 degrees. If necessary, return lobster to pot for 2 minutes, until tail registers 140 degrees.

3. Serve immediately or transfer lobsters to rimmed baking sheet and set aside until cool enough to remove meat (see page 492), about 10 minutes. (Lobster meat can be refrigerated in airtight container for up to 24 hours.)

SCIENCE LESSON

Getting the Lobster into the Pot

The most common method of cooking lobsters is plunging them into boiling water, where they will continue to move about for a short time. Though there's no way to know the extent to which the lobster suffers during this time, most scientists agree that their primitive nervous system prevents processing pain the way we do. Still, putting live lobsters into a pot can be unpleasant. Seeking a way to sedate the lobster before cooking we worked through a number of techniques, including cutting through its head, a soak in clove-scented water, and hypnotization, but landed upon a simple approach: a 30-minute stay in the freezer, which rendered the lobster motionless before it went into the pot.

KEYS TO SUCCESS

- **Seek out hard-shell lobster:** For better flavor and meatier texture

- **Temp the tail:** Ignore charts recommending cooking times and use an instant-read thermometer to ensure your lobster is just cooked through.

NEW ENGLAND LOBSTER ROLLS

Serves: 6
Total Time: 25 minutes

Make sure to use a top-loading hotdog bun—well toasted.

2 tablespoons mayonnaise
2 tablespoons minced celery
1½ teaspoons lemon juice
1 teaspoon minced fresh chives
⅛ teaspoon table salt
  Pinch cayenne pepper
1 pound cooked lobster meat, tail meat cut into ½-inch pieces and claw meat cut into 1-inch pieces
2 tablespoons unsalted butter, softened
6 New England–style hot dog buns
6 leaves Bibb lettuce

1. Whisk mayonnaise, celery, lemon juice, chives, salt, and cayenne together in large bowl. Add lobster and gently toss to combine.

2. Place 12-inch nonstick skillet over low heat. Butter both sides of buns and season to taste with salt. Place buns in skillet, 1 buttered side down, increase heat to medium-low, and cook until crisp and brown, 2 to 3 minutes per side. Transfer buns to large serving platter. Line each bun with 1 lettuce leaf. Spoon lobster salad into buns and serve immediately.

KEYS TO SUCCESS

- **Simple mayo:** Complements the richly flavored lobster

- **A hint of crunch:** Created with a small amount of lettuce and celery

- **Toasting the buns:** Not only adds flavor but also ensures the buns don't get soggy

GRILLED LOBSTERS

Serves: 2
Total Time: 45 minutes, plus 30 minutes freezing

RECIPE OVERVIEW If you're going to grill lobster rather than boil it, you want it to be worth it. This recipe delivers lobster with smoky grill flavor penetrating the sweet meat—not just coloring the shell. Splitting the lobsters in half takes some care, but is the right way to go. Starting the lobsters cut side down and then flipping them after 2 minutes keeps moisture loss to a minimum. To allow the claws to finish cooking at the same time as the tail meat, you need to crack each one before cooking so heat can better reach the meat. A buttery, herby bread-crumb topping that sizzles on the lobsters as they grill brings dressed-up appeal. Make sure the topping is prepped before you start the grill. Don't halve the lobsters until the grill has been started. If you plan to cook more than two lobsters, you will need to cook them in batches so as not to overcrowd the grill. To split and clean lobsters, see page 497.

2   (1½- to 2-pound) live lobsters
¼   cup panko bread crumbs
1   teaspoon vegetable oil
6   tablespoons unsalted butter, melted
2   garlic cloves, minced
2   tablespoons minced fresh parsley
½   teaspoon table salt, divided
¼   teaspoon pepper, divided
    Lemon wedges

1. Place lobsters in large bowl and freeze for 30 minutes. Toss panko with oil in small bowl until evenly coated. Microwave, stirring frequently, until panko is light golden brown, about 2 minutes; set aside.

2A. FOR A CHARCOAL GRILL Open bottom vent completely. Light large chimney starter filled with charcoal briquettes (6 quarts). When top coals are partially covered with ash, pour evenly over grill. Set cooking grate in place, cover, and open lid vent completely. Heat grill until hot, about 5 minutes.

2B. FOR A GAS GRILL Turn all burners to high, cover, and heat grill until hot, about 15 minutes. Leave all burners on high.

3. Meanwhile, combine melted butter and garlic in bowl. Combine toasted panko, parsley, ¼ teaspoon salt, ⅛ teaspoon pepper, and 2 tablespoons garlic butter in second bowl; set aside. Split lobsters in half lengthwise, then clean and devein lobsters. Using meat pounder, pound each claw to crack open slightly. Sprinkle tail meat with remaining ¼ teaspoon salt and remaining ⅛ teaspoon pepper and brush lobster meat evenly with 2 tablespoons garlic butter.

4. Clean cooking grate, then repeatedly brush grate with well-oiled paper towels until grate is black and glossy, 5 to 10 times. Place lobsters, cut side down, on grill and cook (covered if using gas) until tail meat just begins to turn opaque, about 2 minutes.

5. Transfer lobsters, cut side up, to rimmed baking sheet. Divide panko mixture evenly among lobster halves and drizzle with remaining 2 tablespoons garlic butter. Return lobsters, shell-side down, to grill and cook (covered if using gas) until panko mixture begins to bubble and tail meat is opaque and registers 140 degrees, 4 to 6 minutes. Serve lobsters with lemon wedges.

KEYS TO SUCCESS

- **Freeze the lobsters:** To sedate them before splitting them

- **Heat the grill first:** You want to kill the lobsters just before cooking them, so give the grill a head start.

- **Crack the claws:** A meat pounder opens each claw to help it cook at the same rate as the split tail.

LOBSTER AND CORN CHOWDER

Serves: 4 to 6
Total Time: 2 hours, plus 30 minutes freezing

RECIPE OVERVIEW This luxurious chowder is our favorite way to enjoy the summery combination of succulent lobster and sweet corn. Lobster broth gives the soup big lobster flavor. After killing and splitting the lobsters, we sauté the bodies until bright red and lightly browned and then add the classic mirepoix of onion, carrot, and celery along with white wine to fortify a potent broth that we later use to poach the tails and claws. Bacon provides a meaty backbone, while a bit of flour as well as the sweet pulp from the starchy corn cobs give it the body of a chowder. For a final touch of complexity, we add a splash of dry sherry. Do not substitute frozen corn for the fresh corn here; fresh corn is crucial to the flavor of this seasonal soup.

Broth

- 2 (1¼-pound) live lobsters
- 3 tablespoons vegetable oil
- 1 onion, chopped
- 1 carrot, peeled and chopped
- 1 celery rib, chopped
- 2 plum tomatoes, cored and cut into ½-inch pieces
- ⅓ cup dry white wine
- 7 cups water
- 1 bay leaf

Chowder

- 2 ears corn, husks and silk removed
- 2 slices bacon, chopped fine
- 1 onion, chopped fine
- 1 celery rib, chopped fine
- 1 teaspoon minced fresh thyme or ¼ teaspoon dried
- ¼ cup all-purpose flour
- 1 large Yukon Gold potato (10 to 12 ounces), peeled and cut into ½-inch pieces
- ¾ cup heavy cream
- 2 tablespoons minced fresh parsley
- 2 teaspoons dry sherry

1. FOR THE BROTH Place lobsters in large bowl and freeze for 30 minutes. Kill the lobsters following the instructions on page 497, then remove the claws (with arms) and tails; remove rubber bands. Split the bodies in half and discard the innards and gills.

2. Heat oil in Dutch oven over medium-high heat until just smoking. Add cleaned lobster bodies and cook until bright red and lightly browned, 3 to 5 minutes. Stir in onion, carrot, celery, and tomatoes and cook until softened, 5 to 7 minutes. Stir in wine and cook until nearly evaporated, about 1 minute.

3. Stir in water and bay leaf and bring to boil. Add lobster claws and tails, reduce heat to medium-low, and simmer gently until tails register 140 degrees (insert thermometer through underside of tail into thickest part), about 4 minutes. If necessary, return claws and tails to pot for 2 minutes, until tails register 140 degrees. Remove claws and tails from pot and let cool slightly. Once cool enough to handle, remove lobster meat from shells (see page 492), chop coarse, and refrigerate until ready to serve; discard shells.

4. Meanwhile, continue to simmer lobster broth until rich and flavorful, about 45 minutes. Strain broth through fine-mesh strainer, pressing on solids to extract as much liquid as possible. Wipe out pot with paper towels.

5. FOR THE CHOWDER Cut corn kernels off cobs; set aside. Scrape cobs clean of pulp and reserve pulp separately. Cook bacon in pot over medium heat until crisp, 5 to 7 minutes. Stir in onion and celery and cook until softened, about 5 minutes. Stir in thyme and cook until fragrant, about 30 seconds. Stir in flour and cook for 1 minute.

6. Gradually whisk in strained lobster broth, scraping up any browned bits and smoothing out any lumps. Stir in potato and corn cob pulp and bring to boil. Reduce heat to medium-low and simmer gently until potato is nearly tender, 15 to 20 minutes.

7. Stir in corn kernels and simmer until tender, 5 to 7 minutes. Stir in cream and return to brief simmer. Off heat, stir in parsley and sherry and season with salt and pepper to taste. Stir in lobster meat, cover, and let sit until warmed through, about 1 minute. Serve.

KEYS TO SUCCESS

- **Sauté the shells:** When lobster shells are cooked with dry heat they start to brown and undergo the Maillard reaction, developing new and enticing flavor and aroma compounds, the basis for our lobster broth.

- **Don't rush the simmer:** A full 45 minutes is needed to develop the lobster broth's potent flavor.

- **Milk the corn:** Scraping the pulp and milk from spent ears of corn helps develop a soup with deep corn essence.

RESOURCES FOR LOBSTER

CHOOSING LOBSTER

Not all lobsters are created equal. The quality of lobster meat depends to a large extent on where the crustacean is in its molting cycle, during which the hard, old shell is replaced with a soft, new one. Hard-shell lobsters taste better and are meatier. To determine the stage of your lobster, just squeeze. A soft-shell lobster will yield to pressure. Like the roe? Look for a female lobster. Her soft "swim-merets" (appendages under the lowest legs) give her away.

WHY COOK LOBSTERS ALIVE?

Lobsters are the only animals we regularly kill ourselves in the kitchen. Lobsters are cooked alive or immediately after killing for two reasons, related to both flavor and health: First, the instant a lobster dies, enzymes within its body begin to break down the flesh and cause it to turn mushy. Second, like other shellfish, deceased lobsters are vulnerable to bacterial contamination that can cause food poisoning.

TALKING TOMALLEY

When cleaning out a lobster, you'll find a soft green mass; that's the digestive gland known to marine biologists as the hepatopancreas and to lobster fans as the tomalley. The latter group prizes the tomalley for its creamy texture and intensely concentrated lobster flavor. Tomalley of cooked lobster is eaten as is, whisked into sauces, or mixed into a compound butter for toast.

There is some concern that eating tomalley can lead to the contraction of paralytic shellfish poisoning (PSP), the illness caused by red tide. Lobsters do not filter-feed, but they consume infected clams and scallops. The PSP could accumulate in its tomalley. It's fine to eat lobster meat, but it's a good idea to forgo the tomalley when there's a shellfish ban. Otherwise, indulge.

KILLING AND SPLITTING LOBSTERS FOR THE GRILL OR CHOWDER

If we are grilling lobster or using it in a chowder, we do cut through the head of the lobster to kill it. If the thought of splitting a live lobster makes you squeamish, know that this is humane and, of course, the most efficient way to dispatch a lobster. You can still freeze the lobster before doing so to lessen its activity. Don't be surprised if the lobster continues to move after being split; this is the result of twitching nerve fibe.

With the blade of a chef's knife facing the head, plunge the knife into the body at the point where the shell forms a T. Move the blade straight down through the head. Positioning the knife blade so that it faces the tail end, continue to cut through the body toward the tail, making sure to cut all the way through the shell.

Using a spoon, discard the stomach, digestive track, and tomalley (see above for more information). Using a meat pounder, lightly pound each claw to crack it open slightly for cooking.

WHY DO COOKED LOBSTERS TURN RED?

The muscles in lobster, especially the tail, are fast-twitch muscles, only used during sudden movement. Fast-twitch muscles contain very little of the red protein pigment myoglobin (the compound that makes beef or pork red), so the tail muscles of lobster contain very little color in their raw state. The reddish color we see in cooked lobster meat is due to carotenoid pigments that in the raw state are bound together with proteins. But when cooked, the proteins denature and release the carotenoids, allowing them to assume their natural red. This also happens in lobster's shells, turning them from brownish-green in live lobsters to bright red when cooked.

SEAFOOD MEDLEYS

STEVE DUNN

Seafood stews and other dishes containing multiple kinds of fresh seafood are a heady mix of textures and flavors. In this course we go fishing for more than the better-known bouillabaisse and cioppino. We reel in colorful cataplana from Portugal, with its smoky red broth. We find inspiration from Brazilian moqueca, a creamy shrimp and fish stew. We revel in the seafood pasta from Italy known as allo scoglio, rich with the juices from clams and mussels. Lastly we carry a Spanish paella out to the grill where it obtains smoky flavor and a golden crisp crust while it cooks in a large roasting pan.

STEVE'S PRO TIP: *While shellfish need to be bought fresh for these dishes, by all means use frozen fish fillets, shrimp, and squid in these recipes if you wish. Recent advancements in flash-freezing technology yield high-quality frozen seafood well-suited for these meals.*

CATAPLANA

Serves: 4 to 6
Total Time: 1 hour

RECIPE OVERVIEW Hailing from the Algarve, Portugal's sandy and rugged southernmost coast, this simple seafood stew brings together fresh seafood and smoky cured meat in a rich, ruddy broth. Traditionally served in a hammered copper clamshell-shaped pot bearing the same name as the dish itself, cataplana may once have been a lunch-box meal for fishermen, who some say used the vessel to store their catch and transfer it right to the fire when it came time to cook. We draw inspiration from amêijoas na cataplana, or clams in a cataplana, supplementing the clams with juicy shrimp. We start by cooking slices of linguica, rendering fat that we then use to sauté our aromatic vegetables and smoked paprika to build a flavor base. To create a brothy but balanced stew, we include canned tomatoes and white wine, but don't go overboard on either. Instead, we add more liquid in the form of bottled clam juice. Look for small littleneck or Manila clams that are all about 2 inches across so that they cook at the same rate. If linguica sausage is unavailable, you can substitute chouriço or Spanish chorizo. Most linguica sausages are about 1½ inches thick; if yours are narrower, cut them into ¼-inch-thick coins. For more information on cleaning clams, see page 503. Serve with crusty bread.

12 ounces extra-large shrimp (21 to 25 per pound), peeled, deveined, and cut in half crosswise
¾ teaspoon table salt, divided
2 tablespoons extra-virgin olive oil
12 ounces linguica sausage, quartered lengthwise and sliced ¼ inch thick
2 garlic cloves, minced
¾ teaspoon smoked paprika
½ teaspoon red pepper flakes
1 large onion, halved and sliced thin
1 fennel bulb, stalks discarded, bulb halved, cored, and sliced thin lengthwise
1 red bell pepper, stemmed, seeded, and cut into ¼-inch-wide strips
1 (28-ounce) can whole peeled tomatoes, drained and chopped coarse
1 (8-ounce) bottle clam juice
½ cup dry white wine
3 pounds littleneck or Manila clams, scrubbed
½ cup chopped fresh parsley
Lemon wedges

1. Combine shrimp and ¼ teaspoon salt in bowl; refrigerate until needed. Heat oil in large Dutch oven over medium-high heat until shimmering. Add linguica and cook, stirring occasionally, until browned and fat is slightly rendered, about 4 minutes. Stir in garlic, paprika, and pepper flakes and cook until fragrant, about 30 seconds.

2. Add onion, fennel, bell pepper, and remaining ½ teaspoon salt and cook, stirring occasionally, until vegetables are softened, 8 to 10 minutes. Stir in tomatoes, clam juice, and wine. Bring to simmer and cook, stirring occasionally, until thickened slightly, about 5 minutes.

3. Increase heat to high and bring mixture to boil. Stir in clams; cover and cook until clams have opened, 5 to 7 minutes, stirring halfway through cooking. Off heat, stir in shrimp. Cover and let stand off heat until shrimp are opaque and just cooked through, about 5 minutes. Discard any unopened clams. Stir in parsley and season with salt to taste. Transfer to serving bowl, if desired, and serve, passing lemon wedges separately.

KEYS TO SUCCESS

- **Bottled clam juice:** Reinforces the briny taste of the sea and makes for a brothier stew without diluting its flavor as water would

- **Supplement with shrimp:** More than 3 pounds of clam shells would crowd the pot, so we add shrimp for a more seafood-forward stew.

- **Add the shellfish at the end:** To preserve their delicate textures and render them plump, juicy, and tender

MOQUECA

Serves: 6
Total Time: 1¼ hours

RECIPE OVERVIEW One of the most complex-tasting seafood stews you may ever taste, Brazilian moqueca is a masterclass in layering flavors—and how this can be done simply with the right ingredients. Cooks typically marinate fish and/or shellfish in lime juice and garlic, stew the mixture in a clay pot with coconut milk and aromatics, then drizzle on nutty African dendê (palm) oil and a tangy hot pepper sauce. This combination balances creamy richness, bright citrus, aromatic depth, and heat. In our version, instead of marinating the fish, we reserve the lime juice to add at the end for brighter citrus flavor. To balance the richness and sweetness of the coconut milk with the bright, fresh flavor of the aromatics, we blend onion, tomatoes, and cilantro in the food processor, which also adds body, creating a lush stew. We keep the bell peppers diced for contrasting texture and bite. To approximate the hot-tangy sauce made from local malagueta chiles, we pulse vinegar-packed hot cherry peppers with onion and sugar and stir some of it into the stew, then serve more alongside (save any leftovers to punch up eggs, meats, or grains). Black sea bass, haddock, hake, pollock, or other firm-fleshed, flaky whitefish may be substituted for the cod. We use olive oil in place of dendê oil but if you have it available, season individual bowls to taste. Serve with steamed white rice.

Pepper Sauce
4 pickled hot cherry peppers (3 ounces)
½ onion, chopped coarse
¼ cup extra-virgin olive oil
⅛ teaspoon sugar

Stew
1 pound large shrimp (26 to 30 per pound), peeled, deveined, and tails removed
1 pound skinless cod fillets (¾ to 1 inch thick), cut into 1½-inch pieces
3 garlic cloves, minced
1½ teaspoons table salt, divided
¼ teaspoon pepper
1 onion, chopped coarse
1 (14.5-ounce) can whole peeled tomatoes
¾ cup chopped fresh cilantro, divided
2 tablespoons extra-virgin olive oil
1 red bell pepper, stemmed, seeded, and cut into ½-inch pieces
1 green bell pepper, stemmed, seeded, and cut into ½-inch pieces
1 (14-ounce) can coconut milk
2 tablespoons lime juice

1. **FOR THE PEPPER SAUCE** Process all ingredients in food processor until smooth, about 30 seconds, scraping down sides of bowl as needed. Season with salt to taste and transfer to separate bowl. Rinse out processor bowl.

2. **FOR THE STEW** Toss shrimp and cod with garlic, ½ teaspoon salt, and pepper in bowl. Set aside.

3. Process onion, tomatoes and their juice, and ¼ cup cilantro in food processor until finely chopped and mixture has texture of pureed salsa, about 30 seconds.

4. Heat oil in large Dutch oven over medium-high heat until shimmering. Add red and green bell peppers and ½ teaspoon salt and cook, stirring frequently, until softened, 5 to 7 minutes. Add onion-tomato mixture and remaining ½ teaspoon salt. Reduce heat to medium and cook, stirring frequently, until puree has reduced and thickened slightly, 3 to 5 minutes (pot should not be dry).

5. Increase heat to high, stir in coconut milk, and bring to boil (mixture should be bubbling across entire surface). Add seafood mixture and lime juice and stir to evenly distribute seafood, making sure all pieces are submerged in liquid. Cover pot and remove from heat. Let stand until shrimp and cod are opaque and just cooked through, 15 minutes.

6. Gently stir in 2 tablespoons pepper sauce and remaining ½ cup cilantro, being careful not to break up cod too much. Season with salt and pepper to taste. Serve, passing remaining pepper sauce separately.

KEYS TO SUCCESS

- **Process some aromatics:** Blending some to the consistency of a slightly chunky salsa adds body and cuts the coconut milk's richness.

- **Cut the heat:** Shrimp and cod are easy to overcook, so we let the broth reach a full boil before adding the seafood, then turn off the heat.

- **Stir in pepper sauce:** Instead of just serving it alongside to elevate the dish's brightness

LINGUINE ALLO SCOGLIO

Serves: 6
Total Time: 1¾ hours

RECIPE OVERVIEW Italian seafood pastas promise noodles teeming with shellfish and saturated with clean, briny-sweet flavor. In this trattoria classic named for rocky Italian seashores (scoglio means "rock") we show how to create a pasta dish with rich, savory seafood flavor in every bite. We start by making a sauce with clam juice and four minced anchovies, which fortify the juices shed by the shellfish. Cooking the shellfish in a careful sequence ensures that every piece stays plump and tender. We parboil the linguine and then finished cooking it directly in the sauce; the noodles soak up flavor while shedding starches that thicken the sauce. Fresh cherry tomatoes, lots of garlic, fresh herbs,

and lemon made for a bright, complex-tasting sauce. For a simpler version, you can omit the clams and squid and increase the amounts of mussels and shrimp to 1½ pounds each; also increase the amount of salt in step 2 to ¾ teaspoon. A Pinot Grigio or similar dry white wine works well here.

6	tablespoons extra-virgin olive oil, divided
12	garlic cloves, minced
¼	teaspoon red pepper flakes
1	pound littleneck or cherrystone clams, scrubbed
1	pound mussels, scrubbed and debearded
1¼	pounds cherry tomatoes (half of tomatoes halved, remaining tomatoes left whole), divided
1	(8-ounce) bottle clam juice
1	cup dry white wine
1	cup minced fresh parsley, divided
1	tablespoon tomato paste
4	anchovy fillets, rinsed, patted dry, and minced
1	teaspoon minced fresh thyme
½	teaspoon table salt, plus salt for cooking pasta
1	pound linguine
1	pound extra-large shrimp (21 to 25 per pound), peeled and deveined
8	ounces squid, sliced crosswise into ½-inch-thick rings
2	teaspoons grated lemon zest, plus lemon wedges for serving

1. Heat ¼ cup oil in large Dutch oven over medium-high heat until shimmering. Add garlic and pepper flakes and cook until fragrant, about 1 minute. Add clams, cover, and cook, shaking pot occasionally, for 4 minutes. Add mussels, cover, and continue to cook, shaking pot occasionally, until clams and mussels have opened, 3 to 4 minutes. Transfer clams and mussels to bowl, discarding any that haven't opened, and cover to keep warm; leave any broth in pot.

2. Add whole tomatoes, clam juice, wine, ½ cup parsley, tomato paste, anchovies, thyme, and salt to pot and bring to simmer over medium-high heat. Reduce heat to medium and cook, stirring occasionally, until tomatoes have started to break down and sauce is reduced by one-third, about 10 minutes.

3. Meanwhile, bring 4 quarts water to boil in large pot. Add pasta and 1 tablespoon salt and cook, stirring often, for 7 minutes. Reserve ½ cup cooking water, then drain pasta.

4. Add pasta to sauce in Dutch oven and cook over medium heat, stirring gently, for 2 minutes. Reduce heat to medium-low, stir in shrimp, cover, and cook for 4 minutes. Stir in squid, lemon zest, halved tomatoes, and remaining ½ cup parsley; cover and continue to cook until shrimp and squid are just cooked through, about 2 minutes. Gently stir in clams and mussels. Remove pot from heat, cover, and let stand until clams and mussels are warmed through, about 2 minutes. Season with salt and pepper to taste and adjust consistency with reserved cooking water as needed. Transfer to large serving dish, drizzle with remaining 2 tablespoons oil, and serve, passing lemon wedges separately.

KEYS TO SUCCESS

- **Add clam juice:** Boosts the briny seafood essence of the sauce without the need to use a seafood stock

- **Stagger additions:** Add hardier clams and mussels first, reserving shrimp and squid for the final minutes of cooking.

- **Reserve some pasta water:** To adjust the consistency of the sauce while adding more starch to help thicken the sauce

- **Finish cooking the pasta in the sauce:** This infuses the pasta with the briny flavor of the sauce, and makes the sauce viscous enough to cling to the pasta.

Making Linguine allo Scoglio

START SAUCE
Create flavorful sauce base for pasta. Cooking several kinds of shellfish in stages leaves you with potent, briny broth.

FINISH SAUCE
Add remaining sauce ingredients to pot and simmer, stirring gently, until they break down and sauce is reduced.

ADD PASTA
Add parboiled pasta to pot (it should be flexible but not fully cooked). Simmer in sauce mixture, stirring gently, until al dente.

COMBINE EVERYTHING
Combine all ingredients in pot. Adjust consistency of sauce to your liking with reserved pasta cooking water. Toss with tongs to combine everything before serving.

GRILLED PAELLA

Serves: 8
Total Time: 2¼ hours

RECIPE OVERVIEW While many paella recipes are cooked indoors, paella was originally made on the grill. Cooking it over a large live fire gives the dish a subtle smokiness and using a roasting pan offers an extra-large cooking surface that encourages thorough development of the prized caramelized crust known as socarrat. But grilling presents challenges. Delicate proteins can overcook while they wait for heartier items to cook through, and keeping a charcoal fire going strong is tricky. Our technique produces a uniformly crisp, golden crust topped with tender-chewy rice that nestles perfectly cooked moist chicken, sausage, shellfish, and vegetables. The key to even cooking is to create long-lasting heat. While that's easy enough on a gas grill, for a charcoal grill we start with a whopping 7 quarts of charcoal (instead of our usual 6 quarts) and then cover the lit coals with 20 fresh briquettes, which gradually ignite during cooking. We give chicken thighs a head start by browning them directly on the grate and then arrange them around the pan's cooler perimeter to keep them moist. We separately prepare a flavorful broth with garlic, paprika, and saffron. As our roasting pan heats on the grill we cook chopped onion, roasted red peppers, and tomato paste, then add the rice to coat with oil and pour our hot broth mixture over the top. Next, in go the shrimp and clams in the middle of the simmering rice, partially submerged so they won't overcook, and a scattering of chorizo. The final addition: Quick-cooking green peas, at which point we let the paella cook until the rice grains are perfectly plump and the crust sizzles invitingly. You will need a heavy-duty roasting pan that measures at least 14 by 11 inches. If the exterior of your pan is dark, the cooking times will be on the lower side of the ranges given. The recipe can also be made in a 15- to 17-inch paella pan. If littlenecks are unavailable, use 1½ pounds shrimp in step 1 and season them with ½ teaspoon table salt.

1½ pounds boneless, skinless chicken thighs, trimmed and halved crosswise

1¾ teaspoons table salt, divided

1 teaspoon pepper

12 ounces jumbo shrimp (16 to 20 per pound), peeled and deveined

5 tablespoons extra-virgin olive oil, divided

6 garlic cloves, minced, divided

1¾ teaspoons hot smoked paprika, divided

3 tablespoons tomato paste

4 cups chicken broth

⅔ cup dry sherry

1 (8-ounce) bottle clam juice

Pinch saffron threads, crumbled (optional)

1 onion, chopped fine

½ cup jarred roasted red peppers, rinsed, patted dry, and chopped fine

3 cups Arborio rice

1 pound littleneck or cherrystone clams, scrubbed

8 ounces Spanish-style chorizo sausage, cut into ½-inch pieces

1 cup frozen peas, thawed

Lemon wedges

1. Pat chicken dry with paper towels and season both sides with 1 teaspoon salt and pepper. Toss shrimp with 1½ teaspoons oil, ½ teaspoon garlic, ¼ teaspoon paprika, and ¼ teaspoon salt in bowl until evenly coated; set aside.

2. Heat 1½ teaspoons oil in medium saucepan over medium heat until shimmering. Add remaining garlic and cook, stirring constantly, until garlic sticks to bottom of saucepan and begins to brown, about 1 minute. Add tomato paste and remaining 1½ teaspoons paprika and continue to cook, stirring constantly, until dark brown bits form on bottom of saucepan, about 1 minute. Stir in broth, sherry, clam juice, and saffron, if using. Increase heat to high and bring to boil. Remove saucepan from heat and set aside.

3A. FOR A CHARCOAL GRILL Open bottom vent completely. Light large chimney starter mounded with charcoal briquettes (7 quarts). When top coals are partially covered with ash, pour evenly over grill. Using tongs, arrange 20 unlit briquettes evenly over coals. Set cooking grate in place, cover, and open lid vent completely. Heat grill until hot, about 5 minutes.

3B. FOR A GAS GRILL Turn all burners to high, cover, and heat grill until hot, about 15 minutes. Leave all burners on high.

4. Clean and oil cooking grate. Place chicken on grill and cook until both sides are lightly browned, 5 to 7 minutes; transfer chicken to plate and clean cooking grate.

5. Place roasting pan on grill (turning burners to medium-high if using gas) and add remaining ¼ cup oil. When oil begins to shimmer, add onion, red peppers, and remaining ½ teaspoon salt. Cook, stirring frequently, until onion begins to brown, 4 to 7 minutes. Stir in rice (turning burners to medium if using gas) until grains are well coated with oil.

6. Arrange chicken around perimeter of pan. Pour chicken broth mixture and any accumulated chicken juices over rice. Smooth rice into even layer, making sure no rice

sticks to sides of pan or rests atop chicken. When liquid reaches gentle simmer, place shrimp in center of pan in single layer. Arrange clams in center of pan, evenly dispersing them among shrimp and pushing hinge side of clams into rice slightly so they stand up. Distribute chorizo evenly over surface of rice. Cook, moving and rotating pan to maintain gentle simmer across entire surface of pan, until rice is almost cooked through, 12 to 18 minutes. (If using gas, heat can also be adjusted to maintain simmer.)

7. Sprinkle peas over paella, cover grill, and cook until liquid is absorbed and rice on bottom of pan sizzles, 5 to 8 minutes. Uncover and continue to cook, checking frequently, until uniform golden-brown crust forms on bottom of pan, 8 to 15 minutes. (Slide pan around grill as needed for even crust formation.) Remove from grill, cover, and let sit for 10 minutes. Serve with lemon wedges.

KEYS TO SUCCESS

- **A layer of fresh briquettes**: Added to hot coals (if using a charcoal grill), they ensure long, steady heat as they will ignite gradually.

- **Nestle the shellfish in the center**: To allow them to release their flavorful juices into the rice without overcooking

- **Start the chicken first**: Staggering the addition of ingredients ensures everything cooks to perfection.

Making Grilled Paella

COAT RICE
Heat oil in roasting pan on grill and cook onion and roasted red peppers. Add rice and stir until grains are well coated with oil.

ADD CHICKEN AND BROTH
Arrange chicken around edge of pan and pour in broth mixture. Smooth rice into even layer, making sure nothing sticks to sides of pan and no rice rests atop chicken. Bring to simmer.

ADD SHRIMP, CLAMS, CHORIZO, AND PEAS
Arrange shrimp in center of pan. Arrange clams in center of pan, evenly distributing among shrimp and pushing hinge sides of clams into rice slightly. Distribute chorizo evenly over top. When rice is almost cooked, sprinkle peas evenly over paella.

COOK DELICATE SEAFOOD USING RESIDUAL HEAT

To gently and evenly cook the delicate cod and shrimp in our moqueca (page 499), bring the stew to a full boil, then add the seafood and remove the pot from the heat. Letting food cook in residual heat—a technique we've used in several other recipes, such as roast chicken, shrimp salad, and even boiled corn—provides insurance against overcooking. After 15 minutes off the heat, the temperatures of the seafood and the cooking liquid equalize at about 140 degrees, our preferred doneness temperature for whitefish such as cod.

Making sure the stew is at a full boil before adding the cold seafood is key for proper cooking—note the significant drop in temperature at the outset. If the stew wasn't at 212 degrees, the seafood would be undercooked.

The Method:

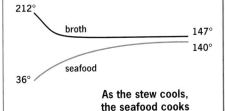

As the stew cools, the seafood cooks

CLEANING AND STORING FRESH HARD-SHELL CLAMS

Fresh clams are sold live, so you'll find them loose or in mesh. Inspect the clams before cooking. They should smell clean like the ocean, their shells tightly closed. Gently tap the shells of any open clams and wait a few seconds; discard those that don't close, along with any that have cracked shells or smell fishy.

CLEANING Scrub the clams with a stiff brush under cold water to remove exterior mud. If you've ever received gritty clams from your fishmonger, we recommend purging them to remove interior sand, a simple and easy process.

ditch the grit

How to purge Dissolve 2 tablespoons kosher salt for every quart of cool water in bowl. Fully submerge clams in saltwater solution. Allow them to sit for 2 hours at cool room temperature, or refrigerate overnight. Carefully lift clams from bowl, leaving grit behind. Rinse again in cool water before using or storing.

STORING Fresh clams must be stored in the refrigerator (except during purging), and storing them over ice will help them last longer. But do not store them directly over the ice, since they will die if the ice melts and they're submerged for too long in fresh water. Our method: Place the clams in a bowl, cover them with a wet paper towel or newspaper that will keep them moist while also allowing them to breathe, and set that bowl in a larger bowl filled with ice. Check the ice daily, replenishing as necessary. Clams stored this way will stay fresh for up to one week.

THE BOOZY HISTORY OF CLAM JUICE

If you woke with a hangover in the early 1900s, you may have downed aspirin with an iced clam juice chaser to cure your ailments. In the same era, the briny blend—made by filtering the salted water used to steam clams—also became popular as a mixer for hot soda-fountain drinks such as the clam and ginger and the malted clamette. Since then, the bivalve-based brew is mainly used to add marine savoriness to seafood soups and stews, though its role in drinks persists in cocktails such as the Bloody Caesar.

BREADS

TWISTED AND TIED ROLLS

LEAH COLINS

In this course we show you how to get the texture of bakery-quality rolls just right and how to form them into distinctive shapes with a professional look. Using plenty of eggs and butter makes crescent rolls suitably rich, and a high-low baking method gives them impressive height. Leaner kaiser rolls have a subtle sweetness and burnished crust; the supple dough is easy to tie into knots. And golden, fruit-filled St. Lucia buns are a Swedish specialty; you'll find that rolling the dough into the classic "S" shape is a snap.

LEAH'S PRO TIP: *When shaping decorative rolls, I tend to roll out the dough about an inch further than specified and wait to let it naturally shrink down to the desired length. If the dough is too stiff and bouncing back, try giving it a rest for a few minutes to relax the gluten before trying again. And if the dough is too soft and supple to work with, try refrigerating it for a few minutes to firm up the dough so that it holds its shape better.*

CRESCENT ROLLS

Makes: 16 rolls
Total Time: 1 hour, plus 13¾ hours rising, resting, and chilling

RECIPE OVERVIEW For crescent rolls that are tender and supple rather than chewy and thick-crusted, all-purpose flour works better than bread flour. Three eggs make these rolls soft and golden, and a full two sticks of butter add richness. The easiest way to incorporate such a large amount of butter is to melt it and add it with the other liquid ingredients. After you let the dough rise and form the rolls, refrigerate them—the longer the better (three days is optimal). This process, called retarding, permits a buildup of acetic acid in the dough, which gives the crescents complex flavor and a stunning, crackled crust. They bake at 425 degrees until they start to color; you'll then lower the temperature to 350. The initial blast of heat provides a dramatic initial increase in size (called oven spring). A burst of steam gives the rolls an even higher rise and turns the crust into a thin and still flakier shell. We developed this recipe using lower-protein flours such as Gold Medal and Pillsbury. If using a higher-protein flour such as King Arthur, reduce the amount to 3½ cups (17½ ounces).

16	tablespoons unsalted butter, cut into 16 pieces
¾	cup skim milk
¼	cup (1¾ ounces) sugar
3	large eggs, plus 1 large white beaten with 1 teaspoon water for brushing
4	cups (20 ounces) all-purpose flour
1	teaspoon instant or rapid-rise yeast
1½	teaspoons table salt

1. Microwave butter, milk, and sugar in 4-cup liquid measuring cup until butter is mostly melted and mixture is warm (110 degrees), about 1½ minutes. Whisk to fully melt butter and dissolve sugar. Beat eggs lightly in medium bowl; whisk in about one-third of warm milk mixture. When bottom of bowl feels warm, whisk in remaining milk mixture until fully combined.

2. Using stand mixer fitted with paddle, mix flour and yeast on low speed until combined, about 15 seconds. Add egg mixture in steady stream and mix until loose, shiny dough forms (you may also see satiny webs as dough moves in bowl), about 1 minute. Increase speed to medium and mix for 1 minute; slowly add salt and continue mixing until stronger webs form, about 3 minutes longer. (Dough will remain loose rather than forming neat, cohesive mass.) Transfer dough to large, lightly greased bowl; cover bowl tightly with plastic wrap and let dough rise at room temperature until doubled in size and surface feels tacky, about 3 hours.

3. Line rimmed baking sheet with plastic. Sprinkle dough with flour (no more than 2 tablespoons) to prevent sticking, and press down gently to deflate. Transfer dough to floured counter and press into rough rectangle shape. Transfer dough rectangle to prepared sheet, cover with plastic, and refrigerate for 8 to 12 hours.

4. Transfer dough rectangle to lightly floured counter and line baking sheet with parchment paper. Roll dough into uniform 20 by 13-inch rectangle. Using pizza wheel or sharp knife, cut dough in half lengthwise, then cut each rectangle into 8 triangles, trimming edges as needed to make uniform triangles. Before rolling into crescents, elongate each triangle of dough, stretching it an additional 2 to 3 inches in length. Starting at wide end, gently roll up dough, ending with pointed tip on bottom, and curve ends toward one another to create crescent shape. Arrange crescents in 4 rows on prepared sheet; wrap sheet with plastic and refrigerate for at least 2 hours or up to 3 days.

5. Remove plastic and slide baking sheet into large plastic garbage bag and tie or fold under to enclose. Let crescents rise at room temperature until they feel slightly tacky and soft and have come to room temperature, 45 minutes to 1 hour.

6. Thirty minutes before baking, adjust oven racks to lower-middle and lowest positions, place second rimmed baking sheet on lower rack, and heat oven to 425 degrees. Bring kettle of water to boil. Lightly brush crescents with egg white mixture. Working quickly, place sheet with crescents on upper rack, then pour 1 cup boiling water into empty sheet in oven. Bake for 10 minutes, then reduce oven temperature to 350 degrees and continue to bake until tops and bottoms of rolls are deep golden brown, 12 to 16 minutes longer. Transfer rolls to wire rack and let cool for 5 minutes. Serve warm.

Variation
MAKE-AHEAD CRESCENT ROLLS

In step 6, bake crescents at 350 degrees for 4 minutes, or until tops and bottoms brown slightly. Transfer rolls to wire rack and let cool completely. Place partially baked rolls in single layer in zipper-lock bag and freeze. When ready to serve, thaw rolls at room temperature on parchment-lined baking sheet, then bake in preheated 350-degree oven for 12 to 16 minutes. Fully baked and cooled rolls can be stored in zipper-lock bag at room temperature for up to 24 hours. Wrapped in aluminum foil before being placed in bag, rolls can be frozen for up to 1 month.

KEYS TO SUCCESS

- **Melt the butter:** Adding the large amount of butter in this recipe piece by piece is tedious; by melting it, you can just pour it in.

- **Skim is fine:** Other ingredients provide enough richness; skim milk prevents the rolls from being heavy.

- **Slow rise:** The longer the dough rests, the more flavor-building acetic acid builds up in the dough.

Shaping Crescent Rolls

ROLL AND CUT
Roll dough into 20 by 13-inch rectangle. Using pizza wheel or sharp knife, cut dough in half lengthwise, then cut 16 triangles.

STRETCH
Before rolling pieces into crescents, stretch each triangle an additional 2 to 3 inches in length with your hands.

ROLL AND CURVE
Starting at wide end, gently roll each piece toward pointed tip, then curve ends toward each other to form crescent shape.

KAISER ROLLS

Makes: 12 rolls
Total Time: 3¼ to 4¼ hours, plus 1 hour cooling time

RECIPE OVERVIEW Originally from Austria, crusty kaiser rolls are perfect for overstuffed sandwiches or for dipping into soup. To re-create the thin, crisp, golden exterior and moist, sturdy crumb of deli-style rolls, use high-protein bread flour. One egg and a bit of vegetable oil add tenderness and richness. Many traditional recipes use malt syrup for sweetness and browning, but white sugar provides a more subtle flavor. An egg wash brushed on before baking gives the rolls a deep golden sheen. Some delis imprint their rolls with a special stamp to create the signature rosette design, but the traditional shaping method is easy with our supple dough, so you won't need special equipment.

- 5 cups (27½ ounces) bread flour
- 4 teaspoons instant or rapid-rise yeast
- 1 tablespoon plus pinch table salt, divided
- 2 cups (16 ounces) plus 1 tablespoon water, room temperature, divided
- 3 tablespoons vegetable oil
- 2 large eggs, room temperature, divided
- 4 teaspoons sugar
- 1 tablespoon poppy seeds (optional)

1. Whisk flour, yeast, and 1 tablespoon salt together in bowl of stand mixer. Whisk 2 cups water, oil, 1 egg, and sugar in 4-cup liquid measuring cup until sugar has dissolved.

2. Using dough hook on low speed, slowly add water mixture to flour mixture and mix until cohesive dough starts to form and no dry flour remains, about 2 minutes, scraping down bowl as needed. Increase speed to medium-low and knead until dough is smooth and elastic and clears sides of bowl but sticks to bottom, about 8 minutes.

3. Transfer dough to lightly floured counter and knead by hand to form smooth, round ball, about 30 seconds. Place dough seam side down in lightly greased large bowl or container, cover tightly with plastic wrap, and let rise until doubled in size, 1 to 1½ hours.

4. Line 2 rimmed baking sheets with parchment paper. Press down on dough to deflate. Transfer dough to clean counter. Press and stretch dough into 12 by 6-inch rectangle, with long side parallel to counter edge. Using pizza cutter or chef's knife, cut dough vertically into 12 (6 by 1-inch) strips and cover loosely with greased plastic.

5. Working with 1 piece of dough at a time (keep remaining pieces covered), stretch and roll into 14-inch rope. Shape rope into U with 2-inch-wide bottom curve and ends facing away from you. Tie ends into single overhand knot, with 1½-inch open loop at bottom. Wrap 1 tail over loop and press through opening from top. Wrap other tail under loop and pinch ends together to seal.

6. Arrange rolls pinched side down on prepared sheets, spaced evenly apart. Cover loosely with greased plastic and let rise until nearly doubled in size and dough springs back minimally when poked gently with your knuckle, 30 minutes to 1 hour.

7. Adjust oven racks to upper-middle and lower-middle positions and heat oven to 350 degrees. Lightly beat remaining egg, remaining 1 tablespoon water, and remaining pinch salt together in bowl. Gently brush rolls with egg mixture and sprinkle with poppy seeds, if using. Bake until golden brown, 30 to 34 minutes, switching and rotating sheets halfway through baking. Transfer rolls to wire rack and let cool completely, about 1 hour, before serving. (Cooled rolls can be stored in zipper-lock bag at room temperature for up to 2 days. Wrapped in aluminum foil before being placed in the bag, rolls can be frozen for up to 1 month. To reheat thawed, frozen rolls, wrap them in foil, place on rimmed baking sheet, and bake in 350-degree oven for 10 minutes.)

KEYS TO SUCCESS

- **Bread flour:** These rolls need the structure that high-protein bread flour provides.

- **Long ropes:** Rolling the dough strips to 14 inches makes it easier to tie a knot.

- **Pinch the ends:** You don't want the knots to come undone as they bake.

Shaping Kaiser Rolls

SHAPE ROPES
Roll each dough strip into 14-inch rope and shape into U with 2-inch-wide bottom curve and ends facing away from you.

TIE KNOT
Tie ends into single overhand knot, with 1½-inch open loop at bottom.

WRAP AND PRESS
Wrap 1 tail over loop and press through opening from top. Wrap other tail under loop and pinch ends together to seal.

SET ON SHEET
Arrange rolls pinched side down on prepared sheets, spaced about 3 inches apart.

EGG WASH
Gently brush rolls with egg mixture and sprinkle with poppy seeds, if using.

ST. LUCIA BUNS

Makes: 16 buns
Total Time: 1¼ hours, plus 3 to 4 hours rising and cooling

RECIPE OVERVIEW Lussebullar, also known as St. Lucia buns, are a staple of St. Lucia Day, which ushers in the Christmas season in Sweden. Just ¼ teaspoon of saffron gives these buns the right balance of flavor, and a small amount of turmeric bolsters the golden color. Steeping the saffron, along with the turmeric, in hot water for 15 minutes helps release the full potential of its water-soluble flavor compounds. One-third cup each of sugar and currants (the customary mix-in) gives the buns just enough sweetness. While the dough can be shaped into a variety of traditional forms, here you'll make the most popular "S," or "cat's tail," shape. Brushing the buns with egg wash and giving each an optional sprinkling of pearled sugar creates a glossy and festive finish. For an accurate measurement of boiling water, bring a full kettle of water to a boil and then measure out the desired amount. If the dough becomes too soft to work with at any point, refrigerate it until it's firm enough to easily handle.

¼ cup (2 ounces) boiling water
¼ teaspoon saffron threads, crumbled
⅛ teaspoon ground turmeric
3½ cups (17½ ounces) all-purpose flour
2 teaspoons instant or rapid-rise yeast
¾ cup (6 ounces) whole milk, room temperature
6 tablespoons (3 ounces) unsalted butter, melted
⅓ cup (2⅓ ounces) granulated sugar
1 large egg, room temperature
1 teaspoon table salt
⅓ cup currants
1 large egg, lightly beaten with 1 tablespoon water and pinch table salt
¼ cup pearled sugar (optional)

1. Combine boiling water, saffron, and turmeric in small bowl and let steep for 15 minutes.

2. Whisk flour and yeast together in bowl of stand mixer. Whisk saffron mixture, milk, melted butter, granulated sugar, and egg in 4-cup liquid measuring cup until sugar has dissolved. Using dough hook on low speed, slowly add milk mixture to flour mixture and mix until cohesive dough starts to form and no dry flour remains, about 2 minutes, scraping down bowl as needed. Cover bowl and let dough stand for 10 minutes.

3. Add salt to dough and knead on medium-low speed until dough is smooth and elastic and clears sides of bowl but sticks to bottom, about 8 minutes. Reduce speed to low, slowly add currants, and mix until incorporated, about 2 minutes.

4. Transfer dough to lightly floured counter and knead by hand to form smooth, round ball, about 30 seconds. Place dough seam side down in lightly greased large bowl or container, cover tightly with greased plastic wrap, and let rise until increased in size by about half, 1½ to 2 hours.

5. Line 2 rimmed baking sheets with parchment paper. Press down on dough to deflate, then transfer to clean counter. Press and roll dough into 16 by 6-inch rectangle, with long side parallel to counter edge. Using pizza cutter or chef's knife, cut rectangle vertically into sixteen 6 by 1-inch strips and cover loosely with greased plastic.

6. Working with 1 dough strip at a time (keep remaining pieces covered), stretch and roll into 16-inch rope. (If dough resists stretching, let it relax for 5 to 10 minutes before trying to stretch it again.) Coil ends of rope in opposite directions to form tight S shape. Arrange buns on prepared sheets, spaced about 2½ inches apart. Cover loosely with greased plastic and let rise until puffy, 30 minutes to 1 hour.

7. Adjust oven racks to upper-middle and lower-middle positions and heat oven to 350 degrees. Gently brush buns with egg mixture and sprinkle with pearled sugar, if using. Bake until golden brown, 15 to 20 minutes, switching and rotating sheets halfway through baking. Transfer rolls to wire rack and let cool completely, about 1 hour, before serving. (Buns can be wrapped in double layer of plastic wrap and stored at room temperature for up to 5 days.)

KEYS TO SUCCESS

- **Steep the spices:** A short rest in hot water blooms the flavor of the saffron and turmeric.

- **Cover the strips:** Keep the remaining dough moist as you shape each bun.

Shaping St. Lucia Buns

MAKE ROPES
Using pizza cutter or chef's knife, cut dough rectangle into sixteen 6 by 1-inch strips. Working with 1 dough strip at a time, stretch and roll into 16-inch ropes.

COIL TIGHTLY
Coil ends of rope in opposite directions to form tight S shape. Arrange buns on prepared sheets, spaced about 2½ inches apart.

BRUSH AND SUGAR
Gently brush buns with egg mixture and sprinkle with pearled sugar, if using.

SHAPED SWEET ENRICHED BREADS

DAN SOUZA

Sweet, enriched yeast breads are good with coffee or tea, for breakfast or anytime, and they look more complicated than they are. Case in point: The classic braid for eggy challah is pretty straightforward once you break it down, which we do for you with step-by-step illustrations. Another simple braiding technique ensures that all the sweet, spicy goodness stays inside our cinnamon swirl bread. And it just takes a few cuts and twists to expose the spirals of smooth almond and brioche-like dough in our coffee cake.

DAN'S PRO TIP: *If you are worried about trying a new shaping technique, reach for the Play-Doh. With it, you can practice any shape over and over to gain confidence before getting your hands on the real dough.*

CHALLAH

Makes: 1 loaf
Total Time: 1¾ hours, plus 7 hours resting and cooling

RECIPE OVERVIEW With a light, eggy interior and a bronzed, braided exterior, challah is an approachable show-stopper. A bit of sugar helps create a tender crumb and nicely browned crust. To create a moist but not sticky dough, you'll use the dough-mixing technique called tangzhong, which employs a simple cooked water-flour paste. Ample amounts of oil and eggs make the baked bread plush. For a beautiful yet fuss-free braid, pointing the four dough strands in different directions, rather than lining them up parallel to each other, makes them easier to keep track of. Brush the loaf with egg wash before baking for an evenly brown, glossy crust. Some friction is necessary for rolling and braiding the ropes, so resist the urge to dust the counter with flour. If your counter is too narrow to stretch the ropes, slightly bend the pieces at the 12 o'clock and 6 o'clock positions. Bake this loaf on two nested baking sheets to keep the bottom from getting too dark.

Flour Paste
- ½ cup water
- 3 tablespoons bread flour

Dough
- 1 large egg plus 2 large yolks
- ¼ cup water
- 2 tablespoons vegetable oil
- 2¾ cups (15⅛ ounces) bread flour
- 1¼ teaspoons instant or rapid-rise yeast
- ¼ cup (1¾ ounces) sugar
- 1 teaspoon table salt
  Vegetable oil spray

Egg Wash
- 1 large egg
  Pinch table salt
- 1 tablespoon sesame seeds or poppy seeds (optional)

1. **FOR THE FLOUR PASTE** Whisk water and flour in bowl until no lumps remain. Microwave, whisking every 20 seconds, until mixture thickens to stiff, smooth, pudding-like consistency that forms mound when dropped from end of whisk into bowl, 40 to 80 seconds.

2. **FOR THE DOUGH** In bowl of stand mixer, whisk flour paste, egg and yolks, water, and oil until well combined. Add flour and yeast. Fit mixer with dough hook and mix on low speed until all flour is moistened, 3 to 4 minutes. Let stand for 20 minutes.

3. Add sugar and salt and mix on medium speed for 9 minutes (dough will be quite firm and dry). Transfer dough to counter and lightly spray now-empty mixer bowl with oil spray. Knead dough briefly to form ball and return it to prepared bowl. Lightly spray dough with oil spray and cover bowl with plastic wrap. Let dough rise until about doubled in volume, about 1½ hours.

4. Line rimmed baking sheet with parchment paper and nest in second rimmed baking sheet. Transfer dough to counter and press into 8-inch square, expelling as much air as possible. Cut dough in half lengthwise to form 2 rectangles. Cut each rectangle in half lengthwise to form 4 equal strips of dough. Roll 1 strip of dough into 16-inch rope. Continue rolling, tapering ends, until rope is 18 inches long. Repeat with remaining dough strips. Arrange ropes in plus-sign shape, with 4 ends overlapping in center by ½ inch. Firmly press center of cross into counter to seal ropes to each other and to counter.

5. Lift rope at 12 o'clock, bring over center, and place in 5 o'clock position. Lift rope at 6 o'clock, bring over center, and place in 12 o'clock position.

6. Lift rope at 9 o'clock, bring over center, and place in 4 o'clock position. Lift rope at 3 o'clock and, working toward yourself, bring over braid and place in 8 o'clock position. Adjust ropes so they are at 12, 3, 6, and 9 o'clock positions.

7. Repeat steps 5 and 6, working toward yourself, until you can no longer braid. Loaf will naturally list to 1 side.

8. Pinch ends of ropes together and tuck both ends under braid. Carefully transfer braid to prepared sheets. Cover loosely with plastic and let rise until dough does not spring back fully when gently pressed with your knuckle, about 3 hours.

9. FOR THE EGG WASH Thirty minutes before baking, adjust oven rack to middle position and heat oven to 350 degrees. Whisk together egg and salt. Brush loaf with egg wash and sprinkle with sesame seeds, if using. Bake until loaf is deep golden brown and registers at least 195 degrees, 35 to 40 minutes. Let cool on sheets for 20 minutes. Transfer loaf to wire rack and let cool completely before slicing, about 2 hours.

Variation
CHALLAH IN THE ROUND
There are many other challah shapes besides the long braid, one of the most common being a braided round. Traditional for Rosh Hashanah (the Jewish New Year), it symbolizes continuity.

1. After rolling dough into four 16-inch ropes, arrange nested sheets so long side is parallel to edge of counter. Place first rope just to left of center of sheets so that its ends hang off rim of sheets. Place second rope perpendicular to first rope, just above center of sheets. Place third rope across second rope, just right of center. (Ropes 1 and 3 should be parallel to each other.) Place final rope below rope 2, making sure that it is on top of rope 3 and beneath rope 1. Adjust ropes to create 1-inch square at center of sheets.

2. Pick up 2 ropes closest to you and loosely cross them right over left. Rotate sheets 90 degrees counterclockwise. Repeat crossing ropes and turning sheets 3 times. Rearrange ends of all ropes so they point at corners of sheets. Rotate sheets until any corner points toward you.

Six Steps to Braiding Challah

Our unconventional braiding method is easier to follow than those of most recipes and produces a loftier loaf.

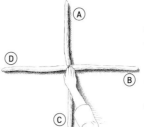

STEP 1
Arrange ropes in plus-sign shape, with 4 ends overlapping in center by ½ inch. Firmly press center of cross into counter to seal ropes to each other and to counter.

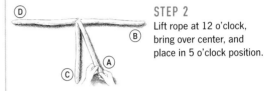

STEP 2
Lift rope at 12 o'clock, bring over center, and place in 5 o'clock position.

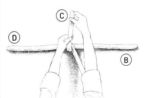

STEP 3
Lift rope at 6 o'clock, bring over center, and place in 12 o'clock position.

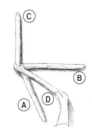

STEP 4
Lift rope at 9 o'clock, bring over center, and place in 4 o'clock position.

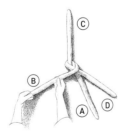

STEP 5
Lift rope at 3 o'clock and, working toward yourself, bring over braid and place in 8 o'clock position. Adjust ropes so they are at 12, 3, 6, and 9 o'clock positions. Repeat steps 2 through 5.

STEP 6
Continue braiding, working toward yourself, until you can no longer braid. Loaf will naturally list to 1 side. Pinch ends of ropes together. Tuck both ends under braid.

3. Pick up 2 ropes closest to you and loosely cross them left over right. Rotate sheets 90 degrees counterclockwise. Repeat crossing ropes and turning sheets 3 times. Rearrange ends of ropes so they point at sides of sheets. Rotate sheets so long side is parallel to edge of counter.

4. Pinch 2 ends closest to you together. Rotate sheets 90 degrees and repeat until all ends are pinched together. Tuck all pinched ends and outer loops under round. Cover loosely with plastic and let rise until dough does not spring back fully when gently pressed with your knuckle, about 3 hours.

KEYS TO SUCCESS

- **Don't dust:** Resist the urge to flour the counter when rolling out and braiding the dough so there will be some friction.

- **Moist but malleable dough:** A short rest during kneading plus a long fermentation builds a sturdy but stretchy gluten network that makes the dough easy to handle. A cooked flour-water paste called tangzhong binds up water in the dough so that it's moist but not sticky.

- **Use an egg wash:** Brushing an egg wash—lightly salted to make the eggs more fluid—over the braided dough encourages rich browning as the loaf bakes.

SCIENCE LESSON | **Making a Moist Dough Handle Like a Dry Dough**

Adding plenty of water to challah dough makes for a supremely soft, moist bread—and usually a very loose, sticky dough. But our challah dough is both well hydrated and easy to handle because we employ a unique bread-baking technique called tangzhong. The key is to cook a portion of the flour and water, which causes the starch molecules to absorb more water than they would at room temperature and form a gel that's then added to the dough. The water trapped in the gel doesn't contribute to stickiness, resulting in a dough that feels drier.

With Gel
The dough is malleable but firm.

Without Gel
The dough is slack and sticky.

CINNAMON SWIRL BREAD

Makes: 2 loaves
Total Time: 2 hours, plus 5½ hours rising and cooling

RECIPE OVERVIEW At its best, this American classic has a fluffy, delicate crumb that's studded with plump raisins and laced with a substantial swirl of gooey cinnamon sugar. Shokupan, a Japanese sandwich bread that's airy and milky-sweet, makes the perfect foil for the cinnamon filling. You'll employ two strategies to prevent the common pitfalls of swirl breads—leaky filling and large gaps. First, use confectioners' sugar and plenty of cinnamon to make the filling sticky, not runny. Second, instead of the traditional swirl, form a simple yet elegant Russian braid: After rolling the filling and dough into a cylinder halve it lengthwise, then stretch the two halves slightly and twist them together, keeping the cut surfaces facing up to expose the nice-looking striations of filling. Any gas that would have been trapped between the layers is able to escape so that the bread bakes up tightly seamed and beautifully marbled.

Dough
  8 tablespoons unsalted butter
3¾ cups (20⅔ ounces) bread flour, divided
  ¾ cup (2¾ ounces) nonfat dry milk powder
  ⅓ cup (2⅓ ounces) granulated sugar
  1 tablespoon instant or rapid-rise yeast
1½ cups (12 ounces) water, heated to 110 degrees
  1 large egg, lightly beaten
1½ teaspoons table salt
1½ cups (7½ ounces) golden raisins

Filling
  1 cup (4 ounces) confectioners' sugar
  3 tablespoons ground cinnamon
  1 teaspoon vanilla extract
  ½ teaspoon table salt

  1 large egg, lightly beaten with pinch table salt

1. FOR THE DOUGH Cut butter into 32 pieces and toss with 1 tablespoon flour; set aside to soften while mixing dough. Whisk remaining flour, milk powder, granulated sugar, and yeast together in bowl of stand mixer fitted with dough hook. Add water and egg and mix on medium-low speed until cohesive mass forms, about 2 minutes, scraping down bowl as needed. Cover mixing bowl with plastic wrap and let stand for 20 minutes.

2. Adjust oven rack to middle position and place loaf or cake pan on bottom of oven. Grease large bowl. Remove plastic from mixer bowl, add salt, and mix on medium-low speed until dough is smooth and elastic and clears sides of bowl, 7 to 15 minutes. With mixer running, add butter a few pieces at a time, and continue to knead until butter is fully incorporated and dough is smooth and elastic and clears sides of bowl, 3 to 5 minutes longer. Add raisins and mix until incorporated, 30 to 60 seconds. Transfer dough to prepared

Cinnamon Swirl Bread, Russian-Style

Forming a Russian braid solves the gapping that plagues swirl breads. The twisted shape tightly seals the pieces of dough together while providing plenty of escape routes for the excess air that would otherwise create tunnels in the loaf.

CUT LENGTHWISE
Using bench scraper or sharp chef's knife, cut filled dough in half lengthwise. Turn halves so cut sides are facing up.

STRETCH
With cut sides up, stretch each half into 14-inch length.

FOLD LEFT OVER RIGHT
Pinch 2 ends of each strip together. To form braid, take left strip of dough and lay it over right strip of dough.

REPEAT AND PINCH
Repeat braiding process, keeping cut sides facing up, until pieces are tightly twisted together. Pinch ends of braid together.

bowl and, using bowl scraper or rubber spatula, fold dough over itself by gently lifting and folding edge of dough toward middle. Turn bowl 90 degrees; fold again. Turn bowl and fold dough 6 more times (total of 8 folds). Cover tightly with plastic and transfer to middle rack of oven. Pour 3 cups boiling water into loaf pan in oven, close oven door, and allow dough to rise for 45 minutes.

3. Remove bowl from oven and gently press down on center of dough to deflate. Repeat folding (making total of 8 folds), re-cover, and return to oven until doubled in volume, about 45 minutes.

4. FOR THE FILLING Whisk all ingredients together in bowl until well combined; set aside.

5. Grease two 8½ by 4½-inch loaf pans. Transfer dough to lightly floured counter and divide into 2 pieces. Working with 1 piece of dough, pat into rough 6 by 11-inch rectangle. With short side facing you, fold long sides in like a business letter to form 3 by 11-inch rectangle. Roll dough away from you into ball. Dust ball with flour and flatten with rolling pin into 7 by 18-inch rectangle with even ¼-inch thickness. Using spray bottle, spray dough lightly with water. Sprinkle half of filling mixture evenly over dough, leaving ¼-inch border on sides and ¾-inch border on top and bottom; spray filling lightly with water. (Filling should be speckled with water over entire surface.) With short side facing you, roll dough away from you into firm cylinder. Turn loaf seam side up and pinch closed; pinch ends closed. Dust loaf lightly on all sides with flour and let rest for 10 minutes. Repeat with second ball of dough and remaining filling.

Making a Sticky Filling That Sticks

The cinnamon sugar swirl isn't just for flavor; it's needed to help hold the pieces of dough together. Here's how we altered the typical formula.

Powdered Sugar
Confectioners' sugar contains cornstarch, which thickens the filling and makes it less runny.

Lots of Cinnamon
Cinnamon contains starches that thicken the filling and help it form a sticky paste.

Spritz of Water
Lightly misting the dough before and after adding the filling creates extra adhesiveness.

6. Working with 1 loaf at a time, use bench scraper to cut loaf in half lengthwise; turn halves so cut sides are facing up. Gently stretch each half into 14-inch length. Line up pieces of dough and pinch 2 ends of strips together. Take piece on left and lay over piece on right. Repeat, keeping cut side up, until pieces of dough are tightly twisted. Pinch ends together. Transfer loaf, cut side up, to prepared loaf pan; push any exposed raisins into seams of braid. Repeat with second loaf. Cover loaves loosely with plastic, return to oven, and allow to rise for 45 minutes. Remove loaves and water pan from oven; heat oven to 350 degrees. Allow loaves to rise at room temperature until almost doubled in size, about 45 minutes (tops of loaves should rise about 1 inch over lip of pans).

7. Brush loaves with egg mixture. Bake until crust is well browned, about 25 minutes. Reduce oven temperature to 325 degrees, tent loaves with aluminum foil, and continue to bake until internal temperature registers 200 degrees, 15 to 25 minutes longer.

8. Transfer pans to wire rack and let cool for 5 minutes. Remove loaves from pans, return to rack, and cool to room temperature before slicing, about 2 hours.

KEYS TO SUCCESS

- **Add air**: A long kneading time, plus two sets of folds, gives the dough more oxygen, which strengthens gluten formation and leads to a light, springy loaf.

- **Hold the flour**: The dough will appear very wet and sticky until the final few minutes of kneading; do not be tempted to add supplemental flour.

ALMOND RING COFFEE CAKES

Makes: 2 rings (serves 12)
Total Time: 1½ hours, plus 3 hours rising and cooling

RECIPE OVERVIEW Like most yeasted coffee cakes, these rings are a variation of eggy, buttery brioche. All-purpose flour lends structure without making the dough too tough. One stick of butter adds just the right level of richness. Using just egg yolks instead of whole eggs adds flavor and tenderness without making the dough too sticky. (Save the whites; they'll come in handy for the garnish.) Honey gives the dough a vaguely caramel-like flavor and adds moisture. For the filling, you'll blend almond paste with cream cheese and confectioners' sugar to smooth and lighten its sticky, dense texture while still delivering intense almond flavor. Rolling, stuffing, and shaping the dough into an attractive, professional-looking ring is quite easy; make sure to use a sharp knife or scissors to make the cuts. With a quick glaze and a garnish of sliced almonds, this coffee cake looks every bit as good as a store-bought version and is a world apart in flavor.

Filling
1   (7-ounce) tube almond paste
4   ounces cream cheese, softened
½   cup (2 ounces) confectioners' sugar

Dough
1⅓ cups warm whole milk (110 degrees)
8   tablespoons unsalted butter, melted and cooled
⅓   cup honey
3   large egg yolks
2   teaspoons vanilla extract
4¾ cups (23¾ ounces) all-purpose flour, plus extra as needed
2¼ teaspoons instant or rapid-rise yeast
2   teaspoons table salt
    Vegetable oil spray

Topping
3   large egg whites, lightly beaten
½   cup sliced almonds
1½ cups (6 ounces) confectioners' sugar
2   ounces cream cheese, softened
2   tablespoons milk
½   teaspoon vanilla extract

1. FOR THE FILLING Using stand mixer fitted with paddle, beat almond paste, cream cheese, and sugar on medium-low speed until smooth, about 2 minutes. Transfer to small bowl, cover, and refrigerate until ready to use.

2. FOR THE DOUGH Whisk milk, melted butter, honey, egg yolks, and vanilla together in 4-cup liquid measuring cup. Using clean, dry mixer bowl and dough hook, mix flour, yeast, and salt together on low speed. Add milk mixture and knead until dough comes together, about 2 minutes.

3. Increase speed to medium and knead until dough is smooth and shiny, 5 to 7 minutes. If after 5 minutes dough is sticking to sides of bowl, add up to ¼ cup extra flour, 1 tablespoon at a time, until dough clears side of bowl but sticks to bottom.

4. Turn dough onto lightly floured counter and knead by hand to form smooth, round ball. Place dough in greased bowl and wrap bowl tightly with plastic. Let dough rise in warm, draft-free place until doubled in size, 1 to 1½ hours.

5. Line 2 rimmed baking sheets with parchment paper. On lightly floured counter, divide dough into 2 equal pieces. Roll 1 dough piece into 18 by 9-inch rectangle with long side facing you. Spread half of filling in 1-inch-wide strip just above bottom edge of dough.

6. Using bench scraper or metal spatula, loosen dough from counter and roll into tight cylinder; pinch seam closed. Transfer cylinder, seam side down, to prepared sheet. Repeat with remaining dough and filling and second prepared sheet.

7. Shape each cylinder into ring. Using kitchen shears or sharp knife, make about 11 cuts around outside of each ring, spaced 1 to 1½ inches apart. Twist each piece cut side up. Mist rings with oil spray, cover loosely with plastic, and let rise in warm place until rings are nearly doubled in size and spring back slowly when indented with your finger, 1 to 1½ hours.

8. FOR THE TOPPING Adjust oven racks to upper-middle and lower-middle positions and heat oven to 375 degrees. Brush rings with egg whites and sprinkle with almonds. Bake until deep brown, about 25 minutes, switching and rotating sheets halfway through baking.

9. Let cakes cool for 1 hour. Whisk sugar, cream cheese, milk, and vanilla in small bowl until smooth, then drizzle over cakes before serving.

Reconstituting Hardened Almond Paste

Almond paste is expensive and seldom used, which means that leftovers often sit around. When faced with rock-hard almond paste, place the paste in a zipper-lock bag along with a slice of bread. Within a day or two, it will be restored to its normal, pliable state.

KEYS TO SUCCESS

- **Use honey:** Not only does honey add great flavor, it also contributes moisture, thanks to its hygroscopic qualities.

- **Just the yolks:** Egg whites contribute little more than moisture and make this dough sticky; using yolks alone adds tenderness.

- **Smooth filling:** Make sure your almond paste is fresh and pliable and your cream cheese is softened to avoid a lumpy filling.

Making a Ring-Shaped Coffee Cake

SPREAD FILLING
After rolling dough into 18 by 9-inch rectangle, spread 1-inch-wide strip of filling about 1 inch above bottom edge of dough.

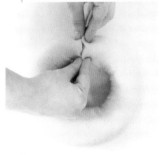

SHAPE INTO RING
Loosen dough from counter with bench scraper (or metal spatula) and carefully roll dough into even cylinder. Pinch seam to seal. Transfer dough cylinder seam side down to parchment-lined baking sheet. Shape dough into ring.

MAKE CUTS
Make about 11 cuts around outside of ring using sharp knife or scissors, spacing them 1 to 1½ inches apart.

ROTATE PIECES AND TOP
Twist each piece of dough cut side up. After dough rises, brush with egg mixture and sprinkle with almonds.

CLASSIC LOAVES WITH SPONGES

BRIDGET LANCASTER

The breads in this course all begin with a sponge, an element that adds time to the dough-making process but pays off in terms of structure and depth of flavor. A sponge is made with water, yeast, and part of the flour used in the bread dough, and it rests for 6 to 24 hours before it's mixed into the dough. During this period the yeast consumes sugars in the flour. This fermentation process, made visible by the rise and collapse of the mixture, helps develop the strong gluten network that supports an open crumb and gives the loaf a slight tang. You'll experience what a sponge brings to pane Francese and a loaf of whole-wheat sandwich bread.

BRIDGET'S PRO TIP: *The difference between bread baked with or without using a starter sponge is like night and day. The tangy, deep flavor comes from mixing a little of the flour, yeast, and water and giving it time. One key is to cover the bowl containing the sponge tightly with plastic wrap to trap in the moisture. I use a Sharpie to write the time I started the sponge right on the plastic.*

THE METHOD
SPONGES

A sponge is a mixture of part of a recipe's flour, yeast, and water that is allowed to ferment, then used to start rustic-style bread recipes.

1 STIR SPONGE INGREDIENTS
Use wooden spoon to stir portion of flour with water and small amount of yeast in 4-cup liquid measuring cup until well combined.

2 LET RISE AND FALL
Cover tightly with plastic wrap and let sit at room temperature until sponge has risen and begins to collapse, about 6 hours (sponge can sit at room temperature for up to 24 hours).

3 WHISK FLOUR AND YEAST
Whisk remaining flour for dough with more yeast in bowl of stand mixer.

4 STIR WATER INTO SPONGE
Stir additional water into sponge with a wooden spoon until well combined; mixture will be quite liquid.

5 ADD SPONGE TO FLOUR
Using dough hook on low speed, slowly add sponge mixture to flour mixture and knead until cohesive dough starts to form and no dry flour remains, about 2 minutes, scraping down bowl as needed.

6 COVER AND REST
Cover bowl tightly with plastic wrap and let dough rest for 20 minutes before continuing to knead.

PANE FRANCESE

Makes: 2 loaves
Total Time: 2¼ hours, plus 11¾ to 12¾ hours cooling time

RECIPE OVERVIEW The Italian cousin to the baguette, pane Francese is a long loaf with a moist and open crumb, nice for sandwiches or just dipping into olive oil. Starting this bread with a sponge adds structure and flavor to the loaf. After preparing this mixture (made with water, yeast, and 20 percent of the bread's total weight of flour), let it sit on the counter for 6 to 24 hours before mixing it into the dough. A repeated series of gentle folds helps develop the gluten structure in the dough even further while also incorporating air for an open interior crumb. You'll use two baker's tools to create this rustic loaf: A heavy linen cloth called a couche helps the wet dough keep its shape while proofing, and a curved-blade lame makes slashes in the dough that bake up with crisp, dramatic raised edges.

Sponge

- ⅔ cup (3⅔ ounces) bread flour
- ½ cup (4 ounces) water, room temperature
- ⅛ teaspoon instant or rapid-rise yeast

Dough

- 2⅔ cups (14⅔ ounces) bread flour
- 1½ teaspoons instant or rapid-rise yeast
- 1¼ cups (10 ounces) water, room temperature
- 1 tablespoon extra-virgin olive oil
- 2¼ teaspoons table salt

1. FOR THE SPONGE Stir all ingredients in 4-cup liquid measuring cup with wooden spoon until well combined. Cover tightly with plastic wrap and let sit at room temperature until sponge has risen and begins to collapse, about 6 hours (sponge can sit at room temperature for up to 24 hours).

2. FOR THE DOUGH Whisk flour and yeast together in bowl of stand mixer. Stir water into sponge with wooden spoon until well combined. Using dough hook on low speed, slowly add sponge mixture to flour mixture and mix until cohesive dough starts to form and no dry flour remains, about 2 minutes, scraping down bowl as needed. Cover bowl tightly with plastic and let dough rest for 20 minutes.

3. Add oil and salt to dough and knead on medium-low speed until dough is smooth and elastic and clears sides of bowl, about 5 minutes. Transfer dough to lightly greased large bowl or container, cover tightly with plastic, and let rise for 30 minutes.

4. Using greased bowl scraper (or your fingertips), fold dough over itself by gently lifting and folding edge of dough toward middle. Turn bowl 45 degrees and fold dough again; repeat turning bowl and folding dough 6 more times (total of 8 folds). Cover tightly with plastic and let rise for 30 minutes. Repeat folding, then cover bowl tightly with plastic and let dough rise until nearly doubled in size, 1 to 1½ hours.

5. Mist underside of couche with water, drape over inverted rimmed baking sheet, and dust evenly with flour. Transfer dough to lightly floured counter. Press and stretch dough into 12 by 6-inch rectangle, deflating any gas pockets larger than 1 inch, and divide in half crosswise. Cover loosely with greased plastic.

6. Gently press and stretch 1 piece of dough (keep remaining piece covered) into 7-inch square. Fold top corners of dough diagonally into center of square and press gently to seal. Stretch and fold upper third of dough toward center and press seam gently to seal.

7. Stretch and fold dough in half toward you to form rough loaf with tapered ends and pinch seam closed. Roll loaf seam side down. Starting at center of dough and working toward ends, gently and evenly roll and stretch dough until it measures 15 inches long by 2½ inches wide. Moving your hands in opposite directions, use back and forth motion to roll ends of loaf under your palms to form sharp points.

8. Gently slide your hands underneath each end of loaf and transfer seam side up to prepared couche. On either side of loaf, pinch couche into pleat, then cover loosely with large plastic garbage bag. Repeat steps 6 through 7 with remaining piece of dough and place on opposite side of 1 pleat. Fold edges of couche over loaves to cover completely, then carefully place sheet inside garbage bag. Tie, or fold under, open end of bag to fully enclose. Let rise until loaves increase in size by about half and dough springs back minimally when poked gently with your knuckle, 30 minutes to 1 hour (remove loaf from bag to test).

9. One hour before baking, adjust oven racks to lower-middle and lowest positions. Place baking stone on upper rack, place 2 disposable aluminum pie plates filled with 1 quart lava rocks each on lower rack, and heat oven to 450 degrees. Line pizza peel with 16 by 12-inch piece of parchment paper, with long edge perpendicular to handle. Bring 1 cup water to boil.

10. Remove sheet with loaves from bag. Unfold couche, pulling from ends to remove pleats. Dust top of loaves with flour. (If any seams have reopened, pinch closed before dusting with flour.) Gently pushing with side of flipping board, roll 1 loaf over, away from other loaf, so it is seam side down. Using your hand, hold long edge of flipping board between loaf and couche at 45-degree angle, then lift couche with your other hand and flip loaf seam side up onto board. Invert loaf seam side down onto prepared pizza peel, about 2 inches from long edge of parchment, then use flipping board to straighten loaf and reshape as needed. Repeat with second loaf, leaving at least 3 inches between loaves.

11. Carefully pour ½ cup boiling water into 1 disposable pie plate of preheated rocks and close oven door for 1 minute to create steam. Meanwhile, holding lame concave side up at 30-degree angle to loaf, make one ½-inch-deep slash with swift, fluid motion lengthwise along top of loaf, starting and stopping about ½ inch from ends. Repeat with second loaf.

12. Working quickly, slide parchment with loaves onto baking stone and pour remaining ½ cup boiling water into second disposable pie plate of preheated rocks. Bake until crust is golden brown and loaves register 205 to 210 degrees, 20 to 25 minutes, rotating loaves halfway through baking. Transfer loaves to wire rack, discard parchment, and let cool completely, about 3 hours, before serving.

KEYS TO SUCCESS

- **Six-hour sponge:** This bread gets most of its flavor from a pre-fermented sponge, so don't undercut the fermentation time.
- **Steam heat:** Preheat pans filled with lava rocks and add water to create a steamy oven, which encourages a crisp crust.

WHAT CAN GO WRONG

PROBLEM You don't have a flipping board.

SOLUTION Make one from cardboard. You don't want to deflate the delicate proofed loaf, so you don't want to pick it up with your hands. A flipping board has a thin edge that you can wedge under the loaf to roll it onto the pizza peel without collapsing the air bubbles. But if you don't have a flipping board, you can fashion one from cardboard: Simply tape two 16 by 4-inch pieces of heavy cardboard together with packaging tape.

PROBLEM The loaf sticks to the couche.

SOLUTION Mist and flour the couche well. Although a linen couche is better than a cotton towel for releasing loaves, it can still stick to very wet doughs. Mist the couche with water and dust it well with flour—2 tablespoons does the trick.

CORE TECHNIQUE **Using a Sponge**

Let the sponge rise for about 2 hours and then begin to fall (another 4 hours); this indicates that the yeast is active and ready to go. At this point the sponge can sit for up to 24 hours at room temperature before using or be refrigerated for several days.

After 2 hours   **After 4 hours**

Forming Pane Francese

PRESS AND STRETCH
Press and stretch dough into 12 by 6-inch rectangle, deflating any gas pockets larger than 1 inch, and divide in half crosswise.

FOLD INTO SQUARE
Gently press and stretch dough into square. Fold top corners of dough into center and press gently to seal. Stretch and fold upper third of dough toward center and seal.

FORM ROUGH LOAF
Stretch and fold dough to form rough loaf with tapered ends. Gently and evenly roll and stretch dough from center to ends. Roll ends of loaf to form sharp points.

TRANSFER TO COUCHE
Transfer loaves seam side up to prepared couche. On either side of each loaf, pinch couche into pleat. Fold edges of couche over loaves to cover completely.

MOVE TO PEEL
Unfold couche. Dust top of loaves with flour. Use flipping board to roll 1 loaf over, seam side down. Lift couche and flip loaf onto board. Invert loaf onto pizza peel; reshape loaf.

SLASH TOPS
Holding lame concave side up at 30-degree angle to loaf, make ½-inch-deep slash with swift, fluid motion lengthwise along top of loaf, starting and stopping about ½ inch from ends.

WHOLE-WHEAT SANDWICH BREAD

Makes: two 8-inch loaves
Total Time: 1¾ hours, plus 10½ hours resting and 3 hours cooling

RECIPE OVERVIEW   This whole-wheat bread balances nutty wheat flavor with a light texture by using 60 percent whole-wheat flour and 40 percent bread flour. A half-cup of wheat germ reinforces the nutty flavor. You'll soak the whole-wheat flour and wheat germ overnight in milk to soften the grain's fiber, keep the dough moist, and coax out some sweetness. You'll also make a sponge, a mixture of flour, water, and yeast left to sit overnight to develop a full range of flavor. Adding honey lends complexity and swapping out some of the butter for vegetable oil cuts the richness. If you don't have a baking stone, bake the bread on an overturned and preheated rimmed baking sheet set on the lowest oven rack. The bread can be wrapped in a double layer of plastic wrap and stored at room temperature for up to three days. Wrapped with an additional layer of aluminum foil, the bread can be frozen for up to one month.

Soaker

- 3 cups (16½ ounces) whole-wheat flour
- 2 cups whole milk
- ½ cup wheat germ

Sponge

- 2 cups (11 ounces) bread flour
- 1 cup water, heated to 110 degrees
- ½ teaspoon instant or rapid-rise yeast

Dough

- 6 tablespoons unsalted butter, softened
- ¼ cup honey
- 2 tablespoons instant or rapid-rise yeast
- 2 tablespoons vegetable oil
- 4 teaspoons table salt

1. **FOR THE SOAKER** Stir flour, milk, and wheat germ in large bowl with wooden spoon until shaggy mass forms. Transfer dough to lightly floured counter and knead by hand until smooth, about 3 minutes. Return soaker to bowl, cover tightly with plastic wrap, and refrigerate for at least 8 hours or up to 24 hours.

2. **FOR THE SPONGE** Stir flour, water, and yeast in 8-cup liquid measuring cup with wooden spoon until well combined. Cover tightly with plastic wrap and let sit at room temperature until sponge has risen and begins to collapse, about 6 hours (sponge can sit at room temperature for up to 24 hours).

3. **FOR THE DOUGH** Tear soaker into 1-inch pieces and place in bowl of stand mixer fitted with dough hook. Add sponge, butter, honey, yeast, oil, and salt and mix on low speed until cohesive dough starts to form, about 2 minutes, scraping down bowl as needed. Increase speed to medium-low and knead until dough is smooth and elastic and clears sides of bowl but sticks to bottom, about 8 minutes. Transfer dough to lightly greased large bowl or container, cover tightly with plastic, and let rise for 45 minutes.

4. Using greased bowl scraper (or your fingertips), fold dough over itself by gently lifting and folding edge of dough toward middle. Turn bowl 45 degrees and fold dough again; repeat turning bowl and folding dough 6 more times (total of 8 folds). Cover tightly with plastic and let rise until nearly doubled in size, 30 minutes to 1 hour.

5. Grease two 8½ by 4½-inch loaf pans. Press down on dough to deflate. Transfer dough to lightly floured counter, divide in half, and cover loosely with greased plastic. Press and stretch 1 piece of dough (keep remaining piece covered) into 8 by 6-inch rectangle, with long side parallel to counter edge.

6. Roll dough away from you into firm cylinder, keeping roll taut by tucking it under itself as you go. Pinch seam closed and place loaf seam side down in prepared pan, pressing dough gently into corners. Repeat with second piece of dough. Cover loosely with greased plastic and let rise until

loaves reach 1 inch above lips of pans and dough springs back minimally when poked gently with your knuckle, 1 to 1½ hours.

7. Adjust oven rack to lower-middle position and heat oven to 350 degrees. Using sharp paring knife or single-edge razor blade, make one ¼-inch-deep slash with swift, fluid motion lengthwise along top of loaf, starting and stopping about ½ inch from ends. Repeat with second loaf.

8. Mist loaves with water and bake until deep golden brown and loaves register 205 to 210 degrees, 40 to 45 minutes, rotating pans halfway through baking. Let loaves cool in pans for 15 minutes. Remove loaves from pans and let cool completely on wire rack, about 3 hours, before serving.

KEYS TO SUCCESS

- **Wheat germ**: Wheat germ adds sweetness and boosts the flavor of the whole-wheat flour.
- **Vegetable oil**: Butter makes the dough a bit too rich; using oil produces a leaner-tasting loaf that works well for sandwiches.

Forming Whole-Wheat Sandwich Bread

PAT INTO RECTANGLE
Halve dough and pat each portion into 17 by 8-inch rectangle.

ROLL AND RISE
Roll each rectangle away from you into tight cylinder, keeping roll taut. Pinch seams to seal. Place loaves seam side down in pans. Let dough rise until almost doubled in size.

SLASH TOP
Using sharp knife or single-edge razor blade, make shallow slash along top of each loaf.

SCIENCE LESSON Soaking Whole-Wheat Flour for Better Bread

When developing the recipe for whole-wheat bread, our goal was to cram as much whole-wheat flour into the dough as possible. But with more than 50 percent whole-wheat, the bread got too heavy and developed off-flavors. Would giving the whole-wheat flour a long soak before creating the final dough allow us to bump up its amount?

THE EXPERIMENT

We baked two loaves, each with a 60:40 ratio of whole-wheat to refined bread flour. We soaked the whole-wheat flour for one loaf overnight in the milk from our recipe before combining it with the other ingredients. For the second loaf, we didn't give the whole-wheat flour any special treatment.

THE RESULTS

The texture and flavor of the bread made with soaked whole-wheat flour was markedly better than those of the loaf with flour that wasn't soaked.

THE EXPLANATION

Soaking has a threefold effect on the loaf. First, it dulls the flour's fibrous bran, blunting its ability to disrupt gluten development and produce a dense crumb. Second, soaking hydrates the whole-wheat flour, preventing it from absorbing too much of the dough's moisture. Finally, this technique activates enzymes in the flour that convert some of the starches into sugars, thereby sweetening the bran's natural bitterness. We were able to pack our bread with roughly 50 percent more whole wheat than most recipes call for and still create a loaf with earthy-sweet flavor and a soft yet hearty crumb.

WHAT CAN GO WRONG

PROBLEM The loaf is dense.

SOLUTION Soak the whole-wheat flour for at least 8 hours to soften the bran so its sharp edges don't cut through strands of gluten. If you don't give the soaker enough time, the bran can compromise the gluten structure, yielding a dense loaf of bread.

PROBLEM The soaker doesn't incorporate.

SOLUTION Tear the soaker into 1-inch pieces. The soaker is fairly stiff once it's time to add the sponge and other dough ingredients. If you try to knead a mass of soaker into the sponge, it will never incorporate properly.

BIG-FLAVOR BREADS

DAN ZUCCARELLO

The three loaves in this course take basic sponge-based doughs to the next level with flavorful add-ins: cheddar cheese, caramelized onions, chewy dried figs. We show you how to add these ingredients for maximum flavor without compromising texture or impeding rise. You'll also learn how to shape the dough into a classic boule, or round loaf, and how to achieve the deeply satisfying crunchy crust of a rustic bread.

DAN'S PRO TIP: *While the slashes on these loaves are primarily functional, allowing for uniform expansion while baking, the pattern is open to embellishment. Once you are comfortable with a basic cross shape, try a square by making four slashes that intersect 1 inch from edges of loaf, or a crescent moon by making a single slash approximately 1 inch from the edge of the loaf.*

THE METHOD
FLAVORED RUSTIC LOAF

Our rustic loaves incorporate their flavorful ingredients in slightly different ways, but the basic method is the same.

1 MAKE SPONGE
Stir water, yeast, and part of flour together, cover, and let rest for at least 6 hours.

2 KNEAD
Combine sponge with remaining dough ingredients. Some or all of the flavoring ingredients are added at this point, depending on the recipe.

3 FOLD TO MIX
After dough has rested, fold dough over on itself in bowl several times to incorporate air for more open crumb.

4 SHAPE INTO BALL
Drag dough in small circles on floured counter, forming it into ball and pulling seams down to bottom. Pinch seams closed.

5 PROOF IN COLANDER
Line colander with damp dish towel and dust towel with flour. Place loaf in colander to help it maintain round shape as it rises.

6 SLASH TOP
Using lame, razor, or sharp knife, cut large X in top of loaf.

7 PREPARE LAVA ROCKS
Pour water over preheated lava rocks to create steam for maximum lift.

8 TEMP FOR DONENESS
When instant-read thermometer inserted into center of loaf registers 205 to 210 degrees, you know it's done.

CHEDDAR AND BLACK PEPPER BREAD

Makes: 1 loaf

Total Time: 4½ hours, plus 13½ hours rising, resting, and cooling

RECIPE OVERVIEW This yeasted cheesy bread is decadent, featuring big cheddar flavor and a lingering finish of zesty black pepper. Its rusticity makes you want to tear it into generous chunks to dunk into a bowl of tomato soup. Making a bread this cheesy isn't as simple as just kneading the generous amount of shredded cheddar into the dough, because the fatty cheese will coat the gluten strands, preventing them from linking up into a strong network. To achieve a sturdy and flavorful crumb with pockets of melted cheese, knead just half of the cheese into the dough and then roll in the remaining cheese jelly roll–style before shaping the dough into a round loaf. Look for a cheddar aged for about one year. (Avoid cheddar aged for longer; it won't melt well.) Use the large holes of a box grater to shred the cheddar. If you own a round banneton, you may use that instead of a towel-lined colander; either way, enclosing the proofing dough in a plastic garbage bag protects it from forming a tough skin. If you don't have a baking peel, use a rimless or overturned baking sheet to slide the bread onto the baking stone. If you don't have a baking stone or steel, you can use a preheated rimless or overturned baking sheet; however, the crust will be less crisp. This recipe uses lava rocks to create steam for a bakery-style loaf. For the best texture and height, we don't recommend omitting them; see page 529 for more information on lava rocks.

Sponge

⅔ cup (3⅔ ounces) bread flour
½ cup water, room temperature
⅛ teaspoon instant or rapid-rise yeast

Dough

2⅓ cups (12¾ ounces) bread flour
1¼ teaspoons instant or rapid-rise yeast
1¼ teaspoons coarsely ground pepper, divided
1 cup water, room temperature
2 teaspoons table salt
8 ounces cheddar cheese, shredded (2 cups), room temperature, divided

1. **FOR THE SPONGE** Stir flour, room-temperature water, and yeast in 4-cup liquid measuring cup with wooden spoon until well combined. Cover tightly with plastic wrap and let sit at room temperature until sponge has risen and begins to collapse, about 6 hours (sponge can sit at room temperature for up to 24 hours).

2. **FOR THE DOUGH** Whisk flour, yeast, and ¾ teaspoon pepper together in bowl of stand mixer. Stir room-temperature water into sponge with wooden spoon until well combined. Using dough hook on low speed, slowly add sponge mixture to flour mixture and mix until cohesive dough starts to form and no dry flour remains, about 2 minutes, scraping down bowl as needed. Cover bowl tightly with plastic and let dough rest for 20 minutes.

3. Add salt to dough and knead on medium-low speed until dough is smooth and elastic and clears sides of bowl, about 5 minutes. Reduce speed to low; slowly add 1 cup cheddar, ¼ cup at a time; and mix until just incorporated, about 30 seconds. Transfer dough to lightly greased large bowl or container, cover tightly with plastic, and let rise for 30 minutes.

4. Using greased bowl scraper (or your fingertips), fold dough over itself by gently lifting and folding edge of dough toward middle. Turn bowl 45 degrees and fold dough again; repeat turning bowl and folding dough 6 more times (total of 8 folds). Cover tightly with plastic and let rise for 30 minutes. Repeat folding and rising every 30 minutes, 3 more times. After fourth set of folds, cover bowl tightly with plastic and let dough rise until nearly doubled in size, 1 to 1½ hours.

5. Mist underside of large linen or cotton tea towel with water. Line 5-quart colander with prepared towel and dust evenly with flour. Transfer dough to lightly floured counter (side of dough that was against bowl should now be against counter). Press and stretch dough into 10-inch square, deflating any gas pockets larger than 1 inch. Sprinkle remaining 1 cup cheddar evenly over dough, leaving ½-inch border. Roll dough away from you into snug cylinder. Pinch seam closed. Turn cylinder seam side up and roll away from you into snug spiral, ending with tail end on bottom. Pinch side seams together to seal. Using your cupped hands, drag dough in small circles on counter until dough feels taut and round and all seams are secured on underside of loaf. (Some cheddar may become exposed.)

6. Place loaf seam side up in prepared colander and pinch any remaining seams closed. Loosely fold edges of towel over loaf to enclose, then place colander in large plastic garbage bag. Tie, or fold under, open end of bag to fully enclose. Let rise until loaf increases in size by about half and dough springs back minimally when poked gently with your knuckle, 30 minutes to 1 hour (remove loaf from bag to test).

7. One hour before baking, adjust oven racks to lower-middle and lowest positions. Place baking stone or steel on upper rack, place 2 disposable aluminum pie plates filled with 1 quart lava rocks each on lower rack, and heat oven to 450 degrees. Bring 1 cup water to boil. Remove colander from bag, unfold edges of towel, and dust top of loaf with flour. (If any seams have reopened, pinch closed before dusting with flour.) Lay 16 by 12-inch sheet of parchment paper on top of loaf. Using 1 hand to support parchment and loaf, invert loaf onto parchment and place on counter. Gently remove colander and towel. Transfer parchment with loaf to baking peel.

8. Carefully pour ½ cup boiling water into 1 disposable pie plate of preheated rocks and close oven door for 1 minute to create steam. Meanwhile, using sharp paring knife or single-edge razor blade, make two 7-inch-long, ½-inch-deep slashes with swift, fluid motion along top of loaf to form cross. Sprinkle top of loaf with remaining ½ teaspoon pepper.

9. Working quickly, slide parchment with loaf onto baking stone and pour remaining ½ cup boiling water into second disposable pie plate of preheated rocks. Bake until crust is dark brown and loaf registers 205 to 210 degrees, 35 to 40 minutes, rotating loaf halfway through baking. Transfer loaf to wire rack, discard parchment, and let cool completely, about 3 hours, before serving.

KEYS TO SUCCESS

- **Grate cheese:** Use the large holes of a box grater to grate the cheddar.
- **Cover to rise:** Enclose the bread in a garbage bag to avoid a tough skin.

Shaping Cheddar Bread

ADD CHEESE
Sprinkle cheddar cheese evenly over dough, leaving ½-inch border. Roll dough away from you into snug cylinder. Pinch seam closed.

ROLL INTO SPIRAL
Turn cylinder seam side up and roll away from you into snug spiral, ending with tail end on bottom. Pinch side seams together to seal.

FORM THE LOAF
Using your cupped hands, drag dough in small circles on counter until dough feels taut and round and all seams are secured on underside of loaf.

CARAMELIZED ONION BREAD

Makes: 1 loaf
Total Time: 1½ hours, plus 12½ to 13½ hours rising, resting, and cooling

RECIPE OVERVIEW Savory-sweet caramelized onions pack this artisan-style loaf with deeply concentrated flavor. You'll start by making a sponge, which is simply a mixture of a portion of the dough's flour, water, and yeast that ferments for around 6 hours to develop more complex flavor; it then gets mixed into the rest of the dough ingredients. You'll load a whopping 3 cups of onions into this bread, first cooking them down with brown sugar, garlic, and thyme to a deep golden brown. Finely chopped onions work best—larger pieces will leave you with soggy pockets of uncooked dough surrounding the onions. A two-pronged approach to incorporating the onions ensures that their flavor permeates every bite: First, mix half of them with the wet ingredients at the beginning of mixing, where they'll break down during kneading. Second, add the remaining half at the end of kneading to provide great textural contrast. Yellow onions offer a good flavor and a firm texture. You can use white or red onions, but the flavor will be different. Vidalia onions have a high water content and will make the dough too wet. If you own a round banneton, you may use that instead of a towel-lined colander; either way, enclosing the proofing dough in a plastic garbage bag protects it from forming a tough skin. If you don't have a baking peel, use a rimless or overturned baking sheet to slide the bread onto the baking stone. If you don't have a baking stone or steel, you can use a preheated rimless or overturned baking sheet; however, the crust will be less crisp. This recipe uses lava rocks to achieve a bakery-style loaf. For the best texture and height, we don't recommend omitting them; see page 529 for more information on lava rocks.

Sponge

- ⅔ cup (3⅔ ounces) bread flour
- ½ cup water, room temperature
- ⅛ teaspoon instant or rapid-rise yeast

Dough

- 2 tablespoons extra-virgin olive oil
- 3 cups finely chopped onions
- 2 garlic cloves, minced
- 2 teaspoons minced fresh thyme or ½ teaspoon dried
- 2 teaspoons packed brown sugar
- 2 teaspoons table salt, divided
- ¼ teaspoon pepper
- 2⅓ cups (12¾ ounces) bread flour
- 1¼ teaspoons instant or rapid-rise yeast
- ¾ cup plus 2 tablespoons water, room temperature

1. **FOR THE SPONGE** Stir flour, room-temperature water, and yeast in 4-cup liquid measuring cup with wooden spoon until well combined. Cover tightly with plastic wrap and let sit at room temperature until sponge has risen and begins to collapse, about 6 hours (sponge can sit at room temperature for up to 24 hours).

2. **FOR THE DOUGH** Heat oil in 12-inch nonstick skillet over medium heat until shimmering. Stir in onions, garlic, thyme, sugar, ½ teaspoon salt, and pepper. Cover and cook, stirring occasionally, until onions are softened and have released their juice, 3 to 5 minutes. Remove lid and continue to cook, stirring often, until juice evaporates and onions are deep golden brown, 10 to 15 minutes. Transfer onion mixture to bowl and let cool completely before using.

3. Whisk flour and yeast together in bowl of stand mixer. Stir room-temperature water and half of onion mixture into sponge with wooden spoon until well combined. Using dough hook on low speed, slowly add sponge mixture to flour mixture and mix until cohesive dough starts to form and no dry flour remains, about 2 minutes, scraping down bowl as needed. Cover bowl tightly with plastic and let dough rest for 20 minutes.

4. Add remaining 1½ teaspoons salt to dough and knead on medium-low speed until dough is smooth and elastic and clears sides of bowl, about 5 minutes. Reduce speed to low; slowly add remaining onion mixture, 1 tablespoon at a time; and mix until mostly incorporated, about 1 minute. Transfer dough to lightly greased large bowl or container, cover tightly with plastic, and let rise for 30 minutes.

5. Using greased bowl scraper (or your fingertips), fold dough over itself by gently lifting and folding edge of dough toward middle. Turn bowl 45 degrees and fold dough again; repeat turning bowl and folding dough 6 more times (total of 8 folds). Cover tightly with plastic and let rise for 30 minutes. Repeat folding and rising. Fold dough again, then cover bowl tightly with plastic and let dough rise until nearly doubled in size, 45 minutes to 1¼ hours.

6. Mist underside of large linen or cotton tea towel with water. Line 5-quart colander with prepared towel and dust evenly with flour. Transfer dough to lightly floured counter (side of dough that was against bowl should now be against counter). Press and stretch dough into 10-inch round, deflating any gas pockets larger than 1 inch. Working around circumference of dough, fold edges toward center until ball forms. Flip dough ball seam side down and, using your cupped hands, drag in small circles on counter until dough feels taut and round and all seams are secured on underside of loaf.

7. Place loaf seam side up in prepared colander and pinch any remaining seams closed. Loosely fold edges of towel over loaf to enclose, then place colander in large plastic garbage bag. Tie, or fold under, open end of bag to fully enclose. Let rise until loaf increases in size by about half and dough springs back minimally when poked gently with your knuckle, 1 to 1½ hours (remove loaf from bag to test).

8. One hour before baking, adjust oven racks to lower-middle and lowest positions. Place baking stone or steel on upper rack, place 2 disposable aluminum pie plates filled with 1 quart lava rocks each on lower rack, and heat oven to 425 degrees. Bring 1 cup water to boil. Remove colander from bag, unfold edges of towel, and dust top of loaf with flour. (If any seams have reopened, pinch closed before dusting with flour.) Lay 16 by 12-inch sheet of parchment paper on top of loaf. Using 1 hand to support parchment and loaf, invert loaf onto parchment and place on counter. Gently remove colander and towel. Transfer parchment with loaf to baking peel.

9. Carefully pour ½ cup boiling water into 1 disposable pie plate of preheated rocks and close oven door for 1 minute to create steam. Using sharp paring knife, single-edge razor blade, or lame make two 7-inch-long, ½-inch-deep slashes with swift, fluid motion along top of loaf to form cross.

10. Working quickly, slide parchment with loaf onto baking stone and pour remaining ½ cup boiling water into second disposable pie plate of preheated rocks. Bake until crust is dark brown and loaf registers 205 to 210 degrees, 45 to 50 minutes, rotating loaf halfway through baking. Transfer loaf to wire rack, discard parchment, and let cool completely, about 3 hours, before serving.

KEYS TO SUCCESS

- **Chopped onions:** Small onion pieces blend into the dough more seamlessly than slices.

- **Repeated folding:** This easy kneading method incorporates air for the signature open crumb of rustic breads.

Forming Caramelized Onion Bread

FOLD EDGES

Working around circumference of dough, fold edges toward center until ball forms. Flip dough ball seam side down and drag in small circles on counter until dough feels taut and round and seams are secured on underside of loaf.

PLACE LOAF IN COLANDER

Place loaf seam side up in prepared colander and pinch any remaining seams closed. Loosely fold edges of towel over loaf to enclose, then place colander in large plastic garbage bag.

REMOVE FROM COLANDER

Using 1 hand to support parchment and loaf, invert loaf onto parchment and place on counter. Gently remove colander and towel. Transfer parchment with loaf to pizza peel.

SLASH TOP

Holding lame concave side up at 30-degree angle to loaf, make two 7-inch-long, ½-inch-deep slashes with swift, fluid motion along top of loaf to form cross.

FIG AND FENNEL BREAD

Makes: 1 loaf
Total Time: 4 hours, plus 11¼ hours rising and cooling

RECIPE OVERVIEW   This company-worthy artisan loaf, with its sophisticated pairing of sweet, earthy dried figs and complementary fennel seeds, is ideal for accompanying cheese and charcuterie plates. Blending some rye flour into the mix along with bread flour adds even more flavor intrigue. Starting the dough with a sponge develops lots of complex flavor, and making a series of folds as the dough rises incorporates air, which gives the bread better structure and a more open crumb. A Dutch oven creates a humid, moist bread-baking environment, which fosters an airy crumb and a beautifully browned, crisp crust on the finished bread. Here you'll go a step further by preheating the Dutch oven before placing the loaf inside. The Dutch oven's heavy cast-iron construction helps the vessel retain heat effectively. In combination with the steamy covered environment, this mimics the use of a baking stone or steel and lava rocks to help achieve the rustic crumb of a bakery-quality bread. Dusting the top of the loaf with cornmeal before baking gives it a rustic finished appearance and a light crunch. While any variety of dried figs will work, we especially like the flavor of Calimyrna figs. Use light or medium rye flour; dark rye flour will be overpowering. Toast the fennel seeds in a dry skillet over medium heat until fragrant (about 1 minute), and then remove the seeds from the skillet so they don't scorch.

Sponge

   1 cup (5½ ounces) bread flour
  ¾ cup water, room temperature
  ⅛ teaspoon instant or rapid-rise yeast

Dough

   1 cup plus 2 tablespoons (6¼ ounces) bread flour
   1 cup (5½ ounces) light or medium rye flour
   1 tablespoon fennel seeds, toasted
   2 teaspoons table salt
 1½ teaspoons instant or rapid-rise yeast
   1 cup water, room temperature
   1 cup dried figs, stemmed and chopped coarse
      Cornmeal

   1. FOR THE SPONGE Stir flour, room-temperature water, and yeast in 4-cup liquid measuring cup with wooden spoon until well combined. Cover tightly with plastic wrap and let sit at room temperature until sponge has risen and begins to collapse, about 6 hours (sponge can sit at room temperature for up to 24 hours).

   2. FOR THE DOUGH Whisk bread flour, rye flour, fennel seeds, salt, and yeast together in bowl of stand mixer. Stir room-temperature water into sponge with wooden spoon until well combined. Using dough hook on low speed, slowly add sponge mixture to flour mixture and mix until cohesive dough starts to form and no dry flour remains, about 2 minutes, scraping down bowl as needed.

3. Increase speed to medium-low and continue to knead until dough is smooth, elastic, and slightly sticky, about 5 minutes. Reduce speed to low; slowly add figs, ¼ cup at a time; and mix until mostly incorporated, about 1 minute. Transfer dough to lightly greased large bowl or container, cover tightly with plastic, and let rise for 30 minutes.

4. Using greased bowl scraper (or your fingertips), fold dough over itself by gently lifting and folding edge of dough toward middle. Turn bowl 45 degrees and fold dough again; repeat turning bowl and folding dough 6 more times (total of 8 folds). Cover tightly with plastic and let rise for 30 minutes. Repeat folding and rising. Fold dough again, then cover bowl tightly with plastic and let rise until nearly doubled in size, 45 minutes to 1¼ hours.

5. Lay 18 by 12-inch sheet of parchment paper on counter, lightly spray with vegetable oil spray, and dust evenly with cornmeal. Transfer dough to lightly floured counter. Using your lightly floured hands, press and stretch dough into 10-inch round, deflating any gas pockets larger than 1 inch.

6. Shape dough into ball by pulling edges into middle, then flip dough ball seam side down and, using your cupped hands, drag in small circles on counter until dough feels taut and round and all seams are secured on underside of loaf. Place loaf, seam side down, in center of prepared parchment and cover loosely with greased plastic. Let rise until loaf increases in size by about half and dough springs back minimally when poked gently with your knuckle, about 30 minutes.

7. Thirty minutes before baking, adjust oven rack to lower-middle position, place Dutch oven (with lid) on rack, and heat oven to 500 degrees. Using sharp paring knife or single-edge razor blade, make two 5-inch-long, ½-inch-deep slashes with swift, fluid motion along top of loaf to form cross. Dust top of loaf with cornmeal.

8. Carefully transfer pot to wire rack and uncover. Using parchment as sling, gently lower loaf into pot. Cover pot, tucking any excess parchment into pot, and return to oven. Reduce oven temperature to 425 degrees and bake loaf for 15 minutes (start timing as soon as bread goes in oven). Remove lid and continue to bake until loaf is deep golden brown and registers 205 to 210 degrees, about 20 minutes.

9. Using parchment sling, remove loaf from pot and transfer to wire rack; discard parchment. Let cool completely, about 3 hours, before serving.

KEYS TO SUCCESS

- **Light rye:** A little light rye flour adds depth of flavor without overtaking the loaf.

- **Toasted fennel:** Toasting increases the savory impact of the tiny seeds.

- **Dutch oven:** Using this kitchen workhorse creates a steamy environment for a crisp crust.

CORE TECHNIQUE | **Slashing a Loaf**

CRISSCROSS

Once loaf is fully risen, use sharp paring knife or single-edge razor blade to make two 5-inch-long, ½-inch-deep slashes with swift, fluid motion along top of loaf to form cross.

TURNING BREAD INTO BOULES

French bakers achieve the symmetrical round loaves of bread known as boules by transferring the dough to shallow, linen-lined woven baskets known as bannetons or brotforms for the last rising step before baking. The cloth-lined basket serves two functions: It retains the round shape of the loaf as it proofs, and its breathable construction wicks away moisture from the dough's surface, for a crispier, browner crust. While an ordinary bowl isn't a suitable substitute, you can still create an improvised banneton at home: Line a metal or plastic colander with a linen dish towel (linen is preferable to cotton, since cotton has microscopic fibers that can stick to dough) and dust it liberally with flour. Place the formed loaf upside down in the colander, fold the cloth loosely over it, and place the colander (which allows in more air than a true banneton) in a loose plastic bag to protect the dough from drafts. The method will produce a beautifully shaped boule that would be impossible to replicate if you simply left the dough to proof on its own.

LAVA ROCKS FOR STEAM

For thick, crisp-crusted, dramatic-looking rustic loaves, a steamy oven is a bread's best friend. Professional bakers use steam-injected ovens for three reasons: First, a moist environment transfers heat more rapidly than dry heat does, allowing the gases inside the loaf to expand quickly in the first few minutes of baking, ensuring maximum volume. At the same time, steam prevents the bread's exterior from drying out too quickly, which would create a rigid structure that limits rise. Finally, moisture converts the exterior starches into a thin coating of gel that eventually results in the glossy, crackly crust that is a hallmark of a great artisan-style loaf.

We've come up with an effective work-around for the home oven: lava rocks. Pouring boiling water over a disposable pan full of preheated lava rocks creates an initial burst of steam; the irregularly shaped rocks absorb and retain heat to continue to produce steam, creating a moist oven environment that helps rustic breads develop a crisp crust. You can find lava rocks, which are also used for gas grills, at many hardware and home-improvement stores. Here's how to use them so the oven stays steamy for the entire time.

Adjust oven rack to lowest position. Fill 2 aluminum pie plates with 1 quart of lava rocks each and place them on rack before heating oven. When bread is ready to bake, pour ½ cup boiling water into 1 plate and close oven door for 1 minute to create initial burst of steam. Then, working quickly, transfer loaf to oven and pour ½ cup boiling water into second plate.

Lava Rock Workaround

We tested multiple ways to create steam in the oven, and nothing turned out crusts as crisp and crackly as our lava rock method. For the best bread, we highly recommend you use them. However, if you don't want to buy lava rocks, you can get satisfactory crust (it will be chewier and less crunchy) by using a water pan. Before baking, place an empty loaf pan or cake pan on the lower rack instead of the pans of lava rocks and bring 1 cup of water to boil. When you slide the loaf onto the baking stone, pour the boiling water into the empty pan and shut the oven door.

USING A COUCHE

Working with a Couche

Professional bakers proof some free-form loaves in the folds of a piece of heavy linen known as a couche. The couche has two core jobs: It helps the loaf hold its shape, and it wicks away moisture, keeping the dough's surface uniformly dry as it proofs and rises, helping develop a thin "skin" that bakes up to the perfect crisp, chewy, attractively floured crust.

USING A BANNETON

Bakers achieve symmetrical round loaves of bread (boules) by transferring the dough to shallow, woven baskets known as bannetons or brotforms for the last rising step before baking. The cloth-lined basket serves two functions: It retains the round shape of the loaf as it proofs, and its breathable construction wicks away moisture from the dough's surface, much like the couche does, for a crispier, browner crust. We've found that you can improvise a banneton at home by lining a 5-quart metal or plastic colander with a linen dish towel and dusting the towel liberally with flour, and we use this simple technique in our recipes. But if you're inclined to purchase these inexpensive baskets, you'll find that they're not just lightweight and convenient; they mark your bread with a beautiful floured spiral. As the dough expands when it proofs, it makes its way into the ridges of the banneton, so the pattern is transferred onto the loaf's surface.

RUSTIC ITALIAN BREADS

KEITH DRESSER

The pair of rustic Italian loaves in this course are made with highly hydrated (i.e., very wet) doughs. This makes the bread delightfully chewy, with an open, airy crumb. Wet, sticky doughs can be hard to handle but we'll show you techniques to tame them and make creating these breads as pleasurable as eating them.

KEITH'S PRO TIP: *When working with high hydration doughs like these, I find a bench scraper to be an invaluable tool. The wide, thin blade is easy to get underneath the slack dough and because it is metal, the sticky dough won't stick to it the same way it will your hands.*

CIABATTA

Makes: 2 loaves
Total Time: 1½ hours, plus 8 to 8½ hours resting and rising and 2 hours cooling

RECIPE OVERVIEW Ciabatta, like many rustic breads, starts with a sponge, but beyond that, ciabatta has unique characteristics. First, the dough is extremely wet—even more hydrated than other rustic breads—which gives this loaf its signature holes. Second, ciabatta has a light, springy texture, achieved in this recipe by using all-purpose flour instead of the bread flour used in most rustic breads. Because this dough is so hydrated, it's necessary to begin kneading with the stand mixer's paddle attachment instead of the dough hook, and to incorporate a series of folds to reinforce the structure and make it easier to work with. A hallmark of ciabatta is an open texture with large holes, but you don't want a loaf with more air than bread. That's why this recipe includes milk; it contains a protein fragment called gluta-thione, which weakens the gluten strands slightly. A small amount of milk reduces the size of the bubbles just enough. As you make this bread, keep in mind that the dough is wet and very sticky. The key to manipulating it is working quickly and gently; rough handling will result in flat, tough loaves. When possible, use a bowl scraper or a large rubber spatula to move the dough. If you have to use your hands, make sure they are well floured. We do not recommend mixing this dough by hand.

Sponge

>   1 cup (5 ounces) all-purpose flour
>   ½ cup (4 ounces) water, room temperature
>   ⅛ teaspoon instant or rapid-rise yeast

Dough

>   2 cups (10 ounces) all-purpose flour
>   1½ teaspoons table salt
>   ½ teaspoon instant or rapid-rise yeast
>   ¾ cup (6 ounces) water, room temperature
>   ¼ cup (2 ounces) whole milk, room temperature

1. FOR THE SPONGE Stir all ingredients in 4-cup liquid measuring cup with wooden spoon until well combined. Cover tightly with plastic wrap and let sit at room temperature until sponge has risen and begins to collapse, about 6 hours (sponge can sit at room temperature for up to 24 hours).

2. FOR THE DOUGH Whisk flour, salt, and yeast together in bowl of stand mixer. Stir water and milk into sponge with wooden spoon until well combined. Using paddle on low speed, slowly add sponge mixture to flour mixture and mix until cohesive dough starts to form and no dry flour remains, about 2 minutes, scraping down bowl as needed. Increase speed to medium-low and continue to mix until dough becomes uniform mass that collects on paddle and pulls away from sides of bowl, 4 to 6 minutes.

3. Remove paddle and fit stand mixer with dough hook. Knead on medium-low speed until dough is smooth and shiny (dough will be very sticky), about 10 minutes. Transfer dough to lightly greased large bowl or container, cover tightly with plastic, and let rise until doubled in size, 30 minutes to 1 hour.

4. Using greased bowl scraper (or rubber spatula), fold dough over itself by gently lifting and folding edge of dough toward middle. Turn bowl 45 degrees and fold dough again; repeat turning bowl and folding dough 6 more times (total of 8 folds). Cover tightly with plastic and let rise for 30 minutes. Repeat folding, then cover bowl tightly with plastic and let dough rise until nearly doubled in size, about 30 minutes.

5. One hour before baking, adjust oven racks to lower-middle and lowest positions. Place baking stone on upper rack and heat oven to 450 degrees. Dust two 12 by 6-inch pieces of parchment paper liberally with flour. Transfer dough to well-floured counter (side of dough that was against bowl should now be against counter). Liberally dust top of dough with flour and divide in half. Turn 1 piece of dough cut side up and dust with flour. Using your well-floured hands, press and stretch dough into 12 by 6-inch rectangle, with short side parallel to counter edge, being careful not to deflate dough completely.

6. Stretch and fold top and bottom thirds of dough over middle like business letter to form rough 7 by 4-inch loaf. Pinch seams closed. Transfer loaf seam side down to 1 sheet of prepared parchment and cover loosely with greased

plastic. Repeat with second piece of dough. Let loaves sit until puffy and surface of loaves develops small bubbles, about 30 minutes.

7. Transfer parchment with loaves to pizza peel. Using your floured fingertips, evenly poke entire surface of each loaf to form 10 by 6-inch rectangle. Mist loaves with water.

8. Working quickly, slide each piece of parchment with loaf onto baking stone. Bake, misting loaves with water twice more during first 5 minutes of baking time, until crusts are deep golden brown and loaves register 210 to 212 degrees, 25 to 30 minutes, rotating loaves halfway through baking. Transfer loaves to wire rack, discard parchment, and let cool completely, about 2 hours, before serving.

KEYS TO SUCCESS

- **Add milk:** The protein in milk weakens gluten slightly, which helps keep the size of the air pockets under control.
- **Hands off:** Use a bowl scraper or spatula when possible and be gentle, to avoid a tough loaf.

Shaping Ciabatta

PRESS AND STRETCH
Liberally dust top of dough with flour and divide in half. Turn 1 piece of dough cut side up and dust with flour. Press and stretch dough into 12 by 16-inch rectangle, with short side parallel to counter edge, being careful not to deflate dough completely.

FOLD INTO LOAF
Stretch and fold top and bottom thirds of dough over middle like business letter to form rough 7 by 4-inch loaf. Pinch seams closed. Transfer loaf seam side down to 1 sheet of prepared parchment.

POKE SURFACE
Transfer parchment with loaves to pizza peel. Using your floured fingertips, evenly poke entire surface of each loaf to form 10 by 6-inch rectangle. Mist loaves with water.

DURUM BREAD

Makes: 1 loaf
Total Time: 1¾ hours, plus 11¾ to 12¼ hours resting, rising, and cooling

RECIPE OVERVIEW Italian loaves made with durum flour boast an open, airy crumb; a warm, golden color; a chewy texture; and a sweet, nutty flavor. Most recipes call for a combination of durum and bread flours; this loaf is made with 60 percent durum flour, which provides the right balance. The hydration level for this dough is 90 percent, which makes for an open, chewy crumb. Though handling this clingy dough can be challenging, after folding it onto itself several times during the initial proofing period, the gluten strands elongate and the dough becomes more supple. To make the shaping process fuss-free, transfer the proofed dough directly onto a piece of floured parchment paper. A simple stretching of the dough with well-floured hands, followed by a couple of folds, yields an elegant slipper-shaped loaf—ready to be split to make panini, sliced into pieces for bruschetta, swabbed through the juicy remnants of a meal, or even dunked into a fruity wine. We do not recommend mixing this dough by hand.

Sponge

- ¾ cup (4⅛ ounces) bread flour
- ½ cup (4 ounces) water, room temperature
- ¼ teaspoon instant or rapid-rise yeast

Dough

- 2 cups (9½ ounces) durum flour
- ½ cup (2¾ ounces) bread flour
- 2½ teaspoons instant or rapid-rise yeast
- 1⅓ cups (10⅔ ounces) water, room temperature
- 1½ teaspoons table salt

1. FOR THE SPONGE Stir all ingredients in 4-cup liquid measuring cup with wooden spoon until well combined. Cover tightly with plastic wrap and let sit at room temperature until sponge has risen and begins to collapse, about 6 hours (sponge can sit at room temperature for up to 24 hours).

2. FOR THE DOUGH Whisk durum flour, bread flour, and yeast together in bowl of stand mixer. Stir water into sponge with wooden spoon until well combined. Using paddle on low speed, slowly add sponge mixture to flour mixture and mix until cohesive dough starts to form and no dry flour remains, about 2 minutes, scraping down bowl as needed. Remove paddle, cover bowl tightly with plastic, and let dough rest for 20 minutes.

3. Fit stand mixer with dough hook. Add salt to dough and knead on medium-low speed until dough is smooth and elastic and clears sides of bowl but sticks to bottom, about 5 minutes. Transfer dough to lightly greased large bowl or container, cover tightly with plastic, and let rise for 30 minutes.

4. Using greased bowl scraper (or rubber spatula), fold dough over itself by gently lifting and folding edge of dough toward middle. Turn bowl 45 degrees and fold dough again; repeat turning bowl and folding dough 6 more times (total of 8 folds). Cover tightly with plastic and let rise for 30 minutes. Repeat folding, then cover bowl tightly with plastic and let dough rise until nearly doubled in size, 1 to 1½ hours.

5. One hour before baking, adjust oven racks to lower-middle and lowest positions. Place baking stone on upper rack, place 2 disposable aluminum pie plates filled with 1 quart lava rocks each on lower rack, and heat oven to 450 degrees. Place 16 by 12-inch piece of parchment paper on counter, with long edge of paper parallel to counter edge, and dust liberally with bread flour. Transfer dough to prepared parchment (side of dough that was against bowl should now be against parchment). Using your well-floured hands, press and stretch dough into 14 by 9-inch rectangle, being careful not to deflate it completely.

6. Stretch and fold top and bottom thirds of dough over middle like business letter to form rough 14 by 4-inch loaf. Pinch seams closed, then flip loaf seam side down. Reshape loaf as needed, tucking edges under to form taut torpedo shape with rounded ends. Transfer parchment with loaf to pizza peel. Cover loosely with greased plastic and let rise until loaf increases in size by about half and dough springs back minimally when poked gently with your knuckle, about 30 minutes. Bring 1 cup water to boil.

7. Carefully pour ½ cup boiling water into 1 disposable pie plate of preheated rocks and close oven door for 1 minute to create steam. Meanwhile, holding lame concave side up at 30-degree angle to loaf, make one ½-inch-deep slash with swift, fluid motion lengthwise along top of loaf, starting and stopping about 1½ inches from ends.

8. Working quickly, slide parchment with loaf onto baking stone and pour remaining ½ cup boiling water into second disposable pie plate of preheated rocks. Bake until crust is deep golden brown and loaf registers 210 to 212 degrees, 30 to 35 minutes, rotating loaf halfway through baking. Transfer loaf to wire rack, discard parchment, and let cool completely, about 3 hours, before serving.

KEYS TO SUCCESS

- **Use durum flour, not semolina flour:** You can find durum flour online or in specialty baking stores.

- **Be gentle:** The key to manipulating this dough is working quickly and gently; rough handling will result in flat, tough loaves. When possible, use a bowl scraper or large rubber spatula to move the dough. For shaping, make sure your hands are well floured.

Shaping Durum Bread

PRESS AND STRETCH
Using your well-floured hands, press and stretch dough into 14 by 9-inch rectangle, being careful not to deflate it completely.

STRETCH AND FOLD
Stretch and fold top and bottom thirds of dough over middle like business letter. Pinch seams closed, then flip seam side down. Reshape loaf as needed, tucking edges under to form taut torpedo shape.

SLASH TOP
Holding lame concave side up at 30-degree angle to loaf, make one ½-inch-deep slash with swift, fluid motion lengthwise along top of loaf, starting and stopping about 1½ inches from ends.

WHAT CAN GO WRONG

PROBLEM The dough sticks.

SOLUTION Use flour liberally. This dough is very wet for a reason—the high hydration level gives the loaf a dramatic chewy, open crumb structure. To work around this, we don't shape this bread like we do other loaves; instead, using very well-floured hands, we stretch and fold it into shape on a very well-floured piece of parchment paper to avoid contact with the counter. Once shaped and proofed, the loaf is slid onto the baking stone with the floured parchment to avoid further handling.

The Science of Hydration

In bread baking, sometimes wetter is better: The more hydrated the dough is, the stronger and more extensible the gluten strands. Strong, extensible gluten strands can support the starch granules and gas bubbles that hydrate and swell as the dough rises and bakes, giving you an airier bread with good chew. During baking, the water within the dough turns to steam, creating hollow pockets as moisture escapes. Extra water also creates a looser dough, which allows the steam bubbles to expand more easily. In drier dough, gas bubbles have a harder time forming and are more likely to collapse. Getting those gas bubbles to hold their shape until the dough has risen and set in the oven is the key to creating an open, airy crumb.

CALCULATING BAKER'S PERCENTAGES

So how do you figure out how much water is actually in a particular bread recipe? Professional bakers use a method called "baker's percentage," in which the quantity of each ingredient is a percentage by weight of the amount of flour, which is always set at 100 percent. This system allows for easy conversion from pounds and ounces to kilograms and grams (or vice versa). And once weights are calculated, scaling recipes up or down is a simple matter of multiplication or division.

Hydration percentage, or the weight of the water (or other liquid) relative to the weight of the flour, is perhaps the most important part of a baker's formula. Sandwich-bread dough with a typical 60 percent hydration (the weight of the liquid is 60 percent of the weight of the flour), for example, yields a loaf with a denser, closed crumb, whereas the 80 percent hydration level of a rustic Italian loaf such as ciabatta (the weight of the liquid is 80 percent of the weight of the flour) is responsible for its airy crumb and large, irregular holes.

To calculate the hydration of a recipe, first weigh the flour and liquid. Divide the weight of the liquid by the weight of the flour and then multiply the result by 100. For example, a recipe containing 1¼ cups of water (10 ounces) and 3 cups of all-purpose flour (15 ounces) will have a 67 percent ($[10 \div 15] \times 100 = 67$) hydration level, indicating a moderately airy crumb. To find the baker's percentage of other ingredients, follow this procedure, weighing the ingredient, dividing it by the total flour weight, and multiplying by 100.

A TOUR OF GRAINS

STEPHANIE PIXLEY

So far in this chapter we've covered a few ways to add flavor to bread: giving the dough a slow, long rise; wrapping the dough around a filling; mixing flavorful ingredients like fruits and vegetables directly into the dough; baking until the crust is dark. The breads in this course come by their varied flavors through the use of different grains—pumpernickel (a kind of rye), spelt, and corn (polenta). Each presents its own challenges but, following our instructions, you'll be able to go beyond basic wheat flour to make some truly special loaves.

STEPH'S PRO TIP: *Don't ever let homemade bread go moldy! At the first sign of staling, cut up the bread into cubes, toss with oil, salt, and pepper, and bake for 10 minutes to create the tastiest croutons.*

PUMPERNICKEL

Makes: 1 loaf
Total Time: 4½ hours, plus 12½ to 13½ hours resting, rising, and cooling

RECIPE OVERVIEW Pumpernickel bread is a slightly sweet, dense, dark-colored German bread often used as the base for canapés of smoked salmon and crème fraîche. Pumpernickel flour is coarsely ground from the whole rye berry and includes the seed coating, bran, and germ. Traditional German pumpernickels use a sourdough starter to provide tang. This recipe uses a simplified process, making a basic sponge with some of the pumpernickel flour. This produces an aromatic and flavorful base for the dough without the planning and time commitment a sourdough starter requires. A combination of 25 percent bread flour and 75 percent pumpernickel flour yields the richest flavor and the ideal chew. Instant espresso powder, cocoa powder, molasses, and caraway seeds enhance the sweet and bitter notes of the loaf, as well as deepen its color. You'll bake this bread low and slow (at 250 degrees for 3 hours) in a Pullman loaf pan to give it the tight, dense crumb that's traditional. You can find pumpernickel flour online or in specialty baking stores. Dark rye flour can be substituted for pumpernickel flour; however, do not use pumpernickel meal, which is a more coarsely ground version of the flour. The more neutral pH of Dutch-processed cocoa powder is important for proper gluten development in this dough; do not substitute natural unsweetened cocoa. The texture of this loaf improves over time, and it is best eaten three days after baking.

Sponge
- 1⅓ cups (7⅓ ounces) pumpernickel flour
- 1 cup (8 ounces) water, room temperature
- ⅛ teaspoon instant or rapid-rise yeast

Dough
- 3½ cups (19¼ ounces) pumpernickel flour
- 1½ cups (8¼ ounces) bread flour
- ¼ cup (¾ ounce) Dutch-processed cocoa powder
- 1 tablespoon caraway seeds
- 1 tablespoon table salt
- 1 teaspoon instant or rapid-rise yeast
- 1 tablespoon instant espresso powder
- 2 cups (16 ounces) water, room temperature
- ¼ cup (3 ounces) molasses
- 2 tablespoons vegetable oil
- 1 large egg, lightly beaten with 1 tablespoon water and pinch table salt

1. FOR THE SPONGE Stir all ingredients in 8-cup liquid measuring cup with wooden spoon until well combined. Cover tightly with plastic wrap and let sit at room temperature until sponge has risen and begins to collapse, about 6 hours (sponge can sit at room temperature for up to 24 hours).

2. FOR THE DOUGH Whisk pumpernickel flour, bread flour, cocoa, caraway seeds, salt, and yeast together in bowl of stand mixer. Dissolve espresso powder in water, then whisk molasses, oil, and espresso powder mixture into sponge until well combined (mixture may look curdled). Using dough hook on low speed, slowly add sponge mixture to flour mixture and mix until cohesive dough starts to form and no dry flour remains, about 2 minutes, scraping down bowl as needed.

3. Increase speed to medium-low and knead until dough is smooth, about 8 minutes. (Dough will resemble cookie dough.)

4. Dust counter with pumpernickel flour. Transfer dough to counter and knead by hand to form smooth, round ball, about 30 seconds. Place dough seam side down in lightly greased large bowl or container, cover tightly with plastic, and let rise until increased in size by about half, 1 to 1½ hours.

5. Grease 13 by 4-inch Pullman loaf pan. Press down on dough to deflate. Lightly dust counter with pumpernickel flour. Turn out dough onto counter (side of dough that was against bowl should now be facing up). Press dough into 12 by 10-inch rectangle, with long side parallel to counter edge.

6. Roll dough away from you into firm cylinder, keeping roll taut by tucking it under itself as you go. Pinch seam closed and place loaf seam side down in prepared pan, pressing dough gently into corners. Cover loosely with greased plastic and let rise until loaf reaches ½ inch below lip of pan and dough springs back minimally when poked gently with your knuckle, 1½ to 2 hours.

7. Adjust oven rack to lower-middle position and heat oven to 250 degrees. Using sharp paring knife or single-edge razor blade, make one ½-inch-deep slash with swift, fluid motion lengthwise along top of loaf, starting and stopping about ½ inch from ends. Gently brush loaf with egg mixture and bake, uncovered, until crust is very dark brown and dry and loaf registers 205 to 210 degrees, about 3 hours, rotating pan halfway through baking. Let loaf cool in pan for 15 minutes. Remove loaf from pan and let cool completely on wire rack, about 4 hours, before serving.

KEYS TO SUCCESS

- **Flour blend:** Use 75 percent pumpernickel flour for flavor and 25 percent bread flour for chew.

- **Go Dutch:** Dutch-processed cocoa has the right pH for gluten development; don't use the more acidic natural cocoa.

Forming Pumpernickel

PRESS INTO RECTANGLE
Press dough into 12 by 10-inch rectangle, with long side parallel to counter edge.

ROLL INTO CYLINDER
Roll dough away from you into firm cylinder, keeping roll taut by tucking it under as you go. Pinch seam closed and place loaf seam side down in pan, pressing gently into corners.

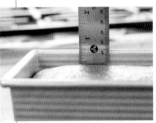

LET RISE
Cover loosely with greased plastic and let rise until loaf reaches ½ inch below lip of pan and dough springs back minimally when poked gently with your knuckle.

SLASH TOP
Make a ½-inch-deep slash with swift, fluid motion lengthwise along top of loaf, starting and stopping about ½ inch from ends. Gently brush loaf with egg mixture and bake.

WHAT CAN GO WRONG

PROBLEM The loaf is underbaked.

SOLUTION Bake for the full 3 hours. It can be difficult to judge the doneness of dark pumpernickel bread, and you should not use temperature as your main guide. You want this heavy dough to dry out fully in the oven, so the 3-hour baking time is critical. Because the loaf is baked for so long and at such a low temperature, it will reach the "proper" temperature range—about an hour or so into the baking time—long before it is fully baked. If you pull the loaf at this time, it will have a soft, brownie-like texture. Make sure the crust is very dark brown and looks dry before you take it out of the oven. And let the loaf cool for the full 4 hours—longer than for other breads—to allow it to continue to dry out and set up.

SAGE-POLENTA BREAD

Makes: 1 loaf
Total Time: 2 hours, plus 8¼ to 8¾ hours resting and rising, and 3 hours cooling

RECIPE OVERVIEW The warm, sunny flavor of corn-meal accented with earthy sage makes this a welcome change from wheat bread. You'll start by cooking coarse-ground polenta for just a few minutes on the stovetop to give the bread a soft, pillowy texture with just the right amount of chew—and no grittiness. Since polenta increases dramatically in volume once it's cooked, don't stir all of it into the dough after kneading. Instead, add the cooked polenta in two stages, incorporating half with the wet ingredients at the beginning of mixing and the remaining half at the end. This method results in pleasant pockets of cooked polenta swirled throughout a hearty loaf. Fresh sage brings out the polenta's savory notes. A dusting of dry polenta on the formed dough gives the bread a crunchy, golden exterior. Do not substitute instant polenta or prepared polenta (sold in a tube) here.

Sponge
- ⅔ cup (3⅔ ounces) bread flour
- ½ cup (4 ounces) water, room temperature
- ¼ teaspoon instant or rapid-rise yeast

Dough
- 1¼ cups plus 2 tablespoons (11 ounces) water, room temperature, divided
- ¼ cup (1¼ ounces) plus 1 tablespoon coarse-ground polenta, divided
- 2⅓ cups (12¾ ounces) bread flour
- 2¼ teaspoons instant or rapid-rise yeast
- 2 tablespoons extra-virgin olive oil
- 4 teaspoons minced fresh sage
- 1½ teaspoons table salt

1. FOR THE SPONGE Stir all ingredients in 4-cup liquid measuring cup with wooden spoon until well combined. Cover tightly with plastic wrap and let sit at room temperature until sponge has risen and begins to collapse, about 6 hours (sponge can sit at room temperature for up to 24 hours).

2. FOR THE DOUGH Bring ¾ cup water and ¼ cup polenta to simmer in small saucepan over medium heat and cook, stirring frequently, until polenta is softened and water is completely absorbed, about 3 minutes; let cool completely before using.

3. Whisk flour and yeast together in bowl of stand mixer. Break cooked polenta into small pieces with wooden spoon. Stir half of polenta and remaining ½ cup plus 2 tablespoons water into sponge until well combined. Using dough hook on low speed, slowly add sponge mixture to flour mixture and mix until cohesive dough starts to form and no dry flour remains, about 2 minutes, scraping down bowl as needed. Cover bowl tightly with plastic and let dough rest for 20 minutes.

4. Add oil, sage, and salt to dough and knead on medium-low speed until dough is smooth and elastic and clears sides of bowl, about 5 minutes. Reduce speed to low, slowly add remaining cooked polenta, 1 tablespoon at a time, and mix until mostly incorporated, about 1 minute. Transfer dough to lightly greased large bowl or container, cover tightly with plastic, and let rise for 30 minutes.

5. Using greased bowl scraper (or your fingertips), fold dough over itself by gently lifting and folding edge of dough toward middle. Turn bowl 45 degrees and fold dough again; repeat turning bowl and folding dough 6 more times (total of 8 folds). Cover tightly with plastic and let rise for 30 minutes. Repeat folding, then cover bowl tightly with plastic and let dough rise until nearly doubled in size, 30 minutes to 1 hour.

6. Mist underside of couche with water and drape over inverted rimmed baking sheet. Dust couche evenly with flour, then sprinkle with remaining 1 tablespoon polenta. Transfer dough to lightly floured counter (side of dough that was against bowl should now be against counter). Press and stretch dough into 10-inch square, deflating any gas pockets larger than 1 inch. Fold top and bottom corners of dough diagonally into center of square and press gently to seal.

7. Stretch and fold upper and bottom thirds of dough toward center and press gently to seal. Stretch and fold dough in half toward you to form rough 12 by 4½-inch diamond-shaped loaf, and pinch seam closed.

8. Gently slide your hands underneath each end of loaf and transfer seam side up to prepared couche. On either side of loaf, pinch couche into pleat, then fold remaining edges of couche over loaf to cover completely. Carefully place sheet inside large plastic garbage bag. Tie, or fold under, open end of bag to fully enclose. Let rise until loaf increases in size by about half and dough springs back minimally when poked gently with your knuckle, about 30 minutes (remove loaf from bag to test).

9. One hour before baking, adjust oven racks to lower-middle and lowest positions. Place baking stone on upper rack, place 2 disposable aluminum pie plates filled with 1 quart lava rocks each on lower rack, and heat oven to 425 degrees. Line pizza peel with 16 by 12-inch piece of parchment paper, with long edge perpendicular to handle. Bring 1 cup water to boil.

10. Remove sheet with loaf from bag. Unfold couche, pulling from ends to remove pleats. Dust top of loaf with flour. (If any seams have reopened, pinch closed before dusting with flour.) Gently pushing with side of flipping board, roll loaf over so it is seam side down. Using your hand, hold long edge of flipping board between loaf and couche at 45-degree angle, then lift couche with your other hand and flip loaf seam side up onto board. Invert loaf seam side down onto prepared pizza peel. Reshape loaf as needed, tucking edges under to form taut diamond shape.

11. Carefully pour ½ cup boiling water into 1 disposable pie plate of preheated rocks and close oven door for 1 minute to create steam. Meanwhile, holding lame concave side up at 30-degree angle to loaf, make three 6-inch-long, ½-inch-deep diagonal slashes with swift, fluid motion across top of loaf, starting and stopping about ½ inch from edges and spacing slashes about 2 inches apart.

12. Working quickly, slide parchment with loaf onto baking stone and pour remaining ½ cup boiling water into second disposable pie plate of preheated rocks. Bake until crust is deep golden brown and loaf registers 205 to 210 degrees, 45 to 50 minutes, rotating loaf halfway through baking. Transfer loaf to wire rack, discard parchment, and let cool completely, about 3 hours, before serving.

KEYS TO SUCCESS

- **Cook the corn:** Briefly cooking some of the polenta prevents grittiness.
- **Add gradually:** Adding the polenta to the dough in stages creates savory pockets in the loaf.

Shaping Sage-Polenta Bread

STRETCH AND FOLD
Stretch and fold upper and bottom thirds of dough toward center and seal. Stretch and fold dough in half toward you to form diamond-shaped loaf, and pinch seam closed.

TRANSFER TO COUCHE
Gently transfer seam side up to couche. On either side of loaf, pinch couche into pleat, then fold remaining edges of couche over loaf.

REMOVE LOAF
Unfold couche. Dust loaf with flour. Gently pushing with side of flipping board, roll loaf seam side down. Hold long edge of board between loaf and couche at angle, then lift couche and flip loaf onto board.

SLASH TOP
Holding lame concave side up at 30-degree angle to loaf, make three diagonal slashes with swift, fluid motion across top of loaf.

WHAT CAN GO WRONG

PROBLEM The loaf is dry and coarse.

SOLUTION Don't use instant polenta.

We tested various polenta varieties for our recipe and found that you can't just use what you have on hand. Instant polenta yielded a very dry, chalky loaf of bread. Why? The grains for instant polenta are ground so fine that they suck up all of the available water in the dough. That water not only moistens the loaf, it helps bolster the gluten structure so the polenta-packed loaf has chew. In addition to using coarse-ground polenta, we found that it's best to cook a portion of the polenta before adding it to the dough for bread with just the right chewy-soft texture.

HONEY-SPELT BREAD

Makes: 1 loaf
Total Time: 1¾ hours, plus 17¾ to 18¼ hours resting, rising, and cooling

RECIPE OVERVIEW Spelt is an ancient grain—it's a cousin of modern wheat but has been cultivated for more than 8,000 years and has recently experienced a resurgence in popularity. Hardier and nuttier than common wheat, spelt lends a rich, sweet flavor to baked goods. Because of its high water solubility, its nutrients are also more quickly absorbed by the body, making it a healthful grain full of fiber, protein, and vitamins. This rustic bread takes advantage of this unique grain's qualities. For superior flavor, you'll make your own spelt flour by soaking whole spelt berries overnight to soften their hard outer shells, then puree them into a mash. Combining the spelt with some bread flour makes a sturdy loaf with wheaty flavor and a pleasant chew. A full quarter cup of honey enhances the spelt's natural sweetness and gives the loaf a deep brown color. You can find whole spelt berries in the natural- or bulk-foods section of the grocery store.

Soaker

- 1¼ cups (8 ounces) spelt berries
- 1 cup (8 ounces) water, room temperature

Sponge

- ¾ cup (4⅛ ounces) bread flour
- ½ cup (4 ounces) water, room temperature
- ¼ teaspoon instant or rapid-rise yeast

Dough

- 1 cup (5½ ounces) bread flour
- 2½ teaspoons instant or rapid-rise yeast
- ¼ cup (3 ounces) honey
- 1 tablespoon extra-virgin olive oil
- 1½ teaspoons table salt

1. **FOR THE SOAKER** Combine spelt berries and water in bowl, cover tightly with plastic wrap, and let sit at room temperature until grains are fully hydrated and softened, at least 12 hours or up to 24 hours.

2. **FOR THE SPONGE** Stir all ingredients in 4-cup liquid measuring cup with wooden spoon until well combined. Cover tightly with plastic wrap and let sit at room temperature until sponge has risen and begins to collapse, about 6 hours (sponge can sit at room temperature for up to 24 hours).

3. **FOR THE DOUGH** Whisk flour and yeast together in bowl of stand mixer. Process soaked spelt berries and remaining soaking liquid in food processor until grains are finely ground, about 4 minutes, scraping down sides of bowl as needed. Stir spelt berry mixture and honey into sponge with wooden spoon until well combined. Using dough hook on low speed, slowly add sponge mixture to flour mixture and mix until cohesive dough starts to form

and no dry flour remains, about 2 minutes, scraping down bowl as needed. Cover bowl tightly with plastic and let dough rest for 20 minutes.

4. Add oil and salt to dough and knead on medium-low speed until dough is smooth and elastic and clears sides of bowl but sticks to bottom, about 5 minutes. Transfer dough to lightly greased large bowl or container, cover tightly with plastic, and let rise for 30 minutes.

5. Using greased bowl scraper (or your fingertips), fold dough over itself by gently lifting and folding edge of dough toward middle. Turn bowl 45 degrees and fold dough again; repeat turning bowl and folding dough 6 more times (total of 8 folds). Cover tightly with plastic and let rise for 30 minutes. Repeat folding, then cover bowl tightly with plastic and let dough rise until nearly doubled in size, 1 to 1½ hours.

6. Mist underside of couche with water, drape over inverted rimmed baking sheet, and dust evenly with flour. Transfer dough to lightly floured counter (side of dough that was against bowl should now be against counter). Press and stretch dough into 10-inch square, deflating any gas pockets larger than 1 inch. Fold top and bottom corners of dough diagonally into center of square and press gently to seal.

7. Stretch and fold upper and bottom thirds of dough toward center and press gently to seal. Stretch and fold dough in half toward you to form rough 12 by 5-inch diamond-shaped loaf, and pinch seam closed.

8. Gently slide your hands underneath each end of loaf and transfer seam side up to prepared couche. On either side of loaf, pinch couche into pleat, then fold remaining edges of couche over loaf to cover completely. Carefully place sheet inside large plastic garbage bag. Tie, or fold under, open end of bag to fully enclose. Let rise until loaf

increases in size by about half and dough springs back minimally when poked gently with your knuckle, about 30 minutes (remove loaf from bag to test).

9. One hour before baking, adjust oven racks to lower-middle and lowest positions. Place baking stone on upper rack, place 2 disposable aluminum pie plates filled with 1 quart lava rocks each on lower rack, and heat oven to 450 degrees. Line pizza peel with 16 by 12-inch piece of parchment paper, with long edge perpendicular to handle. Bring 1 cup water to boil.

10. Remove sheet with loaf from bag. Unfold couche, pulling from ends to remove pleats. Dust top of loaf with flour. (If any seams have reopened, pinch closed before dusting with flour.) Gently pushing with side of flipping board, roll loaf over so it is seam side down. Using your hand, hold long edge of flipping board between loaf and couche at 45-degree angle, then lift couche with your other hand and flip loaf seam side up onto board. Invert loaf seam side down onto prepared pizza peel. Reshape loaf as needed, tucking edges under to form taut diamond shape.

11. Carefully pour ½ cup boiling water into 1 disposable pie plate of preheated rocks and close oven door for 1 minute to create steam. Meanwhile, holding lame concave side up at 30-degree angle to loaf, make three 6-inch-long, ½-inch-deep diagonal slashes with swift, fluid motion across top of loaf, starting and stopping about ½ inch from edges and spacing slashes about 2 inches apart.

12. Working quickly, slide parchment with loaf onto baking stone and pour remaining ½ cup boiling water into second disposable pie plate of preheated rocks. Bake until crust is dark brown and loaf registers 205 to 210 degrees, 30 to 35 minutes, rotating loaf halfway through baking. Transfer loaf to wire rack, discard parchment, and let cool completely, about 3 hours, before serving.

KEYS TO SUCCESS

- **Soak the spelt:** It's important to soften the spelt berries overnight before pureeing them.
- **Plenty of honey:** A full quarter-cup adds flavor and gives the crust a deep brown color.

WHAT CAN GO WRONG

PROBLEM Whole spelt berries are not available.

SOLUTION If you cannot find whole spelt berries for this recipe, you can substitute an equal weight of store-bought spelt flour, though the sweet wheat flavor will be less deep. Soak the flour in the water for the 12 hours specified for the spelt berries, skip processing, and stir the mixture into the sponge as directed in step 3.

Forming Honey-Spelt Bread

PRESS AND STRETCH
Press and stretch dough into 10-inch square, deflating any gas pockets larger than 1 inch. Fold top and bottom corners of dough diagonally into center of square and press gently to seal.

STRETCH AND FOLD
Stretch and fold upper and bottom thirds of dough toward center and press gently to seal. Stretch and fold dough in half toward you to form rough diamond-shaped loaf, and pinch seam closed.

TRANSFER TO COUCHE
Gently slide your hands underneath each end of loaf and transfer seam side up to prepared couche. On either side of loaf, pinch couche into pleat, then fold remaining edges of couche over loaf to cover completely.

REMOVE FROM COUCHE
Unfold couche, pulling from ends to remove pleats. Dust top of loaf with flour. Using flipping board, roll loaf seam side down, then lift couche and flip seam side up onto board. Invert loaf onto peel and reshape as needed.

SLASH TOP
Holding lame concave side up at 30-degree angle to loaf, make three diagonal slashes with swift, fluid motion across top of loaf, starting and stopping about ½ inch from edges and spacing slashes about 2 inches apart.

SOURDOUGH PRO

CHRISTIE MORRISON

Perhaps the ultimate DIY bread, sourdough is a yeast bread that doesn't require buying any yeast. In this course, you'll learn how to make a sourdough culture and, more important, how to keep it going (not as much of a high-maintenance process as you might think). With an understanding of how sourdough culture works, you'll be able to produce an authentic pain au levain with a tangy, chewy crumb and crackly crust.

CHRISTIE'S PRO TIP: *Build the right environment. For the best results, weigh your ingredients and use organic flour (which is richer in microorganisms than conventional flour) and bottled or filtered water (which is free of the chlorine in tap water that can kill those essential microorganisms) to create the starter.*

THE METHOD
SOURDOUGH STARTER

Make and keep alive a home-grown batch of sourdough starter so you can enjoy homemade sourdough bread whenever you want.

1 MIX
Mix flour mixture with room-temperature water in glass bowl. Cover with plastic and let sit at room temperature until bubbly and fragrant, 48 to 72 hours.

2 MEASURE
Measure ¼ cup starter and transfer to clean bowl; discard remaining starter. Stir in another portion of flour mixture and room-temperature water. Cover with plastic and let sit at room temperature for 24 hours.

3 REPEAT
Repeat step 2 every 24 hours until starter is pleasantly aromatic and doubles in size 8 to 12 hours after being fed, 10 to 14 days. At this point, starter is ready for baking or storing.

4 USE
To prepare for baking, measure out ½ cup starter and transfer to clean bowl; discard remaining starter. Stir all-purpose flour and room-temperature water into starter. Cover and let sit at room temperature for 5 hours. Transfer amount needed for recipe to second bowl. Cover and refrigerate for 12 hours to 18 hours. Refrigerate remaining starter.

5 MAINTAIN
Feed stored starter once a week to maintain: Measure out ¼ cup starter and transfer to clean bowl; discard remaining starter. Stir ½ cup all-purpose flour and ¼ cup room-temperature water into starter until no dry flour remains.

SOURDOUGH STARTER

A sourdough starter begins with mixing together flour and water. As the mixture sits, wild yeast and lactic acid–producing bacteria that are already present in the flour wake up and start to multiply, eventually creating the culture of microorganisms that will leaven and flavor your bread. It's okay to occasionally miss a daily feeding in step 2, but don't let it go for more than 48 hours. Leaving the culture at room temperature after each feeding is also key. For the best results, weigh the flour and water and use organic flour and bottled or filtered water to create the starter. Once the starter is mature, use all-purpose flour to maintain it. Placing the starter in a glass bowl allows for easier observation of activity beneath the surface. A starter that is ready for baking will double in size 8 to 12 hours after feeding. To double-check that it's ready, drop a spoonful of starter into a bowl of water. If it floats, the culture is sufficiently active. If it sinks, let your starter sit for another hour or so.

4½ cups (24¾ ounces) whole-wheat flour
5 cups (25 ounces) all-purpose flour, plus extra for maintaining starter
Water, room temperature

1. Combine whole-wheat flour and all-purpose flour in large container. Using wooden spoon, mix 1 cup (5 ounces) flour mixture and ⅔ cup (5⅓ ounces) room-temperature water in glass bowl until no dry flour remains (reserve remaining flour mixture). Cover with plastic wrap and let sit at room temperature until bubbly and fragrant, 48 to 72 hours.

2. TO FEED THE STARTER Measure out ¼ cup (2 ounces) starter and transfer to clean bowl; discard remaining starter. Stir ½ cup (2½ ounces) flour mixture and ¼ cup (2 ounces) room-temperature water into starter until no dry flour remains. Cover with plastic wrap and let sit at room temperature for 24 hours.

3. Repeat step 2 every 24 hours until starter is pleasantly aromatic and doubles in size 8 to 12 hours after being fed, 10 to 14 days. At this point, starter is mature and ready to be baked with, or it can be stored. (If baking right away, use starter once it has doubled in size during 8- to 12-hour window. Use starter within 1 hour after it starts to deflate once reaching its peak.)

4A. TO PREPARE THE STARTER FOR BAKING Measure out ½ cup (4 ounces) starter and transfer to clean bowl; discard remaining starter. Stir 1 cup (5 ounces) all-purpose flour and ½ cup (4 ounces) room-temperature water into starter until no dry flour remains. Cover and let sit at room temperature for 5 hours. Measure out amount of starter called for in recipe and transfer to second bowl. Cover and refrigerate for at least 12 hours or up to 18 hours. Refrigerate and maintain remaining starter.

4B. TO STORE AND MAINTAIN THE MATURE STARTER FOR WEEKLY FEEDINGS Measure out ¼ cup (2 ounces) starter and transfer to clean bowl; discard remaining starter. Stir ½ cup (2½ ounces) all-purpose flour and ¼ cup (2 ounces) room-temperature water into starter until no dry flour remains. Transfer to clean container that can be loosely covered and let sit at room temperature for 5 hours. Cover and transfer to refrigerator. If not baking regularly, repeat process weekly. When using stored starter to bake, start step 4A 18 to 24 hours before baking.

> ### KEYS TO SUCCESS
> - **Remember to feed:** Don't let the starter go for more than 48 hours without feeding it.
> - **Make sure it's active:** To be usable for baking, the starter should double in size in 8 to 12 hours after feeding.

CLASSIC SOURDOUGH BREAD

Makes: 1 large loaf
Total Time: 2 hours, plus 19½ hours rising, resting, and cooling

RECIPE OVERVIEW Nurturing a sourdough starter opens up a delicious universe of bakery-quality breads. This classic pain au levain recipe is a great way to get started, with its open crumb and rustic appearance that makes you want to tear into it. Sifting the whole-wheat flour removes excess bran, ensuring a light and airy loaf. For deeply complex flavor, let the shaped loaf proof overnight in the refrigerator then again in a turned-off oven. To achieve a crackling, bakery-style crust without having to open the oven to spray the loaf with water, bake it in a covered Dutch oven to trap steam. We prefer King Arthur all-purpose flour here, but you may substitute bread flour. If you have a banneton or a lined proofing basket, use that rather than the towel-lined colander in steps 3 and 4. Do not wait until the oven has preheated in step 6 to start timing or the bread will burn.

1 cup (5½ ounces) whole-wheat flour
2 cups (10 ounces) King Arthur all-purpose flour
1¼ cups water, room temperature
1 cup (8 ounces) mature Sourdough Starter (left)
1¾ teaspoons table salt

1. Sift whole-wheat flour through fine-mesh strainer into large bowl; discard bran remaining in strainer. Add all-purpose flour, room-temperature water, and starter and stir with wooden spoon until cohesive dough forms and no dry flour remains. Cover with plastic wrap and let rest at room temperature for 20 minutes. Sprinkle salt over dough and knead gently in bowl until incorporated. Cover with plastic and let rest at room temperature for 30 minutes.

2. Holding edge of dough with your fingertips, fold dough over itself by gently lifting and folding edge of dough toward center. Turn bowl 45 degrees; fold again. Turn bowl and fold dough 6 more times (total of 8 folds). Cover with plastic and let rise for 30 minutes. Repeat folding and rising every 30 minutes, 3 more times. After fourth set of folds, transfer dough to lightly floured counter.

3. Gently press dough into 8-inch disk, then fold edges toward middle to form round. Cover loosely with plastic and let rest for 15 minutes. Meanwhile, line colander with large linen or cotton dish towel and dust liberally with flour. Repeat pressing and folding of dough to form dough on unfloured counter. Loosely cup your hands around dough and, without applying pressure to dough, move your hands in small circular motions. Tackiness of dough against counter and circular motion should work dough into smooth, even ball, but if dough sticks to your hands, lightly dust your fingers with flour.

4. Place dough seam side up on floured towel in colander and loosely fold edges of towel over dough to enclose. Place colander in large plastic garbage bag and tie or fold under to fully enclose. Let rest at room temperature for 1 hour, then refrigerate for 12 to 24 hours.

5. Adjust oven rack to middle position and place loaf pan or cake pan in bottom of oven. Remove colander from refrigerator and place on middle rack; pour 3 cups boiling water into pan below. Close oven door and let dough rise until doubled in size and does not readily spring back when poked with your finger, 2 to 3 hours.

6. Remove colander and water pan from oven. Lay 16 by 12-inch sheet of parchment paper on counter and spray generously with vegetable oil spray. Remove colander from plastic bag, unfold edges of towel, and dust top of loaf with flour. Lay parchment sprayed side down over loaf, then invert colander onto counter. Remove colander and towel. Holding lame at 30-degree angle to loaf, make two 7-inch-long, ½-inch-deep slashes along top of loaf to form cross. Pick up dough by lifting parchment edges and lower into heavy-bottomed Dutch oven. Cover pot and place in oven. Heat oven to 425 degrees. Bake bread for 30 minutes (starting timing as soon as you turn on oven).

7. Remove lid and continue to bake until bread is deep brown and registers 210 degrees, 20 to 30 minutes longer. Carefully remove bread from pot; transfer to wire rack and let cool completely, at least 2 hours, before serving.

KEYS TO SUCCESS

- **Ban the bran:** Sift the whole-wheat flour to rid it of bran, which would interfere with gluten development and impede the loaf's rise.

- **Remove the lid:** For a brown crust, take the cover off the Dutch oven halfway through baking.

Forming Sourdough Bread

ROUND DOUGH

Flip dough ball seam side down and, using your cupped hands, drag in small circles on counter until dough feels taut and round and all seams are secured on underside of loaf.

TRANSFER TO COLANDER

Place loaf seam side up in prepared colander and pinch any remaining seams closed. Loosely fold edges of towel over loaf to enclose, then place colander in large plastic garbage bag.

LET RISE

Let rise still inside plastic bag at warm room temperature until nearly doubled in size and dough springs back minimally when poked gently with your knuckle, 2 to 3 hours.

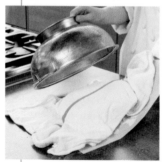

INVERT LOAF

Lay 16 by 12-inch sheet of parchment paper on top of loaf. Using 1 hand to support parchment and loaf, invert loaf onto parchment and place on counter. Gently remove colander and towel. Transfer parchment with loaf to pizza peel.

SLASH TOP

Holding lame concave side up at 30-degree angle to loaf, make two 7-inch-long, ½-inch-deep slashes with swift, fluid motion along top of loaf to form cross.

NURTURE A SOURDOUGH STARTER FOR OLD-WORLD BREAD

If you crave the tang, complexity, and chew of a good homemade sourdough loaf, then it behooves you to make and keep alive a homegrown batch of sourdough starter. Since we crave sourdough too, we've demystified and uncomplicated the process with a straightforward, reliable recipe for creating and maintaining a starter.

A starter is simply a culture of yeast and "good" bacteria, and making one is pretty simple, requiring time but little effort. You start by stirring together flour and water and letting it ferment for a couple of days at room temperature. Natural yeast and bacteria in the flour wake up and start to multiply, and the mixture evolves into a bubbly blob. From here, it grows strong through regular "feedings." After a few weeks, it becomes chock-full of enough yeast and bacteria that a portion of it can leaven and flavor bread. As long as you keep it healthy and alive, you can use it for years to come.

We learned in testing that a 50–50 mix of whole-wheat and all-purpose flours works much faster than all-purpose flour alone, because the whole-wheat flour provides more nutrition for the budding organisms. Using filtered or bottled water is also important, because chlorine in tap water can kill the starter. The first stage is to make sure the microorganisms are alive and consuming nutrients. At this point, the loose, batter-like mixture smells like sour milk, but it's a positive sign that the starter is established. Then feeding begins. Many recipes call for feeding every 12 hours, but every 24 hours is totally sufficient. After about two weeks of feedings, your starter will be pleasantly aromatic and ready for baking.

During the long-term maintenance stage, simply keep your starter healthy through weekly feedings. Discarding some starter before each feeding gets rid of waste that the microorganisms produce as they consume nutrients—and keeps the starter from taking over your fridge. It works best to feed the starter and leave it out for a shorter period of time than typically called for: Five hours is just long enough for the culture to dig in but not so long that it consumes all of the food too quickly. Back in the fridge, your starter continues to feed and grow at a very slow pace, staying healthy all the while.

SOURDOUGH STARTER RESCUE REMEDY

Experienced sourdough bakers know that even a healthy sourdough starter can occasionally lose vigor—either because it hasn't been fed regularly or simply for reasons unknown (which can, and does, happen)—leaving it unable to leaven a loaf of bread. Fortunately, a little love is all it usually takes to revive an ailing starter.

Here's what to do: Feed ¼ cup (2 ounces) starter with ½ cup (2½ ounces) all-purpose flour and ¼ cup (2 ounces) water twice daily (approximately every 12 hours) and let it sit, covered with plastic wrap, at room temperature. It will be ready to use again when it smells pleasantly yeasty and sweet (rather than sour) and doubles in volume 8 to 12 hours after a feeding.

Sadly, this doesn't always work. If the starter doesn't revive at all after a day or two of feedings—it doesn't double in volume even more than 12 hours after a feeding—it is probably beyond saving, and it's time to start a new one from scratch.

SHAPE INTO ROUND
Press and stretch the dough into a round.

FOLD IN EDGES
Working around circumference of dough, fold edges toward center of round until ball forms.

DRAG DOUGH
Flip dough ball seam side down and, using your cupped hands, drag dough in small circles until dough feels taut and round.

BAGUETTES AT HOME

BRYAN ROOF

Perfect for sandwiches, dipping, spreading, or just snacking, the baguette is a must-have in the artisanal baker's repertoire. Learn how to make this French bakery staple with confidence. Once you've mastered the basic technique, you can apply your skill and have fun with the baguette's siblings: narrow, seed-crusted ficelles and wheat stalk–shaped pain d'epi.

BRYAN'S PRO TIP: *Proofing the shaped loaves in a heavy-duty floured linen couche absorbs moisture to form a skin that becomes your super-crackly crust (my favorite part). I use only a moderate amount of flour, and I really work it into the linen; too much flour can give the crust a blotchy surface. The more you use your couche, the less flour you'll need to work in. And while you might want to be a little shy with the flour, you don't have to be with scoring. If your slashes aren't deep enough or don't stick, don't be afraid to reinforce the marks quickly before sending the loaves to the oven. If I don't have a lame, I use a sharp paring knife or a single-edge razor blade.*

BAKERY-STYLE FRENCH BAGUETTES

Makes: 4 loaves
Total Time: 21¼ to 22¼ hours, plus 20 minutes cooling time

RECIPE OVERVIEW A truly great baguette boasts a moist, wheaty interior punctuated with irregular holes and a deeply browned crust so crisp it shatters—an ideal that this recipe will help you achieve. You'll use a hybrid mixing approach: Mix the dough in a stand mixer and then fold the dough several times during the first rise. A 16- to 48-hour rest in the fridge produces the best flavor. Diastatic malt powder boosts exterior browning and flavor; during the dough's long chill, the yeast consumes nearly all of the available sugars, and the malt powder unlocks more sugar by converting starches in the flour. A little whole-wheat flour provides even more depth. For a supercrisp, flavorful crust, cover the bread with stacked disposable roasting pans for the first few minutes of baking so the loaves cook in their own steam. If you can't find King Arthur all-purpose flour, you can substitute bread flour. This recipe makes enough dough for four loaves, which can be baked anytime during the 16- to 48-hour window after placing the dough in the refrigerator in step 3.

- ¼   cup (1⅓ ounces) whole-wheat flour
- 3   cups (15 ounces) King Arthur Unbleached All-Purpose Flour
- 1½ teaspoons salt
- 1   teaspoon instant or rapid-rise yeast
- 1   teaspoon diastatic malt powder (optional)
- 1½ cups (12 ounces) water, room temperature

1. Sift whole-wheat flour through fine-mesh strainer into bowl of stand mixer; discard bran in strainer.

2. Whisk all-purpose flour, salt, yeast, and malt powder, if using, into mixer bowl. Using dough hook on low speed, slowly add water to flour mixture and mix until cohesive dough starts to form and no dry flour remains, 5 to 7 minutes, scraping down bowl as needed. Transfer dough to lightly greased large bowl or container, cover tightly with plastic wrap, and let rise for 30 minutes.

3. Using greased bowl scraper (or your fingertips), fold dough over itself by gently lifting and folding edge of dough toward middle. Turn bowl 45 degrees and fold dough again; repeat turning bowl and folding dough 6 more times (total of 8 folds). Cover tightly with plastic and let rise for 30 minutes. Repeat folding and rising every 30 minutes, 3 more times. After fourth set of folds, cover bowl tightly with plastic and refrigerate for at least 16 hours or up to 48 hours.

4. Transfer dough to lightly floured counter, press into 8-inch square (do not deflate), and divide in half. Return 1 piece of dough to bowl, cover tightly with plastic, and refrigerate (dough can be shaped and baked anytime within 48-hour window). Divide remaining dough in half crosswise, transfer to lightly floured rimmed baking sheet, and cover loosely with greased plastic. Let rest until no longer cool to touch, 30 minutes to 1 hour.

size and dough springs back minimally when poked gently with your knuckle, 30 minutes to 1 hour (remove from bag to test with knuckle).

12. One hour before baking, adjust oven rack to lower-middle position, place baking stone on rack, and heat oven to 500 degrees. Line pizza peel with 16 by 12-inch piece of parchment paper, with long edge of paper perpendicular to handle. Unfold couche, pulling from ends to remove pleats. Gently pushing with side of flipping board, roll 1 loaf over, away from other loaf, so it is seam side down.

13. Using your hand, hold long edge of flipping board between loaf and couche at 45-degree angle, then lift couche with your other hand and flip loaf seam side up onto board.

14. Invert loaf seam side down onto prepared pizza peel, about 2 inches from long edge of parchment, then use flipping board to straighten loaf. Repeat with remaining loaf, leaving at least 3 inches between loaves.

15. Holding lame concave side up at 30-degree angle to loaf, make three 4-inch-long, ½-inch-deep slashes with swift, fluid motion along length of loaf. Repeat with second loaf.

16. Slide parchment with loaves onto baking stone. Cover loaves with 2 stacked inverted disposable roasting pans and bake for 5 minutes. Carefully remove pans and continue to bake until loaves are deep golden brown, 12 to 15 minutes, rotating loaves halfway through baking. Transfer loaves to wire rack, discard parchment, and let cool for 20 minutes. Serve warm or at room temperature. (Baguettes are best eaten within 4 hours of baking.)

KEYS TO SUCCESS

- **Sifted whole-wheat flour:** Sifting adds wheatiness without the tiny bran bits that might turn bitter in the oven.
- **A long ferment:** It improves flavor and makes the dough easier to work with.
- **Couche:** The baguettes are sticky; the couche pulls moisture from the surface.
- **Flipping board:** Using a board helps the fragile baguettes maintain their shape.

WHAT CAN GO WRONG

PROBLEM The bread has a uniform crumb.

SOLUTION Shape the loaves gently. One of the hallmarks of a good French baguette is its open, uneven crumb structure. Be sure to use a gentle hand when following the shaping steps; otherwise, you'll press out the air that forms the irregular, open, airy holes in these loaves.

5. Working with 1 piece of dough at a time (keep remaining piece covered), roll into loose 3- to 4-inch-long cylinder on lightly floured counter. Cover loosely with greased plastic and let rest for 30 minutes.

6. Mist underside of couche with water, drape over second rimmed baking sheet that has been inverted, and dust evenly with flour. Gently press 1 dough cylinder into 6 by 4-inch rectangle on lightly floured counter, with long side parallel to counter edge. Fold upper quarter of dough toward center and press gently to seal. Rotate dough 180 degrees and repeat folding step to form 8 by 2-inch rectangle.

7. Fold dough in half toward you, using thumb of your other hand to create crease along center of dough, sealing with heel of your hand as you work your way along loaf. Without pressing down on loaf, use heel of your hand to reinforce seal (do not seal ends of loaf).

8. Cup your hand over center of dough and roll dough back and forth gently to tighten (it should form dog-bone shape).

9. Starting at center of dough and working toward ends, gently and evenly roll and stretch dough until it measures 15 inches long by 1¼ inches wide. Moving your hands in opposite directions, use back and forth motion to roll ends of loaf under your palms to form sharp points.

10. Transfer loaf seam side up to prepared couche. On either side of loaf, pinch edges of couche into pleat, then cover loosely with large plastic garbage bag.

11. Repeat steps 5 through 10 with remaining piece of dough and place on opposite side of pleat. Fold edges of couche over loaves to cover completely, then carefully place sheet inside garbage bag. Tie, or fold under, open end of bag to fully enclose. Let loaves rise until nearly doubled in

Shaping and Baking Baguettes

Once your dough has gone through the initial rising, folding, and resting stages, it's ready to be shaped.

1. ROLL AND REST
On lightly floured counter, roll 1 piece of refrigerated and rested dough into loose 3- to 4-inch-long cylinder. Cover with plastic and let rest at room temperature for 30 minutes.

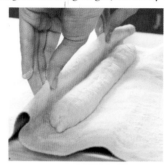

6. PLACE IN COUCHE
Transfer dough to floured couche, seam side up. On either side of loaf, pinch edges of couche into pleat. Cover loosely with large plastic garbage bag.

2. PRESS AND FOLD
Gently press 1 piece of dough into 6 by 4-inch rectangle with long edge facing you. Fold upper quarter of dough toward center and press gently to seal. Rotate dough 180 degrees and repeat folding step to form 8 by 2-inch rectangle.

7. BAG AND RISE
Place second loaf on opposite side of pleat. Fold edges of couche over loaves to cover, then carefully place sheet inside bag, and tie or fold under to enclose. Let rise for 30 minutes to 1 hour. While bread rises, preheat baking stone.

3. CREASE AND SEAL
Fold dough in half toward you, using thumb of your other hand to create crease along center of dough, sealing with heel of your hand as you work your way along the loaf. Do not seal ends of loaf.

8. FLIP ONTO PEEL
Unfold couche. For each loaf, use flipping board to roll loaf over so it is seam side down. Hold long edge of flipping board between loaf and couche at 45-degree angle. Lift couche and flip loaf seam side up onto board. Invert loaf onto parchment-lined peel.

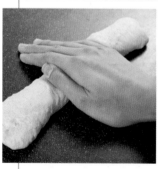

4. ROLL AND STRETCH
Cup your hand over center of dough and roll dough back and forth gently to form dog-bone shape. Working toward ends, gently roll and stretch dough until it measures 15 inches long by 1¼ inches wide.

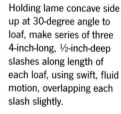

9. SLASH TOP
Holding lame concave side up at 30-degree angle to loaf, make series of three 4-inch-long, ½-inch-deep slashes along length of each loaf, using swift, fluid motion, overlapping each slash slightly.

5. FORM POINTS
Moving your hands in opposite directions, use back and forth motion to roll ends of loaf under your palms to form sharp points.

10. BAKE, COVERED
Transfer loaves, on parchment, to baking stone, cover with stacked inverted disposable pans, and bake for 5 minutes. Carefully remove pans and bake until loaves are evenly browned, 12 to 15 minutes longer, rotating parchment halfway through baking.

PAIN D'EPI

Makes: 4 loaves
Total Time: 21¼ to 22¼ hours, plus 20 minutes cooling time

RECIPE OVERVIEW Pain d'epi is a striking wheat stalk–shaped loaf with a unique, impressive crust. Once you've mastered our Bakery-Style French Baguettes, making pain d'epi doesn't take much extra effort, and adapting our baguette shaping technique is simple; just follow our baguette recipe until it's time to score the loaves. Instead of a lame, you'll use kitchen shears to cut into the loaves at an angle to create attached lobes that resemble stalks of wheat. All those cuts and angles make for a seriously crackly crust. If you can't find King Arthur all-purpose flour, you can substitute bread flour. This recipe makes enough dough for four loaves, which can be baked anytime during the 16- to 48-hour window after placing the dough in the refrigerator in step 3 of the baguette recipe.

1 recipe Bakery-Style French Baguettes (page 546), made through step 11

1. One hour before baking, adjust oven rack to middle position, place baking stone on rack, and heat oven to 500 degrees.

2. Line pizza peel with 16 by 12-inch piece parchment paper with long edge perpendicular to handle. Unfold couche, pulling from ends to remove pleats. Gently pushing with side of flipping board, roll 1 loaf over, away from other loaf, so it is seam side down. Using your hand, hold long edge of flipping board between loaf and couche at 45-degree angle, then lift couche with your other hand and flip loaf seam side up onto board.

3. Invert loaf onto parchment-lined peel, seam side down, about 2 inches from long edge of parchment, then use flipping board to straighten loaf. Repeat with remaining loaf, leaving at least 3 inches between loaves.

4. Using kitchen shears, cut into loaf at 45-degree angle, about 3 inches from end of loaf, nearly but not all the way through loaf.

5. Arrange cut section at 30-degree angle in either direction. Repeat every 3 inches, pulling sections out toward alternating sides to create wheat stalk shape. Repeat with second loaf.

6. Slide parchment with loaves onto baking stone. Cover loaves with 2 stacked inverted disposable roasting pans and bake for 5 minutes. Carefully remove pans and continue to bake until loaves are deep golden brown, 12 to 15 minutes, rotating loaves halfway through baking. Transfer loaves to wire rack, discard parchment, and let cool for 20 minutes. Serve warm or at room temperature. (The pain d'epi are best eaten within 4 hours of baking.)

KEYS TO SUCCESS

- **Use kitchen shears:** Snipping the dough with shears is easier than using a knife.
- **Bake on a stone:** Using a baking stone helps develop a crackly crust.

Forming Pain d'Epi

CUT INTO LOAF
Using kitchen shears, cut into loaf at 45-degree angle, about 3 inches from end of loaf, nearly but not all the way through loaf.

ARRANGE SECTIONS
Arrange cut section at 30-degree angle in either direction. Repeat every 3 inches, pulling sections out toward alternating sides to create wheat stalk shape.

WHAT CAN GO WRONG

PROBLEM The crust is pale and dull-tasting.

SOLUTION During the long proofing time, nearly all the sugars in this dough are consumed by the yeast. Since sugars are responsible for browning and caramelization, this will leave the crust pale and dull-tasting. Adding diastatic malt powder, derived from a naturally occurring enzyme that converts the starches in flour into sugar, guarantees a supply of sugar at baking time and thus a crust that browns and caramelizes. Purchase diastatic malt powder, not plain malt powder or malt syrup.

PROBLEM The loaves are too chewy or tender.

SOLUTION Use the right flour. Although we develop most of our recipes with Gold Medal Unbleached All-Purpose Flour, we call for King Arthur Unbleached All-Purpose Flour in this recipe for the best results. King Arthur all-purpose flour has a higher protein content than most other all-purpose flours, yet it is lower in protein than bread flour. Some of our artisan-style breads get folded for an airier crumb, and given an extended refrigerator rise for great flavor. Both of these techniques also develop more gluten. So if you use high-protein bread flour, your loaves may be too chewy and tough. Conversely, regular all-purpose flour might not give the bread enough structure. If you can't find King Arthur Unbleached All-Purpose Flour, use bread flour.

SEEDED FICELLE

Makes: 4 loaves
Total Time: 3¼ hours, plus 20¼ hours rising, resting, and cooling

RECIPE OVERVIEW The French word "ficelle" means "string," and its namesake loaf resembles a slender baguette made from a "string" of dough. Because it's so skinny, a ficelle maximizes the ratio of crackly crust to chewy interior. This recipe is a scaled-down version of our Bakery-Style French Baguettes, sized to make four slender loaves. As in the baguette recipe, a small amount of diastatic malt powder boosts exterior browning during the loaves' short stint in the oven by converting the flour's starch to sugar. Ficelles are sometimes rolled in seeds before being proofed and baked; here, a mixture of poppy, sesame, and fennel seeds provides just the right crunch and flavor. Although temperature is often used to assess a loaf's doneness, these loaves are so thin that it's difficult to insert the probe into them and get an accurate reading. Instead, you'll rely on a clear visual cue: When the loaves are deep golden brown and the crust is dry and crackly, they're done baking. If you can't find King Arthur all-purpose flour, you can substitute bread flour. This recipe makes enough dough for four loaves, which can be baked anytime during the 16- to 48-hour window after placing the dough in the refrigerator in step 2. The ficelles are best eaten within 4 hours of baking; slice them for hors d'oeuvres, dip them in oil, or cut them down the middle to make elegant sandwiches.

- 2 **cups (10 ounces) King Arthur Unbleached All-Purpose Flour**
- 1 **teaspoon table salt**
- ¾ **teaspoon instant or rapid-rise yeast**
- ¾ **teaspoon diastatic malt powder (optional)**
- 1 **cup water, room temperature**
- 3 **tablespoons poppy seeds**
- 3 **tablespoons sesame seeds**
- 2 **teaspoons fennel seeds**

1. Whisk flour, salt, yeast, and malt powder, if using, together in bowl of stand mixer. Using dough hook on low speed, slowly add room-temperature water to flour mixture and mix until cohesive dough starts to form and no dry flour remains, 5 to 7 minutes, scraping down bowl as needed. Transfer dough to lightly greased large bowl or container, cover tightly with plastic wrap, and let rise for 30 minutes.

2. Using greased bowl scraper (or your fingertips), fold dough over itself by gently lifting and folding edge of dough toward middle. Turn bowl 45 degrees and fold dough again; repeat turning bowl and folding dough 6 more times (total of 8 folds). Cover tightly with plastic and let rise for 30 minutes. Repeat folding and rising every 30 minutes, 3 more times. After fourth set of folds, cover bowl tightly with plastic and refrigerate for at least 16 hours or up to 48 hours.

3. Transfer dough to lightly floured counter, press into 8-inch square (do not deflate), and divide in half. Return 1 piece of dough to bowl, cover tightly with plastic, and refrigerate (dough can be shaped and baked anytime within 48-hour window). Divide remaining dough in half crosswise, transfer to lightly floured rimmed baking sheet, and cover loosely with greased plastic. Let rest until no longer cool to touch, 30 minutes to 1 hour.

4. Working with 1 piece of dough at a time (keep remaining piece covered), roll into loose 3- to 4-inch-long cylinder on lightly floured counter. Cover loosely with greased plastic and let rest for 30 minutes. Combine poppy seeds, sesame seeds, and fennel seeds in bowl. Spread half of seed mixture on second rimmed baking sheet; reserve remaining seed mixture for second half of dough. Mist underside of couche with water, drape over inverted rimmed baking sheet, and dust evenly with flour.

5. Gently press 1 dough cylinder into 6 by 4-inch rectangle on lightly floured counter, with long side parallel to counter edge. Fold upper quarter of dough toward center and press gently to seal. Rotate dough 180 degrees and repeat folding to form 8 by 2-inch rectangle. Fold dough in half toward you, using thumb of your other hand to create crease along center of dough, sealing with heel of your hand as you work your way along loaf. Without pressing down on loaf, use heel of your hand to reinforce seal (do not seal ends of loaf).

6. Cup your hand over center of dough and roll dough back and forth gently to tighten (it should form dog-bone shape). Starting at center of dough and working toward ends, gently and evenly roll and stretch dough until it measures 15 inches long by 1 inch wide. Moving your hands in opposite directions, use back and forth motion to roll ends of loaf under your palms to form sharp points. Mist loaf with water on all sides and roll in seed mixture, pressing gently to adhere.

7. Transfer loaf seam side up to prepared couche. On either side of loaf, pinch couche into pleat, then cover loosely with large plastic garbage bag.

8. Add remaining seed mixture to baking sheet and distribute into even layer. Repeat steps 4 through 7 with remaining piece of dough and place on opposite side of pleat. Fold edges of couche over loaves to cover completely, then carefully place sheet inside plastic bag. Tie, or fold under, open end of bag to fully enclose. Let loaves rise until nearly doubled in size and dough springs back minimally when poked gently with your knuckle, 30 minutes to 1 hour (remove loaves from bag to test).

9. One hour before baking, adjust oven rack to lower-middle position, place baking stone or steel on rack, and heat oven to 500 degrees. Line baking peel with 16 by 12-inch piece of parchment paper, with long edge of parchment perpendicular to handle. Unfold couche, pulling from ends to remove pleats. Gently pushing with side of flipping board, roll 1 loaf over, away from other loaf, so it is seam side down. Using your hand, hold long edge of flipping board between loaf and couche at 45-degree angle, then lift couche with your other hand and flip loaf seam side up

onto board. Invert loaf seam side down onto prepared baking peel, about 2 inches from long edge of parchment, then use flipping board to straighten loaf. Repeat with remaining loaf, leaving at least 3 inches between loaves.

10. Using sharp paring knife or single-edge razor blade, make three 4-inch-long, ½-inch-deep diagonal slashes with swift, fluid motion along length of 1 loaf. Repeat with second loaf. Slide parchment with loaves onto baking stone. Cover loaves with 2 stacked inverted disposable roasting pans and bake for 5 minutes. Carefully remove pans; rotate loaves; and continue to bake until loaves are deep golden brown, 8 to 10 minutes. Transfer loaves to wire rack, discard parchment, and let cool for 15 minutes. Serve warm or at room temperature.

KEY TO SUCCESS

- **Mist:** To ensure an even coating of seeds, mist all sides of the dough with water so that the seeds adhere.

WHAT CAN GO WRONG

PROBLEM The seed coating is uneven.

SOLUTION Spray all sides of the loaf with water. Rolling the ficelle in a mixture of poppy seeds, sesame seeds, and fennel seeds gives these skinny baguettes a distinctive crust. To ensure an even coating of seeds, make sure that you mist all sides of the dough—not just the top— with water so that the seed mixture adheres after you roll the loaves in it.

Coating Ficelle with Seeds

PREPARE SEEDS

Combine poppy seeds, sesame seeds, and fennel seeds in bowl. Spread half of seed mixture on rimmed baking sheet; reserve remaining seed mixture for second half of dough.

ROLL IN SEEDS

Mist loaf with water on all sides and roll in seed mixture, pressing gently to adhere.

BAKERY-STYLE LAMINATED PASTRIES

ANDREA GEARY

The layers of laminated pastries come from repeatedly folding dough around a block of butter. Kouign amann, a specialty from Brittany, France, also happens to be one of the simplest forms of layered pastry that you can make, so it's a good starting point if you're new to the process (and a delicious project for experts as well). Turning out flaky, buttery croissants is arguably the pinnacle of home-baking accomplishments, and one that's within your reach. With our detailed instructions, including freezing directions, you can enjoy a flaky croissant whenever you like.

ANDREA'S PRO TIP: *When making croissants, intermittent chilling of the butter-and-dough package is key to producing thin, delicate layers. When making a kouign amman, it's important to do all the folds in one session. If you try to rest it, the sugar will draw water from the dough, turning it into a sticky mess, so do your best to power through.*

BRETON KOUIGN AMANN

Serves: 8 to 10
Total Time: 2 hours, plus 1¾ hours resting and cooling

RECIPE OVERVIEW This ultrarich Breton pastry boasts a crunchy top, lightly caramelized base, and custardy inner layers that are soaked with butter and melted sugar. It's an afternoon project that impresses like an all-day affair. Not only can you make the series of turns in a single session—rather than resting and refrigerating the dough between turns as you would for croissants—but shaping one large disk of dough is much simpler than cutting, rolling, and resting individual pastries. A lean yeasted dough made with all-purpose flour offers the best combination of strength and workability. To prevent the sugar from tearing the dough, you'll mix it right into the butter for the butter block. Shaping the butter mixture inside a parchment paper "envelope" creates a thin, even rectangle that's easy to roll during lamination. You'll score an elegant, traditional diamond pattern into the surface of the dough, brush it with milk, and shower it with sugar before baking, which renders the top attractively golden and crunchy.

We strongly recommend weighing the flour for this recipe. The butter block should be cool but malleable at the beginning of step 4; if your kitchen is cooler than 70 degrees, you may need to leave the butter block on the counter for up to 20 minutes (it's OK to leave the dough in the freezer for the extended time). Once you begin rolling and folding the dough, you'll want to move swiftly so have your ingredients and equipment in place before you start.

2¼   cups (11¼ ounces) all-purpose flour
1¼   teaspoons table salt, divided
 ½   teaspoon instant or rapid-rise yeast
 1   cup water, room temperature
16   tablespoons salted butter, softened
 ¾   cup (5¼ ounces) plus 1 tablespoon sugar, divided
 1   tablespoon milk

1. Using rubber spatula, stir together flour, ¾ teaspoon salt, and yeast in bowl of stand mixer. Add water and mix until most flour is moistened. Attach dough hook and knead on low speed until cohesive dough forms, about 1 minute. Increase speed to medium-low and knead until dough is smooth and elastic, about 5 minutes. Shape dough into ball (scrape out mixer bowl but do not wash). Flatten into rough 5-inch square and transfer to lightly greased plate. Cover dough and refrigerate for at least 1 hour or up to 24 hours. While dough rests, make butter packet.

2. Fold 18-inch length of parchment in half to create rectangle. Fold over the 3 open sides of rectangle to form 6 by 9-inch rectangle with enclosed sides. Crease folds firmly. Unfold and open parchment packet and set aside. Combine butter, ¾ cup sugar, and remaining ½ teaspoon salt in now-empty mixer bowl. Using paddle, mix on low speed until thoroughly combined, about 1 minute. Transfer butter mixture to prepared parchment rectangle, fold parchment over mixture, and press to ½-inch thickness. Refold parchment at creases to enclose mixture. Turn packet over so flaps are underneath and roll gently until butter mixture fills packet, taking care to achieve even thickness. Refrigerate for at least 45 minutes or up to 24 hours.

3. Transfer butter block to counter. Transfer dough to freezer and freeze for 10 minutes. Meanwhile, adjust oven rack to middle position and heat oven to 375 degrees. Lightly grease 9-inch round cake pan and line with 12-inch parchment square, pleating parchment so it lines bottom and sides of pan.

4. Transfer dough to well-floured counter and roll into 18 by 6½-inch rectangle with short side parallel to counter edge. Unwrap butter block and place in center of dough. Fold upper and lower sections of dough over butter so they meet in center (it's OK to gently stretch dough). Press center seam and side seams closed. Dust counter with more flour if necessary. Place rolling pin at top edge of dough and press gently to make slight depression across top. Lift pin, move it 1 inch closer to you, and press again. Continue pressing and lifting to bottom edge. Turn rolling pin 90 degrees and make similar depressions across width of dough. Roll dough out lengthwise into 21 by 7-inch rectangle (it's OK if it becomes slightly wider). Pop any bubbles that form. Using dry pastry brush, dust off any flour clinging to surface of dough. Starting at bottom of dough, fold into thirds like business letter to form 7-inch square. Turn square 90 degrees. Dust counter with more flour if necessary. Roll out lengthwise into 21 by 7-inch rectangle, and pop any bubbles. Using dry pastry brush, dust off any flour clinging to surface of dough, and fold into thirds.

Making a Butter Block "Envelope"

To form the butter block itself, it helps to enclose and shape the butter mixture in a parchment paper envelope. The parchment keeps the mixture contained, so you end up with a thin, even rectangle that perfectly fits the dimensions of the dough and is easy to roll during lamination.

FOLD IN HALF
Fold 18-inch length of parchment in half to create rectangle.

FOLD SIDES
Fold over 3 open sides of rectangle to form 6 by 9-inch rectangle with enclosed sides. Crease folds firmly.

OPEN
Unfold and open parchment packet. Place butter mixture in center.

FOLD
Fold parchment over mixture and press to ½-inch thickness. Refold parchment at creases to enclose mixture.

TURN
Turn packet over so flaps are underneath and roll until butter fills packet, taking care to achieve even thickness.

5. Dust counter with more flour if necessary. Roll dough into 11-inch square. Fold each corner to center, overlapping slightly, and press to adhere. Push right and left corners toward center, and then push top and bottom corners toward center to form rough, crumpled round. Press top to compress. Flip dough so smoother side is facing up, then tuck edges under to form round. Flatten gently with your hands, then roll dough into 9½-inch round. Transfer to prepared pan (it's OK if dough is slightly sticky), squishing edges to fit.

6. Brush top with milk. Using sharp paring knife, score top of pastry in diamond pattern. Sprinkle evenly with remaining 1 tablespoon sugar. Using paring knife, pierce dough all the way down to pan surface in 4 places to create air vents. Bake until pastry is deeply browned and crisp, 50 minutes to 1 hour. Let cool in pan on wire rack for 10 minutes. Invert, remove parchment, and reinvert. Let cool for at least 30 minutes before serving. (Kouign amann is best eaten on the day it's made, but leftovers can be wrapped well and stored at room temperature for up to 3 days. Warm leftovers gently in oven before serving.)

KEYS TO SUCCESS

- **Add salt:** Adding salt to conventional American salted butter (which is 1.5 to 1.7 percent salt) brings it more in line with the salinity of Breton butter (3 percent salt).

- **Dust with flour:** Use plenty of flour while rolling out the dough to prevent tears, but brush away excess before folding so the layers will adhere.

- **Vent the dough:** Piercing the kouign amann after shaping prevents ballooning that would distort its attractively layered structure.

Butter Block Reform

Incorporating sugar into the folds of the kouign amann dough can be a messy business. Sugar is abrasive, so scattering it over the butter block, enclosing it in the dough, and rolling it out (per the traditional method) causes it to tear large holes in the dough that allow butter to leak out during baking, disrupting lamination. It's also hygroscopic, and if given even a little time, it will draw moisture from the dough, dissolve in that liquid, and make the dough impossibly sticky.

Our solution: Embed the sugar (along with a little extra salt, for pronounced salinity) into the butter block by paddling the ingredients together in a stand mixer. That way, there's minimal contact between the dough and the sugar and thus virtually no risk of tearing or sticking.

CROISSANTS

Makes: 22
Total Time: 2½ hours, plus 8¾ to 9¼ hours resting, rising, and cooling

RECIPE OVERVIEW Part pastry, part bread, croissants have a crisp, flaky, deeply golden crust wrapped around tender, pillow-soft, buttery layers. There are few culinary feats quite as satisfying as making a successful batch of these bronzed beauties in your own kitchen. First, you'll make a basic dough of flour, milk, yeast, sugar, salt, and a small amount of butter. Then, you'll form a larger amount of butter into a block and encase it in the relatively lean dough. This dough-and-butter package is rolled out and folded multiple times (called a "turn") to form paper-thin layers of dough separated by paper-thin layers of butter. These layers are what make baked croissants so flaky. Three turns are enough to produce plenty of layers. Give the dough a 30-minute super chill in the freezer to firm it up before rolling, cutting, and shaping to minimize the risk of tears. After letting the croissants rise until they double in size, brush them with an egg wash and slide them into a very hot oven. If you can't find King Arthur all-purpose flour, you can substitute bread flour, though the dough may be more difficult to roll. Our favorite European-style butter is Plugrá. Do not attempt to make these croissants in a room that is warmer than 80 degrees. This recipe yields 12 baked croissants and 10 croissants for freezing and baking at a later time.

- 4¼ cups (21¼ ounces) King Arthur Unbleached All-Purpose Flour
- 4 teaspoons instant or rapid-rise yeast
- 2 teaspoons table salt
- 1¾ cups (14 ounces) whole milk, room temperature
- ¼ cup (1¾ ounces) sugar
- 3 tablespoons European-style unsalted butter, melted, plus 24 tablespoons (12 ounces) chilled
- 1 large egg, lightly beaten with 1 tablespoon water and pinch table salt

1. Whisk flour, yeast, and salt together in bowl of stand mixer. Whisk milk, sugar, and melted butter in 4-cup liquid measuring cup until sugar has dissolved. Using dough hook on low speed, slowly add milk mixture to flour mixture and mix until cohesive dough starts to form and no dry flour remains, about 2 minutes, scraping down bowl as needed. Increase speed to medium-low and knead for 1 minute. Cover bowl tightly with plastic wrap and let dough rest for 30 minutes.

2. Transfer dough to parchment paper–lined rimmed baking sheet and press into 10 by 7-inch rectangle, about 1 inch thick. Wrap tightly with greased plastic and refrigerate for 2 hours.

3. Meanwhile, fold 24-inch length of parchment in half to create 12-inch rectangle. Fold over the 3 open sides of rectangle to form 8-inch square with enclosed sides. Crease folds firmly. Place chilled butter directly on counter and

Shaping Croissants

1. ROLL OUT DOUGH
After freezing dough for 30 minutes, roll into 18 by 16-inch rectangle. Fold upper half of dough over lower half.

2. MEASURE AND MARK
Using ruler, mark dough at 3-inch intervals along bottom edge. Move ruler to top edge of dough, measure in 1½ inches from left, then use this mark to measure out 3-inch intervals.

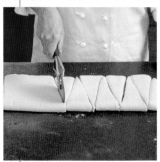

3. CUT
Using pizza wheel or knife, cut dough from mark to mark. You should have 12 triangles and 5 double triangles; discard scraps.

4. SEPARATE
Unfold double triangles and cut into 10 triangles (making 22 equal-size triangles in total).

5. MAKE SLIT
Cut ½-inch slit in center of short side of 1 triangle.

6. STRETCH
Grasp triangle by 2 corners on either side of slit and stretch gently, then stretch bottom point.

7. FOLD EDGES
Place triangle on counter so point is facing you. Fold down both sides of slit.

8. ROLL
Roll top of triangle partway toward point.

9. STRETCH AND ROLL
Gently grasp point and stretch again. Resume rolling, tucking point underneath.

10. CURVE
Curve ends gently toward each other to create crescent.

beat with rolling pin until butter is just pliable but not warm, about 60 seconds, then fold butter in on itself using bench scraper. Beat into rough 6-inch square. Unfold parchment envelope. Using bench scraper, transfer butter to center of parchment, refolding at creases to enclose. Turn packet over so that flaps are underneath, and gently roll until butter fills parchment square, taking care to achieve even thickness. Refrigerate for at least 45 minutes.

4. Transfer dough to freezer and chill for 30 minutes. Transfer dough to lightly floured counter and roll into 17 by 8-inch rectangle, with long side parallel to counter edge. Unwrap butter square and place in center of rectangle. Fold 2 sides of dough over butter so they meet in center. Press seam together with your fingertips. Using rolling pin, press firmly on each open end of dough packet. Roll dough into 24 by 8-inch rectangle, with short side parallel to counter edge. Fold bottom third of dough over middle, then fold upper third over it like business letter to form 8-inch square. Turn dough 90 degrees counterclockwise and repeat rolling and folding into thirds. Return dough to parchment-lined sheet, wrap tightly with greased plastic, and return to freezer for 30 minutes.

5. Transfer dough to lightly floured counter so that top flap of dough is facing right. Roll dough into 24 by 8-inch rectangle, with short side parallel to counter edge, and fold into thirds. Return dough to baking sheet, wrap tightly with plastic, and refrigerate for at least 2 hours or up to 24 hours.

6. Transfer dough to freezer and chill for 30 minutes. Transfer dough to lightly floured counter and roll into 18 by 16-inch rectangle, with long side parallel to counter edge. Fold upper half of dough over lower half. Using ruler, mark dough at 3-inch intervals along bottom edge with bench scraper (you should have 5 marks). Move ruler to top of dough, measure in 1½ inches from left, then use this mark to measure out 3-inch intervals (6 marks).

7. Starting at lower left corner, use pizza cutter or chef's knife to cut dough into triangles from mark to mark. You will have 12 single triangles and 5 double triangles (diamonds); discard scraps. Unfold double triangles and cut into 10 single triangles (making 22 equal-size triangles in total). If dough begins to soften, return to freezer for 10 minutes. Cover all triangles loosely with greased plastic.

8. Cut ½ inch slit in center of short side of 1 dough triangle (keep remaining triangles covered). Grasp triangle by 2 corners on either side of slit and stretch gently. Grasp bottom point of triangle and stretch. Place triangle on counter so point is facing toward you and fold both sides of slit down.

9. Positioning your palms on folds, roll partway toward point. Gently grasp point again and stretch. To finish, continue to roll, tucking point underneath. Curve ends gently toward one another to create crescent shape. Repeat with remaining triangles.

Laminating the Dough

PLACE BUTTER BLOCK
After freezing dough for 30 minutes, roll into 17 by 8-inch rectangle. Place unwrapped butter in center of dough.

FOLD DOUGH
Fold sides of dough over butter so they meet in center. Press seam together with fingertips.

PRESS AND ROLL
With rolling pin, press firmly on each open end of packet. Roll out dough lengthwise into 24 by 8-inch rectangle.

FOLD AND TURN
Starting at bottom of dough, fold into thirds like business letter. Turn dough 90 degrees. Roll and fold into thirds again.

WRAP AND CHILL
Place dough on sheet, wrap with plastic, and return to freezer for 30 minutes. Roll and fold into thirds, then rewrap and refrigerate for 2 hours.

WHAT CAN GO WRONG

PROBLEM The dough is hard to work with.

SOLUTION Put your freezer to work.

Be sure to chill the dough between turns two and three for the full 30 minutes to keep the butter and flour at exactly the same degree of malleability during rolling. And pop the dough in the freezer anytime it becomes too soft to work with.

10. Place 12 croissants on 2 parchment-lined rimmed baking sheets, spaced about 2½ inches apart, 6 croissants per sheet. Cover loosely with greased plastic and let rise until nearly doubled in size, 2½ to 3 hours. (Unrisen croissants can be refrigerated for up to 18 hours; let rise at room temperature for 3 to 3½ hours before baking.) Place remaining 10 croissants on separate parchment-lined rimmed baking sheet, spaced about 1 inch apart. Wrap tightly with greased plastic and freeze until solid, about 2 hours. Transfer frozen croissants from baking sheet to zipper-lock bag and return to freezer. (Frozen croissants can be stored in freezer for up to 2 months. Arrange on 2 sheets as directed and increase rising time by 1 to 2 hours.)

11. Adjust oven racks to upper-middle and lower-middle positions and heat oven to 425 degrees. Gently brush croissants with egg mixture. Place croissants in oven and reduce temperature to 400 degrees. Bake for 12 minutes, then switch and rotate baking sheets. Continue to bake until deep golden brown, 8 to 12 minutes. Transfer croissants to wire rack and let cool for 15 minutes. Serve warm or at room temperature.

Variation
PAIN AU CHOCOLAT
Makes: 16
Total Time: 45 minutes, plus 4 hours freezing, rising, and cooling

The only thing better than waking up to the smell of buttery pastries is waking up to the smell of buttery pastries filled with chocolate. Traditional pain au chocolat uses batons (sticks) of chocolate; to avoid seeking out batons, we line up finely chopped chocolate, which neither interrupts nor punctures the dough layers. This recipe yields eight baked croissants and eight croissants for freezing and baking at a later time.

> 1 recipe Croissants, made through step 5
> 3½ ounces bittersweet chocolate, chopped fine

1. Transfer dough to freezer. After 30 minutes, transfer to lightly floured counter and roll into 18 by 16-inch rectangle with short side of rectangle parallel to counter edge. Using sharp pizza wheel or knife, starting at 1 short side, cut dough into four 4 by 18-inch strips. Then cut dough crosswise into 4 by 4½-inch rectangles (16 rectangles total).

2. With short side of 1 dough rectangle facing you, spread 1 teaspoon chopped chocolate, end to end, in tidy row, ½ inch from bottom. Stretch and fold bottom third of dough over chocolate to center. Spread 1 more teaspoon chocolate end to end along dough seam. Brush top of folded dough

with portion of egg wash. Stretch and fold top third of dough over chocolate until even with bottom edge of dough; gently press seam to seal. Repeat with remaining rectangles.

3. Place 4 croissants each, seam side down, on 2 parchment-lined rimmed baking sheets at least 3 inches apart. Cover loosely with greased plastic. Let rise at room temperature until nearly double in size, 2½ to 3 hours. (Shaped croissants can be refrigerated for up to 18 hours. Remove from refrigerator to rise and add at least 30 minutes to rising time). Place remaining 8 croissants on separate parchment-lined rimmed baking sheet, spaced about 1 inch apart. Wrap tightly with greased plastic and freeze until solid, about 2 hours. Transfer frozen croissants from baking sheet to zipper-lock bag and return to freezer. (Frozen croissants can be stored in freezer for up to 2 months. Arrange on 2 sheets as directed and increase rising time by 1 to 2 hours.)

4. After 2 hours of rising, adjust oven racks to upper-middle and lower-middle positions and heat oven to 425 degrees. Brush croissants with remaining egg wash. Place croissants in oven and reduce temperature to 400 degrees. Bake for 10 minutes, then switch and rotate baking sheets. Continue to bake until deep golden brown, 8 to 12 minutes. Transfer to wire rack and let cool completely, about 1 hour. Serve.

KEYS TO SUCCESS

- **Use high-protein flour:** High-protein all-purpose flour such as King Arthur develops more gluten and is more resistant to tearing.

- **Use European-style butter:** Higher-fat European butter contains less water than domestic butter, thereby creating flakier layers.

- **Freeze the dough:** To ensure that the butter and the dough surrounding it are equally malleable, briefly freeze the packet.

- **Be cool:** Do not attempt to make these croissants in a room that is warmer than 80 degrees.

- **Turn down the heat:** Be sure to reduce the temperature immediately after putting the croissants in the oven.

Shaping Chocolate Croissants

SPREAD CHOCOLATE
With short side of 1 dough rectangle facing you, spread 1 teaspoon chopped chocolate, end to end, in tidy row, ½ inch from bottom.

STRETCH AND FOLD
Stretch and fold bottom third of dough over chocolate to center.

SPREAD MORE CHOCOLATE
Spread 1 more teaspoon chocolate end to end along dough seam.

BRUSH TOP
Brush top of folded dough with egg wash.

STRETCH AND FOLD
Stretch and fold top third of dough over chocolate until even with bottom edge of dough.

PRESS TO SEAL
Gently press seam to seal.

CHAPTER 12

DESSERTS

CLASSIC FLAVORS, NEW COOKIES

MORGAN BOLLING

One of the best things about cookies is that they can be made in an infinite number of forms and flavor combinations, including some classic candy bar and cake flavors. In this course, you'll make peanut butter–filled chocolate cookies, bars that top a crisp shortbread base with caramel and chocolate, a bite-size take on carrot cake, and another classic favorite, the cookie ice cream sandwich (which is not as easy as pressing some ice cream between two cookies). We show you how to reformulate a chocolate chip cookie recipe so the cookies are firm yet tender, even when frozen.

MORGAN'S PRO TIP: *Bringing ice cream sandwiches out at a hot barbecue is a sure party winner. I play up the different ice cream flavors with other coatings in place of the mini chocolate chips. I'll put crushed Oreos around coffee ice cream, rainbow sprinkles around birthday cake ice cream, and fruity crisp rice cereal around strawberry ice cream. They're cute and it makes it easier to tell which flavor is which.*

PEANUT BUTTER–STUFFED CHOCOLATE COOKIES

Makes: 16 cookies
Total Time: 1½ hours, plus 30 minutes cooling

RECIPE OVERVIEW When you take a filling inspired by the creamy core of a peanut butter cup and bake it inside double-chocolate cookie dough, you get the mouthwatering combination of a slightly chewy, intensely chocolaty cookie and a satisfying peanutty center. Making stuffed cookies sounds like a lot more work than unwrapping a peanut butter cup, but it's easier than you'd think, and the reward is worth it. A combination of unsweetened cocoa powder and bittersweet chocolate, plus a good dose of salt, maximizes the dough's chocolaty complexity and balances the cookies' sweetness. Melting a portion of the chopped chocolate for the dough and then folding in the remaining pieces creates luscious molten pockets in the finished cookies. Using both baking soda and baking powder ensures that the cookies will puff and spread just enough to crackle on top, and a combination of vegetable oil and butter creates the perfect amount of chew. Once stirred together, the dough is easy to work with, so you can easily mold it around the filling, a simple stir-together mixture of peanut butter, confectioners' sugar, and salt. A final roll in granulated and confectioners' sugars endows the cookies with the stunning visual contrast of crinkle cookies and adds a crunchy texture to their exteriors.

Filling

½ cup creamy peanut butter

½ cup (2 ounces) confectioners' sugar

¼ teaspoon table salt

Dough

1½ cups (7½ ounces) all-purpose flour

¼ cup (¾ ounce) Dutch-processed cocoa powder

1 teaspoon baking powder

¼ teaspoon baking soda

¾ teaspoon table salt

10 ounces bittersweet chocolate, chopped fine, divided

3 tablespoons vegetable oil

1 tablespoon unsalted butter

1 tablespoon vanilla extract

1 cup (7 ounces) granulated sugar, plus ⅓ cup for rolling

2 large eggs

½ cup confectioners' sugar for rolling

1. **FOR THE FILLING** Combine peanut butter, sugar, and salt in bowl. Using fork or your hands, stir and mash mixture until thoroughly combined and no dry pockets of sugar remain. Divide filling into 16 equal portions (about 2 teaspoons each). Roll each portion into ball and place on large plate. Freeze until firm, about 30 minutes.

2. **FOR THE DOUGH** Meanwhile, adjust oven racks to upper-middle and lower-middle positions and heat oven to 300 degrees. Line 2 rimmed baking sheets with parchment paper.

3. Whisk flour, cocoa, baking powder, baking soda, and salt together in medium bowl. Microwave 6 ounces chocolate, oil, and butter in second medium bowl at 50 percent power, stirring occasionally, until melted, about 3 minutes. Whisk vanilla into melted chocolate mixture until combined.

4. Whisk 1 cup granulated sugar and eggs in large bowl until thoroughly combined. Add melted chocolate mixture and whisk until uniform. Using rubber spatula, fold in flour mixture until combined. Fold in remaining 4 ounces chocolate.

5. Divide dough into 16 equal portions, about scant 3 tablespoons (1⅞ ounces) each; divide any remaining dough evenly among portions. Use your fingers to flatten 1 dough portion into disk with roughly 3-inch diameter. Place 1 ball of filling in center of disk. Wrap edges of dough up and around filling, seal dough, and shape into smooth ball. Repeat with remaining dough portions and filling.

6. Place confectioners' sugar and remaining ⅓ cup granulated sugar in 2 separate shallow dishes. Working in batches, roll dough balls first in granulated sugar, then in confectioners' sugar, to coat. Evenly space dough balls on prepared sheets, 8 dough balls per sheet.

7. Using bottom of drinking glass, flatten dough balls into 2-inch-wide disks. (Dough balls will crack at edges; this is OK. If filling shows through any large cracks, pinch dough together to seal cracks.) Bake until cookies are puffed, edges are just set, and cookies no longer look raw between cracks, about 22 minutes, switching and rotating sheets halfway through baking.

8. Let cookies cool completely on sheets, about 30 minutes. Serve.

KEYS TO SUCCESS

- **Use Dutch process cocoa:** It provides deep chocolate flavor, and its high fat and low starch levels help keep the cookies moist and fudgy.

- **Freeze the filling:** A brief freeze firms the filling enough to make stuffing the cookies easy, not frustrating.

- **Flatten:** Gently flatten the coated dough balls just before baking to make the cookies pleasingly disk-shaped rather than domed.

- **Store cold:** Once baked and cooled, these cookies are best stored in the refrigerator.

Stuffing and Shaping the Cookies

FLATTEN
Use your fingers to flatten 1 dough portion into disk with roughly 3-inch diameter.

ADD FILLING
Place 1 ball of chilled filling in center of disk.

WRAP FILLING
Wrap edges of dough up and around filling, seal dough, shape into smooth ball, and roll in sugar.

FLATTEN AGAIN
Flatten dough balls into 2-inch-wide disks using bottom of drinking glass. Seal any cracks where filling shows through.

CARROT CAKE COOKIES

Makes: 24 cookies

Total Time: 1 hour, plus 30 minutes macerating and 20 minutes cooling

RECIPE OVERVIEW Everything you love about carrot cake—warm spices, sweet raisins, toasted walnuts, and bright orange carrots—is here in miniature form. For a chewy (not cakey or dense) texture, melted butter works better than the oil traditionally called for in carrot cake. Granulated sugar produces crisp edges and prevents the cookies from being too soft. A full 2 cups of shredded carrots provide plenty of flavor but also add moisture that can wreak havoc with the cookies' texture. To extract their excess liquid, we salt and sugar the carrots—a test kitchen trick that draws water out of vegetables—and then wring them out before adding them to the dough. A thick layer of sweet-tangy cream cheese frosting is the perfect finishing touch; spread it to cover the entire cookie.

Cookies

- 12 ounces carrots, peeled and shredded (2 cups)
- 1 teaspoon granulated sugar, plus ½ cup (3½ ounces)
- 1 teaspoon table salt, divided
- 2 cups (10 ounces) all-purpose flour
- 1 teaspoon ground cinnamon
- ½ teaspoon baking soda
- ½ teaspoon ground nutmeg
- 1 cup packed (7 ounces) light brown sugar
- 12 tablespoons unsalted butter, melted and cooled
- 1 large egg plus 1 large yolk
- 2 teaspoons vanilla extract
- 1¾ cups walnuts, toasted and chopped coarse, divided
- ¾ cup golden raisins

Frosting

- 6 tablespoons unsalted butter, softened
- 1½ cups (6 ounces) confectioners' sugar
- 6 ounces cream cheese, cut into 4 pieces and softened
- 1 teaspoon vanilla extract

1. FOR THE COOKIES Adjust oven racks to upper-middle and lower-middle positions and heat oven to 350 degrees. Line 2 baking sheets with parchment paper. Combine carrots, 1 teaspoon granulated sugar, and ½ teaspoon salt in bowl and let sit for 30 minutes. Place carrots in center of clean dish towel, gather ends of towel to form bundle, and twist to remove as much moisture from carrots as possible (you should squeeze off about ¼ cup liquid).

2. Whisk flour, cinnamon, baking soda, nutmeg, and remaining ½ teaspoon salt together in bowl. Whisk brown sugar, melted butter, egg and yolk, vanilla, and remaining ½ cup granulated sugar in separate large bowl until fully combined. Stir flour mixture into butter mixture until just combined. Stir in carrots, 1 cup walnuts, and raisins.

3. Drop 2-tablespoon portions of dough onto prepared sheets, staggering 12 portions per sheet. (Distribute any remaining dough evenly.) Using your fingers, lightly press cookies to even ¾-inch thickness. Bake cookies until edges are set and beginning to brown, 16 to 20 minutes, switching and rotating sheets halfway through baking. Let cookies cool on sheets for 5 minutes. Transfer cookies to wire rack and let cool completely before frosting.

4. FOR THE FROSTING Using stand mixer fitted with paddle, beat butter and sugar on medium speed until light and fluffy, about 2 minutes. Add cream cheese, 1 piece at a time, beating after each addition, until fully incorporated. Add vanilla and mix until no lumps remain.

5. Spread about 1 tablespoon frosting over each cooled cookie and sprinkle cookies with remaining ¾ cup walnuts. Serve. (Cookies can be layered between sheets of parchment paper and stored in airtight container for up to 2 days.)

KEYS TO SUCCESS

- **Grate your own:** Do not use packaged preshredded carrots.
- **Wring thoroughly:** You should get about ¼ cup liquid out of the carrots.
- **Lump-free frosting:** Thoroughly mix the softened butter and confectioners' sugar before adding pieces of softened cream cheese.

Cookie Carrot Prep

Three simple steps enhance natural sweetness and eliminate excess moisture.

SHRED
Using the shredding disk of a food processor makes quick work of grating the carrots.

SALT/SUGAR
Tossing the carrots with salt and sugar and letting them sit helps pull out excess moisture.

SQUEEZE
Wringing the carrots in a dish towel (you should expel about ¼ cup of liquid) gets them as dry as possible.

CHOCOLATE CHIP COOKIE ICE CREAM SANDWICHES

Makes: 12 sandwiches
Total Time: 1½ hours, plus 8 hours freezing

RECIPE OVERVIEW The perfect chocolate chip cookie isn't necessarily perfect for making ice cream sandwiches. To keep them out of jawbreaker territory, the cookies need to be thin and stay soft when frozen. And because freezing temperatures dull flavor, they should also have pronounced toffee notes. Adding water and a bit more fat keeps the dough softer, and baking the cookies at a lower temperature allows them to spread to the right thickness. Browning the butter and using dark brown sugar, plenty of vanilla, and extra salt adds flavor. Mini chocolate chips are easier to bite through than the larger size. As the cookie sandwiches sit in the freezer, the cookies absorb moisture from the ice cream, enhancing their softness. For the best results, weigh the flour and sugar for the cookies. We prefer the deeper flavor of dark brown sugar here, but light brown sugar will also work. Use your favorite ice cream. If using a premium ice cream such as Ben & Jerry's or Häagen-Dazs, which is likely to be harder than a less-premium brand when frozen, let the ice cream soften slightly in the refrigerator before scooping. We like these sandwiches with chocolate chips pressed into the sides, but the garnish is optional.

10	tablespoons unsalted butter
¾	cup packed (5¼ ounces) dark brown sugar
¾	teaspoon table salt
1	cup plus 2 tablespoons (5⅔ ounces) all-purpose flour
¼	teaspoon baking soda
1	large egg
2	tablespoons water
2	teaspoons vanilla extract
½	cup (3 ounces) mini semisweet chocolate chips, plus 1 cup for optional garnish
3	pints ice cream

1. Adjust oven rack to middle position and heat oven to 325 degrees. Melt butter in 10-inch skillet over medium-high heat. Cook, stirring and scraping skillet constantly with rubber spatula, until milk solids are dark golden brown and butter has nutty aroma, 1 to 3 minutes. Immediately transfer to heatproof large bowl. Whisk in sugar and salt until fully incorporated and let mixture cool for 10 minutes. Meanwhile, line 2 rimmed baking sheets with parchment paper. Stir flour and baking soda together in second bowl; set aside.

2. Add egg, water, and vanilla to browned butter mixture and whisk until smooth, about 30 seconds. Using rubber spatula, stir in flour mixture until combined. Stir in ½ cup chocolate chips. (Dough will be very soft.)

3. Using #60 scoop or 1-tablespoon measure, evenly space 12 mounds of dough on each prepared sheet. Bake cookies, 1 sheet at a time, until puffed and golden brown, 9 to 12 minutes, rotating sheet halfway through baking.

SCIENCE LESSON How More Water Makes Softer Frozen Cookies

We made several changes to our Perfect Chocolate Chip Cookies recipe to engineer a frozen cookie that was soft enough to bite through. Our new cookie contains a bit more fat and a bit less sugar, but the real outlier is something rarely considered in cookie composition: water. In fact, our ice cream sandwich cookie dough contains almost twice as much water as our "Perfect" formula. That may sound counterintuitive—you'd think frozen water would make cookies harder—but it works because the sugar in the dough lowers the temperature at which water freezes, keeping it fluid. By increasing the amount of sugary water in the dough, we were able to make the cookies more tender.

Just Add Water
For soft and tender frozen cookies,
add 2 tablespoons of water.

Let cookies cool on sheet for 5 minutes, then transfer to wire rack and let cool completely, about 45 minutes. Place 1 sheet, still lined with parchment, in freezer.

4. Place 4 cookies upside down on counter. Quickly deposit 2-inch-tall, 2-inch-wide scoop of ice cream in center of each cookie. Place 1 cookie from wire rack right side up on top of each scoop. Gently press and twist each sandwich between your hands until ice cream spreads to edges of cookies (this doesn't have to be perfect; ice cream can be neatened after chilling). Transfer sandwiches to sheet in freezer. Repeat with remaining cookies and remaining ice cream. Place 1 cup chocolate chips, if using, in shallow bowl or pie plate.

5. Remove first 4 sandwiches from freezer. Working with 1 sandwich at a time, hold sandwiches over bowl of chocolate chips and gently press chocolate chips into sides of sandwiches with your other hand, neatening ice cream if necessary. Return garnished sandwiches to freezer and repeat with remaining 8 sandwiches in 2 batches. Freeze sandwiches for at least 8 hours before serving. (Sandwiches can be individually wrapped tightly in plastic wrap, transferred to zipper-lock bag, and frozen for up to 2 months.)

KEYS TO SUCCESS
- **Plan ahead:** These sandwiches should be made at least 8 hours before serving.
- **Sweet 16:** If you have it, a #16 scoop works well for portioning the ice cream.

Boosting Flavor in the Cold

Cold temperatures are known for dulling flavor. They diminish the responsiveness of our tastebuds' receptor proteins, hindering our ability to taste, and they slow the movement of aromatic compounds, preventing our noses from detecting them. To compensate for the flavor-zapping effect of freezing our ice cream sandwiches, we use brown sugar instead of white and up the amounts of browned butter, brown sugar, vanilla, and salt. This not only boosts the complex flavors we taste on our tongues but also increases the number of aromatic compounds we smell, resulting in better-tasting cookies.

Filling Cookies Evenly

After placing the ice cream in the center of the overturned cookie and topping it with the second cookie, gently press and twist the sandwiches until the ice cream spreads to the edges.

Blueprint for the Perfect Ice Cream Sandwich

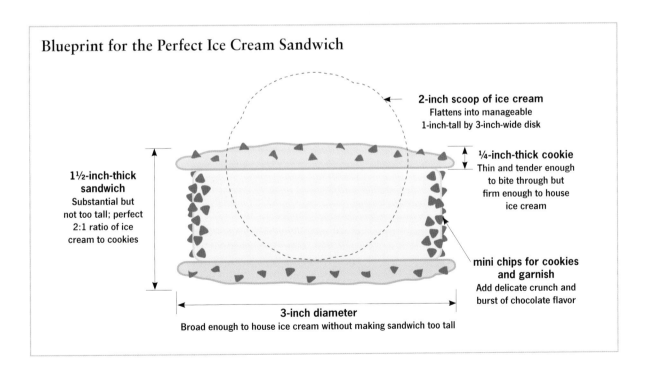

2-inch scoop of ice cream
Flattens into manageable 1-inch-tall by 3-inch-wide disk

¼-inch-thick cookie
Thin and tender enough to bite through but firm enough to house ice cream

1½-inch-thick sandwich
Substantial but not too tall; perfect 2:1 ratio of ice cream to cookies

mini chips for cookies and garnish
Add delicate crunch and burst of chocolate flavor

3-inch diameter
Broad enough to house ice cream without making sandwich too tall

MILLIONAIRE'S SHORTBREAD

Makes: 40 cookies
Total Time: 1¾ hours, plus 1½ hours cooling

RECIPE OVERVIEW Millionaire's shortbread has a lot
going for it: a crunchy shortbread base topped with a chewy,
caramel-like layer, all covered in shiny, snappy chocolate.
Here are the foolproof methods for producing all three
layers: You start by making a quick pat-in-the-pan shortbread with melted butter. For the creamy filling, you cook
a caramel based on sweetened condensed milk and add a
little heavy cream to keep it from separating. Finally, you
use an easy microwave method to temper the chocolate for
a firm, glossy top layer, which makes a suitably elegant
finish for this rich yet refined cookie.

Crust

2½ cups (12½ ounces) all-purpose flour
½ cup (3½ ounces) granulated sugar
¾ teaspoon table salt
16 tablespoons unsalted butter, melted

Filling

1 (14-ounce) can sweetened condensed milk
1 cup packed (7 ounces) brown sugar
½ cup heavy cream
½ cup corn syrup
8 tablespoons unsalted butter
½ teaspoon table salt

Chocolate

8 ounces bittersweet chocolate (6 ounces chopped
fine, 2 ounces grated)

1. FOR THE CRUST Adjust oven rack to lower-
middle position and heat oven to 350 degrees. Make foil
sling for 13 by 9-inch baking pan by folding 2 long sheets
of aluminum foil; first sheet should be 13 inches wide and
second sheet should be 9 inches wide. Lay sheets of foil in
pan perpendicular to each other, with extra foil hanging
over edges of pan. Push foil into corners and up sides of
pan, smoothing foil flush to pan. Combine flour, sugar,
and salt in medium bowl. Add melted butter and stir with
rubber spatula until flour is evenly moistened. Crumble
dough evenly over bottom of prepared pan. Using your
fingertips and palm of your hand, press and smooth dough
into even thickness. Using fork, pierce dough at 1-inch
intervals. Bake until light golden brown and firm to touch,
25 to 30 minutes. Transfer pan to wire rack. Using sturdy
metal spatula, press on entire surface of warm crust to
compress (this will make finished bars easier to cut). Let
crust cool until it is just warm, at least 20 minutes.

2. FOR THE FILLING Stir all ingredients together in large, heavy-bottomed saucepan. Cook over medium heat, stirring frequently, until mixture registers between 236 and 239 degrees (temperature will fluctuate), 16 to 20 minutes. Pour over crust and spread to even thickness (mixture will be very hot). Let cool completely, about 1½ hours.

3. FOR THE CHOCOLATE Microwave chopped chocolate in bowl at 50 percent power, stirring every 15 seconds, until melted but not much warmer than body temperature (check by holding the bowl in palm of your hand), 1 to 2 minutes. Add grated chocolate and stir until smooth, returning to microwave for no more than 5 seconds at a time to finish melting if necessary. Spread chocolate evenly over surface of filling. Refrigerate shortbread until chocolate is just set, about 10 minutes.

4. Using foil overhang, lift shortbread out of pan and transfer to cutting board; discard foil. Using serrated knife and gentle sawing motion, cut shortbread in half crosswise to create two 6½ by 9-inch rectangles. Cut each rectangle in half to make four 3¼ by 9-inch strips. Cut each strip crosswise into 10 equal pieces. (Shortbread can be stored at room temperature, between layers of parchment, for up to 1 week.)

Millionaire's Shortbread Perfected

Most versions of millionaire's shortbread rely on a labor-intensive shortbread layer, and they produce a caramel filling that separates during cooking and a chocolate layer that's dull and soft. Here's how we make a cookie that's easier and a step above.

Quick, Pat-in-the-Pan Shortbread
Opting for melted butter means we need just a bowl and spoon, no food processor or stand mixer.

Filling That Doesn't Break
Supplementing the usual filling ingredients with a little heavy cream prevents the butter from separating out.

Chocolate with Shine and Snap
Grated chocolate and gentle heating in the microwave are the keys to an easy faux-tempered chocolate layer.

KEYS TO SUCCESS

- **Line the pan with foil:** Lifting the bars from the pan is the key to neatly cut bars.

- **Compact the crust:** Pressing the just-baked crust with a spatula compacts it, preventing it from crumbling.

- **Temp the filling:** For a caramel filling with the right texture, monitor the temperature with an instant-read thermometer.

- **Melt the chocolate gently:** You don't want to overheat it.

- **Serrated knife:** For the cleanest cuts, use a serrated knife and a gentle sawing motion.

The Problem with Sweetened Condensed Milk

While developing the caramel filling for our Millionaire's Shortbread, we found that fillings made with some brands of sweetened condensed milk were more prone to breaking—meaning that the butter separated out and pooled on the surface instead of staying emulsified—than others. When we took a closer look at the milks, we noticed that the ones that broke more often were darker in color than the ones that tended to stay emulsified. What was the connection? The temperature used in processing.

Some manufacturers process their milks at high temperatures, speeding up the Maillard reaction, which leads to more browned sugars and proteins, and damaging more whey proteins in the milk, which are key to keeping the fat emulsified. For a foolproof filling that won't break, no matter the brand of sweetened condensed milk, we add fresh dairy. Just ½ cup of cream bolsters the mixture with enough undamaged whey proteins to prevent the butter from separating out.

Bad Break
Sweetened condensed milk's high-heat processing can cause the filling to break. A little fresh dairy is the fix.

COURSE
SWEET CUSTARDS

ELLE SIMONE SCOTT

When done right, a custard is the epitome of both comfort food and sophisticated cuisine. The comfort comes from the creamy taste and texture of dairy, and the sophistication from sugar cooked right to the edge of bittersweet. There's a bit of a learning curve to producing a perfectly smooth custard with just the right amount of body, but this course will get you there. You'll learn three classics—silky crème brûlée, rich Latin flan, and homey yet intense butterscotch pudding—each with a slightly different approach to thickening the custard and caramelizing the sugar, but all equally delicious.

ELLE'S PRO TIP: *When making sweet custards, always use quality ingredients; this takes the guesswork out of how well balanced your flavors will turn out. Also, once you've found ingredients that work best for you, stick with them. This creates a consistent custard experience.*

CRÈME BRÛLÉE
Serves: 6
Total Time: 1¼ hours, plus 6 hours cooling and chilling

RECIPE OVERVIEW Crème brûlée is all about the contrast between the crisp sugar crust and the silky vanilla-scented custard underneath. The texture of the custard should not be firm but rather soft and supple. The secret is using egg yolks—and lots of them—rather than whole eggs. Heavy cream gives the custard a luxurious richness. Scalding the cream, a common custard technique, can result in over-cooking. To avoid this danger, you'll heat only half of the cream in order to extract flavor from the vanilla bean and dissolve the sugar, and use the rest of the cream cold. Crunchy turbinado sugar is easy to distribute over the baked and chilled custards for the crust, and a propane or butane torch works better than the broiler for caramelizing it. Custard is one of the easiest dessert mediums to infuse with flavor. Steeping Irish Breakfast tea bags in the cream makes a custard with warm, distinctive flavor that complements the deeply caramelized crust. Orange blossom water lends an elegant floral, citrus flavor to a second variation.

> 1 vanilla bean
> 3 cups heavy cream, divided
> ½ cup (3½ ounces) granulated sugar
> Pinch table salt
> 9 large egg yolks
> 9 teaspoons turbinado sugar or demerara sugar

 1. Adjust oven rack to lower-middle position and heat oven to 300 degrees. Cut vanilla bean in half lengthwise. Using tip of paring knife or spoon, scrape out vanilla seeds. Combine vanilla bean pod and seeds, 2 cups cream, granulated sugar, and salt in medium saucepan. Bring mixture to boil over medium heat, stirring occasionally to dissolve sugar. Off heat, cover and let steep for 15 minutes.

 2. Stir remaining 1 cup cream into cream mixture. Whisk egg yolks in large bowl until uniform. Whisk about 1 cup cream mixture into yolks, then repeat with 1 cup more cream mixture. Whisk in remaining cream mixture until thoroughly combined. Strain mixture through fine-mesh strainer into 8-cup liquid measuring cup, discarding solids.

 3. Meanwhile, place dish towel in bottom of large baking dish or roasting pan. Set six 4- or 5-ounce ramekins (or shallow fluted dishes) on towel. Bring kettle of water to boil.

 4. Divide cream mixture evenly among ramekins. Set baking dish on oven rack. Taking care not to splash water into ramekins, pour enough boiling water into dish to reach two-thirds up sides of ramekins. Bake until centers of custards are just barely set and register 170 to 175 degrees, 25 to 35 minutes depending on ramekin type, checking temperature 5 minutes early.

 5. Transfer ramekins to wire rack and let custards cool completely, about 2 hours. Set ramekins on rimmed baking sheet, cover tightly with plastic wrap, and refrigerate until cold, about 4 hours.

CUT
Use paring knife to cut vanilla bean in half lengthwise.

SCRAPE
Scrape vanilla seeds out of bean using blade of knife.

6. Uncover ramekins and gently blot tops dry with paper towels. Sprinkle each with 1 to 1½ teaspoons turbinado sugar (depending on ramekin type). Tilt and tap each ramekin to distribute sugar evenly, then dump out excess sugar and wipe rims of ramekins clean. Caramelize sugar with torch until deep golden brown, continually sweeping flame about 2 inches above ramekin. Serve.

Variations

ORANGE BLOSSOM CRÈME BRÛLÉE

Add 2 teaspoons orange blossom water to strained custard before portioning into ramekins.

TEA-INFUSED CRÈME BRÛLÉE

Substitute 10 Irish Breakfast tea bags, tied together, for vanilla bean; after steeping tea in cream, squeeze bags with tongs or press into fine-mesh strainer to extract all liquid. Whisk 1 teaspoon vanilla extract into yolks before adding cream mixture.

KEYS TO SUCCESS

- **The right vessels:** It's important to use 4- to 5-ounce ramekins.
- **Don't let the yolks sit:** Separate the eggs and whisk the yolks after the cream has finished steeping; if left to sit, the surface of the yolks will dry and form a film.
- **Accurate temping:** The best way to judge doneness is with an instant-read thermometer.
- **Serve promptly:** Once the sugar on top is brûléed, serve within 30 minutes or the sugar crust will soften.

Torching Crème Brûlée

SPRINKLE WITH SUGAR
If condensation forms, gently blot tops of custards before sprinkling them with turbinado sugar.

CARAMELIZE
To create caramel crust, keep torch flame 2 inches above ramekin and slowly sweep flame across, starting at perimeter and moving toward middle. Sugar should be bubbling and deep golden brown.

Two Subs

A vanilla bean gives the custard the deepest flavor, but 2 teaspoons of vanilla extract, whisked into the yolks in step 2, can be used instead.

For the caramelized sugar crust, we recommend turbinado or demerara sugar. Regular granulated sugar will work, too, but use only 1 scant teaspoon on each ramekin or 1 teaspoon on each shallow fluted dish.

LATIN FLAN

Serves: 8 to 10
Total Time: 2 hours, plus 12 hours cooling and chilling

RECIPE OVERVIEW Latin flan is far richer and more densely creamy than its European counterparts, with a texture somewhere between that of cheesecake and pudding. It also boasts a more deeply caramelized, toffee-like flavor, thanks to the inclusion of canned milk—evaporated as well as sweetened condensed. The exact texture of a custard mainly depends on the ratio of eggs to dairy: The more the proteins (from the eggs) are diluted with water (from the dairy), the looser the custard's consistency will be. Since canned milks contain less water than fresh milk, they contribute less water and more protein to Latin flan, which can border on dense and stiff. A half-cup of fresh milk, whisked into the egg-and-canned-milk mixture, produces a luxuriously creamy texture. Baked in a cake pan, flan is prone to developing cracks, so we call for a loaf pan, which, as a bonus, creates a taller, more impressive-looking dessert. To ensure that most of the caramel releases from the pan you'll add moisture in two ways: directly to the caramel in the form of a couple tablespoons of warm water, and by letting the flan rest overnight before serving, so that moisture from the flan travels into the caramel. Finally, we've created a few easy flavor variations by infusing the custard with orange and cardamom, as well as with typically Latin flavors: coffee and almond extract. You may substitute 2 percent milk for the whole milk in this recipe; do not use skim milk. We recommend an 8½ by 4½-inch loaf pan. If your pan is 9 by 5 inches, begin checking for doneness after 1 hour.

⅔   cup (4⅔ ounces) sugar
¼   cup water
2   tablespoons warm water
2   large eggs plus 5 large yolks
1   (14-ounce) can sweetened condensed milk
1   (12-ounce) can evaporated milk
½   cup whole milk
1½ tablespoons vanilla extract
½   teaspoon table salt

1. Stir sugar and water in medium saucepan until sugar is completely moistened. Bring to boil over medium-high heat, 3 to 5 minutes, and cook, without stirring, until mixture begins to turn golden, 1 to 2 minutes. Gently swirling pan, continue to cook until sugar is color of peanut butter, 1 to 2 minutes longer. Off heat, swirl pan until sugar is reddish-amber and fragrant, 15 to 20 seconds. Carefully swirl in warm water until incorporated; mixture will bubble and steam. Pour caramel into 8½ by 4½-inch loaf pan; do not scrape out saucepan. Set loaf pan aside.

2. Adjust oven rack to middle position and heat oven to 300 degrees. Line bottom of 13 by 9-inch baking pan with dish towel, folding towel to fit smoothly, and set aside. Bring 2 quarts water to boil.

3. Whisk eggs and yolks in large bowl until combined. Add condensed milk, evaporated milk, whole milk, vanilla, and salt and whisk until incorporated. Strain mixture through fine-mesh strainer into prepared loaf pan.

4. Cover loaf pan tightly with aluminum foil and place in prepared baking pan. Place baking pan in oven and carefully pour all of boiling water into pan. Bake until center of custard jiggles slightly when shaken and custard registers 180 degrees, 1¼ to 1½ hours. Remove foil and leave custard in water bath until loaf pan has cooled completely. Remove loaf pan from water bath, wrap tightly with plastic wrap, and chill overnight or for up to 4 days.

5. To unmold, slide paring knife around edges of pan. Invert serving platter on top of pan and turn pan and platter over. When flan is released, remove loaf pan. Using rubber spatula, scrape residual caramel onto flan. Slice and serve. (Leftover flan may be covered loosely with plastic wrap and refrigerated for up to 4 days.)

Variations
ALMOND LATIN FLAN
Reduce vanilla to 1 tablespoon and whisk 1 teaspoon almond extract into egg-milk mixture in step 3.

COFFEE LATIN FLAN
Whisk 4 teaspoons instant espresso powder into egg-milk mixture in step 3 until dissolved.

ORANGE-CARDAMOM LATIN FLAN
Whisk 2 tablespoons orange zest and ¼ teaspoon ground cardamom into egg-milk mixture in step 3 before straining.

KEYS TO SUCCESS

- **Make ahead:** This recipe should be made at least one day before serving.
- **Bake in a narrow loaf pan:** Makes it easier to unmold the flan without it cracking
- **Use a rimmed platter:** Serve the flan on a serving dish with a raised rim to contain the liquid caramel.

WHAT CAN GO WRONG

PROBLEM The custard is thin and buckles when it is unmolded.

SOLUTION The balance of canned and fresh milk is key in this recipe. The ½ cup of whole milk provides just the right amount of water to balance the protein network that the canned milks provide. If you add too much whole milk as a substitute for the evaporated milk, the custard will be too thin and won't set up correctly.

PROBLEM There is a thin skin on the edges of the custard.

SOLUTION Wrapping the loaf pan in aluminum foil before baking it in the water bath prevents that pesky skin from forming. This helps with the texture of the completed flan, since that skin can feel unpleasant and stiffer than the creamy center of the custard.

Don't Let the Caramel Stick to the Pan

The rich layer of caramel on top of flan is the best part of the dessert—except when most of it sticks to the pan like glue. Adding a couple of tablespoons of water to the syrup after it's caramelized will dissolve some of the sugar and keep it runny. In addition, letting the flan rest overnight allows moisture from the custard to dissolve more of the sugar, ensuring that most of the caramel will release from the pan (and that what's left in the pan is soft and easy to remove).

Clingy Caramel
To prevent the caramel from sticking to the pan, we add a little water.

When Goodness Comes (Mainly) from a Can

The advent of canned milk in Latin America in the late 1800s helped make flan, which was introduced by Spanish conquistadores 300 years earlier, even more popular. Even when refrigeration became widespread and shelf-stable milk was no longer as necessary, the practice of using the canned stuff stuck. And with good reason: Evaporated and sweetened condensed milks give flan a distinctively thick, luxurious texture and caramelized notes. But these milks can also have a negative effect, contributing to a stiff, almost rubbery consistency. This is because they have about twice as much protein as an equivalent amount of fresh dairy, which, when combined with the egg proteins in the custard, can create an overly tight structure. Our solution? Add ½ cup of fresh milk, which loosens the texture without adding much protein of its own or diluting dairy flavor.

EVAPORATED

This canned milk is made by heating pasteurized fresh milk in two stages to drive off nearly half its water, which also triggers some Maillard browning. Once sealed in a can, the milk is sterilized to become shelf-stable, a process that triggers more browning and the creation of subtle carame flavors.

SWEETENED CONDENSED

Adding sucrose or glucose syrups to milk that's been evaporated (and undergone Maillard browning) results in this canned milk. In combination with the lactose naturally present in the milk, these added sugars make up more than 50 percent of its weight, rendering sterilization unnecessary.

BEST BUTTERSCOTCH PUDDING

Serves: 8

Total Time: 50 minutes, plus 3 hours chilling

RECIPE OVERVIEW   Real butterscotch pudding gets its rich, nuanced, slightly bitter character from the complex process known as the Maillard reaction, which takes place when brown sugar and butter are cooked together into a caramel. The sweet spot for optimum caramel flavor—intense, but not bitter—is achieved by cooking it to 300 degrees. Usually, caramel is boiled from start to finish, making it easy to over- or undercook the mixture. Instead, you'll use a gentler approach: Boil the caramel to jump-start the cooking, but then lower the heat and simmer for 12 to 16 minutes until the mixture reaches 300 degrees. This process provides a larger window of time to achieve the right results. When making the custard, you won't need to use the traditional, time-consuming method of stirring part of the hot liquid (the caramel) into egg yolks, milk, and cornstarch and then returning everything to the pot to boil. Instead, simply pour the caramel over the egg yolk mixture and whisk until it's combined and thickened. This risky-sounding approach works for two reasons: First, the yolks are protected by the cornstarch, which absorbs water, swells, and slows down the binding of the egg proteins. Second, the pour-over approach removes the custard from direct heat, thereby eliminating any risk of curdling. The payoff is flawlessly creamy pudding with the bittersweet flavor of butterscotch—and with far less fuss.

12	tablespoons unsalted butter, cut into ½-inch pieces
½	cup (3½ ounces) granulated sugar
½	cup packed (3½ ounces) dark brown sugar
¼	cup water
2	tablespoons light corn syrup
1	teaspoon lemon juice
¾	teaspoon table salt
1	cup heavy cream, divided
2¼	cups whole milk, divided
4	large egg yolks
¼	cup cornstarch
2	teaspoons vanilla extract
1	teaspoon dark rum

1. Bring butter, granulated sugar, brown sugar, water, corn syrup, lemon juice, and salt to boil in large saucepan over medium heat, stirring occasionally to dissolve sugar and melt butter. Once mixture is at full rolling boil, cook, stirring occasionally, for 5 minutes (caramel should register about 240 degrees). Immediately reduce heat to medium-low and gently simmer (caramel should maintain steady stream of lazy bubbles—if not, adjust heat accordingly), stirring frequently, until mixture is color of dark peanut butter, 12 to 16 minutes (caramel should register about 300 degrees and have slight burnt smell).

2. Remove saucepan from heat; carefully pour ¼ cup cream into caramel mixture and swirl to incorporate (mixture will bubble and steam); let bubbling subside.

Whisk vigorously and scrape corners of saucepan until mixture is completely smooth, at least 30 seconds. Return saucepan to medium heat and gradually whisk in remaining ¾ cup cream until smooth. Whisk in 2 cups milk until mixture is smooth, scraping corners and edges of saucepan to remove any remaining bits of caramel.

3. Meanwhile, microwave remaining ¼ cup milk until simmering, 30 to 45 seconds. Whisk egg yolks and cornstarch in large bowl until smooth. Gradually whisk in hot milk until smooth; set aside.

4. Return saucepan to medium-high heat and bring mixture to full rolling boil, whisking frequently. Once mixture is boiling rapidly and beginning to climb toward top of saucepan, working quickly, immediately pour into bowl with yolk mixture in 1 motion (do not add gradually). Whisk thoroughly for 10 to 15 seconds (mixture will thicken after few seconds). Whisk in vanilla and rum.

5. Spray piece of parchment paper with vegetable oil spray and press directly against surface of pudding. Cover and refrigerate until fully set, at least 3 hours or up to 3 days.

6. Whisk pudding until smooth before serving.

KEYS TO SUCCESS

- **Temp correctly:** When taking the temperature of the caramel, tilt the saucepan and move the thermometer back and forth to equalize hot and cool spots.

- **Pour quickly:** Add the hot caramel mixture to the egg yolk mixture all at once.

A New Way to Perfect Caramel

It's easy to over- or undercook the caramel for butterscotch pudding when it's boiled from start to finish (the usual approach). Our more forgiving method: Boil the caramel over medium heat until it reaches 240 degrees, then reduce the heat to medium-low and gently simmer it until it reaches 300 degrees. The simmer phase takes 12 to 16 minutes—plenty of time in which to grab a thermometer and the cream.

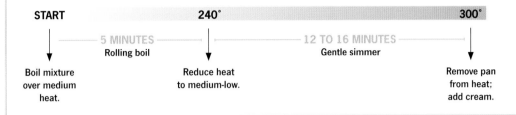

START	240°	300°
—— 5 MINUTES ——	—— 12 TO 16 MINUTES ——	
Rolling boil	Gentle simmer	
Boil mixture over medium heat.	Reduce heat to medium-low.	Remove pan from heat; add cream.

Making Butterscotch Pudding

SIMMER
Simmer caramel mixture gently, stirring often, until it is color of dark peanut butter, 12 to 16 minutes (caramel will register about 300 degrees and have slight burnt smell).

ADD CREAM
Remove pan from heat, carefully pour ¼ cup cream into caramel, and swirl to incorporate (mixture will bubble and steam); let bubbling subside.

WHISK
Vigorously whisk caramel mixture until completely smooth. Return pan to medium heat and gradually whisk in remaining ¾ cup cream and 2 cups milk until smooth.

ADD TO YOLKS
Whisk ¼ cup hot milk into egg yolks and cornstarch. Return caramel mixture to full boil; quickly pour into yolk mixture in 1 motion. Whisk for 10 seconds, then whisk in vanilla and rum.

Smoother Route to Pudding?

Pudding recipes usually call for tempering the yolks and cornstarch (adding some hot dairy to the mixture to gently raise its temperature), adding everything to the remaining dairy in the pot, and stirring constantly as the mixture comes to a boil and thickens. Inevitably, bits of egg still overcook and need to be strained. Was there a better way?

EXPERIMENT
We made one batch of pudding the conventional way and a second with the yolks never seeing the heat of the stove: We added a little warm milk to the yolks and cornstarch, brought the remaining "dairy" (the butterscotch mixture) to a boil, and then dumped this hot liquid over the egg mixture and whisked briefly as the pudding thickened.

RESULTS
The conventional pudding needed straining, while the "no-cook" custard was perfectly smooth and thick.

EXPLANATION
Cornstarch combined with liquid thickens between 144 and 180 degrees, while yolks diluted by liquid coagulate between 180 and 185 degrees—both lower than the boiling point of 212 degrees. Whisking the hot butterscotch mixture into the yolk mixture heated the pudding to 185 degrees— hot enough to thicken but not overcook the yolks.

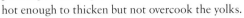

FRUIT PIES

LEAH COLINS

The key to success when baking pies with fresh summer fruits is taming that wonderful juiciness. For fruit fillings with just the right balance of moisture and structure, we show you how to match the thickening agent and technique to the fruit's level of moisture and pectin. The style of top crust also affects the texture of the finished pie filling. Cutting vents or using a lattice allows the proper amount of moisture to evaporate from a fruit pie for the perfect fruit-to-juice ratio. With our step-by-step guides, not only will you weave without fear, but you're guaranteed to get pies that come out of the oven looking as good as when they went in.

LEAH'S PRO TIP: *Have fun and be creative with your decorative lattice, but make sure to keep the pie dough cold yet malleable when shaping. If the dough becomes too soft while shaping, pop it back into the refrigerator for a few minutes on a sheet tray to firm up. I always put my decorative pies back in the refrigerator or freezer for several minutes before baking, to ensure the butter in the pie dough is nice and cold and will puff up immediately when it hits the hot oven. This ensures your finished pie crust will hold its beautiful design without any pie dough sinking or sagging while baking.*

THE METHOD
FRUIT PIE

In these pies, buttery, flaky top and bottom crusts encase mounds of perfectly cooked fruit. The most traditional top crusts either feature sliced vents for moisture to escape or sport a lattice-woven crust.

1 MAKE DOUGH
Process the butter with the flour mixture in two stages, then toss with ice water. Press the dough into two disks and refrigerate.

2 ROLL OUT
Roll out one disk of dough into a circle for the bottom crust and the second disk into a circle or a rectangle, depending on the style of top crust called for in the recipe.

3 FIT IN PAN
Fit the bottom crust into the pan, pressing it into the corners.

4 MAKE FILLING
Prepare the fruit and combine it with the other filling ingredients; cook or let macerate as directed in the recipe.

5 FILL
Fill the pie, making sure the fruit is spread out evenly.

6 COVER THE TOP
Set the top crust on the filling and cut vents if it's a full top crust, or weave a lattice crust, according to the recipe. Pinch the edges together firmly.

7 BAKE
Place the pie on an aluminum foil–lined baking sheet and bake until the crust is deep golden brown and the juices are bubbling.

8 COOL
Let the pie cool for 4 hours so that the filling will be fully set and you can cut neat slices.

STRAWBERRY-RHUBARB PIE

Serves: 8

Total Time: 2¼ hours, plus 5 hours chilling and cooling

RECIPE OVERVIEW The trouble with pairing straw-berries and rhubarb in a pie lies not in their differences, but in a similarity: Both are loaded with water (92 and 95 percent, respectively). During baking, all this water heats up and causes the rhubarb to blow out, releasing its moisture into the filling and collapsing into mush, while the strawberries become bloated. To fix these problems, we microwave the rhubarb with sugar to draw out some liquid and then stir a portion of the strawberries into the warm liquid to soften; we then cook down the liquid with the remaining strawberries to make a jam to fold into the filling. This allows you to use less thickener and more fruit than most pies for an intense filling that is chunky and softly gelled. Eliminating excess liquid in the filling means you can forgo an open lattice in favor of a solid top crust. Brush the dough with water and sprinkle it with a generous amount of sugar for a candy-like shell with a crackly finish.

1   recipe Foolproof All-Butter Double-Crust Pie Dough (page 582)
2   pounds rhubarb, trimmed and cut into ½-inch pieces (7 cups)
1¼ cups (8¾ ounces) sugar plus 3 tablespoons, divided
1   pound strawberries, hulled, halved if less than 1 inch or quartered if more than 1 inch (3 to 4 cups), divided
3   tablespoons instant tapioca, ground

1. Roll 1 disk of dough into 12-inch circle on floured counter. Loosely roll dough around rolling pin and gently unroll it onto 9-inch pie plate, letting excess dough hang over edge. Ease dough into plate by gently lifting edge of dough with your hand while pressing into plate bottom with your other hand. Leave any dough that overhangs plate in place. Wrap dough-lined plate loosely in plastic wrap and refrigerate until firm, about 30 minutes. Roll other disk of dough into 12-inch circle on floured counter, then transfer to parchment paper–lined rimmed baking sheet; cover loosely with plastic and refrigerate until firm, about 30 minutes.

The Runniest of All Pies

Most fruit pies are runny by nature, but the strawberry-rhubarb kind is the worst. That's because the abundant liquid in rhubarb floods the pie during baking, and the berries soak up some of the juice and bloat. We devised specific treatments for each component, resulting in a filling that gels softly and tastes bright. We also fixed rhubarb's mushy texture.

PROBLEMS

Mushy rhubarb Rhubarb in pie fillings tends to "blow out" because its rigid structure can't accommodate the expansion that occurs when the heat of the oven converts the stalk's abundant moisture to steam. The result: pieces that have exploded rather than remained tender and intact.

Bloated berries Strawberries also soften during baking but remain intact because their structure is more flexible and better able to withstand expansion. In fact, strawberries in pie filling not only contain their own juice during baking but also soak up moisture thrown off by the rhubarb, which makes them unappealingly bloated.

SOLUTIONS

Microwave To rid the rhubarb of some water without cooking it too much, we toss the cut-up pieces with sugar (which helps draw out moisture) and briefly microwave them.

Macerate, then drain Resting the sugared rhubarb and some of the berries for 30 minutes draws out even more moisture that can then be drained off.

Reduce We further minimize the juices but retain their flavor by reducing the shed liquid with the rest of the berries until the mixture turns jammy.

2. While dough chills, combine rhubarb and 1 ¼ cups sugar in bowl and microwave for 1 ½ minutes. Stir and continue to microwave until sugar is mostly dissolved, about 1 minute longer. Stir in 1 cup strawberries and set aside for 30 minutes, stirring once halfway through. Drain rhubarb mixture in fine-mesh strainer set over large saucepan. Return drained rhubarb mixture to bowl; set aside. Add remaining strawberries to rhubarb liquid and cook over medium-high heat until strawberries are very soft and mixture is reduced to 1 ½ cups, 10 to 15 minutes. Mash berries with fork (mixture does not have to be smooth). Add strawberry mixture and tapioca to drained rhubarb mixture and stir to combine; set aside.

3. Adjust oven rack to lowest position and heat oven to 425 degrees. Spread filling in dough-lined plate. Loosely roll remaining dough round around rolling pin and gently unroll it onto filling. Trim overhang to ½ inch beyond lip of plate. Pinch edges of top and bottom crusts firmly together. Tuck overhang under itself; folded edge should be flush with edge of plate. Crimp dough evenly around edge of plate. Cut eight 2-inch slits in top of dough. Brush surface thoroughly with water and sprinkle with remaining 3 tablespoons sugar.

4. Place pie on aluminum foil–lined rimmed baking sheet and bake until crust is set and begins to brown, about 25 minutes. Rotate pie and reduce oven temperature to 375 degrees; continue to bake until crust is deep golden brown and filling is bubbling, 30 to 40 minutes longer. Let cool on wire rack until filling has set, about 4 hours. Serve.

KEYS TO SUCCESS

- **Grind the tapioca:** You don't want the filling to be marred by lumps of thickener.

- **Divide and conquer:** Soaking some strawberries in the rhubarb liquid and cooking the rest into a jam adds potent flavor and prevents bloated berries.

- **Vent:** Cut eight vents in the top crust to allow steam to escape.

CORE TECHNIQUE **Venting Guides**

Cutting vents in a pie's top crust allows steam to escape—important for juicy fruit pies such as strawberry-rhubarb. By cutting eight evenly spaced slits in a spoke-like pattern, we also create slicing guidelines that help produce even portions.

PLUM-GINGER PIE

Serves: 8
Total Time: 2½ hours, plus 5 hours chilling and cooling

RECIPE OVERVIEW For a pie with tender bites of plum in a fresh but slightly jammy filling, leave the skins on and cut the plums into ¼-inch-thick slices. Plums, while plenty juicy, release less liquid during baking than fruit such as blueberries or cherries, and they have a fair amount of pectin, so cornstarch is the best thickener. Let the filling rest before adding it to the pie shell; this draws out some of the plums' juices, which ensures that the cornstarch is evenly absorbed with no lumps. A bit of spicy ginger complements the sweetness of the plums. We like our whole-wheat pie crust with the plum filling, but you can use the regular Foolproof All-Butter Double-Crust Pie Dough instead. A lattice top allows excess moisture to evaporate.

1 recipe Whole-Wheat Double-Crust Pie Dough (page 582)
¾ cup (5¼ ounces) sugar
3 tablespoons cornstarch
2 teaspoons grated lemon zest plus 1 tablespoon juice
1 teaspoon grated fresh ginger
¼ teaspoon ground ginger
¼ teaspoon table salt
2½ pounds plums, halved, pitted, and cut into
     ¼-inch-thick wedges
1 large egg, lightly beaten with 1 tablespoon water

1. Roll 1 disk of dough into 12-inch circle on floured counter. Loosely roll dough around rolling pin and gently unroll it onto 9-inch pie plate, letting excess dough hang over edge. Ease dough into plate by gently lifting edge of dough with your hand while pressing into plate bottom with your other hand. Leave any dough that overhangs plate in place. Wrap dough-lined plate loosely in plastic wrap and refrigerate until firm, about 30 minutes.

2. Roll other piece of dough into 13 by 10½-inch rectangle on floured counter, then transfer to parchment paper–lined rimmed baking sheet; cover loosely with plastic and refrigerate until firm, about 30 minutes.

3. Using pizza wheel, fluted pastry wheel, or paring knife, trim ¼ inch dough from long sides of rectangle, then cut lengthwise into eight 1¼-inch-wide strips. Cover loosely with plastic and refrigerate until firm, about 30 minutes. Adjust oven rack to middle position and heat oven to 400 degrees.

4. Whisk sugar, cornstarch, lemon zest, fresh ginger, ground ginger, and salt together in large bowl. Stir in plums and lemon juice and let sit for 15 minutes. Spread plum mixture into dough-lined plate.

5. Remove dough strips from refrigerator; if too stiff to be workable, let sit at room temperature until softened slightly but still very cold. Space 4 strips evenly across top of pie, parallel to counter edge. Fold back first and third strips almost completely. Lay 1 strip across pie, perpendicular to second and fourth strips, keeping it snug to folded edges of dough strips, then unfold first and third strips over top.

Weaving a Lattice Top

LAY FIRST STRIPS
Evenly space 4 dough strips across top of pie, parallel to counter edge.

FOLD BACK STRIPS
Fold back first and third strips almost completely. Lay 1 strip across pie, perpendicular to counter edge.

UNFOLD STRIPS
Unfold first and third strips over top of perpendicular strip.

FOLD BACK STRIPS
Fold back second and fourth strips and add second perpendicular strip. Unfold second and fourth strips.

REPEAT
Repeat, alternating between folding back first and third strips and second and fourth strips and laying remaining strips evenly across pie.

TRIM AND CRIMP
Trim lattice ends, press edges of bottom crust and lattice strips together, and fold under. Crimp dough evenly around edge of pie.

Fold back second and fourth strips and add second perpendicular strip, keeping it snug to folded edge. Unfold second and fourth strips over top. Repeat weaving remaining strips evenly across pie, alternating between folding back first and third strips and second and fourth strips to create lattice pattern. Shift strips as needed so they are evenly spaced over top of pie. (If dough becomes too soft to work with, refrigerate pie and dough strips until firm.)

6. Trim overhang to ½ inch beyond lip of plate. Pinch edges of bottom crust and lattice strips together firmly to seal. Tuck overhang under itself; folded edge should be flush with edge of plate. Crimp dough evenly around edge of plate. (If dough is very soft, refrigerate for 10 minutes before baking.) Brush surface with egg wash.

7. Place pie on aluminum foil–lined rimmed baking sheet and bake until crust is light golden, 20 to 25 minutes. Reduce oven temperature to 350 degrees, rotate sheet, and continue to bake until juices are bubbling and crust is deep golden brown, 30 to 50 minutes longer. Let pie cool on wire rack until filling has set, about 4 hours. Serve.

KEYS TO SUCCESS
- **Don't peel:** The plum skins are tender and add an attractive color to the filling.
- **Double the ginger:** Using both dried and fresh ginger adds a sophisticated spiciness.
- **Macerate:** A 15-minute rest in sugar pulls juices from the plums, which helps dissolve the cornstarch.

For Better Plum Pie, Leave the Skins On

Peeling slippery plums can be maddening, so we were happy to find that our pie actually turned out better when we left the skins on. The thin, tender skins dyed the filling a lovely purply-red, whereas skinned plums produced a filling that looked like peaches. The bitter tannins in the skins also produced a pie that tasted a bit less sweet, which we preferred. Finally, the skins' high concentration of pectin helped create a lightly gelled texture that held the filling together.

Skins

No Skins

BLUEBERRY EARL GREY PIE

Serves: 8
Total Time: 3 hours, plus 5 hours chilling and cooling

RECIPE OVERVIEW The sweet, almost earthy flavor of blueberries is great on its own, but also makes them a perfect match for the citrusy, slightly musky flavor of Earl Grey tea. We grind the tea and add it to the filling, along with just a touch of orange zest to reinforce its citrus notes. As with most fruit pies, achieving a blueberry pie with a firm, glistening filling full of fresh, bright flavor and still-plump fruit requires careful calibration of thickening ingredients and techniques. Here you start by cooking half of the blueberries to reduce some of their liquid. Next, add a peeled and grated Granny Smith apple, which is high in pectin, a type of carbohydrate that acts as a thickener when cooked. Finally, you'll need just a modest 2 tablespoons of instant tapioca to produce a soft, even filling consistency. A lattice crust allows for moisture evaporation as more liquid is released during baking. To elevate this better-than-the-rest blueberry pie even further, make a tea-infused glaze to drizzle over the burnished crust. This recipe was developed using fresh blueberries, but unthawed frozen blueberries will work as well. In step 4, cook half the frozen berries over medium-high heat, without mashing, until reduced to 1¼ cups, 12 to 15 minutes.

- 1 recipe Foolproof All-Butter Double-Crust Pie Dough (page 582)
- 1 large egg, lightly beaten with 1 tablespoon water

Filling
- 30 ounces (6 cups) blueberries, divided
- ¾ cup (5¼ ounces) granulated sugar
- 2 tablespoons instant tapioca, ground
- 2 teaspoons Earl Grey tea leaves, ground
- ⅛ teaspoon grated orange zest
  Pinch table salt
- 1 Granny Smith apple, peeled and shredded
- 2 tablespoons unsalted butter, cut into ¼-inch pieces

Glaze
- 2 tablespoons milk
- 1 teaspoon Earl Grey tea leaves, ground
- 1 cup (4 ounces) confectioners' sugar

1. Roll 1 disk of dough into 12-inch circle on floured counter. Loosely roll dough around rolling pin and gently unroll it onto 9-inch pie plate, letting excess dough hang over edge. Ease dough into plate by gently lifting edge of dough with your hand while pressing into plate bottom with your other hand. Leave any dough that overhangs plate in place. Wrap dough-lined plate loosely in plastic wrap and refrigerate until firm, about 30 minutes.

The Apple of My Pie

When making our blueberry pie filling, we found that if we used more than 2 tablespoons of tapioca, the texture of the filling took on a gummy consistency we didn't like. But 2 tablespoons or less resulted in a filling that was too loose. We wondered if we could solve this problem with pectin, a gentle thickener that occurs naturally in fruit. To find out, we devised a little experiment.

EXPERIMENT

As a control, we thickened one pie with 2 tablespoons of tapioca. We then compared it with a second pie thickened with 2 tablespoons of tapioca and a grated apple, which is high in pectin and has a mild flavor. (We hoped that grating the apple would make its flavor less noticeable in the baked pie.)

RESULTS

As expected, the pie thickened with tapioca alone was loose and soupy. But the pie thickened with tapioca plus an apple had a naturally gelled texture that was just right. The apple bits seemed to melt into the berry filling during baking, boosting fruity flavor but leaving no textural sign of their presence.

EXPLANATION

Pectin creates structure in a plant by helping bind its cell walls together. This same substance is used to thicken jams and jellies. Apples are a great source of pectin because they contain high levels of high-methoxyl pectin, the best natural pectin for making gels. Mashing some of the blueberries and grating the apple released enough pectin from the fruits' cell walls to thicken the pie filling.

On the Loose
Pie filling thickened without enough tapioca won't firm up. But too much tapioca leads to gumminess.

All Firmed Up
A little tapioca plus a grated apple works perfectly.

2. Roll other piece of dough into 13 by 10½-inch rectangle on floured counter, then transfer to parchment paper–lined rimmed baking sheet; cover loosely with plastic and refrigerate until firm, about 30 minutes.

3. Using pizza wheel, fluted pastry wheel, or paring knife, trim ¼ inch dough from long sides of rectangle, then cut lengthwise into eight 1¼-inch-wide strips. Cover loosely with plastic and refrigerate until firm, about 30 minutes.

4. FOR THE FILLING Place 3 cups blueberries in medium saucepan and set over medium heat. Using potato masher, mash blueberries several times to release juice. Continue to cook, stirring often and mashing occasionally, until about half of blueberries have broken down and mixture is thickened and reduced to 1½ cups, about 8 minutes; let cool slightly. Adjust oven rack to middle position and heat oven to 400 degrees.

5. Whisk sugar, tapioca, tea, orange zest, and salt together in large bowl. Place shredded apple in clean dish towel and wring dry. Stir apple, remaining 3 cups blueberries, and cooked blueberries into sugar mixture. Spread mixture into dough-lined pie plate and scatter butter over top.

6. Remove dough strips from refrigerator; if too stiff to be workable, let sit at room temperature until softened slightly but still very cold. Space 4 strips evenly across top of pie, parallel to counter edge. Fold back first and third strips almost completely. Lay 1 strip across pie, perpendicular to second and fourth strips, keeping it snug to folded edges of dough strips, then unfold first and third strips over top. Fold back second and fourth strips and add second perpendicular strip, keeping it snug to folded edge. Unfold second and fourth strips over top. Repeat weaving remaining strips evenly across pie, alternating between folding back first and third strips and second and fourth strips to create lattice pattern. Shift strips as needed so they are evenly spaced over top of pie. (If dough becomes too soft to work with, refrigerate pie and dough strips until firm.)

7. Trim overhang to ½ inch beyond lip of plate. Pinch edges of bottom crust and lattice strips together firmly to seal. Tuck overhang under itself; folded edge should be flush with edge of plate. Crimp dough evenly around edge of plate. (If dough is very soft, refrigerate for 10 minutes before baking.) Brush surface with egg wash.

8. Place pie on aluminum foil–lined rimmed baking sheet and bake until crust is light golden, 20 to 25 minutes. Reduce oven temperature to 350 degrees, rotate sheet, and continue to bake until juices are bubbling and crust is deep golden brown, 30 to 50 minutes longer. Let pie cool on wire rack until filling has set, about 4 hours.

9. FOR THE GLAZE Once pie is cooled, combine milk and tea in bowl. Microwave until steaming, about 30 seconds. Let cool completely, about 10 minutes. Whisk sugar into milk mixture until smooth; let sit until thick but pourable, about 10 minutes. Drizzle glaze attractively over top of cooled pie. Let glaze set for 10 minutes before serving.

FOOLPROOF ALL-BUTTER DOUBLE-CRUST PIE DOUGH

Makes: one 9-inch double crust
Total Time: 35 minutes, plus 2 hours chilling

RECIPE OVERVIEW This is the test kitchen's go-to pie dough. It is supremely supple and very easy to roll out. It produces a buttery, tender, and flaky crust every time.

- 20 tablespoons (2½ sticks) unsalted butter, chilled, divided
- 2½ cups (12½ ounces) all-purpose flour, divided
- 2 tablespoons sugar
- 1 teaspoon table salt
- ½ cup (4 ounces) ice water, divided

1. Grate 4 tablespoons butter on large holes of box grater and place in freezer. Cut remaining 16 tablespoons butter into ½-inch cubes.

2. Pulse 1½ cups flour, sugar, and salt in food processor until combined, 2 pulses. Add cubed butter and process until homogeneous paste forms, 40 to 50 seconds. Using your hands, carefully break paste into 2-inch chunks and redistribute evenly around processor blade. Add remaining 1 cup flour and pulse until mixture is broken into pieces no larger than 1 inch (most pieces will be much smaller), 4 to 5 pulses. Transfer mixture to bowl. Add grated butter and toss until butter pieces are separated and coated with flour.

3. Sprinkle ¼ cup ice water over mixture. Toss with rubber spatula until mixture is evenly moistened. Sprinkle remaining ¼ cup ice water over mixture and toss to combine. Press dough with spatula until dough sticks together. Using spatula, divide dough into 2 equal portions. Transfer each portion to sheet of plastic wrap. Working with 1 portion at a time, draw edges of plastic over dough and press firmly on sides and top to form compact, fissure-free mass. Wrap in plastic and form into 5-inch disk. Refrigerate dough for at least 2 hours or up to 2 days. Let chilled dough sit on counter to soften slightly, about 10 minutes, before rolling. (Wrapped dough can be frozen for up to 1 month. If frozen, let dough thaw completely on counter before rolling.)

Variation
WHOLE-WHEAT DOUBLE-CRUST PIE DOUGH
Substitute 1½ cups (8¼ ounces) whole-wheat flour for first addition of all-purpose flour, using 1 cup all-purpose flour (5 ounces) for second addition of flour.

KEYS TO SUCCESS

- **Box grater:** Use the large holes of a box grater to shred the apple.

- **Use some berries raw:** Cook only half of the blueberries and add the rest to the pie raw to preserve their delicate flavor.

VENTING THE TOP STYLISHLY

A vented top crust allows moisture to evaporate so that juicy fillings, such as blueberry or peach, thicken. An intricate lattice is classic, but these alternatives are equally functional and easy to execute—and they're also visually striking.

FREE-FORM WEDGES

1. Start with 13 by 10½-inch rectangle of chilled dough. Cut into two 10½-inch-long triangles with ½-inch base, two 10½-inch-long triangles with 1-inch base, two 10½-inch-long triangles with 2-inch base, and two 10½-inch-long triangles with 3-inch base. Refrigerate for 30 minutes.

2. Arrange triangles decoratively over filling, with base of each triangle placed at least ½ inch beyond edge of plate (to anchor pieces) and being careful not to overlap more than 2 triangles. Trim overhang to ½ inch beyond lip of plate, then pinch edges of bottom crust and triangles firmly together to seal. Tuck overhang under itself and crimp dough evenly around edge of plate. Brush with egg wash (or water).

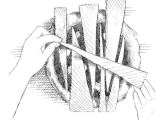

CUTOUTS

- For the clearest visual effect, use cutout crusts on fillings that are flat, not mounded.
- Chill the dough before and after cutting to create sharper, sturdier edges.
- Choose a cutter that measures about 1 inch in diameter; any shape will work.
- Remove one-quarter to one-third of the crust, leaving at least ¾ inch between each cutout and a 1-inch border around the edge.
- Occasionally dip the cutters in flour to prevent them from becoming sticky.

Optional: For more visual appeal, save a few cutouts to decorate intact areas of crust, brushing their undersides with water and pressing gently but firmly to adhere.

FRUIT PECTIN

Many fruits are naturally high in pectin, a complex polysaccharide that acts as a sort of glue, binding mixtures when it comes into contact with liquid. As a fruit dessert cools, the fruit's pectin molecules (which dissolve in the fruit's water during cooking) form a gel that immobilizes the water, resulting in a nicely set filling. It may be hard to resist cutting into a freshly baked fruit pie, but serving before that gel has firmed will cause the filling to run out like hot soup.

IMPORTANT TIPS FOR DECORATING WITH DOUGH

The refrigerator is your best friend. There are chilling steps built into every crust design, from a traditional double crust to the most intricate of lattice-woven tops. But you can also turn to the refrigerator whenever you need or want to. Dough should be firm but malleable during these decorating processes: You don't want butter to melt as your dough will be misshapen, the design won't stay, and overhandled dough won't be flaky once baked. However, you also don't want dough strips to be too cold. You need to do a lot of folding and too-cold dough may crack, ruining your design. The more pie you bake, the easier it will be to get a feel for the perfect dough temperature and texture.

Stay put The easiest way to track your progress on any design is for you, the pie maker, to stay in one place and to instead move the pie plate as needed. When crimping an edge, rotate the pie plate as you go; if you try to move, the crimps will come out crooked. When weaving lattice strips, don't move around the counter; if you stay in the same position vis-à-vis the pie, you'll remember which strips one and three are versus two and four.

Flour as needed If dough sticks to your fingers (or to any implement) while you're working, dip them in a little flour so you can continue working with your hands.

Use an egg wash We don't always use egg wash (for more on wash options, see page 585), but we like it when applying more intricate edging or designs as it highlights those designs, as with the free-form shapes.

Roll out a larger rectangle We always roll out our dough to a rectangle size slightly larger than what we need (usually that means a 13 by 10½-inch rectangle) and then trim ¼ inch from the long sides so that our strips are straight and neat.

MAKING A BRAIDED CRUST

1. Cut 13 by 10-inch dough rectangle into eighteen 13-inch-long by ½-inch-wide strips. Chill for 30 minutes.

2. Working with 3 strips at a time (and refrigerating remaining dough strips while you work), arrange side by side on counter, perpendicular to counter edge, then firmly pinch tops of strips together to seal.

3. Lift and place right dough strip over center dough strip as close to top as possible. Lift and place left dough strip over center dough strip as close to top as possible. Repeat braiding dough strips tightly until you reach bottom of braid.

4. Firmly pinch ends of strips together to secure braid. Return to sheet and chill while braiding remaining strips. (You should have a total of 6 braids.)

5. Fill chilled dough-lined pie plate. Arrange chilled braids evenly over top of filling, then trim overhang to ½ inch beyond lip of plate.

6. Pinch braids and bottom crust together firmly to seal. Tuck overhang under itself; folded edge should be flush with edge of plate. Crimp dough evenly around edge of plate.

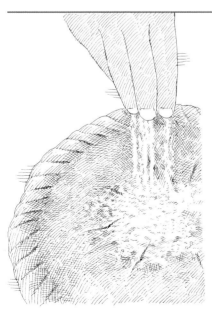

MAKING THE CRUST SHINE AND SPARKLE

Brushing the top crust with egg wash (or water) and sprinkling it with sugar gives the pastry lustrous browning and shimmer—and the effect can be really impressive when you liberally apply both. Thoroughly moistening the dough enables it to grasp lots of sugar, which transforms into a candy-like layer with brilliant sheen, crackly crunch, and notable sweetness that pairs particularly well with tart fruit fillings such as rhubarb, apricot, plum, and sour cherry.

FORMULA FOR 9-INCH PIE

WASH: 1 to 2 tablespoons of beaten egg or roughly 2 tablespoons of water. Add a pinch of salt to the egg wash, which loosens the proteins and makes the wash more fluid and easier to brush evenly over the dough.

SUGAR: 3 tablespoons

CHEESECAKE

NICOLE KONSTANTINAKOS

Say "cheesecake" and the word likely brings to mind a dessert that's gently baked in a water bath and is creamy from edge to edge. New York cheesecake is not that kind. Tall and bronzed, it features gradations of texture—the result of facing the full heat of the oven. That range can be hard to achieve, but we've cracked the code and we share it with you in this course. For fans of crustless, fuss-free cheesecakes, along with a deeply golden exterior (a natural crust) and a smooth and creamy interior, La Viña–style cheesecake is an easy win. And if consistently creamy is really your cheesecake sweet spot, we show you how to make a smooth, luscious, cheesecake—without dairy cheese. Our plant-based pumpkin cheesecake uses mild cashews and coconut oil for a plush, smooth, authentic cheesecake texture.

NICOLE'S PRO TIP: *To ensure the Basque cheesecake cooks properly within the given timeframe, be sure all ingredients are at room temperature (65 to 70 degrees). If you can't wait 1 to 2 hours for your ingredients to come to room temperature, cut the cream cheese into rough 2-inch pieces and place them in a bowl wrapped in a warm damp dish towel. Place whole eggs in a small bowl of warm water (about 110 degrees) for about 5 minutes.*

THE METHOD
NEW YORK CHEESECAKE

Our baking techniques produce a cheesecake with a lush texture, without using a water bath.

1 MAKE CRUST
Process cracker pieces and sugar in food processor until finely ground. Add flour and salt; pulse to combine. Add melted butter; pulse until evenly moistened.

2 PREPARE AND BAKE CRUST
Brush bottom of springform pan with melted butter. Firmly pack crumb mixture into pan bottom. Bake on lower rack until edges brown. Let cool completely on baking sheet. Reduce oven temperature.

3 MAKE FILLING
Using stand mixer and paddle, beat cream cheese, sugar, and other ingredients until combined. Add whole eggs, two at a time, beating until thoroughly combined. Strain mixture into large bowl.

4 ADD FILLING TO CRUST
Pour filling into crust; let sit for 10 minutes. Draw fork across cake to pop air bubbles.

5 BAKE LOW AND SLOW
Bake on lower rack for 3 to 3½ hours. Remove cake from oven. Increase oven temperature to 500 degrees.

6 BAKE HOT AND FASTER
When oven reaches 500 degrees, bake cake on upper rack until evenly browned, then let cool for 5 minutes.

7 REFRIGERATE THEN REMOVE COLLAR
Run paring knife around edge of pan. Let cake cool until barely warm. Wrap in plastic and refrigerate for at least 6 hours. Remove sides of pan; slide thin spatula between crust and pan bottom, then slide cake onto plate. Let sit for 30 minutes, slice, and serve.

FOOLPROOF NEW YORK CHEESECAKE

Serves: 12 to 16
Total Time: 4½ to 5 hours, plus 9 hours chilling and resting

RECIPE OVERVIEW The luxurious texture and bronzed surface of a New York cheesecake is usually achieved by starting it in a very hot oven and then finishing the baking at a low temperature. Depending on how long your oven takes to cool down, this method can yield disappointing results; too quickly and the cheesecake is pallid and under-baked, too slowly and it is dry and overly browned. To ensure consistent results, we turned our original cooking method on its head. Bake the cheesecake at a low temperature, then remove it from the oven, crank the heat to 500 degrees, and return the cheesecake to the upper rack to brown. This method produces the same texture, flavor, and appearance no matter what oven is used. We've also solved a couple other problems: A pastry–graham cracker hybrid crust resists becoming soggy. Pulsing graham crackers, sugar, flour, and salt with melted butter coats the starches, making a crisp crust. Straining and resting the filling releases bubble-producing air pockets and helps make a smooth surface. This cheesecake takes at least 12 hours to make (including chilling), so we recommend making it the day before serving. An accurate oven thermometer and instant-read thermometer are essential. To ensure proper baking, check that the oven thermometer is holding steady at 200 degrees and refrain from frequently taking the temperature of the cheesecake (unless it is within a few degrees of 165), allowing 20 minutes between checking.

Crust

- 6   whole graham crackers, broken into pieces
- ⅓   cup packed (2⅓ ounces) dark brown sugar
- ½   cup (2½ ounces) all-purpose flour
- ¼   teaspoon table salt
- 6½ tablespoons unsalted butter, melted, divided

Filling

- 2½ pounds cream cheese, softened
- 1½ cups (10½ ounces) granulated sugar, divided
- ⅛   teaspoon table salt
- ⅓   cup sour cream
- 2   teaspoons lemon juice
- 2   teaspoons vanilla extract
- 2   large egg yolks plus 6 large eggs
- ½   tablespoon butter, melted

1. FOR THE CRUST Adjust oven racks to upper-middle and lower-middle positions and heat oven to 325 degrees. Process cracker pieces and sugar in food processor until finely ground, about 30 seconds. Add flour and salt and pulse to combine, 2 pulses. Add 6 tablespoons melted butter and pulse until crumbs are evenly moistened, about 10 pulses. Brush bottom of 9-inch springform pan with remaining ½ tablespoon melted butter. Using your hands, press crumb mixture evenly into pan bottom. Using flat bottom of measuring cup or ramekin, firmly pack crust into pan. Bake on lower-middle rack until fragrant and beginning to brown around edges, about 13 minutes. Transfer to rimmed baking sheet and set aside to cool completely. Reduce oven temperature to 200 degrees.

2. FOR THE FILLING Using stand mixer fitted with paddle, beat cream cheese, ¾ cup sugar, and salt at medium-low speed until combined, about 1 minute. Beat in remaining ¾ cup sugar until combined, about 1 minute. Scrape beater and bowl well; add sour cream, lemon juice, and vanilla and beat at low speed until combined, about 1 minute. Add egg yolks and beat at medium-low speed until thoroughly combined, about 1 minute. Scrape bowl and beater. Add whole eggs two at a time, beating until thoroughly combined, about 30 seconds after each addition. Pour filling through fine-mesh strainer set in large bowl, pressing against strainer with rubber spatula or back of ladle to help filling pass through strainer.

3. Brush sides of springform pan with melted butter. Pour filling into crust and set aside for 10 minutes to allow air bubbles to rise to top. Gently draw tines of fork across surface of cake to pop air bubbles that have risen to surface.

4. When oven thermometer reads 200 degrees, bake cheesecake on lower rack until center registers 165 degrees, 3 to 3½ hours. Remove cake from oven and increase oven temperature to 500 degrees.

5. When oven is at 500 degrees, bake cheesecake on upper rack until top is evenly browned, 4 to 12 minutes. Let cool for 5 minutes; run paring knife between cheesecake and side of springform pan. Let cheesecake cool until barely warm, 2½ to 3 hours. Wrap tightly in plastic wrap and refrigerate until cold and firmly set, at least 6 hours.

6. To unmold cheesecake, remove sides of pan. Slide thin metal spatula between crust and pan bottom to loosen, then slide cheesecake onto serving plate. Let cheesecake stand at room temperature for about 30 minutes. To slice, dip sharp knife in very hot water and wipe dry between cuts. Serve. (Leftovers can be refrigerated for up to 4 days.)

WHAT CAN GO WRONG

PROBLEM The batter is lumpy and the cheesecake is dense.

SOLUTION The first step to making this recipe is cutting the cream cheese into small chunks and letting them soften on the counter. If you try to beat the sugar and eggs into cold cream cheese, the batter will be lumpy and curdled looking. In addition, you won't be able to aerate cold cream cheese and the cheesecake will bake up heavy and dense.

PROBLEM The crust is crumbly and soggy.

SOLUTION Make sure to press the crumbs firmly in place—we use the bottom of a dry measuring cup for this step. Compacting the crumbs is the first step to a firm, cohesive crust. In addition, many cheesecake recipes don't bother prebaking the crumb crust. If you skip this step the moisture in the filling will cause the crust to become soggy very quickly. Likewise, the crust won't be very cohesive. Baking makes the crust stronger and firmer.

LA VIÑA–STYLE CHEESECAKE

Serves: 8 to 12
Total Time: 1½ hours, plus 2 hours cooling

RECIPE OVERVIEW The cheesecake developed by Basque Country chef Santiago Rivera, owner of La Viña bar and restaurant in San Sebastián, Spain, is globally celebrated for its exquisite texture and flavor. The center is soft and spoonable, with a perfect balance of milky, tangy, and sweet, while the edges are firmer with hints of warmth and bitterness from the deeply caramelized exterior. Our version stays true to the original recipe while ensuring that you can achieve consistently extraordinary results at home. Your first step to success is to make sure the five ingredients are at room temperature, and you'll use a food processor, not a mixer, to combine them so that the texture is velvety smooth, with no unwanted air mixed in. Line a springform pan with parchment paper, add the custard, and bake in a hot oven until the internal temperature is 155 degrees (the center will still be jiggly). And that's it; the hardest step will be waiting the 2 hours for the cheesecake to cool. If you don't have a large (14-cup) food processor, you can use a large deep bowl and an immersion blender.

7 large eggs, room temperature
2 cups (14 ounces) sugar
2¼ pounds (36 ounces) cream cheese, softened
1 cup heavy cream, room temperature
¼ cup (1¼ ounces) all-purpose flour

1. Adjust oven rack to middle position and heat oven to 425 degrees. Spray or lightly sprinkle 2 approximately 16 by 12-inch pieces of parchment paper evenly with cold water. Crumple each piece of parchment into ball, then gently uncrumple. Overlap parchment pieces slightly to form an approximately 16-inch square. Press parchment into bottom and sides of 9-inch springform pan. Fold overhanging parchment outward, over edge of pan. Using scissors or kitchen shears, trim overhanging parchment to about 1 inch past edge of pan.

2. Process eggs and sugar in large (14-cup) food processor until mixture is frothy and pale yellow, about 1 minute. Add cream cheese, heavy cream, and flour and pulse until cream cheese is broken into large, even pieces, 8 to 10 pulses. Process until mixture is completely smooth, about 2 minutes, scraping down sides of bowl and breaking up any large clumps of cream cheese as needed.

3. Transfer batter to prepared pan and place pan on rimmed baking sheet. Bake until top of cheesecake is deeply browned, edges are set, and center of cheesecake registers 155 degrees, 45 to 55 minutes (center will be very jiggly). Remove cheesecake from oven and transfer to cooling rack. Let cheesecake cool in pan for at least 2 hours.

4. Remove side of pan. Gently peel parchment away from sides of cheesecake until parchment is flush with counter. To slice, dip sharp knife in very hot water and wipe dry after each cut. Serve slightly warm (after 2 hours cooling) or at room temperature. (Cheesecake can be refrigerated for up to 3 days; let sit at room temperature for 1 to 2 hours before serving.)

KEYS TO SUCCESS

- **Real cream cheese:** Don't use cream cheese spread, whipped or low-fat cream cheese, or neufchatel.

- **Room-temp ingredients:** For the cheesecake to cook properly in the time given, all the ingredients should be between 65 and 70 degrees.

- **Large processor:** This recipe requires a 14-cup food processor, although if you don't have one you can use an immersion blender and a large, deep bowl.

- **Crumple the parchment:** Moistening the parchment paper and crumpling it softens it enough to conform to the pan.

PLANT-BASED PUMPKIN CASHEW CHEESECAKE

Serves: 12 to 16
Total Time: 45 minutes, plus 19 hours soaking, cooling, and chilling

RECIPE OVERVIEW To make a plant-based cheesecake that's as irresistible as any dairy rendition, job one is creating a thick, creamy base. Mild cashews, soaked and pureed, make a velvety ricotta-like mixture—a good start. Blotting the pumpkin puree with paper towels before mixing it with the other ingredients helps eliminate some moisture. Melted coconut oil gives this dessert the dense, set-up structure of true cheesecake. Because coconut oil becomes solid at or below room temperature, the cheesecake sets up into a sliceable dessert after a stay in the refrigerator. A small amount of cream cheese (plant-based or dairy) provides tanginess. Not all graham crackers are vegan, so check ingredient lists carefully.

Filling

4	cups (1¼ pounds) raw cashews
1	(15-ounce) can unsweetened pumpkin puree
⅔	cup refined coconut oil, melted and hot
2	tablespoons lemon juice
1½	tablespoons vanilla extract
1⅓	cups (10⅓ ounces) sugar
1	teaspoon ground cinnamon
¾	teaspoon table salt
½	teaspoon ground ginger
¼	teaspoon ground nutmeg
¼	teaspoon allspice
8	ounces plant-based cream cheese, softened

Crust

8	whole graham crackers, broken into 1-inch pieces
1	tablespoon sugar
⅓	cup refined coconut oil, melted

1. FOR THE FILLING Place cashews in bowl and add water to cover by 1 inch. Soak at room temperature for at least 12 hours or up to 24 hours.

2. FOR THE CRUST Adjust oven rack to lower-middle position and heat oven to 325 degrees. Spray bottom and sides of 9-inch springform pan with vegetable oil spray. Line pan bottom with parchment paper and grease parchment.

3. Process graham crackers and sugar in food processor to fine, even crumbs, about 30 seconds. Sprinkle melted oil over top and pulse to incorporate, about 5 pulses. Sprinkle crumbs into prepared pan and press into even layer with bottom of dry measuring cup. Bake until fragrant and edges begin to darken, about 13 minutes. Let cool completely on wire rack, about 1 hour.

4. While crust cools, line baking sheet with triple layer of paper towels. Spread pumpkin puree on paper towels into even layer. Cover pumpkin with second triple layer of paper towels and press firmly until paper towels are saturated. Discard top layer of towels, then transfer pumpkin puree to now-empty food processor bowl.

5. Rinse and drain soaked cashews well. Add cashews, hot melted oil, lemon juice, and vanilla to food processor and process until thoroughly combined and cashews are finely chopped, 2 to 3 minutes, scraping down sides of bowl as needed. Add sugar, cinnamon, salt, ginger, nutmeg, and allspice. Continue to process until thoroughly combined, about 1 minute. Add cream cheese and process until very smooth and creamy, about 3 minutes, scraping down sides of bowl as needed (mixture will be grainy like ricotta cheese).

6. Pour filling into cooled crust and, using offset spatula dipped in hot water and wiped dry, smooth top. Refrigerate for at least 6 hours or up to 24 hours.

7. To unmold cheesecake, run thin knife between cake and sides of pan, then remove sides of pan. Slide thin metal spatula between parchment and crust and carefully slide cheesecake onto plate. To slice, dip sharp knife in hot water and wipe dry between cuts. Serve immediately.

KEYS TO SUCCESS

- **Blot the pumpkin:** Excess moisture from the pumpkin will make the filling too loose.

- **Let it set:** For the best results, chill the cheesecake for the full 24 hours.

- **Serve cool:** If the cheesecake sits at room temperature for more than 1 hour, it will soften too much.

FOUR FAMILIAR FAILURES

A nut-brown surface, puffed-up rim, velvety interior, and buttery graham cracker crust are classic New York cheesecake traits. Unfortunately, so are these common pitfalls.

Cracked
When exposed to high heat for too long, the cheesecake will overbake and develop unsightly fissures.

Burnt
Too much high heat can also cause the cheesecake to burn.

Spotty
Air bubbles that rise to the batter's surface during baking brown faster, giving the facade an undesirably mottled appearance.

Soupy
Even when the exterior is nicely set, the interior can be underdone and runny at the core.

BAKER BEWARE: OVENS COOL DOWN AT DIFFERENT RATES

The textural and visual contrast that defines a New York cheesecake is typically produced by a high-to-low oven method: an initial blast of heat that puffs the sides and browns the top before the temperature is turned way down for the duration of baking to ensure just the right velvety interior. But baking cheesecakes in a variety of test kitchen ovens made us realize that this method works only in ovens that lose heat at a particular rate. If the oven is more thoroughly insulated and the temperature falls too slowly, the cheesecake will overcook; if the oven is less well insulated and the temperature falls too quickly, the beautifully browned exterior of the cheesecake is likely to hide a soupy, raw interior.

We confirmed this theory after monitoring the time it took three different ovens in the test kitchen to fall from 500 to 200 degrees. The results were all over the map. Even more compelling was that in the slowest oven, the temperature took almost 2 hours to reach 200 degrees—45 minutes longer than the recommended baking time for our previous recipe for New York cheesecake.

The Solution To eliminate the drop in oven temperature as a variable, we took the bold step of reversing the typical high-to-low method. We baked the cake in a 200-degree oven until it was completely set, removed it, and then cranked the heat to 500 degrees. Once the oven came up to temperature, we placed the cake on the upper rack, where in just 10 minutes the top browned and the edges puffed, creating that characteristic slope from edge to center.

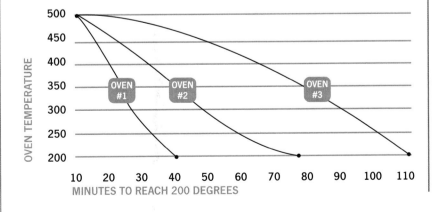

PROBLEM SOLVING: A NON-SOGGY CRUST

Graham cracker crusts turn soggy because the structure of the crushed-up crackers is loose and porous. As a result, moisture from the heavy, wet cream cheese filling seeps into the crevices and saturates the crumbs before the water has a chance to evaporate during baking.

The key to a more moisture-resistant crust is to "waterproof" the crumbs, which we do by working them into a pastry dough. Because the structure of pastry dough is much less porous than a crumb crust—picture a sheet of rock versus the absorbent "sand" of a crumb crust—water from the filling never soaks into it and simply evaporates in the oven. Furthermore, the butter in the dough coats both the crumbs and the starch granules in the flour, making the dough even more resistant to soaking up water.

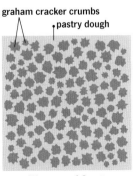

Waterproof Crust

SWEET SOUFFLÉS

JACK BISHOP

Home cooks are wary of attempting soufflés, which have the reputation of being difficult and temperamental and so are relegated to being eaten only in restaurants. In this course, you'll find three recipes that debunk that myth and show that soufflés are relatively easy to make. Skillet Lemon Soufflé proves that you don't necessarily even need a special dish to make a soufflé. It uses an easy base and a stovetop-to-oven method to produce gloriously puffy, golden results. Chocolate Soufflé embodies the seemingly impossible: ethereal lightness combined with deep, resonant chocolate flavor. Grand Marnier Soufflé uses a traditional base of flour and milk called a bouillie.

JACK'S PRO TIP: *If you separate the eggs neatly, a soufflé is actually pretty reliable. Take your time with this step and make sure your eggs are refrigerator-cold. Chilled yolks are firmer and more likely to stay intact as you drain off the whites.*

SKILLET LEMON SOUFFLÉ

Serves: 6
Total Time: 45 minutes

RECIPE OVERVIEW This recipe brings soufflé into the realm of everyday cooking. The heat on the stovetop activates the soufflé batter and ensures an even rise from the egg whites. Rather than making a béchamel or bouillie, here we use a simple base of whipped egg yolks with a little flour added to keep the soufflé creamy. The bright citrus flavor of lemon juice shines through the eggy base. You beat the egg whites separately, adding sugar partway through, fold them into the egg-lemon base, and pour the mixture into a buttered ovensafe skillet. After a few minutes on the stovetop, when the soufflé is just set around the edges and on the bottom, move the skillet to the oven to finish. Minutes later, you'll be rewarded with soufflé that's puffed, golden on top, and creamy in the middle— a successful transformation from fussy to easy.

5	large eggs, separated
¼	teaspoon cream of tartar
⅔	cup (4⅔ ounces) granulated sugar, divided
⅛	teaspoon table salt
⅓	cup juice plus 1 teaspoon grated zest from 2 lemons
2	tablespoons unbleached all-purpose flour
1	tablespoon unsalted butter
	Confectioners' sugar, for dusting

1. Adjust oven rack to middle position and heat oven to 375 degrees. Using stand mixer with whisk attachment, whip egg whites and cream of tartar on medium-low speed until foamy, about 1 minute. Slowly add ⅓ cup granulated sugar and salt, increase mixer speed to medium-high, and continue to whip until stiff peaks form, 3 to 5 minutes. Gently transfer whites to clean bowl and set aside.

2. In now-empty mixer bowl, whip egg yolks and remaining ⅓ cup granulated sugar on medium-high speed until pale and thick, about 1 minute. Whip in lemon juice, zest, and flour until incorporated, about 30 seconds.

3. Fold one-quarter of whipped egg whites into yolk mixture until almost no white streaks remain. Gently fold in remaining egg whites until just incorporated.

4. Melt butter in 10-inch ovensafe skillet over medium-low heat. Swirl pan to coat it evenly with melted butter, then gently scrape soufflé batter into skillet and cook until edges begin to set and bubble slightly, about 2 minutes.

5. Transfer skillet to oven and bake soufflé until puffed, center jiggles slightly when shaken, and surface is golden, 7 to 11 minutes. Using pot holder (skillet handle will be hot), remove skillet from oven. Dust soufflé with confectioners' sugar and serve immediately.

SKILLET CHOCOLATE-ORANGE SOUFFLÉ

Grating the chocolate fine is key here; we find it easiest to use either a rasp grater or the fine holes of a box grater.

Substitute 1 tablespoon grated orange zest for lemon zest and ⅓ cup orange juice for lemon juice. Gently fold 1 ounce finely grated bittersweet chocolate (about ½ cup) into soufflé batter after incorporating whites in step 3.

KEYS TO SUCCESS

- **Use the right skillet:** A traditional (not nonstick) 10-inch skillet is essential for the proper texture and height.

- **Keep the door shut:** Don't open the oven during the first 7 minutes of baking, but do check the soufflé regularly for doneness during its final few minutes.

- **Serve immediately:** Enjoy the souffle while it's still puffy and light.

CHOCOLATE SOUFFLÉ

Serves: 6 to 8
Total Time: 1 hour

RECIPE OVERVIEW Ethereally light and rising to impressively tall heights, a well-made chocolate soufflé is a thing of beauty—and good taste. This chocolate soufflé offers decadent chocolate flavor without compromising the requisite light, creamy texture and dramatic rise. Instead of starting with a classic béchamel base it relies entirely on eggs as its foundation. After beating six egg yolks with sugar, you fold them into a mixture of melted chocolate and butter scented with orange liqueur. Whip the whites to stiff peaks (adding two more for extra volume) and then fold them into the chocolate mixture. The eggs provide enough structure to support an entire half a pound of chocolate, yielding an airy yet decadently chocolaty confection. Soufflé waits for no one, so be ready to serve it immediately. Or see the brilliant make-ahead variation for individual soufflés that can be frozen up to 1 month ahead and go directly from your freezer to the oven.

- 1 tablespoon softened unsalted butter plus 4 tablespoons unsalted butter, cut into ½-inch pieces, divided
- 1 tablespoon plus ⅓ cup (2⅓ ounces) sugar, divided
- 8 ounces bittersweet or semisweet chocolate, chopped
- 1 tablespoon orange-flavored liqueur, such as Grand Marnier
- ½ teaspoon vanilla extract
- ⅛ teaspoon table salt
- 6 large eggs, separated, plus 2 large whites
- ¼ teaspoon cream of tartar

1. Adjust oven rack to lower-middle position and heat oven to 375 degrees. Grease 2-quart soufflé dish with 1 tablespoon softened butter, then coat dish evenly with 1 tablespoon sugar; refrigerate until ready to use.

2. Microwave chocolate and remaining 4 tablespoons butter in large bowl at 50 percent power, stirring occasionally, until melted and smooth, 2 to 4 minutes. Stir in liqueur, vanilla, and salt; set aside.

3. Using stand mixer fitted with paddle, beat egg yolks and remaining ⅓ cup sugar on medium speed until thick and pale yellow, about 3 minutes. Fold into chocolate mixture.

4. Using clean, dry mixer bowl and whisk attachment, whip egg whites and cream of tartar on medium-low speed until foamy, about 1 minute. Increase speed to medium-high and whip until stiff peaks form, 3 to 4 minutes.

5. Using rubber spatula, vigorously stir one-quarter of whipped whites into chocolate mixture. Gently fold remaining whites into chocolate mixture until just incorporated. Transfer mixture to prepared dish. Bake until fragrant, fully risen, and exterior is set but interior is still a bit loose and creamy, about 25 minutes. (Use 2 large spoons to gently pull open top and peek inside.) Serve immediately.

Variation

MAKE-AHEAD CHOCOLATE SOUFFLÉS

Serves: 8

Total Time: 45 minutes, plus 3 hours freezing

This technique only works for the individual chocolate soufflés, which can be made and frozen for up to 2 days before baking. For a mocha-flavored soufflé, add 1 tablespoon instant coffee powder dissolved in 1 tablespoon hot water when adding the vanilla to the chocolate mixture.

Grease eight 1-cup ramekins with 1 tablespoon softened butter, then coat dishes evenly with 1 tablespoon sugar; refrigerate until ready to use. Prepare Chocolate Soufflé. Fill each ramekin almost to rim, wiping excess filling from rim. Cover and freeze until firm, at least 3 hours. Adjust oven rack to lower-middle position and heat oven to 400 degrees. Bake soufflés until fragrant, fully risen, and exterior is set but interior is still a bit loose and creamy, 16 to 18 minutes. (Use 2 large spoons to gently pull open top and peek inside.) Serve immediately.

KEYS TO SUCCESS

- **Use more whites:** Using two extra egg whites in addition to the six whole eggs gives the soufflé the proper volume.

- **The right dish:** A real soufflé dish with straight sides holds the soufflé and prevents spillover.

- **Chill the dish:** For chocolate soufflé, starting with a cold dish ensures a higher rise.

GRAND MARNIER SOUFFLÉ

Serves: 6 to 8

Total Time: 1 hour

RECIPE OVERVIEW With a luxuriously creamy interior and crusty top, our foolproof soufflé is an impressive dessert that can easily be made at home. It begins with a bouillie—a paste of flour and milk. Butter keeps the egginess at bay, and increasing the usual amount of flour prevents frothiness. An equal number of egg whites and yolks is the right proportion for rise versus richness. Adding a little sugar and some cream of tartar to the whites while you whip them stabilizes the whites so that they hold their structure. Add the sugar gradually and partway through the beating process, not at the beginning, or the soufflé will not rise properly and will taste too sweet. Remove the soufflé from the oven while the center is still loose and moist to prevent overcooking. A quick dusting of confectioners' sugar is a nice finishing touch.

Soufflé Dish Preparation

- 1 tablespoon unsalted butter, softened
- ¼ cup sugar
- 2 teaspoons sifted cocoa powder

Soufflé

- 5 tablespoons all-purpose flour
- ½ cup (3½ ounces) sugar, divided
- ¼ teaspoon table salt
- 1 cup whole milk
- 2 tablespoons unsalted butter, at room temperature
- 5 large eggs, separated
- 3 tablespoons Grand Marnier
- 1 tablespoon grated orange zest
- ⅛ teaspoon cream of tartar

1. **TO PREPARE THE SOUFFLÉ DISH** Adjust oven rack to upper-middle position and heat oven to 400 degrees. Grease 1½-quart porcelain soufflé dish with butter, making sure to coat entire interior surface. Stir sugar and cocoa together in small bowl; pour into buttered soufflé dish and shake to coat bottom and sides with thick, even coating. Tap out excess and set dish aside.

2. **FOR THE SOUFFLÉ** Whisk flour, ¼ cup sugar, and salt in a small saucepan. Gradually whisk in milk until smooth and no lumps remain. Bring mixture to boil over high heat, whisking constantly, until thickened and mixture pulls away from sides of pan, about 3 minutes. Scrape mixture into medium bowl; whisk in butter until combined. Whisk in yolks until incorporated; stir in Grand Marnier and orange zest.

3. Using stand mixer fitted with whisk, whip egg whites, cream of tartar, and 1 teaspoon sugar at medium-low speed until combined, about 10 seconds. Increase speed to medium-high and whip until frothy and no longer translucent, about 2 minutes. With mixer running, sprinkle in half of remaining sugar; continue whipping until whites form soft, billowy peaks, about 30 seconds. With mixer still running, sprinkle in remaining sugar and whip until just combined, about 10 seconds. (Whites should form soft peaks when beater is lifted but should not appear Styrofoam-like or dry.)

4. Using rubber spatula, immediately stir one-quarter of beaten whites into soufflé base to lighten until almost no white streaks remain. Scrape remaining whites into base and fold in whites with balloon whisk until mixture is just combined, gently flicking whisk after scraping up sides of bowl to free any of the mixture caught in the whisk. Gently pour mixture into prepared dish and run your index finger through mixture, tracing circumference about ½ inch from side of dish, to help soufflé rise properly. Bake until surface is deep brown, center jiggles slightly when shaken, and soufflé has risen 2 to 2½ inches above rim of dish, 20 to 25 minutes. Serve immediately.

KEYS TO SUCCESS

- **Don't let the whites wait:** Make the soufflé base and immediately begin beating the whites before the base cools too much. Once the whites have reached the proper consistency, they must be used at once.

- **Do not disturb:** Don't open the oven door during the first 15 minutes of baking time; as the soufflé nears the end of its baking, you may check its progress by opening the oven door slightly.

CORE TECHNIQUE

Folding in Egg Whites

If you don't incorporate the beaten egg whites properly into the soufflé base, the finished soufflé may have an uneven texture. Here's our preferred folding method.

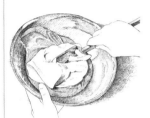

CUT THROUGH CENTER
Using rubber spatula, cut through center of egg whites and down to bottom of bowl.

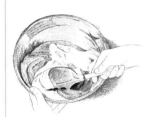

PULL TOWARD YOU
Pull spatula toward you, scraping along bottom and up side of bowl.

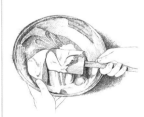

ROTATE SPATULA
Rotate spatula so any egg whites clinging to it fall back onto surface of mixture.

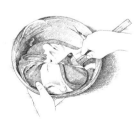

SPIN BOWL
Spin bowl quarter turn and repeat process until whites are incorporated and no visible streaks remain.

COURSE
OLIVE OIL DESSERTS

ANDREA GEARY

You may associate extra-virgin olive oil with savory baked goods, such as focaccia, but its grassy, peppery notes work surprisingly well in sweet baking, too. In this course, you'll start with a deliciously moist snacking cake in which extra-virgin olive oil takes the place of butter. A brightly flavored lemon tart uses oil in both its crust and its lemon curd filling, where the absence of dairy lets the citrus shine. Finally, in a refreshing and unusual ice cream, olive oil acts as a stand-in for heavy cream, lending both body and flavor.

ANDREA'S PRO TIP: *I love robustly flavored olive oil drizzled over broiled fish or whisked into a vinaigrette, but when it comes to baking I stick to a buttery, mild oil. It provides a hint of olive oil flavor but doesn't overpower the other ingredients.*

OLIVE OIL CAKE

Serves: 8 to 10
Total Time: 1½ hours, pus 1½ hours cooling

RECIPE OVERVIEW Olive oil makes a cake with a light, fine-textured, and plush crumb, and the olive oil flavor is subtle but noticeable. Whipping the sugar with the whole eggs, rather than just the whites, produces a fine texture that's airy but sturdy enough to support the olive oil–rich batter. To emphasize the defining flavor, a good-quality extra-virgin olive oil works best; you'll supplement its fruitiness with a tiny bit of lemon zest. A crackly sugar topping adds a touch of sweetness and sophistication. If your springform pan is prone to leaking, place a rimmed baking sheet on the oven floor to catch any drips. Leftover cake can be wrapped in plastic wrap and stored at room temperature for up to three days.

- 1¾ cups (8¾ ounces) all-purpose flour
- 1 teaspoon baking powder
- ¾ teaspoon table salt
- 3 large eggs
- 1¼ cups (8¾ ounces) plus 2 tablespoons sugar, divided
- ¼ teaspoon grated lemon zest
- ¾ cup extra-virgin olive oil
- ¾ cup milk

1. Adjust oven rack to middle position and heat oven to 350 degrees. Grease 9-inch springform pan. Whisk flour, baking powder, and salt together in bowl.

2. Using stand mixer fitted with whisk attachment, whip eggs on medium speed until foamy, about 1 minute. Add 1¼ cups sugar and lemon zest, increase speed to high, and whip until mixture is fluffy and pale yellow, about 3 minutes. Reduce speed to medium and, with mixer running, slowly pour in oil. Mix until oil is fully incorporated, about 1 minute. Add half of flour mixture and mix on low speed until incorporated, about 1 minute, scraping down bowl as needed. Add milk and mix until combined, about 30 seconds. Add remaining flour mixture and mix until just incorporated, about 1 minute, scraping down bowl as needed.

3. Transfer batter to prepared pan; sprinkle remaining 2 tablespoons sugar over entire surface. Bake until cake is deep golden brown and toothpick inserted in center comes out with few crumbs attached, 40 to 45 minutes. Transfer pan to wire rack and let cool for 15 minutes. Remove side of pan and let cake cool completely, about 1½ hours. Cut into wedges and serve.

KEYS TO SUCCESS

- **Use fresh, high-quality extra-virgin olive oil:** A milder olive oil delivers the best savory, complex flavor.

- **A little lemon zest:** Accentuates the olive oil's fruitiness.

Don't Panic When It Puffs

Sprinkling sugar on top of this cake creates a crackly-sweet crust that puffs up during baking. Don't worry; this is just air released by cake batter trapped beneath the layer of melted sugar. It will settle once it cools.

SCIENCE LESSON **Aerating Cake with Eggs**

While butter cakes get their lift from air that's whipped into the butter, our olive oil cake relies on eggs. Whipped whites might be the first thing to come to mind, but you can also whip just yolks or whole eggs. We tried all three in our cake. Whipped whites made it too airy, and our cake collapsed somewhat. Whipped yolks made a squat, dense cake. Whipping whole eggs was the perfect compromise. But why?

The proteins in egg whites are better at unfurling and creating a foam than the proteins in egg yolks are, so whipped whites will be more voluminous than whipped whole eggs and certainly more voluminous than whipped yolks. But the oil in this batter is a factor, too. Oil molecules are able to displace some egg white proteins in whipped whites, which weakens the bubbles. Yolks offer some protection against this; their emulsifiers help keep the oil from interfering with the structure. Thus, whipped whole eggs are the perfect compromise because they provide some lift from the whites as well as a more stable structure from the yolks.

Just Whites
Ultrafluffy egg whites made a cake that was too airy and collapsed.

Just Yolks
Unable to hold much air, egg yolks made a squat, dense cake.

Whole Eggs
Whipping whole eggs provided structure and just enough lift.

LEMON–OLIVE OIL TART

Serves: 8
Total Time: 1¼ hours, plus 2 hours cooling

RECIPE OVERVIEW Most lemon tart recipes feature butter in both the crust and the filling, but here we use extra-virgin olive oil instead. It makes the crust a snap: Just mix flour, sugar, and salt with the oil and a little water until a soft dough forms; crumble it into the tart pan; press it into the sides and bottom; and bake it right away—no rolling or chilling required. Using olive oil in the lemon curd filling doesn't compromise its firmness or sliceability because the filling gets plenty of structure from the protein in the eggs. Olive oil does, however, allow lemons' acidity to come to the fore in a way that butter doesn't. That means we can use a bit less juice and still enjoy plenty of bright lemon flavor. Use a fresh, high-quality extra-virgin olive oil here.

Crust

- 1½ cups (7½ ounces) all-purpose flour
- 5 tablespoons (2¼ ounces) sugar
- ½ teaspoon table salt
- ½ cup extra-virgin olive oil
- 2 tablespoons water

Filling

- 1 cup (7 ounces) sugar
- 2 tablespoons all-purpose flour
- ¼ teaspoon table salt
- 3 large eggs plus 3 large yolks
- 1 tablespoon grated lemon zest plus ½ cup juice (3 lemons)
- ¼ cup extra-virgin olive oil

1. FOR THE CRUST Adjust oven rack to middle position and heat oven to 350 degrees. Whisk flour, sugar, and salt together in bowl. Add oil and water and stir until uniform dough forms. Using your hands, crumble three-quarters of dough over bottom of 9-inch tart pan with removable bottom. Press dough to even thickness in bottom of pan. Crumble remaining dough and scatter evenly around edge of pan, then press crumbled dough into fluted sides of pan. Press dough to even thickness. Place pan on rimmed baking sheet and bake until crust is deep golden brown and firm to touch, 30 to 35 minutes, rotating pan halfway through baking.

2. FOR THE FILLING About 5 minutes before crust is finished baking, whisk sugar, flour, and salt in medium saucepan until combined. Whisk in eggs and yolks until no streaks of egg remain. Whisk in lemon zest and juice. Cook over medium-low heat, whisking constantly and scraping corners of saucepan, until mixture thickens slightly and registers 160 degrees, 5 to 8 minutes.

3. Off heat, whisk in oil until incorporated. Strain curd through fine-mesh strainer set over bowl. Pour curd into warm tart shell.

4. Bake until filling is set and barely jiggles when pan is shaken, 8 to 12 minutes. Let tart cool completely on wire rack, at least 2 hours. Remove outer metal ring of tart pan. Slide thin metal spatula between tart and pan bottom, then carefully slide tart onto serving platter. Cut tart into wedges, wiping knife clean between cuts if necessary, and serve. (Leftovers can be wrapped loosely in plastic wrap and refrigerated for up to 3 days.)

KEYS TO SUCCESS

- **Use nonreactive equipment:** Make sure your saucepan, strainer, and whisk are made of nonreactive metal or the filling may have a metallic flavor.
- **Strain the curd:** Passing the filling through a fine-mesh strainer removes the grated zest and any stray bits of cooked egg, for a perfectly smooth texture.

CORE TECHNIQUE

Forming a Pat-in-Pan Crust

Distributing crumbles of dough around the pan means you won't run out of dough before the edge is complete.

COVER BOTTOM
Crumble three-quarters of dough into bottom of tart pan and press to even thickness.

COVER SIDES
Crumble remaining one-quarter of dough evenly around edge of pan and press into fluted sides.

SMOOTH DOUGH
Press dough across bottom of pan until even and smooth.

PROBLEM The tart shell is so tender it crumbles and falls apart.

SOLUTION Use water in the dough. Unlike olive oil, butter is not pure fat; it's almost 20 percent water. This means that 10 tablespoons of butter is actually 8 tablespoons of fat and 2 tablespoons of water. When using oil, it's important to add the water that would have been naturally present had you used butter, or you will end up with a tart shell that crumbles apart.

PROBLEM The tart filling is gritty.

SOLUTION Strain the curd. Lemon zest contributes a lot of pure lemon flavor to foods, which is why we use both lemon zest and juice in this tart. However, if you skip the step of straining the curd, then small pieces of lemon peel remain and make this tart unpleasantly gritty.

SCIENCE LESSON | Why a Liquid Fat Doesn't Make a Loose Curd

We worried that using olive oil instead of butter in our filling would cause it to be runny, but it was actually beautifully sliceable. That's because the firmness of a curd made with butter is due mainly to the coagulation of the egg proteins, not to the hardening of the butter when it cools. As the curd cooks, the protein molecules in the eggs unwind into long strands, which tangle to make a mesh that traps liquid. The tangling continues as the curd cools, creating a creamy yet firm texture.

Butter or Oil? Both Cut Clean

OLIVE OIL ICE CREAM

Makes: about 1 quart
Total Time: 1 hour, plus 8 hours chilling and freezing

RECIPE OVERVIEW It may sound like an odd combination, but extra-virgin olive oil ice cream is pretty amazing stuff—creamy and sweet, with a hint of grassiness and a pleasant back-of-the-throat burn to balance its refreshing chill. Simply adding olive oil to a regular ice cream base leads to pasty, gummy ice cream. Replacing the heavy cream with water lets you add a full ¾ cup olive oil, producing deep flavor and great texture. A little freshly ground pepper reinforces the oil's peppery notes and gives this ice cream the look of classic vanilla bean ice cream.

- 6 tablespoons (2⅔ ounces) sugar
- ½ cup plus ⅓ cup nonfat dry milk powder
- ½ teaspoon pepper
- ¼ teaspoon kosher salt
- 1¼ cups plus ¼ cup whole milk, divided
- 1 cup water
- ¼ cup corn syrup
- 2 tablespoons plus 2½ teaspoons cornstarch
- ¾ cup extra-virgin olive oil

1. In small bowl, whisk sugar, milk powder, pepper, and salt together. Whisk sugar mixture, 1¼ cups milk, water, and corn syrup together in large saucepan. Cook over medium-high heat until tiny bubbles form around edge of saucepan and mixture registers 190 degrees, whisking frequently to dissolve sugar and break up any clumps, 5 to 7 minutes.

2. Meanwhile, whisk remaining ¼ cup milk and cornstarch together in small bowl.

3. Reduce heat to medium. Whisk cornstarch mixture to recombine, then whisk into milk mixture in saucepan. Cook, constantly scraping bottom of saucepan with rubber spatula, until mixture thickens, about 30 seconds. Immediately pour ice cream base through fine-mesh strainer into large bowl; let cool until no longer steaming, about 20 minutes. Whisk in oil in steady stream until smooth. Cover bowl, transfer to refrigerator, and chill to 40 degrees, at least 6 or up to 8 hours. (Base can be refrigerated overnight. Alternatively, base can be chilled in about 1½ hours by placing it over ice bath of 6 cups ice, ½ cup water, and ⅓ cup salt.)

4. Churn base in ice cream maker until mixture resembles thick soft-serve ice cream and registers 21 degrees. Transfer to airtight container, cover, transfer to freezer, and freeze until hard, at least 2 hours or up to 8 hours.

KEY TO SUCCESS

- **Prechill:** Freeze your ice cream canister for at least 24 hours ahead of use. For self-refrigerating units, run the machine for 5 to 10 minutes before adding the base.

COURSE

CREAM-FILLED PASTRIES

STEPHANIE PIXLEY

In this course, we show you how to make two desserts you'd expect to see only in a refrigerated glass case at a bakery: choux au craquelin (crunchy cream puffs) and napoleons. Learn how to make the basic components for these desserts—silky pastry cream, airy pate a choux, and flaky puff pastry—and you will have mastered the foundation for a myriad of classic French pastries.

STEPH'S PRO TIP: *Keeping the dough and butter cool is the key to success when making puff pastry. Take your time when rolling but be sure to return the dough to the refrigerator if you're at all worried that it's getting too warm.*

THE METHOD
PASTRY CREAM

Learn how to best combine hot milk or cream and egg yolks to make rich and smooth pastry cream.

1 HEAT MILK OR CREAM
After heating milk or cream (one recipe uses sugar with the dairy), whisk egg yolks, cornstarch or flour, and sugar together.

2 TEMPER EGG YOLKS
Temper yolks by gradually pouring some hot milk mixture over them while whisking constantly. Add remaining hot milk to yolk mixture in 3 or 4 batches, whisking constantly until combined.

3 RETURN TO SAUCEPAN
Pour mixture back into saucepan and cook, whisking vigorously, until thickened.

4 WHISK IN BUTTER AND VANILLA
Off heat, whisk in butter and vanilla extract (one recipe uses a vanilla bean) until butter is melted and fully incorporated.

5 COVER AND CHILL
Pour pastry cream into bowl, press plastic wrap or greased parchment directly on surface, and chill.

CHOUX AU CRAQUELIN

Makes: 24

Total Time: 1¾ hours, plus 3 hours chilling and cooling

RECIPE OVERVIEW For choux au craquelin (airy, crispy shells encasing smooth, lush pastry cream), begin by making the pastry cream, which you'll reinforce with a little extra flour so it can be lightened with whipped cream later on. While it chills and sets, mix the craquelin dough—a simple combination of flour, butter, and sugar—and roll it into a thin sheet from which you'll cut 24 disks before freezing the dough. Incorporating both milk and water ensures that the puffs (choux) bake up crisp and brown nicely, and using the food processor makes it easy to incorporate eggs into the choux paste. Before sliding the mounds of batter into the oven, top them with slim disks of the craquelin dough, which transform into crackly shells as the puffs bake. Slit the baked puffs to release steam before returning them to the turned-off oven for 45 minutes to ensure crispness. You'll need a 2-inch round cutter, a pastry bag, and two pastry tips—one with a ¼-inch round opening and one with a ½-inch round opening. This recipe can be made over two days if you like: Make the pastry cream and craquelin on day 1 and the puffs on day 2.

Pastry Cream

- 2½ cups whole milk, divided
- ⅔ cup (3⅓ ounces) all-purpose flour
- ½ cup (3½ ounces) granulated sugar
- ¼ teaspoon table salt
- 6 large egg yolks
- 4 tablespoons unsalted butter, cut into 4 pieces and chilled
- 1 tablespoon vanilla extract

Craquelin

- 6 tablespoons unsalted butter, softened
- ½ cup packed (3½ ounces) light brown sugar
- ¾ cup (3¾ ounces) all-purpose flour
- Pinch table salt

Choux

- 2 large eggs plus 1 large white
- 6 tablespoons water
- 5 tablespoons unsalted butter, cut into ½-inch pieces
- 2 tablespoons milk
- 1½ teaspoons granulated sugar
- ¼ teaspoon table salt
- ½ cup (2½ ounces) all-purpose flour
- 1 cup heavy cream

1. FOR THE PASTRY CREAM Heat 2 cups milk in medium saucepan over medium heat until just simmering. Meanwhile, whisk flour, sugar, and salt in medium bowl until combined. Add egg yolks and remaining ½ cup milk to flour mixture and whisk until smooth. Remove saucepan from heat and, whisking constantly, slowly add ½ cup milk to yolk mixture to temper. Whisking constantly, add tempered yolk mixture to milk in saucepan.

A Customizable Treat

Once you're comfortable with making choux au craquelin, you can customize them to your taste. If you're short on time, skip the pastry cream and fill the puffs with whipped cream or ice cream. Are you a mocha fan? Add instant espresso powder to the pastry cream and cocoa powder to the craquelin dough. Need to match a color theme for a special event? Substitute granulated sugar for the brown sugar in the craquelin and add a bit of food coloring.

2. Return saucepan to medium heat and cook, whisking constantly, until mixture thickens slightly, about 1 minute. Reduce heat to medium-low and continue to simmer, whisking constantly, for 8 minutes. Increase heat to medium and cook, whisking vigorously, until very thick (mixture dripped from whisk should mound on surface), 1 to 2 minutes. Off heat, whisk in butter and vanilla until butter is melted and incorporated. Transfer to wide bowl. Press lightly greased parchment paper directly on surface and refrigerate until set, at least 2 hours or up to 24 hours.

3. FOR THE CRAQUELIN Mix butter and sugar in medium bowl until combined. Mix in flour and salt. Transfer mixture to large sheet of parchment and press into 6-inch square. Cover with second piece of parchment and roll dough into 13 by 9-inch rectangle (it's fine to trim and patch dough to achieve correct dimensions). Remove top piece of parchment and use 2-inch round cutter to cut 24 circles. Leaving circles and trim in place, replace top parchment and transfer to rimless baking sheet. Freeze until firm, at least 30 minutes or up to 2 days.

4. FOR THE CHOUX Adjust oven rack to middle position and heat oven to 400 degrees. Spray rimmed baking sheet with vegetable oil spray and dust lightly and evenly with flour, discarding any excess. Using 2-inch round cutter, mark 24 circles on sheet. Fit pastry bag with ½-inch round tip. Beat eggs and white together in 2-cup liquid measuring cup.

5. Bring water, butter, milk, sugar, and salt to boil in small saucepan over medium heat, stirring occasionally. Off heat, stir in flour until incorporated. Return saucepan to low heat and cook, stirring constantly and using smearing motion, until mixture looks like shiny, wet sand, about 3 minutes (mixture should register between 175 and 180 degrees).

6. Immediately transfer hot mixture to food processor and process for 10 seconds to cool slightly. With processor running, add beaten eggs in steady stream and process until incorporated, about 30 seconds. Scrape down sides of bowl and continue to process until smooth, thick, sticky paste forms, about 30 seconds longer.

7. Fill pastry bag with warm mixture and pipe into 1½-inch-wide mounds on prepared sheet, using circles as guide. Using small, thin spatula, transfer 1 frozen craquelin disk to top of each mound. Bake for 15 minutes; then, without opening oven door, reduce oven temperature to 350 degrees and continue to bake until golden brown and firm, 7 to 10 minutes longer.

8. Remove sheet from oven and cut ¾-inch slit into side of each pastry with paring knife to release steam. Return pastries to oven, turn off oven, and prop open oven door with handle of wooden spoon. Let pastries dry until center is mostly dry and surface is crisp, about 45 minutes. Transfer pastries to wire rack and let cool completely.

Making Choux au Craquelin

You can prepare these puffs over two days: Make the pastry cream and craquelin on day 1 and the puffs on day 2.

COOK
Cook pastry cream and chill for at least 2 hours or up to 24 hours.

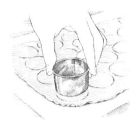

MAKE AND MARK
Make craquelin; roll out and cut 24 circles; freeze for at least 30 minutes. Mark 24 circles on oiled, floured baking sheet using 2-inch round cutter.

COOK
Cook choux paste and pipe into mounds on sheet, using circles as guide.

TOP
Top choux mounds with frozen craquelin disks.

BAKE
Bake pastries (reduce temperature for last 10 minutes), then pierce and allow to dry.

WHIP AND FILL
Whip cream in large bowl and fold in pastry cream to create filling. Pipe filling into buns until cream just starts to appear around opening.

9. **TO SERVE** Fit pastry bag with ¼-inch round tip. In large bowl, whisk cream to stiff peaks. Gently whisk pastry cream until smooth. Fold pastry cream into whipped cream until combined. Transfer one-third of mixture to pastry bag. To fill choux buns, insert pastry tip ¾ inch into opening and squeeze gently until cream just starts to appear around opening, about 2 tablespoons cream per bun. Refill bag as needed. Serve. (Choux are best eaten up to 2 hours after filling. Leftovers can be refrigerated for up to 3 days but will soften over time.)

Variations
COLORFUL CHOUX AU CRAQUELIN
Substitute granulated sugar for brown sugar in craquelin. Add gel or paste food coloring to craquelin dough until desired color is achieved.

MOCHA CHOUX AU CRAQUELIN
Add 5 teaspoons instant espresso powder to hot milk for pastry cream. Decrease flour in craquelin to ⅔ cup and add 1 tablespoon unsweetened cocoa powder.

KEYS TO SUCCESS

- **Extra flour in the pastry cream:** A stiff pastry cream lets you fold in whipped cream for lightness without making the filling too loose.

- **Cut the puffs:** It's important to make a slit in each baked puff and return them to the oven to dry out, so they maintain their shape and aren't soggy.

- **Use a food processor:** It makes adding the eggs to the choux batter simple and quick.

What Craquelin Does for Cream Puffs

A simple craquelin layer not only adds sweetness and lasting crunch to your cream puffs but also controls the expansion of the choux in the oven so that it's more uniformly rounded instead of whimsically shaped. Here's how it works: The craquelin consists of a buttery dough that's cut into disks and frozen before being placed atop the mounds of choux. In the oven, as the craquelin thaws, it blankets the choux, helping smooth out its contours. At the same time, the butter (of which there is a large amount in the dough) melts, creating fissures in the craquelin that widen as the choux expands.

NAPOLEONS
Makes: 8 napoleons
Total Time: 1½ hours, plus 1 hour cooling

RECIPE OVERVIEW You can make perfectly satisfactory napoleons using store-bought puff pastry—or you can make satisfyingly perfect ones with homemade. Puff pastry dough takes time but the process is straightforward and the results are worth it. To achieve level puff pastry layers that can be spread with pastry cream and stacked, you'll roll the dough into an even layer, poke holes in it with a fork, and bake it topped with a weighted sheet pan. Cutting the baked pastry into rectangles and assembling the napoleons individually produces neat, professional results, with no squishing. You'll decorate the tops using two quick glazes to make the classic, simple-yet-stunning design. The napoleons are best enjoyed soon after assembling; they will hold for up to two days but the pastry will not be as crisp.

Puff Pastry
- ½ recipe Puff Pastry Dough (recipe follows)

Chocolate Glaze
- 1 ounce bittersweet or semisweet chocolate, chopped fine
- 2 tablespoons milk
- ¾ cup (3 ounces) confectioners' sugar

Vanilla Glaze
- ¼ cup (1 ounce) confectioners' sugar
- 1½ teaspoons milk
- ⅛ teaspoon vanilla extract

- 1 recipe Vanilla Pastry Cream (page 606)

1. FOR THE PUFF PASTRY Adjust oven rack to middle position and heat oven to 325 degrees. Roll dough into 16 by 12-inch rectangle, about ¼ inch thick, between 2 lightly floured sheets of parchment paper. Remove top sheet of parchment and prick pastry with fork every 2 inches.

2. Replace top sheet of parchment and slide dough onto rimmed baking sheet. Place second rimmed baking sheet on top of dough and weight baking sheet with large ovensafe dish. Bake pastry until cooked through and lightly golden, 50 minutes to 1 hour, rotating baking sheet halfway through baking. Remove weight, top baking sheet, and top sheet of parchment and continue to bake pastry until golden brown, 5 to 10 minutes longer. Let pastry cool completely on baking sheet, about 1 hour.

3. Cut pastry in half lengthwise with serrated knife. Trim edges to make them straight. Cut each pastry half crosswise into 3 rectangles, then cut each rectangle crosswise into 3 small rectangles (you will have 18 rectangles). (Pastry can be wrapped tightly in plastic wrap and stored at room temperature for up to 1 day.)

4. FOR THE CHOCOLATE GLAZE Microwave chocolate at 50 percent power for 15 seconds; stir chocolate, add milk, and continue heating for 10 seconds; stir until smooth. Whisk in confectioners' sugar until smooth.

5. FOR THE VANILLA GLAZE Whisk sugar, milk, and vanilla together in bowl until smooth.

6. Spread chocolate glaze evenly over top of 6 rectangles of pastry and lay them on wire rack set over sheet of parchment (for easy cleanup). Drizzle thin stream of vanilla glaze crosswise over chocolate glaze. Run tip of small knife or toothpick lengthwise through icing to make design. Let icing set, about 20 minutes. Spread about 2½ tablespoons of pastry cream evenly over 6 more rectangles of pastry. Gently top each with one of remaining 6 rectangles and spread remaining pastry cream evenly over tops. Top with glazed rectangles. Serve.

PUFF PASTRY DOUGH

Makes: 2 pounds
Total Time: 45 minutes, plus 9 hours chilling

Puff pastry gets its superflaky, buttery layers from a process called lamination, also known as turning or folding. The multiple turnings create paper-thin sheets of butter, and when the dough is baked, the moisture in the butter evaporates into steam, causing the dough to puff and separate into flaky layers. You'll make the dough in a food processor for even, quick distribution and then chill it to allow it to relax for easier rolling. While the dough chills, you'll make a butter square by gently pounding butter sticks into an even layer. Chill the square so the butter doesn't melt when combined with the dough. You'll need half of this dough (about 1 pound) to make the napoleons.

Making Puff Pastry

FORM BUTTER BLOCK
Lay butter sticks side by side on parchment. Sprinkle flour over butter and cover with second sheet of parchment.

ROLL AND CHILL
Using rolling pin, gently pound flour into butter until softened. Roll into 8-inch square. Wrap and refrigerate for 1 hour.

PLACE ON DOUGH
Roll chilled dough into 13½-inch square on lightly floured counter. Place chilled butter square diagonally in center of dough.

WRAP IT UP
Fold corners of dough square over butter square so that corners meet in middle and pinch dough seams to seal.

FLATTEN SQUARE
Using rolling pin, gently tap dough from center outward until square becomes larger and butter begins to soften. Gently roll dough into 14-inch square, dusting with flour as needed.

FOLD IN THIRDS
Fold dough into thirds like business letter, then fold rectangle into thirds to form square. Wrap dough in plastic and refrigerate for 2 hours.

ROLL AND REPEAT
Repeat rolling and folding twice and let folded square of dough rest in refrigerator for 2 more hours.

Divide the dough after it has chilled in step 6; use one piece of dough as directed and refrigerate the rest for up to two days or freeze, wrapped in plastic wrap and then aluminum foil, for up to one month. A half recipe of this homemade dough is equal to two sheets of frozen puff pastry.

Dough

3	cups (15 ounces) all-purpose flour
1½	tablespoons sugar
1½	teaspoons table salt
2	teaspoons lemon juice
1	cup ice water, divided

Butter Square

24	tablespoons (3 sticks) unsalted butter, chilled
2	tablespoons all-purpose flour

1. **FOR THE DOUGH** Process flour, sugar, and salt in food processor until combined, about 5 seconds. With processor running, add lemon juice, followed by ¾ cup water, in slow steady stream. Add remaining ¼ cup water as needed, 1 tablespoon at a time, until dough comes together and no floury bits remain.

2. Turn dough onto sheet of plastic wrap and flatten into 6-inch square. Wrap tightly in plastic and refrigerate for 1 hour.

3. **FOR THE BUTTER SQUARE** Lay butter sticks side by side on sheet of parchment paper. Sprinkle flour over butter and cover with second sheet of parchment. Gently pound butter with rolling pin until butter is softened and flour is fully incorporated, then roll it into 8-inch square. Wrap butter square in plastic and refrigerate until chilled, about 1 hour.

4. Roll chilled dough into 13½-inch square on lightly floured counter. Place chilled butter square diagonally in center of dough. Fold corners of dough up over butter square so that corners meet in middle and pinch dough seams to seal.

5. Using rolling pin, gently tap dough, starting from center and working outward, until square becomes larger and butter begins to soften. Gently roll dough into 14-inch square, dusting with extra flour as needed to prevent sticking. Fold dough into thirds like business letter, then fold rectangle in thirds to form square. Wrap dough in plastic and let rest in refrigerator for 2 hours.

6. Repeat step 5 twice and let folded square of dough rest in refrigerator for 2 hours more before using.

VANILLA PASTRY CREAM

Makes: about 2 cups
Total Time: 15 minutes, plus 3 hours chilling
You can substitute 1½ teaspoons of vanilla extract for the vanilla bean; add the extract with the butter in step 2.

½	vanilla bean
2	cups half-and-half
½	cup (3½ ounces) sugar, divided
	Pinch table salt
5	large egg yolks
3	tablespoons cornstarch
4	tablespoons unsalted butter, cut into 4 pieces

1. Cut vanilla bean in half lengthwise. Using tip of paring knife, scrape out seeds. Bring vanilla bean and seeds, half-and-half, 6 tablespoons sugar, and salt to simmer in medium saucepan over medium-high heat, stirring occasionally.

2. Meanwhile, whisk egg yolks, cornstarch, and remaining 2 tablespoons sugar together in medium bowl until smooth. Slowly whisk 1 cup simmering half-and-half mixture into egg mixture to temper, then slowly whisk tempered egg mixture into remaining half-and-half mixture. Reduce heat to medium and cook, stirring constantly, until pastry cream is thickened and few bubbles burst on surface, about 30 seconds. Off heat, whisk in butter.

3. Remove vanilla bean and transfer pastry cream to clean bowl. Lay plastic wrap directly on surface of pastry cream and refrigerate until cold and set, about 3 hours. (Pastry cream can be refrigerated for up to 3 days.)

Assembling Napoleons

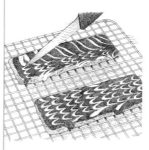

GLAZE

Spread chocolate glaze evenly over top of 6 rectangles, then drizzle thin stream of vanilla glaze crosswise over chocolate glaze. Run tip of small knife or toothpick lengthwise through icing to make design.

STACK

After layering remaining rectangles of pastry with pastry cream to make 6 individual portions, top each portion with glazed pastry rectangle.

BEST PRACTICES FOR WHIPPING CREAM BY HAND

Our Choux au Craquelin recipe (page 602) requires whipping just 1 cup of cream, which hardly warrants dragging out the stand mixer. But whipping cream by hand can be a real chore (and make a mess) if everything isn't just so. Follow these simple guidelines and you may decide to take the manual route more often.

Choose a really big bowl Use a much bigger bowl than you think you'll need (at least eight times the volume of the unwhipped cream); this will give you the freedom to whisk with abandon. Choose stainless steel or glass, which stay colder than plastic does.

Coldness counts The colder the cream, the faster it whips. Chill the cream—and the bowl, too—in the freezer until it's thoroughly chilled. (If the bowl doesn't fit, chill it in the fridge.)

Whisk side to side Whisking from side to side is easier to execute quickly and aggressively than stirring or beating. It's also more effective because it causes more shear force to be applied to the liquid.

Use your sink Transfer your bowl/ cream/whisk setup to the sink; it's easier to whisk at this lower angle, and the sides of the sink will catch any errant drops.

PASTRY BAG TIPS AND TRICKS

A pastry bag fitted with the appropriate-size tip is the most efficient tool for piping uniformly sized mounds of dough for our Choux au Craquelin (page 602) (the mocha variation is pictured below) and filling the baked puffs with cream. If you're new to working with a pastry bag, these tips can help you pipe like a pro—as well as reduce waste.

Prevent leaks Place pastry tip in bag. Twist bag near tip and gently press twisted portion into tip to create temporary barrier. (When ready to pipe, pull on tip to release barrier.)

Fill efficiently Place pastry bag in tall container and fold down sides. Fill halfway (multiple smaller loads, versus a single big load, are easier to manage, especially if you have small hands).

Do the twist Twist upper half of bag closed to push contents down toward tip; twisted upper half will allow you to continue exerting pressure on filling to pipe.

Remove air bubbles Before piping in earnest, press out small amount of filling on parchment paper or other surface; this eliminates air bubbles that can cause filling to spurt unevenly.

Get every last bit When bag is almost empty, lay bag on side and use plastic bowl scraper or credit card (avoid metal tool, since it can tear bag) on outside of bag to press contents toward tip.

Clean and reuse As long as it isn't punctured, even a disposable pastry bag can be reused. To clean, turn bag inside out and scrub gently with warm, soapy water; stand up to air-dry.

SHOWSTOPPING LAYER CAKES

BRIDGET LANCASTER

Nothing says "celebration" quite like a majestic layer cake. Here you'll learn to make four-layer beauties: a buttery coconut cake with Swiss meringue buttercream, a blackberry-filled lemon cake with mascarpone buttercream, and a nutty chocolate-covered dacquoise filled with rich German buttercream. In addition to their multiple layers and creamy frostings, the cakes in this course offer an interplay of textures: springy chiffon, crunchy toasted coconut, juicy fruit jam, crisp and airy meringue.

BRIDGET'S PRO TIP: *Buy a sturdy rotating cake stand. Place each layer on the stand, bend so that your eyes are at the same level as the cake, and rotate to see if the cake looks crooked before and after icing at each step. If you're new to icing cakes, after filling the layers with icing, frost the outside with just enough icing to trap any crumbs. Pop the cake in the fridge for 30 minutes or so, then frost with the remaining icing.*

COCONUT LAYER CAKE

Serves: 10 to 12
Total Time: 2 hours, plus 20 minutes cooling

RECIPE OVERVIEW This coconut cake is an elegant four-layer affair featuring moist, tender cake with a delicate, yielding crumb and silky, gently sweetened frosting covered with a deep drift of downy coconut. You'll use low-protein cake flour for cake layers with a supertender crumb. Using cream of coconut as the liquid in the batter yields more consistent results and fuller coconut flavor than coconut milk. For a light yet rich frosting, make an egg white–based buttercream and flavor it with more coconut extract and cream of coconut. A woolly coating of toasted shredded coconut provides textural interest and delivers a final dose of flavor. Be sure to use cream of coconut (such as Coco López) and not coconut milk here. One 15-ounce can of cream of coconut is enough for both the cake and the frosting.

Cake

- 1 large egg plus 5 large whites
- ¾ cup cream of coconut
- ¼ cup water
- 1 teaspoon coconut extract
- 1 teaspoon vanilla extract
- 2¼ cups (9 ounces) cake flour
- 1 cup (7 ounces) sugar
- 1 tablespoon baking powder

¾ teaspoon table salt
 12 tablespoons unsalted butter, cut into
    12 pieces and softened
  2 cups (6 ounces) sweetened shredded coconut

Frosting
  4 large egg whites
  1 cup (7 ounces) sugar
    Pinch table salt
  1 pound (4 sticks) unsalted butter, each stick
    cut into 6 pieces and softened
  ¼ cup cream of coconut
  1 teaspoon coconut extract
  1 teaspoon vanilla extract

1. FOR THE CAKE Adjust oven rack to lower-middle position and heat oven to 325 degrees. Grease two 9-inch round cake pans, line with parchment paper, grease parchment, and flour pans. Whisk egg and whites together in 4-cup liquid measuring cup. Whisk in cream of coconut, water, coconut extract, and vanilla.

2. Using stand mixer fitted with paddle, mix flour, sugar, baking powder, and salt on low speed until combined. Add butter, 1 piece at a time, until only pea-size pieces remain, about 1 minute. Add half of egg mixture, increase speed to medium-high, and beat until light and fluffy, about 1 minute. Reduce speed to medium-low, add remaining egg mixture, and beat until incorporated, about 30 seconds. Give batter final stir by hand.

3. Divide batter evenly between prepared pans and smooth tops with rubber spatula. Gently tap pans on counter to settle batter. Bake until toothpick inserted in center comes out clean, about 30 minutes, switching and rotating pans halfway through baking.

4. Let cakes cool in pans on wire rack for 10 minutes. Remove cakes from pans, discarding parchment, and let cool completely on rack, about 2 hours. (Cake layers can be stored at room temperature for up to 24 hours or frozen for up to 1 month; defrost cakes at room temperature.) Meanwhile, spread shredded coconut on rimmed baking sheet and toast in oven until shreds are mix of golden brown and white, 15 to 20 minutes, stirring 2 or 3 times; let cool.

5. FOR THE FROSTING Combine egg whites, sugar, and salt in bowl of stand mixer and set over medium saucepan filled with 1 inch barely simmering water, making sure that water does not touch bottom of bowl. Cook, whisking constantly, until mixture is opaque and registers 120 degrees, about 2 minutes.

6. Remove bowl from heat and transfer to stand mixer fitted with whisk attachment. Whip egg white mixture on high speed until glossy, sticky, and barely warm (80 degrees), about 7 minutes. Reduce speed to medium-high and whip in butter, 1 piece at a time, followed by cream of coconut, coconut extract, and vanilla, scraping down bowl as needed. Continue to whip until combined, about 1 minute.

Assembling Coconut Cake

CUT LAYERS
With long serrated knife, cut both cakes in half horizontally so that each cake forms two layers.

ANCHOR CAKE
Put dab of icing on cardboard round cut just larger than cake. Center one cake layer on round.

FROST LAYERS
Place large blob of icing in center of layer and spread it to edges with icing spatula. Hold spatula at 45-degree angle to cake and drag it across surface to level icing. Repeat with remaining cake layers.

FROST SIDES
To ice sides of cake, scoop up large dab of icing with tip of spatula and spread it on sides with short side-to-side strokes.

ADD TOASTED COCONUT
Sprinkle top of cake with toasted coconut, then press coconut into sides of cake, letting excess fall back onto baking sheet.

CORE TECHNIQUE **Toasting Large Quantities of Coconut**

For toasting small amounts of shredded coconut, we like to use the microwave. But to evenly toast 2 cups or more, we turn to the oven.

USE THE OVEN
After baking cake layers, keep oven on and spread coconut on rimmed baking sheet. Toast until shreds are a mix of golden brown and white, 15 to 20 minutes, stirring 2 or 3 times.

7. Using long serrated knife, cut 1 horizontal line around sides of each layer; then, following scored lines, cut each layer into 2 even layers.

8. Line edges of cake platter with 4 strips of parchment to keep platter clean. Place 1 cake layer on platter. Spread ¾ cup frosting evenly over top, right to edge of cake. Repeat with 2 more cake layers, pressing lightly to adhere and spreading ¾ cup frosting evenly over each layer. Top with remaining cake layer and spread remaining frosting evenly over top and sides of cake. Sprinkle top of cake evenly with toasted coconut, then gently press remaining toasted coconut onto sides. Carefully remove parchment strips before serving. (Frosted cake can be refrigerated for up to 24 hours; bring to room temperature before serving.)

KEYS TO SUCCESS

- **Add one yolk:** A whole egg along with five whites gives the cake richness without changing its snow-white color.
- **Make meringue:** Meringue buttercream is silky and less sweet than seven-minute frosting.

Cream of Coconut Versus Coconut Cream

Coconut cream is made using the same method as coconut milk: Shredded coconut meat is steeped in either warm milk or water, the meat is pressed or mashed to release as much liquid as possible, and the mixture is strained. The difference is that while coconut milk uses equal amounts of coconut meat and liquid, coconut cream uses a 4:1 ratio of coconut meat to liquid.

In our Coconut Layer Cake we use another product: cream of coconut. Cream of coconut is a sweetened product based on coconut milk that also contains thickeners and emulsifiers. Cream of coconut and coconut cream are not interchangeable in recipes, as the former is heavily sweetened and the latter is not. In our cake, cream of coconut was the most consistent product, perhaps because there are fewer brands (Coco López being the best known). To accommodate this sweeter product, we cut back on the sugar in our cake recipe. Cakes made with cream of coconut baked up beautifully, featuring appealing burnished exteriors that coconut milk versions lacked, and they had more pronounced coconut flavor as well.

BLACKBERRY-MASCARPONE LEMON CAKE

Serves: 12 to 16
Total Time: 3¼ hours, plus 2 hours 20 minutes cooling and chilling

RECIPE OVERVIEW This strikingly beautiful cake features layers of contrasting flavors and textures: tart lemon, sweet blackberries, and a silky rich mascarpone whipped cream. The lemon chiffon cake has a light, fluffy texture but enough structure to stand four layers tall. For the frosting, you'll start by making an easy, vibrantly flavored blackberry jam. Mascarpone cream is prone to separating when beaten; replacing half of the mascarpone with tangy cream cheese (which has stabilizers to ensure a creamy texture) makes the frosting foolproof. A little gelatin adds structure to the whipped cream, giving the frosting a lighter texture that is still stable enough to be stacked between the cake layers. For a modern look, scrape a thin veil of frosting over the sides of the cake so the lovely layers peek through.

Blackberry Jam
- 1 pound (3¼ cups) blackberries, plus extra for garnish
- 1 cup (7 ounces) granulated sugar

Cake
- 2½ cups (10 ounces) cake flour
- 2 cups (14 ounces) granulated sugar
- 1 tablespoon baking powder
- ½ teaspoon table salt
- 10 large eggs (4 whole, 6 separated), room temperature
- 12 tablespoons unsalted butter, melted and cooled
- ¼ cup water
- 2 teaspoons grated lemon zest plus ¼ cup juice (2 lemons)
- 4 teaspoons vanilla extract

Mascarpone Frosting
- 1 teaspoon unflavored gelatin
- 2 tablespoons water
- 8 ounces (1 cup) mascarpone cheese, room temperature
- 8 ounces cream cheese, softened
- ¼ cup (1 ounce) confectioners' sugar
- 1 teaspoon vanilla extract
- ⅛ teaspoon table salt
- 2 cups heavy cream, chilled

1. **FOR THE BLACKBERRY JAM** Process blackberries in food processor until smooth, about 1 minute; transfer to large saucepan. Stir sugar into blackberries and bring to boil over medium-high heat. Boil mixture, stirring often and adjusting heat as needed, until thickened and measures 1½ cups, 15 to 20 minutes. Transfer jam to bowl and let cool completely. (Jam can be refrigerated for up to 1 week; stir to loosen and bring to room temperature before using.)

2. FOR THE CAKE Adjust oven rack to lower-middle position and heat oven to 325 degrees. Lightly grease two 8-inch round cake pans, line with parchment paper, grease parchment, and flour pans. Whisk 1¼ cups flour, ¾ cup sugar, 1½ teaspoons baking powder, and ¼ teaspoon salt together in large bowl. Whisk in 2 eggs and 3 yolks, 6 tablespoons butter, 2 tablespoons water, 1 teaspoon lemon zest and 2 tablespoons juice, and 2 teaspoons vanilla until smooth.

3. Using stand mixer fitted with whisk attachment, whip 3 egg whites on medium-low speed until foamy, about 1 minute. Increase speed to medium-high and whip whites to soft, billowy mounds, about 1 minute. Gradually add ¼ cup sugar and whip until glossy, soft peaks form, 1 to 2 minutes. Whisk one-third of whites into batter to lighten. Using rubber spatula, gently fold remaining whites into batter in 2 batches until no white streaks remain.

4. Divide batter evenly between prepared pans and smooth tops with rubber spatula. Bake until toothpick inserted in center comes out clean, 30 to 40 minutes, switching and rotating pans halfway through baking.

5. Let cakes cool in pans on wire rack for 10 minutes. Remove cakes from pans, discarding parchment, and let cool completely on rack, about 2 hours. Repeat steps 2 through 5 with remaining cake ingredients to make two more cake layers.

6. **FOR THE MASCARPONE FROSTING** Sprinkle gelatin over water in bowl and let sit until gelatin softens, about 5 minutes. Microwave mixture in 5-second increments until gelatin is dissolved and liquefied.

7. Using clean, dry mixer bowl and whisk attachment, whip mascarpone, cream cheese, sugar, vanilla, and salt on medium speed until light and fluffy, about 30 seconds, scraping down bowl as needed; transfer to large bowl. Using clean, dry mixer bowl and whisk attachment, whip cream on medium-low speed until foamy, about 1 minute. Increase speed to high and whip until soft peaks just begin to form, about 1 minute, scraping down bowl as needed. Slowly pour in gelatin mixture, and continue to beat until stiff peaks form, about 1 minute. Using rubber spatula, stir one-third of whipped cream into mascarpone mixture to lighten; gently fold remaining whipped cream into mixture in 2 batches. Stir room temperature blackberry jam to loosen, then gently fold jam into mascarpone mixture until combined. Refrigerate frosting for at least 20 minutes or up to 24 hours before using.

8. Line edges of cake platter with 4 strips of parchment to keep platter clean and place small dab of frosting in center of platter to anchor cake. Place 1 cake layer on platter. Spread 1 cup frosting evenly over top, right to edge of cake. Repeat with 2 more cake layers, pressing lightly to adhere and spreading 1 cup frosting evenly over each layer. Top with remaining cake layer and spread 1½ cups frosting evenly over top. Spread remaining frosting evenly over sides of cake to cover with thin coat of frosting. Run edge of offset spatula around cake sides to create sheer veil of frosting. (Cake sides should still be visible.) Refrigerate cake for 20 minutes. Garnish with blackberries and carefully remove parchment strips before serving. (Cake can be refrigerated for up to 24 hours; bring to room temperature before serving.)

KEYS TO SUCCESS

- **Add cream cheese:** Mascarpone cheese on its own is prone to breaking; adding more stable cream cheese keeps the filling smooth.
- **Cool the pans:** Let the cake pans cool completely before repeating baking with more batter.

Naked Cakes

One of the biggest trends in cake making is the naked cake—layer cakes with sheer coatings or completely bare sides. At once elegant and rustic, these cakes showcase the juxtaposition of layer and filling to beautiful effect. If you're filling a cake and leaving the sides unfrosted, you'll want to be a bit more graceful in your filling of the cakes, as it will show through the sides. Another option is to scrape frosting along the sides of the cake— just enough to give the cake a thin veil but not so much that you can't see the stacked layers. We use this technique in our Blackberry-Mascarpone Lemon Cake.

Frosting Blackberry-Mascarpone Lemon Cake

SPREAD TOP AND SIDES
After filling cake, spread 1½ cups frosting over top. Spread remaining frosting evenly over sides of cake to cover with thin coat of frosting.

SMOOTH SIDES
Run edge of offset spatula around cake sides to create sheer veil of frosting.

CHOCOLATE-ESPRESSO DACQUOISE

Serves: 10 to 12
Total Time: 3¾ hours, plus 1½ hours cooling and 7 hours chilling

RECIPE OVERVIEW Dacquoise might just be the best and most impressive dessert you ever make. It is a multi-layered showpiece of crisp meringue and rich, silky buttercream coated in a glossy chocolate ganache. It's not an easy dessert to pull off, but we've reworked each component to make it approachable. Instead of individually piped layers of meringue, you'll make a single sheet and bake it at a slightly higher temperature to shorten the usual 4-plus hours of oven time. Instead of a Swiss or French buttercream made with a hot sugar syrup, you'll make a German buttercream: With equal parts pastry cream and butter, this option requires no hot syrup and uses up the egg yolks left over from the meringue. The components in this recipe can easily be prepared in advance. Use a rimless baking sheet or an overturned rimmed baking sheet to bake the meringue. Instant coffee may be substituted for the espresso powder. To skin the hazelnuts, simply place the warm toasted nuts in a clean dish towel and rub gently.

Meringue

- ¾ cup blanched sliced almonds, toasted
- ½ cup hazelnuts, toasted and skinned
- 1 tablespoon cornstarch
- ⅛ teaspoon table salt
- 1 cup (7 ounces) sugar, divided
- 4 large egg whites, room temperature
- ¼ teaspoon cream of tartar

Buttercream

- ¾ cup whole milk
- 4 large egg yolks
- ⅓ cup (2⅓ ounces) sugar
- 1½ teaspoons cornstarch
- ¼ teaspoon table salt
- 2 tablespoons amaretto or water
- 1½ tablespoons instant espresso powder
- 16 tablespoons unsalted butter, softened

Ganache

- 6 ounces bittersweet chocolate, chopped fine
- ¾ cup heavy cream
- 2 teaspoons corn syrup
- 12 whole hazelnuts, toasted and skinned
- 1 cup blanched sliced almonds, toasted

1. **FOR THE MERINGUE** Adjust oven rack to middle position and heat oven to 250 degrees. Using ruler and pencil, draw 13 by 10½-inch rectangle on piece of parchment paper. Grease baking sheet and place parchment on it, marked side down.

2. Process almonds, hazelnuts, cornstarch, and salt in food processor until nuts are finely ground, 15 to 20 seconds. Add ½ cup sugar and pulse to combine, 1 to 2 pulses.

3. Using stand mixer fitted with whisk, whip egg whites and cream of tartar on medium-low speed until foamy, about 1 minute. Increase speed to medium-high and whip whites to soft, billowy mounds, about 1 minute. With mixer running at medium-high speed, slowly add remaining ½ cup sugar and continue to whip until glossy, stiff peaks form, 2 to 3 minutes. Fold nut mixture into egg whites in 2 batches.

Making Meringue for Dacquoise

DRAW TEMPLATE
Draw 13 by 10½-inch rectangle on parchment. Set on greased baking sheet.

PROCESS NUTS
Process nuts, cornstarch, and salt in food processor. Pulse in half of sugar.

MAKE MERINGUE
Using stand mixer and whisk, whip egg whites and cream of tartar. Add remaining sugar and continue to whip until glossy, stiff peaks form. Fold nut mixture into egg whites in 2 batches.

SPREAD AND MIST
Spread meringue evenly into rectangle on parchment. Evenly mist surface of meringue with water until glistening.

BAKE AND COOL
Bake for 1½ hours. Turn off oven and let meringue cool in oven for 1½ hours. Remove from oven and let cool completely, about 10 minutes.

With offset spatula, spread meringue evenly into 13 by 10½-inch rectangle on parchment, using lines on parchment as guide. Using spray bottle, evenly mist surface of meringue with water until glistening. Bake for 1½ hours. Turn off oven and allow meringue to cool in oven for 1½ hours. (Do not open oven during baking and cooling.) Remove from oven and let cool to room temperature, about 10 minutes. (Cooled meringue can be kept at room temperature, tightly wrapped in plastic wrap, for up to 2 days.)

4. FOR THE BUTTERCREAM Heat milk in small saucepan over medium heat until just simmering. Meanwhile, whisk yolks, sugar, cornstarch, and salt in bowl until smooth. Remove milk from heat and, whisking constantly, add half of milk to yolk mixture to temper. Whisking constantly, return tempered yolk mixture to remaining milk in saucepan. Return saucepan to medium heat and cook, whisking constantly, until mixture is bubbling and thickens to consistency of warm pudding, 3 to 5 minutes. Transfer pastry cream to bowl. Cover and refrigerate until set, at least 2 hours or up to 24 hours. Before using, warm gently to room temperature in microwave at 50 percent power, stirring every 10 seconds.

5. Stir together amaretto and espresso powder; set aside. Using stand mixer fitted with paddle, beat butter at medium speed until smooth and light, 3 to 4 minutes. Add pastry cream in 3 batches, beating for 30 seconds after each addition. Add amaretto mixture and continue to beat until light and fluffy, about 5 minutes longer, scraping down bowl thoroughly halfway through mixing.

6. FOR THE GANACHE Place chocolate in heatproof bowl. Bring cream and corn syrup to simmer in small saucepan over medium heat. Pour cream mixture over chocolate and let stand for 1 minute. Stir mixture until smooth. Set aside to cool until chocolate mounds slightly when dripped from spoon, about 5 minutes.

7. Carefully invert meringue and peel off parchment. Reinvert meringue and place on cutting board. Using serrated knife and gentle, repeated scoring motion, trim edges of meringue to form 12 by 10-inch rectangle. Discard trimmings. With long side of rectangle parallel to counter, use ruler to mark both long edges of meringue at 3-inch intervals. Using serrated knife, score surface of meringue by drawing knife toward you from mark on top edge to corresponding mark on bottom edge. Repeat scoring until meringue is fully cut through. Repeat until you have four 10 by 3-inch rectangles. (If any rectangles break during cutting, use them as middle layers.)

8. Place 3 rectangles on wire rack set in rimmed baking sheet. Using offset spatula, spread ¼ cup ganache evenly over surface of each meringue. Refrigerate until ganache is firm, about 15 minutes. Set aside remaining ganache.

9. Using offset spatula, spread top of remaining rectangle with ½ cup buttercream; place on wire rack with ganache-coated meringues. Invert 1 ganache-coated meringue, place on top of buttercream, and press gently to level. Repeat, spreading meringue with ½ cup buttercream and topping with inverted ganache-coated meringue. Spread top with buttercream. Invert final ganache-coated meringue on top of cake. Use 1 hand to steady top of cake and spread half of remaining buttercream to lightly coat sides of cake, then use remaining buttercream to coat top of cake. Smooth until cake resembles box. Refrigerate until buttercream is firm, about 2 hours. (Once buttercream is firm, assembled cake may be wrapped tightly in plastic and refrigerated for up to 2 days.)

10. Warm remaining ganache in heatproof bowl set over barely simmering water, stirring occasionally, until mixture is very fluid but not hot. Keeping assembled cake on wire rack, pour ganache over top of cake. Using offset spatula, spread ganache in thin, even layer over top of cake, letting excess flow down sides. Spread ganache over sides in thin layer (top must be completely covered, but some small gaps on sides are OK).

11. Garnish top of cake with hazelnuts. Holding bottom of cake with 1 hand, gently press almonds onto sides with other hand. Chill on wire rack, uncovered, for at least 3 hours or up to 12 hours. Transfer to platter. Cut into slices with sharp knife that has been dipped in hot water and wiped dry before each slice. Serve.

KEYS TO SUCCESS

- **Cool pastry cream:** Chill the cream thoroughly but then warm it slightly before mixing it with the softened butter.

- **Easy slicing:** Use a gentle scoring motion with a long serrated knife to cut the delicate meringue.

- **Let it flow:** The rewarmed ganache should be fluid so it easily coats the sides of the cake, but not so hot that it melts the buttercream.

Assembling the Dacquoise

Here's how to assemble the three different components of dacquoise—cooled, baked meringue; buttercream; and ganache—into a dessert that looks like it was made in a professional bakery.

TRIM MERINGUE
Using serrated knife and gentle, repeated scoring motion, trim edges of cooled meringue to form 12 by 10-inch rectangle.

CUT INTO STRIPS
With long side of meringue parallel to counter, mark top and bottom edges at 3-inch intervals. Score surface from top mark to corresponding bottom mark until cut through.

SPREAD GANACHE AND BUTTERCREAM
Place 3 strips on wire rack and spread ¼ cup ganache evenly over each. Refrigerate for 15 minutes. Spread remaining strip with ½ cup buttercream.

LAYER STRIPS
Invert one ganache-coated strip on top of buttercream-coated strip and press gently. Spread top with buttercream. Repeat twice to form 4 layers.

COAT SIDES AND TOP
Lightly coat sides of cake with half of remaining buttercream; coat top with remaining buttercream. Smooth edges and surfaces; refrigerate until firm.

COVER WITH GANACHE AND PLACE NUTS
Pour ganache over cake and spread in thin, even layer, letting excess flow down sides. Spread across sides. Place toasted whole hazelnuts in line on top of cake and gently press sliced almonds onto sides.

COURSE
FROZEN DELIGHTS

CHRISTIE MORRISON

Ice cream and other frozen desserts often have deceptively simple ingredient lists— just sugar, cream or milk or water, perhaps some egg yolks, maybe fruit or nuts or vanilla. The flavors are often easy to nail but the bigger challenge is texture, and that is largely determined before the mixture sees the inside of the freezer. In this course, you'll make a trio of frozen desserts— a sorbet, a gelato, and a frozen custard— that demonstrate different ways of priming their ingredients to control ice crystallization and produce smooth, stable, and satisfying scoops. (For a delicious and unusual ice cream recipe, see page 599).

CHRISTIE'S PRO TIP: *Ice crystals are the enemy of a smooth frozen dessert. Since managing crystals depends on a fine balance of water, sugar, and (sometimes) fat, it's important to stick to the precise ratios and ingredients in the recipes (i.e., don't opt for skim milk as a way to "lighten" your frozen custard).*

RASPBERRY SORBET

Serves: 8 (makes 1 quart)
Total Time: 1 hour, plus 1 hour steeping, 2 hours cooling, and 6 hours freezing

RECIPE OVERVIEW To make a light, refreshing raspberry sorbet that is beautifully creamy and smooth, you need to avoid both the jagged, unpleasant ice crystals that often develop in homemade sorbets and the tendency toward crumbly, dull results. Finding the right balance of water and sugar is key; corn syrup helps to create a smooth texture without oversweetening. Freezing a small amount of the base separately and adding it back to the rest helps superchill the mix, making it freeze faster and more smoothly, and keeping ice crystals to a minimum. Added pectin bumps up the raspberries' natural pectin, which gives the sorbet stability both in the freezer and out and helps to keep it from turning into a puddle too quickly at room temperature. Allow the sorbet to sit at room temperature for 5 minutes to soften before serving. Fresh or frozen berries may be used. If using frozen berries, thaw them before proceeding.

  1 cup water
  1 teaspoon Sure-Jell for Less or No Sugar Needed Recipes
  ⅛ teaspoon table salt
1¼ pounds (4 cups) raspberries
  ½ cup (3½ ounces) plus 2 tablespoons sugar
  ¼ cup light corn syrup

  1. Combine water, Sure-Jell, and salt in medium saucepan. Heat over medium-high heat, stirring occasionally, until Sure-Jell is fully dissolved, about 5 minutes. Remove saucepan from heat and allow mixture to cool slightly, about 10 minutes.

2. Process raspberries, sugar, corn syrup, and Sure-Jell mixture in blender or food processor until smooth, about 30 seconds. Strain mixture through fine-mesh strainer, pressing on solids to extract as much liquid as possible. Transfer 1 cup liquid to small bowl and place remaining puree in large bowl. Cover both bowls with plastic wrap. Place large bowl in refrigerator and small bowl in freezer and chill completely, at least 4 hours or up to 24 hours. (Small bowl of base will freeze solid.)

3. Remove bases from refrigerator and freezer. Scrape frozen base from small bowl into large bowl of base. Stir occasionally until frozen base has fully dissolved. Transfer mixture to ice cream maker and churn until mixture has consistency of thick milkshake and color lightens, 15 to 25 minutes.

4. Transfer sorbet to airtight container, pressing firmly to remove any air pockets, and freeze until firm, at least 2 hours. Serve. (Sorbet can be frozen for up to 5 days.)

Variations

RASPBERRY-LIME RICKEY SORBET
Reduce water to ¾ cup. Add 2 teaspoons grated lime zest and ¼ cup lime juice to blender with raspberries.

RASPBERRY-PORT SORBET
Substitute ruby port for water in step 1.

RASPBERRY SORBET WITH GINGER AND MINT
Substitute ginger beer for water in step 1. Add 2-inch piece of peeled and thinly sliced ginger and ¼ cup mint leaves to blender with raspberries. Decrease amount of sugar to ½ cup.

KEYS TO SUCCESS

- **Prechill:** If using a canister-style ice cream maker, be sure to freeze the empty canister for at least 24 hours and preferably 48 hours before churning. For self-refrigerating ice cream makers, prechill the canister by running the machine for five to 10 minutes before pouring in the sorbet mixture.

- **Use the right pectin:** Make certain that you use Sure-Jell engineered for low- or no-sugar recipes (packaged in a pink box) and not regular Sure-Jell (in a yellow box).

- **Right ratio of water to sugar:** Ensures a velvety-smooth sorbet that's easy to scoop

Superchilling Raspberry Sorbet

FREEZE PART OF PUREE
Transfer 1 cup berry puree to small bowl. Cover bowls; freeze small bowl and refrigerate large bowl for at least 4 hours or up to 1 day.

ADD FROZEN PUREE
Scrape frozen base into large bowl. Stir until completely combined. Transfer to ice cream maker and churn until color lightens.

SCIENCE LESSON **Sorbet Science**

The best sorbet has a soft, silky texture that melts in your mouth. The secret to sorbet's texture is sugar. Sugar not only makes sorbet sweet but also makes it smooth and scoopable instead of hard and icy. How? Sugar dissolves in the liquid released from the chopped or processed fruit (which is mostly water). As the fruit-sugar mixture freezes, the dissolved sugar gets in the way of ice crystals forming in the freezing water. This also makes any ice crystals that do form very tiny and helps give your sorbet a smooth texture. In addition, the dissolved sugar lowers the freezing point of the water to below 32 degrees, which makes it more difficult for those ice crystals to form. And fewer ice crystals means more-scoopable sorbet.

PISTACHIO GELATO

Serves: 8 (makes about 1 quart)
Total Time: 1¼ hours, plus 1 hour steeping and 12 hours chilling

RECIPE OVERVIEW Gelato is the Italian version of ice cream, but it's a luxurious, more grown-up cousin. We wanted to make a nutty, elegant treat that was quintessentially Italian, so we turned to buttery pistachios. Many recipes call for pistachio paste, a challenging-to-find specialty Sicilian product made from sweetened ground pistachios and oil. While pistachio paste is generally delicious and intensely flavored, we found that the percentages of sugar and fat varied from brand to brand, which would affect the texture of the gelato. Instead, we turned to raw pistachios.

Grinding the nuts and steeping them in warmed milk and cream released their volatile oils and deeply flavored the base, and straining the solids through cheesecloth ensured a velvety smooth texture. The gelato stayed within the ideal temperature range for up to 6 hours of freezing time, but after that we needed to temper the frozen gelato in the refrigerator until it warmed to the ideal serving temperature of 10 to 15 degrees for a creamy, intensely pistachio-flavored treat, perfect for bringing sunny Sicilian afternoons home. If using a canister-style ice cream maker, be sure to freeze the empty canister for at least 24 hours and preferably for 48 hours before churning. For self-refrigerating ice cream makers, prechill the canister by running the machine for 5 to 10 minutes before pouring in the custard.

2½	cups (11¼ ounces) shelled pistachios
3¾	cups whole milk, divided
¾	cup (5¼ ounces) sugar
⅓	cup heavy cream
⅓	cup light corn syrup
¼	teaspoon table salt
5	teaspoons cornstarch
5	large egg yolks

1. Process pistachios in food processor until finely ground, about 20 seconds. Combine 3½ cups milk, sugar, cream, corn syrup, and salt in large saucepan. Cook, stirring frequently, over medium-high heat until tiny bubbles form around edge of saucepan, 5 to 7 minutes. Off heat, stir in pistachios, cover, and let steep for 1 hour.

2. Line fine-mesh strainer with triple layer of cheesecloth that overhangs edges and set over large bowl. Transfer pistachio mixture to prepared strainer and press to extract as much liquid as possible. Gather sides of cheesecloth around pistachio pulp and gently squeeze remaining liquid into bowl; discard spent pulp.

3. Whisk cornstarch and remaining ¼ cup milk together in small bowl; set aside. Return pistachio-milk mixture to clean saucepan. Whisk in egg yolks until combined. Bring custard to gentle simmer over medium heat and cook, stirring occasionally and scraping bottom of saucepan with rubber spatula, until custard registers 190 degrees, 4 to 6 minutes.

4. Whisk cornstarch mixture to recombine, then whisk into custard. Cook, stirring constantly, until custard thickens, about 30 seconds. Immediately pour custard into bowl and let cool until no longer steaming, about 20 minutes.

5. Cover with plastic wrap and refrigerate for at least 6 hours or up to 24 hours.

6. Whisk custard to recombine, then transfer to ice cream maker and churn until mixture resembles thick soft-serve ice cream and registers 21 degrees, 15 to 30 minutes. Transfer gelato to airtight container, pressing firmly to remove any air pockets, and freeze until firm, at least 6 hours or up to 5 days. Serve. (If frozen for longer than 6 hours, let gelato sit in refrigerator for 1 to 2 hours until it registers 10 to 15 degrees before serving.)

KEYS TO SUCCESS

- **Grind your own:** Using fresh pistachios instead of paste lets you control the sugar and flavor.
- **Corn syrup:** Makes the texture smooth

WHAT CAN GO WRONG

PROBLEM The custard is undercooked and the gelato is not creamy or the custard is overcooked and the eggs curdle.

SOLUTION Using an instant-read thermometer is the easiest way to know that a custard is done. At 190 degrees, the eggs provide the maximum thickening power. A custard may be thick enough to coat a spoon and hold its shape when a line is drawn through it on a spoon, but don't be fooled. These things can happen before the custard has reached 190 degrees.

Ice Cream, Frozen Custard, and Gelato—What's the Difference?

Are frozen custard and gelato simply ice creams by another name? Yes and no. Like ice cream, frozen custard must contain at least 10 percent milk fat (along with milk, cream, sweeteners, flavorings, and so forth). The main difference between them is eggs: While egg yolks are optional in ice cream bases (and occasionally do appear on ingredient lists), they are required in frozen custard, which must contain at least 1.4 percent yolks by weight. The result is that frozen custard is eggier and richer than ice cream.

As for gelato, this Italian ice cream is lower in fat than the ice cream we eat stateside, since it uses mostly milk as opposed to cream. But because the churning process for gelato incorporates less air than for a typical ice cream, gelato tastes creamier. The lower amount of butterfat in gelato allows for more intensity of flavor, as does a slightly higher serving temperature. Gelato is also slightly lower in sugar, often sweetened by the products that define its flavors.

OLD-FASHIONED VANILLA FROZEN CUSTARD

Serves: 8 (makes about 1 quart)
Total Time: 25 minutes, plus 1 to 2 hours chilling and 6 hours freezing

RECIPE OVERVIEW Frozen custard is a rich, supremely creamy frozen treat. While stores use industrial condensers to produce the consistency we know and love, you can achieve supersmooth custard at home without a machine. For the right level of richness, us a combination of heavy cream and whole milk, with a little nonfat dry milk powder added to enhance the dairy flavor. After combining heated cream and egg yolk mixtures, strain the custard to remove any pieces of cooked egg. To achieve the smoothest possible custard, cool the mixture on ice, let it chill in the refrigerator, and then whip it in a stand mixer to add air. This prevents ice crystals from building up and makes the final texture silky and creamy. One teaspoon of vanilla extract can be substituted for the vanilla bean; stir the extract into the strained custard in step 3. Use an instant-read thermometer for the best results.

- 6 large egg yolks
- ¼ cup (1¾ ounces) sugar
- 2 tablespoons nonfat dry milk powder
- 1 cup heavy cream
- ½ cup whole milk
- ⅓ cup light corn syrup
- ⅛ teaspoon salt
- 1 vanilla bean

1. Whisk egg yolks, sugar, and milk powder in bowl until smooth, about 30 seconds; set aside. Combine cream, milk, corn syrup, and salt in medium saucepan. Cut vanilla bean in half lengthwise. Using tip of paring knife, scrape out vanilla seeds and add to cream mixture, along with vanilla bean. Heat cream mixture over medium-high heat, stirring occasionally, until it steams steadily and registers 175 degrees, about 5 minutes. Remove saucepan from heat.

2. Slowly whisk heated cream mixture into yolk mixture to temper. Return cream-yolk mixture to saucepan and cook over medium-low heat, stirring constantly, until mixture thickens and registers 180 degrees, 4 to 6 minutes.

3. Immediately pour custard through fine-mesh strainer set over large bowl; discard vanilla bean. Fill slightly larger bowl with ice and set custard bowl in bowl of ice. Transfer to refrigerator and let chill until custard registers 40 degrees, 1 to 2 hours, stirring occasionally.

4. Transfer chilled custard to stand mixer fitted with whisk and whip on medium-high speed for 3 minutes, or until mixture increases in volume to about 3¾ cups. Pour custard into airtight 1-quart container. Cover and freeze until firm, at least 6 hours, before serving. (Frozen custard is best eaten within 10 days.)

Making Smooth Frozen Custard

TEMPER
Heating the cream mixture before slowly adding it to the cold yolk mixture prevents the eggs from curdling.

STRAIN
Pouring the warm custard through a strainer removes any pieces of cooked egg.

CHILL
Cooling the custard on ice primes it for adding air.

WHIP
Finally, whipping the cooled custard adds air to make the final texture especially creamy.

WHAT CAN GO WRONG

PROBLEM The frozen custard has lots of ice crystals.

SOLUTION Adding sugar and corn syrup to a recipe seems like double trouble, but don't be fooled into thinking you can just up the sugar and omit the corn syrup. The corn syrup helps disrupt the ice crystals that can form when making this frozen custard and yields a smoother, creamier consistency.

PROBLEM The frozen custard is not totally smooth.

SOLUTION During the process of cooking the custard, small curds may form. Straining the custard before it gets cooled and whipped will not only remove bits of curd and the egg's chalaza from your custard base, but will ensure a smooth and silky frozen custard.

A rich and glossy or sweet and fruity sauce makes an everyday dessert special occasion–worthy. Keep a jar of one of these easy sauces on hand in the fridge and you'll have a quick route from plain to fancy.

DARK CHOCOLATE FUDGE SAUCE

Makes: 2 cups
Total Time: 25 minutes

Our classic hot fudge sauce relies on cocoa powder and unsweetened chocolate for complexity and richness. Milk, rather than cream, preserves the intense chocolate flavor; butter thickens the sauce and adds attractive, glossy shine.

- 1¼ cups (8¾ ounces) sugar
- ⅔ cup whole milk
- ¼ teaspoon table salt
- ⅓ cup (1 ounce) unsweetened cocoa powder, sifted
- 3 ounces unsweetened chocolate, chopped fine
- 4 tablespoons unsalted butter, cut into 8 pieces and chilled
- 1 teaspoon vanilla extract

1. Heat sugar, milk, and salt in medium saucepan over medium-low heat, whisking gently, until sugar has dissolved and liquid starts to bubble around edges of saucepan, about 6 minutes. Reduce heat to low, add cocoa, and whisk until smooth.

2. Off heat, stir in chocolate and let sit for 3 minutes. Whisk sauce until smooth and chocolate is fully melted. Whisk in butter and vanilla until fully incorporated and sauce thickens slightly. (Sauce can be refrigerated for up to 1 month; gently warm in microwave, stirring every 10 seconds, until pourable before using.)

Variations

DARK CHOCOLATE–ORANGE FUDGE SAUCE

Bring milk and 8 (3-inch) strips orange zest to simmer in medium saucepan over medium heat. Off heat, cover and let sit for 15 minutes. Strain milk mixture through fine-mesh strainer into bowl, pressing on orange zest to extract as much liquid as possible. Return milk to now-empty saucepan and proceed with recipe as directed.

DARK CHOCOLATE–PEANUT BUTTER FUDGE SAUCE

Increase salt to ½ teaspoon. Whisk ¼ cup creamy peanut butter into sauce after butter.

MEXICAN DARK CHOCOLATE FUDGE SAUCE

Add ¼ teaspoon ground cinnamon and ¼ teaspoon chipotle chile powder to saucepan with milk in step 1.

PEACH-BOURBON SAUCE

Makes: about 2 cups
Total Time: 25 minutes

- 4 tablespoons unsalted butter
- ½ cup packed (3½ ounces) dark brown sugar
- ½ cup water
- ¼ cup bourbon
- ⅛ teaspoon table salt
- 1 pound frozen peaches, cut into ½-inch pieces
- 1 teaspoon vanilla extract

Melt butter in 12-inch skillet over medium heat. Whisk in sugar, water, bourbon, and salt until sugar has dissolved. Add peaches and bring to simmer. Reduce heat to medium-low, cover, and cook for 5 minutes. Uncover and continue to cook until peaches are tender and mixture measures about 2 cups, 5 to 7 minutes. Off heat, stir in vanilla. (Sauce can be refrigerated for up to 2 days; gently warm in microwave, stirring every 10 seconds, until pourable, before using.)

CAJETA

Makes: 3 cups
Total Time: 1¾ hours

This recipe produces a caramel sauce that's suitable for spooning over ice cream or sliced bananas or stirring into coffee. To produce a stiffer confection that's thick enough to spread between cake layers or sandwich between cookies, continue to cook the cajeta, stirring constantly to prevent scorching, until it's reduced to 2 cups. If you substitute cow's milk for goat's milk in this recipe, it may curdle slightly toward the end of cooking, but you can easily restore the smooth consistency by processing the cajeta in a blender or buzzing it with an immersion blender.

8 cups goat's milk
2 cups (14 ounces) sugar
2 teaspoons vanilla extract
¼ teaspoon kosher salt
1 cinnamon stick (optional)
¾ teaspoon baking soda, dissolved in 1 tablespoon water

1. Bring milk, sugar, vanilla, salt, and cinnamon stick, if using, to boil in Dutch oven over medium-high heat, stirring occasionally with rubber spatula.

2. Off heat, stir in baking soda mixture (milk will start to foam). When foaming subsides, return milk mixture to boil. Reduce heat to medium-low and simmer rapidly, adjusting heat as necessary to maintain rapid simmer and stirring occasionally to prevent scorching, until mixture is pale golden brown, 45 minutes to 1 hour.

3. Continue to cook, stirring frequently, until cajeta is caramel-colored and heavily coats back of spoon, about 30 minutes longer. Discard cinnamon stick, if using. If desired, strain cajeta through fine-mesh strainer. Cajeta can be refrigerated in airtight container for up to 2 months.

MIXED BERRY COULIS

Makes: about 1½ cups
Total Time: 15 minutes, plus 1 hour chilling

The amount of sugar added at the end is variable based on the type of berries used and their ripeness. Stir any additional sugar into the warm coulis immediately after straining so that the sugar will readily dissolve.

15 ounces (3 cups) fresh or thawed frozen blueberries, blackberries, and/or raspberries
¼ cup water
5 tablespoons (2¼ ounces) sugar, plus extra if needed
⅛ teaspoon table salt
2 teaspoons lemon juice

1. Bring berries, water, sugar, and salt to gentle simmer in medium saucepan over medium heat and cook, stirring occasionally, until sugar is dissolved and berries are heated through, about 1 minute.

2. Process mixture in blender until smooth, about 20 seconds. Strain through fine-mesh strainer into bowl, pressing on solids to extract as much puree as possible. Stir in lemon juice and season with extra sugar as needed. Cover and refrigerate until well chilled, about 1 hour. Adjust consistency with extra water as needed. (Sauce can be refrigerated for up to 4 days; stir to recombine before using.)

Beyond Ice Cream: More Ways to Use Dessert Sauces

CHOCOLATE
• Use as a dip for fresh fruit and pretzels.
• Cool and use as a filling for crepes.
• Spoon over cheesecake or pound cake.

CARAMEL
• Use as a dip for fresh fruit and pretzels.
• Drizzle over waffles, pancakes, and French toast in place of maple syrup.
• Spoon over cheesecake or pound cake.
• Cool and use as a filling for layered cakes.

FRUIT
• Cool and use as a filling for crepes.
• Drizzle over waffles, pancakes, and French toast in place of maple syrup.
• Use as a flavoring in yogurt smoothies.
• Spoon over cheesecake or pound cake.
• Spread on toast in place of jam.

CANDY MAKING

JULIA COLLIN DAVISON

There are plenty of impressive "project" dessert recipes (many right in this chapter), but none are so much fun as making candy. In this course, you'll learn how to craft confections that will wow any lucky recipient—including yourself. For luxe, fluffy marshmallows that are head and shoulders above the supermarket kind, a sturdy stand mixer does most of the work. Sophisticated salted caramels and crunchy chocolate-covered toffee bark both rely on the magic that happens when you cook sugar. Old-fashioned Needhams, which taste a lot like a popular coconut and chocolate candy bar, use a surprising ingredient for body and an easy tempering method for their glossy chocolate coating.

JULIA'S PRO TIP: *Having an accurate, fast digital thermometer is key when making candy. Before you start cooking, be sure to calibrate your thermometer using ice water (which should register 32° F) and/or boiling water (which should register 212° F).*

FLUFFY VANILLA MARSHMALLOWS

Makes: 48 marshmallows
Total Time: 1 hour, plus 4 hours setting

RECIPE OVERVIEW Marshmallows are easier to make than you think. Armed with a mixer and a thermometer, you'll find them failproof and not as sticky or messy as you'd suspect. All you need to do is cook a sugar syrup to the soft-ball stage (240 degrees), stir in gelatin, and whip a couple egg whites in your mixer before streaming in the hot syrup. The egg whites make the marshmallows lighter and fluffier than store-bought varieties, and a hefty pour of vanilla gives them homemade flavor. Three ¼-ounce envelopes of gelatin will yield the 2½ tablespoons needed for this recipe. You'll need a candy thermometer or another thermometer, such as an instant-read probe model, that registers high temperatures for this recipe. For a cleaner look, you can trim (and snack on) the edges of the marshmallows before cutting them into squares.

1	cup water, divided
2½	tablespoons unflavored gelatin
2	large egg whites
2	cups (14 ounces) granulated sugar
½	cup light corn syrup
¼	teaspoon table salt
1	tablespoon vanilla extract
⅔	cup (2⅔ ounces) confectioners' sugar
⅓	cup (1⅓ ounces) cornstarch

1. Make foil sling for 13 by 9-inch baking pan by folding 2 long sheets of aluminum foil; first sheet should be 13 inches wide and second sheet should be 9 inches wide. Lay sheets of foil in pan perpendicular to each other, with extra foil hanging over edges of pan. Push foil into corners and up sides of pan, smoothing foil flush to pan. Spray foil with vegetable oil spray.

2. Whisk ½ cup water and gelatin together in bowl and let sit until very firm, about 5 minutes. Add egg whites to bowl of stand mixer fitted with whisk attachment.

3. Combine granulated sugar, corn syrup, salt, and remaining ½ cup water in large saucepan. Bring to boil over medium-high heat and cook, gently swirling saucepan occasionally, until sugar has dissolved completely and mixture registers 240 degrees, 6 to 8 minutes. Off heat, immediately whisk in gelatin mixture until gelatin is dissolved.

4. Working quickly, whip whites on high speed until soft peaks form, 1 to 2 minutes. With mixer running, carefully pour hot syrup into whites, avoiding whisk and bowl as much as possible. Whip until mixture is very thick and stiff and bowl is only slightly warm to touch, about 10 minutes. Reduce speed to low and add vanilla. Slowly increase speed to high and mix until incorporated, about 30 seconds, scraping down bowl as needed.

5. Transfer mixture to prepared pan and spread into even layer using greased rubber spatula. Let sit at room temperature until firm, at least 4 hours.

6. Lightly coat chef's knife with oil spray. Whisk confectioners' sugar and cornstarch together in bowl. Lightly dust top of marshmallows with 2 tablespoons confectioners' sugar mixture. Transfer remaining confectioners' sugar mixture to 1-gallon zipper-lock bag. Place cutting board over pan of marshmallows and carefully invert pan and board. Remove pan and peel off foil.

7. Cut marshmallows crosswise into 8 strips, then cut each strip into 6 squares (marshmallows will be approximate 1½-inch squares). Separate marshmallows and add half to confectioners' sugar mixture in bag. Seal bag and shake to coat marshmallows.

8. Using your hands, remove marshmallows from bag and transfer to colander. Shake colander to remove excess confectioners' sugar mixture. Repeat with remaining marshmallows. Marshmallows can be stored in zipper-lock bag or airtight container at room temperature for up to 2 weeks.

Variations
FLUFFY EGGNOG MARSHMALLOWS
Substitute 2 tablespoons dark rum, ⅛ teaspoon ground nutmeg, and pinch ground cinnamon for vanilla.

FLUFFY LEMON-STRAWBERRY MARSHMALLOWS
Grind ½ ounce freeze-dried strawberries to powder in spice grinder. Add ground strawberries with vanilla. Stir in 1 tablespoon grated lemon zest with rubber spatula before transferring marshmallow mixture to prepared pan.

FLUFFY MOCHA MARSHMALLOWS
Add ¼ cup natural unsweetened cocoa powder and 2 tablespoons instant espresso powder with vanilla. Add 2 tablespoons natural unsweetened cocoa powder to confectioners' sugar mixture.

FLUFFY PEPPERMINT SWIRL MARSHMALLOWS
Add ⅛ teaspoon peppermint extract with vanilla. After spreading marshmallow mixture in pan, evenly drop 12 drops red food coloring over marshmallow mixture. Using clean, dry paring knife, swirl food coloring into marshmallow mixture.

KEYS TO SUCCESS
- **Whip it good**: It takes about 10 minutes of whipping in a stand mixer to get the marshmallow mixture to the right consistency.
- **Shake to coat**: A cornstarch and confectioners' sugar mix keeps the marshmallows separate.

Making Marshmallows

MAKE SYRUP
Cook sugar, water, corn syrup, and salt to 240 degrees, or soft-ball stage.

ADD SYRUP TO EGG WHITES
With mixer running, pour syrup into egg whites, avoiding sides of bowl and whisk.

TRANSFER TO PAN
Transfer marshmallow mixture to greased foil-lined pan and smooth top.

CUT
Cut marshmallows into 1½-inch squares using greased knife.

SALTED CARAMELS

Makes: about 50 caramels
Total Time: 1¼ hours, plus 1 hour cooling and 1 hour chilling

RECIPE OVERVIEW Gourmet caramels sprinkled with sea salt are the ultimate in sweet sophistication—and making them from scratch is an alluring prospect. When it comes to cooking the sugar syrup, the most important lesson is not to turn your back on it. It can go from golden amber to dark mahogany to burnt beyond recognition in the blink of an eye. Caramel candies aren't just about the caramelized sugar; you need to add cream so that the caramel has a rich flavor and chewy—not tooth-breaking—texture. When the caramel develops an amber color, add the cream mixture, watch it bubble, and cook the caramel to the right temperature. Transfer the molten mixture to a baking pan, sprinkle it with salt, and let it set before cutting the caramel into candies. If you like, substitute smoked sea salt for the flake sea salt. When taking the temperature of the caramel in steps 3 and 4, it helps to tilt the pan to one side.

  1 vanilla bean
  1 cup heavy cream
  5 tablespoons unsalted butter, cut into ¼-inch pieces
1½ teaspoons flake sea salt, divided
  ¼ cup light corn syrup
  ¼ cup water
1½ cups (9½ ounces) sugar

   1. Cut vanilla bean in half lengthwise. Using tip of paring knife, scrape out seeds. Combine vanilla bean seeds, cream, butter, and 1 teaspoon salt in small saucepan over medium heat. Bring to boil, cover, remove from heat, and let steep for 10 minutes.
   2. Meanwhile, grease 8-inch square baking pan. Fold 2 long sheets of parchment so each is 8 inches wide. Lay sheets of parchment in greased pan perpendicular to each other, with extra parchment hanging over edges of pan. Push parchment into corners and up sides of pan, smoothing parchment flush to pan. Grease parchment; set aside.
   3. Combine corn syrup and water in large saucepan. Pour sugar into center of pan (do not let sugar hit pan sides). Bring to boil over medium-high heat and cook, without stirring, until sugar has dissolved completely and syrup has faint golden color and registers 300 degrees, 7 to 9 minutes. Reduce heat to medium-low and continue to cook, gently swirling pan, until mixture is amber colored and registers 350 degrees, 2 to 3 minutes.
   4. Off heat, slowly and carefully stir in cream mixture (mixture will foam up). Return mixture to medium-high heat and cook, stirring frequently, until caramel reaches 248 degrees, about 5 minutes. Carefully transfer caramel to prepared baking pan. Using greased rubber spatula, smooth surface of caramel, and let cool for 10 minutes. Sprinkle with remaining ½ teaspoon salt and then let cool to room temperature, about 1 hour.

5. Transfer to refrigerator and chill until caramel is completely solid and cold to touch, about 1 hour. Lift parchment sling out of baking pan and place on cutting board. Peel parchment away from caramel. Cut caramel into ¾-inch-wide strips and then crosswise into ¾-inch pieces. Individually wrap pieces in waxed-paper squares, twisting ends of paper to close. Caramels can be refrigerated for up to 3 weeks.

KEYS TO SUCCESS

- **Don't skimp on steeping**: Let the vanilla seeds sit in the cream for 10 minutes to develop their flavor.
- **Get the temp right**: It's important to use an accurate thermometer.

WHAT CAN GO WRONG

PROBLEM The caramel foams up over the sides of the pan.

SOLUTION You might think a smaller saucepan will work here, but the caramel will foam up when you add the cream mixture, leaving you with a sweet version of Mount Vesuvius erupting all over your stovetop.

PROBLEM The sugar crystallizes.

SOLUTION It's important to pour the sugar carefully into the center of the pan, taking care not to get any on the sides of the pot. This prevents crystallization, which will give you grainy caramel.

PROBLEM The caramel burns.

SOLUTION Caramel overcooks in a matter of seconds. The best way to make sure it stays on track is to temp it with a candy thermometer or an instant-read thermometer. You can also watch the bubbles: Early on they are separate and boil vigorously; over time, they become smaller and more delicate, almost foamy. When the sugar mixture reaches 350 degrees, turn the heat down, then add the cream. Turning the heat down here gives you more control and safeguards against burning.

PROBLEM The caramels stick together.

SOLUTION Since the caramels tend to stick together and will get too soft if left at room temperature, it's best to individually wrap them in pieces of waxed paper and store them in the refrigerator to preserve their sharp, smooth edges and sophisticated appearance.

Making Caramel Candy

MAKE SUGAR SYRUP
After combining corn syrup and water in pan, pour sugar into center of pan without letting it hit pan sides. Bring to boil.

DISSOLVE SUGAR
Cook without stirring over medium-high heat until sugar has dissolved, syrup is faint golden color, and temperature registers 300 degrees.

COOK UNTIL AMBER COLORED
Lower heat to medium-low and continue to cook, gently swirling pan, until mixture is amber colored and registers 350 degrees. Tilt pan slightly for most accurate reading.

STIR IN CREAM MIXTURE
Remove from heat, stir in cream mixture (it will foam up), return to medium-high heat, and cook, stirring frequently, until caramel registers 248 degrees.

POUR INTO PAN AND CHILL
Pour into prepared pan and smooth surface with a greased silicone spatula. Refrigerate until thoroughly chilled.

CUT AND WRAP
Lift parchment sling out onto cutting board and peel away parchment. Cut caramel into pieces and wrap in waxed paper for storage.

NEEDHAMS

Makes: 36 candies
Total Time: 40 minutes, plus 2 hours 25 minutes chilling

RECIPE OVERVIEW Also known as potato fudge or potato candy, Needhams are an heirloom chocolate candy from Maine with an unexpected twist: Their creamy, coconut-studded base is built on mashed potatoes. While its flavor is undetectable, the potato does a great job of binding the filling together. Once coated in a silky chocolate shell, the treat is reminiscent of a Mounds candy bar in texture and flavor. As an easier alternative to boiling and then mashing only part of one potato, you'll use dried potato flakes: Just ¼ cup mixed with hot milk and melted butter makes the perfect amount of unseasoned mashed potatoes for the candy base. Stir in confectioners' sugar, sweetened shredded coconut, and vanilla and then let the mixture firm up in the refrigerator before cutting it into bite-size squares. For the bittersweet chocolate coating, it's essential to slowly melt the chocolate so it will recrystallize around the candies to form a shiny, snappy shell that won't melt in your hands. For this you'll use our easy microwave tempering technique, which calls for melting a portion of the chocolate before mixing in the rest.

- 6 tablespoons unsalted butter
- 3 tablespoons whole milk
- ¼ teaspoon table salt
- ¼ cup (½ ounce) plain instant mashed potato flakes
- 1 teaspoon vanilla extract
- 1½ cups (6 ounces) confectioners' sugar
- 1½ cups (4½ ounces) sweetened shredded coconut
- 1 pound bittersweet chocolate (12 ounces chopped fine, 4 ounces grated)

1. Make foil sling for 8-inch square baking pan by folding 1 long sheet of aluminum foil so it is 8 inches wide. Lay foil sheet in pan with extra foil hanging over edges of pan. Push foil into corners and up sides of pan, smoothing foil flush to pan. Grease foil.

2. Microwave butter, milk, and salt in bowl until butter is melted and mixture is bubbling, about 2 minutes. Stir in potato flakes and vanilla until mixture resembles applesauce, about 30 seconds (mixture will look oily). Stir in sugar and coconut until no dry spots remain and mixture forms loose paste.

3. Transfer coconut mixture to prepared pan and, using rubber spatula, press firmly into thin, even layer reaching into corners of pan. Cover with plastic wrap and refrigerate until firm, at least 2 hours or up to 24 hours.

4. Flip coconut mixture onto cutting board; discard foil. Cut into 36 (1-inch) squares (5 horizontal cuts by 5 vertical cuts). Separate squares into 2 batches and keep half refrigerated while working with other half. Line rimmed baking sheet with parchment paper.

5. Microwave finely chopped chocolate in bowl at 50 percent power, stirring often, until about two-thirds melted, 2 to 4 minutes. (Melted chocolate should not be much warmer than body temperature; check by holding bowl in palm of your hand.) Add grated chocolate and stir until smooth, returning to microwave for no more than 5 seconds at a time to finish melting if necessary.

6. Drop several coconut squares into chocolate. Using 2 forks, gently flip squares to coat on all sides. Lift squares one at a time from chocolate with fork. Tap fork against edge of bowl and then wipe underside of fork on edge of bowl to remove excess chocolate from bottom of candy. Use second fork to slide candy onto prepared sheet.

7. Repeat with remaining coconut squares and remaining chocolate, cleaning forks as needed. (As chocolate begins to set, microwave it at 50 percent power for no more than 5 seconds at a time, stirring at each interval, until fluid. Expect to microwave chocolate at least twice during coating process.)

8. Refrigerate candy until chocolate is set, 25 to 30 minutes. Serve. (Candy can be refrigerated for up to 1 week.)

KEYS TO SUCCESS

- **Instant potatoes:** Using instant means you can make just the amount of potatoes you need.

- **Temper:** Tempered chocolate looks better and is snappy, not crumbly.

CHOCOLATE-TOFFEE BARK

Serves: 24 (makes about 1½ pounds)
Total Time: 1½ hours

RECIPE OVERVIEW Crafting candies at home doesn't have to be a fussy affair, and this chocolate-covered toffee is a great example. To prevent sugar crystals that can mar the toffee's consistency, make sure none of the sugar sticks to the sides of the pan as you pour it in, and resist the urge to agitate the pan before the sugar is dissolved. Toffee can quickly turn from lightly browned to burnt, so keep a close watch as it cooks. Once the mixture hits 325 degrees, you'll add chopped pecans and pour it into a pan. Coating both sides of the toffee with semisweet chocolate and more pecans guarantees plenty of rich chocolate flavor and nutty crunch in every bite. When taking the temperature of the toffee in step 2, remove the saucepan from the heat and tilt to one side. Use your thermometer to stir the caramel back and forth to equalize hot and cool spots and make sure you are getting an accurate reading.

8	tablespoons unsalted butter
½	cup water
1	cup (7 ounces) sugar
¼	teaspoon table salt
1½	cups pecans or walnuts, toasted and chopped, divided
8	ounces semisweet chocolate, chopped, divided

1. Make foil sling for 13 by 9-inch baking pan by folding 2 long sheets of aluminum foil; first sheet should be 13 inches wide and second sheet should be 9 inches wide. Lay sheets of foil in pan perpendicular to each other, with extra foil hanging over edges of pan. Push foil into corners and up sides of pan, smoothing foil flush to pan. Grease foil.

2. Heat butter and water in medium saucepan over medium-high heat until butter is melted. Pour sugar and salt into center of saucepan, taking care not to let sugar touch sides of saucepan. Bring mixture to boil and cook, without stirring, until sugar is completely dissolved and syrup is faint golden color and registers 300 degrees, about 10 minutes. Reduce heat to medium-low and continue to cook, gently swirling saucepan, until toffee is amber-colored and registers 325 degrees, 1 to 3 minutes longer. Off heat, stir in ½ cup pecans until incorporated and thoroughly coated. Pour toffee into prepared pan and smooth into even layer with spatula. Refrigerate, uncovered, until toffee has hardened, about 15 minutes.

3. Microwave 4 ounces chocolate in bowl at 50 percent power, stirring occasionally, until melted, 1 to 2 minutes. Pour chocolate over hardened toffee and smooth with spatula, making sure to cover toffee layer evenly and completely. Sprinkle with ½ cup pecans and press lightly to adhere. Refrigerate, uncovered, until chocolate has hardened, about 15 minutes. Line rimmed baking sheet with parchment paper. Using foil sling, invert toffee onto prepared sheet. Discard foil.

4. Microwave remaining 4 ounces chocolate in bowl at 50 percent power, stirring occasionally, until melted, 1 to 2 minutes. Pour chocolate over toffee and smooth with spatula, making sure to cover toffee layer evenly and completely. Sprinkle with remaining ½ cup pecans and press lightly to adhere. Refrigerate, uncovered, until chocolate has hardened, about 15 minutes. Break toffee into rough 2-inch squares and serve. (Toffee can be stored at room temperature for up to 2 weeks.)

KEYS TO SUCCESS

- **Prep the pan:** Line the baking pan with foil and grease it to make removing the toffee easy.

- **Do not disturb:** Let the sugar dissolve on its own to prevent crystals from forming.

Coating with Chocolate

We apply the second layer of chocolate using this easy method.

PREPARE TOFFEE LAYER
Using foil sling, invert chocolate-covered toffee onto parchment-lined sheet. Peel away and discard foil.

COVER TOFFEE LAYER
Microwave remaining 4 ounces chocolate until melted and pour over toffee. Smooth with spatula.

CORE TECHNIQUE

Taking the Temperature of Caramel

We prefer an instant-read thermometer for measuring the temperature of caramel. To ensure an accurate reading, swirl the caramel to even out hot spots and then tilt the pot so that the caramel pools 1 to 2 inches deep. Move the thermometer back and forth for about 5 seconds before taking a reading.

NUTRITIONAL INFORMATION FOR OUR RECIPES

We calculate the nutritional values of our recipes per serving; if there is a range in the serving size, we used the highest number of servings to calculate the nutritional values. We entered all the ingredients, using weights for important ingredients such as most vegetables. We also used our preferred brands in these analyses. We did not include additional salt or pepper for food that's "seasoned to taste."

	CALORIES	TOTAL FAT (G)	SAT FAT (G)	CHOL (MG)	SODIUM (MG)	TOTAL CARB (G)	DIETARY FIBER (G)	TOTAL SUGARS (G)	PROTEIN (G)
CHAPTER 1: COOKING SMARTS									
Green Tomato Chutney	138	0	0	0	408	33	2	31	2
Tahini Sauce	294	26	4	0	284	13	5	1	8
Mint Persillade	185	19	3	3	147	4	2	0	2
Candied Bacon Bits	85	8	3	13	128	1	0	1	2
Za'atar	20	1.5	0	0	5	2	1	0	1
Pistachio Dukkah	60	4	0	0	240	5	2	0	3
Microwave-Fried Shallots	30	2	0	0	2	2	0	1	0
CHAPTER 2: EGGS AND DAIRY									
Perfect Omelet with Cheddar and Chives	380	30	14	602	435	2	0	1	26
Perfect Ham, Pear, and Brie Omelet	533	40	19	650	982	9	1	4	34
Perfect Kale, Feta, and Sun-Dried Tomato Omelet	424	34	17	616	520	6	1	2	24
Fluffy Omelets	341	25	13	413	509	3	0	0	26
Asparagus and Smoked Salmon Filling	60	3	0	5	170	5	2	3	5
Mushroom Filling	45	2	0	0	151	5	1	3	2
Artichoke and Bacon Filling	160	12	4	20	390	9	5	2	6
Classic Spanish Tortilla	340	21	4	250	550	24	1	2	1
with Chorizo and Scallions	572	39	10	397	794	33	4	2	23
Garlic Mayonnaise	104	12	1	18	34	0	0	0	0
Egyptian Eggah with Ground Beef and Spinach	247	14	4	273	553	13	2	3	18
Tunisian Tajine with White Beans	500	29	9	500	800	15	2	2	45
Classic Cheese Quiche	340	25	15	185	390	18	0	3	11
Leek and Goat Cheese Quiche	360	26	16	180	370	20	0	4	11
Spinach and Feta Quiche	350	25	15	185	530	19	1	5	12
Asparagus and Gruyère Quiche	360	25	15	185	400	19	1	5	13
Deep-Dish Quiche Lorraine	607	48	26	291	562	26	1	5	18
Baked Eggs for Sandwiches	140	10	3	370	290	1	0	0	13
Egg, Kimchi, and Avocado Sandwiches	459	27	6	378	616	35	4	2	19
Egg, Smoked Salmon, and Dill Sandwiches	349	14	4	381	636	30	2	5	25

	CALORIES	TOTAL FAT (G)	SAT FAT (G)	CHOL (MG)	SODIUM (MG)	TOTAL CARB (G)	DIETARY FIBER (G)	TOTAL SUGARS (G)	PROTEIN (G)
CHAPTER 2: EGGS AND DAIRY (CONTINUED)									
Egg, Ham, and Pepperoncini Sandwiches	481	23	10	417	978	41	3	10	29
Egg, Salami, and Tomato Sandwiches	520	32	8	408	1034	32	2	2	24
Lemon-Herb Sformati	479	35	20	335	578	20	1	6	21
Roasted Red Pepper Sformati	420	31	17	320	850	15	0	7	19
Spinach Sformati	420	31	17	320	790	16	1	6	20
Cheese Soufflé	355	26	15	250	459	8	0	3	21
Rolled Spinach and Cheese Soufflé for a Crowd	255	17	9	192	367	11	1	3	15
Mayonnaise	257	29	2	31	85	0	0	0	0
Aioli	250	29	5	30	150	0	0	0	0
Smoked Paprika Mayonnaise	250	29	5	30	150	1	0	0	1
Herbed Mayonnaise	250	29	5	30	150	0	0	0	0
Hollandaise Sauce	300	33	20	173	120	0	0	0	2
Mustard-Dill Hollandaise Sauce	300	32	19	170	160	1	0	0	1
Saffron Hollandaise Sauce	300	32	19	170	100	1	0	0	1
Béarnaise Sauce	290	32	19	170	100	0	0	0	1
Eggs Benedict (without Hollandaise)	340	12	4	400	1350	28	0	1	29
Sous Vide Soft-Poached Eggs	38	3	1	99	38	0	0	0	3
Sous Vide Hard-Cooked Eggs	71	5	2	186	71	0	0	0	6
Sous Vide Runny Egg Yolk Sauce	109	9	3	369	123	1	0	0	5
Creamy Ricotta Cheese	300	16	9	50	790	24	0	24	15
Lemon Ricotta Pancakes	280	11	6	115	610	34	0	16	10
Paneer	350	17	10	55	1510	30	0	29	20
Saag Paneer	540	29	15	71	2121	47	6	37	27
Homemade Yogurt	36	0	0	3	51	5	0	5	3
Labneh (per ¼ cup)	70	4	2.5	15	55	6	0	6	4
Lemon-Dill Labneh (per ¼ cup)	80	4	2.5	15	130	6	0	6	4
Honey-Walnut Labneh (per ¼ cup)	130	8	3	15	130	11	0	10	5
Frico	222	15	9	39	780	2	0	0	20
Cheese Fondue	767	38	22	120	888	49	2	5	42
Nacho Cheese Sauce with Gochujang	190	12	8	40	690	10	0	7	10
Grown-Up Stovetop Macaroni and Cheese	520	23	12	55	679	52	2	5	25
Grown-Up Grilled Cheese Sandwiches with Cheddar and Shallot	489	31	18	88	719	30	2	4	21
with Gruyére and Chives	491	31	18	92	753	29	2	4	24
with Asiago and Dates	493	27	17	71	1082	34	3	7	27
with Comté and Cornichon	487	31	18	88	719	29	2	4	21
with Robiola and Chipotle	487	31	18	88	721	29	2	4	21
Soy-Marinated Eggs	113	5	2	186	1823	6	0	4	9
Soy Sauce–Cured Egg Yolks	129	5	2	186	996	10	0	9	8
Salt-Cured Egg Yolks	218	5	2	186	204	38	0	38	6
Bonito and Black Pepper–Cured Egg Yolks	222	5	2	186	214	39	0	38	7

	CALORIES	TOTAL FAT (G)	SAT FAT (G)	CHOL (MG)	SODIUM (MG)	TOTAL CARB (G)	DIETARY FIBER (G)	TOTAL SUGARS (G)	PROTEIN (G)
CHAPTER 3: VEGETABLES									
Beet Muhammara	67	4	1	0	134	8	1	7	1
Carrot-Habanero Dip	80	5	1	0	180	8	2	4	1
Skordalia	160	14	2	0	176	8	2	1	2
Baba Ghanoush	245	22	3	0	475	12	6	5	4
Mushroom Pâté	110	8	5	25	250	6	1	3	3
Boiled Whole Artichokes	12	0	0	0	148	3	1	0	1
Roasted Artichokes	144	10	1	0	657	13	6	1	4
with Lemon Vinaigrette	333	31	4	0	774	16	7	2	4
Roman-Style Stuffed Braised Artichokes	329	28	4	0	807	20	7	3	5
Carciofi alla Giudia	475	47	4	0	118	13	7	1	4
Grilled Artichokes with Lemon Butter	273	24	12	47	731	15	6	2	5
Duck Fat–Roasted Potatoes	319	13	4	13	649	47	6	2	5
Aligot	465	30	18	94	650	31	4	4	20
Pommes Anna	230	9	5	23	432	35	2	1	4
Classic French Fries	410	19	2	0	15	54	0	0	7
Patatas Bravas	1224	122	9	4	764	33	3	2	4
Ultimate Extra-Crunchy Onion Rings	510	21	3	10	1320	66	2	11	12
Asparagus Fries	280	16	3	100	780	24	1	4	8
Gobi Manchurian	530	36	3	0	706	48	4	6	6
Fried Brussels Sprouts	170	14	1	0	25	9	4	2	3
Sriracha Dipping Sauce	120	13	2	5	200	1	0	1	0
Celery Root Puree	156	9	6	28	396	17	3	3	3
Bacon, Garlic, and Parsley Topping	40	4	1	5	65	1	0	0	1
Shallot, Sage, and Black Pepper Topping	35	4	3	10	25	0	0	0	0
Roasted Kohlrabi with Crunchy Seeds	100	8	1	0	310	7	4	3	2
Fried Yuca with Mojo Sauce	498	28	3	0	445	61	4	3	2
Root Vegetable Gratin	331	15	9	45	803	37	5	5	10
Upside-Down Tomato Tart	98	4	2	5	310	15	2	10	2
Beet and Caramelized Onion Turnovers with Beet-Yogurt Sauce	310	19	8	25	570	31	2	6	7
Eggplant and Tomato Phyllo Pie	410	28	8	20	800	28	3	4	10
Erbazzone	468	32	19	95	646	29	3	2	17
Whole Romanesco with Berbere and Yogurt-Tahini Sauce	339	28	12	50	688	12	6	9	13
Roasted King Trumpet Mushrooms	140	11	7	30	300	7	0	5	3
Red Wine–Miso Sauce	100	3	2	10	430	7	0	4	1
Browned Butter–Lemon Vinaigrette	110	11	7	30	180	2	0	1	0
Chile-Rubbed Butternut Squash Steaks	400	15	2	0	900	70	12	15	6
Ranch Dressing	190	20	3	10	260	1	0	0	0
Stuffed Eggplant with Bulgur and Tomatoes	330	19	5	15	530	36	12	13	10
Kousa Mihshi	600	38	11	55	1360	45	6	19	22
Mehshi Bazal	280	9	4	40	430	37	2	17	13
Sautéed Okra	110	8	2	0	285	9	3	2	3

	CALORIES	TOTAL FAT (G)	SAT FAT (G)	CHOL (MG)	SODIUM (MG)	TOTAL CARB (G)	DIETARY FIBER (G)	TOTAL SUGARS (G)	PROTEIN (G)
CHAPTER 3: VEGETABLES (CONTINUED)									
Roasted Okra	58	3	0	0	269	8	4	2	2
Spicy Red Pepper Mayonnaise	109	11	1	4	70	3	1	1	1
Charred Sichuan-Style Okra	360	28	2	0	770	18	4	6	3
Deep-Fried Okra	480	39	3	35	630	30	3	2	5
Cajun Pickled Okra	5	0	0	0	38	1	0	0	0
Okra and Shrimp Stew	302	17	5	108	1474	13	4	3	24
Sauerkraut (per ¼ cup)	15	0	0	0	200	3	1	2	1
Kimchi (per ¼ cup)	30	0	0	0	260	6	1	3	1
Sour Dill Pickles	19	0	0	0	558	4	1	2	1
Beets and Beet Kvass	25	0	0	0	1090	5	2	4	1
CHAPTER 4: SALADS									
Mâche Salad with Cucumber and Mint	120	11	1.5	0	100	5	2	1	2
Herb Salad	107	8	1	0	98	11	6	0	2
Bitter Greens Salad with Olives and Feta	120	10	2.5	10	480	5	3	1	2
Purslane and Watermelon Salad	170	12	4.5	20	220	11	1	8	6
Killed Salad	230	17	6	30	880	13	1	11	6
Wilted Spinach Salad with Strawberries, Goat Cheese, and Almonds	150	13	2.5	5	70	7	2	3	4
Frisée Salad with Warm Browned Butter–Hazelnut Vinaigrette	210	17	9	35	220	11	3	7	4
Pea Green Salad with Warm Apricot-Pistachio Vinaigrette	180	10	1.5	0	140	19	6	11	5
Bitter Greens, Carrot, and Chickpea Salad with Warm Lemon Dressing	410	21	4	10	630	46	9	26	10
Shaved Celery Salad with Honey-Pomegranate Vinaigrette	164	8	3	11	362	19	3	10	6
Shaved Zucchini Salad with Pepitas	110	8	1.5	5	310	5	1	3	4
Shaved Brussels Sprout Salad with Warm Bacon Vinaigrette	170	8	3	15	490	11	4	3	12
Shaved Jicama, Mango, and Cucumber Salad with Pan-Seared Scallops	391	24	4	41	822	22	2	12	24
Fennel, Orange, and Olive Salad	91	7	1	0	178	7	2	5	1
Red Cabbage and Grapefruit Salad	182	12	2	0	404	17	3	10	4
Citrus Salad with Watercress, Dried Cranberries, and Pecans	244	14	2	2	486	32	5	22	3
with Arugula, Golden Raisins, and Walnuts	187	8	1	2	464	30	4	20	2
with Radicchio, Dates, and Smoked Almonds	283	13	1	0	542	42	7	30	5
with Napa Cabbage, Dried Cherries, and Cashews	266	12	2	0	512	38	4	26	4
Mango, Orange, and Jicama Salad	140	0.5	0	0	30	34	6	27	2
Papaya, Clementine, and Chayote Salad	100	0	0	0	30	26	3	16	1
Persimmon and Burrata Salad with Prosciutto	270	16	6	35	420	29	1	2	10
Greek Bread Salad	376	23	6	22	698	33	8	7	12
Fattoush with Butternut Squash and Apple	310	19	2.5	0	460	33	4	7	4
Panzanella with Fiddleheads	303	22	5	11	395	21	1	2	9

	CALORIES	TOTAL FAT (G)	SAT FAT (G)	CHOL (MG)	SODIUM (MG)	TOTAL CARB (G)	DIETARY FIBER (G)	TOTAL SUGARS (G)	PROTEIN (G)
CHAPTER 4: SALADS (CONTINUED)									
Chicken and White Bean Panzanella	620	20	4	65	780	67	11	11	42
Italian Pasta Salad	398	20	7	46	921	37	2	2	17
Couscous Salad with Smoked Trout, Tomatoes, and Pepperoncini	360	16	2.5	30	950	37	3	1	17
Summer Ramen Salad	350	9	1	65	770	48	3	4	21
Chilled Somen Noodle Salad with Shrimp	310	3.5	0.5	70	2570	48	3	4	1
Bun Bo Xao	560	24	6	85	840	58	2	6	30
Wedge Salad with Creamy Black Pepper Dressing	283	26	6	22	617	8	3	5	5
Pai Huang Gua	61	3	0	0	493	9	1	4	2
Shredded Carrot and Serrano Chile Salad	202	13	2	0	439	19	6	10	6
Som Tam	100	2.5	0	0	240	19	3	13	3
Carrot and Beet Salad with Rose Harissa	250	15	2	60	410	22	7	11	6
Rose Harissa	120	11	1.5	0	150	3	2	0	1
Crispy Artichoke Salad with Lemon Vinaigrette	200	12	1.5	0	330	17	4	2	5
Za'atar	20	1.5	0	0	5	2	1	0	1
Crispy Eggplant Salad	560	38	4	0	1330	52	12	31	13
Crispy Rice Salad	290	9	1	5	530	45	1	5	9
Charred Beet Salad	190	14	6	20	830	13	3	9	6
Roasted Butternut Squash Salad with Za'atar and Parsley	250	13	2	0	600	32	5	12	5
Roasted Cauliflower and Grape Salad	340	28	4	0	510	22	6	11	6
Roasted Pattypan Squash Salad with Dandelion Green Pesto	270	20	2.5	0	310	24	4	12	6
Roasted Cipollini and Escarole Salad	290	19	4.5	20	790	21	3	5	10
Grilled Caesar Salad	481	35	7	17	695	31	3	4	11
Grilled Vegetable and Halloumi Salad	251	17	7	34	506	19	4	14	7
Grilled Radicchio Salad with Corn, Cherry Tomatoes, and Pecorino	425	32	6	11	489	34	6	14	9
Grilled Peach and Tomato Salad with Burrata and Basil	342	28	11	49	530	14	2	11	11
Nam Tok	237	10	4	77	556	11	3	4	26
CHAPTER 5: SOUPS									
Chinese Corn and Chicken Soup	208	6	2	79	693	29	2	9	12
Garlic-Chicken and Wild Rice Soup	252	10	2	28	888	26	3	3	18
Artichoke Soup à la Barigoule	210	11	4	10	890	19	3	5	7
Classic Corn Chowder	300	18	8	40	800	32	5	11	8
Mushroom Bisque	192	14	6	76	882	12	2	5	7
Smoky Eggplant Miso Soup	149	4	1	0	2069	23	7	8	9
Best French Onion Soup	505	23	13	65	1686	51	6	14	26
Kimchi, Beef, and Tofu Soup	481	27	8	81	1305	16	5	4	36
Beef and Cabbage Soup	310	19	6	80	840	8	3	4	26
Beef and Vegetable Soup	310	19	6	80	840	8	3	4	26
Beef Yakamein	624	25	8	185	1480	55	4	7	45

	CALORIES	TOTAL FAT (G)	SAT FAT (G)	CHOL (MG)	SODIUM (MG)	TOTAL CARB (G)	DIETARY FIBER (G)	TOTAL SUGARS (G)	PROTEIN (G)
CHAPTER 5: SOUPS (CONTINUED)									
Multicooker Hawaiian Oxtail Soup	520	29	10	170	1090	14	4	4	53
Chilled Borscht	262	17	10	56	564	26	4	21	4
Chilled Fresh Tomato Soup	232	21	3	0	606	12	3	7	2
Spanish Chilled Almond and Garlic Soup	416	35	4	0	484	20	5	4	10
Chilled Cucumber Soup with Mango and Mint	92	2	1	5	508	18	2	14	3
Brown Bean Soup	290	14	2	0	630	31	1	6	8
Minestra di Orzo e Fasio	252	11	3	12	273	31	8	1	9
Moong Dal Soup with Coconut Mik and Spinach	490	19	11	0	750	58	11	5	26
Harira	210	6	2	20	990	21	5	4	18
Harissa	208	21	3	0	75	5	3	1	1
Sweet Potato Soup	216	8	5	20	93	35	5	9	3
Buttery Rye Croutons	77	8	4	15	15	1	0	0	0
Candied Bacon Bits	85	8	3	13	128	1	0	1	2
Maple Sour Cream	33	3	1	7	6	3	0	2	0
Creamy Kohlrabi Soup	239	15	7	24	1072	24	12	11	7
Chestnut Soup with Mushrooms and Baharat	290	8	2	5	590	49	6	15	8
Creamy Hawaij Cauliflower Soup with Zhoug	270	24	4	0	740	12	4	4	4
Green Zhoug	100	11	2	0	75	1	0	0	0
Tanabour	289	15	8	65	686	27	5	6	13
New England Clam Chowder	370	22	12	75	640	29	1	3	15
Shellfish Soup with Leeks and Turmeric	220	7	1	150	840	17	2	4	18
Fregula with Clams and Saffron Broth	401	8	1	2	949	47	3	2	29
Shrimp Bisque	390	23	12	130	800	17	1	5	11
Seafood Bisque	440	24	12	145	980	18	1	5	21
Guay Tiew Tom Yum Goong	516	24	3	105	2122	52	4	18	25
Nam Prik Pao	76	6	0	0	160	5	1	3	1
CHAPTER 6: PASTA AND NOODLES									
Fresh Egg Pasta Dough	280	11	3	245	30	35	0	0	10
Fettuccine with Olivada	680	42	8	375	350	56	0	1	18
Fettuccine with Tomato–Browned Butter Sauce	570	27	11	400	760	62	2	6	16
Tagliatelle with Artichokes and Parmesan Bread Crumbs	520	18	3	5	740	70	4	3	16
Fresh Semolina Pasta Dough	293	1	0	0	281	59	3	0	10
Fresh Saffron Semolina Pasta Dough	293	1	0	0	281	59	3	0	10
Orecchiette alla Norcina	625	30	13	85	534	61	3	4	23
Fileja with 'Nduja Tomato Sauce	310	9	2	15	960	44	3	4	13
Malloreddus with Fava Beans and Mint	322	8	2	9	270	50	5	5	13
Three-Cheese Ravioli with Tomato-Basil Sauce	540	29	11	320	860	40	1	4	26
Short Rib Agnolotti	476	31	15	160	538	26	2	2	22
Squash-Filled Cappellacci	590	36	19	315	440	48	2	3	16
Tortellini in Brodo	250	10	3	93	342	25	1	1	15

	CALORIES	TOTAL FAT (G)	SAT FAT (G)	CHOL (MG)	SODIUM (MG)	TOTAL CARB (G)	DIETARY FIBER (G)	TOTAL SUGARS (G)	PROTEIN (G)
CHAPTER 6: PASTA AND NOODLES (CONTINUED)									
Pork Ragu	550	22	6	190	2920	18	3	11	59
Lamb Ragu	300	18	6	70	850	10	2	5	21
Ultimate Ragu alla Bolognese	370	24	8	115	640	6	0	3	25
Ragu Bianco	480	18	8	110	1140	48	2	4	29
Pasta ai Quattro Formaggi	749	40	25	135	714	68	3	5	28
Cheese and Tomato Lasagna	598	35	18	107	1380	39	5	11	33
Lasagne Verdi alla Bolognese	267	15	8	87	315	21	1	1	12
Pastitsio	541	27	13	101	802	45	3	12	28
Potato Gnocchi with Sage Browned Butter	498	14	8	77	734	84	5	3	12
Potato Gnocchi with Fontina Sauce	378	13	7	67	510	54	3	1	13
Roman Gnocchi	281	15	9	70	366	26	1	5	11
Spinach and Ricotta Gnudi with Tomato-Butter Sauce	427	28	18	87	727	23	3	3	23
Butternut Squash Gnudi with Kale, Parmesan, and Pepitas	662	45	21	81	1173	54	12	9	22
Yakisoba with Beef, Shiitakes, and Cabbage	484	11	3	105	978	69	5	10	27
Shichimi Togarashi	29	2	0	0	2	3	1	0	1
Pad See Ew	561	20	3	202	1511	61	3	10	30
Shrimp Pad Thai	580	25	4	200	1210	67	3	13	24
Shrimp and Tofu Pad Thai	657	31	5	200	1215	70	4	14	30
Sweet Potato Noodles with Shiitakes and Spinach	400	23	2	0	1000	44	5	13	5
Biang Biang Mian	704	37	3	0	2686	81	6	11	15
Phở Gà Miền Bắc	712	32	9	154	2450	60	2	9	44
Phở Gà Miền Nam	291	14	4	66	511	22	1	1	18
Simple Dumplings	190	5	1	90	1380	20	1	3	12
Pork Dumplings	74	3	1	6	93	8	1	1	3
Shu Mai	338	10	2	83	744	40	2	1	21
Tofu Summer Rolls with Spicy Almond Butter Sauce	180	6	1	0	298	28	3	6	6
Gỏi Cuốn	604	21	4	98	771	76	5	8	28
Nước Chấm	54	0	0	0	1770	13	0	11	1
Egg Rolls	260	17	3	25	740	18	1	4	9
Lumpiang Shanghai	390	31	6	66	378	16	1	1	13
CHAPTER 7: RICE, GRAINS, AND BEANS									
Rice and Pasta Pilaf	307	7	4	18	438	52	1	3	7
Herbed Rice and Pasta Pilaf	314	8	4	20	468	52	1	3	8
Rice and Pasta Pilaf with Golden Raisins and Almonds	397	12	4	18	489	63	2	10	10
Rice and Pasta Pilaf with Pomegranate and Walnuts	315	8	4	18	433	53	1	4	7
Arroz con Titoté	522	22	19	0	604	77	1	14	7

	CALORIES	TOTAL FAT (G)	SAT FAT (G)	CHOL (MG)	SODIUM (MG)	TOTAL CARB (G)	DIETARY FIBER (G)	TOTAL SUGARS (G)	PROTEIN (G)
CHAPTER 7: RICE, GRAINS, AND BEANS (CONTINUED)									
Wild Rice Pilaf with Pecans and Dried Cranberries	238	12	11	342	31	31	4	10	6
Plov	570	26	10	83	1002	59	5	9	26
Oat Berry Pilaf with Walnuts and Gorgonzola	139	6	2	8	366	19	2	14	3
Chicken and Spiced Freekeh with Cilantro and Preserved Lemon	569	24	5	91	582	51	8	4	40
Preserved Lemons	50	1	0	0	405	16	5	4	2
Farro and Broccoli Rabe Gratin	400	12	3	4	760	59	12	5	18
Chicken Biryani	599	21	10	181	824	65	3	10	38
Paella de Verduras	519	14	2	6	802	78	9	9	19
Vegetable Bibimbap with Nurungji	595	20	3	124	1223	87	4	13	15
Chicken Posole Verde	520	35	9	190	1050	16	3	4	34
Pork Posole Rojo	480	26	8	105	1130	26	5	7	34
Homemade Corn Tortillas	85	3	0	0	117	14	1	0	2
Tomatillo-Chicken Huaraches	810	28	9	115	1080	90	13	6	52
Cuban-Style Black Beans and Rice	307	22	7	18	597	22	5	3	8
Red Beans and Rice with Okra and Tomatoes	480	7	3	15	910	81	12	5	22
Koshari	410	12	2	0	1250	64	9	9	13
Crispy Onions	90	5	1	0	100	13	2	6	1
Barley and Lentils with Mushrooms and Tahini-Yogurt Sauce	510	21	3	0	890	66	15	3	18
Crispy Lentil and Herb Salad	213	19	3	6	185	8	0	6	4
Vospov Kofte	380	20	7	20	549	42	8	2	12
Palak Dal	276	8	4	16	348	42	8	4	15
Ultimate Hummus	392	20	1	0	382	22	6	4	10
Baharat-Spiced Beef Topping	180	14	2	30	320	2	0	0	10
Crispy Mushroom and Sumac Topping	190	11	2	0	440	17	6	1	8
Falafel Burgers with Herb-Yogurt Sauce	584	24	4	3	526	73	11	12	22
Quick-Pickled Red Onions	20	0	0	0	35	5	0	4	0
Espinacas con Garbanzos	430	25	4	0	1010	36	11	2	15
Pasta e Ceci	536	21	5	15	923	68	13	10	22
Boston Baked Beans	530	20	7	20	1120	70	12	26	19
Gigantes Plaki	390	10	2	0	620	60	16	14	18
Cassoulet	940	41	14	155	1910	77	18	9	59
Feijoada	876	55	17	153	1503	43	11	4	52
Edamame Salad	320	20	2	0	600	19	2	10	18
Succotash Salad with Lima Beans and Cilantro	236	13	2	0	485	27	4	10	6
Vignole	154	3	0	0	717	27	11	11	11
Fava Bean Crostini with Manchego and Pine Nuts	380	11	2	5	400	59	10	14	18
Ta'ameya with Tahini-Yogurt Sauce	470	25	6	50	1180	47	6	8	19
Pink Pickled Turnips	20	0	0	0	580	5	1	3	0

	CALORIES	TOTAL FAT (G)	SAT FAT (G)	CHOL (MG)	SODIUM (MG)	TOTAL CARB (G)	DIETARY FIBER (G)	TOTAL SUGARS (G)	PROTEIN (G)
CHAPTER 8: MEAT									
Butter-Basted Rib Steak	700	61	26	155	690	1	0	0	36
with Coffee-Chile Butter	700	61	26	155	690	1	0	0	36
Spice-Crusted Steaks	595	47	19	148	548	2	1	0	41
Sous Vide Seared Steaks	736	60	17	141	586	0	0	0	45
Red Wine–Peppercorn Pan Sauce	120	8	5	25	115	6	0	3	1
Thick-Cut Porterhouse Steaks	363	19	6	118	740	1	0	0	45
Bistecca alla Fiorentina	360	21	7	135	660	0	0	0	38
Ultimate Charcoal-Grilled Steaks	485	35	14	167	529	0	0	0	40
Pan-Seared Thick-Cut Pork Chops	160	6	2	65	70	0	0	0	26
Grind-Your-Own Sirloin Burger Blend	410	21	11	145	420	0	0	0	49
Grind-Your-Own Ultimate Beef Burger Blend	450	29	12	1.5	155	430	0	0	45
Juicy Pub-Style Burgers	716	47	21	207	663	22	1	3	50
Pub–Style Burger Sauce	323	33	5	17	732	5	0	4	1
Juicy Pub-Style Burgers with Crispy Shallots and Blue Cheese	980	62	21	185	1520	30	3	10	65
Juicy Pub-Style Burgers with Peppered Bacon and Aged Cheddar	1120	76	26	220	1590	28	3	8	70
Juicy Pub-Style Burgers with Pan-Roasted Mushrooms and Gruyère	1030	66	20	190	1480	30	3	10	68
Bistro Burgers with Pâté, Figs, and Watercress	1082	66	29	320	1114	57	4	17	66
Breakfast Pork Burgers	871	57	21	338	884	41	4	9	49
Lamb Burgers with Halloumi and Beet Tzatziki	991	67	29	179	883	33	2	12	44
Braciole	491	28	9	111	896	17	3	7	38
Osso Buco	440	18	3	120	560	13	2	5	40
Porchetta	469	35	10	118	634	4	2	0	34
Pork Tenderloin Roulade with Pancetta, Pear, and Cheddar	360	18	7	129	564	7	1	4	39
Best Prime Rib	520	27	10	185	870	0	0	0	64
Pepper-Crusted Beef Tenderloin Roast	460	26	7	145	570	4	2	1	51
Pomegranate-Port Sauce	85	4	2	10	153	9	0	8	0
Roast Fresh Ham	380	15	5	140	1470	9	0	9	46
Etli Kuru Fasulye	727	47	18	153	1251	25	7	6	51
Jamaican Oxtail	811	52	21	187	1249	26	4	10	58
Alcatra	569	23	8	122	952	11	2	3	60
Bulalo	600	21	5	170	1210	20	1	2	77
Southern-Style Collard Greens with Ham Hocks	208	11	4	54	925	9	5	2	20
Grill-Roasted Beef Tenderloin	420	21	7	160	680	1	0	0	53
Cuban-Style Grill-Roasted Pork	844	36	11	167	1232	77	1	69	52
Mojo Sauce	102	11	1	0	56	1	0	1	0
Grilled Bone-In Leg of Lamb with Charred Scallion Sauce	648	50	17	160	795	4	1	0	44
Texas Thick-Cut Smoked Pork Chops	453	22	7	145	892	18	1	12	45
Texas Barbecue Brisket	470	14	5	235	1160	1	0	0	79

	CALORIES	TOTAL FAT (G)	SAT FAT (G)	CHOL (MG)	SODIUM (MG)	TOTAL CARB (G)	DIETARY FIBER (G)	TOTAL SUGARS (G)	PROTEIN (G)
CHAPTER 8: MEAT (CONTINUED)									
South Carolina Pulled Pork	310	11	4	100	2320	19	1	17	32
Memphis Barbecue Spareribs	840	62	20	210	1850	24	1	19	42
Texas-Smoked Beef Ribs	1040	82	33	245	2710	4	1	0	67
Oklahoma Barbecue Sauce	70	2	0	0	311	13	0	10	1
Texas Barbecue Sauce	143	6	4	15	427	21	1	17	2
Eastern North Carolina–Style Barbecue Sauce	64	0	0	0	1199	13	0	12	0
Lexington-Style Barbecue Sauce	76	0	0	0	441	16	1	11	1
Louisiana Sweet Barbecue Sauce	240	12	7	31	534	31	3	25	2
CHAPTER 9: POULTRY									
Crispy-Skinned Chicken Breasts with Chermoula	620	40	9	175	610	4	2	0	58
Chermoula	80	7	1	0	0	3	1	0	1
Herbed Roast Chicken	670	51	215	215	470	3	1	1	47
Cumin-Coriander Rubbed Cornish Game Hens	853	63	15	384	1484	3	1	0	66
Oregano-Anise Rubbed Cornish Game Hens	848	62	15	384	1481	2	1	0	66
Extra-Crunchy Fried Chicken	820	47	13	200	650	37	0	5	57
Extra-Spicy, Extra-Crunchy Fried Chicken	830	48	13	200	1060	39	1	5	57
Lard Fried Chicken	820	46	16	195	1740	33	0	0	61
Mole Hot Fried Chicken	1000	71	10	140	670	42	1	2	49
Roasted and Glazed Chicken Wings	899	63	19	503	1065	0	0	0	80
Dakgangjeong	440	30	7	150	220	16	0	4	26
Stuffed Turkey Wings	793	49	10	192	1621	24	3	6	61
Classic Chicken Pot Pie	660	38	23	180	820	50	5	8	29
Dutch Oven Chicken Pot Pie with Spring Vegetables	508	22	10	211	1246	38	6	10	40
Chicken B'Stilla	415	24	4	164	438	27	3	4	24
Grilled Chicken with Adobo and Sazón	584	44	11	164	737	3	0	0	41
Sweet and Tangy Barbecued Chicken	860	55	15	255	961	25	1	20	64
Smoked Citrus Chicken	576	43	11	170	568	2	1	0	43
Porchetta-Style Turkey Breast	694	36	10	256	1032	4	2	0	85
Turkey Thigh Confit with Citrus-Mustard Sauce	964	74	24	220	1032	30	3	19	46
Sous Vide Turkey Thigh Confit with Citrus-Mustard Sauce	664	42	14	187	941	28	4	20	47
Holiday Smoked Turkey	538	20	5	251	1269	8	1	6	76
Deep-Fried Turkey	1340	117	20	270	960	3	0	1	70
Duck Breast Salad with Blackberries and Quick-Pickled Fennel	290	8	2	85	980	31	6	22	25
Quick-Pickled Fennel	45	0	0	0	650	11	1	9	0
Orange-Ginger Vinaigrette	35	2	0	0	75	5	0	4	0
Duck Breasts with Port Wine–Fig Sauce	210	5	2	88	605	14	1	12	23
Whole Roast Duck with Cherry Sauce	1900	177	59	340	2230	21	1	18	53
Duck Confit	330	22	6	145	690	0	0	0	32

	CALORIES	TOTAL FAT (G)	SAT FAT (G)	CHOL (MG)	SODIUM (MG)	TOTAL CARB (G)	DIETARY FIBER (G)	TOTAL SUGARS (G)	PROTEIN (G)
CHAPTER 10: SEAFOOD									
Cóctel de Camarón	166	6	1	119	832	15	3	8	15
Mussels Escabèche	201	12	2	32	411	6	0	0	14
Best Crab Cakes	448	26	8	180	924	23	2	5	29
Salt Cod Fritters	170	10	4	65	1290	9	1	1	12
Fish Crudo with Furikake	102	7	1	26	321	2	1	1	8
Furikake	92	7	1	0	70	6	2	3	3
Fish Ceviche with Radishes and Orange	252	11	2	28	548	23	3	8	18
Scallop Ceviche with Cucumber and Grapefruit	287	10	1	18	666	41	4	15	12
Tuna Poke	299	18	2	44	713	4	1	1	30
Oysters on the Half Shell	162	5	1	100	230	10	0	0	19
Lime-and-Soy-Marinated Scallions	4	0	0	0	110	1	0	0	0
Red Wine Vinegar Mignonette Granité	6	0	0	0	2	1	0	0	0
Cocktail Sauce	20	0	0	0	150	4	0	3	0
Butter-Basted Fish Fillets with Garlic and Thyme	366	26	12	119	491	3	1	0	31
Crispy Skin-On Fish Fillets	257	11	1	81	480	1	0	1	37
Green Olive, Almond, and Orange Relish	110	9	1	0	240	6	2	2	3
Oven-Steamed Fish Fillets with Scallions and Ginger	263	10	1	73	759	8	1	3	32
Oil-Poached Fish Fillets with Artichokes and Tomato Vinaigrette	565	44	7	85	727	10	3	2	36
Oven-Poached Side of Salmon	260	12	2	100	250	0	0	0	36
Fresh Tomato Relish	35	3	0	0	0	3	1	2	1
Cucumber-Ginger Relish	217	21	3	0	333	7	2	2	2
Roasted Whole Side of Salmon	390	24	6	100	433	4	0	3	37
Hot-Smoked Whole Side of Salmon	260	15	3	62	278	6	0	6	23
Hot-Smoked Salmon Kedgeree	804	42	13	284	1025	50	2	14	55
Whole Roast Snapper with Citrus Vinaigrette	592	26	4	147	1017	4	2	1	82
Whole Roast Mackerel with Preserved Lemon	653	47	10	179	806	6	2	3	48
Grilled Whole Trout with Orange and Fennel	496	25	5	187	753	2	0	1	62
Salt-Baked Whole Branzino	408	8	2	163	1118	2	0	0	77
Boiled Lobster	437	4	1	720	2398	0	0	0	94
New England Lobster Rolls	244	10	3	108	560	21	1	3	17
Grilled Lobsters	971	43	23	1100	3376	7	1	0	133
Lobster and Corn Chowder	472	24	9	287	1633	26	4	6	37
Cataplana	541	26	8	183	2518	19	4	6	54
Moqueca	409	29	15	128	916	13	3	5	27
Linguine allo Scoglio	686	19	3	229	1500	69	3	3	50
Grilled Paella	897	38	11	204	1792	76	4	5	56

	CALORIES	TOTAL FAT (G)	SAT FAT (G)	CHOL (MG)	SODIUM (MG)	TOTAL CARB (G)	DIETARY FIBER (G)	TOTAL SUGARS (G)	PROTEIN (G)
CHAPTER 11: BREADS									
Crescent Rolls	230	12	7	65	240	25	0	4	5
Kaiser Rolls	230	5	1	30	610	39	2	1	8
St. Lucia Buns	170	5	3	35	170	26	0	7	4
Challah	299	8	1	47	243	48	2	6	9
Cinnamon Swirl Bread	307	8	5	43	242	52	2	21	7
Almond Ring Coffee Cakes	551	22	9	85	394	79	3	35	12
Pane Francese	1008	11	2	0	1089	190	7	1	32
Whole-Wheat Sandwich Bread	318	10	4	16	292	50	5	7	10
Cheddar and Black Pepper Bread	280	9	6	30	770	34	1	0	13
Carmelized Onion Bread	220	4	1	0	590	39	2	3	7
Fig and Fennel Bread	333	2	0	0	347	70	6	9	10
Ciabatta	130	0	0	0	290	26	0	0	4
Durum Bread	220	1	0	0	440	45	3	1	8
Pumpernickel	410	5	1	25	910	82	13	8	12
Sage-Polenta Bread	240	4	1	0	440	41	2	0	7
Honey-Spelt Bread	240	3	0	0	440	48	3	9	8
Classic Sourdough Bread	290	1	0	0	510	60	4	0	10
Bakery-Style French Baguettes	330	0	0	0	880	69	1	0	10
Pain d'Epi	330	0	0	0	880	69	1	0	10
Seeded Ficelle	80	2	0	0	150	14	1	0	3
Breton Kouign Amann	343	19	12	49	224	41	1	16	4
Croissants	240	14	9	45	230	23	0	3	4
Pain au Chocolat	374	23	14	66	236	38	2	8	6
CHAPTER 12: DESSERTS									
Peanut Butter–Stuffed Chocolate Cookies	318	14	5	25	175	48	2	34	5
Carrot Cake Cookies	236	12	7	38	151	31	1	21	2
Chocolate Chip Cookie Ice Cream Sandwiches	467	24	15	70	238	60	2	38	6
Millionaire's Shortbread	198	11	7	26	92	25	1	18	2
Crème Brûlée	580	50	30	410	70	27	0	26	7
Orange Blossom Créme Brûlée	590	50	30	410	70	27	0	26	7
Tea-Infused Créme Brûlée	580	50	30	410	70	27	0	26	7
Latin Flan	252	7	4	62	222	39	0	39	7
Almond Latin Flan	251	7	4	62	222	39	0	39	7
Coffee Latin Flan	252	7	4	62	223	39	0	39	7
Orange-Cardamom Latin Flan	253	7	4	62	223	39	0	39	7
Best Butterscotch Pudding	442	33	20	186	272	34	0	30	4

	CALORIES	TOTAL FAT (G)	SAT FAT (G)	CHOL (MG)	SODIUM (MG)	TOTAL CARB (G)	DIETARY FIBER (G)	TOTAL SUGARS (G)	PROTEIN (G)
CHAPTER 12: DESSERTS (CONTINUED)									
Strawberry-Rhubarb Pie	648	31	14	46	300	85	4	43	6
Plum-Ginger Pie	589	31	19	100	378	76	6	36	8
Blueberry Earl Grey Pie	700	34	16	77	326	90	4	49	7
Foolproof All-Butter Double-Crust Pie Dough	410	28	18	75	290	35	0	3	5
Foolproof New York Cheesecake	518	38	21	213	359	37	0	29	9
La Viña–Style Cheesecake	550	37	24	235	410	42	0	37	10
Plant-Based Pumpkin Cashew Cheesecake	548	40	20	18	227	44	3	28	9
Skillet Lemon Soufflé	177	6	3	160	108	26	0	23	6
Skillet Chocolate-Orange Soufflé	254	10	5	160	110	37	1	33	6
Chocolate Soufflé	290	19	10	160	105	27	0	22	7
Make-Ahead Chocolate Soufflés	290	19	10	160	105	27	0	22	7
Grand Marnier Soufflé	206	8	4	131	131	25	0	20	6
Olive Oil Cake	372	18	3	58	237	47	1	28	5
Lemon–Olive Oil Tart	443	22	3	70	247	57	1	33	6
Olive Oil Ice Cream	281	20	5	14	109	22	0	20	4
Choux au Craquelin	205	13	8	97	80	18	0	9	3
Colorful Choux au Craquelin	210	13	8	97	79	19	0	10	3
Mocha Choux au Craquelin	204	13	8	97	80	18	0	9	3
Napoleons	510	31	19	195	270	51	0	32	6
Puff Pastry Dough	230	17	11	45	220	18	0	1	2
Vanilla Pastry Cream	220	15	9	150	60	18	0	15	4
Coconut Layer Cake	782	53	37	127	361	73	1	55	6
Blackberry-Mascarpone Lemon Cake	633	37	21	241	367	67	2	49	9
Chocolate-Espresso Dacquoise	555	42	18	124	111	41	4	34	9
Raspberry Sorbet	130	0	0	0	45	33	5	27	1
Raspberry–Lime Rickey Sorbet	136	0	0	0	45	35	5	29	1
Raspberry-Port Sorbet	153	0	0	0	45	35	5	29	1
Raspberry Sorbet with Ginger and Mint	130	1	0	0	55	33	5	27	1
Pistachio Gelato	480	28	8	140	140	48	4	39	14
Fluffy Vanilla Marshmallows	54	0	0	0	18	13	0	13	0
Fluffy Eggnog Marshmallows	54	0	0	0	18	13	0	13	0
Flluffy Lemon-Strawberry Marshmallows	54	0	0	0	18	13	0	13	0
Fluffy Mocha Marshmallows	55	0	0	0	18	14	0	13	1
Fluffy Peppermint Swirl Marshmallows	54	0	0	0	18	13	0	13	0
Salted Caramels	52	3	2	10	34	7	0	7	0
Needhams	296	18	12	13	74	38	2	34	2
Chocolate-Toffee Bark	160	11	5	10	25	15	1	14	1
Dark Chocolate Fudge Sauce	515	24	15	33	172	74	6	64	6
Dark Chocolate–Orange Fudge Sauce	518	24	15	33	172	75	7	64	6
Dark Chocolate –Peanut Butter Fudge Sauce	611	32	17	33	320	78	7	66	10
Mexican Dark Chocolate Fudge Sauce	515	24	15	33	177	75	6	64	6
Cajeta	121	3	2	9	100	20	0	20	3
Mixed Berry Coulis	40	0	0	0	25	10	1	9	0

CONVERSIONS AND EQUIVALENTS

Some say cooking is a science and an art. We would say that geography has a hand in it, too. Flours and sugars manufactured in the United Kingdom and elsewhere will feel and taste different from those manufactured in the United States. So we cannot promise that the loaf of bread you bake in Canada or England will taste the same as a loaf baked in the States, but we can offer guidelines for converting weights and measures. We also recommend that you rely on your instincts when making our recipes. Refer to the visual cues provided. If the dough hasn't "come together in a ball" as described, you may need to add more flour—even if the recipe doesn't tell you to. You be the judge.

The recipes in this book were developed using standard U.S. measures following U.S. government guidelines. The charts below offer equivalents for U.S. and metric measures. All conversions are approximate and have been rounded up or down to the nearest whole number.

EXAMPLE

1 teaspoon = 4.9292 milliliters, rounded up to 5 milliliters

1 ounce = 28.3495 grams, rounded down to 28 grams

VOLUME CONVERSIONS

U.S.	METRIC
1 teaspoon	5 milliliters
2 teaspoons	10 milliliters
1 tablespoon	15 milliliters
2 tablespoons	30 milliliters
¼ cup	59 milliliters
⅓ cup	79 milliliters
½ cup	118 milliliters
¾ cup	177 milliliters
1 cup	237 milliliters
1¼ cups	296 milliliters
1½ cups	355 milliliters
2 cups (1 pint)	473 milliliters
2½ cups	591 milliliters
3 cups	710 milliliters
4 cups (1 quart)	0.946 liter
1.06 quarts	1 liter
4 quarts (1 gallon)	3.8 liters

WEIGHT CONVERSIONS

OUNCES	GRAMS
½	14
¾	21
1	28
1½	43
2	57
2½	71
3	85
3½	99
4	113
4½	128
5	142
6	170
7	198
8	227
9	255
10	283
12	340
16 (1 pound)	454

CONVERSIONS FOR COMMON BAKING INGREDIENTS

Baking is an exacting science. Because measuring by weight is far more accurate than measuring by volume, and thus more likely to produce reliable results, in our recipes we provide ounce measures in addition to cup measures for many ingredients. Refer to the chart below to convert these measures into grams.

INGREDIENT	OUNCES	GRAMS
Flour		
1 cup all-purpose flour*	5	142
1 cup cake flour	4	113
1 cup whole-wheat flour	5½	156
Sugar		
1 cup granulated (white) sugar	7	198
1 cup packed brown sugar (light or dark)	7	198
1 cup confectioners' sugar	4	113
Cocoa Powder		
1 cup cocoa powder	3	85
Butter†		
4 tablespoons (½ stick or ¼ cup)	2	57
8 tablespoons (1 stick or ½ cup)	4	113
16 tablespoons (2 sticks or 1 cup)	8	227

* U.S. all-purpose flour, the most frequently used flour in this book, does not contain leaveners, as some European flours do. These leavened flours are called self-rising or self-raising. If you are using self-rising flour, take this into consideration before adding leaveners to a recipe.

† In the United States, butter is sold both salted and unsalted. We generally recommend unsalted butter. If you are using salted butter, take this into consideration before adding salt to a recipe.

OVEN TEMPERATURES

FAHRENHEIT	CELSIUS	GAS MARK
225	105	¼
250	120	½
275	135	1
300	150	2
325	165	3
350	180	4
375	190	5
400	200	6
425	220	7
450	230	8
475	245	9

CONVERTING TEMPERATURES FROM AN INSTANT-READ THERMOMETER

We include doneness temperatures in many of the recipes in this book. We recommend an instant-read thermometer for the job. Use this simple formula to convert Fahrenheit degrees to Celsius:

Subtract 32 degrees from the Fahrenheit reading, then divide the result by 1.8 to find the Celsius reading.

EXAMPLE

"Roast chicken until thighs register 175 degrees."

TO CONVERT:
175°F − 32 = 143°
143° ÷ 1.8 = 79.44°C, rounded down to 79°C

INDEX

Note: Page references in *italics* indicate photographs.

A

Achiote
Sazón, 432
Adobo and Sazón, Grilled Chicken with, *430*, 430–32
Aioli, 66
Aioli, Preserved-Lemon, 20
Alcatra, *382*, 382–83
Aleppo pepper
about, 14
Harissa, 225
Aligot, *111*, 111–12
Almond Butter Sauce, Tofu Summer Rolls with, 294–95
Almond(s)
Chicken B'stilla, 428–29
Chocolate-Espresso Dacquoise, *613*, 613–15
and Garlic Soup, Spanish Chilled (White Gazpacho), 220–21, *221*
and Golden Raisins, Rice and Pasta Pilaf with, 304
Green Olive, and Orange Relish, 474
Latin Flan, 572
Ring Coffee Cakes, *514*, 514–15
Skordalia, 97–98, *98*
Smoked, Radicchio, and Dates, Citrus Salad with, 168
Anise-Oregano Rubbed Cornish Game Hens, 413
Apple and Butternut Squash, Fattoush with, 171, *171*
Apricot-Pistachio Vinaigrette, Warm, Pea Green Salad with, 160–61
Aquafaba, science lesson, 338
Aromatics, smashing, 237
Arroz con Titoté, 304–5
Artichoke(s)
anatomy of, 109
and Bacon Omelet, 40
boiled, how to eat, 109
Boiled Whole, *104*, 104–5
Carciofi alla Giudia, 106–7, *107*
fresh, buying, 109
Grilled, with Lemon Butter, 108, *108*
and Parmesan Bread Crumbs, Tagliatelle with, 243–44
preparing, method for, 102, *103*
processed, buying, 207
resources for, 109
Roasted, *104*, 105

Artichoke(s) (cont.)
Roasted, with Lemon Vinaigrette, 105
Roman-Style Stuffed Braised, 105–6
Salad, Crispy, with Lemon Vinaigrette, 182
science lesson, 108
Soup à la Barigoule, 206–7, *207*
and Tomato Vinaigrette, Oil-Poached Fish Fillets with, *475*, 475–76
Vignole, 346, *346*
Arugula
Edamame Salad, 344
Golden Raisins, and Walnuts, Citrus Salad with, 168
Asparagus
Dutch Oven Chicken Pot Pie with Spring Vegetables, *427*, 427–28
Fries, 118–19
and Gruyère Quiche, 51
and Smoked Salmon Omelet, *39*, 40
Vignole, 346, *346*
Avocado oil, 18
Avocado(s)
Cóctel de Camarón, *458*, 459
Egg, and Kimchi Sandwiches, 55
Summer Ramen Salad, 176

B

Baba Ghanoush, 98–99
Bacon
and Artichoke Omelet, 40
Bits, Candied, 21, 227
Deep-Dish Quiche Lorraine, 51–53, *52*
Eggs Benedict, 68
Garlic, and Parsley Celery Root Topping, 123
Killed Salad, 158
Peppered, and Aged Cheddar, Juicy Pub-Style Burgers with, 363
Pork Tenderloin Roulade with Pancetta, Pear, and Cheddar, 372–73, *373*
Vinaigrette, Warm, Shaved Brussels Sprout Salad with, 164, *164*
Wedge Salad with Creamy Black Pepper Dressing, 178
Baguettes, Bakery-Style French, 546–48, *547*
Baharat
and Mushrooms, Chestnut Soup with, 228–29
-Spiced Beef Hummus Topping, 335, *335*

Bakeware
advanced, list of, 7
basic, list of, 5
Banneton, working with a, 529
Barbecue Sauces
Eastern North Carolina–Style, 403, *403*
Kansas City, 402
Lexington-Style, 403
Louisiana Sweet, 403
for Memphis Barbecue Spareribs, 399
Oklahoma, 402
for South Carolina Pulled Pork, 397
for Sweet and Tangy Barbecued Chicken, 432–33
Texas, 402–3
for Texas Thick-Cut Smoked Pork Chops, 392
Bar cookies
doneness cues, 25
Millionaire's Shortbread, *568*, 568–69
Bark, Chocolate-Toffee, 627
Barley
and Bean Soup (Minestra di Orzo e Fasio), 223–24
and Lentils with Mushrooms and Tahini-Yogurt Sauce, 330–31
and Yogurt Soup, Armenian (Tanabour), 231, *231*
Basil
Gỏi Cuốn, 295–96
Tofu Summer Rolls with Spicy Almond Butter Sauce, 294–95
-Tomato Sauce, Three-Cheese Ravioli with, *252*, 252–53
Bean(s)
baked, 340–43
Black, and Rice, Cuban-Style, *324*, 324–25
Boston Baked, 340–41
Brown, Soup, 223
Cassoulet, 342
dried, soaking, 327
Edamame Salad, 344
Etli Kuru Fasulye, 380–81
Farro and Broccoli Rabe Gratin, *309*, 309–10
Fava, and Mint, Malloreddus with, 249
Fava, Crostini with Manchego and Pine Nuts, 347
fava, prepping, 249
Feijoada, 343, *343*
fresh fava, preparing, 346
Gigantes Plaki, *341*, 341–42

E

F

H

Ham
Egg, and Pepperoncini Sandwiches, 56
fresh, buying, 379
Fresh, Roasted, *377,* 377–78
hocks, removing meat from, 384
Hocks, Southern-Style Collard Greens
with, 384
Okra and Shrimp Stew, 144
Pear, and Brie Omelet, Perfect, 36–37
Harira, 225, *225*
Harissa, 225
Harissa, Rose, 181
Hawaij, 230
Hazelnut(s)
Chocolate-Espresso Dacquoise, *613,*
613–15
Short Rib Agnolotti, *252,* 253–54
–Warmed Browned Butter Vinaigrette,
Frisée Salad with, 159–60, *160*
Herb(s)
chopping and mincing, 13
and Crispy Lentil Salad, 331, *331*
delicate, about, 13
edible parts, 13
eight to try, 12
fresh, making the most of, 12–13
hearty, about, 13
Herbed Mayonnaise, 66
Herbed Rice and Pasta Pilaf, 304
Herbed Roast Chicken, 410–12, *411*
measuring, 13
Salad, *154,* 155
storing, 13
washing and drying, 13
–Yogurt Sauce, Falafel Burgers with,
336, 337
see also specific herbs
Hoisin Sauce, Tangy, 20
Hollandaise Sauce, 67–68
Eggs Benedict, 68
Mustard-Dill, 67
Saffron, 67
ways to use, 68
Hominy
about, 316
Chicken Posole Verde, 316–17
dried, soaking and cooking, 317
Pork Posole Rojo, 317
Honey
-Spelt Bread, *538,* 538–39
Spicy, 21
-Walnut Labneh, 83

Horseradish
Cocktail Sauce, 469
Cream Sauce with Chives, 482
Huaraches, Tomatillo-Chicken, 321–22, *323*
Hummus, Ultimate, 334–35, *335*

I

Ice
bath, working with, 73
crushed, preparing, 471
serving seafood on, 471
Ice Cream
Olive Oil, 599
Sandwiches, Chocolate Chip Cookie, *566,*
566–67
Instant-read thermometer, 25
Italian Pasta Salad, *174,* 174–75

J

Jamaican Oxtail, *381,* 381–82
Jicama
Mango, and Orange Salad, 169
Shaved, Mango, and Cucumber Salad
with Pan-Seared Scallops, 165, *165*

K

Kaiser Rolls, 507–8
Kale
Feta, and Sun-Dried Tomato Omelet,
Perfect, 37
Parmesan, and Pepitas, Butternut
Squash Gnudi with, 272–73, *273*
Kansas City Barbecue Sauce, 402
Kedgeree, Hot-Smoked Salmon, 484–85, *485*
Ketchup-based sauces
Cocktail Sauce, 469
Cóctel de Camarón sauce, *458,* 459
Lexington-Style Barbecue Sauce, 403
Memphis Barbecue Spareribs sauce,
399
Oklahoma Barbecue Sauce, 402
Sweet and Tangy Barbecued Chicken
sauce, 432–33
Kimchi, 148–49, *149*
Beef, and Tofu Soup, 213, *213*
Egg, and Avocado Sandwiches, 55
Knives
advanced, list of, 7
basic, list of, 4
caring for, 10–11
cleaning, 11
storing, 10

Kofte, Vospov, *332,* 332–33
Kohlrabi
peeling, 123
Roasted, with Crunchy Seeds, 123
Soup, Creamy, 228, *228*
Koji
Fried Chicken, *437,* 437–38
Shio, 436
Turkey, 438, *439*
Korean Chile Sauce, 21
Koshari, 327–28, *329*
Kouign Amann, Breton, *552,* 552–54
Kousa Mihshi, 137–39, *138*
Kvass, Beet, 150, *151*

L

Labneh, 83, *83*
Honey-Walnut, 83
Lemon-Dill, 83
Lamb
Bone-in Leg of, Grilled, with Charred
Scallion Sauce, *390,* 390–91
Burgers with Halloumi and Beet
Tzatziki, 366, *366*
Harira, 225, *225*
internal cooking temperatures, 24
Kousa Mihshi, 137–39, *138*
leg, temping, 391
Ragu, 259
Lasagna, Cheese and Tomato, 263, 263–64
Lasagne Verdi alla Bolognese, 264–66, *265*
Latin Flan, *572,* 572–73
Almond, 572
Coffee, 572
Orange-Cardamom, 572
Lavender, 12
La Viña–Style Cheesecake, 589
Leek(s)
Dutch Oven Chicken Pot Pie with Spring
Vegetables, *427,* 427–28
and Goat Cheese Quiche, 50
Microwave-Fried, 21
and Turmeric, Shellfish Soup with, *233,*
233–34
Legumes. *See* **Bean(s); Lentil(s)**
Lemon(s)
–Browned Butter Vinaigrette, 135
Butter, Grilled Artichokes with, 108, *108*
Cake, Blueberry-Mascarpone,
610–12, *611*
-Dill Labneh, 83
Gremolata, 370
-Herb Sformati, *60,* 60–61
–Olive Oil Tart, 598–99
Preserved, 309

P

S

T

Ta'ameya with Tahini-Yogurt Sauce, 347–48, *349*

Tahini
Sauce, 20
-Yogurt Sauce, Ta'ameya with, 347–48, *349*
-Yogurt Sauce and Berbere, Whole Romanesco with, 134–35
-Yogurt Sauce and Mushrooms, Barley and Lentils with, 330–31

Tamales Two Ways, 319–21, *320*

Tamarind paste, about, 277

Tanabour, 231, *231*

Tarragon
Béarnaise Sauce, 67
Herbed Roast Chicken, 410–12, *411*
-Lemon Gremolata, 20

Tartar Sauce, Classic, 462

Tarts
Chicken B'stilla, 428–29
Lemon–Olive Oil, 598–99
resources for, 133
Tomato, Upside-Down, *128*, 128–29

Tea
Blueberry Earl Grey Pie, 581–82, *583*
-Infused Crème Brûlée, 571

Texas Barbecue Brisket, *394*, 395–96

Texas Barbecue Sauce, 402–3

Texas-Smoked Beef Ribs, 400

Texas Thick-Cut Smoked Pork Chops, *391*, 391–92

Thermometers
instant-read, 25
oven, 23

Thyme
and Garlic, Butter-Basted Fish Fillets with, 472–73, *473*
Porchetta, *371*, 371–72
Porchetta-Style Turkey Breast, 440–42, *442*
Za'atar, 21, 182–83

Toasted sesame oil, 18

Toffee-Chocolate Bark, 627

Tofu
Kimchi, and Beef Soup, 213, *213*
and Shrimp Pad Thai, 278
Smoky Eggplant Miso Soup, 209–10
Summer Rolls with Spicy Almond Butter Sauce, 294–95

Togarashi, Shichimi, 275

Tomatillo(s)
-Chicken Huaraches, 321–22, *323*
Chicken Posole Verde, 316–17

Tomato(es)
-Basil Sauce, Three-Cheese Ravioli with, *252*, 252–53
Braciole, *368*, 368–69
-Browned Butter Sauce, Fettuccine with, 243
and Bulgur, Stuffed Eggplant with, 137
-Butter Sauce, Spinach and Ricotta Gnudi with, 270–71
and Cheese Lasagna, *263*, 263–64
Cherry, Corn, and Pecorino, Grilled Radicchio Salad with, 192
Chicken and White Bean Panzanella, 173, *173*
Egg, and Salami Sandwiches, 56, *56*
and Eggplant Phyllo Pie, 131
Etli Kuru Fasulye, 380–81
Gigantes Plaki, *341*, 341–42
Green, Chutney, 20
Kousa Mihshi, 137–39, *138*
Lamb Ragu, 259
Linguine allo Scoglio, 500–501
'Nduja Sauce, Fileja with, 248, *248*
and Okra, Red Beans and Rice with, 325–27, *326*
and Peach, Grilled, Salad with Burrata and Basil, 193
plum, coring and seeding, 129
Pork Posole Rojo, 317
Pork Ragu, 258–59
Relish, Fresh, 482
Roasted Pattypan Squash Salad with Dandelion Green Pesto, 188–89
Seafood Bisque, 236
Shrimp Bisque, *235*, 235–36
Smoked Trout, and Pepperoncini, Couscous Salad with, 175
Soup, Chilled Fresh, 219–20, *220*
Tart, Upside-Down, *128*, 128–29
Vinaigrette and Artichokes, Oil-Poached Fish Fillets with, *475*, 475–76
Wedge Salad with Creamy Black Pepper Dressing, 178

Tools
advanced, list of, 8–9
basic, list of, 5

Tortillas, Corn, Homemade, 318–19

Trout
Grilled Whole, with Orange and Fennel, 488, *488*
Smoked, Tomatoes, and Pepperoncini, Couscous Salad with, 175
whole, buying, 491

Tuna
internal cooking temperatures, 24
Poke, 468, *468*

Tunisian Tajine with White Beans, 46–47, *47*

Turchetta, 440–42, *442*

Turkey
Breast, Porchetta-Style, 440–42, *442*
buying, 449
Deep-Fried, *447*, 447–48
frying, safety tips, 449
Koji, 438, *439*
resources for, 449
Smoked, Holiday, *445*, 445–46
spatchcocking, 446
Thigh Confit, Sous Vide, with Citrus-Mustard Sauce, 444
Thigh Confit with Citrus-Mustard Sauce, 443–45
thighs, carving, 443
Wings, Stuffed, 423–24, *424*

Turmeric
Hawaij, 230
and Leeks, Shellfish Soup with, *233*, 233–34

Turnips, Pink Pickled, 348, *349*

Turnovers, Beet and Caramelized Onion, with Beet-Yogurt Sauce, 130, *130*

Tzatziki, Beet, and Halloumi, Lamb Burgers with, 366, *366*

V

Vanilla
beans, removing seeds from, 571
Frozen Custard, Old-Fashioned, 619
Marshmallows, Fluffy, 622–23, *623*
Pastry Cream, 606

Veal
Lasagne Verdi alla Bolognese, 264–66, *265*
Osso Buco, *370*, 370–71
Ultimate Ragu alla Bolognese, 260, 260–61

Vegetable oil, 18

Vegetable(s)
and Beef Soup, 214–15
Bibimbap with Nurungji, 313–14, *314*
blanching, 100
deep frying, method for, 114, *115*
fermented, 146–50
and Halloumi, Grilled, Salad, *191*, 191–92
modern crudités, 100–101, *101*
Root, Gratin, 125
science lesson, 134
see also specific vegetables

Vignole, 346, *346*

Vinaigrettes
Browned Butter–Lemon, 135
Orange-Ginger, 451

Vospov Kofte, *332*, 332–33

W

Y

Z